WRITING ABOUT WRITING

A College Reader

THIRD EDITION

WRITING ABOUT WRITING

A College Reader

ELIZABETH WARDLE
Miami University

DOUG DOWNS
Montana State University

bedford/st.martin's
Macmillan Learning
Boston | New York

FOR BEDFORD/ST. MARTIN'S

Vice President, Editorial, Macmillan Learning Humanities: Edwin Hill
Editorial Director, English: Karen S. Henry
Senior Publisher for Composition, Business and Technical Writing,
    Developmental Writing: Leasa Burton
Executive Editor: John E. Sullivan III
Executive Development Manager: Jane Carter
Developmental Editor: Leah Rang
Production Editor: Pamela Lawson
Media Producer: Rand Thomas
Production Manager: Joe Ford
Executive Marketing Manager: Joy Fisher Williams
Project Management: Jouve
Text Permissions Researcher: Mark Schaefer
Permissions Editor: Kalina Ingham
Photo Researcher: Susan Doheny
Senior Art Director: Anna Palchik
Text Design: Laura Shaw Design, Inc.
Cover Design: John Callahan
Composition: Jouve
Printing and Binding: LSC Communications

Manufactured in the United States of America.

1   0   9   8   7
f   e   d   c   b

For information, write: Bedford/St. Martin's, 75 Arlington Street,
Boston, MA 02116   (617-399-4000)

ISBN 978-1-319-03276-0 (Student Edition)
ISBN 978-1-319-06231-6 (Instructor's Edition)

ACKNOWLEDGMENTS

Text acknowledgments and copyrights appear at the back of the book on pages 903–906, which constitute an extension of the copyright page. Art acknowledgments and copyrights appear on the same page as the art selections they cover.

PREFACE FOR INSTRUCTORS

Writing about Writing is part of a movement that continues to grow. As composition instructors, we have always focused on teaching students how writing works and on helping them develop ways of thinking that would enable them to succeed as writers in college. We found ourselves increasingly frustrated, however, teaching traditional composition courses based on topics that had nothing to do with writing. It made far more sense to us to have students really engage with writing in the writing course; the best way to do this, we decided, was to adopt a "writing about writing" approach, introducing students directly to what writing researchers have learned about writing and challenging them to respond by writing and doing research of their own. After years of experimenting with readings and assignments, and watching our colleagues do the same, we developed *Writing about Writing*, a textbook for first-year composition students that presents the subjects of composition, discourse, and literacy as its content. Here's why we think *Writing about Writing* is a smart choice for composition courses.

Writing about Writing engages students in a relevant subject. One of the major goals of the writing course, as we see it, is to move students' ideas about language and writing from the realm of the automatic and unconscious to the forefront of their thinking. In conventional composition courses, students are too often asked to write about an arbitrary topic unrelated to writing. In our experience, when students are asked to read and interact with academic scholarly conversations about writing and test their opinions through their own research, they become more engaged with the goals of the writing course and — most important — they learn more about writing.

Writing about Writing engages students' own areas of expertise. By the time they reach college, students are expert language users with multiple literacies: They are experienced student writers, and they're engaged in many other discourses as well — blogging, texting, instant messaging, posting to social networking sites like Facebook and Snapchat, and otherwise using language and writing on a daily basis. *Writing about Writing* asks students to work from their own experience to consider how writing works, who they are as writers, and how they use (and don't use) writing. Students might wonder, for example, why they did so poorly on the SAT writing section or why some groups of people use writing that is so specialized it seems intended to leave others out. This book encourages students to discover how others — including Sondra Perl, Deborah Brandt, James Paul Gee, their instructors, and their classmates — have answered these questions and then to find out more by doing meaningful research of their own.

***Writing about Writing* helps students transfer what they learn.** Teachers often assume that students can automatically and easily "apply" what they learn in a writing course to all their other writing — or at the very least, to other college writing. This assumption sees writing and reading as "basic" universal skills that work the same regardless of situation. Yet research on transfer of learning suggests that there is nothing automatic about it: Learning transfer researchers David Perkins and Gavriel Salomon found that in order to transfer knowledge, students need to explicitly create general principles based on their own experience and learning; to be self-reflective, so that they keep track of what they are thinking and learning as they do it; and to be mindful — that is, alert to their surroundings and to what they are doing rather than just doing things automatically and unconsciously. A writing course that takes language, writing, reading, and literacy as its subjects can help students achieve these goals by teaching them to articulate general principles such as "Carefully consider what your audience needs and wants this document to do." In addition, it teaches them to reflect on their own reading, writing, and research processes.

***Writing about Writing* has been extensively class tested — and it works.** The principles of this writing-about-writing approach have been well tested and supported by the experience of writing instructors and thousands of students across the country. *Writing about Writing* was formally class tested in a pilot at the University of Central Florida, an experiment that yielded impressive outcomes in comparative portfolio assessment with more traditional composition courses. Assessment results suggest, among other things, that the writing-about-writing approach had a statistically significant impact on higher-order thinking skills — rhetorical analysis, critical thinking about ideas, and using and integrating the ideas of others. The writing-about-writing approach also had a significant impact on how students and teachers engaged in writing as a process. The first and second editions of *Writing about Writing* were used in a variety of composition programs across the country, and based on positive feedback from those users, we have even greater confidence that this approach — and this third edition — is successful.

Features of *Writing about Writing*

FRAMED AROUND THRESHOLD CONCEPTS ABOUT WRITING

Writing about Writing is organized around concepts and principles from Writing Studies with which we think students should become familiar; we identify these as "threshold concepts," and we spend the entire first chapter discussing them in detail, and engaging students in activities to think about how they apply to their lives. Threshold concepts are concepts that learners must become acquainted with in order to progress in that area of study — they are gateways to learning. Naming and using threshold concepts is an approach that has been used in the United Kingdom and now increasingly in the United States and other countries to improve teaching and learning in various disciplines and programs, including Writing Studies (for example, see the 2015 publication *Naming What We Know: Threshold Concepts of Writing Studies*). Because they are central to work in a particular field but are often assumed and unstated, threshold concepts when explicitly identified can better help students come to understand ideas that are central to that field or phenomenon.

Researchers Ray Land and Jan (Erik) Meyer have argued that threshold concepts are often troublesome and can conflict with common knowledge about a phenomenon. We think that this is particularly true when it comes to writing. Much of what we have learned as a field about writing conflicts with commonly held assumptions about writing. For example, many people believe that "good writers" are people for whom writing is easy, while research about writing suggests that "good writers" are people who persist, revise, and are willing to learn from their failures.

Threshold concepts are the organizing theme for the third edition of *Writing about Writing*, and we've arranged them in a sequence that we believe assists understanding of each subsequent concept:

- **Chapter 1, "Threshold Concepts: Why Do Your Ideas about Writing Matter?"** introduces and defines threshold concepts and describes some central concepts about writing that conflict with common ideas of writing in popular culture.

- **Chapter 2, "Literacies: How Is Writing Impacted by Our Prior Experiences?"** engages the threshold concept that *our prior experiences deeply impact our writing and literacy practices*, or in simpler terms, that our reading and writing past will shape our reading and writing present.

- **Chapter 3, "Individual in Community: How Does Writing Help People Get Things Done?"** engages the threshold concept that people use texts and discourse in order to *do something*, to *make meaning*. And the texts and language they create *mediate meaningful activities*. People construct meaning through texts and language, and texts construct meaning as people use them.

- **Chapter 4, "Rhetoric: How Is Meaning Constructed in Context?"** explores the threshold concepts that *writing helps people make meaning and get things done*, that *"good" writing is dependent on writers, readers, situation, technology, and use*, and therefore that *there are always constraints on writing*.

- **Chapter 5, "Processes: How Are Texts Composed?"** engages several threshold concepts about writing, including that *writing is a process*, *all writers have more to learn*, and *writing is not perfectible*.

CHALLENGING AND ENGAGING READINGS

Because our intention in putting this book together was to invite students directly into scholarly conversations about writing, most readings in the book are articles by rhetoric and composition scholars. We looked for work that was readable by undergraduates, relevant to student experience, effective in modeling how to research and write about writing, and useful for helping students frame and analyze writing-related issues. We drew not only on our own experience with students but also on feedback from a nationwide network of faculty using writing-about-writing approaches to composition and on the feedback of teachers who used the first two editions of the book. The articles in this edition expose students to some of the longest-standing questions and some of the most interesting work in our field, encouraging them to wrestle with concepts we're all trying to figure out.

Of course, we don't expect first-year students to read these texts like graduate students or scholars would — that is, with a central focus on the content of the readings, for the purposes of critiquing them and extending their ideas. Instead, we intend for them to be used as springboards to exploration of students' own writing and reading experiences. The readings — and thus this book — are not the center of the course; instead, they help students develop language and ideas for thinking through the threshold concepts identified above, and begin exploring them by considering their own experiences with writing, discourse, and literacy, and their (and the field's) open questions.

While most readings are scholarly, we include a number of other sorts of texts throughout this edition. There are new pieces written directly for the student readers of this book, including Chapter 1, with readings on genre theory and rhetorical reading written by us, and an introduction to rhetoric by **Doug Downs** and a discussion of document design and social justice written by **Natasha Jones** and **Stephanie Wheeler** (both in Chapter 4); short pieces by fiction and nonfiction writers (including **Anne Lamott**, **Sandra Cisneros**, **Barbara Mellix**, and **Malcolm X**); and a research report by the Writing in Digital Environments (WIDE) Research Group led by **Jeff Grabill** and **Bill Hart-Davidson**. These readings, combined with the others in the book, help students approach the threshold concepts about writing from a variety of perspectives.

REAL STUDENT WRITING

Writing about Writing also includes student voices, with eight pieces of student writing. We have continued to draw from *Young Scholars in Writing*, the national peer-reviewed journal of undergraduate research in Writing Studies and rhetoric, and from *Stylus*, the University of Central Florida Writing Program's peer-reviewed first-year student publication. Given their nature as reprinted scholarly articles, we have treated the student essays the same as we have treated the professional essays: They are framed and introduced and accompanied by questions and activities. We want the students who use this book to see other students as participants in the ongoing conversations about writing; we hope this will enable them to see themselves as potential contributors to these conversations. This time around, rather than placing all the student readings at the end of the chapter, we have integrated them into the chapters where we thought they best fit into the conversation.

SCAFFOLDED SUPPORT FOR LEARNING

The material presented in this book is challenging. We've found that students need guidance in order to engage with it constructively, and many instructors appreciate support in teaching it. Therefore, we've scaffolded the material in ways that help make individual readings more accessible to students and that help them build toward mastery of often complex rhetorical concepts.

- The book begins with a chapter written directly to a student audience. **Chapter 1** not only explains the purpose of the book, but explains why and how the book is organized around threshold concepts of Writing Studies and provides extended explanation of these concepts. This chapter also provides an introduction to genre theory and rhetorical reading in order to help students engage in the readings of this book (and the rest of their college experience). We outline some reading strategies and an overview of John Swales's CARS model of research introductions to assist with this. There you will also find a reading by Stuart Greene that asks students to think about this class and book as inquiry, and a reading by Richard Straub that helps prepare students for responding to each other's writing. Reflective activities throughout the chapter as well as sections of reading support and tips on "Using This Book" — including a descriptive guide to the Reading Assist Tags feature — prepare students to engage with *Writing about Writing*.

- Chapters 2–5 begin with a **chapter introduction** that explains the chapter's threshold concepts, summarizes the chapter's content and goals, and overviews each reading and its central ideas by placing it in the larger conversation at play within the chapter. These introductions are robust discussions of background knowledge and principles that help students better approach the threshold concepts the chapter includes.

- Each reading begins with a **Framing the Reading** section offering background on the author and the text as well as **Getting Ready to Read** suggestions for activities to do *before* reading and questions to ask *during* reading.

- Each reading is followed by two sets of questions: **Questions for Discussion and Journaling**, which can be used in class or for homework, and **Applying and Exploring Ideas**, which recommends medium-scale reading-related writing activities (both individual and group). A **Meta Moment** concludes the post-reading question set and asks students to reflect on the selection's ideas in the context of the chapter's threshold concept and of their own writing experiences. These questions and activities are designed to make teachers' jobs easier by providing a variety of prompts that have been class tested by others.

- Each chapter ends with the **Writing Assignments** section. Building on one or more of the readings from the chapter, assignments are designed to help students achieve the goals outlined in the chapter introduction. Though these assignments hardly scratch the surface of what's possible, these have proven to be favorites with us, our students, and other teachers.

- The book includes a **glossary** of technical terms in composition that students will encounter in their readings. Terms in the glossary, such as **rhetorical situation** and **discourse**, are noted in the chapter and reading introductions via bold print.

A note on citation styles. While the selection introductions reflect current MLA style from the eighth edition of the *MLA Handbook* (2016) in citation and documentation, other material in the book, all previously published, remains written in the citation styles used by the journals and books in which they were originally published, current at those times. This means you should expect to see a great deal of variation from current MLA, APA, CMS, or journal-specific style guidelines — a decision that we hope will provide instructors with an excellent starting point for conversation about how citation actually works in the "real world" of academic publication over time.

New to the Third Edition

DIVERSE AND RELEVANT NEW READINGS

The third edition features eight new professional essays. Selections by authors such as **Sandra Cisneros** ("Only Daughter"), popular in many first-year writing courses, are offered through a writing-about-writing lens to promote and understand literacy. Now integrated throughout Chapters 2–5, readings on multimodality and on technology in writing, such as **Jim Ridolfo** and **Dànielle Nicole DeVoss**'s "Composing for Recomposition: Rhetorical Velocity and Delivery" and **Stacey Pigg**'s "Coordinating Constant Invention: Social Media's Role in Distributed Work," relate to our evolving conceptions of writing in a networked and digital age. Other notable new additions include **Vershawn Ashanti Young**'s "'Naw, We Straight': An Argument Against Code Switching"; **James M. Corder**'s "Argument as Emergence, Rhetoric as Love"; and **Liane Robertson**, **Kara Taczak**, and **Kathleen Blake Yancey**'s "Notes toward a Theory of Prior Knowledge."

Six of the eight student essays in this edition are also new. Now dispersed through each chapter to show the importance and relevance of students' engagement with Writing Studies, these student texts present topics relevant to students today: explorations of literacy by rejecting labels of "remedial" writing (**Arturo Tejada, Jr.** et al.), rhetorical analyses of social media and library catalog pages (**Komysha Hassan**), studies of bilingual writing processes (**Lucas Pasqualin** and **Alcir Santos Neto**), and more.

A MORE ACCESSIBLE AND TEACHABLE INTRODUCTION TO THRESHOLD CONCEPTS, GENRE, AND RHETORICAL READING

The new **Chapter 1, "Threshold Concepts: Why Do Your Ideas about Writing Matter?,"** explains the ideas and rationale of the writing-about-writing approach to students directly. Students are introduced to the threshold concepts that frame the chapters in *Writing about Writing* with relatable examples and conversational language. A new section introduces genre and rhetorical reading as threshold concepts that assist academic reading and writing, providing a foundation for students as they engage with articles of Writing Studies scholarship. The *Write Reflectively* and *Try Thinking Differently* activities get students writing and thinking actively about each threshold concept, and *Questions for Discussion and Journaling* and *Applying and Exploring Ideas* allow students to reflect on the entire chapter and their conceptions of writing from the beginning of the course.

READING ASSIST TAGS

Chapters 2–5 each present one foundational or challenging selection as a **Tagged Reading**. These selections feature two types of Reading Assist Tags: *Genre Cues* to help students see and understand genre conventions and rhetorical moves, and *Reading Cues* such as "Look Ahead" and "Reread" to help students find and understand the key points of each article. A fresh design color-codes the two different tags and provides extended commentary for each cue below the main text, but remains in the margins to allow annotation and flexibility for working with the readings. A two-page chart in Chapter 1 (pages 58–59) explains each tag's meaning and function and serves as a useful reference for students throughout the course.

AN UPDATED GLOSSARY

New and revised glossary terms such as *ecology*, *embodiment*, and *velocity* present more coverage of key concepts of writing, both the concepts presented in this edition's reading selections as well as terminology from the evolving field of Writing Studies.

NEW IDEAS FOR WRITING ASSIGNMENTS

This edition features seven new **Writing Assignments**, now designed to be more clearly visible at the end of each chapter. These engaging projects are class-tested favorites that respond to the concepts presented in the new reading selections and include a challenge to students to explore their conceptions about writing, reading, and research; a reflection on gaining authority in new discourse communities; and an analysis of rhetorical velocity in social media.

MORE SUPPORT IN THE INSTRUCTOR'S EDITION OF *WRITING ABOUT WRITING*

Some teachers won't need any supplements at all, including the discussion questions and major assignment options. But we have designed the book to be as accessible and supportive as possible to composition instructors with a wide range of experience, including new graduate students and very busy adjuncts. Toward that end, we provide a revised instructor's resource manual written by Matt Bryan, which builds on the previous two editions written by Deborah Weaver and Lindee Owens. All three of these instructors are teacher-trainers at the University of Central Florida, who themselves piloted an early version of this book and taught the material in it to a number of other composition teachers there. This material, bound together with the student text in a special Instructor's Edition, includes the following:

- frequently asked questions

- sample course calendars

- chapter overviews

- lists of key vocabulary for each chapter

- key student outcomes for each chapter

- a list of readings that can help teach key student outcomes

- summaries and take-home points for each reading

- supplemental activities that help teach to each outcome

The manual is also available for download on the instructor's resources tab on the catalog page for *Writing about Writing* at **macmillanlearning.com**.

Acknowledgments

We came to writing-about-writing independently of one another, in different ways, and became better at it as a result of working together. David Russell was a mentor for us both. Elizabeth came to writing-about-writing as a result of her dissertation research, which Russell chaired and supported. Doug came to it as a result of questions about building better research pedagogy, directly fueled by Russell's work on the history of college research-writing instruction and his chapter in Joseph Petraglia's *Reconceiving Writing*. Initially, Elizabeth's interest was theoretical ("this might be an interesting idea") while Doug's was quite practical (he designed and studied a writing-about-writing class for his dissertation). We discovered each other's common interest through dialog on the WPA-L listserv, two independent clauses and a long-term collaboration was born. It is fair to say that neither of us would have written this book without the other, as we both seem to get a lot more done when working collaboratively. (We remember vividly two hours in the sunshine at the University of Delaware, at the 2004 WPA conference, when we took our first steps at figuring out collaboration.) So, if it's not too corny, we would like to acknowledge collaboration in general, our collaboration in particular, and tenure and promotion systems at our institutions that have recognized collaborative work for the valid, challenging, and rewarding process it is.

To many, many people — colleagues, mentors, and friends — we owe a deep debt of gratitude for putting the ideas grounding *Writing about Writing* "in the air." In addition, over the five years that it took to build the first edition of this book, and the three years we planned and wrote the second edition, and in the year and a half it took to write the third edition, we met many wonderful teacher-scholars who inspired us to keep going. Over many dinners, SIGs, conference panels, e-mail discussions, and drinks, we learned and are still learning a lot from them. A partial list of people who helped us start on this path or rethink it and make it better includes Linda Adler-Kassner, Anis Bawarshi, Barb Bird, Shannon Carter, Dana Driscoll, Heidi Estrem, Michelle LaFrance, Moriah McCracken, Susan McLeod, Laurie McMillan, Michael Michaud, Michael Murphy, Sarah Read, Jan Rieman, David Russell, Betsy Sargent, Jody Shipka, David Slomp, Susan Thomas, Jennifer Wells, Kathi Yancey, and Leah Zuidema.

Each of us is also deeply indebted to the wonderful teachers, scholars, and students at our own institutions who have worked with this curriculum and pushed our thinking on what is possible in a writing-about-writing classroom. At UCF, some of these people include Matt Bryan, Angela Rounsaville, Debbie Weaver, Lindee Owens, Mark Hall, Dan Martin, Matt McBride, Adele Richardson, Nichole Stack, Mary Tripp, and Thomas Wright. At Montana State, some of these people include Jean Arthur, Jess Carroll, Glen Chamberlain, Jill Davis, ZuZu Feder, Jake Henan, Kimberly Hoover, Katie Jo LaRiviere, Miles Nolte, Ashley Rives, Kiki Rydell, Mark Schlenz, and Aaron Yost.

Many of these people are now on the FYC as Writing Studies listserv; members of the Writing about Writing Network founded by Betsy Sargent; participants in or leaders of the CCCC standing group, the Writing about Writing Development Group; or contributors to a forthcoming edited collection of research on the approach edited by Doug Downs, Moriah McCracken, Barb Bird, and Jan Rieman. Through such interaction, they continue to develop research projects, create conference presentations and workshops, and inspire us — and one another — with their curricular creativity. Writing-about-writing students have also been given a national platform to publish their work, thanks to the editorial board of the national, peer-reviewed undergraduate journal of Writing Studies, *Young Scholars in Writing*. Editor Laurie Grobman created a First-year Writing Feature (continued as the Spotlight on First-year Writing under the editorship of Jane Greer) co-edited over time by Shannon Carter, Doug Downs, David Elder, Heidi Estrem, Patti Hanlon-Baker, Holly Ryan, Heather Bastian, and Angela Glotfelter.

We are grateful to those instructors who gave us valuable feedback as we worked on this new edition: Rebecca Day Babcock, University of Texas–Permain Basin; Matthew Bryan, University of Central Florida; Ellen C. Carillo, University of Connecticut; Colin Charlton, University of Texas–Pan American; Jonikka Charlton, University of Texas–Pan American; Geoffrey Clegg, Arkansas State University; E. Dominguez Barajas, University of Arkansas; Dana Driscoll, Oakland University; Carolyn Fitzpatrick, University of Maryland; Alanna Frost, University of Alabama, Huntsville; Gina Hanson, California State University; Krystal Hering, Des Moines Area Community College; Kim Hoover, Montana State University; Michael D. Johnson, Ohio University; Joseph Jones, University of Memphis; Erik Juergensmeyer, Fort Lewis College; Jessica Kester, Daytona State College; Cat Mahaffey, University of North Carolina–Charlotte; Jill McCracken, University of South Florida–St. Petersburg; Janine Morris, University of Cincinnati; Melissa Nicolas, University of Nevada; Miles Nolte, Montana State University; Juli Parrish, University of Denver; Pegeen Reichert Powell, Columbia College; Rhonda Powers, University of Memphis; Sarah Read, DePaul University; Jan Rieman, University of North Carolina–Charlotte; Gregory Robinson, Nevada State College; Kevin Roozen, University of Central Florida; Albert Rouzie, Ohio University; John H. Whicker, Fontbonne University; Gail York, Appalachian State University; Sarah Zurhellen, Appalachian State University.

We owe a massive thank you to Bedford/St. Martin's, and to Leasa Burton and Joan Feinberg in particular, who had the vision to believe that this book might really find an audience if they published it. To all the Bedford crew who made it real the first time and improved it the second and third times, we are deeply grateful. We are grateful to John Sullivan, our second edition editor, who unfailingly believed (and continues to believe) in our ideas and vision, and encouraged others to trust us when our ideas might not immediately seem possible; his mentorship and advocacy on the second edition helped push this book to a new place. This third go-round, Leah Rang had the unenviable task of corralling us along the revision path while we struggled with many other competing commitments. To her we owe the follow-through to make the reading assist tags and improved design a reality.

Ultimately, our students deserve the most acknowledgment. They have inspired us to keep teaching writing about writing. They have demonstrated that the focus is one that continues to excite and motivate, and their ideas continue to inspire and teach us.

ELIZABETH WARDLE

DOUG DOWNS

With Bedford/St. Martin's, You Get More

At Bedford, providing support to teachers and their students who use our books and digital tools is our top priority. The Bedford/St. Martin's English Community is now our home for professional resources, featuring Bedford *Bits*, our popular blog site with new ideas for the composition classroom. Join us to connect with our authors and your colleagues at **community.macmillan.com** where you can download titles from our professional resource series, review projects in the pipeline, sign up for webinars, or start a discussion. In addition to this dynamic online community and book-specific instructor resources, we offer digital tools, custom solutions, and value packages to support both you and your students. We are committed to delivering the quality and value that you've come to expect from Bedford/St. Martin's, supported as always by the power of Macmillan Learning. To learn more about or to order any of the following products, contact your Bedford/St. Martin's sales representative or visit the website at **macmillanlearning.com**.

CHOOSE FROM ALTERNATIVE FORMATS OF *WRITING ABOUT WRITING*

Bedford/St. Martin's offers affordable formats — a paperback version and an electronic version — allowing students to choose the one that works best for them. For details about popular e-book formats from our e-book partners, visit **macmillanlearning.com /ebooks**.

SELECT VALUE PACKAGES

Add value to your text by packaging one of the following resources with *Writing about Writing.* To learn more about package options for any of the following products, contact your Bedford/St. Martin's sales representative or visit **macmillanlearning .com**.

Writer's Help 2.0 is a powerful online writing resource that helps students find answers whether they are searching for writing advice on their own or as part of an assignment.

- **Smart search.** Built on research with more than 1,600 student writers, the smart search in Writer's Help 2.0 provides reliable results even when students use novice terms, such as *flow* and *unstuck*.

- **Trusted content from our best-selling handbooks.** Choose *Writer's Help 2.0, Hacker Version,* or *Writer's Help 2.0, Lunsford Version,* and ensure that students have clear advice and examples for all of their writing questions.

- **Diagnostics that help establish a baseline for instruction.** Assign diagnostics to identify areas of strength and areas for improvement on topics related to grammar and reading and to help students plan a course of study. Use visual reports to track performance by topic, class, and student as well as comparison reports that track improvement over time.

- **Adaptive exercises that engage students.** Writer's Help 2.0 includes LearningCurve, game-like online quizzing that adapts to what students already know and helps them focus on what they need to learn.

Student access is packaged with *Writing about Writing* at a significant discount. Order ISBN 978-1-319-10777-2 for *Writer's Help 2.0, Hacker Version,* or ISBN 978-1-319-10780-2 for *Writer's Help 2.0, Lunsford Version,* to ensure your students have easy access to online writing support. Students who rent a book or buy a used book and instructors can purchase access to Writer's Help 2.0 at **macmillanlearning.com /writershelp2.**

LaunchPad Solo for Readers and Writers allows students to work on whatever they need help with the most. At home or in class, students learn at their own pace, with instruction tailored to each student's unique needs. *LaunchPad Solo for Readers and Writers* features:

- **Pre-built units that support a learning arc.** Each easy-to-assign unit is comprised of a pre-test check, multimedia instruction and assessment, and a post-test that assesses what students have learned about critical reading, writing process, using sources, grammar, style, and mechanics. Dedicated units also offer help for multilingual writers.

- **Diagnostics that help establish a baseline for instruction.** Assign diagnostics to identify areas of strength and areas for improvement on topics related to grammar and reading and to help students plan a course of study. Use visual reports to track performance by topic, class, and student as well as comparison reports that track improvement over time.

- **A video introduction to many topics.** Introductions offer an overview of the unit's topic, and many include a brief, accessible video to illustrate the concepts at hand.

- **Adaptive quizzing for targeted learning.** Most units include LearningCurve, game-like adaptive quizzing that focuses on the areas in which each student needs the most help.

- **The ability to monitor student progress.** Use our gradebook to see which students are on track and which need additional help with specific topics.

LaunchPad Solo for Readers and Writers can be packaged at a significant discount. Order ISBN 978-1-319-10761-1 to ensure your students can take full advantage. Visit **macmillanlearning.com/readwrite** for more information.

INSTRUCTOR RESOURCES

You have a lot to do in your course. Bedford/St. Martin's wants to make it easy for you to find the support you need — and to get it quickly.

Instructor's Manual for Writing about Writing, **Third Edition,** is available as a PDF that can be downloaded from the Bedford/St. Martin's online catalog at the page for *Writing about Writing.* In addition to chapter overviews and teaching tips, the instructor's manual includes answers to Frequently Asked Questions, sample syllabi, key vocabulary and student learning objectives for each chapter, summaries of reading selections, and classroom activities.

ABOUT THE AUTHORS

Elizabeth Wardle is Howe Professor of English and Director of the Roger and Joyce Howe Center for Writing Excellence at Miami University (OH). She was Chair of the Department of Writing and Rhetoric at the University of Central Florida (UCF), and Director of Writing Programs at UCF and University of Dayton. These experiences fed her interest in how students learn and repurpose what they know in new settings. With Linda Adler-Kassner, she is co-editor of *Naming What We Know: Threshold Concepts of Writing Studies*, winner of the WPA Award for Outstanding Contribution to the Discipline (2016).

Doug Downs is Associate Professor of Writing Studies as well as Director of the Core Writing Program in the Department of English at Montana State University (Bozeman). His interests are in writing, research, and reading instruction at the college level, especially related to first-year composition and under-graduate research. He is currently editor of *Young Scholars in Writing*, the national peer-reviewed journal of undergradu-ate research on writing and rhetoric. His most recent research projects focus on students' reading practices in an age of screen-based literacy, and on learning transfer from first-year writing courses to students' writing in their majors.

CONTENTS

CHAPTER 3
Individual in Community: How Does Writing Help People Get Things Done? 270

CHAPTER 4
Rhetoric: How Is Meaning Constructed in Context?   447

CHAPTER 5
Processes: How Are Texts Composed?   706

WRITING ABOUT WRITING
A College Reader

CHAPTER 1

THRESHOLD CONCEPTS:
Why Do Your Ideas about Writing Matter?

Stephanie Pilick/picture-alliance/dpa/AP Images

An image of writing in the twenty-first century: digital, networked, collaborative, screen-based, and interactive.

Before you read this chapter, jot down your ideas about the following:

- Writing is . . . .
- Research is . . . .
- Good writers do or are . . . .
- Good writing is . . . .

At the end of the chapter we will ask you to revisit your ideas to see if they have changed. In fact, throughout the book, we will ask you to note how and what you think about writing so that you can return to your ideas, track how they change, and, most importantly, see whether they impact what you do as a writer.

Introduction to the Conversation

Have you ever wondered why every teacher seems to have a different set of rules for writing? Or why writing seems to be more difficult for some people than for others? Or why some people use big words when they don't have to? This book invites you to explore questions such as these by reading research about writing, comparing your own writing experiences with those of others, and finding your own answers by conducting research of your own through your own research and writing.

This book does not tell you how to write. It does not contain step-by-step advice about how to draft your paper or how to conduct research. Instead, it introduces you to research about writing conducted in the field of **writing studies**,[1] much as your textbooks in biology or psychology introduce you to the research of those fields. Writing studies researchers study how writing works, how people write, and how best to teach writing. From this book, then, you'll learn *about* the subject — writing — just as you would learn about biology from a biology textbook or about psychology from a psychology textbook. *Writing about Writing* asks you to think about writing as something we *know about*, not just something we *do*. It offers you these kinds of learning:

- Deeper understanding of what's going on with your own writing and how writing works
- Knowledge about writing that you can take with you to help you navigate other writing situations
- Experience engaging with scholarly articles and other research
- The ability to conduct inquiry-driven research on unanswered questions

WHY STUDY WRITING?

Why is it helpful to learn *about* writing rather than simply be told *how* to write? What good will this do you as a writer?

We think that changing what you know *about* writing can change *the way* you write. Much of the research in this book questions everyday assumptions about writing — such as the idea that you can't use your own **voice** in writing for school, or that writing is just easy for some people and hard for others, or that **literacy** is only about how well you can read. If you change your ideas about what writing is *supposed* to be, you're likely to do things differently — more effectively — when you write.

There are additional advantages to studying writing in a writing course:

- Writing is *relevant* to all of us. Most of us do it every day, and all of us live in a world in which writing, reading, and other related uses of language are primary means of communication.
- What you learn about writing now will be directly *useful* to you long after the class ends. In college, at work, and in everyday life, writing well can have a measurable impact on your current and future success.
- You already have a great deal of *experience* with writing and reading, so you are a more knowledgeable investigator of these subjects than you might be of a lot of others.
- Doing research on writing will give you the opportunity to **contribute** *new knowledge* about your subject, not simply gather and repeat what many other people have already said.

---

[1]**Boldface** terms are further defined in the Glossary (p. 885).

TWO STORIES ABOUT WRITING

You might be thinking that we're making writing harder than it has to be: Can't people just tell you how to write for any new situation or task? Even if studying about writing can help you write differently and better, wouldn't it be more direct to simply *tell you the rules* and let you practice and memorize them?

That would work if the traditional story about writing that most of us learn in school were accurate. In that traditional story, "writing" is a basic grammatical skill of transcribing speech to print, a skill that can **transfer** (be used again) unaltered from the situation in which you learn it (high school and college English classes, usually) to any other writing situation. Because, that story goes, the rules of English don't change. English is English, whether you're in a chemistry class or the boardroom of a bank. And, according to that story, what makes good writing is following all the rules and avoiding errors: *Just don't do anything wrong* and your writing will be okay. According to this view of writing, people who are good at writing are people who break the fewest rules and write with the greatest ease; writing is hard because following the rules is hard; so if you can learn the rules, you can write more easily and thus be a good writer. That's the story that the majority of high school graduates seem to have learned. It's likely that no one stood in front of you and told you this story directly; but instead, it is a story that you learned by watching how people around you modeled this behavior. For example, when teachers read your papers and ignored your ideas but corrected your grammatical mistakes, they were telling you this story: Writing is nothing but error-avoidance. When you took standardized tests (like the SAT) and were given a prompt you had never seen before and told to write about it in 30 minutes, and then a stranger read it and ignored your ideas and facts and instead rated you on correctness and organization, they were telling you this story: Writing is not about content; it is about correctness. If you think about the views of writing that you see on the news ("Kids today can't write! Texting is ruining their spelling!") or what you saw teachers and test-makers model, you will start to recognize how widespread this story of writing is.

But there's more than one story about writing. You'll find the college writing instructor who assigned this book probably believes a very different story, one based not on teachers' rulebooks but rather on observation of successful writers and how writing, reading, language, and texts actually work — how people actually experience them. In this other story, "writing" is much fuller and richer. Writing is not just what you say (*content*) but also how you say something (*form*), how you come up with your ideas (*invention*), how you go through the act of thinking and writing (*process*), and whether what you've said and how you've said it successfully meet the current situation (*rhetoric*). In this story, avoiding errors that get in the way of the readers' understanding is only one small part of writing. Writing is about communicating in ways that work, that *do something* in the world. Writing is much more than grammar, and it's also much more than the final text you create; writing is the whole process of creating that text. In this story, there is not one universal set of rules for writing correctly, but rather many sets of *habits* adopted by groups of people using particular texts to accomplish particular ends or activities. For example, the habits and conventions of engineers' writing are vastly different than the habits and conventions of lawyers' writing or your writing for your history class. That means there is *no easily transferable set of rules* from one writing situation to another. What transfers is not *how to write*, but *what to ask about writing*.

This second, alternative story about writing is one you have also been exposed to, but maybe not in school. When you text your friends, for example, you already know that what you say and how you say it matter, and that the text will be successful if your friend reads it and understands it and responds somehow. If your friend ignores it or finds it insulting or can't quite decipher the new shorthand you devised, then it's not "good writing." You also know that when you go to your English class or write a letter to your mother, you can't write the same way you do when you are texting your friends. You know these things even if no one has ever told them to you directly.

This second story about writing — the one that writing scholars believe — is why we think it would not be very helpful to write a book that tries to teach you "how to write." After all, in a "how to write" book you would have to respond to every piece of advice by asking, "How to write *what*, for *whom*, in order to be used *in what way*?" This book doesn't give you easy, quick, or limited advice about how to write, but it instead shows you ways of thinking about how writing works, and how to make informed and effective choices for yourself in each new writing situation.

As a writer you have likely been experiencing the two competing stories about, or "conceptions of," writing throughout much of your life. This might have led to confusing and frustrating experiences with writing. Teachers might have said they want to hear your personal voice and heartfelt opinion on something and then respond only to spelling and comma splices in your papers. School might have turned into a place where writing is simply an opportunity for you to be told that you've made mistakes. But at the same time, you might have a rich writing life through texting and Facebooking, writing fanfiction, writing on gaming chatboards, writing songs or poetry. In those worlds, writing is used to communicate, to share ideas, to get things done. These competing experiences with writing are enacting different conceptions of what writing is, and those conceptions of writing lead you to do different things. If you think that writing is avoiding error, it is unlikely you will spend much time developing ideas. If you think that a reader is going to respond and react to your ideas, you are quite likely to spend a lot of time developing them and thinking about your reader's possible reactions.

Part of the purpose of this book is to give you the language and the ideas to figure out what conceptions of writing you are experiencing and which ones might be most accurate, and what to do about that.

CONCEPTIONS: WITH OUR THOUGHTS WE MAKE THE WORLD

We all have conceptions about writing that come from our life experiences. A **conception** is a belief, an idea about something. For example, you might think that you aren't a very good writer. If we asked you why, you might say because you don't do well on timed writing tests like the SAT or school assessments. Or you might think that good writing is writing that doesn't have any grammatical errors in it. Where did that idea come from? Probably from an English teacher who used a red pen to mark every error in your papers — but gave no feedback on what you were actually writing *about*.

Our conceptions of writing — the stories we tell ourselves about it, what we assume about it — really matter. What you believe about writing directly impacts what you do or are willing to do. If you think you are a bad writer because you struggle with timed writing tests, you might not be willing to try other kinds of writing, or you might not recognize how good you are at coming up with smart ideas when you have a lot of time to think them over. If you think that good writing is writing with no errors, you might struggle to put words on paper (or on the screen) as you attempt to avoid errors. And in the process, you might forget what you wanted to say, or get so frustrated that you give up, or write much less than you would have otherwise.

Many of the readings in this book suggest that some of our cultural beliefs about reading and writing aren't exactly right, and our lives as readers and writers would make a lot more sense if we could see these beliefs as *misconceptions* — that is, as ideas and stories about writing that don't really hold up to interrogation and research. Readings in this book are intended to challenge your everyday ideas about writing; they suggest that writing is much more complicated (and interesting) when we actually pay close attention to how texts work and what readers and writers are doing when they engage them. These readings also suggest that, as a writer and a reader, you usually have a great deal more power, and are less controlled by universal, mysterious rules, than you might have been taught. You can construct different ideas about writing, and you can construct meaning for yourself in ways that can empower you as a writer. And you can choose to operate using different constructions (conceptions) of writing.

Our ideas matter: As Buddha said, "With our thoughts we make the world." Writers *construct* texts by using words and images to develop ideas, and readers *construct* a variety of meanings for a text by bringing their personal experiences and understandings to a text. In this usage, *construct* is a verb. It suggests actions that writers and readers take. But *construct* is not only a verb (conSTRUCT); it is also a noun (CONstruct). **Constructs** (noun) are mental frameworks that people build in order to make sense of the world around them.

So in large part this book intends to help you become aware of and explore your ideas about writing — your conceptions about writing that construct your world — and to put you in touch with other people's ideas and research about writing. Our goal is to help you have robust, healthy, research-based ideas about writing that will make you a more successful writer. "Research-based" ideas are important ideas that have actually been studied and tested, and they have been demonstrated to work for experienced writers.

Considering constructs about writing and assessing whether your ideas about writing are misconceptions might be difficult at times and will require you to be willing to think through ideas that might be uncomfortable.

Threshold Concepts of Writing

Some conceptions of writing matter more than others. Recently, researchers from the United Kingdom, Ray Meyer and Jan Land, identified what they call **threshold concepts** — ideas that are so central to understanding a particular subject that a learner can't move forward in that area without grasping them. However, grasping threshold concepts is hard because they are based in the research of particular fields or areas of study, and that research is often in conflict with popular, commonsense ideas about topics that haven't been tested or thought through carefully.

For example, one of us has been doing a research project with some historians and was surprised to learn that professional historians don't think that studying history is about dates, events, or learning lessons for the future. Rather, the historians said that studying history is about learning to recognize multiple narratives and to see each narrative as an interpretation that must be understood in context. These historians were frustrated that the History Channel and common conversations about history lead people to misunderstand what history is and how to study it. When students engage in their history classes, the historians have to spend a lot of time (years, sometimes) helping students understand what narratives are, what it means to see narratives as someone's interpretation of past events, and how to research the context of the narratives. Until students can do these things, they can't move forward in their study of history at the college level.

As the history example illustrates, when learners are introduced to threshold concepts in different disciplines, they often find them troublesome, and it can take a long time to really grasp them. While learners are struggling with the ideas, they find themselves in a *"liminal" space* — a space where they move back and forth, start to get a handle on the ideas, then realize they don't really have a handle on them. Learning in this liminal space can be quite uncomfortable because learners have to examine their previous ideas and experiences and try to understand something that might conflict with those ideas.

But when learners finally do grasp these threshold concepts, the way they see things is changed — *transformed*, likely for good. Different ideas and experiences make sense and seem related in ways they hadn't before — in other words, learning threshold concepts is what Meyer and Land call an *integrative experience*. When history students understand that history is made up of a set of competing narratives that interpret events in different ways, and that these narratives and events must be understood in context, they start to question everything they see. If they see a news story about the Confederate flag, for example, they recognize that people who take opposing views of it have competing narratives, are examining different pieces of the historical record, and interpreting that historical record in different ways. Instead of asking who is right and who is wrong, new questions emerge — for example, how groups of people can interpret the past in such different ways. These are the kinds of questions that motivate historians to conduct and publish research. When history students finally grasp central threshold concepts, they see and understand the world differently, and find interesting research possibilities through their new perspective.

Threshold concepts of writing are no different than other threshold concepts in their troublesomeness. In some ways, writing threshold concepts may be even more troublesome to learn than threshold concepts in other disciplines. Because everyone writes, and writing is so common in our schools, lives, and daily experiences, by the time we get to a place where we are actually studying writing (usually in college writing classes) we've had a long time to solidify our non-research-based views about writing.

WRITING IS NOT JUST SOMETHING PEOPLE DO, BUT SOMETHING PEOPLE STUDY

In order to really engage with threshold concepts about writing, there is one basic underlying concept that you'll need to grapple with first: that writing is not just something that you *do*, but also something that people *study*. Usually in high school, students write about literature, and instruction in writing is often limited to things like grammar, style, and form. But there is a lot more to writing than that, and there are scholars who study writing for a living. Writing can be studied because it is a complex activity about which little is actually known. (In contrast, in earlier schooling, writing is often treated as a fairly basic, fundamental skill. As you'll learn in the class in which you're using this book, there is *nothing* "basic" about writing.)

Writing scholars want to know things like how we learn to write, how we can teach writing well, how technologies affect our writing processes, and how we use writing to accomplish our goals, communicate, and persuade one another. The study of persuasion goes back a long way, to Aristotle (c. 350 BCE) and before. The formal study of how writing works, though, is more recent, beginning sometime in the 1950s. The activity of writing is difficult to study because people use it for so many different things and go about it in so many different ways. And compared with many other academic fields, the field of writing studies has had only a short time to get started on that research. At first, most study of writing concentrated on student writers, but it gradually became apparent that writing assignments didn't look a lot like writing outside of school, so writing research had to be expanded to more sites and scenes. Throughout this time, some of the main research questions have been fairly stable, and you will find them discussed in various chapters in this book:

- What do we believe to be true about writing, and where do these beliefs come from?
- Do writers think of what to say in their writing through inspiration or through the world around them, or both (in what balance)?
- How does meaning depend on context?
- How does the shape a text takes depend on its rhetorical situation?
- How do writers actually get writing done?
- How can we tell the difference between writing and other kinds of communication such as photo-essays and pictorial instruction manuals? What counts as writing?

While all these are still open questions (requiring more research), there is also much we do know now about writing, and this research can help us better understand what we do as writers, what we need to do, what works, and what doesn't. In other words, if we can recognize that writing isn't just something we *do*, but something we can also learn more *about*, we can be empowered to change our ideas about writing and, in turn, change our writing practices.

We have used the questions of writing studies to guide the content in this book; the answers are, in effect, some of the threshold concepts resulting from these many decades of study about writing. We will next introduce you to the threshold concepts about writing you will encounter in this book. We don't expect you to thoroughly understand these threshold concepts here, in Chapter 1 — and it's likely you are not going to "master" any of them in this class, as they take a long time to enact and understand. But we want you to start to think about them and question the conceptions you are bringing with you, as you delve into these ideas about writing.

TC Writing Is Impacted by Prior Experiences

As we have already illustrated in this chapter, how and why you write, what you think about writing, and how you make sense of texts are impacted by all that you've done and experienced. Your experiences with writing and with literacy (reading and writing) are part of who you are, part of your identity. As Kathleen Blake Yancey explains it, "each writer is a combination of the collective set of different dimensions and traits and features that make us human."[2]

---

[2]Adler-Kassner, Linda, and Elizabeth Wardle, editors. *Naming What We Know: Threshold Concepts of Writing Studies.* Utah State UP, 2015, p. 52.

ACTIVITY 1A | Write Reflectively

Spend about ten minutes writing freely about your most important memories of reading, writing, and speaking. What were your experiences at home and outside school? What were your experiences in school? How do these impact what you believe, feel, and do with writing and reading today?

Our experiences with writing and language start very early — in our homes, with our families — and then are impacted by activities, events, and groups — from clubs, library visits, and religious organizations to online interactions, hobbies, and schooling. We bring this rich, varied, and extensive history of reading and writing practices with us whenever we read, write, or receive feedback on our writing, or give feedback to someone else. When we encounter a new and challenging writing situation or task, we bring all of our previous experiences to bear. Who we are, where we've been, what we've done, the technologies we've used or been exposed to (or not) are all involved in our writing practices, attitudes, strengths, and weaknesses.

Andrea Lunsford, writing researcher and former director of Stanford University's writing program, conducted a study of people's early writing memories, and found that many people "reported something painful associated with writing: being made to sit on their left hands so they had to write right-handed" or "being made to write 'I will not X' a hundred times in punishment for some mistake."[3] Prior experiences with writing create negative or positive feelings about writing, and those attitudes and feelings remain with people throughout their lives. Feelings and ideas can change, of course, but we are all always an accumulation of everything we have experienced and done. If our experiences happen to be those that are valued by the dominant (schooled) culture, we tend to have easier and more positive literacy experiences. But if our experiences do not mirror those of the dominant culture, we can often have very negative feelings about reading, writing, school, and/or ourselves. For example, if we come from a white, English-speaking, middle-class, Midwestern family that had a variety of books at home, we likely started school in the United States with a leg up on reading and speaking the dominant version of English. But if we come from an immigrant family, and our parents speak, for example, Spanish or Portuguese, and we had no books written in English at home, we likely started school without the literacy experiences that teachers expect, speaking and writing with an accent that set us apart.

Remember the earlier claim of this chapter, that thoughts make the world? We might modify that here to say that our thoughts and experiences make our own

---

[3]Adler-Kassner and Wardle, editors. *Naming What We Know*, p. 54.

literate worlds. Thus the accumulation of our experiences with reading and writing impact what we think about writing and what we do as readers and writers, and how we feel about ourselves as writers. We may never have stopped to think why reading and writing in school has been easy or hard for us, why teachers singled us out for praise or criticism, why we loved writing online with friends in Wattpad but dreaded writing for our teachers. But if we stop to think through our experiences with literacy, our feelings and experiences can begin to make more sense. We can be empowered to own and explain them, and to take control of them. For example, instead of feeling like a victim if a teacher criticizes your accent, you might learn to take pride in the fact that you speak several languages, and that you can choose just the right word in any of those languages to express how you feel.

ACTIVITY 1B | Try Thinking Differently

Think of a reading or writing situation when your usual habits didn't work to complete the task or communicate effectively, when you were made to feel like an outsider. Instead of denigrating yourself, ask where your ideas and feelings and practices came from, and how they compared with those of the people around you at the time. Was there something others could have learned to do or understand differently from you and your experiences? Explain.

TC **Writing Helps People Make Meaning and Get Things Done, But There Are Always Constraints**

People use writing to get things done, and they use writing and language to make meaning together. This might seem obvious, but when we have spent the majority of our lives writing for school tasks, as has been the case for most students, we can forget the power that writing has to actually accomplish something with other people. School writing can often be what writing researcher Joseph Petraglia calls "pseudotransactional" — in other words, school writing tasks often pretend (that's the *pseudo* part) to be the kind of writing that communicates with other people (that's the *transactional* part), but really it is often just that: pretend.

ACTIVITY 2A | Write Reflectively

Spend ten minutes writing about a time when you wrote something and it didn't work at all — people didn't understand it, thought you had made terrible mistakes, ignored it, etc. Describe the experience and your feelings about it.

In the rest of our lives outside of school — at work, online, at church, and so on — we know that writing helps us communicate and make meaning with others, and get things done. We know this without being told because we use writing like this all the time. If you are feeling lonely, you might text three friends and see if they want to meet you at the gym later. They text you back and negotiate the activity (maybe they need to study instead, so suggest meeting at the library) and the time (they have a sorority meeting at 6, but could meet you at 8). Together you make meaning and get things done, and your ideas create the world and its activities through the writing you are doing together.

This same principle holds true for all kinds of writing that takes place within and between groups of people. At work, three or four people might be on a deadline to finish a report, and they negotiate how to write that report together; when they turn it in, they may find that their working group gets more funding next year than they had last year. In our sororities, we have written guidelines and rituals that help us know who we are and what we stand for. If we write fanfiction online in Wattpad, hundreds or thousands of people might read and comment on what we write, and we know how to write fanfiction because we have read the examples others have written on Wattpad, and have seen how readers there commented on those examples.

Writing helps people get things done, which makes writing powerful. But how and why particular writing does (or does not) work depends on who the people are, where they come from, what their goals are, what technologies they have available to them, and the kinds of texts (**genres**) they are writing.

There are rules for how groups of people use writing together, and these rules con-strain what writers and readers can do. Sometimes those rules are spoken or written down, sometimes they aren't. But for people to use writing successfully, they have to learn these rules. Think about the example above, of texting your friends to see if they want to join you at the gym later. When you got your first phone and started texting, you didn't receive a list of rules about how to do it. You and your friends learned what worked and what didn't. You learned the shorthand texts that people would understand, and the ones they wouldn't. You learned that it can be easy to mis-interpret some things in text messages, so you probably learned to be more cautious about how you write your texts. You also probably figured out that some goals can't be accomplished through texting (like applying for a job), and that some people don't respond well to texting (like your great-grandmother). Every writing situation has its own rules, and writers must learn them in order to use writing effectively to get things done. The rules might seem arbitrary to outsiders (for example, someone might read your texts and think you are being mean or sloppy, not realizing that you've written a joke acceptable in texting your friends), but those rules are rarely arbitrary. For example, when surgeons write or talk about their work, they have a very specialized vocabulary that helps them be extremely precise and accurate. There is a hierarchy regarding who can say, do, and write when in the hospital, and that hierarchy helps ensure that everyone knows what their job is, and patients are protected.

The same is true in college. As you move to different subjects, you'll find the rules are different for how and what you write, and what you can do with writing. These rules might seem arbitrary, but they aren't. The writing that historians do looks and sounds a certain way in order to help them accomplish their goals as part of an academic discipline. Their writing looks very different from the writing of biologists, whose goals and purposes for writing are quite different.

So writing helps people get things done and make meaning together. But as groups of people spend more and more time together, how and why they use writing in particular ways can be increasingly difficult for outsiders to comprehend. If you know this, and you understand what is happening, you can have an easier time as a newcomer to a situation or a particular form of writing. You'll understand that there are certain questions you need to ask, and you'll need to watch what other people do — and try to discover who does what and when.

ACTIVITY 2B | Try Thinking Differently

In Activity 2A, you reflected on a time when something you wrote didn't work. Go back to that activity and think about the rules for writing that are established when groups of people use writing to help accomplish their goals. Were there unspoken rules that help explain what went wrong in that writing situation for you? Why or why not?

The next time you are in a class and you feel like you can't understand the language or the rules for what you are reading or writing, step back and ask some bigger questions: What is the subject ("discipline" or "field") like? What do the people who participate in that subject study? What do they value? What are they trying to do with their writing? If you don't know, who can you ask? Can understanding these things help you better understand why you're confused?

TC "Good" Writing Is Dependent on Writers, Readers, Situation, Technology, and Use

Whether or not writing is good depends on whether it gets things done, and whether it accomplishes what the writer (and readers) need the writing to accomplish. This threshold concept of writing likely conflicts with a lot of what school writing situations have led you to believe. In school, it's easy to believe that good writing is writing that doesn't have grammatical errors or that follows the directions. But just by looking at examples from your own life, you can start to test and prove that such school-based ideas about writing are not accurate.

ACTIVITY 3A | Write Reflectively

Try to remember a time when a rule or rules you were taught about writing by one authority (teacher, parent, boss) were changed or contradicted by another authority. What was the rule? Did you understand the reason for the change or contradiction at the time? Were you bothered by it? How well was the difference (and the reason for it) explained to you?

Consider what makes writing work when you are texting your friends. Do they think your texts are good if you use full sentences, correct grammar, and spell all words correctly? Probably not — and quite likely, the opposite. If you did those things, texting would take a long time, and your friends might make fun of you. Why? Because good writing is writing that is appropriate to the situation, your purpose as a writer, and the technology you use to write (in this case, typing on a phone makes it inefficient to spell out all the words and write in complete sentences).

Of course, you can't use the rules of good texting when you write job application letters, your history exam, fanfiction, or poetry in your journal. Sometimes, the rules about writing you learned in school do hold true; when you apply for a job, for example, you want to show that you have a good grasp of formal language, that you can punctuate sentences and write clearly, and that you pay attention to details and go back and edit what you've written before sharing it with someone who could choose whether or not to hire you.

But even in cases where more formal and "correct" writing is appropriate, what counts as formal and correct can differ widely across contexts. For example, scientists often write using the passive voice. (In other words, their sentences don't necessarily tell readers who did the action; for example, they may write "Tests were conducted.") One major reason is that scientists value objectivity and group discovery, so the passive voice helps focus on what was done or learned, rather than individuals who did it. But in the humanities, writers are very often discouraged from using the passive voice and told to write to emphasize the action and the person doing the acting. For example, you might hear, "Shakespeare plays with the meaning of words" in a literature class. This is because in fields such as literature and history and philosophy and art, it really does matter who performed an action. Or, to provide another example, think of an investigative reporter with a secret source. The reporter wouldn't write, "John Jones revealed that Hillary Clinton destroyed her e-mails" if the reporter was protecting her sources. One way of concealing the source would be to use passive voice: "Hillary Clinton was accused of destroying her e-mails." So even though both passive and active sentences are grammatically correct, they may be appropriate or inappropriate depending on the situation and readers for whom you are writing.

As you might have guessed by now, the writer isn't the only person making meaning from writing. Readers make meaning, too, based on their own prior experiences, the purpose of the writing, the situation in which they are reading it, and their values and the values of the group(s) they belong to. Your history teacher might find the language you use to write a lab report so unappealing that he or she can't really make a lot of sense of it, and your great-grandmother might find your text messages offensive or incoherent. Readers of the reporter's story on Hillary Clinton might build all sorts of speculation around the passive sentence that doesn't reveal its source: They might think the reporter is dishonest and making it up, or they might conclude that a political opponent is planting an untrue story, or that the newspaper is politically biased — or something else, depending on their experiences, politics, etc. So when you write, it's important to remember not just what you want to say, but who you want to make meaning for and with.

And, of course, today your writing might circulate among many different groups of people whom you may never have thought about as a result of social media and other online platforms. Something you wrote for one purpose and audience might be really effective initially but might not work at all once it is communicated to a different audience at another time. Many a politician or business executive, for example, makes one statement privately to a narrow set of constituents, such as close staff or shareholders — as happened to Mitt Romney, who in the 2012 presidential campaign was secretly recorded calling out 47 percent of voters as people who don't take responsibility for their lives — only to have that private statement become public, and find they must explain it when it is circulated online to an unintended and unsympathetic audience.

This **"contingency"** of writing — the fact that what makes writing good depends on circumstances — can be a hard threshold concept to learn because you've been in school for so long, being taught rules that were treated as universal even though they were actually only contingent — specific to that time and place. However, if you test this threshold concept against your daily experiences writing across different contexts and technologies, you can quickly start to see how accurate it is. And if you can understand this threshold concept, it can help you start to make sense of things that may otherwise really frustrate you. Instead of being upset that your history teacher and your biology teacher want you to write differently, and being confused about "who's right," you can recognize that the differences stem from different ideas about what good writing is — and these ideas are related to what historians and biologists do with writing. They aren't trying to frustrate you; they are trying to help you write like historians or biologists, and sound credible when you do. In other words, understanding this threshold concept can really empower you to see that many kinds of writing can be good, and that you may be better at some kinds than others.

ACTIVITY 3B | Try Thinking Differently

Writing researchers frequently hear students say that they dislike writing for school because it seems to be mostly about following rules and structures, and being judged for failure to observe all the rules correctly. In contrast, students often report preferring self-sponsored writing outside of school (sometimes they call it "creative" writing, sometimes "personal" writing) because they are free to write whatever they like without being constrained by rule structures.

Try this thought experiment: What would your school writing look like if you could approach it as you do "home" or personal writing, and if you could expect the same kind of responses that you receive to your home and school writing? What would you do differently in your school writing? Would you spend more time on it or treat it differently? How would your writing itself change?

TC **Writing Is a Process, All Writers Have More to Learn, and Writing Is Not Perfectible**

In considering that "good" writing depends on a lot of different variables, you start to imagine what you are able to do with writing, and to recognize that you are able to do some things better than others. You might have a pretty easy time writing lab reports, job application letters, and texts to your friends, but a much harder time writing a paper about *Moby Dick* or writing a poem. One reason for this is the threshold concept that what you do and who you are as a writer is informed by your prior experiences. You might have had more practice with certain kinds of writing, you might be fact-oriented, you might have read a lot of nonfiction books but not many novels. There are many reasons why some kinds of writing come more easily to you than other kinds.

ACTIVITY 4A | Write Reflectively

Think of something about writing (not related to grammar or "flow") that you wish you were more confident about. (Grammar and flow are two things students commonly say they want to work on; we want to push you to consider other elements and aspects of writing.) When you've come up with the thing you'd like to work on, explain why: What makes you uncomfortable with what you know about it or how you write right now? What do you imagine you could be doing differently or better?

The good news is that this threshold concept is true for everyone: *all writers* have more to learn. And this concept will remain true for each writer's entire life: Writers *always* have more to learn. Learning is the key — and writers *can always learn to be a little better* at writing something that is not their strong suit. You should feel a kind of freedom in this realization: If you feel like you have a lot more to learn about writing, you're not "behind" or lacking; you're normal.

Writing is a process. It takes time and practice. Writing things that are new to you, writing longer texts, and writing with new kinds of technology all take practice. And no matter how much you practice, what you write will never be perfect. This is, in large part, due to what we discussed in the previous threshold concept: Readers make meaning out of what you write, and the situation in which your writing is read makes a difference in how effective the writing is. There is no such thing as perfect writing; writing is not in the category of things that are perfectible. Rather, it can grow, change, be different, and work for better or worse for the purposes for which you are trying to use it. Still, there are strategies and habits that can help you write more easily, more quickly, more effectively — and asking for feedback is, of course, always a good way to improve.

This understanding of writing should be very liberating because it helps you recognize that good writers aren't born that way; they're made through practice and circumstance. Someone might be a good writer at one kind of thing (like writing horror novels) but not very good at another kind of thing (like writing grant proposals or poems). How you feel about yourself as a writer, and what you do as a writer, can change a lot for the better if you realize that no writers are perfect, good writing depends on the situation, all writers have more to learn, and you can learn things about writing and how to write that can help you write more effectively. If you can stop thinking of yourself as a "bad writer" or a person "who just can't write," you can be freed up to try new things with writing.

ACTIVITY 4B | Try Thinking Differently

If writing is *not perfectible*, then writing is not about "getting it right" (either the first time, or in later tries). If writing is not about "getting it right," then what *is* it about? If you're not prioritizing *perfection* in your writing, what are you prioritizing instead? Try to keep this in mind when you write from now on. How will this change in focus impact how you write and how you feel about yourself as a writer?

Threshold Concepts That Assist Academic Reading and Writing

Many of the readings in this book are about research, and almost all of the individual pieces in this book have been published someplace else before. In most cases, they were published in scholarly journals and books — where expert writing researchers are telling each other about studies they've conducted on writing (as well as literacy, language, discourse, and technology) and what they've found.

Reading texts that are written by expert researchers for other experts is not easy even for your instructor, and such writing won't be easy or quick reading for you at first, either. So we will next introduce you to two threshold concepts that will explicitly help you work with the material in the rest of this book — and in the rest of your academic life. These threshold concepts are about **genres** (recurring kinds of texts) and about the kind of reading that you will do in this book. By learning some principles of genre, you'll be able to more quickly recognize patterns in what even hard-to-read texts are doing, which helps you know what they mean. And by reading *rhetorically*, understanding the readings as people talking to one another in ongoing conversations, you'll have strategies to help you make the most sense you can out of unfamiliar material.

Throughout the rest of this chapter, we'll use the term **rhetorical** more and more. Its meaning, which is complex, will gradually become clearer to you the more we (and you) use it, both here as well as later in the book (especially Chapter 4). For now, we'll simply say that when you see the word "rhetorical" you should think *communication* — anything that has to do with the way people interact, communicate, and persuade each other (make up their minds, and change them). A **rhetorical situation** is any moment in which people are communicating. So why don't we just call it a "communication situation"? Because communication is the *activity* that people are engaged in, but **rhetoric** is the set of principles they're using (often unconsciously) to do it — to shape their communication and make decisions about it. To remind ourselves that writers and speakers are using these principles of rhetoric and doing rhetorical work, we often call them **rhetors**. Remember that these boldface terms all appear in the glossary at the end of this book, which you can turn to any time you need a refresher or additional clarification on how we're using a term.

TC Genres: Writing Responds to Repeating Situations through Recognizable Forms

In this book you will find types of readings and texts you may never have encountered before. These strange encounters happen to you not just in this class, of course, but throughout your life. There are many different ways to write about things, and as you encounter new situations and groups of people who use writing in different ways to accomplish their goals, you will always encounter new kinds of texts that you haven't encountered before. Sometimes this can be fun (as in the earlier example of getting your first phone and learning about texting, or finding Wattpad and learning about fanfiction), sometimes it can be frustrating (maybe reading a novel from an earlier time period), and sometimes it can seem easy but then turn out to be difficult (as with resumes and cover letters).

All of these different kinds of texts have names because they are kinds of writing that recur, happening over and over because they facilitate particular functions in life. Resumes, wedding invitations, birthday cards, parking tickets, textbooks, novels, text messages, magazine cover stories — these are all constantly recurring kinds of writing. In other words, if a particular writing situation and resulting need for communication happens again and again, prompting writers to respond (for example, a need to apply for a job), then certain kinds of writing come into existence to respond to that recurring situation (like resumes). We call such recurring text-types *genres*, which are "typified rhetorical actions in response to recurrent situations or situation-types."[4]

ACTIVITY 5A | Write Reflectively

Take out the syllabi that you've collected from your different classes during the first week or two of school this year. Look at them all and then answer these questions:

- What *situation* calls for the syllabus to be written?
- What *content* is typically contained in a syllabus?
- What does a syllabus *look like; what shape* does a syllabus take?
- How is a syllabus *organized*?
- What *tone* is used? Is the language *formal* or *informal*?

You'll notice that although syllabi are similar, they can be very different, too. What is the *common denominator* — what do you think makes a syllabus a syllabus, even though individual syllabi differ?

Genres do a lot of work for you as a writer. Think about the situation we discussed before the activity: People have to apply for jobs all the time, and they have a pretty good idea of how to do this through resumes and cover letters because so many other people before them have done the same thing. But what if there was no agreed upon way for people to apply for jobs? What if no conventions for doing that had ever come into being? You as a job seeker would have no idea what you should do when you want a job; actually, much worse, every single option would be open to

---

[4]Freedman, Aviva. "Situating 'Genre' and Situated Genres: Understanding Student Writing from a Genre Perspective." *Genre and Writing: Issues, Arguments, Alternatives*, edited by Wendy Bishop and Hans Ostrom, Boynton/Cook Publishers, 1997, pp. 179–89. Also referenced in this section: Bazerman, Charles. "The Life of Genre, the Life in the Classroom." *Genre and Writing: Issues, Arguments, Alternatives*, pp. 19–26.

you. You could sing a song, write a haiku, send a carrier pigeon, make a painting . . . really, you could do anything, and you'd have no way to know what option was best. It would take a really long time to do anything. This wouldn't be efficient, and it would be very stressful for you as a rhetor.

So genres emerge because rhetors start to find ways to respond to the recurring situation that seem to work pretty well, and other rhetors keep using them and tweaking them. Because job seekers found that listing all their previous jobs on a piece of paper was helpful, and because employers found this helpful too, people kept doing it. There are a lot of ways to make a resume (check out the range of templates for resumes in your word-processing software), but there are some limitations that at least make it easier for you as a resume writer to know that you could do *this* (for example, organize by date) or *this* (for example, organize by skill) but *not that* (for example, write a haiku). In the movie *The Patriot*, Mel Gibson teaches his children to shoot, telling them, "Aim small, miss small." In a way, this is what genres help you do when you write; they give you a limited area to aim for so that you have a better chance of success.

There are a lot of reasons to think about this threshold concept that *writers over time create "typical" or expected responses to situations* that come up again and again. For one thing, understanding this helps you look for patterns when you encounter new situations and new kinds of texts. The genre might look strange and new to you, but if it's a typical or expected response to a recurring situation, then that means you can find out what the recurring situation is and what previous responses have looked like. In other words, you aren't completely on your own in a strange world. There are maps, if you know to look for them and can figure out how to read them.

Think for a minute about this idea of genres as maps to new situations. For maps to work, you have to ask certain questions. *Where am I and where do I want to go?* If you don't know these things, you'll find yourself looking at a map of the entire world that is simply not helpful in your current situation. If you know that you are in Orlando and you want to go to Key West, then you know that there are maps for this situation. You'll want a map of Florida, particularly southeast Florida. But you also need to know what to look for on the map and what the various symbols mean. You'll need to know how to read this map. You'll need to know north from south, east from west, highways from back roads, toll roads from free roads. When you first start driving, you might end up getting lost a few times before you can make sense of the map.

The other thing to remember about maps is that they change. They change for all sorts of reasons, including technology. You might never have used a paper map before, since today's maps are on smartphones. You might never have had to look at a paper map and its key to figure out what you are seeing, because your smartphone does this for you. Maps change, and people have to figure out how to read new kinds of maps. Ask your parents or grandparents whether they find it easier to read paper maps or maps on their smartphones, and you'll see that what seems easy to you is not easy or obvious to everyone else. What's on the maps changes across time (as roads have been paved, as federal highways have been created) and for different purposes (sailors use completely different maps than vacationers, and both sailors and vacationers use maps that are completely different from those used by forest rangers).

Maps on smartphones that tell you what to do have some advantages over paper maps — they make you do less work, there is less for you to figure out, you can drive and listen to directions at the same time. But relying too much on your smartphone can have serious disadvantages as well. For example, if your phone dies or you lose service, you won't have any idea where you are. You might not know north from south, or what to do with the paper map that you have to stop and buy at the gas station in the middle of the Everglades. So relying on them without thinking for yourself can leave you stranded and lost. Genres are the same way. They are maps, but not maps that you should rely on rigidly without thinking for yourself about what to do in any writing situation.

Genres, just like maps, are extremely helpful *if* you know how to read them and remember that they change across time and for different purposes. Like maps, genres aren't rigid and formulaic. You can always do something different with writing, just like you can choose a different kind of map, or a different route on your map: "Rules of a genre do not specify precisely how a rhetorical act is to be performed. *A genre is not formulaic*; there is always another strategy that a rhetor can use to meet the requirements of the situation. *But a genre establishes bounded options for rhetors in situations.*"[5]

What questions should you ask when you encounter a new genre? Try to discern the similarities in rhetorical situations (the situations calling for the genre you are encountering) and the rhetoric constructed in response to those situations (the genre itself). According to Sonja Foss, there are four kinds of questions to ask when looking at a new or unfamiliar genre:

- *Questions about situational elements:* What conditions (situations) call for the genre? What prompts this sort of document to be written? What is the **exigence** — the need or reason for a given action or communication?
- *Questions about substantive characteristics (content):* What sort of content (substance) is typically contained in this genre? What do these texts tend to talk about or say?
- *Questions about stylistic characteristics (form):* What form does this sort of genre take? What does it look like? How is it organized? What language does it use? What tone does it take?

---

[5]Foss, Sonja. *Rhetorical Criticism: Exploration and Practice*. 4th ed., Waveland Press, 2008, pp. 231, 255.

- *Questions about the organizing principle:* What makes this genre what it is? What are the common denominators of the genre? What makes a resume a resume, for example? Of each characteristic that you identify in the first three questions above, you might ask, "If I took out this characteristic, would it still be recognizable as this genre?"

GENRE FEATURES OF SCHOLARLY ARTICLES: JOHN SWALES'S "CREATE A RESEARCH SPACE" (CARS) MODEL OF RESEARCH INTRODUCTIONS

Researcher John Swales, who worked on genre analysis of scholarly articles like the ones in this book, looked at thousands of examples of the articles that researchers write to see what their introductions might share in common. He found that introductions contain similar "moves" that you as a reader can look for in order to help orient yourself when you start reading. On the next few pages, we provide a summary of his research specifically to help you navigate some of the scholarly articles you will encounter.

Sometimes getting through the introduction of a research article can be the most difficult part of reading it. In his CARS model, which we have adapted from his book *Genre Analysis,*[6] Swales describes three "moves" that almost all research introductions make. We're providing a summary of Swales's model here as a kind of shorthand to help you in both reading research articles and writing them. Identifying these moves in introductions to the articles you read in this book will help you understand the authors' projects better from the outset. When you write your own papers, making the same moves yourself will help you present your own arguments clearly and convincingly. So read through the summary now, but be sure to return to it often for help in understanding the selections in the rest of this book.

Move 1: Establishing a Territory

In this move, the author sets the context for his or her research, providing necessary background on the topic. This move includes one or more of the following steps:

Step 1: Claiming Centrality

The author asks the **discourse community** (the audience for the paper) to accept that the research about to be reported is part of a lively, significant, or well-established research area. To claim centrality the author might write:

"Recently there has been a spate of interest in . . ."

"Knowledge of X has great importance for . . ."

---

[6]Swales, John M. *Genre Analysis: English in Academic and Research Settings.* Cambridge UP, 1990.

This step is used widely across the academic disciplines, though less in the physical sciences than in the social sciences and the humanities.

and/or

Step 2: Making Topic Generalizations

The author makes statements about current knowledge, practices, or phenomena in the field. For example:

> "The properties of X are still not completely understood."

> "X is a common finding in patients with . . ."

and/or

Step 3: Reviewing Previous Items of Research

The author relates what has been found on the topic and who found it. For example:

> "Both Johnson and Morgan claim that the biographical facts have been misrepresented."

> "Several studies have suggested that . . . (Gordon, 2003; Ratzinger, 2009)."

> "Reading to children early and often seems to have a positive long-term correlation with grades in English courses (Jones, 2002; Strong, 2009)."

In citing the research of others, the author may use *integral citation* (citing the author's name in the sentence, as in the first example above) or *nonintegral citation* (citing the author's name in parentheses only, as in the second and third examples above). The use of different types of verbs (e.g., *reporting verbs* such as "shows" or "claims") and verb tenses (past, present perfect, or present) varies across disciplines.

Move 2: Establishing a Niche

In this move, the author argues that there is an open "niche" in the existing research, a space that needs to be filled through additional research. The author can establish a niche in one of four ways:

Option 1. Counter-Claiming

The author refutes or challenges earlier research by making a counter-claim. For example:

> "While Jones and Riley believe X method to be accurate, a close examination demonstrates their method to be flawed."

Option 2. Indicating a Gap

The author demonstrates that earlier research does not sufficiently address all existing questions or problems. For example:

> "While existing studies have clearly established X, they have not addressed Y."

Option 3. Question-Raising

The author asks questions about previous research, suggesting that additional research needs to be done. For example:

> "While Jones and Morgan have established X, these findings raise a number of questions, including . . ."

Option 4. Continuing a Tradition

The author presents the research as a useful extension of existing research. For example:

> "Earlier studies seemed to suggest X. To verify this finding, more work is urgently needed."

Move 3: Occupying a Niche

In this move, the author turns the niche established in Move 2 into the *research space* that he or she will fill; that is, the author demonstrates how he or she will substantiate the counterclaim made, fill the gap identified, answer the question(s) asked, or continue the research tradition. The author makes this move in several steps, described below. The initial step (1A or 1B) is obligatory, though many research articles stop after that step.

Step 1A: Outlining Purposes

The author indicates the main purpose(s) of the current article. For example:

> "In this article I argue . . ."
>
> "The present research tries to clarify . . ."

or

Step 1B: Announcing Present Research

The author describes the research in the current article. For example:

> "This paper describes three separate studies conducted between March 2008 and January 2009."

Step 2: Announcing Principal Findings

The author presents the main conclusions of his or her research. For example:

> "The results of the study suggest . . ."
>
> "When we examined X, we discovered . . ."

Step 3: Indicating the Structure of the Research Article

The author previews the organization of the article. For example:

"This paper is structured as follows . . ."

ACTIVITY 5B | Try Thinking Differently

Many students have been taught a rigid formula for how to write an essay for school. One extremely common formula is the "five paragraph essay" (intro, three body paragraphs, conclusion). Some students have also been taught a formula for what sentences each *paragraph* should contain. In a "Schaeffer" paragraph, for instance, you would have been taught to use five sentences: topic, concrete detail, commentary, commentary, and closing.

Consider whether you've been taught a specific formula for writing essays; then try actively changing the formula, moving from a (false) universal "rule" about what the essay must contain to a more genre-like sense of "mapping" where you have a guideline that can be shaped to fit specific circumstances. For example, if you were taught a rule about where the "thesis statement" must go in an essay, think about how you could *change* that rule if you knew it didn't always apply. What would happen if you put the thesis statement someplace else? What would happen if you turned the thesis statement into a focused question? What's your rule, how would you change it, and why?

Look Forward to the Rest of This Book

Try asking questions we borrowed from Sonja Foss (pp. 20–21) about genres when you approach new situations and genres, including in this class and in this book: Why were these texts written and for whom? What content do they usually seem to contain? What do they tend to look like? How do they tend to be organized? Many of the readings in this book are long and somewhat difficult because they are written for audiences such as teachers and researchers. Don't be alarmed by this. Recognize that scholarly articles are a genre, and each instance of a genre has similarities with other instances of that genre, even across apparent differences. Pick a few of the scholarly articles in this book and ask the above questions about them before you dive into reading one in depth.

TC **Rhetorical Reading: Texts Are People Talking**

This book asks you to read some complicated, difficult, perhaps "dry" texts — the same kinds that Swales explains with his CARS model in the previous section. He analyzes the genre-based ("generic") paths that scholarly articles follow in establishing a territory, establishing a niche, and occupying the niche in order to *contribute* to knowledge in a field. Most of the readings in this book do that. In this section, we want you to think more about *why* the CARS model exists, and works, because considering this will help you greatly in making sense of and finding value in the texts in this book. It will also introduce you to the threshold concept, broadly applicable beyond school, that *when we read texts, we are interacting with other people.* Texts are people talking.

ACTIVITY 6A | Write Reflectively

First, make a list of some kinds of texts that you easily think of as people talking to each other (example: texting). Second, make a list of some texts that you haven't thought about before as people talking (example: textbooks). Try to systematically think through all the kinds of texts you regularly encounter in your everyday life.

When you've made these two lists, try to explain why you see the texts this way. What do the texts that you see as people talking have in common? How about the texts you haven't thought of as people talking before? In particular, why do you think the texts on the nonconversation list don't seem to be about people communicating with each other?

The CARS model works because scholarly texts represent turns in an *ongoing conversation* — they are people talking back and forth to each other. At first that idea might sound obvious — *of course* texts are people talking. But stop and think about how we actually act around texts every day, and you'll see that we're much more likely to treat "school" writing — textbooks, articles, reference materials such as encyclopedias and dictionaries, anything you could be tested on — as *information* that *just exists*, rather than as *people testing new ideas out on each other.* When was the last time you read a dictionary definition — or a textbook — and thought, "Someone is trying to *talk to me* to *persuade me* of these ideas"? When was the last time you tried to picture the actual writer of a *WebMD* article, or considered the hobbies of whoever wrote the last *Wikipedia* article you read? Most of us never give these writers a second thought. Have you noticed the names of any of the authors of the textbooks in your classes this term — or did you just think of the words as coming from a book, not from people? Given how we usually interact with school texts, we think you will agree that it is not such a commonsense idea to say that scholarly texts are people speaking to each other in an ongoing conversation. But that is what is happening.

When you're in a face-to-face conversation, human instinct is to know or find out who you're talking to, and why they want to talk. But as readers we've been taught to think differently about some written texts — not to pay attention to who's talking, or why. Early schooling tends to teach us to think of facts and information as existing independent of *people* — to suggest that knowledge is independent of the people thinking about it. One of the threshold concepts we want you to encounter in your college writing class is a new way of thinking about texts: that *texts are people talking;* that rather than texts having a single fixed meaning, *readers construct a text's meaning from interaction between the words of the text, the ideas already in the reader's mind, and the context* in which the text is written and read. *People* are where the meaning in texts comes from — not from the texts themselves. As rhetors, we *construct* a meaning for each text we read. This is different from the typical assumption that meaning exists *in the text* and when we read we simply "absorb" or "pick up" that preexisting meaning.

How do we know that a fixed meaning isn't "in" writing texts? Just as is the case with writing, reading is something people not only do, but *study*. The "physics" of reading are pretty fascinating. For example, when we track readers' eyes moving across the page they're reading, we discover that fluent readers don't actually read word by word. They treat texts like parkour experts treat buildings, covering ground (encountering words) in big leaps (reading whole phrases or lines at a time) and using their momentum (fast reading) to glide over "sketchy" areas where the footing isn't good (where the meaning isn't immediately clear).

And just as with writing, we have explanations (*theories*) of reading that help us make sense of the research. One theory and term that helps us remember the actual nature of reading as constructing meaning is *rhetorical reading*. The term "rhetorical" emphasizes the way that human interaction depends on context and situation — using this term reminds us that meaning comes from *interaction* between text, context, writers, and readers with specific backgrounds in specific situations. To better prepare you for reading the selections in this book, and how reading is rhetorical, we can start by asking, why does it matter and what does it mean that "texts are people talking"?

People Have Motives

Nonfiction texts say what they say because their writers are motivated by a variety of purposes. If you've written a resume, you already know this: Part of your choice of how to write the resume is based on your motivation for writing it (presumably, getting a job you want). So we will say the resume is a *motivated* text. If you were to click through every nonfiction text you can think of, you wouldn't be able to find a nonmotivated one. Thus, you will construct one meaning if you ignore the motivated nature of a text — what its writer's particular motives and purposes were in shaping it as they did — and you will construct another, richer and wiser, meaning if you do pay attention to motive. You'll also construct different meanings of a text if you ascribe different motivations to it. Does "It's cold in here!" mean the speaker is complaining, or asking for the heat to be turned up? Whether you think it means one, the other, or both will depend heavily on what you think motivates the statement to begin with.

Texts Are Called into Being by a Need Shared between Writers and Readers

One important concept for reading rhetorically (and one which Keith Grant-Davie's piece in Chapter 4 explains further) is **exigence**, or whatever need for the text to exist is built into the rhetorical situation. The exigence for a *Wikipedia* article on "space-flight" is not too complicated: (1) spaceflight is a concept in need of explaining;

(2) *Wikipedia* tries to be a thorough and complete source of explanations of concepts; so (3) *Wikipedia* needs an article on spaceflight. The "situation" in which people use *Wikipedia* to gain a quick understanding of a huge range of subjects "calls" the space-flight article into being. Exigence is not quite the same as a writer's motives, though exigence and motives can overlap. In this example, the motives of the writer of the spaceflight article might be (1) to show what they know about spaceflight, (2) to write a really nicely done article on spaceflight, and (3) to make *Wikipedia* more complete. There are interesting gaps between the way the situation calls the article into being, and the writer's motives for "answering" that call. As with motives themselves, when readers seek out the exigence for a given text — why is there a text at all, since texts don't write themselves and it is easier not to write than to write — they construct a different and fuller meaning of the text than when they don't consider exigence at all.

Readers Have Needs, Values, and Expectations of Texts

Readers of resume or *Wikipedia* genres meet those texts with at least four kinds of knowledge or ideas already formed. The first is simply the experiential background knowledge they have of the world as a whole and of how texts and reading work. Circles are round, trees grow upward, there's no air in space, etc. And again as with writing, your current practices and expectations of reading are shaped by your past reading experiences. If you are used to a particular genre being dull and loathsome, you will expect another example of that genre to keep being so . . . and your mind will make it so.

The other three kinds of knowledge readers bring to texts are much more specific to the interaction, or conversation, they and the text are taking part in:

- The reader has a particular *need* related to that text. They need a resume in order to help them make a hire, so they need the resume to convey a particular range of information.
- The reader has specific sets of *values* — some readers, for example, might value conciseness while others might more highly value depth of information.
- The reader has specific *expectations* for what the text will do and be, many of which are genre-based. A resume should look like a resume, a *Wikipedia* article should work like a *Wikipedia* article. Some other expectations come with a given situation and context. If you're reading a *Wikipedia* article on spaceflight in 2015, you expect it to talk about not just the 1960s NASA moonflight program, but about current private endeavors like SpaceX and SpaceShipOne.

What do readers' needs, values, and expectations mean for reading as conversation, and for reading the articles in this book? Most writers and readers who have graduated from high school have an instinctive awareness that writers shape their texts to meet their readers' expectations. When you write a resume, you spell-check it extensively. Why? Because, as you read earlier in this chapter, that writing context sees "good" writing as including extremely careful attention to detail in order to create typo-free writing. You know that readers *expect* a resume to be free of typos, that readers don't *value* the work of job applicants without this attention to detail, and that readers believe they *need* this genre to help assess whether an applicant is capable of that kind of attention to detail. So as the writer, you proofread the resume — *anticipating* the reader's needs, values, and expectations, and trying to meet them.

In turn, as a reader, part of the way you're constructing the meaning of a text is by trying to get a sense of *how* the writer has anticipated the reader. Texts carry traces of this anticipation. For example, academics are very skeptical readers and don't like overstatements or overgeneralizations. Knowing this, writers for academic readers tend to *hedge* their claims by using *qualifiers* such as "might," "may," "probably," "sometimes," "perhaps," and other words to indicate they're not claiming certainty. That's a trace of a writer anticipating a reader's values and accommodating them.

Context Shapes the Construction of a Text's Meaning

Context tells you even more about how the writer probably tried to anticipate the reader. An extended example: 2015 and 2016 saw a terrible string of police shootings of unarmed or already-arrested suspects. Increasingly, such shootings are captured on video that is released to the public before investigations of the shootings are completed. The videos, news coverage, and endless public commentary create a specific context into which official investigative reports of a shooting are later released. If readers of the report know of this context in which the report was written, they can use that context to make some educated guesses about why some aspects of the report are written the way they are — because the writers anticipate the context as well, and shape their text to meet it. If a video makes it look to the viewing public as if the shooting victim was raising his hands, and that belief has entered the context of the overall dispute, then a report finding that the victim was reaching for a weapon will anticipate the counterargument already in the context and be written to address that specific context. As a reader, when you construct the meaning of such a report, you'll construct different meanings if you look for ways the text has been written to fit its context, versus if you just assume that the text has no context at all and that the writers didn't think so either.

That example leads us to a final principle of rhetorical reading: That the meaning we construct of texts depends in part on their contexts. In the same way that the utterance "It's really cold in here" means "Please turn up the heat" in one context (a physically cold room where people have access to climate controls), "I wish we could turn up the heat" in another context (same room, but no access to climate controls), and "Wow, the people in this room really don't like each other!" in a third context (where the room is not cold at all but people are visibly "chilly" toward one another or have a public history of disliking one another), a text's context shapes the meaning we construct of the text. Put again in terms of conversation: Context shapes what the conversation means.

ACTIVITY 6B | Try Thinking Differently

Most of us, in our everyday approaches to reading, assume that meaning "lives in" the text we're reading, and that we just "absorb" or "extract" or "see" the meaning that's there. When you read, try thinking instead that you're *making* the meaning of the text, building it from the ground up. To help you see from this perspective, ask these questions of what you're reading:

- Who is the writer of this text? What are the writer's motives for writing it?
- How does this text emerge from some "need" in the situation shared between you as the reader and the text's writer?
- What needs, values, and expectations do you bring to the text you're reading?
- How is context — the situation in which the text is written and that in which it will be read, its history, and your history as a reader — shaping the meaning you build from the text?
- How can this text be understood as a "turn" in a conversation? Can you see yourself as talking with, interacting with, its writer?

Look Forward to the Rest of This Book

A number of texts in this book focus explicitly on reading or connect to it. Reading these selections and considering their ideas is one way that you will continue to stretch your thinking about how reading works. But we also want to encourage you to look for places in all the readings where authors refer to other authors in this book or elsewhere. Start making notes when you see authors directly or indirectly responding to something that another author has written. You'll start to see this happening frequently, especially (but not only) at the beginning of scholarly articles when they are making the moves that John Swales called "establishing a territory" and "establishing a niche." See if this helps you see that the articles you are reading aren't really as "dry" as you might have feared they would be. We've included author photos with each reading to make it even easier for you to imagine the words you are reading being spoken by actual people, who are talking to other actual people, some of whom you have read, and whose faces you can see. We've also included images of the book or journal covers where the readings originally appeared to give you a sense of the publication context.

A Different Kind of Research, Argument, and Reading

One of the biggest differences between the readings in this book and what you might encounter in a traditional textbook is that very little of what you'll read here could be considered *fact*. Rather, it's *argument*. But not the kind of argument you have with a sibling over whose turn it is to take out the trash, and not the kind of argument frustrated people might have over whose fault it is that their cars collided in an intersection.

The readings here are doing a kind of research we call *scholarly inquiry*. It is, and *means to be*, imperfect, incomplete, inconclusive, and provisional. It doesn't offer easy or full answers. It is question- and problem-driven. It includes a great deal of personal opinion rather than clear, objective facts.

How can this be? The point of most scholarly inquiry isn't to gather and transmit *existing* knowledge; rather, in scholarly inquiry, researchers come together to try a lot of different approaches to the same problem, and then, through argument *as conversation*, gradually develop consensus about what the best explanation of, or solution to, the problem is.

Stuart Greene's piece "Argument as Conversation" (p. 31) will help you see how the selections in the rest of the book argue differently than texts you might be more familiar with. We offer this selection as an introduction to the ongoing scholarly conversations about writing, research, and inquiry — conversations in which they, and now you, are an essential part. Greene is asking you to read academic arguments rhetorically, as conversations, in the ways that we just outlined in the rhetorical reading section (pp. 24–29). After Greene, Richard Straub, in "Responding — Really Responding — to Other Students' Writing" (p. 44), asks you to think similarly about reading the texts written by your classmates. Whatever you are reading, whether published or unpublished, whether a first draft or a last draft, try to imagine people in conversation with one another, trying to make meaning.

Writers and researchers don't work alone. They need readers, other writers, and other researchers to give them feedback. Part of your journey in this class will probably be to help your classmates as they research and write, and engage them in a conversation so that they can get better at what they are trying to do. Thus, this class will likely ask you to read not only the scholarly texts in this book, but the drafts created by your classmates. To help you with the kind of reading necessary to give feedback that helps your classmates develop their drafts, we've included Straub's piece, which is written directly to students regarding how to respond to their classmates' writing.

Argument as Conversation

The Role of Inquiry in Writing a Researched Argument

Stuart Greene

STUART GREENE

Framing the Reading

In "Argument as Conversation," Stuart Greene explains how scholarly inquiry is a different kind of research and argument from the kinds we encounter in our everyday lives or (for most of us) in earlier schooling. The principles that Greene discusses — research as *conversational inquiry*, where an *issue* and *situation* contribute to *framing* a problem a particular way, and where researchers seek not to collect information but to generate new knowledge in *a social process* — are the ideas and activities that drive the entire college or university where you're studying right now. They work in every field where scholarly research is happening, from anthropology to zoology.

In this book, you'll apply these principles specifically in terms of research on writing, literacy, language, communication, and related fields. As Greene suggests in his discussion of context, you'll "weave" your experiences with research that's already been done on questions and issues related to them. The research you do on your own may even offer new insights into long-running questions about these subjects.

Getting Ready to Read

Before you read, do at least one of the following activities:

- Think about how you define *argument*. How is the word used in everyday conversation? What do you think the word means in an academic setting? What's the difference between the two?

Greene, Stuart. "Argument as Conversation: The Role of Inquiry in Writing a Researched Argument." *The Subject Is Research,* edited by Wendy Bishop and Pavel Zemliansky, Boynton/Cook Publishers, 2001, pp. 145–64.

- Have a conversation with a classmate on the following topic: How would you say *argument* and *conversation* relate to each other? Can some arguments be conversational and some conversations argumentative, or is no crossover possible? Provide examples, and be sure to explain your terms as precisely as possible.

As you read, consider the following questions to help you focus on particularly important parts of the article:

- Who is Greene's audience? Who, in other words, is the "you" he addresses? How do you know?
- How does Greene structure his article? If you were to pull out the major headings, would the outline created from them be useful in any way?
- What kinds of support does Greene use for his claims? What other texts does he refer to? Is this support relevant to his claims and sufficient to prove them?

ARGUMENT IS VERY MUCH a part of what we do every day: We confront 1 a public issue, something that is open to dispute, and we take a stand and support what we think and feel with what we believe are good reasons. Seen in this way, argument is very much like a conversation. By this, I mean that making an argument entails providing good reasons to support your viewpoint, as well as counterarguments, and recognizing how and why readers might object to your ideas. The metaphor of conversation emphasizes the social nature of writing. Thus inquiry, research, and writing arguments are intimately related. If, for example, you are to understand the different ways others have approached your subject, then you will need to do your "homework." This is what Doug Brent (1996) means when he says that research consists of "the looking-up of facts in the context of other worldviews, other ways of seeing" (78).

In learning to argue within an academic setting, such as the one you probably 2 find yourself in now, it is useful to think about writing as a form of inquiry in which you convey your understanding of the claims people make, the questions they raise, and the conflicts they address. As a form of inquiry, then, writing begins with problems, conflicts, and questions that you identify as important. The questions that your teacher raises and that you raise should be questions that are open to dispute and for which there are not prepackaged answers. Readers within an academic setting expect that you will advance a scholarly conversation and not reproduce others' ideas. Therefore, it is important to find out who else has confronted these problems, conflicts, and questions in order to take a stand within some ongoing scholarly conversation. You will want to read with an eye toward the claims writers make, claims that they are making with respect to you, in the sense that writers want you to think and feel in a certain way. You will want to read others' work critically, seeing if the reasons writers use to support their arguments are what you would consider good reasons. And finally, you will want to consider the possible counterarguments to the claims writers make and the views that call your own ideas into question.

> *The questions that your teacher raises and that you raise should be questions that are open to dispute and for which there are not prepackaged answers.*

Like the verbal conversations you have with others, effective arguments never take place in a vacuum; they take into account previous conversations that have taken place about the subject under discussion. Seeing research as a means for advancing a conversation makes the research process more *real*, especially if you recognize that you will need to support your claims with evidence in order to persuade readers to agree with you. The concept and practice of research arises out of the specific social context of your readers' questions and skepticism.

Reading necessarily plays a prominent role in the many forms of writing that you do, but not simply as a process of gathering information. This is true whether you write personal essays, editorials, or original research based on library research. Instead, as James Crosswhite suggests in his book *The Rhetoric of Reason*, reading "means making judgments about which of the many voices one encounters can be brought together into productive conversation" (131).

When we sit down to write an argument intended to persuade someone to do or to believe something, we are never really the first to broach the topic about which we are writing. Thus, learning how to write a researched argument is a process of learning how to enter conversations that are already going on in written form. This idea of writing as dialogue—not only between author and reader but between the text and everything that has been said or written beforehand—is important. Writing is a process of balancing our goals with the history of similar kinds of communication, particularly others' arguments that have been made on the same subject. The conversations that have already been going on about a topic are the topic's historical context.

Perhaps the most eloquent statement of writing as conversation comes from Kenneth Burke (1941) in an oft-quoted passage:

> Imagine that you enter a parlor. You come late. When you arrive, others have long preceded you, and they are engaged in a heated discussion, a discussion too heated for them to pause and tell you exactly what it is about. In fact the discussion had already begun long before any of them got there, so that no one present is qualified to retrace for you all the steps that had gone before. You

listen for a while, until you decide that you have caught the tenor of the argument; then you put in your oar. Someone answers; you answer him; another comes to your defense; another aligns himself against you, to either the embarrassment or gratification of your opponent, depending on the quality of your ally's assistance. However, the discussion is interminable. The hour grows late, you must depart, with the discussion still vigorously in progress. (110–111)

As this passage describes, every argument you make is connected to other arguments. Every time you write an argument, the way you position yourself will depend on three things: which previously stated arguments you share, which previously stated arguments you want to refute, and what new opinions and supporting information you are going to bring to the conversation. You may, for example, affirm others for raising important issues, but assert that they have not given those issues the thought or emphasis that they deserve. Or you may raise a related issue that has been ignored entirely.

ENTERING THE CONVERSATION

To develop an argument that is akin to a conversation, it is helpful to think of writing as a process of understanding conflicts, the claims others make, and the important questions to ask, not simply as the ability to tell a story that influences readers' ways of looking at the world or to find good reasons to support our own beliefs. The real work of writing a researched argument occurs when you try to figure out the answers to the following:

- What topics have people been talking about?
- What is a relevant problem?
- What kinds of evidence might persuade readers?
- What objections might readers have?
- What is at stake in this argument? (What if things change? What if things stay the same?)

In answering these questions, you will want to read with an eye toward identifying an *issue*, the *situation* that calls for some response in writing, and framing a *question*.

Identify an Issue

An issue is a fundamental tension that exists between two or more conflicting points of view. For example, imagine that I believe that the best approach to educational reform is to change the curriculum in schools. Another person might suggest that we need to address reform by considering social and economic concerns. One way to argue the point is for each writer to consider the goals of education that they share, how to best reach those goals, and the reasons why their approach might be the best one to follow. One part of the issue is (*a*) that some people believe that educational reform should occur through changes in the curriculum; the second part is (*b*) that some people believe that reform should occur at the socioeconomic level. Notice that in defining different parts of an issue, the conflicting claims may not necessarily invalidate each other. In fact, one could argue that reform at the levels of curriculum and socioeconomic change may both be effective measures.

Keep in mind that issues are dynamic and arguments are always evolving. One of my students felt that a book he was reading placed too much emphasis on school-based learning and not enough on real-world experience. He framed the issue in this way: "We are not just educated by concepts and facts that we learn in school. We are educated by the people around us and the environments that we live in every day." In writing his essay, he read a great deal in order to support his claims and did so in light of a position he was writing against: "that education in school is the most important type of education."

Identify the Situation

It is important to frame an issue in the context of some specific situation. Whether curricular changes make sense depends on how people view the problem. One kind of problem that E. D. Hirsch identified in his book *Cultural Literacy* is that students do not have sufficient knowledge of history and literature to communicate well. If that is true in a particular school, perhaps the curriculum might be changed. But there might be other factors involved that call for a different emphasis. Moreover, there are often many different ways to define an issue or frame a question. For example, we might observe that at a local high school, scores on standardized tests have steadily decreased during the past five years. This trend contrasts with scores during the ten years prior to any noticeable decline. Growing out of this situation is the broad question, "What factors have influenced the decline in standardized scores at this school?" Or one could ask this in a different way: "To what extent have scores declined as a result of the curriculum?"

The same principle applies to Anna Quindlen's argument about the homeless in her commentary "No Place Like Home," which illustrates the kinds of connections an author tries to make with readers. Writing her piece as an editorial in the *New York Times*, Quindlen addresses an issue that appears to plague New Yorkers. And yet many people have come to live with the presence of homelessness in New York and other cities. This is the situation that motivates Quindlen to write her editorial: People study the problem of homelessness, yet nothing gets done. Homelessness has become a way of life, a situation that seems to say to observers that officials have declared defeat when it comes to this problem.

Frame a Good Question

A good question can help you think through what you might be interested in   12
writing; it is specific enough to guide inquiry and meets the following criteria:

- It can be answered with the tools you have.
- It conveys a clear idea of who you are answering the question for.
- It is organized around an issue.
- It explores "how," "why," or "whether," and the "extent to which."

A good question, then, is one that can be answered given the access we have to
certain kinds of information. The tools we have at hand can be people or other
texts. A good question also grows out of an issue, some fundamental tension that
you identify within a conversation. Through identifying what is at issue, you
should begin to understand for whom it is an issue—who you are answering
the question for.

FRAMING AS A CRITICAL STRATEGY FOR WRITING, READING, AND DOING RESEARCH

Thus far, I have presented a conversational model of argument, describing   13
writing as a form of dialogue, with writers responding to the ways others have
defined problems and anticipating possible counterarguments. In this section,
I want to add another element that some people call framing. This is a strategy
that can help you orchestrate different and conflicting voices in advancing your
argument.

   Framing is a metaphor for describing the lens, or perspective, from which   14
writers present their arguments. Writers want us to see the world in one way as
opposed to another, not unlike the way a photographer manipulates a camera
lens to frame a picture. For example, if you were taking a picture of friends in
front of the football stadium on campus, you would focus on what you would
most like to remember, blurring the images of people in the background. How
you set up the picture, or frame it, might entail using light and shade to make
some images stand out more than others. Writers do the same with language.

   For instance, in writing about education in the United States, E. D. Hirsch   15
uses the term *cultural literacy* as a way to understand a problem, in this case
the decline of literacy. To say that there is a decline, Hirsch has to establish the
criteria against which to measure whether some people are literate and some
are not. Hirsch uses *cultural literacy* as a lens through which to discriminate
between those who fulfill his criteria for literacy and those who do not. He
defines *cultural literacy* as possessing certain kinds of information. Not all educators agree. Some oppose equating literacy and information, describing literacy as

an *event* or as a *practice* to argue that literacy is not confined to acquiring bits of information; instead, the notion of literacy as an *event or practice* says something about how people use what they know to accomplish the work of a community. As you can see, any perspective or lens can limit readers' range of vision: readers will see some things and not others.

In my work as a writer, I have identified four reasons to use framing as a strat- 16
egy for developing an argument. First, framing encourages you to name your position, distinguishing the way you think about the world from the ways others do. Naming also makes what you say memorable through key terms and theories. Readers may not remember every detail of Hirsch's argument, but they recall the principle—cultural literacy—around which he organizes his details. Second, framing forces you to offer both a definition and description of the principle around which your argument develops. For example, Hirsch defines *cultural literacy* as "the possession of basic information needed to thrive in the modern world." By defining your argument, you give readers something substantive to respond to. Third, framing specifies your argument, enabling others to respond to your argument and to generate counterarguments that you will want to engage in the spirit of conversation. Fourth, framing helps you organize your thoughts, and readers', in the same way that a title for an essay, a song, or a painting does.

To extend this argument, I would like you to think about framing as a strategy 17
of critical inquiry when you read. By critical inquiry, I mean that reading entails understanding the framing strategies that writers use and using framing concepts in order to shed light on our own ideas or the ideas of others. Here I distinguish *reading as inquiry* from *reading as a search for information*. For example, you might consider your experiences as readers and writers through the lens of Hirsch's conception of cultural literacy. You might recognize that schooling for you was really about accumulating information and that such an approach to education served you well. It is also possible that it has not. Whatever you decide, you may begin to reflect upon your experiences in new ways in developing an argument about what the purpose of education might be.

Alternatively, you might think about your educational experiences through a 18
very different conceptual frame in reading the following excerpt from Richard Rodriguez's memoir, *Hunger of Memory*. In this book, Rodriguez explains the conflicts he experienced as a nonnative speaker of English who desperately sought to enter mainstream culture, even if this meant sacrificing his identity as the son of Mexican immigrants. Notice how Rodriguez recalls his experience as a student through the framing concept of "scholarship boy" that he reads in Richard Hoggart's 1957 book, *The Uses of Literacy*. Using this notion of "scholarship boy" enables him to revisit his experience from a new perspective.

As you read this passage, consider what the notion of "scholarship boy" helps 19
Rodriguez to understand about his life as a student. In turn, what does such a concept help you understand about your own experience as a student?

Motivated to reflect upon his life as a student, Rodriguez comes across Richard Hoggart's book and a description of "the scholarship boy."

His initial response is to identify with Hoggart's description. Notice that Rodriguez says he used what he read to "frame the meaning of my academic success."

The scholarship boy moves between school and home, between moments of spontaneity and reflectiveness.

Rodriguez uses Hoggart's words and idea to advance his own understanding of the problem he identifies in his life: that he was unable to find solace at home and within his working-class roots.

For weeks I read, speed-read, books by modern educational theorists, only to find infrequent and slight mention of students like me. . . . Then one day, leafing through Richard Hoggart's *The Uses of Literacy*, I found, in his description of the scholarship boy, myself. For the first time I realized that there were other students like me, and so I was able to frame the meaning of my academic success, its consequent price—the loss.

Hoggart's description is distinguished, at least initially, by deep understanding. What he grasps very well is that the scholarship boy must move between environments, his home and the classroom, which are at cultural extremes, opposed. With his family, the boy has the intense pleasure of intimacy, the family's consolation in feeling public alienation. Lavish emotions texture home life. *Then*, at school, the instruction bids him to trust lonely reason primarily. Immediate needs set the pace of his parents' lives. From his mother and father the boy learns to trust spontaneity and nonrational ways of knowing. *Then*, at school, there is mental calm. Teachers emphasize the value of a reflectiveness that opens a space between thinking and immediate action.

Years of schooling must pass before the boy will be able to sketch the cultural differences in his day as abstractly as this. But he senses those differences early. Perhaps as early as the night he brings home an assignment from school and finds the house too noisy for study.

He has to be more and more alone, if he is going to "get on." He will have, probably unconsciously, to oppose the ethos of the health, the intense gregariousness of the working-class family group. . . . The boy has to cut himself off mentally, so as to do his homework, as well as he can. (47)

In this excerpt, the idea of framing highlights the fact that other people's texts can 20
serve as tools for helping you say more about your own ideas. If you were writing
an essay using Hoggart's term *scholarship boy* as a lens through which to say something about education, you might ask how Hoggart's term illuminates new aspects
of another writer's examples or your own — as opposed to asking, "How well does
Hoggart's term *scholarship boy* apply to my experience?" (to which you could answer,
"Not very well"). Further, you might ask, "To what extent does Hirsch's concept
throw a more positive light on what Rodriguez and Hoggart describe?" or "Do my
experiences challenge, extend, or complicate such a term as *scholarship boy*?"

Now that you have a sense of how framing works, let's look at an excerpt from 21
a researched argument a first-year composition student wrote, titled "Learning
'American' in Spanish." The assignment to which she responded asked her to do
the following:

> Draw on your life experiences in developing an argument about education
> and what it has meant to you in your life. In writing your essay, use two of
> the four authors (Freire, Hirsch, Ladson-Billings, Pratt) included in this unit
> to frame your argument or any of the reading you may have done on your
> own. What key terms, phrases, or ideas from these texts help you teach your
> readers what you want them to learn from your experiences? How do your
> experiences extend or complicate your critical frames?
>
> In the past, in responding to this assignment, some people have offered an
> overview of almost their entire lives, some have focused on a pivotal experience,
> and others have used descriptions of people who have influenced them. The
> important thing is that you use those experiences to argue a position: for
> example, that even the most well-meaning attempts to support students can
> actually hinder learning. This means going beyond narrating a simple list
> of experiences, or simply asserting an opinion. Instead you must use — and
> analyze — your experiences, determining which will most effectively convince
> your audience that your argument has a solid basis.

As you read the excerpt from this student's essay, ask yourself how the writer uses
two framing concepts — "transculturation" and "contact zone" — from Mary Louise
Pratt's article "Arts of the Contact Zone." What do these ideas help the writer bring
into focus? What experience do these frames help her to name, define, and describe?

Jennifer Farrell

The writer has not yet
named her framing concept;
but notice that the concrete
details she gathers here set
readers up to expect that
she will juxtapose

Exactly one week after graduating from high
school, with thirteen years of American education
behind me, I boarded a plane and headed for a
Caribbean island. I had fifteen days to spend on an
island surrounded with crystal blue waters, white
sandy shores, and luxurious ocean resorts.

the culture of Guayabal and the Dominican Republic with that of the United States.

The writer names her experience as an example of Pratt's conception of a "contact zone." Further, the writer expands on Pratt's quote by relating it to her own observations. And finally, she uses this frame as a way to organize the narrative (as opposed to ordering her narrative chronologically).

With beaches to play on by day and casinos to play in during the night, I was told that this country was an exciting new tourist destination. My days in the Dominican Republic, however, were not filled with snorkeling lessons and my nights were not spent at the blackjack table. Instead of visiting the ritzy East Coast, I traveled inland to a mountain community with no running water and no electricity. The bus ride to this town, called Guayabal, was long, hot, and uncomfortable. The mountain roads were not paved and the bus had no air-conditioning. Surprisingly, the four-hour ride flew by. I had plenty to think about as my mind raced with thoughts of the next two weeks. I wondered if my host family would be welcoming, if the teenagers would be friendly, and if my work would be hard. I mentally prepared myself for life without the everyday luxuries of a flushing toilet, a hot shower, and a comfortable bed. Because Guayabal was without such basic commodities, I did not expect to see many reminders of home. I thought I was going to leave behind my American ways and immerse myself into another culture. These thoughts filled my head as the bus climbed the rocky hill toward Guayabal. When I finally got off the bus and stepped into the town square, I realized that I had thought wrong: There was no escaping the influence of the American culture.

In a way, Guayabal was an example of what author Mary Louise Pratt refers to as a contact zone. Pratt defines a contact zone as "a place where cultures meet, clash, and grapple with each other, often in contexts of highly asymmetrical relations of power" (76). In Guayabal, American culture and American consumerism were clashing with the Hispanic and Caribbean culture of the Dominican Republic. The clash came from the Dominicans' desire to be American in every sense, and especially to be consumers of American products. This is nearly impossible for Dominicans to achieve due to their extreme poverty. Their poverty provided the "asymmetrical relation of power" found in contact zones, because it impeded not only the Dominican's ability to be

The writer provides concrete evidence to support her point.

consumers, but also their ability to learn, to work, and to live healthily. The effects of their poverty could be seen in the eyes of the seven-year-old boy who couldn't concentrate in school because all he had to eat the day before was an underripe mango. It could be seen in the brown, leathered hands of the tired old man who was still picking coffee beans at age seventy.

The writer offers an illustration of what she experienced, clarifying how this experience is similar to what Pratt describes. Note that Pratt's verb *clash*, used in the definition of *contact zone*, reappears here as part of the author's observation.

The moment I got off the bus I noticed the clash between the American culture, the Dominican culture, and the community's poverty. It was apparent in the Dominicans' fragmented representation of American pop culture. Everywhere I looked in Guayabal I saw little glimpses of America. I saw Coca-Cola ads painted on raggedy fences. I saw knockoff Tommy Hilfiger shirts. I heard little boys say, "I wanna be like Mike" in their best English, while playing basketball. I listened to merengue house, the American version of the traditional Dominican merengue music. In each instance the Dominicans had adopted an aspect of American culture, but with an added Dominican twist. Pratt calls this transculturation. This term is used to "describe processes whereby members of subordinated or marginal groups select and invent from materials transmitted by a dominant or metropolitan culture" (80). She claims that transculturation is an identifying feature of contact zones. In the contact zone of Guayabal, the marginal group, made up of impoverished Dominicans, selected aspects of the dominant American culture, and invented a unique expression of a culture combining both Dominican and American styles. My most vivid memory of this transculturalization was on a hot afternoon when I heard some children yelling, "Helado! Helado!" or "Ice cream! Ice cream!" I looked outside just in time to see a man ride by on a bicycle, ringing a hand bell and balancing a cooler full of ice cream in the front bicycle basket. The Dominican children eagerly chased after him, just as American children chase after the ice-cream truck.

The author adds another layer to her description, introducing Pratt's framing concept of "transculturation."

Here again she quotes Pratt in order to bring into focus her own context here. The writer offers another example of transculturation.

Although you will notice that the writer does not challenge the framing terms 22 she uses in this paper, it is clear that rather than simply reproducing Pratt's ideas and using her as the Voice of Authority, she incorporates Pratt's understandings to enable her to say more about her own experiences and ideas. Moreover, she uses this frame to advance an argument in order to affect her readers' views of culture. In turn, when she mentions others' ideas, she does so in the service of what she wants to say.

CONCLUSION: WRITING RESEARCHED ARGUMENTS

I want to conclude this chapter by making a distinction between two different 23 views of research. On the one hand, research is often taught as a process of collecting information for its own sake. On the other hand, research can also be conceived as the discovery and purposeful use of information. The emphasis here is upon *use* and the ways you can shape information in ways that enable you to enter conversations. To do so, you need to demonstrate to readers that you understand the conversation: what others have said in the past, what the context is, and what you anticipate is the direction this conversation might take. Keep in mind, however, that contexts are neither found nor located. Rather, context, derived from the Latin *contexere*, denotes a process of weaving together. Thus your attempt to understand context is an active process of making connections among the different and conflicting views people present within a conversation. Your version of the context will vary from others' interpretations.

Your attempts to understand a given conversation may prompt you to do 24 research, as will your attempts to define what is at issue. Your reading and inquiry can help you construct a question that is rooted in some issue that is open to dispute. In turn, you need to ask yourself what is at stake for you and your reader other than the fact that you might be interested in educational reform, homelessness, affirmative action, or any other subject. Finally, your research can provide a means for framing an argument in order to move a conversation along and to say something new.

If you see inquiry as a means of entering conversations, then you will under- 25 stand research as a social process. It need not be the tedious task of collecting information for its own sake. Rather, research has the potential to change readers' worldviews and your own.

Works Cited

Bartholomae, David, and Anthony Petrosky. 1996. *Ways of Reading: An Anthology for Writers*. New York: Bedford Books.

Brent, Doug. 1996. "Rogerian Rhetoric: Ethical Growth Through Alternative Forms of Argumentation." In *Argument Revisited; Argument Redefined: Negotiating Meaning in a Composition Classroom*, 73–96. Edited by Barbara Emmel, Paula Resch, and Deborah Tenney. Thousand Oaks, CA: Sage Publications.

Burke, Kenneth. 1941. *The Philosophy of Literary Form*. Berkeley: University of California Press.

Crosswhite, James. 1996. *The Rhetoric of Reason: Writing and the Attractions of Argument*. Madison, WI: University of Wisconsin Press.

Freire, Paulo. 1970. *Pedagogy of the Oppressed*. New York: Continuum.

Hirsch, E. D. 1987. *Cultural Literacy*. New York: Vintage Books.

Ladson-Billings, Gloria. 1994. *The Dreamkeepers: Successful Teachers of African American Children*. New York: Teachers College Press.

Pratt, Mary Louise. "Arts of the Contact Zone." *Profession* 91 (1991): 33–40.

Quindlen, Anna. 1993. "No Place Like Home." In *Thinking Out Loud: On the Personal, the Public, and the Private*, 42–44. New York: Random House.

Rodriguez, Richard. 1983. *Hunger of Memory: The Education of Richard Rodriguez*. New York: Bantam Books.

Acknowledgment

I wish to thank Robert Kachur and April Lidinsky for helping me think through the notions of argument as conversation and framing.

- -

Responding — Really Responding — to Other Students' Writing

Photo Courtesy of Ron Lunsford

RICHARD STRAUB

Framing the Reading

Richard Straub was an associate professor of English at Florida State University prior to his untimely death in 2002. His special area of research interest was responding to student writing. He wrote a number of articles and books on how teachers can respond effectively to student writing in order to help students grow and improve. The short piece you will read here takes what Straub learned about responding to writing and explains it directly to students. It was originally published in a textbook for first-year students, so you'll see that he speaks directly to you, giving you explicit advice about what to do. As you read this selection, keep in mind what you have been learning in this chapter about reading. As you read the texts drafted by your classmates during the semester or quarter ahead, remember to read them as turns in a conversation that are attempting to make meaning with others, including with you.

Getting Ready to Read

Before you read, do the following activity:

- Consider your experiences with "peer review." What has gone wrong? What has gone well? What is your attitude about peer review?

As you read, consider the following questions:

- Does Straub's advice set up peer review differently than your previous experiences did?
- How can you understand and better participate in peer review if you understand your task as reading rhetorically and making meaning with another author?

Straub, Richard. "Responding — Really Responding — to Other Students' Writing." *The Subject Is Writing,* edited by Wendy Bishop and James Strickland, Heinemann/Boynton-Cook Publishers, 2005, pp. 136–46.

OKAY. YOU'VE GOT a student paper you have to read and make comments on 1
for Thursday. It's not something you're looking forward to. But that's alright, you
think. There isn't really all that much to it. Just keep it simple. Read it quickly
and mark whatever you see. Say something about the introduction. Something
about details and examples. Ideas you can say you like. Mark any typos and
spelling errors. Make your comments brief. Abbreviate where possible: *awk.
Good intro, give ex, frag.* Try to imitate the teacher. Mark what he'd mark and
sound like he'd sound. But be cool about it. Don't praise anything really, but no
need to get harsh or cut throat either. Get in and get out. You're okay. I'm okay.
Everybody's happy. What's the problem?

This is, no doubt, a way of getting through the assignment. Satisfy the 2
teacher and no surprises for the writer. It might just do the trick. But say you
want to do a *good* job. Say you're willing to put in the time and effort — though
time is tight and you know it's not going to be easy — and help the writer
look back on the paper and revise it. And maybe in the process learn something
more yourself about writing. What do you look for? How do you sound? How
much do you take up? What exactly are you trying to accomplish? Here are some
ideas.

HOW SHOULD YOU LOOK AT YOURSELF AS A RESPONDER?

Consider yourself a friendly reader. A test pilot. A roommate who's been asked 3
to look over the paper and tell the writer what you think. Except you don't just
take on the role of The Nice Roommate or The Ever-faithful Friend and tell her
what she wants to hear. *This all looks good. I wouldn't change a thing. There are a
couple places that I think he might not like, but I can see what you're doing there.
I'd go with it. Good stuff.* You're supportive. You give her the benefit of the doubt
and look to see the good in her writing. But friends don't let friends think their
writing is the best thing since *The Great Gatsby* and they don't lead them to think
that all is fine and well when it's not. Look to help this friend, this roommate
writer — okay, this person in your class — to get a better piece of writing. Point
to problems and areas for improvement but do it in a constructive way. See what
you can do to push her to do even more than she's done and stretch herself as a
writer.

WHAT ARE YOUR GOALS?

First, don't set out to seek and destroy all errors and problems in the writing. 4
You're not an editor. You're not a teacher. You're not a cruise missile. And don't
rewrite any parts of the paper. You're not the writer; you're a reader. One of many.
The paper is not yours; it's the writer's. She writes. You read. She is in charge of

what she does to her writing. That doesn't mean you can't make suggestions. It doesn't mean you can't offer a few sample rewrites here and there, as models. But make it clear they're samples, models. Not rewrites. Not edits. Not corrections. Be reluctant at first even to say what you would do if the paper were yours. It's not yours. Again; Writers write, readers read and show what they're understanding and maybe make suggestions. What to do instead: Look at your task as a simple one. You're there to play back to the writer how you read the paper: what you got from it; what you found interesting; where you were confused; where you wanted more. With this done, you can go on to point out problems, ask questions, offer advice, and wonder out loud with the writer about her ideas. Look to help her improve the writing or encourage her to work on some things as a writer.

HOW DO YOU GET STARTED?

Before you up and start reading the paper, take a minute (alright, thirty seconds) 5 to make a mental checklist about the circumstances of the writing, the context. You're not going to just read a text. You're going to read a text within a certain context, a set of circumstances that accompany the writing and that you bring to your reading. It's one kind of writing or another, designed for one audience and purpose or another. It's a rough draft or a final draft. The writer is trying to be serious or casual, straight or ironic. Ideally, you'll read the paper with an eye to the circumstances that it was written in and the situation it is looking to create. That means looking at the writing in terms of the assignment, the writer's particular interests and aims, the work you've been doing in class, and the stage of drafting.

- *The assignment:* What kind of writing does the assignment call (or allow) for? Is the paper supposed to be a personal essay? A report? An analysis? An argument? Consider how well the paper before you meets the demands of the kind of writing the writer is taking up.

- *The writer's interests and aims:* What does the writer want to accomplish? If she's writing a personal narrative, say, is she trying to simply recount a past experience? Is she trying to recount a past experience and at the same time amuse her readers? Is she trying to show a pleasant experience on the surface, yet suggest underneath that everything was not as pleasant as it seems? Hone in on the writer's particular aims in the writing.

- *The work of the class:* Try to tie your comments to the concepts and strategies you've been studying in class. If you've been doing a lot of work on using detail, be sure to point to places in the writing where the writer uses detail effectively or where she might provide richer detail. If you've been working on developing arguments through examples and sample cases, indicate where the writer might use such methods to strengthen her arguments. If you've been considering various ways to sharpen the style of your sentences, offer places where the writer can clarify her sentence structure or arrange a sentence for maximum impact. The best comments will ring familiar even as they lead the writer to try to do something she hasn't quite done before, or done in quite the same way. They'll be comforting and understandable even as they create some need to do more, a need to figure out some better way.

• *The stage of drafting:* Is it an early draft? A full but incomplete draft? A nearly final draft? Pay attention to the stage of drafting. Don't try to deal with everything all at once if it's a first, rough draft. Concentrate on the large picture: the paper's focus; the content; the writer's voice. Don't worry about errors and punctuation problems yet. There'll be time for them later. If it's closer to a full draft, go ahead and talk, in addition to the overall content, about arrangement, pacing, and sentence style. Wait till the final draft to give much attention to fine-tuning sentences and dealing in detail with proofreading. Remember: You're not an editor. Leave these sentence revisions and corrections for the writer. It's her paper. And she's going to learn best by detecting problems and making her own changes.

WHAT TO ADDRESS IN YOUR COMMENTS?

Try to focus your comments on a couple of areas of writing. Glance through the paper quickly first. Get an idea whether you'll deal mostly with the overall content and purpose of the writing, its shape and flow, or (if these are more or less in order) with local matters of paragraph structure, sentence style, and correctness. Don't try to cover everything that comes up or even all instances of a given problem. Address issues that are most important to address in this paper, at this time. 6

WHERE TO PUT YOUR COMMENTS?

Some teachers like to have students write comments in the margins right next to the passage. Some like to have students write out their comments in an end note or in a separate letter to the writer. I like to recommend using both marginal comments and a note or letter at the end. The best of both worlds. Marginal comments allow you to give a quick moment-by-moment reading of the paper. They make it easy to give immediate and specific feedback. You still have to make sure you specify what you're talking about and what you have to say, but they save you some work telling the writer what you're addressing and allow you to focus your end note on things that are most important. Comments at the end allow you to provide some perspective on your response. This doesn't mean that you have to size up the paper and give it a thumbs up or a thumbs down. You can use the end comment to emphasize the key points of your response, explain and elaborate 7

47

on issues you want to deal with more fully, and mention additional points that you don't want to address in detail. One thing to avoid: plastering comments all over the writing; in between and over the lines of the other person's writing—up, down, and across the page. Write in your space, and let the writer keep hers.

HOW TO SOUND?

Not like a teacher. Not like a judge. Not like an editor or critic or shotgun. 8 (Wouldn't you want someone who was giving you comments not to sound like a teacher's red pen, a judge's ruling, an editor's impatience, a critic's wrath, a shotgun's blast?) Sound like you normally sound when you're speaking with a friend or acquaintance. Talk to the writer. You're not just marking up a text; you're responding to the writer. You're a reader, a helper, a colleague. Try to sound like someone who's a reader, who's helpful, and who's collegial. Supportive. And remember: Even when you're tough and demanding you can still be supportive.

HOW MUCH TO COMMENT?

Don't be stingy. Write most of your comments out in full statements. Instead 9 of writing two or three words, write seven or eight. Instead of making only one brief comment and moving on, say what you have to say and then go back over the statement and explain what you mean or why you said it or note other alternatives. Let the writer know again and again how you are understanding her paper, what you take her to be saying. And elaborate on your key comments. Explain your interpretations, problems, questions, and advice.

IS IT OKAY TO BE SHORT AND SWEET?

No. At least not most of the time. Get specific. Don't rely on general statements 10 alone. How much have generic comments helped you as a writer? "Add detail." "Needs better structure." "Unclear." Try to let the writer know what exactly the problem is. Refer specifically to the writer's words and make them a part of your comments. "Add some detail on what it was like working at the beach." "I think we'll need to know more about your high school crowd before we can understand the way you've changed." "This sentence is not clear. Were *you* disappointed or were *they* disappointed?" This way the writer will see what you're talking about, and she'll have a better idea what to work on.

DO YOU PRAISE OR CRITICIZE OR WHAT?

Be always of two (or three) minds about your response to the paper. You like the 11 paper, but it could use some more interesting detail. You found this statement interesting, but these ideas in the second paragraph are not so hot. It's an alright paper, but it could be outstanding if the writer said what was really bothering her. Always be ready to praise. But always look to point to places that are not working well or that are not yet working as well as they might. Always be ready to expect more from the writer.

HOW TO PRESENT YOUR COMMENTS?

Don't steer away from being critical. Feel free—in fact, feel obliged—to tell the writer what you like and don't like, what is and is not working, and where you think it can be made to work better. But use some other strategies, too. Try to engage the writer in considering her choices and thinking about possible ways to improve the paper. Make it a goal to write two or three comments that look to summarize or paraphrase what the writer is saying. Instead of *telling* the reader what to do, *suggest* what she might do. Identify the questions that are raised for you as you the reader: 12

- Play back your way of understanding the writing:
  This seems to be the real focus of the paper, the issue you seem
    most interested in.
  So you're saying that you really weren't interested in her
    romantically?

- Temper your criticisms:
  This sentence is a bit hard to follow.
  I'm not sure this paragraph is necessary.

- Offer advice:
  It might help to add an example here.
  Maybe save this sentence for the end of the paper.

- Ask questions, especially real questions:
  What else were you feeling at the time?
  What kind of friend? Would it help to say?
  Do you need this opening sentence?
  In what ways were you "daddy's little girl"?

- Explain and follow up on your initial comments:
  You might present this episode first. This way we can see what you
    mean when you say that he was always too busy.
  How did you react? Did you cry or yell? Did you walk away?
  This makes her sound cold and calculating. Is that what you want?

- Offer some praise, and then explain to the writer why the writing works:
  Good opening paragraph. You've got my attention.
  Good detail. It tells me a lot about the place.
  I like the descriptions you provide—for instance, about your grand-
    mother cooking, at the bottom of page 1; about her house, in
    the middle of page 2; and about how she said her rosary at night:
    "quick but almost pleading, like crying without tears."

HOW MUCH CRITICISM? HOW MUCH PRAISE?

Challenge yourself to write as many praise comments as criticisms. When you 13 praise, praise well. Think about it. Sincerity and specificity are everything when it comes to a compliment.

HOW MUCH SHOULD YOU BE INFLUENCED BY WHAT YOU KNOW ABOUT THE WRITER?

Consider the person behind the writer when you make your comments. If 14 she's not done so well in class lately, maybe you can give her a pick-me-up in your comments. If she's shy and seems reluctant to go into the kind of personal detail the paper seems to need, encourage her. Make some suggestions or tell her what you would do. If she's confident and going on arrogant, see what you can do to challenge her with the ideas she presents in the paper. Look for other views she may not have thought about, and find ways to lead her to consider them. Always be ready to look at the text in terms of the writer behind the text.

Good comments, this listing shows, require a lot from a reader. But you 15 don't have to make a checklist out of these suggestions and go through each one methodically as you read. It's amazing how they all start coming together when you look at your response as a way of talking with the writer seriously about the writing, recording how you experience the words on the page and giving the writer something to think about for revision. The more you see examples of thoughtful commentary and the more you try to do it yourself, the more you'll get a feel for how it's done.

Here's a set of student comments on a student paper. They were done in the 16 last third of a course that focused on the personal essay and concentrated on helping students develop the content and thought of their writing. The class had been working on finding ways to develop and extend the key statements of their essays (by using short, representative details, full-blown examples, dialogue, and multiple perspectives) and getting more careful about selecting and shaping parts of their writing. The assignment called on students to write an essay or an autobiographical story where they looked to capture how they see (or have seen) something about one or both of their parents—some habits, attitudes, or traits their parents have taken on. They were encouraged to give shape to their ideas and experiences in ways that went beyond their previous understandings and try things they hadn't tried in their writing. More a personal narrative than an essay, Todd's paper looks to capture one distinct difference in the way his mother and father disciplined their children. It is a rough draft that will be taken through one or possibly two more revisions. Readers were asked to offer whatever feedback they could that might help the writer with the next stage of writing (Figure 1).

Figure 1

Jeremy
Todd
ENG 1
Rick Straub
Assign 8b

"Uh, oh"

When I called home from the police station I was praying that my *I like this paragraph. It*
father would answer the phone. He would listen to what I had to say *immediately lets the*
and would react comely, logical, and in a manner that would keep *reader relate to you and*
my mother from screaming her head off. If my Mother was to answer *also produces a picture*
the phone, I would have to explain myself quickly in order to keep her *in the reader's mind*
from having a heart attached.

When I was eleven years old I hung out with a group of boys that
were almost three years older than me. The five of us did all the things
that young energetic kids did playing ball, riding bikes, and getting in *Good point, makes*
to trouble. [Because they were older they worried less about getting in *it more unlikely that*
trouble and the consequences of there actions than I did.]—————— *you should be the*
one to get caught

My friends and I would always come home from school, drop our
backpacks off and head out in the neighborhood to find something to do. *What other things*
Our favorite thing to do was to find construction cites and steal wood *did you do to get*
to make tree forts in the woods or skateboard ramps. So one day, coming *into trouble? Or is it*
home from school, we noticed a couple new houses being built near our *irrelevant?*
neighborhood. It was a prime cite for wood, nails, and anything else we
could get our hands on. We discussed our plan on the bus and decided that
great passage really we would all meet there after dropping our stuff off at home. [I remember
lets the reader being a little at hesitant first because it,was close to my house but beyond
know what you were the boundaries my parents had set for me. Of course I went because I
thinking didn't want to be the odd man out and have to put up with all the name
calling.] I dropped my bag off and I headed to the construction cite.

I meet my friends there and we began to search the different
houses for wood and what not. We all picked up a couple of things
and were about to leave when one of my friends noticed what looked
to be a big tool shed off behind of the houses. It looked promising so
we decided that we should check it out. Two of the boys in the group
said that they had all the wood they could carry and said they were
going home. The rest of us headed down to the shed to take a look.

was there a reason
Once there we noticed that the shed had been broken in to previ- *you were there first*
ously. The lock on it had been busted on the hinges were bent. I opened *or did it just happen*
the door to the shed and stepped inside to take a look around while my *that way*
friends waited outside. It was dark inside but I could tell the place had
been ransacked, there was nothing to take so I decided to leave. I heard my
friends say something so turned back around to site of them running away.

(continued)

This is a full and thoughtful set of comments. The responder, Jeremy, creates 17
himself not as a teacher or critic but first of all as a reader, one who is intent on
saying how he takes the writing and what he'd like to hear more about:

> Good point. Makes it more unlikely that you should be the one to get
> caught. Great passage. Really lets the reader know what you were thinking.
> Was there a reason you were first or did it just happen that way? Would he
> punish you anyway or could you just get away with things?

He makes twenty-two comments on the paper—seventeen statements in the
margins and five more in the end note. The comments are written out in full
statements, and they are detailed and specific. They make his response into a
lively exchange with the writer, one person talking with another about what
he's said. Well over half of the comments are follow-up comments that explain,
illustrate, or qualify other responses.

(continued)   Figure 1

I thought that they were playing a joke on me so I casually walked out only to see a cop car parked near one of the houses under construction. As soon as I saw that cop car I took off but was stopped when a big hand pulled at the back of my shirt. I watched my friends run until they were out of cite and then I turned around.

The cop had me sit in the cop car while he asked my questions. He asked me if I know those kids that ran off and I said "Nnnnnooooooooo". He asked me if I had broken into that shed and I said "Nnnnnnooooo". The cop wrote down what I was saying all the while shaking his head. Then he told me that I wasn't being arrested but I would have to go down to the station to call parents and have them pick me up. Upon hearing that I nearly soiled my undershorts. "My God, I'm dead. My mom is going to kill me".

what else happened at the police station? how long were you there?

At the station the officer showed me the whole station, jail cells and everything. An obvious tactic to try and scare me, which worked. That plus the thought of my mom answering the phone and my trying to explain what happened nearly made me sick.

"Wwwwhhhaatttt! You're where?" She would say.

"The police station mom," uh oh, hear it comes.

"Ooooohhhh my God, my son is a criminal," so loud I would have to pull the phone away from my ear.

maybe you could say more as to why you think your mom is like this

She had this uncanny ability to blow things out of proportion right from the start. She would assume the worse and then go from there. This was a classic example of why I could never go to her if I had any bad news. She would start screaming, get upset, and then go bitch at my father. My father is a pretty laid back but when ever my mother started yelling at him about me, he would get angry and come chew me out worse than if I had just gone to him in the first place.

If my father were to answer the phone he would respond with out raising his voice. He would examine the situation in a logical manner and make a decision from there.

"Uhmmm (long pause). You're at the police station."

"Yeah dad. I didn't get arrested they just had me come down here so I had to tell you."

Did your Dad get into trouble as a kid so he knows what it's like? Explain why he reacts as he does

"Uhm, so you didn't get arrested (long pause). Well (long pause), I'll come pick you up and will talk about then."

I feel like I can relate to my father much better than I can to my mother. He has a cool and collective voice that can take command of any situation. I always feel like he understands me, like he knows what I'm thinking all the time. This comes in real handy when I get in trouble.

I like the way you use dialogue in this section to illustrate how each of your parents would react and then explain to the reader what each of them are like, it works well.

would he punish you anyway or could you just get away with things

(continued)

The comments focus on the content and development of the writing, in line with the assignment, the stage of drafting, and the work of the course. They also view the writing rhetorically, in terms of how the text has certain effects on readers. Although there are over two dozen wording or sentence-level errors in the paper, he decides, wisely, to stick with the larger matters of writing. Yet even as he offers a pretty full set of comments he doesn't ever take control over the text. His comments are placed unobtrusively on the page, and he doesn't try to close things down or decide things for the writer. He offers praise, encouragement, and direction. What's more, he pushes the writer to do more than he has already

18

(continued) **Figure 1**

I called home. Sweet beading on my lip.

"Hello", my mom said. Oh geez, I'm dead.

"Mom can I talk to dad?"

"Why, what's wrong?"

"Oh, nothing, I just need to talk to him," yes, this is going to work!

"Hold on," she said.

"Hello," my father said.

"Dad, I'm at the police station," I told him the whole story of what happened. He reacted exactly as I expect he would.

"Uhmm (long pause). You're at the police station..........

I really like the ending, it tells the reader what is going to happen without having to explain it step, by step. Good paper, I like the use of dialogue. Perhaps more on your understanding of why your parents react as they do.

done, to extend the boundaries of his examination. In keeping with the assignment and the larger goals of the course, he calls on Todd in several comments to explore the motivations and personalities behind his parents' different ways of disciplining:

> Maybe you could say more as to why you think your mom is like this. Did your dad get into trouble as a kid so he knows what it's like? Explain why he reacts as he does.

He is careful, though, not to get presumptuous and make decisions for the writer. Instead, he offers options and points to possibilities:

> Perhaps more on your understanding of why your parents react as they do.
> What other things did you do to get into trouble? Or is it irrelevant?

From start to finish he takes on the task of reading and responding and leaves the work of writing and revising to Todd.

Jeremy's response is not in a class by itself. A set of comments to end all commentary on Todd's paper. He might have done well, for instance, to recognize how much this paper works because of the way Todd arranges the story. He could have done more to point to what's not working in the writing or what could be made to work better. He might have asked Todd for more details about his state of mind when he got caught by the policeman and while he was being held at the police station. He might have urged him more to make certain changes. He might even have said, if only in a brief warning, something about the number of errors across the writing. But this is moot and just. Different readers are always going to pick up on different things and respond in different ways, and no one reading or response is going to address everything that might well be addressed, in the way it might best be addressed. All responses are incomplete and provisional—one reader's way of reading and reacting to the text in front of him. And any number of other responses, presented in any number of different ways, might be as useful or maybe even more useful to Todd as he takes up his work with the writing.

All this notwithstanding, Jeremy's comments are solid. They are full. They are 20 thoughtful. And they are respectful. They take the writing and the writer seriously and address the issues that are raised responsibly. His comments do what commentary on student writing should optimally do. They turn the writer back into his writing and lead him to reflect on his choices and aims, to consider and reconsider his intentions as a writer and the effects the words on the page will have on readers. They help him see what he can work on in revision and what he might deal with in his ongoing work as a writer.

SHARING IDEAS

- What are your experiences with responding to other students' writing? 21 Have you done so in other classes? How did that work out? Were you able to discuss your responses? In small groups or large groups? Which situation did you like best?
- Do you have any papers where others have responded to your writing? Collect one or more and see how the responses stack up against Rick's guidelines. Having read his essay, what would you say your respondent did well and needs to learn to do better?
- In the same way, after everyone in your small group responds to a first paper, go over those papers/responses together in a group and look at what was done and what could be done to improve the quality of responses. In addition, you might try to characterize each of you as a responder: What are your habits? What character/persona do you take on? Would you like to be responded to by the responder you find you are through this group analysis?
- How do my suggestions for response to student writers sound the same or different from Rick's suggestions? Do we come from the same "school" of responding or do we suggest different approaches? Characterize the differences or similarities you find.
- Rick shows you a responder—Jeremy—and the comments he wrote on Todd's paper. If you were Todd, how would you feel about Jeremy's responses? Do you agree with Rick's analysis of Jeremy's comments? What three or four additional things would you tell Todd about his paper?

- What are your insights into responding? What has worked for you? What do you wish people would do or not do when they respond to your writing? What would make you most inclined to listen to responses and use them to change your work?

- -

Using This Book

Reading texts that are written by expert researchers for other experts is not easy even for your instructors, and it won't be easy or quick reading for you at first, either. We've created *Writing about Writing* to make sure that the time you spend with the readings is worthwhile and will lead you to new insights and more successful writing experiences. To help you, we have some concrete advice and suggestions about how to approach the readings in the following chapters.

GETTING THE MOST OUT OF YOUR READINGS

- **Leave plenty of time for reading.** These aren't pieces that you'll be able to sit down and skim in fifteen minutes, as you may be able to with material in a traditional textbook. Know that you'll need an hour or two, so give yourself that time. You'll find yourself less frustrated with the time reading can take if you *expect* it to take that time.

- **Consciously connect at least *some* part of each piece you read to your own experience as a writer.** The readings have been chosen specifically to allow you to do that. You'll understand them best in the moments you can say, "Oh, that sounds like what I do" — or, "That's actually not what I do at all; I do this instead."

- **Read the backstory of each piece, which you'll find in the "Framing the Reading" sections.** These introductions give you background knowledge necessary to understand the pieces themselves more fully.

- **Look up any boldface terms in the glossary before you dive into the reading.** Terms that we anticipate you'll need background on we include in bold in the chapter introduction or the "Framing the Reading" section so that you know you can find information on them in the glossary. Don't forget the glossary is there for you!

- **Use the activities and questions in the "Getting Ready to Read" section** to help you focus your reading and develop additional background knowledge that may help you make the clearest sense of the texts. Often we've chosen these to get your brain turning on a specific subject so that when you encounter it in the reading, you've already been thinking about it.

- **Look over the "Questions for Discussion and Journaling," "Applying and Exploring Ideas," and "Meta Moments" *before* you read,** so that you can get a further sense of where we suggest you focus your attention. This should help you be *selective* in your attention, rather than trying to read every word in the article in equal depth.

- **Read with your favorite search engine and *Wikipedia* open** so you can get instant definitions and background, and so that you can learn more about the authors by quickly researching them.
- **Don't feel like you're doing poorly just because you don't understand the piece well.** Your instructors encounter readings *all the time* that they have difficulty understanding — that's how you know you're stretching your knowledge and growing. It's okay not to have complete clarity; if we couldn't accept that, we'd never be able to learn anything new. What you really want is to finish a piece, having worked hard on it, and be able to say "Here are the parts that made sense to me, and here are the parts I still don't understand and want to talk about more." Even if you write down only a few things that you understood and many more that you didn't, that's okay — you're doing what you're supposed to, and you *are* learning. Remember that sometimes you only learn things, or realize you've learned them, long after the initial encounter. In other words, when you finish a text with a certain level of understanding, you can expect that as you go on and read other texts, ideas in them will continue to clarify aspects of the first text that you hadn't understood yet. That, too, is a natural part of learning.

READING ASSIST TAGS

Four readings in the book include Assist Tags to help you get the most from the reading. Consider the Assist Tags direct messages from us, things we would tell you to help you out if we were reading with you. Not every tagged reading will have all the tags described below, but most of the tagged readings will use several of them. When we tag a reading, the tags will be quite brief.

- Chapter 2 – Deborah Brandt, "Sponsors of Literacy" (p. 68)
- Chapter 3 – James Paul Gee, "Literacy, Discourse, and Linguistics: Introduction" (p. 274)
- Chapter 4 – Keith Grant-Davie, "Rhetorical Situations and Their Constituents" (p. 484)
- Chapter 5 – Sondra Perl, "The Composing Processes of Unskilled College Writers" (p. 738)

On the next two pages is a detailed explanation of what each tag means. Mark this reading assist tag guide so that you can refer to it when you are looking at a tagged reading later.

Assist Tags Guide

GENRE CUES

These tags will alert you to the kinds of genre moves a text is making, like those we explained earlier in this chapter. (Be sure to read the Swales section on pages 21–24 if you haven't already done so.) These tags will appear in the left margin of a selection as numbers that correspond to the explanations at the bottom of the same page.

CARS: Territory — This tag marks an area where a writer is establishing a territory, a particular area of existing inquiry or conversation.

CARS: Niche — This tag marks part of the reading where a writer is establishing a niche or gap in the territory — where current knowledge is insufficient or problematic.

CARS: Occupy — This tag marks a moment in the reading where a writer is moving to occupy the niche they've created by explaining their approach to researching the problem or question they've demonstrated.

Conversation — Sometimes a writer will organize a series of sources so that they're in conversation with each other and the writer. These are particularly helpful moments for readers to become familiar with the conversation the writing is engaging. This tag marks such conversations among sources.

Extending — Often writers use a source in order to create a "jumping-off point" or a point of departure for their own ideas. We use this tag to mark moments in the reading where writers extend their own ideas from an idea in a source's work.

Forecasting — Writers will sometimes offer metacommentary (text *about* the text itself) that explains where their writing is going next, or outlines the organization of their piece, or explains how different parts of the piece fit together. We've used this tag to identify such moments.

Framework — Some sources provide an explanation or analytical pattern that writers will apply to what they're studying. This pattern or explanatory theory creates a framework that writers use to interpret their own data. We use this tag to mark the appearance of such frameworks.

Making Knowledge — Every piece in this book creates new knowledge rather than simply transmitting existing information. We use this tag to mark particularly clear or decisive moments in a piece where writers are saying either (1) *how* they've made this new knowledge (usually a methodological explanation or claim) or (2) *what* the new knowledge is that they're contributing to the conversation.

Research Question — One common way of creating a CARS niche is to state the research problem as a question. This tag identifies research questions that focus and organize the rest of the text.

So What? — In their conclusions, and frequently in their introductions, writers will discuss the implications of their work — why their research problems, and their findings, actually matter. They answer the implicit questions "So what?" and "Who cares?" This tag marks those moments of discussion.

READING CUES

These tags will give you suggestions about *how* to read — like speeding up, rereading, or coming back to part of the text later. They will appear in the right margin of assisted texts, and sometimes with additional guidance at the bottom of the page.

At some moments in a reading, it helps to page through the text looking at the structure to understand where the text will go next. It's a kind of pre-viewing that can help you make more sense of the text you're currently reading. One example of such moments is when the author seems to be starting a list — you might want to overview the items on the list briefly before coming back to read each one in depth. You should also usually look ahead at the headings throughout an article, so that you know the structure of the main sections of the piece — in other words, so that you will know where you are going. The "Look Ahead" tag points to places where seeing the structure that lies ahead will help you understand the current point in the text.

Plan to reread some parts of the article once or twice. That's good, responsible reading, not a lack of ability or success. Your brain works by hooking new knowledge to existing knowledge. If *all* the knowledge in a piece is new, you need to read a piece to make some of it "old" in order to have a place to hang the rest of the new knowledge. The "Reread" tag identifies sections that students often need to read several times.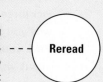

Sometimes a reading will make more sense if you read it out of order. When reading a typical social-science research report, experienced readers will often read the introduction and then skip to the conclusion, then read the discussion section immediately prior to the conclusion, and only then read the methods section that comes after the introduction. This is because readers want to know the findings first, and if they are still interested, they want to know how the research was conducted. When you see a "Read Later" tag, skip ahead to the next section or to the conclusion, and then come back to this section later.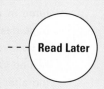

When you get bogged down in phrases, lines, or paragraphs that you just can't make sense of, try *reading more quickly*. Often, when you can't make sense of a particular line, it's because you don't yet have enough information on the new subject to "connect" it to. If you skim ahead to a point in the article where things start to make sense to you again, you can more quickly build that "big picture" that will let you make more sense of the individual lines that are hard for you. "Speed Up" tags alert you to points in the text where it may help you to read faster the first time through if the meaning isn't clear to you.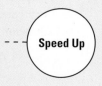

Reflecting on the Ideas of Chapter 1

Questions for Discussion and Journaling

1. What surprised you most in this chapter? Why?
2. What confused you most? Why?
3. Did anything you read give you a sense of relief, or lead you to have an "aha moment"? Why?
4. If you were going to pick one of the threshold concepts we have talked about in this chapter and study it in depth this semester, which would it be? Why? How would you go about trying to learn more about this concept?
5. Briefly explain the idea of "genre" and how it can help you undertake your in-school and out-of-school writing tasks.
6. Draw on Greene, Straub, and the section about rhetorical reading (pp. 24–29) and write a short explanation of how to read rhetorically.
7. What is the relationship between reading and writing, as you understand it after reading this chapter?

Applying and Exploring Ideas

1. Make a list of key terms from this chapter. If you aren't sure you understand them, reread the explanation and/or read their definitions in the glossary. Pick three that seem especially important and write a few paragraphs about why you think they are important to you as a writer or reader.
2. Have you encountered and successfully grappled with a threshold concept about writing in an English or writing class before? (A different college course, or a high school course?) Based on the descriptions of threshold concepts in this chapter, try to identify a threshold concept you've encountered in your earlier writing instruction, give it a name, and write a half-page description of it that addresses these questions: What did you know or believe about writing *before* you learned the concept? What experiences helped you cross that threshold? How did your knowledge or understanding after crossing the threshold make it difficult or impossible to think in your old way again?
3. Try naming some threshold concepts that you've encountered in *other* fields or subjects, such as history or biology or art or math. Do the same with one of these other fields' concepts as instructed in the previous question.

4. Make an "inventory" of how you usually read assignments for school by listing out the steps you usually go through, from the time you get the assignment to the time you finish the reading. Now compare the way you usually read with the advice for reading given in the "Using This Book" section (p. 55) or in the Greene and Straub readings (pp. 31 and 44). Make a list of the differences and similarities between your typical reading process and the suggestions given in this chapter. For each difference, write a paragraph about what is different, why you do what you do, and what might happen if you tried the strategies we suggest.

WRITING ABOUT THRESHOLD CONCEPTS: MAJOR WRITING ASSIGNMENT

To help you learn and explore the ideas in this chapter, we suggest an assignment option for a larger writing task to challenge and explore your conceptions about writing, reading, and research.

CHALLENGING AND EXPLORING YOUR CONCEPTIONS ABOUT WRITING, READING, AND RESEARCH

Jot down your ideas about the following:

- Writing is . . . .
- Research is . . . .
- Reading is . . .
- Good writers do or are . . . .
- Good writing is . . . .

Now pull out what you wrote about these ideas before you read this chapter. How are they different or the same now? Trade your pre- and post-reading ideas with another student and ask them to help you consider ways in which your ideas have changed or remained the same.

Pick one of the above ideas that you would like to think more about, then write a one-paragraph explanation of your idea (about writing, research, reading, good writers, good writing). Next, gather examples from your daily life and experiences, as well as those of your friends, to support the explanation that you have given. We have done this throughout the chapter, so you can go back to our various discussions if you need some models.

Planning, Drafting, and Revising.   Without realizing it, you have been planning and drafting for this writing task throughout this chapter. You explored your ideas before you started, and several times throughout the chapter you stopped to check how your ideas were changing and to consider some examples from your own experience. You can now go back to your notes from the chapter in order to help you begin this more formal writing task. Ideally, this is how you will approach writing tasks in this class and in college. You'll write as you are learning, and you'll continue to reflect on and modify your ideas.

Collect your ideas and draft a three- to five-page exploratory essay in which you define the idea you have been developing (about writing, research, reading, good writers, etc.). Be sure to explain the idea, define your terms, provide examples that support your position, and explain in some detail any aspect of this idea that might conflict with common conceptions about it. (For example, if you believe that school-based notions of "good writing" are too limited and do not stand up to what research and everyday experience show us about good writing, you will need to guide readers through that line of thinking, as if they haven't done the reading and thinking you've been doing in this chapter.)

What genre you will write in depends on all of the above. We want you to use what you learned in this chapter about genres and about how good writing is context-dependent in order to figure that out. Who do you want to share your claim and examples with? Why? What do those people expect? Where do they get their information? What are they likely to read? What do those texts look like? For example, you might decide that you would like to share your changing and research-based ideas about good writing with your high school teacher, because she constantly marked up your paper for grammar and ignored your ideas. How would you communicate with her? Possibly in a letter or a formal e-mail, in which case you'd need to look at examples before writing up your final draft that way.

What Makes It Good?   This writing task has two primary purposes. First, to help you deeply reflect and consider your ideas about writing, reading, and research and how they hold up to what you are learning in this class and what you do in your daily life. Second, to try to make a thoughtful claim that you can support through inquiry-based examples. So ensuring that what you are writing is thoughtful and supported by meaningful examples is the first priority for writing well here. You will then need to decide who you want to communicate this information with, and why. If you write appropriately for the audience and purpose you have in mind, and if you reflect and make a thoughtful and well-supported claim, you will have accomplished your goals.

CHAPTER 2

LITERACIES:
How Is Writing Impacted by Our Prior Experiences?

Mike Burley/Telegraph Herald/Associated Press

If **you are** reading this textbook, you are a literate person. You went to school, learned to read and write, and were admitted to the college where you are now being asked to write new and different kinds of texts. Experts who study **literacy** typically think about more than the ability to read and write. They refer broadly to fluency or expertise in communicating and interacting with other people in many different ways. Thus, it's more accurate to speak about *literacies* when thinking about what it means to be a literate person. This book asks you to think broadly about what it means to be literate. What is writing? What is reading? How do you communicate and compose? How have you been taught to engage with texts and how has this influenced your understanding of writing and your relationship with writing? This

All of us have what Deborah Brandt will call "literacy sponsors." You see here a barber from Iowa who gave free back-to-school haircuts to kids who would read him a book. In this way, he helped them engage in and value reading, even if they hadn't found this same value at home.

chapter focuses on how individuals develop literacies and become literate learners. It asks you to think about what your literacies and your attitudes about literacies are, how they developed, how they influence one another, and who you are as a literate person. The purpose of doing so, of course, is to help you deeply engage with one of the *threshold concepts* we discussed in Chapter 1 — that our prior experiences deeply impact our writing and literacy practices.

In thinking about literacies, it might help you to start by considering your daily life. For example, every day you read and write all kinds of things that you probably rarely talk about in school and that you might not think about as literacy practices or forms of literacy: You check your Facebook account, you text friends, you Skype. You interpret thousands of visual images every time you turn on the television, read a magazine, or go to the mall. You also have literacies particular to your interests — you may know everything there is to know about a particular baseball player's RBIs, for example, or you may have advanced to an impressively high level in a complex, massively multiplayer online role-playing game like *World of Warcraft*. And, of course, you have home literacies that may be very different from school or hobby-related literacies. You may come from a family where languages other than English are spoken, or you may live in a community that values collaborative literacy practices (such as storytelling) that school often does not.

Researchers in the discipline of Writing Studies are particularly interested in these more complex ideas about literacy because they want to understand how people acquire literacies and what literacies a society should assist people in acquiring. For example, in contemporary U.S. culture, schools don't educate students in highly specialized literacies — for example, those related to most hobbies, like radio-controlled vehicles or gaming. Computer literacy was once in this category; as the use of computers went mainstream in the 1980s and 1990s, however — and particularly as it grew in importance in the workplace — the school system realized it needed to commit significant resources toward educating students in computer and information literacy.

The readings in this chapter ask you to consider what counts as "literacy," how people become literate, how cultures support and value various forms of literacy, and how we use (or adapt and change) literacy practices across contexts (or what Chapter 3 will describe as *discourse communities*). Deborah Brandt's "Sponsors of Literacy" will provide some starting definitions of literacy and some questions about how we acquire the literacies that we do. All of the other readings in the chapter can be understood in some ways as demonstrating the ideas that Brandt talks about in her piece — literacy, access to literacy, and the power that literacy can provide. The excerpts from Sandra Cisneros's, Malcolm X's, and Victor Villanueva's autobiographies are short but poignant examples of how an individual's family situation, financial situation, race, home language and culture, gender, and similar identifiers influence lifelong literacies, access to education, economic status, and the like. Arthur Tejada et al., a group of students who were labeled as "remedial" writers, ask you to consider how labels influence who you believe you are and what you believe you can do; they illustrate the power that institutions and teachers have in encouraging or discouraging students from all backgrounds to embrace their literacy and language practices. In two other selections, Vershawn Ashanti Young and Barbara Mellix specifically ask you to consider language use and how and why various forms of English are valued differently — and how those values affect writers.

The readings in this chapter also help you explicitly to consider how people use what they have learned in one setting when they are interacting in another setting. Liane Robertson, Kara Taczak, and Kathleen Black Yancey look at how students draw on (or don't draw on) prior knowledge in order to complete new literacy tasks. Nancy Sommers and Donald Murray write narrative pieces that demonstrate the ways that our identities and experiences inform what we write, how we write, and how we think of things to write in the first place. Lucas Pasqualin, a student, reflects on many of these ideas as he revisits his experiences as a young child from Brazil entering school in the United States. Finally, Jeff Grabill and his colleagues ask you to remember that technologies and media are part of the fabric of your experience as a literate learner.

Before you begin reading, take a few minutes to consider how you became the literate person you are today. No two people have exactly the same literacies, and yours are peculiar to your own personal history — your family, your geographic location, your culture, your hobbies, your religious training, your schooling, and so on. Consider, for example, the following questions:

- When and how did you learn to read?
- What did you read?
- Were there things you were not allowed to read?
- Where did you first or most memorably encounter texts as a child — for example, at home, at school, at a church or synagogue, at day care, at a friend's or relative's house?
- Did you write or draw as a child? Was this encouraged or discouraged?
- What languages or different forms of the same language do you speak at home and elsewhere?
- What technologies (from pencils to phones to social media platforms and desktop software) impact your literacy practices?

The **threshold concept** this chapter addresses is that your experiences have shaped your literacy practices — both what they are, and what they are not — so your answers will not be the same as other people's. All of us were shaped by what Brandt calls **literacy sponsors** — people, ideas, or institutions that helped us become literate, but literate in specific ways. If you attended private school instead of public school, for example, what were you exposed to and what literate experiences did you not have that public school students might have had?

As you reflect on your own experiences, consider both the texts you were exposed to and those you were not exposed to, or the ones that you were explicitly denied. When you learned to write, what motivated you to want to write? Who helped you — or did not? What kinds of things did you write, and for whom? As you grew older, did your interest in writing change? What factors impacted those changes — friends? teachers? parents? new hobbies?

This brief reflection on your literacy history should illustrate the point we are trying to make: You are a literate person; you are an expert on your own literacy practices and history; you have been shaped by many factors including home language, class, race, geographical location, and much more. You come to this chapter knowing a lot, and through the readings and activities you'll find here, we hope to help you uncover more of what you know, in addition to learning some things that you did not know before. We hope you will be able to see your past experiences living in your current experiences, and draw on them in creative and useful ways. We hope you will consciously consider what it means to be literate (and who decides what "literate" means), and what it means to read and write in various contexts and cultures — and by so doing broaden your understandings in new ways.

CHAPTER GOALS

- To understand the concepts of *literacy* and *multiple literacies*
- To consider how different forms of language and literacy are valued and by whom — and what the consequences are
- To acquire additional vocabulary for talking about yourself as a writer and reader
- To come to greater awareness of the forces that have shaped you as a writer and reader
- To consider how you use your literacy practices across different settings, what that means for you, and what it reveals about our culture at large
- To understand ways of conducting contributive research and writing about literacy that can be shared with an audience
- To strengthen your ability to read complex, research-based texts more confidently
- To gain experience writing from readings and citing sources

Sponsors of Literacy

DEBORAH BRANDT

Steve Wajda

Framing the Reading

Deborah Brandt is a professor emerita in the Department of English at the University of Wisconsin–Madison. She has written several books about literacy, including *Literacy as Involvement: The Acts of Writers, Readers and Texts* (Southern Illinois University Press, 1990); *Literacy in American Lives* (Cambridge University Press, 2001); and *Literacy and Learning: Reading, Writing, Society* (Jossey-Bass, 2009). Her most recent book is *The Rise of Writing: Redefining Mass Literacy* (Cambridge University Press, 2015). She has also written a number of scholarly research articles about literacy, including the one you are about to read here, "Sponsors of Literacy," which describes some of the data she collected when writing *Literacy in American Lives*. In that book, Brandt examined the way literacy learning changed between 1895 and 1985, noting that literacy standards have risen dramatically. In "Sponsors of Literacy" she discusses the forces that shape our literacy learning and practices.

Brandt's breakthrough idea in this piece is that people don't become literate on their own; rather, literacy is *sponsored* by people, institutions, and circumstances that both make it possible for a person to become literate and shape the way the person actually acquires literacy. And this is, of course, the threshold concept this chapter is emphasizing. In interviewing a large number of people from all ages and walks of life, Brandt began recognizing these literacy sponsors everywhere, and thus her article here (and the book that the same research led to) is crammed with examples of them, ranging from older siblings to auto manufacturers and World War II.

While we think of the term *sponsor* as suggesting support or assistance, Brandt doesn't confine her discussion to the supportive aspects of literacy sponsors. Her research shows ways in which, while opening some doors, literacy sponsors may close others. Literacy sponsors are not always (or even, perhaps, usually) altruistic — they have self-interested reasons for sponsoring literacy, and very often only some kinds of literacy

Brandt, Deborah. "Sponsors of Literacy." *College Composition and Communication*, vol. 49, no. 2, May 1998, pp. 165–85.

will support their goals. (If you've ever wondered why schools encourage you to read, but seem less than thrilled if you'd rather read the *Hunger Games* series than Ernest Hemingway, Brandt's explanation of literacy sponsorship may provide an answer.) Brandt also discusses cases where people "misappropriate" a literacy sponsor's intentions by using a particular literacy for their own ends rather than for the sponsor's.

Brandt's portrayal of the tension between people and their literacy sponsors illustrates one more important point in thinking about literacy acquisition and how each of us has become literate. We claim in the chapter introduction that you have a combination of literacies that make you unique. While this is true, people also share many of the *same* literacy experiences. Brandt can help us understand this, too. Some literacy sponsors are organizations or institutions, such as a public school system or a major corporation, whose sponsorship affects large numbers of people. During the Middle Ages prior to the invention of the printing press, the biggest literacy sponsor in Western civilization was the Roman Catholic Church, which shaped the literacies of virtually every person in feudal Europe as well as vast native populations around the world. Remember, literacy sponsors are not necessarily empowering; they can also disempower and *prevent* people from becoming literate in some ways while fostering other literacies. "Big" literacy sponsors such as these have likely influenced your literacy narrative in the same way they've influenced many others, giving you something in common with others around you even as your particular literacies are unique to you.

This reading is tagged in order to help you navigate it. Remember that the tags are explained in more detail in Chapter 1 (p. 58). You may want to quickly read about or review the tags there before you begin.

Getting Ready to Read

Before you read, do at least one of the following activities:

- Compare notes with a roommate or friend about what your school literacy experience was like. What books did the school encourage you to read and discourage you from reading? What events and activities supported reading?

- Make a list of the ways you've seen U.S. culture and your own local community encourage and emphasize reading. What are the reasons usually given for being a good reader and writer, and who gives those reasons?

As you read, consider the following questions:

- What are Brandt's primary terms, in addition to *literacy sponsor*, and how do they apply to you?

- Where do you see yourself in the examples Brandt gives, and where do you not? Keep your early literacy experiences in mind as you read.

- What are implications of Brandt's idea of literacy sponsors for your education *right now* as a college student?

IN HIS SWEEPING HISTORY of adult learning in the United States, Joseph Kett describes the intellectual atmosphere available to young apprentices who worked in the small, decentralized print shops of antebellum America. Because printers also were the solicitors and editors of what they published, their workshops served as lively incubators for literacy and political discourse. By the mid-nineteenth century, however, this learning space was disrupted when the invention of the steam press reorganized the economy of the print industry. Steam presses were so expensive that they required capital outlays beyond the means of many printers. As a result, print jobs were outsourced, the processes of editing and printing were split, and, in tight competition, print apprentices became low-paid mechanics with no more access to the multi-skilled environment of the craft-shop (Kett 67–70). While this shift in working conditions may be evidence of the deskilling of workers induced by the Industrial Revolution (Nicholas and Nicholas), it also offers a site for reflecting upon the dynamic sources of literacy and literacy learning. The reading and writing skills of print apprentices in this period were the achievements not simply of teachers and learners nor of the discourse practices of the printer community. Rather, these skills existed fragilely, contingently within an economic moment. The pre-steam press economy enabled some of the most basic aspects of the apprentices' literacy, especially their access to material production and the public meaning or worth of their skills. Paradoxically, even as the steam-powered penny press made print more accessible (by making publishing more profitable), it brought an end to a particular form of literacy sponsorship and a drop in literate potential.

1 The apprentices' experience invites rumination upon literacy learning and teaching today. Literacy looms as one of the great engines of profit and competitive advantage in the 20th century: a lubricant for consumer desire; a means for integrating corporate

GENRE CUES

1 — CARS: Territory The opening narrative has been an example of the overall problem the article will discuss.

markets; a foundation for the deployment of weapons and other technology; a raw material in the mass production of information. As ordinary citizens have been compelled into these economies, their reading and writing skills have grown sharply more central to the everyday trade of information and goods as well as to the pursuit of education, employment, civil rights, status. At the same time, people's literate skills have grown vulnerable to unprecedented turbulence in their economic value, as conditions, forms, and standards of literacy achievement seem to shift with almost every new generation of learners. How are we to understand the vicissitudes of individual literacy development in relationship to the large-scale economic forces that set the routes and determine the worldly worth of that literacy?

The field of writing studies has had much to say about individual literacy development. Especially in the last quarter of the 20th century, we have theorized, researched, critiqued, debated, and sometimes even managed to enhance the literate potentials of ordinary citizens as they have tried to cope with life as they find it. Less easily and certainly less steadily have we been able to relate what we see, study, and do to these larger contexts of profit making and competition. This even as we recognize that the most pressing issues we deal with—tightening associations between literate skill and social viability, the breakneck pace of change in communications technology, persistent inequities in access and reward—all relate to structural conditions in literacy's bigger picture. When economic forces are addressed in our work, they appear primarily as generalities: contexts, determinants, motivators, barriers, touchstones. But rarely are they systematically related to the local conditions and embodied moments of literacy learning that occupy so many of us on a daily basis.[1]

GENRE CUES

2 — CARS: Territory This broad question establishes the territory. It's not yet describing a "niche," the specific research question, but rather the overall subject.

3 — CARS: Niche

4 — CARS: Niche

This essay does not presume to overcome the analytical failure completely. But it does offer a conceptual approach that begins to connect literacy as an individual development to literacy as an economic development, at least as the two have played out over the last ninety years or so. The approach is through what I call sponsors of literacy. Sponsors, as I have come to think of them, are any agents, local or distant, concrete or abstract, who enable, support, teach, model, as well as recruit, regulate, suppress, or withhold literacy—and gain advantage by it in some way. Just as the ages of radio and television accustom us to having programs *brought* to us by various commercial sponsors, it is useful to think about who or what underwrites occasions of literacy learning and use. Although the interests of the sponsor and the sponsored do not have to converge (and, in fact, may conflict) sponsors nevertheless set the terms for access to literacy and wield powerful incentives for compliance and loyalty. Sponsors are a tangible reminder that literacy learning throughout history has always required permission, sanction, assistance, coercion, or, at minimum, contact with existing trade routes. Sponsors are delivery systems for the economies of literacy, the means by which these forces present themselves to—and through—individual learners. They also represent the causes into which people's literacy usually gets recruited.[2]

For the last five years I have been tracing sponsors of literacy across the 20th century as they appear in the accounts of ordinary Americans recalling how they learned to write and read. The investigation is grounded in more than 100 in-depth interviews that I collected from a diverse group of people born roughly between 1900 and 1980. In the interviews, people

GENRE CUES

⑤ CARS: Occupy Often, as here, writers mark their contribution to the conversation with an "I" statement.

⑥ Framework Endnotes often give details on conversations a writer joins or history on the source of an idea. Check them!

⑦ Research Questions Even without question marks, you can infer Brandt's research questions from her methods statement here.

explored in great detail their memories of learning to read and write across their lifetimes, focusing especially on the people, institutions, materials, and motivations involved in the process. The more I worked with these accounts, the more I came to realize that they were filled with references to sponsors, both explicit and latent, who appeared in formative roles at the scenes of literacy learning. Patterns of sponsorship became an illuminating site through which to track the different cultural attitudes people developed toward writing vs. reading as well as the ideological congestion faced by late-century literacy learners as their sponsors proliferated and diversified (see my essays on "Remembering Reading" and "Accumulating Literacy"). In this essay I set out a case for why the concept of sponsorship is so richly suggestive for exploring economies of literacy and their effects. Then, through use of extended case examples, I demonstrate the practical application of this approach for interpreting current conditions of literacy teaching and learning, including persistent stratification of opportunity and escalating standards for literacy achievement. A final section addresses implications for the teaching of writing.

8

SPONSORSHIP

Intuitively, *sponsors* seemed a fitting term for the figures who turned up most typically in people's memories of literacy learning: older relatives, teachers, priests, supervisors, military officers, editors, influential authors. Sponsors, as we ordinarily think of them, are powerful figures who bankroll events or smooth the way for initiates. Usually richer, more knowledgeable, and more entrenched than the sponsored, sponsors nevertheless enter a reciprocal relationship with those they underwrite. They lend their resources or credibility to the sponsored but also stand to gain benefits from their success,

6

GENRE CUES

8— Forecasting

whether by direct repayment or, indirectly, by credit of association. *Sponsors* also proved an appealing term in my analysis because of all the commercial references that appeared in these 20th-century accounts—the magazines, peddled encyclopedias, essay contests, radio and television programs, toys, fan clubs, writing tools, and so on, from which so much experience with literacy was derived. As the 20th century turned the abilities to read and write into widely exploitable resources, commercial sponsorship abounded.

In whatever form, sponsors deliver the ideological freight that must be borne for access to what they have. Of course, the sponsored can be oblivious to or innovative with this ideological burden. Like Little Leaguers who wear the logo of a local insurance agency on their uniforms, not out of a concern for enhancing the agency's image but as a means for getting to play ball, people throughout history have acquired literacy pragmatically under the banner of others' causes. In the days before free, public schooling in England, Protestant Sunday Schools warily offered basic reading instruction to working-class families as part of evangelical duty. To the horror of many in the church sponsorship, these families insistently, sometimes riotously demanded of their Sunday Schools more instruction, including in writing and math, because it provided means for upward mobility.[3] Through the sponsorship of Baptist and Methodist ministries, African Americans in slavery taught each other to understand the Bible in subversively liberatory ways. Under a conservative regime, they developed forms of critical literacy that sustained religious, educational, and political movements both before and after emancipation (Cornelius). Most of the time, however, literacy takes its shape from the interests of its sponsors. And, as we will see below, obligations toward one's sponsors run deep, affecting what, why, and how people write and read.

The concept of sponsors helps to explain, then, a range of human relationships and ideological pressures that turn up at the

7

8

scenes of literacy learning—from benign sharing between adults and youths, to euphemized coercions in schools and workplaces, to the most notorious impositions and deprivations by church or state. It also is a concept useful for tracking literacy's material: the things that accompany writing and reading and the ways they are manufactured and distributed. Sponsorship as a sociological term is even more broadly suggestive for thinking about economies of literacy development. Studies of patronage in Europe and *compadrazgo* in the Americas show how patron-client relationships in the past grew up around the need to manage scarce resources and promote political stability (Bourne; Lynch; Horstman and Kurtz). Pragmatic, instrumental, ambivalent, patron-client relationships integrated otherwise antagonistic social classes into relationships of mutual, albeit unequal dependencies. Loaning land, money, protection, and other favors allowed the politically powerful to extend their influence and justify their exploitation of clients. Clients traded their labor and deference for access to opportunities for themselves or their children and for leverage needed to improve their social standing. Especially under conquest in Latin America, *compadrazgo* reintegrated native societies badly fragmented by the diseases and other disruptions that followed foreign invasions. At the same time, this system was susceptible to its own stresses, especially when patrons became clients themselves of still more centralized or distant overlords, with all the shifts in loyalty and perspective that entailed (Horstman and Kurtz 13–14).

In raising this association with formal systems of patronage, I do not wish to overlook the very different economic, political, and educational systems within which U.S. literacy has developed. But where we find the sponsoring of literacy, it will be useful to look for its function within larger political and economic arenas. Literacy, like land, is a valued commodity in this economy, a key resource in gaining profit and edge. This value helps to explain, of course, the lengths people will go to secure literacy for themselves

9

or their children. But it also explains why the powerful work so persistently to conscript and ration the powers of literacy. The competition to harness literacy, to manage, measure, teach, and exploit it, has intensified throughout the century. It is vital to pay attention to this development because it largely sets the terms for individuals' encounters with literacy. This competition shapes the incentives and barriers (including uneven distributions of opportunity) that greet literacy learners in any particular time and place. It is this competition that has made access to the right kinds of literacy sponsors so crucial for political and economic well-being. And it also has spurred the rapid, complex changes that now make the pursuit of literacy feel so turbulent and precarious for so many.

(9) In the next three sections, I trace the dynamics of literacy sponsorship through the life experiences of several individuals, showing how their opportunities for literacy learning emerge out of the jockeying and skirmishing for economic and political advantage going on among sponsors of literacy. Along the way, the analysis addresses three key issues: **(10)** (1) how, despite ostensible democracy in educational chances, stratification of opportunity continues to organize access and reward in literacy learning; (2) how sponsors contribute to what is called "the literacy crisis," that is, the perceived gap between rising standards for achievement and people's ability to meet them; and (3) how encounters with literacy sponsors, especially as they are configured at the end of the 20th century, can be sites for the innovative rerouting of resources into projects of self-development and social change.

10

SPONSORSHIP AND ACCESS

A focus on sponsorship can force a more explicit and substantive link between literacy learning and systems of opportunity and access. A statistical correlation between high literacy achievement and high socioeconomic, majority-race status

11

GENRE CUES

9 — Forecasting

10 — Research Questions

routinely shows up in results of national tests of reading and writing performance.[4] These findings capture yet, in their shorthand way, obscure the unequal conditions of literacy sponsorship that lie behind differential outcomes in academic performance. Throughout their lives, affluent people from high-caste racial groups have multiple and redundant contacts with powerful literacy sponsors as a routine part of their economic and political privileges. Poor people and those from low-caste racial groups have less consistent, less politically secured access to literacy sponsors—especially to the ones that can grease their way to academic and economic success. Differences in their performances are often attributed to family background (namely education and income of parents) or to particular norms and values operating within different ethnic groups or social classes. But in either case, much more is usually at work.

As a study in contrasts in sponsorship patterns and access to literacy, consider the parallel experiences of Raymond Branch and Dora Lopez, both of whom were born in 1969 and, as young children, moved with their parents to the same, mid-sized university town in the midwest.[5] Both were still residing in this town at the time of our interviews in 1995. Raymond Branch, a European American, had been born in southern California, the son of a professor father and a real estate executive mother. He recalled that his first-grade classroom in 1975 was hooked up to a mainframe computer at Stanford University and that, as a youngster, he enjoyed fooling around with computer programming in the company of "real users" at his father's science lab. This process was not interrupted much when, in the late 1970s, his family moved to the midwest. Raymond received his first personal computer as a Christmas present from his parents when he was twelve years old, and a modem the year after that. In the 1980s, computer hardware and software stores began popping up within a bicycle-ride's distance from where he lived. The stores were serving the university community and, increasingly, the high-tech industries that were becoming established in that vicinity. As an adolescent,

12

Raymond spent his summers roaming these stores, sampling new computer games, making contact with founders of some of the first electronic bulletin boards in the nation, and continuing, through reading and other informal means, to develop his programming techniques. At the time of our interview he had graduated from the local university and was a successful freelance writer of software and software documentation, with clients in both the private sector and the university community.

Dora Lopez, a Mexican American, was born in the same year as Raymond Branch, 1969, in a Texas border town, where her grandparents, who worked as farm laborers, lived most of the year. When Dora was still a baby her family moved to the same midwest university town as had the family of Raymond Branch. Her father pursued an accounting degree at a local technical college and found work as a shipping and receiving clerk at the university. Her mother, who also attended technical college briefly, worked part-time in a bookstore. In the early 1970s, when the Lopez family made its move to the midwest, the Mexican-American population in the university town was barely one per cent. Dora recalled that the family had to drive seventy miles to a big city to find not only suitable groceries but also Spanish-language newspapers and magazines that carried information of concern and interest to them. (Only when reception was good could they catch Spanish-language radio programs coming from Chicago, 150 miles away.) During her adolescence, Dora Lopez undertook to teach herself how to read and write in Spanish, something, she said, that neither her brother nor her U.S.-born cousins knew how to do. Sometimes, with the help of her mother's employee discount at the bookstore, she sought out novels by South American and Mexican writers, and she practiced her written Spanish by corresponding with relatives in Colombia. She was exposed to computers for the first time at the age of thirteen when she worked as a teacher's aide in a federally-funded summer school program for the children of migrant workers. The computers were being used to help the children to be brought up to grade level in their

13

reading and writing skills. When Dora was admitted to the same university that Raymond Branch attended, her father bought her a used word processing machine that a student had advertised for sale on a bulletin board in the building where Mr. Lopez worked. At the time of our interview, Dora Lopez had transferred from the university to a technical college. She was working for a cleaning company, where she performed extra duties as a translator, communicating on her supervisor's behalf with the largely Latina cleaning staff. "I write in Spanish for him, what he needs to be translated, like job duties, what he expects them to do, and I write lists for him in English and Spanish," she explained.

In Raymond Branch's account of his early literacy learning we are able to see behind the scenes of his majority-race membership, male gender, and high-end socioeconomic family profile. There lies a thick and, to him, relatively accessible economy of institutional and commercial supports that cultivated and subsidized his acquisition of a powerful form of literacy. One might be tempted to say that Raymond Branch was born at the right time and lived in the right place—except that the experience of Dora Lopez troubles that thought. For Raymond Branch, a university town in the 1970s and 1980s provided an information-rich, resource-rich learning environment in which to pursue his literacy development, but for Dora Lopez, a female member of a culturally unsubsidized ethnic minority, the same town at the same time was information- and resource-poor. Interestingly, both young people were pursuing projects of self-initiated learning, Raymond Branch in computer programming and Dora Lopez in biliteracy. But she had to reach much further afield for the material and communicative systems needed to support her learning. Also, while Raymond Branch, as the son of an academic, was sponsored by some of the most powerful agents of the university (its laboratories, newest technologies, and most educated personnel), Dora Lopez was being sponsored by what her parents could pull from the peripheral service systems of the university (the mail room, the bookstore, the second-hand technology market). In these accounts

14

we also can see how the development and eventual economic worth of Raymond Branch's literacy skills were underwritten by late-century transformations in communication technology that created a boomtown need for programmers and software writers. Dora Lopez's biliterate skills developed and paid off much further down the economic-reward ladder, in government-sponsored youth programs and commercial enterprises, that, in the 1990s, were absorbing surplus migrant workers into a low-wage, urban service economy.[6] Tracking patterns of literacy sponsorship, then, gets beyond SES shorthand to expose more fully how unequal literacy chances relate to systems of unequal subsidy and reward for literacy. These are the systems that deliver large-scale economic, historical, and political conditions to the scenes of small-scale literacy use and development.

⑪

This analysis of sponsorship forces us to consider not merely how one social group's literacy practices may differ from another's, but how everybody's literacy practices are operating in differential economies, which supply different access routes, different degrees of sponsoring power, and different scales of monetary worth to the practices in use. In fact, the interviews I conducted are filled with examples of how economic and political forces, some of them originating in quite distant corporate and government policies, affect people's day-to-day ability to seek out and practice literacy. As a telephone company employee, Janelle Hampton enjoyed a brief period in the early 1980s as a fraud investigator, pursuing inquiries and writing up reports of her efforts. But when the breakup of the telephone utility reorganized its workforce, the fraud division was moved two states away and she was returned to less interesting work as a data processor. When,

⑫

15

GENRE CUES

⑪— Making Knowledge Read this endnote for a direct statement of one point Brandt wishes to make in her article.

⑫— Making Knowledge Brandt likes to show a lot of data and then swoop her knowledge-making into a short summary statement like this.

which, for a number of reasons, is becoming a key requirement for literacy learning at the end of the 20th century.

The following discussion will consider two brief cases of literacy diversion. Both involve women working in subordinate positions as secretaries, in print-rich settings where better-educated male supervisors were teaching them to read and write in certain ways to perform their clerical duties. However, as we will see shortly, strong loyalties outside the workplace prompted these two secretaries to lift these literate resources for use in other spheres. For one, Carol White, it was on behalf of her work as a Jehovah's Witness. For the other, Sarah Steele, it was on behalf of upward mobility for her lower-middle-class family. 28

Before turning to their narratives, though, it will be wise to pay some attention to the economic moment in which they occur. Clerical work was the largest and fastest-growing occupation for women in the 20th century. Like so much employment for women, it offered a mix of gender-defined constraints as well as avenues for economic independence and mobility. As a new information economy created an acute need for typists, stenographers, bookkeepers, and other office workers, white, American-born women and, later, immigrant and minority women saw reason to pursue high school and business-college educations. Unlike male clerks of the 19th century, female secretaries in this century had little chance for advancement. However, office work represented a step up from the farm or the factory for women of the working class and served as a respectable occupation from which educated, middle-class women could await or avoid marriage (Anderson, Strom). In a study of clerical work through the first half of the 20th century, Mary Christine Anderson estimated that secretaries might encounter up to 97 different genres in the course of doing dictation or transcription. They routinely had contact with an array of professionals, including lawyers, auditors, tax examiners, and other government overseers (52–53). By 1930, 30% of women office workers used machines other than typewriters (Anderson 76) and, in contemporary offices, clerical workers have 29 often been the first employees to learn to operate CRTs and personal computers and to teach others how to use them. Overall, the daily duties of 20th-century secretaries could serve handily as an index to the rise of complex administrative and accounting procedures, standardization of information, expanding communication, and developments in technological systems.

With that background, consider the experiences of Carol White and Sarah Steele. An Oneida, Carol White was born into a poor, single-parent household in 1940. She graduated from high school in 1960 and, between five maternity leaves and a divorce, worked continuously in a series of clerical positions in both the private and public sectors. One of her first secretarial jobs was with an urban firm that produced and disseminated Catholic missionary films. The vice-president with whom she worked most closely also spent much of his time producing a magazine for a national civic organization that he headed. She discussed how typing letters and magazine articles and occasionally proofreading for this man taught her rhetorical strategies in which she was keenly interested. She described the scene of transfer this way:

> [My boss] didn't just write to write. He wrote in a way
> to make his letters appealing. I would have to write what
> he was writing in this magazine too. I was completely
> enthralled. He would write about the people who were
> in this [organization] and the different works they were
> undertaking and people that died and people who were sick
> and about their personalities. And he wrote little anecdotes.
> Once in a while I made some suggestions too. He was a man
> who would listen to you.

The appealing and persuasive power of the anecdote became especially important to Carol White when she began doing door-to-door missionary work for the Jehovah's Witnesses, a pan-racial, millennialist religious faith. She now uses colorful anecdotes to prepare demonstrations that she performs with other women at weekly service meetings at their Kingdom Hall.

30

These demonstrations, done in front of the congregation, take the form of skits designed to explore daily problems through Bible principles. Further, at the time of our interview, Carol White was working as a municipal revenue clerk and had recently enrolled in an on-the-job training seminar called Persuasive Communication, a two-day class offered free to public employees. Her motivation for taking the course stemmed from her desire to improve her evangelical work. She said she wanted to continue to develop speaking and writing skills that would be "appealing," "motivating," and "encouraging" to people she hoped to convert.

Sarah Steele, a woman of Welsh and German descent, was born in 1920 into a large, working-class family in a coal mining community in eastern Pennsylvania. In 1940, she graduated from a two-year commercial college. Married soon after, she worked as a secretary in a glass factory until becoming pregnant with the first of four children. In the 1960s, in part to help pay for her children's college educations, she returned to the labor force as a receptionist and bookkeeper in a law firm, where she stayed until her retirement in the late 1970s. 31

Sarah Steele described how, after joining the law firm, she began to model her household management on principles of budgeting that she was picking up from one of the attorneys with whom she worked most closely. "I learned cash flow from Mr. B_____," she said. "I would get all the bills and put a tape in the adding machine and he and I would sit down together to be sure there was going to be money ahead." She said that she began to replicate that process at home with household bills. "Before that," she observed, "I would just cook beans when I had to instead of meat." Sarah Steele also said she encountered the genre of the credit report during routine reading and typing on the job. She figured out what constituted a top rating, making sure her husband followed these steps in preparation for their financing a new car. She also remembered typing up documents connected to civil suits being brought against local businesses, teaching her, she said, which firms never to hire for home repairs. "It just changes the way you think," she 32 observed about the reading and writing she did on her job. "You're not a pushover after you learn how business operates." .

The dynamics of sponsorship alive in these narratives expose important elements of literacy appropriation, at least as it is practiced at the end of the 20th century. In a pattern now familiar from the earlier sections, we see how opportunities for literacy learning—this time for diversions of resources—open up in the clash between long-standing, residual forms of sponsorship and the new: between the lingering presence of literacy's conservative history and its pressure for change. So, here, two women—one Native American and both working-class—filch contemporary literacy resources (public relations techniques and accounting practices) from more-educated, higher-status men. The women are emboldened in these acts by ulterior identities beyond the workplace: Carol White with faith and Sarah Steele with family. These affiliations hark back to the first sponsoring arrangements through which American women were gradually allowed to acquire literacy and education. Duties associated with religious faith and child rearing helped literacy to become, in Gloria Main's words, "a permissable feminine activity" (579). Interestingly, these roles, deeply sanctioned within the history of women's literacy— and operating beneath the newer permissible feminine activity of clerical work—become grounds for covert, innovative appropriation even as they reinforce traditional female identities.

Just as multiple identities contribute to the ideologically hybrid character of these literacy formations, so do institutional and material conditions. Carol White's account speaks to such hybridity. The missionary film company with the civic club vice president is a residual site for two of literacy's oldest campaigns— Christian conversion and civic participation—enhanced here by 20th-century advances in film and public relations techniques. This ideological reservoir proved a pleasing instructional site for Carol White, whose interests in literacy, throughout her life, have

33

(19)

34

GENRE CUES

 19— Making Knowledge

been primarily spiritual. So literacy appropriation draws upon, perhaps even depends upon, conservative forces in the history of literacy sponsorship that are always hovering at the scene of acts of learning. This history serves as both a sanctioning force and a reserve of ideological and material support.

At the same time, however, we see in these accounts how individual acts of appropriation can divert and subvert the course of literacy's history, how changes in individual literacy experiences relate to larger-scale transformations. Carol White's redirection of personnel management techniques to the cause of the Jehovah's Witnesses is an almost ironic transformation in this regard. Once a principal sponsor in the initial spread of mass literacy, evangelism is here rejuvenated through late-literate corporate sciences of secular persuasion, fund-raising, and bureaucratic management that Carol White finds circulating in her contemporary workplaces. By the same token, through Sarah Steele, accounting practices associated with corporations are, in a sense, tracked into the house, rationalizing and standardizing even domestic practices. (Even though Sarah Steele did not own an adding machine, she penciled her budget figures onto adding-machine tape that she kept for that purpose.) Sarah Steele's act of appropriation in some sense explains how dominant forms of literacy migrate and penetrate into private spheres, including private consciousness. At the same time, though, she accomplishes a subversive diversion of literate power. Her efforts to move her family up in the middle class involved not merely contributing a second income but also, from her desk as a bookkeeper, reading her way into an understanding of middle-class economic power.

TEACHING AND THE DYNAMICS OF SPONSORSHIP

It hardly seems necessary to point out to the readers of *CCC* that we haul a lot of freight for the opportunity to teach writing. Neither rich nor powerful enough to sponsor literacy on our own terms, we serve instead as conflicted brokers between

35

36

literacy's buyers and sellers. At our most worthy, perhaps, we show the sellers how to beware and try to make sure these exchanges will be a little fairer, maybe, potentially, a little more mutually rewarding. This essay has offered a few working case studies that link patterns of sponsorship to processes of **(20)** stratification, competition, and reappropriation. How much these dynamics can be generalized to classrooms is an ongoing empirical question.

I am sure that sponsors play even more influential roles at the scenes of literacy learning and use than this essay has explored. I have focused on some of the most tangible aspects — material supply, explicit teaching, institutional aegis. But the ideological pressure of sponsors affects many private aspects of writing processes as well as public aspects of finished texts. Where one's sponsors are multiple or even at odds, they can make writing maddening. Where they are absent, they make writing unlikely. Many of the cultural formations we associate with writing development — community practices, disciplinary traditions, technological potentials — can be appreciated as make-do responses to the economics of literacy, past and present. The history of literacy is a catalogue of obligatory relations. That this catalogue is so deeply conservative and, at the same time, so ruthlessly demanding of change is what fills contemporary literacy learning and teaching with their most paradoxical choices and outcomes.[9]

In bringing attention to economies of literacy learning I am not advocating that we prepare students more efficiently for the job markets they must enter. What I have tried to suggest is that as we assist and study individuals in pursuit of literacy, we also recognize how literacy is in pursuit of them. When this process stirs ambivalence, on their part or on ours, we need to be understanding.

37

38

GENRE CUES

 So What?

Acknowledgments

This research was sponsored by the NCTE Research Foundation and the Center on English Learning and Achievement. The Center is supported by the U.S. Department of Education's Office of Educational Research and Improvement, whose views do not necessarily coincide with the author's. A version of this essay was given as a lecture in the Department of English, University of Louisville, in April 1997. Thanks to Anna Syvertsen and Julie Nelson for their help with archival research. Thanks too to colleagues who lent an ear along the way: Nelson Graff, Jonna Gjevre, Anne Gere, Kurt Spellmeyer, Tom Fox, and Bob Gundlach.

Notes

1. Three of the keenest and most eloquent observers of economic impacts on writing, teaching, and learning have been Lester Faigley, Susan Miller, and Kurt Spellmeyer.

2. My debt to the writings of Pierre Bourdieu will be evident throughout this essay. Here and throughout I invoke his expansive notion of "economy," which is not restricted to literal and ostensible systems of money making but to the many spheres where people labor, invest, and exploit energies — their own and others' — to maximize advantage, see Bourdieu and Wacquant, especially 117–120 and Bourdieu, Chapter 7.

3. Thomas Laqueur (124) provides a vivid account of a street demonstration in Bolton, England, in 1834 by a "pro-writing" faction of Sunday School students and their teachers. This faction demanded that writing instruction continue to be provided on Sundays, something that opponents of secular instruction on the Sabbath were trying to reverse.

4. See, for instance, National Assessments of Educational Progress in reading and writing (Applebee et al.; and "Looking").

5. All names used in this essay are pseudonyms.

6. I am not suggesting that literacy that does not "pay off" in terms of prestige or monetary reward is less valuable. Dora Lopez's ability to read and write in Spanish was a source of great strength and pride, especially when she was able to teach it to her young child. The resource of Spanish literacy carried much of what Bourdieu calls cultural capital in her social and family circles. But I want to point out here how people who labor equally to acquire literacy do so under systems of unequal subsidy and unequal reward.

7. For useful accounts of this period in union history, see Heckscher; Nelson.

8. Marcia Farr associates "essayist literacy" with written genres esteemed in the academy and noted for their explicitness, exactness, reliance on reasons and evidence, and impersonal voice.

9. Lawrence Cremin makes similar points about education in general in his essay "The Cacophony of Teaching." He suggests that complex economic and social changes since World War Two, including the popularization of schooling and the penetration of mass media, have created "a far greater range and diversity of languages, competencies, values, personalities, and approaches to the world and to its educational opportunities" than at one time existed. The diversity most of interest to him (and me) resides not so much in the range of different ethnic groups there are in society but in the different cultural formulas by which people assemble their educational — or, I would say, literate — experience.

Works Cited

Anderson, Mary Christine. "Gender, Class, and Culture: Women Secretarial and Clerical Workers in the United States, 1925–1955." Diss. Ohio State U, 1986.

Applebee, Arthur N., Judith A. Langer, and Ida V. S. Mullis. *The Writing Report Card: Writing Achievement in American Schools.* Princeton: ETS, 1986.

Bourdieu, Pierre. *The Logic of Practice.* Trans. Richard Nice. Cambridge: Polity, 1990.

Bourdieu, Pierre, and Loic J. D. Wacquant. *An Invitation to Reflexive Sociology.* Chicago: Chicago UP, 1992.

Bourne, J. M. *Patronage and Society in Nineteenth-Century England.* London: Edward Arnold, 1986.

Brandt, Deborah. "Remembering Reading, Remembering Writing." *CCC* 45 (1994): 459–79.

———. "Accumulating Literacy: Writing and Learning to Write in the 20th Century." *College English* 57 (1995): 649–68.

Cornelius, Janet Duitsman. '*When I Can Ready My Title Clear*': Literacy, Slavery, and Religion in the Antebellum South.* Columbia: U of South Carolina P, 1991.

Cremin, Lawrence. "The Cacophony of Teaching." *Popular Education and Its Discontents.* New York: Harper, 1990.

Faigley, Lester. "Veterans' Stories on the Porch." *History, Reflection and Narrative: The Professionalization of Composition, 1963–1983.* Eds. Beth Boehm, Debra Journet, and Mary Rosner. Norwood: Ablex, 1999. 23–38.

Farr, Marcia. "Essayist Literacy and Other Verbal Performances." *Written Communication* 8 (1993): 4–38.

Heckscher, Charles C. *The New Unionism: Employee Involvement in the Changing Corporation.* New York: Basic, 1988.

Horstman, Connie, and Donald V. Kurtz. *Compadrazgo in Post-Conquest Middle America.* Milwaukee: Milwaukee-UW Center for Latin America, 1978.

Kett, Joseph F. *The Pursuit of Knowledge Under Difficulties: From Self Improvement to Adult Education in America 1750–1990.* Stanford: Stanford UP, 1994.

Laqueur, Thomas. *Religion and Respectability: Sunday Schools and Working Class Culture 1780–1850.* New Haven: Yale UP, 1976.

Looking at How Well Our Students Read: The 1992 National Assessment of Educational Progress in Reading. Washington: US Dept. of Education, Office of Educational Research and Improvement, Educational Resources Information Center, 1992.

Lynch, Joseph H. *Godparents and Kinship in Early Medieval Europe.* Princeton: Princeton UP, 1986.

Main, Gloria L. "An Inquiry into When and Why Women Learned to Write in Colonial New England." *Journal of Social History* 24 (1991): 579–89.

Miller, Susan. *Textual Carnivals: The Politics of Composition.* Carbondale: Southern Illinois UP, 1991.

Nelson, Daniel. *American Rubber Workers and Organized Labor, 1900–1941.* Princeton: Princeton UP, 1988.

Nicholas, Stephen J., and Jacqueline M. Nicholas. "Male Literacy, 'Deskilling,' and the Industrial Revolution." *Journal of Interdisciplinary History* 23 (1992): 1–18.

Resnick, Daniel P., and Lauren B. Resnick. "The Nature of Literacy: A Historical Explanation." *Harvard Educational Review* 47 (1977): 370–85.

Spellmeyer, Kurt. "After Theory: From Textuality to Attunement with the World." *College English* 58 (1996): 893–913.

Stevens, Jr., Edward. *Literacy, Law, and Social Order.* DeKalb: Northern Illinois UP, 1987.

Strom, Sharon Hartman. *Beyond the Typewriter: Gender, Class, and the Origins of Modern American Office Work, 1900–1930.* Urbana: U of Illinois P, 1992.

Questions for Discussion and Journaling

1. How does Brandt define *literacy sponsor*? What are the characteristics of a literacy sponsor?

2. How does Brandt support her claim that sponsors always have something to gain from their sponsorship? Can you provide any examples from your own experience?

3. How do the sponsored sometimes "misappropriate" their literacy lessons?

4. Consider Brandt's claim that literacy sponsors "help to organize and administer stratified systems of opportunity and access, and they raise the literacy stakes in struggles for competitive advantage" (para. 27). What does Brandt mean by the term *stratified*? What "stakes" is she referring to?

5. Giving the examples of Branch and Lopez as support, Brandt argues that race and class impact how much access people have to literacy sponsorship. Summarize the kinds of access Branch and Lopez had — for example, in their early education, access to books and computers, and parental support — and decide whether you agree with Brandt's claim.

Applying and Exploring Ideas

1. Compare your own literacy history with that of Branch and of Lopez, using categories like those in discussion question 5 above. Then consider who your primary literacy sponsors were (people, as well as institutions such as churches or clubs or school systems) and what literacies they taught you (academic, civic, religious, and so on). Would you consider the access provided by these sponsors adequate? What literacies have you not had access to that you wish you had?

2. Have you ever had literacy sponsors who withheld (or tried to withhold) certain kinds of literacies from you? For example, did your school ban certain books? Have sponsors forced certain kinds of literacies on you (for example, approved reading lists in school) or held up some literacies as better than others (for example, saying that certain kinds of books didn't "count" as reading)? Were you able to find alternative sponsors for different kinds of literacy?

3. Interview a classmate about a significant literacy sponsor in their lives, and then discuss the interview in an entry on a class wiki or blog, a brief presentation, or a one-page report. Try to cover these questions in your interview:

   a. Who or what was your literacy sponsor?

   b. What did you gain from the sponsorship?

   c. Did you "misappropriate" the literacy in any way?

   d. What materials, technologies, and so forth were involved?

   In reflecting on the interview, ask yourself the following:

   a. Did the sponsorship connect to larger cultural or material developments?

   b. Does the sponsorship let you make any hypotheses about the culture of your interviewee? How would you test that hypothesis?

   c. Does your classmate's account have a "So what?" — a point that might make others care about it?

- -

META MOMENT Review the goals for this chapter (p. 67): For which goals is Brandt's article relevant? Are there experiences you're currently having that Brandt's ideas help to explain?

- -

Only Daughter

SANDRA CISNEROS

David Livingston/Getty Images

Framing the Reading

Sandra Cisneros is a successful and prolific writer of poetry, novels, stories, children's books, and even a picture book for adults. Some of her best-known work includes *The House on Mango Street* (1984) and *Woman Hollering Creek and Other Stories* (1991). She returns frequently to the theme of Chicana identity in her writing. She has won numerous awards for her work, including the MacArthur Fellowship, two National Endowment for the Arts fellowships, and a Texas Medal of Arts. Born to Mexican American parents, she grew up in Chicago with six brothers and now lives in Mexico.

The following short narrative describes the struggle she faced to gain her father's approval for her writing. This narrative illustrates Brandt's idea of literacy sponsorship, including ways that sponsors seek to promote certain kinds of literacy experiences and not others, and the way that the sponsored can "misappropriate" the literacy experiences available to them toward ends other than those intended by the sponsor. Cisneros's text also asks you to think about what it means to be multilingual, and how literacy experiences differ (and are valued differently) across different cultural contexts. These ideas will be taken up in other ways later in this chapter.

Getting Ready to Read

Before you read, do at least one of the following activities:

- Refresh your memory regarding Brandt's definition of literacy sponsor in the previous reading.
- Google Sandra Cisneros and learn a little more about what she has written.

As you read, consider the following questions:

- How do Cisneros's experiences illustrate the idea of literacy sponsorship?
- In what ways are your experiences with literacy and family similar to and different from Cisneros's?

Cisneros, Sandra. "Only Daughter." *Glamour*, Nov. 1990, pp. 256–57.

ONCE, SEVERAL YEARS AGO, when I was just starting out my writing career, 1
I was asked to write my own contributor's note for an anthology I was part of. I
wrote: "I am the only daughter in a family of six sons. *That* explains everything."

Well, I've thought about that ever since, and yes, it explains a lot to me, but 2
for the reader's sake I should have written: "I am the only daughter in a *Mexican*
family of six sons." Or even: "I am the only daughter of a Mexican father and
a Mexican American mother." Or: "I am the only daughter of a working-class
family of nine." All of these had everything to do with who I am today.

I was/am the only daughter and *only* a daughter. Being an only daughter in 3
a family of six sons forced me by circumstance to spend a lot of time by myself
because my brothers felt it beneath them to play with a *girl* in public. But that
aloneness, that loneliness, was good for a would-be writer—it allowed me time
to think and think, to imagine, to read and prepare myself.

Being only a daughter for my father meant my destiny would lead me to 4
become someone's wife. That's what he believed. But when I was in fifth grade and
shared my plans for college with him, I was sure he understood. I remember my
father saying, "*Que bueno, mi'ja*, that's good." That meant a lot to me, especially
since my brothers thought the idea hilarious. What I didn't realize was that my
father thought college was good for girls—for finding a husband. After four
years in college and two more in graduate school, and still no husband, my
father shakes his head even now and says I wasted all that education.

In retrospect, I'm lucky my father believed daughters were meant for hus- 5
bands. It meant it didn't matter if I majored in something silly like English. After
all, I'd find a nice professional eventually, right? This allowed me the liberty to
putter about embroidering my little poems and stories without my father inter-
rupting with so much as a "What's that you're writing?"

But the truth is, I wanted him to interrupt. I wanted my father to under- 6
stand what it was I was scribbling, to introduce me as "My only daughter,
the writer." Not as "This is my only daughter.
She teaches." *El maestra*—teacher. Not even
profesora.

> I wanted my father to under-
> stand what I was scribbling,
> to introduce me as "My only
> daughter, the writer."

In a sense, everything I have ever written has 7
been for him, to win his approval even though I
know my father can't read English words, even
though my father's only reading includes the
brown-ink *Esto* sports magazines from Mexico
City and the bloody *¡Alarma!* magazines that feature yet another sighting of *La
Virgen de Guadalupe* on a tortilla or a wife's revenge on her philandering husband by bashing his skull in with a *molcajete* (a kitchen mortar made of volcanic
rock). Or the *fotonovelas*, the little picture paperbacks with tragedy and trauma
erupting from the characters' mouths in bubbles.

My father represents, then, the public majority. A public who is uninterested 8
in reading, and yet one whom I am writing about and for, and privately trying
to woo.

When we were growing up in Chicago, we moved a lot because of my father. 9
He suffered periodic bouts of nostalgia. Then we'd have to let go our flat, store
the furniture with mother's relatives, load the station wagon with baggage and
bologna sandwiches, and head south. To Mexico City.

We came back, of course. To yet another Chicago flat, another Chicago 10
neighborhood, another Catholic school. Each time, my father would seek out
the parish priest in order to get a tuition break, and complain or boast: "I have
seven sons."

He meant *siete hijos*, seven children, but he translated it as "sons." "I have 11
seven sons." To anyone who would listen. The Sears Roebuck employee who
sold us the washing machine. The short-order cook, where my father ate his
ham-and-eggs breakfasts. "I have seven sons." As if he deserved a medal from
the state.

My papa. He didn't mean anything by that mistranslation, I'm sure. But 12
somehow I could feel myself being erased. I'd tug my father's sleeve and whisper:
"Not seven sons. Six! and *one daughter.*"

When my oldest brother graduated from medical school, he fulfilled my 13
father's dream that we study hard and use this—our heads, instead of this—our
hands. Even now my father's hands are thick and yellow, stubbed by a history of
hammer and nails and twine and coils and springs. "Use this," my father said,
tapping his head, "and not this," showing us those hands. He always looked tired
when he said it.

Wasn't college an investment? And hadn't I spent all those years in college? 14
And if I didn't marry, what was it all for? Why would anyone go to college and
then choose to be poor? Especially someone who had always been poor.

Last year, after ten years of writing professionally, the financial rewards started 15
to trickle in. My second National Endowment for the Arts Fellowship. A guest
professorship at the University of California, Berkeley. My book, which sold to
a major New York publishing house.

At Christmas, I flew home to Chicago. The house was throbbing, same as 16
always; hot *tamales* and sweet *tamales* hissing in my mother's pressure cooker,
and everybody—mother, six brothers, wives, babies, aunts, cousins—talking
too loud and at the same time, like in a Fellini film, because that's just how
we are.

I went upstairs to my father's room. One of my stories had just been trans- 17
lated into Spanish and published in an anthology of Chicano writing, and I
wanted to show it to him. Ever since he recovered from a stroke two years ago,
my father likes to spend his leisure hours horizontally. And that's how I found
him, watching a Pedro Infante movie on Galavision and eating rice pudding.

There was a glass filmed with milk on the bedside table. There were several 18
vials of pills and balled Kleenex. And on the floor, one black sock and a plastic
urinal that I didn't want to look at but looked at anyway. Pedro Infante was
about to burst into song, and my father was laughing.

I'm not sure if it was because my story was translated into Spanish, or because 19
it was published in Mexico, or perhaps because the story dealt with Tepeyac, the
colonia my father was raised in, but at any rate, my father punched the mute
button on his remote control and read my story.

I sat on the bed next to my father and waited. He read it very slowly. As if he 20
were reading each line over and over. He laughed at all the right places and read
lines he liked out loud. He pointed and asked questions: "Is this So-and-so?"
"Yes," I said. He kept reading.

When he was finally finished, after what seemed like hours, my father looked 21
up and asked: "Where can we get more copies of this for the relatives?"

Of all the wonderful things that happened to me last year, that was the most 22
wonderful.

- -

Questions for Discussion and Journaling

1. At the beginning of this piece, Cisneros writes several sentences about herself that she says "explain everything." List those sentences. Why does she
   think these aspects of her identity and experience are so powerful? Now write
   several sentences about yourself that you think might "explain everything"
   in a similar way. Why are these aspects of your identity and experience so
   powerful?

2. Cisneros's father supported her in attending college, but for very different
   reasons than her own. Explain how her father and college were what Brandt
   terms "literacy sponsors" (p. 72), and how Cisneros "misappropriated" the
   college literacy sponsorship that her father intended.

3. Cisneros's father had his own literacy sponsors, some of which are mentioned in this reading. What are they? How do you think they impacted what
   he expected of his daughter? How do they differ from his daughter's literacy
   sponsors?

4. Cisneros and her father have different ideas about what it means to be successful. How and why do they differ?

5. Cisneros has achieved extensive recognition for her writing, but she says that
   her father's approval of one story was "the most wonderful" thing that happened to her the year before she wrote this narrative (para. 22). Why? What
   about that particular story helped her bridge the divide between what she valued and what her father valued?

6. Cisneros speaks one language with her family and uses another language in her professional life and writing, at least most of the time. What does this multilingual experience provide Cisneros that a monolingual experience would not? What challenges does it present her?

Applying and Exploring Ideas

1. In your own family, how is literacy understood? Which literacy practices are frequently engaged in? Which literacy practices are valued, and which are not?

2. In question 4 above, you listed some of Cisneros's father's literacy sponsors. Now think about your own parents and list some of their literacy sponsors. How are these similar to or different from your own? How did those sponsors show up in your house and impact your own literacy?

3. Do you speak different languages at home, school, and work? If so, what language(s) do you speak in which settings? What do you think you gain from being able to draw on these various languages in different contexts? Are there any times when these multiple languages present a challenge for you? If you speak the same language in all contexts, reach out to a classmate or friend who is multilingual, and ask them the above questions.

- -

META MOMENT How does Cisneros's experience help you understand yourself and your own literacy sponsors differently?

- -

Learning to Read

MALCOLM X

Framing the Reading

Malcolm X was born Malcolm Little in Omaha, Nebraska, in 1925. Essentially orphaned as a child, he lived in a series of foster homes, became involved in criminal activity, and dropped out of school in eighth grade after a teacher told him his race would prevent him from being a lawyer. In 1945, he was sentenced to prison, where he read voraciously. After joining the Nation of Islam, he changed his last name to "X," explaining in his autobiography that "my 'X' replaced the white slavemaster name of 'Little.'" A strong advocate for the rights of African Americans, Malcolm X became an influential leader in the Nation of Islam but left the organization in 1964, becoming a Sunni Muslim and founding an organization dedicated to African American unity. Less than a year later, he was assassinated.

In this chapter we excerpt a piece from *The Autobiography of Malcolm X*, which he narrated to Alex Haley shortly before his death. We see Malcolm X's account as exemplifying many of the principles that Deborah Brandt introduces in "Sponsors of Literacy" (p. 68). For example, Malcolm X's account of how he came to reading is remarkable for how clearly it shows the role of motivation in literacy and learning: When he had a reason to read, he read, and reading fed his motivation to read further. His account also demonstrates the extent to which literacies shape the worlds available to people and the experiences they can have, as well as how literacy sponsors affect the kinds of literacy we eventually master.

We expect that reading Malcolm X's experiences in coming to reading will bring up your own memories of this stage in your life, which should set you thinking about what worlds your literacies give you access to and whether there are worlds in which you would be considered "illiterate." We think you'll find a comparison of your experiences and Malcolm X's provocative and telling.

X, Malcolm. *The Autobiography of Malcolm X*. Edited by Alex Haley, Ballantine Books, 1965.

Getting Ready to Read

Before you read, do at least one of the following activities:

- Do some reading online about Malcolm X and his biography.
- Start a discussion with friends, roommates, family, or classmates about whether, and how, "knowledge is power."

As you read, consider the following questions:

- How would Malcolm X's life have been different if his literacy experiences had been different?
- How was Malcolm X's literacy inextricably entangled with his life experiences, his race, and the religion he chose?
- How do Malcolm X's early literacy experiences and literacy sponsors compare with your own?

IT WAS BECAUSE OF MY LETTERS that I happened to stumble upon starting to acquire some kind of a homemade education. 1.

I became increasingly frustrated at not being able to express what I wanted 2 to convey in letters that I wrote, especially those to Mr. Elijah Muhammad. In the street, I had been the most articulate hustler out there—I had commanded attention when I said something. But now, trying to write simple English, I not only wasn't articulate, I wasn't even functional. How would I sound writing in slang, the way I would *say* it, something such as "Look, daddy, let me pull your coat about a cat, Elijah Muhammad—"

Many who today hear me somewhere in person, or on television, or those 3 who read something I've said, will think I went to school far beyond the eighth grade. This impression is due entirely to my prison studies.

It had really begun back in the Charlestown Prison, when Bimbi first made 4 me feel envy of his stock of knowledge. Bimbi had always taken charge of any conversation he was in, and I had tried to emulate him. But every book I picked up had few sentences which didn't contain anywhere from one to nearly all of the words that might as well have been in Chinese. When I just skipped those words, of course, I really ended up with little idea of what the book said. So I had come to the Norfolk Prison Colony still going through only book-reading motions. Pretty soon, I would have quit even these motions, unless I had received the motivation that I did.

> In the street, I had been the most articulate hustler out there—I had commanded attention when I said something. But now, trying to write simple English, I not only wasn't articulate, I wasn't even functional.

I saw that the best thing I could do was get hold of a dictionary—to study, to 5
learn some words. I was lucky enough to reason also that I should try to improve
my penmanship. It was sad. I couldn't even write in a straight line. It was both
ideas together that moved me to request a dictionary along with some tablets
and pencils from the Norfolk Prison Colony school.

I spent two days just riffling uncertainly through the dictionary's pages. I'd 6
never realized so many words existed! I didn't know *which* words I needed to
learn. Finally, just to start some kind of action, I began copying.

In my slow, painstaking, ragged handwriting, I copied into my tablet 7
everything printed on that first page, down to the punctuation marks.

I believe it took me a day. Then, aloud, I read back, to myself, everything 8
I'd written on the tablet. Over and over, aloud, to myself, I read my own
handwriting.

I woke up the next morning, thinking about those words—immensely proud 9
to realize that not only had I written so much at one time, but I'd written words
that I never knew were in the world. Moreover, with a little effort, I also could
remember what many of these words meant. I reviewed the words whose meanings I didn't remember. Funny thing, from the dictionary first page right now,
that "aardvark" springs to my mind. The dictionary had a picture of it, a long-
tailed, long-eared, burrowing African mammal, which lives off termites caught
by sticking out its tongue as an anteater does for ants.

I was so fascinated that I went on—I copied the dictionary's next page. And 10
the same experience came when I studied that. With every succeeding page, I
also learned of people and places and events from history. Actually the dictionary is like a miniature encyclopedia. Finally the dictionary's A section had filled
a whole tablet—and I went on into the B's. That was the way I started copying
what eventually became the entire dictionary. It went a lot faster after so much
practice helped me to pick up handwriting speed. Between what I wrote in my
tablet, and writing letters, during the rest of my time in prison I would guess I
wrote a million words.

I suppose it was inevitable that as my word-base broadened, I could for 11
the first time pick up a book and read and now begin to understand what the
book was saying. Anyone who has read a great deal can imagine the new world
that opened. Let me tell you something: from then until I left that prison, in
every free moment I had, if I was not reading in the library, I was reading on
my bunk. You couldn't have gotten me out of books with a wedge. Between
Mr. Muhammad's teachings, my correspondence, my visitors—usually Ella and
Reginald—and my reading of books, months passed without my even thinking
about being imprisoned. In fact, up to then, I never had been so truly free in
my life.

The Norfolk Prison Colony's library was in the school building. A variety of 12
classes was taught there by instructors who came from such places as Harvard

and Boston universities. The weekly debates between inmate teams were also held in the school building. You would be astonished to know how worked up convict debaters and audiences would get over subjects like "Should Babies Be Fed Milk?"

Available on the prison library's shelves were books on just about every general subject. Much of the big private collection that Parkhurst had willed to the prison was still in crates and boxes in the back of the library—thousands of old books. Some of them looked ancient: covers faded, old-time parchment-looking binding. Parkhurst, I've mentioned, seemed to have been principally interested in history and religion. He had the money and the special interest to have a lot of books that you wouldn't have in general circulation. Any college library would have been lucky to get that collection. 13

As you can imagine, especially in a prison where there was heavy emphasis on rehabilitation, an inmate was smiled upon if he demonstrated an unusually intense interest in books. There was a sizable number of well-read inmates, especially the popular debaters. Some were said by many to be practically walking encyclopedias. They were almost celebrities. No university would ask any student to devour literature as I did when this new world opened to me, of being able to read and *understand*. 14

I read more in my room than in the library itself. An inmate who was known to read a lot could check out more than the permitted maximum number of books. I preferred reading in the total isolation of my own room. 15

When I had progressed to really serious reading, every night at about ten P.M. I would be outraged with the "lights out." It always seemed to catch me right in the middle of something engrossing. 16

Fortunately, right outside my door was a corridor light that cast a glow into my room. The glow was enough to read by, once my eyes adjusted to it. So when "lights out" came, I would sit on the floor where I could continue reading in that glow. 17

At one-hour intervals the night guards paced past every room. Each time I heard the approaching footsteps, I jumped into bed and feigned sleep. And as soon as the guard passed, I got back out of bed onto the floor area of that light-glow, where I would read for another fifty-eight minutes—until the guard approached again. That went on until three or four every morning. Three or four hours of sleep a night was enough for me. Often in the years in the streets I had slept less than that. 18

The teachings of Mr. Muhammad stressed how history had been "whitened"—when white men had written history books, the black man simply had been left out. Mr. Muhammad couldn't have said anything that would have struck me much harder. I had never forgotten how when my class, me and all of those whites, had studied seventh-grade United States history back in Mason, 19 the history of the Negro had been covered in one paragraph, and the teacher had gotten a big laugh with his joke, "Negroes' feet are so big that when they walk, they leave a hole in the ground."

This is one reason why Mr. Muhammad's teachings spread so swiftly all over the United States, among *all* Negroes, whether or not they became followers of Mr. Muhammad. The teachings ring true—to every Negro. You can hardly show me a black adult in America—or a white one, for that matter—who knows from the history books anything like the truth about the black man's role. In my own case, once I heard of the "glorious history of the black man," I took special pains to hunt in the library for books that would inform me on details about black history. [20]

I can remember accurately the very first set of books that really impressed me. I have since bought that set of books and have it at home for my children to read as they grow up. It's called *Wonders of the World.* It's full of pictures of archeological finds, statues that depict, usually, non-European people. [21]

I found books like Will Durant's *Story of Civilization.* I read H. G. Wells' *Outline of History. Souls of Black Folk* by W. E. B. Du Bois gave me a glimpse into the black people's history before they came to this country. Carter G. Woodson's *Negro History* opened my eyes about black empires before the black slave was brought to the United States, and the early Negro struggles for freedom. [22]

J. A. Rogers' three volumes of *Sex and Race* told about race-mixing before Christ's time; about Aesop being a black man who told fables; about Egypt's Pharaohs; about the great Coptic Christian Empires; about Ethiopia, the earth's oldest continuous black civilization, as China is the oldest continuous civilization. [23]

Mr. Muhammad's teaching about how the white man had been created led me to *Findings in Genetics* by Gregor Mendel. (The dictionary's G section was where I had learned what "genetics" meant.) I really studied this book by the Austrian monk. Reading it over and over, especially certain sections, helped me to understand that if you started with a black man, a white man could be produced; but starting with a white man, you never could produce a black man—because the white gene is recessive. And since no one disputes that there was but one Original Man, the conclusion is clear. [24]

During the last year or so, in the *New York Times*, Arnold Toynbee used the word "bleached" in describing the white man. (His words were: "White (i.e., bleached) human beings of North European origin. . . .") Toynbee also referred to the European geographic area as only a peninsula of Asia. He said there is no such thing as Europe. And if you look at the globe, you will see for yourself that America is only an extension of Asia. (But at the same time Toynbee is among those who have helped to bleach history. He has written that Africa was the only continent that produced no history. He won't write that again. Every day now, the truth is coming to light.) [25]

I never will forget how shocked I was when I began reading about slavery's 26 total horror. It made such an impact upon me that it later became one of my favorite subjects when I became a minister of Mr. Muhammad's. The world's most monstrous crime, the sin and the blood on the white man's hands, are almost impossible to believe. Books like the one by Frederick Olmstead opened my eyes to the horrors suffered when the slave was landed in the United States. The European woman, Fannie Kimball, who had married a Southern white slave-owner, described how human beings were degraded. Of course I read *Uncle Tom's Cabin*. In fact, I believe that's the only novel I have ever read since I started serious reading.

Parkhurst's collection also contained some bound pamphlets of the 27 Abolitionist Anti-Slavery Society of New England. I read descriptions of atrocities, saw those illustrations of black slave women tied up and flogged with whips; of black mothers watching their babies being dragged off, never to be seen by their mothers again; of dogs after slaves, and of the fugitive slave catchers, evil white men with whips and clubs and chains and guns. I read about the slave preacher Nat Turner, who put the fear of God into the white slavemaster. Nat Turner wasn't going around preaching pie-in-the-sky and "non-violent" freedom for the black man. There in Virginia one night in 1831, Nat and seven other slaves started out at his master's home and through the night they went from one plantation "big house" to the next, killing, until by the next morning 57 white people were dead and Nat had about 70 slaves following him. White people, terrified for their lives, fled from their homes, locked themselves up in public buildings, hid in the woods, and some even left the state. A small army of soldiers took two months to catch and hang Nat Turner. Somewhere I have read where Nat Turner's example is said to have inspired John Brown to invade Virginia and attack Harper's Ferry nearly thirty years later, with thirteen white men and five Negroes.

I read Herodotus, "the father of History," or, rather, I read about him. And 28 I read the histories of various nations, which opened my eyes gradually, then wider and wider, to how the whole world's white men had indeed acted like devils, pillaging and raping and bleeding and draining the whole world's non-white people. I remember, for instance, books such as Will Durant's story of Oriental civilization, and Mahatma Gandhi's accounts of the struggle to drive the British out of India.

Book after book showed me how the white man had brought upon the 29 world's black, brown, red, and yellow peoples every variety of the sufferings of exploitation. I saw how since the sixteenth century, the so-called "Christian trader" white man began to ply the seas in his lust for Asian and African empires, and plunder, and power. I read, I saw, how the white man never has gone among the non-white peoples bearing the Cross in the true manner and spirit of Christ's teachings — meek, humble, and Christ-like.

I perceived, as I read, how the collective white man had been actually nothing   30
but a piratical opportunist who used Faustian machinations to make his own
Christianity his initial wedge in criminal conquests. First, always "religiously,"
he branded "heathen" and "pagan" labels upon ancient non-white cultures and
civilizations. The stage thus set, he then turned upon his non-white victims his
weapons of war.

I read how, entering India — half a *billion* deeply religious brown people —   31
the British white man, by 1759, through promises, trickery and manipulations,
controlled much of India through Great Britain's East India Company. The par-
asitical British administration kept tentacling out to half of the subcontinent. In
1857, some of the desperate people of India finally mutinied — and, excepting
the African slave trade, nowhere has history recorded any more unnecessary bes-
tial and ruthless human carnage than the British suppression of the non-white
Indian people.

Over 115 million African blacks — close to the 1930s population of the   32
United States — were murdered or enslaved during the slave trade. And I read
how when the slave market was glutted, the cannibalistic white powers of Europe
next carved up, as their colonies, the richest areas of the black continent. And
Europe's chancelleries for the next century played a chess game of naked exploitation and power from Cape Horn to Cairo.

Ten guards and the warden couldn't have torn me out of those books. Not   33
even Elijah Muhammad could have been more eloquent than those books were
in providing indisputable proof that the collective white man had acted like
a devil in virtually every contact he had with the world's collective non-white
man. I listen today to the radio, and watch television, and read the headlines
about the collective white man's fear and tension concerning China. When the
white man professes ignorance about why the Chinese hate him so, my mind
can't help flashing back to what I read, there in prison, about how the blood
forebears of this same white man raped China at a time when China was trust-
ing and helpless. Those original white "Christian traders" sent into China millions of pounds of opium. By 1839, so many of the Chinese were addicts that
China's desperate government destroyed twenty thousand chests of opium. The
first Opium War was promptly declared by the white man. Imagine! Declaring
war upon someone who objects to being narcotized! The Chinese were severely
beaten, with Chinese-invented gunpowder.

The Treaty of Nanking made China pay the British white man for the   34
destroyed opium; forced open China's major ports to British trade; forced China
to abandon Hong Kong; fixed China's import tariffs so low that cheap British
articles soon flooded in, maiming China's industrial development.

After a second Opium War, the Tientsin Treaties legalized the ravaging opium   35
trade, legalized a British-French-American control of China's customs. China
tried delaying that Treaty's ratification; Peking was looted and burned.

"Kill the foreign white devils!" was the 1901 Chinese war cry in the Boxer 36
Rebellion. Losing again, this time the Chinese were driven from Peking's choicest areas. The vicious, arrogant white man put up the famous signs, "Chinese and dogs not allowed."

Red China after World War II closed its doors to the Western white world. 37
Massive Chinese agricultural, scientific, and industrial efforts are described in a book that *Life* magazine recently published. Some observers inside Red China have reported that the world never has known such a hate-white campaign as is now going on in this non-white country where, present birth-rates continuing, in fifty more years Chinese will be half the earth's population. And it seems that some Chinese chickens will soon come home to roost, with China's recent successful nuclear tests.

Let us face reality. We can see in the United Nations a new world order 38
being shaped, along color lines—an alliance among the non-white nations. America's U.N. Ambassador Adlai Stevenson complained not long ago that in the United Nations "a skin game" was being played. He was right. He was facing reality. A "skin game" *is* being played. But Ambassador Stevenson sounded like Jesse James accusing the marshal of carrying a gun. Because who in the world's history ever has played a worse "skin game" than the white man?

Mr. Muhammad, to whom I was writing daily, had no idea of what a new 39
world had opened up to me through my efforts to document his teachings in books.

When I discovered philosophy, I tried to touch all the landmarks of philo- 40
sophical development. Gradually, I read most of the old philosophers, Occidental and Oriental. The Oriental philosophers were the ones I came to prefer; finally, my impression was that most Occidental philosophy had largely been borrowed from the Oriental thinkers. Socrates, for instance, traveled in Egypt. Some sources even say that Socrates was initiated into some of the Egyptian mysteries. Obviously Socrates got some of his wisdom among the East's wise men.

I have often reflected upon the new vistas that reading opened to me. I knew 41
right there in prison that reading had changed forever the course of my life. As I see it today, the ability to read awoke inside me some long dormant craving to be mentally alive. I certainly wasn't seeking any degree, the way a college confers a status symbol upon its students. My homemade education gave me, with every additional book that I read, a little bit more sensitivity to the deafness, dumbness, and blindness that was afflicting the black race in America. Not long ago, an English writer telephoned me from London, asking questions. One was, "What's your alma mater?" I told him, "Books." You will never catch me with a free fifteen minutes in which I'm not studying something I feel might be able to help the black man.

Yesterday I spoke in London, and both ways on the plane across the Atlantic 42
I was studying a document about how the United Nations proposes to insure

the human rights of the oppressed minorities of the world. The American black man is the world's most shameful case of minority oppression. What makes the black man think of himself as only an internal United States issue is just a catch-phrase, two words, "civil rights." How is the black man going to get "civil rights" before first he wins his *human* rights? If the American black man will start thinking about his *human* rights, and then start thinking of himself as part of one of the world's great peoples, he will see he has a case for the United Nations.

I can't think of a better case! Four hundred years of black blood and sweat 43 invested here in America, and the white man still has the black man begging for what every immigrant fresh off the ship can take for granted the minute he walks down the gangplank.

But I'm digressing. I told the Englishman that my alma mater was books, a 44 good library. Every time I catch a plane, I have with me a book that I want to read — and that's a lot of books these days. If I weren't out here every day battling the white man, I could spend the rest of my life reading, just satisfying my curiosity — because you can hardly mention anything I'm not curious about. I don't think anybody ever got more out of going to prison than I did. In fact, prison enabled me to study far more intensively than I would have if my life had gone differently and I had attended some college. I imagine that one of the biggest troubles with colleges is there are too many distractions, too much panty-raiding, fraternities, and boola-boola and all of that. Where else but in a prison could I have attacked my ignorance by being able to study intensely sometimes as much as fifteen hours a day?

- -

Questions for Discussion and Journaling

1. Who seems to be Malcolm X's intended audience? How do you know?

2. How does Malcolm X define *literacy*? How does this definition compare with school-based literacy?

3. Drawing on Deborah Brandt's definition of *literacy sponsor*, list as many of Malcolm X's literacy sponsors as you can find. (Remember that sponsors don't have to be people; they can also be ideas or institutions, which can withhold literacy as well as provide it.) Which sponsors were most influential? What were their motivations?

4. Brandt explains that people often subvert or misappropriate the intentions of their sponsors (see paras. 7 and 27). Was this ever the case with Malcolm X? If so, how?

5. Like Malcolm X, many readers have memories in which a reference work like a dictionary or an encyclopedia figures significantly. Did his account bring back any such memories for you? If so, what were they?

6. Malcolm X asserts that his motivation for reading — his desire to understand his own experiences — led him to read far more than any college student. Respond to his claim. Has a particular motivation helped you decide what, or how much, to read?

7. What was the particular role for *writing* that Malcolm X describes in his account of his literacy education? How do you think it helped him read? Can you think of ways that writing helped *you* become a better reader?

Applying and Exploring Ideas

1. Both Deborah Brandt and Malcolm X wrote before much of the technology that you take for granted was invented. How do you think technologies such as the Internet, text messaging, and Skype shape what it means to be "literate" in the United States today?

2. Write a one-page narrative about the impact of an early literacy sponsor on your life. Recount as many details as you can and try to assess the difference that sponsor made in your literate life.

3. Malcolm X turned to the dictionary to get his start in acquiring basic literacy. If you met a person learning to read today, what primary resource would you suggest to them? Would it be print (paper) or electronic? How would you tell them to use it, and how do you think it would help them?

- -
META MOMENT   What is the most important idea for you to take away from the Malcolm X text?
- -

Excerpt from *Bootstraps: From an American Academic of Color*

Victor Villanueva

VICTOR VILLANUEVA

Framing the Reading

You've probably noticed, consciously or unconsciously, that some languages or dialects tend to be dominant in particular settings, while others seem marginalized. In many cases, language users have the ability to change their language for different audiences and purposes — that is, to "code-switch" or "code-mesh" (ideas taken up in more detail by Young later in this chapter [p. 148], and by Gee in Chapter 3 [p. 274]). Changing language use in this way might be as simple as speaking differently in a place of worship versus at work or school. Or it could be as complicated as speaking one language with your parents and grandparents, and another with your friends and teachers. There are many variations of a language; there is not just one "English" but many Englishes that are spoken and written to great effect by people from different countries, regions of a country, ethnicities, classes, and even genders.

The ability to move among different versions of a language, or different languages altogether, can be helpful in communicating effectively and powerfully in different circumstances. But moving and changing language like this can also require speakers and writers to give up something that is important to who they are. This is because to be human is to be aware of the interplay among languages and how they mark power, identity, status, and potential. In circumstances where individuals use a form of language that is not the dominant or powerful one in that context, they have choices to make: Should they use (or learn to use) the dominant and powerful language? Can they do so effectively (a question that Gee takes up [p. 274])? If

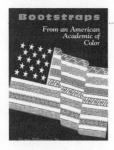

Villanueva, Victor. *Bootstraps: From an American Academic of Color.* National Council of Teachers of English, 1993, pp. 66–77.

so, when, where, and how much should they use it? What do they give up and gain by doing so (a question taken up by Young [p. 148])? Making decisions about what language practices to use is not just a matter of learning something new, but of becoming someone else.

Victor Villanueva's book *Bootstraps: From an American Academic of Color* is a narrative and an analysis of his own experience with this struggle. Villanueva grew up as a Puerto Rican in the Hell's Kitchen area of New York City, with parents who had emigrated from Puerto Rico with Spanish as their first language. As an adult, he became a successful professor of rhetoric, focusing on questions of race, language, and power. *Bootstraps* tells the story of his evolution, and the excerpt that you'll read here focuses specifically on his movement from the U.S. Army into an English degree and graduate school. It's a literacy narrative that captures the feelings of confusion and frustration, as well as elation and satisfaction, experienced by one member of a group whose language and ethnicity are not in the majority as he learns to participate in an academic community that requires its participants to use very different language practices. Villanueva's story, like the other literacy narratives included in this chapter, demonstrates the complexity of what it means to be "literate" — and who has the authority to decide what forms of literacy are understood as powerful or "legitimate." Villanueva's experiences illustrate what it might look like to try out new language practices in a new place; it also describes the frustrations of learning to write in school settings like the one you are in now.

Villanueva is Regents Professor and Edward R. Meyer Distinguished Professor of Liberal Arts at Washington State University. In his work, he describes and theorizes the relationship between language and power, especially the ways that language is used as a tool of racism. He has won a wide range of honors and awards both from the field of writing studies and the universities in which he's taught, researched, and administered.

Getting Ready to Read

Before you read, do at least one of the following activities:

- Find out more about this writer and his experiences through a quick online search.
- Think back to when you first considered going to college, whatever age that was. Did you think, back then, you could do it? If you didn't feel confident, what prevented that confidence?

As you read, consider the following questions:

- What school-writing experiences have you encountered that resemble any described by Villanueva?
- What do you know about affirmative action in higher education, and how is this reading matching up with that knowledge?

I WANTED TO TRY my hand at college, go beyond the GED. But college 1
scared me. I had been told long ago that college wasn't my lot.

He drives by the University District of Seattle during his last days in the mili- 2
tary and sees the college kids, long hair and sandals, baggy short pants on the
men, long, flowing dresses on the women, some men in suits, some women in
high heels, all carrying backpacks over one shoulder. There is both purpose and
contentment in the air. Storefronts carry names like Dr. Feelgood and Magus
Bookstore, reflecting the good feelings and magic he senses. A block away is
the University, red tiles and green grass, rolling hills and tall pines, apple and
cherry blossoms, the trees shading modern monoliths of gray concrete and
gothic, church-like buildings of red brick. And he says to himself, "Maybe in
the next life."

He must be content with escaping a life at menial labor, at being able to 3
bank on the skills in personnel management he had acquired in the Army. But
there are only two takers. The large department-store chain would hire him
as a management trainee—a shoe salesman on commission, no set income,
but a trainee could qualify for GI Bill benefits as well as the commissions. Not
good enough, not getting paid beyond the GI Bill; and a sales career wasn't
good enough either, the thought of his mother's years as a saleslady, years lost,
still in memory. A finance corporation offers him a job: management trainee.
The title: Assistant Manager. The job: bill collector, with low wage, but as a
trainee, qualified to supplement with the GI Bill. The combined pay would
be good, but he would surely lose his job in time, would be unable to be righ-
teously indignant like the bill collectors he has too often had to face too often
are, unable to bother people like Mom and Dad, knowing that being unable
to meet bills isn't usually a moral shortcoming but most often an economic
condition.

The GI Bill had come up again, however, setting the "gettinover" wheels in 4
motion. The nearby community college charges ninety dollars a quarter tuition,
would accept him on the strength of his GED scores. That would mean nearly
four hundred dollars a month from the GI Bill, with only thirty dollars a month
for schooling ("forgetting" to account for books and supplies). What a get-over!
There would be immediate profit in simply going to school. And if he failed,
there would be nothing lost. And if he succeeded, an Associate degree in something. He'd be better equipped to brave the job market again.

So he walks onto the community college campus in the summer of 1976. It's 5
not the campus of the University of Washington. It's more like Dominguez High
School in California. But it is a college. Chemistry: a clumsiness at the lab, but
relative grace at mathematical equations and memorization. French is listening
to audiotapes and filling out workbooks. History is enjoyable stories, local lore
from a retired newsman, easy memorization for the grade.

Then there is English. There are the stories, the taste he had always had for read- 6
ing, now peppered with talk of philosophy and psychology and tensions and tex-
tures. Writing is 200 words on anything, preceded by a sentence outline. He'd write
about Korea and why *The Rolling Stone* could write about conspiracies of silence, or
he'd write about the problems in trying to get a son to understand that he is Puerto
Rican when the only Puerto Ricans he knows are his grandparents; he'd write about
whatever seemed to be on his mind at the time. The night before a paper would be
due, he'd gather pen and pad, and stare. Clean the dishes. Stare. Watch an "I Love
Lucy" rerun. Stare. Then sometime in the night the words would come. He'd write;
scratch something out; draw arrows shifting paragraphs around; add a phrase or
two. Then he'd pull out; the erasable bond, making changes even as he typed, frantic
to be done before school. Then he'd use the completed essay to type out an outline,
feeling a little guilty about having cheated in not having produced the outline first.

The guilt showed one day when Mrs. Ray, the Indian woman in traditional 7
dress with a Ph.D. in English from Oxford, part-time instructor at the community college, said there was a problem with his writing. She must have been able
to tell somehow that he was discovering what to write while writing, no prior
thesis statement, no outline, just a vague notion that would materialize, magically, while writing. In her stark, small office she hands him a sheet with three
familiar sayings mimeoed on it; instructs him to write on one, right there, right
then. He writes on "a bird in the hand is worth two in the bush." No memory
of what he had written, probably forgotten during the writing. Thirty minutes
or so later, she takes the four or five pages he had written; she reads; she smiles;
then she explains that she had suspected plagiarism in his previous writings. She
apologizes, saying she found his writing "too serious," too abstract, not typical
of her students. He is not insulted; he is flattered. He knew he could read; now
he knew he could write well enough for college.

English 102, Mr. Lukens devotes a portion of the quarter to Afro-American 8
literature. Victor reads Ishmael Reed, "I'm a Cowboy in the Boat of Ra." It begins,

I am a cowboy in the boat of Ra,
sidewinders in the saloons of fools
bit my forehead   like   O
the untrustworthiness of Egyptologists
Who do not know their trips. Who was that
dog faced man? they asked, the day I rode
from town.

School marms with halitosis cannot see
the Nefertitti fake chipped on the run by slick
germans, the hawk behind Sonny Rollins' head or
the ritual beard of his axe; a longhorn winding
its bells thru the Field of Reeds.

There was more, but by this point he was already entranced and excited. Poetry has meaning, more than the drama of Mark Antony's speech years back.

Mr. Lukens says that here is an instance of poetry more for effect (or maybe 9 *affect*) than for meaning, citing a line from Archibald MacLeish: "A poem should not mean / But be." But there *was* meaning in this poem. Victor writes about it. In the second stanza, the chipped Nefertitti, a reference to a false black history, with images from "The Maltese Falcon" and war movies. The "School marms" Reed mentions are like the schoolmasters at Hamilton, unknowing and seeming not to know of being unknowing. Sonny Rollins' axe and the Field of Reeds: a saxophone, a reed instrument, the African American's links to Egypt, a history whitewashed by "Egyptologists / Who do not know their trips." He understood the allusions, appreciated the wordplay. The poem had the politics of Bracy, the language of the block, TV of the fifties, together in the medium Mr. D had introduced to Victor, Papi, but now more powerful. This was fun; this was politics. This was Victor's history, his life with language play.

Years later, Victor is on a special two-man panel at a conference of the Modern 10 Language Association. He shares the podium with Ishmael Reed. Victor gives a talk on "Teaching as Social Action," receives applause, turns to see Ishmael Reed looking him in the eye, applauding loudly. He tries to convey how instrumental this "colleague" had been in his life.

He'll be an English major. Mr. Lukens is his advisor, sets up the community 11 college curriculum in such a way as to have all but the major's requirements for a BA from the University of Washington out of the way. The University of Washington is the only choice: it's relatively nearby, tuition for Vietnam veterans is $176 a quarter. "Maybe in this life."

His AA degree in his back pocket, his heart beating audibly with exhilaration 12 and fear, he walks up the campus of the University of Washington, more excited than at Disneyland when he was sixteen. He's proud: a regular transfer student, no special minority waivers. The summer of 1977.

But the community is not college in the same way the University is. The 13 community college is torn between vocational training and preparing the unprepared for traditional university work. And it seems unable to resolve the conflict (see Cohen and Brawer).[1] His high community-college GPA is no measure of what he is prepared to undertake at the University. He fails at French 103, unable to carry the French conversations, unable to do the reading, unable to do the writing, dropping the course before the failure becomes a matter of record. He starts again. French 101, only to find he is still not really competitive with the white kids who had had high school French. But he cannot fail,

---

[1]Cohen, Arthur M., and Florence B. Brawer. *The American Community College.* 2nd ed., Jossey-Bass, 1989.

and he does not fail, thanks to hour after hour with French tapes after his son's in bed.

English 301, the literature survey, is fun. Chaucer is a ghetto boy, poking fun 14 at folks, the rhyming reminding him of when he did the dozens on the block; Chaucer telling bawdy jokes: "And at the wyndow out she putte hir hole . . . 'A berd, a berd!; quod hende Nicholas." So this is literature. Chaucer surely ain't white. At least he doesn't sound white, "the first to write poetry in the vernacular," he's told. Spenser is exciting: images of knights and damsels distressing, magic and dragons, the *Lord of the Rings* that he had read in Korea paling in the comparison. Donne is a kick: trying to get laid when he's Jack Donne, with a rap the boys from the block could never imagine; building church floors with words on a page when he's Dr. John Donne. Every reading is an adventure, never a nod, no matter how late into the night the reading. For his first paper, Victor, the 3.8 at Tacoma Community College, gets 36 out of a possible 100 — "for your imagination," written alongside the grade.

I was both devastated and determined, my not belonging was verified but I 15 was not ready to be shut down, not so quickly. So to the library to look up what the Professor himself had published: *Proceedings of the Spenser Society.* I had no idea what the Professor was going on about in his paper, but I could see the pattern: an introduction that said something about what others had said, what he was going to be writing about, in what order, and what all this would prove; details about what he said he was going to be writing about, complete with quotes, mainly from the poetry, not much from other writers on Spenser; and a "therefore." It wasn't the five-paragraph paper Mr. Lukens had insisted on, not just three points, not just repetition of the opening in the close, but the pattern was essentially the same. The next paper: 62 out of 100 and a "Much better." Course grade: B. Charity.

I never vindicated myself with that professor. I did try, tried to show that I 16 didn't need academic charity. Economic charity was hard enough. I took my first graduate course from him. This time I got an "All well and good, but what's the point?" alongside a "B" for a paper. I had worked on that paper all summer long.

I have had to face that same professor, now a Director of Freshman Writing, at 17 conferences. And with every contact, feelings of insecurity well up from within, the feeling that I'm seen as the minority (a literal term in academics for those of us of color), the feeling of being perceived as having gotten through *because* I am a minority, an insecurity I face often. But though I never got over the stigma with that professor (whether real or imagined), I did get some idea on how to write for the University.

Professorial Discourse Analysis became a standard practice: go to the library; 18 see what the course's professor had published; try to discern a pattern to her writing; try to mimic the pattern. Some would begin with anecdotes. Some

> *I was both devastated and determined, my not belonging was verified but I was not ready to be shut down, not so quickly. So to the library to look up what the Professor himself had published:* Proceedings of the Spenser Society. *I had no idea what the Professor was going on about in his paper, but I could see the pattern.*

would have no personal pronouns. Some would cite others' research. Some would cite different literary works to make assertions about one literary work. Whatever they did, I would do too. And it worked, for the most part, so that I could continue the joy of time travel and mind travel with those, and within those, who wrote about things I had discovered I liked to think about: Shakespeare and work versus pleasure, religion and the day-to-day world, racism, black Othello and the Jewish Merchant of Venice; Dickens and the impossibility of really getting into the middle class (which I read as "race," getting into the white world, at the time), pokes at white folks (though the Podsnaps were more likely jabs at the middle class); Milton and social responsibility versus religious mandates; Yeats and being assimilated and yet other (critically conscious with a cultural literacy, I'd say now); others and other themes. And soon I was writing like I had written in the community college: some secondary reading beforehand, but composing the night before a paper was due, a combination of fear that nothing will come and faith that something would eventually develop, then revising to fit the pattern discovered in the Professorial Discourse Analysis, getting "A's" and "B's," and getting comments like "I never saw that before."

There were failures, of course. One professor said my writing was too formulaic. One professor said it was too novel. Another wrote only one word for the one paper required of the course: "nonsense." But while I was on the campus I could escape and not. I could think about the things that troubled me or intrigued me, but through others' eyes in other times and other places. I couldn't get enough, despite the pain and the insecurity. 19

School becomes his obsession. There is the education. But the obsession is as much, if not more, in getting a degree, not with a job in mind, just the degree, just because he thinks he can, despite all that has said he could not. His marriage withers away, not with rancor, just melting into a dew. The daily routine has him taking the kid to a daycare/school at 6:00 a.m., then himself to school, from school to work as a groundskeeper for a large apartment complex; later, a maintenance man, then a garbage man, then a plumber, sometimes coupled with other jobs: shipping clerk for the library, test proctor. From work to pick up the kid from school, prepare dinner, maybe watch a TV show with the kid, tuck him into bed, read. There are some girlfriends along the way, and he studies them too: the English major who won constant approval from the same professor who had given him the 36 for being imaginative; the art major who 20 had traveled to France (French practice); the fisheries major whose father was an executive vice president for IBM (practice at being middle class). Victor was going to learn—quite consciously—what it means to be white, middle class. He didn't see the exploitation; not then; he was obsessed. There were things going on in his classes that he did not understand and that the others did. He didn't know what the things were that he didn't understand, but he knew that even those who didn't do as well as he did, somehow did not act as foreign as he felt. He was the only colored kid in every one of those classes. And he hadn't the time nor the racial affiliation to join the Black Student Union or Mecha. He was on his own, an individual pulling on his bootstraps, looking out for number one. He's not proud of the sensibility, but isolation—and, likely, exploitation of others—are the stuff of racelessness.

There were two male friends, Mickey, a friend to this day, and Luis el Loco. 21 Luis was a *puertoriceño*, from Puerto Rico, who had found his way to Washington by having been imprisoned in the federal penitentiary at MacNeal Island, attending school on a prison-release program. Together, they would enjoy talking in Spanglish, listening to *salsa*. But Luis was a Modern Languages major, Spanish literature. Nothing there to exploit. It's a short-lived friendship. Mickey was the other older student in Victor's French 101 course, white, middle class, yet somehow other, one who had left the country during Vietnam, a disc jockey in Amsterdam. The friendship begins with simply being the two older men in the class, longer away from adolescence than the rest; the friendship grows with conversations about politics, perceptions about America from abroad, literature. But Victor would not be honest with his friend about feeling foreign until years later, a literary bravado. Mickey was well read in the literary figures Victor was coming to know. Mickey would be a testing ground for how Victor was reading, another contact to be exploited. Eventually, Mickey and his wife would introduce Victor to their friend, a co-worker at the post office. This is Carol. She comes from a life of affluence, and from a life of poverty, a traveler within the class system, not a journey anyone would volunteer for, but one which provides a unique education, a path not unlike Paulo Freire's. From her, there is the physical and the things he would know of the middle class, discussed explicitly, and there is their mutual isolation. There is love and friendship, still his closest friend, still his lover.

But before Carol there is simply the outsider obsessed. He manages the BA. He 22 cannot stop, even as the GI Bill reaches its end. He will continue to gather credentials until he is kicked out. Takes the GRE, does not do well, but gets into the graduate program with the help of references from within the faculty—and with the help of minority status in a program decidedly low in numbers of minorities. "Minority," or something like that, is typed on the GRE test results in his file, to be seen while scanning the file for the references. His pride is hurt, but he remembers All Saints, begins to believe in the biases of standardized tests: back in the eighth grade, a failure top student; now a near-failure, despite a 3.67 at the competitive Big University of State. Not all his grades, he knew, were matters of charity. He had earned his GPA, for the most part. Nevertheless, he is shaken.

More insecure than ever, there are no more overnight papers. Papers are writ- 23 ten over days, weeks, paragraphs literally cut and laid out on the floor to be pasted. One comment appears in paper after paper: "Logic?" He thinks, "Yes." He does not understand. Carol cannot explain the problem. Neither can Mickey. He does not even consider asking the professors. To ask would be an admission of ignorance, "stupid spic" still resounding within. This is his problem.

Then by chance (exactly how is now forgotten), he hears a tape of a conference 24 paper delivered by the applied linguist Robert Kaplan. Kaplan describes contrastive rhetoric. Kaplan describes a research study conducted in New York City among Puerto Ricans who are bilingual and Puerto Ricans who are monolingual in English, and he says that the discourse patterns, the rhetorical patterns which include the logic, of monolingual Puerto Ricans are like those of Puerto Rican bilinguals and different from Whites, more Greek than the Latin-like prose of American written English. Discourse analysis takes on a new intensity. At this point, what this means is that he will have to go beyond patterns in his writing, become more analytical of the connections between ideas. The implications of Kaplan's talk, for him at least, will take on historical and political significance as he learns more of rhetoric.

About the same time as that now lost tape on Kaplan's New York research (a 25 study that was never published, evidently), Victor stumbles into his first rhetoric course.

The preview of course offerings announces a course titled "Theories of 26 Invention," to be taught by Anne Ruggles Gere. His GRE had made it clear that he was deficient in Early American Literature. Somewhere in his mind he recalls reading that Benjamin Franklin had identified himself as an inventor; so somehow, Victor interprets "Theories of Invention" as "Theories of Inventors," an American lit course. What he discovers is Rhetoric.

Not all at once, not just in that first class on rhetoric, I discover some things 27 about writing, my own, and about the teaching of writing. I find some of modern composition's insights are modern hindsights. I don't mind the repetition. Some things bear repeating. The repetitions take on new significance and are elaborated upon in a new context, a new time. Besides, not everyone who teaches writing knows of rhetoric, though I believe everyone should.

I read Cicero's *de Inventione*. It's a major influence in rhetoric for centuries. 28 The strategies he describes on how to argue a court case bears a remarkable resemblance to current academic discourse, the pattern I first discovered when I first tried to figure out what I had not done in that first English course at the University.

Janet Emig looks to depth psychology and studies on creativity and even 29
neurophysiology, the workings of the brain's two hemispheres, to pose the case
that writing is a mode of learning. She explains what I had been doing with my
first attempts at college writing, neither magic nor a perversion. Cicero had said
much the same in his *de Oratore* in the first century BCE (Before the Common
Era, the modern way of saying BC):

> *Writing* is said to be *the best and most excellent modeler and teacher of ora-*
> *tory;* and not without reason; for if what is meditated and considered
> easily surpasses sudden and extemporary speech, a constant and diligent
> habit of writing will surely be of more effect than meditation and consid-
> eration itself; since all the arguments relating to the subject on which we
> write, whether they are suggested by art, or by a certain power of genius
> and understanding, will present themselves, and occur to us, while we
> examine and contemplate it in the full light of our intellect and all the
> thoughts and words, which are the most expressive of their kind, must of
> necessity come under and submit to the keenness of our judgment while
> writing; and a fair arrangement and collocation of the words is effected
> by writing, in a certain rhythm and measure, not poetical, but oratorical.
> (*de Oratore* I.cxxxiv)

Writing is a way of discovering, of learning, of thinking. Cicero is arguing the
case for literacy in ways we still argue or are arguing anew.

David Bartholomae and Anthony Petrosky discuss literary theorists like 30
Jonathan Culler and the pedagogical theorist Paulo Freire to come up with a
curriculum in which reading is used to introduce basic writers, those students
who come into the colleges not quite prepared for college work, to the ways of
academic discourse. Quintilian, like others of his time, the first century CE, and
like others before his time, advocates reading as a way to come to discover the
ways of language and the ways of writing and the ways to broaden the range of
experience.

Kenneth Bruffee, Peter Elbow, and others, see the hope of democratizing the 31
classroom through peer-group learning. So did Quintilian:

> But as emulation is of use to those who have made some advancement of
> learning, so, to those who are but beginning and still of tender age, to imi-
> tate their schoolfellows is more pleasant than to imitate their master, for the
> very reason that it is more easy; for they who are learning the first rudiments
> will scarcely dare to exalt themselves to the hope of attaining that eloquence
> which they regard as the highest; they will rather fix on what is nearest to
> them, as vines attached to trees fain the top by taking hold of the lower
> branches first (23–24).

Quintilian describes commenting on student papers in ways we consider new:

> [T]he powers of boys sometimes sink under too great severity in correction; for they despond, and grieve, and at last hate their work; and what is most prejudicial, while they fear everything; they cease to attempt anything. . . . A teacher ought, therefore, to be as agreeable as possible, that remedies, which are rough in their nature, may be rendered soothing by gentleness of hand; he ought to praise some parts of his pupils' performances, tolerate some, and to alter others, giving his reasons why the alterations are made. (100)

Richard Haswell recommends minimal scoring of student papers, sticking to one or two items in need of correction per paper. Nancy Sommers warns against rubber-stamp comments on student papers, comments like "awk;" she says comments ought to explain. Both have more to say than Quintilian on such matters, but in essence both are Quintilian revisited.

Edward P. J. Corbett looks to Quintilian, Cicero, and others from among the 32 ancients, especially Aristotle, to write *Classical Rhetoric for the Modern Student.* In some ways, the book says little that is different from other books on student writing. But the book is special in its explicit connections to ancient rhetorical traditions.

Without a knowledge of history and traditions, we risk running in circles 33 while seeking new paths. Without knowing the traditions, there is no way of knowing which traditions to hold dear and which to discard. Self evident? Maybe. Yet the circles exist.

For all the wonders I had found in literature—and still find—literature 34 seemed to me self-enveloping. What I would do is read and enjoy. And, when it was time to write, what I would write about would be an explanation of what I had enjoyed, using words like *Oedipal complex* or *polyvocal* or *anxiety* or *unpacking,* depending on what I had found in my discourse-analytical journeys, but essentially saying "this is what I saw" or "this is how what I read took on a special meaning for me" (sometimes being told that what I had seen or experienced was nonsense). I could imagine teaching literature—and often I do, within the context of composition—but I knew that at best I'd be imparting or imposing one view: the what I saw or the meaning for me. The reader-response theorists I would come to read, Rosenblatt, Fish, Culler, and others, would make sense to me, that what matters most is what the reader finds. Bakhtin's cultural and political dimension would make even more sense: that all language is an approximation, generated and understood based on what one has experienced with language. In teaching literature, I thought, there would be those among students I would face who would come to take on reading, perhaps; likely some who would appreciate more fully what they had read. But it did not seem to me that I could somehow make someone enjoy. Enjoyment would be a personal matter: from the self, for the self.

And what if I did manage a Ph.D. and did get a job as a professor? I would 35 have to publish. A guest lecturer in a medieval lit course spoke of one of the important findings in his new book: medieval scribes were conscious of the thickness of the lozenge, the medieval version of the comma. He found that thinner lozenges would indicate a slight pause in reading; thicker lozenges, longer pauses. Interesting, I reckon. Surely of interest to a select few. But so what, in some larger sense? What would I write about?

Then I stumbled onto rhetoric. Here was all that language had been to me. 36 There were the practical matters of writing and teaching writing. There were the stylistic devices, the tricks of language use that most people think about when they hear the word *rhetoric;* "Let's cut through the rhetoric." It's nice to have those devices at one's disposal — nice, even important, to know when those devices are operating. But there is more. Rhetoric's classic definition as the art of persuasion suggests a power. So much of what we do when we speak or write is suasive in intent. So much of what we receive from others — from family and friends to thirty-second blurbs on TV — is intended to persuade. Recognizing how this is done gives greater power to choose. But rhetoric is still more.

Rhetoric is the conscious use of language: "observing in any given case the 37 available means of persuasion," to quote Aristotle (I.ii). As the conscious use of language, rhetoric would include everything that is conveyed through language: philosophy, history, anthropology, psychology, sociology, literature, politics — "the use of language as a symbolic means of inducing cooperation in beings that by nature respond to symbols," according to modern rhetorician Kenneth Burke (46).[2] The definition says something about an essentially human characteristic: our predilection to use symbols. Language is our primary symbol system. The ability to learn language is biologically transmitted. Burke's definition points to language as ontological, part of our being. And his definition suggests that it is epistemological, part of our thinking, an idea others say more about (see Leff).[3]

So to study rhetoric becomes a way of studying humans. Rhetoric becomes 38 for me the complete study of language, the study of the ways in which peoples have accomplished all that has been accomplished beyond the instinctual. There were the ancient greats saying that there was political import to the use of language. There were the modern greats saying that how one comes to know is at least mediated by language, maybe even constituted in language. There were the pragmatic applications. There was the possibility that in teaching writing and in teaching rhetoric as conscious considerations of language use I could help others like myself: players with language, victims of the language of failure.

---

[2]Burke, Kenneth. *A Rhetoric of Motives.* U of California P, 1969, p. 46.
[3]Leff, Michael C. "In Search of Ariadne's Thread: A Review of the Recent Literature on Rhetorical Theory." *Central States Speech Journal*, no. 29, 1978, pp. 73–91.

Questions for Discussion and Journaling

1. This account shifts back and forth between the first person ("I") and the third person ("Victor," "he"). What effects does that shifting create? Does it break any rules you've been taught?

2. How does Villanueva define *rhetoric*? What else does he say that studying rhetoric helps you study?

3. Have you ever tried observing and imitating the writing moves that other writers make, as Villanueva describes doing with his English teachers ("Professorial Discourse Analysis")? If so, what was your experience doing so? If not, what would you need to look for in order to do the kind of imitation Villanueva describes?

4. In paragraph 6, Villanueva describes his college writing process as, "The night before a paper was due, he'd gather pen and pad, and stare. Clean the dishes. Stare. Watch an 'I Love Lucy' rerun. Stare. Then sometime in the night the words would come." What elements of this process resemble your own? How is yours different?

5. Villanueva is describing his own experience of encountering affirmative action — how he benefited from it, and how it also had some negative effects. Was this an account you might have expected to hear? If not, how did it differ from your perceptions of affirmative action?

6. In telling the story of his writing process and being called into Mrs. Ray's office (para. 7), Villanueva suggests that he expected Mrs. Ray would take issue with his writing style of "discovering what to write by writing, no prior thesis statement, no outline, just a vague notion of what would materialize, magically, while writing." What are some of your own experiences of being taught how you are supposed to plan and write?

7. Did you attend other colleges before attending the one at which you're using this book? Villanueva describes the difference between his community college and the University of Washington (paras. 5–21). If you've attended both two-year and four-year schools, what differences do you see? If you've attended different schools of the same sort, what were the differences? Can you see your experiences at different schools as acquiring different "literacies"?

8. In a number of places in this excerpt, Villanueva talks not just about "literacy sponsors" but about authors whose ideas about writing and teaching writing shaped his own. Before coming to college, what authors had you read that shaped your thinking about writing?

Applying and Exploring Ideas

1. Villanueva writes that "school became my obsession," and yet he describes struggling with writing for school. In other words, he ran the risk of being barred from doing the thing he loved because of his writing. Consider the activities you most love being part of: Was there ever a moment where language or

writing threatened to (or did) bar your access to them? Or where language or writing provided your gateway to them? Write a two- to three-page descriptive narrative (imitate Villanueva's style, if you like) about that situation.

2. Analyze Villanueva's piece using Brandt's notion of literacy sponsorship. What literacy sponsors appear in Villanueva's literacy narrative? (Start by making as complete a list as you can.) What did these sponsors allow and limit?

3. Do some Professorial Discourse Analysis of two college or high school teachers you've had. What did they each expect from your writing? Did they agree or differ in their expectations? Describe their expectations in two to three pages, and give specific examples of what each expected.

4. Look up information about Robert Kaplan's "contrastive rhetoric." Write a two-to-three-page explanation describing contrastive rhetoric and explaining why it might have helped a student like Villanueva make sense of his own experiences in college.

- -

META MOMENT   After reading Villanueva, what is your understanding of the relationship between language, identity, and power? How can this understanding help you better understand your own experiences or those of others?

- -

Challenging Our Labels

Rejecting the Language of Remediation

ARTURO TEJADA, JR.
ESTHER GUTIERREZ
BRISA GALINDO
DESHONNA WALLACE
SONIA CASTANEDA

Brisa Galindo

Esther Gutierrez

Brisa Galindo

Brisa Galindo and DeShonna Wallace

Esperanza Castaneda

Framing the Reading

This article was written by five first-year composition students at California State University, San Bernardino, as part of their "rebellion" against being labeled "remedial" writers due to a standardized, timed test they took prior to entering college.

The issues these students raise here should be ones with which you can relate. Even if you were never labeled remedial, you likely had to take (and be judged by your performance on) timed writing tests. You've probably been labeled in some form, and then encountered specific treatment and experience based on those labels. You've probably encountered teachers whose perceptions of you colored your feelings about yourself and your ability. And certainly the type of school you attended determined the kinds of experiences and resources to which you were exposed.

This article illustrates many of the threshold concepts discussed in this book, and also many of the claims made by other scholars in this chapter. For example, Tejada

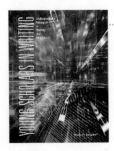

Tejada, Arturo, Jr., et al. "Challenging Our Labels: Rejecting the Language of Remediation." *Young Scholars in Writing*, vol. 11, 2014, pp. 5–16.

et al. talk a great deal about how words, ideas, and labels made them who they are. In other words, that thoughts and ideas make reality, as we explained in Chapter 1 (p. 5). Their experiences illustrate what happens to students when the two stories about writing that we discussed in that chapter collide: Their administrators and high school teachers seem to be acting out of a traditional story about writing as error avoidance, while their college writing teacher seems to see writing as much richer than that. These writers illustrate repeatedly the ways that their writing (and their sense of themselves) is impacted by their prior experiences, that it is possible to see writing as a powerful way to get things done and take action (in this case, as rebellion against labels they don't want to accept), and that all writers have more to learn — thus, it's problematic to label any particular group of students as "remedial."

Getting Ready to Read

Before you read, do at least one of the following activities:

- Do you have any experience being tested and then "placed" into a writing or English class? If so, what was that experience like?
- Conduct an Internet search for "remediation" and "remedial writer" and see what you find.
- Google the "EPT California placement test" so that you understand what it is when the writers here refer to it.

As you read, consider the following questions:

- Where do you relate to the authors' feelings and experiences?
- Are there any unfamiliar terms, particularly those related to testing, placement, and orientation, at their school? You may want to bring these up in class.

EVEN THOUGH MOST California State University campuses no longer offer 1 remedial English courses, the university's system-wide English Placement Test (EPT) continues to designate between 50–80% of first-year students enrolled on its twenty-three campuses as remedial writers, although sometimes using the label "not yet proficient." English departments have resisted these categories in various ways, and now most of them have adopted local enactments of what Arizona State University calls "stretch" programs (Glau) in which students do substantive text work that is not, and is not named, remedial. On our campus, students are directed to one-, two-, or three-quarter first-year writing (FYW) courses in which they are taught in the same cohort by the same instructor.

However, on our campus, as on many others, despite these curricular and 2 pedagogical changes, the language of remediation has continued to be imposed by institutional structures in both official communications and campus conversation — again, even though our English department has not offered remedial writing courses for several years.

Based on our EPT scores, we five FYW students were categorized as remedial. 3 The implications of that assessment became clear to us in unexpected and conflicting ways. For example, although documents from the Chancellor's Office as well as communications from our home campus personnel used the term *remedial*, we were assigned to a three-quarter (thirty-week) FYW "stretch" course, listed by the English department as nonremedial. In fact, far from being remedial in either its topics or its pedagogy, our coursework helped us to challenge the language of remediation that continues to mark students like us and our writing.

Elizabeth Wardle and Doug Downs's *Writing about Writing* unmasked the 4 language of remediation for us and for our professors, class TAs, and writing center tutors, pushing us all not only to stretch our own ideas about labeled writing populations but also to speak out to the academic community about how institutional language constructs students and shapes their relationships with their families, with other students, with professors, and within the professions they plan to enter.

As we read Deborah Brandt's work on literacy sponsorship and Jean Anyon's 5 descriptions of socioeconomic-status (SES) differentiated high school curricula and pedagogy, we began to challenge CSU's administrative labeling practices, showing how these labels isolate and limit students. This has come to matter enormously to us, and thus we offer the following narratives, which have helped us to better understand the importance of language and labels. We hope to challenge others to think about how the language they use each day shapes writers and the writing that takes place in their spaces. We begin by explaining how we came to *feel* remedial and how that constructed us as students and writers, then show how those perceptions clashed with our experiences in our FYW class. Next we describe our research into labels and labeling. We conclude by showing some of the impact we believe our work has had locally and by challenging others to join in this work in their own spaces. We especially hope that we can encourage students who have been labeled remedial to realize that they are not alone and that they don't have to accept someone else's label.

WHY DID WE FEEL REMEDIAL WHEN WE WERE NOT IN A REMEDIAL COURSE?

Even "remedial" students can read signs! Even before we arrived on campus, 6 we knew that we were remedial. And if we didn't, we quickly learned who we "really" were, and it wasn't pretty.

Sonia: As a first-generation college student, I had been told by my parents that they would always try their best to support me and to help me reach my goals, so receiving an acceptance letter from a four-year university was the best feeling ever. My parents were beyond excited and proud of me. Any chance they had, they told people that I got accepted to a four-year university and that not many people can get in, but I did because I worked hard for it. Two weeks later, when I received my EPT results, I was confused. I didn't know what my scores meant until I went to orientation and found out that I was placed in what they called a remedial course for English. I was speechless. The word *remedial* hit me like a brick. I knew I was being accepted by Cal State, but when I found out that I was placed in a remedial English course I began to question myself—if I were worthy of their sponsorship. I didn't have the courage to tell my parents that their daughter needed to take a "remedial" course. Just the word itself was disappointing and made me feel embarrassed. That was two years ago. Even though I have successfully passed my English course and Cal State no longer labels me remedial, my parents still don't know that I was in a remedial class, and I don't know if they ever will.

Esther: Like Sonia, once I received my acceptance letter I was proud of myself that I had made it—against all odds I had made it. In fact, I was not aware of what the term *remedial* even meant until I came to orientation at CSUSB. But I quickly learned. As I sat through the dean of the natural sciences' speech, I heard him use it about classes that were not "college level." I remember the dean making specific remarks about these courses, that if you had to take any remedial classes you were already behind on being able to graduate in four years. This meant if you were not enrolled in Math 110 or English 107, you were behind. As I sat there looking at my paper that had on it the classes I was eligible to enroll in, I felt ashamed. My paper had 102 for English, while everyone around me had a 107 on theirs. I felt so embarrassed. I had never wanted to run and hide so much as I did at this moment. Already behind, and I had not even started? Hearing this come from someone of such power made me feel as though I was no match for all the other students who had placed into "college-level" English. My first thought after hearing this was, "Oh, great, now I must take high school English all over again." Being labeled remedial shook my confidence as a student because all my life I had been told that going to college was basically not an option for me. Then once I finally made it, I had to carry with me this "remedial" label which shows people that I wasn't good enough to be a regular college student, that I was underprepared and needed fixing. Feeling accepted and welcomed to the university is very important as an incoming freshman. Once I left that orientation, I knew I would still have to demonstrate to the university administrators as well as myself that I belonged at CSUSB. The feeling of not belonging created an unnecessary barrier for me as a student because of the negative impact the label "remedial" carries.

Arturo: When I went to orientation, I was extremely confident because my 9 hard work in high school, resulting in a high GPA, allowed me to gain acceptance into every school I applied to, and I chose Cal State, San Bernardino. When I received my schedule, I saw that I had an English 102 class and a Math 90 class. I had no idea what those meant, but the orientation instructor told us that students who were placed below Math 110 or below English 107 were in "remedial classes" and had one year to pass them or else they were kicked off the campus. Like the others here, these words stung so much because I had worked so hard to get here, only to find myself at the bottom of the food chain, which meant being looked down upon by everyone. I felt like I did not belong at this school.

As soon as I got home and told others about my classes, they scrutinized 10 me intensely. My father even told me to go to a community college because he thought that I should not be in Cal State if I was a "remedial" student and that I would be discriminated against there. However, when he left me at my Cal State dorm, he said, "I know you are better than the label, but now you just have to prove to them how much you want it."

My first reaction to the orientation adviser's warning about finishing our 11 "remedial" classes within one year or being kicked out was shock. The next was shame. But then I began to feel afraid—afraid that he was right to segregate me, that I would never be good enough to fit in. This fear either makes or breaks students because they can carry it for the rest of their college career, creating a sense of helplessness that may ultimately cause them to drop out: if they'll never measure up, what point is there in continuing? Luckily, I instead used fear as motivation. I allowed it to consume me and become an obsession, the reason I got up every morning. My fear and anger of never measuring up in the eyes of my peers and superiors, due to the discrimination that came with the "remedial" label, made me want to do my absolute best to prove them wrong by working that much more on my craft—because in my eyes, failure was not an option.

Being discriminated against is painful, especially when it jeopardizes people's 12 futures. It's been three years since I was labeled, and I've accomplished so much during that time. However, despite my accomplishments, the label still stings as much as it did at first. That fear of never measuring up, never being good enough, still consumes me to my very core. It shows up in my school-work, even in my day-to-day behavior. I'm constantly second-guessing myself; the question *Do I belong here?* will probably be in the back of my mind for the rest of my college career and maybe even my professional career. Much like so many others, no matter how much I fight against it, trying to prove that I'm not "remedial," that label has become part of my identity because of the internal scars it's inflicted. Not everyone has the good fortune to be stubborn in facing and enduring the label, in trying to prove it wrong, which is why all of us feel so keenly about this project.

Brisa: When I started college, I did know what remediation meant because of an explanation from my high school AVID (Advancement via Individual Determination, a college-readiness program) teacher. He said, "When you place in remedial it means that you have to take extra English classes in order to be considered a 'real college student.'" That shocked me because I had worked so hard to get into a university, only to find out that I was not a "real college student" after all. Like Sonia, I was too embarrassed to tell anyone in my family that I was remedial because I felt guilty. I almost felt ashamed when I told people what school I was going to because I didn't know if one small move could jeopardize my university standing. I couldn't enjoy my first year in college because the thought of being kicked out of the university followed my every move. If I had any doubts about what the university thought about me, they flew out the window when I was sitting in my philosophy class and another student asked the professor a question about the *Crito*. He answered, "It's not like you are remedial!" That made me feel ashamed, lower than the other philosophy majors. I'm not saying that professors should watch every word they say in their classes, but it was another reminder that even though I was sitting in the same classroom with "regular" students, I would still be looked down upon if anyone discovered that I was remedial. I hoped no one would find out, and I wondered whether the philosophy major was off limits to people like me. It made me sad but also mad. I never knew how much a simple word could affect me until I was labeled remedial; I still feel the loss of that pride I had when I was first admitted. Instead of identifying as a legitimate student with my school—which is an important element in persistence—I still sometimes feel like a fake, as if someone will discover that I don't really belong. I think that even when I receive my diploma, I'll still be looking for the attachment that reads "provisional" or somehow not-real. 13

DeShonna: When I was graduating from high school, the majority of the teachers pushed students into going to a junior college not only because of price but because we would learn more there in order to transfer to a four-year university as "equals." Already I felt remedial because I could see that going into college meant going into a hierarchy. You take a placement test and find out where you fall in that hierarchy. Then once I got my results and saw that I would be taking remedial courses, I knew for sure that I was not considered college level. Shocking, because no one had said that this test would rank us as remedial or not; it was instead described as showing whether or not students should take a freshman English class. I did not want to skip that class and didn't think that I would be looked down on for taking it. 14

Having graduated high school with honors and thus gained admission to any CSU campus I chose, I thought as time went on that maybe I had escaped 15

CSUSB's hierarchy. But once I got to campus, the orientation session let me know that although I may have had a great past, the EPT made me remedial now. The counselors placed me in a thirty-week English class and emphasized that failing to complete remedial classes in my first year would get me kicked out of school. As a pre-nursing student, they stressed, I had no room for failure. I began to feel less and less sure of myself. They actually told me that because I had to take remedial courses, most likely I would in fact not even make it into the nursing major. This bothered me because the orientation staff, without knowing anything about me, judged my lifetime capabilities by one inaccurately described placement test. Although they may have thought they were doing a good deed in being realistic and welcoming students to "the real world," they were only increasing the odds that I would fail by *predicting* that I would fail. The remedial title somehow also entered into the social fabric of the school, so that even in places like the writing center, I felt that some tutors treated me differently from other students once they found out what English class I was in — even if I came with work from another class like philosophy. So for most of that year, I went into the writing center only to fulfill assignments for my English class.

So — we all had plenty of people to tell us that we were remedial and exactly 16 what that meant: not-good, fake, damaged, unlikely to succeed. We were embarrassed; we felt marginal, inferior, and alienated. Some of us were angry, but more of us just decided that we had to play the university's game. However, the labels mattered so much to our identities that when other students asked us what "English" we were taking, we avoided the questions or we lied.

AND THEN WE SHOWED UP FOR OUR FIRST "NOT-REMEDIAL REMEDIAL" ENGLISH CLASS

We came through the door not knowing what to expect, but expecting it not to 17 be good — and again we were confused. Our professor didn't seem to have heard that we were remedial. When we began reading and writing, she kept pestering us about "exigency," which didn't seem like something we remedial students should have. It didn't seem like something that went along with the Google definition of remedial as "1. Giving or intended as a remedy or cure. 2. Provided or intended for students who are experiencing learning difficulties." What we were called and what we were actually doing in class just didn't add up, so we spent a lot of time wondering what we were being cured of, and exactly what "learning difficulties" had placed us in what the university, at least, thought was a remedial English course.

Sonia: I can still remember how nervous I was that first day of our class; my 18 heart was pounding so fast that I thought I might explode as I sat there looking around. The classroom little by little started to fill in, and the professor came in and gave us our syllabus and explained what we would be doing for the quarter. I was shocked when I started reading the syllabus. I thought it would have a lot of grammar lessons or basic instructions on how to do an essay, but it didn't. It had a lot of reading passages and articles by scholars like Michel Foucault, Peter Elbow, James Paul Gee, and many more. Why were we reading these scholars if this was a remedial course?

What surprised me the most was the professor. She never treated us like 19 remedial students. She believed in us and knew from the beginning that we had a lot of potential. She gave us work that many other professors wouldn't give their first-year students. At the end of class, I knew that I wasn't a remedial student and neither were my classmates. We were labeled by the school, but our work said something else. It showed that we were capable of being scholars.

Arturo: Coming into my FYW class, I was so furious that the only thing I 20 was interested in was proving to Professor Hanson that I could write just as well as, if not better than, any one of her students in the non-"remedial" ten-week course. I refused to accept the mediocrity, the failure, the being looked down on that I felt the university was assigning me. I was determined to prove not just to my professors and everyone around me but especially to myself that I belonged, that I was an equal, normal college student. But as we began to read John Swales, James Paul Gee, Deborah Brandt, Ann Johns, Sherman Alexie, bell hooks, Mike Rose, and others, I noticed that Professor Hanson believed in us, saw us as normal, and

> At the end of the class I knew that I wasn't a remedial student and neither were my classmates. We were labeled by the school, but our work said something else. It showed that we were capable of being scholars.

challenged us. One way she did this — beyond having us read difficult, "real" work — was by asking us, surprisingly, what we would say back to them, and how they might speak to us in response. She challenged us to prove we were not the label by first using the work to prove it to ourselves. She assigned us work that even graduate students did, and then had us apply those concepts in everyday life in order to prove to others that we were not "remedial." I started to feel more confident — even proud. My dad was right: we were better than our labels, and now we had to work harder to challenge the entire structure of academia and prove who we really were — which, ironically enough, we discovered in our "remedial" class.

Esther: As I stepped into my remedial English class, I was so sure I would 21 be going over exactly the same material I had gone through in high school — because obviously I did not learn it the first time and I needed to go over it some more in order to be ready for "college-level" English. I was shocked when our professor did not hand out a grammar book and start teaching us how to construct sentences or how to properly use a comma. Instead she began by having us read scholarly journals and think critically about them. These journals were a new genre of writing we had never been exposed to. It was difficult to understand exactly what the authors were saying, but class discussion brought the meaning clearer and clearer as we began to adapt.

I was even more surprised when we began to read Jean Anyon's essay "Social 22 Class and the Hidden Curriculum of Work." She writes about the difference in the teaching methods elementary teachers use, differences that depend on the economic status and social class of the community in which a school is placed. The "executive elite" method of teaching is for schools in wealthy communities, where students are imagined as leaders, to learn to challenge and remake others' rules rather than just follow them. "In the executive elite school," Anyon writes, "work is developing one's analytical intellectual powers" (83). As we read Anyon, I could see that in K-12 I had been taught to be a follower, an obeyer; but in my FYW class, I was finally being challenged to think in more depth about the assignments, not just follow grammar rules. As the class proceeded and the level at which I was being challenged increased, I began to wonder who exactly decided this class was remedial. No one in our class needed to be cured of anything, and as far as I could see, no one had learning difficulties. We were all able to keep up, and we all worked together to unpack the readings. The term *remedial* implies that we are not at the college level, but in my "remedial" class all we ever did from the first day was college-level work.

Brisa: I took the remedial class, but to me it felt nothing like I thought a 23 remedial class would be. We were reading everything from Gee to Foucault, and we were breaking the high school habit of Jane Schaffer paragraphs by writing college essays. I didn't feel like a remedial student because of all the difficult reading that I was doing; when I asked my peers, none of them were reading what I was. I began to enjoy doing difficult work, to read in between the lines, to think critically, and to feel confident in my writing. I no longer felt that my essay was controlling me. I knew what I wanted to say, and I knew how to translate it into my paper; I controlled what I wrote.

DeShonna: When I entered the opening ten weeks of our thirty-week English 24 course, I thought this would be easy, especially since I had graduated high school with honors. However, my professor did not do the expected grammar drills but instead told us this class would be no different from the English class that any incoming college students take, except that our class was stretched over a longer span. We would get a chance to learn in more depth, she said, which would help us excel in college. As the weeks went by, we learned a lot about the academic community and read articles that graduate students said they were having difficulty with. This led me to question why we were considered "not yet proficient" by the English department and remedial by everyone else, especially when my English class pedagogy was more advanced than some of the classes I saw "proficient" students taking. After icebreakers in class, I finally felt that I could speak on remediation without feeling ashamed. I began to wonder why over half of Cal State students were being labeled remedial, why the majority of the students who are defined as remedial are minorities, and why students who start off being classified as remedial and not yet proficient end up with lower retention rates (Tierney and Garcia 2).

However, exigency took on life when our professor offered us extra credit to attend the Celebration of Writing for FYW and said that she hoped we might get excited about entering the contest ourselves. Us? Remedial students earning writing awards? It became even more confusing when during the awards ceremony, one of her colleagues in the composition department gave a speech celebrating the successful elimination of remedial classes on our campus. "What?" we demanded during our next class. How could she make that claim when we were all acutely aware of our own remedial status and the remedial status of our stretch class? Yes, we had begun not to feel remedial while we were actually in class, but we sure knew we were outside of it.

WE DID RESEARCH ON LABELS AND REMEDIATION AND BECAME EVEN MORE CONFUSED

Our professor didn't have any answers that satisfied us, but she agreed that we could take it on for our winter-quarter research project. Because we found the disjunction between what the institution said about us, what we were learning in class, and what we thought about ourselves puzzling, irritating, and at times enraging, we decided that we needed to look beyond our own experiences to the work of those we were now describing as "other scholars." We were especially attracted to Brandt's work on literacy sponsors, Gee's on identity kits, Anyon's on how different educations prepare and predestine students, Elbow's and Rose's on the effects of remediation and labeling, and that of some of our fellow CSUSB students.

Brisa: Things just didn't add up. I learned while researching my remediation paper that over 60% of students place into some kind of remedial class in CSUSB (California State University). This shocked me when I thought about my philosophy professor's comment about remedial students: didn't he know about the 60%? Had my adviser missed the prerequisite for philosophy majors that said, "No remedial students permitted"?

I also was confused when I read Elbow's comment that "the teachers of remedial classes are often the least well paid and the least respected" (588). When we discussed this in class, it seemed to us that if professors had the option of teaching a remedial class or a "regular" writing class, most often they would pick the regular class. How is that supposed to help us with our confidence, knowing we aren't usually first choice? We enter as remedial students, so since we are considered unprepared, wouldn't it make sense to have the most prepared professors teaching us? Although our professor was new, we were lucky in the sense that she actually wanted to teach our class. She wanted to teach our class because she was excited about us all learning together. Had she and my philosophy professor ever met?

Arturo: I was so furious when I began our class that I hardly could believe 29 Professor Hanson when she told us that she did not see any of us as "remedial students." I was amazed when she asked us if we wanted to do a paper on the topic of "remediation" for our term paper. I thought if I was going to prove that I wasn't a remedial student, I would need to interview as many students, professors, and administrators that were directly associated with the label as I could, so I did just that. I interviewed over a hundred college students, most of whom said a lot of the same things that my peers and I said: remediation means that you don't really belong, are doing "basic" work, and are less smart and less likely to succeed. When I asked the composition professors who have direct contact with students, they said that they don't look at incoming freshmen as anything but developing writers. Even the chair said, "The content of the courses in our stretch program is university level and not remedial." So why were we being labeled?

To find out I spoke to one of the college deans. He argued that, while it is not 30 good that there is a negative connotation to being in certain classes, "the fact of the matter is that students in these classes need additional help in these subjects." When I asked him whether the EPT is flawed, he said that every test has some flaw in it, but the EPT is an "adequate" test that has been working for a long time, and there is no reason to discontinue its use. He said that there could be improvements to better evaluate students coming out of high school, but he had to work within the framework of the budget, and as of now the EPT is the best way to evaluate students.

The EPT was created many years ago to help the university place students in 31 FYW classes that would give them the best chance to succeed as college students; that was its only purpose. However, this two-part exam—a multiple-choice grammar, usage, and critical thinking test, plus a thirty-minute essay—has become much more than that. Now it is seen as a proficiency test, one students can fail. Worse, it uses predicted outcomes to designate a system-wide "failure" rate of 50% or higher, depending on the population of individual campuses.

Further, the language the Educational Testing Service (ETS) website uses and 32 the way the CSU system interprets the test conflict in how they present information about the test to incoming students. ETS tells students that the test is not for admission but simply helps determine which courses best match their level of performance in English (ETS). Prior to the test, I was told how insignificant and easy it was. The ETS website even tells people not to stress about the test, so when I went to take it, I was extremely confident. I followed the advice and relaxed—until none of the test was as I expected. The multiple-choice section asked questions unlike anything that I had seen before, even on the SATs and AP tests. The essay question took awhile just to figure out what I was being asked to write about — which wasn't even being looked at by the graders, who were looking more at grammar. I did not finish the test because it took me a long time to figure out how I wanted to tackle the topic. When I write, it takes me hours just to write the first draft, which usually has numerous grammatical errors. How could I have been accurately evaluated by a test that eliminated that normal, extended writing process? Even more irritating was how my results hinged on the performance of others taking the test that day via the system's predetermined "failure" rate.

Only after I had taken the test did I realize the importance of the very differ- 33
ent language employed by the CSU campuses. They look at it as an evaluation as opposed to how the ETS presents it. There the language of remediation and the costs of failure are alive and well. I learned that EPT scores like mine result in students being unjustly labeled and prejudged prior to stepping foot inside a classroom of the university — to which they were already admitted prior to the test.

I was astonished to find out that even on our campus there was a huge dif- 34
ference in opinion regarding the topic of remediation depending on who you talked to and their ranking in academe. However, I was less surprised when I read Rose's statements about how academics get their ideas about students:

> There's not a lot of close analysis of what goes on in classrooms, [and] the cognitive give and take of instruction and what students make of it. . . . We don't get much of a sense of the texture of students' lives . . . but even less of a sense of the power of learning things and through that learning redefining who you are. Student portraits when we do get them are too often profiles of failure rather than of people with dynamic mental lives. (12)

Maybe the administrators should talk to the professors and the students and get some of that texture into their definitions. And maybe they should be reading what we read in our research.

Sonia: College students see themselves partly through the images and frame- 35
works that are constructed by their literacy sponsors. Brandt defines literacy sponsors as "any agents, local or distant, concrete or abstract, who enable, support, teach, model, as well as recruit, regulate, suppress, or withhold literacy — and gain advantage by it in some way" (334). Students might be sponsored by a scholarship, a sport, or their parents. The support they receive varies depending on the type of sponsors they have. Reading Brandt helped us reflect on our sponsors. Our families believed in us, but when they learned that we were remedial (that is, if we told them), some were afraid and warned us to scale down our hopes. They didn't want us to take on higher goals until we were ready for them.

Many family members and friends assumed that our placement was remedial for a reason. Most of our high school sponsors were like DeShonna's, who said that after high school we were meant to either get jobs or go to community colleges. Brandt argues that some kinds of literacy sponsorship, in privileging one kind of literacy, actually suppress others. Cal State's sponsorship was mixed: the administration was sponsoring us as somehow special or different, which wasn't a vote of confidence, but our professor saw us as smart and capable. At first we weren't sure whether to believe her, but since Professor Hanson was pretty powerful in her belief, we began to trust in what she and other scholars said about us. So our parents supported us in our literacy goals even though the EPT shook their faith; our high school and college administrators regulated and in some ways suppressed or even withheld literacy; and our professor and her colleagues and department modeled literacy and enabled us as literate persons.

Esther: Reading Anyon's "Social Class and the Hidden Curriculum of Work" 36 was shocking and revealing. It was discouraging to discover that social and economic class differentiates teaching, so the school you attend can determine how well you become prepared to either go into the workforce or attend college. Anyon spent a full year researching five schools with different economic backgrounds. She found that although the same material was being taught throughout the five different schools, *how* the students were being taught had a huge impact. Coming from a "working-class" school, I have been taught since I was a child how to follow rules and regulations. These are the steps working-class students are taught because we are expected to go into the workforce once we are done with high school as opposed to attending college. We especially don't learn that we are on the bottom rung of a ladder on which some other students are taught to become our thinkers and managers.

Students who come from a working-class school face a hard battle every day. 37 By the ways we are taught and labeled, we face the oppression of being told we will not make it to college. Ever since I was little, I was told that people like me will find a job after high school, ending their schooling. When a high school teacher asked what I planned to do after high school, I told him I was hoping to go to CSU. He looked at me and said that if I wanted to go to a four-year university, I was in the wrong school. Our high school prepares students to go into the workforce or community college.

DeShonna: The disjunction between schools that Esther's high school teacher 38 was pointing out is a function of what Gee calls "Discourses," and these differences also help explain validity problems with the EPT. A Discourse, according to Gee, "is a sort of 'identity kit', which comes complete with instructions on how to talk, act, and write as taking on a particular social role that others will recognize" (484). High school and college are two very different Discourses. When I entered college it bothered me that the community identified students as remedial based on invalid reasons—invalid because the EPT measures of critical thinking and college writing skills can, as Esther uses Anyon to point out, also be shaped by your socioeconomic status. As Anyon says, a major difference between elite and working-class schools can be instruction in critical thinking and writing. Working-class students may not be prepared to write as college students because they are not expected to go to college, having instead mostly been taught to follow directions so they can join the workforce. These different ways of teaching are creating students who work within different Discourses, and why would we expect valid test results on potential for accomplishment in a Discourse many students haven't even been taught yet?

There are two other reasons that labeling incoming college students remedial 39 is a bad idea. First, many universities, including some Ivy League schools, offer all students thirty weeks of writing instruction without any negative connotation. However, for many public schools, budget cuts discourage any course over ten weeks, which resonates with Anyon's assertions about socioeconomic status and education. This limitation contributes to the negative stereotype of students in the stretch programs. Second, psychology suggests that a critical period of identity formation occurs between the ages of thirteen and twenty, during which people (including the majority of first-year college students) clarify their values and try to experience success. They are also developing a sense of individuality, connectedness, and critical thinking. It's not the time to critically undermine student self-efficacy with spurious labels.

In my own case, the remedial label affected my identity formation in that 40 the university's doubt whether I was a "real" college student weakened my own sense of identity and belonging as a college student. I started to feel like I had not accomplished anything in high school, and I felt powerless and confused, lacking confidence—and silenced, as I worried about telling other students and campus offices that I was in the stretch program. Gee argues that an identity kit for a role includes clothes, attitudes, language—both oral and print—and ways of interacting with others. Labeled a remedial writer, I started to wonder, "Well, am I remedial in my other classes as well? Will the teachers be able to tell I am a remedial writer? Can I even write a paper and get a good grade?"

OUR REBELLION

Scholarship had helped us understand the issues. However, all the work we 41 read was written by professors and other scholars, not by students who have actually lived with the stigma of being labeled remedial. We wanted our voices heard, so first we presented our work at the 2012 International Writing Centers Association (IWCA) Conference, which helped us complicate our thinking about institutional, tutor, and student language. Then Arturo entered his remediation research project into our campus's FYW Celebration of Writing and took home the first prize, which helped us believe in ourselves and our words. And then we proposed and presented a session at the 2013 Conference on College Composition and Communication (CCCC), where the audience response encouraged us to reach farther with our ideas. So we began writing, hoping to someday publish our work. That was our rebellion against the unfair label. In rebelling we came to believe we do belong in college. We believe that our work shows how student-initiated and carefully theorized resistance to institutional language helped us, and our professors, to reexamine our own acceptance of institutional labeling as well as to challenge administrators and faculty to label students accurately: as writers.

One of our favorite class quotes is from Albert Einstein: "Everybody is a   42 genius. But if you judge a fish by its ability to climb a tree, it will live its whole life believing that it is stupid." Gee's theory of identity formation speaks power-fully to labeling students as remedial, and it is why a university should put extra effort into understanding the effects of remedial labels on its writers. This could go a long way toward keeping students from feeling put down; they would be more motivated to meet the common goals of the other students in the univer-sity and not feel they are worth less than their colleagues. After all, college writ-ing is very different from high school writing. There is no way students should be condemned for not exhibiting characteristics of a style they have never been taught.

Fortunately for the incoming students who followed us, prior to our speak-   43 ing out, numerous faculty members had already been laying the foundation to resolve the injustice done to us; all we did was bring it out in the open. In a sense, it was the perfect storm. The following year, things did end up changing at CSUSB, due in part to the implementation of a new initiative, directed self-placement (DSP), which gave students the opportunity to choose their own English placement. So throughout that year, our sophomore year, we asked numerous first-year students if any of them felt a "remedial" stigma related to writing; much to our surprise, they had no idea what we were talking about. Some even asked us to define the term. When we explained it and the effect it has had on us as university students, many were shocked. In speaking to them about the past, we felt as if we were telling a mythical tale because to them, last year was a page in an old history book. It was hard for them to believe because the present is so different.

Also in our sophomore year, though, the CSU system implemented the Early   44 Start Program, a mandatory experience for students designated as "underpre-pared" by the EPT. They are required to attend a four-day class to "prepare" them for college-level writing. When we came to college, our university told us that our four years of high school hadn't prepared us for college writing, yet they now believe four days will prepare new students. According to the composition faculty who have been working with us on this project, CSUSB and other CSU campuses with Stretch Composition and DSP have asked to be exempt from

Early Start, but their requests have been denied. So now, even though several professors have commented that the work that came out of our class unmasked the harmful language regarding remediation and influenced both the professor-training materials and the ways Early Start classes are conducted on our campus, students in this year's Early Start are still being discriminated against based on their EPT scores. Although they seem to have no awareness of the remedial label, they do know that their EPT scores were what required them to come to campus in the summer for the Early Start session. And while our faculty has worked hard to find and erase the language of remediation in our campus documents, it remains unchanged on the CSU and ETS websites.

We have helped to change the landscape, and even though Early Start may be 45 the new obstacle that keeps students from equality, we are optimistic that it can be overcome as long as people keep speaking up. We hope that our class doing so will have some effect on other universities' use of the remedial label. Seeing the interest in our presentations at the 2012 IWCA and the 2013 CCCC conferences gave us courage, and we encourage others to speak out. Being engaged as FYW students doing research that matters to us positioned us not just as research subjects for "real" writing scholars to study, but as scholars ourselves who can create knowledge and rewrite the terms of our own education.

As more of us let our voices be heard, there may come a time when all students are treated as normal. The scarring of the past need not continue in the 46 future—a future which will be determined not just by administrators but by brave students who speak out and start making a difference.

Works Cited

Anyon, Jean. "Social Class and the Hidden Curriculum of Work." *Journal of Education* 162.1 (1980): 67–92. Print.

Brandt, Deborah. "Sponsors of Literacy." *College Composition and Communication* 49 (1998): 165–85. Rpt. in Wardle and Downs 332–50. Print.

The California State University (CSU). "Analytic Studies: CSU Proficiency." 15 April 2013. Web. 8 Oct. 2013.

Elbow, Peter. "Response to Glynda Hull, Mike Rose, Kay Losey Fraser, and Marisa Castellano, 'Remediation as Social Construct.'" *College Composition and Communication* 44 (1993): 587–88. Print.

ETS. "CSU: About the CSU Placement Tests." 2013. Web. 8 Oct. 2013.

Gee, James Paul. "Literacy, Discourse, and Linguistics: Introduction." *Journal of Education* 171.1 (1989): 5–17. Rpt. in Wardle and Downs 482–95. Print.

Glau, Gregory. "The 'Stretch Program': Arizona State University's New Model of University-Level Basic Writing Instruction." *WPA: Writing Program Administration* 20.1–2 (1996): 79–91. Print.

Rose, Mike. "Rethinking Remedial Education and the Academic-Vocational Divide." *Mind, Culture, and Activity* 19 (2012): 1–16. Print.

Tierney, William G., and Lisa D. Garcia. "Preparing Underprepared Students for College: Remedial Education and Early Assessment Programs." *Journal of At-Risk Issues* 14.2 (2008): 1–7. Print.

Wardle, Elizabeth, and Doug Downs. *Writing about Writing: A College Reader.* Boston: Bedford/ St. Martin's, 2011. Print.

- -

Questions for Discussion and Journaling

1. What is a "remedial" writer, according to the definitions you researched prior to reading, and according to Tejada et al.?

2. What do you think Tejada et al. mean when they say that reading this book (*Writing about Writing*) "unmasked the language of remediation" for them? Is there anything in your experience of reading this book so far that might help you to understand and question what it means to be called a "remedial" writer?

3. The writers talk about the shame of what Esther calls "carrying this remedial label" (para. 8). Arturo's father warned him that this label would cause him to be discriminated against at the university, and told him that he had to prove to university administrators that he was "better than the label" (para. 10). And Arturo argues that no matter how many successes he has had, the label of remedial has become a part of his identity. Why do you think labels have so much power to shape how people feel about themselves and even who they are?

4. Tejada and the other writers here were placed into their college writing course based on the California EPT placement test. How were you placed into your writing class? If you don't know, do a little research to find out.

5. DeShonna talks about the "hierarchy" in education. Think back to your experiences with reading and writing throughout your school experience. What hierarchies were at play? How were you slotted into reading and writing groups, experiences, and classes? How did those experiences serve as "literacy sponsors" for you? Did these experiences increase the odds that you would fail or succeed by predicting that you would do so, as DeShonna argues?

6. The student writers here talk about the power of their teacher, who "seemed not to have heard that they were remedial" and who assigned them difficult work that showed they "were capable of being scholars" (para. 19). What experiences have you had with the power of teachers who either believed in you or did not? How have those experiences impacted you?

7. Brisa says that in her college writing class she finally felt that her essay was no longer controlling her. What do you think she means? Can you relate to her feeling of being "controlled" by your writing?

8. These authors demonstrate the difficulty of completing a timed essay. What's your own experience with timed writing? Do you think such tests are a good way to judge your abilities as a writer? Why or why not?

Applying and Exploring Ideas

1. Bring a set of index cards to class. With your classmates, fill the index cards with any of the labels that you have been given in your life, both academic and nonacademic. Post the labels on the board. Then as a class engage in the following activities:

   - Discuss who has had the power to assign these labels and write their names on the cards.
   - Consider how the labels have impacted what you could do, were willing to do, and have become. Next to each label write terms to explain how those labels affected you (for example, "limited," "encouraged," "hurt," "created self-doubt").
   - Decide which labels you would like to reject and then remove them from the board.
   - Decide which new labels you might want to name and choose for yourselves, and add them to the board.

2. Write a short manifesto about the power of labels, how labels impact your identity and your writing, and the labels you would like to claim for yourself.

3. Google and read the Jean Anyon article, "Social Class and the Hidden Curriculum of Work" that the writers mention here. Write a short explanation of her argument, and then identify the social-class designation of the schools you have attended using her categories (working class, middle-class, affluent professional, or executive elite). Then explain whether the kinds of tasks engaged in at your schools were similar to the kinds of tasks Anyon outlines (for example, "following steps of a procedure" or "getting the right answer," "creative activity carried out independently," or "developing one's analytical intellectual powers"). Finally, consider how the type of school you attended and its activities have "sponsored" your literacy and expanded or limited what you were asked to do and learned to do.

4. Do some research on the relationship of remediation to social class and race. What do you find? Given what you have learned so far from this book and from the activities you engaged in above, try to write an explanation of why so many minority students are classified as remedial.

- -
META MOMENT   How would you like to label yourself as a writer? What labels have been given to you by others that you want to reject?
- -

"Nah, We Straight"

An Argument Against Code Switching

VERSHAWN ASHANTI YOUNG

Vershawn Ashanti Young

Framing the Reading

Vershawn Ashanti Young describes himself as a trans-disciplinary scholar and teacher. He studies and writes about the language issues that he discusses in this article, as well as about masculinity and representations of race in art, film, and literature. He has written and performed plays, and served as an anti-racism consultant, and he has been a high school teacher, an elementary school principal, and a school board administrator. He is currently an associate professor of drama and speech communication at the University of Waterloo in Canada.

In this article he describes a phenomenon that linguists call "code switching," which is the act of using different versions of a language in different situations. In the United States, some scholars and teachers have argued for teaching code switching in schools, particularly to African American students. Young zargues vigorously against this practice, suggesting that no one form of English is superior to any other form and that arguing that any student's language is inferior is harmful and a form of segregation.

Young's argument and analysis is another way of illustrating the threshold concept you've been learning about in this chapter — that our literacy practices are impacted by prior experience. In this case, Young argues that our identity is deeply informed by our language and literacy practices, and that minority students have a right to see their various uses of language (and thus themselves) as valuable and equal to the more dominant forms.

Young, Vershawn Ashanti. "'Nah, We Straight': An Argument Against Code Switching." *JAC*, vol. 29, no.1, 2009, pp. 49–76.

Getting Ready to Read

Before you read, do at least one of the following activities:

- Google "African American English" and write a short definition.
- Google "code switching" and write a short definition.

As you read, consider the following questions:

- What ideas, terms, and phrases are unfamiliar to you? Make a note of these to ask about in class.
- Highlight places where Young's phrasing and tone surprise you, or seem unusual for an academic article.

PRESIDENT BARACK OBAMA GARNERS as much media attention for his embodied performance of black culture as he does for being America's first national leader of African descent. Comments about his swagger, his growing affinity for Hip Hop, and especially his public use of African American English (hereafter AAE), swiftly travel the airwaves and Internet. The primary title of this essay is excerpted, in fact, from a popular YouTube video that features a dialogue between Obama and a waitress at a pre-inaugural lunchtime stop at Ben's Chili Bowl, a popular diner in Washington, D.C. In a crowded room, over the voices of people from many different races, the waitress asks Obama if he wants the change from the twenty dollar bill he'd given her. "Nah, we straight," he replies (Henderson). 1

I do not intend this opening example to suggest that I will conduct a sociolin- guistic analysis of Obama's speech habits, nor do I wish to indicate that this essay is mostly about him. Instead I forefront Obama's undeniable use of AAE in the mainstream public to exemplify my primary argument—an argument against code switching. Code switching may be defined as the use of more than one language or language variety concurrently in conversation (Auer). Spanglish, the simultaneous linguistic production of Spanish and English in the same discourse, is an example of this kind of code switching. Spanglish, according to writer Santiago Vaquera-Vasquez, is "not that game played in that translation of the first chapter of *Don Quixote*. . . . Spanglish is not inserting words here y there, aveces inserting certain jerga to give it that toque nice y cool"; it is a real hybrid language. 2

Another example of code switching as hybrid language performance is Barack Obama's blending of AAE and so-called standard English to produce what some linguists call Black Standard English (Hoover). Like Vaquera-Vasquez's clarification of Spanglish, Princeton political scientist Melissa Harris-Lacewell observes 3

149

that Obama's black speech and cultural performance are less a product of dog-whistle politics, words dropped here, mannerisms employed there, to appeal to blacks for votes. It is instead an example, as she puts it, of "'his blackness kind of squishing out of the edges. It's not the same thing as deploying [words and phrases] like Bush did'" (qtd. in Henderson).

However, Spanglish and Black Standard English do not typify, nor do they exemplify, the prevailing definition of code switching that language educators promote as the best practice for teaching speaking and writing to African Americans and other "accent- and dialect-speakers" of English. The prevailing definition, the one most educators accept, and the one I'm against, advocates language substitution, the linguistic translation of Spanglish or AAE into standard English. This unfortunate definition of code switching is not about accommodating two language varieties in one speech act. It's not about the practice of language blending. Rather it characterizes the teaching of language conversion. 4

In *Code Switching: Teaching Standard English in Urban Classrooms* (2006), linguist Rebecca S. Wheeler and elementary teacher Rachel Swords encourage teachers to employ the translation model of code switching. Indeed, they represent themselves as fellow teachers, writing that the job of language educators is to "help our students *transition* from home grammar to school grammar in the classroom" (11, emphasis added). Code switching for them is acquiring the facility to transition from one language variety to a different one. They are not promoting what I see as the better alternative — code meshing: blending dos idiomas or copping enough standard English to really make yo' AAE be Da Bomb. 5

Wheeler and Swords also urge teachers to ignore race when teaching and discussing code switching. Even though they write, "We focus our discussion and draw our examples from African American English," in their conclusion, they advise: "We suggest that you refrain from referring to race when describing code-switching. It's not about race" (161). My first response to this blatant contradiction is: "Huh? What tha . . . ?! Code switching is nothing if it ain't about race! How can you draw on the experiences of African Americans, then render them invisible, extract their historical and contemporary racial experience from the discussion?" My second response is this article. 6

The body of this essay is divided into two segments. In Part I, I seek to illustrate how code switching is all about race; how it is steeped in a segregationist, racist logic that contradicts our best efforts and hopes for our students. I do this by placing code switching within the discursive context of what sociologist W.E.B. Du Bois deemed the problem of double consciousness. In the second part, I discuss code switching within the context of the 1974 "The Students' Right to Their Own Language" resolution and further expose code switching as a strategy to negotiate, side-step and ultimately accommodate bias against the working-class, women, and the ongoing racism against the language habits of blacks and other non-white peoples. In the end, I promote code meshing, the 7 blending and concurrent use of American English dialects in formal, discursive products, such as political speeches, student papers, and media interviews.

PART I: THE PROBLEM OF LINGUISTIC DOUBLE CONSCIOUSNESS

> It's a peculiar sensation, this double consciousness. . . . The history of the American Negro is the history of this strife—this longing . . . to merge his double self into a better and truer self.
>
> —W.E.B. Du Bois

> Double-consciousness has a history and should not be manufactured in the composition classroom.
>
> —Catherine Prendergast

> Linguistic integration is preferable to segregation.
>
> —Gerald Graff

Seven years after the Supreme Court legalized racial segregation (*Plessey v.* 8 *Ferguson*, 1896), upholding the right of individual states to restrict and prohibit black people's public (and private) interaction with whites, sociologist W.E.B. Du Bois published *Souls of Black Folks* (1903). *Souls* is an analysis and critique of the effects of Jim Crow on blacks in America. During this period when blacks were deemed a separate and inferior race in relation to whites, Du Bois used the term "double consciousness" to describe the psychological impact this judgment had on blacks. He borrows the term from medical terminology that was used to diagnose patients suffering from split-personality disorder. Du Bois believed that legal segregation produced a similar, if metaphorical, mental disorder in blacks—racial schizophrenia.[1]

The doubling of one's racial self-consciousness is produced, he writes, from 9 having to "always look at one's self through the eyes of others" (2), from being recognized as an American citizen while simultaneously being denied the rights of citizenship, from trying to reconcile how one's racial heritage justifies legal and social subordination not only to whites but to non-citizens residing in the United States (Thomas 58).[2] Du Bois's statement in the epigraph above illustrates blacks' "longing" to resolve double consciousness, "to merge his double self" (2), the American and black selves, into a unified identity that would be better than either could ever be alone, divided, unmerged.

Yet more than a century later blacks still contend with double consciousness, 10 despite the fact that the Supreme Court reversed its earlier sanctioning of segregation with its 1954 decision in *Brown v. The Board of Education,* in Topeka, Kansas. What's so strange about the present circumstances of double consciousness is that it has been adopted and translated into an instructional strategy that is used, like legal segregation, to govern blacks' social interactions in public, paradoxically in an era where allegedly, as linguist John McWhorter opines, "racism is quickly receding" (266).

Double consciousness shows up in one of its most pronounced and pernicious forms in both the theory and practice of teaching oral and written communication to black students, where code switching is offered as the best strategy. Code switching is a strategy whereby black students are taught contrastive analysis—a method comparing black English to standard English so that they can learn to switch from one to the other in different settings. The description on the back of Wheeler and Sword's co-authored textbook reads: "The authors recommend teaching [black] students to recognize the grammatical differences between home speech and school speech so that they are then able to choose the language style most appropriate to the time, place, audience, and communicative purpose." 11

On the surface this instructional method sounds fair because it appears to allow black students to have their racial identity and speak it too. Yet in truth, to teach students that the two language varieties cannot mix and must remain apart belies the claim of linguistic equality and replicates the same phony logic behind Jim Crow legislation—which held that the law recognized the equality of the races yet demanded their separation. Indeed, the arguments used to support code switching are startlingly and undeniably similar to those that were used to support racial separation. 12

Justice Billings Brown, who delivered the majority opinion in the case upholding segregation, wrote that the "assumption that the enforced separation of the two races stamps the colored race with a badge of inferiority" was a false and mistaken view. He continues: "If this be so, it is not by reason of anything found in act, but solely because the colored race chooses to put that construction upon it" (Thomas 33). In dispute of this notion, Justice Thurgood Marshall argued 58 years later in the case that opened the way for desegregation that "separate is inherently unequal." The badge of inferiority that was stamped upon blacks racially and that remains attached to black speech was and is not contrived by blacks. The evidence that they were considered racially inferior then as their speech is now resides in their experience in school where, as Graff writes, they are "urged to use Black English on the streets and formal English in school while keeping these languages separate" (27). Graff believes code switching is a misguided approach and argues: "Linguistic integration is better than segregation" (27). 13

Similarly, literacy scholar Catherine Prendergast substantiates Graff's view in her study *Literacy and Racial Justice: The Politics of Learning after Brown v. The Board of Education* (2003), which uncovers the segregationist practices that still inform the instruction of black students. As she explains, educational institutions still constitute a "site of racial injustice in America" (2), making literacy teachers accomplices, often unwittingly, in the continuation of racial inequality. 14

Literacy and Racial Justice is a conceptual enlargement of Prendergast's earlier   15
essay, "Race: The Absent Presence in Composition Studies," where she focuses
on writing instruction at the college level and uses Du Bois's complaint about
double consciousness to "describe the experience of domination and exclusion
within a society which professes equality and integration" (39). While analyzing the writing of minority law professors (e.g. Derrick Bell, Richard Delgado,
and Patricia Williams), she points out how, like Du Bois, their writing reflects
double consciousness because they view themselves as residing both inside and
outside the legal profession. Their two-ness doesn't stem from any insecurity
on their parts, nor are they uncomfortable being lawyers. To the contrary, it
arises from the way that everyday legal practices reflect a segregationist ideology,
which recognizes the existence of minorities but often excludes their experience
from legal discourse and decisions. Prendergast cautions writing teachers against
imposing a segregationist logic on students by creating models of instruction,
like code switching, out of double consciousness, which, as she puts it, "has a
history and should not be manufactured in the composition classroom" (51).

Yet double consciousness is continually manufactured in writing classrooms.   16
In fact, it's commonly reproduced at all levels of literacy instruction because so
many educators, including many blacks, promote it. This is so even though
double consciousness stems from the legacy of
racism and generates the very racial schizophrenia Du Bois condemned. To be clear, educators
who support code switching are not all conscious
proponents of racism. Thus I am not suggesting
that self-described anti-racist advocates of code

> Double consciousness is
> continually manufactured in
> writing classrooms.

switching are really intentional racists. Nevertheless, the inherent racism of code
switching cannot be denied.

Racism is the belief that race is the primary determinant of human traits and   17
abilities and that the different behaviors and capacities among distinct groups of
people (e.g., blacks and whites) produce a racial taxonomy: One group's behaviors are understood to be superior while another group's abilities are perceived as
inferior. Although racism is slowly being unhinged by our current understanding that race is not a naturally occurring biological fact but is rather a social
construction, advocates of code switching apply old-time racial thinking to their
current understanding of culture and language.

If, as linguists propose, standard English arises primarily from the speech hab-   18
its of middle- and upper-class whites, and students who speak black English are
required to give up their variety and switch to standard English in public and in
school, then students are simultaneously required to recognize the superiority of
standard English and the people associated with it. The response that Wheeler,
Swords and teachers who promote language changing provide to this perspective
is that neither black English nor standard English is superior. They say both are

equal; each has prestige in their respective, separate sites (standard English in school, black English at home). This reasoning reflects the false logic of equality that permitted people to support legal segregation. It's reasoning that doesn't hold up when the two varieties meet in the public domain or in "formal settings." Since black English is restricted in school and the mainstream public, it is, in effect, rendered inferior, even if it is euphemistically described by Wheeler and Swords as "appropriate for other settings, times, situations" (read: "ineffective" and "inappropriate" in formal communication[3]).

Therefore while many advocates of code switching also claim to be anti- 19
racists who would never seek to reinstitute racial subordination, they nonetheless translate the racist logic of early twentieth century legal segregation into a linguistic logic that undergirds twenty-first century language instruction. Toni Cook, the outspoken member of the Oakland School Board who helped persuade other members "to unanimously support the nation's first education policy recognizing Ebonics as the 'primary language' of many students," personifies this paradox (Perry and Delpit 172). In an interview after the Oakland School Board's decision, Cook was asked: "Why don't children automatically know Standard English, since they hear it all the time on television and at school?" She responded:

> African Americans whose economic status and exposure is closer to that
> of the Huxtables have the exposure to work with the youngsters and teach
> them about the 'two-ness' of the world they're involved in. But some schools
> are located in very depressed areas, have a primary population of African
> Americans on a fixed income. They see very little, the young people are
> exposed to very little, and there isn't a whole lot of reason in the home—this
> is just my guess—to adopt the behavior of duality (Perry and Delpit 176).

Cook's observation of the "two-ness of the world" apparently refers to the vestiges of segregation that blacks must still negotiate. It's illegal, of course, to restrict blacks from integration based on their "color." But it's currently legal to discriminate on the basis euphemistically called "the content of their character," which in this context is manifested by whether or not they talk black in public.

In Cook's view, blacks should develop a dual personality, acting and speaking 20
one way with whites, another with blacks in recognition of "the two-ness of the world their involved in." From this perspective, what's really wrong with code switching is that it seeks to transform double consciousness, the very product of racism, into a linguistic solution to racial discrimination. Thus the real irony of Cook's belief that black people should "adopt the behavior of duality" is that the very anti-racist, liberal-minded individuals who claim to oppose racial discrimination are the same ones who unconsciously perpetuate it. Instead of attacking racism, they attempt to teach black folks how to cope with it. As school retention

rates and test scores indicate, they fail quite miserably at convincing the majority of black students to embrace double consciousness as a coping strategy, but succeed at allowing the residue of racism to remain.

Double consciousness and the related belief in the value of code switching 21 are so widespread that both are unfortunately encouraged by even prominent black linguists John Russell Rickford and Geneva Smitherman — two admirable scholars, who tirelessly pursue racial justice and the validation of black English. *Spoken Soul: The Story of Black English,* a book Rickford co-authored with his son, journalist Russell John Rickford, and for which Smitherman wrote the foreword, ends with a section titled "The Double Self." This last section has only one chapter, "The Crucible of Identity." The Rickfords begin it with the same epigraph from Du Bois' *Souls* that I use above. And they close it with four strong "suggestions": (1) Accept black English as a language. (2) Reject linguistic shame. (3) Urge black youth to "become proficient in Standard English, *especially the black Standard English*" (229, emphasis added). And, the last suggestion is worth quoting at some length:

> Don't ever shun or jeer a brother or sister because of the way he or she speaks. It is only when we have claimed both Spoken Soul and Standard English as our own, *empowering our youth to appreciate and articulate each in their respective forums,* that we will have mastered the art of merging our double selves into a better and truer self. Remember: to become an accomplished pianist (jazz and classical), you've got to be able to work both the ebonies and the ivories. (229, emphasis added)

Although they pursue very noble work in their book, Rickford and Rickford 22 end with a fallacious claim. They believe that code switching can help one master the art of merging linguistic double selves. But how can the meshing occur if each self is restricted to "their respective forums," each limited to its own environment? If the two languages are not used together, at the same time, in the same place, no merging will materialize. Really, how could one ever really learn to speak the "black Standard English" they say black youth must learn, the language that so many black leaders have used, the very product of code meshing, if we can't combine the dialects together?

Even their ending music metaphor is at odds with code switching and actu- 23 ally supports code meshing. For pianists don't use only white keys to perform classical music nor only the black ones to create jazz. Pianists use "both the ebonies and the ivories" all the time, in all cases, in classical, the blues, jazz, and hip hop to access a range a harmonic combinations and possibilities that make genres and styles of music. As the Rickfords themselves state in their introduction, to "abandon Spoken Soul and cleave only to Standard English is like proposing that we play only the white keys of a piano" (10). Their own comparison illustrates that the white keys, representing standard English, and the black keys, representing Spoken Soul, are always already co-existent. No music is created playing only white keys and none playing only black. To attempt to compose music or even speech for that matter using only one set of keys would mean consciously and strategically ignoring and avoiding the other set of keys. A sheer impossibility! Yet this is the very arduous feat that code switching depicts. Both sets of keys must be used simultaneously to compose music. Likewise, both dialects should be used to communicate in all sites.

As a matter of fact, the Rickfords' *Spoken Soul* itself is a beautiful composition using both the black and white keys. Note these examples: (1) The title of their first chapter "What's Going On?" is adapted from black cultural discourse (Marvin Gaye's musical critique of the Vietnam War in the title song of his hit R & B album *What's Going On?* 1971); (2) In the second chapter where they discuss how various writers employ black English in literature, they write: "Charles Chesnutt and Alice Walker could have hung with [poet Stephen] Henderson" (15). Their use of "could have hung" follows the standard English grammatical formulation for the informal "hang out with," which in black English means to leisurely loiter around with a group of like-minded people. And (3) in the conclusion, they write that Spoken Soul should be embraced in order for blacks "to determine for ourselves what's good and what's bad, even what's *baaad*" (228). This use of "baaad" is a superlative expression meaning very amazing, the exact opposite of the standard English "bad." It signifies cultural triumph and strength, especially in the face of mainstream oppression (remember Melvin Van Peeble's film, *Sweet Sweetback's Baadasss Song,* 1971). These authors mix and mingle black English and standard dialect. They code mesh.

Smitherman's "Foreword" is even more exemplary in its meshing (as is most of her writing). Her two short pages are replete with meshings of black English and standard dialect, beginning with her opening statement: "It's been a long time coming, as the old song goes, but the change done come" (ix). In this sentence, like the Rickfords, she appeals to the black musical tradition to empower her rhetoric. The old song she refers to is Sam Cooke's posthumous hit single *A Change Is Gonna Come* (1964), which was a score often used to exemplify the 1960's civil rights movement. On the same page, she explains: "In writing that is rich and powerful—and funky and bold when it bees necessary—they dissect black writing and black speech . . ." (ix). Smitherman uses "bees," an emphasized version of the verb "be" from the grammar of AAE, instead of the standard verb form "is." And she later praises the Rickfords' effort to discuss language, culture, race, and American history and offers their example to others, by writing: "To get it right, you have to do what the Rickfords have done. You have to represent" (x). In AAE "represent" means to be an outstanding example. In this case, the Rickfords exemplify both careful scholarship and cultural critique, doing both while also using black English. They indeed did represent.

Supporting linguistic segregation is fundamentally at odds with the social 26 justice work the Rickfords and Smitherman seek to accomplish and even contradicts their very own writing. So why would such erudite intellectuals back code switching? I have argued elsewhere that the most unlikely people accept code switching because American racial logic exaggerates the differences between black and white people, which leads to exaggerations between black and white languages. Exaggerated perceptions of racial difference lead the very people who would never accept the idea that black and white people are bio-logically different to zealously displace that difference onto a vision of black and white language (Young, "Your Average Nigga" and *Your Average Nigga*). It makes sense then that code switching takes place in the mind, is essentially ide-ological, and that code meshing is what happens in actual practice—because in reality the languages aren't so disparate after all. The ideology of code switch-ing eclipses the wonderful code meshing that occurs in black people's speech and writing. And it's this pervasive ideology that needs to be critiqued, as the following cases typify.

While attending a session on the relationship between black English and 27 academic writing at the *Race and the Writing Center Conference* held at the University of Illinois at Chicago (1 March 2008), a youngish white male writing professor, who identified himself as gay, and a young black female elementary school teacher, both proclaimed code switching as best for getting black students to shuttle between black and standard languages. I listened as the woman spoke about her difficulties learning standard English, while attending the same school where she now teaches on the South Side of Chicago, and how her students must learn to do as she did. I enjoyed the wonderful ring of black English in her speech, and asked her boldly but privately later if she wanted her students to give up that which she possesses. "Yes," she said. "I want better for them." We had a lively discussion about what I see as a contradiction in her ideology. She is a teacher of language arts, who can't help but mesh identifiably black language patterns with her standardized language use, even in the academic setting of the conference. Yet she wants her students to somehow learn to turn off black language and use only standard, when she can't herself. After I highlighted this observation, she gave a final "tsk" and walked away.

Later I spotted the white male and asked if he thought our nation should 28 more fully implement the "Don't Ask, Don't Tell" policy for gay people, if gays should be forced to carry out their lives as if their identities were confined to a set of habits carried out in private, in the bedroom? He looked aghast (I sup-pose by my seeming political incorrectness), but I pressed the issue. "What if linguists were to codify the speech habits of gay men, identifying the stereotyp-ical lisp as a common feature, highlighting the rhetorical importance of camp, insults, and undercutting among gays," I asked. "And then what if they devel-oped approaches for gay men to avoid speaking 'gay' in public, at school, and at work and restricted them only to speaking gay at home and among other gay people?" He walked away.

Both teachers' very own linguistic performances refute the code switching 29 ideology and practice they choose to impose on their students. I offered to them what I will further explain below—how code meshing allows black people to play both the black and white keys on the piano at the very same time, creating beautiful linguistic performances that will hopefully help relieve double consciousness and facilitate the merging Du Bois actually hoped for.

PART II: CODE MESHING, NOT CODE SWITCHING

> If a student has a right to his own language, we have no right to change
> it at any point, and if we suggest helping him change it solely for the
> practical purposes of getting a job, we are advocating the cheapest form
> of hypocrisy and the most difficult sleight of hand act in the history of
> language, the development of a dual language for use at home and at
> work.
>
> —Allen N. Smith

The opposing stakes of the minority language debate have remained constant 30 since 1974 when they were most notably carved out in the well-known resolution "On the Students' Right to Their Own Language" (STROL). That resolution "affirm[s] the students' right to their own language—to the dialect that expresses their family and community identity, the idiolect that expresses their unique personal identity" ("Resolution"). Thus those who support this resolution promote students' expression of their diverse dialects, while others argue that students' futures are put at risk unless they learn the accepted forms of language performance. This debate has continued because code switching has been accepted by both sides. However, the logic of code switching contradicts the very issue that sparked this debate (the legitimate use of so called "nonstandard" dialects).

The major contradiction that code switching presents to STROL is acutely 31 summarized by Allen N. Smith. Commenting on the inconsistency he observed among those supporting STROL at an English conference he attended, he writes: "The conference opened with an amusing and thoughtful statement by Robert Hogan, Executive Secretary of NCTE, who advocated students' right to their own language. His keynote address was followed by a panel which concerned itself with 'How and When Do We Change the Student from His Own Dialect to Standard English?'" (155–56).

"The strange thing," Smith points out, "was that no one appeared to rec- 32 ognize that the panel's goal was at cross purposes with the basic thrust of the opening address" (156). As noted in the epigraph, Smith finds the very goal of code switching—developing "a dual language for use at home and at work" (156)—to be hypocritical and ideologically at odds with efforts to support linguistic rights. For him, as his title imparts, "No One Has a Right to His Own Language." This does not mean what some supporters of code switching might like it to mean—that teaching standard English poses no threat to students' dialects and identities since they have no fundamental claim to them in regard to the project of schooling, which is supposed to change everybody's language. For Smith it doesn't mean a change from home dialect to standard English, since, according to him, "there is no such standard." The very concept of standard English, he says, "is mythical" (155).

What I believe he means, and what I expressly accept as true, is that American 33 dialects of English are already building blocks of standard English. That is to say, dialects are part and parcel of standard English and standard English has strong elements in dialects. In this vein, Smith reasons that "no body of men and no computer, can survey, analyze and synthesize the speaking and writing of over 200 million delightfully varied American Citizens" (155). By way of elaboration, he adds that there is no "textbook or grammar which does in fact offer the definitive and comprehensive standard to apply in each and every individual choice of expression" (155). Still, there are those who put stock in "definitive" instruction, and who miss the point: to require folks to parse out the parts of their dialect that are standard and attempt to codify those into a form of acceptable public expression and then to parse the parts of their speech and writing that are "nonstandard" and codify those into a form of private, informal expression is both illogical and profoundly problematic.

On this front, many teachers have found, as linguist A. Suresh Canagarajah 34 reports, that students resist the request to fork their tongues when producing formal written and oral communication. In his essay "The Place of World Englishes in Composition" (2006), Canagarajah writes: "Though [code switching] is a pragmatic resolution that is sensitive to the competing claims in this debate . . . I have experienced certain difficulties in implementing this approach. I have found that minority students are reluctant to hold back their Englishes even for temporary reasons" (597). Unlike so many others, he abandoned code switching in his literacy instruction and now advocates code meshing.

Unlike code switching, code meshing does not require students to "hold back 35 their Englishes" but permits them to bring them more forcefully and strategically forward. The ideology behind code meshing holds that peoples' so-called "nonstandard" dialects are already fully compatible with standard English. Code meshing secures their right to represent that meshing in all forms and venues where they communicate. This understanding becomes all the more important if we consider that many folks may not have as big of a choice as we believe they have in choosing the ways they speak and write.

To clarify, if from a linguistic perspective, we accept that black and white 36
Englishes are different dialects, even if complementary and compatible, then
the familiar linguistic concept of accent helps explain why substituting one version of English for another may be impossible and why code meshing is inevitable. Some linguists theorize that around five or six years old, efforts to learn
a new language become more difficult, although certainly attainable. Still the
first, native, or home language will always impact, that is, be present and heard
within, the target language. This is how someone's, say, African, Spanish, Polish,
or Russian accent and heritage are identified when they are speaking English.
Their native language is breaking through the target language and becomes an
inextricable feature of their communication. Although this breakthrough is
undeniable in speech, some believe it also occurs just as frequently in writing
(Coleman). So trying to separate the two languages for some is virtually impossible, and makes requirements to do so appear tyrannical, oppressive. Wouldn't
it be better to promote integrating them?

There's enough cultural, educational, and linguistic evidence to challenge and 37
hopefully end code switching. And, since teachers point to the world outside
of school as the biggest obstacle to accepting language integration, it's important to point out how code switching is out of sync with the social, racial, and
political progress our nation has achieved and is pursuing. Without a doubt, the
extraordinary 2008 presidential campaign points up just how retrograde code
switching is.

In that election, for the first time in history, the final candidates for the 38
Democratic presidential nomination were a white woman, Senator Hillary
Clinton, and a black man, Senator Barack Obama. The contest between the two
was itself positive proof that our nation may finally really be ready to value and
respect all of its citizens, regardless of how different they may be from the white,
male, heterosexual, middle-class façade often portrayed as the guardian image
of American democracy. Even Senator John McCain, the Republican nominee
signified hope in this regard—after all, at 72, many considered him a senior citizen. His age, Clinton's gender, and Obama's race reflect a triumph *of* Affirmative
Action, or, as some might say (too swiftly I think), a triumph *over* the need for
Affirmative Action. Either way, in aggregate, the candidates represent indisputable progress towards respect for diversity.

Yet despite this obvious progress neither Clinton nor Obama believe that 39
their candidacies stand as the iconic image of racial and gender equity. In his
speech on race (March 2008), Obama flat-out contradicts colorblind ideologies
that suggest race is no longer a central American concern. "Race is an issue that
I believe this nation cannot afford to ignore right now," he says. In an effort to
convince the American people that race is important in everyday concerns not
just when someone is called a spic, a chink, a nigger, or hangs a noose or sports a
Swastika, he explains that "the complexities of race in this country" have "never

really [been] worked through—a part of our union that we have yet to perfect. And if we walk away now, if we simply retreat into our respective corners, we will never be able to come together and solve challenges like health care, or education."

Similarly, in her speech of concession to Obama (June 2008), Clinton 40 addresses those she calls the "Eighteen million of you, from all walks of life . . . women and men, young and old, Latino and Asian, African-American and Caucasian . . . rich, poor, and middle-class, gay and straight." She says to them

> Senator Obama and I achieved milestones essential to our progress as a nation. . . . [However] on a personal note, when I was asked what it means to be a woman running for president, I always gave the same answer, that I was proud to be running as a woman . . . [but] like millions of women, I know there are still barriers and biases out there, often unconscious, and I want to build an America that respects and embraces the potential of every last one of us.

In the following statement, Senator Clinton asks the American people in general terms the same thing I ask of literacy teachers in specific educational terms: "Let us resolve and work toward achieving very simple propositions: There are no acceptable limits, and there are no acceptable prejudices in the 21st century in our country."

Code switching does not—neither as ideology nor pedagogy—match nor 41 advance the achievements in diversity that are reflected in the presidential campaign. Nor does it aid us in achieving the propositions Clinton promotes or the coming together that Obama says is required in order to solve educational challenges that racism produces. Instead it reinforces notions of "acceptable limits" and "acceptable prejudices" by telling people of dialect difference that there is an acceptable way to communicate in this nation, and their way isn't it—at least not in official, graded school assignments, in public, or at work. It gives teachers permission to fail students who display linguistic difference in their speech and writing. It gives employers permission to place limitations on workers' promotional opportunities or permits them not to hire diverse speakers—certainly not for important positions. And it sanctions accent discrimination and pronunciation prejudice.

Code meshing, on the other hand, while also acknowledging standard prin- 42 ciples for communication, encourages speakers and writers to fuse that standard with native speech habits, to color their writing with what they bring from home. It has the potential to enlarge our national vocabulary, multiply the range of available rhetorical styles, expand our ability to understand linguistic difference and make us in the end multidialectical, as opposed to monodialectical.

161

"Ah," some might say, "but aren't Obama and Clinton examples of what our students can be if they learn standard English? And don't their examples offer enough proof to support teaching it?" Indeed, both Clinton and Obama are outstanding role models for young and old people. They've done something truly "remarkable," as Clinton expressed in her concession speech; they've made it now "unremarkable" for a black person or a woman to successfully run for the highest office of the Free World. Yet, perceptions of their language use illustrate the very trouble code switching presents to our students—and our nation. 43

For instance, Obama was often parodied in mainstream media for being too "professorial" in his rhetorical delivery and too "polysyllabic" in his usage. His linguistic performance might be compared to what Jay Semel, associate vice president for research at the University of Iowa, observes during a radio segment on black middle-class performance. Semel says he was intrigued as a Jewish college student by the verbal performance of his black professors, many of whom he knew came from urban cities, but spoke impeccable English—with a British clip! To boot, he says, they even regularly dressed to the nines—in full suits—when teaching. They stood in stark contrast to the white professors who were no match to them in dress and speech and who didn't care or need to be. The conclusions Semel draws regarding his professors might also apply to Obama—that they hyper-performed standard language mastery as a way to (over) compensate for the stigma of their race (*Know the Score*). 44

On the surface, code switching may seem like a good thing for Obama. Not using too much AAE in the campaign, code switching advocates would say, helped him win the presidency. But the fact that he had to code switch is the problem; the fact that AAE is still subject to racism is the issue to correct, not the people who speak it. Furthermore, code switching also restricts how expressive he could be. Perhaps his earlier, stilted, professorial style was produced by being forced in the face of racial perceptions to keep the most expressive parts of his language out of the public's ear. Perhaps what linguist Elaine Richardson calls "stereotype threat" set it and his language became neither expressive standard nor expressive AAE but a stilted middle brow discourse (2004). He faces the same problem other African Americans face who are forced to extract AAE from their speech: If they do give up AAE, they're damned for being affected, over-formal, artificial, even by those who require the extraction. But if they do use AAE, they're damned for being too black, too radical, too militant, profiled as ignorant. Being damned in both directions stems from not being able to blend the two together. 45

Consider, for example, that Michelle Obama's use of AAE has had an endearing effect on African Americans but an alienating effect on whites when she referred to Obama as her "babies' daddy" and her use of ain't ("Ain't no black people in Iowa") after he won the first primary caucus. Her language use adds fuel to the political fire regarding her patriotism, spurred by her use of a black 46 rhetorical sentiment after Obama's initial primary victories: "This is the first time I'm proud of my country." While Obama may have engaged code switching, the problem is the racial disparity. Had he employed more AAE, he would not have been perceived in the same way as, say, President George W. Bush, who, although often called stupid, has not suffered major consequences for his abuse of standard English and rhetoric. Instead, if Obama spoke more black English in public, it would likely instigate already circulating insinuations that he's anti-American and unpatriotic. And no doubt Obama's speech performance forms part of the basis for the trite speculations about whether he is "too black or not black enough."

As a woman, Clinton has not been spared this linguistic catch-22. Some have 47 said that the emotions she displayed in her concession speech should have been demonstrated much earlier, that it might have softened her, made her more feminine, and may have helped her clinch the nomination. She faces the "too feminine/ not feminine enough" predicament. It was said that she tried too hard to perform a masculine rhetorical style, a style no doubt many believed she had to take on to be viable in a country that is still unaccustomed to women's ways of knowing and speaking. So while Obama is criticized for a rhetorical style that is too professional, too stiff and unemotional, Clinton is criticized for not being emotional enough. Yes, both Clinton and Obama represent progress, but criticisms of their rhetorical styles also represent the problem: the progress we have yet to make.[4]

Code switching produces such racial and gender prejudice because it fosters 48 linguistic confusion: What's the right way to speak/write? Code switching suggests that women speak an incompatibly different language from blacks, who are believed to utter a completely different speech from white men — and the biggest lie of all is that there is one, set, specific, appropriate, formal way to communicate in America. Code switching, in short, fortifies language barriers. Those who appeal to code switching as a way to negotiate racism and sexism actually end up supporting a linguistic basis for facilitating them. If we're to capitalize on the progress exemplified in the 2008 presidential election, then we should abandon code switching. And for this to happen requires a movement.

Indeed, concerned linguists and educational theorists have pursued efforts to 49 make something like code meshing a national policy and an established pedagogy for some thirty years. Note the following excerpt from Geneva Smitherman's *Talkin' and Testifyin'*:

> An ultimate goal would be for teachers to struggle for a national public policy on language which would reassert the legitimacy of languages other than English, and American dialects other than standard. If these goals seem farfetched, teachers have only to reflect on the tremendous power potential of their teacher unions and professional educational organizations — such structures could form the massive political units needed to extend the concept of linguistic-cultural diversity and legitimacy beyond the classroom. (240-1)

Smitherman recognized the need for "a national public policy" on language integration in 1977. The same is needed now. The fact that no such policy currently exists is not because there are no examples of code meshing or because it's unintelligible, but because it stems from and supports dominant language ideology otherwise known as standard language ideology.

Standard language ideology is, according to linguist Rosina Lippi-Green, 50 "a bias toward an abstracted, idealized, homogenous spoken language which is imposed and maintained by the dominant bloc institutions and which names as its model the written language, but which is drawn primarily from the spoken language of the upper middle class" (64). In other words, commercial, business, and educational institutions perpetuate and perpetrate the belief that there is a single dominant race (read as white), dominant culture (read as white middle/upper class), and that the way these speakers communicate forms the bases for standard modes of public expression.

The really big rub in standard language ideology is this: It doesn't mean that 51 white middle and upper class people actually speak standard English! (Think President George W. Bush.) But dominant language ideology persuades us to imagine they do. It demands that we participate in a fantasy that white middle class folks are entitled speakers of public English. And we're asked to ignore those who regularly and glaringly muck up the standard grammar, since the consequences for their illiteracy are far less severe than for those outside of the supposed dominant culture.

Smitherman shares a revealing example of dominant language ideology: 52

> I was trying to solicit support for a study of attitudes of potential employers toward black speech. This white research man . . . contended that such a study would only prove the obvious since everybody knew that you had to speak the King's English to get ahead in America. With my research proposal thus dismissed, I started to leave. As I did so, the research division head turned to his assistant and said, "Listen, can you stay a few minutes? You and me have some work to do." Now, me bein me, I had to correct my man's, "bad grammar," I said, "Hey, watch yo' dialect—it's you and I have some work to do." He turned fifty shades o' red, and I split. Naturally, that siggin of mine had shonuff blowed the possibility of me gitten any grant money! (*Talkin'* 199).

The dominant language ideology behind code switching contends that minoritized dialect speakers must learn the accepted standard because it's necessary for them to communicate in the public and at work. Yet Smitherman's encounter shows that even whites, supposedly the majority of non-dialect speakers, don't communicate in the accepted standard—and acquire and maintain good jobs without doing so. To underscore this point, the matter of illiteracy and middle-class white folks has come into the public, confirming what scholars have long observed—that Americans tend to believe that whites speak and write better than others when they really don't. Consequently, whites are often led to believe their speech is standard when really it's not.

This state of affairs is being exposed because of its negative consequences for 53 literacy practices in the workplace. The writing ineptitude of most corporate workers has long been notorious and recently made the front page of the *New York Times.* According to one report "millions of employees must write more frequently on the job than previously. And many are making a hash of it." The report concludes "that a third of employees in the nation's blue-chip companies wrote poorly and that businesses were spending as much as $3.1 billion annually on remedial training" (Dillon 1). The tendency to exaggerate the writing competence of middle-class (or even upper-class) white people leads to the prevailing fallacy that they enjoy a higher level of literacy.[5]

Even university presidents and highly regarded English professors don't 54 always speak and write in the dominant standard, even when they believe they are doing so. Former Duke English Department Chair and Dean of the College of Liberal Arts and Sciences at the University of Illinois at Chicago, Stanley Fish, publicly criticized the grammar of former Harvard President Lawrence Summers in a 2002 article in the *Chronicle of Higher Education.* Summers, who gained some notoriety for challenging the accessible nature of then Harvard professor and public intellectual Cornel West's scholarship, offered an apology when the media publicized the encounter: "I regret any faculty member leaving a conversation feeling they are not respected" (qtd. in van Der Werf A30). It's this apology Fish critiques, writing: "In a short, 13-word sentence, the chief academic officer of the highest ranked university in the country, and therefore in the entire world, has committed three grammatical crimes, failure to mark the possessive case, failure to specify the temporal and causal relationships between the conversations he has and the effects he regrets, and failure to observe noun-pronoun agreement" (Fish).

> *Even university presidents and highly regarded English professors don't always speak and write in the dominant standard, even when they believe they are doing so.*

The three mistakes Fish finds in Summers' one sentence are the same kinds 55 of mistakes that English teachers believe African American students make when they use AAE. But what's really interesting is that Fish's correction of Summers' sentence is also incorrect, according to a grammar evaluation by Professor Kyoko Inoue, a Japanese American linguist from Fish's same university. According to Inoue, Summers' usage is acceptable, if not correct, since "what the writer/speaker says (means) often controls the form of the sentence" (Unpublished).

Although in these examples, dominant language ideology is biting (albeit 56 mildly) its perpetrators in the butt for once, the point of including them is to show the racial disparity that's propagated by code switching. The ideology of code switching insists a minority student will never become an Ivy League English Department chair or president of Harvard University if she doesn't perfect their mastery of standard English. At the same time the ideology instructs that white men will gain such positions, even with a questionable handle on standard grammar and rhetoric. And even though this is the current state of our country, it doesn't mean we should accept it. We should combat it not only so people can become prominent political figures, but so they can just get a good job.

At the same *Race and the Writing Center Conference* where I encountered the 57 gay man and the dialect speaking woman who supported code switching, there was a white, middle-aged, female, college professor who was distraught after my talk on code meshing. She reported that she and her colleagues were interviewing candidates to teach freshman writing. The committee was enamored with a black woman, but decided not to hire her because she conjugated one subject with the wrong verb ("he don't"). The committee doubted her ability to correct her would-be students' grammar if she couldn't follow standard conjugation in her own speech during the interview. The female professor recounting the episode admitted that her committee may have been wrong, but she then asked, "What else can I do except teach my students to avoid such mistakes?"

"You should have resisted the language prejudice (I wanted to say racism) of 58 the committee with tooth and nail!" I said. I then asked: "Have you or any of your colleagues mismatched a subject with a verb or made a pronoun/antecedent disagreement?" She said, "Yes, I'm sure we have," then made the obvious point that she's not black. She was, of course, proving my point that race is the biggest culprit, not the woman's grammar. Still, I followed up by asking if she'd ever read Joseph Williams' essay "The Phenomenology of Error" where he shows how our ideological frameworks diminish even the most obvious errors of some writers (and I added speakers too) and makes us hyper-aware of some others' mistakes based on how we perceive them socially. When grammar and usage are viewed too narrowly through the lens of social performance our understanding of "error" is based "less on a handbook definition," Williams writes, "than on the reader's [or listener's] response, because it is that response [most often negatively constituted] that defines the seriousness of the error and its expected amendment" (164).

Williams' essay explains what happened to the black woman, whose one ver- 59 bal (natural) mishap cost the opportunity to obtain a good job. It wasn't so much the conjugation error that caused the negative response; it was the stigma of her race reeling back into play when her language usage failed to assuage that stigma for the committee. Her failure was less about linguistic aptitude and more about her racial performance. She was not hyper-conscious enough about her verbs to over-compensate for her race. Had the white female committee member resisted the actions of the other committee members, she would have sounded a wake-up call, made an effort in the struggle to show how dominant language ideology intensifies and magnifies the error of blacks but reduces or ignores those of the dominant group. So teaching code switching to avoid errors in standard grammar won't work because all writers and speakers make errors.

As a brief concession to a discussion of teaching standard English grammar, 60 I return to the Fish/Summers example. After Summers uttered his "errors," Fish mandated that writing instructors at his university, then the University of Illinois at Chicago, where I was still a graduate student, teach more grammar. In response Inoue writes: "I believe that grammar training for academic writing is necessary, but it is not sufficient. . . . What is most important in writing is selecting the linguistic expressions that will convey exactly what the writer intends to say" ("Linguist's Perspective").

I agree with Inoue that "grammar" if it is to be taught should be done "in con- 61 junction with semantics and rhetoric (what linguists calls pragmatics), showing how and in what ways grammatical structures convey meanings and influence the rhetorical force of written work" ("Linguist's Perspective" 2). This should not be misunderstood as a case for teaching the grammar of standard English. To the contrary, if anything, it's an appeal to literacy educators to teach how the semantics and rhetoric of AAE are compatible/combinable with features of standard English. This way the rhetorical force of students' written work and oral fluency will come from a combination of the two—not from translating one from the other, but from allowing them both to mingle together with vim and vigor.

It's clear that my case has been to eliminate code switching as both an ideolog- 62 ical and pedagogical feature within literacy instruction and to replace it with code meshing. Code switching spells failure for most students—and worse, it's covered in the residue of racism. Code meshing is a better resolution to the minority language debate because it allows minoritized people to become more effective communicators by doing what we all do best, what comes naturally: blending, merging, meshing dialects. Code meshing is so very important to our work with minoritized peoples, to those who can not or will not extract their dialects from their use of standard English, to folks who speak and write with accents, really, to the majority of American citizens and English speakers across the globe.

POST SCRIPT: RETURN TO OBAMA

I want to end with a speculation—a little further food for thought. As we think 63 about Obama's language practice during his campaign and accept for the sake of argument that he played the code switching game (I say for the sake of argument, because some believe that he is heard differently by whites and blacks), then what if, just what if, he played the game to end the game? Not so only he could have the luxury to use AAE more freely after the election, both in informal settings, like Ben Chili's referenced up top, and in formal settings, as he did in one interview with Diane Sawyer, where he says he "hipped" his personal aide Reggie Love to Aretha Franklin and John Coltrane, but so nobody else, no other AAE speakers would have to put on a show just to prove their worth (Sawyer). What if he played the game not to endorse the game but to show that the stigma against AAE in formal settings and academic writing is stupid? What if he played the game to end the game so that he could be free to show his black cultural and linguistic heritage and not have to worry about containing his blackness because it's, as Harris-Lacewell describes, "squishing out of the edges?" If this were so, and I believe it is, then when teachers are asked to teach code switching and when students are urged to code switch, both groups should respond as Obama did to the waitress when she asked if he wanted his change; they too could say: "Nah, we straight."

Notes

1. For an extended discussion of Du Bois, double-consciousness and racial schizophrenia in the context of African American English, see Chapter 6, "To Be A Problem," in my *Your Average Nigga: Performing Race, Literacy, and Masculinity.* For more on double-consciousness as a synonym for schizophrenia, see the insightful analyses of Bruce, Jr., Early, and Wells.

2. Thomas explains that in *Plessey v. Ferguson* the only justice to oppose the decision based his dissent in part on what he considered to be a legal irony: that although Chinese immigrants were ineligible for U.S. citizenship, they were not subject to separate but equal laws, while black citizens were segregated.

3. It should be noted that Wheeler and Swords' discussion of language has to do with pitting one language variety against another. When describing how they settled on using the unraced terms "informal English versus formal English," they report they considered *"nonstandard versus standard"*; *"community English versus Standard English; Everyday English versus Standard"* (emphasis in original, 19–20).

4. For an insightful critique of the way standard English and academic discourse perpetuate patriarchal relations, particularly the domination of women, see Bleich.

5. This discussion of standard language ideology is adapted from Chapter 5, "Casualties of Literacy," in my *Your Average Nigga: Performing Race, Literacy, and Masculinity*, 2007.

Works Cited

Auer, Peter. *Code-Switching in Conversation: Language, Interaction and Identity.* New York: Routledge, 1988.

Bleich, David. "Genders of Writing." *JAC* 9 (1989): 10–25.

Bruce, Dickson D., Jr. "W. E. B. Du Bois and the Dilemma of Race." *American Literary History* 7 (1995): 334–343.

Canagarajah, A. Suresh. "The Place of World Englishes in Composition: Pluralization Continued." *College Composition and Communication* 57 (2006): 586–619.

Clinton, Hillary. "HillaryClintonEndorsesBarackObama.CNN.com. 8 June 2008. 11 Jan 2010. <http://wwwnytimes.com/2008/06/07us/politics/07text-clinton.html>. Transcript.

Coleman, Charles F. "Our Students Write With Accents—Oral Paradigms for ESD Students." *College Composition and Communication* 48 (Dec. 1997): 486–500.

Dillon, Sam. "What Corporate America Can't Build: A Sentence." *New York Times* 7 December 2004: 1.

Du Bois, W. E. B. *The Souls of Black Folk.* New York: Dover Thrift Edition, 1994.

Early, Gerald. *Lure and Loathing: Essays on Race, Identity, and the Ambivalence of Assimilation.* New York: Penguin, 1993.

Fish, Stanley. "Say It Ain't So." *Chronicle of Higher Education* 21 June 2002. 11 Jan 2010 <http://chronicle.com/article/Say-It-Ain-tSo/46137>.

Graff, Gerald. *Clueless in Academe: How Schooling Obscures the Life of the Mind.* New Haven: Yale UP, 2003.

Henderson, Nia-Malika. "Blacks, Whites Hear Obama Differently." Politico. 3 Mar 2009.11 Jan 2010. <http://www.cbsnews.com/stories/2009/03/03/politics/politico/main4840223.shtml?source=RSSattr=HOME_4840223>.

Hoover, Mary Rhodes. "Community Attitudes Toward Black English." *Language in Society* 7(1978): 65–87.

Inoue, Kyoko. Unpublished Grammar Note. University of Illinois at Chicago. October, 2002.

———. "A Linguist's Perspective on Teaching Grammar." Unpublished paper. University of Illinois at Chicago. October 2002.

Know the Score. KSUI-FM 91.7, University of Iowa Radio. Clear Lake/Mason City, Iowa. 2 Nov. 2007.

Lippi-Green, Rosina. *English with an Accent: Language, Ideology and Discrimination in the United States.* London: Routledge, 1997.

McWhorter, John. *Losing the Race: Self-Sabotage in Black America.* New York: Free, 2001.

My.Barack.Obama.com. Organizing for America. 11 Jan 2010. <http://my.barackobama.com/page/content/hisownwords>

Obama, Barack. "A More Perfect Union." Speech. Philadelphia, PA. March 18, 2008.

Perry, Theresa, and Lisa Delpit, eds. *The Real Ebonics Debate: Power, Language, and the Education of African-American Children.* Boston: Beacon, 1998.

Prendergast, Catherine. *Literacy and Racial Justice: The Politics of Learning After Brown v. Board of Education.* Carbondale: Southern Illinois UP, 2003.

———. "Race: The Absent Presence in Composition Studies." *College Composition and Communication* 50 (1998): 36–53.

"Resolution on the Students' Right to Their Own Language." NCTE Position Statement, 1974. 12 January 2010. <http://www.ncte.org/positions/statements/righttoownlanguage>.

Richardson, Elaine B. "Coming from the Heart: African American Students, Literacy Stories, and Rhetorical Education." *African American Rhetoric(s): Interdisciplinary Perspectives.* Ed. Richardson, E. B. and R. L. Jackson II. Carbondale: Southern Illinois UP, 2004. 155–69.

Rickford, John Russell, and Russell John Rickford. *Spoken Soul: The Story of Black English.* New York: Wiley, 2000.

Sawyer, Diane. "Person of the Week: Reggie Love." World News with Diane Sawyer. ABCNews.com. 23 Jan 2009. 12 Jan 2010. <http://media.abcnews.com/WN/PersonOfWeek/Story?id=6717051&page=2>.

Smith, Allen N. "No One Has a Right to His Own Language." *College Composition and Communication* 27 (1976): 155–59.

Smitherman, Geneva. Foreword. *Spoken Soul: The Story of Black English.* Ed. John Russell Rickford and Russell John Rickford. New York: Wiley, 2000. ix–x.

———. *Talkin' and Testifyin': The Language of Black America.* Detroit: Wayne State UP, 1977.

Thomas, Brook. *Plessy v. Ferguson: A Brief History With Documents.* St. Martins, 1996.

Van Der Werf, Martin. "Lawrence Summers and His Tough Questions." *Chronicle of Higher Education* April 26, 2002: A29–A32.

Vaquera-Vásquez, Santiago. "Meshed America: Confessions of a Mercacirce." *Code Meshing As World English: Policy, Pedagogy, Performance.* Eds. Vershawn Ashanti Young and Aja Y. Martinez. Urbana: National Council of Teachers of English, forthcoming.

Wells, Susan. "Discursive Mobility and Double Consciousness in S. Weir Mitchell and W. E. B. Du Bois." *Philosophy and Rhetoric* 35 (2002): 120–137.

Wheeler, Rebecca S., and Rachel Swords. *Code-Switching: Teaching Standard English in Urban Classrooms.* Urbana: National Council of Teachers of English, 2006.

Williams, Joseph M. "The Phenomenology of Error." *Composition in Four Keys: Inquiring into the Field.* Ed. M. Wiley, B. Gleason, and L. Wetherbee Phelps. London: Mayfield, 1996.

Young, Vershawn Ashanti. "Your Average Nigga." *College Composition and Communication* 55 (2004): 693–715.

———. *Your Average Nigga: Performing Race, Literacy, and Masculinity.* Detroit: Wayne State UP, 2007.

- -

Questions for Discussion and Journaling

1. Explain the difference between code switching and code meshing that Young describes.

2. Explain Du Bois's idea of double consciousness. How does Young extend this idea to what he calls "linguistic double consciousness"?

3. Young describes prevailing definitions of the translation model of code switching as "language conversion" (para. 4). What does he mean by this understanding, and why is he against it?

4. Young summarizes Catherine Prendergast's argument that literacy teachers are "accomplices, often unwittingly, in the continuation of racial inequality" (para. 14), and he argues that "double consciousness is continually manufactured in writing classrooms . . . [and] commonly reproduced at all levels of literacy instruction" (para. 16). Explain what you think they mean.

5. Young argues that asking black students to use a different language at school than they do at home is a form of racial segregation. Explain this argument.

6. Earlier, we asked you to mark places where Young's phrasing and tone surprised you during your reading. List some of these. Why did he use these? How do they help support and illustrate the argument he is making?

7. Young conveys Jay Semel's story about his black professors at the University of Iowa who, although they came from urban backgrounds, spoke impeccable formal English and dressed in suits. Semel argues that they "hyper-performed standard language to (over) compensate for the stigma of their race" (para. 44).

Explain what you think this means, and then see if you can think of times when you or someone else engaged in this kind of overcompensation, and why.

8. Young points out that George W. Bush did not suffer any major political consequences for his "abuse of standard English and rhetoric," but that if Barack Obama had spoken "more black English in public," he would have been accused even more vehemently of being "anti-American and unpatriotic" (para. 46). Given what you've thought about so far in relation to language and identity, and the ways that different people are judged for using language, do you agree? If so, what do you think accounts for this different judgment of Bush's and Obama's uses of language?

9. What is "standard language ideology," according to Young? How does this concept help explain the different reactions to Bush and Obama, if it does?

Applying and Exploring Ideas

1. Young argues that in reality, "black and white languages . . . aren't so disparate" (para. 26). He gives examples from the Rickford book that he criticizes in order to partially demonstrate this point. Today as you engage in your daily activities (talking with friends, listening to music, checking out at the store, working your job), listen to people's spoken language and write down every example you hear that merges "black and white languages." Once you have compiled this list, consider whether you agree with Young's claim.

2. Young cites Smith, who argues that there really is no such thing as one "standard" English. What does this mean? As you were making your list of phrases and examples for question 1 above that merge "black and white language," did you at any point notice the wide variety of dialects and grammatical variations, beyond just "black" and "white"? If so, what were some of the examples you heard? If not, try the exercise again and listen for these variations. Once you've done this, write a short argument for or against this claim: There is no single, identifiable, standard English in spoken practice.

3. Young is essentially arguing what other authors in this chapter, and in the next chapter, also argue: that language use is inextricably bound up with identity. Explore your ideas about this by first thinking about the examples you've read so far in this book, as well as examples in your own life and in those of your friends. Then write a 1- to 2-page reflection on your ideas about how language and identity are related, drawing on the examples you read and thought about.

4. Google the 1974 statement "Students' Right to Their Own Language" that Young references and read it. What is your reaction to this statement? What was happening in 1974 that might have motivated teachers to write this statement? Does this statement help you better understand Young's claims?

- -

META MOMENT Does Young help you think differently about how you judge people based on their language use? How?

- -

From Outside, In

BARBARA MELLIX

Barbara Mellix is an African American woman born and raised in South Carolina who went on to earn a B.A. in English and M.F.A. in creative writing from the University of Pittsburgh. She has since taught, worked as an assistant dean, and served as director of the advising center there.

In this essay, Mellix explores her experiences and conflicts with black English and standard English. We have included her essay here because she illustrates many of the conflicts and experiences that led Young, in the previous essay (p. 148), to argue against requiring minority speakers to engage in "code switching." If you haven't read Young, we recommend that you do so before reading Mellix. Mellix's essay illustrates the many ways that language is bound up with identity, and how literacy practices are always informed by prior experiences. Who she is as a writer, and how she feels about writing and the language she uses when she writes, are all colored by her experiences in a particular place and time — experiences that include home, school, extended family, geographical location, race, class, and more.

Getting Ready to Read

Before you read, do at least one of the following activities:

- Think about the ways you speak and write in different situations.
- Consider the ways that your family and schooling have shaped how you speak, and what kind of speech is considered "correct" in school and professional settings.

Mellix, Barbara. "From Outside, In." *The Georgia Review*, vol. 41, no.2, Summer 1987, pp. 258–67.

As you read, consider the following questions:

- How do Mellix's experiences relate to Young's claims in the previous article?
- Which part of Mellix's experiences can you identify with, and which seem difficult to identify with?

TWO YEARS AGO, when I started writing this paper, trying to bring order 1 out of chaos, my ten-year-old daughter was suffering from an acute attack of boredom. She drifted in and out of the room complaining that she had nothing to do, no one to "be with" because none of her friends were at home. Patiently I explained that I was working on something special and needed peace and quiet, and I suggested that she paint, read, or work with her computer. None of these interested her. Finally, she pulled up a chair to my desk and watched me, now and then heaving long, loud sighs. After two or three minutes (nine or ten sighs), I lost my patience. "Looka here, Allie," I said, "you too old for this kinda carryin' on. I done told you this is important. You wronger than dirt to be in here haggin' me like this and you know it. Now git on outta here and leave me off before I put my foot all the way down."

I was at home, alone with my family, and my daughter understood that this 2 way of speaking was appropriate in that context. She knew, as a matter of fact, that it was almost inevitable; when I get angry at home, I speak some of my finest, most cherished black English. Had I been speaking to my daughter in this manner in certain other environments, she would have been shocked and probably worried that I had taken leave of my sense of propriety.

Like my children, I grew up speaking what I considered two distinctly dif- 3 ferent languages—black English and standard English (or as I thought of them then, the ordinary everyday speech of "country" coloreds and "proper" English)—and in the process of acquiring these languages, I developed an understanding of when, where, and how to use them. But unlike my children, I grew up in a world that was primarily black. My friends, neighbors, minister, teachers—almost everybody I associated with every day—were black. And we spoke to one another in our own special language: *That sho is a pretty dress you got on. If she don't soon leave me off I'm gon tell her head a mess. I was so mad I could'a pissed a blue nail. He all the time trying to low-rate somebody. Ain't that just about the nastiest thing you ever set ears on?*

Then there were the "others," the "proper" blacks, transplanted relatives and 4 one-time friends who came home from the city for weddings, funerals, and vacations. And the whites. To these we spoke standard English. "Ain't?" my mother would yell at me when I used the term in the presence of "others." "You *know* better than that." And I would hang my head in shame and say the "proper" word.

I remember one summer sitting in my grandmother's house in Greeleyville, 5
South Carolina, when it was full of the chatter of city relatives who were home
on vacation. My parents sat quietly, only now and then volunteering a comment
or answering a question. My mother's face took on a strained expression when
she spoke. I could see that she was being careful to say just the right words in just
the right way. Her voice sounded thick, muffled. And when she finished speaking, she would lapse into silence, her proper smile on her face. My father was
more articulate, more aggressive. He spoke quickly, his words sharp and clear.
But he held his proud head higher, a signal that he, too, was uncomfortable. My
sisters and brothers and I stared at our aunts, uncles, and cousins, speaking only
when prompted. Even then, we hesitated, formed our sentences in our minds,
then spoke softly, shyly.

My parents looked small and anxious during those occasions, and I waited 6
impatiently for leave-taking when we would mock our relatives the moment
we were out of their hearing. "Reeely," we would say to one another, flexing
our wrists and rolling our eyes, "how dooo you stan' this heat? Chile, it just too
h*yooo*-mid for words." Our relatives had made us feel "country," and this was our
way of regaining pride in ourselves while getting a little revenge in the bargain.
The words bubbled in our throats and rolled across our tongues, a balming.

As a child I felt this same doubleness in uptown Greeleyville where the whites 7
lived. "Ain't that a pretty dress you're wearing!" Toby, the town policeman, said
to me one day when I was fifteen. "Thank you very much," I replied, my voice
barely audible in my own ears. The words felt wrong in my mouth, rigid, foreign. It was not that I had never spoken that phrase before—it was common
in black English, too—but I was extremely conscious that this was an occasion
for proper English. I had taken out my English and put it on as I did my church
clothes, and I felt as if I were wearing my Sunday best in the middle of the week.
It did not matter that Toby had not spoken grammatically correct English. He
was white and could speak as he wished. I had something to prove. Toby did not.

Speaking standard English to whites was our way of demonstrating that we 8
knew their language and could use it. Speaking it to standard-English-speaking
blacks was our way of showing them that we, as well as they, could "put on
airs." But when we spoke standard English, we
acknowledged (to ourselves and to others—but
primarily to ourselves) that our customary way
of speaking was inferior. We felt foolish, embarrassed, somehow diminished because we were
ashamed to be our real selves. We were reserved,
shy in the presence of those who owned and/or
spoke *the* language.

> When we spoke standard
> English we acknowledged . . .
> that our customary way of
> speaking was inferior. We
> felt . . . diminished because
> we were ashamed to be our
> real selves.

My parents never set aside time to drill us in 9
standard English. Their forms of instruction were

less formal. When my father was feeling particularly expansive, he would regale us with tales of his exploits in the outside world. In almost flawless English, complete with dialogue and flavored with gestures and embellishment, he told us about his attempt to get a haircut at a white barbershop; his refusal to acknowledge one of the town merchants until the man addressed him as "Mister"; the time he refused to step off the sidewalk uptown to let some whites pass; his airplane trip to New York City (to visit a sick relative) during which the stewardesses and porters—recognizing that he was a "gentleman"—addressed him as "Sir." I did not realize then—nor, I think, did my father—that he was teaching us, among other things, standard English and the relationship between language and power.

My mother's approach was different. Often, when one of us said, "I'm gon 10 wash off my feet," she would say, "And what will you walk on if you wash them off?" Everyone would laugh at the victim of my mother's "proper" mood. But it was different when one of us children was in a proper mood. "You think you are so superior," I said to my oldest sister one day when we were arguing and she was winning. "Superior!" my sister mocked. "You mean I'm acting 'biggidy'?" My sisters and brothers sniggered, then joined in teasing me. Finally, my mother said, "Leave your sister alone. There's nothing wrong with using proper English." There was a half-smile on her face. I had gotten "uppity," had "put on airs" for no good reason. I was at home, alone with the family, and I hadn't been prompted by one of my mother's proper moods. But there was also a proud light in my mother's eyes; her children were learning English very well.

Not until years later, as a college student, did I begin to understand our 11 ambivalence toward English, our scorn of it, our need to master it, to own and be owned by it—an ambivalence that extended to the public school classroom. In our school, where there were no whites, my teacher taught standard English but used black English to do it. When my grammar-school teachers wanted us to write, for example, they usually said something like, "I want y'all to write five sentences that make a statement. Anybody git done before the rest can color." It was probably almost those exact words that led me to write these sentences in 1953 when I was in the second grade:

The white clouds are pretty.
There are only 15 people in our room.
We will go to gym.
We have a new poster.
We may go out doors.

Second grade came after "Little First" and "Big First," so by then I knew the implied rules that accompanied all writing assignments. Writing was an occasion for proper English. I was not to write in the way we spoke to one another: The white clouds pretty; There ain't but fifteen people in our room; We going to gym; We got a new poster; We can go out in the yard. Rather I was to use the language of "other": clouds *are,* there *are,* we *will,* we *have,* we *may.*

My sentences were short, rigid, perfunctory, like the letters my mother wrote   12
to relatives:

> Dear Papa,
>   How are you? How is Mattie? Fine I hope. We are fine. We will come
> to see you Sunday. Cousin Ned will give us a ride.
>   Love,
>   Daughter

The language was not ours. It was something from outside us, something we used for special occasions.

But my coloring on the other side of that second-grade paper is different. I   13
drew three hearts and a sun. The sun has a smiling face that radiates and envelops everything it touches. And although the sun and the world are enclosed in a circle, the colors I used — red, blue, green, purple, orange, yellow, black — indicate that I was less restricted with drawing and coloring than I was with writing standard English. My valentines were not just red. My sun was not just a yellow ball in the sky.

By the time I reached the twelfth grade, speaking and writing standard   14
English had taken on new importance. Each year, about half of the newly gradu-ated seniors of our school moved to large cities — particularly in the North — to live with relatives and find work. Our English teacher constantly corrected our grammar: "Not 'ain't,' but 'isn't.'" We seldom wrote papers, and even those few were usually plot summaries of short stories. When our teacher returned the papers, she usually lectured on the importance of using standard English: "I *am;* you *are;* he, she, or it *is,*" she would say, writing on the chalkboard as she spoke. "How you gon git a job talking about 'I is,' or 'I isn't' or 'I ain't'?"

In Pittsburgh, where I moved after graduation, I watched my aunt and   15
uncle — who had always spoken standard English when in Greeleyville — switch from black English to standard English to a mixture of the two, according to where they were or who they were with. At home and with certain close relatives, friends, and neighbors, they spoke black English. With those less close, they spoke a mixture. In public and with strangers, they generally spoke standard English.

In time, I learned to speak standard English with ease and to switch smoothly   16
from black to standard or a mixture, and back again. But no matter where I was, no matter what the situation or occasion, I continued to write as I had in school:

> Dear Mommie,
>   How are you? How is everybody else? Fine I hope. I am fine. So are
> Aunt and Uncle. Tell everyone I said hello. I will write again soon.
>   Love,
>   Barbara

At work, at a health insurance company, I learned to write letters to customers. I studied form letters and letters written by co-workers, memorizing the phrases and the ways in which they were used. I dictated:

> Thank you for your letter of January 5. We have made the changes in your coverage you requested. Your new premium will be $150 every three months. We are pleased to have been of service to you.

In a sense, I was proud of the letters I wrote for the company: they were proof of my ability to survive in the city, the outside world—an indication of my growing mastery of English. But they also indicated that writing was still mechanical for me, something that didn't require much thought.

Reading also became a more significant part of my life during those early 17 years in Pittsburgh. I had always liked reading, but now I devoted more and more of my spare time to it. I read romances, mysteries, popular novels. Looking back, I realize that the books I liked best were simple, unambiguous: good versus bad and right versus wrong with right rewarded and wrong punished, mysteries unraveled and all set right in the end. It was how I remembered life in Greeleyville.

Of course I was romanticizing. Life in Greeleyville had not become very 18 uncomplicated. Back there I had been—first as a child, then as a young woman with limited experience in the outside world—living in a relatively closed-in society. But there were implicit and explicit principles that guided our way of life and shaped our relationships with one another and the people outside— principles that a newcomer would find elusive and baffling. In Pittsburgh, I had matured, become more experienced. I had worked at three different jobs, associated with a wider range of people, married, had children. This new environment with different prescripts for living required that I speak standard English much of the time and slowly, imperceptibly, I had ceased seeing a sharp distinction between myself and "others." Reading romances and mysteries, characterized by dichotomy, was a way of shying away from change, from the person I was becoming.

But that other part of me—that part which took great pride in my abil- 19 ity to hold a job writing business letters—was increasingly drawn to the new developments in my life and the attending possibilities, opportunities for even greater change. If I could write letters for a nationally known business, could I not also do something better, more challenging, more important? Could I not, perhaps, go to college and become a school teacher? For years, afraid and a little embarrassed, I did no more than imagine this different me, this possible me. But sixteen years after coming north, when my youngest daughter entered kindergarten, I found myself unable—or unwilling—to resist the lure of possibility. I enrolled in my first college course: Basic Writing, at the University of Pittsburgh.

For the first time in my life, I was required to write extensively about myself. 20 Using the most formal English at my command, I wrote these sentences near the beginning of the term:

> One of my duties as a homemaker is simply picking up after others. A day seldom passes that I don't search for a mislaid toy, book, or gym shoe, etc. I change the Ty-D-Bol, fight "ring around the collar," and keep our laundry smelling "April fresh." Occasionally, I settle arguments between my children and suggest things to do when they're bored. Taking telephone messages for my oldest daughter is my newest (and sometimes most aggravating) chore. Hanging the toilet paper roll is my most insignificant.

My concern was to use "appropriate" language, to sound as if I belonged in a college classroom. But I felt separate from the language—as if it did not and could not belong to me. I couldn't think and feel genuinely in that language, couldn't make it express what I thought and felt about being a housewife. A part of me resented, among other things, being judged by such things as the appearance of my family's laundry and toilet bowl, but in that language I could only imagine and write about a conventional housewife.

For the most part, the remainder of the term was a period of adjustment, a 21 time of trying to find my bearings as a student in a college composition class, to learn to shut out my black English whenever I composed, and to prevent it from creeping into my formulations; a time for trying to grasp the language of the classroom and reproduce it in my prose; for trying to talk about myself in that language, reach others through it. Each experience of writing was like standing naked and revealing my imperfection, my "otherness." And each new assignment was another chance to make myself over in language, reshape myself, make myself "better" in my rapidly changing image of a student in a college composition class.

But writing became increasingly unmanageable as the term progressed, and 22 by the end of the semester, my sentences sounded like this:

> My excitement was soon dampened, however, by what seemed like a small voice in the back of my head saying that I should be careful with my long awaited opportunity. I felt frustrated and this seemed to make it difficult to concentrate.

There is a poverty of language in these sentences. By this point, I knew that the clichéd language of my Housewife essay was unacceptable, and I generally recognized trite expressions. At the same time, I hadn't yet mastered the language of the classroom, hadn't yet come to see it as belonging to me. Most notable is the lifelessness of the prose, the apparent absence of a person behind the words. I wanted those sentences—and the rest of the essay—to convey the anguish of yearning to, at once, become something more and yet remain the same. I had the sensation of being split in two, part of me going into a future the other part didn't believe possible. As that person, the student writer at that moment, I was essentially mute. I could not—in the process of composing—use the language of the old me, yet I couldn't imagine myself in the language of "others."

I found this particularly discouraging because at midsemester I had been writing in a much different way. Note the language of this introduction to an essay I had written then, near the middle of the term: 23

> Pain is a constant companion to the people in "Footwork." Their jobs are physically damaging. Employers are insensitive to their feelings and in many cases add to their problems. The general public wounds them further by treating them with disgrace because of what they do for a living. Although the workers are as diverse as they are similar, there is a definite link between them. They suffer a great deal of abuse.

The voice here is stronger, more confident, appropriating terms like "physically damaging," "wounds them further," "insensitive," "diverse"—terms I couldn't have imagined using when writing about my own experience—and shaping them into sentences like, "Although the workers are as diverse as they are similar, there is a definite link between them." And there is the sense of a personality behind the prose, someone who sympathizes with the workers: "The general public wounds them further by treating them with disgrace because of what they do for a living."

What caused these differences? I was, I believed, explaining other people's thoughts and feelings, and I was free to move about in the language of "others" so long as I was speaking *of* others. I was unaware that I was transforming into my best classroom language my own thoughts and feelings about people whose experiences and ways of speaking were in many ways similar to mine. 24

The following year, unable to turn back or let go of what had become something of an obsession with language (and hoping to catch and hold the sense of control that had eluded me in Basic Writing), I enrolled in a research writing course. I spent most of the term learning how to prepare for and write a research paper. I chose sex education as my subject and spent hours in libraries, searching for information, reading, taking notes. Then (not without messiness and often-demoralizing frustration) I organized my information into categories, wrote a thesis statement, and composed my paper—a series of paraphrases and quotations spaced between carefully constructed transitions. The process and 25 results felt artificial, but as I would later come to realize I was passing through a necessary stage. My sentences sounded like this:

> This reserve becomes understandable with examination of who the abusers are. In an overwhelming number of cases, they are people the victims know and trust. Family members, relatives, neighbors and close family friends commit seventy-five percent of all reported sex crimes against children, and parents, parent substitutes and relatives are the offenders in thirty to eighty percent of all reported cases. While assault by strangers does occur, it is less common, and is usually a single episode. But abuse by family members, relatives and acquaintances may continue for an extended period of time. In cases of incest, for example, children are abused repeatedly for an average of eight years. In such cases, "the use of physical force is rarely necessary because of the child's trusting, dependent relationship with the offender. The child's cooperation is often facilitated by the adult's position of dominance, an offer of material goods, a threat of physical violence, or a misrepresentation of moral standards."

The completed paper gave me a sense of profound satisfaction, and I read it 26 often after my professor returned it. I know now that what I was pleased with was the language I used and the professional voice it helped me maintain. "Use better words," my teacher had snapped at me one day after reading the notes I'd begun accumulating from my research, and slowly I began taking on the language of my sources. In my next set of notes, I used the word "vacillating"; my professor applauded. And by the time I composed the final draft, I felt at ease with terms like "overwhelming number of cases," "single episode," and "reserve," and I shaped them into sentences similar to those of my "expert" sources.

If I were writing the paper today, I would of course do some things differ- 27 ently. Rather than open with an anecdote—as my teacher suggested—I would begin simply with a quotation that caught my interest as I was researching my paper (and which I scribbled, without its source, in the margin of my notebook): "Truth does not do so much good in the world as the semblance of truth does evil." The quotation felt right because it captured what was for me the central idea of my essay—an idea that emerged gradually during the making of my paper—and expressed it in a way I would like to have said it. The anecdote, a hypothetical situation I invented to conform to the information in the paper, felt forced and insincere because it represented—to a great degree—my teacher's understanding of the essay, *her* idea of what in it was most significant. Improving upon my previous experiences with writing, I was beginning to think and feel in the language I used, to find my own voices in it, to sense that how one speaks influences how one means. But I was not yet secure enough, comfortable enough with the language to trust my intuition.

Now that I know that to seek knowledge, freedom, and autonomy means   28
always to be in the concentrated process of becoming—always to be venturing
into new territory, feeling one's way at first, then getting one's balance, negotiating, accommodating, discovering one's self in ways that previously defined
"others"—I sometimes get tired. And I ask myself why I keep on participating
in this highbrow form of violence, this slamming against perplexity. But there is
no real futility in the question, no hint of that part of the old me who stood outside standard English, hugging to herself a disabling mistrust of a language she
thought could not represent a person with her history and experience. Rather,
the question represents a person who feels the consequence of her education,
the weight of her possibilities as a teacher and writer and human being, a voice
in society. And I would not change that person, would not give back the good
burden that accompanies my growing expertise, my increasing power to shape
myself in language and share that self with "others."

"To speak," says Frantz Fanon, "means to be in a position to use a certain   29
syntax, to grasp the morphology of this or that language, but it means above all
to assume a culture, to support the weight of a civilization."* To write means
to do the same, but in a more profound sense.
However, Fanon also says that to achieve mastery means to "get" to a position of power, to
"grasp," to "assume." This, I have learned—both
as a student and subsequently as a teacher—can
involve tremendous emotional and psychological
conflict for those attempting to master academic
discourse. Although as a beginning student
writer I had a fairly good grasp of ordinary spo-

> To write . . . can involve
> tremendous emotional and
> psychological conflict for
> those attempting to master
> academic discourse.

ken English and was proficient at what Labov calls "code switching" (and what
John Baugh in *Black Street Speech* terms "style shifting"), when I came face to
face with the demands of academic writing, I grew increasingly self-conscious,
constantly aware of my status as a black and a speaker of one of the many black
English vernaculars, a traditional outsider. For the first time, I experienced
my sense of doubleness as something menacing, a built-in enemy. Whenever
I turned inward for salvation, the balm so available during my childhood, I
found instead this new fragmentation which spoke to me in many voices. It
was the voice of my desire to prosper, but at the same time it spoke of what I
had relinquished and could not regain: a safe way of being, a state of powerless-
ness which exempted me from responsibility for who I was and might be. And
it accused me of betrayal, of turning away from blackness. To recover balance,
I had to take on the language of the academy, the language of "others." And to

Black Skin, White Masks (1952, rpt. New York: Grove Press, 1967), pp. 17–18.

do that, I had to learn to imagine myself a part of the culture of that language, and therefore someone free to manage that language, to take liberties with it. Writing and rewriting, practicing, experimenting, I came to comprehend more fully the generative power of language. I discovered—with the help of some especially sensitive teachers—that through writing one can continually bring new selves into being, each with new responsibilities and difficulties, but also with new possibilities. Remarkable power, indeed. I write and continually give birth to myself.

- -

Questions for Discussion and Journaling

1. Mellix argues that Toby, the Greeleyville town policeman, did not need to speak grammatically correct English because "He was white and could speak as he wished." Mellix herself, on the other hand, "had something to prove. Toby did not" (para. 7). Explain what she means.

2. Young (p. 148) makes similar arguments regarding why Barack Obama needed to speak more correctly than George W. Bush, and why the black professors at the University of Iowa spoke what Jay Semel called the "hyper-performed standard language" (para. 44). Now that you've read several arguments and illustrations of this felt need, try to explain it. Why does this happen? Why do Obama, the professors, Mellix, and others who don't speak "*the* language" (or what Gee (p. 274) will call the "dominant Discourse") feel this pressure?

3. Mellix says that "speaking standard English to whites was our way of demonstrating that we knew their language and could use it . . . . But when we spoke standard English, we acknowledged . . . that our customary way of speaking was inferior" (para. 8). What does she mean by this? How would Young explain the damage this dual speaking was causing?

4. Young talked about the ways that school teaches children standard English. Where did Mellix learn standard English? Where have you learned standard English? Do you speak it in every situation or just some?

5. For many years, having to write in standard English made writing feel "mechanical" to Mellix, and she says she felt "separate from the language" (paras. 16, 20). Do you feel like your spoken, home, or social English is the same as the kind of English you are expected to use in school and workplace writing? If not, do you think that has an impact on your writing, as it did on Mellix's writing? Is there anything about your home/social and spoken language(s) you feel you have to "shut out" when you write?

6. Go back to Young and review his idea of "double consciousness." Does that idea describe Mellix's experiences? Why? How?

Applying and Exploring Ideas

1. Mellix says she was "shy in the presence of those who owned and/or spoke *the* language" (para. 8). Drawing on what you've learned from Young and/or others in this chapter, write 2–3 pages in which you explain what "*the* language" is, why it is seen as "*the* language," how that is determined, and why certain people are seen to own it.

2. Young argues that asking black students to use a different language at school than they do at home is a form of racial segregation. Write 1–2 pages about whether you agree or disagree with Young, and support your argument by drawing on Mellix's experiences.

3. Young argues vehemently against code switching, arguing that it is dangerous and damaging to people who have to engage in it. Most of Mellix's essay seems to suggest she would agree with him; however, at the end she seems to change her position. How do you think Mellix would respond to Young's claims? Write a short dialogue between Young and Mellix on the subject of code switching.

4. Conduct short interviews with three people you know from different areas of your life. Try to ensure these people are as different from one another as possible. Ask those people the following questions:

   - Do you speak the same way in every situation?
   - Do you feel like the way you speak at home with your family is the way you speak at school and/or at work?
   - If not, what are some of the differences? Can you give examples?
   - Do you feel like one of the ways you speak is valued more highly than the others? How do you know?

   Summarize your results in 2–3 pages, and then share them with your classmates. What are some themes or trends that you find as a class? What questions does this raise for you? Do any of the answers you received relate to any of the readings you've done so far in this book?

- -

META MOMENT   How can Mellix help you understand your feelings about the way that you and others speak? When your feelings or judgments about language varieties (your own or others') arise in the future, how can you respond to and reflect on them differently as a result of reading Mellix?

- -

Notes toward a Theory of Prior Knowledge

LIANE ROBERTSON

KARA TACZAK

KATHLEEN BLAKE YANCEY

Framing the Reading

These authors take up a topic that researchers refer to as **transfer** — the ability of learners to draw on what they already know or have learned in order to do something new, or something in a new context. This research area has been very complicated for a long time (over a hundred years), as researchers have repeatedly had trouble seeing evidence of people applying what they've learned in one setting to another setting. This is a pretty major problem for school, since the expectation is that what students learn in school will be useful to them elsewhere. But transfer researchers have found that very often people don't use what they already know, don't see it as relevant, or can't figure out how to use it in helpful ways. There are ways to teach that are better at encouraging this use of prior knowledge than others. The researchers who wrote this article have been conducting studies on that very topic — how to help writing teachers "teach for transfer," so that what students learn about writing in their courses can be useful to them in the many other settings where they will write.

Kathleen Blake Yancey is the Kellogg W. Hunt Professor of English and Distinguished Research Professor at Florida State University. Liane Robertson and Kara Taczak were her doctoral students there. Now, Robertson is an assistant professor of English at William Paterson University, and Taczak is a Teaching Professor in the writing program at the University of Denver. Together they

Robertson, Liane, et al. "Notes Toward a Theory of Prior Knowledge and Its Role in College Composers' Transfer of Knowledge and Practice." *Composition Forum*, vol. 26, Fall 2012, compositionforum.com/issue/26/prior-knowledge-transfer.php.

published a book on the topic of teaching to encourage transfer called *Writing across Contexts: Transfer, Composition, and Sites of Writing*, which won the 2015 Research Impact Award from the Conference on College Composition and Communication.

So far in this chapter, the articles have examined prior experience and knowledge in terms of literacy broadly understood — in particular, how early experiences with reading, writing, and language use are central to people's identities and to how they fare (and are treated) in school and other contexts. In this article, the focus shifts a little to look specifically at **how** people write is useful to them when they try to write in new situations. And, of course, everything you've read about so far is still relevant here. Robertson et al. note that students draw on their prior knowledge in various ways. What they don't say, but you can likely guess from what you've been reading, is that students' prior literacy experiences, culture, class, language use, and sense of self all impact how they are going to use and transfer prior knowledge.

Getting Ready to Read

Before you read, do at least one of the following activities:

- Think of those times when teachers expected you to be able to complete a writing task by drawing on what you already knew. How did that go? Were you successful or unsuccessful?
- Google "mindfulness" and see what you find.
- Google "self-efficacy" and see what you find.

As you read, consider the following questions:

- Do you see yourself in the students they describe?
- Are there terms and ideas you don't understand? Make a note to ask about them in class.

DURING THE LAST DECADE, especially, scholars in composition studies have investigated how students "transfer" what they learn in college composition into other academic writing sites. Researchers have focused, for example, on exploring with students how they take up new writing tasks (e.g., McCarthy, Wardle); on theorizing transfer with specific applicability to writing tasks across a college career (e.g., Beaufort); and on developing new curricula to foster such transfer of knowledge and practice (e.g., Dew, Robertson, Taczak). Likewise, scholars have sought to learn what prior knowledge from high school first-year students might draw on, and how, as they begin college composition (e.g., Reiff and Bawarshi). To date, however, no study has actively documented or theorized precisely how students *make use of* such prior knowledge as they find themselves in new rhetorical situations, that is, on how students draw on and employ what they already know and can do, and whether such knowledge and practice is efficacious in the new situation or not. In this article, we take up this task, within a specific view of transfer as a dynamic activity through which students, like all composers, actively make use of prior knowledge as they respond to new writing tasks. More specifically, we theorize that students actively make use of prior knowledge and practice in three ways: by *drawing on* both knowledge and practice and employing it in ways almost identical to the ways they have used it in the past; by *reworking* such knowledge and practice as they address new tasks; and by *creating new knowledge and practices* for themselves when students encounter what we call a setback or critical incident, which is a failed effort to address a new task that prompts new ways of thinking about how to write and about what writing is.

In this article, then, we begin by locating our definition of transfer in the general literature of cognition; we then consider how students' use of prior knowledge has been represented in the writing studies literature. Given this context and drawing on two studies, we then articulate our theory of students' use of prior knowledge, in the process focusing on student accounts to illustrate how they make use of such knowledge as they take up new writing tasks.[1] We then close by raising questions that can inform research on this topic in the future.[2]

MODELS OF TRANSFER

Early transfer research in the fields of psychology and education (Thorndike, Prather, Detterman) focused on specific situations in which instances of transfer occurred. Conducted in research environments and measuring subjects' ability to replicate specific behavior from one context to another, results of this research suggested that transfer was merely accidental, but it did not explore transfer in contexts more authentic and complex than those simulated in a laboratory.

In 1992, Perkins and Salomon suggested that researchers should consider the conditions and contexts under which transfer might occur, redefining transfer according to three subsets: near versus far transfer, or how closely related a new situation is to the original; high-road (or mindful) transfer involving knowledge abstracted and applied to another context, versus low-road (or reflexive) transfer involving knowledge triggered by something similar in another context; and positive transfer (performance improvement) versus negative transfer (performance interference) in another context. With consideration of the complexity of transfer and the conditions under which it may or may not occur, Perkins and Salomon suggest deliberately teaching for transfer through *hugging* (using approximations) and *bridging* (using abstraction to make connections) as strategies to maximize transfer (7).

In composition studies, several scholars have pursued "the transfer ques- 5
tion." Michael Carter, Nancy Sommers and Laura Saltz, and Linda Bergmann
and Janet Zepernick, for example, have theorized that students develop toward
expertise, or "write into expertise" (Sommers and Saltz 134), when they understand the context in which the writing is situated and can make the abstrac-
tions that connect contexts, as Perkins and Salomon suggest (6). David Russell
likewise claims that writing happens within a context, specifically the "activity
system" in which the writing is situated, and that when students learn to make
connections between contexts, they begin to develop toward expertise in understanding writing within any context, suggesting that transfer requires contextual
knowledge (Russell 536). In a later article, Russell joins with Arturo Yañez to
study the relationship of genre understanding to transfer, finding, in the case
of one student, that students' prior genre knowledge can be limited to a single
instance of the genre rather than situated in a larger activity system; such limited
understanding can lead to confusion and subsequent difficulty in writing (n.p.).

Other research has contributed to our understanding of the complexity of 6
transfer as well, notably of the role that motivation and metacognition play in
transfer. For instance, Tracy Robinson and Tolar Burton found that students
are motivated to improve their writing when they understand that the goal is
to transfer what they learn between contexts, an understanding also explored
by Susan Jarratt et al. in a study involving interview research with students in
upper-division writing courses to determine what might have transferred to those
contexts from the first-year composition experience. Results of the research offer
three categories from which students accounted for transfer: (1) active transfer,
which requires the mindfulness that Perkins and Salomon define as high-road
transfer, (2) unreflective practice, in which students cannot articulate why they
do what they do, and (3) transfer denial, in which students resist the idea of
transfer from first-year composition or don't see the connection between it and
upper-division writing (Jarratt et al. 3). The Jarratt et al. study, perhaps most
importantly, suggests that metacognition students develop before transfer occurs
can be prompted; students may not necessarily realize that learning has occurred
until they are prompted, but this is the point at which transfer can occur (6).

Metacognition as a key to transfer is identified by Anne Beaufort as well: in 7
College Writing and Beyond, Beaufort suggests conceptualizing writing according
to five knowledge domains, which together provide a frame within which writers
can organize the context-specific knowledge they need to write successfully in
new situations. These domains — writing process knowledge, rhetorical knowledge, genre knowledge, discourse community knowledge, and content knowledge — provide an analytical framework authors can draw on as they move from
one context to another. Using this conceptual model, students can learn to write
in new contexts more effectively because they understand the inquiry necessary
for entering the new context. Beaufort suggests that the expertise students need

to write successfully involves "mental schema" they use to organize and apply knowledge about writing in new contexts (17).

More recent scholarship about transfer, including the "writing about writ-   8 ing" approach advocated by Douglas Downs and Elizabeth Wardle, suggests that teaching students about concepts of writing will help foster transfer through a curricular design based on reading and writing as scholarly inquiry such that students develop a rhetorical awareness (553). This writing-as-writing-course-content approach dismisses the long-held misconception that content doesn't matter, and others are pursuing this same end although with different curricular models (e.g., Sargent and Slomp; Bird; Dew; Robertson; and Taczak).

A little-referenced source of research on transfer that is particularly relevant to   9 this study on how students use prior knowledge in new situations, however, is the National Research Council volume *How People Learn: Mind, Brain, Experience, and School*. Here transfer "is best viewed as an active, dynamic process rather than a passive end-product of a particular set of learning experiences" (53). As important, according to this generalized theory of transfer, all "new learning involves transfer based on previous learning" (53). All such prior learning is not efficacious, however; according to this theory, prior knowledge can function in one of three ways. First, an individual's prior knowledge can match the demands of a new task, in which case a composer can draw from and build on that prior knowledge; we might see this use of prior knowledge when a first-year compos-ition student thinks in terms of audience, purpose, and genre when entering a writing situation in another discipline. Second, an individual's prior knowledge might be a bad match, or at odds with, a new writing situation; in FYC, we might see this when a student defines success in writing as creating a text that is grammatically correct without reference to its rhetorical effectiveness. And third, an individual's prior knowledge—located in a community context—might be at odds with the requirements of a given writing situation; this writing classroom situation, in part, seems to have motivated the Vander Lei-Kyburz edited collection documenting the difficulty some FYC students experience as a function of their religious beliefs coming into conflict with the goals of higher education. As this brief review suggests, we know that college students call on prior knowledge as they encounter new writing demands; the significant points here are that students actively use their prior knowledge and that some prior knowledge provides help for new writing situations, while other prior knowledge does not.

> *College students call on prior knowledge as they encounter new writing demands; the significant points here are that students actively use their prior knowledge and that some prior knowledge provides help for new writing situations, while other prior knowledge does not.*

This interest in how first-year students use   10 prior knowledge in composing, however, has not been taken up by composition scholars until very recently. During the last four years, Mary Jo Reiff and Anis Bawarshi have undertaken this task. Their 2011 article, Tracing Discursive Resources: How Students Use Prior Genre Knowledge to Negotiate New Writing Contexts in First-Year Composition, provides a compilation of this research, which centers on if and how students' understanding and use of genre facilitates their transition from high school to college writing situations. Conducted at the University of Washington and the University of Tennessee, Reiff and Bawarshi's study identified two kinds of students entering first year comp: first, what they call boundary crossers, "those students who were more likely to question their genre knowledge and to break this knowledge down into useful strategies and repurpose it"; and second, boundary guarders, "those students who were more likely to draw on whole genres with certainty, regardless of task" (314). In creating these student prototypes, the researchers drew on document-based interviews focused on students' use of genre knowledge early in the term, first as they composed a "preliminary" essay and second, as they completed the first assignment of the term:

> Specifically, we asked students to report on what they thought each writing task was asking them to do and then to report on what prior genres they were *reminded of* and *drew on* for each task. As students had their papers in front of them, we were able to point to various rhetorical conventions and ask about how they learned to use those conventions or why they made the choices that they made, enabling connections between discursive patterns and prior knowledge of genres. (319)

Based on this study, Reiff and Bawarshi identify two kinds of boundary- 11 guarding students, and key to their definition is the use of what they call "not talk":

> The first, what might be called "strict" boundary guarding, includes students who report no "not" talk (in terms of genres or strategies) and who seem to maintain known genres regardless of task. The second kind of boundary guarding is less strict in that students report some strategy-related "not" talk and some modification of known genres by way of adding strategies to known genres. (329)

These students, in other words, work to maintain the boundary marking their 12 prior knowledge, and at the most add only strategies to the schema they seek to preserve. By way of contrast, the boundary crossing student accepts noviceship, often as a consequence of struggling to meet the demands of a new writing task. Therefore, this writer seems to experience multiple kinds of flux—such as uncertainty about task, descriptions of writing according to what genre it is not, and the breakdown and repurposing of whole genres that may be useful to students entering new contexts in FYC (329).

What's interesting here, of course, isn't only the prototypes, but how those pro- 13 totypes might change given other contexts. For example, what happens to students as they continue learning in the first term of FYC? What happens when students move on to a second term and take up writing tasks outside of first-year composition? Likewise, what difference might both curriculum and pedagogy make? In other words, what might we do to motivate those students exhibiting a boundary-guarding approach to take up a boundary-crossing one? And once students have boundary-crossed, what happens then? How can we support boundary-crossers and help them become more confident and competent composers?[3]

WHERE MANY STUDENTS BEGIN: ABSENT PRIOR KNOWLEDGE

As documented above, it's a truism that students draw on prior knowledge when 14 facing new tasks, and when that acquired knowledge doesn't fit the new situation, successful transfer is less likely to occur; this is so in writing generally, but it's especially so as students enter first-year composition classrooms in college. At the same time, whether students are guarding or crossing, they share a common high school background. Moreover, what this seems to mean for virtually all first-year college composition students, as the research literature documents but as we also learned from our students, is that as students enter college writing classes, there's not only prior knowledge, but also an *absence* of prior knowledge, and in two important areas: (1) key writing concepts and (2) non-fiction texts that serve as models. In part, that's because the "writing" curricula at the two sites—high school and college—don't align well. As Arthur Applebee and Judith Langer's continuing research on the high school English/Language Arts curriculum shows, the high school classroom is a literature classroom, whereas the first-year writing classroom—which despite the diverse forms it takes, from first-year seminars to WAC-based approaches to cultural studies and critical pedagogy approaches (see Fulkerson; *Delivering College Composition*)—is a writing classroom. The result for our students—and, we think, others like them—is that they enter college with very limited experience with the conceptions and kinds of writing and reading they will engage with during the first year of postsecondary education.

In terms of how such an absence might occur, the Applebee and Langer 15 research is instructive, especially in its highlighting of two dimensions of writing in high school that are particularly relevant in terms of absent prior knowledge. First is the emphasis that writing receives, or not, in high school classrooms; their studies demonstrate an emphasis placed on literature with deleterious effects for writing instruction:

> In the English classes observed, 6.3% of time was focused on the teaching of explicit writing strategies, 5.5% on the study of models, and 4.2% on evaluating writing, including discussion of rubrics or standards. (Since multiple

things were often going on at once, summing these percentages would overestimate the time devoted to writing instruction.) To put the numbers in perspective, in a 50-minute period, students would have on average just over three minutes of instruction related to explicit writing strategies, or a total of 2 hours and 22 minutes in a nine-week grading period. ("A Snapshot" 21)

Second, and as important, is the way that writing is positioned in the high 16 school classes Applebee and Langer have studied: chiefly as preparation for test-taking, with the single purpose of passing a test, and the single audience of Britton's "teacher-as-examiner." Moreover, this conclusion echoes the results of the University of Washington Study of Undergraduate Learning (SOUL) on entering college writers, which was designed to identify the gaps between high school and college that presented obstacles to students. Their findings suggest that the major gaps are in math and writing, and that in the latter area, writing tests themselves limit students' understanding of and practice in writing. As a result, writing's purposes are truncated and its potential to serve learning is undeveloped. As Applebee and Langer remark, "Given the constraints imposed by high-stakes tests, writing as a way to study, learn, and go beyond—as a way to construct knowledge or generate new networks of understandings   is rare" (26). One absence of prior knowledge demonstrated in the scholarship on the transition from high school to college is thus a conception and practice of writing for authentic purposes and genuine audiences.

Writers are readers as well, of course. In high school, the reading is largely (if 17 not exclusively) of imaginative literature, whereas in college, it's largely (though not exclusively) non-fiction, and for evidence of impact of such a curriculum, we turn to our students. What we learned from them, through questionnaires and interviews, is that their prior knowledge about texts, at least in terms of what they *choose* to read and in terms of how such texts represent good *writing*, is located in the context of imaginative literature, which makes sense given the school curriculum. When asked "What type of authors represent your definition of good writing?" these students replied with a list of imaginative writers. Some cited writers known for publishing popular page-turners—Michael Crichton, James Patterson, and Dan Brown, for instance; others pointed to writers of the moment—Jodi Picoult and Stephenie Meyer; and still others called on books that are likely to be children's classics for some time to come: Harry Potter, said one student, "is all right." Two other authors were mentioned—Frey, whose *A Million Little Pieces*, famously, was either fiction or non-fiction given its claim to truth (or not); and textbook author Ann Raimes. In sum, we have a set of novels, one "memoir," and one writing textbook—none of which resembles the non-fiction reading characteristic of first-year composition and college more generally. Given the students' reading selections, what we seem to be mapping here, based on their interviews, is a second absence of prior knowledge.

Of course, the number of students is small, their selections limited. These data 18 don't prove that even these students, much less others, have no prior knowledge about non-fiction. But the facts (1) that the curricula of high schools are focused on imaginative literature and (2) that none of the students pointed to even a single non-fiction book—other than the single textbook, which identification may itself be part of the problem—suggest that these may not have models of non-fiction to draw on when writing their own non-fiction. Put another way, when these students write the non-fiction texts characteristic of the first-year composition classroom, they have neither pre-college experience with the reading of non-fiction texts nor mental models of non-fiction texts, which together constitute a second absence of prior knowledge.

Perhaps not surprisingly, what at least some students do in this situation is 19 draw on and generalize their experience with imaginative texts in ways that are at odds with what college composition instructors expect, particularly when it comes to concepts of writing.[4] When we asked students how they wrote and how they defined writing, for example, we saw a set of contradictions. On the one hand, students reported writing in various genres, especially outside of school. Moreover, unlike the teenagers in the well-known Pew study investigating teenagers' writing habits and understandings—for whom writing inside school is writing and writing outside school is not writing but communication—the students we interviewed do understand writing both inside and outside school as *writing*. More specifically, all but one of the students identified writing outside school as a place where they "use writing most," for example, with all but one identifying three specific practices—taking notes, texting, and emailing—as frequent (i.e., daily) writing practices. In addition, two writers spoke to particularly robust writing lives; one of them noted, for instance, writing

> [i]nside school. Taking notes. Inside the classroom doing notes. If not its
> writing assignments. Had blog for a while; blog about everyday life [she and
> three friends]; high school sophomore through senior year; fizzled out b/c of
> life; emails; hand written letters to family members.

A second one described a similar kind of writing life, his located particularly in the arts: "Probably [it would] be texting . . . the most that I write. I also write a little poetry; I'm in a band so I like to write it so that it fits to music; a pop alternative; I play the piano, synth and sing."

On the other hand, given that many of these texts—emails and texts, for 20 example—are composed to specific audiences and thus seem in that sense to be highly rhetorical, it was likewise surprising that every one of the students, when asked to define writing, used a single word: *expression*. One student thus defined writing as a "way to express ideas and feelings and to organize my thoughts," while another summarized the common student response: "I believe writing is, um, a way of expressing your thoughts, uh, through, uh, text." In spite of their own experience as writers *to others*, these students see writing principally as a vehicle for authorial expression, not as a vehicle for dialogue with a reader or an opportunity to make knowledge, both of which are common conceptions in college writing environments. We speculate that this way of seeing writing—universally as a means of expression in different historical and intellectual contexts—may be influenced by the emphasis on imaginative authorship in the high school literature curriculum, in which students read poets', novelists', and dramatists' writing as forms of expression. Likewise, the emphasis on reading in high school, at the expense of writing, means that it's likely that reading exerts a disproportionate influence on how these students understand writing itself, especially since the writing tasks, often a form of literary analysis, are also oriented to literature and literary authorship. And more generally, what we see here—through these students' high school curricula, their own reading practices, and their writing practices both in but mostly out of school—is reading culture-as-prior-experience, an experience located in pre-college reading and some writing practices, but one missing the conceptions, models, and practices of writing as well as practices of reading that could be helpful in a new postsecondary environment emphasizing a rhetorical view of both reading and writing. Or: absent prior knowledge.

A TYPOLOGY OF PRIOR KNOWLEDGE, TYPE ONE: ASSEMBLAGE

While we speculate that college students, like our students, enter college with 21 an absence of prior knowledge relevant to the new situation, how students *take up* the new knowledge relative to the old varies; and here, based on interview data, writing assignments, and responses to the assignments, we describe three models of uptake. Some students, like Eugene, seem to take up new knowledge in a way we call assemblage: by grafting isolated bits of new knowledge onto a continuing schema of old knowledge. Some, like Alice, take up new knowledge in ways we call remix: by integrating the new knowledge into the schema of the old. And some, like Rick, encounter what we call a critical incident—a failure to meet a new task successfully—and use that occasion as a prompt to re-think writing altogether.

Eugene, who seems to be an example of Reiff and Bawarshi's border guard- 22 ers, believes that what he is learning in FYC is very similar to what he learned in high school. How he makes use of prior knowledge and practice about writing is what we call *assemblage*: such students maintain the concept of writing they brought into college with them, breaking the new learning into bits, atomistically, and grafting those isolated "bits" of learning onto the prior structure without either recognition of differences between prior and current writing conceptions and tasks, or synthesis of them. Such bits may take one or both of two forms: key

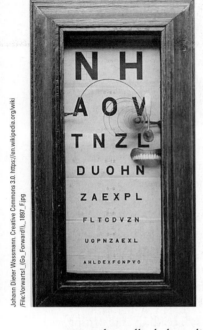

terms and strategies. Taken together, the conception of writing that students develop through an assemblage model of prior knowledge is very like the assemblage "Vorwarts!" in its remaking of the earlier structure of the eye chart: the new bits are added to it, but are not integrated *into* it but rather on top of it, such that the basic chart isn't significantly changed at all.

When Eugene, a successful AP student in high 23 school whose score enabled him to exempt the first of the two first-year composition courses at Florida State, entered English 1102, the second-term, research and argument course, he articulated a dualistic view of writing—for writing to be successful, "you have the right rhetoric and the right person in the right manner," he observed—and believed that writing operates inside a transmission model through which his writing would allow him "to get his message across." Interestingly, he believed that he was "really prepared for college": "[in high school] we were doing a lot of papers that talked about literary devices so I basically knew a lot of literacy devices so there wasn't a lot more to learn necessarily, I guess more fine-tuning of what I had already learned." And what there was to learn, Eugene didn't find worthwhile, in part because it fell outside what he did know: "I don't like research papers because I don't know how they work very well and collecting sources and analyzing." He noted that he was better at "evaluating an article and finding a deeper meaning," which is the purpose, of course, of the literary analysis texts he wrote in high school.

As he begins his college writing career, then, Eugene establishes a three-part 24 pattern that continues throughout English 1102 and the next term: (1) he confuses and conflates the literary terms of high school and the literacy and rhetorical terms and practices of college; (2) he continues to believe that "there wasn't a lot more to learn"; and (3) he relies on his prior knowledge of writing, one located chiefly in the role of the unconscious in writing process. As he analyzes his progress in terms of writing, for example, he notes the central role of the unconscious:

> my main point is that writing is unconsciously understanding that certain genres that have certain formalities where I have progressed and so where I have progressed is I can put names and places to genres; writing is pretty much unconscious how you are adjusting the person you are talking to and how you are writing.

In this case, the unconscious element of writing provides the central element of Eugene's concept of writing, and as English 1102 continues and in the semester that follows, Eugene struggles to find terms that he can comfortably graft onto that central understanding.

During the course of two semesters, Eugene was interviewed four times, each time nominating his key terms for composing, and in this data set, we can also see Eugene struggling to make his prior conception of writing work with the new conception of writing to which he is being introduced. In all, he nominated 18 terms: audience and genre were both mentioned three times (once each in three of the four interviews), with other terms each suggested once: reflection, tone, purpose, theme, exigence, diction, theory of writing, imagination, creativity, and rhetorical situation. Some of the terms—rhetorical situation and exigence, for instance—came from his first-year composition class, while others—diction and imagination—were terms located in his high school curriculum. As he continued into the semester following English 1102, Eugene held on to genre, saying in one interview immediately following English 1102 that "I still have to go with genre [as] important and everything else is subcategories," in the next that genre was still important but not something he needed to think about, as he worked "unconsciously": 25

> A lot of my writing is like unconsciously done because it's been ingrained in me to how writing is done. Even though I probably think of genre I don't really think of it. Writing just kind of happens for me.

And in the final interview, Eugene retrospectively notes that what he gained was a "greater appreciation" of genre, "for the role genre plays in writing. [I]t went from being another aspect of writing to the most important part of writing as a result of ENC 1102." Genre for Eugene, then, seems to be mapped assemblage-like onto a fundamental and unchanging concept of writing located in expression and the unconscious.

In the midst of trying to respond to new tasks like the research project and unable to frame them anew, Eugene defaults to two strategies that he found particularly helpful. One of these was multiple drafting, not to create a stronger draft so much, however, as to have the work scaffolded according to goals: "Most useful was the multiple drafts, being able to have smaller goals to work up to the bigger goal made it easier to manage." The second strategy Eugene adopted both for English 1102 and for writing tasks the next semester was "reverse outlining," a practice in which (as its name suggests) students outline a text once it's in draft form to see if and how the focus is carried through the text. This Eugene found particularly helpful: "something new I hadn't experienced before was the reverse outline because it helped me to realize that my paragraphs do have main points and it helps me realize where I need main points." Interestingly, the parts-is-parts approach to writing Eugene values in the smaller goals leading to larger ones in the multiple drafting process is echoed in his appreciation of reverse outlining, 26 where he can track the intent of *each* paragraph rather than how the paragraphs relate to *each other*, a point he makes explicitly as English 1102 closes:

> Um, my theory of writing when I first started the class was very immature. I remember describing it as just putting your emotions and thoughts on the paper I think was my first theory of writing and I think from the beginning of fall it's gotten to where I understand the little parts of writing make up the important part of writing, so I think in that way it's changed.

As the study concludes and Eugene is asked to comment retrospectively on 27 what he learned in English 1102, he re-states not what he learned, but rather the prior knowledge on writing that he brought with him to college. He observes that, "For me, there wasn't much of a difference between high school and college writing" and

> Like I came from a really intensive writing program in high school, so coming into [the first-year comp] class wasn't that different, so, um, I mean obviously any writing that I do will help me become better and hopefully I will progress and become better with each piece that I write, so in that regard I think it was helpful.

What thus seems to help, according to Eugene, is simply the opportunity to write, which will enable him to progress naturally through "any writing that I do."

And not least, as the study closes, Eugene, in describing a conception of 28 writing developed through an assemblage created by grafting the new key term "genre" onto an unconscious process resulting in writing that is dichotomously "good" or "bad," repeats the definition he provided as English 1102 commenced:

> I mean writing is, like, when you break it down it's a lot more complex than what you describe it to me. I mean you can sit all day and talk about literary devices but it comes down to writing. Writing is, um, it's more complex, so, it's like anything, if you are going to break down, it's going to be more complex than it seems. Writing is emotionally based. Good writing is good and bad writing is bad.

Writing here is complex, something to be analyzed, much like literature, "when you break it down." But it's also a practice: "you can sit all day and talk about literacy devices but it comes down to writing." Likewise, the strategies Eugene appreciated—revising toward larger goals and reverse outlining to verify the points of individual paragraphs—fit with the assemblage model as well: they do not call into question an "unconscious" approach, but can be used to verify that this approach is producing texts whose component parts are satisfactory. Of course, this wasn't the intent of the teacher introducing either the multiple drafting process or the reverse outlining strategy. But as Eugene makes use of prior knowledge, in an assemblage fashion, the conceptual model of unconscious writing he brought to college with him shapes his uptake of the curriculum more broadly, from key terms to process strategies.

TYPE TWO: REMIX

Students who believe that what they are learning differs from their prior knowledge in some substantive way(s) and value that difference behave differently. They begin to create a revised model of writing we characterize as a *remix:* prior knowledge revised synthetically to *incorporate* new concepts and practices into the prior model of writing. Remix, in this definition, isn't a characteristic of hip-hop only or of modernism more generally, but a feature of invention with a long history: 29

> Seen through a wider lens . . . remix — the combining of ideas, narratives, sources — is a *classical means of invention,* even (or perhaps especially) for canonical writers. For example, . . . as noted in *Wikipedia,* Shakespeare arguably "remixed" classical sources and Italian contemporary works to produce his plays, which were often modified for different audiences. Nineteenth century poets also utilized the technique. Examples include Samuel Taylor Coleridge's "Rime of the Ancient Mariner," which was produced in multiple, highly divergent versions, and John Keats' La Belle Dame sans Merci, which underwent significant revision between its original composition in 1819 and its republication in 1820 (Remix). In sum, remixing, both a practice and a set of material practices, is connected to the creation of new texts (Yancey, Re-designing 6).

Here, we use remix with specific application to writing: a set of practices that links past writing knowledge and practice to new writing knowledge and practice, as we see in the experience of Alice.

Alice entered English 1102 with a conception of writing influenced by three sets of experience: preparing for and taking the Florida K-12 writing exams, known as the FCAT; completing her senior AP English class; and taking her English 1101 class, which she had completed in the summer before matriculating at Florida State. Alice had literally grown up as an "FCAT writer," given that the writing curriculum in the state is keyed to these essay exams and for many if not most students, the writing exam is the curriculum (e.g., Scherff and Piazza). In her senior year, however, Alice enrolled in an AP English class, where she learned a different model of text that both built on and contrasted with her experience as an FCAT writer: "[my senior English teacher] explained his concept as instead of writing an intro, listing your three points, then the conclusion, to write like layers of a cake. Instead of spreading out each separate point . . . 30

197

layer them." The shift here, then, is one of remix: the arrangement of texts was to remain the same, while what happened *inside* the texts was to be changed, with Alice's explanation suggesting that the shift was from a listing of points to an analysis of them. During the third experience, in the summer before her first year in college, Alice learned a new method of composing: she was introduced to "process writing," including drafts, workshops and peer reviews.

When Alice entered English 1102, she defined writing as a Murray-esque 31 exercise: "Writing," Alice said, "is a form of expression that needs to have feeling and be articulate in order to get the writer's ideas across. The writing also needs to have the author's own unique voice," an idea that provided something of a passport for her as she encountered new conceptions of writing located in key terms like rhetorical situation, context, and audience. In Alice's retrospective account of English 1102, in fact, she focuses particularly on the conception of rhetorical situation as one both new to her and difficult to understand, in part because it functioned as something of a meta-concept: "Rhetorical situation had a lot of things involved in that. It was a hard concept for me to get at first but it was good." By the end of the course, however, Alice was working hard to create an integrated model of writing that included three components: her own values, what she had learned during the summer prior to English 1102, and what she had learned in English 1102:

> I still find writing to be a form of expression, it should have the author's
> own voice and there should be multiple drafts and peer reviews in order to
> have the end result of a good and original paper. Along with that this year I
> learned about concepts such as rhetorical situation. . . . This opened me up
> to consider audience, purpose, and context for my writing. I need to know
> why I am writing and who I am writing to before I start. The context I am
> writing in also brings me to what genre I'm writing in.

Alice's conception of writing here seems to rely on the layering strategy recommended by her AP teacher: voice, mixed with process, and framed rhetorically, defined here layer by layer.

As Alice continues into the term after she completes English 1102, two 32 writing-related themes emerge for her. One: a key part of the process for Alice that begins to have new salience for her is reflecting on her writing, both *as* she drafts and *after* she completes a text. Two: she finds that the study itself has helped her develop as a writer but that she needs more time and more writing activity to make sense of all that she's been offered in English 1102.

In English 1102, Alice had been asked to reflect frequently: in the midst 33 of drafting; at the end of assignments; and at the end of the course itself in a reflection-in-presentation where she summarized what she had learned and also theorized about writing. These reflective practices she found particularly helpful and, in the next term, when she wrote assignments for her humanities and meteorology classes, she continued to practice a self-sponsored reflection: it had become part of her composing process. As she explains, her own sense is that through reflection, she is able to bring together the multiple factors that contribute to writing:

> I do know that I really liked reflection, like having that because I haven't done that before. And whatever term was writing with a purpose and I like that so I guess writing with some purpose. Like when you are done writing you do reflection because before I would be done with a writing and go to the next one and so then in between we go over each step or throughout.

As the study concluded, Alice linked reflection and rhetorical situation as the two most important concepts for writing that she learned in English 1102, but as she did earlier, she also includes a value of her own, in this case "being direct," into a remixed model of writing:[5] 34

> Two of the words I would use to describe my theory of writing would be the key terms, rhetorical situation, reflection and the last that isn't would just be being direct. Rhetorical situation encompasses a lot about anybody's theory of writing. It deals with knowing the purpose of my writing, understanding the context of my writing, and thinking about my audience. I chose being direct for lack of a better term. I don't think my writing should beat around the bush. It should just say what needs to be said and have a purpose. As for reflection that's something we do in life and not just writing. In the context of writing it really helps not just as a review of grammar or spelling errors but as a thought back on what I was thinking about when I wrote what I wrote, and that could change as I look back on my writing.

Being direct, of course, was Alice's contribution to a curricular-based model of writing informed by reflective practice and rhetorical situation. Reflection she defines as a "thought back," a variation of the "talk backs" that students were assigned in English 1102, here a generalized articulation of a meta-cognitive practice helping her "change as I look back on my writing." In addition, Alice works toward making reflection her own as she theorizes about it — "that's something we do in life and not just writing" — in the process seeing it as a life-practice as well as a writing practice. More generally, what we see here is that Alice is developing her own "remixed" model of composing, combining her values with curricular concepts and practices. Not least, reflection was thus more than an after-the-fact activity for Alice; rather, it provided a mechanism for her to understand herself as a learner and prepare for the future whether it was writing or another activity. 35

Alice, however, is also aware of the impact of the study and of the need for more time to integrate what she has learned in English 1102 into her model and 36 practice of writing. On the one hand, she seems to appreciate the study since, in her view, it functions as a follow-up activity extending the class itself, which is particularly valuable as she takes up new writing tasks the next semester:

> I feel as though I forget a lot about a class after I take it. I definitely don't remember everything about my English class, but I feel I remember what will help me the most in my writing and I think that information will stay with me. This study has helped me get more from the class than just taking it and after not thinking about it anymore. The study helped me in a way to remind me to think about what we went over in English as I wrote for my other classes.

On the other hand, Alice understands that she has been unable to use all that was offered in English 1102:

> I feel like I haven't used everything; there were a lot of terms that we went over I don't use and there are some that I do and those are the ones that [the teacher] used the most anyways. I feel like this has helped me remember those that I will use and I feel like this has helped me retain a lot of information and now I have had to write a lot more besides our class and the stuff I gave to you. I was still thinking about what we did in that comp class, so it has really helped me. But I still think I could use a lot more experiences with writing papers and getting more from a college class, I mean like getting away from the FCAT sound. I wrote like that until 10th grade.

Alice hopes that she has identified the best terms from the class and thinks 37 that she has, given that "those are the ones that the teacher used the most," which repetition was, as she observes, one reason she probably remembers them. But because of the interviews, she "was still thinking about what we did in the comp class": she is continuing to think about the terms more intentionally than she might have had no interviews taken place. But as important, Alice believes that she "could use a lot more experiences with writing papers and getting more from a college class," here pointing to the need to get "away from the FCAT." Given that Alice "wrote like that until 10th grade," "getting away from the FCAT sound" is more difficult than it might first appear.

In sum, there is much to learn from Alice's experience. Through her integra- 38 tion of her own values, prior knowledge, and new knowledge and practice, we see how students develop a remix model of composing, one that may change over time but that remains a remix. We see as well how a composing practice like reflection can be generalized into a larger philosophy of reflection, one more characteristic of expertise. And, not least, we see, through a student's observations, how a term that we see as a single concept functions more largely, as a meta-concept, and we see as well how hard it can be to remix prior knowledge, especially when that prior knowledge is nearly deterministic in its application and impact.[6]

CRITICAL INCIDENTS: MOTIVATING NEW CONCEPTIONS AND PRACTICES OF COMPOSING

Often students, both in first-year composition and in other writing situations, 39 encounter a version of what's called, in fields ranging from air traffic control and surgery to teaching, a "critical incident": a situation where efforts either do not succeed at all or succeed only minimally. What we have found is that writing students also encounter critical incidents, and some students can be willing or able to let go of prior knowledge as they re-think what they have learned, revise their model and/or conception of writing, and write anew. In other words, the set-backs motivated by critical incidents can provide the opportunity for conceptual breakthroughs, as we shall see in the case of Rick.

The surgeon Atul Gawande describes critical incidents as they occur in sur- 40 gery and how they are later understood in his account of medical practice titled *Complications*. Surgical practice, like air traffic control, routinely and intentionally engages practitioners in a collective reviewing of what went wrong—in surgery, operations where the patient died or whose outcome was negative in other ways; in air traffic control, missteps large (e.g., a crash) and small (e.g., a near miss)—in the belief that such a review can reduce error and thus enhance practice. Accordingly, hospital-based surgeons meet weekly for the Morbidity and Mortality Conference, the M&M for short, its purpose both to reduce the incidence of mistakes and to make knowledge. As Gawande explains,

> There is one place, however, where doctors can talk candidly about their mistakes, if not with the patients, then at least with one another. It is called the Morbidity and Mortality Conference—or, more simply, M & M—and it takes place, usually once a week, at nearly every academic hospital in the country. . . . Surgeons, in particular, take the M & M seriously. Here they can gather behind closed doors to review the mistakes, untoward events, and deaths that occurred on their watch, determine responsibility, and figure out what to do differently next time. (57–58)

The protocol for the M&M never varies. The physician in charge speaks for the 41 entire team, even if she or he wasn't present at the event under inquiry. In other words, a resident might have handled the case, but the person responsible—called, often ironically, the attending physician—speaks. First presented is information about the case: age of patient, reason for surgery, progress of surgery. Next the surgeon outlines what happened, focusing on the error in question; that there was an error is not in question, so the point is to see if that error might have been discerned more readily and thus to have produced a positive outcome. The surgeon provides an analysis and responds to questions, continuing to act as a spokesperson for the entire medical team. The doctor members of the team, regardless of rank, are all included but do not speak; the other members of the medical team, including nurses and technicians, are excluded, as are patients. The presentation concludes with a directive about how such prototypic cases should be handled in the future, and it's worth noting that, collectively, the results of the M&Ms have reduced error.

Several assumptions undergird this community of practice, in particular 42 assumptions at odds with those of compositionists. We long ago gave up a focus on error, for example, in favor of the construction of a social text. Likewise, we might find it surprising that the M&M is so focused on what went wrong when just as much might be learned by what went right, especially in spite of the odds, for instance, on the young child with a heart defect who surprises by making it through surgery. Still, the practice of review in light of a critical incident suggests that even experts can revise their models when prompted to do so.

This is exactly what happened to Rick, a first-year student with an affection 43 for all things scientific, who experienced a misfit between his prior knowledge and new writing tasks as he entered English 1102. Rick identified as a novice writer in this class, in part because he was not invested in writing apart from its role in science. A physics and astrophysics major, he was already working on a faculty research project in the physics laboratory and was planning a research career in his major area. He professed:

> I am a physics major so I really like writing about things I think people
> should know about that is going on in the world of science. Sometimes it's
> a challenge to get my ideas across to somebody that is not a science or math
> type, but I enjoy teaching people about physics and the world around them.

Rick credited multiple previous experiences for his understanding of writing, including his other high school and college courses; in addition, he mentioned watching YouTube videos of famous physicists lecturing and reading Einstein's work. He also believed that reading scientific materials had contributed to his success in writing scientific texts: "I think I write well in my science lab reports because I have read so many lectures and reports that I can just kind of copy their style into my writing."[7]

Rick's combination of prior knowledge and motivation, however, didn't prove 44 sufficient when he began the research project in English 1102. He chose a topic with which he was not only familiar but also passionate, quantum mechanics, his aim to communicate the ways in which quantum mechanics benefits society. He therefore approached the research as an opportunity to share what he knew with others, rather than as inquiry into a topic and discovery of what might be significant. He also had difficulty making the information clear in his essay, which he understood as a rhetorical task: "The biggest challenge was making sure the language and content was easy enough for someone who is not a physics major to understand. It took a long time to explain it in simple terms, and I didn't want to talk down to the audience." In this context, Rick understood the challenge of expressing the significance of his findings to his audience, which he determined was fellow college students. But the draft he shared with his peers was confusing to them, not because of the language or information, as Rick had anticipated, but instead because of uncertainty about key points of the essay and about what they as readers were being asked to do with this information.

As a self-identified novice, however, Rick reported that this experience taught   45 him a valuable lesson about audience. "I tried to make it simple so . . . my class-mates would understand it, but that just ended up messing up my paper, focusing more on the topic than on the research, which is what mattered. I explained too much instead of making it matter to them." Still, when the projects were returned, he admitted his surprise at the evaluation of the essay but was not willing to entertain the idea that his bias or insider knowledge about quantum mechanics had prevented his inquiry-based research:

> After everyone got their papers back, I noticed that our grades were based more on following the traditional conventions of a research paper, and I didn't follow those as well as I could have. I don't really see the importance of following specific genre conventions perfectly.

In the next semester, however, these issues of genre and audience came   46 together in a critical incident for Rick as he wrote his first lab report for chemistry. Ironically, Rick was particularly excited about this writing because, unlike the writing he had composed in English 1102, this was science writing: a lab report. But as it turned out, it was a lab report with a twist: the instructor specified that the report have a conclusion to it that would link it to "everyday life":

> We had to explain something interesting about the lab and how that relates to everyday life. I would say it is almost identical to the normal introduction one would write for a paper, trying to grab the reader's attention, while at the same time exploring what you will be talking about.

Aware of genre conventions and yet in spite of these directions for modifica-   47 tion, Rick wrote a standard lab report. In fact, in his highlighting of the data, he made it *more* lab-report-like rather than less: "I tried to have my lab report stick out from the others with better explanations of the data and the experiment." The chemistry instructor noticed, and not favorably: Rick's score was low, and he was more than disappointed. Eager to write science, he got a lower grade than he did on his work in English 1102, and it wasn't because he didn't know the content; it was because he hadn't followed directions for writing.

This episode constituted a critical incident for Rick. Dismayed, he went to   48
talk to the teacher about the score; she explained that he indeed needed to write
the lab report not as the genre might strictly require, but as she had adapted
it. Chastened, he did so in all the next assigned lab reports, and to good effect:
"My lab reports were getting all the available points and they were solid too,
very concise and factual but the conclusions used a lot of good reflection in
them to show that the experiments have implications on our lives." The ability
to adapt to teacher directions in order to get a higher grade, as is common for
savvy students, doesn't in and of itself constitute a critical incident; what makes
it so here is Rick's response *and* the re-seeing that Rick engages in afterwards. Put
differently, he begins to see writing as synthetic and genres as flexible, and in the
process, he begins to develop a more capacious conception of writing, based in
part on his tracing similarities and differences across his own writing tasks past
and present.

This re-seeing operates at several units of analysis. On the first level, Rick   49
articulates a new appreciation for the value of the assignment, especially the new
conclusion, and the ways he is able to theorize it: "I did better on the conclusions
when I started to think about the discourse community and what is expected
in it. I remembered that from English 1102, that discourse community dictates
how you write, so I thought about it." On another level, while Rick maintains
that the genres were different in the lab courses than in 1102, as in fact they are,
he is able to map similarities across them:

> One similarity would be after reading an article in 1102 and writing a cri-
> tique where we had to think about the article and what it meant. This is very
> similar to what we do in science: we read data and then try to explain what it
> means and how it came about. This seems to be fundamental to the under-
> standing of anything really, and is done in almost every class.

This theorizing, of course, came after the fact of the critical incident, and one   50
might make the argument that such theorizing is just a way of coming to terms
with meeting the teacher's directions. But as the term progressed, Rick was able
to use his new understanding of writing—located in discourse communities *and*
genres and keyed to reading data and explaining them—as a way to frame one
of his new assignments, a poster assignment. His analysis of how to approach
it involved his taking the terms from English 1102 and using them to frame
the new task:

> I have this poster I had to create for my chemistry class, which tells me what
> genre I have to use, and so I know how to write it, because a poster should
> be organized a certain way and look a certain way and it is written to a
> specific audience in a scientific way. I wouldn't write it the same way I would
> write a research essay – I'm presenting the key points about this chemistry

project, not writing a lot of paragraphs that include what other people say about it or whatever. The poster is just the highlights with illustrations, but it is right for its audience. It wasn't until I was making the poster that I realized I was thinking about the context I would present it in, which is like rhetorical situation, and that it was a genre. So I thought about those things and I think it helped. My poster was awesome.

Here we see Rick's thinking across tasks, genres, and discourse communities as he maps both similarities and differences across them. Moreover, as he creates the chemistry poster, he draws on new prior knowledge, that prior knowledge he developed in his English 1102 class, this a rhetorical knowledge keyed to three features of rhetorical situations generally: (1) an understanding of the genre in which he was composing and presenting, (2) the audience to whom he was presenting, and (3) the context in which they would receive his work. Despite the fact that this chemistry poster assignment was the first time he had composed in this genre, he was successful at creating it, at least in part because he drew on his prior knowledge in a useful way, one that allowed him to see where similarities provided a bridge and differences a point of articulation.[8]

All this, of course, is not to say that Rick is an expert, but as many scholars in composition, including Sommers and Saltz, and Beaufort, as well as psychologists like Marcia Baxter-Magolda argue, students need the opportunity to be novices in order to develop toward expertise. This is exactly what works for Rick when the challenges in college writing, in both English 1102 and more particularly in chemistry, encourage him to think of himself as a novice and to take up new concepts of writing and new practices. Moreover, the critical incident prompts Rick to develop a more capacious understanding of writing, one in which genre is flexible and the making of knowledge includes application. Likewise, this new understanding of writing provides him with a framework that he can use as he navigates new contexts and writing tasks, as he does with the chemistry poster.

If indeed some college students are, at least at the beginning of their postsecondary career, boundary guarders, and others boundary crossers, and if we want to continue using metaphors of travel to describe the experience of college writers, then we might say that Rick has moved beyond boundary crossing: as a college writer, he has taken up residence.

CONCLUDING THOUGHTS

Our purpose in this article is both to elaborate more fully students' uses of prior knowledge and to document how such uses can detract from or contribute to efficacy in student writing. As important, this analysis puts a face on what transfer in composition as "an active, dynamic process" looks like: it shows students working with such prior knowledge in order to respond to new situations and to create their own new models of writing. As documented here, both in the research literature and in the students' own words, students are likely to begin college with absent prior knowledge, particularly in terms of conceptions of writing and models of non-fiction texts. Once in college, students tap their prior knowledge in one of three ways. In cases like Eugene's, students work within an assemblage model, grafting pieces of new information—often key terms or process strategies—onto prior understandings of writing that serve as a foundation to which they frequently return. Other students, like Alice, work within a remix model, blending elements of both prior knowledge and new knowledge with personal values into a revised model of writing. And still other students, like Rick, use a writing setback, what we call a critical incident, as a prompt to re-theorize writing and to practice composing in new ways.

The prototype presented here is a basic outline that we hope to continue devel- 55 oping; we also think it will be helpful for both teaching and research. Teachers, for example, may want to ask students about their absent prior knowledge and invite them to participate in creating a knowledge filling that absence. Put differently, if students understand that there is an absence of knowledge that they will need—a perception which many of them don't seem to share—they may be more motivated to take up a challenge that heretofore they have not understood. Likewise, explaining remix as a way of integrating old and new, personal and academic knowledge and experience into a revised conception and practice of composing for college may provide a mechanism to help students understand how writing development, from novice to expertise, works and, again, how they participate in such development. Last but not least, students might be alerted to writing situations that qualify as critical incidents; working with experiences like Rick's, they may begin to understand their own setbacks as opportunities. Indeed, we think that collecting experiences like Rick's (of course, with student permissions) to share and consider with students may be the most helpful exercise of all.

There is more research on student uptake of prior knowledge to conduct as 56 well, as a quick review of Rick's experience suggests. The critical incident motivates Rick to re-think writing, as we saw, but it's also so that Rick is a science major and, as he told us, science not only thrives on error, but also progresses on the basis of error. Given his intellectual interests, Rick was especially receptive to a setback, especially—and it's worth noting this—when it occurred in his preferred field, science. For one thing, Rick identifies as a scientist, so he is motivated to do well. For another and more generally, failure in the context of science is critical to success. Without such a context, or even an understanding of the context as astute as Rick's, other students may look upon such a setback as a personal failure (and understandably so), which view can prompt not a re-thinking, but rather resistance. In other words, we need to explore what difference a student's major, and the intellectual tradition it represents, makes in a student's use of prior knowledge. Likewise, we need to explore other instantiations of the assemblage model of prior knowledge uptake as well as differentiations in the remix model. And we need to explore the relationship between these differentiations and efficacy: surely some are more efficacious than others. And, not least, we need to explore further what happens to those students, like Rick, who through critical incidents begin to take up residence as college composers.

Notes

1. In this article, we draw on two studies of transfer, both connected to a Teaching for Transfer composition curriculum for first-year students: Liane Robertson's "The Significance of Course Content in the Transfer of Writing Knowledge from First-Year Composition to other Academic Writing Contexts" and Kara Taczak's "Connecting the Dots: Does Reflection Foster Transfer?"

2. A more robust picture includes an additional dimension of prior knowledge: what we call a point of departure. We theorize that students make progress, or not, in part relative to their past performances as writers—as represented in external benchmarks like grades and test scores. See *Writing Across Contexts: Transfer, Composition, and Cultures of Writing*.

3. The travel metaphor in composition has been variously used and critiqued: for the former, see Gregory Clark; for the latter, see Nedra Reynolds. Regarding the use of such a metaphor in the transfer literature in college composition, it seems first to have been used by McCarthy in her reference to students in strange lands. Based on this usage and on our own studies, we theorize that what students bring with them to college, by way of prior knowledge, is a passport that functions as something of a guide. As important, when students use the guide to reflect back rather than to cast forward, it tends to replicate the past rather than to guide for the future, and in that sense, Reynolds's observations about many students replicating the old in the new are astute. See our *Writing Across Contexts: Transfer, Composition, and Cultures of Writing*, forthcoming.

4. According to *How People Learn*, prior knowledge can function in three ways, as we have seen. But when the prior knowledge is a misfit, it may be because the "correct" prior knowledge, or knowledge that is more related, isn't available, which leads us to conceptualize absent prior knowledge. For a similar argument in a very different context, materials science, see Krause et al.

5. Alice's interest in "being direct," of course, may be a more specific description of her voice, whose value she emphasized upon entering English 1102.

6. Ironically, the function of such tests, according to testing advocates, is to help writers develop; here the FCAT seems to have mis-shaped rather than to have helped, as Alice laments.

7. Rick's sense of the influence of his reading on his conception of text, of course, is the point made above about students' reading practices.

8. This ability to read across patterns, discerning similarities and differences, that we see Rick engaging in, is a signature practice defining expertise, according to *How People Learn*.

Works Cited

Applebee, Arthur, and Judith Langer. "What's Happening in the Teaching of Writing?" *English Journal* 98.5 (2009): 18–28. Print.

——. "A Snapshot of Writing Instruction in Middle Schools and High Schools." *English Journal* 100.6 (2011): 14–27. Print.

Baxter-Magolda, Marcia B. *Making Their Own Way: Narratives for Transforming Higher Education to Promote Self-Development.* Sterling, VA: Stylus, 2001. Print.

Beaufort, Anne. *College Writing and Beyond: A New Framework for University Writing Instruction.* Logan: Utah State UP, 2007. Print.

Bergmann, Linda S., and Janet S. Zepernick. "Disciplinarity and Transference: Students' Perceptions of Learning to Write." *WPA: Writing Program Administration* 31.1/2 (2007): 124–49. Print.

Beyer, Catharine Hoffman, Andrew T. Fisher, and Gerald M. Gillmore. *Inside the Undergraduate Experience, the University of Washington's Study of Undergraduate Learning.* Bolton, MA: Anker Publishing, 2007. Print.

Bird, Barbara. "Writing about Writing as the Heart of a Writing Studies Approach to FYC: Response to Douglas Downs and Elizabeth Wardle, 'Teaching about Writing/Righting Misconceptions' and to Libby Miles et al., 'Thinking Vertically'." *College Composition and Communication* 60.1 (2008): 165–71. Print.

Bransford, John D., James W. Pellegrino, and M. Suzanne Donovan, eds. *How People Learn: Brain, Mind, Experience, and School: Expanded Edition.* Washington, DC: National Academies P, 2000. Print.

Britton, James, et al. *The Development of Writing Abilities (11–18),* London: MacMillan Education, 1975. Print.

Carter, Michael. "The Idea of Expertise: An Exploration of Cognitive and Social Dimensions of Writing." *College Composition and Communication* 41.3 (1990): 265–86. Print.

Clark, Gregory. "Writing as Travel, or Rhetoric on the Road." *College Composition and Communication* 49.1 (1998): 9–23. Print.

Detterman, Douglas K., and Robert J. Sternberg, eds. *Transfer on Trial: Intelligence, Cognition, and Instruction.* New Jersey: Ablex, 1993. Print.

Dew, Debra. "Language Matters: Rhetoric and Writing I as Content Course." *WPA: Writing Program Administration* 26.3 (2003): 87–104. Print.

Downs, Douglas, and Elizabeth Wardle. "Teaching about Writing, Righting Misconceptions: (Re) Envisioning 'First-Year Composition' as Introduction to Writing Studies." *College Composition and Communication* 58.4 (2007): 552–84. Print.

Fulkerson, Richard. "Summary and Critique: Composition at the Turn of the Twenty-first Century." *College Composition and Communication* 56.4 (2005): 654–87. Print.

Gawande, Atul. *Complications: A Surgeon's Notes on an Imperfect Science.* New York: Holt/Picador, 2002. Print.

Jarratt, Susan, et al. "Pedagogical Memory and the Transferability of Writing Knowledge: an Interview-Based Study of Juniors and Seniors at a Research University." *Writing Research Across Borders Conference.* University of California Santa Barbara. 22 Feb 2008. Presentation.

Krause, Steve, et al. "The Role of Prior Knowledge on the Origin and Repair of Misconceptions in an Introductory Class on Materials Science and Engineering Materials Science." *Proceedings of the Research in Engineering Education Symposium 2009,* Palm Cove, QLD. Web.

Langer, Judith A., and Arthur N. Applebee. *How Writing Shapes Thinking: A Study of Teaching and Learning.* Urbana, IL: NCTE P, 1987. Print.

Lenhart, Amanda, et al. *Writing, Technology, and Teens.* Washington, D.C.: Pew Internet and American Life Project, April 2008. Web. 12 Jan 2012.

McCarthy, Lucille. "A Stranger in Strange Lands: A College Student Writing across the Curriculum." *Research in the Teaching of English* 21.3 (1987): 233–65. Print.

Perkins, David N., and Gavriel Salomon. "Transfer of Learning." *International Encyclopedia of Education.* 2nd ed. Oxford: Pergamon P, 1992. 2–13. Print.

Prather, Dirk C. "Trial and Error versus Errorless Learning: Training, Transfer, and Stress." *The American Journal of Psychology* 84.3 (1971): 377–86. Print.

Reiff, Mary Jo, and Anis Bawarshi. "Tracing Discursive Resources: How Students Use Prior Genre Knowledge to Negotiate New Writing Contexts in First-Year Composition." *Written Communication* 28.3 (2011): 312–37. Print.

Reynolds, Nedra. *Geographies of Writing: Inhabiting Places and Encountering Difference.* Southern Illinois UP, 2004. Print.

Robertson, Liane. "The Significance of Course Content in the Transfer of Writing Knowledge from First-Year Composition to other Academic Writing Contexts." Diss. Florida State University, 2011. Print.

Robinson, Tracy Ann, and Vicki Tolar Burton. "The Writer's Personal Profile: Student Self Assessment and Goal Setting at Start of Term." *Across the Disciplines* 6 (Dec 2009). Web. 12 Jan 2012.

Russell, David R. "Rethinking Genre and Society: An Activity Theory Analysis." *Written Communication* 14.4 (1997): 504–54. Print.

Russell, David R., and Arturo Yañez. "'Big Picture People Rarely Become Historians': Genre Systems and the Contradictions of General Education." *Writing Selves/Writing Societies: Research From Activity Perspectives.* Ed. Charles Bazerman and David R. Russell. Fort Collins, CO: WAC Clearinghouse and Mind, Culture and Activity, 2002. Web. 12 Jan 2012.

Scherff, Lisa, and Carolyn Piazza. "The More Things Change, the More They Stay the Same: A Survey of High School Students' Writing Experiences." *Research in the Teaching of English* 39.3 (2005): 271–304. Print.

Slomp, David H., and M. Elizabeth Sargent. "Responses to Responses: Douglas Downs and Elizabeth Wardle's 'Teaching about Writing, Righting Misconceptions.'" *College Composition and Communication* 60.3 (2009): 595–96. Print.

Sommers, Nancy, and Laura Saltz. "The Novice as Expert: Writing the Freshman Year." *College Composition and Communication* 56.1 (2004): 124–49. Print.

Taczak, Kara. "Connecting the Dots: Does Reflection Foster Transfer?" Diss. Florida State University, 2011. Print.

Thorndike, E. L., and R. S. Woodworth. "The Influence of Improvement in One Mental Function upon the Efficiency of Other Functions." *Psychological Review* 8 (1901): 247–61. Print.

Vander Lei, Elizabeth, and Bonnie Lenore Kyburz, eds. *Negotiating Religious Faith in the Composition Classroom.* Portsmouth: Boynton/Cook, 2005. Print.

Wardle, Elizabeth. "Understanding 'Transfer' from FYC: Preliminary Results of a Longitudinal Study." *WPA: Writing Program Administration* 31.1–2 (2007), 65–85. Print.

Wikipedia contributors. "William Shakespeare." *Wikipedia, The Free Encyclopedia.* 4 Jan. 2012. Web. 12 Jan. 2012.

Yancey, Kathleen Blake, Ed. *Delivering College Composition: The Fifth Canon.* Portsmouth: Boynton/Cook, 2006. Print.

——. "Re-designing Graduate Education in Composition and Rhetoric: The Use of Remix as Concept, Material, and Method." *Computers and Composition* 26.1 (2009): 4–12. Print.

——, Laine Robertson, and Kara Taczak. *Writing Across Contexts: Transfer, Composition, and Cultures of Writing.* Utah State UP, 2014.

- -

Questions for Discussion and Journaling

1. Drawing on what you learned in this article, write a definition of *transfer*.

2. What are the three subsets of transfer that Perkins and Salomon offered? Can you think of an example for each of these kinds of transfer in your own experience? For example, can you think of a time when you mindfully drew on prior knowledge to complete a new task?

3. The authors here draw on research to suggest that most entering college students lack knowledge about key writing concepts and how to write nonfiction texts for anything other than taking tests. Think back on your high school writing experience. Do you share this lack of prior knowledge? If not, where did you learn these things? Do you feel there is prior knowledge about writing that you find yourself lacking in college? How can you go about gaining that absent knowledge?

4. Try to explain in your own words what you think Reiff and Bawarshi mean by boundary crossers and boundary guarders. Which do you think you are? Draw on some examples to support your claim about yourself.

5. Explain the three ways (assemblage, remix, critical incident) that students use prior knowledge, according to Robertson et al. You can draw on examples from the three students they describe: Eugene, Alice, and Rick. Which student — and which approach to using prior knowledge about writing — do you think best describes your approach to writing in college so far?

Applying and Exploring Ideas

1. Robertson et al. emphasize the importance of conceptions of writing, which we also have emphasized heavily in this book, especially in Chapter 1. Try to write 2–3 paragraphs in which you explain what you think writing is. If you completed the major writing assignment at the end of Chapter 1, compare what you wrote here with what you wrote there, and see if your ideas have changed.

2. With your classmates, divide up into groups of three. Bring with you a text that you have written at any point in recent memory where something went wrong or did not succeed. As a group, conduct your own "M&M" or critical incident review. First, present information about the case — what you were writing, for whom, under what circumstances. Second, explain what happened, focusing

specifically on what went wrong or what mistakes you made. Then, take questions from your two group members. Finally, as a group, consider what you might have done to see the problem or mistake sooner, and how you might have avoided it. Once all of you have completed your presentation and analysis, together write a 1–2 page group reflection on what you just did together. Was it helpful? Was it uncomfortable? Did you learn anything? How did it make you feel to focus on the negative? Is there anything from this critical incident review that you would like to do in the future? How can you see your apparent setbacks as opportunities?

- -

META MOMENT   Given what you've read here, explain how mindfulness can help students more usefully draw on their prior knowledge. How might the "meta moments" assigned in this book after each reading assist with mindfulness?

- -

I Stand Here Writing

NANCY SOMMERS

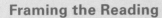

Nancy Sommers teaches and researches at Harvard University, where she has served a number of roles over nearly three decades, including directing Harvard's Expository Writing Program and several other programs, and launching the Harvard Study of Undergraduate Writing, which tracked four hundred students throughout their college experience in order to investigate what they were writing and how.

Throughout her career, Sommers's work has focused on the development of high school and college students' literacies and writing. She has been a significant advocate and practitioner of empirical research on writing: interviewing writers directly, getting them to write about writing, and studying what they say, and collecting (often at great expense) and reading the writing they actually produce. Her work has been of tremendous value to other writing researchers. In this piece, however, Sommers works more reflectively, examining her own practices as a reader, thinker, and writer in order to consider the role of reading and "sources" in **invention** — how writers come up with what to say in their writing.

As you've already read in this chapter, our prior experiences, sense of self, literacy sponsors, language practices, and much more all impact who we are as writers. Here Sommers directly looks at how prior experience comes to bear on how we come up with things to write. If you hadn't already stopped to think about it, this question about where our words come from seems to be an important one for writers — so important (and complicated) that many researchers can study that question from many angles for many years without fully answering it. The topic of how we write, and where our ideas come from, is taken up again in Chapter 5.

Sommers, Nancy. "I Stand Here Writing." *College English*, vol. 55, no. 4, Apr. 1993, pp. 420–28.

Getting Ready to Read

Before you read, do at least one of the following activities:

- Consider where your ideas come from when you write.
- Consider whether as you write you are aware of how who you are and what you've experienced impact what you are thinking about and doing?

As you read, consider the following questions:

- Is Sommers discussing any familiar ideas? What ideas are new to you? Is she looking in a new or different way at some ideas you've thought about before?

I STAND IN MY KITCHEN, wiping the cardamom, coriander, and cayenne 1
off my fingers. My head is abuzz with words, with bits and pieces of conversation. I hear a phrase I have read recently, something about "a radical loss of certainty." But, I wonder, how did the sentence begin? I search the air for the rest of the sentence, can't find it, shake some more cardamom, and a bit of coriander. Then, by some play of mind, I am back home again in Indiana with my family, sitting around the kitchen table. Two people are talking, and there are three opinions; three people are talking, and there are six opinions. Opinions grow exponentially. I fight my way back to that sentence. Writing, that's how it begins: "Writing is a radical loss of certainty." (Or is it uncertainty?) It isn't so great for the chicken when all these voices start showing up, with all these sentences hanging in mid-air, but the voices keep me company. I am a writer, not a cook, and the truth is I don't care much about the chicken. Stories beget stories. Writing emerges from writing.

The truth. Has truth anything to do with the facts? All I know is that no mat- 2
ter how many facts I might clutter my life with, I am as bound to the primordial drama of my family as the earth is to the sun. This year my father, the son of a severe Prussian matriarch, watched me indulge my daughters, and announced to me that he wished I had been his mother. This year, my thirty-ninth, my last year to be thirty-something, my mother—who has a touch of magic, who can walk into the middle of a field of millions of clovers and find the *one* with four leaves—has begun to think I need help. She sends me cards monthly with four-leaf clovers taped inside. Two words neatly printed in capital letters—GOOD LUCK!! I look at these clovers and hear Reynolds Price's words: "Nobody under forty can believe how nearly everything's inherited." I wonder what my mother knows, what she is trying to tell me about the facts of my life.

When I was in high school studying French, laboring to conjugate verbs, the 3
numerous four-leaf clovers my mother had carefully pressed inside her French dictionary made me imagine her in a field of clovers lyrically conjugating verbs

of love. This is the only romantic image I have of my mother, a shy and conservative woman whose own mother died when she was five, whose grandparents were killed by the Nazis, who fled Germany at age thirteen with her father and sister. Despite the sheer facts of her life, despite the accumulation of grim knowable data, the truth is my mother is an optimistic person. She has the curious capacity always to be looking for luck, putting her faith in four-leaf clovers, ladybugs, pennies, and other amulets of fortune. She has a vision different from mine, one the facts alone can't explain. I, her daughter, was left, for a long time, seeing only the ironies; they were my defense against the facts of my life.

In this world of my inheritance in which daughters can become their fathers' 4 mothers and mothers know their daughters are entering into a world where only sheer good luck will guide them, I hear from my own daughters that I am not in tune with their worlds, that I am just like a 50s mom, that they are 90s children, and I should stop acting so primitive. My children laugh uproariously at my autograph book, a 1959 artifact they unearthed in the basement of my parents' home. "Never kiss by the garden gate. Love is blind, but the neighbors ain't," wrote one friend. And my best friend, who introduced herself to me on the first day of first grade, looking me straight in the eye—and whispering through her crooked little teeth "the Jews killed Jesus"—wrote in this autograph book: "Mary had a little lamb. Her father shot it dead. Now she carries it to school between two slices of bread."

My ten-year-old daughter, Rachel, writes notes to me in hieroglyphics and 5 tapes signs on the refrigerator in Urdu. "Salaam Namma Man Rachaal Ast" reads one sign. Simply translated it means "Hello, my name is Rachel." Alex, my seven-year-old daughter, writes me lists, new lists each month, visibly reminding me of the many things I need to buy or do for her. This month's list includes a little refrigerator filled with Coke and candy; ears pierced; a new toilet; neon nail polish and *real* adult make-up.

How do I look at these facts? How do I embrace these experiences, these 6 texts of my life, and translate them into ideas? How do I make sense of them and the conversations they engender in my head? I look at Alex's list and wonder what kind of feminist daughter I am raising whose deepest desires include neon nail polish and *real* adult make-up. Looking at her lists a different way, I wonder if this second child of mine is asking me for something larger, something more permanent and real than adult make-up. Maybe I got that sentence wrong. Maybe it is that "Love (as well as writing) involves a radical loss of certainty."

Love is blind, but the neighbors ain't. Mary's father shot her little lamb dead, 7 and now she carries it to school between two slices of bread. I hear these rhymes today, and they don't say to me what they say to my daughters. They don't seem so innocent. I hear them and think about the ways in which my neighbors in Indiana could only see my family as Jews from Germany, exotic strangers who ate tongue, outsiders who didn't celebrate Christmas. I wonder if my daughter Rachel needs to tell me her name in Urdu because she thinks we don't share a common language. These sources change meaning when I ask the questions in a different way. They introduce new ironies, new questions.

I want to understand these living, breathing, primary sources all around me. 8 I want to be, in Henry James's words, "a person upon whom nothing is lost." These sources speak to me of love and loss, of memory and desire, of the ways in which we come to understand something through difference and opposition. Two years ago I learned the word *segue* from one of my students. At first the word seemed peculiar. Segue sounded like something you did only on the Los Angeles freeway. Now I hear that word everywhere, and I have begun using it. I want to know how to segue from one idea to the next, from one thought to the fragment lying beside it. But the connections don't always come with four-leaf clovers and the words GOOD LUCK neatly printed beside them.

My academic need to find connections sends me to the library. There are 9 eleven million books in my University's libraries. Certainly these sanctioned voices, these authorities, these published sources can help me find the connections. Someone, probably some three thousand someones, has studied what it is like to be the child of survivors. Someone has written a manual on how the granddaughter of a severe Prussian matriarch and the daughter of a collector of amulets ought to raise feminist daughters. I want to walk into the fields of writing, into those eleven million books, and find the one book that will explain it all. But I've learned to expect less from such sources. They seldom have the answers. And the answers they do have reveal themselves to me at the most unexpected times. I have been led astray more than once while searching books for the truth.

> *I want to walk into the fields of writing, into those eleven million books, and find the one book that will explain it all. But I've learned to expect less from such sources. They seldom have the answers.*

Once I learned a lesson about borrowing someone else's words and losing 10 my own.

I was fourteen, light years away from thirty-something. High school debate 11 teams across the nation were arguing the pros and cons of the United States Military Aid Policy. It all came back to me as I listened to the news of the Persian Gulf War, as I listened to Stormin' Norman giving his morning briefings, an eerie resonance, all our arguments, the millions of combative words—sorties— fired back and forth. In my first practice debate, not having had enough time to assemble my own sources, I borrowed quote cards from my teammates. I attempted to bolster my position that the U.S. should limit its military aid by reading a quote in my best debate style: "W. W. Rostow says: 'We should not give military aid to India because it will exacerbate endemic rivalries.'"

Under cross-examination, my nemesis, Bobby Rosenfeld, the neighbor kid,   12
who always knew the right answers, began firing a series of questions at me without stopping to let me answer:

"Nancy, can you tell me who W. W. Rostow is? And can you tell me why he   13
might say this? Nancy, can you tell me what 'exacerbate' means? Can you tell
me what 'endemic rivalries' are? And exactly what does it mean to 'exacerbate
endemic rivalries'?"

I didn't know. I simply did not know who W. W. Rostow was, why he might   14
have said that, what "exacerbate" meant, or what an "endemic rivalry" was.
Millions of four-leaf clovers couldn't have helped
me. I might as well have been speaking Urdu. I
didn't know who my source was, the context of
the source, nor the literal meaning of the words I
had read. Borrowing words from authorities had
left me without any words of my own.

> Borrowing words from authorities had left me without words of my own.

My debate partner and I went on that year to   15
win the Indiana state championship and to place third in the nationals. Bobby
Rosenfeld never cross-examined me again, but for twenty years he has appeared
in my dreams. I am not certain why I would dream so frequently about this
scrawny kid whom I despised. I think, though, that he became for me what the
Sea Dyak tribe of Borneo calls a *ngarong*, a dream guide, someone guiding me to
understanding. In this case, Bobby guided me to understand the endemic rivalries
within myself. The last time Bobby appeared in a dream he had become a woman.

I learned a more valuable lesson about sources as a college senior. I was the   16
kind of student who loved words, words out of context, words that swirled
around inside my mouth, words like *exacerbate, undulating, lugubrious,* and
zeugma. "She stained her honour or her new brocade," wrote Alexander Pope. I
would try to write zeugmas whenever I could, exacerbating my already lugubrious prose. Within the English department, I was known more for my long hair,
untamed and untranslatable, and for my long distance bicycle rides than for my
scholarship.

For my senior thesis, I picked Emerson's essay "Eloquence." Harrison   17
Hayford, my advisor, suggested that I might just get off my bicycle, get lost in
the library, and read all of Emerson's essays, journals, letters. I had picked one
of Emerson's least distinguished essays, an essay that the critics mentioned only
in passing, and if I were not entirely on my own, I had at least carved out new
territory for myself.

I spent weeks in the library reading Emerson's journals, reading newspa-   18
per accounts from Rockford and Peoria, Illinois, where he had first delivered
"Eloquence" as a speech. Emerson stood at the podium, the wind blowing his
papers hither and yon, calmly picking them up, and proceeding to read page 8

followed by page 3, followed by page 6, followed by page 2. No one seemed to know the difference. Emerson's Midwestern audience was overwhelmed by this strange man from Concord, Massachusetts, this eloquent stranger whose unit of expression was the sentence.

As I sat in the library, wearing my QUESTION AUTHORITY T-shirt, I 19 could admire this man who delivered his Divinity School Address in 1838, speaking words so repugnant to the genteel people of Cambridge that it was almost thirty years before Harvard felt safe having him around again. I could understand the Midwestern audience's awe and adulation as they listened but didn't quite comprehend Emerson's stunning oratory. I had joined the debate team not to argue the U.S. Military Aid Policy, but to learn how to be an orator who could stun audiences, to learn a personal eloquence I could never learn at home. Perhaps only children of immigrant parents can understand the embarrassing moments of inarticulateness, the missed connections that come from learning to speak a language from parents who claim a different mother tongue.

As an undergraduate, I wanted to free myself from that mother tongue. Four- 20 leaf clovers and amulets of oppression weighed heavy on my mind, and I could see no connection whatsoever between those facts of my life and the untranslatable side of myself that set me in opposition to authority. And then along came Emerson. Like his Midwest audience, I didn't care about having him whole. I liked the promise and the rhapsodic freedom I found in his sentences, in his invitation to seize life as our dictionary, to believe that "Life was not something to be learned but to be lived." I loved his insistence that "the one thing of value is the active soul." I read that "Books are for the scholar's idle time," and I knew that he had given me permission to explore the world. Going into Emerson was like walking into a revelation; it was the first time I had gone into the texts not looking for a specific answer, and it was the first time the texts gave me the answers I needed. Never mind that I got only part of what Emerson was telling me. I got inspiration, I got insight, and I began to care deeply about my work.

Today I reread the man who set me off on a new road, and I find a different 21 kind of wisdom. Today I reread "The American Scholar," and I don't underline the sentence "Books are for the scholar's idle time." I continue to the next paragraph, underlining the sentence "One must be an inventor to read well." The second sentence doesn't contradict the one I read twenty years ago, but it means more today. I bring more to it, and I know that I can walk into text after text, source after source, and they will give me insight, but not answers. I have learned too that my sources can surprise me. Like my mother, I find myself sometimes surrounded by a field of four-leaf clovers, there for the picking, waiting to see what I can make of them. But I must be an inventor if I am to read those sources well, if I am to imagine the connections.

As I stand in my kitchen, the voices that come to me come by way of a life- 22 time of reading, they come on the waves of life, and they seem to be helping me translate the untranslatable. They come, not at my bidding, but when I least expect them, when I am receptive enough to listen to their voices. They come when I am open.

If I could teach my students one lesson about writing it would be to see 23 themselves as sources, as places from which ideas originate, to see themselves as Emerson's transparent eyeball, all that they have read and experienced—the dictionaries of their lives—circulating through them. I want them to learn how sources thicken, complicate, enlarge writing, but I want them to know too how it is always the writer's voice, vision, and argument that create the new source. I want my students to see that nothing reveals itself straight out, especially the sources all around them. But I know enough by now that this Emersonian ideal can't be passed on in one lesson or even a semester of lessons.

Many of the students who come to my classes have been trained to collect 24 facts; they act as if their primary job is to accumulate enough authorities so that there is no doubt about the "truth" of their thesis. They most often disappear behind the weight and permanence of their borrowed words, moving their pens, mouthing the words of others, allowing sources to speak through them unquestioned, unexamined.

At the outset, many of my students think that personal writing is writing 25 about the death of their grandmother. Academic writing is reporting what Elizabeth Kübler-Ross has written about death and dying. Being personal, I want to show my students, does not mean being autobiographical. Being academic does not mean being remote, distant, imponderable. Being personal means bringing their judgments and interpretation to bear on what they read and write, learning that they never leave themselves behind even when they write academic essays.

Last year, David Gray came into my essay class disappointed about everything. 26 He didn't like the time of the class, didn't like the reading list, didn't seem to like me. Nothing pleased him. "If this is a class on the essay," he asked the first day, "why aren't we reading real essayists like Addison, Steele, and Lamb?" On the second day, after being asked to read Annie Dillard's "Living Like Weasels," David complained that a weasel wasn't a fit subject for an essay. "Writers need big subjects. Look at Melville. He needed a whale for *Moby-Dick*. A weasel— that's nothing but a rodent." And so it continued for a few weeks.

I kept my equanimity in class, but at home I'd tell my family about this 27 kid who kept testing me, seizing me like Dillard's weasel, and not letting go. I secretly wanted him out of my class. But then again, I sensed in him a kindred spirit, someone else who needed to question authority.

I wanted my students to write exploratory essays about education, so I asked 28 them to think of a time when they had learned something, and then a time when they had tried to learn something but couldn't. I wanted them to see what ideas and connections they could find between these two very different experiences and the other essays they were reading for the class. I wanted the various sources to work as catalysts. I wanted my students to find a way to talk back to those other writers. The assigned texts were an odd assortment with few apparent connections. I hoped my students would find the common ground, but also the moments of tension, the contradictions, and the ambiguities in those sources.

David used the assigned texts as a catalyst for his thinking, but as was his 29 way, he went beyond the texts I offered and chose his own. He begins his essay, "Dulcis Est Sapientia," with an account of his high school Latin class, suggesting that he once knew declensions, that he had a knack for conjugations, but has forgotten them. He tells us that if his teacher were to appear suddenly today and demand the perfect subjunctive of *venire*, he would stutter hopelessly.

About that Latin class, David asks, "What is going on here? Did I once know 30 Latin and forget it through disuse? Perhaps I never learned Latin at all. What I learned was a bunch of words which, with the aid of various ending sounds, indicated that Gaius was either a good man delivering messages to the lieutenant or a general who struck camp at the seventh hour. I may have known it once, but I never learned it." The class never gave David the gift of language. There was something awry in the method.

What is learning? That's what David explores in his essay as he moves from his 31 Latin lesson to thinking about surrealist paintings, to thinking about barriers we create, to Plato, to an airplane ride in which he observed a mother teaching her child concepts of color and number, all the time taking his readers along with him on his journey, questioning sources, reflecting, expanding, and enriching his growing sense that learning should stress ideas rather than merely accumulating facts and information.

David draws his essay to a close with an analysis of a joke: A man goes to a 32 cocktail party and gets soused. He approaches his host and asks, "Pardon me, but do lemons whistle?"

The host looks at him oddly and answers, "No, lemons don't whistle." 33

"Oh dear," says the guest, "then I'm afraid I just squeezed your canary into 34 my gin and tonic."

David reflects about the significance of this joke: "One need not be an orni- 35 thologist to get the joke, but one must know that canaries are yellow and that they whistle. . . . What constitutes the joke is a connection made between two things . . . which have absolutely nothing in common except for their yellowness. It would never occur to us to make a comparison between the two, let alone to confuse one with the other. But this is the value of the joke, to force into our consciousness the ideas which we held but never actively considered. . . . This knocking down of barriers between ideas is parallel to the process that occurs in all learning. The barriers that we set . . . suddenly crumble; the boundaries . . . are extended to include other modes of thought." Learning, like joking, David argues, gives us pleasure by satisfying our innate capacity to recognize coherence, to discern patterns and connections.

David's essay, like any essay, does not intend to offer the last word on its subject. 36 The civilizing influence of an essay is that it keeps the conversation going, chronicling an intellectual journey, reflecting conversations with sources. I am confident that when David writes for his philosophy course he won't tell a joke anywhere in his essay. But if the joke—if any of his sources—serves him as a catalyst for his thinking, if he makes connections among the sources that circulate within him, between Plato and surrealism, between Latin lessons and mother-child lessons— the dictionaries of *his* life—then he has learned something valuable about writing.

I say to myself that I don't believe in luck. And yet. Not too long ago Rachel 37 came home speaking with some anxiety about an achievement test that she had to take at school. Wanting to comfort her, I urged her to take my rabbit's foot to school the next day. Always alert to life's ironies, Rachel said, "Sure, Mom, a rabbit's foot will really help me find the answers. And even if it did, how would I know the answer the next time when I didn't have that furry little claw?" The next day, proud of her ease in taking the test, she remained perplexed by the one question that seized her and wouldn't let go. She tried it on me: "Here's the question," she said. "Can you figure out which of these sentences cannot be true?"

(a) We warmed our hands by the fire.

(b) The rain poured in and around the windows.

(c) The wind beckoned us to open the door.

Only in the mind of someone who writes achievement tests, and wants to close the door on the imagination, could the one false sentence be "The wind beckoned us to open the door." Probably to this kind of mind, Emerson's sentence "Life is our dictionary" is also not a true sentence.

But life *is* our dictionary, and that's how we know that the wind can beckon 38 us to open the door. Like Emerson, we let the wind blow our pages hither and yon, forcing us to start in the middle, moving from page 8 to page 2, forward to page 7, moving back and forth in time, losing our certainty.

Like Emerson, I love basic units, the words themselves, words like carda- 39 mom, coriander, words that play around in my head, swirl around in my mouth. The challenge, of course, is not to be a ventriloquist—not to be a mouther of words—but to be open to other voices, untranslatable as they might be. Being open to the unexpected, we can embrace complexities: canaries and lemons, amulets and autograph books, fathers who want their daughters to be their mothers, and daughters who write notes in Urdu—all those odd, unusual conjunctions can come together and speak through us.

The other day, I called my mother and told her about this essay, told her that 40 I had been thinking about the gold bracelet she took with her as one of her few possessions from Germany — a thin gold chain with three amulets: a mushroom, a lady bug, and, of course, a four-leaf clover. Two other charms fell off years ago — she lost one, I the other. I used to worry over the missing links, thinking only of the loss, of what we could never retrieve. When I look at the bracelet now, I think about the Prussian matriarch, my grandmother, and my whole primordial family drama. I think too of Emerson and the pages that blew in the wind and the gaps that seemed not to matter. The bracelet is but one of many sources that intrigues me. Considering them in whatever order they appear, with whatever gaps, I want to see where they will lead me, what they tell me.

With writing and with teaching, as well as with love, we don't know how the 41 sentence will begin and, rarely ever, how it will end. Having the courage to live with uncertainty, ambiguity, even doubt, we can walk into all of those fields of writing, knowing that we will find volumes upon volumes bidding *us* enter. We need only be inventors, we need only give freely and abundantly to the texts, imagining even as we write that we too will be a source from which other readers can draw sustenance.

- -

Questions for Discussion and Journaling

1. How would you state the "problem" that this article addresses? In other words, why is Sommers writing it? What issue is she taking up here, and why?

2. When Sommers says that texts "will give me insight, but not answers" (para. 21), what distinction is she drawing between the two things? In your own experience, have you been encouraged to look at texts as sources of insight or sources of answers? Why do you think this is?

3. Consider Sommers's distinctions among *personal, academic,* and *autobiographical*: "Being personal, I want to show my students, does not mean being autobiographical. Being academic does not mean being remote, distant, imponderable . . ." (para. 25). What's your understanding of the distinctions she's making between these terms? Do you feel like you know how to be "personally academic" or "academically personal" or how to be personal without being autobiographical? How academic does Sommers's piece itself feel to you? Why?

4. In paragraph 23, Sommers starts a new section with the line, "If I could teach my students one lesson about writing it would be to see themselves as sources, as places from which ideas originate, to see themselves as Emerson's transparent eyeball, all that they have read and experienced — the dictionaries of their lives — circulating through them." Do you see yourself like this, as a source of ideas with all that you "have read and experienced . . . circulating" through you? Have any other pieces in this chapter helped you see yourself like this? If you don't see yourself like this, how do you see yourself?

5. Sommers describes reading a text by Emerson at two very different times in her life and finding different lines in the text to be meaningful to her at each time. How have you seen the passage of time affecting what *you* find most meaningful in the things you read?

6. Early in the essay, we get Sommers's account of "a lesson about borrowing someone else's words and losing my own" (para. 10). Has this ever happened to you? If you read Young's piece in this chapter (p. 148), can you relate Sommers's claim to his?

7. If you read Robertson et al.'s piece in this chapter (p. 184), what resonances did you encounter between their thinking about *prior knowledge* and Sommers's account of her changing ideas as a writer?

Applying and Exploring Ideas

1. Choose another reading you've encountered in this chapter that reminds you most of Sommers's piece. What connections do you find between the pieces? Now get in a small group and see how other students answered this question and why. What connections are you all seeing across the readings in this chapter?

2. Where does *your* writing usually come from? In other words, how do you tend to come up with ideas? Look at the last two or three memorable writing projects you've done and write two to three pages explaining where your ideas come from. Then get into a small group with other students and compare your findings. What is similar across your various experiences, and what is different?

3. Sommers gives an example of how puzzled her daughter was about a question on a standardized achievement test, and argues that "only in the mind of someone who writes achievement tests, and wants to close the door on imagination, could the one false sentence be 'The wind beckoned us to open the door'" (para. 37). How does this experience compare with your own experiences on standardized writing tests you took throughout school? In what ways did those tests encourage or discourage your imagination as a writer? Were there any ways in which those tests were helpful to your thinking and writing?

4. Review the pieces you've read so far in this chapter. How many of them seem to be making some use of "the personal," as Sommers describes it? Write two to three pages in which you describe some of the pieces in this chapter that use "the personal" and try to identify patterns in when and why the authors use it.

- -

META MOMENT   What would change about your invention process for writing if you took Sommers's argument seriously that writers should value their own experiential and reading knowledge by "mak[ing] connections among the sources that circulate within [us]" (para. 36)?

- -

All Writing Is Autobiography

© Gary Samson, University of New Hampshire

DONALD M. MURRAY

Framing the Reading

By the time you've gotten to college, it's very likely that at least one teacher has told you not to use "I" in your school papers. Push the question, and you might be told that academic writing (especially if it uses research) isn't supposed to be "personal" — rather, you should strive to be as objective as possible. The paper, after all, isn't about you — so you shouldn't be in it. But after reading the other pieces in this chapter — about how personal experience and prior knowledge seeps into what we know, how we speak, what we invent to write about, and so on — you should be starting to question such teachers.

Donald M. Murray probably had the same voices echoing in his head when he wrote this article for the writing teachers who read *College Composition and Communication* — and he did not accept what they had to say. Having made his living as a writer (including winning a Pulitzer Prize as a newspaper columnist, writing textbooks, and publishing a range of poetry and fiction), Murray knew that prior personal experience should and must impact writing. Writing, he thought, is *always* personal, whatever else it is. So he sat down to catalog the various ways that writing of any sort *includes the writer* — the ways that, in a sense, all writing is **autobiography**. This article is one result of his thinking on this topic.

Some readers object to Murray's argument because they misunderstand his use of the term *autobiography*, assuming he's referring to all writing as books in which people tell the stories of their lives. Murray makes it clear, though, that he's not thinking that research papers and workplace memos are autobiographies. Rather, Murray is referring to the autobiographical *nature* of texts, all of which necessarily contain traces of their creators. If you understand autobiography in this sense, it will be easier to fairly weigh Murray's arguments.

Murray, Donald M. "All Writing Is Autobiography." *College Composition and Communication*, vol. 42, no. 1, Feb. 1991, pp. 66–74.

Murray's arguments are explicitly about writing, but his broader focus is *all* literacy activities, as we've been discussing them in this chapter. He is really arguing for the threshold concept that all our past literacy experiences inform our present literacy experiences — how we write, what language we use, even (he suggests in the end) how we read. Traces of our literate pasts unavoidably emerge in our writing.

As we discussed in Chapter 1, this book is also about how actual research about writing challenges many of the commonsense "rules" or ideas or conceptions we're taught about writing as young people. In this case, Murray is challenging the ideas that you can keep yourself out of your writing, and (as Sommers also argued in the previous essay [p. 212]) that research writing is purely factual and objective. Murray is sharing a more complicated conception about writing that does a better job explaining the actual writing we do and see around us.

Getting Ready to Read

Before you read, try the following activity:

- Think back to what you've been taught about how "personal" your school or work writing (that is, not your diary, journal, poetry, songwriting, or other "expressive" writing) can be. What kinds of rules or guidance did you get? If you have friends or classmates around, compare notes with them.

As you read this article, consider the following questions:

- What reasons does Murray give for his contention that all writing is autobiography?
- What **genres** (kinds) of writing does Murray discuss? Why? Does he leave any out?
- Why did Murray choose to write *as* he did (for example, by using poetry), *where* he did (in the scholarly journal *College Composition and Communication*), and *for whom* he did? (You may need to do some research to answer this question.) What did he hope to accomplish?

I PUBLISH IN MANY FORMS — poetry, fiction, academic article, essay, 1 newspaper column, newsletter, textbook, juvenile nonfiction and I have even been a ghost writer for corporate and government leaders — yet when I am at my writing desk I am the same person. As I look back, I suspect that no matter how I tuned the lyre, I played the same tune. All my writing — and yours — is autobiographical.

To explore this possibility, I want to share a poem that appeared in the 2
March 1990 issue of *Poetry.*

At 64, Talking Without Words

The present comes clear when rubbed
with memory. I relive a childhood
of texture; oatmeal, the afternoon rug,
spears of lawn, winter finger tracing
frost on window glass, August nose
squenched against window screen. My history
of smell: bicycle oil, leather catcher's
mitt, the sweet sickening perfume of soldiers
long dead, ink fresh on the first edition.
Now I am most alone with others, companioned
by silence and the long road at my back,
mirrored by daughters. I mount the evening
stairs with mother's heavy, wearied
step, sigh my father's long complaint.
My beard grows to the sepia photograph
of a grandfather I never knew. I forget
if I turned at the bridge, but arrive
where I intended. My wife and I talk
without the bother of words. We know Lee
is 32 today. She did not stay twenty
but stands at each room's doorway. I place
my hand on the telephone. It rings.

What is autobiographical in this poem? I was 64 when I wrote it. The child- 3
hood memories were real once I remembered them by writing. I realized I was
mirrored by daughters when the line arrived on the page. My other daughter
would have been 32 on the day the poem was written. Haven't you all had the
experience of reaching for the phone and hearing it ring?

There may even be the question of autobiographical language. We talk about 4
our own language, allowing our students their own language. In going over this
draft my spellcheck hiccupped at "squenched" and "companioned." As an academic I gulped; as a writer I said, "Well they are now."

Then Brock Dethier, one of the most perceptive of the test readers with 5
whom I share drafts, pointed out the obvious—where all the most significant information is often hidden. He answered my question, "What is autobiographical in this poem?" by saying, "Your thinking style, your voice." Of
course.

We are autobiographical in the way we write; my autobiography exists in the 6 examples of writing I use in this piece and in the text I weave around them. I have my own peculiar way of looking at the world and my own way of using language to communicate what I see. My voice is the product of Scottish genes and a Yankee environment, of Baptist sermons and the newspaper city room, of all the language I have heard and spoken.

> We are autobiographical in the way we write; my autobiography exists in the examples of writing I use in this piece and in the text I weave around them.

In writing this paper I have begun to under- 7 stand, better than I ever have before, that all writing, in many different ways, is autobiographical, and that our autobiography grows from a few deep taproots that are set down into our past in childhood.

Willa Cather declared, "Most of the basic material a writer works with is 8 acquired before the age of fifteen." Graham Greene gave the writer five more years, no more: "For writers it is always said that the first 20 years of life contain the whole of experience — the rest is observation."

Those of us who write have only a few topics. My poems, the novel I'm writ- 9 ing, and some of my newspaper columns keep returning to my family and my childhood, where I seek understanding and hope for a compassion that has not yet arrived. John Hawkes has said, "Fiction is an act of revenge." I hope not, but I can not yet deny the importance of that element in my writing. Revenge against family, revenge against the Army and war, revenge against school.

Another topic I return to is death and illness, religion and war, a great tangle 10 of themes. During my childhood I began the day by going to see if my grandmother had made it through the night; I ended my day with, "Now I lay me down to sleep, I pray the Lord my soul to keep. If I should die before I wake, I pray the Lord my soul to take."

I learned to sing "Onward Christian Soldiers Marching as to War," and still 11 remember my first dead German soldier and my shock as I read that his belt buckle proclaimed God was on *his* side. My pages reveal my obsession with war, with the death of our daughter, with that territory I explored in the hours between the bypass operation that did not work and the one that did.

Recently, Boynton/Cook/Heinemann published *Shoptalk*, a book I began in 12 Junior High School that documents my almost lifelong fascination with how writing is made. I assume that many people in this audience are aware of my obsession with writing and my concern with teaching that began with my early discomfort in school that led to my dropping out and flunking out. My academic writing is clearly autobiographical.

Let's look now at a Freshman English sort of personal essay, what I like to 13 call a reflective narrative. I consider such pieces of writing essays, but I suppose others think of them in a less inflated way as newspaper columns. I write a column, *Over Sixty*, for the *Boston Globe*, and the following one was published October 10th of 1989. It was based on an experience I had the previous August.

Over sixty brings new freedoms, a deeper appreciation of life and the time to celebrate it, but it also brings, with increasing frequency, such terrible responsibilities as sitting with the dying.

Recently it was my turn to sit with my brother-in-law as he slowly left us, the victim of a consuming cancer.

When I was a little boy, I wanted—hungered—to be a grown-up. Well, now I am a grown-up. And when someone had to sit with the dying on a recent Saturday, I could not look over my shoulder. I was the one. My oldest daughter will take her turn. She is a grown-up as well, but those of us over sixty have our quota of grown-upness increase. Time and again we have to confront crisis: accident, sickness, death. There is no one else to turn to. It is our lonely duty.

Obligation has tested and tempered us. No one always measures up all the time. We each do what we can do, what we must do. We learn not to judge if we are wise, for our judgments boomerang. They return. At top speed and on target.

Most of us, sadly and necessarily, have learned to pace ourselves. We have seen friends and relatives destroyed by obligation, who have lost themselves in serving others. There is no end to duty for those who accept it.

And we have seen others who diminish by shirking responsibility. When we call them for help the door is shut. We hear silence.

We grow through the responsible acceptance of duty, obligation balanced by self-protection. We teeter along a high wire trying to avoid guilt or sancrimoniousness as we choose between duty and avoidance.

And so my mind wanders as Harry sleeps, blessedly without pain for the moment, moving steadily toward a destination he seems no longer to fear.

He would understand that as we mourn for him, we mourn for ourselves. Of course. We are learning from his dying how to live. We inevitably think of what he did that we can emulate and what we should try to avoid.

And we learn, from his courage and his example, not to fear death. I remember how horrified I was years ago when a mother of a friend of mine, in her late eighties, feeling poorly in the middle of the night, would get up, change into her best nightgown, the one saved for dying, and go back to sleep.

Now I understand. During my last heart attack I had a volcanic desire to live but no fear of dying. It was not at all like my earlier trips to the edge.

Harry continues my education. He did not want trouble while he lived and now he is dying the same way, causing no trouble, trying to smile when he wakes, trying to entertain me.

227

He needs the comfort of sleep and I leave the room, turning outside his door to see how quickly his eyes close. He wants nothing from us now. Not food, not drink, not, we think, much companionship. He accepts that his road is lonely and he does not even show much impatience at its length.

It is not a happy time, alone in the house with a dying man, but it is not a dreadful time either. I pat the cat who roams the house but will not go to the room where Harry lies; I read, write in my daybook, watch Harry, and take time to celebrate my living.

This house, strange to me, in an unfamiliar city, is filled with silence. No music, no TV, just the quiet in which I can hear his call. But he does not call. I cannot hear his light breathing. Every few minutes I go to the door to see if the covers still rise and fall.

He would understand as I turn from him to watch the tree branch brush the roof of the house next door, as I spend long moments appreciating the dance of shadows from the leaves on the roof, then the patterns of sunlight reflected up on the ceiling of the room where I sit, as I celebrate my remaining life.

Again I stand at the edge of the door watching, waiting, and take instruction from his dying. We should live the hours we have in our own way, appreciating their passing. And we should each die in our own way. I will remember his way, his acceptance, his not giving trouble, his lonely, quiet passing.

This is simple narrative with the facts all true, but it is really not that simple; few things are in writing or in life. The details are selective. A great deal of family history is left out. A great many details about the day, the illness, where it was taking place and why were left out. In fact, I wrote it in part for therapy, and it began as a note to myself several weeks after the experience to help me cut through a jungle of thoughts and emotions, to try to recover for myself what was happening that day. Later I saw that it might speak to others, give comfort or form to their own autobiographies. I did not write the whole truth of that day, although the facts in the piece are accurate; I wrote a limited truth seeking a limited understanding, what Robert Frost called "a momentary stay of confusion." 14

Yes, I confess it, I wrote, and write, for therapy. Writing autobiography is my way of making meaning of the life I have led and am leading and may lead. 15

Let's look at another autobiographical poem, one of my favorites, which, I suppose, means that it was one I especially needed to write for no autobiographical reason I can identify. It has not yet been published, although a great many of the best poetry editors in the country have failed in their obligation to Western culture by rejecting it. 16

BLACK ICE

On the first Saturday of winter, the boy
skated alone on Sailor's Home Pond, circling
from white ice to black, further each time
he rode the thin ice, rising, dipping, bending
the skin of the water until the crack raced
from shore to trick him but he heard, bent
his weight to the turn, made it back in time.

That winter he saw the fish frozen in ice,
its great unblinking eye examining him
each time he circled by. He dreamt that eye
all summer, wondered if Alex had seen
the fish eye before he rode the black ice,
did not hear the crack sneak out from shore,
imagined he learned to skate on water.

At night, after loving you, I fall back
to see that fish eye staring down, watch
Alex in shoe skates and knickers from below
as he skates overhead, circling faster, faster,
scissor legs carrying him from white ice
to black. His skates sing their cutting song,
etching larger, larger circles in my icy sky.

It is true that the boy, myself, skated on thin ice and that he skated at Sailor's 17
Home Pond in Quincy, Massachusetts, although the thin ice may not have been
on that pond. He did not, however, see a fish in the ice until he wrote the poem,
although he was obsessed with the eyes of the fish, haddock and cod, that followed him when he went to Titus's fish store in Wollaston. Readers believe that
Alex is my brother, although I was an only child. There was no Alex; no one I
knew had drowned by falling through the ice until I received the poem; I did
not, after loving, stare up to see him skating above me until after I wrote the
poem. I do now. The poem that was for a few seconds imaginary has become
autobiographical by being written.

Ledo Ivo, the Latin American writer, said, "I increasingly feel that my writing 18
creates me. I am the invention of my own words" (*Lives on the Line,* Ed. Doris
Meyer, U of California P, 1988). Don DeLillo explains, "Working at sentences
and rhythms is probably the most satisfying thing I do as a writer. I think after a
while a writer can begin to know himself through his language. He sees someone
or something reflected back at him from these constructions. Over the years it's
possible for a writer to shape himself as a human being through the language he
uses. I think written language, fiction, goes that deep. He not only sees himself

but begins to make himself or remake himself" (*Anything Can Happen,* Ed. Tom LeClair and Larry McCaffery, U of Illinois P, 1988).

We become what we write. That is one of the great magics of writing. I am   19 best known as a nonfiction writer, but I write fiction and poetry to free myself of small truths in the hope of achieving large ones. Here are the first pages from a novel I am writing.

> Notebook in his lap, pen uncapped, Ian Fraser sat in the dark green Adirondack chair studying the New Hampshire scene that had so often comforted him as he put in his last years in his Washington office. The green meadow sloping unevenly over granite ledge to the lake and the point of land with its sentinel pine that marked the edge of his possession, and across the lake the hills rising into mountains touched with the reds, oranges, yellows that would flame into autumn this week or next. He was settled in at last and ready to begin the book he had so long delayed, but he could not write until he scanned this quiet scene with his infantryman's eyes for it still was, as were all his landscapes, a field of fire.
>
> He had to know where to dig in, where the enemy would attack, what was at his back. He supposed it was what had attracted him to this old farmhouse, he could hold this position, he had a good field of fire. First he scanned the lake. Left to right, far edge to near, not one boat or canoe, nothing breaking the surface, no wind trail or wake. Now right to left to see what might be missed. Nothing.
>
> The point of land, his furthest outpost. Scraggly pines, hulking ledge, ideal cover. He studied it close up, knew the pattern of shadows, where the ledge caught the light, where crevice was always dark. This is ridiculous, he thought, an old man whose wars are all over, but he could not stop the search for the enemies that had been there at the edge of other fields so long ago, so recent in memory.
>
> The woods left, on the other side from sentinel point. Sweep his eyes at the woods a half a field away, open ground any enemy would have to cross. He made himself still; anyone watching would not know his eyes were on patrol. He could have hidden a platoon in these woods, tree and bush, ledge and rock wall, but there was no shadow that moved, no unexpected sound, no leaves that danced without wind.
>
> And yet, Ian felt a presence as if he, the watcher, were being watched. He scanned the woods on the left again, moving from lake edge up. Nothing.
>
> Now the woods on the right, he had cut back from the house when he bought it, saying he needed sun for vegetables. He needed open field. More hardwoods here, more openness, the road unseen beyond. It was where someone would come in. His flood lights targeted these woods,

but it was not night. He examined these familiar woods, suddenly looking high in the old oak where a pileated woodpecker started his machine
gun attack. Ian studied squirrel and crow, the pattern of light and dark,
followed the trail of the quiet lake breeze that rose through the woods and
was gone.

Now the field of fire itself, where a civilian would think no-one could
hide. He smiled at the memory of a young paratrooper, himself, home on
leave, telling Claire, who would become his first wife, to stand at the top
of the field and spot him if she could as he crept up the slope, taking cover
where there seemed no cover. She was patient with his soldiering—then. She
knew her quarry and did not laugh as this lean young man crawled up the
slope moving quickly from ledge to slight hollow to the cover of low bush
blueberries that July in 1943.

He never knew if she saw him or not.

Do I have a green lawn that reaches down to a New Hampshire lake? No. Do 20
I still see when I visit a new place, forty-six years after I have been in combat, a
good field of fire? Yes. Did I have another wife than Minnie Mae? Yes. Was her
name Claire? No. Did I play that silly game in the field when I was home on
leave? Yes. Is the setting real? Let Herman Melville answer, "It is not down on
any map: true places never are."

What is true, what is documentally autobiographical, in the novel will not 21
be clear to me when I finish the last draft. I confess that at my age I am not
sure about the source of most of my autobiography. I have written poems
that describe what happened when I left the operating table, looked back and
decided to return. My war stories are constructed of what I experienced, what I
heard later, what the history books say, what I needed to believe to survive and
recover—two radically different processes.

I dream every night and remember my dreams. Waking is often a release 22
from a greater reality. I read and wear the lives of the characters I inhabit. I
do not know where what I know comes from. Was it dreamt, read, overheard,
imagined, experienced in life or at the writing desk? I have spun a web more
coherent than experience.

But of course I've been talking about fiction, a liar's profession, so let us turn 23
to the realistic world of nonfiction. That novel from which I have quoted is
being written, more days than not, by a technique I call layering that I describe
in the third edition of *Write to Learn:*

> One technique, I've been using, especially in writing the novel, is to layer my
> writing. Once I did quite a bit of oil painting and my pictures were built up,
> layer after layer of paint until the scene was revealed to me and a viewer. I've
> been writing each chapter of the novel the same way, starting each day at the

beginning of the chapter, reading and writing until the timer bings and my daily stint is finished. Each day I lay down a new layer of text and when I read it the next day, the new layer reveals more possibility.

There is no one way the chapters develop. Each makes its own demands, struggles towards birth in its own way. Sometimes it starts with a sketch, other times the first writing feels complete [next day's reading usually shows it is not]; sometimes I race ahead through the chapter, other times each paragraph is honed before I go on to the next one. I try to allow the text to tell me what it needs.

I start reading and when I see—or, more likely, hear—something that needs doing, I do it. One day I'll read through all the written text and move it forward from the last day's writing; another time I'll find myself working on dialogue; the next day I may begin to construct a new scene [the basic element of fiction]; one time I'll stumble into a new discovery, later have to set it up or weave references to it through the text; I may build up back-ground description, develop the conflict, make the reader see a character more clearly; I may present more documentation, evidence, or exposition, or hide it in a character's dialogue or action.

Well, that is academic writing, writing to instruct, textbook writing. It is 24 clearly nonfiction, and to me it is clearly autobiography. And so, I might add, is the research and scholarship that instructs our profession. We make up our own history, our own legends, our own knowledge by writing our autobiography.

This has enormous implications for our students, or should have. In *Notebooks* 25 *of the Mind* (U of New Mexico P, 1985), a seminal book for our discipline, Vera John-Steiner documents the importance of obsession. "Creativity requires a *continuity of concern*, an intense awareness of one's active inner life combined with sensitivity to the external world." Again and again she documents the importance of allowing and even cultivating the obsessive interest of a student in a limited area of study. I read that as the importance of encouraging and supporting the exploration of the autobiographical themes of individual students—and the importance of allowing ourselves to explore the questions that itch our lives.

I do not think we should move away from personal or reflective narrative in 26 composition courses, but closer to it; I do not think we should limit reflective narrative to a single genre; I do not think we should make sure our students write on many different subjects, but that they write and rewrite in pursuit of those few subjects which obsess them.

But then, of course, I am writing autobiographically, telling other people to 27 do what is important to me.

And so all I can do is just rest my case on my own personal experience. I 28 want to read my most recent poem in which the facts are all true. I had not seen as clearly before I wrote the poem the pattern of those facts, the way I—and a generation of children in the United States and Germany and Britain and Japan

and China and Spain and France and Italy and Russia and so many other countries—was prepared for war. This piece of writing is factually true but watch out
as you hear it. Writing is subversive and something dangerous may happen as
you hear my autobiography.

A woman hearing this poem may write, in her mind, a poem of how she was 29
made into a docile helpmate by a society that had its own goals for her. A black
may write another autobiography as mine is heard but translated by personal
history. A person who has been mistreated in childhood, a person who is a Jew,
a person whose courage was tested at the urging of jeering peers on a railroad
bridge in Missouri, will all hear other poems, write other poems in their mind
as they hear mine.

WINTHROP 1936, SEVENTH GRADE

December and we comb our hair wet,
pocket our stocking caps and run,
uniformed in ice helmets,

to read frost etched windows:
castle, moat, battlements, knight,
lady, dragon, feel our sword

plunge in. At recess we fence
with icicles, hide coal in
snow balls, lie freezing

inside snow fort, make ice balls
to arc against the enemy; Hitler.
I lived in a town of Jews,

relatives hidden in silences,
letters returned, doors shut,
curtains drawn. Our soldier

lessons were not in books taught
by old women. In East Boston,
city of Mussolinis, we dance

combat, attack and retreat, sneak,
hide, escape, the companionship
of blood. No school, and side

staggered by icy wind we run
to the sea wall, wait
for the giant seventh wave

to draw back, curl mittens
round iron railing, brace
rubber boots, watch

the entire Atlantic rise
until there is no sky. Keep
mittens tight round iron rail,

prepare for the return of ocean,
that slow, even sucking back,
the next rising wave.

I suspect that when you read my poem, you wrote your own autobiography. 30 That is the terrible, wonderful power of reading: the texts we create in our own minds while we read—or just after we read—become part of the life we believe we lived. Another thesis: all reading is autobiographical.

- -

Questions for Discussion and Journaling

1. Remember that one of the goals of this book is to help you consider threshold concepts about writing that help you rethink how writing actually works. Pick one of the threshold concepts that Murray addresses and write a paragraph that explains your evolving ideas about it.

2. Murray argues that "all writing, in many different ways, is autobiographical, and that our autobiography grows from a few deep taproots that are set down into our past childhood" (para. 7). He lists a variety of ways that writing is autobiographical. What are they?

3. Other writers in this chapter have been making similar arguments to Murray's, that writing "grows from a few deep taproots" set in our past (para. 7). What are some ways that others in this chapter have suggested that our writing and language use are influenced by our past?

4. Murray writes, " . . . at my age I am not sure about the source of most of my autobiography" (para. 21). But we suspect this is true for most writers, at any age. Before reading the pieces in this chapter, had you thought about the experiences that had shaped you as a writer? Now that you have done so, do you understand your writing, language use, and writing processes any differently than before? Why or why not?

5. Murray's article was published in a peer-reviewed, scholarly journal, yet it does not share the typical features of that genre. Murray's writing is more informal, more "literary," and easier to read in some ways. Make a list of the ways that Murray's article is different from the other scholarly articles in this chapter. Then consider some reasons why Murray would have wanted to break out of the usual "rules" for writing in the scholarly article genre.

6. If you've answered question 5, you have already considered the ways in which this piece is unusual for a scholarly article. Now consider the opposite question: Make a list of the features that mark Murray's article as belonging to the genre of "scholarly article."

7. Consider the implications of Murray's arguments: If he's right, how do his ideas change the way you think about writing? Would they encourage you to write any differently than you currently do?

8. Consider the last few texts that you have written, whether for school, work, or personal reasons. Consider the ways that these texts are — or are not — autobiography in the sense that Murray describes.

Applying and Exploring Ideas

1. In question 5 above you listed some ways that Murray's writing departs from typical "academic" writing. But other authors in this chapter have done the same. Make a list of what you expect academic writing to be and sound like. Then go back to some of the other pieces you've read in this chapter and list ways they conform to those expectations of academic writing, and the ways they differ from those expectations. Once you've made this list, write one to two pages arguing for or against this claim: All academic writing sounds the same and uses the same conventions.

2. Write a one- to two-page response to Murray that explains your reaction to his piece and gives reasons for your thinking. You could write your piece a number of different ways: as a letter to Murray, or to a friend; as an article in the same style as Murray's; or as a review of the article (like a review of a new album or movie).

3. If you've heard before that writing — especially academic writing — should be impersonal and keep the writer out, Murray's article might inspire you to argue against that point of view. Take one to two pages and freewrite comments you might make to a teacher or other authority figure who told you in the past to write "objectively" and keep yourself out of the text.

4. Near the end of this piece, Murray offers a second thesis, that all reading is auto-biographical as well. In order to test this claim, talk with a classmate about how they responded to another piece that you've read in this chapter so far (Malcolm X, Sandra Cisneros, and Vershawn Ashanti Young would be good choices). As they share their reactions with you, ask them some probing questions, such as:

    *   Why do you think you read it that way instead of this way?
    *   What experiences have you had in the past that helped you read this or made it harder for you to understand?
    *   When you struggled with a particular idea, can you point to a reason in your own experience that would explain why that was hard for you?

    Once you've heard their responses, compare them with your own. Now write one to two pages explaining Murray's claim that all reading is autobiography, and then arguing for or against that claim.

- -

META MOMENT   Name two or three ways that understanding Murray's claims here can have a positive impact on you as a writer and/or on your attitude about writing.

- -

"Don't Panic: A Hitchhiker's Guide to My Literacy"

Lucas Pasqualin

LUCAS PASQUALIN

Framing the Reading

Lucas Pasqualin was a first-year student at the University of Central Florida when he wrote this piece. As you will learn in his narrative, he was born in São Paulo, Brazil, and moved to South Florida when he was young. The literacy struggles associated with that move form the backbone of his piece. His story illustrates quite a few of the ideas covered in this chapter related to languages spoken in different settings, to literacy sponsorship, to the power that teachers and schools have to label and limit students, and to the ways that students can take control of their own literacy experiences and identities when given the opportunity.

Getting Ready to Read

Before you read, do at least one of the following activities:

- Google Douglas Adams's *A Hitchhiker's Guide to the Galaxy*. If you are not familiar with it, read a quick overview of it, as it provides the title for Pasqualin's piece.
- Google Sherman Alexie's "The Joy of Reading and Writing." It's very short, so read it if you can find it, as Pasqualin finds himself relating to Alexie.
- Google Sun Tzu's *The Art of War*, if you are not familiar with it.
- Take a quick peek at Tony Mirabelli in the next chapter (p. 298) in order to get a sense of his argument about **multiliteracies**, which Pasqualin references.

Pasqualin, Lucas. "Don't Panic: A Hitchhiker's Guide to My Literacy." *Stylus*, vol. 4, no. 2, Fall 2013, pp. 1–5.

WHITE BLEACHED WALLS — that was the first thing I saw as I stepped into my room. Walls scrubbed clean of Sharpied poems, lyrics, and quotes; walls which were completely void of my Crayola stick figures, Woodstock posters, maps, and pictures of completely everything and absolutely nothing. There were no more clothes on the floor, old locks hanging from my curtains, or messages scribbled here and there from all of the people who had passed through my room and my life. I wonder if Malcolm X ever meant his phrase "bleached history" to be taken literally (356)? Despite that all of this had been taking place, and even when I was forced to take down everything from my walls, or when the painters came in, or when I came home to find my bed had been taken, I still had not realized *that* room was no longer *my* room until I had to pack away the last of my belongings into boxes for storage. Out of the thousands of books I had read, the relatively small amount I could keep was now packed into two neat rows, each stacked three boxes high.

As I was packing I looked up above my door, where a sign used to read, "Don't Panic." I thought—quite dramatically, if I might add—that a more fitting sign would probably have been, "Abandon all hope ye who enter here." My door swung open and the smile quickly dropped from my lips as my mom entered the room in a hurry. "There is no way you are keeping *another box* of books," she said. The words escaped from her lips with her breath as she dropped a box on the floor: "We do not have room for any more of your junk." I had a decision to make. I could sit here and argue that my stuff was not junk, or I could stay quiet and live to fight another day. Silence prevailing, my mom arched her eyebrows in a way that said, "Get rid of it," before she hurried back out.

I went over to the opened box she'd dropped off and took a look inside. She must have been dreaming. Did she really believe I could ever have gotten rid of *A Hitchhiker's Guide to the Galaxy* or the entire Harry Potter series? How could I possibly give up my *National Forensics League Rule Book, The Art of War,* or any of the countless treasures I had hidden inside? She had to understand, it wasn't possible. How is it that she could only see junk where I saw my entire life story?

LUCAS PASQUALIN AND THE SORCERER'S STONE

By the time I was in the first grade, I was lugging around books that were almost 4 too heavy for me to lift. Writer Sherman Alexie described my predicament

> By the time I was in the first grade, I was lugging around books that were almost too heavy for me to lift.

exactly: "[I] read books at recess, then during lunch, and in the minutes left after I had finished my classroom assignments" (365). Out of all the hundreds of books I've read, I can say with confidence that I really wouldn't be the same person I am today without J.K. Rowling.

The story goes that, at a time when I was 5 just developing my literacy, my sister began to read me a story. Definitely not just any bedtime story, the over three hundred-page *Sorcerer's Stone* was teased and spoon-fed to me in bite-sized pieces. Poor Amanda. It wasn't until much later that I discovered she was just trying to get me to fall asleep. She couldn't have made a bigger mistake. When the time came that I finally couldn't take the anticipation any longer, I decided to pick up the book myself and struggle my way through. I can remember reading that book until once again, just like Sherman Alexie, "I could barely keep my eyes open" (365).

Even though they might not have known it, Amanda and J.K. Rowling served 6 as perfect examples of Deborah Brandt's theory about literacy sponsors. While they gave me my initial hunger for reading, perhaps a more important sponsor would be the person who literally made it all possible — my mother. I arrived in the United States from Brazil not knowing a word of English, so as you can imagine I was quite surprised when I was placed in classrooms in the United States and expected to read. Granted, most students in those early years were just getting a grasp on language, but the expectations put on me at that time had implications that lasted well into my life. I don't remember exactly what I did, but what I do remember is the general sense of being the "stupid kid." I wasn't expected to know how to read, so I just shuffled through the school system not really gaining any knowledge. I specifically remember times when the teachers would talk about me right in front of my face. Someone should have mentioned how close "idiot" is to "idiota."

As tragic as that may sound, my story would completely change when I got 7 home from school. When I was home, I was expected to be smart; I was expected not to complain, and most of all I was expected to be equal parts *Abduch* (my middle name as well as my mother's family's name) and *Pasqualin,* which to my family meant never giving up. I was on the verge of failing in school until my mother took time off her busy schedule to help me study. I remember she would set up these wild games involving crazy chases through the house just to match a picture to the correct spelling of a word. While I did not realize it at the time, these games and her attention are probably the reasons why I took to reading as quickly as I did. While my actual love affair with reading and writing did not start until much later, I'd be lying if I said I didn't love the looks on the faces of the other kids when they saw me reading books they couldn't dream of understanding. But what spurred me on even more than that was ultimately the pride I could hear in my mother's voice when she chided me about reading so much. Forever and always I will think of my mother as Professor McGonagall. My mother is tough as rocks, but also incredibly loving and caring. She is some-one who will always be regarded as my strongest literacy sponsor, even if she did want me to throw away all my stuff.

THE HITCHHIKER'S GUIDE TO THE GALAXY

While I have said before it would be hard to single out a book as my favorite, 8 Douglas Adam's *A Hitchhiker's Guide to the Galaxy* definitely would not miss the mark by much. To understand just exactly what this book means to me you need some background knowledge of what I was going through at the time I picked it up. While there really is no short and sweet version—I was a melodramatic teen-ager—let's just say I was in a position where I felt depressed and alone in a world that no longer made sense to me. My parents were on the verge of a divorce, my brother was on the edge of being deported, and our entire family was about to go bankrupt. And, just to top it all off, my best friend had moved to another country, and it seemed like all my other friends had deserted me right as I was coming of age.

I felt like the two old women in *A Hitchhiker's Guide to the Galaxy.* Sitting on 9 a bench by the Pacific, one turns to the other and complains that she thought it would be bigger. I could relate in that I felt growing up was certainly not all that it had been built up to be. But, then again, I could relate anything in my life to that book. In fact my motto—the same motto written on the cover of any copy of *A Hitchhiker's Guide to the Galaxy*—is "Don't Panic." I learned from Douglas Adams that, while I didn't understand why my brother continued to get into trouble, or why my parents didn't want to be together anymore, or why it seemed I was left alone, it was all okay; things didn't always need to make sense.

If J.K. Rowling gave me a hunger for reading, Adams is who made me respect 10 literacy as a force to be reckoned with. After all, it took Malcolm X from behind bars and turned him into the leader of a movement. It took a poor Indian child from a reservation and turned him into Sherman Alexie—winner of the World Heavyweight Poetry Bout, writer of screenplays, and much more. And it turned out to also be the vehicle of my escape.

BUSBOY

My family's financial situation wasn't really getting better over time, and 11 my curiosity was growing almost as fast as my list of extracurricular activ-ities, so by the time I graduated high school I was definitely well-versed in several different multiliteracies. Mirabelli would have a field day researching my experiences.

For example, the first job I held was busing tables, so I was totally astonished 12 to read in Mirabelli's article, "Learning to Serve: The Language and Literacy of Food Service Workers," that the National Skills Labor Board had labeled waiting tables as a "low skilled profession" (540). As young as I was at the time (around fifteen-years-old), there was still a host of definitions, protocols, and norms I had to learn. Just as Mirabelli described in his article, I experienced firsthand that answering a question most of the time did not only require knowledge of what words meant on the menu, but also of the specific process my restaurant used in making the food they served. Likewise, since a big portion of my job included getting drink orders, knowing the distinctions between wines and what they meant was essential to my job experience.

One thing Mirabelli did not mention was the role physical communication 13 plays in the service industry. People do not like being pestered while they eat and they do not want to be watched, yet they want their own private appetites fulfilled without having to ask. As a busboy, I found it was important I not only understood technical knowledge about the food and wine, but it was just as important that I had a really keen eye and an acute understanding of body language. It takes practice to know the numerous signals people use to communicate they're ready for their check, they are finished with their plates, or they would like to order dessert.

PET DETECTIVE

Another way I became multiliterate was by working as a sales associate for Pet 14 Supermarket. You'd be surprised just how much discourse goes on between sales associates and customers. Similar to food service, at Pet Supermarket there were also two parts to that literacy: first, the technical knowledge, and, second, the knowledge about the customers. Just in the fish department alone, for example, it was necessary to know words like pH, ammonia, nitrates, cichlids, and gobies. And while these words are more objective in their meaning, there is an entire process that goes into pinpointing your customers' problems, and then actually convincing them you can fix them. Mirabelli wrote of a waiter who when questioned about the menu, "would make it sound so elaborate that they would just leave it up to [him] . . ." (546). While I was always trying to help my customers, the best strategy sometimes involved doing the same thing. Just as the waiter used his superiority in the restaurant literacy to control the flow of the conversation, I would use my pet store literacy to convince customers I knew what I was talking about.

While working as a busboy the most I would talk to someone was maybe a 15 couple of minutes. However, a big sale at Pet Supermarket could literally go on and on for days. I knew it was pertinent in retail to know how to spot a customer who has needs you can fill, instead of one just looking for a petting zoo. And even then I would still have to discern how much they wanted to pay and what products they needed. If someone was very adamant about a pet, and, for example, referred to pets like children, then most likely that individual would end up wanting the security of having paid a higher price for pet products. I also learned how to tell if customers were ready to buy something just by the physical contact they had with the product.

THE DEBATE TEAM AND THE ART OF WAR

Ah, debate. Like modern day linguistic gladiator fights. This is where literacies come to battle it out and, in some cases, even die. I joined the debate team really early in my high school career, and if I had not held a wide range of multiliteracies by then, I would have developed them at that time. Obviously, I needed very clear communication skills just to be able to compete. The ability to write ten minute speeches, or, for that matter, even four minute speeches, is not something everyone possesses. But the intricacies, the "kill words," the strategies that would upstage Sun Tzu — it is in those skills where the real literacy of debate lies. While there is no instruction manual on winning a debate, doing so requires a very clear understanding of what your judges want to hear, what your adversary is actually communicating (and not just what he wants to communicate), and much, much more. 16

"Always" (just to name one from the dozens) was a kill word. Since it's not often something is "always" true, using that word by accident or on purpose usually meant that an adversary could "kill" you on that claim. But that's just where it starts. Sometimes people would bait others with kill words just to pull attention from other weaker claims they were using. Or better yet, cite untrustworthy sources just so their opponents could waste the rest of the remaining time citing the dozens they had to back them up. Mirabelli speaks about the struggle for control in the interactions between waiter and customer. As can be seen, this struggle for control is manifested in the debate world in a much more tangible way. Hand signals, changes in pitch, even moments of silence are all used to gain control of the debate, just as a soccer player fights for control of a ball. 17

The best debaters were also literate in the signals someone made when they were bluffing on a claim, or better yet when they were about to break down. Losing your cool in a debate, screaming, or using language that was a little too passionate usually resulted in that person losing. One important strategy in any debate is spotting a weak point and then striking that weak point until your opponent is frantic, all the while making sure it still appears you are amicable to the judge. Being literate in this kind of knowledge actually prepared me for 18 watching the presidential debates. I knew exactly what Biden was doing when he was laughing at Paul Ryan's arguments. When Obama stayed quiet while Romney was arguing with him, I knew he was just baiting him to look foolish. On a much larger scale, the literacy of the private struggle for power in communication has also allowed me to spot those kinds of situations in my own life.

> Now, whenever I write, there is always a little voice inside my head asking for evidence, checking for loopholes in my arguments, and really just being a general nuisance.

A lot of what I learned from debate has also 19 gone into my writing. When I was writing claims for debate, I had to have all these strategic elements in mind. Not supporting any one claim was a failure of biblical proportions, a failure that would undoubtedly crucify me in front of the judges. It was that serious. Now, whenever I write, there is always a little voice inside my head asking for evidence, checking for loopholes in my arguments, and really just being a general nuisance.

DON'T PANIC

Sitting alone in my room and looking through that box of books, it was crazy to 20 think about just how much reading had positively impacted my life. I'm curious to know if other people have had the same kind of experiences as me. What kind of impact does not just reading but also developing many different kinds of multiliteracies actually have on people long-term? It would be interesting to study whether there is a correlation between developing various multiliteracies early in childhood and success later in life, just as I believe there has been in my life. Would my grades have been the same without all of my sponsors? Would I still have been accepted to UCF without the many literacies I have acquired? Would I still have been that same kid, sitting in my room alone and scared as all hell of leaving home?

What life and literacy have shown me so far is that you can't abandon hope. I've 21 learned that the world can be a very confusing place, especially if you're not versed in all of its literacies. I've also learned to keep that in mind, and when life throws me in a new direction, I try to embrace that. Life and literacy have taught me that when your walls are painted blank, you should let them represent a new page in your life. When it's three a.m., and you've been stuck on the same sentence for the past three hours, and your paper is due in the morning, you can't abandon hope. And when your adversaries drive you into a corner, when you feel like everyone around you is speaking a foreign language, when everything is going wrong, and especially when you're going to a new place with sure to be alien literacies, I've learned the best thing you can do is to take it all in, remember to pick up your towel, and never, never ever forget that motto — don't panic.

Works Cited

Alexie, Sherman. "The Joy of Reading and Writing: Superman and Me." Wardle and Downs 362–65. Print.

Brandt, Deborah. "Sponsors of Literacy." Wardle and Downs 332–50. Print.

Mirabelli, Tony. "Learning to Serve: The Language and Literacy of Food Service Workers." Wardle and Downs 538–54. Print.

Wardle, Elizabeth, and Doug Downs, eds. *Writing about Writing: A College Reader.* Boston: Bedford/St. Martin's, 2011. Print.

X, Malcolm. "Learning to Read." Wardle and Downs 354–60. Print.

- -

Questions for Discussion and Journaling

1. Pasqualin lists and describes a number of his formative literacy experiences and sponsors. Do the same for yourself.

2. Earlier, we asked you to mark places where Pasqualin references other readings in this book. Go back to your markings and consider how he used those sources. What did he do with them? Why did he use them? How do they help introduce his own ideas? Are there any places where Pasqualin's use of other sources seems like a stretch to you?

3. Pasqualin covers a lot of ground here. However, there is much that he does not say. Are there aspects of his story you wish he had written more about? Why? How can you use this feeling as a reader in order to help you figure out when to say more as a writer?

4. Have you ever had a job that required using specialized language? If so, how did you learn the specialized literacies required there?

5. Pasqualin describes the varied strategies employed by successful debaters, and then he explains how that knowledge translated into an ability to better understand what is happening in presidential debates and to better use evidence when he writes. Can you think of a specialized literacy you have in one area that is useful elsewhere? If you read Robertson et al. in this chapter (p. 184), draw on their ideas to help explain this use of prior knowledge in new settings.

6. Pasqualin ends by talking about the fear of going to a new place with "alien literacies" (para. 21). Can you think of a time when you encountered an alien literacy? What happened? Did you conquer it? Why or why not?

Applying and Exploring Ideas

1. Take one of the literacy experiences or sponsors you listed for question 1 above and turn it into a short narrative, using Pasqualin's story as a model.

2. In question 6 above, you considered a time when you encountered an alien literacy. Develop this experience and write about it in one to two pages.

3. Pasqualin begins with a descriptive narrative of himself sorting out his room, preparing to move. How effective was this narrative as a way of opening his piece? Write an alternate opening, and explain why you think it is more or less effective than Pasqualin's.

- -

META MOMENT   How do your various language and literacy experiences impact what you are willing and able to do with writing? Is there anything you'd like to change about your writing? Why?

- -

Revisualizing Composition

Mapping the Writing Lives of First-Year College Students

Jeff Grabill

JEFF GRABILL
WILLIAM HART-DAVIDSON
STACEY PIGG
MICHAEL McLEOD
PAUL CURRAN
JESSIE MOORE
PAULA ROSINSKI
TIM PEEPLES
SUZANNE RUMSEY
MARTINE COURANT RIFE
ROBYN TASAKA
DUNDEE LACKEY
BETH BRUNK-CHAVEZ

William Hart-Davidson

Stacey Pigg

Framing the Reading

Jeff Grabill is a professor and Bill Hart-Davidson is an associate professor in the Department of Writing, Rhetoric, and American Cultures at Michigan State University. Stacey Pigg was a doctoral student at Michigan State when she coauthored this article, and she is currently an assistant professor of scientific and technical communication at North Carolina State University. Together with the other authors, they are part of a large team of researchers that make up the Writing in Digital Environments (WIDE) Research Center, which Grabill and Hart-Davidson co-direct. This research center looks at a variety of questions about digital communication. It explores questions about what first-year college students are writing, what writing they most value, and what technologies are mediating their writing.

....

Grabill, Jeff, et al. "Revisualizing Composition: Mapping the Writing Lives of First-Year College Students." WIDE Research Center, Michigan State University, 7 Sept. 2010, www2.matrix.msu.edu/wp-content/uploads/2013/08/WIDE_writinglives_whitepaper.pdf.

So far, the readings in this chapter have suggested a variety of factors and experiences that impact you as a literate person. This reading asks you to expand your thinking in that regard to imagine how technologies are also a part of your literate self and inform what Murray would imagine as your autobiography.

Getting Ready to Read

Before you read, do at least one of the following activities:

- Make a quick list of the technologies that you think have had the most impact on your literacy "autobiography."
- Do a Google search for the Writing in Digital Environments (WIDE) Research Center. What is this group? Who is involved? What do they study? If you can find this paper on their website, take a look at the studies they published before and after this one.
- In Section 3, the authors explain that the type of college or university students attend is a good predictor of which genres students have written. You may not have thought very much before about the kind of college or university you are attending — at least not using the categories that the WIDE researchers assign: the Carnegie classification system (explained briefly in their "About This Study" section). Do a quick Google search to discover what the Carnegie classification system is, and then find out what Carnegie category your college or university falls under.

As you read, consider the following questions:

- How do the findings of WIDE researchers compare with your own experiences?
- Keep your school's Carnegie classification in mind and see whether your experience seems to correlate with the type of school you attend, as the WIDE researchers suggest it will in sections 3.1 and 3.2.

SUMMARY OF FINDINGS

This white paper reports initial findings from a Writing in Digital Environments (WIDE) Research Center study entitled Revisualizing Composition: Mapping the Writing Lives of First-Year College Students. These initial findings are drawn from a survey of students enrolled in writing classes at a sample of US postsecondary institutions. 1

Writing practices and technologies have changed considerably over recent years. Given these changes, we know that contemporary college students are highly 2 literate, but we lack clear and comprehensive portraits of how writing works in their lives. The primary aim of this study is to generate a large and uniform data set that leads to a better understanding of the writing behaviors of students across a variety of institutions and locations. Working from the assumption that students lead complex writing lives, this study is interested in a broad range of writing practices and values both for the classroom and beyond it, as well as the technologies, collaborators, spaces, and audiences they draw upon in writing. Initial findings include the following:

> *Working from the assumption that students lead complex writing lives, this study is interested in a broad range of writing practices and values both for the classroom and beyond it, as well as the technologies, collaborators, spaces, and audiences they draw upon in writing.*

- SMS texts (i.e., texts using short message services on mobile devices), emails, and lecture notes are three of the most frequently written genres (or types) of writing
- SMS texts and academic writing are the most frequently valued genres
- Some electronic genres written frequently by participants, such as writing in social networking environments, are not valued highly
- Students' write for personal fulfillment nearly as often as for school assignments
- Institution type is related in a meaningful way to the writing experiences of participants, particularly what they write and the technologies used
- Digital writing platforms — cell phones, Facebook, email — are frequently associated with writing done most often
- Students mostly write alone, and writing alone is valued over writing collaboratively

These findings, along with others reported in this white paper, shed light on the writing practices and values of contemporary college students. In particular, these findings point to the pervasiveness of writing in the lives of our participants and the importance of hand-held devices like mobile phones as a writing platform. 3

Our findings also raise a number of questions related to how students experience, use, and value new writing technologies and environments in the larger context of their writing lives. We hope the findings in this report raise questions for further research and scholarship. 4

ABOUT THE SURVEY

This report is based on the findings of a survey (n = 1366) distributed to students enrolled in a first-year writing class during April-June of the Spring 2010 5

247

semester. Students at seven institutions completed the survey (Elon University [Elon, North Carolina]; Indiana University-Purdue University at Fort Wayne [Ft. Wayne, Indiana]; Lansing Community College [Lansing, Michigan]; Leeward Community College [Pearl City, Hawaii]; Michigan State University [East Lansing, Michigan]; the University of North Carolina at Pembroke [Pembroke, North Carolina]; the University of Texas at El Paso [El Paso, Texas]).

These institutions represent a range of institution types according to the Carnegie classification system, including Research University, very high activity, Michigan State University; Research University, high activity, the University of Texas at El Paso; Master's Colleges and University, Medium, Indiana University-Purdue University at Fort Wayne and the University of North Carolina at Pembroke; Master's Colleges and Universities, Small, Private, Elon University; Associate's Public Rural-serving, Large, Lansing Community College; and Associate's Public 2-year Colleges under 4-year Universities, Leeward Community College. Of the 2110 students who began the survey, 1366 completed it, for a completion rate of 65% (see Methodology for more details). 6

The survey asked for demographic information and included a series of questions related to what participants write. Participants were first asked to identify types of writing that they do based on a list of 30 writing types. Then participants were asked to rank order the five types of writing that they do most often. Next they were asked to rank order the types of writing that they value the most. For each type of writing, participants were asked to detail why, where, with whom, for whom, and with what technologies they typically write. The meaning of "writing" in this survey included a wide range of practices, from lists to research papers to texting to multi-media compositions. . . . 7

SECTION 1: WHAT ARE STUDENTS WRITING IN AND OUT OF SCHOOL?

1.1: SMS Texts, Emails, and Lecture Notes Are Three of the Most Frequently Written Genres

The genres—or types—of writing that participants report writing most frequent are SMS text messages, emails, and lecture notes. Texting and emailing were ranked highly by participants when asked to identify all of their writing practices and by participants when asked to rank their most frequent writing practices. This finding reinforces common perceptions that texting and email have become commonplace writing practices. This finding also highlights the importance of the phone as a platform for writing. However, in highlighting the importance of a practice like texting, this finding may challenge other common perceptions of what counts as "writing." 8

When considering the simple ranking of writing practices, we find that 91% of participants selected texting from the thirty choices available of all writing 9 that they have done, and 78% said that texting was one of the five kinds of writing they do most often. In fact, nearly half of all participants (46%) indicated that texting was the kind of writing that they performed more than any other. A greater percentage of participants overall (94%) selected email as a type of writing practice they had performed in the past, but fewer placed it within their top five types of writing done most often (57%), and less than ten percent selected it as the genre they write the most (9%).

A number of academic writing practices 10 were highly ranked, which is not surprising given the participants and sampling approach. 78% of participants selected lecture notes as a type of writing they have done, while 93% and 82% chose research and academic papers respectively (meaning, in turn, that almost 7% and 20% respectively report having not written academic or research papers).

We utilized a statistical weighting method 11 for the ranked lists of most frequent and valued writing practices for our findings that accounted for the placement of a given writing practice somewhere in the top 5 listings for frequency and value. We believe that this method provides a stronger measure of both frequency and value. When considering the weighted ranking of writing practices, the top 10 most frequently written genres are as follows:

1. Texting
2. E-mail
3. Lecture notes
4. Academic papers
5. Research papers
6. Lists
7. Instant messaging

Beyond the Data:
Cell Phones: The New Pencil for Personal Life?

Cell phones have become a prominent writing technology for students for self-sponsored writing. Students use phones most often for SMS texting, but they also use them for a range of other digital writing, including emails, status message updates, instant messaging, and comments on status messages or posts. Cell phones are also frequently used for lists, and even occasionally for academic genres including lecture notes, reading notes, research papers, academic papers, and outlines. We have had students report using their phones to compose academic essays.

8. Comments on status messages or posts

9. Status message updates

10. Reading notes

We see in this list a range of traditional academic genres along with types of writing that we think of as "helpers" for larger tasks (e.g., notes). We see as well a number of genres that are a function of networked communication technologies. They have a clear place in the writing lives of these participants.

1.2: As Expected, Students Frequently Write Traditional School Genres Including Academic Papers and Research Papers

The top five most often used types of writing include the academic and research 12 paper, as well as more informal types of writing that often support the academic and research paper such as lecture and reading notes, lists, and even email and texting. Additional inquiry is needed to explore how, whether, and how often the more informal types of writing are used (or not) to support traditional school writing such as the academic and research paper.

1.3: Several Digital Genres Are Written by Almost All Participants, but Several Others Are Practiced by Less Than Half of Participants

As described above, half of the ten genres that participants report writing most 13 frequently are digital genres. Along with email and texting, which we detail above, instant messaging was practiced by 83% of participants, and status message updates (65%) and comments on status message updates (75%) were likewise prominent, indicating the importance of social media in the writing lives of these participants. However, other types of electronic communication were not as pervasive. Chat rooms had been utilized previously by just over half of all students. A total of 49% of participants reported writing for websites, and 39% of students reported writing for blogs.

1.4: Gender Is a Relevant Factor in What Students Write but in a Limited Number of Genres

For many types of writing, gender is not significantly related to frequency in our 14 sample. For the fifteen genres where gender is significantly related to frequency, only three categories skewed male, and only one of these in a strong way: websites, with over half of males (53%) and less than half of females (45%) reporting writing this genre. The other, business writing, was reported by 25% of males and 20% of females. Female respondents were significantly more likely than males to use academic "helper" genres: outlines, reading notes, lecture notes, and lists.

SECTION 2: HOW DO STUDENTS VALUE THE WRITING THEY DO?

2.1: SMS Texts and Academic Writing Are the Most Frequently Valued Genres

Participants were asked to rank how they valued 30 genres of writing by selecting the five most valuable types of writing to them. When considering the simple ranking of writing practices, we find that students ranked the following five genres most frequently as one of their top five most valued: Texting (47%), Academic Paper (45%), Lecture Notes (43%), Email (43%), and Research Paper (41%).

The weighted scores for value results in the following list of most valued genres of writing:

1. Texting
2. Academic Paper
3. Lecture Notes
4. Research Paper
5. Email
6. Resume
7. List
8. Letter
9. Journal/Diary
10. Forms

School-sponsored genres are valued highly by survey participants: academic paper and research paper ranked second and fourth, respectively. Lecture notes ranked third. As Figure 1 indicates, 21% of participants ranked academic papers as their

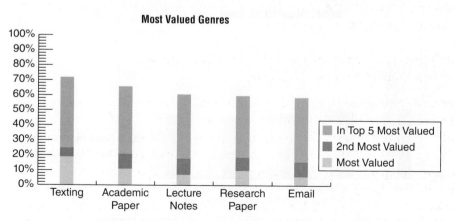

Figure 1 Display of top five most valued genres based on un-weighted rankings.

251

first or second most valued genre. 19% of students ranked research papers as their first or second most valued genre. Finally, for those who selected lecture notes, 19% of participants ranked lecture notes as their first or second most valued genre.

2.2: Some Less Frequently Written Genres Are Valued Highly by Student Writers

Among the ten most valued genres, four genres are valued highly but written 17 relatively infrequently. Resumes ranked 6th for value, but 20th for frequency. Journal/diary ranked 9th for value, but 12th for frequency. Letters ranked 8th for value, but 14th for frequency. Finally, poetry ranked 12th for value, but 15th for frequency.

2.3: Some Electronic Genres Written Frequently by Participants Are Not Valued Very Highly

There are a number of electronic genres that rank higher among participants 18 for use than for value. Notably, while texting ranked as most valued and most frequently used among all genres, participants do not value this form of writing at the same level that they practice it. As Figure 2 indicates, while 1049 participants (78%) selected texting as one of their top five most frequently used genres, only 641 participants (47%) ranked it in their top five most valued genres. Similarly, email was the second most frequently used genre (776 students, 57%), but it ranked 5th for value (586 students, 43%).

Several electronic genres which are used frequently did not rank in the top 19 ten most valued. Comments on status messages or posts in social software environments were ranked 8th for frequency but ranked 21st for value. Instant

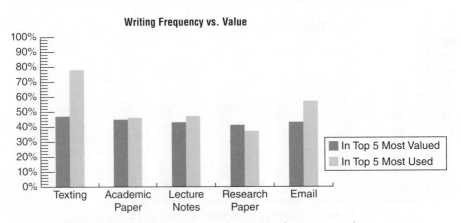

Figure 2 Top five most valued genres compared with their frequency numbers.

messaging ranked 7th for frequency but 15th for value. Finally status message updates were ranked 9th for frequency, but 18th for value.

SECTION 3: DO STUDENTS FROM DIFFERENT INSTITUTION TYPES COMPOSE AND VALUE DIFFERENT KINDS OF WRITING?

3.1: Institution Type Is a Meaningful Predictor of the Writing Experiences of Participants

In our sample, institution was statistically significant in predicting what gen- [20] res participants at different types of institutions had written. Participants who attended research universities were significantly more likely than participants from Master's or Associates institutions to have engaged in play/screenwriting and website writing. Survey participants who attended associate-granting institutions were significantly more likely to have written cover letters. Participants who attend master's-granting institutions were significantly more likely to have written many genres, including academic genres (academic papers, research papers, lab reports), helper academic genres (reading notes, outlines, lecture notes, peer responses), digital genres (texting, status message updates and responses, emails, instant messages), and more (poetry, journal, lists, letters, forms).

3.2: Use of Digital Genres Differed Across Institution Types

Each institution type was significantly more likely to write a set of particular [21] digital genres. Master's University students were most likely to use email at least

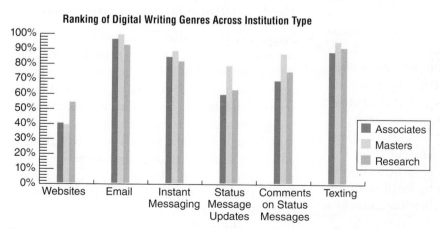

Figure 3 Percentage of students at each institution type reporting having written digital genres. Relationships shown are statistically significant.

Beyond the Data:
Facebook . . . meh

Our results show that Facebook is used frequently among first-year college students, and they use it to write a broad range of genres. The reasons why students do not report valuing this writing as highly are unclear, but it likely means that when faced with a list of types of writing, they still attach a lot of value to traditional print forms such as research papers and academic writing vs. shorter, born-digital forms such as status messages and instant messages.

Most of the writing students report doing on Facebook is directly related to interpersonal messaging. Though many think of social networking platforms as places where people write indulgently about themselves, our survey shows participants who more often comment on the posts and status updates of others than post things to their own profile. They also use Facebook to send messages: texts, IM, and email. Participants also report using the platform for writing everything from lists to screenplays to poetry.

once, followed by Associate's College students and then Research University students. More participants enrolled in Associate's Colleges used chat rooms, but these participants were least likely to make status updates or comment on status updates. Participants enrolled in Master's Universities were most likely to email, use instant messenger, write status message updates, comment on status messages, and to text. Participants enrolled in Research Universities were most likely to write for websites and least likely to use instant messenger. These findings suggest that we need further investigation into how students at different kinds of institutions incorporate digital genres into their writing lives.

SECTION 4: WHY DO PARTICIPANTS WRITE WHAT THEY WRITE?

4.1: Participants Are Most Often Motivated by the Need to Complete School Assignments

Half (50%) of all frequently written and most valued genres were associated with writing for school, 97% of participants reported that one of their most valued or most often completed genres was done to fulfill a school assignment. 22

4.2: Participants Write for Personal Fulfillment Nearly as Often as for School Assignments

Nearly half (44%) of all valued and frequently written genres were associated with personal fulfillment. 93% of participants said that one of their most valued or most often completed genres was done for personal fulfillment. This finding is especially interesting given the fact that participants were solicited through academic avenues (e.g., college email addresses, course websites) and sometimes took the survey in college classrooms, where we might expect them to focus on school-sponsored motivations for writing. 23

4.3: Participants Associate Their Writing with Entertainment, Civic Participation, and for Their Jobs Much Less Often Than for School or Personal Fulfillment

After writing for school and personal fulfillment, writing for entertainment was   24
the next most frequently identified motivation for the writing participants to do most often and value most highly. Almost a third (31%) of the most frequently written and most valued genres were associated with entertainment. Writing for civic participation (16%) and writing to fulfill the requirements of a job (12%) were associated much less frequently with participants' writing. Notably, although writing for civic participation and for the job were related less frequently to most of the types of writing participants identified, over half of students associated these motivations with at least one of their most frequent or valued kinds of writing. 61% of participants reported writing for civic participation at least once among their most often written and valued genres, and 55% reported writing for the job at least once, suggesting that these motives are present in the lives of many participants, even if less pervasively.

SECTION 5: WHAT ARE PARTICIPANTS WRITING WITH PARTICULAR TECHNOLOGIES?

5.1: Participants Who Associate Particular Technologies with at Least One of Their Most Frequently or Valued Genres Use That Technology Frequently

As Figure 4 shows, 90% of participants associate word processors with at   25
least one of their most frequently or valued written genres. Word processing

	% USED AT LEAST ONCE	% MOST OFTEN USED
Word Processor	90%	91%
Notebook or Paper	89%	94%
Cell Phone	86%	98%
Pencil	80%	92%
Email	76%	90%
Facebook	67%	95%

Figure 4 Percentage of students who associated each technology at least once with the writing they do, and the percentage of students who associated each technology with a most often written genre.

technologies are used most often to write academic or research papers, but they also are used often for outlines, lecture notes, and emails. Users also rate word processing technologies as the technology most often associated with their most valued writing (79%).

5.2: Blogs, Twitter, and Wikis Are Not Used by Many Participants, but Among Those Participants Who Use These Technologies, They Are Used Frequently

In contrast to how often they are associated with writing done most often, these [26] technologies are only moderately or minimally associated with valued writing. This inverse relationship may reinforce the popular perception that a small percentage of people write the majority of blog, twitter, and wiki posts. This data also suggests that use of these technologies is not age specific or always connected to or influenced by writing in a school setting.

Beyond the Data:
Students are often writing alone and for personal fulfillment motives. But what does this mean?

Our findings suggest that students are doing a great deal of personal writing. They report writing alone and for personal fulfillment quite often. We hope that this finding helps us better understand the nature of personal writing for contemporary students. While they are often doing personal writing, we do not think that this writing is always private. For example, students are frequently writing alone when using cell phones, though they are frequently using them to connect to others through texting and social media platforms.

SECTION 6: WITH WHOM ARE PARTICIPANTS WRITING?

6.1: Participants Do Much of Their Most Common and Valued Writing Alone

While participants write with friends or classmates, [27] writing with these two groups is not valued nearly as much as writing alone.

6.2: Only 245 Participants Report Collaborating with Writing Center Consultants for Their Most Valued or Frequently Written Genres (One of the Lowest Ranked Collaborators, Behind Only "Other")

When compared with all of the other types of [28] collaborators, the fewest number of participants worked with writing center consultants while writing their most frequent and valued genres. Among those participants who report working with writing center consultants, they list it as their least used collaboration. Further, participants identified

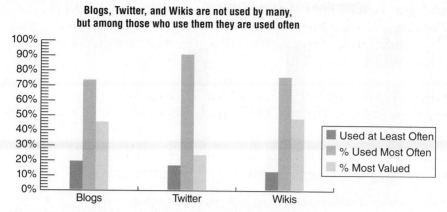

Figure 5 Percentage of students who associated each technology at least once with the writing they do, and the percentage of students who associated each technology with a most often written genre.

collaborating with writing center consultants as least valued (second only to "Other").

6.3: Writing with Work Colleagues Is Reported Less Often and Not Highly Valued

38% of participants report collaborating with work colleagues to write at least 29 one of their most frequent of valued genres. While 33% associate work colleagues with one of their most often written genres, only 12% of participants associate it with a most valued genre.

METHODOLOGY

Sampling

In this study, we constructed a purposive, stratified sample in an attempt to 30 match the demographic profile of US college students (those enrolled in both four-year and two-year institutions in 2010). We identified institutions for recruitment that had enabled us to construct a reasonable sample of US institutions of higher education. With regard to data analysis, in order to arrive at the findings in this report, two similar tests were utilized. Fisher's Exact Test was used to determine relationships between variables when possible (i.e., when results formed a 2 × 2 contingency table). Chi-square tests were used in all other situations. Results were considered significant at the .05 level.

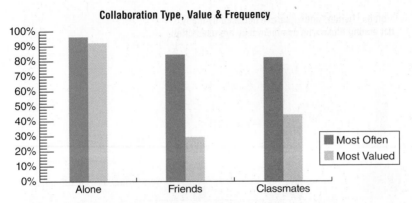

Figure 6 Percentage of students who associate each collaborator with their most frequently written and valued genres.

Our sampling resulted in the following profile: 31

- Age: The vast majority of participants (90%) were a "traditional" age for US institutions of higher education (18–23). Half of all participants were 19 years old, indicating that they had enrolled in college immediately after graduating from high school.

- Institution: 58% of participants attended a research university, 20% of participants attend a master's granting institution, and 11% of participants attend a Community college.

- Race and ethnicity: 43% of our sample was non-white, with 5% Black, 28% Hispanic, 8% Asian, and 2% Native American.

Comparison to Race and Ethnicity Profiles of Students in Higher Education

To further assess our sample, we compared the demographic data of those 32 completing our survey with both the 1999–2000 and the 2003–2004 "National Postsecondary Student Aid Study: Profile of Undergraduates in U.S. Postsecondary Education institutions" report issued by the U.S. National Center for Education Statistics (NCES).

The 2003–2004 version of the NCES report included a special focus on two- 33 year institutions, and so in its 2004 report of demographic data the center breaks out community colleges and 4-year institutions. The figure below shows how our sample compares with the NCES numbers:

As Figure 7 shows, we likely oversampled Hispanic students and, to a lesser 34 degree, Asian students. We undersampled African American students. That our sample includes a slightly higher percentage of non-white participants than

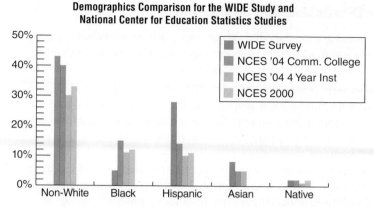

Figure 7 Race and ethnicity breakdown for Revisualizing Composition and two National Centers for Education Statistics Studies.

the NCES demographic profile of college students reflects a concerted effort on our part to construct a diverse student profile. The participation of the University of Texas, El Paso and Leeward Community College, respectively, contributed in large measure to the numbers in all of the minority population categories above with the exception of African American students. For future surveys, we should focus more carefully on ways to sample African American students at a level consistent with their numbers in the overall demographic profile (12–15%).

Survey Distribution

Distribution methods varied by institution based on local IRB recommenda- 35 tions. The survey was distributed via email to all students in first-year composition classes at Michigan State University, University of Texas, El Paso, and Leeward Community College. At Lansing Community College and the University of North Carolina, Pembroke, writing program faculty who teach first-year composition were contacted via email with the online survey link and distributed the survey link to students enrolled in their courses, some of which included first-year business and technical writing classes. At IPFW, the survey was distributed to all students enrolled in any writing course during the spring of 2010, including advanced writing and technical writing students, and a majority of students enrolled in first-year and intermediate composition courses. At Elon University, the survey was sent via email to all first-year students who matriculated in 2009 and were still enrolled in Spring 2010.

Questions for Discussion and Journaling

1. What research questions did the WIDE researchers ask here, and what research methods did they use to answer those questions? How do their research methods differ from those used by other authors in this chapter?

2. The WIDE researchers, along with other writing scholars in this chapter and throughout this book, understand writing broadly. The WIDE authors found that 78 percent of student respondents said that texting was one of the five most common types of writing they have done. However, they note that texting challenges "common perceptions of what counts as 'writing'" (para. 7). Drawing on your own experiences with texting and considering what you have read so far in this book, write a few sentences exploring your opinion of texting and how it fits into your developing understanding of what "writing" is.

3. The WIDE authors made a list of the top ten genres most frequently written by students. Make your own top-ten list based on your own experience. How does it compare with the WIDE findings? If there are differences, what do you think accounts for them? Now consider how these types of writing (and the technologies needed for engaging in them) impact who you are as a literate person. How would things be different if you didn't have access to those technologies?

4. The WIDE researchers found that students valued texting the most, but the next three genres they valued most were academic. When the WIDE researchers asked students what kind of writing they valued, how do you think students were defining "value"? Do you think they value texting and research papers in the same way? Consider the list of genres you write (that you made for question 3, above). How are these different genres valuable to you? What is it about them that makes them valuable? Is it easy for you to compare and rank the kinds of value that each of those genres has for you, or is it like comparing apples and oranges?

5. Where do you think your perception of what is "valuable" comes from? Drawing on what you've learned so far in this book, is there any reason to question the kinds of writing you see as valuable and make room for other kinds of writing, or other ways of valuing that writing?

6. In addition to the genres that students write, WIDE also organizes findings by the purposes for which students write: school, work, entertainment, personal fulfillment, civic participation. Think about the genres that you and other students write. Do they take on different kinds of value and different conventions depending on the purpose and context? For example, is an e-mail always an e-mail, or do e-mails differ a lot if they are written for work, school, and entertainment?

7. Before this reading, we asked you to research and identify the type of institution you attend. Why do you attend this type of school? What in your history led you here, versus to another kind of institution? How does the experience of being here, along with the previous experiences that led you here, shape your literate self? What might be different if you had attended different kinds

of institutions? Imagine those types of institutions as what Brandt calls *literacy sponsors*. How have they sponsored you? What various literacy practices have they pushed you toward and away from?

Applying and Exploring Ideas

1. The WIDE researchers found that students write alone quite frequently, but that their technologies and genres are actually linking them to others. Write several pages imagining how you think technology has changed what it means to write alone. For example, is posting on Facebook while you are alone in your dorm room the same as writing in your diary while alone in an isolated farmhouse in 1872? How has technology changed the way writing connects people? If you want, you could try writing a page as your current self, and then a page as the self you might have been if you were writing in 1872 or 1972.

2. Because this study involves surveying college students about the kinds of writing in which they regularly engage, it invites you to compare your own experiences with their findings and to follow up with your own research projects. Work with a partner to identify two or three research questions you would like to explore further as a result of what you read here and elsewhere in this chapter. What are you interested in learning about — what people's literacy experiences are, what has shaped those experiences, what technologies, goals, and values impact their literacy, and so on?

3. How would you go about finding answers to the questions you posed above in question 2?

4. The authors state that they are "working from the assumption that students lead complex writing lives" (para. 2). They then go on to all of the ways that students' writing lives are complex. Make a list of the various ways that your writing life is and has been complex, using their discussion as a model.

5. Conduct an informal survey of your classmates, your roommates, fraternity or sorority, or some other group in order to come up with a list of all the technologies Grabill et al. use to engage with writing, using the list in Section 5 as a starting point. Then research the technologies people used to engage in writing 20 or 40 years ago, perhaps by interviewing your parents, grandparents, older cousins, or people at work. Once you have the two lists, write two to three pages that outline the different technologies used in different time periods, and explore how you think those technologies impact writers' identities, behaviors, and values.

META MOMENT   If you haven't thought before now about the ways that technology and writing are deeply intertwined, keep it in mind as you write going forward. Ask yourself what would happen if you used a different technology to complete the writing task, or if you valued writing in various modes differently than you have in the past.

WRITING ABOUT LITERACIES: WRITING ASSIGNMENTS

To help you learn and explore the ideas in this chapter, we are suggesting three Assignment Options for larger writing projects: Literacy Narrative, Group Analysis of Literacy History, and Linguistic Observation and Analysis, an extensive synthesis of some of the activities in this chapter.

LITERACY NARRATIVE

Drawing on what you have read in this chapter, examine your own literacy history, habits, and processes. The purpose of this inquiry is to get to know yourself better as a reader and writer. As Malcolm X argued, awareness gives power and purpose: The more you know about yourself as a reader and writer, the more control you are likely to have over these processes.

Invention, Research, and Analysis   Start your literacy narrative by considering your history as a reader and writer. Try to get at what your memories and feelings about writing/reading are and how you actually write/read now. Do not make bland generalizations ("I really love to write"), but go into detail about how you learned to write/read. Mine your memory, thinking carefully about where you've been and where you are as a reader and writer. You might begin by answering questions such as these:

- How did you learn to write and/or read?
- What kinds of writing/reading have you done in the past?
- How much have you enjoyed the various kinds of writing/reading you've done?
- What are particularly vivid memories that you have of reading, writing, or activities that involved them?
- What is your earliest memory of reading and of writing?
- What sense did you get, as you were learning to read and write, of the *value* of reading and writing, and where did that sense come from?
- What frustrated you about reading and writing as you were learning and then as you progressed through school? By the same token, what pleased you about them?
- What kind of writing and reading do you do most commonly?
- What is your favorite kind of writing and reading?
- What are your current attitudes, feelings, or stance toward reading and writing?

- Where do you think your feelings about and habits of writing and reading come from? How did you get to where you are as a writer/reader? What in your past has made you the kind of writer/reader you are today?
- Who are some people in your life who have acted as literacy sponsors?
- What are some institutions and experiences in your life that have acted as literacy sponsors?
- What technologies impact you as a writer? When, where, and why did you start using them?
- What have any of the readings in this chapter reminded you about from your past or present as a reader and writer?

Questions such as these help you start thinking deeply about your literate past. You should try to come up with some answers for all of them, but it's unlikely that you'll actually include all the answers to all those questions in your literacy narrative itself. Right now you're just thinking and writing about what reading and writing was like for you. When you plan the narrative, you'll select from among all the material you've been remembering and thinking about. The question then becomes, how will you decide what to talk about out of everything you *could* talk about? This depends in part on your analysis of what you're remembering.

As you consider what all these memories and experiences suggest, you should be looking for an overall "so what?" — a main theme, a central "finding," an overall conclusion that your consideration leads you to draw. It might be an insight about why you read and write as you do today based on past experience. It might be an argument about what works or what doesn't work in literacy education, on the basis of your experience. It might be a resolution to do something differently, or to *keep* doing something that's been working. It might be a description of an ongoing conflict or tension you experience when you read and write — or the story of how you resolved such a conflict earlier in your literacy history. (It could also be a lot of other things.)

Planning and Drafting Your consideration and analysis of your previous experience, one way or another, will lead you to a *main point* that your literacy narrative will demonstrate and support. That main point is what you've learned in your analysis; the literacy narrative then explains why you think what you do about that main point. It draws in whatever stories, experiences, moments, and descriptions help explain the point. Because your literacy narrative tells the particular story of a particular person — you — its shape will depend on the particular experiences you've had and the importance you attach to them. Therefore, it's difficult to suggest a single structure for the literacy narrative that will work for all writers. The structure that you use should support your particular intention and content.

Headings or sections (such as Part I or Act I or "Early Literacy Memories"), may be helpful, but your content may better lend itself to write one coherent, unbroken essay. Do what works for you, given the material you want to include. Just be sure to organize and make some sort of point (or points).

Because your literacy narrative is about you, you may find it difficult to write without talking about yourself in the first person. Using "I" when you need to will make the piece feel somewhat informal, which is appropriate to this kind of writing.

If you wish, include pictures or artifacts with your narrative. You could bring in your first spelling test or the award you won for the essay contest or the article in the school newspaper about your poem. If your circumstances make it appropriate, write this narrative in some mode other than alphabet-on-paper: for example, write it as a blog entry on your website and incorporate multimedia, or write it as a performed or acted presentation, or make it a PowerPoint presentation, a YouTube video, a poster, or whatever else works to reach the audience you want to and to help you make your point.

What Makes It Good?   This assignment asks you to carefully think about your history as a reader and writer, to tell a clear story that helps make a point, and to write a readable piece. So, be sure your piece (1) tells a story or stories about your literacy history, (2) talks about where you are now as a writer and reader and how your past has shaped your present, and (3) makes some overall point about your literacy experiences. Of course, this essay should also be clear, organized, interesting, and well-edited. The strongest literacy narratives will incorporate ideas and concepts from the readings in this chapter to help frame and explain your experiences.

GROUP ANALYSIS OF LITERACY HISTORY

Collaborate with a group of classmates on a formal research study of some theme that emerges when everyone's literacy experiences are compared. You can use the following instructions to guide the writing of this kind of study, which lends itself to answering "bigger" questions or making larger points than a single literacy narrative really can.

Conduct a Self-Study   Post your answers to the following questions on the class blog, wiki, website, or learning management system:

- How did you learn to write and/or read?
- What kinds of writing/reading have you done in the past?
- How much have you enjoyed the various kinds of writing/reading you've done?
- What are particularly vivid memories that you have of reading, writing, or activities that involved them?
- What is your earliest memory of reading and your earliest memory of writing?
- What sense did you get, as you were learning to read and write, of the *value* of reading and writing, and where did that sense come from?

- What frustrated you about reading and writing as you were learning and then as you progressed through school? By the same token, what pleased you about them?

- What kind of writing/reading do you do most commonly?

- What is your favorite kind of writing/reading?

- What are your current attitudes, feelings, or stance toward reading and writing?

- Where do you think your feelings about and habits of writing and reading come from?

- How did you get to where you are as a writer/reader? What in your past has made you the kind of writer/reader you are today?

- Who are some people in your life who have acted as literacy sponsors?

- What are some institutions and experiences in your life that have acted as literacy sponsors?

- What have any of the readings in this chapter reminded you about from your past or present as a reader and writer?

Discuss and Code the Self-Studies   In your group, read the answers to the self-interviews. Look together for common themes, recurring trends, or unique experiences, and determine which of these might be most interesting to further research and write about. What data will you need to collect to explore these themes? (For example, do you need to interview some classmates further? Interview people outside the class?) Common themes that emerge from this sort of study include the role of technology in literacy, hobbies as literacy sponsors, motivations for literacy learning, privilege and access, and help overcoming literacy struggles.

Collaborate to Write about Emergent Themes   Pair up with another student by choosing an emergent theme to write a paper about. As a pair, pinpoint a specific research question related to your theme and gather whatever further data is necessary. Drawing on terms and ideas from this chapter's readings, you can then write your analysis of and findings on this theme.

Planning and Drafting   Before beginning to write, the group as a whole should consider the audience and genre appropriate for this paper. Discuss the following questions together:

- Who should be the audience for what you write? How can you best reach them?

- How would you like to write about your findings? In a somewhat formal, scholarly way? In a more storytelling, narrative way?

- What content and format would make this narrative most effective? Paper, text-only? Paper, text, and images? Online text and images? Online text, images, and video?

As you analyze and begin to write with your partner, you should consider the following questions:

- What is your research question?
- What answers to this question do your research and analysis suggest?
- What data support each of these answers?

These questions will actually help you arrange your paper, too, in most cases. That is, the paper includes an introduction that poses your research question and explains the value of it. It goes on to explain how you attempted to answer the question — what methods you used to gather the data you gathered to try to reach answers. Next, you talk about that data and what answers it led you to. The paper concludes with your sense of "so what?" — the implications that your findings seem to suggest. What have you learned about this emergent theme from your research, and what does it mean for the rest of us?

If you haven't written collaboratively before, you may find it a bit of a challenge to coordinate schedules with your co-author, to decide how to break up the work of writing the piece, and to make sure you both always have current information and the other writer's most up-to-date ideas so that you can write the part of the piece you need to when you need to. You'll also find that you rewrite each other's material a bit — this will help it sound like the piece was written by a single voice or mind rather than two people.

What Makes It Good? A good analysis of an issue emerging from your group's literacy history may take a number of different shapes but will tend to have these traits in common:

- A clear, directly stated research question
- A detailed description of what methods you used to try to answer the question
- A clear explanation of what you found in your research and what conclusions it leads you to
- An explanation of "so what?" — why your findings might matter
- The usual: readable, fluent prose; transitions that make the paper easy to follow; and editing and proofreading that keep the paper from distracting readers with typos and goofs

LINGUISTIC OBSERVATION AND ANALYSIS

In this chapter, Young and Mellix illustrate that there are a variety of "Englishes," and that different varieties of English are valued differently. People who learn and speak the dominant "standard" version of English at home have power, authority, and privilege that those who learn other versions do not. However, Young also argues that different versions of English really aren't so different, and that in our culture people are more often than not borrowing freely from different forms of English in their daily interactions, resulting in what he calls "code meshing." If you read Young and Mellix, you likely conducted some quick field research in order to test their claims. Here, you will continue that research in order to reach some conclusions about what it means to "speak English" and what forms of English have power — and in what settings.

Observations and Interviews First, choose three different sites where you can expect to find people of different ages, occupations, genders, races, interests, linguistic backgrounds, etc. — for example, outside a movie theater, in your sorority, at a convenience store, at a bar or restaurant, in an office. Consult with your teacher and classmates about sites that would be appropriate for observation. You want to be cautious about conducting observations in sites where you might make people uncomfortable. As a result, it might be easiest to choose sites where you regularly interact.

Arrange for one to two hours where you can sit in each setting and listen and observe people interacting. Get permission if the site isn't public. Take careful notes. Who are you seeing? What are you hearing? Write down phrases, words, notes about tone and loudness, etc.

Next, conduct interviews with three people who are different from one another in some significant ways — age, race, gender, class, occupation, where they were raised, etc. Be respectful of people and their time when you set up the interviews. Ask them these questions:

- Do you speak the same way in every situation?
- Do you feel like the way you speak at home with your family is the way you speak at school and/or at work?
- If not, what are some of the differences? Can you give examples?
- Do you feel like one of the ways you speak is valued more highly than the others? How do you know?

Caution: When you interview and observe, record *what people actually say*, not what you *expect* them to say. It will be easy to stereotype and to turn stereotypes into expectations. Listening to people and really hearing them must precede making conclusions or judgments. Ask yourself as you are listening to people whether your stereotypes and expectations are getting in the way of collecting data.

Analyzing Data   Take a look at the data that you collected. Lay out your interview notes and transcripts and read them carefully, annotating as you go. Then ask yourself the following questions:

- What are you seeing?
- Do you see everyone (or anyone) speaking one clear version of a standard English? If not, what are some of the variations?
- Do you see people switching back and forth between different versions of English? Do they do this within one setting, or in different settings? What are some examples?
- Do you think they are code switching, code meshing, or both?
- What do your interviewees say about their experiences changing language forms?
- What forms of language seem to have power or authority, and in what situations? How do you know?

Considering What You Think   Given what you read in this chapter, what you saw in your research, and what you've experienced in your own life, what do you have to say about the following questions:

- Is there one standard form of English?
- Are some forms of English inherently "superior" to other forms? If not, are some forms of English *treated as though* they are inherently "superior" to other forms?
- How can you tell when a certain form of English has power and authority? What happens to suggest that this is the case?
- How do you think those forms of English gained that power and authority?
- How have you personally been impacted by people's attitudes about appropriate and dominant forms of English?
- What did you *expect* to hear and find going into this study?
- Did your expectations make it difficult for you to really listen to people without stereotyping them?
- What does your experience trying to listen and observe suggest about the difficulties of conducing "unbiased" research?

Write a Reflection   It will not be possible or desirable for you to write a definitive argument-driven research essay about what you found. In order to do that, you would need much more data, collected across wider varieties of sites, and much more training in how to conduct linguistic analysis. Instead, we want to engage here in a formal, data- and research-driven reflection about what you are learning, think-ing, and struggling with around issues of language use.

Write a five- to six-page reflection that explores your growing understanding of what it means to "speak English," what it means in practice for people to speak differ-ent forms of English, how power is enacted through various versions of English, and how your own expectations and experiences impact your ability to conduct research.

As you reflect and take positions, draw on the data that you've collected, as well as your own experiences. As you've learned in this chapter, your own experiences are always going to shape what you think and understand, and will inevitably shape your writing. This is why it's important for you to also reflect on yourself, your expec-tations of what you would find, and how your expectations impacted your ability to collect and analyze data.

In a project like this, you should be cautious about trying to speak authorita-tively about other people's experience. The purpose of this assignment is to grow and expand your thinking on difficult questions by gathering data and reflecting on what you find when you really listen to other people in order to interrogate your ideas and assumptions. Be cautious about assuming that your language variation is "normal" or superior to what you are hearing from the people you observe and speak with.

What Makes It Good? This is what writing scholars would call a "writing to learn" assignment. The primary goal is for you to think about, reflect on, and grapple with ideas about language that you may not have considered before, and to learn how to try to collect some data in order to test out ideas and assumptions.

In assessing whether your completed reflection is successful, consider the follow-ing questions:

- Have you integrated ideas and terms from relevant readings in this chapter?

- Have you collected data and used it to inform your ideas?

- Have you written about your ideas and reflected on them in ways that readers (likely your classmates and teacher) will be able to follow?

- Have you supported your thinking with data from readings and from your research?

- Have you been careful to reflect on what you actually heard when you listened to others and to avoid stereotyping people and their languages?

- Have you thought about your own positionality and the history and expec-tations you brought to this project?

If you've done these things, and demonstrated that you are trying hard to think through questions that are difficult, then you've written a good reflection.

CHAPTER 3

INDIVIDUAL IN COMMUNITY:

How Does Writing Help People Get Things Done?

Start your drive

$10 can provide up to $90 worth of food!

The Second Harvest Food Bank virtual food drive is a representational web-based tool that allows individuals and organizations to hold an online food drive. While we love donations in any form, our virtual food drive allows us to serve more clients, more efficiently. It's fast, easy and fun!

© Second Harvest Food Bank of Central Florida

In the previous chapter, you explored your own literacy history and considered how individuals' literate pasts influence their current literacy practices and attitudes. In this chapter, you will broaden your scope to consider how groups and communities influence readers, writers, and texts. People don't write in a vacuum. Their literate histories influence their current writing practices, but their purposes for writing texts, and the people to and with whom they write, also influence how they write, what they write, how their texts are used, and how users make meaning of their texts. The central idea, the **threshold concept**, in this chapter is that people use texts and discourse in order to *do something*, to *make meaning*. And the texts and language they create **mediate** *meaningful activities*. (*Mediate* here means something like "intervene to shape an experience" — see the Glossary entry for more.) People construct meaning through texts and language, and texts construct meaning as people use them.

In the photo on the previous page, the Second Harvest Food Bank of Central Florida is using their website to encourage possible donors to host a "virtual" food drive. Here they use text to explain how a virtual food drive works, and they use visuals, alphabetic text, numbers, and colors. They create these materials for the possible food drive hosts to use so that they don't have to create anything themselves. This page serves multiple purposes: to encourage people to host virtual food drives, to convince them that doing so is easy, and to provide the needed materials for doing so — and those materials can be "recomposed" and reused in another setting, to encourage others to sponsor food drives for the hungry (the virtual food drive materials gain what Jim Ridolfo and Dànielle Nicole DeVoss in the next chapter call "rhetorical velocity" [p. 512]). The text here is all about getting things done — helping readers make meaning about hunger, and helping them take action to feed the hungry.

Consider another related example from the perspective of the writer and the site in which she is writing. Another way for food banks to raise money to feed the hungry is through "appeal letters" that they might send out to all past volunteers and donors at Christmas. How the staff person who writes the letter does so is influenced by her understanding of the ideas and interests of the people reading it — what they need, want, and value — as well as by her own training as a fundraiser, all of her past writing experiences, her supervisor's expectations, and her own and other staff members' experiences with past fundraising letters. The letter the staff person writes mediates the activities of fundraising and feeding the hungry. It is read by many people who have very different reactions to it (some will throw it away, others will set it aside and forget about it, others will volunteer but not donate money, others will donate money).

Readers' responses to this letter will continue to shape the work of the food bank, and the food bank and its donors and volunteers and clients all shape how future fundraising letters are written. The fundraising letter, in turn, shapes the work of the food bank — how it is understood, or whether it can be done at all. If this letter is not effective, the food bank might have to cut back services, and it will surely revise how future fundraising letters are written or distributed. The people who read the letter might start thinking about hunger and poverty differently as a result of what they read. Meaning and activities about hunger, poverty, fundraising, and so on are constructed through the fundraising letter. For example, the writer might want to help possible donors think about hungry children, and thus include a photo of a child in the letter — not the stereotypical "homeless person" that might first come to people's minds — and emphasize the number of hungry children in the area. In doing so, he is shaping meaning for the readers.

This chapter asks you to take a close look at how texts are constructed as a result of the needs and activities of various groups, and how groups of people use communication to achieve their shared goals and purposes. In this chapter, you'll learn one or more theoretical terms that will help you look at and understand groups: **Discourses** (that's from Gee, p. 274), **discourse communities** (that's from Johns, p. 319), and **activity systems** (that's from Kain and Wardle, p. 395). You'll consider how the texts construct meaning for the people who read, write, and otherwise use them. You'll consider the expectations, norms, histories, and people who influence, construct, and interpret texts, and you'll consider how texts help groups get work done and achieve shared goals — or impede work when they are not successful. And you'll think carefully about the language — the discourse(s) — that help or hinder people in their efforts to make meaning, get work done, accomplish goals, and become part of new groups (or not).

The authors whose work appears in this chapter are describing something you do every day: When you go to your dorm and interact with your roommates, for example, you are in one discourse community; when you go to biology class, you are in another. And most of us are amazingly efficient at navigating multiple discourse communities: What you learn in biology about evolution might conflict with what you are taught in your Bible study course, for example, but most of you learn to manage that tension and figure out how to talk and interact differently in different settings. The language and texts you use in each discourse community help you accomplish your collective purposes there.

As you examine texts through the analytical lenses described in this chapter, you'll want to begin thinking of texts as **genres**, a term we explained in Chapter 1 (see pages 17–21), and which is referenced in this chapter by several of the authors. A reminder here about what genres are: If you see a particular text and you recognize it as having a particular name and expected characteristics or conventions that respond to recurring situations, it is a *genre*. Scholar Carolyn Miller tells us that genres arise in response to repeated **rhetorical situations** (a term described more fully in Chapter 4). As a familiar example, people do nice things for others repeatedly and recipients of the kindness need to do something in return; thus, the genre of thank-you cards came into being. These cards make easier the task of responding the next time someone does something nice for you; instead of having to think through all the ways you could respond, you can just buy a thank-you card and write the standard words of gratitude you were likely taught as a child. As you've already considered in Chapter 1, syllabi are another example you'll recognize: Each time you go into a new classroom, you need to know what is expected of you. Teachers over time came to respond to this situation similarly by providing students with a syllabus. There are thousands of examples of these kinds of texts: horoscopes, obituaries, job application letters, etc. All of them arose in response to the fact that certain situations happened again and again and were easier to respond to with recognizable forms.

Genres are interesting because, although they are recognizable due to their common features across texts, no two examples of a genre are ever exactly the same, and their features change over time. So one teacher's syllabus is not exactly like the next teacher's syllabus. And the syllabi teachers give out today are different than the ones teachers gave out a hundred years ago — which might not even have been called a "syllabus." The point is that genres help people get things done as they engage in different activities. Having a syllabus means that students have to guess a lot less than they would without a syllabus, and teachers don't have to repeat instructions as much. In other words, genres help *mediate* the activities in which groups of people (in this example, teachers and students) engage.

This chapter presents three lenses for analyzing how texts mediate work in communities: discourse theory (Gee), discourse community theory (Johns), and activity theory (Kain and Wardle). For each theory, you will first read an explanation and description, and then examples of how scholars and students use that theory.

CHAPTER GOALS

- To understand the threshold concept that language and texts (genres) mediate group activities
- To define and understand key terms related to that threshold concept, including *Discourse, discourse community, activity system,* and *genre*
- To gain tools for examining the discourse and texts used by various communities
- To gain tools for conducting primary research
- To conduct research and write about it for various audiences
- To understand writing and research as processes
- To improve as readers of complex, research-based texts

Literacy, Discourse, and Linguistics

Introduction

JAMES PAUL GEE

Framing the Reading

James Paul Gee (his last name is pronounced like the "gee" in "gee whiz") is a Regents' Professor and Mary Lou Fulton Presidential Professor of Literacy Studies at Arizona State University. Gee has taught linguistics at the University of Wisconsin at Madison, Stanford University, Northeastern University, Boston University, and the University of Southern California. His book *Sociolinguistics and Literacies* (1990) was important in the formation of the interdisciplinary field known as "New Literacy Studies," and he's published a number of other works on literacy as well, including *Why Video Games Are Good for Your Soul* (2005). Based on his research, he's a widely respected voice on literacy among his peers.

In this article, Gee introduces his term **Discourses**, which he explains as "saying (writing)-doing-being-valuing-believing combinations" that are "ways of being in the world." (The capital D is important for Gee, to make a *Discourse* distinct from *discourse*, or "connected stretches of language" that we use every day to communicate with each other.) Gee spends a lot of time working to make these definitions clear, using a variety of examples. A number of other terms crop up as well in his work: *dominant* and *nondominant* Discourses, *primary* and *secondary* Discourses, **literacy**, **apprenticeship**, **metaknowledge**, and **mushfake**, among others. Probably the most useful way to read this article for the first time is to try to (1) define terms and (2) apply what Gee is saying to your own experience by trying to think of related examples from your own life.

Gee, James Paul. "Literacy, Discourse, and Linguistics: Introduction." *Journal of Education*, vol. 171, no.1, 1989, pp. 5–17.

As you read, think back to the underlying threshold concepts of this chapter: that people use texts and Discourse in order to *do something*, to *make meaning*; that the texts and language they create *mediate meaningful activities*; and that people construct meaning through texts and language, and texts construct meaning as people use them. Ask yourself how the Discourses that Gee talks about are tools for helping people make meaning or not, get things done or not.

You'll find one particularly controversial argument in the article. Gee insists that you can't "more or less" embody a Discourse — you're either recognized by others as a full member of it, or you're not. Many readers can't make this argument line up with their perceptions of their own experiences in acquiring new Discourses; they haven't experienced this "all-or-nothing" effect. It's also possible to read Gee's article as undermining itself: He explains that we are never "purely" members of a single Discourse, but rather, that a given Discourse is influenced by other Discourses of which we're also members. By this reasoning, there may be no such thing as embodying a Discourse fully or perfectly.

The important thing is this: When you encounter that subargument, or others you might have trouble accepting, your job as a reader is to stay engaged in the *overall* argument while "setting aside" the particular argument you're not sure about. As you know from your own experience, people can be wrong about smaller points while still being right about bigger ones. Further, scholarly arguments are made very precisely with very careful language; Gee's argument might work if you read it exactly as he intended it to be understood, without trying to apply it too broadly.

Gee's text is one we have chosen to tag, partially because of its complexity. Before you begin, review the explanation of the reading tags in Chapter 1 (pp. 58–59) in order to get the most from them.

Getting Ready to Read

Before you read, do at least one of the following activities:

- Google the term *mushfake*. What comes up?

- Consider two or three activities you take part in that are very different from each other, having different languages and purposes (for example, college, volunteering, and a hobby like gaming). Does one influence the way you do the others, or do they remain distinctly separate in your life? Explain.

As you read, consider the following questions:

- Why is Gee so concerned with how people learn Discourses? What does it have to do with education?

- Are there alternative explanations for the knowledge Gee describes? Could we have similar knowledge for some reason *other than* that there are Discourses?

- Does Gee's discussion of Discourses sound similar to ideas you've encountered in other chapters in this book? If so, which ones?

WHAT I PROPOSE in the following papers, in the main, is a way of talking about literacy and linguistics. I believe that a new field of study, integrating "psycho" and "socio" approaches to language from a variety of disciplines, is emerging, a field which we might call literacy studies. Much of this work, I think (and hope), shares at least some of the assumptions of the following papers. These papers, though written at different times, and for different purposes, are, nonetheless, based on the claim that the focus of literacy studies or applied linguistics should not be language, or literacy, but social practices. This claim, I believe, has a number of socially important and cognitively interesting consequences.

"Language" is a misleading term; it too often suggests "grammar." It is a truism that a person can know perfectly the grammar of a language and not know how to use that language. It is not just *what* you say, but *how* you say it. If I enter my neighborhood bar and say to my tattooed drinking buddy, as I sit down, "May I have a match please?" my grammar is perfect, but what I have said is wrong nonetheless. It is less often remarked that a person could be able to use a language perfectly and *still* not make sense. It is not just *how* you say it, but what you *are* and *do* when you say it. If I enter my neighborhood bar and say to my drinking buddy, as I sit down, "Gime a match, wouldya?," while placing a napkin on the bar stool to avoid getting my newly pressed designer jeans dirty, I have said the right thing, but my "saying-doing" combination is nonetheless all wrong.

Look Ahead

GENRE CUES

1 — CARS: Territory

2 — Conversation

3 — CARS: Occupy

4 — So What? Because this article introduces a collection of others, its organization is unusual. Instead of explaining the consequences covered in all the articles right here, Gee next transitions to explaining the problem they all work on.

READING CUES

Look Ahead As an introduction, this piece doesn't have sections and headings. Scan for transition words at the beginning of paragraphs, like "So," "Now," "Furthermore," "Finally," "First," "Second," and "But."

F. Niyi Akinnaso and Cheryl Ajirotutu (1982) present "simulated job interviews" from two welfare mothers in a CETA job training program. The first woman, asked whether she has ever shown initiative in a previous job, responds: "Well, yes, there's this Walgreen's Agency, I worked as a microfilm operator, OK. And it was a snow storm, OK. And it was usually six people workin' in a group . . ." and so forth (p. 34). This woman is simply using the wrong grammar (the wrong "dialect") for this type of (middle-class) interview. It's a perfectly good grammar (dialect), it just won't get you this type of job in this type of society.

The second woman (the authors' "success" case) responds to a similar question by saying " . . . I was left alone to handle the office. I didn't really have a lot of experience. But I had enough experience to deal with any situations that came up . . . and those that I couldn't handle at the time, if there was someone who had more experience than myself, I asked questions to find out what procedure I would use. If something came up and if I didn't know who to really go to, I would jot it down . . . on a piece of paper, so that I wouldn't forget that if anyone that was more qualified than myself, I could ask them about it and how I would go about solving it. So I feel I'm capable of handling just about any situation, whether it's on my own or under supervision" (p. 34). This woman hasn't got a real problem with her grammar (remember this is *speech*, not *writing*), nor is there any real problem with the *use* to which she puts that grammar, but she is expressing the *wrong values*. She views being left in charge as just another form of supervision, namely, supervision by "other people's" knowledge and expertise. And she fails to characterize her own expertise in the overly optimistic form called for by such interviews. Using this response as an example of "successful training" is only possible because the authors, aware that language is more than grammar (namely, "use"), are unaware that communication is more than language use.

At any moment we are using language we must say or write the right thing in the right way while playing the right social role and (appearing) to hold the right values, beliefs, and attitudes.

277

5 Thus, what is important is not language, and surely not grammar, but *saying (writing)-doing-being-valuing-believing combinations*. These combinations I call "Discourses," with a capital "D" ("discourse" with a little "d," to me, means connected stretches of language that make sense, so "discourse" is part of "Discourse"). Discourses are ways of being in the world; they are forms of life which integrate words, acts, values, beliefs, attitudes, and social identities as well as gestures, glances, body positions, and clothes.

6 A Discourse is a sort of "identity kit" which comes complete with the appropriate costume and instructions on how to act, talk, and often write, so as to take on a particular role that others will recognize. Being "trained" as a linguist meant that I learned to speak, think, and act like a linguist, and to recognize others when they do so. Some other examples of Discourses: (enacting) being an American or a Russian, a man or a woman, a member of a certain socioeconomic class, a factory worker or a boardroom executive, a doctor or a hospital patient, a teacher, an administrator, or a student, a student of physics or a student of literature, a member of a sewing circle, a club, a street gang, a lunchtime social gathering, or a regular at a local bar. We all have many Discourses.

7 How does one acquire a Discourse? It turns out that much that is claimed, controversially, to be true of second language acquisition or socially situated cognition (Beebe, 1988; Dulay, Burt, & Krashen, 1982; Grosjean, 1982; Krashen, 1982, 1985a, 1985b; Krashen & Terrell, 1983; Lave, 1988; Rogoff & Lave, 1984) is, in fact, more obviously true of the acquisition of Discourses. Discourses are not mastered by overt instruction (even less so than languages, and hardly anyone ever fluently acquired a second language sitting in a classroom), but by enculturation ("apprenticeship") into social practices through scaffolded and supported

GENRE CUES

5 — **Making Knowledge** Gee differentiates previous knowledge from new by emphasizing his concept. The "I" statement says he is contributing new knowledge to the conversation.

6 — Conversation

7 — Extending

interaction with people who have already mastered the Discourse (Cazden, 1988; Heath, 1983). This is how we all acquired our native language and our home-based Discourse. It is how we acquire all later, more public-oriented Discourses. If you have no access to the social practice, you don't get in the Discourse, you don't have it. You cannot overtly teach anyone a Discourse, in a classroom or anywhere else. Discourses are not bodies of knowledge like physics or archeology or linguistics. Therefore, ironically, while you can overtly teach someone *linguistics*, a body of knowledge, you can't teach them *to be a linguist*, that is, to use a Discourse. The most you can do is to let them practice being a linguist with you.

The various Discourses which constitute each of us as persons are changing and often are not fully consistent with each other; there is often conflict and tension between the values, beliefs, attitudes, interactional styles, uses of language, and ways of being in the world which two or more Discourses represent. Thus, there is no real sense in which we humans are consistent or well integrated creatures from a cognitive or social viewpoint, though, in fact, most Discourses assume that we are (and thus we do too, while we are in them).

All of us, through our *primary socialization* early in life in the home and peer group, acquire (at least) one initial Discourse. This initial Discourse, which I call our *primary Discourse*, is the one we first use to make sense of the world and interact with others. Our primary Discourse constitutes our original and home-based sense of identity, and, I believe, it can be seen whenever we are interacting with "intimates" in totally casual (unmonitored) social interaction. We acquire this primary Discourse, not by overt instruction, but by being a member of a primary socializing group (family, clan, peer group). Further, aspects and pieces of the primary Discourse become a "carrier" or "foundation" for Discourses acquired later in life. Primary Discourses differ significantly across various social (cultural, ethnic, regional, and economic) groups in the United States.

After our initial socialization in our home community, each of us interacts with various non-home-based social institutions—

GENRE CUES

8 — Making Knowledge

institutions in the public sphere, beyond the family and immediate kin and peer group. These may be local stores and churches, schools, community groups, state and national businesses, agencies and organizations, and so forth. Each of these social institutions commands and demands one or more Discourses and we acquire these fluently to the extent that we are given access to these institutions and are allowed apprenticeships within them.

(9) | Such Discourses I call *secondary Discourses*.

We can also make an important distinction between *dominant Discourses* and *nondominant Discourses*. Dominant Discourses are secondary Discourses the mastery of which, at a particular place and time, brings with it the (potential) acquisition of social "goods" (money, prestige, status, etc.). Nondominant Discourses are secondary Discourses the mastery of which often brings solidarity with a particular social network, but not wider status and social goods in the society at large. **11**

Finally, and yet more importantly, we can always ask about how much *tension or conflict* is present between any two of a person's Discourses (Rosaldo, 1989). We have argued above that some degree of conflict and tension (if only because of the discrete historical origins of particular Discourses) will almost always be present. However, some people experience more overt and direct conflicts between two or more of their Discourses than do others (for example, many women academics feel conflict between certain feminist Discourses and certain standard academic Discourses such as traditional literary criticism). I argue that when such conflict or tension exists, it can deter acquisition of one or the other or both of the conflicting Discourses, or, at least, affect the fluency of a mastered Discourse on certain occasions of use (e.g., in stressful situations such as interviews). **12**

(10) |

Very often dominant groups in a society apply rather constant "tests" of the fluency of the dominant Discourses in which their **13**

GENRE CUES

9 — Making Knowledge

10 — Making Knowledge

power is symbolized. These tests take on two functions: they are tests of "natives" or, at least, "fluent users" of the Discourse, and they are *gates* to exclude "non-natives" (people whose very conflicts with dominant Discourses show they were not, in fact, "born" to them). The sorts of tension and conflict we have mentioned here are particularly acute when they involve tension and conflict between one's primary Discourse and a dominant secondary Discourse.

Discourses, primary and secondary, can be studied, in some ways, like languages. And, in fact, some of what we know about second language acquisition is relevant to them, if only in a metaphorical way. Two Discourses can *interfere* with one another, like two languages; aspects of one Discourse can be *transferred* to another Discourse, as one can transfer a grammatical feature from one language to another. For instance, the primary Discourse of many middle-class homes has been influenced by secondary Discourses like those used in schools and business. This is much less true of the primary Discourse in many lower socio-economic black homes, though this primary Discourse has influenced the secondary Discourse used in black churches.   14

Furthermore, if one has not mastered a particular secondary Discourse which nonetheless one must try to use, several things can happen, things which rather resemble what can happen when one has failed to fluently master a second language. One can fall back on one's primary Discourse, adjusting it in various ways to try to fit it to the needed functions; this response is very common, but almost always socially disastrous. Or one can use another, perhaps related, secondary Discourse. Or one can use a simplified, or stereotyped version of the required secondary Discourse. These processes are similar to those linguists study under the rubrics of *language contact*, *pidginization*, and *creolization*.   15

 I believe that any socially useful definition of "literacy" must be couched in terms of the notion of Discourse. Thus, I   16

GENRE CUES

 CARS: Niche Gee uses his preceding discussion of Discourse to open a new niche for conversation about *literacy*, which he raises here for the first time.

define "*literacy*" as *the mastery of or fluent control over a second-ary Discourse.* Therefore, literacy is always plural: *literacies* (there are many of them, since there are many secondary Discourses, and we all have some and fail to have others). If we wanted to be rather pedantic and literalistic, then we could define "literacy" as "mastery of or fluent control over secondary Discourses *involving print*" (which is almost all of them in a modern society). But I see no gain from the addition of the phrase "involving print," other than to assuage the feelings of people committed (as I am not) to reading and writing as decontextualized and isolable skills. We can talk about *dominant literacies* and *nondominant literacies* in terms of whether they involve mastery of dominant or nondominant secondary Discourses. We can also talk about a literacy being *liberating* ("powerful") if it can be used as a "meta-language" (a set of meta-words, meta-values, meta-beliefs) for the critique of other literacies and the way they constitute us as persons and situate us in society. Liberating literacies can reconstitute and resituate us.

My definition of "literacy" may seem innocuous, at least to someone already convinced that decontextualized views of print are meaningless. Nonetheless, several "theorems" follow from it, theorems that have rather direct and unsettling consequences.

 First theorem: Discourses (and therefore literacies) are not like languages in one very important regard. Someone can speak English, but not fluently. However, someone cannot engage in a Discourse in a less than fully fluent manner. You are either in it or you're not. Discourses are connected with displays of an identity; failing to fully display an identity is tantamount to announcing you don't have that identity, that at best you're a pretender or a beginner. Very often, learners of second languages "fossilize" at a stage of development significantly short of fluency. This can't happen with Discourses. If you've fossilized in the acquisition of

17

18

GENRE CUES

— CARS: Occupy

— So What?

 — **Making Knowledge** Gee's theorems are claims, not facts, so is it strange to call them "knowledge"? No. New knowledge is always first a claim to be tested by readers.

a Discourse prior to full "fluency" (and are no longer in the process of apprenticeship), then your very lack of fluency marks you as a non-member of the group that controls this Discourse. That is, you don't have the identity or social role which is the basis for the existence of the Discourse in the first place. In fact, the lack of fluency may very well mark you as a *pretender* to the social role instantiated in the Discourse (an *outsider* with pretensions to being an *insider*).

There is, thus, no workable "affirmative action" for Discourses: you can't be let into the game after missing the apprenticeship and be expected to have a fair shot at playing it. Social groups will not, usually, give their social goods—whether these are status or solidarity or both—to those who are not "natives" or "fluent users" (though "mushfake," discussed below, may sometimes provide a way for non-initiates to gain access). While this is an *empirical* claim, I believe it is one vastly supported by the sociolinguistic literature (Milroy, 1980, 1987; Milroy & Milroy, 1985).

19

This theorem (that there are no people who are partially literate or semiliterate, or, in any other way, literate but not fluently so) has one practical consequence: notions like "functional literacy" and "competency-based literacy" are simply incoherent. As far as literacy goes, there are only "fluent speakers" and "apprentices" (metaphorically speaking, because remember, Discourses are not just ways of talking, but ways of talking, acting, thinking, valuing, etc.).

20

Second theorem: Primary Discourses, no matter whose they are, can never really be liberating literacies. For a literacy to be liberating it must contain both the Discourse it is going to critique and a set of meta-elements (language, words, attitudes, values) in terms of which an analysis and criticism can be carried out. Primary Discourses are initial and contain only themselves. They can be embedded in later Discourses and critiqued, but they can never serve as a meta-language in terms of which a critique of secondary Discourses can be carried out. Our second theorem is not likely to be very popular. Theorem 2 says that all primary Discourses are limited. "Liberation" ("power"), in the sense I am using the term here, resides in acquiring at least one more

21

15

Discourse in terms of which our own primary Discourse can be analyzed and critiqued.

This is not to say that primary Discourses do not contain critical attitudes and critical language (indeed, many of them contain implicit and explicit racism and classism). It is to say that they cannot carry out an *authentic* criticism, because they cannot verbalize the words, acts, values, and attitudes they use, and they cannot mobilize explicit meta-knowledge. Theorem 2 is quite traditional and conservative — it is the analogue of Socrates's theorem that the unexamined life is not worth living. Interestingly enough, Vygotsky (1987, chapter 6) comes very closely to stating this theorem explicitly.

22

Other theorems can be deduced from the theory of literacy here developed, but these two should make clear what sorts of consequences the theory has. It should also make it quite clear that the theory is *not* a neutral meta-language in terms of which one can argue for *just any* conclusions about literacy.

23

Not all Discourses involve writing or reading, though many do. However, all writing and reading is embedded in some Discourse, and that Discourse always involves more than writing and reading (e.g., ways of talking, acting, valuing, and so forth). You cannot teach anyone to write or read outside any Discourse (there is no such thing, unless it is called "moving a pen" or "typing" in the case of writing, or "moving one's lips" or "mouthing words" in the case of reading). Within a Discourse you are always teaching more than writing or reading. When I say "teach" here, I mean "apprentice someone in a master-apprentice relationship in a social practice (Discourse) wherein you scaffold their growing ability to say, do, value, believe, and so forth, within that Discourse, through demonstrating your mastery and supporting theirs even when it barely exists (i.e., you make it look as if they can do what they really can't do)." That is, you do much the same

24

(16)

GENRE CUES

 16 — **CARS: Occupy** Here Gee shifts to another theme of this piece, *how to teach* Discourses.

thing middle-class, "super baby" producing parents do when they "do books" with their children.

Now, there are many Discourses connected to schools (different ones for different types of school activities and different parts of the curriculum) and other public institutions. These "middle-class mainstream" sorts of Discourses often carry with them power and prestige. It is often felt that good listeners and good readers ought to pay attention to *meaning* and not focus on the petty details of mechanics, "correctness," the superficial features of language. Unfortunately, many middle-class mainstream status-giving Discourses often *do* stress superficial features of language. Why? Precisely because such superficial features are the *best* test as to whether one was apprenticed in the "right" place, at the "right" time, with the "right" people. Such superficial features are exactly the parts of Discourses most impervious to overt instruction and are only fully mastered when everything else in the Discourse is mastered. Since these Discourses are used as "gates" to ensure that the "right" people get to the "right" places in our society, such superficial features are ideal. A person who writes in a petition or office memo: "If you cancel the show, all the performers would have did all that hard work for nothing" has signaled that he or she isn't the "right sort of person" (was not fully acculturated to the Discourse that supports this identity). That signal stays meaningful long after the content of the memo is forgotten, or even when the content was of no interest in the first place.

Now, one can certainly encourage students to simply "resist" such "superficial features of language." And, indeed, they will get to do so from the bottom of society, where their lack of mastery of such superficialities was meant to place them anyway. But, of

25

26

GENRE CUES

17 — **Conversation** With this passive voice construction ("It is often felt that . . ."), Gee cites a conversation without naming its participants, whom Gee's original readers will know. This conversation extends through the next few paragraphs.

18 — **Conversation** Gee uses quotation-marked but uncited phrases to separate his own language from that of other researchers that he is calling into question.

course, the problem is that such "superficialities" cannot be taught in a regular classroom in any case; they can't be "picked up" later, outside the full context of an early apprenticeship (at home and at school) in "middle-class-like" school-based ways of doing and being. That is precisely why they work so well as "gates." This is also precisely the tragedy of E. D. Hirsch, Jr.'s much-talked-about book *Cultural Literacy* (1987), which points out that without having mastered an extensive list of trivialities people can be (and often are) excluded from "goods" controlled by dominant groups in the society. Hirsch is wrong in thinking that this can be taught (in a classroom of all places!) apart from the socially situated practices that these groups have incorporated into their homes and daily lives. There is a real contradiction here, and we ignore it at the peril of our students and our own "good faith" (no middle-class "super baby" producing parents ignore it).

Beyond changing the social structure, is there much hope? No, there is not. So we better get on about the process of changing the social structure. Now, whose job is that? I would say, people who have been allotted the job of teaching Discourses, for example, English teachers, language teachers, composition teachers, TESOL teachers, studies-skills teachers. We can pause, also, to remark on the paradox that even though Discourses cannot be overtly taught, and cannot readily be mastered late in the game, the University wants teachers to overtly teach and wants students to demonstrate mastery. Teachers of Discourses take on an impossible job, allow themselves to be evaluated on how well they do it, and accept fairly low status all the while for doing it.

So what can teachers of Discourses do? Well, there happens to be an advantage to failing to master mainstream Discourses, that is, there is an advantage to being socially "maladapted." When we have really mastered anything (e.g., a Discourse), we have little or no conscious awareness of it (indeed, like dancing, Discourses wouldn't work if people were consciously aware of what they were doing while doing it). However, when we come across a situation where we are unable to accommodate or adapt (as many minority students do on being faced, late in the game, with having to

27

28

acquire mainstream Discourses), we become consciously aware of what we are trying to do or are being called upon to do. Let me give an example that works similarly, that is, the case of classroom second language learning. Almost no one really acquires a second language in a classroom. However, it can happen that exposure to another language, having to translate it into and otherwise relate it to your own language, can cause you to become consciously aware of how your first language works (how it means). This "meta-knowledge" can actually make you better able to manipulate your first language.

Vygotsky (1987) says that learning a foreign language "allows the child to understand his native language as a single instanti-ation of a linguistic system" (p. 222). And here we have a clue. Classroom instruction (in language, composition, study skills, writing, critical thinking, content-based literacy, or whatever) can lead to metaknowledge, to seeing how the Discourses you have already got relate to those you are attempting to acquire, and how the ones you are trying to acquire relate to self and society. Metaknowledge is liberation and power, because it leads to the ability to manipulate, to analyze, to resist while advancing. Such metaknowledge can make "maladapted" students smarter than "adapted" ones. Thus, the liberal classroom that avoids overt talk of form and superficialities, of how things work, as well as of their socio-cultural-political basis, is no help. Such talk can be pow-erful so long as one never thinks that in talking about grammar, form, or superficialities one is getting people to actually acquire Discourses (or languages, for that matter). Such talk is always political talk.

But, the big question: If one cannot acquire Discourses save through active social practice, and it is difficult to compete with the mastery of those admitted early to the game when one has entered it as late as high school or college, what can be done to see to it that metaknowledge and resistance are coupled with

29

30

GENRE CUES

19 — **Extending** Gee signals that he is about to carry Vygotsky's insight into this other area of learning.

Discourse development? The problem is deepened by the fact that true acquisition of many mainstream Discourses involves, at least while being in them, active complicity with values that conflict with one's home- and community-based Discourses, especially for many women and minorities.

The question is too big for me, but I have two views to push nonetheless. First, true acquisition (which is always full fluency) will rarely if ever happen. Even for anything close to acquisition to occur, classrooms must be active apprenticeships in "academic" social practices, and, in most cases, must connect with these social practices as they are also carried on outside the "composition" or "language" class, elsewhere in the University.

31

Second, though true acquisition is probably not possible, "mush-fake" Discourse is possible. Mack (1989) defines "mushfake," a term from prison culture, as making "do with something less when the real thing is not available. So when prison inmates make hats from underwear to protect their hair from lice, the hats are mush-fake. Elaborate craft items made from used wooden match sticks are another example of mushfake." "Mushfake Discourse" means partial acquisition coupled with metaknowledge and strategies to "make do" (strategies ranging from always having a memo edited to ensure no plural, possessive, and third-person "s" agree-ment errors to active use of black culture skills at "psyching out" interviewers, or to strategies of "rising to the meta-level" in an interview so the interviewer is thrown off stride by having the rules of the game implicitly referred to in the act of carrying them out).

32

20

"Mushfake," resistance, and metaknowledge: this seems to me like a good combination for successful students and successful social change. So I propose that we ought to produce "mushfak-ing," resisting students, full of metaknowledge. But isn't that to

33

21

GENRE CUES

20 — **Framework** Gee will make Mack's notion of *mushfake* a major means of structuring his own argument through the rest of the piece.

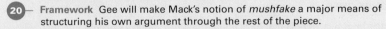

21 — CARS: Occupy

288

politicize teaching? A Discourse is an integration of saying, doing, and *valuing*, and all socially based valuing is political. All successful teaching, that is, teaching that inculcates Discourse and not just content, is political. That too is a truism.

As a linguist I am primarily interested in the functioning of language in Discourses and literacies. And a key question in this sort of linguistics is how language-within-Discourses is acquired (in socially situated apprenticeships) and how the languages from different Discourses transfer into, interfere with, and otherwise influence each other to form the linguistic texture of whole societies and to interrelate various groups in society. To see what is at stake here, I will briefly discuss one text, one which clearly brings out a host of important issues in this domain. The text, with an explanation of its context, is printed below. The text is demarcated in terms of "lines" and "stanzas," units which I believe are the basis of speech:

CONTEXT OF TEXT A young middle-class mother regularly reads storybooks to both her 5- and 7-year-old daughters. Her 5-year-old had had a birthday party, which had had some problems. In the next few days the 5-year-old has told several relatives about the birthday party, reporting the events in the language of her primary Discourse system. A few days later, when the mother was reading a storybook to her 7-year-old, the 5-year-old said she wanted to "read" (she could not decode), and *pretended* to be reading a book, while telling what had happened at her birthday party. Her original attempt at this was not very good, but eventually after a few tries, interspersed with the mother reading to the other girl, the 5 year-old produced the following story, which is not (just) in the language of her primary Discourse system:

STANZA ONE (Introduction)

1. This is a story
2. About some kids who were once friends
3. But got into a big fight
4. And were not

STANZA TWO (Frame: Signalling of Genre)

5. You can read along in your storybook

6. I'm gonna read aloud

[story-reading prosody from now on]

STANZA THREE (Title)

7. "How the Friends Got Unfriend"

STANZA FOUR (Setting: Introduction of Characters)

8. Once upon a time there was three boys 'n three girls

9. They were named Betty Lou, Pallis, and Parshin, were the girls

10. And Michael, Jason, and Aaron were the boys

11. They were friends

STANZA FIVE (Problem: Sex Differences)

12. The boys would play Transformers

13. And the girls would play Cabbage Patches

STANZA SIX (Crisis: Fight)

14. But then one day they got into a fight on who would be which team

15. It was a very bad fight

16. They were punching

17. And they were pulling

18. And they were banging

STANZA SEVEN (Resolution 1: Storm)

19. Then all of a sudden the sky turned dark

20. The rain began to fall

21. There was lightning going on

22. And they were not friends

STANZA EIGHT (Resolution 2: Mothers punish)

23. Then um the mothers came shooting out 'n saying

24. "What are you punching for?

25. You are going to be punished for a whole year"

STANZA NINE (Frame)

26. The end
27. Wasn't it fun reading together?
28. Let's do it again
29. Real soon!

This text and context display an event, which I call *filtering*, "in the act" of actually taking place. "Filtering" is a process whereby aspects of the language, attitudes, values, and other elements of certain types of secondary Discourses (e.g., dominant ones represented in the world of school and trans-local government and business institutions) are *filtered* into primary Discourse (and, thus, the process whereby a literacy can influence home-based practices). Filtering represents *transfer* of features from secondary Discourses into primary Discourses. This transfer process allows the child to practice aspects of dominant secondary Discourses in the very act of acquiring a primary Discourse. It is a key device in the creation of a group of elites who appear to demonstrate quick and effortless mastery of dominant secondary Discourses, by "talent" or "native ability," when, in fact, they have simply *practiced* aspects of them longer.

The books that are part of the storybook reading episodes surrounding this child's oral text encode language that is part of several specific secondary Discourses. These include, of course, "children's literature," but also "literature" proper. Such books use linguistic devices that are simplified analogues of "literary" devices used in traditional, canonical "high literature." These devices are often thought to be natural and universal to literary art, though they are not. Many of them have quite specific origins in quite specific historical circumstances (though, indeed, some of them are rooted in universals of sense making and are devices that occur in nonliterary talk and writing).

One device with a specific historical reference is the so-called "sympathetic fallacy." This is where a poem or story treats natural

35

22

36

37

events (e.g., sunshine or storms) as if they reflected or were "in harmony" or "in step" with (sympathetic with) human events and emotions. This device was a hallmark of 19th-century Romantic poetry, though it is common in more recent poetry as well.

Notice how in the 5-year-old's story the sympathetic fallacy is not only used, but is, in fact, the central organizing device in the construction of the story. The fight between the girls and boys in stanza 6 is immediately followed in stanza 7 by the sky turning dark, with lightning flashing, and thence in line 22: "and they were not friends." Finally, in stanza 8, the mothers come on the scene to punish the children for their transgression. The sky is "in tune" or "step" with human happenings.

38

The function of the sympathetic fallacy in "high literature" is to equate the world of nature (the macrocosm) with the world of human affairs (the microcosm) as it is depicted in a particular work of art. It also suggests that these human affairs, as they are depicted in the work of literary art, are "natural," part of the logic of the universe, rather than conventional, historical, cultural, or class-based.

39

In the 5-year-old's story, the sympathetic fallacy functions in much the same way as it does in "high literature." In particular, the story suggests that gender differences (stanza 4: boy versus girl) are associated with different interests (stanza 5: Transformers versus Cabbage Patches), and that these different interests inevitably lead to conflict when male and female try to be "equal" or "one" or sort themselves on other grounds than gender (stanza 6: "a fight on who would be which team").

40

The children are punished for transgressing gender lines (stanza 8), but *only after* the use of the sympathetic fallacy (in stanza 7) has suggested that *division by gender*, and the conflicts which transgressing this division lead to, are sanctioned by nature—are "natural" and "inevitable" not merely conventional or constructed in the very act of play itself.

41

23 Notice, then, how the very form and structure of the language, and the linguistic devices used, carry an *ideological message*. In

42

GENRE CUES

 23— So What?

mastering this aspect of this Discourse, the little girl has unconsciously "swallowed whole," ingested, a whole system of thought, embedded in the very linguistic devices she uses. This, by the way, is another example of how linguistic aspects of Discourses can never be isolated from nonlinguistic aspects like values, assumptions, and beliefs.

Let's consider how this text relates to our theory of Discourse and literacy. The child had started by telling a story about her birthday to various relatives, over a couple of days, presumably in her primary Discourse. Then, on a given day, in the course of repeated book reading episodes, she reshapes this story into another genre. She incorporates aspects of the book reading episode into her story. Note, for example, the introduction in stanza 1, the frame in stanza 2, the title in stanza 3, and then the start of the story proper in stanza 4. She closes the frame in stanza 9. This overall structure shapes the text into "storybook reading," though, in fact, there is no book and the child can't read. I cannot help but put in an aside here: note that this girl is engaged in an apprenticeship in the Discourse of "storybook reading," a mastery of which I count as a literacy, though in this case there is no book and no reading. Traditional accounts of literacy are going to have deep conceptual problems here, because they trouble themselves too much over things like books and reading.

Supported by her mother and older sister, our 5-year-old is mastering the secondary Discourse of "storybook reading." But this Discourse is itself an aspect of apprenticeship in another, more mature Discourse, namely "literature" (as well as, in other respects, "essayist Discourse," but that is *another* story). This child, when she goes to school to begin her more public apprenticeship into the Discourse of literature, will look like a "quick study" indeed. It will appear that her success was inevitable given her native intelligence and verbal abilities. Her success was inevitable, indeed, but because of her earlier apprenticeship. Note too how her mastery of this "storybook reading" Discourse leads to the incorporation of

43

44

READING CUES

Reread Look again at the line of arguments Gee made to reach this conclusion.

a set of values and attitudes (about gender and the naturalness of middle-class ways of behaving) that are shared by many other dominant Discourses in our society. This will facilitate the acquisition of other dominant Discourses, ones that may, at first, appear quite disparate from "literature" or "storybook reading."

It is also clear that the way in which this girl's home experience interpolates primary Discourse (the original tellings of the story to various relatives) and secondary Discourses will cause *transfer* of features from the secondary Discourse to the primary one (thanks to the fact, for instance, that this is all going on at home in the midst of primary socialization). Indeed, it is *just such* episodes that are the *locus* of the process by which dominant secondary Discourses filter from public life into private life.

45

The 5-year-old's story exemplifies two other points as well. First, it is rather pointless to ask, "Did she really intend, or does she really know about such meanings?" The Discourses to which she is apprenticed "speak" *through her* (to other Discourses, in fact). So, she can, in fact, "speak" quite beyond herself (much like "speaking in tongues," I suppose). Second, the little girl ingests an ideology whole here, so to speak, and not in any way in which she could analyze it, verbalize it, or critique it. This is why this is not an experience of learning a liberating literacy.

46

To speak to the educational implications of the view of Discourse and literacy herein, and to close these introductory remarks, I will leave you to meditate on the words of Oscar Wilde's Lady Bracknell in *The Importance of Being Earnest*. "Fortunately, in England, at any rate, education produces no effect whatsoever. If it did, it would prove a serious danger to the upper classes, and probably lead to acts of violence in Grosvenor Square" (quoted in Ellman, 1988, p. 561).

47

References

Akinnaso, F. N., & Ajirotutu, C. S. (1982). Performance and ethnic style in job intervews. In J. J. Gumperz (Ed.), *Language and social identity* (pp. 119–144). Cambridge: Cambridge University Press.

Beebe, L. M. (Ed.) (1988). *Issues in second language acquisition: Multiple perspectives*. New York: Newbury House.

Cazden, C. (1988). *Classroom discourse: The language of teaching and learning.* Portsmouth, NH: Heinemann.

Dulay, H., Burt, M., & Krashen, S. (1982). *Language two.* New York: Oxford University Press.

Ellman, R. (1988). *Oscar Wilde.* New York: Vintage Books.

Grosjean, F. (1986). *Life with two languages.* Cambridge: Harvard University Press.

Heath, S. B. (1983). *Ways with words: Language, life, and work in communities and classrooms.* Cambridge: Cambridge University Press.

Hirsch, E. D. (1987). *Cultural literacy: What every American needs to know.* Boston: Houghton Mifflin.

Krashen, S. (1982). *Principles and practice in second language acquisition.* Hayward, CA: Alemany Press.

Krashen, S. (1985a). *The input hypothesis: Issues and implications.* Harlow, U.K.: Longman.

Krashen, S. (1985b). *Inquiries and insights.* Hayward, CA: Alemany Press.

Krashen, S., &. Terrell, T. (1983). *The natural approach: Language acquisition in the classroom.* Hayward, CA: Alemany Press.

Lave, J. (1988). *Cognition in practice.* Cambridge: Cambridge University Press.

Mack, N. (1989). The social nature of words: Voices, dialogues, quarrels. *The Writing Instructor,* 8, 157–165.

Milroy, J., & Milroy, L. (1985). *Authority in language: Investigating language prescription and standardisation.* London: Routledge & Kegan Paul.

Milroy, L. (1980). *Language and social networks.* Oxford: Basil Blackwell.

Milroy, L. (1987). *Observing and analysing natural language.* Oxford: Basil Blackwell.

Rogoff, B., & Lave, J. (Eds.). (1984). *Everyday cognition: Its development in a social context.* Cambridge: Harvard University Press.

Rosaldo, R. (1989). *Culture and truth: The remaking of social analysis.* Boston: Beacon Press.

Vygotsky, L. S. (1987). *The collected works of L. S. Vygotsky, Volume 1: Problems of general psychology. Including the volume thinking and speech* (R. W. Rieber & A. S. Carton, Eds.). New York: Plenum.

Questions for Discussion and Journaling

1. What does Gee mean when he says that you can speak with perfect grammar and yet be "wrong nonetheless" (para. 2)? Does this conflict with what you've been taught in school about grammar?

2. Gee argues that you can say something in the right way but do the wrong thing, which he calls the "saying-doing combination" (para. 2). What does this mean? How does this impact people's ability to make meaning together?

3. Explain Gee's distinction between *Discourse* with a capital *D* and *discourse* with a lowercase *d*. Does it make sense to you? Why or why not?

4. What does Gee mean by the terms *primary Discourse, secondary Discourse, dominant Discourse,* and *nondominant Discourse*?

5. What does it mean to say that "Discourses are connected with displays of identity" (para. 18)? What are the implications of this claim, if it is true?

6. Gee argues that reading and writing never happen, and thus can't be taught, apart from some Discourse. Further, he argues, teaching someone to read or write also means teaching them to "say, do, value, and believe" as members of that Discourse do (para. 24). How is this connected to his claims about the relationship between Discourse and identity?

7. Gee argues that members of dominant Discourses apply "constant 'tests'" (para. 13) to people whose primary Discourse is not the dominant one. Later, he explains that members of dominant Discourses often pay close attention to how mechanically "correct" others' language is because these features are the "best test as to whether one was apprenticed in the 'right' place, at the 'right' time, with the 'right' people" (para. 25). What is Gee talking about here? Can you think of an example you have seen or experienced that illustrates what Gee is describing?

8. Why do you think dominant Discourse "tests" happen? What is the benefit to members of the dominant Discourse? What goals (and whose goals) are being *mediated* through such Discourse tests?

9. How does Gee define *literacy*? What is his attitude toward print-based literacy, specifically?

10. How does Gee define *enculturation*?

11. What is *metaknowledge* and what is its value, according to Gee?

12. Consider a Discourse that you believe you are already a part of. How do you *know* you are a part of it? How did you become a part of it?

13. Consider a Discourse to which you do not belong but want to belong — a group in which you are or would like to be what Gee calls an *apprentice*. What is hardest about learning to belong to that Discourse? Who or what aids you the most in becoming a part? Do you ever feel like a "pretender"? If so, what marks you as a pretender?

Applying and Exploring Ideas

1. Write a description of the "saying (writing)-doing-being-valuing-believing" of your own primary Discourse (the one you were enculturated into at birth). Be sure to note things like grammatical usage, common phrases, tone of voice, formality of speech, and values related to that Discourse. Once you have done this, write a description of the "saying (writing)-doing-being-valuing-believing" of *academic* Discourse as you have encountered it so far. Finally, discuss sources of transfer (overlap) and sources of conflict between these two Discourses.

2. Gee argues that English teachers are the ones who have to do something about the fact that people from nondominant Discourses can't join dominant Discourses late in life. Write a letter to one of your high school or college English teachers in which you explain what Discourses are, describe the difference between dominant and nondominant Discourses, and ask the teacher to take some specific action of your choosing to better help students from nondominant Discourses.

3. Gee notes that there are often conflicts and tensions between Discourses. Consider different Discourses you belong to that have different values, beliefs, attitudes, language use, etc. How do you navigate between or among these Discourses?

- -

META MOMENT   What have you learned from Gee that you can usefully apply elsewhere in your life? How does Gee help you understand your experiences (or those of other people) better? Finally, how does Gee help you better understand the threshold concepts of this chapter: that people use texts and discourse in order to *do something*, to *make meaning*, and that the texts and language they create *mediate meaningful activities*?

- -

Learning to Serve

The Language and Literacy of Food Service Workers

TONY MIRABELLI

Tony Mirabelli

Framing the Reading

Tony Mirabelli earned a Ph.D. in Education in Language, Literacy, and Culture from the University of California, Berkeley, in 2001 and is currently a lecturer in the Graduate School of Education at that same institution. He is also the Coordinator of the Tutorial Program for the Athletic Study Center there, as well as a graduate advisor for the Cultural Studies of Sport in Education Program and an academic specialist who works with athletes who have special academic needs.

Mirabelli's article focuses on theories about language use in communities to examine how workers in a diner use language and texts to interact. He is interested in the language and literacy practices of blue-collar service workers. In fact, he introduces the concept of **multiliteracies** to argue that these workers do not just read texts: They also read people and situations.

If you read James Gee earlier in this chapter (p. 274), this argument should be familiar to you. Gee, you will remember, argues that there is too much focus on textual literacies and that print-based literacies cannot be separated from what he called the "saying (writing)-doing-being-valuing-believing" within **Discourses**. The connection between Gee and Mirabelli is not accidental. Mirabelli relies on assumptions from an academic area called New Literacy Studies, which Gee was instrumental in establishing. As you might expect, knowing this, Mirabelli cites Gee when defining his theoretical terms. (And if you look at the publication information for the book in which Mirabelli's article appears, you'll find that Gee reviewed that book for the publisher.) Remember that in Chapter 1 we challenged you to see written academic

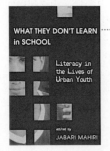

Mirabelli, Tony. "The Language and Literacy of Food Service Workers." *What They Don't Learn in School*, edited by Jabari Mahiri, Peter Lang, 2004, pp. 143–62.

texts as conversations between people. Mirabelli's article provides a good place for you to test this way of seeing texts.

Mirabelli's focus on the everyday literacies of a diner should illustrate the underlying threshold concepts of this chapter in very clear ways. The people in the diner use texts and discourse in order to *do something* and to *make meaning*. The texts (for example, the menu) and specialized language they create and use together *mediate the activities* they are trying to accomplish in the diner.

Getting Ready to Read

Before you read, do at least one of the following activities:

- Think back to your first job. What was it like learning to do it? What did you have to learn? In particular, what terms, language, and vocabulary did you have to learn? What texts helped you do the work of that job (remember to consider even mundane texts like notes, menus, and so on)? How difficult did you find it? Why?

- Find some friends who have worked in food service, and have them compare notes: Are there different Discourses for different kinds of food service?

As you read, consider the following questions:

- How do you understand the notion of Discourses differently depending on which (or what kind of) Discourse is being studied and analyzed?

- How many kinds of literacies do you imagine there are? Is there a literacy for *every* kind of reading? How many kinds of reading are there?

- How do Discourses avoid stereotyping people? Is that possible? What are the consequences of this kind of stereotyping?

BITTERWAITRESS.COM IS ONE of the newest among a burgeoning number of worker-produced websites associated with the service industry.[1] The menu on the first page of this website offers links to gossip about celebrity behavior in restaurants, gossip about chefs and restaurant owners, accounts from famous people who were once waitresses,[2] and customer-related horror stories. There is also a forum that includes a "hate mail" page that posts email criticisms of the website itself, as well as general criticisms of waitressing, but the criticisms are followed by rebuttals usually from past or present waitresses. Predictably, most of the criticisms either implicitly or explicitly portray waitresses as ignorant and stupid. One email respondent didn't like what he read on the customer horror story page and sent in this response:

> If you find your job [as a waitress] so despicable, then go get an education and get a REAL job. You are whining about something that you can fix. Stop being such a weakling, go out and learn something, anything, and go make a real contribution to society. . . . Wait, let me guess: you do not have any marketable skills or useful knowledge, so you do what any bumbling fool can do, wait on tables. This is your own fault.

This response inspired a number of rebuttals of which the following two best 2 summarize the overall sentiment expressed in response to the rant above. The first is from the webmaster of bitterwaitress.com:

> Is it possible that I have an education, maybe I went to, oh say, Duke, and I just waitressed for some free time? Or that there are very many people in the industry who do this so that they CAN get an education? Not all of us were born with a trust fund. — There is, I might add, considerably more or less to a job than a "clear cut" salary. If you . . . live in New York, . . . you'll know that empty stores and un-crowded subways are half the reason to work at night. By the way, what are the three Leovilles? What are the two kinds of tripe? Who was Cesar Ritz' partner? What is the JavaScript for a rollover? I guess I would have to ask a bumbling fool those questions. So, tell me then.

The second is from a mother of four: 3

> I might not have a college education, but I would love to see those so called intelligent people get a big tip out of a bad meal, or from a person who is rude and cocky just because that's the way they are — that takes talent and its not a talent you can learn at any university. So, think about it before you say, "poor girl — too dumb to get a real job. . . ."

Assumptions that waitresses (and waiters) are ignorant and stupid and that waiting on tables contributes little to society are not new. The rebuttals to commonplace, pejorative understandings of the food service industry suggest, however, that there is complexity and skill that may go unrecognized by the general public or institutions such as universities.

Assumptions that waitresses (and waiters) 4 are ignorant and stupid and that waiting on tables contributes little to society are not new. The rebuttals to commonplace, pejorative understandings of the food service industry suggest, however, that there is complexity and skill that may go unrecognized by the general public or institutions such as universities. Indeed institutions, particularly government and corporate entities in the United States, like the Bureau of Labor Statistics or the National Skills Labor Board, define waiting on tables as a low skilled profession. By defining this kind of work as low skilled, there is a concomitant implication that the more than one-third of America's workforce who do it are low skilled.

Service occupations, otherwise known as "in-person" services (Reich, 1992) 5 or "interactive services" (Leidner, 1993; MacDonald and Sirianni, 1996), include any kind of work which fundamentally involves face-to-face or voice-to-voice interactions and conscious manipulation of self-presentation. As distinguished from white-collar service work, this category of "emotional proletariat" (MacDonald and Sirianni, 1996) is comprised primarily of retail sales workers, hotel workers, cashiers, house cleaners, flight attendants, taxi drivers, package delivery drivers, and waiters, among others. According to the U.S. Bureau of Labor Statistics (1996), one-fifth of the jobs in eating, drinking, and grocery store establishments are held by youth workers between the ages of 16 and 24. While this kind of work is traditionally assumed to be primarily a stop-gap for young workers who will later move up and on to other careers, it also involves youths who will later end up in both middle- and working-class careers. It should not be forgotten that more than two thirds of the workers involved in food service are mature adults — many or most who began their careers in the same or similar industries. Interactive service work is a significant part of the economy in the U.S. today, and the Bureau of Labor Statistics predicts that jobs will be "abundant" in this category through 2006.

Economists such as Peter Drucker (1993) suggest that interactive service 6 workers lack the necessary education to be "knowledge" workers. These economists support general conceptions that service work is "mindless," involving routine and repetitive tasks that require little education. This orientation further suggests that these supposedly low skilled workers lack the problem identifying, problem solving, and other high level abilities needed to work in other occupations. However, relatively little specific attention and analysis have been given to the literacy skills and language abilities needed to do this work. My research investigates these issues with a focus on waiters and waitresses who work in diners. Diner restaurants are somewhat distinct from fast food or fine-dining restaurants, and they also epitomize many of the assumptions held about low skilled workplaces that require interactive services. The National Skills Standard Board, for instance, has determined that a ninth-grade level of spoken and written language use is needed to be a waiter or a waitress. Yet, how language is spoken, read, or written in a restaurant may be vastly different from how it is used in a classroom. A seemingly simple event such as taking a customer's food order can become significantly more complex, for example, when a customer has a special request. How the waitress or waiter understands and uses texts such as the menu and how she or he "reads" and verbally interacts with the customer reflect carefully constructed uses of language and literacy.

This chapter explores these constructed ways of "reading" texts (and cus- 7 tomers) along with the verbal, "performances" and other manipulations of self-presentation that characterize interactive service work. In line with MacDonald and Sirianni (1996), I hope this work will contribute to the development of understandings and policies that build more respect and recognition for service work to help ensure it does not become equated with servitude.

LITERACY AND CONTEMPORARY THEORY

In contrast to institutional assessments such as the National Skills Standards 8 Board (1995), current thinking in key areas of education, sociology, anthropology and linguistics views language, literacy, and learning as embedded in social practice rather than entirely in the minds of individuals (Street, 1984; Gee, 1991; Lave and Wenger, 1991; Kress, 1993; Mahiri and Sablo, 1996; New London Group, 1996; Gee, Hull, and Lankshear, 1996). As earlier chapters in this book have noted, Gee (1991: 6) — a key proponent of this conception of literacy — explains that to be literate means to have control of "a socially accepted association among ways of using language, of thinking, and of acting that can be used to identify oneself as a member of a socially meaningful group or 'social network.'" In a similar fashion, research work located explicitly within workplace studies proposes that literacy is "a range of practices specific to groups and individuals of different cultures, races, classes and genders" (Hull et al., 1996: 5).

In most societal institutions, however, literacy continues to be defined by 9 considerations of achievement and by abstract, standardized tests of individual students. Also, there is a decided focus on printed texts over other mediums of communication like visual and audio. Such a focus limits our understanding of literacy in terms of its use in specific situations in multiple modes of communication. The New Literacy Studies orientation that shapes the work reported in this book argues that literacy extends beyond individual experiences of reading and writing to include the various modes of communication and situations of any socially meaningful group or network where language is used in multiple ways. The New London Group (1996), for example, claims that due to changes in the social and economic environment, schools too must begin to consider language and literacy education in terms of "multiliteracies." The concept of multiliteracies supplements traditional literacy pedagogy by addressing the multiplicity of communications channels and the increasing saliency of cultural and linguistic diversity in the world today. Central to this study is the understanding that literate acts are embedded in specific situations and that they also extend beyond the printed text involving other modes of communication including both verbal and nonverbal. In this chapter, I illustrate something of the character of literacies specific to the "social network" of waiting on tables and show how they are distinct from the conceptions of literacy commonly associated with formal education. This is not simply to suggest that there is a jargon specific to the work, which of course there is, but that there is something unique and complex about the ways waiters and waitresses in diners use language and literacy in doing their work.

METHODOLOGY

Taken together, extant New Literacies Studies research makes a formidable argument for the need to re-evaluate how we understand literacy in the workplace—particularly from the perspective of interactive service workers. The research reported here is modeled after Hull and her colleagues' groundbreaking ethnographic study of skill requirements in the factories of two different Silicon Valley computer manufacturing plants (1996). Instead of studying manufacturing plants, the larger research study I conducted and that underpins the study reported here involves two diner restaurants—one that is corporately owned and one that is privately owned. In this chapter, however, I focus only on the one that is privately owned to begin addressing the specific ways that language use and literacy practices function in this kind of workplace. 10

To analyze the data, I relied on some of the methodological tools from the work of Hull and her colleagues (1996). In short, I looked at patterns of thought and behavior in the setting; I identified key events taking place; I did conversational analysis of verbal interactions; and I conducted sociocultural analyses of key work events. 11

The data used in this chapter came from direct participation, observation, field notes, documents, interviews, tape recordings, and transcriptions, as well as from historical and bibliographic literature. I myself have been a waiter (both part-time and full-time over a ten-year period), and I was actually employed at the privately owned restaurant during my data collection period. In addition to providing important insights into worker skills, attitudes, and behaviors, my experience and positioning in this setting also enabled access to unique aspects of the work that might have otherwise gone unnoticed. The primary data considered in this chapter were collected during eight-hour periods of participant observation on Friday and/or Saturday nights in the restaurant. I chose weekend nights because they were usually the busiest times in the diner and were therefore the most challenging for the workers. Weekend shifts are also the most lucrative for the restaurant and the workers. 12

LOU'S RESTAURANT

Lou's Restaurant[3] is a modest, privately owned diner restaurant patterned in a style that is popular in the local region. It has an open kitchen layout with a counter where individual customers can come and sit directly in front of the cooks' line and watch the "drama" of food service unfold while enjoying their 13 meals. The food served at Lou's is Italian-American and it includes pastas, seafood, and a variety of sautéed or broiled poultry, beef, and veal. As is often the case with diner restaurants, Lou's has over ninety main course items, including several kinds of appetizers and salads, as well as a number of side dishes. The primary participants focused on in this chapter are three waiters at Lou's: John, Harvey, and myself.

After finishing my master's degree in English literature and deciding to move 14 out of the state where I taught English as a Second Language at a community college, I ended up working as a waiter for two years at Lou's. This work allowed me to survive financially while further advancing my academic career. At the time I began my study at this site, the only waiter to have worked longer than two years at Lou's was John. Like myself, John began working in the restaurant business to earn extra money while in school after he had been discharged from the Marines, where he had been trained as a radio operator, telephone wireman, and Arabic translator. Two days after his honorable discharge, he started working in the restaurant that four years later would become Lou's. He subsequently has worked there for ten years. John also is the most experienced waiter at Lou's, and although the restaurant does not have an official "head" waiter, John is considered by his peers to be the expert. In an interview, he noted that it took almost ten years before he felt that he had really begun to master his craft.

Harvey might also be considered a master waiter, having been in the profes- 15 sion for over thirty years. However, at the beginning of the study he had been with Lou's for only two weeks. He was initially reticent to participate in the study because he said he lacked experience at this restaurant, and "didn't know the menu." Having left home when he was 14 years old to come "out West," over the years he had done a stint in the Air Force, held a position as a postal clerk, worked as a bellhop and bartender, and even had the opportunity to manage a local cafe. He decided that he did not like managerial work because he missed the freedom, autonomy, and customer interaction he had as a waiter and took a position at Lou's.

THE MENU

Harvey's concern over not knowing the menu was not surprising. The menu is 16 the most important printed text used by waiters and waitresses, and not knowing it can dramatically affect how they are able to do their work. The menu is the key text used for most interactions with the customer, and, of course, the contents of menus vary greatly from restaurant to restaurant. But, what is a menu and what does it mean to have a literate understanding of one?

The restaurant menu is a genre unto itself. There is regularity and predicta- 17 bility in the conventions used such as the listing, categorizing, and pricing of individual, ready-made food items. The menu at Lou's contains ninety main course items, as well as a variety of soups, salads, appetizers, and side dishes. In addition, there are numerous selections where, for example, many main course items offer customers a choice of their own starch item from a selection of four: spaghetti, ravioli, french fries, or a baked potato. Some of the main course items, such as sandwiches, however, only come with french fries—but if the customer prefers something such as spaghetti, or vegetables instead of fries, they can substitute another item for a small charge, although this service is not listed in the menu. In addition to the food menu, there is also a wine menu and a full service bar meaning that hard liquor is sold in this restaurant. There are twenty different kinds of wine sold by the glass and a selection of thirty-eight different kinds of wine sold by the bottle, and customers can order most other kinds of alcoholic beverages.

In one context, waitresses and waiters' knowing the meaning of the words in the menus means knowing the process of food production in the restaurant. But this meaning is generally only used when a customer has a question or special request. In such situations the meaning of the words on the page are defined more by the questions and the waiters or waitresses' understanding of specific food preparation than by any standard cookbook or dictionary. For example, the *Better Homes and Gardens New Cook Book* (1996) presents a recipe for marinara sauce calling for a thick sauce all sautéed and simmered for over thirty minutes. At Lou's, a marinara sauce is cooked in less than ten minutes and is a light tomato sauce consisting of fresh tomatoes, garlic, and parsley sautéed in olive oil. At a similar restaurant nearby—Joe's Italian Diner—marinara sauce is a seafood sauce, albeit tomato based. Someone who is familiar with Italian cooking will know that marinara sauce will have ingredients like tomatoes, olive oil, and garlic, but, in a restaurant, to have a more complete understanding of a word like *marinara* requires knowing how the kitchen prepares the dish. Clearly, the meanings of the language used in menus are socially and culturally embedded in the context of the specific situation or restaurant. To be literate here requires something other than a ninth-grade level of literacy. More than just a factual, or literal interpretation of the words on the page, it requires knowledge of specific practices—such as methods of food preparation—that take place in a particular restaurant.

On one occasion Harvey, the new but experienced waiter, asked me what "pesto" sauce was. He said that he had never come across the term before, and explained that he had never worked in an Italian restaurant and rarely eaten in one. Pesto is one of the standard sauces on the menu, and like marinara, is commonly found on the menus of many Italian-American restaurants. I explained that it comprised primarily olive oil and basil, as well as garlic, pine nuts, Parmesan cheese, and a little cream. Harvey then told me that a customer had asked him about the sauce, and since he could not explain what it was, the customer did not order it.

18

19

305

On another occasion a mother asked Harvey if her child could have only car- 20 rots instead of the mixed vegetables as it said in the menu. Although he initially told her this was not possible, explaining that the vegetables were premixed and that the cooks would have to pick the carrots out one by one, the mother persisted. After a few trips from the table to the cooks' line, Harvey managed to get the carrots, but the customer then declined them because everyone had finished eating. Later, I explained to Harvey that it would have been possible to go to the back of the restaurant where he could find the vegetables in various stages of preparation. While the cooks only have supplies of premixed vegetables on the line, Harvey could have gone to the walk-in refrigerator and picked up an order of carrots himself to give to the cooks.

Harvey's interactions with his customers highlight how much of what he 21 needs to know to be a good waiter is learned within the specific situations and social networks in which that knowledge is used. The instantiation of the meaning of words like *pesto* and *marinara* often occurs in the interaction between co-workers as well as with customers. Conversation becomes a necessary element in achieving an appropriately literate understanding of the menu.

Harvey's understanding and use of the menu and special requests also involves 22 more than his knowledge of food preparation. It involves the manipulation of power and control. Sociocultural theories of literacy consider the role of power and authority in the construction of meaning (Kress, 1993). From his perspective, the order of carrots was not simply an order of carrots, but a way of positioning one's self in the interaction. The customer saw her desire for the carrots as greater than what was advertised in the menu and thus exercised authority as a customer by requesting them despite Harvey's attempt to not make the carrots an option. While such a request might seem fairly innocuous in isolation, when considered in the specific situation of Lou's at that time — that is, peak dinner hour — it becomes more complex.

Special requests and questions can extend the meaning of the menu beyond 23 the printed page and into the conversation and interaction between the waiter or waitress and the customer. Furthermore, special requests and questions can be as varied as the individual customers themselves. The general public shares a diner restaurant menu, but it is used by each individual patron to satisfy a private appetite. How to describe something to an individual customer and satisfy their private appetite requires not only the ability to *read* the menu, but also the ability to *read* the customer. This is achieved during the process of the dinner interaction, and it includes linguistic events such as greeting the customer or taking food orders and involves both verbal and non-verbal communication. In such events the meaning of the menu is continually reconstructed in the interaction between the waitress or waiter and the individual customer, and as a text functions as a "boundary object" that coordinates the perspectives of various constituencies for a similar purpose (Star and Griesmer, 1989); in this case the satisfaction of the individual patron's appetite. The degree to which private appetite is truly satisfied is open to debate, however. Virtually everyone who has eaten at a restaurant has his or her favorite horror story about the food and/or the service, and more often than not these stories in some way involve the menu and an unfulfilled private appetite.

In addition to being a text that is shared by the general public and used by 24 the individual patron to satisfy a private appetite, the menu is also a text whose production of meaning results in ready-made consumable goods sold for profit. The authors of a printed menu, usually the chefs and owners of the restaurant, have their own intentions when producing the hard copy. For example, it is common practice to write long extensively itemized menus in diner restaurants like Lou's. As was pointed out earlier, Lou's menu has over ninety selections from which to choose, and many of these can be combined with a range of additional possible choices. Printing a large selection of food items gives the appearance that the customer will be able to make a personal — and *personalized* — selection from the extensive menu. In fact, it is not uncommon for patrons at Lou's to request extra time to read the menu, or ask for recommendations before making a choice. The authors of the printed menu at Lou's constructed a text that appears to be able to satisfy private appetites, but they ultimately have little control over how the patron will interpret and use the menu.

The waiters and waitresses, however, do have some control. While customers 25 certainly have their own intentions when asking questions, waitresses and waiters have their own intentions when responding. When customers ask questions about the menu, in addition to exercising their own authority, they also introduce the opportunity for waiters and waitresses to gain control of the interaction. A good example of how this control could be manipulated by a waiter or waitress comes from Chris Fehlinger, the web-master of bitterwaitress.com, in an interview with *New Yorker* magazine:

> "A lot of times when people asked about the menu, I would make it sound so elaborate that they would just leave it up to me," he said, "I'd describe, like, three dishes in excruciating detail, and they would just stutter, 'I, I, I can't decide, you decide for me.' So in that case, if the kitchen wants to sell fish, you're gonna have fish." He also employed what might be called a "magic words" strategy: "All you have to do is throw out certain terms, like guanciale, and then you throw in something like saba, a reduction of the unfermented must of the Trebbiano grape. If you mention things like that, people are just, like, 'O.K.!'" (Teicholz, 1999)

The use of linguistic devices like obfuscating descriptions and "magic words" 26 is not unusual — particularly for waiters in fine dining restaurants. In *The World of the Waiters* (1983), Mars and Nicod examined how English waiters use devices to "get the jump" and gain control of selecting items from the menu.

Their position of authority is further substantiated in fine dining restaurants by the common practice of printing menus in foreign languages, such as French, because it shifts the responsibility of food ordering from the customer, who often will not understand the language, to the waiter.

While diner restaurants generally do not print their menus in incomprehen- 27 sible terms, they do, as at Lou's, tend to produce unusually long ones that can have a similar effect. But, diner menus like Lou's which offer Italian-American cuisine do use some language that is potentially unfamiliar to the clientele (e.g., *pesto*). The combination of menu length and potentially confusing language creates frequent opportunities for waiters and waitresses to get a jump on the customer. Customers at Lou's tend to ask questions about the meaning of almost every word and phrase in the menu. Not being able to provide at least a basic description of a menu item, as shown by Harvey's unfamiliarity with pesto, usually results in that item not being ordered.

Knowing what a customer wants often goes beyond simply being able to 28 describe the food. It also involves knowing which descriptions will more likely sell and requires being able to apply the menu to the specific situation. For instance, in the following transcription I approach a table to take a food order while one customer is still reading the menu (Customer 3b). She asks me to explain the difference between veal scaloppini and veal scaloppini sec.

TONY: (to Customer 3a and Customer 3b) hi

CUSTOMER 3B: what's the difference between scaloppini and scaloppini sec?

TONY: veal scaloppini is a tomato based sauce with green onions and mushrooms/veal scaloppini sec is with marsala wine green onions and mushrooms

CUSTOMER 3B: I'll have the veal scaloppini sec.

TONY: ok/would you like it with spaghetti/ravioli/french fries

CUSTOMER 3B: ravioli

CUSTOMER 3A: and/I'll get the tomato one/the veal scaloppini with mushrooms

TONY: with spaghetti/ravioli/french fries

CUSTOMER 3A: can I get steamed vegetables

TONY: you want vegetables and no starch?/it already comes with vegetables/(.) (Customer 3a nods yes) ok/great/thank you

CUSTOMER 3A: thanks

The word *sec* functions not unlike one of Fehlinger's "magic" words. 29 Customers who are interested in ordering veal frequently ask questions about the distinctions between the two kinds of scaloppini. I discovered over time that my description of the veal scaloppini sec almost always resulted in the customer ordering the dish. It seemed that mentioning marsala wine piqued customer interest more than tomato sauce did. One customer once quipped that marsala is a sweet wine and wanted to know why the word *sec*—meaning *dry*—was used. I replied that since no fat was used in the cooking process, it was considered "dry" cooking. In situations like this the menu is situated more in a conversational mode than a printed one. The transition from print to spoken word occurs due to the customer's inability to understand the menu, and/or satisfy his or her private appetite which results in a request for assistance. As a result the waiter or waitress can become the authority in relation to not only the printed text, but within the interaction as well. Eventually, I began to recommend this dish when customers asked for one, and the customers more often than not purchased it.

This particular food-ordering event also is interesting with regard to the cus-   30
tomer's request for steamed vegetables. When I asked what kind of pasta she would like with her meal, she asked for steamed vegetables. The menu clearly states that vegetables are included with the meal along with the customer's choice of spaghetti, ravioli, or french fries. When she requested steamed vegetables, I simply could have arranged for her to have them and persisted in asking her which pasta she would like, but instead I anticipated that she might not want any pasta at all. I knew that, while it was not printed on the menu, the kitchen could serve her a double portion of steamed vegetables with no pasta. Most importantly, this customer's ability to order food that would satisfy her private appetite depended almost entirely upon my suggestions and understanding of the menu. Mars and Nicod (1984: 82), discussing a situation in a similar restaurant, noted a waiter who would say, "You don't really need a menu . . . I'm a 'walking menu' and I'm much better than the ordinary kind . . . I can tell you things you won't find on the menu." Examples like this illustrate not only how waitresses and waiters gain control of their interactions with customers, but also how other modes of communication—such as conversations—are used to construct complex forms of meaning around printed texts like menus. Thus, the meaning of words in a menu are embedded in the situation, its participants, and the balance of power and authority, and this meaning manifests itself in more than one mode of communication.

Reading menus and reading customers also involves a myriad of cultural dis-   31
tinctions. Although there is not the space to discuss them here, age, gender, race, and class are all relevant to interactions between customers and waiter or waitress. The argument can be made that diner restaurants like Lou's promote a friendly, family-like atmosphere. Historically diners in the U.S. have been recognized as being places where customers can find a familial environment. Popular media today support this characteristic—particularly via television—where restaurant chains explicitly advertise that their customers are treated like family, and a number of television situation comedies have long used restaurants, diners, bars, and cafés as settings where customers and employees interact in very personal and intimate ways. This cultural atmosphere can have a tremendous

impact on interactions with the customers. There is sometimes miscommuni-
cation or resistance where a customer may or may not want to be treated like
family, or the waitress or waiter may or may not want to treat a customer like
family. At Lou's, in addition to having an intimate understanding of food production and being able to describe it to a customer in an appealing fashion,
reading a menu and taking a customer's food order also requires the ability to
perform these tasks in a friendly, familial manner.

The following example reveals the complexity of meanings involved in taking 32
a customer's food order and the expression of "family." Al is a regular customer
who almost always comes in by himself and sits at the counter in front of the
cooks' line. He also always has the same thing to eat, a side order of spaghetti
marinara, and never looks at the menu. Perhaps more important to Al than the
food he eats are the people he interacts with at Lou's. He will sit at the counter
and enjoy the badinage he shares with the other customers who sit down next
to him at the counter, the waitresses and waiters as they pass by his seat, and
the cooks working just across the counter. On this particular evening, however,
he was joined by his son, daughter-in-law, and young adult granddaughter, and
rather than sitting at the counter, he sat in a large booth. Although I immediately recognized Al, I had never waited on him and his family before, and I was
not sure how informal he would like the interaction to be. So I began with a
fairly formal greeting saying "hello" instead of "hi" and avoided opportunities to
make small talk with Al and his family:

TONY: hello::=

CUSTOMER 2D: =hello

AL: hey(.) what they put in the water?/I don't know/is it the ice or what is it?

CUSTOMER 2S: (chuckles from Customer 2d, Customer 2s, and Customer 2c)

TONY: does the water taste strange?

CUSTOMER 2S: no

TONY: do you want me to get you another water?

AL: no/I don't want any water

TONY: ok

AL: I had a couple of drinks before I came

CUSTOMER 2S: (chuckles)=

TONY: (in reference to the water tasting strange) =it could be/it could be/I
don't know

CUSTOMER 2D: (to Customer 2s) are you having anything to drink?

CUSTOMER 2S: I'll have a beer/American beer/you have Miller draft?

TONY: (while writing down the order) Miller Genuine

CUSTOMER 2D: and I'll have a tequila sunrise

AL: (to Customer 2d) what are you having?

CUSTOMER 2D: tequila sunrise

AL: oh/you should fly/you should fly

TONY: (to Customer 2a) Al/you want anything?

CUSTOMER 2S: (to Customer 2a) a beer?/or anything?

AL: no/I've had too much already

CUSTOMER 2S: are you sure

CUSTOMER 2D: we'll get you a coffee later

TONY: (nod of affirmation to daughter-in-law)

AL: I've been home alone drinking

TONY: ugh ogh::/(chuckles along with Customer 2s)

Al's comment about the water tasting funny and his drinking at home alone 33
both provided opportunities for me to interact more intimately with Al and his
family, but instead I concerned myself solely with taking their drink orders. Al's
desire for me to interact in a more familial manner became more apparent when
I returned to take their food order.

CUSTOMER 2D: (as the drinks are delivered) ah/great/thank you

TONY: (placing drinks in front of customers) there you go/you're welcome

AL: (to Customer 2s) so we're flying to Vegas (mumbles)

TONY: all right/you need a few minutes here?

CUSTOMER 2S: no/(to Customer 2a) are you ready or do you want to wait?

CUSTOMER 2D: you made up your mind yet?

AL: (mumble) made up my mind yet

CUSTOMER 2D: oh/ok

TONY: al/what can I get for you?

AL: I said I haven't made up my mind yet

TONY: oh/ok (everyone at the table chuckles except Al)

AL: I always have pasta you know/I would walk out there (points to the
counter) the guy says/I know what you want

TONY: ok / I'll be back in a few minutes

CUSTOMER 2D: come back in a few minutes/thanks

While I misunderstood Al when I asked if he was ready to order, for him the 34 greater transgression was simply asking if he was ready to order. Al expected me to know what he was going to eat because he's a regular; he's like family. He wanted a side order of spaghetti marinara and didn't want to have to speak regarding his food order. To be successful in fulfilling Al's private appetite required more than the ability to describe food according to individual customer preferences. A side order of spaghetti marinara represents not merely a food item on a menu, nor a satisfying mix of pasta and tomatoes, but also, depending on the way it is ordered and served, a gesture of friendliness: "I always have pasta you know/ I would walk out there (points to the counter) the guy says/I know what you want." To be literate with a menu also means knowing when and how to express emotion (or not express emotion) to a customer through its use.

Being able to take a customer's order without him or her reading the menu 35 are important ways of expressing friendliness and family at Lou's. John, the most experienced waiter on staff, often can be found running to get an order of home-made gnocchi from the back freezer and delivering them to the cooks when they are too busy to get back there themselves. Or, he might step in behind the bar to make his own cappuccino when the bartender is busy serving other custom-ers. On one occasion, like many others, John had a customer request a special order called *prawns romano*, a pasta dish consisting of fettuccine with prawns in a white sauce with green onions, tomatoes, and garlic. This is not listed on any menu in the restaurant, but it is something that the cooks occasionally offer as an evening special. John politely asked whether or not the cooks could accom-modate his customer's request, and they complied. One can frequently hear John greeting many of his customers with some variation of, "Can I get you the usual?" Alternatively, in the case of special requests, some variant of, "That's no problem" is an often used phrase. Just like a friend for whom it would be no problem, John attempts to satisfy his customer's special requests in a similar fashion.

Yet, friendliness is often a feigned performance. Being friendly is an experi- 36 ential phenomenon that is learned through participation. To be a good waitress or waiter generally requires being able to perform friendliness under any num-ber of circumstances. To be successful at the practice of being friendly requires performing certain techniques over and over until they can be performed on an unconscious level. Referred to as *emotional labor* (Hochschild, 1983: 6–7), this kind of work "requires one to induce or suppress feeling in order to sustain the outward countenance that produces the proper state of mind in others." Emotional labor also is an integral part to how a waitress constructs meaning in a menu. While emotional labor may not yield the same monetary results in res-taurants like Lou's, it is still essential to the work. For example, John is masterful in the way he utilizes emotional labor. On one particularly busy evening John was trapped in a line at the bar waiting to place his drink order. He was clearly anxious, and was looking at his food order tickets to see what he needed to do next. The crowd of customers waiting to be seated spilled out of the foyer and into the aisle near where the waitresses and waiters were waiting to place their drink orders. One customer, who recognized John, caught his attention:

JOHN: hi=

CUSTOMER: =hi can I get a glass of wine

JOHN: sure (.) what do you want

CUSTOMER: are you busy

JOHN: NO (.) I got it (.) what do you want

John's friendly "hi" and overemphatic "no" were intended to suggest to the 37 customer that he was not busy, when he clearly was. As he later explained, he knew that the customer knew he was really busy, but he also knew that if he was friendly and accommodating, the customer probably would give him a nice tip for his trouble, which the customer did. His feigned amiability in agreeing to get the customer a drink was more or less a monetary performance. John had learned to use language for financial gain. One should not be fooled by the apparent simplicity in the preceding interaction. While it may be brief, being able to be friendly and accommodating under extreme circumstances like the "dinner rush" requires years of practice in a real work setting learning to be able to say, "hi—sure—NO, I got it."

Although interactions with customers have been presented individually, the 38 reality of how these events occur is quite different. Unlike fine-dining restaurants where the dinner experience can extend over a few hours, diners operate on high volume, serving to a great number of patrons in a short amount of time. George Orwell, reflecting on the difficulty involved in this work, wrote, "I calculated that [a waiter] had to walk and run about 15 miles during the day and yet the strain of the work was more mental than physical. . . . One has to leap to and fro between a multitude of jobs—it is like sorting a pack of cards against the clock" (Orwell, 1933). Because one person may be serving as many as ten tables or more at one time, the process of serving each individual table will overlap with the others. Food orders are taken numerous times in a half-hour period during busy dinner hours at Lou's. The preceding transcriptions were taken from tape-recorded data collected on Friday evenings around 7 o'clock. My own interactions were recorded during a period when I had what is referred to as a *full station,* meaning that all of the tables under my supervision were filled with customers. By this point in the evening I had two customers at the counter, a party of four and six parties of two, for a total of eighteen customers—all of whom were in the process of ordering their meals within the same half-hour to forty-five minute period.

Literacy practices in this environment are nothing like those found in tra- 39 ditional classrooms, but they might be more comparable to those found in the emergency ward of a hospital or an air-traffic controller's tower. Interaction with texts and participants takes place in a rapid succession of small chunks. During the dinner hours, there are no long drawn out monologues. Time is of the essence during the busiest dinner hours for all participants involved: from the waiters and waitresses to the cooks, bartenders, and busboys. In two hundred lines of transcribed dialogue during a busy dinner period, for example, I never paused longer than thirty-nine seconds, and no participant spoke more than forty-one words in one turn. Even these pauses were usually the result of other work being completed, such as preparing a salad or waiting to order a drink. During this period, virtually all the conversation, reading, and writing were related to the immediate situational context. As this research has shown, language use was far more complex than one might assume in situations and events that involve taking a customer's food order. In addition to knowing how food is prepared, what will appeal to specific customers, and how to present this information in a friendly manner, the waiter or waitress must also remain conscious of the number of other tables waiting to have their orders taken and the amount of time that will take. Reading menus and reading customers requires the ability to think and react quickly to a multitude of almost simultaneously occurring literate events.

CONCLUSION

Menus at Lou's are texts that are catalysts for interaction between staff and cus- 40 tomers, and their meaning is firmly embedded in this interaction. Meaning is constructed from the menu through more than one mode of communication and between a variety of participants. This process involves knowledge of food preparation, use of specific linguistic devices like magic words and other ways of describing food, the ability to read individual customers' tastes and preferences, the general expectation to perform in a friendly manner, and all during numerous virtually simultaneous and similar events. Yet, there is much left unconsidered in this chapter, particularly regarding the nature of power and control. While waitresses and waiters are frequently able to manipulate control over customer decisions while taking a food order, this control is often tenuous and insignificant beyond the immediate interaction.

Little also has been said in this chapter about the role of management. 41 Extensive research has already been done in the area of management control, literacy, and worker skills (Braverman, 1974; Hochschild, 1983; Kress, 1993; Leidner, 1993; Hall, 1993; Hull et al., 1996; MacDonald and Sirianni, 1996; Gee, Hull, and Lankshear, 1996). These researchers consider how literacy practices are manipulated by management to maintain control over the worker. Whether it be scientific management where workers are deskilled and routinized, or Fast Capitalism where forms of control are more insidious and shrouded in the guise of "empowering" the worker, there is little research on interactive service work beyond the fast food industry that explores how this rhetoric plays itself out in a real world situation. This leaves open to debate questions regarding the effectiveness of Fast Capitalism as a form of control over the worker. While my research has shown that waiters and waitresses can exercise some level of authority, skill, and wit through their use of language with customers, they must also interact with management and other staff where authority and control play out in different ways.

In the end, however, the customer has ultimate authority over the waiter or 42
waitress. Diner waitressing has a long history of prejudice dating back to the beginning of the industrial revolution and involves issues of gender regarding our general perceptions and ways of interacting (Cobble, 1991; Hall, 1993). Waitressing is integrally tied to domesticated housework and likewise has historically been treated as requiring little skill or ability. In fact, the stigma of servitude that plagues waitressing and other similar kinds of work are not only the result of less than respectable treatment from management, but from customers as well. In her sociological study of diner waitresses in New Jersey, Greta Paules sums it up best:

> That customers embrace the service-as-servitude metaphor is evidenced by
> the way they speak to and about service workers. Virtually every rule of
> etiquette is violated by customers in their interactions with the waitress:
> the waitress can be interrupted; she can be addressed with the mouth full;
> she can be ignored and stared at; and she can be subjected to unrestrained
> anger. Lacking status as a person, she, like the servant, is refused the most
> basic considerations of polite interaction. She is, in addition, the subject of
> chronic criticism. Just as in the nineteenth century servants were perceived
> as ignorant, slow, lazy, indifferent, and immoral (Sutherland 1981), so in the
> twentieth century service workers are condemned for their stupidity, apathy,
> slowness, incompetence, and questionable moral character. (1991:138–39)

The low status of waitressing and waitering belies the complex nature of this 43
kind of work and the innovative and creative ways in which such workers use language.

Notes

1. Some of the more than 20 websites I have found so far like waitersrevenge.com are award winning. They include sites for taxi drivers, hotel workers, and the like.

2. How to appropriately refer to waitresses and waiters is not a simple decision. Terms like *server* and *food server* are alternatives, but all are problematic. I personally do not like *server* or *food*

server because they are too closely related to the word *servitude*. The waiter/waitress distinction is problematic not simply because it differentiates genders, but also because it is associated with a kind/class of service. Often in fine-dining restaurants today both men and women are referred to as waiters, but it is more commonly the practice in the "diner" style restaurant to maintain the distinctive terms. This is historically connected to the diner waitressing being regarded as inferior to fine-dining waitering because it was merely an extension of the domesticated duties of the household.

3. Pseudonyms have been used throughout this chapter.

Works Cited

Better homes and gardens new cook book. (1996). New York: Better Homes and Gardens.

Braverman, H. (1974). *Labor and monopoly capital: The degradation of work in the twentieth century.* New York: Monthly Review Press.

Bureau of Labor Statistics. (1996). Washington, D.C.: U.S. Department of Labor.

Cobble, S. (1991). *Dishing it out: Waitresses and their unions in the 20th century.* Urbana: University of Illinois Press.

Drucker, P. (1993). *Innovation and entrepreneurship: Practice and principles.* New York: Harper-business.

Gee, J. (1991). *Sociolinguistics and literacies: Ideology in discourses.* New York: Falmer.

Gee, J., Hull, G., and Lankshear, C. (1996). *The new work order: Behind the language of the new capitalism.* Sydney: Allen & Unwin.

Gowen, S. (1992). *The politics of workplace literacy.* New York: Teachers College Press.

Hall, E. (1993). Smiling, deferring, and good service. *Work and occupations, 20* (4), 452–471.

Hochschild, A. (1983). *The managed heart.* Berkeley: University of California Press.

Hull, G. (Ed.). (1997). *Changing work, changing workers: Critical perspectives on language, literacy, and skills.* New York: State University of New York Press.

Hull, G. et al. (1996). *Changing work, changing literacy? A study of skills requirements and development in a traditional and restructured workplace. Final Report.* Unpublished manuscript. University of California at Berkeley.

Kress, G. (1993). Genre as social process. In B. Cope and M. Kalantzis (Eds.), *The powers of literacy: A genre approach to teaching writing* (pp. 22–37). London: Falmer.

Kress, G. (1995). *Writing the future: English and the making of a cultural innovation.* London: NATE.

Lave, J. and Wenger, E. (1991). *Situated learning: Legitimate peripheral participation.* New York: Cambridge University Press.

Leidner, R. (1993). *Fast food, fast talk: Service work and the routinization of everyday life.* Berkeley: University of California Press.

MacDonald, C. and, Sirianni, C. (Eds.). (1996). *Working in the service society.* Philadelphia: Temple University.

Mahiri, J. and Sablo, S. (1996). Writing for their lives: The non-school literacy of California's urban African American youth. *Journal of Negro Education, 65* (2), 164–180.

Mars, G. and Nicod, M. (1984). *The world of waiters.* London: Unwin Hyman.

New London Group. (1996). A pedagogy of multiliteracies: Designing social futures. *Harvard Educational Review,* 66 (1), 60–92.

NSSB (National Skills Standards Board). (1995). *Server skill standards: National performance criteria in the foodservice industry.* Washington, DC: U.S. Council on Hotel, Restaurant and Institutional Education.

Orwell, G. (1933). *Down and out in Paris and London.* New York: Harcourt Brace.

Paules, G. (1991). *Dishing it out: Power and resistance among waitresses in a New Jersey restaurant.* Philadelphia: Temple University Press.

Reich, R. (1992). *The work of nations.* New York: Vintage.

Star, L. and Griesmer, J. (1989). Institutional ecology, translations and boundary objects: Amateurs and professionals in Berkeley's Museum of Vertebrate Zoology, 1907–1939. *Social Studies of Science,* 19.

Street, B. (1984 April 5). *Literacy in theory and practice.* London: Cambridge University Press.

- -

Questions for Discussion and Journaling

1. How does Mirabelli begin his article? What can you infer from it about his intended audience(s) and purpose(s) from the way he begins? What are the effects for his audience of the way he begins?

2. Mirabelli chooses to focus on participation in a restaurant Discourse. Why? What is he contributing to the conversation on Discourses by doing so?

3. What is the "traditional" view of literacy, according to Mirabelli, and what is the view of literacy that New Literacy Studies takes? What are *multiliteracies*?

4. What seems to be Mirabelli's research question and where does he state it? What kind of data did Mirabelli collect to analyze the diner discourse community? What seem to be his primary findings in answer to his research question?

5. Mirabelli spends a good deal of his analysis focusing on the genre of the menu, and in doing so, he also discusses the diner's lexis and methods of intercommunication. Why does Mirabelli focus on the genre of the menu? Is this an effective focus for him as he attempts to answer the research question you identified above? Why or why not?

6. Mirabelli argues that literacy in the diner includes not only reading the menu but also reading the customers. Do you agree that reading customers is a form of literacy? Why or why not?

7. Do you now or have you ever participated in a discourse community that is strongly stereotyped in the ways that restaurant work is stereotyped (for example, a football team or a sorority)? What are the stereotypes? Using Mirabelli, consider the various "multiliteracies" of this discourse community.

Applying and Exploring Ideas

1. Consider a non-school Discourse that you are a member of, and answer the following questions about it:

   a. What are the shared goals of the community; why does this group exist, what does it do?

   b. What mechanisms do members use to communicate with each other (for example, meetings, phone calls, email, text messages, newsletters, reports, evaluation forms)?

   c. What are the purposes of each of these mechanisms of communication (for example, to improve performance, make money, grow better roses, share research)?

   d. Which of the above mechanisms of communication can be considered *genres* (textual responses to recurring situations that all group members recognize and understand)?

   e. What kinds of **lexis** (specialized language) do group members use? Provide some examples.

   f. Who are the "old-timers" with expertise? Who are the newcomers with less expertise? How do newcomers learn the appropriate language, genres, and knowledge of the group?

2. Select a Discourse you're interested in and develop a research question about it. What would you want to know, for example, about how the Discourse works, what it takes to enculturate or gain membership in it, and how it differs from other Discourses?

META MOMENT   What did you learn from Mirabelli that can help you make sense of situations in your own life, both seemingly mundane situations like your part-time job, as well as more complex situations like learning to write in your major? How has Mirabelli helped you better understand the threshold concepts of this chapter: that people use texts and discourse in order to *do something*, to *make meaning*, and that the texts and language they create *mediate meaningful activities*?

Discourse Communities and Communities of Practice

Membership, Conflict, and Diversity

Ann M. Johns

ANN M. JOHNS

Framing the Reading

Ann M. Johns, like Gee, is a well-known linguist. While she was at San Diego State University, Johns directed the American Language Institute, the Writing Across the Curriculum Program, the Freshman Success Program, and the Center for Teaching and Learning, and she still found time to research and write twenty-three articles, twenty-two book chapters, and four books (including *Genre in the Classroom* [2001] and *Text, Role, and Context*, from which the following reading is taken). Since retiring from San Diego State, Johns continues to write articles and consult around the world.

Discourse community is the second of three frames for analysis that this chapter provides in order to help you consider how people use texts and language to accomplish work together. Johns gives you some things to look for and consider when trying to figure out what is happening in any situation where language and texts play a part: What are people doing here? Do they have shared goals? How do they communicate with one another? How do newcomers learn what to do here?

Johns doesn't simply explain discourse communities, but focuses on how and why conflicts occur in them. In doing so, she focuses primarily on *academic* discourse communities. She talks about some of the "expected" **conventions** of discourse in the academy (what she calls "uniting forces"), and then describes sources of contention. Johns brings up issues of rebellion against discourse community conventions, change within conventions of communities, the relationship of **identity** to discourse

Text, Role, and Context

Developing Academic Literacies

Ann M. Johns

Johns, Ann M. "Discourse Communities and Communities of Practice: Membership, Conflict, and Diversity." *Text, Role, and Context: Developing Academic Literacies*, Cambridge UP, 1997, pp. 51–70.

community membership, and the problems of **authority** and control over acceptable community discourse. Johns's exploration of conflicts within discourse communities should remind you that such communities are always changing and are not
static. Thus, even though newcomers may be expected to **enculturate**, they can also
make change within communities — and change the way that people get work done
and make meaning together. As always, this reading will be easier for you if you can
try to relate what Johns describes to your own experiences or to things you have
witnessed or read about elsewhere.

Getting Ready to Read

Before you read, do at least one of the following activities:

- If you've read other articles in this chapter already, make a list of the
  difficulties or problems you've had with concepts related to discourses so far.
  What have you not understood? What has not made sense? What questions
  have you been left with?

- Write a quick note to yourself about *membership*: What does the idea of
  membership mean to you? When you hear that word, what do you associate
  it with? What memories of it do you have? Do you often use it or hear it?

As you read, consider the following questions:

- What does it mean to have *authority* in relation to texts and discourse
  communities?

- How does trying to become a member of a discourse community impact
  your sense of self? Do you feel your "self" being compressed or pressured,
  or expanding?

- How are discourse communities related to *identity*?

---

*If there is one thing that most of [the discourse community definitions] have in
common, it is an idea of language [and genres] as a basis for sharing and holding
in common: shared expectations, shared participation, commonly (or commu-
nicably) held ways of expressing. Like audience, discourse community entails
assumptions about conformity and convention (Rafoth, 1990, p. 140).*

*What is needed for descriptive adequacy may not be so much a search for the
conventions of language use in a particular group, but a search for the varieties
of language use that work both with and against conformity, and accurately reflect
the interplay of identity and power relationships (Rafoth, 1990, p. 144).*

A SECOND IMPORTANT CONCEPT in the discussion of socioliteracies is *discourse* 1
community. Because this term is abstract, complex, and contested,[1] I will approach it
by attempting to answer a few of the questions that are raised in the literature, those
that seem most appropriate to teaching and learning in academic contexts.

1. Why do individuals join social and professional communities? What
   appear to be the relationships between communities and their genres?
2. Are there levels of community? In particular, can we hypothesize a general
   academic community or language?
3. What are some of the forces that make communities complex and varied? What forces work against "shared participation and shared ways of
   expressing?" (Rafoth, 1990, p. 140).

I have used the term discourse communities because this appears to be the 2
most common term in the literature. However, *communities of practice*, a related
concept, is becoming increasingly popular, particularly for academic contexts
(see Brown & Duguid, 1995; Lave & Wenger, 1991). In the term *discourse communities*, the focus is on texts and language, the genres and lexis that enable
members throughout the world to maintain their goals, regulate their membership, and communicate efficiently with one another. Swales (1990, pp. 24–27)
lists six defining characteristics of a discourse community:

1. [It has] a broadly agreed set of common public goals.
2. [It has] mechanisms of intercommunication among its members (such as
   newsletters or journals).
3. [It] utilizes and hence possesses one or more genres in the communicative
   furtherance of its aims.
4. [It] uses its participatory mechanisms primarily to provide information
   and feedback.
5. In addition to owning genres, [it] has acquired some specific lexis.
6. [It has] a threshold level of members with a suitable degree of relevant
   content and discoursal expertise.

The term communities of practice refers to genres and lexis, but especially 3
to many practices and values that hold communities together or separate them
from one another. Lave and Wenger, in discussing students' enculturation into
academic communities, have this to say about communities of practice:

As students begin to engage with the discipline, as they move from exposure
to experience, they begin to understand that the different communities on
campus are quite distinct, that apparently common terms have different

321

meanings, apparently shared tools have different uses, apparently related objects have different interpretations. . . . As they work in a particular community, they start to understand both its particularities and what joining takes, how these involve language, practice, culture and a conceptual universe, not just mountains of facts (1991, p. 13).

Thus, communities of practice are seen as complex collections of individuals who share genres, language, values, concepts, and "ways of being" (Geertz, 1983), often distinct from those held by other communities.

In order to introduce students to these visions of community, it is useful to 4 take them outside the academic realm to something more familiar, the recreational and avocational communities to which they, or their families, belong. Thus I begin with a discussion of nonacademic communities before proceeding to issues of academic communities and membership.

COMMUNITIES AND MEMBERSHIP

Social, Political, and Recreational Communities

People are born, or taken involuntarily by their families and cultures, into some 5 communities of practice. These first culture communities may be religious, tribal, social, or economic, and they may be central to an individual's daily life experiences. Academic communities, on the other hand, are selected and voluntary, at least after compulsory education. Therefore, this chapter will concentrate on communities that are chosen, the groups with which people maintain ties because of their interests, their politics, or their professions. Individuals are often members of a variety of communities outside academic life: social and interest groups with which they have chosen to affiliate. These community affiliations vary in terms of individual depth of interest, belief, and commitment. Individual involvement may become stronger or weaker over time as circumstances and interests change.

Nonacademic communities of interest, like "homely" genres, can provide a 6 useful starting point for student discussion. In presenting communities of this type, Swales uses the example of the Hong Kong Study Circle (HKSC),[2] of which he is a paying member, whose purposes are to "foster interest in and knowledge of the stamps of Hong Kong" (1990, p. 27). He was once quite active in this community, dialoging frequently with other members through HKSC publications.[3] However, at this point in his life, he has other interests (birds and butterflies), and so he is now an inactive member of HKSC. His commitments of time and energy have been diverted elsewhere.

> Why do individuals join social and professional communities? Are there levels of community? What are some of the forces that make communities complex and varied?

Members of my family are also affiliated with several types of communities. 7
We are members of cultural organizations, such as the local art museum and
the theater companies. We receive these communities' publications, and we
attend some of their functions, but we do not consider ourselves to be active.
We also belong to a variety of communities with political aims. My mother, for
example, is a member of the powerful lobbying group, the American Association
of Retired Persons (AARP). The several million members pay their dues because
of their interests in maintaining government-sponsored retirement (Social
Security) and health benefits (Medicare), both of which are promoted by AARP
lobbyists in the U.S. Congress. The AARP magazine, *Modern Maturity*, is a
powerful organ of the association, carefully crafted to forward the group's aims.
Through this publication, members are urged to write to their elected representatives about legislation, and they are also informed about which members of
Congress are "friends of the retired." However, members are offered more than
politics: Articles in the magazine discuss keeping healthy while aging, remaining
beautiful, traveling cheaply, and using the Internet. AARP members also receive
discounts on prescription drugs, tours, and other benefits.[4]

Recently, my husband has become very active in a recreational discourse com- 8
munity, the international community of cyclists.[5] He reads publications such as
Bicycling ("World's No. 1 Road and Mountain Bike Magazine") each month for
advice about better cyclist health ("Instead of Pasta, Eat This!"),[6] equipment to
buy, and international cycling tours. Like most other communities, cycling has
experts, some of whom write articles for the magazines to which he subscribes,
using a register that is mysterious to the uninitiated: "unified gear triangle";
"metal matrix composite." Cyclists share values (good health, travel interests),
special knowledge, vocabulary, and genres, but they do not necessarily share
political or social views, as my husband discovered when conversing with other
cyclists on a group trip. In publications for cyclists, we can find genres that
we recognize by name but with community-related content: editorials, letters
to the editor, short articles on new products, articles of interest to readers (on
health and safety, for example), advertisements appealing to readers, and essay/
commentaries. If we examine magazines published for other interest groups, we
can find texts from many of the same genres.

As this discussion indicates, individuals often affiliate with several commu- 9
nities at the same time, with varying levels of involvement and interest. People
may join a group because they agree politically, because they want to socialize, or
because they are interested in a particular sport or pastime. The depth of an individual's commitment can, and often does, change over time. As members come
and go, the genres and practices continue to evolve, reflecting and promoting
the active members' aims, interests, and controversies.

Studying the genres of nonacademic communities, particularly those with 10
which students are familiar, helps them to grasp the complexity of text production

and processing and the importance of understanding the group practices, lexis, values, and controversies that influence the construction of texts.

Professional Communities

Discourse communities can also be professional; every major profession has its organizations, its practices, its textual conventions, and its genres. Active community members also carry on informal exchanges: at conferences, through e-mail interest groups, in memos, in hallway discussions at the office, in laboratories and elsewhere, the results of which may be woven intertextually into public, published texts. However, it is the written genres of communities that are accessible to outsiders for analysis. We need only to ask professionals about their texts in order to collect an array of interesting examples. One of the most thoroughly studied professional communities is the law. In his *Analysing Genre: Language Use in Professional Settings* (1993), Bhatia discusses at some length his continuing research into legal communities that use English and other languages (pp. 101–143). He identifies the various genres of the legal profession: their purposes, contexts, and the form and content that appear to be conventional. He also contrasts these genres as they are realized in texts from various cultures.

However, there are many other professional discourse communities whose genres can be investigated, particularly when students are interested in enculturation. For example, students might study musicians who devote their lives to pursuing their art but who also use written texts to dialogue with others in their profession. To learn more about these communities, I interviewed a bassoonist in our city orchestra.[7] Along with those who play oboe, English horn, and contrabassoon, this musician subscribes to the major publication of the double-reed community, *The International Double Reed Society Journal.* Though he has specialized, double-reed interests, he reports that he and many other musicians also have general professional aims and values that link them to musicians in a much broader community. He argues that all practicing musicians within the Western tradition[8] share knowledge; there is a common core of language and values within this larger community. Whether they are guitarists, pianists, rock musicians, or bassoonists, musicians in the West seem to agree, for example, that the strongest and most basic musical intervals are 5–1 and 4–1, and that other chord intervals are weaker. They share a basic linguistic register and an understanding of chords and notation. Without this sharing, considerable negotiation would have to take place before they could play music together. As in other professions, these musicians have a base of expertise, values, and expectations that they use to facilitate communication. Thus, though a musician's first allegiance may be to his or her own musical tradition (jazz) or instrument (the bassoon), he or she will still share a great deal with other expert musicians — and much of this sharing is accomplished through specialized texts.

What can we conclude from this section about individual affiliations with 13 discourse communities? First, many people have chosen to be members of one or a variety of communities, groups with whom they share social, political, professional, or recreational interests. These communities use written discourses that enable members to keep in touch with each other, carry on discussions, explore controversies, and advance their aims; the genres are their vehicles for communication. These genres are not, in all cases, sophisticated or intellectual, literary or high-browed. They are, instead, representative of the values, needs, and practices of the community that produces them. Community membership may be concentrated or diluted; it may be central to a person's life or peripheral. Important for the discussion that follows is the juxtaposition of generalized and specialized languages and practices among these groups. Musicians, lawyers, athletes, and physicians, for example, may share certain values, language, and texts with others within their larger community, though their first allegiance is to their specializations. Figure 1 illustrates this general/specific relationship in communities.

In the case of physicians, for example, there is a general community and a 14 set of values and concepts with which most may identify because they have all had a shared basic education before beginning their specializations. There are publications, documents, concepts, language, and values that all physicians can, and often do, share. The same can be said of academics, as is shown in the figure. There may be some general academic discourses,[9] language, values, and concepts

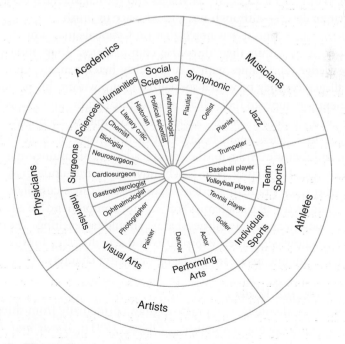

Figure 1 Levels of Community

that most academics share. Thus faculty often identify themselves with a college or university and its language and values, as well as with the more specialized areas of interest for which they have been prepared.

This broad academic identification presents major problems for scholars and literacy practitioners, for although it is argued that disciplines are different (see Bartholomae, 1985; Belcher & Braine, 1995; Berkenkotter & Huckin, 1995; Carson et al., 1992; Lave & Wenger, 1991, among others), many faculty believe that there is a general academic English as well as a general set of critical thinking skills and strategies for approaching texts. 15

Because this belief in a general, shared academic language is strong and universal, the next section of this chapter is devoted to this topic. 16

Academic Communities

What motivates this section more than anything else is its usefulness as a starting point in the exploration of academic literacies and its accessibility to students at various levels of instruction who need to become more aware of the interaction of roles, texts, and contexts in academic communities. Many literacy faculty have mixed classes of students from a number of disciplines or students just beginning to consider what it means to be an academic reader and writer. For these students, and even for some of the more advanced, a discussion of what are considered to be general academic languages and textual practices is a good place to start their analyses—although not a good place to finish. 17

In the previous section it was noted that professionals may affiliate at various levels of specificity within their discourse communities. They often share language, knowledge, and values with a large, fairly heterogeneous group, though their first allegiances may be with a specialized group within this broader "club." This comment can apply to individuals in academic communities as well. Faculty have their own discipline-specific allegiances (to biology, chemistry, sociology, engineering); nonetheless, many believe that there are basic, generalizable linguistic, textual, and rhetorical rules for the entire academic community that can apply. 18

Discipline-specific faculty who teach novices at the undergraduate level, and some who teach graduate students as well, sometimes complain that their students "do not write like academics" or "cannot comprehend" academic prose, arguing that these are general abilities that we should be teaching. The discussion that follows acknowledges their complaints and sets the stage for discussions of more specific academic issues and pedagogies in later chapters. 19

Language, Texts, and Values

This section on academic textual practices draws principally from three sources: "Reflections on Academic Discourse" (Elbow, 1991); *Words and Lives: The Anthropologist as Author* (Geertz, 1988); and *The Scribal Society: An Essay on* 20

Literacy and Schooling in the Information Age (Purves, 1990) (see also Dudley-Evans, 1995). Elbow and Purves are well-known composition theorists from different theoretical camps who were cited in Chapter I. Geertz, an anthropologist, has studied academic communities and their genres for many years. All three of these experts live in the United States, and this may affect their views; however, in many universities in the world in which English is employed, these beliefs about general text features are also shared, except perhaps in literature and some of the humanities disciplines. Following is a composite of the arguments made by the three academics about the nature, values, and practices in general expository academic prose, including some commentary on each topic.

1. *Texts must be explicit.* Writers should select their vocabulary carefully and use it wisely. In some cases, such as with certain noun compounds, paraphrase is impossible because specialized academic vocabulary must be used. Citation must be constructed carefully. Data analysis should be described and discussed explicitly. The methodology should be stated so clearly that it is replicable. Ambiguity in argumentation should be avoided. 21

Comment. Faculty often complain that students are "careless" in their use of vocabulary, in their citation practices, and in their argumentation and use of data. Because many literacy classes value the personal essay and because many readings in literacy classes are in story form or are adapted or specially written for these classes, students are not exposed to the exactness of some academic prose. One of our responsibilities in developing socioliterate practices is to expose students to authentic academic texts and to analyze these texts for their specificity. 22

2. *Topic and argument should be prerevealed in the introduction.* Purves says that experienced academics, particularly when writing certain kinds of texts, should "select a single aspect of [a] subject and announce [their] theses and purposes as soon as possible" (1990, p. 12). 23

Comment. Finding the argument in a reading and noticing how data, examples, or narration are used to support this argument are essential academic abilities that are praised by faculty from many disciplines. In like manner, understanding and presenting a clear argument that is appropriate to a genre are writing skills that appear high on faculty wish lists for students, particularly for those who come from diverse rhetorical traditions (see Connor, 1987). Most faculty require that arguments and purposes appear early, generally in an introduction. One of the discipline-specific faculty with whom I work tells her students not to "spend much time clearing their throats." She wants them to "get right down to the argument." 24

We must be aware, however, that the pressure to reveal topic, purposes, and argumentation early in a written text may be a culture-specific value and apply only to certain kinds of texts within specific communities. There is considerable discussion in the contrastive rhetoric and World Englishes literature about the 25 motivations for text organization and content and the necessity (or lack thereof) for prerevealing information. Local cultures and first languages, as well as academic disciplines, can influence how and where arguments appear.

3. *Writers should provide "maps" or "signposts" for the readers throughout the* 26 *texts, telling the readers where they have been in the text and where they are going.* By using a variety of tactics, writers can assist readers in predicting and summarizing texts and in understanding the relationships among topics and arguments. Most of these tactics fall under the metadiscourse rubric.

Comment. Metadiscourse is defined in the following way: 27

It is writing about reading and writing. When we communicate, we use metadiscourse to name rhetorical actions: *explain, show, argue, claim, deny, suggest, add, expand, summarize;* to name the part of our discourse, *first, second . . . in conclusion;* to reveal logical connections, *therefore . . . if so . . .* to guide our readers, *Consider the matter of* (Williams, 1989, p. 28).

Literacy textbooks for both reading and writing often emphasize the understanding and use of metadiscourse in texts. However, it is important to note that language and culture can have considerable influence on the ways in which metadiscourse is used. For example, in countries with homogeneous cultures, academic written English may have fewer metadiscoursal features (Mauranen, 1993) than in heterogeneous, "writer-responsible" cultures (see Hinds, 1987) such as the United States, Great Britain, or Australia. As in the case of all texts, academic discourses are influenced by the cultures and communities in which they are found, often in very complicated ways.

4. *The language of texts should create a distance between the writer and the text* 28 *to give the appearance of objectivity.* Geertz (1988) speaks of academic, expository prose as "author-evacuated"; the author's personal voice is not clearly in evidence, because the first person pronoun is absent and arguments are muted. He compares author-evacuated prose with the "author-saturated" prose of many literary works, in which individual voice pervades. As mentioned earlier, this "author-evacuation" is particularly evident in pedagogical genres, such as the textbook. One way to create the evacuated style is to use the passive, a common rhetorical choice for the sciences, but there are other ways as well.

Comment. Discipline-specific faculty sometimes tell us that students are 29 unable to write "objectively" or to comprehend "objective" prose.[10] These students have not mastered the ability to clothe their argumentation in a particular register, to give it the kind of objective overlay that is valued in academic circles. When I asked one of my first-year university students to tell the class what he had learned about academic English, he said: "We can't use 'I' anymore. We have to pretend that we're not there in the text." In many cases, he is right. Literacy teachers need to help students to analyze texts for their author-evacuated style, and to discuss the particular grammatical and lexical choices that are made to achieve the appearance of objectivity and distance.

5. *Texts should maintain a "rubber-gloved" quality of voice and register.* They must show a kind of reluctance to touch one's meanings with one's naked fingers (Elbow, 1991, p. 145). 30

Comment. For some academic contexts, writers appear to remove themselves emotionally and personally from the texts, to hold their texts at arms' length (metaphorically). The examination of texts in which this "rubber-gloved quality" is evident will provide for students some of the language to achieve these ends. What can students discover? Many academic writers abjure the use of emotional words, such as *wonderful* and *disgusting;* they hide behind syntax and "objective" academic vocabulary. 31

6. *Writers should take a guarded stance, especially when presenting argumenta-tion and results.* Hedging through the use of modals (*may, might*) and other forms (*It is possible that . . .*) is perhaps the most common way to be guarded. 32

Comment. Hedging appears to be central to some academic discourses, par-ticularly those that report research. In a study of two science articles on the same topic published for two different audiences, Fahenstock (1986) found that the article written for experts in the field was replete with hedges ("*appear to* hydro-lyze," "*suggesting* that animal food"), as scientists carefully reported their findings to their peers. However, the article written for laypersons was filled with "facts," much like those in the textbooks described in Chapter 3. For these and other reasons, we need to introduce students to expert and nonexpert texts; we need to expose them at every level to the ways in which genre, context, readers, writers, and communities affect linguistic choices. 33

7. *Texts should display a vision of reality shared by members of the particular discourse community to which the text is addressed (or the particular faculty member who made the assignment).* 34

Comment. This may be the most difficult of the general academic require-ments, for views of reality are often implicit, unacknowledged by the faculty themselves and are not revealed to students. Perhaps I can show how this "reality vision" is so difficult to uncover by discussing my research on course syllabi. I have been interviewing faculty for several years about the goals for their classes, goals that are generally stated in what is called a syllabus in the United States, but might be called a class framework or schedule of assignments in other coun-tries. These studies indicated that most faculty tend to list as goals for the course the various topics that will be studied. The focus is exclusively on content. They do not list the particular views of the world that they want students to embrace, or the understandings that they want to encourage. In a class on "Women in the Humanities," for example, the instructor listed topics to be covered in her syl-labus, but she did not tell the students that she wanted them to analyze images of women in cultures in order to see how these images shape various cultural 35 contexts. In a geography class, the instructor listed topics to be covered, but he did not tell his students about his goals for analysis and synthesis of texts. Why are the critical-thinking goals and disciplinary values hidden by most faculty? I don't know. Perhaps instructors believe that students should intuit the values, practices, and genres required in the course; or the faculty have difficulty explicitly stating goals that are not related to content. Certainly content is the most commonly discussed issue at discipline-specific (DS) curriculum meetings, and this may influence faculty choices. In a later chapter I will discuss one of the questionnaires that I use to elicit from faculty the "views of reality" or "ways of being" that my students and I would like to see stated explicitly in the syllabi.

In contrast to DS faculty, we literacy faculty are often most interested 36 in processes and understandings, in developing students metacognition and metalanguages — and these interests are often reflected in our syllabi. [Following,] for example, are the student goals for a first-year University writing class developed by a committee from my university's Department of Rhetoric and Writing Studies:[11]

    a. To use writing to clarify and improve your understanding of issues and texts

    b. To respond in writing to the thinking of others and to explore and account for your own responses

    c. To read analytically and critically, making active use of what you read in your writing

    d. To understand the relationships between discourse structure and the question at issue in a piece of writing, and to select appropriate structures at the sentence and discourse levels

    e. To monitor your writing for the grammar and usage conventions appropriate to each writing situation

    f. To use textual material as a framework for understanding and writing about other texts, data or experiences

No matter what kind of class is being taught, faculty need to discuss critical- 37 thinking and reading and writing goals frequently with students. They need to review why students are given assignments, showing how these tasks relate to course concepts and student literacy growth.

8. *Academic texts should display a set of social and authority relations; they* 38 *should show the writer's understanding of the roles they play within the text or context.*[12]

Comment. Most students have had very little practice in recognizing the 39 language of social roles within academic contexts, although their experience with language and social roles outside the classroom is often quite rich. Some students cannot recognize when they are being talked down to in textbooks, and they cannot write in a language that shows their roles vis-à-vis the topics studied or the faculty they are addressing. These difficulties are particularly evident among ESL/EFL students; however, they are also found among many other students whose exposure to academic language has been minimal. One reason for discussing social roles as they relate to texts from a genre, whether they be "homely" discourses or professional texts, is to heighten students' awareness of the interaction of language, roles, and contexts so that they can read and write with more sophistication.

9. *Academic texts should acknowledge the complex and important nature of intertextuality, the exploitation of other texts without resorting to plagiarism.* Students need to practice reformulation and reconstruction of information so that they do not just repeat other texts by "knowledge telling" (Bereiter & Scardamalia, 1989) but rather use these texts inventively for their purposes (called "knowledge transforming"; Bereiter & Scardamalia, 1989). 40

Comment. Carson (1993), in a large study of the intellectual demands on undergraduate students, found that drawing from and integrating textual sources were two of the major challenges students face in attaining academic literacy. And no wonder. Widdowson (1993, p. 27) notes that 41

> When people make excessive and unacknowledged use of [another's text], and are found out, we call it plagiarism. When people are astute in their stitching of textual patchwork, we call it creativity. It is not easy to tell the difference. . . . If a text is always in some degree a conglomerate of others, how independent can its meaning be?

Drawing from sources and citing them appropriately is the most obvious and most commonly discussed aspect of intertextuality. As a result, Swales and Feak (1994) claim that citation may be the defining feature of academic discourses. However, there are other, more subtle and varied borrowings from past discourses, for, as Widdowson notes, "Any particular text is produced or interpreted in reference to a previous knowledge of other texts" (1993, p. 27). 42

10. *Texts should comply with the genre requirements of the community or classroom.* 43

Comment. This, of course, is another difficult challenge for students. As mentioned earlier, pedagogical genres are often loosely named and casually described by DS faculty. It is difficult to identify the conventions of a student research paper, an essay examination response, or other pedagogical genres because, in fact, these vary considerably from class to class. Yet DS faculty expect students to understand these distinctions and to read and write appropriately for their own classes. My students and I often ask faculty: "What is a good critique for your class?" or "What is a good term paper?" We request several student-written 44 models and, if possible, interview the faculty member about their assigned texts and tasks.

This section has outlined what may be some general rules for academic liter-   45
acy, most of which are refined within each discipline and classroom. Although it would be difficult to defend several of these beliefs because of the wide range of academic discourses and practices, listing and discussing these factors can prepare students for an examination of how texts are socially constructed and whether some of the points made here are applicable to specific texts.

Of course, we also need to expose students to texts that contradict these rules   46
for academic discourse. We should examine literary genres, which break most of the rules listed. We should look at specialized texts that have alternative require-ments for register. In any of our pedagogical conversations, the objective should not be to discover truths but to explore how social and cultural forces may influ-ence texts in various contexts.

COMMUNITY CONFLICTS AND DIVERSITY

So far, the discussion of communities and their genres has focused on the unit-   47
ing forces, particularly the language, practices, values, and genres that groups may share. It has been suggested that people can join communities at will and remain affiliated at levels of their own choosing. For a number of reasons, this is not entirely accurate. In some cases people are excluded from communities because they lack social standing, talent, or money, or because they live in the wrong part of town. In other cases, community membership requires a long initiatory process, and even then there is no guarantee of success. Many students work for years toward their doctoral degrees, for example, only to find that there are no faculty positions available to them or that their approach to research will not lead to advancement.

Even after individuals are fully initiated, many factors can separate them.   48
Members of communities rebel, opposing community leaders or attempting to change the rules of the game and, by extension, the content and argumentation in the texts from shared genres. If the rebellion is successful, the rules may be changed or a new group may be formed with a different set of values and aims. There may even be a theoretical paradigm shift in the discipline. In academic communities, rebellion may result in the creation of a new unit or department, separate from the old community, as has been the case recently in my own university.[13] Even without open rebellion, there is constant dialogue and argument within communities as members thrash out their differences and juggle for power and identity, promot-ing their own content, argumentation, and approaches to research.

Although much could be said about factors that affect communities outside   49
the academic realm, the following discussion will focus on a few of the rich and complex factors that give academic communities their character.

The Cost of Affiliation

If students want to become affiliated with academic discourse communities, or 50 even if they want to succeed in school, they may have to make considerable sacrifices. To become active academic participants, they sometimes must make major trade-offs that can create personal and social distance between them and their families and communities. Students are asked to modify their language to fit that of the academic classroom or discipline. They often must drop, or at least diminish in importance, their affiliations to their home cultures in order to take on the values, language, and genres of their disciplinary culture. The literature is full of stories of the students who must make choices between their communities and academic lives (see, for example, Rose's *Lives on the Boundary*, 1989). In an account of his experiences, Richard Rodriguez (1982, p. 56), a child of Mexican immigrant parents, wrote the following:

> What I am about to say to you has taken me more than twenty years to admit: a primary reason for my success in the classroom was that I couldn't forget that schooling was changing me and separating me from the life I had enjoyed before becoming a student. . . . If because of my schooling, I had grown culturally separated from my parents, my education has finally given me ways of speaking and caring about that fact.

Here Rodriguez is discussing his entire schooling experience; however, as stu- 51 dents advance in schools and universities, they may be confronted with even more wrenching conflicts between their home and academic cultures and languages. In her story of a Hispanic graduate student in a Ph.D. sociology program in the United States, Casanave (1992) tells how the tension between this student's personal values and language and her chosen department's insistence on its own scientific language and genres finally drove her from her new academic community. When she could no longer explain her work in sociology in everyday language to the people of her primary communities (her family and her clients), the student decided to leave the graduate program. The faculty viewed her stance as rebellious, an open refusal to take on academic community values. By the time she left, it had become obvious to all concerned that the faculty were unable, or unwilling, to bend or to adapt some of their disciplinary rules to accommodate this student's interests, vocation, and language.

A graduate student from Japan faced other kinds of affiliation conflicts when 52 attempting to become a successful student in a North American linguistics program (Benson, 1996). This student brought from her home university certain social expectations: about faculty roles, about her role as a student, and about what is involved in the production of texts. She believed, for example, that the faculty should provide her with models of what was expected in her papers; she felt that they should determine her research topics and hypotheses. This had been the case in her university in Japan, and she had considerable difficulty understanding why the American faculty did not conform to the practices of her home country. She tried to follow her professors' instructions with great care, but they chastised her for "lacking ideas." In her view, the faculty were being irresponsible; however, some faculty viewed her as passive, unimaginative, and dependent. What she and many other students have found is that gaining affiliation in graduate education means much more than understanding the registers of academic language.

These examples are intended to show that full involvement or affiliation in academic discourse communities requires major cultural and linguistic tradeoffs from many students. Faculty expect them to accept the texts, roles, and contexts of the discipline, but acceptance requires much more sacrifice and change than the faculty may imagine. In our literacy classes, we can assist academic students in discussing the kinds of problems they encounter when attempting to resolve these conflicts. However, we can also assist our faculty colleagues, who often are unaware of their students' plight, through workshops, student presentations, and suggestions for reading.

Issues of Authority

What happens after a person has become an academic initiate, after he or she has completed the degree, published, and been advanced? There are still community issues to contend with, one of which relates to authority (Bakhtin, 1986 p. 88) noted that "in each epoch, in each social circle, in each small world of family, friends, acquaintances and comrades in which a human being grows and lives, there are always authoritative utterances that set the tone."

In academic circles, these "authoritative utterances" are made by journal or e-mail interest-group editors, by conference program planners, and by others. At the local level, this authority can be held by department chairs or by chairs of important committees. Prior (1994, p. 522) speaks of these academically powerful people as "an elite group that imposes its language, beliefs and values on others through control of journals, academic appointments, curricula, student examinations, research findings and so on." It is important to note that Prior extends his discussion beyond authority over colleagues to broad authority over students through curricula and examinations. This type of pedagogical authority is very important, as all students know, so it will be discussed further.

In many countries, provincial and national examinations drive the curricula, and theoretical and practical control over these examinations means authority over what students are taught. In the People's Republic of China, for example, important general English language examinations have been based for years on word frequency counts developed in several language centers throughout the country. Each "band," or proficiency level on the examination, is determined by "the most common 1,000 words," "the most common 2,000 words," and so on.[14] Although features of language such as grammar are tested in these examinations, it is a theory about vocabulary, based on word frequency, that is central. It is not surprising, then, that most Chinese students believe that vocabulary is the key to literacy, particularly the understanding of "exact" meanings of words. When I have worked with teachers in China, I have frequently been asked questions such as "What is the exact meaning of the term 'discourse'? What does 'theory' mean?" These teachers requested a single definition, something I was often unable to provide.

The centralized power over important examinations in China, over the 57 TOEFL and graduate entrance examinations in the United States, and over the British Council Examinations in other parts of the world gives considerable authority within communities to certain test developers and examiners. This authority permits little pedagogical latitude to teachers preparing students for these "gate-keeping" examinations. As practitioners, we can use test preparation pedagogies, or we can critique these examinations (Raimes, 1990), as we should; but we cannot institute large-scale change until we gain control and authority over the examination system.

With students at all academic levels, we practitioners should raise the issues of 58 authority, status, and control over community utterances in literacy classes. About their own social groups, we can ask: "Who has status in your clubs and why? Who has status in your ethnic or geographical communities and why? How do they exert control over people, over utterances, and over publications?" When referring to academic situations and authority, we can ask: "Who wrote this textbook? What are the authors' affiliations? Are they prestigious? How does the language of the textbook demonstrate the author's authority over the material and over the students who read the volume?" We can also ask: "Who writes your important examinations? What are their values?" Or we can ask: "Who has status in your academic classrooms? Which students have authority and why?" And finally, we might ask: "How can you gain authority in the classroom or over texts?"

Throughout a discussion of authority relationships, we need to talk about 59 communities, language, and genres: how texts and spoken discourses are used to gain and perpetuate authority. We can assist students to analyze authoritative texts, including those of other students, and to critique authority relationships. Our students need to become more aware of these factors affecting their academic lives before they can hope to produce and comprehend texts that command authority within academic contexts.

Conventions and Anticonventionalism

There are many other push and pull factors in academic communities, factors 60 that create dialogue, conflict, and change. Communities evolve constantly, though established community members may attempt to maintain their power and keep the new initiates in line through control over language and genres. A student or a young faculty member can be punished for major transgressions from the norm, for attempting to move away from what the more established, initiated members expect. In order to receive a good grade (or be published), writers often must work within the rules. Understanding these rules, even if they are to be broken, appears to be essential.

As individuals within an academic community become more established 61 and famous, they can become more anticonventional, in both their texts and their lives. Three famous rule breakers come to mind, though there are others. Stephen J. Gould, a biologist, has written a series of literate essays for the general public, principally about evolution, that look considerably different from the scientific journal article. Gould has broken his generic traditions to "go public" because he already has tenure at Harvard, he likes to write essays, and he enjoys addressing a public audience (see Gould, 1985). Deborah Tannen, an applied linguist, has also "gone public," publishing "pop books" about communication between men and women that are best-sellers in the United States (see Tannen, 1986, 1994). She continues to write relatively conventional articles in journals, but she also writes often for the layperson. Clifford Geertz, the anthropologist, refuses to be pigeon-holed in terms of topic, argumentation, or genre. Using his own disciplinary approaches, he writes texts on academic cultures as well as the "exotic" ones that are typical to anthropologists (see Geertz, 1988). Gould, Tannen, and Geertz have established themselves within their disciplines. Now famous, they can afford to defy community conventions as they write in their individual ways.

Rule breaking is a minefield for many students, however. They first need to 62 understand some of the basic conventions, concepts, and values of a community's genres. Learning and using academic conventions is not easy, for many students receive little or no instruction. To compound the problems, students need constantly to revise their theories of genres and genre conventions (see Bartholomae, 1985). Some graduate students, for example, often express confusion about conventions, anticonventions, and the breaking of rules, for faculty advice appears to be idiosyncratic, based not on community conventions but on personal taste. Some faculty thesis advisers, particularly in the humanities, require a careful review of the literature and accept nothing else; others may insist on "original"[15] work without a literature review. For some advisers there is a "cookie cutter" macrostructure that all papers must follow; others may prefer a more free-flowing, experimental text. Graduate students complain that discovering or breaking these implicit rules requires much research and many visits to faculty offices, as well as many drafts of their thesis chapters (see Schneider & Fujishima, 1995).

It should be clear from this discussion that we cannot tell students "truths" 63 about texts or community practices. However, we can heighten student awareness of generic conventions, and we can assist students in formulating questions that can be addressed to faculty. In our literacy classes, we are developing researchers, not dogmatists, students who explore ideas and literacies rather than seek simple answers.

Dialogue and Critique

In any thriving academic community, there is constant dialogue: disagreements 64 among members about approaches to research, about argumentation, about topics for study, and about theory. The journal *Science* acknowledges this and accepts two types of letters to the editor to enable writers to carry out informal dialogues. In other journals, sections are set aside for short interchanges between two writers who hold opposing views (see the *Journal of Second Language Writing*, for example). Most journals carry critiques of new volumes in book review sections, and many published articles are in dialogue with other texts. Academic communities encourage variety and critique (within limits), because that is how they evolve and grow.

Most professional academics know the rules for dialogue: what topics are cur- 65 rently "hot," how to discuss these topics in ways appropriate for the readers of their genres, how far they can go from the current norms, and what they can use (data, narratives, nonlinear texts) to support their arguments. Some professionals who understand the rules can also break them with impunity. They can push the boundaries because they know where the discipline has been and where it may be going, and how to use their authority, and the authority of others, to make their arguments. In a volume on academic expertise, Geisler (1994) comments that there are three "worlds" with which expert academics must be familiar before they can join, or contravene, a disciplinary dialogue: the "domain content world" of logically related concepts and content; the "narrated world" of everyday experience; and the "abstract world" of authorial conversation. Academic experts must manipulate these worlds in order to produce texts that can be in dialogue or conflict with, yet appropriate to, the communities they are addressing.

This discussion has suggested that communities and their genres are useful 66 to study not only because they can share conventions, values, and histories but because they are evolving: through affiliation of new, different members; through changes in authority; through anticonventionalism, dialogue, and critique. Students know these things about their own communities; we need to draw from this knowledge to begin to explore unfamiliar academic communities and their genres.

This chapter has addressed some of the social and cultural factors that influ- 67 ence texts, factors that are closely related to community membership. Although there is much debate in the literature about the nature of discourse communities and communities of practice, it can be said with some certainty that community affiliations are very real to individual academic faculty. Faculty refer to themselves as "chemists," "engineers," "historians," or "applied linguists"; they read texts from community genres with great interest or join in heated debates with their peers over the Internet. They sometimes recognize that the language, values, and genres of their communities (or specializations) may differ from those of another academic community, though this is not always the case. At a promotions committee made up of faculty from sixteen departments in which I took part, a member of the quantitative group in the Geography Department said of a humanities text, "We shouldn't accept an article for promotion without statistics." And we all laughed, nervously.

Academics, and others, may belong to several communities and have in com- 68 mon certain interests within each. Thus, faculty may have nothing in common with other faculty in their disciplines but the discipline itself; their social, political, and other interests can, and often do, vary widely. In one department, for example, musical interests can be diverse. There may be country-western fans, opera fans, jazz enthusiasts, and those whose only musical experiences consist of listening to the national anthem at baseball games. Recreational interests may also differ. Among faculty, there are motorcyclists and bicyclists, hikers and "couch potatoes," football fans and those who actually play the sport.

A complex of social, community-related factors influences the socioliteracies 69 of faculty and the students who are in their classes. As literacy practitioners, we need to help our students examine these factors by bringing other faculty and students, and their genres, into our classrooms, as well as drawing from our own students' rich resources.

Notes

1. Some of the contested issues and questions are: "How are communities defined?" (Rafoth, 1990); "Do discourse communities even exist?" (Prior, 1994); "Are they global or local? Or both?" (Killingsworth, 1992); "What is the relationship between discourse communities and genres?" (Swales, 1988b, 1990).

2. Note that most communities use abbreviations for their names and often for their publications. All community members recognize these abbreviations, of course.

3. These written interactions are impossible for the noninitiated to understand, I might point out.

4. When I asked my mother to drop her AARP membership because of a political stand the organization took, she said, "I can't, Ann. I get too good a deal on my medicines through my membership."

5. Those of us who are outsiders call them "gearheads." Often, terms are applied to insiders by community outsiders.

6. Brill, D. (1994, November). What's free of fat and cholesterol, costs 4 cents per serving, and has more carbo than pasta? Rice! *Bicycling*, pp. 86–87.

7. I would like to thank Arlan Fast of the San Diego Symphony for these community insights.

8. Knowledge is also shared with musicians from other parts of the world, of course. However, some of the specific examples used here apply to the Western musical tradition.

9. For example, *The Chronicle of Higher Education* and several pedagogical publications are directed to a general academic audience.

10. "Objective" appears in quotation marks because, though academic writing may have the appearance of being objective, all texts are biased.

11. Quandahl, E. (1995). Rhetoric and writing studies 100: A list of goals. Unpublished paper, San Diego State University, San Diego, CA.

12. When I showed this point to Virginia Guleff, a graduate student, she said, "So students have to know their place!" Perhaps we should put it this way: They need to know different registers in order to play different rules. The more people use these registers, the more effective they can become and, not incidentally, the more power they can have over the situation in which they are reading or writing.

13. San Diego State's new Department of Rhetoric and Writing Studies is composed of composition instructors who asked to leave the Department of English, as well as of faculty from the previously independent Academic Skills Center.

14. "Most common" appears in quotation marks because what is most common (other than function words) is very difficult to determine. These lists are influenced by the type of language data that is entered into the computer for the word count: whether it is written or spoken, its register etc. If data are varied, other vocabulary become common.

    At one point in my career, I attempted to develop low-proficiency English for Business textbooks for adults using a famous publisher's list of most common words. I failed because the data used to establish the frequency lists were taken from children's books. The common words in children's language and those most common in business language are considerably different (Johns, 1985).

15. Since I am arguing here that all texts rely on other texts, I put "original" in quotation marks.

References

Bakhtin, M. M. (1986). *Speech genres and other late essays.* (V. W. Mc Gee, Trans.). C. Emerson & M. Holquist (Eds.). Austin: University of Texas Press.

Bartholomae, D. (1985). Inventing the university. In M. Rose (Ed.), *When a writer can't write: Studies in writer's block and other composing process problems* (pp. 134–165). New York: Guilford Press.

Belcher, D., & Braine, G. (Eds.). (1995). *Academic writing in a second language: Essays on research and pedagogy.* Norwood, NJ: Ablex.

Benson, K. (1996). *How do students and faculty perceive graduate writing tasks? A case study of a Japanese student in a graduate program in linguistics.* Unpublished manuscript, San Diego State University.

Bereiter, C., & Scardamalia, M. (1989). Intentional learning as a goal of instruction. In J. Resnick (Ed.), *Knowing, learning* (pp. 361–392). Hillsdale, NJ: Lawrence Erlbaum.

Berkenkotter, C., & Huckin, T. (1995). *Genre knowledge in disciplinary communities.* Hillsdale, NJ: Lawrence Erlbaum.

Bhatia, V. J. (1993). *Analyzing genre: Language use in professional settings.* London & New York: Longman.

Brill, D. (1994, November). What's free of fat and cholesterol, costs 4 cents per serving, and has more carbo than pasta? Rice! *Bicycling, 86–87.*

Brown, J. S., & Duguid, P. (1995, July 26). Universities in the digital age. *Xerox Palo Alto Paper.* Palo Alto, CA: Xerox Corporation.

Carson, J. G. (1993, April). *Academic literacy demands of the undergraduate curriculum: Literacy activities integrating skills.* Paper presented at the International TESOL Conference, Atlanta, GA.

Carson, J. G., Chase, N., Gibson, S., & Hargrove, M. (1992). Literacy demands of the undergraduate curriculum. *Reading Research and Instruction, 31,* 25–50.

Casanave, C. P. (1992). Cultural diversity and socialization: A case study of a Hispanic woman in a doctoral program in Sociology. In D. Murray (Ed.), *Diversity as a resource: Redefining cultural literacy* (pp. 148–182). Arlington, VA: TESOL.

Connor, U. (1987). Argumentative patterns in student essays: Cross-cultural differences. In U. Connor & R. B. Kaplan (Eds.), *Writing across languages: Analysis of L2 text* (pp. 57–71). Reading, MA: Addison-Wesley.

Dudley-Evans, T. (1995). Common-core and specific approaches to teaching academic writing. In D. Belcher & G. Braine (Eds.), *Academic writing in a second language: Essays on research and pedagogy* (pp. 293–312). Norwood, NJ: Ablex.

Elbow, P. (1991). Reflections on academic discourse. *College English, 53(2),* 135–115.

Fahenstock, J. (1986). Accommodating science. *Written Communication, 3,* 275–296.

Geertz, C. (1983). *Local knowledge: Further essays in interpretive anthropology.* New York: Basic Books.

Geertz, C. (1988). *Words and lives: The anthropologist as author.* Palo Alto, CA: Stanford University Press.

Geisler, C. (1994). Literacy and expertise in the academy. *Language and Learning Across the Disciplines, 1,* 35–57.

Gould, S. J. (1985). *The flamingo's smile.* New York: Norton.

Hinds, J. (1987). Reader versus writer responsibility: A new typology. In U. Connor & R. B. Kaplan (Eds.), *Writing across languages: An analysis of L2 texts* (pp. 141–152). Reading, MA: Addison-Wesley.

Johns, A. M. (1985). The new authenticity and the preparation of commercial reading texts for lower-level ESP students. *CATESOL Occasional Papers, 11,* 103–107.

Killingsworth, M. J. (1992). Discourse communities—local and global. *Rhetoric Review, 11,* 110–122.

Lave, J., & Wenger, E. (1991). *Situated learning: Legitimate peripheral participation.* New York: Cambridge University Press.

Mauranen, A. (1993). Contrastive ESP rhetoric Metatext in Finnish-English economic texts. *English for Specific Purposes, 12,* 3–22.

Prior, P. (1994). Response, revision and disciplinarity: A microhistory of a dissertation prospectus in sociology. *Written Communication, 11,* 483–533.

Purves, A. C. (1990). *The scribal society: An essay on literacy and schooling in the information age.* New York: Longman.

Rafoth, B. A. (1990). The concept of discourse community: Descriptive and explanatory adequacy. In G. Kirsch & D. H. Roen (Eds.), *A sense of audience in written communication* (pp. 140–152). *Written Communication Annual, Vol. 5.* Newbury Park, CA: Sage.

Raimes, A. (1990). The TOEFL Test of Written English: Some causes for concern. *TESOL Quarterly, 24,* 427–442.

Rodriguez, R. (1982). *Hunger of memory: The education of Richard Rodriguez.* New York: Bantam Books.

Rose, M. (1989). *Lives on the boundary: The struggles and achievements of America's underprepared.* New York: Free Press.

Schneider, M., & Fujishima, N. K. (1995). When practice doesn't make perfect: The case of a graduate ESL student. In D. Belcher & G. Braine (Eds.), *Academic writing in a second language: Essays on research & pedagogy* (pp. 3–22). Norwood, NJ: Ablex.

Swales, J. M. (1988b). Discourse communities, genres and English as an international language. *World Englishes, 7,* 211–220.

Swales, J. M. (1990). *Genre analysis: English in academic and research settings.* New York: Cambridge University Press.

Swales, J. M., & Feak, C. B. (1994). *Academic writing for graduate students: Essential tasks and skills.* Ann Arbor: University of Michigan Press.

Tannen, D. (1986). *That's not what I meant: How conversational style makes or breaks your relations with others.* New York: W. Morrow.

Tannen, D. (1994). *Talking from 9–5: How women's and men's conversational styles affect who gets heard, who gets credit, and what gets done at work.* New York: W. Morrow.

Widdowson, H. G. (1993). The relevant conditions of language use and learning. In M. Krueger & F. Ryan (Eds.), *Language and content: Discipline- and content-based approaches to language study* (pp. 27–36). Lexington, MA: D. C. Heath.

Williams, J. (1989). *Style: Ten lessons in clarity and grace.* (3rd. ed.). Glenview, IL: Scott Foresman.

- -

Questions for Discussion and Journaling

1. What are some of the complications Johns outlines related to joining a discourse community?

2. Johns notes that people joining a new discourse community can rebel against some of its conventions, and in so doing actually change the discourse community. Explain what this means and try to think of some historical examples where this has happened. If you read Gee (p. 274), compare Johns's view of *change* in discourse communities with Gee's view.

3. Have you ever felt that learning to write or speak in a new discourse community conflicted with your sense of self, your values, your beliefs? If so, what happened? If not, why do you think you have been exempt from this sort of conflict?

4. Johns cites a number of examples to argue that learning to write and speak in new ways is not just a cognitive matter, but also impacts values and identity. She says, "full involvement or affiliation . . . requires major cultural and linguistic trade-offs" (para. 53). Draw on some examples of your own to explain what you think this means. Do you agree or disagree with her claim here? Why?

5. How do you feel about your *authority* over the kinds of texts you have been asked to write so far in college?

6. Why is rule breaking a "minefield" for students, but not for the more "famous" or established academic writers Johns cites? Have you ever been punished or rewarded for rule breaking related to texts? What happened?

Applying and Exploring Ideas

1. In paragraph 58, Johns outlines a number of questions that teachers should discuss with their students regarding authority and control of language in their classrooms. Go through and answer her list of questions in as much detail as you can. When you are finished, reread your answers and use them to help you write a letter to an incoming student in which you explain the concepts of *discourse communities*, *authority*, and *control*, and explain the relationships among them. Then, explain why having an explicit understanding of these concepts is useful and give specific examples from your own experiences to illustrate what you are saying.

2. Plan an insurrection in your writing classroom. What are some writing rules you'd like to break? Do these rules represent the values or authority of a particular discourse community? How would breaking these rules impact your membership in the discourse community, and your own identity? Try writing a Declaration of Independence from the particular rule or rules in question, and then see if your classmates are persuaded by it to vote in favor of revolution.

- -

META MOMENT   How would understanding what Johns is writing about help you in becoming a member of new discourse communities? In other words, how can you apply what you learned from her to situations outside your writing class? How does Johns help you better understand the underlying threshold concepts of this chapter?

- -

Learning the Language

PERRI KLASS

Adrian Mihai

Perri Klass holds an M.D. from Harvard and is currently professor of journalism and pediatrics at New York University, where she is the Director of the Arthur L. Carter Journalism Institute. She is also the National Medical Director for Reach Out and Read, work for which she received the 2007 American Academy of Pediatrics Education Award. The Reach Out and Read organization incorporates books in pediatric care and encourages families to read aloud together. Dr. Klass wrote a monthly column for the *New York Times* called 18 and Under, and another column for that newspaper called Hers, which chronicled her life as a mother going through medical school. She has also written several novels and nonfiction books. The following excerpt is taken from her book of essays recording her life as a medical student.

We have included this short essay here because it illustrates many of the concepts described theoretically elsewhere in this chapter — namely, that groups of people (discourse communities) use language and texts in specialized ways as they work to accomplish their goals together. Their specialized **lexis** helps to mediate their activities (in this case, it not only helps doctors treat patients, but also helps doctors be more detached about the life and death situations they face on a daily basis). Klass's piece also illustrates Johns's claim that belonging to a discourse community is not just a matter of **cognition**, but also impacts values and identity, that "full involvement or affiliation . . . requires major cultural and linguistic trade-offs."

Klass, Perri. *A Not Entirely Benign Procedure: Four Years as a Medical Student.* Putnam Books, 1987.

Getting Ready to Read

Before you read, do at least one of the following activities:

- If you or someone close to you has ever been in the hospital, try to remember some of the language or special phrasing that you heard the doctors and nurses use. How did that language make you feel?

- Think of a club, group, or workplace you are a part of and write down as many specialized words and phrases used there as you can think of. What purpose do these specialized words serve?

As you read, do the following:

- Highlight or underline every place where Klass explains the purposes, benefits, or consequences of using specialized language.

- Star or circle every place where Klass's examples help you understand Gee's or Johns's theories a little better — or at least places where you think the examples relate to Gee or Johns.

"MRS. TOLSTOY IS YOUR BASIC LOL in NAD, admitted for a soft rule- 1 out MI," the intern announces. I scribble that on my patient list. In other words, Mrs. Tolstoy is a Little Old Lady in No Apparent Distress who is in the hospital to make sure she hasn't had a heart attack (rule out a Myocardial Infarction). And we think it's unlikely that she has had a heart attack (a *soft* rule-out).

If I learned nothing else during my first three months of working in the hos- 2 pital as a medical student, I learned endless jargon and abbreviations. I started out in a state of primeval innocence, in which I didn't even know that "s̄ CP, SOB, N/V" meant "without chest pain, shortness of breath, or nausea and vomiting." By the end I took the abbreviations so much for granted that I would complain to my mother the English professor, "And can you believe I had to put down *three* NG tubes last night?"

"You'll have to tell me what an NG tube is if you want me to sympathize 3 properly," my mother said. NG, nasogastric — isn't it obvious?

I picked up not only the specific expressions but also the patterns of speech 4 and the grammatical conventions; for example, you never say that a patient's blood pressure fell or that his cardiac enzymes rose. Instead, the patient is always the subject of the verb: "He dropped his pressure." "He bumped his enzymes." This sort of construction probably reflects the profound irritation of the intern when the nurses come in the middle of the night to say that Mr. Dickinson has disturbingly low blood pressure. "Oh, he's gonna hurt me bad tonight," the intern might say, inevitably angry at Mr. Dickinson for dropping his pressure and creating a problem.

When chemotherapy fails to cure Mrs. Bacon's cancer, what we say is, 5 "Mrs. Bacon failed chemotherapy."

"Well, we've already had one hit today, and we're up next, but at least we've got 6 mostly stable players on our team." This means that our team (group of doctors and medical students) has already gotten one new admission today, and it is our turn again, so we'll get whoever is admitted next in emergency, but at least most of the patients we already have are fairly stable, that is, unlikely to drop their pressures or in any other way get suddenly sicker and hurt us bad. Baseball metaphor is pervasive. A no-hitter is a night without any new admissions. A player is always a patient—a nitrate player is a patient on nitrates, a unit player is a patient in the intensive care unit, and so on, until you reach the terminal player.

It is interesting to consider what it means to be winning, or doing well, in this 7 perennial baseball game. When the intern hangs up the phone and announces, "I got a hit," that is not cause for congratulations. The team is not scoring points; rather, it is getting hit, being bombarded with new patients. The object of the game from the point of view of the doctors, considering the players for whom they are already responsible, is to get as few new hits as possible.

This special language contributes to a sense of closeness and professional spirit 8 among people who are under a great deal of stress. As a medical student, I found it exciting to discover that I'd finally cracked the code, that I could understand what doctors said and wrote, and could use the same formulations myself. Some people seem to become enamored of the jargon for its own sake, perhaps because they are so deeply thrilled with the idea of medicine, with the idea of themselves as doctors.

I knew a medical student who was referred to by the interns on the team as 9 Mr. Eponym because he was so infatuated with eponymous terminology, the more obscure the better. He never said "capillary pulsations" if he could say "Quincke's pulses." He would lovingly tell over the multinamed syndromes— Wolff-Parkinson-White, Lown-Ganong-Levine, Schönlein-Henoch—until the temptation to suggest Schleswig-Holstein or Stevenson-Kefauver or Baskin-Robbins became irresistible to his less reverent colleagues.

And there is the jargon that you don't ever want to hear yourself using. You 10 know that your training is changing you, but there are certain changes you think would be going a little too far.

The resident was describing a man with devastating terminal pancreatic can- 11 cer. "Basically he's CTD," the resident concluded. I reminded myself that I had resolved not to be shy about asking when I didn't understand things. "CTD?" I asked timidly.

The resident smirked at me. "Circling The Drain." 12

The images are vivid and terrible. "What happened to Mrs. Melville?" 13

"Oh, she boxed last night." To box is to die, of course. 14

Then there are the more pompous locutions that can make the beginning 15
medical student nervous about the effects of medical training. A friend of mine
was told by his resident, "A pregnant woman with sickle-cell represents a failure
of genetic counseling."

Mr. Eponym, who tried hard to talk like the doctors, once explained to me, 16
"An infant is basically a brainstem preparation." The term "brainstem preparation," as used in neurological research, refers to an animal whose higher brain
functions have been destroyed so that only the most primitive reflexes remain,
like the sucking reflex, the startle reflex, and the rooting reflex.

And yet at other times the harshness dissipates into a strangely elusive euphe- 17
mism. "As you know, this is a not entirely benign procedure," some doctor will
say, and that will be understood to imply agony, risk of complications, and
maybe even a significant mortality rate.

The more extreme forms aside, one most important function of medical 18
jargon is to help doctors maintain some distance from their patients. By reformulating a patient's pain and problems into a language that the patient doesn't
even speak, I suppose we are in some sense tak-
ing those pains and problems under our jurisdic-
tion and also reducing their emotional impact.
This linguistic separation between doctors and
patients allows conversations to go on at the
bedside that are unintelligible to the patient.
"Naturally, we're worried about adeno-CA," the
intern can say to the medical student, and lung
cancer need never be mentioned.

> The more extreme forms aside, one most important function of medical jargon is to help doctors maintain some distance from their patients.

I learned a new language this past summer. 19
At times it thrills me to hear myself using it. It enables me to understand my
colleagues, to communicate effectively in the hospital. Yet I am uncomfortably
aware that I will never again notice the peculiarities and even atrocities of medical language as keenly as I did this summer. There may be specific expressions I
manage to avoid, but even as I remark them, promising myself I will never use
them, I find that this language is becoming my professional speech. It no longer
sounds strange in my ears — or coming from my mouth. And I am afraid that as
with any new language, to use it properly you must absorb not only the vocabulary but also the structure, the logic, the attitudes. At first you may notice the
new and alien assumptions every time you put together a sentence, but with
time and increased fluency you stop being aware of them at all. And as you lose
that awareness, for better or for worse, you move closer and closer to being a
doctor instead of just talking like one.

Questions for Discussion and Journaling

1. Klass describes entering the hospital as a medical student "in a state of primeval innocence" but quickly learning all the "endless jargon and abbreviations" (para. 2). What she is describing is the process of enculturating into a discourse community. How does this kind of enculturation happen in general?

2. Klass explains that doctors always make patients the subject of the verb: "He dropped his pressure" or "Mrs. Bacon failed chemotherapy" (paras. 4–5). What is the difference between talking about patients in that way, versus saying "His blood pressure fell" or "chemotherapy did not help her"? What role does the phrasing give to the patient? What role does the phrasing give the doctor? What purpose does this kind of phrasing serve for doctors working every day in a hospital setting?

3. Klass alludes to the title of her book, *A Not Entirely Benign Procedure*, explaining how that phrase is used to describe a procedure that is painful and perhaps life-threatening. Why would doctors use phrases like this? And why do you think that Klass chose this phrase as the title for her book?

Applying and Exploring Ideas

1. Make a list of all the reasons that Klass provides for why doctors use what she calls "medical jargon."

2. Take the list of reasons for using medical jargon that you compiled in answering question 1 above. Now write a page or two in which you draw on these examples to explain and illustrate the threshold concepts of this chapter: texts and language *mediate meaningful activities*, and people construct meaning through texts and language.

3. Klass and Johns both talk about how joining and participating in new discourse communities requires a change in identity. In particular, Klass explains that to use any new language properly, "you must absorb not only the vocabulary but also the structure, the logic, the attitudes." As this happens, she says, "you move closer and closer to being a doctor instead of just talking like one" (para. 19). Before you read Klass, you were asked to think of a club, group, or workplace you are a part of and write down as many specialized words and phrases used there as you can think of. Go back to that list, and then draw on it to write a short essay modeled after Klass's in which you describe the process of learning to talk in that setting, and how learning the language helped you take on the identity of that club/group/workplace. Before you conclude, be sure to talk about the trade-offs involved in that enculturation.

META MOMENT   How does Klass help you better understand the underlying threshold concepts of this chapter? What is one thing you learned from Klass that you can use/apply elsewhere in your experience?

A Stranger in Strange Lands

A College Student Writing across the Curriculum

LUCILLE P. McCARTHY

Framing the Reading

Lucille McCarthy earned her Ph.D. from the University of Pennsylvania, and she is currently a professor of English at the University of Maryland, Baltimore County, where she has taught since 1988. Her many articles and books demonstrate her interest in pedagogies that help promote student learning and writing. Five of her six books and many of her articles focus on student classroom experiences and have won awards such as the James N. Britton Award for Research in the English Language Arts and a National Council of Teachers of English award for Research Excellence in Technical and Scientific Communication. Her books include *John Dewey and the Challenge of Classroom Practice* (1998), *John Dewey and the Philosophy and Practice of Hope* (2007), and *Whose Goals? Whose Aspirations? Learning to Teach Underprepared Writers across the Curriculum* (2002), all co-authored with her frequent collaborator, philosopher Stephen Fishman; and *Thinking and Writing in College: A Naturalistic Study of Students in Four Disciplines* (1991; with Barbara Walvoord).

McCarthy published the article reprinted here in 1987. At that time, researchers in other fields had used **case studies** and **ethnographic research** extensively, but researchers in the field of Writing Studies had only begun to consider what we could learn about writing by using those methods. In writing this article, McCarthy notes that researchers know that writing is strongly influenced by **social context** — that some people write well in one setting (e.g., at home alone) and not very well in another (e.g., on a timed exam), or that some people write well in one genre (e.g.,

McCarthy, Lucille P. "A Stranger in Strange Lands: A College Student Writing across the Curriculum." *Research in the Teaching of English*, vol. 21, no. 3, 1987, pp. 233–65.

poetry) but not very well in another (e.g., a literary criticism essay). But McCarthy wanted to know more about *how* writing is influenced by social settings; in particular, she wanted to know how college writers and their writing are influenced by their different classroom settings.

At the time that McCarthy conducted her study, no one else had followed individual students as they wrote across the university. Since McCarthy published her study, a number of such **longitudinal studies** have been published. While no single case study can produce results that are **generalizable**, a number of case studies taken together can do so. Thus, if you are interested in making claims about how writers write in college, you should read the longitudinal studies that followed McCarthy.

McCarthy followed a student named "Dave" as he wrote in three different classes (or discourse communities) — composition, biology, and poetry. Dave got good grades in the first two classes, but struggled in poetry. McCarthy tried to find out why Dave was so unsuccessful in poetry and ultimately concluded that even though the writing tasks across all the classes had some similarities, Dave *thought* they were very different, and he had very different kinds of support for the writing in each of the classes.

We have included McCarthy's study here because she demonstrates one way to understand the threshold concept that individuals participate in community activities (like college courses) through the use of texts and language. In particular, she demonstrates what can happen when newcomers do or don't understand and share the values and conventions of a new discourse community in which they are participating. She also demonstrates what happens when the "old-timers" in a community (like teachers) aren't able to successfully share conventions, strategies, and values with "newcomers" (like students). If you've read Johns on discourse communities, you can consider how Dave's experiences across various classes is like visiting a variety of discourse communities, some of which use texts in ways that seem very strange to him.

Getting Ready to Read

Before you read, try the following activity:

- Consider a class where you have an easy time writing, and a class where the writing is hard for you. Think about why you might have different levels of success with these writing tasks.

As you read, consider the following questions:

- What research question(s) does McCarthy set out to answer?

- What major findings does McCarthy discover in answer to her research question(s)?

DAVE GARRISON, A COLLEGE JUNIOR and the focus of the present study, 1
was asked how he would advise incoming freshmen about writing for their college courses. His answer was both homely and familiar.

"I'd tell them," he said, "first you've got to figure out what your teachers want. 2
And then you've got to give it to them if you're gonna get the grade." He paused
a moment and added, "And that's not always so easy."

No matter how we teachers may feel about Dave's response, it does reflect 3
his sensitivity to school writing as a social affair. Successful students are those
who can, in their interactions with teachers during the semester, determine
what constitutes appropriate texts in each classroom: the content, structures,
language, ways of thinking, and types of evidence required in that discipline and
by that teacher. They can then produce such a text. Students who cannot do this,
for whatever reason — cultural, intellectual, motivational — are those who fail,
deemed incompetent communicators in that particular setting. They are unable
to follow what Britton calls the "rules of the game" in each class (1975, p. 76).
As students go from one classroom to another they must play a wide range of
games, the rules for which, Britton points out, include many conventions and
presuppositions that are not explicitly articulated.

In this article, writing in college is viewed as a process of assessing and adapt- 4
ing to the requirements in unfamiliar academic settings. Specifically, the study
examined how students figured out what consti-
tuted appropriate texts in their various courses
and how they went about producing them.
And, further, it examined what characterized the
classroom contexts which enhanced or denied
students' success in this process. This study was
a 21-month project which focused on the writing experiences of one college student, Dave, in
three of his courses, Freshman Composition in
the spring of his freshman year, and, in his sophomore year, Introduction to Poetry in the fall
and Cell Biology in the spring. Dave, a biology/
pre-med major, was typical of students at his
college in terms of his SAT scores (502 verbal;
515 math), his high school grades, and his white,
middle-class family background.

> Successful students are those who can, in their interactions with teachers during the semester, determine what constitutes appropriate texts in each classroom: the content, structures, language, ways of thinking, and types of evidence required in that discipline and by that teacher.

As I followed Dave from one classroom writing situation to another, I came to 5
see him, as he made his journey from one discipline to another, as a stranger in
strange lands. In each new class Dave believed that the writing he was doing was
totally unlike anything he had ever done before. This metaphor of a newcomer
in a foreign country proved to be a powerful way of looking at Dave's behaviors

as he worked to use the new languages in unfamiliar academic territories. Robert Heinlein's (1961) science fiction novel suggested this metaphor originally. But Heinlein's title is slightly different; his stranger is in a *single* strange land. Dave perceived himself to be in one strange land after another.

BACKGROUND TO THE STUDY

The theoretical underpinnings of this study are to be found in the work of 6 sociolinguists (Hymes, 1972a, 1972b; Gumperz, 1971) and ethnographers of communication (Basso, 1974; Heath, 1982; Szwed, 1981) who assume that language processes must be understood in terms of the contexts in which they occur. All language use in this view takes place within speech communities and accomplishes meaningful social functions for people. Community members share characteristic "ways of speaking," that is, accepted linguistic, intellectual, and social conventions which have developed over time and govern spoken interaction. And "communicatively competent" speakers in every community recognize and successfully employ these "rules of use," largely without conscious attention (Hymes, 1972a, pp. xxiv–xxxvi).

A key assumption underlying this study is that writing, like speaking, is a 7 social activity. Writers, like speakers, must use the communication means considered appropriate by members of particular speech or discourse communities. And the writer's work, at the same time, may affect the norms of the community. As students go from one class to another, they must define and master the rules of use for written discourse in one classroom speech community after another. And their writing can only be evaluated in terms of that particular community's standards.

Some recent practical and theoretical work in writing studies has emphasized 8 that writers' processes and products must be understood in terms of their contexts, contexts which are created as participants and settings interact (Bazerman, 1981; Bizzell, 1982; Cooper, 1986; Faigley, 1985; Whiteman, 1981). Studies of writing in non-academic settings have shown just how complex these writing environments are and how sophisticated the knowledge — both explicit and tacit — is that writers need in order to operate successfully in them (Odell & Goswami, 1985). And classrooms offer no less complex environments for writing. As Ericson (1982) points out, the classroom learning environment includes not only the teacher and the student, but also the subject matter structure, the social task structure, the actual enacted task, and the sequence of actions involved in the task. In addition, in many classrooms students may be provided with too few instructional supports to help them as they write (Applebee, 1984). Specifically, college classroom contexts for writing, Herrington (1985) argues, must be thought of in terms of several speech communities, viewed "in relation not only to a school community, but also to the intellectual and social conventions of professional forums within a given discipline" (p. 333). These overlapping communities influence the ways students think and write and inter-act in college classrooms, and will shape their notions of what it means to be, for example, an engineer or a biologist or a literary critic.

Research which has directly examined particular classroom contexts for writ- 9 ing has provided insight into their diversity (Applebee, 1984; Calkins, 1980; Florio & Clark, 1982; Freedman, 1985; Herrington, 1985; Kantor, 1984). Though these studies suggest that an individual student is likely to encounter a number of quite different classroom writing situations, there is also evidence that individual student writers may employ consistent patterns across tasks as they interpret assignments, reason, and organize their knowledge (Dyson, 1984; Langer, 1985, 1986).

What has not yet been done, however, is to follow individual college students 10 as they progress across academic disciplines. In this study I offer information about how one college student fares in such a journey across the curriculum. That is, I detail how this student's behavior changed or remained constant across tasks in three classroom contexts and how those contexts influenced his success. Though this study is limited in scope to the experiences of a single student as he wrote for three college courses, it addresses questions central to much writing across the curriculum scholarship:

1. What are the tasks students encounter as they move from one course to another?

2. How do successful students interpret these tasks? Further, how do students determine what constitutes appropriate texts in that discipline and for that teacher, and how do they produce them?

3. What are the social factors in classrooms that foster particular writing behaviors and students' achievement of competence in that setting?

The ultimate aim of this study is to contribute to our understanding of how students learn to write in school. Findings from this study corroborate the notion that learning to write should be seen not only as a developmental process occurring within an individual student, but also as a social process occurring in response to particular situations.

METHODS

The research approach was naturalistic. I entered the study with no hypothe- 11 ses to test and no specially devised writing tasks. Rather, I studied the writing that was actually being assigned in these classrooms, working to understand and describe that writing, how it functioned in each classroom, and what it meant to people there. My purpose was to get as rich a portrait as possible of Dave's writing and his classroom writing contexts. To this end I combined four research tools: observation, interviews, composing-aloud protocols, and text analysis. The data provided by the protocols and text analysis served to add to, cross-check, and refine the data generated by observation and interviews. Using this triangulated approach (Denzin, 1978), I could view Dave's writing experiences through several windows, with the strengths of one method compensating for the limitations of another.

The Courses

The college is a private, co-educational, liberal arts institution located in a large, 12 northeastern city. Of its 2,600 students nearly half are business, accounting, and computer science majors. Yet over half of students' courses are required liberal arts courses, part of the core curriculum. Two of Dave's courses in this study are core courses: Freshman Composition and Introduction to Poetry. The third, Cell Biology, is a course taken by biology majors; it was Dave's third semester of college biology. All three were one-semester courses. In the descriptions of these courses that follow, I use pseudonyms for the teachers.

In Freshman Composition, which met twice a week for 90 minutes, students 13 were required to write a series of five similarly structured essays on topics of their choice. These two- or four-page essays were due at regular intervals and were graded by the professor, Dr. Jean Carter. Classes were generally teacher-led discussions and exercises, with some days allotted for students to work together in small groups, planning their essays or sharing drafts. Dr. Carter held one individual writing conference with each student at mid semester.

Introduction to Poetry is generally taken by students during their sophomore 14 year, and it, like Freshman Composition, met for 90 minutes twice a week. In this class students were also required to write a series of similar papers. These were three-to-six page critical essays on poems that students chose from a list given them by their professor, Dr. Charles Forson. These essays, like those in Freshman Composition, were due at regular intervals and were graded by the professor. The Poetry classes were all lectures in which Dr. Forson explicated poems. However, one lecture early in the semester was devoted entirely to writing instruction.

Cell Biology, which Dave took in the spring of his sophomore year, met three 15 times a week, twice for 90-minute lectures and once for a three-hour lab. In this course, like the other two, students were required to write a series of similar short papers, three in this course. These were three-to-five page reviews of journal articles which reported current research in cell biology. Students were to summarize these articles, following the five-part scientific format in which the experiment was reported. They were then to relate the experiment to what they were doing in class. These reviews were graded by the professor, Dr. Tom Kelly.

The Participants

The participants in this study included these three professors, Drs. Carter, 16
Forson, and Kelly. All were experienced college teachers who had taught these
courses before. All talked willingly and with interest about the writing their
students were doing, and both Dr. Carter and Dr. Forson invited me to observe
their classes. Dr. Kelly said that it would not be productive for me to observe in
his Cell Biology course because he spent almost no time talking directly about
writing, so pressed was he to cover the necessary course material.

The student participants in this study were Dave and two of his friends. I first 17
met these three young men in Dr. Carter's Freshman Composition class where I
was observing regularly in order to learn how she taught the course, the same one
I teach at the college. As I attended that course week after week, I got to know
the students who sat by me, Dave and his friends, and I realized I was no longer
as interested in understanding what my colleague was teaching as I was in understanding what these students were learning. As the study progressed, my focus nar-
rowed to Dave's experiences, although none of the three students knew this. The
contribution of Dave's friends to this study was to facilitate my understanding of
Dave. At first, in their Freshman Composition class, these students saw my role as
a curious combination of teacher and fellow student. As the study progressed, my
role became, in their eyes, that of teacher/inquirer, a person genuinely interested in
understanding their writing. In fact, my increasing interest and ability to remember details of his writing experiences seemed at times to mystify and amuse Dave.

At the beginning of this study Dave Garrison was an 18-year-old freshman, 18
a biology pre-med major who had graduated the year before from a parochial
boys' high school near the college. He described himself as a "hands-on" person who preferred practical application in the lab to reading theory in books.
Beginning in his sophomore year, Dave worked 13 hours a week as a technician
in a local hospital, drawing blood from patients, in addition to taking a full
course load. He "loved" his hospital work, he said, because of the people and the
work, and also because difficulties with chemistry has made him worry about
being accepted in medical school. In the hospital he was getting an idea of a
range of possible careers in health care. The oldest of four children, Dave lived at
home and commuted 30 minutes to campus. He is the first person in his family
to go to college, though both of his parents enjoy reading, he said, and his father
writes in his work as an insurance salesman. When Dave and I first met, he told
me that he did not really like to write and that he was not very good, but he
knew that writing was a tool he needed, one that he hoped to learn to use better.

Instrumentation and Analytic Procedures

I collected data from February 1983 through November 1985. A detailed, 19
semester by semester summary is presented in Table 1.

TABLE 1 DATA COLLECTION RECORD

OBSERVATION
Freshman Composition (Freshman year. Spring, 1983) • Participant observation in 1 class per week for 9 weeks. • All class documents were collected and analyzed.
Introduction to Poetry (Sophomore year. Fall, 1983) • Observation of the 90-minute lecture devoted to writing instruction. • All class documents were collected and analyzed.
Cell Biology (Sophomore year. Spring, 1984) • Observation of a lab session for 15 minutes.
INTERVIEWS
Freshman Composition • Frequent conversations and 2 hour-long interviews with the professor, Dr. Carter. • Frequent conversations with the students before and after class.
Poetry • 1 hour-long interview with the professor, Dr. Forson. • 4 hour-long interviews with the students at one-month intervals.
Cell Biology • 2 hour-long interviews with the professor, Dr. Kelly. • 4 hour-long interviews with the students at one-month intervals.
Junior Year Follow-up (Fall, 1984) • 2 hour-long interviews with the students.
PROTOCOLS WITH RETROSPECTIVE INTERVIEWS
Freshman Composition • 1 protocol and interview audiotaped as Dave composed the first draft of his fourth (next to last) essay.
Poetry • 1 protocol and interview audiotaped as Dave composed the first draft of his third (last) paper.
Cell Biology • 1 protocol and interview audiotaped as Dave composed the first draft of his third (last) review.

(Continued)

TABLE 1 DATA COLLECTION RECORD (*continued*)

TEXT ANALYSIS
Freshman Composition • Dave's fourth essay with the teacher's responses was analyzed. All drafts of all essays were collected.
Poetry • Dave's third paper with the teacher's responses was analyzed. All drafts of all essays were collected.
Cell Biology • Dave's third review with the teacher's responses was analyzed. All drafts of all essays were collected.

Observation

I observed in all three classes in order to help me understand the contexts for [20] writing in which Dave was working. During the observation I recorded field notes about the classroom activities and interactions I was seeing, and as soon as possible after the observation I read my notes and fleshed them out where possible. Returning to fill out the notes was particularly important when I had participated in the classroom activities as I did in Freshman Composition. In that class I participated in Dave's small group discussions of drafts and did the in-class writing exercises along with the students. I wrote my field notes on the right-side pages of a spiral notebook, leaving the pages opposite free for later notes.

Interviews

I interviewed Dave, his two friends, and the three professors in order to elicit [21] their interpretations of the writing in each class. Questions were often suggested by the participants' earlier comments or by emerging patterns in the data that I wanted to pursue. Interviews with professors generally took place in their offices and centered on their assignments, their purposes for having students write, and the instructional techniques they used to accomplish their purposes.

The interviews with the students took place in my office on campus and [22] lasted one hour. I chose to interview Dave and his friends together in a series of monthly interviews because I believed I could learn more from Dave in this way. The students often talked to and questioned each other, producing more from Dave than I believe I ever could have gotten from one-on-one sessions with him. I did on two occasions, however, interview Dave alone for one hour when I wanted to question him in a particularly intensive way.

During all interviews I either took notes or made audiotapes which I later 23
transcribed and analyzed. All hour-long interviews with the students were taped.

Analysis of the Observation and Interviews
I read and reread my field notes and the interview transcripts looking for pat- 24
terns and themes. These organized the data and suggested the salient features
of writing in each context, its nature and meaning, and of Dave's experiences
there. These patterns and themes then focused subsequent inquiry. I was guided
in this process by the work of Gilmore and Glatthorn (1982) and Spradley
(1979, 1980).

Composing-Aloud Protocols and Retrospective Interviews
Late in each of the three semesters, I audiotaped Dave as he composed aloud the 25
first draft of a paper for the course we had focused on that semester. Dave wrote
at the desk in my office, his pre-writing notes and his books spread out around
him, and I sat nearby in a position where I could observe and make notes on his
behaviors. The protocols lasted 30 minutes and were followed by a 30-minute
retrospective interview in which I asked Dave to tell me more about the process
he had just been through. I reasoned that in the retrospective interviews Dave's
major concerns would be reemphasized, whereas the smaller issues that may
have occupied him during composing would be forgotten. Because I followed
Dave across time and collected all his written work for each assignment, I could
examine what preceded and what followed the composed-aloud draft. I could
thus see how the protocol draft related to Dave's entire composing process for
a task.

The information provided by the protocols generally corroborated what he 26
had said in the interviews. Of particular interest, however, were the points at
which the protocol data contradicted the interview data. These points spurred
further inquiry. Though composing-aloud was never easy for Dave, who characterized himself as a shy person, he became more and more comfortable with it
as the semesters progressed. He did produce, in each of the protocol sessions, a
useful first draft for his final paper in each course.

Analysis and Scoring of the Protocols and Retrospective Interviews
I analyzed the transcripts of the protocols and interviews, classifying and count- 27
ing what I called the *writer's conscious concerns*. These concerns were identified
as anything the writer paid attention to during composing as expressed by (1)
remarks about a thought or behavior or (2) observed behaviors. I chose to focus
on Dave's conscious concerns because I expected that they would include a broad
range of writing issues and that they would reflect the nature and emphases of
the classrooms for which he was writing. The protocols would thus provide the

supporting information I needed for this study. In identifying and classifying the writer's conscious concerns, I was guided by the work of Berkenkotter (1983), Bridwell (1980), Flower and Hayes (1981), Perl (1979), and Pianko (1979).

The analysis of the transcripts was carried out in a two-part process. First I [28] read them several times and drew from them four general categories of writer's concerns, along with a number of subcategories. Then, using this scheme, I classified and counted the writer's remarks and behaviors. The first protocol was, of course, made during Dave's writing for Freshman Composition. The categories from that composing session were used again in analyzing the protocols from Poetry and Cell Biology. To these original categories were added new ones to describe the concerns Dave expressed as he composed for the later courses. In this way I could identify both concerns that were constant across courses as well as those that were specific to particular classroom writing situations.

I carried out the analyses of the protocols alone because of the understanding [29] of the writing context that I brought to the task. I viewed this knowledge as an asset in identifying and classifying Dave's writing concerns. Thus, instead of agreement between raters, I worked for "confirmability" in the sense of agreement among a variety of information sources (Cuba, 1978, p. 17).

Text Analysis

The final window through which I looked at Dave's writing experiences was text [30] analysis. I analyzed the completed papers, with the professors' comments on them, of the assignments Dave had begun during the protocol sessions. If Dave is understood to be a stranger trying to learn the language in these classroom communities, then his teachers are the native-speaker guides who are training him. In this view, students and teachers in their written interactions share a common aim and are engaged in a cooperative endeavor. Their relationship is like that of people conversing together, the newcomer making trial efforts to communicate appropriately and the native speaker responding to them.

Thus, in order to examine the conventions of discourse in each classroom [31] and get further insight into the interaction between Dave and his professors, I drew upon the model of conversation proposed by Grice (1975). Grice says that conversants assume, unless there are indications to the contrary, that they have a shared purpose and thus make conversational contributions "such as are required . . . by the accepted purpose or direction of the talk exchange in which they are engaged" (p. 45). He terms this the "Cooperative Principle." From the Cooperative Principle Grice derives four categories or conditions which must be fulfilled if people are to converse successfully: Quality, Quantity, Relation, and Manner. When conversation breaks down, it is because one or more of these conditions for successful conversation have been violated, either accidentally or intentionally. On the other hand, people conversing successfully fulfill these conditions, for the most part without conscious attention. Grice's four conditions for conversational cooperation provided my text analysis scheme. They are

1. *Quality.* Conversants must speak what they believe to be the truth and that for which they have adequate evidence.

2. *Quantity.* Conversants must give the appropriate amount of information, neither too much nor too little.

3. *Relation.* The information that conversants give must be relevant to the aims of the conversation.

4. *Manner.* The conversants must make themselves clear, using appropriate forms of expression.

In my examination of Dave's last paper for each course, I considered both his 32 work and his professor's response as conversational turns in which the speakers were doing what they believed would keep the Cooperative Principle in force. Dave's written turns were taken to display the discourse he believed was required in each setting so he would be deemed cooperative. I identified which of Grice's four conditions for successful conversation Dave paid special attention to fulfilling in each context. In this process I drew from the interview and protocol data as well as from the texts. I then counted and categorized Dave's teachers' written responses to his papers according to these same four conditions. A response was identified as an idea the teacher wanted to convey to Dave and could be as short as a single mark or as long as several sentences. Of particular interest were, first, the extent to which Dave and each teacher agreed upon what constituted cooperation, and, second, what the teacher pointed out as violations of the conditions of cooperation, errors that jeopardized the Cooperative Principle in that setting. Further, the form and language of each teacher's response provided insight into the ways of speaking in that particular discipline and classroom.

The text analysis data added to and refined my understanding of Dave's 33 classroom writing situations. And, conversely, my analyses of Dave's texts were informed by what I knew of the classroom writing situations. For this reason, I again elected to work alone with the texts.

Validity of the findings and interpretations in this study were ensured by 34 employing the following techniques. (1) Different types of data were compared. (2) The perspectives of various informants were compared. (3) Engagement with the subject was carried on over a long period of time during which salient factors were identified for more detailed inquiry. (4) External checks on the inquiry process were made by three established researchers who knew neither Dave nor the professors. These researchers read the emerging study at numerous points and questioned researcher biases and the bases for interpretations. (5) Interpretations were checked throughout with the informants themselves.

(See Lincoln & Guba, 1985, for a discussion of validity and reliability in naturalistic inquiry.)

RESULTS AND DISCUSSION

Information from all data sources supports three general conclusions, two concerning Dave's interpretation and production of the required writing tasks and one concerning social factors in the classrooms that influenced him as he wrote. First, although the writing tasks in the three classes were in many ways similar, Dave interpreted them as being totally different from each other and totally different from anything he had ever done before. This was evidenced in the interview, protocol, and text analysis data. [35]

Second, certain social factors in Freshman Composition and Cell Biology appeared to foster Dave's writing success in them. Observation and interview data indicated that two unarticulated aspects of the classroom writing contexts influenced his achievement. These social factors were (1) the functions that writing served for Dave in each setting, and (2) the roles that participants and students' texts played there. These social factors were bound up with what Dave ultimately learned from and about writing in each class. [36]

Third, Dave exhibited consistent ways of figuring out what constituted appropriate texts in each setting, in his terms, of "figuring out what the teacher wanted." Evidence from the interviews and protocols shows that he typically drew upon six information sources, in a process that was in large part tacit. These information sources included teacher-provided instructional supports, sources Dave found on his own, and his prior knowledge. [37]

The Writing Assignments: Similar Tasks, Audiences, and Purposes

My analysis of the assignments, combined with the observation and interview data, showed that the writing in the three classes was similar in many ways. It was, in all cases, informational writing for the teacher-as-examiner, the type of writing that Applebee found comprised most secondary school writing (1984). More specifically, the task in Cell Biology was a summary, and in Freshman Composition and Poetry it was analysis, closely related informational uses of writing. Dave's audiences were identified as teacher-as-examiner by the fact that all assignments were graded and that Dave, as he wrote, repeatedly wondered how his teacher would "like" his work. [38]

Further similarities among the writing in the three courses included the purpose that the professors stated for having their students write. All three said that the purpose was not so much for students to display specific information, but rather for students to become competent in using the thinking and language of their disciplines. Dr. Kelly, the biologist, stated this most directly when he explained to me why he had his students write reviews of journal articles: [39]

"I want students to be at ease with the vocabulary of Cell Biology and how experiments are being done. . . . Students need to get a feeling for the journals, the questions people are asking, the answers they're getting, and the procedures they're using. It will give them a feeling for the excitement, the dynamic part of this field. And they need to see that what they're doing in class and lab is actually *used* out there." Students' summaries of journal articles in Cell Biology were, in other words, to get them started speaking the language of that discourse community.

Learning the conventions of academic discourse was also the purpose of students' writing in Freshman Composition. Dr. Carter was less concerned with the content of the students' five essays than she was with their cohesiveness. She repeatedly stated that what would serve these students in their subsequent academic writing was the ability to write coherent prose with a thesis and subpoints, unified paragraphs, and explicitly connected sentences. In an interview she said, "Ideas aren't going to do people much good if they can't find the means with which to communicate them. . . . When these students are more advanced, and the ability to produce coherent prose is internalized, then they can concentrate on ideas. That's why I'm teaching the analytic paper with a certain way of developing the thesis that's generalizable to their future writing." Dr. Carter's goal was, thus, to help students master conventions of prose which she believed were central to all academic discourse. ⁴⁰

And likewise in Poetry the purpose of students' writing was to teach them how people in literary studies think and write. In his lecture on writing, early in the semester, Dr. Forson stated this purpose and alluded to some of the conventions for thinking and writing in that setting. He told students, "The three critical essays you will write will make you say something quite specific about the meaning of a poem (your thesis) and demonstrate how far you've progressed in recognizing and dealing with the devices a poet uses to express his insights. You'll find the poem's meaning in the poem itself, and you'll use quotes to prove your thesis. Our concern here is for the *poem,* not the poet's life or era. Nor are your own opinions of the poet's ideas germane." ⁴¹

Dr. Forson then spent 20 minutes explaining the mechanical forms for quoting poetry, using a model essay that he had written on a poem by Robert Herrick. He ended by telling students that they should think of their peers as the audience for their essays and asking them not to use secondary critical sources from the library. "You'll just deal with what you now know and with the poetic devices that we discuss in class. Each group of poems will feature one such device: imagery, symbolism, and so forth. These will be the tools in your tool box." ⁴²

Thus in all three courses Dave's tasks were informational writing for the teacher-as-examiner. All were for the purpose of displaying competence in using the ways of thinking and writing appropriate to that setting. And in all three courses Dave wrote a series of similar short papers, due at about three-week ⁴³

intervals, the assumption being that students' early attempts would inform their subsequent ones, in the sort of trial-and-error process that characterizes much language learning. Further, the reading required in Poetry and Cell Biology, the poems and the journal articles, were equally unfamiliar to Dave. We might expect, then, that Dave would view the writing for these three courses as quite similar, and, given an equal amount of work, he would achieve similar levels of success. This, however, is not what happened.

Dave's Interpretation of the Writing Tasks

The Writer's Concerns While Composing.   In spite of the similarities among 44 the writing tasks for the three courses, evidence from several sources shows that Dave interpreted them as being totally different from each other and totally different from anything he had ever done before. Dave's characteristic approach across courses was to focus so fully on the particular new ways of thinking and writing in each setting that commonalities with previous writing were obscured for him. And interwoven with Dave's conviction that the writing for these courses was totally dissimilar was his differing success in them. Though he worked hard in all three courses, he made B's in Freshman Composition, D's and C's in Poetry, and A's in Cell Biology.

The protocol data explain in part why the writing for these classes seemed so 45 different to Dave. Dave's chief concerns while composing for each course were very different. His focus in Freshman Composition was on textual coherence. Fifty-four percent of his expressed concerns were for coherence of thesis and subpoints, coherence within paragraphs, and sentence cohesion. By contrast, in Poetry, though Dave did mention thesis and subpoints, his chief concerns were not with coherence, but with the new ways of thinking and writing in that setting. Forty-four percent of his concerns focused on accurately interpreting the poem and properly using quotes. In Cell Biology, yet a new focus of concerns is evident. Seventy-two percent of Dave's concerns deal with the new rules of use in that academic discipline. His chief concerns in Biology were to accurately understand the scientific terms and concepts in the journal article and then to accurately rephrase and connect these in his own text, following the same five-part structure in which the published experiment was reported. It is no wonder that the writing for these classes seemed very different to Dave. As a newcomer in each academic territory, Dave's attention was occupied by the new conventions of interpretation and language use in each community. (See Table 2.)

The same preoccupations controlled his subsequent work on the papers. In 46 each course Dave wrote a second draft, which he then typed. In none of these second drafts did Dave see the task differently or make major changes. He is, in this regard, like the secondary students Applebee (1984) studied who were unable, without teacher assistance, to revise their writing in more than minor ways. And Dave revised none of these papers after the teachers had responded.

TABLE 2 CONCERNS EXPRESSED DURING COMPOSING-ALOUD PROTOCOLS AND RETROSPECTIVE INTERVIEWS

	PERCENT OF COMMENTS		
	Freshman Composition	*Poetry*	*Cell Biology*
Concerns Expressed in All Three Courses			
Features of Written Text			
Coherent thesis/subpoint structure	22	18	0
Coherent paragraph structure	15	13	3
Cohesive sentences	17	8	3
Editing for mechanical correctness	9	3	3
Communication Situation (assignment, reader-writer roles, purpose)	8	6	5
On-Going Process	18	6	12
Emerging Text	11	2	2
Concerns Specific to Poetry			
Appropriately using quotes from poem	0	32	0
Making a correct interpretation of the poem	0	12	0
Concerns Specific to Cell Biology			
Following the 5-part scientific guidelines	0	0	20
Correctly understanding the content of the article being summarized	0	0	37
Rephrasing & connecting appropriate parts of the article	0	0	15
Total	100	100	100
Number of comments	64	62	60

We can further fill out the pictures of Dave's composing for the three classes 47 by combining the protocol findings with the observation and interview data. In his first protocol session, in April of his freshman year, Dave composed the first draft of his fourth paper for Freshman Composition, an essay in which he chose to analyze the wrongs of abortion. To this session Dave brought an outline of this thesis and subpoints. He told me that he had spent only 30 minutes writing it the night before, but that the topic was one he had thought a lot about. As he composed, Dave was most concerned with and apparently very dependent upon, his outline, commenting on it, glancing at it, or pausing to study it 14 times during the 30 minutes of composing. Dave's next most frequently expressed concerns were for coherence at paragraph and sentence levels, what Dr. Carter referred to as coherence of mid-sized and small parts. These were the new "rules of use" in this setting. Dave told me that in high school he had done some "bits and pieces" of writing and some outlines for history, but that he had never before written essays like this. The total time Dave spent on his abortion essay was five hours.

In Dave's Poetry protocol session seven months later, in November of his 48 sophomore year, he composed part of the first draft of his third and last paper for that class, a six-page analysis of a poem called "Marriage" by contemporary poet Gregory Corso. To this session he brought two pages of notes and his *Norton Anthology of Poetry* in which he had underlined and written notes in the margins beside the poem. He told me that he had spent four hours (of an eventual total of 11) preparing to write: reading the poem many times and finding a critical essay on it in the library. During his pre-writing and composing, Dave's primary concern was to get the right interpretation of the poem, "the true meaning" as he phrased it. And as Dave wrote, he assumed that his professor knew the true meaning, a meaning, Dave said, that "was there, but not there, not just what it says on the surface." Further, Dave knew that he must argue his interpretation, using not his own but the poet's words; this was his second most frequently expressed concern.

As Dave composed, he appeared to be as tied to the poem as he had been 49 to his outline in Freshman Composition the semester before. He seemed to be almost *physically* attached to the *Norton Anthology* by his left forefinger as he progressed down the numbers he had marked in the margins. He was, we might say, tied to the concrete material, the "facts" of the poem before him. Dave never got his own essay structure; rather, he worked down the poem, explicating from beginning to end. In the retrospective interview he said, "I didn't really have to think much about my thesis and subs because they just come naturally now. . . . But anyway it's not like in Comp last year. Here my first paragraph is the introduction with the thesis, and the stanzas are the subpoints." Dave's preoccupation with the poem and the new conventions of interpreting and quoting poetry resulted in a paper that was not an analysis but a summary with some interpretation along the way. His focus on these new rules of use appeared to limit his ability to apply previously learned skills, the thesis-subpoint analytical structure, and kept him working at the more concrete summary level.

This domination by the concrete may often characterize newcomers' first 50 steps as they attempt to use language in unfamiliar disciplines (Williams, 1985). Dave's professor, Dr. Forson, seemed to be familiar with this phenomenon when he warned students in his lecture on writing: "You must remember that the poet ordered the poem. *You* order your essay with your own thesis and subtheses. Get away from 'Next. . . . Next'." But if Dave heard this in September, he had forgotten it by November. Dave's experience is consonant with Langer's (1984) finding that students who know more about a subject as they begin to write are likely to choose analysis rather than summary. And these students receive higher scores for writing quality as well.

In his writing for Cell Biology the following semester, Dave's concerns were 51 again focused on the new and unfamiliar conventions in this setting. Before writing his last paper, a four-page review of an experiment on glycoprotein reported in *The Journal of Cell Biology,* Dave spent three hours preparing. (He eventually spent a total of eight hours on the review.) He had chosen the article in the library from a list the professor had given to students and had then read the article twice, underlining it, making notes, and looking up the definitions of unfamiliar terms. To the protocol session Dave brought these notes, the article, and a sheet on which he had written what he called "Dr. Kelly's guidelines," the five-part scientific experiment format that Dr. Kelly wanted students to follow: Background, Objectives, Procedures, Results, and Discussion.

In his composing aloud, Dave's chief concerns in Biology were, as in Poetry 52 the semester before, with the reading, in this case the journal article. But here, unlike Poetry, Dave said the meaning was "all out on the table." In Poetry he had had to interpret meaning from the poem's connotative language; in Biology, by contrast, he could look up meanings, a situation with which Dave was far more comfortable. But as he composed for Biology, he was just as tied to the journal article as he had been to the poem or to his outline in previous semesters. Dave paused frequently to consult the article, partially covering it at times so that his own paper was physically closer to what he was summarizing at that moment.

Dave's first and second most commonly expressed concerns during the 53 Biology protocol session were for rephrasing and connecting parts of the article and for following Dr. Kelly's guidelines. These were, in essence, concerns for coherence and organization, what Dave was most concerned with in Freshman Composition. But the writing for Biology bore little relation in Dave's mind to what he had done in Freshman Composition. In Biology he was indeed concerned about his organization, but here it was the five-part scientific format he had been given, very different, it seemed to him, than the thesis/subpoint organization he had had to create for his freshman essays. In fact, until I questioned him about it at the end of the semester, Dave never mentioned the freshman thesis/subpoint structure. And the concerns for coherence at paragraph and sentence levels that had been so prominent as he wrote for Freshman Composition were replaced in Biology by his concern for rephrasing the article's already coherent text. In Freshman Composition Dave had talked about trying to get his sentences and paragraphs to "fit" or "flow" together. In Biology, however, he talked about trying to get the article into his own words, about "cutting," "simplifying," and "combining two sentences." Again, it is no wonder that Dave believed that this writing was totally new. It took one of Dave's friend's and my prodding during an interview to make Dave see that he had indeed written summaries before. Lots of them.

The Nature of Cooperation in the Three Courses.   The text analysis data 54 provide further insight into why Dave perceived the writing in these courses as so dissimilar. The data provide information about what was, in Grice's terms, essential to maintaining the Cooperative Principle in these written exchanges. Analyses of the teachers' responses to Dave's papers show that his concerns in each class generally did match theirs. Put differently, Dave had figured out, though not equally well in all classes, what counted as "cooperation" in each context, and what he had to do to be deemed a competent communicator there. (See Table 3.)

Analysis of Dave's finished essay for Freshman Composition suggests that 55 his concerns for textual coherence were appropriate. Dave knew that to keep the Cooperative Principle in force in Dr. Carter's class, he had to pay special attention to fulfilling the condition of *Manner,* to making himself clear, using appropriate forms of expression. He succeeded and was deemed cooperative by Dr. Carter when she responded to his contribution with a telegraphic reply on the first page: "18/20." Apart from editing two words in Dave's text, she made no further comments, assuming that Dave and she shared an understanding of what constituted cooperation in her class and of what her numbers meant. (She

TABLE 3 TEACHERS' RESPONSES TO DAVE'S PAPERS

	NUMBER OF RESPONSES INDICATING VIOLATIONS OF CONDITIONS FOR COOPERATION				
	Quality	*Quantity*	*Relevance*	*Manner*	*Grade*
Composition	0	0	0	2	18/20
Poetry	8	0	0	11	C+
Cell Biology	0	0	0	14	96

had explained to students that she was marking with numbers that semester in an attempt to be more "scientific," and she had defined for them the "objective linguistic features of text" to which her numbers referred.) Dave did understand the grade and was, of course, very pleased with it.

In an interview, Dr. Carter explained her grade to me. "Though his content 56 isn't great," she said, "his paper is coherent, not badly off at any place. . . . He gave a fair number of reasons to develop his paragraphs, he restated his point at the end, and there is no wasted language. It's not perfectly woven together, but it's good." Though Dr. Carter mentioned the "reasons" Dave gave as evidence for his contentions, she was concerned not so much with their meaning as with their cohesiveness. Cooperation in this setting thus depended upon fulfilling the condition of *Manner*. Dave knew this and expected only a response to how well he had achieved the required form, not to the content of his essay.

In his writing for Poetry the following semester, Dave was attempting to keep 57 the Cooperative Principle in force by paying special attention to two conditions, *Quality* and *Manner*. That is, first he was attempting to say what was true and give adequate evidence, and, second, he was attempting to use proper forms of expression. This is evidenced in the interview and protocol as well as the text data. Analysis of Dr. Forson's 19 responses to Dave's paper shows that Dave's concerns matched those of his teacher, that Dave had figured out, though only in part, what counted as cooperation in that setting. Dr. Forson's responses all referred to violations of the same conditions Dave had been concerned with fulfilling, *Quality* and *Manner*. In seven of his eight marginal notes and in an endnote, Dr. Forson disagreed with Dave's interpretation and questioned his evidence, violations of the *Quality* condition. Mina Shaughnessy (1977) says that such failure to properly coordinate claims and evidence is perhaps the most common source of misunderstanding in academic prose. The ten mechanical errors that Dr. Forson pointed out were violations of the condition of *Manner*, violations which may jeopardize the Cooperative Principle in many academic settings. Dave's unintentional violations in Poetry of the *Quality* and *Manner* conditions jeopardized the Cooperative Principle in that exchange, resulting in the C+ grade.

Dr. Kelly's responses to Dave's writing in Biology were, like those in Freshman 58 Composition, much briefer than Dr. Forson's. Dr. Kelly's 14 marks or phrases all pointed out errors in form, unintentional violations of the Gricean condition of *Manner*. But these were apparently not serious enough to jeopardize the aims of the written conversation in Biology; Dave's grade on the review was 96.

This application of Grice's rubric for spoken conversation to student-teacher 59 written interaction gives further insight into the differences in these classroom contexts for writing. It is evident that successfully maintaining the Cooperative Principle was a more complicated business in Poetry than in Freshman Composition or Biology. In Biology, Dave was unlikely to violate the condition of *Quality*, as he did in Poetry, because he was only summarizing the published experiment and thus only had to pay attention to the condition of *Manner*. In Poetry, by contrast, he was called upon to take an interpretive position. This assumed that he had already summarized the poem. He had not. Thus his analytical essay took the form of a summary, as we have seen. In Biology, on the other hand, the writing was supposed to be a summary that then moved to a comparison of the summarized experiment to what was going on in class.

For Dave, the latter assignment was more appropriate. Novices in a field may 60 need the simpler summary assignment that helps them understand the new reading, the new language that they are being asked to learn. They may then be ready to move to analysis or critique. One wonders if Dave's success in Poetry would have been enhanced if he had been asked to write out a summary of the poem first. He could then have worked from that summary as he structured his own critical essay.

Similarly, in Freshman Composition, Dave was unlikely to violate the condi- 61 tion of *Quality*, to say something untrue or provide inadequate evidence for his claim. Though Dave did have to provide evidence for his subpoints, he was not evaluated for his content, and thus he concentrated on the condition of *Manner*. Further, the writing in Freshman Composition did not require Dave to master unfamiliar texts as it did in both Poetry and Biology. And for Dave the task of integrating new knowledge from his reading into his writing in those courses was his salient concern, as we have seen.

The apparent absence of attention paid in any of these classes to fulfilling 62 the conditions of *Quantity* or *Relation* is puzzling. Perhaps Dave's prior school writing experience had trained him to include the right amount of information (*Quantity*) and stay on topic (*Relation*).

The text analysis data, then, show that what counted as cooperation in these 63 three classes was indeed quite different. Dr. Forson, in his extensive responses, apparently felt it necessary to reteach Dave how people think and write in his community. This is understandable in light of Dave's numerous unintentional violations of the Cooperative Principle. Further, though Dr. Forson told students that he was being objective, finding the meaning of the poem in the text, he told me that his responses to students' papers were to argue his interpretation of the poem and, thus, to justify his grade.

The differing language and forms of these professors' responses probably also 64 added to Dave's sense that in each classroom he was in a new foreign land. Response style may well be discipline-specific as well as teacher-specific, with responses in literary studies generally more discursive than in the sciences. Further, Dr. Forson's responses were in the informal register typically used by an authority speaking to a subordinate (Freedman, 1984). His responses to Dave's paper included the following: "You misfire here." "I get this one. Hurrah for me!" "Pardon my writing. I corrected this in an automobile." The informality, and the word "corrected" in particular, leave little doubt about the authority differential between Dr. Forson and Dave. By contrast, Dave seemed to interpret the numerical grade in Biology as more characteristic of a conversation between equals. In a comment that may say more about their classroom interaction than their written interaction, Dave spoke of Dr. Kelly's brief responses to his review: "Yeah. He's like that. He treats us like adults. When we ask him questions, he answers us." Dave's apparent mixing of his spoken and written interaction with Dr. Kelly emphasizes the point that students' and teachers' writing for each other in classrooms is as fully contextualized as any other activity that goes on there.

Before Dave turned in his last papers in Poetry and Biology, I asked him to 65 speculate about the grade he would get. When he handed in his six-page paper on the Corso poem, "Marriage," on which he had spent eleven hours, he told me that he hoped for an A or B: "I'll be really frustrated on this one if the grade's not good after I've put in the time on it." A week later, however, he told me in a resigned tone and with a short laugh that he'd gotten a C+. By contrast, when he turned in his last review in Biology, he told me he knew he would get an A. When I questioned him, he replied, "I don't know how I know. I just do." And he was right: his grade was 96. Dave obviously understood far better what constituted cooperation in Biology than he did in Poetry.

Social Aspects of the Classrooms That Influenced Dave's Writing

Why was Dave's success in writing in these classrooms so different? The answers 66 to this question will illuminate some of the dimensions along which school writing situations differ and thus influence student achievement. It would be a mistake to think that the differing task structure was the only reason that Dave was more successful in Biology and Freshman Composition than he was in Poetry. Assignments are, as I have suggested, only a small part of the classroom interaction, limited written exchanges that reflect the nature of the communication situation created by participants in that setting. Two unarticulated qualities in the contexts for writing in Freshman Composition and Biology appeared to foster Dave's success in those classes. These were (1) the social functions Dave's writing served for him in those classes, and (2) the roles played by participants and by students' texts there.

The Functions Dave Saw His Writing as Accomplishing.   It has been argued 67 that the social functions served by writing must be seen as an intrinsic part of the writing experience (Clark & Florio, 1983; Hymes, 1972a, 1972b; Scribner & Cole, 1981). Evidence from interviews and observations indicate that the writing in Freshman Composition and Biology was for Dave a meaningful social activity, meaningful beyond just getting him through the course. Further, Dave and his teachers in Freshman Composition and Biology mutually understood and valued those functions. This was not the case in Poetry. The data show a correlation not only between meaningful social functions served by the writing and Dave's success with it, but also between the writing's social meaning and Dave's ability to remember and draw upon it in subsequent semesters.

In Freshman Composition Dave's writing served four valuable functions for 68 him. He articulated all of these.

1. Writing to prepare him for future writing in school and career
2. Writing to explore topics of his choice
3. Writing to participate with other students in the classroom
4. Writing to demonstrate academic competence

In Biology Dave also saw his writing as serving four valuable functions:

1. Writing to learn the language of Cell Biology, which he saw as necessary to his career
2. Writing to prepare him for his next semester's writing in Immunology
3. Writing to make connections between his classwork and actual work being done by professionals in the field
4. Writing to demonstrate academic competence

Evidence from interviews and observation shows that Dr. Carter and Dr. Kelly saw writing in their classes as serving the same four functions that Dave did.

On the other hand, in Poetry, though Dave's professor stated four functions 69 of student writing, Dave saw his writing as serving only one function for him: writing to demonstrate academic competence. Dave, always the compliant student, did say after he had received his disappointing grade in Poetry that the writing in Poetry was probably good for him: "Probably any kind of writing helps you." Though he may well be right, Dave actually saw his writing for Poetry as serving such a limited function—evaluation of his skills in writing poetry criticism for Dr. Forson—that he was not really convinced (and little motivated by the notion) that this writing would serve him in any general way.

Dave contended that any writing task was easy or difficult for him according 70 to his interest in it. When I asked him what he meant by interesting, he said, "If it has something to do with my life. Like it could explain something to me or give me an answer that I could use now." Writing must have, in other words, meaningful personal and social functions for Dave if it is to be manageable, "easy," for him. These functions existed for Dave in Freshman Composition and Biology, providing the applications and personal transaction with the material that may be generally required for learning and forging personal knowledge (Dewey, 1949; Polanyi, 1958).

Dave's Poetry class, however, served no such personally meaningful functions. 71
Six weeks after the Poetry course was finished, I asked Dave some further questions about his last paper for that course, the discussion of the Corso poem on which he had worked 11 hours. He could remember almost nothing about it. When I asked him to speculate why this was, he said, "I guess it's because I have no need to remember it." By contrast, when I asked Dave in the fall of his junior year if his Cell Biology writing was serving him in his Immunology course as he had expected, he said, "Yes. The teacher went over how to write up our labs, but most of us had the idea anyway from last semester because we'd read those journal articles. We were already exposed to it."

Of course the functions of his writing in Biology served Dave better than 72
those in Poetry in part because he was a biology major. The writing for Cell Biology fit into a larger whole: his growing body of knowledge about this field and his professional future. The material in Cell Biology was for Dave a comprehensible part of the discipline of Biology which was in turn a comprehensible part of the sciences. Dave was, with experience, gradually acquiring a coherent sense of the language of the discipline, how biologists think and speak and what it is they talk about. And his understanding of the language of biology was accompanied by an increasing confidence in his own ability to use it. Both of these are probably necessary foundations for later, more abstract and complex uses of the language (Piaget, 1952; Perry, 1970; Williams, 1985).

In the required one-semester Poetry class, however, the poems seemed to 73
Dave to be unrelated to each other except for commonly used poetic devices, and his writing about them was unrelated to his own life by anything at all beyond his need to find the "true meaning" and get an acceptable grade. Dave's different relationship to the languages of these disciplines was shown when he said, "In Biology I'm using what I've *learned*. It's just putting what I've learned on paper. But in Poetry, more or less each poem is different, so it's not *taught* to you. You just have to figure it out from that poem itself and hope Dr. Forson likes it." Nor, in Poetry, was Dave ever invited to make personally meaningful connections with the poems. And he never did it on his own, no doubt in part because he was so preoccupied with the new ways of thinking and speaking that he was trying to use.

In Freshman Composition the social function of writing that was perhaps 74
most powerful for Dave was writing to participate with other students in the classroom. In his peer writing group Dave, for the first time ever, discussed his writing with others. Here he communicated personal positions and insights to his friends, an influential audience for him. That an important social function was served by these students' work with each other is suggested by their clear memory, a year and a half later, both of their essays and of each others' reactions to them.

The four social functions that Dave's writing in Freshman Composition 75
accomplished for him enhanced his engagement with and attitude toward the

writing he did in that class. This engagement is reflected in Dave's memory not only of his essays and his friends' reactions to them, but also in his memory and use of the ideas and terms from that course. When Dave talked about his writing during his sophomore and junior years, he used the process terms he had learned in Freshman Composition: prewriting, revision, and drafts. He also used other language he had learned as a freshman, speaking at times about his audience's needs, about narrowing his topic, about connecting his sentences, providing more details, and choosing his organizational structure. This is not to say that Dave had mastered these skills in every writing situation nor that he always accurately diagnosed problems in his own work. In fact, we know that he did not. It is to say, however, that Dave did recognize and could talk about some of the things that writing does involve in many situations. Thus, the value of this course for Dave lay not so much in the thesis/subpoint essay structure. Rather, Dave had, as a result of his experiences in Freshman Composition, learned that writing is a process that can be talked about, managed, and controlled.

Thus the social functions that writing served for Dave in each class were viewed 76 as an intrinsic part of his writing experiences there. Where these functions were numerous and mutually understood and valued by Dave and his teacher, Dave was more successful in figuring out and producing the required discourse. And then he remembered it longer. In Poetry, where his writing served few personally valued ends, Dave did less well, making a C on the first paper, a D on the second, and a C+ on the third. It should be noted, in addition, that grades themselves serve a social function in classrooms: defining attitudes and roles. Dave's low grades in Poetry probably further alienated him from the social communication processes in that classroom community and helped define his role there.

The Roles Played by the Participants and by Students' Texts. Other social 77 aspects of these classroom contexts for writing which affected Dave's experiences were the roles played by the people and texts in them. Such roles are tacitly assigned in classroom interaction and create the context in which the student stranger attempts to determine the rules of language use in that territory. Here we will examine (1) Dave's role in relation to the teacher, (2) Dave's role in relation to other students in the class, and (3) the role played by students' texts there.

Dave's Role in Relation to the Teacher. This is a particularly important role 78 relationship in any classroom because it tacitly shapes the writer-audience relation that students use as they attempt to communicate appropriately. In all three classes Dave was writing for his teachers as pupil to examiner. However, data from several sources show that there were important variations in the actual "enactments" (Goffman, 1961) of this role-relationship.

In Composition, both Dave and his professor played the role of writer. 79 Throughout the semester Dr. Carter talked about what and how she wrote, the long time she spent in prewriting activities, the eight times she typically revised her work, and the strategies she used to understand her audience in various situations. She spoke to students as if she and they were all writers working together, saying such things as "I see some of you write like I do," or "Let's work together to shape this language." And, as we have seen, she structured the course to provide opportunities for students to play the role of writer in their peer groups. She also asked them to describe their writing processes for several of their essays. Dave told me in an interview during his junior year, "In high school I couldn't stand writing, but in Comp I started to change because I knew more what I was doing. I learned that there are steps you can go through, and I learned how to organize a paper." As a freshman, Dave understood for the first time something of what it feels like to be a writer.

In Biology both Dave and his teacher, Dr. Kelly, saw Dave as playing the role 80 of newcomer, learning the language needed for initiation into the profession. Dr. Kelly played the complementary role of experienced professional who was training Dave in the ways of speaking in that discipline, ways they both assumed Dave would learn in time.

In Poetry, on the other hand, Dave played the role of outsider in relation- 81 ship to his teacher, the insider who knew the true meanings of poetry. And Dave stayed the outsider, unable ever to fully get the teacher's "true meaning." This outsider/insider relationship between Dave and Dr. Forson was created by a number of factors: (1) Their spoken and written interaction, (2) the few meaningful social functions served for Dave by the writing in that class, (3) the demanding nature of the analytic task, combined with (4) the limited knowledge Dave commanded in that setting, (5) the limited number of effective instructional supports, and (6) the low grades Dave got, which further alienated him from the communication processes in that class. (To the instructional supports provided in Poetry we will return below.) Because Dave's outsider role was not a pleasant one for him, he seemed increasingly to separate his thinking from his writing in Poetry, saying several times that he had the right ideas, the teacher just did not like the way he wrote them.

Dave's Role in Relationship to Other Students.   Students' relationships with 82 each other, like those between students and teachers, are created as students interact within the classroom structures the teacher has set up. These classroom structures grow out of teachers' explicit and tacit notions about writing and learning. What specifically were the relationships among students in Freshman Composition, Biology, and Poetry?

In Composition, as we have seen, students shared their writing and responded 83 to each other's work. The classroom structure reflected Dr. Carter's perhaps tacit notion that writing is a social as well as intellectual affair. However, in neither Poetry nor Biology was time built into the class for students to talk with each other about their writing. Dave lamented this as he wrote for Poetry early in his sophomore year, because, he said, he now realized how valuable the small group sessions had been in Freshman Composition the semester before.

In Biology, Dave told me students did talk informally about the journal articles they had selected and how they were progressing on their summaries. Dr. Kelly, who circulated during lab, was at times included in these informal talks about writing. And it is no surprise that students discussed their writing in this way in Biology in light of Dr. Kelly's notions about writing. It is, he believes, an essential part of what scientists do. He told me that it often comes as a rude shock to students that the way biologists survive in the field is by writing. He said, "These students are bright, and they can memorize piles of facts, but they're not yet good at writing. They know what science *is*," he told me, "but they don't know what scientists *do*." Thus, writing up research results is seen by Dr. Kelly as an integral part of a biologist's lab work. No wonder his students talked about it.

In Poetry, however, there was little talk of any kind among students. Classes were primarily lectures where Dr. Forson explicated poems and explained poetic devices. Only occasionally did he call on one of the 22 students for an opinion. This lack of student interaction in Poetry was in line with the image of the writer that Dr. Forson described for students, an image that may be widely shared in literary studies: A person alone with his or her books and thoughts. Dr. Forson did, however, tell students that he himself often got his ideas for writing from listening to himself talk about poems in class. Yet, in conversation with me, he said that he did not want students discussing the poems and their writing with each other because he feared they would not think for themselves. Dave picked up on this idea very clearly. It was not until the fall of his junior year that he admitted to me that he and his girlfriend had worked together on their papers. They had discussed the interpretations of the poems and how they might best write them, but, he told me, they had been careful to choose different poems to write about so that Dr. Forson wouldn't know they had worked together. This absence of student interaction in Poetry may have contributed to the outsider role that Dave played in that class.

Throughout this study I was amazed at the amount of talk that goes on all the time outside class among students as they work to figure out the writing requirements in various courses. What Dave's experience in Poetry may suggest is that where student collaboration in writing is not openly accepted, it goes on clandestinely.

The Roles Played by Students' Texts.   What were students' texts called and how were they handled? Interview and observation data show that students' texts were treated quite differently in these three courses, and this affected how Dave saw the assignments, and, perhaps more important, how he saw himself as writer.

In Freshman Composition Dave wrote what he referred to as "essays"; in Biology, "reviews"; in Poetry, "papers." This latter term is commonly used, of course, but it is one that Emig (1983, p. 173) says suggests a low status text: "Paper"—as if there were no words on the sheet at all. In Poetry the high status texts, the ones that were discussed and interpreted, were the poems. Students' works were just more or less successful explications of those. Furthermore, in Poetry the one model essay the students read was written by the teacher. Though students were told they should think of their peers as their audience, in fact they never read each other's essays at all. Students' texts were, rather, passed only between student and teacher as in a private conversation. 88

In Biology, student texts enjoyed a higher status. Excellent student reviews were posted and students were encouraged to read them; they were to serve as models. Some student writers were thus defined as competent speakers in this territory, and the message was clear to Dave: This was a language that he too could learn given time and proper training. 89

And in Freshman Composition, of course, student texts were the *objects* of study. The class read good and flawed student texts from former semesters and from their own. This not only helped Dave with his writing, it also dignified student writing and elevated his estimation of his own work. Student texts were not, in short, private affairs between teacher and student; they were the subject matter of this college course. 90

Thus the roles that were enacted by teachers, students, and students' texts were quite different in each classroom and were an integral part of Dave's writing experiences there. The participants' interaction and the social functions that writing serves are important factors working to create the communication situation. And this communication situation, it has been suggested, is the fundamental factor shaping the success of writing instruction (Langer & Applebee, 1984, p. 171). 91

The Information Sources Dave Drew Upon

In a process that was in large part tacit, Dave drew upon six sources for information about what constituted successful writing in Freshman Composition, Poetry, and Biology. These included teacher-provided instructional supports, sources Dave found on his own, and his prior experience. Many of these have been mentioned above. They are summarized in Table 4. 92

Of particular interest are the information sources Dave drew upon (or failed to draw upon) in Poetry, the course in which the writing assignment was the most demanding and in which Dave did least well in assessing and producing the required discourse. The information source that Dr. Forson intended to be most helpful to students, the instructional support on which he spent a great deal of time, was his response to their papers. However, his extensive comments 93

TABLE 4 INFORMATION SOURCES DAVE DREW UPON IN ASSESSING REQUIRED DISCOURSE

INFORMATION SOURCES	FRESHMAN COMPOSITION	POETRY	CELL BIOLOGY
What teachers said in class about writing	Constant lectures & exercises about process & products	• One lecture • General statements to the class about their papers when returning them	• Ten minutes giving "guidelines" when returning 1st set of reviews of reviews • Informal comments in lab
Model texts	Many, including flawed models	• One, written by teacher • One, written by professional (from library)	• The articles being summarized served as models. • Posted student reviews
Talk with other students	Frequent groups in class	With friend outside class	Informal, in class
Teachers' written responses to writing	Read responses & revised early essays accordingly	Read. No revision required	Read. No revision required
Dave's prior experience	The extent to which Dave drew upon prior experience is difficult to say. In each class he believed he had no prior experience to draw from. However, we know he had had related prior experience.		
Personal talk with teacher	One conference with teacher	None	None

did not help Dave a great deal in learning how to communicate in that setting. Dave said that the comments on his first paper did help him some with his second, but he really did not refer to Dr. Forson's responses on the second paper as he wrote the third. Nor did Dave use the comments on the third paper when preparing for the essay question on the final exam. Dr. Forson required no revision in direct response to his comments, and the expected carry-over of his responses from one paper to the next did not occur. Rather, Dave repeated similar mistakes again and again. The assumption that trial and error will improve students' writing across a series of similar tasks did not hold true for Dave's work in Poetry.

Neither was the model text in Poetry, Dr. Forson's analysis of the Herrick poem that he went over in lecture, as useful an information source for Dave as Dr. Forson had hoped it would be. Dave told me that though he had looked at Dr. Forson's model critical essay as he wrote his first paper, it had not helped him 94 a great deal. "Seeing how someone else did it," he said, "is a lot different than doing it yourself." In Freshman Composition and Biology, however, the model texts, both excellent and flawed ones, were more numerous. And in Biology, the model provided by the article Dave was summarizing was virtually inescapable. Model texts are, it seems reasonable, particularly important to newcomers learning the conventions of discourse in a new academic territory.

An information source which Dave was not adept at using in any course 95 was direct questioning of the professor, the native-speaker expert in each setting. Dave never voluntarily questioned a teacher, though in October of his sophomore year, when he was doing poorly in Poetry, he did make an attempt to speak with Dr. Forson at his office. But when Dr. Forson was not there, Dave waited only a short time and then left—relieved, he said. He did not return. In Freshman Composition, however, Dave was required to interact with Dr. Carter individually in his mid-semester conference. That interview provided an additional information source upon which Dave could draw as he assessed and adapted to the writing requirements in that class.

DISCUSSION

What, then, can we learn from Dave's experiences? First, this study adds to exist- 96 ing research which suggests that school writing is not a monolithic activity or global skill. Rather, the contexts for writing may be so different from one classroom to another, the ways of speaking in them so diverse, the social meanings of writing and the interaction patterns so different, that the courses may be for the student writer like so many foreign countries. These differences were apparent in this study not only in Dave's perceptions of the courses but in his concerns while writing and in his written products.

Second, the findings of this study have several implications for our under- 97 standing of writing development. This study suggests that writing development is, in part, context-dependent. In each new classroom community, Dave in many ways resembled a beginning language user. He focused on a limited number of new concerns, and he was unable to move beyond concrete ways of thinking and writing, the facts of the matter at hand. Moreover, skills mastered in one situation, such as the thesis-subpoint organization in Freshman Composition, did not, as Dave insisted, automatically transfer to new contexts with differing problems and language and differing amounts of knowledge that he controlled. To better understand the stages that students progress through in achieving competence in academic speech communities, we need further research.

Dave's development across his freshman and sophomore years, where he was 98 repeatedly a newcomer, may also be viewed in terms of his attitude toward writing. Evidence over 21 months shows that his notion of the purpose of school writing changed very little. Though there were, as we have seen, other functions accomplished for Dave by his writing in Freshman Composition and Biology, he always understood the purpose of his school writing as being primarily to satisfy a teacher-examiner's requirements. A change that did occur, however, was Dave's increased understanding of some of the activities that writers actually engage in and an increased confidence in his writing ability. As a freshman, he had told me that he did not like to write and was not very good, but by the fall of his junior year he sounded quite different. Because of a number of successful classroom experiences with writing, and an ability to forget the less successful ones, Dave told me, "Writing is no problem for me. At work, in school, I just do it."

Whether Dave will eventually be a mature writer, one who, according to Britton's (1975) definition, is able to satisfy his own purposes with a wide range of audiences, lies beyond the scope of this study to determine. We do know, however, that Dave did not, during the period of this study, write for a wide range of audiences. Nor did he, in these classes, define his own audiences, purposes, or formats, though he did in Freshman Composition choose his topics and in Poetry and Biology the particular poems and articles he wrote about. What this study suggests is that college undergraduates in beginning-level courses may have even less opportunity to orchestrate their own writing occasions than do younger students. Balancing teachers' and students' purposes is indeed difficult in these classrooms where students must, in 14 weeks, learn unfamiliar discourse conventions as well as a large body of new knowledge. 99

The findings of this study have several implications for the teaching of writing. They suggest that when we ask what students learn from and about writing in classrooms, we must look not only at particular assignments or at students' written products. We must also look at what they learn from the social contexts those classrooms provide for writing. In Freshman Composition, Dave learned that writer was a role he could play. In Biology, writing was for Dave an important part of a socialization process; he was the newcomer being initiated into a profession in which, he learned, writing counts for a great deal. From his writing in Poetry, Dave learned that reading poetry was not for him and that he could get through any writing task, no matter how difficult or foreign. This latter is a lesson not without its value, of course, but it is not one that teachers hope to teach with their writing assignments. 100

This study also raises questions about how teachers can best help student "strangers" to become competent users of the new language in their academic territory. Because all writing is context-dependent, and because successful writing requires the accurate assessment of and adaptation to the demands of particular writing situations, perhaps writing teachers should be explicitly training students in this assessment process. As Dave researched the writing requirements in his classroom, he drew upon six information sources in a process that was for him largely tacit and unarticulated. But Dave was actually in a privileged position in terms of his potential for success in this "figuring out" process. He had, 101 after all, had years of practice writing in classrooms. Furthermore, he shared not only ethnic and class backgrounds with his teachers, but also many assumptions about education. Students from diverse communities may need, even more than Dave, explicit training in the ways in which one figures out and then adapts to the writing demands in academic contexts.

For teachers in the disciplines, "native-speakers" who may have used the language in their discipline for so long that it is partially invisible to them, the first challenge will be to appreciate just how foreign and difficult their language is for student newcomers. They must make explicit the interpretive and linguistic conventions in their community, stressing that theirs is one way of looking at reality and not reality itself. As Fish (1980) points out, "The choice is never between objectivity and interpretation, but between an interpretation that is unacknowledged as such and an interpretation that is at least aware of itself" (p. 179). Teachers in the disciplines must then provide student newcomers with assignments and instructional supports which are appropriate for first steps in using the language of their community. Designing appropriate assignments and supports may well be more difficult when the student stranger is only on a brief visit in an academic territory, as Dave was in Poetry, or when the student comes from a community at a distance farther from academe than Dave did. 102

Naturalistic studies like the present one, Geertz says, are only "another country heard from . . . nothing more or less." Yet, "small facts speak to large issues" (1973, p. 23). From Dave's story, and others like it which describe actual writers at work in local settings, we will learn more about writers' processes and texts and how these are constrained by specific social dynamics. Our generalizations and theories about writing and about how people learn to write must, in the final analysis, be closely tied to such concrete social situations. 103

References

Applebee, A. (1984). *Contexts for learning to write: Studies of secondary school instruction*. Norwood, NJ: Ablex.

Basso, K. (1974). The ethnography of writing. In R. Bauman and J. Sherzer (Eds.), *Explorations in the ethnography of speaking* (pp. 425–432). New York: Cambridge University Press.

Bazerman, C. (1981). What written knowledge does: Three examples of academic discourse. *Philosophy of the Social Sciences, 11*, 361–387.

Berkenkotter, C. (1983). Decisions and revisions: The planning strategies of a publishing writer. *College Composition and Communication, 34*, 156–169.

Bizzell, P. (1982). Cognition, convention, and certainty: What we need to know about writing. *PRE/TEXT, 3*, 213–243.

Bridwell, L. (1980). Revising strategies in twelfth grade students' transactional writing. *Research in the Teaching of English, 14*, 197–222.

Britton, J., Burgess, T., Martin, N., McLeod, A., & Rosen, H. (1975). *The development of writing abilities 11–18*. London: Macmillan.

Calkins, L. (1980). Research update: When children want to punctuate: Basic skills belong in context. *Language Arts, 57,* 567–573.

Clark, C., & Florio, S., with Elmore, J., Martin, J., & Maxwell, R. (1983). Understanding writing instruction: Issues of theory and method. In P. Mosenthal, L. Tamor, & S. Walmsley (Eds.), *Research on writing: Principles and methods* (pp. 236–264). New York: Longman.

Cooper, M. (1986). The ecology of writing. *College English, 48,* 364–375.

Denzin, N. (1978). *Sociological methods.* New York: McGraw-Hill.

Dewey, J. (1949). *The child and the curriculum and the school and society.* Chicago: University of Chicago Press.

Dyson, A. (1984). Learning to write/learning to do school: Emergent writers' interpretations of school literacy tasks. *Research in the Teaching of English, 18,* 233–264.

Emig, J. (1983). *The web of meaning: Essays on writing, teaching, learning, and thinking.* Upper Montclair, NJ: Boynton/Cook.

Ericson, F. (1982). Taught cognitive learning in its immediate environments: A neglected topic in the anthropology of education. *Anthropology & Education Quarterly, 13*(2), 148–180.

Faigley, L. (1985). Nonacademic writing: The social perspective. In L. Odell & D. Goswami (Eds.), *Writing in nonacademic settings* (pp. 231–248). New York: Guilford Press.

Fish, S. (1980). Interpreting the Variorium. In J. Tompkins (Ed.), *Reader response criticism: From formalism to post-structuralism.* Baltimore: Johns Hopkins University Press.

Florio, S., & Clark, C. (1982). The functions of writing in an elementary classroom. *Research in the Teaching of English, 16,* 115–130.

Flower, L., & Hayes, J. (1981). The pregnant pause: An inquiry into the nature of planning. *Research in the Teaching of English, 15,* 229–244.

Freedman, S. (1984). The registers of student and professional expository writing: Influences on teachers' responses. In R. Beach & L. Bridwell (Eds.), *New directions in composition research* (pp. 334–347). New York: Guilford Press.

Freedman, S. (1985). *The acquisition of written language: Response and revision.* New York: Ablex.

Geertz, C. (1973). *The interpretation of cultures.* New York: Basic Books.

Gilmore, P., & Glatthorn, A. (1982). *Children in and out of school: Ethnography and education.* Washington, DC: Center for Applied Linguistics.

Goffman, E. (1961). *Encounters: Two studies in the sociology of interaction.* New York: Bobbs-Merrill.

Grice, H. (1975). *Logic and conversation.* 1967 William James Lectures, Harvard University. Unpublished manuscript, 1967. Excerpt in Cole and Morgan (Eds.), *Syntax and semantics, Vol. III: Speech acts* (pp. 41–58). New York: Academic Press.

Guba, E. (1978). *Toward a method of naturalistic inquiry in educational evaluation.* Los Angeles: Center for the Study of Evaluation, University of California at Los Angeles.

Gumperz, J. (1971). *Language in social groups.* Stanford, CA: Stanford University Press.

Heath, S. B. (1982). Ethnography in education: Defining the essentials. In P. Gilmore & A. Glatthorn (Eds.), *Children in and out of school: Ethnography and education* (pp. 33–55). Washington, DC: Center for Applied Linguistics.

Heinlein, R. (1961). *Stranger in a strange land.* New York: Putnam.

Herrington, A. (1985). Writing in academic settings: A study of the contexts for writing in two college chemical engineering courses. *Research in the Teaching of English, 19,* 331–359.

Hymes, D. (1972a). Introduction. In C. Cazden, V. P. John, & D. Hymes (Eds.), *Functions of language in the classroom* (pp. xi–lxii). New York: Teachers College Press.

Hymes, D. (1972b). Models of the interaction of language and social life. In J. Gumperz & D. Hymes (Eds.), *Directions in sociolinguistics* (pp. 35–71). New York: Holt, Rinehart, & Winston.

Kantor, K. (1984). Classroom contexts and the development of writing intuitions: An ethnographic case study. In R. Beach & L. Bridwell (Eds.), *New directions in composition research* (pp. 72–94). New York: Guilford.

Langer, J. (1984). The effects of available information on responses to school writing tasks. *Research in the Teaching of English, 18,* 27–44.

Langer, J. (1985). Children's sense of genre: A study of performance on parallel reading and writing tasks. *Written Communication, 2,* 157–188.

Langer, J. (1986). Reading, writing, and understanding: An analysis of the construction of meaning. *Written Communication, 3,* 219–267.

Langer, J., & Applebee, A. (1984). Language, learning, and interaction: A framework for improving the teaching of writing. In A. Applebee (Ed.), *Contexts for learning to write: Studies of secondary school instruction* (pp. 169–182). Norwood, NJ: Ablex.

Lincoln, Y., & Guba, E. (1985). *Naturalistic inquiry.* Beverly Hills, CA: Sage Publications.

Odell, L., & Goswami, D. (1985). *Writing in nonacademic settings.* New York: Guilford Press.

Perl, S. (1979). The composing process of unskilled college writers. *Research in the Teaching of English, 13,* 317–336.

Perry, W. G. (1970). *Forms of intellectual and ethical development in the college years.* New York: Holt, Rinehart, and Winston.

Piaget, J. (1952). *The origins of intelligence in children.* New York: International Universities Press.

Pianko, S. (1979). A description of the composing processes of college freshman writers. *Research in the Teaching of English, 13,* 5–22.

Polanyi, M. (1958). *Personal knowledge: Towards a post-critical philosophy.* Chicago: University of Chicago Press.

Scribner, S. & Cole, M. (1981). Unpackaging literacy. In M. F. Whiteman (Ed.), *Variation in writing: Functional and linguistic-cultural differences* (pp. 71–88). Hillsdale, NJ: Lawrence Erlbaum.

Shaughnessy, M. (1977). *Errors and expectations.* New York: Oxford University Press.

Spradley, J. (1979). *The ethnographic interview.* New York: Holt, Rinehart and Winston.

Spradley, J. (1980). *Participant observation.* New York: Holt, Rinehart and Winston.

Szwed, J. (1981). The ethnography of literacy. In M. F. Whiteman (Ed.), *Variation in writing: Functional and linguistic-cultural differences* (pp. 13–23). Hillsdale, NJ: Lawrence Erlbaum.

Whiteman, M. F. (1981). *Variation in writing: Functional and linguistic-cultural differences.* Hillsdale, NJ: Lawrence Erlbaum.

Williams, J. (1985, March). *Encouraging higher order reasoning through writing in all disciplines.* Paper presented at the Delaware Valley Writing Council-PATHS Conference, Philadelphia.

Questions for Discussion and Journaling

1. What are McCarthy's research questions? What research methods did she use to find answers to these questions? What were her primary findings? How might her findings have been shaped by her methods? What other methods might she have used, and how might they have altered her findings?

2. McCarthy analyzed Dave's experiences using Grice's "Cooperative Principle." Explain what this principle is and how it helped McCarthy understand Dave's struggles and successes.

3. Why did Dave struggle in his poetry class? What might Dave and his teacher have done to improve Dave's chances of success in that class?

4. Earlier in this chapter, Ann M. Johns described the importance of discourse communities for the ways that people do — and don't — use language, and the difficulties that can occur when students attempt to use academic language. How does the concept of discourse community shed light on Dave's experiences?

5. How do you see McCarthy's work related to the threshold concept emphasized in this chapter that texts and the language discourse communities they create *mediate meaningful activities*?

6. How does Dave's experience writing in college compare with your own? What aspects of writing in college frustrate or puzzle you? What has been hardest for you about writing in college? Why?

7. Do you find the same variance in expectations of your writing from class to class that Dave experiences, or are the expectations you encounter more consistent? What have been your strategies so far for handling any differing expectations you're finding? Does McCarthy's work give you any ideas for different strategies?

Applying and Exploring Ideas

1. For several weeks, keep a writer's journal about your experiences writing in different classrooms. What are you asked to write? What instructions are you given? What feedback are you given? Do you talk with others about the assignments? What genres are you asked to write? How well do you do? Do you understand the grades and comments your teachers give you? At the end of the weeks of journaling, write about your findings and share them with the class.

2. Write a plan for setting up a study like McCarthy's that examines your own experiences across classrooms. Draw on Johns to help you think about designing the study. What do you want to know, and why? What data will you collect and analyze? Write a two-page paper in which you outline the answers to these questions. Note that you aren't *conducting* a study, just imagining how you would *plan* to do so.

- -

META MOMENT   What have you learned from McCarthy that can help you in your own college classroom experiences? How does McCarthy's study help you understand the ways that language and texts help people make meaning together — or get in the way of people's efforts to do that?

- -

Coaches Can Read, Too

An Ethnographic Study of a Football Coaching Discourse Community

SEAN BRANICK

University of Dayton Athletics

Framing the Reading

Sean Branick was a first-year student in Elizabeth Wardle's composition class at the University of Dayton when he wrote this paper. He was enrolled in a special pilot two-semester composition sequence that allowed him to work on this ethnography for a full academic year. His paper was chosen as one of the best from two such courses and published in a one-time-only university publication called *Looking for Literacy: Reporting the Research*. Branick's interest in the discourse community of football coaches arose from his own experience as a high school football player and as a student coach in college. He later served as a student football coach at the University of Hawaii at Mānoa and a defensive line intern at Ohio State University, and he is now an AP U.S. history teacher.

We are including Branick's paper here because he applies Johns's concept of discourse community to a community that many people do not immediately think of as including literacy: football. In this way, his view of literacy is as expansive as Gee's and Mirabelli's. He begins by explaining the characteristics of effective football coaches, and then explains in detail why he believes that coaches constitute a discourse community. But he doesn't stop there. He goes on to identify some special "literacies" that he believes effective coaches possess. Like Mirabelli, Branick's interest in "mundane" sports texts and literacies should help you better understand the underlying threshold concepts of this chapter: football players and coaches use texts and discourse to *make meaning* in order to *do something*. Their texts and the language they create and use together *mediate activities* that are meaningful to them and their fans.

Getting Ready to Read

Before you read, do the following activity:

- Ask yourself whether you agree that football coaches constitute a *discourse community* according to Johns's definition.

As you read, consider the following question:

- In his introduction, Branick includes the three "moves" that Swales identifies in his CARS model of research introductions (see pp. 22–24) — establishing the territory, establishing a niche, and explaining how he will fill that niche. Using the tags we explained in Chapter 1 (p. 58) and demonstrated in Gee, try tagging the genre moves in Branick's essay.

THE PROFESSION OF COACHING football is one of the most influential 1 professions that exists in today's world. It is a profession essential to the game whether it is a third-grade team or a pro team. Coaches may range from parents volunteering with a child's youth program to people who dedicate every waking hour to the game. Coaches are made up of both everyday Joes and legends that will live in memory as long as the game is played. It is a profession that requires putting the athletes first: "The main responsibility of the coach is to enable their athletes to attain levels of performance not otherwise achievable" (Short "Role," S29). It is a profession very visible to the public yet it has many behind-the-scenes factors that may be often overlooked that directly relate to success. Among these are the idea of goal-focused coaching, coaching with confidence, and the characteristics of effective coaches.

GOAL-FOCUSED COACHING

Whether on the football field or off the football field, people have always used 2 the process of setting and chasing goals to achieve a desired outcome. A goal is often the universal starting point in many things, including football. Anthony Grant, a sport psychologist, takes an in-depth look at the process of effectively setting a goal in order to achieve a desired result. He talks about how the coach should help facilitate the entire process of using goals, which consists of the following: "an individual sets a goal, develops a plan of action, begins action, monitors his or her performance (through observation and self-reflection), evaluates his or her performance (thus gaining insight) and, based on this evaluation, changes his or her actions to further enhance performance, and thus reach his or her goal" (751).

Grant explains that there are five important parts to this goal-focused coach- 3 ing concept. The first part is setting good goals. The coach must help the player set goals that coincide with his values, are well defined, and are realistically achievable. The second part is developing a strong working relationship between the coach and player. This means that a coach must work to develop an honest relationship to help create an environment conducive to growth where the player will feel comfortable being open and honest with the coach. The third aspect is developing a solution focus, which means helping the athlete develop solutions to help him achieve his goals. The fourth part is managing process. This includes developing action steps and holding the athlete accountable for completing the agreed steps. The fifth and final aspect is achieving the desired outcome.

CHARACTERISTICS OF AN EFFECTIVE COACH

While successful coaches have been exposed to the spotlight throughout history, 4 certain personal qualities of these coaches have emerged as essential to success in the coaching business. Sports psychologist Sandra Short explores five specific qualities of effective coaches. The first of these qualities is being a teacher. This is important because coaches must be able to teach their players about the game and what to do during competition.

The second quality is being organized. Being organized is typically a behind- 5 the-scenes job but it is important because a coach must be organized to keep track of players, competitions, and practice schedules. It is important to organize a plan for success and be able to stick to it. Coaches in team sports must be organized before stepping onto the playing field so that they will know how to handle specific situations such as substitutions and timeout management.

The third quality is being competitive. Coaches must have an inner desire to 6 compete and work to instill that desire to compete in their athletes. Being competitive must be a foundational quality in athletes. It doesn't matter how gifted an athlete is or how much he knows, if he does not have the desire to compete then he will not be successful.

The fourth quality is being a learner. Coaches must continue to learn every 7 day they are on the job. They must learn about their players' personality and they must learn about the newest trends, philosophies, and strategies in the sport that they coach.

The fifth and final quality mentioned is being a friend and mentor. It is impor- 8 tant to be a positive role model for their players to look up to. A coach should also offer support and counseling when a player may need it. Fulfilling this role can bring about a deeper level of satisfaction for both the coach and the athlete.

CONFIDENCE IN COACHING

Another aspect of coaching that has been studied is coaching confidence and its 9 relationship with imagery. Sports psychologist Sandra Short argues that imagining being confident helps increase real confidence and the feeling of effectiveness. During pregame preparations, if a coach pictures himself as a confident, successful coach, he is more likely to exude real confidence.

Another point Short made is that coaches who use imagery to put together 10 game plans feel more comfortable with the plans that they come up with. Coaches who make their plans and play out the game using their imaginations are more likely to see strengths and weaknesses in their plans and adjust their plans accordingly.

A third point made is that coaches who imagine in a "cognitive specific way," 11 that is through clear specific examples, will have more confidence in their teaching abilities. In other words, coaches who specifically imagine teaching skills and techniques will acquire confidence in teaching these attributes and therefore be more effective teachers: "The confidence a coach portrays affects the confidence athletes feel. . . . The coach acting confident is one of the most effective strategies coaches can use to increase athletes' 'feelings of efficacy' " (Short, "Relationship" 392).

There have been many articles written on the X's and the O's (specific strate- 12 gies) of the game. Seminars have been held on the newest strategies. Books have been written on the characteristics of good coaches. Studies have been done on confidence in coaching, the method of setting goals, and the role of the coach in coach-athlete relationships; however scholars have yet to study a coach's ability to read his players and the game as a form of literacy. Many people may think that literacy is not part of the responsibilities that go with coaching. However, they couldn't be farther from the truth. Tony Mirabelli gives an unorthodox definition of literacy, arguing that "Literacy extends beyond individual experiences of reading and writing to include the various modes of communication and situations of any socially meaningful group" (146). He talks about reading people and knowing when to do something to help them as forms of literacy.

This idea of multiple literacies can be applied to football coaching staff as 13 well. Coaches need to be able to do so much more than just read. They need to know how to read people. They need to know how to read their players so that they can find out how to get the most out of them. They must also know how to read and teach the plays. The coaches must know their plays because many plays have certain "reads" or "progressions" that the coach must be able to teach the players. Coaches also must be able to read the game so that they can call the best plays that suit certain situations properly.

Coaching as a complex literacy practice has not been examined. How do foot- 14 ball coaches, as members of a specific discourse community, go about reading their players and the game in order to get optimal performance and a positive end result? To figure this out, I conducted an ethnographic study on how the coaches at the University of Dayton go about reading people and reading the game.

METHODS

I recorded football coaches at the University of Dayton during their pregame 15 speeches and interviewed those coaches afterwards; I also interviewed a coaching graduate assistant at the University of Cincinnati via email. The recording of the pregame speeches took place before a home game on a Saturday afternoon. In the pregame speeches, Coach Kelly and Coach Whilding attempted to bring out the best in their players. I conducted an interview with Coach Whilding, the offensive coordinator, the following week, and with Coach Kelly, the head coach at the time, during the winter of the following season. Each interview took place in the coaches' offices. The email interview with Coach Painter, the graduate assistant at the University of Cincinnati, took place in the winter as well. In it, I asked similar questions to those used for the University of Dayton coaches. (Interview questions are attached as Appendix A.) I asked questions about how coaches go about reading their players and the game and also about the coach's personal history and motivation for coaching.

I used these methods because they allowed me to take a direct look at what the coaches were saying and then get a look at the thought process behind it. The interviews involved open-ended questions that helped bring out coaching philosophies on many different issues, including the issue of reading their players and the game. This idea of reading players and the game is directly reflective of Tony Mirabelli's idea of multiple literacies. 16

I analyzed the data collected by applying John Swales's six characteristics of a discourse community. The characteristics I focused on are the set of common goals, the genres, and the specific lexis used. 17

RESULTS

Because we are studying the multiple literacies of football coaches by looking at coaching as a discourse community, it will be clearest to separate the results for the characteristics of a discourse community and the results for multiple literacies. 18

Characteristics of a Discourse Community

A football coaching staff is an excellent example of a discourse community. The characteristics are clearly defined and easy to recognize. The clearest characteristics to pick up on are the goals, lexis, and genres. 19

Goals. Coach Kelly and Coach Whilding helped make up one of the most successful coaching staffs in the history of division 1 college football. This is mainly due to their ability to set and achieve goals, both team and personal goals. There is always the goal of winning the game. The University of Dayton had goal charts with a list of about 10 goals for every game, for offense, defense, and special teams. They use these charts with stickers to help monitor how well they achieve these goals and figure out the goals they need to work on. 20

Coaches also have many individual goals. Many of these goals include getting the most out of their players physically and mentally. Coaches always strive to make their players push themselves to heights that they never thought they 21 could reach. Coaches also have the goal of seeing their players develop as people. Coach Whilding talked about how he enjoyed seeing his players succeed in real-life situations after football: "It's good to see those guys mature and go on and get good jobs and raise families and be very responsible people in their communities."

Along with these goals, there are many rewards. While many big time college coaches may receive a hefty paycheck, Coach Whilding explained that some of the rewards are not monetary: "I know guys who just hate to get up in the morning and hate to go to work, and I have just never felt that way." 22

Lexis. Another important characteristic of discourse communities is that there is a specialized lexis, or set of terms that is unique to the community. There are many terms that are involved in football coaching communities that may not make sense to most people but, among a team, make perfect sense and help the community better do its work and achieve its goals. 23

Some of the more common terms might make more sense to the public, such as touchdown or tackle. There are, however, terms that might not make sense to anybody outside the team. Examples of these may be passing routes such as "Y corner," "Follow," or "Green Gold." They could also be things like blocking schemes such as "Bob," "Sam," or "Combo." There are terms for everything, and it takes many repetitions during practice to learn all of this lexis. The lexis helps save time because one word may describe several actions. This lexis is also important because the lexis varies from team to team, so if the opposing team hears it, they will not know what it means. Without many hours spent preparing and practicing, the players and the coaches would not have this advantage in communication. 24

Genres. A genre is a text that helps facilitate communication between people, and in this example all communication takes place within the discourse community. There are certain genres that help a football team and football coaching staff operate efficiently. Genres often use the unique lexis that was previously mentioned. 25

Perhaps the most essential genre is the playbook. The playbook is created by the coaches and shows all the plays that they plan on running and the proper way that the players are supposed to run them. The players get the playbooks at the beginning of the season and need to learn the plays before they are "installed" during practice. The players must guard these books and make sure that no members from opposing teams get the information. The playbook is essential to success because there are many plays and without a playbook the players would become confused and make mistakes that could be disastrous to the outcome of the football game. 26

Another genre is a scouting report. The scouting report is also made up by the coaches for the players. It shows the other team's personnel, what plays they like to run, and when they like to run them. It helps the players know what to expect 27 going into the game so they can prepare accordingly. The coaches will usually spend the day after a game putting together a scouting report and distribute the report to their players at the beginning of the week.

A third genre is a play-calling sheet. This is made up by the coaches and is only for the coaches, mainly the offensive coordinator. The play-calling sheet helps the coach remember all the plays that they have and what situation that the plays are favorable in. Without a play-calling sheet, the coach would have to remember the names of all the plays on his own, and that is something that could be a distraction to calling the proper plays, and could effectively cost a team a game. 28

Now that we understand what exactly a football coaching discourse community is and what it is made up of, we can learn exactly how the concept of literacy applies to this group. 29

Multiple Literacies

Many people do not see the concept of literacy as something that would apply to a football coaching staff. However, Mirabelli defines literacy as not just reading and writing but things such as reading people. He uses the example of a waiter reading his customers in his article. This same idea can be applied to a football coaching discourse community. 30

Interpersonal Literacies

One of the literacies for a football coach is the ability to read the players. This can be described as an interpersonal literacy. There are two types of reading the coach needs to do. First, coaches must be able to read players to know when they are ready to play; second, coaches must be able to read their players to know how to motivate them properly to get the most out of them. 31

There are different characteristics to look for when it comes to knowing when players are ready to play. Two are comfort and knowledge. Coach Painter from Cincinnati emphasized player comfort: "Knowing their personality is a big part of reading them. When a player is ready to play they will be in a comfortable mode. Whether that is listening to music, jumping around, or even reading, when a player is loose and comfortable they are ready to compete." Coach Kelly emphasized knowledge of the game: "Do they have the knowledge to perform? What we try to do is put them in as many stressful situations as possible from a mental point of view to see if they can handle that in practice. If they can handle that in practice . . . then we cut 'em loose and let 'em play." He went on to state that another way of finding out whether or not a player has that knowledge and is ready to play is by sitting down one on one with him. Coach Kelly elaborates, "I can get a good feel for a young man when I'm sitting in a room with him, watching practice or game tape, asking him questions. . . . If there is a lot of hesitation or if they are totally off then I know we're not there yet." 32

Coaches must be able to read their players in order to motivate them properly. 33 Every coach emphasized that each player is unique and will respond to different types of motivation in different ways. This can be done by taking an emotional, fiery approach or a calm and collected approach. Coach Kelly emphasized the importance of motivation, explaining,

> That's a key element in becoming a coach. Can they motivate? Can they identify what makes this guy go? Can you hit that button and how fast can you hit that button? The sooner you find that motivational tool the better off you're going to be. You can tell immediately if it works or not.

Finding out what motivates each individual is no easy task, but Coach 34 Whilding explains, "You have to be able to understand 'How do I reach that player . . . that young man?' And there are a lot of ways to do that. Through the years, you figure it out." He went more in depth and explained that you have to be able to reach everybody as an individual player and that there are many types of players: "There are some that like to yell and scream and get excited. There are others who don't play well like that, who are a little quieter and keep it within themselves but are still very motivated." Coach Painter from Cincinnati points out the balance between these two opposing motivational styles: "You have to use both and know when to use them. . . . Too much fire and you will lose the team and its effectiveness. Too much calm and you will lose control over the environment."

These explanations show that reading players to know when they are ready to 35 play and reading players to know how to motivate them are two very difficult parts of the coaching profession. They require balance, patience, and persever-ance. Coach Whilding sums it up, saying, sometimes "it just doesn't work and you find out you have to just use another method."

Situational Literacies

A second essential coaching literacy is being able to read a game. The coaches 36 must be able to actively read a game in order to put their players in the best possible situations to attempt to win the game. Reading a game can be broken down into two categories: pregame and in-game.

The week leading up to a game is a week filled with preparation. Preparation 37 is important because it "will allow you the ability to put players in the places they need to be at the times they need to be there to make plays. From there it's out of your hands" (Painter). Coaches study the opposing team in and out and then formulate a game plan. They consolidate this game plan along with information on the opposition into a packet, make copies of the packet, and distribute the copies to the team. This helps players stay on the same page as the coaches and prepare mentally for the game. This mental preparation will make players feel more comfortable as to what to expect during the game: "You do a lot of preparation during the week, getting ready for the week. We watch a lot of tape. You have to have an idea of what their base defense is, what their coverage is going to be, when they're going to blitz, what down they're going to blitz, what are their favorite ones" (Whilding). Coach Kelly elaborated on the importance of preparation by explaining that you have to get a good idea of what the coach likes to do in certain situations and when you feel like you know the opposing coach, it becomes a game of feel: "It's really important to me to know what's going on in that coach's mind" (Kelly).

It is also important to be able to read the game in real time. Ways of read- 38 ing and reacting during the game may be as simple as knowing when to call timeouts, call certain plays, or make substitutions, or may be more complicated such as knowing what type of halftime adjustments to make. Coach Whilding explains that a key aspect of making these adjustments is that "You have to get a feel on the field for what is working, and I think that's something you develop through the years . . . and it changes from week to week, from year to year some- times, depending on your personnel. You have to know your personnel. What you're good at, what you're not good at."

Because coaches don't always have the best view and are not in a position to 39 be heard by all the players when they are on the field, sometimes they will dele- gate this responsibility to their players. Coach Painter explains, "Our players are allowed a small amount of freedom on the fly. We ask our quarterback to check us out of plays when necessary, but we have established what and when he can make such checks." These checks (changing the play at the line) give the team a better chance of calling a play that will be more likely to be successful.

Halftime adjustments are also very important. Sometimes a team will come out 40 in the first half and do something that was not expected or maybe a certain strategy is not working the way the coach expected it to. The coaches will come together at the end of the half and discuss possible changes that might help the team. They then use halftime to explain these changes and make sure everyone is on the same page. This can turn into a chess match because sometimes one team will adjust to something that another team does, but at the same time the other team changes up what they were doing. Coach Painter explains it best by saying, "Your opponent is going to adjust, if you do not then you will be at a disadvantage. No matter how much preparation you have put in, there are going to be things you did not expect. This is where your on the field adjustments give you the final edge."

Relationship Between Textual, Situational, and Interpersonal Literacies

Coaching functions as a discourse community that uses a variety of complex 41 literacies — textual, interpersonal, and situational. All of these literacies can be seen functioning together in a game situation.

Before the game the coach had to spend time evaluating his players and ⁤ 42
deciding who was going to play. To do this he used interpersonal literacies. Now
fast forward to a game situation. Let's say that the team we are looking at is on
offense. While the players are playing the game, there are assistant coaches in the
press box watching to see how the defense reacts to what the offense does. They
are looking for any keys or tips that could give the offense an advantage. This is
an example of situational literacies. The assistant coaches in the press box will
then communicate what they see to the coach calling the offense. This process
involves using lexis. The coach will then process what the assistant coaches told
him and will look at his play-calling sheet and decide what play to run. The play-
calling sheet is an example of a genre. He will then tell the quarterback what play
to run. The name of the play consists of lexis as well. The quarterback will tell
the team the play and then they will line up. The quarterback will then look at
the defense and see if anything needs to be changed. This is an example of situational literacies. If he decides to "check" (change) the play based on what he sees
in the defense, he will use lexis to do so. The quarterback will then call "hike"
(lexis) and the ball will be snapped and the play will be run with the hopes of
scoring a touchdown, which is the goal on any given play.

CONCLUSION

The world of coaching is more complicated than it may seem to the public eye. ⁤ 43
Whether it is looking at some of the characteristics of a coaching community
or looking at the tasks that coaches partake in, such as reading players and the
game, there are still many characteristics and responsibilities that are unexplored
to those outside of these communities. After looking in depth at some of the
behind-the-scenes factors that go into coaching, I hope to have helped increase
knowledge on the literacy aspects involved in coaching. I hope this helps spark
interest in the connection between literacy and sports. This connection will now
help people have a better sense of empathy with what the coaches are thinking
when they make a specific call on the field or partake in an action off the field,
and hopefully I have brought people closer to being able to answer the common
question asked at any sporting event: "What was that coach thinking?!"

Works Cited

Grant, Anthony M. "The Goal-Focused Coaching Skills Questionnaire: Preliminary Findings."
Social Behavior & Personality: An International Journal 35.6 (2007): 751–60. Print.

Hasbrouck, Jan and Carolyn Denton. "Student-Focused Coaching: A Model for Reading
Coaches." *Reading Teacher* 60.7 (2007): 690–93. Print.

Mirabelli, Tony. "Learning to Serve: The Language and Literacy of Food Service Workers." *What
They Don't Learn in School.* Ed. Jabari Mahiri. New York: Peter Lang, 2004: 143–62. Print.

Short, Sandra E. "Role of the Coach in the Coach-Athlete Relationship." Spec. issue of *Lancet* 366 (2005): S29–S30. Print.

———. "The Relationship Between Efficacy Beliefs and Imagery Use in Coaches." *The Sport Psychologist* 19.4 (2005): 380–94. Print.

Swales, John. "The Concept of Discourse Community." *Genre Analysis: English in Academic and Workplace Settings*. Boston: Cambridge UP, 1990: 21–32. Print.

APPENDIX A: INTERVIEW QUESTIONS FOR COACHES

Interpersonal Literacies

1. How do you tell when a player is ready or not ready to play? Are there specific things that you look for (body language and attitude, etc.) or is it more intuitive?

2. In what ways do you go about motivating your players? Do you prefer a calm or a fiery approach? How did your coaches go about motivating you when you played? Do you feel like you have become an effective motivator?

3. Do you focus more on motivating players during the week or during a pregame speech? When do you think it is more effective? Are there any specific examples that stick out when you made an attempt to motivate a player and it was either very successful or unsuccessful? If you were unsuccessful how did you change your approach?

4. Would you consider your approach to correcting athletes more of positive reinforcement or negative reinforcement? Do you think that players respond better to one method than the other? Is it better to correct mistakes publicly or privately? How do the players react to each method?

Situational Literacies

1. What do you feel are the most important factors to reading and calling a game? Do you use any specific methods to help you mediate reading the game (scripting plays, play-calling sheet with specific situations)?

2. Do you put any of this on your players (system of checks or audibles, plays that are run differently depending on the defense's look)?

3. How much of the outcome of a game do you feel is attributed to pregame coaching preparations (game planning, watching film)?

4. How important are in-game decisions such as halftime adjustments, substitutions, and when to gamble on big plays? Do you go with the overall feel of the game or do you look for specific details when it comes to making a game-time decision?

Questions for Discussion and Journaling

1. Before you began to read, you were asked to consider whether you think foot-ball coaches are a discourse community. After reading Branick's paper, have you changed your opinion in any way? If so, what did he say that got you to think differently?

2. Branick's methods include analyzing the coaches' discourse community using John Swales's six characteristics of a discourse community. How effectively does he conduct this analysis? What, if anything, would you change or expand, and why?

3. Branick claims, "There have been many articles written on the X's and O's . . . of the game . . . however scholars have yet to study a coach's ability to read his players and the game as a form of literacy" (para. 12). Does Branick convince you that these abilities are, in fact, a form of literacy? Explain why or why not.

Applying and Exploring Ideas

1. Brainstorm some groups that you think might be discourse communities but which, like football coaches, might not immediately come to mind as such. Why do you think they wouldn't be immediately understood as discourse communities?

2. Pick one of the groups you listed in question 1 and try to sketch out quickly, with a partner or by yourself, whether they meet Swales's six characteristics of a discourse community as described by Branick.

3. Listing characteristics of a discourse community is only the first step in a project. The next step is identifying a genuine question about some aspect of the discourse community, as Branick does here. What else would you like to explore about the discourse community you identified in question 2?

- -

META MOMENT How does Branick help you see the relevance of your work in this class to parts of your life that you had not thought about as being related to writing and literacy? Does he share any conclusions or insights that you can apply to your own experiences?

- -

Activity Theory:
An Introduction for
the Writing Classroom

DONNA KAIN
ELIZABETH WARDLE

Nkosi Shanga

Framing the Reading

Elizabeth Wardle is one of the authors of *Writing about Writing* as well as the Howe Professor and Director of the Howe Center for Writing Excellence at Miami University. Donna Kain is an associate professor at East Carolina University. Wardle and Kain were Ph.D. candidates together at Iowa State University, where they wrote this piece for their undergraduate students around 2001 or 2002. At the time, they taught writing classes in which they asked students to consider how texts worked in context — who used them, how they got written, what they accomplished or didn't, how people learned to write them. In other words, they were trying to teach students the threshold concept that this chapter emphasizes. Kain and Wardle found that activity theory was often a helpful lens for thinking about writing, but that there was no explanation of activity theory appropriate for undergraduates. So they wrote this for their own students, and they have been using it ever since. In 2005 they published an article together in the journal *Technical Communication Quarterly* describing how they use activity theory with their students; that article won the 2006 NCTE Best Article of the Year in Teaching of Technical and Scientific Communication.

Activity theory is the third "lens" that this chapter shares with you to help you analyze how texts, language, and discourse help mediate the activities and meaning that people try to create together in groups. Activity theory, as you will learn in the following reading, "was originally a psychological theory that sees all aspects of activity as shaped by people's social interactions with each other and the tools [including writing and language] that they use" (para. 1 of the reading). Activity theory gives you a lens for looking at an object or event and understanding it in new ways, just as all theories do. Scholars in many different fields, as well as workplace consultants, use the lens of activity theory to look at groups of people doing work together, which they call **activity systems**, and consider what their common motives are and how they try to achieve those common motives. When people are unable to achieve their common motives, activity theory provides a method for examining where the breakdowns might have happened. Activity theory takes into account not only what is happening now, but also the histories that impact what is happening now. In other words, activity theory helps you consider what a particular group (such as people creating and using the food bank we mentioned in the chapter introduction) is trying to accomplish, how it has gone about trying to accomplish that work in the past, and how it is doing so now. In looking at the food bank's activities, the lens of activity theory encourages us to look at the rules or conventions adhered to by the group, how the work (the labor) is divided up within the group, and the tools (including texts and language) that help (or impede) the group in working toward their shared motives.

Activity theory is a useful lens because it acknowledges the importance of the histories, including literacy histories that you studied in Chapter 2, that individuals bring with them when they act as part of an activity system. It is also useful because it helps you take a close look at the actual texts that you or others are writing, reading, and using and ask key questions: How do these work? What are they doing? Who created them? Why are they like this? Activity theory can give you a perspective on texts and groups of people using texts that can assist you in your school, professional, and extracurricular literate lives. You'll learn even more about how to analyze texts in the next chapter on rhetoric. Victoria Marro's student essay in this chapter (p. 426) uses activity theory to look at the genres of her sorority in new ways.

Both Kain and Wardle use activity theory in their own research. In another article in this chapter ("Identity, Authority, and Learning to Write in New Workplaces," p. 407) you will see how Wardle used activity theory to understand the difficulties that a new employee experienced when writing and working. In her current work, she uses activity theory to help explain how and why students do or do not learn and transfer writing-related knowledge learned in school settings. Donna Kain uses activity theory to further her understanding of emergency communication and risk management (particularly related to hurricanes), as well as accommodations for people with disabilities.

Getting Ready to Read

Before you read, do at least one of the following activities:

- List a few groups (formal or informal) in which you participate, and ask yourself what your shared common goals are.

- Pick one of those groups and make a quick list of all of the texts you read, write, or use in order to try to achieve the goals of that group.

- Pick one of those texts, and make a quick list of all of the people who have a hand in or an influence on how it is written and used.

(If you can do the above, you are already on your way to being able to conduct an activity analysis!)

As you read, consider the following questions:

- Are there unfamiliar terms here that you need to spend a little more time thinking about? Are there familiar terms that seem to be used in new or unfamiliar ways? If so, make a list of these terms and try to define them for yourself before your next class.

- Keep in mind the groups you listed before you started reading, and use them to help you imagine examples as Kain and Wardle explain the components of an activity system.

PEOPLE MEET SOCIAL NEEDS by working and learning together over 1
time to achieve particular goals or to act on particular motives. To facilitate their activities, people also develop and use tools. These tools include not only things like hammers or computers, but also language—probably the most complex tool of all. As people refine their tools and add new ones to solve problems more effectively, the activities they perform using those tools can change—and vice versa: as their activities change, people use their tools differently and modify their tools to meet their changing needs. Activity theory, which has its roots in Russia in the early 20th century, was originally a psychological theory that sees all aspects of activity as shaped over time by people's social interactions with each other and the tools they use.

As a society, we differentiate types of activities by the specific knowledge, 2
tools, and repertoires of tasks that people use to achieve particular outcomes. For instance, we recognize the practice of medicine by its goal of meeting people's health-care needs; its participants, including doctors, nurses, and patients; its body of knowledge about human physiology, disease, and treatment options; and its tools, for instance medicines and surgical instruments. We recognize the university by its goal of facilitating learning, its participants, including teachers, students, and administrators; and its tools, including textbooks and chalkboards.

Activity theory gives us a helpful lens for understanding how people in 3
different communities carry out their activities. For those of us interested in rhetorical theory, the most helpful aspect of activity theory is the way it helps us see more fully all the aspects of a situation and community that influence how people use the tools of language and genre. While it is easy enough to say that "context" influences how people write, saying this does not particularly help us know how to write differently when we find ourselves in a new situation. Activity theory provides us with very specific aspects of context to look at as we consider the various factors that influence and change the tool of writing.

WHAT ARE ACTIVITY SYSTEMS?

The most basic activity theory lens, or unit of analysis, is the *activity system,* 4 defined as a group of people who share a common object and motive over time, as well as the wide range of tools they use together to act on that object and realize that motive. David Russell (1997) describes an activity system as "any ongoing, object-directed, historically conditioned, dialectically structured, tool-mediated human interaction" (p. 510). That's a mouthful to be sure; let's look a bit more closely at what Russell means:

> *Activity theory provides us with very specific aspects of context to look at as we consider the various factors that influence and change the tool of writing.*

- **Ongoing.**   The study of activity systems is concerned with looking at how systems function over time. For instance, the university is an activity system of long duration that began in the past and will continue into the future. We can trace the university's activity over time and consider how it might evolve in the future.

- **Object-directed.**   The types of activities that activity theory is concerned with are directed toward specific goals. Continuing with the example of the university, the object of its activity is learning, which is accomplished through instruction and research.

- **Historically conditioned.**   Activity systems come into being because of practices that have a history. At any point that we begin to study how a system works, we need to consider how it came to function in a particular way. For instance, ways that the university carries out its activities developed over time. Many things we do today can be explained by the history of the university's mission as well as the history of western educational institutions.

- **Dialectically structured.**   The term "dialectic" describes a type of relationship in which aspects of a process, transaction, or system are mutually dependent. When one aspect changes, other aspects change in response. Some of these changes we can anticipate; others we can't. For example, when the university began to use computers as a tool in education, the ways that teachers, researchers, and students accomplished tasks related to the activity of learning began to change in response.

- **Tool-mediated.**   People use many types of tools to accomplish activities. These may be physical objects, such as computers, or systems of symbols, such as mathematics. At the university, we use textbooks, syllabi, lab equipment, computers, and many other tools to accomplish our goal of learning. The types of tools we use mediate, or shape, the ways we engage in activity and the ways we think about activity. For example, if we think about the course syllabus as a tool, we might say that it organizes the work in the classroom for both the instructor and the students, which affects how we participate in learning activities.

- **Human interaction.**   Studies of activity systems are concerned with more than the separate actions of individuals. Activity theory is concerned with how people work together, using tools, toward outcomes. In the university, teachers, students, researchers, administrators, and staff interact with each other and with tools to achieve the outcomes of learning.

Activity systems are also constrained by divisions of labor and by rules. In the   5 university, for instance, the labor is divided among the participants—students are responsible for completing assignments; instructors are responsible for grading assignments; administrators are responsible for making sure grades appear on students' transcripts. In the university, we also operate with a set of rules for participating in classroom and laboratory learning. The rules in many respects are our mutual agreement about how the activity will be carried out so we can all progress toward the outcome of learning.

One way that activity theory helps you more fully understand the "context" of a   6 community and its tools is by providing a diagram outlining the important elements and their relationships. Figure 1 shows the conventions activity theory researchers use to present what they view as the critical components of every activity system. The "nodes" in the system are the points on the triangle—think of these as the specific aspects of a "context" that activity theory can help you consider more fully. The arrows indicate the reciprocal relationships among these various aspects. The labels we've provided describe some of the components of each node in the system.

HOW ARE PARTS OF AN ACTIVITY SYSTEM RELATED?

The **Subject(s)** of an activity system is the person or people who are directly   7 participating in the activity you want to study. The subject provides a point of view for studying the activity. The **Motives** direct the subject's activities. Motives include the **Object** of the activity, which is fairly immediate, and the **Outcome**, which is more removed and ongoing. The **Subject(s)** use **Tools** to accomplish their **Object(ives)** and achieve their intended **Outcomes.** They are motivated to use these tools because they want to accomplish something and the tools will help them do so. The **Tools** that mediate the activity system include both physical tools such as computers, texts, and other artifacts, as well as non-physical tools such as language (written and oral) and skills. Activity theorists also refer to this category as "artifacts." When people first learn to use a particular tool, they use it on the level of conscious *action;* they must think about how to use the tool and what they want it to accomplish. Once they have used the tool to perform a particular action over a period of time, the use of that tool becomes *operationalized,* largely uncon-scious. Tool use only moves back to the realm of conscious action if something goes wrong or if the user is presented with a new action to perform with that tool.

The terms at the base of the triangle, **Rules, Community,** and **Division of** 8 **Labor,** make up what Engeström (1999) refers to as the "social basis" of the activity system. The social basis situates the activity in a broader context that allows us to account for the influences that shape the activity.

The **Community** is the larger group which the subject is a part of and from 9 which participants "take their cues." The community's interests shape the activity. Community members divide up the work needed to accomplish their object(ives). The **Division of Labor** describes how tasks are distributed within the activity sys-tem. People might disagree about how labor should be divided or how valuable various positions within that division are, causing conflicts within the activity sys-tem. **Rules** are one way of attempting to manage or minimize these conflicts within activity systems. Rules are defined not only as formal and explicit dos and don'ts, but also as norms, conventions, and values. "Rules shape the interactions of subject and tools with the object" (Russell, "Looking"). These rules understandably change as other aspects of the system change—or as the rules are questioned or resisted—but the rules allow the system to be stabilized-for-now in the face of internal conflicts. These rules affect how people use tools. Of most interest to you will be the ways in which the rules affect how people use the tool of written language.

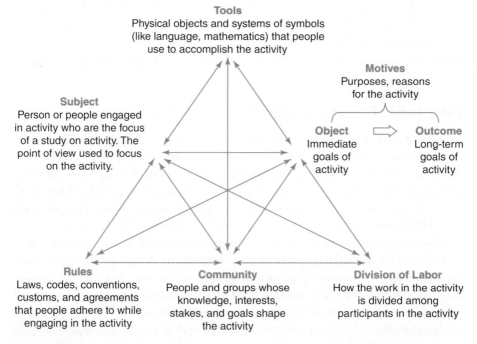

Figure 1 Activity System

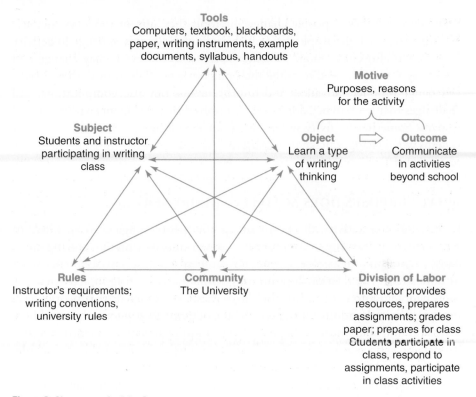

Figure 2 Class as an Activity System

To provide an example that we're familiar with, Figure 2 depicts the class as 10 an activity system.

HOW DO ACTIVITY SYSTEMS CHANGE?

Activity systems consist of the interactions among all of the factors that come to 11 bear on an activity at a given point in time. Cole and Engeström (1993; see also Engeström 1999) suggest that the relationship among the factors in an activity system is a "distribution of cognition," or a sharing of knowledge and work, across all the elements in the system. In this way, activity systems can be thought of as communal.

But activity systems are also very dynamic and, as Russell points out, "best 12 viewed as complex formations" (1997 p. 9). Change is the quality that makes activity systems—and really all human interactions—dynamic. As people participating in activity systems learn, and as new people join the activity, they refine their tools and create new ones. Or one activity system may be influenced by developments in other activity systems. For instance tools developed by computer science may be adopted in other systems, for instance the university or the health care system. As people change the tools they use, or the ways they use existing tools, changes ripple through their activity systems. Change in activity systems can also come about for other reasons. Social needs may change and activity systems may need to refine their outcomes or goals to meet those needs.

Change produces advances and improvements, but also complications and 13 challenges that need to be addressed and resolved by participants within activity systems. Sometimes activity systems are even abandoned or absorbed into other systems when changes make them obsolete (consider for example the fate of the pony express).

WHAT PURPOSES DOES ACTIVITY THEORY SERVE?

Researchers use activity theory to study how people engage in all kinds of 14 activities from learning at a university, to working in a manufacturing company, to shopping in a grocery store. Researchers who use activity theory want to understand the relationships among people participating in activities, the tools people use to accomplish their activities, and the goals that people have for the activity. In addition, researchers use activity theory to understand how historical and social forces shape the way people participate in activities and how change affects activities. Three important goals of activity theory include:

- Accounting for aspects of a system to better understand the nature of activity.
- Analyzing how the parts of a system work together to better anticipate participants' needs and goals.
- Isolating problems to develop solutions.

HOW CAN YOU USE ACTIVITY THEORY TO ANALYZE TEXTS?

You can use the basic tenets of activity theory and the activity theory triangle 15 to help you better understand not only how texts function but also why texts used within a particular system of activity contain certain content and specific conventions, such as formatting, style, and organization. For example, if you are in a business communication course, you may be interested in learning how grant proposals are constructed in your field. You may want to ask, "What are grant proposals like in non-profit social service organizations? What kinds of information do they include? How are they formatted?" If you were performing a rhetorical analysis, you could look at a proposal and name its textual features—length, content, layout, type of language used—and name the rhetorical situation as far as you were able to understand it from looking at the document: writer, audience, purpose. While this sort of analysis is quite useful, there are many things it cannot tell you. For example, it cannot tell you *why* the document is a particular length, *why* it contains certain types of content and not others. A rhetorical analysis also doesn't help you understand who does what tasks pertaining to the document: does only one person write it? Do several people contribute information? Why do certain people become involved in writing the proposal and not others? A rhetorical analysis also won't remind you that the proposal genre has likely changed within a specific social service organization—or suggest that you explore whether the features of the proposal genre as embodied in the text you are examining are uncontested.

So how do you begin your activity theory analysis? First, consider the activity theory triangle (we've included a worksheet-type triangle [p. 404] for you to work with). Of the aspects on the triangle where you could begin your analysis, you (as a rhetorician) will likely begin with specific texts used within a specific activity system; for example, you might gather all the examples of proposals you can find written by people at a particular company or working within a particular field. These texts, then, are tools for achieving goals. At this point, using the triangle, a number of questions should present themselves to you: 16

- What is the immediate object(ive) of using this tool? Do all the members of the community seem to agree on this/these objects?

- What is the long-term purpose (outcome) of using this tool and others like it?

- Why are the people here doing what they are doing? What is motivating them to take the time to use this tool and achieve their short-term object(ives) and long-term outcomes?

- Which people (subjects) are directly involved in using this tool?

- What world does this tool function for? Who constitutes the community that uses and benefits from the use of this tool? Are the readers part of this community or are they participants in a different (but obviously related) activity system?

- If the readers of the text (the tool) are not part of the community/activity system, does this cause conflict or misunderstanding? Do the readers have different expectations about the object(ives) of the tool than the writers do?

- Who is responsible for what part of this tool? How is the work pertaining to this tool divided up? Are there conflicts about how the work is divided up?

- What seem to be the rules, guidelines, conventions (spoken and unspoken, formal and informal) governing the use of this tool? Does everyone in the community seem to have the same idea about what these rules are? What happens when people break any of these rules?

Activity System Worksheet

Use this worksheet to help you begin thinking about the elements of the activity system you are considering and their relationship.

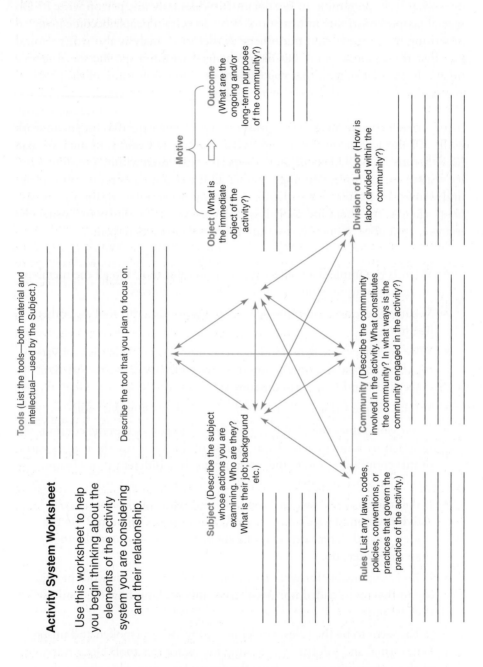

Tools (List the tools—both material and intellectual—used by the Subject.)

Describe the tool that you plan to focus on.

Subject (Describe the subject whose actions you are examining. Who are they? What is their job; background etc.)

Object (What is the immediate object of the activity?)

Motive

Outcome (What are the ongoing and/or long-term purposes of the community?)

Rules (List any laws, codes, policies, conventions, or practices that govern the practice of the activity.)

Community (Describe the community involved in the activity. What constitutes the community? In what ways is the community engaged in the activity?)

Division of Labor (How is labor divided within the community?)

Clearly, you won't be able to answer all these questions (and others that occur 17 to you) just by looking at the text. You are going to need to talk with people who use the tool of proposals and possibly even watch them at work. Often, people can't tell you what the rules governing tool use are in their community because they are only aware of them subconsciously. Remember that when a person uses a tool for a long time, it becomes operationalized, unconscious—what is often called "tacit knowledge." So in order for you to begin to see how and why the tool gets used, you may have to do some watching and guessing, in addition to asking.

As you fill in the triangle, remember that some things about activity theory 18 aren't obviously present on the triangle: remember, for example, that actions are ongoing—they have occurred in the past and will likely continue in some form in the future. Remember that actions are historically conditioned and dialectically structured—texts look the way they do because past events have shaped them and they will continue to change as the other aspects of the activity system change. So, as you write your activity theory analysis, you may also want to see what you can find out about your document's history and see if you can identify aspects of the activity system that could be sources of conflict. Sources of conflict pertaining to the creation or use of the document will likely cause the documents to change again.

When you are finished with your activity theory analysis, you should have a 19 better understanding not only of what particular tools (in this case texts, genres, language) look like, but also why they look that way, what they are being used to accomplish, who uses them, how they have changed over time, and how they might continue to change in the future. Keep in mind, however, that an outsider—someone who is not a part of a particular activity system—can never fully grasp the hows and whys of that system. Some things will remain a mystery to you; some things, in fact, even remain a mystery to insiders. Perhaps you've heard people say, "I don't know why we do it that way, we just do." However, if you are constantly asking the questions activity theory presents to you, you will be far less likely to say something like this. You will be more likely to recognize rules (whether stated or not) and to understand why you are doing something. In this way, you will become a much savvier communicator.

Works Cited

Cole, M., & Engeström, Y. (1993). A cultural-historical approach to distributed cognition. In G. Salomon (Ed.), Distributed cognitions: Psychological and educational considerations (pp. 1–46), Cambridge, UK: Cambridge University Press.

Engeström, Y. (1999). "Activity theory and individual and social transformation." In *Perspectives on Activity Theory.* Eds. Yrjö Engstrom, Reijo Miettinen, and Raija-Leena Punämaki. New York: Cambridge UP.

Russell, D. (1997). "Rethinking genre in school and society: An activity theory analysis." *Written Communication, 14(4),* 504–554.

Russell, D. (2002). Looking beyond the interface: Activity theory and distributed learning. In *Distributed learning: Social and cultural approaches to practice.* Eds. Mary R. Lea and Kathy Nicoll. London, UK: Routledge Falmer, pp. 64–83.

- -

Questions for Discussion and Journaling

1. Explain in your own words what an *activity system* is, and give three examples of activity systems with which you are familiar. For each of these systems, explain what its common motives and goals are.

2. Pick one of the activity systems you chose in response to question 1, and explain how its activities are "ongoing," "object-directed," and "historically conditioned" (para. 4).

3. Focus on that same activity system, and make a list of all of the tools that are used to help the participants in the system achieve their common goals. Remember that tools can be physical objects or symbol systems (para. 4).

4. Can you think of times when one of these tools you listed in response to question 3 was not effective in helping the group achieve its goals? What happened? Did the group change the tool or the way they use the tool?

5. What are some ways that activity theory relates to the threshold concept emphasized in this chapter that the texts and language that discourse communities create mediate meaningful activities?

Applying and Exploring Ideas

1. Work with a partner to choose an activity system that interests you and to which you have access. Using the activity triangle worksheet (p. 404), and the questions in paragraph 16 of the reading, try to discern the object, purpose, tools, community, division of labor, and rules for this activity system. In particular, focus on the textual tools that this group uses in order to try to accomplish its common purposes. In order to do this task, you will need to speak to members of the activity system and collect some examples of the texts (tools) the activity system participants use.

2. Present your activity triangle worksheet to the class, and explain what this analysis has helped you understand differently about writing and how texts are used to accomplish work (mediate meaningful activity and make meaning).

- -

META MOMENT   How can what you learned from this article help you the next time you interact in a new activity system?

- -

Identity, Authority, and Learning to Write in New Workplaces

ELIZABETH WARDLE

Nkosi Shanga

Framing the Reading

Elizabeth Wardle is the Howe Professor and Director of the Howe Center for Writing Excellence at Miami University. She was finishing her Ph.D. at about the time that Ann M. Johns was retiring; you can thus think of her work as growing from the work of the scholars you have read so far. She is interested in how people learn to write, not as children but as adults moving among different discourse communities or activity systems. The following article is one that she researched as a Ph.D. student. While in graduate school, Wardle was asked to use language that did not feel "right" or "natural" to her. She struggled to find the right **register** and **lexis** for her writing, and writing in "academic" ways seemed to stifle her creative voice. You can see, then, why she would be interested in researching someone else who was struggling to enculturate in a new activity system.

This article is the result of that study. It describes a new employee, fresh out of college, trying to communicate with a new workplace community and failing — miserably. The reasons he failed included a lack of authority in the new activity system, a specific form of rebellion against the values of that activity system that Wardle calls *non-participation*, and a sense of identity that conflicts with the new activity system. Wardle applies the frame of activity theory explained in the previous reading, "Activity Theory: An Introduction for the Writing Classroom." If you haven't read that piece, you might find this reading easier if you went back and skimmed it first.

Like Mirabelli, McCarthy, and Branick in this chapter, Wardle is applying theory to a common situation in order to help readers better understand how people use texts and discourse to make meaning together, and where and why they sometimes run into trouble trying to do that. In particular, Wardle uses the frame provided by activity theory to help explain the problems that the new employee, Alan, had when he began a new job.

Wardle, Elizabeth. "Identity, Authority, and Learning to Write in New Workplaces." *Enculturation*, vol. 5, no. 2, 2004, www.enculturation.net/5_2/wardle.html.

least one of the following activities:

er your time in college and write a few paragraphs about whether
ur identity has been changed by your college experiences to date, and, if it
has, *how* it has changed. How can you explain the changes (or lack of change)?

- Make a list of terms or phrases you're using now that you weren't at the beginning of your college experience. Do you associate any of this new language with participation in new groups (discourse communities or activity systems)?

As you read, consider the following questions:

- How does Wardle describe being a "newcomer" to an activity system? Is there anything familiar about her description that you recognize from your own experience?

- How is the idea of an *activity system* different from *Discourse* and *discourse communities*, as discussed in the previous readings?

DESPITE THE MEDIA'S CONTINUED representation of communication as "utilitarian and objective" (Bolin), and the acceptance of this view by much of the public and even by many academics, research in rhetoric and composition over the past twenty years has moved toward a much more complex view of communication. Of particular interest to professional communication specialists is research suggesting that learning to write in and for new situations and workplaces is complex in ways that go far beyond texts and cognitive abilities.

> *Learning to write in and for new situations and workplaces is complex in ways that go far beyond texts and cognitive abilities.*

This research posits that for workers to be successfully enculturated into new communities of practice[1] (Lave and Wenger) or activity systems (Engeström; Russell, "Rethinking" and "Activity Theory"), including learning to write in ways that are appropriate to those new communities, neophytes must learn and conform to the conventions, codes, and genres of those communities (Bazerman; Berkenkotter, Huckin, and Ackerman; Berkenkotter and Huckin; Bizzell). However, *when and how much* each neophyte must conform largely depends on how much authority and cultural capital[2] the neophyte possesses or cultivates to accomplish work effectively. Additionally, issues of identity and values are important factors in neophytes' abilities and willingness to learn to write in and for new workplaces, as they must choose between ways of thinking and writing with which they are comfortable and new ways that seem foreign or at odds with their identities and values (Doheny-Farina; Doheny-Farina and Odell). Researchers who examine issues of identity and authority as important aspects of communicating in workplace settings find that workers' identities are bound up in myriad ways with the genres they are asked to appropriate (Dias et al.; Dias and Paré; Paré). According to Anis Bawarshi, "a certain genre replaces or . . . adds to the range of possible selves that writers have available to them" (105).

As composition widens its focus beyond academic writing, it is increasingly 2 important to consider what it means to write in the workplace. Not only will such knowledge help us prepare students for the writing beyond the classroom, but, as Bolin points out, those of us working in rhetoric and composition must continue to respond to complaints by the media and general public that we have not fulfilled our responsibilities and "polished" students' language use so that they can convey information "clearly." We can respond to these complaints more effectively when we better understand the ways in which writing is bound up with issues of identity and authority. While we recognize the importance of identity and authority issues in the process of enculturating new workers, we do not always fully understand how these issues influence their writing.

Here I first outline theories of identity and authority that are useful in under- 3 standing how newcomers learn to write in and for new situations. The socio-historic theoretical perspective I offer draws on research from two groups: compositionists who focus on cultural-historical activity theory[3] (Russell, "Rethinking" and "Activity Theory"; Prior; Dias et al.) and sociologists who study apprenticeship (Lave and Wenger; Wenger). Combined, these lines of research expand genre theory (Bawarshi; Russell, "Rethinking") and describe the complexities of learning to write, both in school and the workplace (Dias et al.; Dias and Paré; Prior). The socio-historic view usefully illuminates the construction of subject positions and subjectivities specifically within institutions and disciplines.

Second, I illustrate some of the difficulties inherent in writing and identity 4 formation by telling the story of one new worker who struggled with written conventions and codes in his new workplace largely because of issues of identity and authority: how he saw himself versus how other members of this workplace community saw him. Most importantly, I argue that rather than assisting in the new worker's enculturation, members of the community expected a type of servitude: they perceived him not as a community member but as a tool, an identity that he fought strongly against.

IDENTITY

To tease out relationships between identity and writing in the workplace, we 5 need theories that consider the workplace as a legitimate and important influence on subject formation. Socio-historic theories provide one such perspective and describe identity construction within institutions. Like other postmodern theories, socio-historic theories see identity—the "subject"—as a complex "construction of the various signifying practices . . . formed by the various discourses, sign systems, that surround her" (Berlin 18). However, socio-historic theories view the subject as not only *constructed* by signifying practices but also as *constructing* signifying practices: "writers' desires are [not] completely determined, as evidenced by the fact that textual instantiations of a genre are rarely if ever exactly the same" (Bawarshi 91). Socio-historic theories also provide specific tools for analyzing the "levers" within institutions, allowing for a detailed examination of power and the formation of subject positions. Activity theory (Cole; Cole and Engeström; Cole and Scribner; Engeström; Russell, "Rethinking" and "Activity Theory"), for example, which focuses on the relationships among shared activities within communities and individual participants' sometimes competing understandings of motives, conventions, and divisions of labor for carrying out the activities, provides a framework for understanding the interactions of individuals, groups, and texts that enables researchers to illustrate the complex interactions among various aspects of an activity system (see Figure 1).

Activity theorists such as David Russell have also argued the importance of 6 the relationship between writing and identity: as we encounter genres mediating new activity systems, we must determine whether we can and/or must appropriate those genres, thus expanding our involvement within those systems. We must also consider whether expanding involvement in one system forces us away from other activity systems we value—away from "activity systems of family, neighborhood, and friends that construct ethnic, racial, gender, and class identit(ies)" ("Rethinking" 532). Writers can sometimes "challenge the

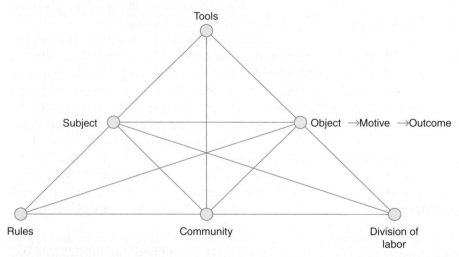

Figure 1 Activity System Triangle (*Based on Engeström: Learning by Expanding*)

genre positions and relations available to them," thus changing genres rather than choosing between the genres and their various activity systems (Bawarshi 97). However, socio-historic theories do not view such resistance as the result of self-will or "inherent forces within each human being that love liberty, seek to enhance their own powers or capacities, or strive for emancipation" (Rose 35), but rather suggest that "resistance arises from the contradictions individuals experience in their multiple subject positions" (Bawarshi 100). As writers shape and change genres, the power of those genres also shapes and enables writers' identities (Bawarshi 97).

Sociologist Etienne Wenger's theory of communities of practice (shaped, ini-   7
tially, with Jean Lave) is particularly useful for describing workplace enculturation as it is affected by and as it affects written practices. Wenger specifically
focuses on matters of identity within *workplace* groups and activities, describing
identity as a "negotiated experience . . . a layering of events of participation and
reification by which our experience and its social interpretation inform each
other" (149). According to Wenger, "layers build upon each other to produce
our identity as a very complex interweaving of participative experience and rei-
ficative projections" (151). To "find their own unique identities" within new
organizations (Wenger 156), newcomers must choose levels and types of engagement; they must find modes of belonging. Wenger describes three interrelated
modes of belonging: engagement, imagination, and alignment.

- *Engagement* entails defining a "common enterprise" that newcomers and
  old-timers pursue together to develop "interpersonal relationships" and
  "a sense of interacting trajectories that shape identities in relation to one
  another" (184). While engagement can be positive, "a lack of mutuality
  in the course of engagement creates relations of marginality that can
  reach deeply into [newcomers'] identities" (193).

- *Imagination,* "a process of expanding . . . self by transcending . . . time
  and space and creating new images of the world and [self]" (176),
  entails newcomers "locating [their] engagement in a broader system . . .
  defining a trajectory that connects what [they] are doing to an extended
  identity . . . [and] assuming the meaning of foreign artifacts and actions"
  (185). While imagination can lead to a positive mode of belonging, it
  can also "be disconnected and ineffective . . . it can be so removed from
  any lived form of membership that it detaches [newcomers'] identit[ies]
  and leaves [them] in a state of uprootedness." Newcomers can lose "touch
  with the sense of social efficacy by which [their] experience of the world
  can be interpreted as competence" (178).

- *Alignment* entails "negotiating perspectives, finding common ground . . .
  defining broad visions and aspirations . . . [and] walking boundaries . . .

411

reconciling diverging perspectives" (186–87). Alignment "requires shareable artifacts/boundary objects able to create fixed points around which to coordinate activities. It can also require the creation and adoption of broader discourses that help reify the enterprise and by which local actions can be interpreted as fitting within a broader framework" (187). However, alignment "can be a violation of [a person's] sense of self that crushes [their] identity" (181).

To fully participate, according to Wenger, new workers must find ways to 8 engage in the work that other community members do, including the writing they do; newcomers must be able to imagine their own work — and writing — as being an important part of a larger enterprise. And they must be comfortable that the larger enterprise and its smaller components — down to the writing conventions of that community — are compatible with the identities they envision for themselves. Joining new workplace communities, then, is not simply a matter of learning new skills but also of fielding new calls for identity construction. This understanding of identity suggests that people *enact* and *negotiate* identities in the world over time: "Identity is dynamic (Hecht, 1993), and it is something that is presented and re-presented, constructed and reconstructed in interaction (including written communication)" (Rubin 9).

At times, however, participation in new communities requires accepting for 9 oneself identities that are at odds with the values of other communities to which one belongs (Lave and Wenger; Russell, "Rethinking"). One way newcomers reconcile the competing demands of various communities is to choose to participate in some aspects of a new community and not others. Such choices are a source of power in that "power derives from belonging as well as from exercising control over what we belong to" (Wenger 207). In addition, choices about participation impact newcomers' emerging identities within communities of practice. For example, the choice of non-participation can lead to marginalization within the workplace (Wenger 167). Identity formation in any new community, then, is a negotiation in which newcomers have some measure of "control over the meanings in which [they] are invested" and can "assert [their] identities as productive of meaning" (Wenger 188, 208) — even if they do so by refusing to participate in some workplace activities.

Achieving enculturation in workplace communities requires neophytes to 10 engage in new practices — including new *written* practices. Some new written practices may be opposed to newcomers' values and ethics; others may simply be foreign to them; still others may ask them to give up some measure of authority to which they believe they are entitled. The resultant struggles will often be visible in their written practices. If new workers fail to write in ways that a workplace community of practice recognizes as effective and appropriate, the reasons may be related to identity rather than ability: "Stylistic options 'leak' clues about writers' social identities. Rhetorical choices help writers construct the social identities they wish to project in given writing episodes" (Rubin 4). Thus, failing to write in ways communities establish as appropriate can be a form of resistance that "does not arise from ignorance of standard forms [but rather] entails considerable language awareness" (Rubin 7). On the other hand, new workers may not be consciously aware that their writing choices are matters of identification: "marking social identity in writing is . . . oftentimes quite below the focal awareness of the writer" (8). Because each individual "is heterogeneously made up of various competing discourses, conflicted and contradictory scripts . . . our consciousness [is] anything but unified" (Berlin 18).

AUTHORITY

As Wenger's theory implies, authority (like identity) is continually negotiated 11 within communities of practice. Authority is bestowed by institutions, can be just as easily withdrawn by those same institutions or its members, and must be maintained through appropriate expressions of authority (Bourdieu). Bruce Lincoln argues that authority is best understood in relational terms "as the effect of a posited, perceived, or institutionally ascribed asymmetry between speaker and audience that permits certain speakers to command not just the attention but the confidence, respect, and trust of their audience, or . . . to make audiences act *as if* this were so" (4). When speakers possess authority, exercising that authority "need not involve argumentation and may rest on the naked assertion that the identity of the speaker warrants acceptance of the speech" (5). Those listening accept the speaker's pronouncement because the speaker *is who she is.* At any given time, however, faith in a speaker's authority can be suspended (either momentarily or forever) if "an explanation is requested . . ." because "the relation of trust and acceptance characteristic of authority is suspended, at least temporarily, in that moment" (6). Authority, then, is an intangible quality granted to persons through institutions, which renders their pronouncements as accepted by those in that institution's communities of practice, but which must be maintained through individuals' speech and actions.

Conversely, a person can understand clearly how to speak in ways that are 12 acceptable in particular circumstances, but if not endowed with some recognized institutional authority, all the relevant and appropriate words in the world will not command it: "authority comes to language from outside. . . . Language at most represents this authority, manifests and symbolizes it" (Bourdieu 109). Bourdieu, while not specifically explaining enculturation, suggests that authority may be a kind of "social magic," dependent upon the "social position of the speaker," and reinforced by her ability to appropriately adjust her speech acts:

> Most of the conditions that have to be fulfilled in order for a performative utterance to succeed come down to the question of the appropriateness

> of the speaker—or, better still, his social function—and of the discourse
> he utters . . . it must be uttered by the person legitimately licensed to so
> do . . . it must be uttered in a legitimate situation . . . in front of legitimate
> receivers . . . [and] it must be enunciated according to the legitimate forms
> (syntactic, phonetic, etc.). (Bourdieu 111–12)

Thus, if the neophyte is granted some measure of authority by an institu-   13
tion but does not quickly learn the appropriate speech conventions of her new
community of practice, she may soon lose the authority with which she began.
While newcomers to a community normally experience a "grace period" for
adopting community practices, it does not last forever and soon the neophyte
must express her authority in her new community appropriately: "[L]earning to
become a legitimate participant in a community involves learning how to talk
(and be silent) in the manner of full participants" (Lave and Wenger 105).

If we understand writing as one tool among many through which knowledge,   14
identity, and authority are continually negotiated, then we must view learning
to write in new ways as a complex and often messy network of tool-mediated
human relationships best explored in terms of the social and cultural practices
that people bring to their shared uses of tools. If we accept these assumptions,
we find ourselves faced with several questions: What happens when new workers
find that to "get along" in a new workplace they must accept basic assumptions
about what is valuable and appropriate that are contrary to their own—or that,
in fact, degrade them to the status of an object or tool? What happens when a
new worker's assumptions are frequently made obvious to the community, and
those assumptions fly in the face of accepted ways of doing things?

LEARNING TO WRITE IN A NEW WORKPLACE: ALAN'S STORY

My story of "Alan"—a computer support specialist who did not learn/choose   15
to write in ways his humanities department colleagues (primarily professors
and graduate students) found appropriate and legitimate—illustrates answers
to some of the questions about identity and authority as they intersect with
writing in the workplace. For seven months, I observed and interviewed Alan,
a new computer specialist in a humanities department at a large Midwestern
university. I also collected 140 email messages he wrote and many others that
were written to him and spent time in public computer labs listening as people
discussed their computer problems with Alan. Finally, near the end of the study,
I conducted a written survey with all members of the humanities department
regarding their use of computers and technology and their awareness of various
initiatives Alan had discussed with them via email.

Alan and the other members of the humanities department were constantly   16
at cross purposes—he did not write in ways the community members saw as
appropriate, and he did not view their conventions as ones he should adopt,

given his position in the community. Most importantly, the community of practice did not appear to view him as a fledgling member but rather as an object—a tool enabling them to get work done. His discursive choices can be viewed as an attempt to reject the identity of tool and to appropriate authority for himself. Thus, Alan's story serves to illustrate some of the complexities associated with learning to write in new workplaces.

Who Is Alan and What Is His Place in the Humanities Department?

Alan was a 23-year-old white male who received a B.A. in art and design from a   17
large Midwestern university. He became interested in computers as an undergraduate and as his interest in computers grew, he performed two computer-related work-study jobs on campus. He decided he liked working with computers and looked for a computer job when he graduated. Alan's first professional position was as computer support specialist responsible for several thousand "users" in various locations at the same university from which he graduated. He was unhappy in this position, primarily because he felt his supervisor did not give him enough responsibility, instead assigning the most difficult tasks to student workers who had been in the department for a long time. He left this job for another in an academic humanities department within the same university, again as a computer support specialist.

In the academic department, Alan was the sole computer support special-   18
ist, surrounded by faculty members with varying computer abilities. While no one else performed a job similar to his, the department included other support staff—all women, primarily administrative assistants—and Alan supervised one student worker several hours per week. Alan's supervisor, the department chair (a white male in his early fifties with a Ph.D. and numerous publications and awards), initially left most computer-related decisions to Alan, though the chair's collaborative administrative style made the division of labor unclear to newcomers. A Computer Resources Committee also interacted regularly with Alan, but whether they had authority over him was unclear. The mentoring he received was fairly hands-off, resembling what Lave and Wenger call "benign community neglect" (93), a situation that left Alan to find his own way, which he saw as a vote of confidence.

What Was Alan's View of Himself and His Authority?

Alan's sense of what it meant to fill a support staff position was very different   19
from the faculty's sense. He left his previous position because it had not allowed him much responsibility, his supervisors "relied on students' work more than" his, and he felt he "was getting no respect." This previous experience strongly informed his understanding of his current job. Because Alan had some measure of institutional authority by way of the cultural capital associated with technical

knowledge, Alan did not initially have to prove himself knowledgeable or competent in the ways many new workers do. He was immediately ascribed authority and respect due to his assumed technical expertise in a place where such expertise was rare. When I asked Alan to name and describe his position he replied: "I am basically a systems administrator, which means I am God here. Anywhere in this department. Except for with the department chair." This continued to be Alan's attitude during his tenure in the department. He often indicated that there was no one "above him" but the department chair. During his fourth week in the position, Alan told me he "couldn't believe how much authority" he had, "how high up in the computer world responsibility-wise" he was. He stressed that his title put "only one other person above" him in the university or the department.

Alan's sense of his level of authority was evident in the way he talked about the faculty members in the department. He described the faculty members as "just users; nobodies [who] use the computers I set up." He indicated they were beneath him: "I put myself down on their level." To Alan, the faculty were simply "users" of his tools. He did not seem to understand—or care about—the faculty members' work or how his tools enabled them to do that work. His focus was on what *he* did: making machines work. His comments illustrate his attempt to find a mode of belonging through imagination; unfortunately, he imagined an identity for himself fairly removed from the reality of the situation. 20

In reality, he was hired in a support staff position, as a "tool" to fix things the faculty needed. The faculty clearly viewed Alan as support personnel. They were happiest when things worked smoothly and when Alan's work hummed along invisibly and successfully behind the scenes. When his assistance was required, they expected him to appear immediately; some faculty even went so far as to copy email messages to the chair and computer resources committee to ensure that Alan knew there would be repercussions if he did not appear when called upon. Alan's view of everyone else as "just users" came across clearly in his writing (which primarily took place via email) and eventually called his competence into question such that department members often failed to respond to him, were ignorant of his initiatives to help them, and laughed at him and his emails. This misalignment between Alan's imagined role for himself and the role imagined for him by others led to a lack of the positive engagement Wenger argues may help newcomers enculturate; Alan and the other members of the humanities department were not actively engaging or mutually negotiating their work together. 21

How Did Alan Relate to the Department in Writing?

A number of discourse conventions existed in the department that could have afforded Alan further authority. Had he adopted these conventions, Alan could have achieved alignment with the department, for example using emails 22 as "boundary objects able to create fixed points around which to coordinate activities" (Wenger 187). Alan did not adopt the conventions of the department, however. Although it is possible for writers "to enact slightly different intentions" and "resist the ideological pull of genres in certain circumstances," their resistance will only be "recognized and valued as resistance and not misinterpretation, or worse, ignorance" if it is "predicated on one's knowledge of a genre" (Bawarshi 92). Alan's written interactions with the department were seen not as resistance but as ignorance, and identified him as an outsider without authority.

One of the conventions Alan did not follow when he wrote involved the 23 department's approximately 15 or 20 listservs, each reaching a specific audience. Tailoring emails to a particular audience was an accepted writing convention in the activity system. During the beginning of each fall semester, listserv addresses were sent out and department members were encouraged to use the list that most directly reached their message's audience. Alan chose to use the list that reached all department members for nearly every email he wrote—despite the fact that he administered all the lists and knew lists more tailored to his messages existed. His email activity did not "fit within [the] broader structures," demonstrating his lack of alignment with the department (Wenger 173)

A survey of the department I conducted indicated that Alan's lack of audience 24 awareness and tailoring had negative consequences for his identity in the department: most people were unaware of his efforts to better their computer system because they either did not read or did not remember reading the information he sent out via email. In other words, the members of the department did not see Alan as engaged in work with and for them. For example, much of his time was spent setting up a new departmental computer network that would benefit all department members by providing them private, disk-free storage space. He discussed this in emails many times, but usually in emails that mentioned a number of other items directed at more specialized audiences. As a result, over half the survey respondents did not know he was setting up a new network. People indicated on the survey that they stopped reading an email if the first item of business did not relate to them.

Other accepted departmental conventions governed the content and style 25 of emails. The community members were highly literate, hyper-aware language users, in the traditional sense of the terms, who valued professional, grammatically correct, Standard English in written communication. The unspoken convention that email within the department be grammatically correct was pervasive and widely practiced in the community. Abiding by this convention was difficult for Alan, who explicitly said on several occasions that he felt his writing abilities were not good. His emails show a number of grammatical errors including sentence fragments, double negatives, and misplaced punctuation. In addition, Alan's emails often contained directives about the use of computers and labs; he frequently implied that people should respect his authority and position in the department by doing what he asked. His utterances were intended to be "*signs of authority* . . . to be believed and obeyed" (Bourdieu 66). However, he sent these emails to many irrelevant audiences and his grammar, punctuation, and sentence structure often undermined his authority as understood by audience members.

Although Alan was institutionally authorized to speak about technology, and recognized as a technical authority, he was not able to "speak in a way that others . . . regard[ed] as acceptable in the circumstances" (Thompson 9). Survey respondents' comments suggested that people dismissed Alan's legitimacy because of his writing choices. While he appeared to feel this dismissal, he did not change his writing behavior and his institutional authority began to erode. 26

What Was the Outcome?

The fact that Alan, a newcomer, used email in ways that old-timers saw as inappropriate — and that this use of email caused conflict — is not surprising; after all, newcomers are expected to make missteps. But rather than adapting and changing to communicate more effectively in his new workplace, Alan resisted and clung to his own ways of writing, causing conflict and breakdowns in the community of practice. Members of the department were similarly unwilling to change their view of what they found acceptable in email. They insisted on what Bourdieu calls "the dominant competence" and imposed their idea of linguistic competence as "the only legitimate one" (56). The community didn't negotiate or compromise its idea of linguistic competence for Alan; the only real possibility for negotiation had to come from Alan — and it did not. 27

Because our identities are shaped to some extent by the communities in which we choose to participate — as well as by those settings we inhabit and in which we choose *not* to participate (Wenger 164) — workers such as Alan may also be demonstrating their desire to identify with communities of practice other than the primary ones in which they work by refusing to appropriate new ways of writing. By refusing to participate in communication conventions adopted by the majority of members of the community, Alan attempted to assert the identity he imagined for himself (powerful network administrator) and to resist the one imposed on him by the workplace. Pushing past resistance to work effectively with others requires people to relinquish aspects of their desired primary identities: "[L]egitimate participation entails the loss of certain identities even as it enables the construction of others" (Hodges 289). Clearly, Alan did not feel this was an acceptable proposition. The result for Alan, as Wenger might predict, was increasing marginalization. His emails were not only the butt of cruel and constant jokes in the department, but they also failed to garner support and convey necessary information. People ignored his emails or laughed at them, and neither response was conducive to getting work done. Ultimately, Alan's 28 choice of non-participation resulted in "disturbances and breakdowns in work processes" (Hasu and Engeström 65).

Socio-historic activity theory argues that such situations can lead to positive developments because breakdowns can potentially serve as catalysts for change: "Discoordination and breakdown often lead to re-mediation of the performance and perspectives, sometimes even to re-mediation of the overall activity system in order to resolve its pressing inner contradictions" (Hasu and Engeström 65). However, for a breakdown to lead to positive change, those involved must be willing to consider and negotiate various perspectives and everyone must be willing to appropriate some new ways of seeing and doing. This did not happen in Alan's case. He clung to his own ways of writing and communicating, which demonstrated that he was not engaging, aligning, and imagining a role for himself as a member of the humanities department. Other members of the humanities department no more changed to accommodate Alan than Alan did to fit in with them. 29

After a year and a half, Alan left and found employment elsewhere. 30

DISCUSSION

Clearly, Alan's enculturation into the humanities department was not successful. He was an outsider, a worker unlike the other community members in age, education, occupation, linguistic abilities, and concern for conventions. Since new workers are often different in these ways and still manage to negotiate communication strategies that are effective and acceptable enough so that work can be done, what might account for Alan's resistance to writing in ways that his new community saw as legitimate and appropriate? 31

One reason for his resistance was that Alan and other members of his department had a different understanding of the division of labor in the department and, thus, a different view of Alan's authority. Alan might have viewed changing his writing habits as an admission that he did not play the role he imagined for himself within the department. Despite his vocal assertions to the contrary, he was not "God" in the department. While he entered the department with some measure of authority by virtue of his technical expertise, he had to prove himself and create his *ethos* continually through language—perhaps even more than through action for this particular workplace. This was something he could not or would not do. 32

However, a socio-linguistic analysis I conducted of Alan's writing suggests that he did not feel as much authority as he claimed to have, even from the beginning of his time in the department when he had the most cooperation and respect because of his technical capital. Of 150 sentences I studied for the analysis, only 39 were directives. While all of Alan's emails were usually sent to department-wide listservs, the overwhelming majority of his directives (28 of 33

419

the 39) were addressed to graduate students alone. Only 3 were written to faculty or staff members, and 6 were written to the department as a whole. Alan's use of directives suggests that while he claimed to have authority and see the faculty as simply "users," he did not, in fact, feel much authority over them, so he confined most of his directives to graduate students. Even then, Alan used hedges over two-thirds of the time, suggesting that his felt sense of authority was shaky. This understanding best matched the department's understanding. He could make technical changes and monitor and limit operations; however, he could not force people to act in the ways he wanted them to or prohibit them from using equipment, as he threatened in more than one email.

Given the limitations of his actual authority—which conflicted with his 34 desired authority—Alan's refusal to change his writing might have been one way of claiming an identity he wanted, one that included the authority and autonomy to which he felt entitled. However, his refusal to write in ways seen as acceptable by the department had the opposite effect: his method of writing stripped him of the institutional authority originally invested in him. Although Alan's words could be understood, they were not "likely to be listened to [or] recognized as acceptable." He lacked "the competence necessary in order to speak the legitimate language," which could have granted him "linguistic capital . . . a profit of distinction" (Bourdieu 55). Since authoritative language is useless "without the collaboration of those it governs," Alan's initial authority was lessened with each utterance seen by the department as illegitimate (Bourdieu 113). We should keep in mind that Alan's choices are unlikely to have been conscious; quite often linguistic action is not "the outcome of conscious calculation" (Thompson 17).

A second reason for Alan's failure to adopt community writing conventions 35 might have been his resistance to being used as a tool. As a support person, Alan joined this activity system as one of its tools, not as a community member. As a technical worker with a B.A. in a university humanities department filled with people who had M.A.s and Ph.D.s, he and the other members of the workplace were not mutually engaged. Rather, the community members used him as a tool to help achieve goals Alan did not share or value. Computer system administrators (like many other workers) are used as tools to do work that others cannot. As a result of his position, Alan was not part of the community of practice; rather, his ability to maintain computer networks figured in as one of many pieces of the humanities community: the community members needed him and his activity to use their computers.

Though Alan was hired to function as a tool, he did not sit quietly like a ham- 36 mer or wrench until he was needed, he did not perform exactly the same way each time he was needed, and he did not remain silent when his work was complete. As a person, Alan didn't always choose to perform his tasks when and how community members wanted. In addition, he initiated and responded to dialogue, and (most frustrating for members of the humanities department) chose to do so in ways contrary to the community expectations. Alan's refusal to write in ways that the faculty felt he should was, perhaps, one means of flouting their linguistic authority, demonstrating that he was not a servant or tool to be used at will. Rather than quietly performing the tasks asked of him, and writing about them in the ways the community members saw as legitimate, Alan resisted the department by seeing *them* as *his* tools and by choosing non-participation over acquiescence to their written conventions. Alan's method of resistance did bring him to the conscious attention of department members; they quickly came to see him as a human being who did not silently serve them in response to their every need or desire. However, his method of resistance did not enable Alan to complete his own work successfully, nor did it lead the humanities department to include him as a human member of their community. Thus, Alan's method of resistance in this case was successful on one level, but detrimental to both himself and the workplace on other levels.

Alan's example illustrates that learning to write in new communities entails 37 more than learning discrete sets of skills or improving cognitive abilities. It is a process of involvement in communities, of identifying with certain groups, of choosing certain practices over others; a process strongly influenced by power relationships a process, in effect, bound up tightly with identity, authority, and experience. Alan's case also suggests that enculturation theories have overlooked an important point: not all new workers are expected, or themselves expect, to enculturate into a community. Some, perhaps many in our service-oriented society, are present in communities of practice not as members but as tools. Given these points, those of us interested in how people learn to write in new environments, in school and beyond, and those of us struggling to teach new ways of writing to students who resist what we ask of them, must continue to study and consider the importance of factors beyond texts and cognitive ability.

Acknowledgments

Thanks to Rebecca Burnett (Iowa State University) and Charie Thralls (Utah State University) for encouraging this study and responding to early drafts; to David Russell (Iowa State University) and Donna Kain (Clarkson University) for responding to later drafts; and to Lisa Coleman and Judy Isaksen, *Enculturation* guest editor and board member respectively, for their helpful reviews.

Notes

1. "A community of practice is a set of relations among persons, activity, and world, over time and in relation with other tangential and overlapping communities of practice" (Lave and Wenger 98).

2. "Knowledge, skills, and other cultural acquisitions, as exemplified by educational or technical qualifications" (Thompson 14).

421

3. Though relatively new to many in our field, activity theory is used more and more widely within composition studies; see, for example, Bazerman and Russell; Berkenkotter and Ravotas; Dias, et al.; Dias and Paré; Grossman, Smagorinsky and Valencia; Harms; Hovde; Kain; Russell, "Rethinking" and "Activity Theory"; Smart; Spinuzzi; Wardle; Winsor. Activity theory's implications for composition instruction are outlined in Russell's "Activity Theory and Its Implications for Writing Instruction" and in Wardle's *Contradiction, Constraint, and Re-Mediation: An Activity Analysis of FYC* and "Can Cross-Disciplinary Links Help Us Teach 'Academic Discourse' in FYC?"

Works Cited

Bawarshi, Anis. *Genre and the Invention of the Writer: Reconsidering the Place of Invention in Composition.* Logan: Utah State UP, 2003. Print.

Bazerman, Charles. *Shaping Written Knowledge: The Genre and Activity of the Experimental Article in Sciences.* Madison: U of Wisconsin P, 1988. Print.

Bazerman, Charles, and David Russell. *Writing Selves/Writing Societies: Research from Activity Perspectives.* Fort Collins: The WAC Clearinghouse and *Mind, Culture, and Activity*, 2002. Print.

Berkenkotter, Carol, Thomas Huckin, and Jon Ackerman. "Conversations, Conventions, and the Writer." *Research in the Teaching of English* 22 (1988): 9–44. Print.

Berkenkotter, Carol, and Thomas Huckin. "Rethinking Genre from a Sociocognitive Perspective." *Written Communication* 10 (1993): 475–509. Print.

Berkenkotter, Carol, and Doris Ravotas. "Genre as a Tool in the Transmission of Practice and across Professional Boundaries." *Mind, Culture, and Activity* 4.4 (1997): 256–74. Print.

Berlin, James. "Poststructuralism, Cultural Studies, and the Composition Classroom: Postmodern Theory in Practice." *Rhetoric Review* 11 (1992): 16–33. Print.

Bizzell, Patricia. "Cognition, Convention, and Certainty: What We Need to Know about Writing." *Pre/Text* 3 (1982): 213–43. Print.

Bolin, Bill. "The Role of the Media in Distinguishing Composition from Rhetoric." *Enculturation* 5.1 (Fall 2003): n. pag. Web. 1 July 2004.

Bourdieu, Pierre. *Language and Symbolic Power.* Ed. John B. Thompson. Trans. Gino Raymond and Matthew Adamson. Cambridge: Harvard UP, 1991. Print.

Cole, Michael. *Cultural Psychology.* Cambridge: Harvard UP, 1996. Print.

Cole, Michael, and Yrgo Engeström. "A Cultural-Historical Approach to Distributed Cognition." Ed. Gavriel Salomon. *Distributed Cognitions: Psychological and Educational Considerations.* Cambridge: Cambridge UP, 1993. 1–46. Print.

Cole, Michael, and Sylvia Scribner. *The Psychology of Literacy.* Cambridge: Harvard UP, 1981. Print.

Dias, Patrick, and Anthony Paré, eds. *Transitions: Writing in Academic and Workplace Settings.* Cresskill: Hampton, 2000. Print.

Dias, Patrick, Aviva Freedman, Peter Medway, and Anthony Paré. *Worlds Apart: Acting and Writing in Academic and Workplace Contexts.* Mahwah: Lawrence Erlbaum, 1999. Print.

Doheny-Farina, Stephen. "A Case Study of an Adult Writing in Academic and Non-Academic Settings." *Worlds of Writing: Teaching and Learning in Discourse Communities at Work.* Ed. Carolyn B. Matalene. New York: Random, 1989. 17–42. Print.

Doheny-Farina, Stephen, and Lee Odell. "Ethnographic Research on Writing: Assumptions and Methodology." *Writing in Nonacademic Settings*. Eds. Lee Odell and Dixie Goswami. New York: Guilford, 1985. 503–35. Print.

Engeström, Yrgo. *Learning by Expanding: An Activity-Theoretical Approach to Developmental Research*. Helsinki: Orienta-Konsultit, 1987. Print.

Grossman, Pamela L., Peter Smagorinsky, and Sheila Valencia. "Appropriating Tools for Teaching English: A Theoretical Framework for Research on Learning to Teach." *American Journal of Education* 108 (1999): 1–29. Print.

Harms, Patricia. *Writing-across-the-Curriculum in a Linked Course Model for First-Year Students: An Activity Theory Analysis*. Ames: Iowa State UP, 2003. Print.

Hasu, Mervi, and Yrgo Engeström. "Measurement in Action: An Activity-Theoretical Perspective on Producer-User Interaction." *International Journal of Human-Computer Studies* 53 (2000): 61–89. Print.

Hodges, Diane. "Participation as Dis-Identification With/In a Community of Practice." *Mind, Culture, and Activity* 5 (1998): 272–90. Print.

Hovde, Marjorie. "Tactics for Building Images of Audience in Organizational Contexts: An Ethnographic Study of Technical Communicators." *Journal of Business and Technical Communication* 14.4 (2000): 395–444. Print.

Kain, Donna J. *Negotiated Spaces: Constructing Genre and Social Practice in a Cross-Community Writing Project*. Ames: Iowa State UP, 2003. Print.

Lave, Jean, and Etienne Wenger. *Situated Learning: Legitimate Peripheral Participation*. New York: Cambridge UP, 1991. Print.

Lincoln, Bruce. *Authority: Construction and Corrosion*. Chicago: U of Chicago P, 1994. Print.

Paré, Anthony. "Genre and Identity: Individuals, Institutions, and Ideology." *The Rhetoric and Ideology of Genre*. Eds. Richard Coe, Lorelei Lingard, and Tatiana Teslenko. Cresskill: Hampton, 2002. Print.

Prior, Paul. *Writing/Disciplinarity: A Sociohistoric Account of Literate Activity in the Academy*. Mahwah: Lawrence Erlbaum, 1998. Print.

Rose, Nikolas. *Inventing Ourselves: Psychology, Power, and Personhood*. Cambridge: Cambridge UP, 1996. Print.

Rubin, Donald L. "Introduction: Composing Social Identity." *Composing Social Identity in Written Language*. Ed. Donald Rubin. Hillsdale: Lawrence Erlbaum, 1995. 1–30. Print.

Russell, David. "Rethinking Genre in School and Society: An Activity Theory Analysis." *Written Communication* 14 (1997): 504–39. Print.

———. "Activity Theory and Its Implications for Writing Instruction." *Reconceiving Writing, Rethinking Writing Instruction*. Ed. Joseph Petraglia. Mahwah: Lawrence Erlbaum, 1995. 51–77. Print.

Smart, Graham. "Genre as Community Invention: A Central Bank's Response to Its Executives' Expectations as Readers." *Writing in the Workplace: New Research Perspectives*. Ed. Rachel Spilka. Carbondale: Southern Illinois UP, 1993. 124–40. Print.

Spinuzzi, Clay. "Pseudotransactionality, Activity Theory, and Professional Writing Instruction." *Technical Communication Quarterly* 5.3 (1996): 295–308. Print.

Thompson, John B. "Editor's Introduction." *Language and Symbolic Power*. By Pierrie Bourdieu. Cambridge: Harvard UP, 1999. 1–31. Print.

Wardle, Elizabeth. *Contradiction, Constraint, and Re-Mediation: An Activity Analysis of FYC*. Ames: Iowa State UP, 2003. Print.

———. "Can Cross-Disciplinary Links Help Us Teach 'Academic Discourse' in FYC?" *Across the Disciplines* 1 (2004): n. pag. Web. 1 July 2004.

Wenger, Etienne. *Communities of Practice: Learning, Meaning, and Identity.* New York: Cambridge UP, 1998. Print.

Winsor, Dorothy. "Genre and Activity Systems: The Role of Documentation in Maintaining and Changing Engineering Activity Systems." *Written Communication* 16.2 (1999): 200–24. Print.

- -

Questions for Discussion and Journaling

1. Drawing on Wardle (who cites Wenger), what are the three ways that newcomers try to belong in a new community? Give a specific example to illustrate each "mode of belonging." Then consider why a newcomer might choose *not* to participate in some aspect of a new community.

2. Wardle quotes Rubin as saying that "stylistic options 'leak' clues about writers' social identities" (para. 10). Explain what this means. Do you have examples from your own experience?

3. Wardle quotes Hasu and Engeström, well-known activity theory scholars, as saying that conflict and breakdown can actually be positive (para. 29), helping to reshape how a community does things in ways that are more productive. However, the conflicts between Alan and his work community did not have positive results. Why do you think this is? How could his conflicts have been handled so that they *did* result in positive change?

4. Toward the end of the article, Wardle quotes Thompson as saying that the choices we make with language are very often unconscious (para. 34); that is, we might be using language in resistant ways unintentionally. Do you agree that this is possible, or do you think that people are usually making conscious choices when they use language?

5. Wardle seems to be arguing that Alan did not successfully join his new workplace community because he was resisting it: He did not want to adopt the identity that people in that community imagined for him. James Gee (p. 274) would likely have a very different opinion; he would most likely argue that Alan could not have joined the Humanities Department activity system even if he had wanted to. Take a look at Gee's article and then consider whether you agree more with Wardle or with Gee.

6. Think of all the people you know who have some sort of institutionally ascribed authority. (Hint: One of them probably assigned this reading!) Can you think of a time when one or more of them lost their authority in your eyes or someone else's through their linguistic actions or behaviors? If so, what happened?

Applying and Exploring Ideas

1. Write a reflective essay of just a few pages in which you (first) define what it means to have authority over texts and within activity systems, and (second) discuss your feelings about your own authority (or lack of it) within any activity system you would like to focus on. Consider, for example, how you know whether you have authority there and how you gained text and discourse authority there (if you did); alternatively, consider how it feels to be at the mercy of someone else's authority in an activity system. Ann M. Johns also talks about authority in this chapter, so if you are having trouble, you might return to her article (p. 319).

2. Make a list of all the tools that mediate the activities of this writing class. How do they help you do the work of the class? How would the work be different if the tools were different? Do you think there are tools that could make the class more effective that are currently not used?

- -

META MOMENT   Why do you think the readings in this chapter seem to refer to *authority* so much? How might thinking about sources of authority help you as a writer on the job, in college, or in your personal writing? How does the concept of authority relate to the threshold concept that this chapter has been asking you to consider?

- -

The Genres of Chi Omega

An Activity Analysis

VICTORIA MARRO

Framing the Reading

Victoria "Tori" Marro was a student in Elizabeth Wardle's Honors Composition II course at the University of Central Florida (UCF). In that class, the students worked on research projects related to literacies in their own lives. Tori was actively involved with her sorority and interested in the ways that her sorority used texts to help chapters in different states achieve some consistent identities and activities. She wrote a draft of the text you see here as her final project, and then later submitted it to UCF's peer-reviewed journal of first-year writing, *Stylus.* The paper was accepted and underwent additional revision with help from the *Stylus* editors prior to publication in the Spring 2012 issue. The version you see here is the version published in *Stylus*. This article received an award during UCF's Third Annual Knights Write Showcase. Tori plans to attend medical school.

In this article, Tori uses activity theory, as well as **genre theory** (described in Chapter 1 and at the beginning of this chapter), in order to explore how her sorority activity system, which is both local and national, finds coherence and is better able to achieve its goals through the use of its various genre "tools." Her analysis should help you understand the threshold concepts of this chapter in a deeper way, exploring how genres help groups of people accomplish their goals together and maintain a coherent identity that helps them make meaning together.

Marro, Victoria. "The Genres of Chi Omega: An Activity Analysis." *Stylus: A Journal of First-Year Writing*, vol. 3, no. 1, 2012, pp. 25–32, writingandrhetoric.cah.ucf.edu /stylus/files/3_1/stylus_3_1_Marro.pdf.

Getting Ready to Read

Before you read, do at least one of the following activities:

- Jot down the definition of *genre* as you understand it.

- Quickly consider what you think genres do and why they exist.

- Think about some genres that are used in an activity system in which you participate. How do they help you and the other members understand the "identity" of people in that activity system?

As you read, consider the following questions:

- Does your initial understanding of genres match Marro's understanding?

- Does what she is describing about the genres, rules, and division of labor in her sorority help you think similarly about those in an activity system you are a part of?

INTRODUCTION

Sororities have existed for over 100 years and have maintained their values even as time passes and chapters become farther apart. One way these organizations have been able to keep these traditions is through the use of various genres. According to the work of writing researchers such as Amy Devitt, genres are flexible responses to fit the needs of a discourse community or social setting. A discourse community is a group with agreed upon goals, communication, the use of genres, feedback, a threshold level of membership and specified language (Johns). Researchers Amy Devitt, Anis Bawarshi and Mary Jo Reiff have looked at the way that genres serve the needs of juries, doctors' offices, and classrooms. According to these researchers, "genre study allows students and researchers to recognize how 'lived textuality' plays a role in the lived experience of a group" (Bawarshi, Devitt, and Reiff 542).

One community that plays a big part in my life and in the lives of 300,000 other women is my sorority, Chi Omega. Usually, research done on Greek life involves eating disorders and problems with hazing, but such issues should not define these organizations. Not enough research has been done on the complex genre systems, or genre sets, used by sororities and fraternities. A genre set, as defined by Charles Bazerman, is a group of several genres that predictably recur inside a domain-specified community (Honig 91). A genre system, as defined by Amy Devitt, is a "set of genres interacting to achieve an overarching function within an activity system" (Bawarshi and Reiff 87). Genre sets

1

2

> *I will look at the genres used within Chi Omega and how the use of the genre systems help the 173 collegiate chapters of Chi Omega function both independently and together as one activity system.*

and systems are important with regard to social action and interact to further the purposes of a group. By analyzing these, social roles and progress become much clearer within activity systems: "A genre system includes genres from multiple genre sets, over time, and can involve the interaction of users with different levels of expertise and authority, who may not all have equal knowledge of or access to all" (Bawarshi and Reiff 88). In an organization as large as Chi Omega, this is incredibly important because the levels of authority and expertise of members varies so greatly. Bazerman has previously looked at the use of genre systems in classrooms and in the US patent application process (Bawarshi and Reiff 88). In this paper, I will look at the genres used within Chi Omega and how the use of genre systems help the 173 collegiate chapters of Chi Omega function both independently and together as one activity system. For the purposes of this paper, an activity system functions in a similar fashion to a discourse community, with laid out purposes, tools, rules, subject, community and a division of labor. This will be further explained in my discussion. I will look at the different genres that are used, as well as the different ways that the same genre may be used by different chapters, examining the ways that the same tool can serve completely different purposes for different chapters. I will specifically look at the genres we use in my chapter today, and how these genres are utilized to further the goals of Chi Omega.

METHODS

I interviewed two sisters in other Chi Omega chapters, including Emily, an active 3 sister in the Eta Delta chapter at the University of Florida and Summer, an active sister of the Psi Kappa chapter at Clemson University. Their names have been changed. These sisters were asked what technologies their executive boards used to communicate with them; about genres used by chapters such as a weekly newsletter, Billhighway and the GIN system; and their opinion on the effectiveness of said genres. These sisters were asked their opinions on the importance of writing and ritual to Chi Omega nationally, and about the national magazine, *The Eleusis.*

An interview was also conducted with Brittany, an alum from the Psi Mu 4 chapter of Chi Omega at the University of Central Florida. Her name has been changed as well. She was asked how the executive board communicated with the sisters during her time in the chapter, about a weekly newsletter, the GIN system, and her opinion on the effectiveness of these genres. She was asked about her involvement in an alumnae chapter and the genres that were used within that chapter. She was also asked about the national magazine, *The Eleusis.*

The Psi Mu chapter secretary, Allison, was interviewed about the writing 5 she does for the chapter and the way she became versed in these genres. She was asked her opinion on the effectiveness of the GIN system and the problems with this system. Other questions included her opinions on the importance of writing to the national organization and whether or not she reads *The Eleusis*.

I also interviewed Psi Mu chapter president, Nicole. Nicole was asked about 6 how the GIN system came into effect and what methods of communication were used prior to this system. She was asked about the ritual text, but at the request of the chapter secretary, these responses will not be included. Like in all of the other interviews, she was asked if she read *The Eleusis*. As the chapter president, she was asked about her communication with other chapters and with nationals, and her opinion on the importance of writing and written communication to the organization as a whole.

Over twenty genres were collected and analyzed including the GIN system, 7 *The Eleusis,* the weekly newsletter, announcements, files and others. The importance of genres that could not be accessed, such as the written rituals and the Book of Rules, were analyzed as well. Activity triangles were constructed for Chi Omega as a national organization, as well as for individual chapters and genres. Database searches were conducted and previous research was synthesized to support findings.

Activity triangles were constructed to analyze the activity systems, Chi 8 Omega nationally, the Psi Mu, Psi Kappa, and Eta Delta chapters, and the GIN system. Activity theory, which says that people write as part of an activity system, can be displayed in a triangle, with tools at the top, subject on the middle left, object on the middle right, rules in the lower left, the community in the lower middle, and division of labor in the lower right-hand corner. A series of arrows inside the triangle shows how each portion is connected to the others (see Figure 1).

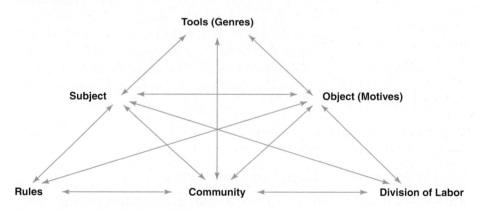

Figure 1 Organization of an Activity System

RESULTS AND DISCUSSION

Through activity analysis, I found that the chapters of Chi Omega all write in 9 different genres; however, all of the chapters share the same goals, which are laid out in the mission statement, a shared genre. I found that this mission statement is broken up into six parts, and each of those has a director, which makes up the cardinal cabinet. Each director works with a specific genre set, and these together make up a genre system. In the Psi Mu chapter, one supergenre encompasses all of these genres sets and works as a genre system within that genre.

Chi Omega sorority was founded in 1895 by Dr. Charles Richardson, Ina 10 May Boles, Jean Vincenheller, Jobelle Holcombe, and Alice Simonds. Chi Omega has initiated over 300,000 members and has 173 collegiate chapters. The tools used by Chi Omega nationally are the written rituals, established by Dr. Charles Richardson when the sorority was founded; the Book of Rules, which lists all rules for members; the Chi Omega Symphony and mission statement, which summarize the organization's purposes; the chapter rosters; ChiOmega.com; and *The Eleusis,* the national magazine. In a letter from the national president that came with the latest issue of *The Eleusis,* she states the purpose of the magazine is "to connect our members to the national organization by sharing experiences, spotlighting successes, and providing tools for the development of our members" (Fulkerson). The written ritual provides the lexis, or specialized language, of the discourse community. The rituals are confidential and therefore will not be further explained. The motives or objects of the activity system are to promote friendship, integrity, scholarship, community service, involvement in the community and career and personal development. These purposes make up the mission statement of Chi Omega. The rules are determined by the Book of Rules and, in individual chapters, the bylaws. The community is all of the sisters and new members of Chi Omega in all of the chapters, both collegiate and alumni. The division of labor in each chapter is determined by the slating process, in which sisters nominate other sisters for a position, other sisters give their input, and then another sister is nominated for that position as well. All of the input is recorded along with all of the sisters nominated for positions and at the end of the day the executive board is chosen based on that information. The idea of slating is that the position seeks the woman, not the other way around. Those who tell people they would like to be slated are ineligible to hold an executive position (see Figure 2). This activity system can be applied to each of the 173 collegiate chapters, and although in most cases more genres are used as well, it keeps all of the chapters in line with the same values and purposes.

Using Different Tools to Achieve the Same Motives

Chi Omega is such a large organization that it would be incredibly diffi- 11 cult to use only a few genres and have every chapter using the same genres.

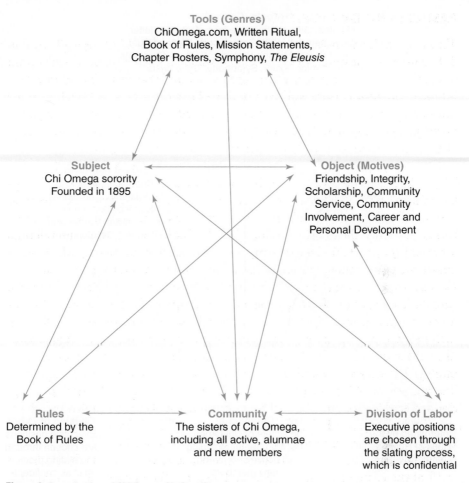

Tools (Genres)
ChiOmega.com, Written Ritual,
Book of Rules, Mission Statements,
Chapter Rosters, Symphony, *The Eleusis*

Subject
Chi Omega sorority
Founded in 1895

Object (Motives)
Friendship, Integrity,
Scholarship, Community
Service, Community
Involvement, Career and
Personal Development

Rules
Determined by the
Book of Rules

Community
The sisters of Chi Omega,
including all active, alumnae
and new members

Division of Labor
Executive positions
are chosen through
the slating process,
which is confidential

Figure 2 Organization of Chi Omega Nationally

According to Carolyn Miller, the amount of genres used by a group is dependent on how complex and diverse the group is (Devitt 575). This statement in itself shows the complexity and diversity of Chi Omega, and the reasoning behind how different chapters use different genres to mediate the same goals. In UCF's Psi Mu chapter (see Figure 3) alone, there are over twenty genres, with more being added all the time. These genres function together as a genre system to make the organization work. Some of these genres have been used since the sorority's founding in 1895 and others have come into being much more recently in response to situations in which the genres being used were not working efficiently. For example, one new genre used is the GIN system, which can be looked at as a genre system within itself. The Eta Delta chapter also uses

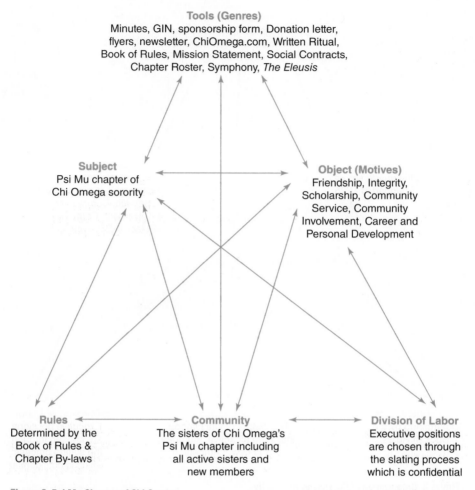

Tools (Genres)
Minutes, GIN, sponsorship form, Donation letter,
flyers, newsletter, ChiOmega.com, Written Ritual,
Book of Rules, Mission Statement, Social Contracts,
Chapter Roster, Symphony, *The Eleusis*

Subject
Psi Mu chapter of
Chi Omega sorority

Object (Motives)
Friendship, Integrity,
Scholarship, Community
Service, Community
Involvement, Career and
Personal Development

Rules
Determined by the
Book of Rules &
Chapter By-laws

Community
The sisters of Chi Omega's
Psi Mu chapter including
all active sisters and
new members

Division of Labor
Executive positions
are chosen through
the slating process
which is confidential

Figure 3 Psi Mu Chapter of Chi Omega

the GIN system (see Figure 4). The GIN system as a genre will be looked at in more detail later.

In Brittany's interview, she explained to me that when she was in the chapter, they had a website, but nothing like the GIN system. She told me that the executive board would rarely post to the chapter website because they did not believe it was secure. Announcements were sent through mass emails. Summer told me that her chapter does not use the GIN system and, like Brittany's chapter, the executive board rarely uses the chapter website. The Psi Kappa (see Figure 5) chapter uses Survey Monkeys, an online type of questionnaire, in the way that the Psi Mu chapter uses the question function on the GIN system. This shows how different genres are able to mediate the same goal for different

12

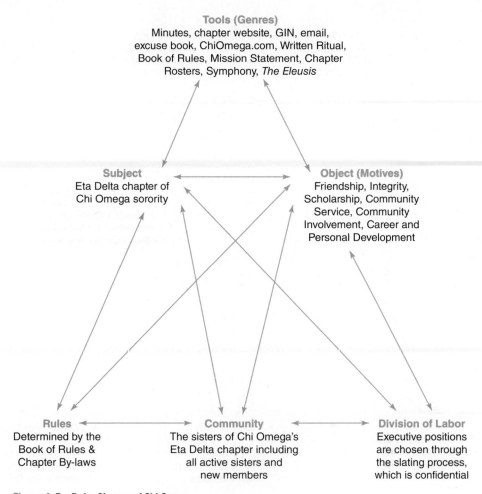

Tools (Genres)
Minutes, chapter website, GIN, email,
excuse book, ChiOmega.com, Written Ritual,
Book of Rules, Mission Statement, Chapter
Rosters, Symphony, *The Eleusis*

Subject
Eta Delta chapter of
Chi Omega sorority

Object (Motives)
Friendship, Integrity,
Scholarship, Community
Service, Community
Involvement, Career and
Personal Development

Rules
Determined by the
Book of Rules &
Chapter By-laws

Community
The sisters of Chi Omega's
Eta Delta chapter including
all active sisters and
new members

Division of Labor
Executive positions
are chosen through
the slating process,
which is confidential

Figure 4 **Eta Delta Chapter of Chi Omega**

chapters. As was the case when Brittany was a sister, Summer's chapter sends mass emails for announcements.

A Genre System within a Genre

The activity triangle laid out simply for the GIN system (see Figure 6) shows [13] that even inside one genre, an entire genre system can be taking place. The Psi Mu chapter's GIN system uses are announcements, questions, files, and an event calendar. These tools help the chapter to accomplish its goals. The system even categorizes the information posted based on the urgency indicated by the person posting. If the message should be read immediately, it is posted on the wall and a text message is sent to all the sisters. If it should be read soon, an email is sent

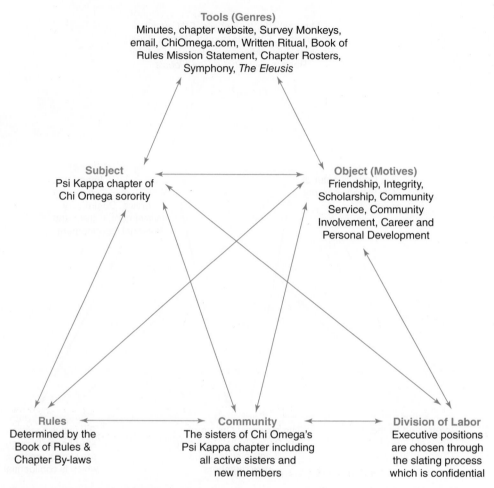

Figure 5 **Psi Kappa Chapter of Chi Omega**

and it is posted on the wall. If it just needs to be read before the next chapter meeting, it is only posted on the wall.

The GIN system contains questions regarding purchasing merchandise and announcements about money that is due, which then function as a genre set with BillHighway.com, a website through which sisters pay their dues, fees, and also pay for any merchandise they order from the chapter. This genre set is particularly important because the chapter would not be able to accomplish its goals without a budget. Another genre set is formed by the GIN questions and announcements regarding volunteer events and the spreadsheet that keeps track of the community service hours, which is posted on the GIN system as a file. This genre set is mediated by the director of community service. Another genre set is made up by the questions, announcements and calendar posts regarding

14

Figure 6 The Psi Mu Chapter of Chi Omega's GIN System

study sessions, a goal GPA, and the spreadsheet posted with all of the scholarship points. This set is mediated by the vice-president, who also serves as the scholarship chair. A question is posted weekly about how often sisters work out. This question, along with links posted to internships and gym classes, makes up the genre set used by the directors of career and personal development. GIN questions and announcements posted about socials function in a genre set with social contracts, mediated by the director of friendship and social. The announcements on GIN as well as in the weekly newsletter about sisterhood events function with the attendance questions in the genre set mediated by the director of sisterhood and personnel. The campus activities director mediates a genre set which includes interest questions about the events put on by other organizations, as well as files and announcements about these events. All of these genre sets together make the genre system within the GIN system.

The Psi Mu chapter began using the GIN system in the spring of 2009. Prior 15 to this system, the chapter was contacted through emails and signup sheets in chapter. Consistent with activity theory, which "illuminates the affordances offered to us by technology" (Levine), the GIN system was found to be a better alternative. By utilizing the GIN system, the chapter was able to keep everything organized and in one place. This genre came into being to "respond appropriately to situations that writers encounter repeatedly" (Devitt 576). The writers of Chi Omega, meaning the sisters in positions of authority, found a new genre that could work more efficiently in the situations they constantly found themselves in, such as how to announce a meeting to the entire chapter, and how to remind sisters to pay their dues. The GIN system provides a means of feedback and communication, two of the defining characteristics of a discourse community (Johns).

SOME FINAL THOUGHTS

In the words of Amy Devitt, "all genres exist through and depend on human 16 action" (Bawarshi, Devitt and Reiff 548). The genres I described in the previous paragraphs are able to further the goals of the chapter because they are well maintained. The chapter secretary checks every post on the GIN system to make sure they are appropriate and the treasurer constantly checks BillHighway to make sure sisters have paid the money they owe to the chapter. Without this maintenance, these genres would not be what they are. For example, I was once shown a fraternity's GIN system. The layout of the website was the same. There was a section for files, announcements, questions, and a calendar; however, where on the Chi Omega GIN system these sections would have many links, their GIN system was quite empty. The brother showing me this GIN system told me that nobody ever used the website and he rarely checked it. The only thing that was really used on this fraternity's GIN system was the list of phone numbers and emails for the brothers. Their announcements were sent out in mass emails and text messages, and their questions were asked in chapter, answers were recorded after a show of hands. This shows how the same tool can serve completely different purposes for different chapters. Most genres are fluid rather than rigid, and can be modified to fit the situation (Devitt 579).

As I said earlier, one of the six characteristics of a discourse community is a 17 threshold level of membership (Johns). In Chi Omega, members go through a recruitment process specific to their university and are given a bid. Upon acceptance of this bid, they become new members. In order "to be successfully enculturated into new communities of practice or activity systems . . . [one] must learn and conform to the conventions, codes and genres of those communities" (Wardle). As a new member, things such as the GIN system and the other genres used by the chapter can be quite confusing, and generally require observation before using them regularly. In her research, Devitt acknowledges that "knowing the genre . . . means knowing such things as appropriate subject matter, level of detail, tone and approach as well as the usual layout and organization" (Devitt 577). This explains the need for observation when becoming enculturated into a community, to learn things such as tone, level of detail, approach and subject matter.

Without various genres, large organizations such as Chi Omega would not be 18 able to function the way that they do. There is a different genre for everything: a spreadsheet to keep track of volunteer hours, a GIN system for questions and announcements, formal letters for donations, and most importantly, the written ritual that has been used to initiate over 300,000 Chi Omega sisters. Having this genre connects each sister to all of the others, even if they've never met. Similar genres mediate the activity of Chi Omega chapters everywhere so that they are able to work together as a whole.

Works Cited

Bawarshi, Anis, Amy J. Devitt, and Mary Jo Reiff, "Materiality and Genre in the Study of Discourse Communities." *College English* 65 (2003): 541–58. *EBSCOhost.* Web. 2 Nov. 2011.

Bawarshi, Anis S., and Mary Jo Reiff. *Genre: An Introduction to History, Theory, Research, and Pedagogy.* Ed. Charles Bazerman. West Lafayette: Parlor, 2010. Print.

Berkenkotter, Carol, and Thomas N. Huckin. "Rethinking Genre from a Sociocognitive Perspective." *Written Communication* 10 (1993): 475–509. *EBSCOhost.* Web. 2 Nov. 2011.

Devitt, Amy. "Generalizing About Genre: New Conceptions of an Old Concept." *College Composition and Communication 44.4* (1993): 573–86. Eric EBSCOhost. Web. 2 Nov. 2011.

Fulkerson, Letitia. Letter to Chi Omega Parents. Oct. 2011. MS. 3395 Players Club Parkway, Memphis, TN.

Honig, Sheryl. "What Do Children Write in Science? A Study of the Genre Set in a Primary Science Classroom." *Written Communication* 27.1 (2010): 87–119. *EBSCOhost.* Web. 7 Nov. 2011.

"Interview of Eta Delta sister." E-mail interview. 24 Oct. 2011.

"Interview of Psi Kappa sister." E-mail interview. 24 Oct. 2011.

"Interview of Psi Mu Chapter President." E-mail interview. 24 Oct. 2011.

"Interview of Psi Mu Chapter Secretary." E-mail interview. 24 Oct. 2011.

"Interview of Psi Mu sister alum." E-mail interview. 24 Oct. 2011.

Johns, Ann M. "Discourse Communities and Communities of Practice: Membership, Conflict, and Diversity." *Text, Role, and Context: Developing Academic Literacies.* Cambridge: Cambridge UP, 1997. 51–70. Print.

Levine, Thomas H. "Tools for the Study and Design of Collaborative Teacher Learning: The Affordances of Different Conceptions of Teacher Community and Activity Theory." *Teacher Education Quarterly* 37.1 (2010): 109. Print.

"Quick Facts about Chi Omega." *Chi Omega.* Chi Omega. Web. 16 Oct. 2011.

Wardle, Elizabeth. "Identity, Authority, and Learning to Write in New Workplaces." *Enculturation* 5.2 (2004): n. pag. Web. 2 Nov. 2011.

Questions for Discussion and Journaling

1. Return to the definition of *genre* that you wrote before you read this piece, and to the explanation of genre offered in Chapter 1 (page 17). Then consider how Marro's definitions of *genre, genre sets*, and *genre systems* compare with those definitions. How has your understanding of genre changed or expanded in reading this piece?

2. In Marro's exploration of how her sorority and another fraternity used the GIN system, how does she help you understand how genres are created by those who use them; reflect their users' values, goals, and needs; and impact the work of those who use them?

3. How do new members of activity systems learn the conventions, codes, and genres of that system?

4. Marro seems to suggest that the genres used by various Chi Omega chapters help the sisters across those chapters maintain a consistent identity. She does not tell you what that identity is, though. By considering the genres they use, the way they use them, and their motives and rules, can you make an informed guess about Chi Omega sisters' values and identities?

Applying and Exploring Ideas

1. Name a nonschool activity system that you participate in and make a list of the important genres that activity system uses and produces to mediate their activities and goals. Then consider the division of labor for using those genres and accomplishing the system's activities and goals.

2. List the texts involved in the genre set of a typical classroom in your major. What are the sorts of goals and activities that these texts help students and teachers accomplish? Consider the division of labor for using those genres and accomplishing the system's activities and goals.

3. Compare the two lists you made for questions 1 and 2 above. What identities are the two activity systems asking you to take? In other words, who and what are you expected to be in each of those systems? How do you know? What happens if you do not adopt that identity?

META MOMENT   How can Marro's analysis help you understand and prepare for writing, reading, speaking, and acting in new activity systems, both in and out of school? What concepts or ideas did she bring up that help you understand and see things differently than before?

WRITING ABOUT INDIVIDUALS IN COMMUNITY: WRITING ASSIGNMENTS

To help you learn and explore the ideas in this chapter, here are four assign-ment options for larger writing projects: an Analysis of Gee's Claims, a Discourse Community Ethnography Report, an Activity Analysis, and a Reflection on Gaining Authority in New Discourse Communities. Each of these stems from the activities and exploration you have already done in this chapter.

ANALYSIS OF GEE'S CLAIMS

Write a four- to five-page essay exploring some of Gee's claims about Discourses *empirically* — that is, by doing your own firsthand research and comparing what you observe with what Gee's theory *predicts* you'll observe. The point of your essay is to compare his theory and your observations.

Reconsidering the Theory   In Gee's article on Discourses (p. 274), he makes a distinction between *dominant* and *nondominant* Discourses. Mastering dominant Discourses, he claims, can bring money, prestige, and status. What does Gee mean by "dominant Discourse"? Is he referring to the language used by people of a par-ticular social class or race? Create a working definition of "dominant Discourse," making absolutely certain that your working definition builds on Gee's and is con-sistent with his actual claims.

Gee claims that once you have "fossilized" into a Discourse without becoming fully fluent in it, you "can't be let into the game" (para. 19). He claims that "true acquisition is probably not possible" and people who are not a part of the dominant Discourse can only "mushfake" it (para. 32). Gee appears to be claiming that people who don't become fluent in the dominant Discourse early are never able to become a part of that Discourse. His claim seems to contradict what is commonly seen as the "American Dream" — the idea that in the United States anyone who works hard can become whatever they want. Using your working definition of dominant Discourse, challenge or support Gee's claim here. If you need additional help, you might want to read some of the research by the sociolinguists that Gee references (Milroy, for example).

Conducting Research   Spend a few hours hanging out with or near a dis-course community of your choice — sorority, store, gaming community, etc. Write down every use of specialized language that you hear — whether it is an unusual word or phrase, or simply an unusual use of a fairly common word or phrase.

Once you have a good list of terms, conduct a short interview with an "old-timer" in that discourse community. Ask the person about using different words: Why do you use this word or phrase instead of a different one? What does this word or phrase mean? Why do you think this group uses this word or phrase? How does it help you achieve your objectives better than using a different word or phrase?

Planning and Drafting Begin drafting your essay by explaining your understanding of Gee's theory of Discourse (whatever aspects of it you have found interesting to test with your research) and then show how your own findings relate to the theory. Do your findings support his theory, contradict it, or do some of both? Can you see places where, according to your research, Gee is likely right, and where he may be wrong? As an example, Gee's theory predicts that Discourses will have specialized languages. Based on your observations, do they?

You can also use your observations to add to or build on Gee's theory. For example, if you do find specialized language in the Discourse you observe, you might consider whether or not specialized language is intended to exclude people, whether it serves a more practical function, or whether it does both.

What Makes It Good? You can see in the various elements of the analysis the basic ideas for what will really make your piece work. Since it's supposed to summarize and explain Gee's theory, the best pieces will do that very well: accurately, concisely, and with good insight into both what Gee *says* and what the implications of his Discourse theory are. At the same time, the analysis won't overreach, by (for example) trying to cover everything in Gee's theory in four or five pages, or trying to make unsupportable claims. Since the analysis is supposed to test Gee's theory against actual observations you make, the best pieces will have very good observations and *explanations* of those observations. And then, in the hardest move of the piece, the best of these analyses will be able to compare the observation and theory in ways that help us understand each better. As always, the best of these pieces will also be well written in terms of fluent and readable sentences, good organization and flow, and careful editing and proofreading.

DISCOURSE COMMUNITY ETHNOGRAPHY REPORT

Choose a *discourse community* that has made an impact on you or one that interests you and explore its goals and characteristics. Then choose a particular point of interest within that discourse community to consider in more detail. Write a five- to eight-page report that describes the discourse community and explores the particular point of interest (or research question) that you want to focus on. Use the data you collect to make and support your claims.

Collecting Data   Choose a discourse community to study, and get permission to do so from the people involved in it. Then do the following:

- *Observe members of the discourse community* while they are engaged in a shared activity; take detailed notes. (What are they doing? What kinds of things do they say? What do they write? How do you know who is "in" and who is "out"?)

- *Collect anything people in that community read or write* (their genres) — even short things like forms, sketches, notes, IMs, and text messages.

- *Interview at least one member of the discourse community.* Record audio and transcribe the interview. You might ask questions like: How long have you been here? Why are you involved? What do X, Y, and Z words mean? How did you learn to write A, B, or C? How do you communicate with other people (on your team, at your restaurant, etc.)?

Data Analysis   First, try analyzing the data you collect using the six characteristics of a discourse community found in Johns (p. 319) and Branick (pp. 383–394):

- What are the shared goals of the community? Why does this group exist? What does it do?

- What mechanisms do members use to communicate with each other (meetings, phone calls, e-mails, text messages, newsletters, reports, evaluation forms, etc.)?

- What are the purposes of each of these mechanisms of communication (to improve performance, make money, grow better roses, share research, etc.)?

- Which of the above mechanisms of communication can be considered *genres* (textual responses to recurring situations that all group members recognize and understand)?

- What kinds of specialized language (*lexis*) do group members use in their conversation and in their genres? Name some examples — ESL, on the fly, 86, etc. What communicative function does this lexis serve (e.g., why say "86" instead of "we are out of this")?

- Who are the "old-timers" with expertise? Who are the newcomers with less expertise? How do newcomers learn the appropriate language, genres, knowledge of the group?

The above will give you an overall picture of the discourse community. Now you want to focus in on what you've learned to find something that is especially interesting, confusing, or illuminating. You can use Johns, Branick, McCarthy, Wardle and

441

Kain, and Marro to assist you in this. In trying to determine what to focus on, you might ask yourself questions such as:

- Are there conflicts within the community? If so, what are they? Why do the conflicts occur? Do texts mediate these conflicts and make them worse in some way?

- Do any genres help the community work toward its goals especially effectively — or keep the community from working toward its goals? Why?

- Do some participants in the community have difficulty speaking and writing there? Why?

- Who has authority here? How is that authority demonstrated in written and oral language? Where does that authority come from?

- Are members of this community stereotyped in any way in regard to their literacy knowledge? If so, why?

Planning and Drafting As you develop answers to some of the above questions, start setting some priorities. Given all you have learned above, what do you want to focus on in your writing? Is there something interesting regarding goals of the community? Are there conflicts in the community? What do you see in terms of the lexis and mediating genres? Do you see verbal and written evidence of how people gain authority and/or enculturate in the community?

At this point you should stop and write a refined research question for yourself that you want to address in your writing. Now that you have observed and analyzed data, what question(s) would you like to explore in your final report? (Consult the articles by Wardle, McCarthy, Mirabelli, Marro, and Branick in this chapter for examples of how you might do this.)

If your teacher has assigned you to write a fairly formal research report, then your final text ought to have the following parts, or you should make the following moves (unless there's a good reason not to):

- Begin with a very brief **literature review** of the existing literature (published research) on the topic: "We know X about discourse communities" (citing Johns and others as appropriate).

- Name a niche ("But we don't know Y" or "No one has looked at X").

- Explain how you will occupy the niche.

- Describe your research methods.

- Discuss your findings in detail. (Use Wardle, McCarthy, and Mirabelli as examples of how to do this — quote from your notes, your interview, the texts you collected, etc.)

- Include a works cited page.

What Makes It Good?   Your assignment will be most successful if you've collected and analyzed data and explored the way that texts mediate activities within a particular discourse community. The assignment asks you to show a clear understanding of what discourse communities are and to demonstrate your ability to analyze them carefully and thoughtfully. It also asks that you not simply list the features of your discourse community but that you also explore in some depth a particularly interesting aspect of that community. Since this assignment asks you to practice making the moves common to academic research articles, it should be organized, readable, fluent, and well edited.

ACTIVITY ANALYSIS

For this assignment, you will continue the analysis of activity systems that you engaged in after reading the articles by Kain and Wardle and by Marro. You will focus on and gather additional data from a specific activity system in order to examine how the primary and minor genres of those systems mediate activity, create and reinforce particular identities and values, and create authority for particular individuals. Write a description of the system, analyzing its motives and tools, and then reflect on what you have learned from doing so.

Collecting Data   Begin by choosing an activity system of importance to you (currently, in the past, or potentially in the future) to focus on. This might be a church group, sorority, family, profession, classroom, club, football team, gaming community, or dorm floor. Just ensure that the activity system holds a personal interest for you and that you have access to its members and its texts.

Next, using the activity triangle worksheet from Kain and Wardle (p. 399) and the questions from paragraph 16 of that article, try to sketch out the object, purpose, tools, community, division of labor, and rules for this activity system. In particular, focus on the textual tools that this group uses in order to try to accomplish its common purposes.

Now determine what data you need to collect.

- You will likely need to interview several members of that activity system and ask them about their activities, purposes, conventions, texts, and so on.

- You will also need to collect some texts that the members commonly read, write, or use in other ways.

- And you will likely need to conduct text-based interviews with some of the system participants in order to ask them about the texts they use. For example, you might ask why they organize the texts as they do, why they use certain phrases or tones instead of others, who writes the texts, who reads them, and so on.

You will also need to set up several opportunities to observe the system members in action, either through observation, shadowing, or in some cases, participant-observation. (For example, if you are a member of the football team, you might participate as you normally do but then take frequent breaks to jot down notes about what you see.)

We suggest taking time with your teacher and classmates to plan out the data collection in more detail. For example, you and your teacher might want to discuss the specific interview questions you will ask. Also, before you contact members of the activity system, talk with your teacher about appropriate ways to approach research participants and gain their permission to engage in your research project.

Analyzing Data   Once you have collected all your data, go back to the activity system worksheet that you drafted before you collected the data. It is now time to rethink what you wrote there. Work through the data that you collected in order to consider anew the motives of the system, the genres (tools) that mediate their work, the rules (conventions) of the system, and so on. As you work through these, make notes about where in your data you found the answers. Was it from what interview subjects said? From the texts you examined? From what you saw while you observed?

Now is also the time to analyze the genres you collected. What are they? Who writes them? Who uses them? What specialized lexis do you see in them? How are they organized? How are they distributed?

Once you feel you have solidly considered the components of the activity system, focus on what is interesting or complicated here. Do community members agree on the motives and purpose of their activities? Do the genres being used effectively facilitate the work of that community? What sorts of values do the genres suggest that the system has? Who has authority in this system? How is that authority affirmed (or questioned) in the genres and activities?

Planning and Drafting   Step back from the data analysis that you just did and ask yourself what you learned. What's interesting here? What's complicated? What's puzzling? What do you know now that you did not know before you collected and analyzed data? Who would care about this?

Now consider the text you want to write. What do you want to focus on? And who do you want to share your information with? Given the answers to these questions, talk with your teacher and classmates about what your text should look like. Do you want to write a formal research report that adds to the conversations that scholars have had about activity systems and texts? Do you want to write to your sister and let her know that the profession she thinks she's interested in probably doesn't suit her? Do you want to write an analysis for the activity system itself that demonstrates why some genres are less effective than others in meeting the system's goals? Do you want to write a reflection to yourself that considers what you've learned and what that means to you personally?

The text you write, and even how you go about planning and writing it, will depend on the answers to the previous questions. Consider the main claim(s) you want to make and the evidence that you need to make that claim and the conventions of the genre you want to write, relevant to the audience you want to write for. Next, make a plan and start drafting. You might need to make an outline first, or you might just want to write down all of the ideas you have and then go back and try to organize them.

Once you feel you have a readable draft, share it with your teacher and classmates. Tell them your point, your desired audience, and the type of genre you were trying to write. Ask them to provide feedback on how well you accomplished your goals and how you might improve. Then revise.

What Makes It Good?   Your text will be good if you learned to collect and analyze data, and then used that data to learn something new and share it in a manner that is engaging and appropriate for your audience and text type. Have you framed your claims and supported them? Do you cite sources where you need to? Do your readers know what your "so what?" is?

REFLECTION ON GAINING AUTHORITY IN NEW DISCOURSE COMMUNITIES

This assignment asks you to continue the reflection you began after reading Kain and Wardle in this chapter in order to (first) define what it means to have authority over texts and within discourse communities or activity systems, and (second) analyze your own experiences gaining authority (or not) within any discourse community or activity system you would like to focus on.

Defining Terms and Explaining Ideas   First, revisit Kain and Wardle, Johns, Gee, and/ or Klass in this chapter in order to write a working definition of what it means to have *authority* when it comes to reading, writing, speaking, and using texts in a new community. Once you've done this, use those same sources and any others you find helpful from this chapter to draft an explanation of how people become competent in this community, and then how they gain authority there (in other words, how they *enculturate*).

Analyzing Your Own Experiences   Drawing on the definitions and explanations you have already drafted, turn to your own experience in any discourse community or community of practice, and answer the following questions, drawing on specific examples and experiences to support your answers. Who has authority with texts and language in your chosen community? What does that look like? How do you know? Do you have authority with texts and language there? If so, how did you gain it? If not, why not?

Planning and Drafting   It may help you to begin by outlining your text and then drafting three different sections:

- Defining authority and discourse communities
- Explaining how newcomers enculturate and gain authority in new discourse communities
- Analyzing your experiences with authority in a particular discourse community

Once you have drafted each of those sections, try to write a conclusion that focuses on the "so what?" Here, you can talk about why thinking about these things matters, and what others can learn from your experiences and analysis.

What Makes It Good?   Your analysis and reflection here will be good if you carefully think through the complicated ideas and terms, drawing on readings to assist you, and if you use those to help you carefully reflect on and analyze your experience. Equally important is the ending, where it is essential that you help readers (in this case, most likely your classmates) consider what they can learn from your analysis.

CHAPTER 4

RHETORIC:
How Is Meaning Constructed in Context?

So far in this book, you've encountered research on threshold concepts of writing (Chapter 1), how our individual literacy histories impact our conceptions and habits of writing (Chapter 2), and how groups use texts to mediate activity (Chapter 3). Now in Chapter 4, we'll examine how people make meaning of texts in relation to their **context**. A central theoretical lens that Writing Studies uses to understand writing is **rhetorical theory**, which helps explain these aspects of writing:

- how writers, texts, readers, and contexts interact
- how writers come up with what to say
- how texts construct knowledge
- how people make up their minds, and change them

This chapter focuses on rhetorical theory because it is so central to building accurate conceptions of writing as well as resisting misconceptions of it. Here we take up most directly the **threshold concepts** that *writing helps people make meaning and get things done*, that *"good" writing is dependent on writers, readers, situation, technology, and use*, and therefore that *there are always constraints on writing*.

Texts take much, if not all, of their meaning from context. If you're a North American reader of this text, you're probably very familiar with the upper image and the meaning it represents. But look at how a similar sign changes meaning in the lower image: The same familiar sign, but now appearing in a completely different context, one complete with a Grim Reaper and very serious looking minions. Now the sign doesn't mean "bring your vehicle to a halt at this sign." The wording on the lower sign translates to "new Higher Education Act." So what does the sign mean in its new context, and how does the Reaper costume provide further context for the sign's meaning?

artpartner-images/Getty images
(top); AP Photo/Bernd Kammerer
(bottom)

To be clear, when we talk about a **theory**, we're referring to a framework of ideas that offers a systematic explanation for some aspect of our lived experience and observation. The better or stronger a theory is, the more completely it accounts for existing phenomena (experiences, events, and objects) and the more accurately it makes testable predictions about future events. For example, a theory that tries to explain how people make up or change their minds has to be able to account for existing observations on the question *and* predict what will happen in future instances. **Rhetoric** attempts to explain or help us understand how people interact through language and other **symbols**, and to predict what will create more and less successful interaction in the future.

Overview of Rhetorical Principles

The first reading in this chapter, Doug Downs's "Rhetoric: Making Sense of Human Interaction and Meaning-Making," offers a broad overview of rhetorical theory, including several descriptions of rhetoric. You'll quickly realize that *rhetoric* is a very hard term to understand quickly because it refers to many different things. To try to help you keep it all in perspective, we want to outline a few principles for you to use when trying to define rhetoric.

The term *rhetoric* actually refers to one of three different things, depending on how it is used: a *field of knowledge*, a *theoretical construct*, and a *performance art*.

- *Rhetoric as a field of knowledge* refers to a body of principles about human interaction and persuasion (that makes it a field of knowledge, like chemistry or history).
- *Rhetoric as a theoretical construct* refers to a theory (as defined above) that provides a systematic explanation of human interaction through language and other symbols.
- *Rhetoric as performance art* refers to how people perform rhetorical principles and concepts in their acts of communication. In this sense, any human interaction follows principles of rhetoric and is thus an "act of" rhetoric.

Rhetoric is thus both the *art* of human interaction (including persuasion) through language and other symbols, as well as the *study* of that interaction. Saying that human action happens through symbols might sound confusing, but it's a fairly simple idea. Humans often take one idea and have it "stand" for another idea; for example, a red light hanging in the street is literally just a red light hanging in the street, but in our culture we have made it into a symbol that we all understand to mean "stop." Language and words are also symbols where we have determined that signs mean something else. For example, the letters "d-o-g" don't necessarily and literally mean or stand for anything — they are just inscriptions on a page. However, we have determined that these three inscriptions form a word that we all understand to represent a four-legged creature that barks. Rhetoric both describes and enables the interaction that we have when using symbols.

The use of symbols to make meaning involves a movement or interaction: A signal must be created, and it must be perceived and interpreted. Therefore, this act of meaning-making usually involves at least two people. (Because you interact with yourself all the time, this interaction *can* be in your head alone.) In other words, rhetoric does not just involve one person "sending" signals to another in a one-way transmission that is "received" and creates an exact copy in another person's mind. Rather, rhetoric involves an interchange of meaning where *each* person — as well as other elements in the interaction — makes signals to be interpreted. The meaning one person makes of those signals is never identical to the meaning another person makes, and meaning is never just transmitted in one direction only. A **rhetor** (any person interacting with other people) can therefore use rhetoric both to *create* interaction and meaning, and to *interpret* and *make meaning of* interaction. For example, if you're sitting around a table eating dinner with friends, everyone at the table is both making meaning as they interpret the signals that others are sending, and creating more signals that others use to make meaning of. Rhetoric is *all* of this, not just the signal-creating or signal-interpreting on their own.

You might already guess, then, that rhetoric has to do with behavior broadly, not just oral or written communication. Rhetoric is also about being and doing particular things that help contribute to the overall signals and meaning a person is trying to create. For instance, when you wanted to be admitted to your college and needed to convince the admissions office that you'd do well at that school, you had to present an overall image of someone who would be a good fit for the school. Part of presenting that image was in what you *said* in your admissions essay, but a larger part was in knowing who and how you needed to appear to be in your application. The principles of rhetoric let us predict this.

The attempts by rhetors to make meaning with their audience through both words and actions require them to find common ground, or **identification**, with their audience; in other words, it requires them to think of what both they and their audience might share as common *foundational values*. Maybe you're trying to convince your city to expand its homeless shelter. In order to solve that problem, you'll first need to find out what values you share (like limiting human suffering or taking care of the indigent) that will build common ground with the city in order to solve shared problems or meet shared needs (which we'll talk about as **exigence** later on). In your college admissions essay, consciously or not, you were trying to explain values that you and the school you were applying to have in common.

Rhetoric: Explaining How People Communicate and Make Meaning

Rhetoric attempts to explain how people communicate, how they make up their minds through interacting with each other, and how they change their minds. We can see some of rhetoric's explanatory principles when we look at examples of such communication. We'll talk about seven explanatory principles here:

- Meaning depends on context.
- Meaning-making is purposeful and motivated.
- Readers and writers interact to make meaning.
- Readers and writers interact to actually make new knowledge.
- Rhetorical interaction is embodied and material.
- Rhetoric is shaped by technology.
- Good writing and communication are contingent on situation, not universal.

These principles will sound a lot like the key threshold concepts this chapter takes up, because so many threshold concepts have to do with gaining a fuller understanding of rhetorical theory.

MEANING DEPENDS ON CONTEXT

You've probably been in situations where the same words had different meanings. If your mom is unloading groceries from the car and says, "Help me," you know what that means because the meaning is clear in the situation. Now suppose you're at the pool and your mom has been swimming laps and you know she's been feeling sick the last couple days and suddenly she stops in the lane and says, "Help me." You know right away that the same words mean something completely different, and you will respond differently. Why is that? It's because the situations in which we use language shape the meaning of the language we use.

Situations also influence what it makes sense to say: It would be a very strange thing for you to go up to the counter at the Department of Motor Vehicles and say, "I need your permission to join a circus." That's because the words don't fit the situation. Because the meaning of language and the things we choose to say depend so much on what situation we're in, one explanatory principle of rhetoric is that human interaction and discourse is **situated** (in time and in space). That's an important principle in rhetoric: When we say something is **rhetorical**, part of what we mean is that it is *situated*. If you've read texts from Chapters 2 or 3 of this book, you already know that discourse communities and activities are also situated. So discourse communities are, in this sense, rhetorical. You can learn more about why it's important that communication is always situated by reading, in this chapter, Keith Grant-Davie's article "Rhetorical Situations and Their Constituents."

Situatedness can be more complicated than it first sounds. The best way to under-stand rhetorical situation is as an **ecology**, where all the elements an interaction involves — people, events, circumstances, material objects, history, time, place, and space — form a *network* by which every element touches or influences and ultimately emerges from every other element. (You can read more about rhetorical ecology in Downs's piece.) This idea of ecology can help us understand rhetorical interchanges which seem *un*situated or multi-situated, like a Skype call with participants in five different countries around the world, or a multi-participant online comment thread stretched out over many months.

MEANING-MAKING IS PURPOSEFUL AND MOTIVATED

When was the last time you saw someone write or say something when they *truly* had no point or purpose? You know that guy who's always at your parties who talks on and on about stuff and yet never seems to have any reason for saying it? It's like he just can't stop talking even though everybody wants him to. Even then, to him, his talk has a purpose — he's trying to say something funny or interesting, he's trying to fill a silence, he's trying to get attention, he's trying to impress people. Even when people don't seem to have a point in what they say, they still have *motives* for say-ing it. There pretty much isn't any speech or writing in the world, in fact, that doesn't have *some* motive.

This is most true of writing, because writing takes a lot more effort than speaking; it's much less natural. When you see a piece of writing, you know the writer had some motive in producing it. (And remember, if you've read any of the Chapter 2 or 3 readings on activity systems or literacy histories, that there are goals, objectives, and motives in people's actions more broadly.) You should also recognize that not only writers have motives — so do readers. So do institutions in the writers' and readers' ecologies. (When a police officer writes you a speeding ticket, she has a motive, but so does the State that created the ticket form and the county court that will receive the ticket.) Even words themselves seem to have motives independent of the rhetors who use them.

A major principle of rhetoric, then, for explaining human interaction, is that texts and discourse are always **motivated** by particular purposes, needs, and values. And because a given discourse (talk or writing) always carries specific motivations, it can never be "objective" in the sense of "neutral" or "unbiased." Discourse is always and inevitably slanted because it is always motivated. So one thing you know, if you know rhetoric, is that when people claim not to have any motive in saying something, it isn't actually true. You can learn more about how communication is always moti-vated: read, in this chapter, Margaret Kantz's article on "Helping Students Use Textual Sources Persuasively" (p. 579). And for an example of how people's motivations may not always be clear, even to themselves, read Annalise Sigona's "Impression Management on Facebook and Twitter" (p. 619).

451

READERS AND WRITERS INTERACT TO MAKE MEANING

So far, then, two central principles of rhetoric are that communication is always *situated* and *motivated*. What can be easy to overlook is how these two principles suggest a third, which is that speech or writing gets its meaning not just from the speaker and not just from the listener, but in the *interaction* between speaker and listener. This principle is fairly easy to see in conversation: A shared meaning of the conversation as a whole emerges from the many back-and-forth interchanges between the speakers. But the way meaning arises through interaction can be harder to see in writing, because the interchange between writing-rhetors and reading-rhetors usually isn't physical and immediate — a text can be read a long time after it's written, in a completely different place. It is exactly this principle of *interaction* that explains why a text can be understood one way if it is read near to the time and place where the author writes it, but it will usually be understood differently when it's read in a different time and place. The text's meaning is established by how the writer (through the text) interacts with the reader and his or her situation; neither the writer nor the reader alone makes meaning.

Several readings in this chapter are based on this principle. For example, in "Digital Literacy and the Making of Meaning" (p. 674), Komysha Hassan studies how college students interact with the search interface on their campus library's home page, finding that the meaning the students make depends both on the text they're given (the search interface) and how they've made meaning of similar texts in the past — that is, the meaning they bring to the interface. Similarly, Natasha Jones and Stephanie Wheeler's "Document Design and Social Justice" (p. 654) explores how different readers interact differently with a given text based on their own bodies, so that different meanings emerge from the interaction. If you read Christina Haas and Linda Flower's "Rhetorical Reading Strategies and the Construction of Meaning" (p. 559), you'll encounter further underlying principles for how readers construct meaning by interacting with texts.

There's a further, special kind of interaction in meaning-making that happens *between texts themselves*, an interaction scholars call **intertextuality**. You'll find more about interaction and intertextuality in this chapter in James Porter's "Intertextuality and the Discourse Community" (p. 542).

READERS AND WRITERS MAKE KNOWLEDGE

So far, these ideas suggest that texts don't "contain" meaning and knowledge; readers and writers of texts interact to *construct* meaning and knowledge *from* them. Now we're approaching a fourth central principle of rhetoric: Human interaction and communication don't simply pass existing knowledge from place to place; they actually make *new* knowledge. You can see this happen when you're reading a text or listening to someone talk and something they say gives you a new idea — you find yourself thinking something *because* of what they said that *isn't* what they said. If you've ever had an argument with your parents or your own children, this knowledge-creating effect was probably happening: They said, "You have to do this thing you don't want to!" and you thought instead of all the reasons why you really *don't* have to do it. Your interaction created ideas that neither of you had had until the moment of that interaction. Or think of the last really difficult piece of writing you did for school. Did you have exactly the same ideas before you wrote it as you had after you wrote it? Probably not. What happens in writing moments like that is that as we write we think of things to say that we didn't know *before* we started writing.

There's a technical term for activities that create new knowledge: **epistemic**. Rhetorical activities are epistemic — they have to do with making new knowledge. You can read more about this idea in this chapter in Christina Haas and Linda Flower's "Rhetorical Reading Strategies and the Construction of Meaning" (p. 559) and in Margaret Kantz's "Helping Students Use Textual Sources Persuasively" (p. 579). They explain why your conception about "what writing is and how it works" matters. You do different things when you think "writing is just putting down ideas you already had" versus when you think "writing is *building* knowledge that didn't yet exist when you began writing."

RHETORICAL INTERACTION IS EMBODIED AND MATERIAL

For centuries, philosophers and scientists made a rigorous distinction between minds and bodies, and insisted that bodies don't matter all that much to intellectual work and creative discovery. Many theories of rhetoric, however, have maintained that there is no clear separation between mindful knowledge and bodily knowledge, that both are important to rhetoric, and that rhetoric is at least as much about materiality as about intellect. Therefore, in contemporary rhetoric, we always stress that rhetoric is material and embodied — it happens not simply in intellectual interaction but in the interaction of bodies situated in times and spaces. This idea matters because bodies, and their ecological situations, shape the meanings that emerge in rhetorical interactions: Different bodies have had different experiences and abilities; those experiences shape meaning-making. Different bodies have different expectations placed on them by culture and the people around them; those expectations shape meaning-making. Different bodies *feel* differently and thus *know* differently, which again shapes meaning-making. (Right now you should be thinking of examples of each one of these points, and it shouldn't be too difficult.)

You'll get a chance to learn and think more about material embodiment and its impact on meaning-making and human interaction if you read either Jim Corder's piece "Argument as Emergence, Rhetoric as Love" (p. 600) or Natasha Jones and Stephanie Wheeler's "Document Design and Social Justice" (p. 654).

RHETORIC IS SHAPED BY TECHNOLOGY

We can imagine a time in prehistory, before writing, painting, or tools, when rhetoric did not involve technology, but we have no record of it. Records require writing, writing is a technology, and this technology has been with us for thousands of years now. It's been a very long time since rhetoric was independent of technology in cultures that communicate through written language or drawing or other instruments.

You may be used to thinking of writing as being *done with* technology, which you probably first think of as screens and electricity. But we actually mean that writing (and therefore written rhetoric) *is* a technology — it is the human use of tools to accomplish a task. There is no writing without tools. Dennis Baron explains this idea in greater depth in his piece "From Pencils to Pixels" (p. 632), which talks about pencils as high technology.

Because such a large majority of our rhetorical interactions are now **mediated** by writing technologies of one kind or another, when we think about rhetoric we need to think about the impacts various technologies create on a.given rhetorical interaction. Different technologies lead to different rhetorical effects by creating unique combinations of **modes** such as language, sound, music, still image, moving image, and color. Even the simplest "writing" is **multimodal**, combining, at least, language, sound (when the language is read aloud), color, and material (the type of object that is written on). This principle that technology shapes rhetoric is so central to rhetorical theory that several of the pieces in this chapter consider it. The articles by Ridolfo and DeVoss, Porter, Sigona, Baron, Jones and Wheeler, and Hassan will all get you thinking about how rhetoric is shaped by the technologies with which we compose, inscribe, and share it.

"GOOD" WRITING AND COMMUNICATION IS CONTINGENT

This principle of rhetoric doesn't show up in just one or two readings; you can actually find it in nearly every reading in this book. It emerges when we put the previous six principles together. You'll see it in play when we ask this question: Which writing is better, the Declaration of Independence or the Gettysburg Address? Your first reaction might well be, "How is that question even *answerable*? Doesn't it *depend* on what criteria you use?" That's a reasonable response. Whether a text or discourse is good does depend on certain criteria; the word for that is **contingent**. You've probably heard people use that word: "Our weekend plans are contingent on the weather" or "You're admitted to this college contingent on completing your high school degree." In these uses, *contingent* means almost literally *depending on*.

If you walk through campus and ask various people, "What makes writing good?," you're likely to get a range of answers. Some will say, good proofreading and no errors. Others might say active verbs, or conciseness, or descriptive language, or clear organization, or a strong thesis. But the ones who are being *really* thoughtful will say something like, "That depends on what you're writing" or "That depends on what it's being used for." Why? Because of all of the principles we've just outlined above: Communication is situated in particular circumstances; motivated by specific goals; interactional by nature; epistemic, creating new knowledge through that interaction; and shaped by the bodies, materialities, and technologies that create it. Thus, the quality of any instance of rhetoric really must depend on all those factors. What makes it good will depend on its circumstances and context, and *that* means there can be few universal rules for what makes communication good. This is perhaps rhetoric's most significant principle: Qualities of good communication are contingent, not universal.

We've included a more compact statement of each of these principles in the definition of **rhetoric** in the glossary (p. 896) so that you can reference it quickly whenever you find yourself needing to return to these ideas. It will take a long time to think through all the implications of these principles — your class will only be the beginning of your understanding of rhetoric, because it's too big to understand all at once. Expect your understanding to be initially hazy and a bit confused; that's okay. More understanding will emerge with more reading, more examples, and more time.

Why Study Rhetoric?

You might be wondering how any of this helps you as a writer. Why is it useful to understand principles of rhetoric like these? What will you know after you read these articles and consider these ideas? Here are some reasons why principles of rhetoric matter to writers:

- The principles that writing is *situated* and *contingent* remind us to always be asking, "What in this situation and context will help me predict what will make this writing good?" These principles will also keep you from believing that criteria for writing that worked in *some other* situation will automatically work in your current one.
- The principle that writing is always *motivated* will help you remember, when you read texts, that they were designed specifically to accomplish something, and that their purpose inevitably gives them a slant and bias. It will help you remember as a writer to make sure you've considered your own motives in writing the piece, and that you're writing a piece that best embodies and enacts those motives.
- The principle that writing makes meaning through *interaction* will keep you from believing that just because you've written something, your readers should or must understand it easily and without complication. It helps you remember that your readers are always bringing their own background, experiences, and language to your writing, and that to know how they'll make meaning of the text, you have to try to anticipate what it is they bring. This principle also reminds you that texts make meaning by connecting to other existing texts, and helps you think about to what extent you're required to be "original" in a given piece of writing.
- The principle that rhetoric is *material and embodied* will help you remember that rhetoric is not merely a mind-game, but that it emerges from, is shaped by, and in turn influences bodies and material objects. Meaning-making

happens in, through, and to bodies and other tangible objects — not apart from or in spite of them.

- The principle that writing (as a form of rhetoric) is *epistemic* helps you remember that you'll never just be "transmitting information" by writing ideas that your readers "receive" unaltered. As you think more about this principle, you'll learn to anticipate ways that you'll learn from your own writing, and that it will build new ideas even as you're drafting.
- The principle that rhetoric is *shaped by technology* will remind you that the technologies you use to compose, inscribe, and share texts and discourses are never neutral or value-free — the technologies that create your rhetoric constrain your rhetoric.

The readings in this chapter help you see *why* and *how* these principles work, and they therefore should help you make your own conceptions of writing consistent with them. If you believe there's one right way or one best way to write, these readings will challenge you. If you already want to answer every writing question with "it depends," these readings will give you reasons with which you can explain that answer to others. If you believe that the best way to write is to figure out everything you want to say *before* you write and then just get it all written down unaltered, never looking back, then some of the readings in this chapter show that you might write more successfully if you think about writing as discovering and making new meaning *while* you write rather than just recording ideas you already knew.

Because rhetoric offers a systematic explanation of how people make knowledge and meaning from interaction through language — helping us see how we make up our minds and how we change them — it's excellent for helping writers know what to write, and helping us as humans better understand how we *actually* work to persuade each other to accept our ideas. There's great power in this kind of knowledge. As you start seeing the rhetorical principles from these readings in action around you, you'll understand better why your writing works as it does.

CHAPTER GOALS

- To understand the basic outlines of rhetorical theory and its relation to writing and human interaction
- To understand the concept of *rhetorical situation* (and *ecology*) and be able to apply it to reading and writing situations
- To understand how writers construct texts persuasively (or not)
- To understand how readers construct meaning from texts
- To understand what it means to say that knowledge is *constructed*
- To understand some approaches to rhetorically analyzing texts

Rhetoric: Making Sense of Human Interaction and Meaning-Making

Courtesy of Doug Downs

DOUG DOWNS

Framing the Reading

There is a genre within rhetoric studies that summarizes broad swaths of rhetorical theory into relatively compact, coherent accounts. This selection by Doug Downs — one of the editors of *Writing about Writing* — is one of these. It was composed specifically for this book to create a guide to rhetoric that would work for readers new to the study of rhetorical theory. The reading goes deeper into some of the principles discussed in the introduction to the chapter. This means that unlike most other pieces in this book, this selection is primarily addressed to readers like you — not writing scholars.

Downs's article uses an extended example of grant-writers for a nonprofit organization to walk readers through many of rhetoric's main principles. It integrates concepts from classical (Greek) rhetoric such as **rhetorical situation**, the rhetorical canons, **kairos**, and the **pisteis** (you might know them as *logos*, *ethos*, and *pathos*) with late twentieth and twenty-first century rhetorical principles such as rhetorical **ecology**, **embodiment** and felt sense, **narrative** ways of knowing, informal logic, and identification. (To the extent the paper's subject is interesting to you, you may want to pay more attention than normal to the footnotes, which include suggestions for additional reading on these various principles.)

Many of the ideas overviewed in this piece are addressed in greater depth in other readings in the chapter. If you find yourself losing track, in some other readings, of how what they talk about relates to rhetoric and writing as a whole, you may find it helpful to turn back to this reading and see how the concept fits in to the larger whole of rhetorical theory. Two particular ideas in this paper — ecology and embodiment — *aren't* addressed as such in other readings (though they are presented in the chapter introduction). Take in what you can about them here so you'll be able to see how these ideas connect to those you'll encounter later in the chapter.

Downs is an associate professor of writing studies at Montana State University, where he also directs the university's Core Writing Program and serves as editor of *Young Scholars in Writing*, the national journal of undergraduate research in rhetoric and writing studies. He studies the teaching of reading and research in writing classes, and he has published widely on writing-about-writing pedagogy.

Getting Ready to Read

Before you read, do at least one of the following activities:

- Write a definition of *rhetoric* as you understand it right now. What does the word mean to you? How do you usually hear it used?

- Look up the word *ecology.* Your definition will probably talk about relationships between organisms and their surroundings. Make a list of the ecologies that you personally participate in. Start thinking about what it means to be a part of an ecology — what kind of networks you participate in, and how the various elements of that network influence each other.

- Think about someone you know who is famous for their rhetoric or their abilities with oratory. What is the person you thought of famous for? What was memorable about their rhetoric?

As you read, consider the following questions:

- How does what Downs is saying connect with what you already knew about rhetoric?

- What concepts discussed in this selection do you wish you could learn more about right away?

THIS GUIDE WALKS YOU through *rhetoric*, a set of principles for human interaction that most people know unconsciously but don't think much about. Rhetorical principles organize and explain much of human communication, interaction, and experience. But most high school and college students don't study them in much depth, and in fact, in earlier schooling most have been taught ideas that conflict with principles of rhetoric. (Many come to believe, for example, that there are rules of writing that are true in all writing situations; rhetoric suggests there are not.) The pages that follow synthesize more than 2,500 years of rhetorical theory—so buckle up! When you know rhetoric, you know how people make up their minds and how they change them. You know how people make meaning of the world around them. You know how people come to believe that an idea is true, that it counts as "knowledge." When you know rhetoric, you gain a kind of "signal intelligence" that makes you a more powerful reader and writer.

Usually, by the term "rhetoric" western culture means something different than any of that. Common conceptions of rhetoric include the following:

- *"Calculated political BS"* (as in, "The congressman's rhetoric is just grand-standing to make it look like his opponents want to kill puppies").

- *"Dressing up a bad idea in convincing words"* (as did Hitler).
- *"Style lacking in substance"* (as in "That environmental activist's speech is very moving but it's just rhetoric").
- *Asking a rhetorical question* that everyone already knows the answer to just to make a point (as in, "You took my car out and now the fender's crumpled—how do you think that happened?").
- *Persuasive tactics* (as when Aristotle said that rhetoric is the art of seeing "the available means of persuasion in each case").

Those five uses of the word "rhetoric" constitute the total knowledge of most people on the subject. This guide will cover different ground about "what rhetoric is."

Rhetoric explains why I started this piece by saying what it isn't. There's a principle of human interaction that if readers have one idea about a concept (like "rhetoric is political BS") and a writer wants to present a contrasting idea, she needs to first explain that her idea comes from a much different place than where the readers are starting. Otherwise, readers may not realize the writer is using a different "lens" and, trying to interpret the writer's text just through their own lens, may not get a good understanding of what she's trying to say. "Rhetoric" refers both to such principles of meaning-making, and to the use of those principles in a given interaction.

WHAT DOES THE TERM "RHETORIC" APPLY TO?

One frustrating aspect of studying rhetoric is that the word has so many meanings. That makes it hard to get a grip on what "rhetoric" refers to, which is not a comfortable feeling for most people. When it comes to rhetoric, though, this fuzziness is normal, and gradually it diminishes. In the beginning, it helps to think about what rhetoric "does."

Consider this comparison: The term *rhetoric* is like the term *gravity*—a set of principles that explain and predict how chunks of matter interact. (Remember Newton's laws of gravity?) But "gravity" also refers to that interaction itself, the universal condition ("force") in which matter is attracted to other matter. In computer or gamer terms, we could say that gravity is an "operating system" for the interaction of matter—it sets the rules and structures for how everything will interact. Now, a lot of people—skiers, skydivers, astronauts, auto racers, high-jumpers, airplane pilots, gymnasts, scuba divers—aren't just "subject to" gravity but are *artful users* of gravity. They take this independently existing force that is simply written into the nature of matter and which all matter, including humans, is thus subject to—and they strategically apply it to make their activities possible.

In a similar way, the term *rhetoric* refers to *a set of principles that explain* 6
and predict how people make meaning and interact. But like "gravity," "rhetoric"
applies not only to the principles for human interaction but to that interaction
itself, the embodied expression of those principles. So, *rhetoric is an operating sys-*
tem for human interaction and meaning-making. Rhetoric also refers to the *artful*
use of those ever-present rhetorical principles. Some people learn to be rhetorical
experts who can take those underlying principles shaping human interaction
and finesse them in specific activities. The most obvious of these experts include
counselors, comedians, lawyers, judges, advertisers, journalists, writers, and dip-
lomats. But there are almost no human activities that don't involve interaction
with other humans, which means that there is almost no activity you might be
involved in that you can't do better as an aware user of rhetoric. Nurses and
surgeons specialize in working on and healing people's bodies, but insofar as
that work requires communicating with other doctors and nurses and with their
patients, a nurse or surgeon who is a rhetoric super-user will probably get better
results than those who aren't. Engineers? Same story. They aren't hired for their
communication ability, but the engineers who can't write wind up working for
the ones who can. Mathematicians are in the same situation. Most of what they
do with math is rhetorical—including debating with other mathematicians
about the best ways of doing math.

So start here: Rhetoric is pervasive. Given that it is an operating system for 7
human meaning-making and interaction, any time we are making meaning
and interacting—otherwise known as "being human"—we are using rhetoric.
There isn't any way to communicate without using rhetoric or "being rhetorical." Communication is inevitably rhetorical. You can't choose whether or not
to use rhetoric. The only question is *how* you'll use it when you're more aware
of how it works.

Another good place to begin is recognizing the ways rhetoric can help us. 8
Since rhetoric helps us understand human communication, there are a variety of
problems or questions that rhetoric can help us
make sense of. From its ancient roots as a study
of persuasive speech, rhetoric offers explanations
for *how we make up our minds and how we change*
them. Because rhetoric has to do with how we
make meaning of our experiences, it also gives us
some keys to understanding *how we know what*
we know. (The technical term for this subject is
epistemology.) The rhetorical principles discussed
here can even reveal something about *who we*
are likely to admire and befriend. In its narrowest
application, rhetoric lets us study *how we can most effectively communicate.* In
its broadest, it shows us *ways of being* and ways of *recognizing the being of others.*

> *Given that it is an operating*
> *system for human meaning-*
> *making and interaction, any*
> *time we are making meaning*
> *and interacting—otherwise*
> *known as "being human"—*
> *we are using rhetoric.*

BEGINNING WITH BODIES

Rhetoric begins in the biology of how sentient bodies[1] experience information and interaction via signals and symbols. Kenneth Burke, one of the premier rhetorical theorists of the 20th century, showed that rhetoric always involves symbolic acts, in which meaning is made when one idea or object stands for another. Such substitution is the entire basis of language, in which sounds stand for (symbolize) ideas and objects. But language of course is not the only symbol system we encounter as humans; humans can turn *anything* into a symbol. We make symbols of clothing, jewelry, objects like cars and homes, animals (mascots), and human behaviors from winks to jumps. (Like in *Game of Thrones* where "bending the knee" symbolizes kneeling which in turn symbolizes accepting a ruler.) As babies leave infanthood they learn that crying symbolizes physical needs (food, warmth, changing, comfort) to their caretakers. Children quickly associate one particular stomach sensation with hunger (we say that feeling is "a sign of" hunger) and a different stomach feeling with illness. You use symbols every time you encounter a green light hanging above the intersection of two streets, and know that this means "go," or a red octagon on a street corner, and know that this means "stop." Making one object or concept stand for some otherwise unrelated concept or object is one of our most basic human ways of making meaning.

Rhetoric begins with this very basic element of sentient (self-aware) embodiment. While we most often focus on *language* as the vehicle for symbolizing, communication scholars have shown that the majority of human communication and nearly the entirety of human/animal communication is nonverbal. Eyes, faces, the tilt of a head, hands, limbs, stance, posture, gait, demeanor, perspiration, voice and tone — our bodies create myriad signals that reveal to others a wide range of information about us. Add to this list the signals your body creates that can only be sensed by you — like the butterflies in your stomach when you show up for a first date (though your date may be able to read something similar on your face!). But to the extent you attend to your felt senses throughout an experience, those feelings and sensations are a crucial root of the meaning you make of each moment.[2]

Our bodies not only generate the signals which we and others interpret, but also contain our embodied sensory apparatus for perceiving and filtering both those signals and all the other signals our physical surroundings generate. What in an everyday sense we take as first-hand, direct experience is in fact filtered by our limited senses and then by perceptual interpretation of the resulting signal. Does

9

10

11

---

[1] We usually think of rhetoric as a human activity, but it's not difficult to identify rhetorical activity among a wide variety of animal species, as both George Kennedy and Natasha Seegart have demonstrated.

[2] Perhaps the most extensive writing on this subject is by Sondra Perl in her 2004 book *Felt Sense*.

cilantro taste like soap? We actually don't know. About 10 percent of the population thinks so, and the rest don't perceive it that way. The reality that is cilantro is impossible for us to encounter except through the filters of our senses. Our ears and eyes similarly give us access to only a portion of reality. Our eyes, which account for about 40 percent of our brains' sensory processing bandwidth, have a "frame rate" of 16 to 20 images per second—we don't actually see "continuously" as it appears to us that we do. Instead, our eyes take many still images per second and our brains "fill in" the gaps to create our perception of seeing moving images.

Our senses, then, are essentially filters that give us partial information, which 12 our brains must interpret into a sensible whole. Happily, our brains are pretty good at stitching that incomplete information together. We do that through another basic brain operation, *association*: we make sense of new information by connecting it to (associating it with) known information. If a friend tells you they're going to go deposit a check, you can reasonably "know" that they're going to a bank—because prior knowledge and past experience tell you (1) what "deposit" is, (2) what "check" is, and (3) where one usually needs to go in order to "deposit" a "check." If it weren't for your brain's ability to create vast "neural networks" that make and recall associations between new objects and ideas and those you've previously learned, you wouldn't be able to accomplish much. All this perception and interpretation, though, wreaks havoc with tasks like eyewitness testimony in courtrooms. Study after study has demonstrated that in high-stress situations like witnessing a crime, what people report seeing afterward is usually more what they would have *expected* to see (that business about making sense of new information by associating it with and interpreting it in light of prior knowledge) than with what they could actually have witnessed.

Not all of our interpretation of signals is driven by our bodies, but much of the 13 meaning we make ultimately is. Linguists George Lakoff and Mark Johnson use a study of metaphor to show just how much of our everyday language is driven by bodily, physical comparisons. For example, our culture believes that *a mind is a brittle object*, as exemplified by language like "His ego is very *fragile*," "She just *snapped*," "He *broke* under cross-examination," "she is easily *crushed*," "the experience *shattered* him," and "I'm *going to pieces*" (28). Metaphor links our bodily experience to many concepts. Bodily, *up* is generally good and *down* is generally bad, as we associate "down" with illness, depression, unconsciousness, and death and "up" with health, energy, vigor, "sharpness," and vitality. Lakoff and Johnson then show that we also associate *up* with having control, force, or power: "I have control *over* her. I am *on top of* the situation. He's in a *superior* position. He's at the *height* of his power. . . . He is *under* my control. He *fell* from power. His power is on the *decline*. . . . He is *low man* on the totem pole" (15). This everyday metaphorical function of language is evidence that much of our meaning-making relates to bodily experience.

Human interaction and meaning-making is at heart, then, the experience of 14 encountering a vast range of sensory signals and interpreting them by associating them with networks of our existing knowledge. Your average human is a genius at assembling a stream of disparate signals into a sensible whole, and this is the physical reality that rhetoric works with. A colleague of mine, Kimberly Hoover, accordingly describes rhetoric as "signal intelligence," because rhetoric is ultimately about the ways that we make sense of and respond to the many signals in our experience of a moment — signals from other people, from our surroundings, and from our own bodies. Rhetorical theorist George Kennedy suggests the parallel term *energy*: "the emotional energy that impels the speaker to speak, the physical energy expended in the utterance, the energy level encoded in the message, and the energy experienced by the recipient in decoding the message" (106).

All this biology and physics together have the following implications for rhet- 15 oric: First, *bodies matter* to knowing, meaning-making, and interaction. So *rhetoric must be about bodies as much as minds*, and about the material as much as the conceptual. Which may be counterintuitive, because western culture since at least Descartes ("I think, therefore I am") has a tradition of, incorrectly, radically separating the mind and body. Contemporary rhetoric, particularly feminist rhetorical theory, makes clear the centrality of the body in making meaning, knowledge, and rhetoric (Kirsch and Royster, Wenger).

Second, because our knowledge, filtered through sensory perception, can 16 only ever be partial and selective, *human interaction can never be based on complete, objective knowledge.* Objectivity is not physically or biologically possible for humans: we are limited to selectivity and partiality, which makes bias (literally *slanting*) inevitable. We can be *more* or *less* objective by trying to get the most complete view of a situation or experience possible, but we can never *achieve* objectivity. Rhetoric must therefore not rely on, or be about the achievement of, objectivity. Rather, it must have something to do with letting people interact *without* objectivity — as subjective beings.

Third, because we make meaning by interpreting filtered sensory informa- 17 tion, we cannot think about events directly; we can only think about our *interpretation of* events. You can experience a moment, but as soon as you reflect on that moment, try to put it in language, or look at a picture of it, you're no longer in that moment or talking about that moment; you're talking about your interpretation of it. The implication is that human interaction is always interpreted: what I say *next* depends on my *interpretation* of what you said *last*, and only unreflected-upon bodily experience can be (briefly) uninterpreted. So *rhetoric must be a system for and art of interpreting other people's actions.*

Fourth, our bodies' ways of making meaning by putting new information in 18 terms of known information (symbolism) or figuring out its relation to known information (association) suggest that *rhetoric is always a matter of the symbolic.* If a phenomenon is, or can be made into, a symbol, it is rhetorical. *Where there are people, there is, inevitably, rhetoric.*

A RHETORICAL GUIDE TO HUMAN INTERACTION

Most moments of rhetorical action stem from people trying to do things with or 19 to each other, cooperatively or agonistically (in competition). People work on a Golden Gate bridge or a rocket to the moon. People farm a field or run cattle on a ranch. People clean up tidal marshes after an oil spill. People try to impose their religion on others by war. People become lovers. People run a school board. In every such scene, people work with, for, through, and against each other, every bit of that work happening according to a web of rhetorical principles entangled with and always leading back to one another. In this section, I'll overview some of those principles and how they fit with one another by telling the story of Maria, Ian, and Jayla, grant writers at Reading Rivers, a nonprofit center for children's literacy in the rural West.

Rhetorical Elements

Motivation
Ecology
    Rhetors / Network
    Context
    Exigence
    Kairos / The Moment
    Interaction and Collaboration
Knowledge Making
    Narrative / Making Present
    Values (Pathos Appeals and Mythos)
    Reasoning (Logos Appeals)
Identification
    Ethos Appeals
    Adherence
Canons (Rhetorical Arts)

Motivation

As grant writers, Maria, Ian, and 20 Jayla come to Reading Rivers each day with a particular motive: to raise money from government agencies, charitable donors, and corporations—money to buy books for children, to support local libraries, and to host literacy events for kids from poor families in remote areas of the western United States that lack much funding for public arts and social services. The entirety of the grant writer's fundraising work is done through rhetorical interaction with people all over the country, and one starting point of that interaction is always the team members' motives *for* interacting. *Rhetoric is always motivated.* People in rhetorical interactions—writers and readers—are always having those interactions for particular reasons that relate to what they want or need from the interaction. As discussed in the previous section, human biology makes objectivity impossible; we are always subjective, partial, and biased. Our *motives* are another aspect of that subjectivity.

In this case, the grant team's most obvious motives are to raise money for 21 the cause they work for: helping children in poverty to become better readers and writers. But other motives are in play as well. The team members are paid by Reading Rivers to bring in funds; if they don't succeed in doing so, they might lose their jobs. Suppose that Maria grew up in poverty, and she sees literacy as a powerful way to combat it; one of her motives might be getting children out of poverty. Perhaps Jayla cares about social justice and is trying to provide poor people the same opportunities as wealthier people. Ian might like developing public funding for the arts and can use this job as a way to do so.

We cannot attend only the motives of the writers in the interaction, though. 22 With some reflection, it should be obvious that a listener's or reader's purposes or desires and the reasons for them (motives) shape the interaction, too. Our grant writers have to care about their readers' motives and resulting subjectivities. Grant reviewers are motivated to follow the correct process in awarding grants; they're also motivated by their interpretations of what will make the best use of grant funds to meet the purpose of the grant. And beyond writers and readers, there will be other nonhuman agents that bring motives to the interaction. The shared root of *motive*, *motivate*, *motivation*, and *motion* (Latin *motivus*, from *movere*) is *to move*. To say that rhetorical interaction is always "motivated" is to say that it is always moved by forces, causes, and desires. Some of these may be human and conscious; others may be human and unconscious. Others may not be human at all. In the same way that we can say water "wants" to run downhill, or that water is "motivated" (forced) to run downhill, we could for example say that government funds "want" (by nature of being what they are) to be spent rather than be saved. This motive of the funds themselves matters for grant writers. If our writers are applying for a grant for a library, it matters that libraries have particular motives (for example, to build collections of books). In this way, rhetorical theorists like Laura Micciche argue that it is not just human rhetors who have agency in rhetorical interactions; other entities that influence and constrain interactions can be understood as motivated and controlling as well.

Ultimately, the motives in rhetorical interaction are extremely complex, and 23 many will be hidden or unknown—but all are central to the interaction. The better you understand all of the motives playing into a given interaction, the more likely you are to be an effective rhetor in that interaction.

Ecology

It's obvious that a rhetorical interaction has to take place somewhere (or multiple 24 somewheres) in space and time. We could call it a scene (invoking a sense of drama, as Burke does), a site (invoking a bounded sense of physical space), a setting (invoking a sense of story), or a situation (invoking a sense of "state of affairs" or circumstances). The most common term is *rhetorical situation*, used by theorists like Lloyd Bitzer and Keith Grant-Davie. But probably the best current term for rhetorical situations, pioneered by a number of scholars including Marilyn Cooper and Jenny Edbauer, is *ecology*, because it invokes a sense of *a place defined by a network of myriad interconnecting and almost inseparable elements that all shape the rhetorical interaction and meaning that emerges from them.*

In the case of Jayla, Maria, and Ian at Reading Rivers, any given grant proposal they write has its own ecology. Common elements across all their grants would be the writers and Reading Rivers itself. Each element is a rhetor, an actor in a given rhetorical ecology who influences, creates, encounters, or reads the text or discourse in question.[3] One grant proposal Jayla and Maria are working on is a U.S. Department of Education grant for after-school programs. Those two writers are the main producers of the grant proposal. But the proposal has many other contributing rhetors who are, in essence, also authors. The first of these are the people in the USDE who created the grant program, solicited proposals, and will read them during proposal review. These are the people who wrote the instructions for how the grant proposal is to be completed — so in many respects they are telling Jayla and Maria *what to write, and how.* They aren't the "authors," per se, but as the proposal's readers, they help constitute the ecology, the network of influences and actors, that is the environment in which Jayla and Maria are writing. Writers and readers — you might imagine that's the end of the list of rhetors. But also in this rhetorical ecology are the people whom the grant is *for*, rural schoolchildren and their teachers and families. If Reading Rivers is doing its job well, the organization has asked these people exactly what they need and would like in their after-school program — so these kids and parents have contributed to the design of what Jayla and Maria are seeking funds for, and that makes them "writers" of the grant proposal as well. Even if they hadn't contributed, that they will be *affected by* the grant proposal makes them a part of the rhetorical ecology and therefore rhetors just the same. What emerges in any rhetorical ecology, then, is a *network* of rhetors, many people with a variety of connections to each other.

Using the term *ecology* reminds us to look beyond *people* for even more elements influencing the writing. Can machines be rhetors? Imagine Maria's computer crashing as she drafts, the hard-drive eating itself and taking her draft and supporting documents with it. Maria has to start over — which we can expect will lead to writing of a different shape than it would otherwise have been. So in the rhetorical ecology leading to a given text or discourse, yes, a machine is

[3]Traditionally, rhetorical theory separates *rhetors* into "speaker" and "audience." The shortcoming of these terms is in suggesting that speakers don't listen while they speak and audiences don't speak while they listen, when in fact people in rhetorical interaction are constantly simultaneously speaking and listening. It's more accurate to speak of all involved as rhetors and emphasize their various *roles* of writing and reading, or speaking and listening, as needed.

a rhetor. Scholars like Thomas Rickert in his work on "ambient rhetoric" trace a wide range of environmental conditions that contribute to a rhetorical interchange, all interacting to give our discourse whatever shape it ends up taking. In a rhetorical ecology there may be pets, food and drink, furniture, even lights, colors, and music which become rhetorical agents in this fashion.

Another way of understanding a rhetorical ecology is as the overall context in 27 which a rhetorical interaction (or set of interactions) takes place. Importantly, this context includes the exigence of the interaction, which Keith Grant-Davie defines as the *need* for a given rhetorical interaction to occur to begin with. What needs, desires, and motives in the rhetorical ecology, we can ask, *"call" the interaction into being to begin with*? If the ecology spans what Grant-Davie calls *compound rhetorical situations*, there will be multiple exigencies. For Maria and Ian, for example, one exigence is *that* the USDE has created this grant to begin with, and a proposal is required to secure funding from it. But another exigence is *why* the grant was created in the first place: a difficulty in providing literacy education in poor, rural areas. We know that each grant writer has their own motivations for participating in this grant writing; we could think of *exigence* as the ecology's own "motivations" for creating a rhetorical interaction to begin with.

We must also consider *events* in the ecology, for which we have an ancient 28 (Greek) rhetorical term, *kairos*, which translates to something like "timely good fortune" or simply "lucky timing." *Kairos* is the principle that rhetors have far-from-complete control of their texts and discourses, because circumstances beyond their control can intervene to change the moment and *what it makes sense to say* in that moment. As I wrote the first draft of this paper, Michigan Governor Rick Snyder was set to deliver his annual "State of the State" address. Rather than solely trumpeting his successes as governor, circumstances forced him to focus extensively on the poisoned water supply of Flint, Michigan, which became contaminated with lead due to a decision he supported to attempt to save a small amount of money on the water supply. Snyder was supposed to be the rhetor "in control" of his own speech, but *kairos* dictated much of what the speech would be about and what Snyder could say in it.

The same power of circumstances and "being in the right place at the right 29 time" (or not) will shape the work of our grant writers at Reading Rivers. If while they're working on their grant proposal, news is released of a significant drop in reading test scores in the area their after-school program will serve, they would suddenly have an additional reason in support of the need for funding their program. *Kairos* reminds us that many aspects of a rhetorical ecology to which we must respond are well outside our control as rhetors.

Not only does the notion of a rhetorical ecology help us know to look for as 30 many influences and factors shaping a text or discourse as we can find (either as its writers or its readers), but it reminds us that *writers neither write alone nor have perfect control of their texts*. Though it is usually portrayed as such in the movies, writing is not a solo activity. Recognizing rhetorical *ecologies* helps make clear the *interconnectedness* and blurred boundaries among various rhetorical agents, showing us how an interaction is shaped not by a single rhetor but by many, and the shape of the resulting text or discourse depends on (is contingent on) the exact interplay among those agents. Rhetorical interaction is therefore inevitably collaborative and shared.

Knowledge Making

Much of what rhetorical theory devotes its attention to is the many ways people 31 have of making a point. This is the place Ian, Maria, and Jayla find themselves, if they have thoughtfully taken account of the rhetorical ecology in which they find themselves on this grant proposal project, and if they're well aware of their own motives as rhetors. *What are they actually going to say* to explain their program, show the need for and value of it, and make the best possible case for getting grant funds for their project? It may initially seem strange to see this question characterized by the heading *knowledge making*, but that is quite literally what these rhetors need to do. They need to build their readers' knowledge of what they're proposing and why it's a good idea. To do this, they don't simply "transmit" existing knowledge to other rhetors. Instead, their interaction with other rhetors actually makes new knowledge for those other rhetors, knowledge that hadn't existed before. Rhetorical interaction always makes new knowledge.

Narrative

The first important rhetorical principle here is that of narrative. One line of 32 thought in rhetorical theory is that humans know by storytelling—that we are, in the words of communication scholar Walter Fisher, *homo narrans*, storytelling people. Fisher, and others such as Jim W. Corder in "Argument as Emergence, Rhetoric as Love," argue that we know ourselves and the world around us through story, and that when people argue against each other, what we are actually hearing is *contending narratives*, different storylines that conflict with each other. For Corder, people *themselves* are narratives. Certainly, we know that even the most scientific knowledge-making (rhetoric) proceeds by storytelling. Any science journal article you might pick up will narrate a story:[4] "We wanted to

---

[4]If you associate storytelling with *fiction* ("made up"), this idea might initially be hard. But remember that factual accounts in everything from courtroom narratives ("Let me tell you the story of the attack on this victim") to news reports ("Did you see the story on that oil train derailment?!") are normally referred to as stories. "Stories" need not be fiction. (Or, reaching the same place from the opposite direction, because we cannot recognize or create objective stories, perhaps even the most factually accurate stories are nonetheless a kind of fiction.)

find out X so we took steps A, B, and C, and then looked at the results and saw that L, M, and N. From that, we didn't learn X but we do know Y and Z." From a rhetorical perspective, then, it behooves writers and readers to imagine just about any text or discourse as a narrative or a story, and to frame the work of rhetors as storytelling—creating an account of some knowledge to be shared between writing and reading rhetors.

So is Jayla and Maria's grant proposal an act of storytelling? Absolutely. The 33 proposal reviewers in Washington, DC, need to understand the story of the rural children who will benefit from these grant funds, and they need to read the story of *how* the grant will make a difference.

Not only do the reviewers need to encounter this narrative, but the grant 34 writers need to find a way to use their writing to turn their program from a mental abstraction into a flesh-and-blood event shaping real people's lives. One powerful possibility of narratives—recognized by rhetorical theorists from Aristotle to Chaim Perelman in the mid-twentieth century—is the ability of stories to make abstract concepts *present*, to "bring them before the eyes" of rhetors encountering the narrative. Perhaps the most powerful recent example of such presence in 2016 is the widely seen image of a drowned Syrian refugee boy lying on a beach. The effect of this narrated image (the photo always appears with a caption or news story explaining what it portrays) is *precisely* that "making present" of an abstract idea. It is easier not to care about "refugees" when you've never been forced to *look* at one. (Just as it is easier, for example, to mock and fear gay people if you believe none of your family or neighbors are gay—which is to say, if none are *present* to you.) Jayla and Maria would be wise, therefore, to try writing a narrative that brings the children their program will affect "before the eyes" of the grant reviewers.

Rhetorical Appeals

Narrative and presence are just two of many tools rhetors have for making 35 knowledge. Several others are kinds of *appeals*, in the typical sense of "things I can say to try to get you to see things my way." Aristotle observed that people usually make three overall kinds of appeals (*pisteis*, in Greek): to logic (*logos*), to emotion (*pathos*), and to a rhetor's credibility (*ethos*). We still use these categories, although the ensuing 2,500 years of rhetorical theory have given us more to say about them.

Most decision-making is ultimately based on *values*, deeply held (sometimes 36 entirely unconscious) beliefs about what is desirable, necessary, important, pleasurable, and valuable, as well as what is dangerous, destructive, contrary to self-interest, painful, or unpleasant. Maslow's hierarchy of needs (see Figure 1, p. 470) is a good set of categories of human values (physiological, safety, love and belonging, self-esteem, and self-actualization). If we like or desire a thing, we have a value for it, or for what it represents; if we dislike or reject a thing, we

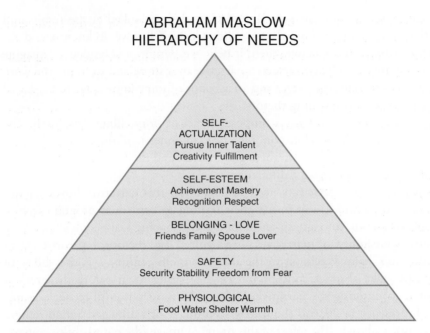

ABRAHAM MASLOW
HIERARCHY OF NEEDS

SELF-
ACTUALIZATION
Pursue Inner Talent
Creativity Fulfillment

SELF-ESTEEM
Achievement Mastery
Recognition Respect

BELONGING - LOVE
Friends Family Spouse Lover

SAFETY
Security Stability Freedom from Fear

PHYSIOLOGICAL
Food Water Shelter Warmth

Figure 1 Maslow's Hierarchy of Needs Maslow, Abraham. *Motivation and Personality.*
2nd ed. Harper and Row, 1970.

have a value against it or what it represents. Human interaction is relentlessly based on and driven by values. Something as simple as asking your roommate to turn on a light relies on a range of values: the security value of preferring light to darkness, the esteem value of assuming you're worthy of asking other people for help, the altruism value of knowing that your roommate will be happy to offer such assistance. If your desire for the light, or the light your roommate chooses to turn on, go beyond the pure utility of lighting a dark space and is a decorative or artful light, then your request also engages aesthetic values and a desire for beautiful pleasures.

Social-issues discussions are hugely value-driven, as George Lakoff has demonstrated in his book *Moral Politics.* He argues that much of politics on the left and right in the United States can be attributed to two value sets: a conservative "strong father" set that values self-reliance, "tough love," "rugged individualism," and (therefore) private solutions to problems; and a liberal "nurturing parent" set that values inter-reliance, taking care of others, communality, and (therefore) public solutions to problems. What seem to us the best ways to address child poverty, apportion public lands for multiple uses, develop energy to power our lifestyles, maintain public safety, and explore outer space—all depend on our value sets. We will be attracted to solutions and policies that accord with our values, and we'll think that solutions and policies that

37

contradict our values — our deepest beliefs about how the world does, can, and should work — are bad ideas.

Values are not always in conflict, of course. Most human interaction and soci-   38
ety is actually based on values held in common. *Culture* is simply the sum of a community's shared values. Together, these values, and the common knowledge they're based on, fuse into stories that ancient Greek rhetors referred to as *mythos*, accounts of how the world works that are shared by entire peoples. Unlike today's derivate English word *myth*, which in everyday speech means a fantasy or fiction, *mythos* spoke to the deepest foundational beliefs a people could share. According to philosopher Robert Pirsig in *Zen and the Art of Motorcycle Maintenance*, mythos is the sum of a culture's shared knowledge, "the huge body of common knowledge that unites our minds as cells are united in the body" (350). Today our mythos includes a heliocentric solar system in which planets revolve around the sun, which is one member of one galaxy among billions speeding through an expand-ing universe. Our mythos includes the notion that lifeforms are comprised of cells whose shape and functions are determined by DNA and constant adaptation and mutation. Part of our mythos, in other words, is physical information and our interpretations of it. Another part is "common sense": Take an umbrella when you're going out on a rainy day. Avoid sick people to help keep from getting sick yourself. Eat a balanced diet. (Now if we only knew what counted as "balanced.") And one kind of common sense is our deepest foundational values. Killing pup-pies is bad. Treasure innocence. Protect the weak. How deep does mythos run? Pirsig argues that it is our rock-bottom definition of *sanity*: to believe something other than your culture's mythos is to appear insane to your fellow humans. Or from a different direction, if you want to map our mythos, look at what counts as sanity by seeing what counts as its opposite, insanity.

This feels, maybe, a long way from Ian, Jayla, and Maria's grant writing for   39
Reading Rivers, but it's not. Look at the roles mythos and values play in their grant proposal:

> *Mythos*: Literacy, as reading and writing ability, is one of the most important kinds of knowledge a person can have.
>
> *Value*: One good use of tax dollars is to provide for needy people in difficult economic circumstances.
>
> *Mythos*: Caring is demonstrated, and problem-solving is facilitated, by directing shared resources or spending to people who lack it.
>
> *Mythos*: Extraordinary resources should be devoted to the care of children.
>
> *Mythos*: Every American is supposed to have an equal opportunity to live a "good life" of economic success.
>
> *Value*: Public funds should be used to support arts-related experiences.

The difference between *mythos* and *values* is simply what proportion of the public believes, and how deeply they believe, the particular story being told. But in all these cases, our grant writers' *reasons* for arguing for a grant come down to shared cultural *beliefs*—their *mythos* and *values*—about what is good and valuable for members of society.

Traditional rhetorical theory talked not about appeals to values but to *emotion*, via the *pisti* of *pathos*. What's the connection? Emotional appeals—usually portrayed as tear-jerking or emotionally manipulative claims—are in essence direct appeals to *mythos*, because emotions are the body's way of expressing our most deeply held underlying values and desires. The bodily sensations we construct as emotions arise from the intersection of signals and values. Anger, fear, joy, shame, love—you literally feel these in your guts, and you might also choke up, break out in a sweat, blush, have your mouth go dry, cry, or tingle. Emotions unite our deepest feelings and the values they're based on, and express these through bodily means. You feel rage when powerful people take advantage of helpless people. You feel terror when you encounter a threat to your life. You feel joy when something *so right* happens—it is "so right" because it aligns with your deepest values for the best of life. Emotions therefore are evidence of the immediate and visceral interpretation of experience (sensory signals) through underlying values,[5] and they are some of our most powerful motivators. Nineteenth-century rhetorician George Campbell recognized this when he distinguished between *convincing* and *persuasion*. It's very easy, he said, to get people to *believe* things with their *minds*—say, in our own times, that it's really very sad that children in some nations of the world die of starvation simply because the rich nations won't help them. But to *move* people to *action*, Campbell said, they can't just *think*—they have to *feel*, literally in their guts, the problem. Persuasion, he argued, goes beyond convincing by actually moving people to action through feelings. We can't just convince your mind that kids are dying of starvation; we are most likely to move you to spend money on the problem by making you *feel bad* about it. (Cue pictures of skeletal kids.)

It's a question that Maria and Jayla need to keep in mind as they write their grant: what will their proposal do to get reviewers not just to *think* about the problem they're trying to solve—which does not make the problem sufficiently present to move the reviewers to action—but how to *feel* the problem? Because reviewers that both think and feel the problem will be more likely to want to try to find solutions to the problem. The knowledge that Maria and Jayla have to make for their reviewers isn't just informational, it's emotional—they need to

40
41

---

[5]Donna Strickland considers the relationship between body knowledge, felt sense, emotion, knowledge, and belief in her article "Before Belief: Embodiment and the 'Trying Game.'"

find a way to associate the problem and solution they're advocating with their reviewers' existing knowledge of values, their *mythos*.[6]

One major set of values the reviewers have is for *reasoning*, for careful, logi- 42 cal analysis, what Aristotle called *logos*.[7] Reasoning is a culture's set of rules for how to draw conclusions based on inference. Formal logic is one set of rules for doing so, but in most western cultures, we actually use more informal kinds of reasoning because they are quicker and in many ways more reliable. The statement "It's raining, I'd better take my umbrella" isn't actually logical, but it makes perfect sense to anyone who understands what "rain" and "umbrella" mean. (It's not logical because it leaves out too many premises to permit the leap the statement makes. Formal logic has to state *all* of its premises. Which is why so few people use it; it feels inhuman.) We start with a *claim*, "I'd better take my umbrella," and we're given one *reason*, because "it's raining." The *warrants*, or unstated premises, that connect the reason to the claim are numerous. Rain makes you wet. Rain happens outside. You're going outside, into the rain. Being wet is unpleasant and you don't want the rain to make you wet. Umbrellas can help keep you dry because they can keep rain from hitting you. As soon as we write out all these warrants, they turn into reasons if the audience already agrees with them, or into claims if the audience doesn't automatically agree. But most listeners *would* automatically agree with all these premises, so why state them to begin with? By treating them as warrants which can go unstated, we save time by relying on listeners' "common sense."

In western rationality, the vast majority of our reasoning is of this informal 43 sort, in which we rely on the shared prior knowledge of other rhetors to "complete" most of our arguments. When we say "Don't drink and drive, because it raises your chances of getting in an accident!" we don't *also* have to say "And car accidents are bad and they might even kill you!" — we all know that already. In most arguments, we're actually just disputing what one rhetor thinks is a warrant but other rhetors want to treat as a claim that requires support. There is actually a Flat Earth Society, for example, that argues against the notion that Earth is round-ish. Most of us treat "the earth is round" as a warrant — we simply take it for granted, as having been incontrovertibly proven long ago. But as Margaret Kantz demonstrates, a *fact* is simply a claim that a community has agreed is true.

---

[6]Those readers raised in or familiar with western cultures may object; rhetoric's insistence that emotions not only *do* matter but *should* matter to our decision-making is certainly a minority viewpoint. Most of us are taught that arguments should *not* rely on emotional appeals for their power, and that those which do are suspect. But this objection would be more convincing if those who most often raise it didn't get so emotional about it.

[7]In Greek, *logos* means both "words" and "reasoning," a fascinating association, when you think about it.

Flat Earth Society adherents change the warrant to a claim and contest the evidence that most people already think *proves* the earth is round.[8]

What kind of reasoning will Maria and Jayla use in their Reading Rivers 44
grant proposal? Their claims will likely include that the children their grant will support are disadvantaged in ways that the grant could help, and that helping these disadvantaged kids with after-school programs to boost reading and literacy is a good investment. To support those claims, they'll need evidence both of the problem they're claiming exists and for the assertion that the after-school program they propose will help solve that problem. They might also need to demonstrate how necessary *these* grant funds really are—that they can't just get the money from someplace else. And, of course, they'll need to be aware of their warrants—relying on them heavily when they believe the grant reviewers will share them, and exposing and converting warrants to supported claims when the grant writers think that the reviewers may not share their warrants. They also need to understand that warrants are how *values* (including *mythos*) connect into *reasoning*. In fact, a great proportion of warrants *are* values. In their grant proposal, Jayla and Maria will probably rely on the warrant that taxpayer funds are an optimal source of money for educational work. They can assume that their reviewers, who are employed for the very purpose of designating taxpayer funds for education, will share this underlying value, so much that the writers won't even need to make this point. Everyone will just assume it.

At the beginning of my discussion of reasoning, I asserted that reasoning is 45
actually a *value* for most people in western cultures. By using modes of reasoning they anticipate their reviewers will respect, Maria and Jayla can actually turn their reasoning appeals into value appeals, which are more powerful. They can expect their reviewers to value, for instance, specific examples of general statements they make. Example is one of the main ways we have of offering evidence for our claims. Similarly, Maria and Jayla can predict that their reviewers will value evidence which is well documented and generally agreed as factual. It is important that their grant proposal engage both reasoning and values that the reviewers will recognize and respect.

We are moving *very* quickly through some rhetorical principles that help 46
rhetors predict the most successful ways of interacting with other rhetors, and that help them interpret what other rhetors are offering in the interaction. There

---

[8]Aristotle divided discourse into arguments which could be proved with certainty and those which could only be supported to a *probability* of truth. The latter, he said, were the purview of rhetoric. Today, most rhetorical theorists claim that *no* argument can be proved to certainty independent of the rhetors' own beliefs, so *all* discourse is in rhetoric's purview. This article has treated this claim as a warrant (taking it for granted and thus leaving it unstated) until now.

remains one significant principle to finish the explanation of how Jayla and Maria might write the best possible grant proposal, and it returns again to having their values recognized by their reviewers.

Identification

If we were to ask Jayla and Maria, "What are you trying to achieve in writing this document?" one response might be "We're trying to gain funding for this after-school program." But there's a much more powerful answer than that. What the grant writers are trying to achieve is *identification* with their proposal reviewers. They're trying to get their reviewers to see, feel, believe, and think what the writers themselves do. They want their reviewers to identify with them and their argument so completely that the only thing that makes sense to the reviewers is to fund the proposal. But what is identification, and how do rhetors achieve it with one another?   47

Aristotle recognized the basic truth that whether people listen to rhetors depends on whether they find them credible, and he classified appeals to credibility as related to *ethos*, Greek for something like "one's accustomed place or habit of being"—the idea that you know someone by where they dwell, by their "haunts."[9] He suggested that rhetors get a sense of each other's ethos in three ways: by assessing their expertise, their moral character, and their goodwill toward other rhetors—their willingness to put others' interests first. We are likely to find a rhetor who shows us authority, character, and goodwill, trustworthy. *Ethos* ultimately addresses the question, how does *who you are* influence *what you're saying* and *how others should respond?*   48

But how do we gauge a rhetor's expertise, morality, and goodwill? We have to compare them to our *own sense of* what is authoritative, in good character, and in our best interests. We are holding the image that the rhetor presents up to the mirror of *our own values,* and what we want to see is *ourselves* looking back. When we trust a rhetor deeply, it is because we see some important aspect of ourselves in them. This is what rhetorical theorists mean by the term *identification*. As Kenneth Burke put it, "*A* is not identical with his colleague, *B*. But insofar as their interests are joined, A is *identified with* B. Or he may *identify himself* with B even when their interests are not joined, if he assumes that they are, or is persuaded to believe so" (544). Rhetoric, Burke says, is "the speaker's attempt to identify himself favorably with his audience" (561).   49

How, though, do we know "who" a rhetor "is"? *Identification* relies first on *identity*, both of speakers and listeners. Jayla and Maria want to use their   50

---

[9]Many have discussed this concept, but my main encounter with it is through Nedra Reynolds's *Rhetoric Review* article "Ethos as Location."

grant application to attempt to build identification with their reviewers, which requires them to have some sense of who those reviewers are. The work of John Ramage, a contemporary rhetoric theorist, suggests that Jayla and Maria have three ways of understanding their reviewers' identities. The first, Ramage calls *given*: identity that derives from the physical and social characteristics we're born with, such as sex, shape, ableness, ethnicity, place of birth, and status of parents. The second, Ramage says, are *readymades*—cultural identity "containers" which others apply to us. If you've seen *The Breakfast Club*, you know the student readymades in it were jock, geek, beauty queen, basket case, and criminal. Readymades are too often stereotypes, but some others are not terribly inaccurate. Jayla and Maria will apply some readymades to their reviewers, who will be "academics" or professor-types (who the Department of Education asks to review grants), and their areas of expertise will be literacy and education. These readymades tell Maria and Jayla *a lot* about their reviewers' needs, values, and expectations—what kinds of evidence they are likely to find convincing, what situations the reviewers are likely to be in as they review, what the reviewers are likely to have read and be familiar with—what they already know, and what the grant writers will need to "teach" them in their application. Ramage's third identity category, *constructed* identities, are those that people build for themselves by blending givens, readymades, and their own interests and unique ways of being. (I, for example, am a professor of rhetoric and writing who is also a techie-gearhead and grooves on motorsports racing and building loud stereo systems, which makes me both a very predictable professor in some ways and a fairly unusual one in others.)

Maria and Jayla's grant reviewers will similarly be trying to build a sense of the writers' identities, in part because the reviewers are trying to decide whether approving the Reading Rivers proposal will be a *safe investment*: Do the people who are writing the grant actually seem qualified and able to do what they're promising to do with the grant funds? This depends in part on who the writers are. So the grant proposal rules will require applicants to include their professional resumes to demonstrate their track-records with similar projects, and the reviewers will be trying to build a sense of Jayla and Maria's professional identities.[10]

If Maria and Jayla's grant proposal is successful, it will be because reviewers "identify with" them as credible grant writers, with their project as sharing the interests that the grant is meant to support, and with the people whom the grant

---

[10]Some grant proposals — and most reputable scholarly publications — are reviewed "blind," with reviewers not knowing who the writers are. This prevents bias for or against a writer based on reputation, which can be necessary; but it also limits the quality of information reviewers have about who is doing the work, which has its own cost.

will benefit. That is, the reviewers will see in the grant proposal, its subjects, and its writers, the reviewers' own needs, values, and expectations for the grant reflected back at them. Jayla and Maria will have *made knowledge* for the reviewers of how their proposal does these things.

A final point about rhetoric as knowledge making. While "persuasion" is certainly one popular term for what rhetorical interaction is often attempting to achieve, philosopher Chaim Perelman gave us a better term back in the 1970s: *adherence*. (Like the adhesive on a Post-It note.) Perelman said, in everyday reality, we don't so much experience identification as all-or-nothing, or absolute. Rather, we experience it as other people more-or-less going along with us, to varying degrees.[11] It is more reasonable to seek adherence than conversion. Of course, Jayla and Maria want their grant reviewers' *complete* adherence to their ideas; but what might actually happen could be a judgment by the reviewers that "we really like your idea but this isn't the right grant to fund it; apply to that other one instead and see what happens," or "we really like your idea but we only have enough funds to give you some of what you asked for." The notion of *adherence* helps us understand responses like these. It more accurately reflects what human knowledge is actually like: provisional, evolving, partial, and variable.

RHETORICAL COMPOSITION AND INSCRIPTION: FIVE CANONS

What remains to explore in this paper is rhetoric's explanation of the various aspects of creating discourses and texts. Aristotle identified five rhetorical arts or *canons*[12] involved in the making of any text or discourse:

- **Invention**: coming up with what to say, developing the material for your piece. The grant writing team has to come up with the arguments and examples they'll use in their proposal. They "invent" the material in the piece.

- **Arrangement**: deciding what order that material should go in and what parts your piece needs. It's not enough for the grant writers to know *what* to say; they also have to know what parts their proposal will have, and what order the parts will go in, and what of their invented material will go in each part. (The instructions for the grant proposal will usually tell them some of this.)

---

[11]Lorraine Code describes one aspect of rhetorical identity as a rhetor's *affectivity*, their "commitments, enthusiasms, desires, and interests" (46). This aspect of identity is what interfaces with a given set of ideas (or another rhetor as a whole) to create adherence.

[12]"Canon" in the sense of "a body of rules or principles which are agreed upon as fundamental to an art."

- **Style**: crafting the particular expressions of your material to make it best suit the ecology. Our grant writers need to know what grant proposals of the kind they're writing *sound like*, and create that sound style. Within that sound, they have to decide the best words and sentence patterns to use to express their ideas and voices.
- **Memory**: recording your arranged, styled material in biological, technological, or cultural forms. The grant proposal will have specific "memory" requirements, such as what file formats to save the proposal in.
- **Delivery**: publishing your composition for other rhetors to encounter via specific modalities. The grant writers have to know how to send their proposal to reviewers, and in what form reviewers will need to work with the proposal.

Aristotle was thinking primarily of oratory when he named these activities, but they continue to work well centuries later in describing writing on paper, writing electronically for screens and audio, and writing in networked digital spaces of instant sharing and collaboration. The main distinction we would add to the canons is that invention, arrangement, and style deal primarily with *composing*, while memory and delivery deal with *inscribing* the composition, making a more or less permanent and portable "recording" of the ideas in the composition.[13] It is via inscription, whether by voice, writing, or other visual means, that rhetoric gains its *interactional* character by rendering private thought as a shareable, *material* experience.

Because the canons cover the main functions of composing a text or discourse, they may appear to present a firm process leading from one canon to the next and then on to the next. Remember, however, that because rhetoric is *interaction*, composing a text is itself a rhetorical interchange, at least with yourself as a rhetor but also usually with other rhetors — people you talk to along the way, bounce ideas off of, ask for help from, get directions from, ask to read a draft of your piece, etc. Because it's an interaction, both in your own mind and with others, it won't go "in order." Imagine our grant writers handling invention and arrangement: part of their deciding what to say is deciding what order to put it in. But there is more: Style is invented, and how they say a thing will change what they say. In our current technological state, where you have to care about what modalities you present your discourse in (Face-to-face? Paper? Screen? Verbal? Visual? Aural?), delivery influences invention — what you want to create partially shapes what you find it important to say, and vice versa. Our grant writers will say different things in a Word document than they would

---

[13]This is a distinction best made by Paul Prior in his book chapter "Tracing Process: How Texts Come into Being."

say in a spreadsheet or a graphical presentation. Each canon interweaves and interlocks with the others. Rhetors need to be comfortable with (or find ways to tolerate) this inevitable flux.

Current technology also requires comfort with a wide range of ways of work- 56
ing on each canon. Take invention: The Greeks understood invention as looking in various *places* in one's memory, and in cultural knowledge, for existing wisdom in *topics* that applied to what one wanted to say.[14] The nineteenth-century romantics believed invention was essentially the opposite: unique inspiration that let a speaker say something that had never been heard before. At the beginning of the twenty-first century, we have an unimaginable network of inscribed compositions, the Internet, which makes much of our invention an act of *curation*: managing existing ideas and remixing them into new expressions.[15] Or consider arrangement: Our word-processing technologies make it incredibly easy to move pieces around in our documents, and even to keep track of separate versions of our document and compare changes among them. Yet it is comparatively difficult to see two widely separated places in a document at the same time when it's on screen. That kind of vision of a work requires printed pages. (Or multiple monitors and copies of documents.) And delivery: technology can make rhetorical interaction *immediate* rather than sequential. Aristotle imagined rhetors completely composing speeches and *then* delivering them. Today, multiple writers can simultaneously edit a document, and speeches can be composed on social media in the very act of delivering them to a world of readers. Making knowledge through rhetorical interaction is indeed a shared, collaborative, and in-the-moment activity.

SUMMING UP

At the beginning of this article, I said that rhetoric offers principles of human 57
interaction — it shows us how we make up our minds, how we change them, how we make meaning, how we know what we know, and how to help people identify with us. I also said this set of principles, when set in motion, is incredibly entangled — every rhetorical principle seems to link to every other rhetorical principle. It's a lot to keep track of. By following the explanations and the example of the grant writers, you've gotten at least a glimpse of how these things

---

[14]The word *topic* shares its root with *topography*, "the lay of the land"; in Greek, *topos* means "place." Aristotle created a list of "common topics," the *Topoi*, which was essentially a list of the *mythos* of his day that related to reasoning. It included definition, comparison, relationship, and other categories of reasoning one could use to understand a subject they were arguing about. Today we would call them a special set of *warrants*.

[15]For example, by memes or by sampling (in music). Thanks to my MSU student Andy Meyer for calling my attention to curation as it relates to rhetorical invention.

could actually be—what some of these rhetorical principles are, and how they actually come into play when we try to make decisions, decide who and what to believe, consider how to present ourselves to others, and try to understand where other people are coming from and why our interactions with them take the shape that they do.

If it hasn't happened already, you'll probably eventually get tired of hearing the term *rhetorical* applied to everything—and the more you think about it, the more you'll probably also start applying it to everything yourself. So let me finish by trying to say more about what that term actually implies and requires. When we say that something is *rhetorical*, we're saying that it has the qualities of rhetoric, which are these: This "rhetorical" thing is *situated*, meaning that it happens in a particular place, time, and moment, and therefore that it cannot be universalized. It is *motivated*, meaning that there is some motive behind it, that therefore it is subjective rather than objective, and that our interpretation of it will depend in part on our understanding what motivates it, its exigence. It is *contingent*, meaning that its shape depends on the situation, exigence, and motivations that call it into being, and that it must be unique to its situation, not purely determined by pre-existing, universal rules. It is *interactional*, meaning that it can only exist in the interaction between itself and the rhetors who shape its meaning. It is *epistemic*, meaning that it creates knowledge for the rhetors interacting with it, rather than merely transmitting pre-existing knowledge unaltered from one rhetor to another. And it is *embodied*, meaning that it takes material form and that its material form shapes the interaction and rhetors' interpretations of it; it cannot be "just ideas." 58

As one who is still learning to understand rhetoric after twenty years of study, and who needed more than ten years of that study just to come to the description in the previous paragraph (and all twenty to come to the totality of this paper), I don't expect everything in that last paragraph to make sense to you right now. I offer it instead as a jumping off point for things you should be trying to understand as you continue to study rhetoric. 59

Works Cited

Aristotle. *Rhetoric*. Translated by George Kennedy, Oxford UP, 1991.

Bitzer, Lloyd. "The Rhetorical Situation." *Philosophy and Rhetoric*, vol. 1, no. 1, Jan. 1968, pp. 1–14.

Burke, Kenneth. *A Grammar of Motives and A Rhetoric of Motives*. Meridian Books, The World Publishing Company, 1962.

Campbell, George. *The Philosophy of Rhetoric*. Harper & Brothers, New York, 1841. Facsimile ed., *Scholars' Facsimiles and Reprints*, 1992.

Code, Lorraine. *What Can She Know? Feminist Theory and the Construction of Knowledge*. Cornell UP, 1991.

Cooper, Marilyn. "Rhetorical Agency as Emergent and Enacted." *College Composition and Communication*, vol. 62, no. 3, Feb. 2001, pp. 420–49.

Corder, Jim W. "Argument as Emergence, Rhetoric as Love." *Rhetoric Review*, vol. 4, no. 1, Sept. 1985, pp. 16-32.

Edbauer, Jenny. "Unframing Models of Public Distribution: From Rhetorical Situation to Rhetorical Ecologies." *Rhetoric Society Quarterly*, vol. 35, no. 4, Fall 2005, pp. 5–24.

Fisher, Walter R. "Narration as a Human Communication Paradigm: The Case of Public Moral Argument." *Communication Monographs*, vol. 51, no. 1, Mar. 1984, pp. 1–22.

Grant-Davie, Keith. "Rhetorical Situations and Their Constituents." *Rhetoric Review*, vol. 15, no. 2, Spring 1997, pp. 264–79.

Kennedy, George. "A Hoot in the Dark: The Evolution of General Rhetoric." *Philosophy and Rhetoric*, vol. 25, no. 1, 1992, pp. 1–21.

Kirsch, Gesa E., and Jacqueline J. Royster. "Feminist Rhetorical Practices: In Search of Excellence." *College Composition and Communication*, vol. 61, no. 4, June 2010, pp. 640–72.

Lakoff, George. *Moral Politics: How Liberals and Conservatives Think.* U of Chicago P, 2002.

Lakoff, George, and Mark Johnson. *Metaphors We Live By.* 2nd ed., U of Chicago P, 2003.

Micciche, Laura R. "Writing Material." *College English*, vol. 76, no. 6, July 2014, pp. 488–505.

Perelman, Chaim. *The Realm of Rhetoric.* U of Notre Dame P, 1990.

Perl, Sondra. *Felt Sense.* Boynton/Cook Publishers, 2004.

Pirsig, Robert. *Zen and the Art of Motorcycle Maintenance: An Inquiry into Values.* HarperPerennial Modern Classics edition, HarperCollins Publishers, 1999.

Prior, Paul. "Tracing Process: How Texts Come into Being." *What Writing Does and How It Does It: An Introduction to Analyzing Texts and Textual Practices*, edited by Charles Bazerman and Paul Prior, Routledge, 2003. 167–200.

Ramage, John. *Rhetoric: A User's Guide.* Pearson/Longman, 2006.

Reynolds, Nedra. "Ethos as Location: New Sites for Understanding Discursive Authority." *Rhetoric Review*, vol. 11, no. 3, Spring 1993, pp. 325–38.

Rickert, Thomas. *Ambient Rhetoric: The Attunements of Rhetorical Being.* U of Pittsburgh P, 2013.

Seegart, Natasha. "Play as Sniffication: Coyotes Sing in the Margins." *Philosophy and Rhetoric*, vol. 47, no. 2, 2014, pp. 158–78.

Strickland, Donna. "Before Belief: Embodiment and the 'Trying Game.'" *The Journal for the Assembly for Expanded Perspectives*, vol. 15, no. 1, Winter 2009–2010, pp. 78–86.

Wenger, Christy. *Yoga Minds, Writing Bodies: Contemplative Writing Pedagogy.* Parlor Press, 2015.

- -

Questions for Discussion and Journaling

1. Compare how you've thought of rhetoric in the past to how it appears to you after this reading. Have you shared one of the conceptions listed in the beginning of the article on pages 458–59? What differences between your previous thinking and what you think now are most obvious? Are there similarities?

2. Using your own words, explain what the term *epistemic* means. What is the difference if rhetoric is epistemic versus if it is not?

3. What difference does it make to think about rhetorical interaction in terms of an ecological network rather than in terms of isolated writers creating texts on their own for isolated readers, everyone independent of their surroundings?

4. What are at least three reasons why bodies, not just minds, matter to rhetorical interaction?

5. Are you surprised to see this guide explain emotions and feelings as central to making knowledge rather than as contrary to it? How does this guide's explanation of the role of emotion and feeling in rhetorical interaction line up with what your culture says their role should be?

6. What are *warrants* and why are they important to rhetorical interaction?

7. Given how Downs describes rhetoric, do you think music and artistic works are rhetorical? Why?

8. Try explaining the concept of *adherence* in your own words. Is it a different way for you to think about human interaction and persuasion?

9. When Aristotle laid out five canons of rhetoric, public speaking was more common than public writing (because writing was expensive and time-consuming). If you were coming up with a list of "canons of rhetoric" today, when writing shared electronically is normal, what do you think the canons would be?

Applying and Exploring Ideas

1. Take an aspect of rhetorical theory discussed in this guide, like ecology or embodiment or one of the canons, and apply it to the hottest topic of discussion in your world this particular day. Does the rhetorical principle help you better understand why the discussion is happening as it is?

2. Rhetorical theory and its implications are usually very hard for people to describe to each other as they first start learning about it. The best way to learn is to give it a try. Suppose a friend or family member who you enjoy talking to asked "What are you studying?" and you said "rhetoric" and they said "What's that?" Write a two- to three-paragraph response that describes rhetoric as best you can right now and helps your friend know what's important about it.

3. Rhetoric is situated and contingent (para. 57), meaning that its use, what works best, or what it looks like, will vary depending on the situation. Make a list of implications of that principle: What does it mean for human communication to be contingent on the situation? For example, what does it mean for *teaching and learning* rhetoric if rhetoric varies according to the situation?

4. Returning to the extended example used throughout this reading of the grant writers working on a grant proposal, create an overall map of this example's rhetorical ecology. What does the network of rhetorical actors and interactions include? Who are all the "players" in this ecology? What does it look like if you draw it? What elements can you think of that would be in the ecology even if the article doesn't mention them?

5. Get a group of three to four fellow students together and have this discussion: Of the three *pisteis* (*logos, ethos, pathos*), which seems most important? Keep lists of the reasons each might be argued to be most important; then make a separate list of which reasons allow all of you to reach a consensus.

- -

META MOMENT   What is one principle you learned from this overview of rhetoric that you can see yourself using a lot in the future? What makes it so important to you?

- -

Tagged Reading

Rhetorical Situations and Their Constituents

KEITH GRANT-DAVIE

Courtesy of Keith Grant-Davie

Framing the Reading

Keith Grant-Davie is an English professor at Utah State University in Logan, "a rural town in the Rocky Mountains." He has studied how readers and writers interact from a number of angles: what readers say writers are trying to do, how writers repeat themselves to make themselves clearer to readers, and how writing and speech are shaped by the context in which they take place and the context(s) to which they respond. When he wrote this article, Grant-Davie was directing the graduate program in USU's English department.

We've referenced the term **rhetorical situation** in earlier chapters, and it appears in this chapter's introduction as well as in the previous selection by Downs. You'll encounter it frequently throughout the rest of this chapter. The term is not an easy one to pin down, however, so you may still be wondering exactly what a rhetorical situation is. Composition theorists like Grant-Davie call an activity, an event, or a situation *rhetorical* when it's shaped by language or communication — also called **discourse** — that tries to get people to *do* something. In order to understand rhetoric, it's necessary to understand the motivations — the purposes, needs, values, and expectations — of the **rhetors** — that is, the people who generate it.

Advertisements are obvious examples of rhetorical communication. In advertising, a business communicates with its **audience** — potential customers — in order to persuade them to buy a product: For example, the Coca-Cola corporation hires basketball star LeBron James to command us, "Obey your thirst — drink Sprite!" But rhetorical situations don't have to be strategically planned and constructed *as* rhetoric: In fact, we encounter them every day, in ordinary, unplanned, un-self-conscious

Grant-Davie, Keith. "Rhetorical Situations and Their Constituents." *Rhetoric Review*, vol. 15, no. 2, Spring 1997, pp. 264–79.

interactions. Imagine, for example, sitting in your kitchen with a friend who says, "Boy, I'm really cold." In both the advertisement and your friend's declaration, language *does* things: It convinces us to buy something or to turn up the heat. Such communication is therefore *rhetorical* — that is, it's persuasive or *motivated* communication — and the situations in which it happens would be *rhetorical situations*.

Grant-Davie's article examines the elements of rhetorical situations and may help you better understand and respond to their rhetoric. Why, for example, didn't the Coca-Cola corporation simply bypass the celebrity and the ad agency and issue a statement telling us they'd like us to drink Sprite? Why didn't your chilly friend ask directly, "Can you please turn up the heat?" We need to explore the rhetorical situations of both examples in order to respond intelligently. To use an everyday example: If your little sister walks into your room yelling at the top of her lungs, you won't know how to respond until you understand what's happened and why she's yelling — is she angry, hurt, or excited? Understanding the rhetorical situation of her outburst will help you understand what's at stake and guide you in making an appropriate response.

The idea of a rhetorical situation might not be completely clear to you right away — most people need to encounter the idea in several different ways before they really start to get a handle on it. In fact, for most students, *rhetorical situation* — particularly the aspect of **exigence** — is a threshold concept. It takes some time to understand and completely changes your understanding of writing once you do. Grant-Davie explains exigence a few different ways, but the simplest explanation for it is a *problem* or *need* that can be addressed by communication. In the case of the Sprite ad, the exigence of the communication is complex: It includes the corporation's desire to sell and the consumer's desire for a product that will fill one or more needs (thirst quenching but also identification with a popular celebrity). In the case of your chilly friend, the exigence is more straightforward: Your friend wants to be warmer, but doesn't want to appear pushy or offend you by directly stating her desire for a thermostat adjustment.

You'll also encounter the term **stases**, which is a pattern or set of questions that helps explain what's at issue in a given rhetorical situation — a problem of *fact*, of *value*, or of *policy*. (The classic journalist's questions — Who? What? Where? When? How? Why? — are actually stases that attempt to establish fact.) Finally, you'll encounter the concept of **constraints**, which are factors that limit or focus the response to the exigence (problem or need) in a given situation. (In the case of your chilly friend, her desire to be perceived as friendly, not pushy, is a primary constraint.) These and other concepts in Grant-Davie's article will become clearer as you see them used in other readings.

Remember, when we identify language or communication as rhetorical, we're saying that it is *doing* something. So we could ask of Grant-Davie's article, what does it *do*? Keep that question in mind as you read.

This reading is tagged in order to help you navigate it. Remember that the tags are explained in more detail in Chapter 1 (pp. 58–59). You may want to quickly review the tags there before you begin.

Getting Ready to Read

Before you read, do at least one of the following activities:

- Ask one or more roommates or friends to describe the last serious argument or debate they had. Get them to describe the situations in which the debates took place in as much detail as they can. Make a list of what was "in the situation," following the reporter's "five Ws": Who was there? What was it about? When and where did it happen? Why did it happen (that is, what were the motivations of the arguers)?

- Watch a television commercial and look for how it "sets the scene" — how it very quickly puts viewers in the middle of one situation or another (like a family riding in a car or people eating in a restaurant or a sick person talking with a doctor). Make some notes about how the commercial uses scenery, particular language, or text to help explain "where you are" as a viewer, and ask yourself how important understanding that "scene" or situation is to understanding what's being advertised.

As you read, consider the following questions:

- What rhetorical situation gave rise to Grant-Davie's article — that is, why did he write it in the first place? Who is his intended audience? Who else has been talking about this problem/question? What text(s) is he responding to?

- Are there places in the article you would have expected to see an Assist Tag and didn't? Make a note of each such place, and what tag you would have used there, in order to compare with other readers later.

- Can you use the examples Grant-Davie gives to help you find examples of rhetorical situations and their components (*exigence, rhetors, audience,* and *constraints*) in your own life?

KEN BURNS'S DOCUMENTARY FILM, *The Civil War*, has mesmerized viewers since it first aired on PBS in 1990. Among its more appealing features are the interviews with writers and historians like Shelby Foote and Barbara Fields, who provide the background information and interpretation necessary to transform battles, speeches, and letters from dry historical data into a human drama of characters, intentions, and limitations. In effect, their commentaries explain the rhetorical situations of the events, pointing out influential factors within the broader contexts that help explain why decisions were made and why things turned out as they did. Their analyses of these rhetorical situations show us that some events might easily have turned out otherwise, while the outcomes of other events seem all but inevitable when seen in light of the situations in which they occurred. When we study history, our first question may be "what happened?" but the more important question, the question whose answer offers hope of learning for the future as well as understanding the past, is "why did it happen?" At a fundamental level, then, understanding the rhetorical situations of historical events helps satisfy our demand for causality—helps us discover the extent to which the world is not chaotic but ordered, a place where actions follow patterns and things happen for good reasons. Teaching our writing students to examine rhetorical situations as sets of interacting influences from which rhetoric arises, and which rhetoric in turn influences, is therefore one of the more important things we can do. Writers who know how to analyze these situations have a better method of examining causality. They have a stronger basis for making composing decisions and are better able, as readers, to understand the decisions other writers have made.

Scholars and teachers of rhetoric have used the term *rhetorical situation* since Lloyd Bitzer defined it in 1968. However, the concept has remained largely underexamined since Bitzer's seminal

1

2

GENRE CUES

1 — So What?

2 — CARS: Territory

3 — CARS: Niche

487

4

5

article and the responses to it by Richard Vatz and Scott Consigny in the 1970s. We all use the term, but what exactly do we mean by it and do we all mean the same thing? My purpose in this essay is to review the original definitions of the term and its constituents, and to offer a more thoroughly developed scheme for analyzing rhetorical situations. I will apply the concept of a rhetorical situation to reading or listening situations as well as to writing or speaking situations, and to what I call "compound" rhetorical situations—discussions of a single subject by multiple rhetors and audiences.[1]

3

Bitzer defines a rhetorical situation generally as "the context in which speakers or writers create rhetorical discourse" (382).[2] More specifically he defines it as "a complex of persons, events, objects, and relations presenting an actual or potential exigence which can be completely or partially removed if discourse, introduced into the situation, can so constrain human decision or action as to bring about the significant modification of the exigence" (386).[3] In other words, a rhetorical situation is a situation where a speaker or writer sees a need to change reality and sees that the change may be effected through rhetorical discourse. Bitzer argues that understanding the situation is important because the situation invites and largely determines the form of the rhetorical work that responds to it. He adds that "rhetorical discourse comes into existence as a response to situation, in the same sense that an answer comes into existence in response to a question, or a solution in

6

response to a problem" (385–86). Richard Vatz challenges Bitzer's assumption that the rhetor's response is controlled by the situation. He contends that situations do not exist without rhetors, and that rhetors create rather than discover rhetorical situations (154). In effect, Vatz argues that rhetors not only answer the question, they also ask it.[4]

GENRE CUES

4 — Research Question

5 — CARS: Occupy

6 — Conversation

7   Scott Consigny's reply to Bitzer and Vatz suggests that each of   4
them is both right and wrong, that a rhetorical situation is partly,
but not wholly, created by the rhetor. Supporting Vatz, Consigny
argues that the art of rhetoric should involve "integrity"—the
ability to apply a standard set of strategies effectively to any situation the rhetor may face. On the other hand, supporting Bitzer,
he argues that rhetoric should also involve "receptivity"—the
ability to respond to the conditions and demands of individual
situations. To draw an analogy, we could say that carpentry has
integrity inasmuch as carpenters tackle most projects with a limited set of common tools. They do not have to build new tools
for every new task (although the evolution of traditional tools
and the development of new ones suggest that integrity is not a
static property). Conversely, carpentry might also be said to have
receptivity if the limited set of tools does not limit the carpenter's
perception of the task. A good carpenter does not reach for the
hammer every time.

8   Looking at these articles by Bitzer, Vatz, and Consigny together,   5
we might define a rhetorical situation as a set of related factors
whose interaction creates and controls a discourse. However, such
a general definition is better understood if we examine the constituents of situation. Bitzer identifies three: exigence, audience, and
constraints. Exigence is "an imperfection marked by urgency; it is
a defect, an obstacle, something waiting to be done, a thing which
is other than it should be" (386). A rhetorical exigence is some
kind of need or problem that can be addressed and solved through
rhetorical discourse. Eugene White has pointed out that exigence
need not arise from a problem but may instead be cause for celebration (291). Happy events may create exigence, calling for
epideictic rhetoric. Bitzer defines the audience as those who can
help resolve the exigence: "those persons who are capable of being
influenced by discourse and of being mediators of change" (387),

GENRE CUES

7— Conversation

8— **Making Knowledge** Grant-Davie finds the "common denominator" among
Bitzer's, Consigny's, and Vatz's definitions that none of them had stated.

489

while constraints are "persons, events, objects, and relations which are parts of the situation because they have the power to constrain decision and action needed to modify the exigence" (388).

Bitzer's three-way division of rhetorical situations has been valuable, but to reveal the full complexity of rhetorical situations, I think we need to develop his scheme further. I propose three amendments. First, I believe exigence, as the motivating force behind a discourse, demands a more comprehensive analysis. Second, I think we need to recognize that rhetors are as much a part of a rhetorical situation as the audience is. Bitzer mentions in passing that when a speech is made, both it and the rhetor become additional constituents of the situation (388), but he does not appear to include the rhetor in the situation that exists *before* the speech is made. And third, we need to recognize that any of the constituents may be plural. Bitzer includes the possibility of multiple exigences and constraints, but he seems to assume a solitary rhetor and a single audience. In many rhetorical situations, there may be several rhetors, including groups of people or institutions, and the discourse may address or encounter several audiences with various purposes for reading. The often complex interaction of these multiple rhetors and audiences should be considered. What follows, then, are definitions and discussions of the four constituents I see in rhetorical situations: exigence, rhetors, audiences, and constraints.

EXIGENCE — THE MATTER AND MOTIVATION OF THE DISCOURSE

Bitzer defines rhetorical exigence as the rhetor's sense that a situation both calls for discourse and might be resolved by

---

GENRE CUES

9 — **Extending** Rather than abandon Bitzer's work completely, Grant-Davie will develop it more fully.

10 — **Making Knowledge**

11 — **Making Knowledge**

12 — **Forecasting**

discourse. According to this definition, the essential question addressing the exigence of a situation would be "Why is the discourse needed?" However, in my scheme I propose that this question be the second of three that ask, respectively, what the discourse is about, why it is needed, and what it should accomplish. I derive the logic for this order of questions from the version of stasis theory explained by Jeanne Fahnestock and Marie Secor, who argue that the stases provide a natural sequence of steps for interrogating a subject. This sequence proceeds from questions of fact and definition (establishing that the subject exists and characterizing it) through questions of cause and effect (identifying the source of the subject and its consequences) and questions of value (examining its importance or quality) to questions of policy or procedure (considering what should be done about it) ("The Stases in Scientific and Literary Argument" 428–31; "The Rhetoric of Literary Criticism" 78–80). Sharon Crowley, too, has suggested stasis theory as a good tool for analyzing rhetorical situations (33).

What is the discourse about? This question addresses the first two stases, fact and definition, by asking what the discourse concerns. The question may be answered at quite a concrete level by identifying the most apparent topic. A speech by a politician during an election year may be about mandatory school uniforms, Medicare, an antipollution bill, the fight against terrorism, or any of a host of other topics. However, what the discourse is about becomes a more interesting and important question, and a source of exigence, if asked at more abstract levels — in other words, if the question becomes "What fundamental issues are represented by the topic of the discourse?" or "What values are at stake?" Political speeches often use specific

GENRE CUES

13 — Making Knowledge

14 — Framework Grant-Davie will take a theory developed separately and bring it into his article to make a "skeleton" around which to grow his own theory of exigence.

topics to represent larger, more enduring issues such as questions of civil rights, public safety, free enterprise, constitutionality, separation of church and state, morality, family values, progress, equality, fairness, and so forth. These larger issues, values, or principles motivate people and can be invoked to lead audiences in certain directions on more specific topics. A speech on the topic of requiring school uniforms in public schools may engage the larger issue of how much states should be free from federal intervention—an issue that underlies many other topics besides school uniforms. In the first episode of *The Civil War,* historian Barbara Fields draws a distinction between the superficial matter of the war and what she sees as the more important, underlying issues that gave it meaning:

> For me, the picture of the Civil War as a historic phenomenon is not on the battlefield. It's not about weapons, it's not about soldiers, except to the extent that weapons and soldiers at that crucial moment joined a discussion about something higher, about humanity, about human dignity, about human freedom.

On the battlefield, one side's ability to select the ground to be contested has often been critical to the outcome of the engagement. In the same way, rhetors who can define the fundamental issues represented by a superficial subject matter—and persuade audiences to engage in those issues—are in a position to maintain decisive control over the field of debate. A presidential candidate may be able to convince the electorate that the more important issues in a debate about a rival's actions are not the legality of those specific actions but questions they raise about the rival's credibility as leader of the nation ("He may have been exonerated in a court of law, but what does the scandal suggest about his character?"). Attorneys do the same kind of thing in a courtroom, trying to induce the jury to see the case in terms of issues that favor their client. Granted, these examples all represent traditional, manipulative rhetoric—the verbal equivalent of a physical contest—but I believe the same principle is critical to the success of the kind of ethical argument Theresa Enos describes, where the aim is not victory over the opponent but a state of identification, where writer and reader are able to meet in the audience identity the writer has created within the discourse (106–08). In these kinds of argument, establishing acceptable issues would seem to be an essential stage, creating an agenda that readers can agree to discuss.

I am proposing stasis theory be used as an analytic tool, an organizing principle in the sequence of questions that explore the exigence of a situation, but defining the issues of a discourse also involves determining the stases that will be contested in the discourse itself. The presidential candidate in the example mentioned above is abandoning the stasis of definition and choosing instead to take a stand at the stasis of value. Asking what the discourse is about, then, involves identifying the subject matter or topic at the most obvious level, but also determining issues that underlie it and the stases that should be addressed—in short, asking "what questions need to be resolved by this discourse?"

Why Is the Discourse Needed? The second question about exigence addresses both the third and fourth stases (cause and value). It addresses cause by asking what has prompted the discourse, and why *now* is the right time for it to be delivered. This aspect of exigence is related, as William Covino and David Jolliffe have observed, to the concept of *kairos*—"the right or opportune time to speak or write" (11, 62). Exigence may have been created by events that precede the discourse and act as a catalyst for it; and the timing of the discourse may also have been triggered by an occasion, such as an invitation to speak. A presidential speech on terrorism may be prompted both by a recent act of terrorism but also by a timely opportunity to make a speech. In the case of letters to the editor of a newspaper, the forum is always there—a standing invitation to address the newspaper's readership. However, letter writers are usually prompted by a recent event or by the need to reply to someone else's letter.

GENRE CUES

15— Making Knowledge

While addressing the stasis of cause, the question "why is the discourse needed?" also addresses the value stasis in the sense that it asks why the discourse matters—why the issues are important and why the questions it raises really need to be resolved. The answer to this question may be that the issues are intrinsically important, perhaps for moral reasons. Alternatively, the answer may lie in the situation's implications. Exigence may result not from what has already happened but from something that is about to happen, or from something that might happen if action is not taken—as in the case of many speeches about the environment.

11

What Is the Discourse Trying to Accomplish? Finally, exigence can be revealed by asking questions at the stasis of policy or procedure. What are the goals of the discourse? How is the audience supposed to react to the discourse? I include objectives as part of the exigence for a discourse because resolving the exigence provides powerful motivation for the rhetor. The rhetor's agenda may also include primary and secondary objectives, some of which might not be stated in the discourse. The immediate objective of a presidential campaign speech might be to rebut accusations made by a rival, while a secondary objective might be to clarify the candidate's stance on one of the issues or help shape his image, and the broader objective would always be to persuade the audience to vote for the candidate when the time comes.

12

Reread

GENRE CUES

 — Making Knowledge

 — Making Knowledge Grant-Davie says the exigence is *not* identical to the rhetor's motivation but leads to it.

READING CUES

Reread The concept of exigence is an easy one to misunderstand especially when the concept of *stases* is new to you. Mark this section to return to once you've finished the entire article (and read the glossary definition of exigence and/or the explanation in the chapter opener or in Downs's article) so you have more perspective and resources to help clarify the concept.

RHETOR(S) — THOSE PEOPLE, REAL OR IMAGINED, RESPONSIBLE FOR THE DISCOURSE AND ITS AUTHORIAL VOICE

Bitzer does not include the rhetor as a constituent of the rhetorical situation before the discourse is produced, although he includes aspects of the rhetor under the category of constraints. Vatz only points out the rhetor's role in defining the situation, yet it seems to me that rhetors are as much constituents of their rhetorical situations as are their audiences. Their roles, like those of audiences, are partly predetermined but usually open to some definition or redefinition. Rhetors need to consider who they are in a particular situation and be aware that their identity may vary from situation to situation. Neither Bitzer nor Vatz explores the role of rhetor in much depth, and an exhaustive analysis of possible roles would be beyond the scope of this essay, too; but in the following paragraphs, I will touch on some possible variations.

First, although for syntactic convenience I often refer to the rhetor as singular in this essay, situations often involve multiple rhetors. An advertisement may be sponsored by a corporation, written and designed by an advertising agency, and delivered by an actor playing the role of corporate spokesperson. Well-known actors or athletes may lend the ethos they have established through their work, while unknown actors may play the roles of corporate representatives or even audience members offering testimony in support of the product. We can distinguish those who originated the discourse, and who might be held legally responsible for the truth of its content, from those who are hired to shape and deliver the message, but arguably all of them involved in the sales pitch share the role of rhetor, as a rhetorical team.

GENRE CUES

18 — Making Knowledge

19 Second, even when a rhetor addresses a situation alone, the 15
answer to the question "Who is the rhetor?" may not be simple.
As rhetors we may speak in some professional capacity, in a volunteer role, as a parent, or in some other role that may be less readily
identifiable—something, perhaps, like Wayne Booth's "implied
author" or "second self"—the authorial identity that readers can
infer from an author's writing (70–71). Roger Cherry makes a
contrast between the ethos of the historical author and any persona created by that author (260–68). Cherry's distinction might
be illustrated by the speech of a presidential candidate who brings
to it the ethos he has established through his political career and
uses the speech to create a persona for himself as president in the
future. Then again, a rhetor's ethos will not be the same for all
audiences. It will depend on what they know and think of the
rhetor's past actions, so the "real" or "historical" author is not a
stable "foundation" identity but depends partly on the audience
in a particular rhetorical situation. Like exigence, then, audience
can influence the identity of the rhetor.

Rhetors may play several roles at once, and even when they 16
try to play just one role, their audience may be aware of their
other roles. A Little League baseball umpire might, depending on
his relationship with local residents, receive fewer challenges from
parents at the game if he happens also to be the local police chief.
The range of roles we can play at any given moment is certainly
constrained by the other constituents of the rhetorical situation
and by the identities we bring to the situation. However, new rhetorical situations change us and can lead us to add new roles to
our repertoire. To use Consigny's terms, rhetors create ethos partly
through integrity—a measure of consistency they take from situation to situation instead of putting on a completely new mask to
suit the needs of every new audience and situation; and they also
need receptivity—the ability to adapt to new situations and not
rigidly play the same role in every one.

GENRE CUES

19— Making Knowledge

AUDIENCE — THOSE PEOPLE, REAL OR IMAGINED, WITH WHOM RHETORS NEGOTIATE THROUGH DISCOURSE TO ACHIEVE THE RHETORICAL OBJECTIVES

Audience as a rhetorical concept has transcended the idea of a homogenous body of people who have stable characteristics and are assembled in the rhetor's presence. A discourse may have primary and secondary audiences, audiences that are present and those that have yet to form, audiences that act collaboratively or as individuals, audiences about whom the rhetor knows little, or audiences that exist only in the rhetor's mind. Chaïm Perelman and Lucie Olbrechts-Tyteca point out that unlike speakers, writers cannot be certain who their audiences are, and that rhetors often face "composite" audiences consisting either of several factions or of individuals who each represent several different groups (214–17).

In Bitzer's scheme audience exists fairly simply as a group of real people within a situation external to both the rhetor and the discourse. Douglas Park has broadened this perspective by offering four specific meanings of audience: (1) any people who happen to hear or read a discourse, (2) a set of readers or listeners who form part of an external rhetorical situation (equivalent to Bitzer's interpretation of audience), (3) the audience that the writer seems to have in mind, and (4) the audience roles suggested by the discourse itself. The first two meanings assume that the audience consists of actual people and correspond to what Lisa Ede and Andrea Lunsford have called "audience addressed" (Ede and Lunsford 156–65). Park's third and fourth meanings are more abstract, corresponding to Ede and Lunsford's "audience invoked." Park locates both those meanings of audience within the text, but I would suggest that the third resides not so much in the text as in the writer before and during composing, while the fourth is

17

18

20

21

GENRE CUES

 — Framework

 — Conversation

derived from the text by readers. Since writers are also readers of their own texts, they can alternate between the third and fourth meanings of audience while composing and rereading; so they might draft with a sense of audience in mind, then reread to see what sense of audience is reflected in the text they have created. In some instances writers may be their own intended audiences. One example would be personal journals, which writers may write for themselves as readers in the future, or for themselves in the present with no more awareness of audience as separate from self than they have when engaging in internal dialogue.

Instead of asking "Who is the audience?," Park recommends we ask how a discourse "defines and creates contexts for readers" (250). As an example of such a context, he offers Chaïm Perelman's notion of the universal audience, which Perelman defines in *The New Rhetoric* as an audience "encompassing all reasonable and competent men" (157). Appealing to the universal audience creates a forum in which debate can be conducted. Likewise, Park argues, a particular publication can create a context that partly determines the nature of the audience for a discourse that appears in it.

22 | Like the other constituents of rhetorical situations, the roles of rhetor and audience are dynamic and interdependent. As a number of theorists have observed, readers can play a variety of roles during the act of reading a discourse, roles that are not necessarily played either before or after reading. These roles are negotiated with the rhetor through the discourse, and they may change during the process of reading (Ede and Lunsford 166–67; Long 73, 80; Park 249; Perelman and Olbrechts-Tyteca 216; Phelps 156–57; Roth 182–83). Negotiation is the key term here. Rhetors' conceptions of audiences may lead them to create new roles for themselves—or adapt existing roles—to address those audiences. Rhetors may invite audiences to accept new identities for themselves, offering readers a vision not of who they are but of

19

20

GENRE CUES

 22— Making Knowledge

who they could be. Readers who begin the discourse in one role may find themselves persuaded to adopt a new role, or they may refuse the roles suggested by the discourse. I may open a letter from a charity and read it not as a potential donor but as a rhetorician, analyzing the rhetorical strategies used by the letter writer. In that case I would see my exigence for reading the letter, and my role in the negotiation, as quite different from what the writer appeared to have had in mind for me.[5]

Rhetorical situations, then, are not phenomena experienced only by rhetors. As Stephen Kucer and Martin Nystrand have argued, reading and writing may be seen as parallel activities involving negotiation of meaning between readers and writers. If reading is a rhetorical activity too, then it has its own rhetorical situations. So, if we prefer to use *writing situation* as a more accessible term than *rhetorical situation* when we teach (as some textbooks have — e.g., Pattow and Wresch 18–22; Reep 12–13), we should not neglect to teach students also about "reading situations," which may have their own exigencies, roles, and constraints.

CONSTRAINTS — FACTORS IN THE SITUATION'S CONTEXT THAT MAY AFFECT THE ACHIEVEMENT OF THE RHETORICAL OBJECTIVES

Constraints are the hardest of the rhetorical situation components to define neatly because they can include so many different things. Bitzer devotes just one paragraph to them, defining them as "persons, events, objects, and relations which are parts of the situation because they have the power to constrain decision and action needed to modify the exigence." Since he assumes that rhetors are largely controlled by situations and since he observes "the power of situation to constrain a fitting response" (390), his use of the term *constraints* has usually been interpreted to mean limitations on the rhetor — prescriptions or proscriptions controlling what can be said, or how it can be said, in a given situation. A rhetor is said to work within the constraints of the situation. However, this commonly held view of constraints as obstacles or restrictions has obscured the fact that Bitzer defines constraints more as aids to the rhetor

21

22

than as handicaps. The rhetor "harnesses" them so as to constrain the audience to take the desired action or point of view. This view of constraints seems useful, so I see them as working either for or against the rhetor's objectives. I refer to the kind that support a rhetor's case as positive constraints, or assets, and those that might hinder it as negative constraints, or liabilities.

Bitzer goes on to divide constraints along another axis. Some, which he equates with Aristotle's inartistic proofs, are "given by the situation." These might be "beliefs, attitudes, documents, facts, traditions, images, interests, motives and the like" — presumably including beliefs and attitudes held by the audience. Other constraints, equivalent to Aristotle's artistic proofs, are developed by the rhetor: "his personal character, his logical proofs, and his style" (388). To paraphrase, Bitzer defines constraints very broadly as all factors that may move the audience (or disincline the audience to be moved), including factors in the audience, the rhetor, and the rhetoric. Such an all-inclusive definition would seem to threaten the usefulness of constraints as a distinct constituent of rhetorical situations, so I propose excluding the rhetor and the audience as separate constituents and making explicit the possibility of both positive and negative constraints. I would define constraints, then, as all factors in the situation, aside from the rhetor and the audience, that may lead the audience to be either more or less sympathetic to the discourse, and that may therefore influence the rhetor's response to the situation — still a loose definition, but constraints defy anything tighter.

With the rhetor and the audience excluded from the category of constraints, it is tempting to exclude the other artistic proofs too, thereby simplifying the category further by drawing a distinction between the rhetorical situation and the discourse that arises from it. However, clearly the situation continues after the point at which the discourse begins to address it. A rhetor continues to define, shape, reconsider, and respond to the rhetorical situation

GENRE CUES

 — Making Knowledge

 — Making Knowledge

throughout the composing process, and at any given point during that process, the rhetor may be highly constrained by the emerging discourse. If we are to be coherent, what we have already written must constrain what we write next.

If constraints are those other factors in rhetorical situations, besides rhetors and audiences, that could help or hinder the discourse, what might they be? I have already included the emerging text of the discourse as a constraint on what a rhetor can add to it. To this we can add linguistic constraints imposed by the genre of the text or by the conventions of language use dictated by the situation. Other constraints could arise from the immediate and broader contexts of the discourse, perhaps including its geographical and historical background. Such constraints could include recent or imminent events that the discourse might call to readers' minds, other discourses that relate to it, other people, or factors in the cultural, moral, religious, political, or economic climate — both local and global — that might make readers more or less receptive to the discourse. Foreign trade negotiations, a domestic recession, a hard winter, civil disturbances, a sensational crime or accident — events like these might act as constraints on the rhetorical situation of an election campaign speech, suggesting appeals to make or avoid making. Every situation arises within a context — a background of time, place, people, events, and so forth. Not all of the context is directly relevant to the situation, but rhetors and audiences may be aware of certain events, people, or conditions within the context that *are* relevant and should be considered part of the situation because they have the potential to act as positive or negative constraints on the discourse. The challenge for the rhetor is to decide which parts of the context bear on the situation enough to be considered constraints, and what to do about them — for instance, whether the best rhetorical strategy for a negative constraint would be to address it directly and try to disarm it — or even try to turn it into a positive constraint — or to say nothing about it and hope that the audience overlooks it too.

25

(Reread)

READING CUES

- - **Reread** Grant-Davie packs a lot of detail into his arguments about constraints, so read the constraints section again to pick up more of them.

Some of my examples have complicated the roles of rhetor and audience, but all so far have looked at discourses in isolation and assumed that situations are finite. It seems clear that a situation begins with the rhetor's perception of exigence, but when can it be said to have ended? Does it end when the exigence has been resolved or simply when the discourse has been delivered? I favor the latter because it establishes a simpler boundary to mark and it limits rhetorical situations to the preparation and delivery of discourses, rather than extending them to their reception, which I consider to be part of the audience's rhetorical situation. Also, as I have tried to show, exigence can be quite complex and the point at which it can be said to have been resolved may be hard to identify. The same exigence may motivate discourses in many quite different situations without ever being fully resolved. Major sources of exigence, like civil rights, can continue to motivate generations of rhetors.

To say that a rhetorical situation ends when the discourse has been delivered still leaves us with the question of how to describe discourse in a discussion. Dialogue challenges the idea of rhetorical situations having neat boundaries. When participants meet around a table and take turns playing the roles of rhetor and audience, are there as many rhetorical situations as there are rhetors — or turns? Or should we look at the whole meeting as a single rhetorical situation? And what happens when the participants in a discussion are not gathered together at one place and time, engaged in the quick give and take of oral discussion, but instead debate a topic with each other over a period of weeks — for example, by sending and replying to letters to the editor of a newspaper? To look at a meeting as a single rhetorical situation recognizes that many of the constituents of the situation were common to all participants, and it emphasizes Bitzer's view that situations are external to the rhetor; whereas to look at each person involved in the discussion as having his or her own rhetorical situation — or each contribution to the discussion having its own situation — would seem to lean toward Vatz's view that rhetorical situations are constructed by rhetors. Both views, of course, are right. Each rhetor has a different perspective and enters the debate at a different time

25

(especially in the case of a debate carried on through a newspaper's editorial pages), so each addresses a slightly different rhetorical situation; but the situations may interlace or overlap extensively with those addressed by other rhetors in the discussion. It may be useful, then, to think of an entire discussion as a compound rhetorical situation, made up of a group of closely related individual situations. Analyzing a compound situation involves examining which constituents were common to all participants and which were specific to one or two. For example, some sources of exigence may have motivated all participants, and in these common factors may lie the hope of resolution, agreement, or compromise. On the other hand, the divisive heat of a debate may be traced to a fundamental conflict of values — and thus of exigence — among the participants.

Examples of this kind of compound rhetorical situation can be found whenever public debate arises, as it did recently in the editorial pages of a local newspaper in a rural community in the Rocky Mountains. The debate was sparked when the newspaper printed a front-page story about a nearby resort hotel, Sherwood Hills, that had erected a 46-foot, illuminated Best Western sign at the entrance to its property. Such a sign on a four-lane highway would not normally be remarkable, but the setting made this one controversial. Sherwood Hills lies hidden in trees at the end of a long driveway, off a particularly scenic stretch of the highway. There are no other residences or businesses nearby, and the area is officially designated a forest-recreation zone, which usually prohibits businesses and their signs. Several months earlier, the resort owners had applied to the county council for a permit and been told that some kind of sign on the road might be allowed, but the application had not been resolved when the sign went up.

28

The newspaper ran several stories reporting the resort owners' rationale (they felt they had applied in good faith and waited long enough) and the council members' reaction (they felt indignant

29

GENRE CUES

 — Making Knowledge

that the owners had flouted the law and were now seeking for-giveness rather than permission). The newspaper also berated the resort owners' actions in an editorial. What might have been a minor bureaucratic matter resolved behind closed doors turned into a town debate, with at least 15 letters to the editor printed in the weeks that followed. From a rhetorical perspective, I think the interesting question is why the incident sparked such a brushfire of public opinion, since not all controversial incidents covered by the newspaper elicit so many letters to the editor. Looking at the debate as a compound rhetorical situation and examining its con-stituents helps answer that question.

The rhetors and audiences included the resort owners, the county council, the county planning commission, the Zoning Administrator, the newspaper staff, and assorted local citizens. Their debate was nominally about the sign—whether it was illegal (a question at the stasis of definition) and what should be done about it (a question at the policy stasis). These questions were sources of exigence shared by all participants in the debate. However, even greater exigence seems to have come from ques-tions at the stasis of cause/effect—what precedent might the sign create for other businesses to ignore local ordinances?—and at the stasis of value—were the sign and the act of erecting it without a permit (and the ordinance that made that act illegal) good or bad? For most of the letter writers, the debate revolved around the issue of land use, one of the more frequently and hotly contested issues in the western United States, where the appropriate use of both public and private land is very much open to argument.

30

Critics of the sign generally placed a high value on unspoiled wilderness. For them the sign symbolized the commercial devel-opment of natural beauty and challenged laws protecting the appearance of other forest-recreation zones in the area. Those in favor of the sign, on the other hand, saw it not as an eyesore but as a welcome symbol of prosperity erected in a bold and

31

READING CUES

Look Ahead The article begins an extended example without saying so. Skim ahead to see where this one ends so that you can read it as one unit.

justified challenge to slow-moving bureaucracy and unfair laws, and as a blow struck for private property rights. Underlying the issue of land use in this debate, then, and providing powerful exigence, was the issue of individual or local freedom versus government interference—another issue with a strong tradition in the western U.S. (as in the case of the "sagebrush rebellions"— unsuccessful attempts to establish local control over public lands). The tradition of justified—or at least rationalized—rebellion against an oppressive establishment can of course be traced back to the American Revolution, and in the 1990s we have seen it appear as a fundamental source of exigence in a number of anti-government disputes in various parts of the nation.

Exigence and constraints can be closely related. For the critics of Sherwood Hills, the breaking of the law was a source of exigence, motivating them to protest, but the law itself was also a positive constraint in the situation, giving them a reason to argue for the removal of the sign. Certainly the law constrained the council's response to the situation. On the other hand, the law was apparently a less powerful constraint for the owners of Sherwood Hills and for many of their supporters who felt that the law, not the sign, should be changed. For many on that side of the debate, the tradition of rebelling against what are perceived to be unfair government restrictions provided both exigence and a positive constraint. The feeling that private property owners' rights had been violated was what motivated them to join the discussion, but it also gave them an appeal to make in their argument. The rhetor's sense of exigence, when communicated successfully to the audience, can become a positive constraint, a factor that helps move the audience toward the rhetor's position. 32

Precedents always create constraints. In the Sherwood Hills debate, several participants mentioned comparable business signs, including one recently erected at another local resort, also in a forest-recreation area. The existence of that sign was a positive constraint for supporters of the Sherwood Hills sign. However, it was also a negative constraint since the other resort had followed the correct procedure and received a permit for its sign, and since the sign was smaller and lower than the Sherwood Hills sign, had 33 no illumination, and had been designed to harmonize with the landscape.

Other constraints emerged from local history. The highway past Sherwood Hills had recently been widened, and the dust had not yet settled from the dispute between developers and environmentalists over that three-year project. Even before the road construction, which had disrupted traffic and limited access to Sherwood Hills, the resort had struggled to stay in business, changing hands several times before the present owners acquired it. The sign, some supporters suggested, was needed to ensure the new owners' success, on which the prosperity of others in the community depended too. The owners were also praised as upstanding members of the community, having employed local people and contributed to local charities. Two letter writers argued from this constraint that the community should not bite the hand that feeds it. 34

This analysis of the Sherwood Hills sign debate as a compound situation only scratches the surface, but understanding even this much about the situation goes a long way toward explaining why the incident generated such an unusual wave of public opinion. The conclusion of a compound rhetorical situation may be harder to determine than the end of a single-discourse situation, particularly if the subject of discussion is perennial. This particular dispute ended when the exchange of letters stopped and the Sherwood Hills owners reached a compromise with the county council: Both the sign and the ordinance remained in place, but the sign was lowered by ten feet. 35

26

As my discussion and examples have shown, exigence, rhetor, audience, and constraints can interlace with each other, and the further one delves into a situation the more connections between them are likely to appear. However, while the boundaries between the constituents will seldom be clear and stable, I do think that pursuing them initially as if they were discrete constituents helps a rhetor or a rhetorician look at a situation from a variety of 36

GENRE CUES

 26— Making Knowledge

perspectives. My efforts in the preceding pages have been to discuss the possible complexities of rhetorical situations. Teaching student writers and readers to ask the same questions, and to understand why they are asking them, will help them realize their options, choose rhetorical strategies and stances for good reasons, and begin to understand each other's roles.[6]

Notes

1. I thank *Rhetoric Review* readers John Gage and Robert L. Scott, whose careful reviews of earlier drafts of this essay helped me improve it greatly.

2. Bitzer's definition does not distinguish *situation* from *context*. The two terms may be used interchangeably, but I prefer to use *context* to describe the broader background against which a rhetorical situation develops and from which it gathers some of its parts. I see situation, then, as a subset of context.

3. In "The Rhetorical Situation" and "Rhetoric and Public Knowledge," Bitzer uses the terms *exigence* and *exigency* synonymously. I have used *exigence* in this essay mostly for reasons of habit and consistency with the original Bitzer/Vatz/Consigny discussion. I consider it an abstract noun like *diligence, influence,* or *coherence.* While cohesion can be located in textual features, coherence is a perception in the reader. In the same way, exigence seems to me to describe not so much an external circumstance as a sense of urgency or motivation within rhetors or audiences. It is they who recognize (or fail to recognize) exigence in a situation and so the exigence, like the meaning in literary works, must reside in the rhetor or audience as the result of interaction with external circumstances. Although Bitzer calls those circumstances exigences, I prefer to think of them as *sources* of exigence.

4. This fundamental disagreement between Bitzer and Vatz parallels the debate within literary theory over the location of meaning: whether meaning exists in the text, independent of the reader, or whether it is largely or entirely brought by the reader to the text. Bitzer's view looks toward formalism, Vatz's toward reader-response theories, and mine toward the position that meaning is a perception that occurs in the reader but is (or should be) quite highly constrained by the text.

5. Taking poststructuralist approaches to the roles of rhetor and audience, Louise Wetherbee Phelps and Robert Roth further challenge any assumption of a static, divided relationship between the two. Phelps uses Mikhail Bakhtin's idea of heteroglossia to deconstruct the idea of a boundary between author and audience.

GENRE CUES

— So What?

She argues that the other voices an author engages through reading and conversation while composing are inevitably present in the text, inextricably woven with the author's voice, and that this intertextuality of the text and the author makes a simple separation of text and author from audience impossible (158–59). Roth suggests that the relationship between writers and readers is often cooperative, not adversarial (175), and that a writer's sense of audience takes the form of a shifting set of possible reading roles that the writer may try on (180–82). Neither Phelps nor Roth argue that we should abandon the terms *rhetor* and *audience*. Phelps acknowledges that although author and audience may not be divisible, we routinely act as if they were (163), and she concludes that we should retain the concept of audience for its heuristic value "as a usefully loose correlate for an authorial orientation—whoever or whatever an utterance turns toward" (171). Like Phelps, Roth recognizes that the free play of roles needs to be grounded. "What we really need," he concludes, "is a continual balancing of opposites, both openness to a wide range of potential readers and a monitoring in terms of a particular sense of audience at any one moment or phase in the composing process" (186).

6. I have summarized my analysis in a list of questions that might be used by writers (or adapted for use by audiences) to guide them as they examine a rhetorical situation. Space does not allow this list to be included here, but I will send a copy to anyone who mails me a request.

Works Cited

Bitzer, Lloyd F. "The Rhetorical Situation." *Philosophy and Rhetoric* 1 (1968): 1–14. Rpt. *Contemporary Theories of Rhetoric: Selected Readings*. Ed. Richard L. Johannesen. New York: Harper, 1971. 381–93.

———. "Rhetoric and Public Knowledge." *Rhetoric, Philosophy, and Literature: An Exploration*. Ed. Don M. Burks. West Lafayette, IN: Purdue UP, 1978. 67–93.

Booth, Wayne C. *The Rhetoric of Fiction*. 2nd ed. Chicago: U of Chicago P, 1983.

Cherry, Roger D. "Ethos Versus Persona: Self-Representation in Written Discourse." *Written Communication* 5 (1988): 251–76.

Consigny, Scott. "Rhetoric and Its Situations." *Philosophy and Rhetoric* 7 (1974): 175–86.

Covino, William A., and David A. Jolliffe. *Rhetoric: Concepts, Definitions, Boundaries*. Boston: Allyn, 1995.

Crowley, Sharon. *Ancient Rhetorics for Contemporary Students*. New York: Macmillan, 1994.

Ede, Lisa, and Andrea Lunsford. "Audience Addressed/Audience Invoked: The Role of Audience in Composition Theory and Pedagogy." *College Composition and Communication* 35 (1984): 155–71.

Enos, Theresa. "An Eternal Golden Braid: Rhetor as Audience, Audience as Rhetor." Kirsch and Roen 99–114.

Fahnestock, Janne, and Marie Secor. "The Rhetoric of Literary Criticism." *Textual Dynamics of the Professions*. Ed. Charles Bazerman and James Paradis. Madison: U of Wisconsin P, 1991. 76–96.

———. "The Stases in Scientific and Literary Argument." *Written Communication* 5 (1988): 427–43.

Fields, Barbara. Interview. *The Civil War*. Dir. Ken Burns. Florentine Films, 1990.

Kirsch, Gesa, and Duane H. Roen, eds. *A Sense of Audience in Written Communication*. Newbury Park, CA: Sage, 1990.

Kucer, Stephen L. "The Making of Meaning: Reading and Writing as Parallel Processes." *Written Communication* 2 (1985): 317–36.

Long, Russell C. "The Writer's Audience: Fact or Fiction?" Kirsch and Roen 73–84.

Moore, Patrick. "When Politeness Is Fatal: Technical Communication and the Challenger Accident." *Journal of Business and Technical Communication* 6 (1992): 269–92.

Nystrand, Martin. "A Social-Interactive Model of Writing." *Written Communication* 6 (1988): 66–85.

Park, Douglas. "The Meanings of 'Audience.'" *College English* 44 (1982): 247–57.

Pattow, Donald, and William Wresch. *Communicating Technical Information: A Guide for the Electronic Age*. Englewood Cliffs, NJ: Prentice, 1993.

Perelman, Chaïm. *The New Rhetoric: A Theory of Practical Reasoning*. Trans. E. Griffin-Collart and O. Bird. *The Great Ideas Today*. Chicago: Encyclopedia Britannica, Inc., 1970. Rpt. *Professing the New Rhetorics: A Sourcebook*. Ed. Theresa Enos and Stuart C. Brown. Englewood Cliffs, NJ: Prentice, 1994, 145–77.

Perelman, Chaïm, and L. Olbrechts-Tyteca. *The New Rhetoric*. Trans. John Wilkinson and Purcell Weaver. U. of Notre Dame P, 1969: 1–26. Rpt. *Contemporary Theories of Rhetoric: Selected Readings*. Ed. Richard L. Johannesen. New York: Harper, 1971, 199–221.

Phelps, Louise Wetherbee. *Audience and Authorship: The Disappearing Boundary*. Kirsch and Roen 153–74.

Reep, Diana C. *Technical Writing: Principles, Strategies, and Readings*. 2nd ed. Boston: Allyn, 1994.

Roth, Robert G. *Deconstructing Audience: A Post-Structuralist Rereading*. Kirsch and Roen 175–87.

Vatz, Richard. "The Myth of the Rhetorical Situation." *Philosophy and Rhetoric* 6 (1973): 154–61.

White, Eugene E. *The Context of Human Discourse: A Configurational Criticism of Rhetoric*. Columbia: U of South Carolina P, 1992.

Questions for Discussion and Journaling

1. Have you ever thought of writers as negotiating with their audiences? As a writer, what is the difference between imagining yourself *talking* to and *negotiating* with your audience? What would you do differently if you were doing the latter?

2. How would you define *exigence*? Why does exigence matter in rhetorical situations? (What difference does it make?)

3. Grant-Davie opens with a discussion of historical documentaries and the difference between asking "What happened?" and asking "Why did it happen?" Which question, in your view, does analyzing rhetorical situations answer? What makes you think so?

4. What are *constraints*? To help you work this out, consider what Grant-Davie's constraints might have been in drafting this piece. Bitzer, you learned in this piece, argues that we should think of constraints as *aids* rather than *restrictions*. How can that be?

5. As a writer, how would it help you to be aware of your rhetorical situation and the constraints it creates?

6. Grant-Davie seems to want us to use the idea of rhetorical situation mostly in an *analytical* way, to understand why existing discourses have taken the shape they have. In other words, he seems to be talking to us as *readers*. In what ways is the idea also useful for writers? That is, how is it useful to understand the rhetorical situation you're "writing into"?

7. Grant-Davie suggests that we have to ask three questions to understand the exigence of a rhetorical situation: what a discourse is about, why it's needed, and what it's trying to accomplish. What's the difference between the second question and the third question?

8. What happens if we imagine everyone in a rhetorical situation to be *simultaneously* a rhetor and an audience? How does imagining a *writer* as simultaneously rhetor and audience make you think differently about writing?

9. Based on the rhetorical situation for which Grant-Davie was writing, would you say you are part of the audience he imagined, or not? Why?

10. Other writers (Bitzer, Vatz, Consigny) have tried to explain the concept of the *rhetorical situation* before. Why does Grant-Davie think more work is needed?

Applying and Exploring Ideas

1. (a) Write a brief (one- to two-page) working definition of *rhetorical situation*. Be sure to give some examples of rhetorical situations to illustrate your definition.

(b) Complicate your working definition by examining how Grant-Davie, Bitzer, Vatz, and Consigny see the rhetorical situation similarly or differently from one another. You may write this as a straightforward compare-and-contrast discussion if you would like, or, to spice things up a little, write it as a dialogue and create the situation in which it occurs. (Is it an argument? A dinner-table discussion? A drunken brawl?) Where does it happen, how does it go, and what do the participants say?

2. Write a two- to three-page analysis of the rhetorical situation of Grant-Davie's own article, using the elements the article explains.

3. Identify an argument that's currently going on at your school. (Check your school newspaper or website if nothing springs to mind.) In a short (two-to three-page) analysis, briefly describe the argument. After describing the argument, analyze the rhetorical situation. Then conclude by noting whether or how your understanding of the argument changed after you analyzed the rhetorical situation.

4. Look at three course syllabi and/or three academic handouts you've received this semester or in previous semesters. What rhetorical situation does each instructor seem to be imagining? Why do you think so? Do the instructors seem to imagine their rhetorical situations differently? If so, why do you think they do this?

5. Watch a few TV commercials and notice how quickly they establish a rhetorical situation *within* the ad. (Not, that is, the rhetorical situation of you as audience and the company as rhetor, but the rhetorical situation inside the commercial, where actors or characters play the roles of rhetors and audiences.) Write a two- to three-page analysis that describes three commercials, the rhetorical situations they create, and whether or not you consider them to be persuasive.

- -
META MOMENT   Why do you think that your teacher assigned this article? How might this article help you achieve the goals of this chapter? How can understanding the concept of *rhetorical situation* potentially be useful to you in school and in your life?
- -

Composing for Recomposition

Rhetorical Velocity
and Delivery

Udi Tirosh

JIM RIDOLFO
DÀNIELLE NICOLE DEVOSS

Peter Johnston, 2014

Framing the Reading

Rhetorical theory in the western hemisphere was established
by the Greeks before writing was common, so it focused
mostly on oratory — speeches by one man (women were usu-
ally excluded) to a large assembly of other men — in courtroom argument, legislative
debate, or public celebrations and funerals. Plato actually argued that writing was
damaging to philosophical discussion because a written document cannot answer
questions asked of it — and for Plato, the development of knowledge required *dialectic*, a spoken interchange usually based on questions and responses.

Writing as a knowledge-making mode of human discourse created problems for
the Greek notion of **rhetorical situation** that were largely ignored until the late twentieth century (see Grant-Davie in this chapter). Oratory, as a mode of delivery, can
be situated in a tightly controlled, singular rhetorical moment — one person talking
to several people in a room — but written texts offer no such stability. As scholars
like Grant-Davie (p. 484) recognize, the portability of writing to different times and
places than those in which it is originally composed means that we can no longer
accurately speak of single audiences for a piece of writing. Nonetheless, we have
mostly continued to do so. Following a Romantic eighteenth-century conception of
writers as singular, inspired, original thinkers, rhetorical theory until very recently

Ridolfo, Jim, and Dànielle Nicole DeVoss. "Composing for Recomposition: Rhetorical
Velocity and Delivery." *Kairos: A Journal of Rhetoric, Technology, and Pedagogy*,
vol. 13, no. 2, Spring 2009, kairos.technorhetoric.net/13.2/topoi/ridolfo_devoss/index
.html.

has relied on the idea of a single author writing for a single immediate purpose to a single immediate audience.

This article from *Kairos*, an online journal of rhetoric and technology, was "born digital" as a webtext that never appeared in print. (As such, we've had to modify it some to make it readable in a paper format.) Creating a webtext allowed authors Jim Ridolfo and Dànielle Nicole DeVoss to take "rhetorical situation" into twenty-first-century scenes of online writing, dealing with the challenges created for writers by new writing technologies that span time and space. Both Ridolfo, an assistant professor and Director of Composition at the University of Kentucky, and DeVoss, a professor at Michigan State University, have longstanding interests in digital rhetorics and technological literacies, among other topics. Ridolfo and DeVoss make the startling observation that writers in electronic textual cultures need to think not simply in terms of creating their own "locked," perfect, finished text, but rather of creating "open" texts that make themselves available for others to borrow from, remix, and transform into new works. Wise writers, Ridolfo and DeVoss argue, should learn to build texts strategically to attempt to shape how the text can later be "remixed" — that is, appropriated, reconfigured, and combined with other texts — by third-party writers. It is hard to overstate how different a conception of writing this is than that of the "finished," stand-alone text that most of us were raised to expect.

Along with a sense of rhetorical **ecology**, then, Ridolfo and DeVoss's notion of rhetorical **velocity** is important to building a full and realistic account of the threshold concepts that writing helps people make meaning and get things done and that "good" writing is dependent on writers, readers, situation, technology, and use. Ridolfo and DeVoss give us a way to think about rhetorical *situatedness* as including "distance, travel, speed, and time" (para. 4).

Getting Ready to Read

Before you read, do at least one of the following activities:

- Google Jim Ridolfo and Dànielle Nicole DeVoss to find what their most recent work focuses on, in order to help build your sense of who these rhetors are.

- Think about something you've written (and probably posted online) that has been used later on by another writer to create a new text. (For instance, when one of your Instagrams or Facebook posts has been shared.) Think as well of a time when you've appropriated someone else's writing (for example, by generating a meme from an existing image).

- Search online for "press releases" and look at several examples of the genre in order to see what its common textual features are and what work it does. This will help you better understand what Ridolfo and DeVoss are doing with their article.

As you read, consider the following questions:

- What other "remixes" can you remember encountering, and do you pay attention to them *as* remixes — that is, do you compare them to the original, or take them as "stand-alone" creations in their own right?

- Is the organization of this piece clear and easy to follow? Even though it's written as a series of press releases, can you track the standard academic moves, such as a **review of the literature,** that it's making?

- How much do Ridolfo and DeVoss actually *explain* the term "rhetorical velocity"? In what places throughout the article do they say "this is what we mean by this term" or make similar moves?

FOR IMMEDIATE RELEASE   **Contact:** Jim Ridolfo and Dànielle Nicole DeVoss

PEER-REVIEWED WORK   **Phone:** 517-555-2400

January 15, 2009, 09:01 AM EST   **E-mail:** ridolfoj@msu.edu and devossda@msu.edu

COMPOSING FOR RECOMPOSITION: RHETORICAL VELOCITY AND DELIVERY

East Lansing, MI – In this webtext, we propose that new concepts are needed 1
to discuss increasingly common rhetorical practices that are, we think, not closely aligned with the ways in which rhetorical delivery has historically been situated. We are specifically interested in situations where composers anticipate and strategize future third-party remixing of their compositions as part of a larger and complex rhetorical strategy that plays out across physical and digital spaces. We find this type of thinking—the asking of "how might the text be rewritten?" and "why, where, and for whom might this text be rewritten?" — an increasingly important set of questions in a digital age characterized, for instance, by swift, easy, and deep web searching and by copying and pasting practices.

We introduce a new conceptual consideration in this webtext, what Jim Ridolfo 2
has called "rhetorical velocity," and we explore the rhetorical possibilities of *composing for strategic recomposition*. We propose that the field needs an even greater

--more--

lexicon to explain the sort of rhetorical moves made by increasingly complex strategies of delivery.

In professional writing, an archetypical example of this sort of strategizing is 3 the press advisory and media release—a document specifically and deliberately strategized by a writer or writers with inventive considerations conscious of third-party recomposing. We chose a press release design for this article because it is distributed as analog and digital, with specific strategic use and importance associated with each of these physicalities; it also demonstrates an implicit consideration and structure for its recomposition. Certainly, a press release is not the flashiest or most compelling example of rhetorical velocity in digital spaces, but we think this genre is a useful place to begin thinking about the strategic appropriation of compositions. This genre, though constrained by rigid formatting conventions, offers a useful starting point for thinking about how such strategizing may predate and also change shape with the widespread adaptation of digital composing literacies. Additionally, this genre—with its disposition to alphabetic text—offers quick, easily locatable research examples for discussion and comparison (see the Defense Department example we've included elsewhere in this webtext). This genre scaffolds well into classroom conversations, and challenges students and researchers to find, argue for, and discuss other instances and mediums where ideas change shape, gather speed, and are elsewhere delivered.

The term *rhetorical velocity*, as we deploy it in this webtext, means a conscious 4 rhetorical concern for distance, travel, speed, and time, pertaining specifically to theorizing instances of strategic appropriation by a third party. In thinking about the concept, we drew from several definitions:

1. Rapidity or speed of motion; swiftness.
2. *Physics*: A vector quantity whose magnitude is a body's speed and whose direction is the body's direction of motion.
3. The rate of speed of action or occurrence.

Combining these definitions allowed us to create a term (i.e., rhetorical velocity) that allows us to wrestle with some of the issues particular to digital delivery, along with layering in a concern for *telos*.

> "We are proposing the beginning of a field conversation about how composers strategically design texts for re-appropriation by third parties," said Jim Ridolfo, a PhD Candidate in Rhetoric and Writing at Michigan State University.

--more--

"When a rhetorician has successfully produced and strategized the third-party use of boilerplate files, text, images, and videos by a third party, a strategic type of 'plagiarism' becomes the desirable 'end'," said Jim Porter and Dànielle Nicole DeVoss, faculty in Professional Writing at Michigan State University.

For more information visit http://kairos.technorhetoric.net/13.2/topoi /ridolfo-devoss/index.html.

REMIX, APPROPRIATION, AND COMPOSITION

Sergio Polano and Pierpaolo Vetta (1993) argued, "true innovation is one that is rightly able to link the adaptive history embodied in any artifact with the changes of production tools whenever they occur" (p. 30). At the 2005 CCCC in San Francisco, Lawrence Lessig opened his featured talk by defining remix as "what we do when we mix together culture or knowledge, and then give others the opportunity to re-express that which we have mixed . . . culture is remix, knowledge is remix, politics is remix. **Remix is how we as humans live and everyone within our society engages in this act of creativity**." Remixing—or the process of taking old pieces of text, images, sounds, and video and stitching them together to form a new product—is how individual writers and communities build common values; it is how composers achieve persuasive, creative, and parodic effects. Remix is perhaps the premier contemporary composing practice. To situate remix more appropriately and accurately, however, we need to leave behind what we think are the two dominant views of remix: (1) remix as simply cutting and pasting, and (2) remix as anchored and only related to music. We want to add another, less visible and less discussed aspect of remix here: that is, composing *for* remix, composing *for* recomposition. 5

A few months after his CCCC talk, speaking at Wikimania 2006, Lessig shifted his focus slightly to talk not just about remix culture, but of "rewrite culture." And at Linuxworld 2006, Lessig again emphasized that "writing is how we remix culture." At both venues, he spoke of the new technologies that have created "tools of creativity," "tools of speech"—and, importantly, tools of rhetoric. Appropriately for this audience, he lauded the success of Wikipedia as an ideal democratic space in which users take culture, remix culture, rewrite culture, and thus make culture. He noted that the success—the growth and, we would argue, the velocity—of Wikipedia was not possible with 20th century technologies. The velocity of Wikipedia is impressive; within 24 hours of September 27, the number of English-written news articles in Wikinews topped 10,000. Now, less than 6 months later, that number is more than 11,500. More than 2.5 million articles are included in the English-language area of Wikipedia. 6

--more--

We start with this discussion of Lessig's work because we think it speaks power- 7
fully to the context in which writers currently compose. His arguments offer us
much to wrestle with in the ways in which we approach remix and understand
the potentials of digital meaning-making tools. Although Lessig comes to his
work with a background in law, composition studies has certainly wrestled with
remix for quite some time now. We might, for instance, identify patchwriting
as remix; composition teachers have always encouraged students to remix their
own work, copying, pasting, merging, and moving their own words and sentences as they reorganize and revise.

A new element, however, enters the mix when we situate remix in today's digi- 8
tal culture; **more elements and others' elements become much more readily
available to mix, mash, and merge**. And, in fact, processes of mixing are valued
across these spaces, where savvy mixers are recognized as their YouTube channels
hit the top ten and as their videos are streamed across hundreds of servers. What
is obvious here is that composing in the digital age is *different* than traditional
practices of composing. **Rhetorical practices in a digital age are *different*
than traditionally conceived**. Electronic copying-and-pasting, downloading,
and networked filesharing change the dynamics of writing and, importantly, of
delivery.

Siva Vaidhyanathan (2003) noted "that's how creativity happens. Artists col- 9
laborate over space and time, even if they lived centuries and continents apart.
Profound creativity requires maximum exposure to others' works and liberal
freedoms to reuse and reshape others' material" (p. 186). Vaidhyanathan also
argues that we need to focus not on An Author—with its romantic connotations and narrow, textual associations—but on producers, the "unromantic
authors" (p. 10). When academics uphold distinctions between author and
producer, we are left in an uncomplicated, often acontextual space that does
not provide the tools we need to best negotiate the ways in which production
and authorship become more slippery in digital spaces and within remix projects. Freedom from romantic authorship is crucial to rhetorical velocity, and
the speed with which artifacts can move and be remixed across networks, audiences, and contexts. In fact, the romantic author figure stands in opposition to
rhetorical velocity.

Lev Manovich (2002) created a telling picture of remix and velocity that links 10
both directly to changes in delivery:

> If a traditional twentieth century model of cultural communication
> described movement of information in one direction from a source to a

--more--

receiver, now the reception point is just a temporary station on information's path. If we compare information or media object with a train, then each receiver can be compared to a train station. Information arrives, gets remixed with other information, and then the new package travels to other destination where the process is repeated.

What Manovich is getting at here are the ways in which delivery happens in remix culture. Instead of a single author producing solitary work in isolation and that work being attributed to that single, solitary author and delivered in a one-way fashion, we have distributed, shared views of authorship—think of spaces like Wikipedia, for instance, where work and authorial agency are attributed often in diverse, diffuse ways.

In our day, writing often requires composers to draw upon multiple modes of meaning-making. Computers and robust networks allow writers to choreograph audio, video, other visual elements, text, and more. Writers engage in taking the old and making new. Appropriating words and images. Taking pieces, splicing ideas, compiling fragments. Transforming existing work. Transformation occurs when the rhetor delivers a text into a new context; collects the text with others to make a new compilation; adds additional materials to the text; and more (Mendelson, 2002; Porter & DeVoss, 2006). Most importantly here, transformation occurs as and when the composer remixes—visit the "Chocolate Rain" original and remixes below. 11

"Chocolate Rain" by Tay Zonday
https://youtu.be/EwTZ2xpQwpA

"Chocolate Rain Sung by McGruff the Crime Dog"
https://youtu.be/fsdM2oMSUbM

"Chocolate Rain: The Music Video"
https://youtu.be/PxJ1iX7LIJo

"Chocolate Rain" by Tre Cool
https://youtu.be/eyDuGwlrFRs

--more--

"Chocolate Rain" by Chad Vader
https://youtu.be/P6dUCOS1bM0

"Vanilla Snow" by Peppergod
https://youtu.be/nTQOpibv_OA

"Fast Food Chain" by snedge45
https://youtu.be/Q1DcavXVK5Y

The "Chocolate Rain" original and remixes are interesting and at times innova- 12
tive examples of remix. Likely, however, Tay Zonday did not write and produce
his original piece with remix in mind. So what does it mean to take future composing and re-composition into strategic consideration while composing? That
is, what does it mean to compose with re-composition in mind? This is a question key to this webtext, and one we return to later. Before turning to that question,
however, we want to situate our work further in the history of delivery and in
contemporary approaches to delivery in rhetoric and composition studies.

DELIVERY: RHETORIC HISTORY AND THEORY

From the texts of Cicero, rhetorical scholars have learned the story of the Greek 13
Demosthenes. When Demosthenes was asked his opinion of what constituted
the most important element of rhetoric, he three times repeated one word:
"delivery, delivery, delivery" (Duncan, 2006, p. 84). Nothing additional has sur-
vived regarding Demosthenes' thinking on delivery, and his answer remains a
mystery in terms of what may have informed his conclusion as to the critical
nature of delivery. In *De Oratore*, Cicero meditated on Demosthenes' assertion;
Cicero noted that he had observed how "many poor speakers have often reaped
the rewards of eloquence because of a dignified delivery, and many eloquent
men have been considered poor speakers because of awkward delivery" (p. 347).
Based on Demosthenes' observation, Cicero theorized that "If, then, there can
be no eloquence without this [delivery], and this without eloquence is so important, certainly its role in oratory is very large" (p. 347). In this work, delivery is
clearly of foundational importance to rhetoric.

--more--

In Aristotle's *Rhetoric*, delivery is presented as an important component of oral 14
delivery, but one not regarded as a virtuous area of study. According to Aristotle,
"No systematic treatise upon the rules of delivery has yet been composed; indeed,
even the study of language made no progress till late in the day. Besides, delivery
is — very properly — not regarded as an elevated subject of inquiry" (p. 120). In
this respect, Aristotle both notes the critical nature of delivery, but undercuts its
study when removed from other subjects. What Aristotle does do, however, is
put forward commentary that stigmatizes the study of rhetorical delivery, even
within the realm of orality where it has been relegated: "It is those who do bear
them [the concerns of delivery] in mind who usually win prizes in the dramatic
contests; and just as in drama the actors now count for more than the poets, so
it is in the contests of public life, owing to the defects of our political institutions" (p. 119–120). In this sense, from Aristotle's ethical distinction of delivery
something remains true today: its consideration remains paramount in much
of political life. This fact alone should elevate rhetorical delivery to a higher status, particularly when its study or analytical application — bringing in a theory
of rhetorical delivery for complex rhetorical analyses — leads to social action.
This delivery-toward-action is not developed in Aristotle's *Rhetoric*; rather, much
of the conversation focuses on the technical particulars of delivery, which, as
Edward Corbett suggested, are a "concern for the management of the voice and
for gestures (*actio*)" (p. 28). According to Aristotle, there are three things that
greatly affect the success of a speech,

> But hitherto the subject has been neglected. Indeed, it was long before it
> found a way into the arts of tragic drama and epic recitation: at first poets
> acted their tragedies themselves. It is plain that delivery has just as much to
> do with oratory as with poetry. It is, essentially, a matter of the right man-
> agement of the voice to express the various emotions — of speaking loudly,
> softly, or between the two; of high, low, or intermediate pitch; of the various
> rhythms that suit various subjects. These are the three things — volume of
> sound, modulation of pitch, and rhythm — that a speaker bears in mind.
> (p. 119)

It is no mystery, then, that a rhetorical treatise on delivery does not seem to 15
exist which includes as its primary subject matter stories of carrier pigeons, mes-
sengers, scrolls, and complex narratives of oral circulation. Aristotle (and much
of the Roman and Medieval rhetorical theory responding to Aristotle) does not
leave very much room for this sort of rhetorical theory. And we think we would
be better able to theorize complex practices of delivery today if there was this
type of room.

--more--

It can no longer be assumed, even in a contemporary instance of oral deliv- 16 ery, that the time, place, and medium of delivery will necessarily be the same for both the speaker and the speaker's audiences. As John Trimbur noted in "Composition and the Circulation of Writing" (2000), a "focus solely on oral rhetoric, absent of other technologies, is not sustainable as a theory of rhetoric. Public forums are diffuse, fragmented, and geographically separated. Speech is both literally and metaphorically broadcast through expanded means of com- munication" (p. 190). We agree with Trimbur's analysis and also think that many of the concepts for and activities of delivery in active use today are not currently theorized in attempts to understand rhetorical delivery. Our project in this article is to introduce one of these theories and begin to expand the rhetori- cal toolbox for additional concepts of delivery.

DELIVERY: CONTEMPORARY COMPOSITION STUDIES

In this section, we survey a few occurrences of how rhetorical delivery is dis- 17 cussed by different scholars in rhetoric and composition studies. Obviously, the need to rethink delivery is felt not only in rhetoric and composition studies (although, we would argue, our field has been most attentive in reconsidering delivery in light of changing technologies and shifting trends, especially tech- nological trends). Jeff Rice (2003; 2006) has reminded us that folks like Walter Ong and Marshall McLuhan, for instance, were reconceiving delivery in the 1960s. In *The Medium is the Massage* (1967), for instance, McLuhan and his collaborator, graphic artist Quentin Fiore, explored electronic delivery systems. They opened the text with this comment: "The medium, or process, of our time — electric technology — is reshaping and restructuring patterns of social interdependence and every aspect of our personal life . . . Societies have always been shaped more by the nature of the media by which men communicate than by the content of the communication" (p. 8). *The Medium is the Massage* is part textbook, part manifesto, and part guidebook for media students and scholars in a changing world. It is thick with grand claims (e.g., "'Time' has ceased, 'space' has vanished" (p. 63)) and compelling, provocative graphical content (e.g., a photograph from the interior of a car where we sit in the driver's seat racing through a tunnel, with a cut-out of a horse and buggy in the rear-view mirror).

Two of the perhaps most compelling claims made in the text were "Our official 18 culture is striving to force the new media to do the work of the old" (repeated throughout the text) and "electric technology fosters and encourages unification

--more--

and involvement" (p. 8). McLuhan's work deserves much, much more than this brief mention here. We certainly don't want to dismiss the importance of McLuhan's work, and we want to pause — as many others have done — to assert the ways in which McLuhan's work resonates so loudly and profoundly today, almost a half-century after the publication of his work. (For readers who want to follow this particular path, we suggest, specifically, Rice's work, especially his 2003 "Writing about Cool," where he describes digital writing in the context of hypertext, juxtaposition, and cool, and his 2006 "The Making of Ka-Knowledge, " where Rice extends the work of Ong and McLuhan in terms of sound and the nature of knowledge.)

In what follows, we attend not to the work of McLuhan or other communica- 19 tions scholars but instead present a review of work anchored to composition studies, because we think it is necessary to base our understanding of rhetorical delivery on existing field conversations, specifically those that make use of the term. We do not focus on conversations of medium theory, which, although extremely relevant to rhetorical delivery, we view as historically distinct within our discipline from conversations of classical rhetorical delivery. As is clear from the dates on these recent field conversations in rhetorical delivery, a flurry of scholarship over the past 20 years has re-evaluated delivery in light of radical changes to modes of production, delivery, and distribution. Within the context of these changes to the means of distribution, field conversations in rhetoric and composition have surfaced that specifically ask how classical rhetorical concepts such as delivery are impacted by changes to the means of distribution.

We are interested in expanding considerations of rhetorical delivery to include 20 complex elements of strategy, and are interested in introducing one specific concept in light of some of these changes, *rhetorical velocity*, which we will discuss in a following section. For now, we review how recent field conversations in rhetorical delivery discuss changes in the means of distribution. One early discussion occurred in 1993, where Sheri Helsley wrote:

> Rhetorical delivery is enormously important in an electronic age. Word processing and desktop publishing, for example, are now readily available to student writers, and classical rhetoric prompts us to address the use and adaptation of these powerful post-typewriter presentation technologies. When we interpret delivery as presentation or secondary orality, we do important things for ourselves and our students. We restore the recursiveness and synthesis originally envisioned in the interaction of the five rhetorical canons. We move into important discussions of inevitable technologies and new structures of consciousness in the electronic age. We expose our students

--more--

to the power of presentation in both encoding and decoding—an issue that has been largely ignored in contemporary education. (p. 158)

Helsley was one of the first to make the argument that the canon of rhetorical delivery would become increasingly important in the digital age. In addition, she also noted how considerations of delivery in composition education are critical to the writing classroom. With a broader, more corporeal sense of concern, Virginia Skinner-Linnenberg's 1997 book *Dramatizing Writing: Reincorporating Delivery into the Classroom* also echoed these concerns.

Skinner-Linnenberg's book is an important work for delivery studies because 21 it provides the field with the most comprehensive historical survey of rhetorical delivery to date. Additionally, her book develops a rich understanding of how rhetorical delivery can be theorized as corporeal, bringing a host of new concerns to the writing classroom. Skinner-Linnenberg noted that in "dramatizing writing, students employ both their physicality and their noetic processes, whether they are the writers or the audience" (p. 109), and theorized extensively how teachers might make the composition classroom a more oral, physical, corporeal environment to study, write, and deliver: "Delivery in the classroom through dramatizing writing aids students to use their bodies and minds in their writing. With delivery, students can, with the help of others, study themselves, hear themselves, and see themselves as users of language" (p. 111). Theorizing that the dramaturgical elements of delivery—elements she reads as once existing in classical rhetoric—have been lost to the contemporary classroom, she challenged the field to consider "where does *ethos* fit into dramatizing writing?" (p. 110). In this sense, Skinner-Linnenberg is early in asking—rather, returning to—Aristotle's question about the ethics of rhetorical delivery.

Kathleen Welch (1999) also participates in this conversation in her *Electric* 22 *Rhetoric: Classical Rhetoric, Oralism, and a New Literacy*. Welch argued that there is an even greater political imperative to delivery at the end of the 20th century:

It is crucial to an understanding of Western literacy at the newly electrified turn of the millennium to recognize that the disappearance of memory and delivery is not a benign removal. Rather, it is part of a larger movement in the United States to pablumize the humanities in general, and to vitiate writing in particular, by behaving (especially in our educational institutions) as if it were a mere skill, craft, or useful tool. The colonizing of memory and delivery reproduces the form/content binary that drives the movement to

--more--

regulate writing to skills and drills and perpetuates the status quo of racism and sexism. (pp. 144–145)

For Welch, there is a clear political imperative for the teaching of memory and delivery, because she implies that to not do so is to debilitate the efficacy of the writer. According to Welch, "The elimination of memory and delivery in the majority of student writing textbooks constitutes the removal of student-written language from the larger public arena" (p. 145). This concern for delivery and student-written language is also picked up by John Trimbur (2000) in "Composition and the Circulation of Writing."

Trimbur advanced that "neglecting delivery has led writing teachers to equate   23
the activity of composing with writing itself and to miss altogether the complex delivery systems through which writing circulates" (pp. 189–190). He adopts a Marxist approach to delivery, one that equates rhetorical delivery with Marx's notion of circulation because

> delivery can no longer be thought of simply as a technical aspect of public discourse. It must be seen also as ethical and political—a democratic aspiration to devise delivery systems that circulate ideas, information, opinions and knowledge and thereby expand the public forums in which people deliberate on the issues of the day. (p. 190)

Additionally, Trimbur argued that the "isolation of writing from the material   24
conditions of production and delivery" should be a concern for compositionists (p. 189). In this sense, both Trimbur and Welch see a call to delivery as a necessity at a similar technological and political moment. Trimbur's analysis of the material circulation of delivery is that

> students' sense of what constitutes the production of writing by tracing its circulation in order to raise questions about how professional expertise is articulated to the social formation, how it undergoes rhetorical transformations (or "passages of form"), and how it might produce not only individual careers but also socially useful knowledge. (p. 214)

Across the work of Skinner-Linnenberg, Welch, and Trimbur, there is a consis-   25
tent thread of technological changes alongside a re-examination of delivery in the wake of its movement into the realm of the electric. A more recent piece of scholarship by Dànielle Nicole DeVoss and James Porter (2006) acutely addresses issues of ethics, file sharing, and delivery. In "Why Napster Matters to Writing," the authors called attention to changes in the means of distribution: "The new

--more--

digital ethic is characterized by drastic changes in delivery, and reminds us of the power of delivery" (p. 36). DeVoss and Porter argue that a change in the infrastructure and systems of cultural delivery and distribution is affecting students' attitudes toward the composition and delivery of writing.

DeVoss and Porter supplement their discussion of electronic delivery with a 26 heuristic of what might constitute a rubric for considering digital delivery and distribution. They make use of the Napster controversy as an example to argue for an "expanded notion of delivery, one that embraces the politics and economics of publishing: the politics of technology development as they impact production and distribution; the politics of information" (DeVoss & Porter, p. 25) in an ever-unfolding and ever-present digital landscape. In addition, their article provided a highly useful list of criteria to help composition scholars think about digital delivery and contemporary theories of delivery:

> The choice of tools for production and the choice of medium for distribution—a.k.a, publishing practices—that is, the technical and human methods of production, reproduction, and distribution of digital "information" (broadly understood to include audio and video, as well as graphic and textual data);

> Knowledge of the systems which govern, constrain, and promote publishing practices—including public policy, copyright laws and other legislation, technology design and development, publishing conventions and economic models (both micro and macro);

> Awareness of the ethical and political issues that impact publishing practices—that is, who decides? What policies best serve the interests of society? What constitutes "digital fair use"? How should content producers be credited for their work? (DeVoss & Porter, p. 26)

"Why Napster Matters" indirectly expands on Trimbur's discussion of deliv- 27 ery, with a call for economic analysis synonymous with Trimbur's discussion. Further, both works of scholarship bring attention to a base-motivating factor for the movement of rhetoric, one that has hitherto not been included in 2,000 years of scholarship on rhetorical delivery.

Recent work by Doug Eyman (2007) in *Digital Rhetoric: Ecologies and Economies* 28 *of Circulation* also examines methodological considerations for doing rhetorical research. In his recent dissertation, he sought to examine how "the interactions of texts and contexts can yield a more comprehensive picture of interaction

--more--

than the traditional approach of rhetorical invention, composition, and delivery; it can also provide a map of the relationships between work and activity that are often hidden because we simply don't have the means to uncover them" (pp. 8–9). Eyman provides a wealth of methodological approaches for scholars interested in studying the overall circulation of a composition, from conference proposals, seminar papers, web texts, and more.

Nancy Welch (2005) raises a concern similar to Eyman's for both delivery and [29] economics. In "Living Room Rhetoric: Teaching Writing in a Post-Publicity Era," Welch discusses a seminar she taught while the second U.S.-Iraqi war began in the spring of 2003. Her article covered issues of audience, circulation, and delivery, specifically how these concepts "add to the growing body of work that has the potential to reorient us from regarding rhetoric as a specialized *techne*—the property of a small economic and political elite—to understanding and teaching rhetoric as a *mass, popular art*" (p. 474).

Her work provides an account of Katie, a student activist involved in the com- [30] position and delivery of writing in opposition to the approaching war. Welch noted that a central compositional consideration for Katie was how she might circulate her work: "I want these poems to be *out there*, not just in a chapbook where my friends will read them and say, 'Oh, Katie wrote a poem. Isn't that nice'" (p. 472). This concern echoed Trimbur's call to see delivery as "inseparable from the circulation of writing and the widening diffusion of socially useful knowledge" (p. 191). Welch discusses how public spaces for sharing, posting, and hosting information (e.g., parks, telephone poles) have been locked down to prohibit communication and maintain a tidy public face. She advocates that rhetorical education should include a greater exposure to the rhetoric of mass struggle, because it offers the opportunity to learn about strategies of action. But perhaps most interesting is how her student, Katie, revisits her strategy of rhetorical delivery and distribution. By the end of the article, Katie decided that the poem needed to be hand-delivered, and this form of delivery seemed better suited for her writing and the occasion than her initial strategy of tacking the poem on telephone poles or utility boxes.

Similar to the approaches advocated by Skinner-Linnenberg, Nancy Welch lists [31] a number of additional corporeal concerns dealing primarily with the legal status and physical safety of the rhetor involved in public acts of rhetorical delivery. According to Welch, "as students and teachers ponder in the fullest way possible the rhetorical canon of delivery, there might even be (as one student suggested at the end of the women's studies seminar) training in civil disobedience or at the very least a guest lecturer from the ACLU" (Welch, p. 478). The list and example

--more--

Welch offers provides rhetoric and composition studies with a fine theoretical synthesis of both the corporeal and the growing focus on emerging concerns for delivery, place, and location.

In the next section we would like to add to the several areas of rhetorical theory dealing with delivery (the corporeal, the legal, the composition classroom, the digital) and introduce a conversation involving the anticipation of remixing, or the strategic composing for future acts of recomposition as part of a rhetorical objective or series of objectives. We introduce this concept first as a conceptual tool useful for thinking about complex strategies of rhetorical delivery, and later as one practical for classroom discussions (an analytic) focused on the recomposition of writing as part of what Daniel Kimmage and Kathleen Ridolfo (2007) call "the amplification effect." We see this concept of rhetorical velocity as adding to the growing body of literature focused around rethinking rhetorical delivery within rhetoric and composition studies. 32

RHETORICAL VELOCITY AND THE AMPLIFICATION EFFECT

In the July 2007 Radio Free Europe/Radio Liberty special report on Iraqi insurgent media titled *The War of Images and Ideas: How Sunni Insurgents in Iraq and Their Supporters Worldwide are Using the Media,* Daniel Kimmage and Kathleen Ridolfo (2007) investigated how Sunni insurgent groups are strategizing the delivery and circulation of their media for local and international audiences. The RFE/RL report did a unique job of surveying "the products, producers, and delivery channels of the Sunni Insurgency's media network" (p. 4); the authors, in addition, documented how the insurgent groups are carefully examining and crafting their messages, along with gauging both potential and ideal impacts of those messages. Although the main purpose of the report was to bring "Iraqi insurgent media from the margins to center stage so that outsiders without a command of Arabic can glimpse the 'other half' of what is happening in Iraq as it is presented by the other side" (p. 6), the report also provides important examples for theorizing how the fifth canon should be reconsidered in terms of how texts are delivered, recomposed, and delivered again. According to Kimmage and Ridolfo, "the Internet is more versatile than traditional delivery platforms because it can serve as a vehicle for those [traditional] platforms in addition to Internet-specific information platforms like websites" (p. 35), and the pair noted that: 33

> Insurgents' willingness to forego a centralized brick-and-mortar production
> infrastructure and their reliance on the Internet as the primary distribution

--more--

527

channel for their media products have led to the emergence of a decentralized, building-block production model in which virtually any individual
or group can design a media product to serve insurgent aims and goals. As
the preceding overview of insurgent media products shows, both text and
audiovisual products begin with simple units and proceed to more complex
creations. For text products, the basic building blocks are operational press
releases and topical statements; for audiovisual products, footage of insurgent
activities and statements recorded by prominent insurgents and sympathiz-
ers. Of these building blocks, only the footage of insurgent activities and
statements by insurgent leaders need be recorded on location in Iraq. One or
more individuals working anywhere in the world can create everything else.
(pp. 34–35)

We are specifically interested as compositionists in this report in terms of how 34
the notion of "building blocks" is discussed regarding strategic and rhetorical
affordances. The observations in this report should direct our field's attention
to an increasingly common and widespread compositional moment: strategically composing for the express, deliberate purpose of providing materials for
future potential acts of appropriation and re-composition by others. Certainly,
boilerplates and templates abound in corporate contexts, for instance, but the
difference here is that these recomposers are perhaps unknown to the initial
composer or creator of video and text—existing elsewhere across digital and
sneaker networks, and potentially across the globe. These third parties may very
well be news agencies or brick and mortar organizations, but they may also be
much more dispersed: Using the example of "attack videos," Krimmage and
Ridolfo explain how the production and re-composition of content is diffused,
and allude to a process of circulation that affords composers the ability to conceive of how their work may be recomposed:

> In the case of short attack videos, only the footage of the actual attack need
> come from Iraq. Once an affiliated individual has received that footage and
> basic accompanying information, which can be transferred over the Internet
> or by mobile phone, he has only to add the insurgent group's logo, a short
> title sequence, and perhaps a soundtrack with a motivational song. He then
> uploads the resulting video product to a free upload-download site and posts
> an announcement to a forum. The video-editing software required to pro-
> duce such a video is cheap and readily available. (p. 35)

According to Krimmage and Ridolfo, the amplification effect is the way in 35
which the media infrastructure serves "to amplify the message of the Sunni

--more--

insurgency by using insurgent press releases and statements as the basis for their coverage of events in Iraq" (p. 61). In addition, emergent digital media infra-structure affords

> a variety of means for amplifying the insurgent message. Materials posted to insurgent group homepages are regularly picked up and posted to broader forms. A message or video posted to one form is then reposted to other forms, thereby amplifying the message to potentially thousands of Internet users. From there, mainstream Arab media access the materials and use them in their print and broadcast reports. For example, Al-Jazeera often runs video clips from insurgent attacks in its newscasts. (p. 61)

What we see in this report, then, is a study of how composing practices are increasingly taking delivery into consideration in particular ways. Although this can occur in oral rhetoric, we see emerging in the variety of compositional medi-ums available an increase in this sort of thinking about delivery: How will the press advisory I write be recomposed by the reporters I have a working relation-ship with? How will my media packet be utilized in the production of broadcast news? From the perspective of the compositionist as rhetorician, we think of this concept as composing with rhetorical velocity in mind. 36

RHETORICAL VELOCITY

Rhetorical velocity is, simply put, a strategic approach to composing for rhetori-cal delivery. It is both a way of considering delivery as a rhetorical mode, aligned with an understanding of how texts work as a component of a strategy. In the inventive thinking of composing, rhetorical velocity is the strategic theorizing for how a text might be recomposed (and *why* it might be recomposed) by third parties, and how this recomposing may be useful or not to the short- or long-term rhetorical objectives of the rhetorician. In this sense, the rhetorician weighs the positive and negative possibilities of different types of textual appropriation against desired objectives: "If I release the video in this format, could the video be used *in this way,* and *would it be worth their time to do this? And would it be supportive of my objectives* for them *to do that?*" And in this sense, the theorizing of the question of "is it worth the time to do this" calls into question a set of economic and material concerns. 37

As a set of practices rhetorical velocity is, secondly, a term that describes an understanding of how the speed at which information composed to be recom-posed travels—that is, it refers to the understanding and rapidity at which 38

--more--

information is crafted, delivered, distributed, recomposed, redelivered, redistributed, etc., across physical and virtual networks and spaces. Thinking with rhetorical velocity in mind requires one to have an idea about the working conditions of the third party and what type of text it would be useful (or not) to provide: What document format should a file be sent in for certain types of future remixing? What resolution should images be released in if they are to be reprinted in a print publication? What level of quality and format should video be released in if it were to be cut up into additional tapes? What segments of these texts may be useful, and to whom, and for what sorts of media production? In each of these strategic questions rhetorical velocity requires on the part of rhetors a careful consideration of the future time (and particular moments) and place(s) of where, how, and potentially into what texts may be recomposed — and what this may mean.

For example, the rhetorician may strategically consider these temporal elements: 39 "What is the publication cycle of this newspaper? How long does the television station keep its video archives online? How long until Google indexes the mailing list archives?" as part of thinking with rhetorical velocity in mind. A classic example of composing with rhetorical velocity in mind is the press release — a mingling of boilerplate text and specific, deliberate, targeted text written to be used and often directly recomposed by local or national television stations, newspapers, or broadcast news. As the diagram below (p. 531) shows, in the theory and composing state rhetoricians may balance the future possibilities in terms of possible positive, negative, and neutral outcomes for recomposing, remixing, and appropriation. The rhetorician writing the press release may, for example, acquire institutional knowledge based on experiential outcomes between theory-composing and how anticipated future possibilities actually turned out. In this sense we highlight in the diagram the epistemic nature of composing with considerations of rhetorical velocity and highlight the knowledge production that is taking place between the theory and practice, particularly when contrasted between multiple strategies, experiences of rhetorical delivery, and composing with a sense of rhetorical velocity in mind.

--more--

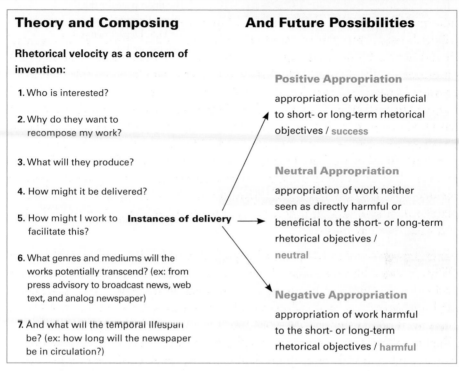

Theory and Composing

And Future Possibilities

Rhetorical velocity as a concern of invention:

1. Who is interested?

2. Why do they want to recompose my work?

3. What will they produce?

4. How might it be delivered?

5. How might I work to **Instances of delivery** facilitate this?

6. What genres and mediums will the works potentially transcend? (ex: from press advisory to broadcast news, web text, and analog newspaper)

7. And what will the temporal lifespan be? (ex: how long will the newspaper be in circulation?)

Positive Appropriation

appropriation of work beneficial to short- or long-term rhetorical objectives / success

Neutral Appropriation

appropriation of work neither seen as directly harmful or beneficial to the short- or long-term rhetorical objectives / neutral

Negative Appropriation

appropriation of work harmful to the short- or long-term rhetorical objectives / harmful

Figure 1 **Rhetorical Velocity as a Concern of Invention**

An example of using rhetorical velocity as an analytic to discuss appropriation across a three-day time span can be drawn from a 2008 United States Department of Defense media release. 40

The main page for the U.S. Department of Defense web site.

--more--

The main page for the "News Releases" area of the U.S. Department of Defense web site.

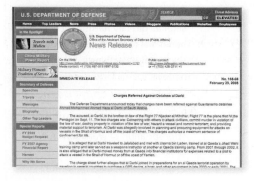

A February 29, 2008 (No. 168-08) news release, "Charges Referred Against Detainee al Darbi."

The results of a Google search of the detainee, using quotation marks to limit the search: "Ahmed Mohammed Ahmed Haza al Darbi of Saudi Arabia" (268 instances of that particular phrase found).

A story dated March 2, 2008, based on the original U.S. Department of Defense media release.

--more--

As we can see from this example, past text has been utilized for future instances of 41 writing (not simply an RSS feed), based on the boilerplate text of the press advisory. This sort of analysis, which we discuss as an assignment in the next section, attempts to understand what has happened in instances of rhetorical delivery by initial authors and by third parties. We see this as also a knowledge-generating research approach to delivery, one where research questions may be discussed, examined, and addressed by analyzing the size, scope, and strategy of how texts are delivered.

We do not know if the writers of the press advisory explicitly anticipated these par- 42 ticular instances of appropriation, but we think it is probable and certainly worth discussing the possibility. We think this strategizing is complimentary to the genre of the press advisory—the genre we have chosen for this webtext—to think in such ways. This one example is typical of how it is possible to learn how a process of rhetorical delivery occurs (and how delivery is knowledge-producing). In the example above, this is evidenced by the textual interactions different news organizations have had with a particular press release. Further study could yield partial institutional patterns of rhetorical delivery, as well as forms and ranges for various types of appropriation, recomposition, and remixing by different composers, such as the interaction between the DefenseLink and blogs, web sites, and news agencies

COMPOSING FOR THE FUTURE AND TEACHING RHETORICAL VELOCITY

> "Today, we are witnessing . . . a writing public made plural . . . Whatever the exchange value may be for these writers—and there are millions of them, here and around the world—it's certainly not grades. Rather, the writing seems to operate in an economy driven by use value" (Yancey, 2005, p. 301).

Along with Helsley, Skinner-Linnenberg, Welch, Trimbur, and others whose 43 work we have cited here, Kathi Yancey has also addressed digital delivery. In the print version of her 2003 Conference on College Composition and Communication chair's address, "Made Not Only in Words: Composition in a New Key," Yancey (2005) speaks of the circulation of texts, and points toward ways in which we might better equip students to approach issues of digital delivery as an often rhizomatic process. She also wrote regarding *deicity*—the now and then of texts, and the ways in which texts change shape as they circulate in digital spaces. She spoke, in rich, eloquent, and illustrated ways, about the "proliferation of writings outside the academy" (p. 298).

Writing happens—and happens a lot—and lives in digital spaces like fan 44 fiction sites, YouTube comments, blogs, and other spaces, and, Yancey notes,

--more--

this writing dramatically counterpoints the writing done within the academy. Students are writing. A lot. They're sharing. A lot. They're circulating texts. A lot and across multiple spaces. As citizens and as professionals, they may be engaging in the strategic acts of composing-for-appropriation and composing-for-remix that Kimmage and Ridolfo (2007) describe. And this isn't the sort of writing we're asking them to do. And we certainly aren't often enough asking them to think about rhetorical velocity, about how their texts might change shape in digital realms, and about how delivery shifts in networked spaces.

We have long known that students enter our classrooms with rich, established, accumulated, multimodal literacy practices (Brandt, 1998; New London Group, 1996; Cope & Kalantzis, 2000). This is nothing new—this was as true 50 years ago as it is today. What is new, however, are the spaces, surfaces, and interfaces in which and through which literacy practices are shaped and rhetoric happens. Jay David Bolter (1991) called our time—or at least the time 17 years ago, Jurassic in light of the rapidly evolving digital spaces in which we now compose—the "late age of print" (p. 150). We don't think it's time to say goodnight to print, but we do feel a need to recognize that "print," "text," "composing," and, importantly, "delivery" change shape in different realms, and that, as composition instructors, we must grapple with those realms and what transformations occur in/through/with writing in these spaces.

The texts Yancey notes we typically ask students to produce are defined in the most traditional, narrow, and academic sense: white paper, black ink, 12-point font, one-inch margins, an appropriately linear approach to topic and development, writing toward conclusions and claims, etc. These conditions were the product of certain approaches to writing, certain values, certain understandings of delivery. And these approaches to writing are expanding, and the values that shape what writing is and what writing does are shifting—at least in the spaces in which many of our students write and deliver their texts. We initially wrote this conclusion on Thursday, March 6, 2008, and that day's context was this:

- As of 2:16pm CST, 4,150 photos had been uploaded to Flickr in the previous 60 seconds. In the last 24 hours, some of the "hottest" tags include aolm (Adventures of Lego Man), ie8, lpruck (uploaded and tagged as part of a Lonely Planet photo challenge), and mix08. The all-time most-popular tags include family, party, japan, and wedding.

- Six months and two hours prior, at noon on Thursday, September 27, the very first of the MySpace / MTV presidential candidate interviews aired, marking the first time that viewers—dispersed across space,

--more--

time, and technologies — could immediately and automatically respond to a candidate's response to questions. Viewers submitted questions through MySpaceIM, mobile devices, and email while watching the event, and online reactions and feedback were gathered and aired during the event.

- Within the past 24 hours, the number of English-written news articles in Wikinews topped 11,500. More than 2,290,000 articles are included in the English-language area of Wikipedia, up 300,000 from six months prior.

- More than 150,000 new users are signing up daily on Facebook, founded in February 2004 and opened to public user accounts in September 2006; Tom has 226,983,254 friends on MySpace, up 2.4 million since about 5 months prior. Friendster, launched in 2002, is considered near-defunct.

- Members of librarything have catalogued more than twenty-four million books, up six million titles from 6 months prior.

- On LiveJournal, users/writers have posted more than 199,259 entries in the past 24 hours.

- Users/creators on worth1000 have contributed to more than 8000 galleries and 318,000+ original images.

We don't mean to imply that these bits and bytes speak for themselves, but we do 47 see these as compelling evidence of the ways in which writers and composers are remixing, rewriting, rescripting, and redelivering work in digital spaces. Each of these moments and the texts created within these moments and spaces point to the landscape of digital composing practices.

Yancey calls attention to the ways in which our classroom writing approaches 48 are out of sync with the ways students are writing in the world. She encouraged us to think about the ways in which we can better situate students to be citizens writing in and to the world — members of a "writing public" (p. 31). Importantly, she also notes that we should better attend to medium and address issues of delivery — and the multiple ways in which a piece of writing can be shared "in those different media, to different audiences" (p. 311).

We see ourselves challenged, then, at the end of this article but still at the begin- 49 nings of this field conversation, to provide teaching materials that help foster these emerging conversations in our first-year classes, undergraduate courses, and graduate seminars. This is important because we think that in the next

--more--

10 years the canon of delivery will be reconstructed with an emergent range of concepts, and the best examples of these will likely begin in classroom conversations, where it is the coming generations who will be the most immersed in this type of remix activity. We propose the following exercise as just one route toward discussing issues of rhetorical velocity in the classroom:

- **Step One:** Go to a government news release site such as www .defenselink.mil or a corporate public relations newswire such as www .prnewswire.com or www.i-newswire.com.

- **Step Two:** Select a recent press advisory or release from the list (from within the last seven days). A highly popular or an event-specific story may be a good place to start.

- **Step Three:** Select and search for phrases (in word groups of three, preferably including one proper name) on both the web and the Google news aggregate site (www.google.com/news). Use quotation marks to perform a more honed search. So, rather than searching for a string of terms, search for an exact phrase from the original release, for instance: "three U.S. servicemen, missing from World War II, have been identified and will be returned to their families for burial with full military honors." The quotation marks will direct the search engine to search for that particular phrase, rather than for web pages that happen to have individual words (e.g., families, burial, honors) within their content.

- **Step Four:** If you've located some hits, analyze the results and compare what you have found to the original press release. In what different types of documents has the press release content been used? For what purposes? For what audiences? Are there any authors listed on the original release? On the new documents you have found? What can we learn about the compositional use of the original release?

- **Step Five:** To launch discussion, ask students to ponder the degree to which is it strategically plausible to think that experienced writers in this genre anticipate or strategize the re-composition of their work. You might also ask students to think about contexts in their professional lives in which they will likely do this sort of recomposing, or in which they will likely be the original writers of documents written to be recomposed.

We have integrated versions of the activity above in first-year courses and 50 in undergraduate courses in professional writing. Drawing on the work of

--more--

Jim Ridolfo (2005), Doug Eyman (2005) has also developed undergraduate teaching materials explicitly around a concept of rhetorical velocity. In an assignment titled "Rhetorical Velocity: (Press Release)" for his introduction to professional writing course taught at Michigan State University (a course oriented toward first-year and sophomore students), Eyman facilitated conversations around strategizing and delivery by working through the lens of economics, circulation, and delivery. His assignment offers a range of classroom possibilities:

1. Collect a minimum of six press releases (we'll call this our "corpus" for the following analysis). Looking at the examples you found, identify the common elements of the press release as a genre. Make sure that you look at textual construction, visual representation, and the activities supported by the release (that is, what does a press release *do*? What is the activity or activities embedded in the genre of the document?). You should write this as a brief report, using appropriate headings and organization of your findings. Include the URLs for the press releases as an appendix.

2. Imagine that you are in charge of an event or activity that you would like covered in the press. Write a press release for this event or activity, using the generic features you identified in Part 1 (that is, engage in the same practices that you see as contributing to a successful press release).

3. Taking into account the cycle of (re)appropriation outlined in the definition of "rhetorical velocity" above, write a memo that explains the decisions you made when you drafted the press release—what elements did you include or exclude? How did you hope to facilitate appropriation by the media? (Eyman, 2005)

We see surfacing in the ideas of rhetorical velocity an emergent, conceptual 51 approach to rhetorical delivery, one that will surely yield many new heuristics and approaches to the fifth canon over the next decade. We are in agreement with Paul Prior and his colleagues (2007) that "the canon of delivery does not focus attention on the possible rhetorical configurations of distribution, mode, and other mediations." We think, however, that delivery is a highly useful container and category to think from as a conceptual space. But there is work to be done to make the fifth canon useful as a classroom heuristic to talk about practice, and we see promise in these sorts of assignments.

--more--

537

References

For more information, please see the following sources.

Aristotle. (2004). *Rhetoric*. North Chelmsford, MA: Courier Dover Publications.

Bolter, Jay David. (1991). *Writing space: The computer, hypertext, and the history of writing*. Mahwah, NJ: Lawrence Erlbaum Associates.

Brandt, Deborah. (1998). Sponsors of literacy. *College Composition and Communication, 49*(2), 165–185.

Cicero. (1939). *Brutus. Orator*. Cambridge, MA: Harvard University Press.

Cope, Bill, & Kalantzis, Mary. (Eds.). (2000). *Multiliteracies: Literacy learning and the design of social futures*. New York: Routledge.

Corbett, Edward P. (1990). *Classical rhetoric for the modern student*. New York: Oxford University Press.

DeVoss, Dànielle Nicole, & Porter, James. (2006). Why Napster matters to writing: Filesharing as a new ethic of digital delivery. *Computers and Composition, 23*(2), 178–210.

Duncan, Anne. (2006). *Performance and Identity in the Classical World*. New York: Cambridge University Press.

Eyman, Douglas. (2005). Modules. WRA 202: Introduction to Professional Writing. Retrieved January 9, 2008, from http://www.msu.edu/~eymandou/wra202/mods.html

Eyman, Douglas. (2007). *Digital rhetoric: Ecologies and economies of circulation*. Unpublished dissertation. East Lansing: Michigan State University.

Helsley, Sheri. (1993). A special afterword to graduate students in rhetoric. In John Frederick Reynolds (Ed.), *Rhetorical memory and delivery: Classical concepts for contemporary composition and communication* (pp. 157–160). Hillsdale, NJ: Lawrence Erlbaum.

Kimmage, Daniel, & Ridolfo, Kathleen. (2007, July). *The war of images and ideas: How Sunni insurgents in Iraq and their supporters worldwide are using the media*. Radio Free Europe/Radio Liberty. Retrieved July 20, 2007, from http://www.rferl.org/featuresarticle/2007/06/830debc3-e399-4fa3-981c-cc44badae1a8.html

Lessig, Lawrence. (1999). *Code and other laws of cyberspace*. New York: Basic Books.

Lessig, Lawrence. (2002). *The future of ideas: The fate of the commons in a connected world*. New York: Random House.

Lessig, Lawrence. (2004). *Free culture: How big media uses technology and the law to lock down culture and control creativity*. New York: The Penguin Press.

Lessig, Lawrence. (2005, March). *Remix culture*. Presentation at the Conference on College Composition and Communication, San Francisco, CA.

Lessig, Lawrence. (2005, April). *Who owns culture?* Presentation at the New York Public Library, New York, NY.

Lessig, Lawrence. (2006, August 4). The ethics of the free culture movement. Presentation at Wikimania. Retrieved July 20, 2007, from http://video.google.com/videoplay?docid=-1926631993376203020

Lessig, Lawrence. (2006, August 15). Free culture: What we need from you. Presentation at Linuxworld. Retrieved July 20, 2007, from http://www.linuxworld.com/events/keynotes/lwsf06-lessig.html

--more--

Manovich, Lev. (2002). Who is the author?: Sampling/remixing/open source. Retrieved December 30, 2005, from http://www.manovich.net/DOCS/models_of_authorship.doc

McLuhan, Marshall, & Fiore, Quentin. (1967). *The medium is the massage*. New York: Bantam Books.

Mendelson, Michael. (2002). *Many sides: A Protagorean approach to the theory, practice, and pedagogy of argument*. Dordrecht, Netherlands: Kluwer.

New London Group. (1996). A pedagogy of multiliteracies: Designing social futures. *Harvard Educational Review, 66*(1), 60–92.

Polano, Sergio, & Vetta, Pierpaolo. (1993). On Aldo Novarese. *Emigre, 26*, pp. 30–37.

Porter, James E., & DeVoss, Dànielle Nicole. (2006, April). Rethinking plagiarism in the digital age: Remixing as a means for economic development. Presentation at the WIDE Research Center Writing: Digital Knowledge Conference, East Lansing, MI.

Prior, Paul, et al. (2007). Re-situating and re-mediating the canons: A cultural-historical remapping of rhetorical activity. *Kairos: A Journal of Rhetoric, Technology, and Pedagogy, 11*(3). Retrieved January 2, 2008, from http://kairos.technorhetoric.net/11.3/index.html

Rice, Jeff. (2003). Writing about cool: Teaching hypertext as juxtaposition. *Computers and Composition, 20*(3), 221–236.

Rice, Jeff. (2006). The making of ka-knowledge: Digital aurality. *Computers and Composition, 23*(3), 266–279.

Ridolfo, Jim. (2005). *Rhetoric, economy and the technologies of activist delivery*. Unpublished Master's Thesis. East Lansing: Michigan State University.

Skinner-Linnenberg, Virginia. (1997). *Dramatizing writing: Reincorporating delivery in the classroom*. Mahwah, NJ: Lawrence Erlbaum.

Trimbur, John. (2000). Composition and the circulation of writing. *College Composition and Communication, 52*(2), 188–219.

Welch, Kathleen E. (1999). *Electric rhetoric: Classical rhetoric, oralism, and a new literacy*. Cambridge: MIT Press.

Welch, Nancy. (2005). Living room: Teaching public writing in a post-publicity era. *College Composition and Communication, 56*(3), 470–492.

Vaidhyanathan, Siva. (2003). *Copyrights and copywrongs: The rise of intellectual property and how it threatens creativity*. New York: New York University Press.

Vaidhyanathan, Siva. (2004). The state of copyright activism. *First Monday, 9*(4). Retrieved January 10, 2006, from http://www.firstmonday.dk/issues/issue9_4/siva/index.html

Yancey, Kathleen Blake. (2004). Made not only in words: Composition in a new key. *College Composition and Communication, 56*(2), 297–328.

###

Questions for Discussion and Journaling

1. If you've read Grant-Davie's article on rhetorical situation (p. 484), how does Ridolfo and DeVoss's definition of rhetorical velocity as concerned with "distance, travel, speed, and time" (para. 4) differ from or add to what Grant-Davie emphasizes about rhetorical situation?

2. Why do Ridolfo and DeVoss think it's important to consider the *speed* (rate of occurrence) aspect of rhetorical velocity? How is speed or rate a factor in "instances of strategic appropriation by a third party" (para. 4)?

3. Do you agree with Ridolfo and DeVoss's characterization of third-party appropriation of writing as "a strategic type of 'plagiarism'" (para. 6)? Why do you think they use that term for the kind of appropriation they're talking about?

4. How is this article using the term "romantic" (for example, in its first two sections)? What are the differences between what the term refers to and how we commonly use the term "romantic" today as having to do with love?

5. In the "Remix" section, Ridolfo and DeVoss argue that "freedom from romantic authorship is crucial to rhetorical velocity" (para. 11). Why?

6. Is the "amplification" effect that Ridolfo and DeVoss discuss in the article an inevitable effect or result of rhetorical velocity? Or is it simply something that composing a text with rhetorical velocity in mind *makes possible*?

Applying and Exploring Ideas

1. Ridolfo and DeVoss quote Vaidhyanathan as saying that writers are more like "producers" than like romantic "authors" (para. 11). Research and extend this claim by writing a short paper that explains what a *producer* is in entertainment or art enterprises, what they do, and why it makes sense (if it does) to understand a modern writer more as a producer than a traditional author.

2. Look up "Transformation (law)" on Wikipedia and build your understanding of how the term "transformative" applies to written or artistic works. Then find an example of a work that you would consider a transformative appropriation of other, earlier works. Write a two- to three-page analysis of *how* the new work transforms the earlier works. When you show your analysis to your classmates, how much do they agree on what counts as "transformation" of the old works?

3. In three sections of this article ("Delivery: Rhetoric History and Theory," "Delivery: Contemporary Composition Studies," and "Rhetorical Velocity and the Amplification Effect"), Ridolfo and DeVoss trace roots of their idea of *rhetorical velocity* that appear in previous rhetorical theory and scholarship. Would you call *their own* writing an example of transformative reuse of this previous scholarship? Why or why not? Prepare two sets of debate notes: one arguing that it *is* an instance of rhetorical velocity through transformative appropriation, and one arguing that their use of scholarship is something else. Use your notes to conduct this debate in class with other students.

4. Consider the last formal writing assignment you turned in for one of your college classes. How would the piece be different if you had considered rhetorical velocity when you wrote it? For example, what would you have done with the piece to make it more easily shareable or reusable by other writers later on? Would any strategies you used get you in trouble with traditional-thinking teachers?

- -

META MOMENT How would your composing process change if you started thinking about rhetorical velocity in all your writing projects?

- -

Intertextuality and the Discourse Community

JAMES E. PORTER

Framing the Reading

Two of the deepest conceptions of writing that our culture holds are (1) that writing must be *original* and (2) that if a writer "borrows" ideas from other writing without acknowledging that borrowing, the writer is *plagiarizing*. In the following study, James Porter argues that these common ideas about **authorship, originality,** and **plagiarism** don't account for how texts actually work and how writers actually write. Porter calls into question how original writers can actually be in constructing texts and, following from that question, also wonders how we should define plagiarism if true originality is so difficult to find.

The principle Porter explores in asking these questions is **intertextuality** — that is, the idea that *all* texts contain "traces" of other texts and that there can be no text that does not draw on *some* ideas from some other texts. You may rightly be skeptical of such a broad claim, so follow along carefully as Porter explains why he thinks this is true. You may be particularly interested in the section in which Porter demonstrates his argument by looking at how the Declaration of Independence was written, as he claims, collaboratively, by a number of different authors.

If you read Ridolfo and DeVoss's piece on rhetorical velocity earlier in this chapter (p. 512), you have already been thinking about intertextuality from another angle. While those two authors consider how one aspect of twenty-first-century writing should be writers *anticipating* how their own texts will become intertextual with later texts, Porter's work in this piece helps us understand how even writers who aren't thinking about intertextuality, or using it strategically, are always already being intertextual.

Porter, James E. "Intertextuality and the Discourse Community." *Rhetoric Review*, vol. 5, no. 1, Autumn 1986, pp. 34–47.

The implications of Porter's study are significant for how you understand writing and how you understand yourself as a writer. Most of us have been taught that writers are *autonomous* — that is, that they're free to do whatever they want with their texts, and also that they're solely responsible for what's in those texts. Porter's research on actual writing and writers challenges this construct. If Porter is correct, then we need a *different* construct of the *author*, one that acknowledges the extent to which communities shape what a writer chooses to say; the extent to which writers say things that have already been said (even when they believe they're being original); and the extent to which texts are constructed by many different people along the way, as readers feed ideas back to the writer. In this way, Porter returns us to the threshold concept that *there are always constraints* in rhetorical situations and composing processes that make writing more complicated than a single writer writing for one particular situation.

Getting Ready to Read

Before you read, do at least one of the following activities:

- Write a paragraph on what, in your mind, is the difference between an *author* and a *writer*. When would you choose the first term to describe the person/people behind a text, and when would you choose the second?

- Make a list of all the ways you get "help," of any kind, in your writing. Where do you get ideas, advice, feedback, and assistance?

- Find one or two friends or family members who write a great deal, either for a living, as a major part of their jobs, or as a hobby. Interview them about who or what they see contributing to their writing. To what extent do they see themselves doing their writing "on their own"?

As you read, consider the following questions:

- Watch for how Porter poses questions about writers' *autonomy* and *originality*. Does he finally decide that autonomy and originality are impossible?

- Do you think Porter is *criticizing* the Declaration of Independence? Thomas Jefferson? Explain your answer.

- If you haven't seen the Pepsi commercial that Porter discusses, try to find a version of it to watch online. Does Porter's reading of the commercial match yours, or do you understand it differently?

AT THE CONCLUSION OF Eco's *The Name of the Rose*, the monk Adso of 1
Melk returns to the burned abbey, where he finds in the ruins scraps of parch-
ment, the only remnants from one of the great libraries in all Christendom. He
spends a day collecting the charred fragments, hoping to discover some meaning
in the scattered pieces of books. He assembles his own "lesser library . . . of fragments, quotations, unfinished sentences, amputated stumps of books" (500).
To Adso, these random shards are "an immense acrostic that says and repeats
nothing" (501). Yet they are significant to him as an attempt to order experience.

We might well derive our own order from this scene. We might see Adso as 2
representing the writer, and his desperate activity at the burned abbey as a model
for the writing process. The writer in this image is a collector of fragments, an
archaeologist creating an order, building a framework, from remnants of the
past. Insofar as the collected fragments help Adso recall other, lost texts, his
experience affirms a principle he learned from
his master, William of Baskerville: "Not infrequently books speak of books" (286). Not
infrequently, and perhaps ever and always,
texts refer to other texts and in fact rely on
them for their meaning. All texts are interdependent: We understand a text only insofar as
we understand its precursors.

> *All texts are interdependent: We understand a text only insofar as we understand its precursors.*

This is the principle we know as intertextuality, the principle that all writing 3
and speech—indeed, all signs—arise from a single network: what Vygotsky
called "the web of meaning"; what poststructuralists label Text or Writing
(Barthes, *écriture*)*;* and what a more distant age perhaps knew as *logos*. Examining
texts "intertextually" means looking for "traces," the bits and pieces of Text which
writers or speakers borrow and sew together to create new discourse.[1] The most
mundane manifestation of intertextuality is explicit citation, but intertextuality
animates all discourse and goes beyond mere citation. For the intertextual critics, Intertext is Text—a great seamless textual fabric. And, as they like to intone
solemnly, no text escapes intertext.

Intertextuality provides rhetoric with an important perspective, one currently 4
neglected, I believe. The prevailing composition pedagogies by and large cultivate the romantic image of writer as free, uninhibited spirit, as independent,
creative genius. By identifying and stressing the intertextual nature of discourse,
however, we shift our attention away from the writer as individual and focus
more on the sources and social contexts from which the writer's discourse arises.
According to this view, authorial intention is less significant than social context;
the writer is simply a part of a discourse tradition, a member of a team, and a
participant in a community of discourse that creates its own collective meaning.
Thus the intertext *constrains* writing.

My aim here is to demonstrate the significance of this theory to rhetoric, by 5 explaining intertextuality, its connection to the notion of "discourse community," and its pedagogical implications for composition.

THE PRESENCE OF INTERTEXT

Intertextuality has been associated with both structuralism and poststructural- 6 ism, with theorists like Roland Barthes, Julia Kristeva, Jacques Derrida, Hayden White, Harold Bloom, Michel Foucault, and Michael Riffaterre. (Of course, the theory is most often applied in literary analysis.) The central assumption of these critics has been described by Vincent Leitch: "The text is not an autonomous or unified object, but a set of relations with other texts. Its system of language, its grammar, its lexicon, drag along numerous bits and pieces—traces—of history so that the text resembles a Cultural Salvation Army Outlet with unaccountable collections of incompatible ideas, beliefs, and sources" (59). It is these "unaccountable collections" that intertextual critics focus on, not the text as autonomous entity. In fact, these critics have redefined the notion of "text": Text *is* intertext, or simply Text. The traditional notion of the text as the single work of a given author, and even the very notions of author and reader, are regarded as simply convenient fictions for domesticating discourse. The old borders that we used to rope off discourse, proclaim these critics, are no longer useful.

We can distinguish between two types of intertextuality: iterability and pre- 7 supposition. Iterability refers to the "repeatability" of certain textual fragments, to citation in its broadest sense to include not only explicit allusions, references, and quotations within a discourse, but also unannounced sources and influences, clichés, phrases in the air, and traditions. That is to say, every discourse is composed of "traces," pieces of other texts that help constitute its meaning. (I will discuss this aspect of intertextuality in my analysis of the Declaration of Independence.) Presupposition refers to assumptions a text makes about its referent, its readers, and its context—to portions of the text which are read, but which are not explicitly "there." For example, as Jonathan Culler discusses, the phrase "John married Fred's sister" is an assertion that logically presupposes that John exists, that Fred exists, and that Fred has a sister. "Open the door" contains a practical presupposition, assuming the presence of a decoder who is capable of being addressed and who is better able to open the door than the encoder. "Once upon a time" is a trace rich in rhetorical presupposition, signaling to even the youngest reader the opening of a fictional narrative. Texts not only refer to but in fact *contain* other texts.[2]

An examination of three sample texts will illustrate the various facets of inter- 8 textuality. The first, the Declaration of Independence, is popularly viewed as the work of Thomas Jefferson. Yet if we examine the text closely in its rhetorical milieu, we see that Jefferson was author only in the very loosest of senses.

A number of historians and at least two composition researchers (Kinneavy, *Theory* 393–49; Maimon, *Readings* 6–32) have analyzed the Declaration, with interesting results. Their work suggests that Jefferson was by no means an original framer or a creative genius, as some like to suppose. Jefferson was a skilled writer, to be sure, but chiefly because he was an effective borrower of traces.

To produce his original draft of the Declaration, Jefferson seems to have 9 borrowed, either consciously or unconsciously, from his culture's Text. Much has been made of Jefferson's reliance on Locke's social contract theory (Becker). Locke's theory influenced colonial political philosophy, emerging in various pamphlets and newspaper articles of the times, and served as the foundation for the opening section of the Declaration. The Declaration contains many traces that can be found in other, earlier documents. There are traces from a First Continental Congress resolution, a Massachusetts Council declaration, George Mason's "Declaration of Rights for Virginia," a political pamphlet of James Otis, and a variety of other sources, including a colonial play. The overall form of the Declaration (theoretical argument followed by list of grievances) strongly resembles, ironically, the English Bill of Rights of 1689, in which Parliament lists the abuses of James II and declares new powers for itself. Several of the abuses in the Declaration seem to have been taken, more or less verbatim, from a *Pennsylvania Evening Post* article. And the most memorable phrases in the Declaration seem to be least Jefferson's: "That all men are created equal" is a sentiment from Euripides which Jefferson copied in his literary commonplace book as a boy; "Life, Liberty, and the pursuit of Happiness" was a cliché of the times, appearing in numerous political documents (Dumbauld).

Though Jefferson's draft of the Declaration can hardly be considered his in 10 any exclusive sense of authorship, the document underwent still more expropriation at the hands of Congress, who made eighty-six changes (Kinneavy, *Theory* 438). They cut the draft from 211 lines to 147. They did considerable editing to temper what they saw as Jefferson's emotional style: For example, Jefferson's phrase "sacred & undeniable" was changed to the more restrained "self-evident." Congress excised controversial passages, such as Jefferson's condemnation of slavery. Thus, we should find it instructive to note, Jefferson's few attempts at original expression were those least acceptable to Congress.

If Jefferson submitted the Declaration for a college writing class as his own 11 writing, he might well be charged with plagiarism.[3] The idea of Jefferson as author is but convenient shorthand. Actually, the Declaration arose out of a cultural and rhetorical milieu, was composed of traces—and was, in effect, team written. Jefferson deserves credit for bringing disparate traces together, for helping to mold and articulate the milieu, for creating the all-important draft. Jefferson's skill as a writer was his ability to borrow traces effectively and to find appropriate contexts for them. As Michael Halliday says, "[C]reativeness does not consist in producing new sentences. The newness of a sentence is a quite unimportant—and unascertainable—property and 'creativity' in language lies in the speaker's ability to create new meanings: to realize the potentiality of language for the indefinite extension of its resources to new contexts of situation. . . . Our most 'creative' acts may be precisely among those that are realized through highly repetitive forms of behaviour" (*Explorations* 42). The creative writer is the creative borrower, in other words.

Intertextuality can be seen working similarly in contemporary forums. Recall this scene from a recent Pepsi commercial: A young boy in jeans jacket, accompanied by dog, stands in some desolate plains crossroads next to a gas station, next to which is a soft drink machine. An alien spacecraft, resembling the one in Spielberg's *Close Encounters of the Third Kind*, appears overhead. To the boy's joyful amazement, the spaceship hovers over the vending machine and begins sucking Pepsi cans into the ship. It takes *only* Pepsis, then eventually takes the entire machine. The ad closes with a graphic: "Pepsi. The Choice of a New Generation." 12

Clearly, the commercial presupposes familiarity with Spielberg's movie or, at least, with his pacific vision of alien spacecraft. We see several American clichés, well-worn signs from the Depression era: the desolate plains, the general store, the pop machine, the country boy with dog. These distinctively American traces are juxtaposed against images from science fiction and the sixties catchphrase "new generation" in the coda. In this array of signs, we have tradition and counter-tradition harmonized. Pepsi squeezes itself in the middle, and thus becomes the great American conciliator. The ad's use of irony may serve to distract viewers momentarily from noticing how Pepsi achieves its purpose by assigning itself an exalted role through use of the intertext. 13

We find an interesting example of practical presupposition in John Kifner's *New York Times* headline article reporting on the Kent State incident of 1970: 14

> Four students at Kent State University, two of them women, were shot to death this afternoon by a volley of National Guard gunfire. At least 8 other students were wounded.
>
> The burst of gunfire came about 20 minutes after the guardsmen broke up a noon rally on the Commons, a grassy campus gathering spot, by lobbing tear gas at a crowd of about 1,000 young people.

From one perspective, the phrase "two of them women" is a simple statement of fact; however, it presupposes a certain attitude—that the event, horrible enough as it was, is more significant because two of the persons killed were women. It might be going too far to say that the phrase presupposes a sexist attitude ("women aren't supposed to be killed in battles"), but can we imagine the phrase "two of them men" in this context? Though equally factual, this wording would have been considered odd in 1970 (and probably today as well) because it presupposes a cultural mindset alien from the one dominant at the time. "Two 15

547

of them women" is shocking (and hence it was reported) because it upsets the sense of order of the readers, in this case the American public.

Additionally (and more than a little ironically), the text contains a number of 16 traces which have the effect of blunting the shock of the event. Notice that the students were not shot by National Guardsmen, but were shot "by a volley of . . . gunfire"; the tear gas was "lobbed"; and the event occurred at a "grassy campus gathering spot." "Volley" and "lobbed" are military terms, but with connections to sport as well; "grassy campus gathering spot" suggests a picnic; "burst" can recall the glorious sight of bombs "bursting" in "The Star-Spangled Banner." This pastiche of signs casts the text into a certain context, making it distinctively American. We might say that the turbulent milieu of the sixties provided a distinctive array of signs from which John Kifner borrowed to produce his article.

Each of the three texts examined contains phrases or images familiar to its 17 audience or presupposes certain audience attitudes. Thus the intertext exerts its influence partly in the form of audience expectation. We might then say that the audience of each of these texts is as responsible for its production as the writer. That, in essence, readers, not writers, create discourse.

THE POWER OF DISCOURSE COMMUNITY

And, indeed, this is what some poststructuralist critics suggest, those who prefer 18 a broader conception of intertext or who look beyond the intertext to the social framework regulating textual production: to what Michel Foucault calls "the discursive formation," what Stanley Fish calls "the interpretive community," and what Patricia Bizzell calls "the discourse community."

A "discourse community" is a group of individuals bound by a common 19 interest who communicate through approved channels and whose discourse is regulated. An individual may belong to several professional, public, or personal discourse communities. Examples would include the community of engineers whose research area is fluid mechanics; alumni of the University of Michigan; Magnavox employees; the members of the Porter family; and members of the Indiana Teachers of Writing. The approved channels we can call "forums." Each forum has a distinct history and rules governing appropriateness to which members are obliged to adhere. These rules may be more or less apparent, more or less institutionalized, more or less specific to each community. Examples of forums include professional publications like *Rhetoric Review, English Journal,* and *Creative Computing;* public media like *Newsweek* and *Runner's World;* professional conferences (the annual meeting of fluid power engineers, the 4C's); company board meetings; family dinner tables; and the monthly meeting of the Indiana chapter of the Izaak Walton League.

A discourse community shares assumptions about what objects are appro- 20 priate for examination and discussion, what operating functions are performed on those objects, what constitutes "evidence" and "validity," and what formal conventions are followed. A discourse community may have a well-established *ethos*; or it may have competing factions and indefinite boundaries. It may be in a "pre-paradigm" state (Kuhn), that is, having an ill-defined regulating system and no clear leadership. Some discourse communities are firmly established, such as the scientific community, the medical profession, and the justice system, to cite a few from Foucault's list. In these discourse communities, as Leitch says, "a speaker must be 'qualified' to talk; he has to belong to a community of scholarship; and he is required to possess a prescribed body of knowledge (doctrine). . . . [This system] operates to constrain discourse; it establishes limits and regularities. . . . who may speak, what may be spoken, and how it is to be said; in addition [rules] prescribe what is true and false, what is reasonable and what foolish, and what is meant and what not. Finally, they work to deny the material existence of discourse itself" (145).

A text is "acceptable" within a forum only insofar as it reflects the community 21 episteme (to use Foucault's term). On a simple level, this means that for a manuscript to be accepted for publication in the *Journal of Applied Psychology*, it must follow certain formatting conventions: It must have the expected social science sections (i.e., review of literature, methods, results, discussion), and it must use the journal's version of APA documentation. However, these are only superficial features of the forum. On a more essential level, the manuscript must reveal certain characteristics, have an *ethos* (in the broadest possible sense) conforming to the standards of the discourse community: It must demonstrate (or at least claim) that it contributes knowledge to the field, it must demonstrate familiarity with the work of previous researchers in the field, it must use a scientific method in analyzing its results (showing acceptance of the truth-value of statistical demonstration), it must meet standards for test design and analysis of results, it must adhere to standards determining degree of accuracy. The expectations, conventions, and attitudes of this discourse community — the readers, writers, and publishers of *Journal of Applied Psychology* — will influence aspiring psychology researchers, shaping not only how they write but also their character within that discourse community.

The poststructuralist view challenges the classical assumption that writing is 22 a simple linear, one-way movement: The writer creates a text which produces some change in an audience. A poststructuralist rhetoric examines how audience (in the form of community expectations and standards) influences textual production and, in so doing, guides the development of the writer.

This view is of course open to criticism for its apparent determinism, for 23 devaluing the contribution of individual writers and making them appear merely tools of the discourse community (charges which Foucault answers in "Discourse on Language"). If these regulating systems are so constraining, how can an individual emerge? What happens to the idea of the lone inspired writer and the sacred autonomous text?

Both notions take a pretty hard knock. Genuine originality is difficult within 24 the confines of a well-regulated system. Genius is possible, but it may be constrained. Foucault cites the example of Gregor Mendel, whose work in the nineteenth century was excluded from the prevailing community of biologists because he "spoke of objects, employed methods and placed himself within a theoretical perspective totally alien to the biology of his time. . . . Mendel spoke the truth, but he was not *dans le vrai* (within the true)" (224). Frank Lentricchia cites a similar example from the literary community: Robert Frost "achieved magazine publication only five times between 1895 and 1912, a period during which he wrote a number of poems later acclaimed . . . [because] in order to write within the dominant sense of the poetic in the United States in the last decade of the nineteenth century and the first decade of the twentieth, one had to employ a diction, syntax, and prosody heavily favoring Shelley and Tennyson. One also had to assume a certain stance, a certain world-weary idealism which took care not to refer too concretely to the world of which one was weary" (197, 199).

Both examples point to the exclusionary power of discourse communities and 25 raise serious questions about the freedom of the writer: chiefly, does the writer have any? Is any writer doomed to plagiarism? Can any text be said to be new? Are creativity and genius actually possible? Was Jefferson a creative genius or a blatant plagiarist?

Certainly we want to avoid both extremes. Even if the writer is locked into a 26 cultural matrix and is constrained by the intertext of the discourse community, the writer has freedom within the immediate rhetorical context.[4] Furthermore, successful writing helps to redefine the matrix—and in that way becomes creative. (Jefferson's Declaration contributed to defining the notion of America for its discourse community.) Every new text has the potential to alter the text in some way; in fact, every text admitted into a discourse community changes the constitution of the community—and discourse communities can revise their discursive practices, as the Mendel and Frost examples suggest.

Writing is an attempt to exercise the will, to identify the self within the con- 27 straints of some discourse community. We are constrained insofar as we must inevitably borrow the traces, codes, and signs which we inherit and which our discourse community imposes. We are free insofar as we do what we can to encounter and learn new codes, to intertwine codes in new ways, and to expand our semiotic potential—with our goal being to effect change and establish our identities within the discourse communities we choose to enter.

THE PEDAGOGY OF INTERTEXTUALITY

Intertextuality is not new. It may remind some of Eliot's notion of tradition, 28 though the parameters are certainly broader. It is an important concept, though. It counters what I see as one prevailing composition pedagogy, one favoring a romantic image of the writer, offering as role models the creative essayists, the Sunday Supplement freelancers, the Joan Didions, E. B. Whites, Calvin Trillins, and Russell Bakers. This dashing image appeals to our need for intellectual heroes; but underlying it may be an anti-rhetorical view: that writers are born, not made; that writing is individual, isolated, and internal; not social but eccentric.

This view is firmly set in the intertext of our discipline. Our anthologies glorify the individual essayists, whose work is valued for its timelessness and creativity. Freshman rhetorics announce as the writer's proper goals personal insight, originality, and personal voice, or tell students that motivations for writing come from "within." Generally, this pedagogy assumes that such a thing as the writer actually exists — an autonomous writer exercising a free, creative will through the writing act — and that the writing process proceeds linearly from writer to text to reader. This partial picture of the process can all too readily become *the* picture, and our students can all too readily learn to overlook vital facets of discourse production. 29

When we romanticize composition by overemphasizing the autonomy of the writer, important questions are overlooked, the same questions an intertextual view of writing would provoke: To what extent is the writer's product itself a part of a larger community writing process? How does the discourse community influence writers and readers within it? These are essential questions, but are perhaps outside the prevailing episteme of composition pedagogy, which presupposes the autonomous status of the writer as independent *cogito*. Talking about writing in terms of "social forces influencing the writer" raises the specter of determinism, and so is anathema. 30

David Bartholomae summarizes this issue very nicely: "The struggle of the student writer is not the struggle to bring out that which is within; it is the struggle to carry out those ritual activities that grant our entrance into a closed society" (300). When we teach writing only as the act of "bringing out what is within," we risk undermining our own efforts. Intertextuality reminds us that "carrying out ritual activities" is also part of the writing process. Barthes reminds us that "the 'I' which approaches the text is already itself a plurality of other texts, of codes which are infinite" (10). 31

Intertextuality suggests that our goal should be to help students learn to write for the discourse communities they choose to join. Students need help developing out of what Joseph Williams calls their "pre-socialized cognitive states." According to Williams, pre-socialized writers are not sufficiently immersed in their discourse community to produce competent discourse: They do not know what can be presupposed, are not conscious of the distinctive intertextuality of the community, may be only superficially acquainted with explicit conventions. (Williams cites the example of the freshman whose paper for the English teacher begins "Shakespeare is a famous Elizabethan dramatist.") Our immediate goal is 32

551

to produce "socialized writers," who are full-fledged members of their discourse community, producing competent, useful discourse within that community. Our long-range goal might be "post-socialized writers," those who have achieved such a degree of confidence, authority, power, or achievement in the discourse community so as to become part of the regulating body. They are able to vary conventions and question assumptions—i.e., effect change in communities—without fear of exclusion.

Intertextuality has the potential to affect all facets of our composition ped- 33 agogy. Certainly it supports writing across the curriculum as a mechanism for introducing students to the regulating systems of discourse communities. It raises questions about heuristics: Do different discourse communities apply different heuristics? It asserts the value of critical reading in the composition class-room. It requires that we rethink our ideas about plagiarism: Certainly *imitatio* is an important stage in the linguistic development of the writer.

The most significant application might be in the area of audience analysis. 34 Current pedagogies assume that when writers analyze audiences they should focus on the expected flesh-and-blood readers. Intertextuality suggests that the proper focus of audience analysis is not the audience as receivers per se, but the intertext of the discourse community. Instead of collecting demographic data about age, educational level, and social status, the writer might instead ask questions about the intertext: What are the conventional presuppositions of this community? In what forums do they assemble? What are the methodological assumptions? What is considered "evidence," "valid argument," and "proof"? A sample heuristic for such an analysis—what I term "forum analysis"—is included as an appendix.

A critical reading of the discourse of a community may be the best way to 35 understand it. (We see a version of this message in the advice to examine a jour-nal before submitting articles for publication.) Traditionally, anthologies have provided students with reading material. However, the typical anthologies have two serious problems: (1) limited range—generally they overemphasize literary or expressive discourse; (2) unclear context—they frequently remove readings from their original contexts, thus disguising their intertextual nature. Several recently published readers have attempted to provide a broader selection of read-ings in various forums, and actually discuss intertextuality. Maimon's *Readings in the Arts and Sciences*, Kinneavy's *Writing in the Liberal Arts Tradition*, and Bazerman's *The Informed Writer* are especially noteworthy.

Writing assignments should be explicitly intertextual. If we regard each writ- 36 ten product as a stage in a larger process—the dialectic process within a dis-course community—then the individual writer's work is part of a web, part of a community search for truth and meaning. Writing assignments might take the form of dialogue with other writers: Writing letters in response to articles is one kind of dialectic (e.g., letters responding to *Atlantic Monthly* or *Science* articles). Research assignments might be more community oriented rather than topic oriented; students might be asked to become involved in communities of researchers (e.g., the sociologists examining changing religious attitudes in American college students). The assignments in Maimon's *Writing in the Arts and Sciences* are excellent in this regard.

Intertextual theory suggests that the key criteria for evaluating writing should 37 be "acceptability" within some discourse community. "Acceptability" includes, but goes well beyond, adherence to formal conventions. It includes choosing the "right" topic, applying the appropriate critical methodology, adhering to standards for evidence and validity, and in general adopting the community's discourse values—and of course borrowing the appropriate traces. Success is measured by the writer's ability to know what can be presupposed and to borrow that community's traces effectively to create a text that contributes to the maintenance or, possibly, the definition of the community. The writer is constrained by the community, and by its intertextual preferences and prejudices, but the effective writer works to assert the will against those community constraints to effect change.

The Pepsi commercial and the Kent State news article show effective uses of 38 the intertext. In the Kent State piece, John Kifner mixes picnic imagery ("grassy campus gathering spot," "young people") with violent imagery ("burst of gunfire") to dramatize the event. The Pepsi ad writers combine two unlikely sets of traces, linking folksy depression-era American imagery with sci-fi imagery "stolen" from Spielberg. For this creative intertwining of traces, both discourses can probably be measured successful in their respective forums.

CODA

Clearly much of what intertextuality supports is already institutionalized (e.g., 39 writing-across-the-curriculum programs). And yet, in freshman comp texts and anthologies especially, there is this tendency to see writing as individual, as isolated, as heroic. Even after demonstrating quite convincingly that the Declaration was written by a team freely borrowing from a cultural intertext, Elaine Maimon insists, against all the evidence she herself has collected, that "Despite the additions, deletions, and changes in wording that it went through, the Declaration is still Jefferson's writing" (*Readings* 26). Her saying this presupposes that the reader has just concluded the opposite.

When we give our students romantic role models like E. B. White, Joan 40 Didion, and Lewis Thomas, we create unrealistic expectations. This type of writer has often achieved post-socialized status within some discourse community (Thomas in the scientific community, for instance). Can we realistically expect our students to achieve this state without first becoming socialized, without learning first what it means to write within a social context? Their role models ought not be only romantic heroes but also community writers like Jefferson, the anonymous writers of the Pepsi commercial—the Adsos of the world, not just the Aristotles. They need to see writers whose products are more evidently part of a larger process and whose work more clearly produces meaning in social contexts.

Notes

1. The dangers of defining intertextuality too simplistically are discussed by Owen Miller in "Intertextual Identity," *Identity of the Literary Text*, ed. Mario J. Valdés and Owen Miller (Toronto: U of Toronto P, 1985), 19–40. Miller points out that intertextuality "addresses itself to a plurality of concepts" (19).

2. For fuller discussion see Jonathan Culler, *The Pursuit of Signs* (Ithaca: Cornell UP, 1981), 100–16. Michael Halliday elaborates on the theory of presupposition somewhat, too, differentiating between exophoric and endophoric presupposition. The meaning of any text at least partly relies on exophoric references, i.e., external presuppositions. Endophoric references in the form of cohesive devices and connections within a text also affect meaning, but cohesion in a text depends ultimately on the audience making exophoric connections to prior texts, connections that may not be cued by explicit cohesive devices. See M. A. K. Halliday and Ruqaiya Hasan, *Cohesion in English* (London: Longman, 1976).

3. Miller cautions us about intertextuality and *post hoc ergo propter hoc* reasoning. All we can safely note is that phrases in the Declaration also appear in other, earlier documents. Whether or not the borrowing was intentional on Jefferson's part or whether the prior documents "caused" the Declaration (in any sense of the word) is not ascertainable.

4. Robert Scholes puts it this way: "If you play chess, you can only do certain things with the pieces, otherwise you are not playing chess. But those constraints do not in themselves tell you what moves to make." See *Textual Power* (New Haven: Yale UP. 1985), 153.

Works Cited

Barthes, Roland. *S/Z*. Trans. Richard Miller. New York: Hill and Wang, 1974.

Bartholomae, David. "Writing Assignments: Where Writing Begins." *fforum*. Ed. Patricia L. Stock. Upper Montclair, NJ: Boynton/Cook, 1983.

Bazerman, Charles. *The Informed Writer*. 2nd ed. Boston: Houghton Mifflin, 1985.

Becker, Carl. *The Declaration of Independence*. 2nd ed. New York: Random, Vintage, 1942.

Bizzell, Patricia. "Cognition, Convention, and Certainty: What We Need to Know about Writing." *PRE/TEXT* 3 (1982): 213–43.

Culler, Jonathan. *The Pursuit of Signs*. Ithaca: Cornell UP, 1981.

Dumbauld, Edward. *The Declaration of Independence*. 2nd ed. Norman: U of Oklahoma P, 1968.

Eco, Umberto. *The Name of the Rose*. Trans. William Weaver. San Diego: Harcourt Brace Jovanovich, 1983.

Fish, Stanley. *Is There a Text in This Class?* Cambridge: Harvard UP, 1980.

Foucault, Michel. *The Archaeology of Knowledge and the Discourse on Language*. Trans. A. M. Sheridan Smith. New York: Harper & Row, 1972.

Halliday, M. A. K. *Explorations in the Functions of Language.* New York: Elsevier, 1973.

Halliday, M. A. K., and Ruqaiya Hasan. *Cohesion in English.* London: Longman, 1976.

Kifner, John. "4 Kent State Students Killed by Troops." *New York Times* 5 May 1970: 1.

Kinneavy, James L. *A Theory of Discourse.* Englewood Cliffs: Prentice-Hall, 1971.

———, et al. *Writing in the Liberal Arts Tradition.* New York: Harper & Row, 1985.

Kuhn, Thomas S. *The Structure of Scientific Revolutions.* 2nd ed. Chicago: U of Chicago P, 1970.

Leitch, Vincent B. *Deconstructive Criticism.* New York: Cornell UP, 1983.

Lentricchia, Frank. *After the New Criticism.* Chicago: U of Chicago P, 1980.

Maimon, Elaine P., et al. *Readings in the Arts and Sciences.* Boston: Little, Brown, 1984.

———, *Writing in the Arts and Sciences.* Cambridge: Winthrop, 1981.

Miller, Owen. "Intertextual Identity." *Identity of the Literary Text.* Ed. Mario J. Valdés and Owen Miller. Toronto: U of Toronto P, 1985, 19–40.

Scholes, Robert. *Textual Power.* New Haven: Yale UP, 1985.

Williams, Joseph. "Cognitive Development, Critical Thinking, and the Teaching of Writing." Conference on Writing, Meaning, and Higher Order Reasoning, University of Chicago, 15 May 1984.

Appendix

Forum Analysis

Background

— Identify the forum by name and organizational affiliation.

— Is there an expressed editorial policy, philosophy, or expression of belief? What purpose does the forum serve? Why does it exist?

— What is the disciplinary orientation?

— How large is the forum? Who are its members? Its leaders? Its readership?

— In what manner does the forum assemble (e.g., newsletter, journal, conference, weekly meeting)? How frequently?

— What is the origin of the forum? Why did it come into existence? What is its history? Its political background? Its traditions?

— What reputation does the forum have among its own members? How is it regarded by others?

Discourse Conventions

Who Speaks/Writes?

— Who is granted status as speaker/writer? Who decides who speaks/writes in the forum? By what criteria are speakers/writers selected?

—What kind of people speak/write in this forum? Credentials? Disciplinary orientation? Academic or professional background?

—Who are the important figures in this forum? Whose work or experience is most frequently cited?

—What are the important sources cited in the forum? What are the key works, events, experiences that it is assumed members of the forum know?

To Whom Do They Speak/Write?

—Who is addressed in the forum? What are the characteristics of the assumed audience?

—What are the audience's needs assumed to be? To what use(s) is the audience expected to put the information?

—What is the audience's background assumed to be? Level of proficiency, experience, and knowledge of subject matter? Credentials?

—What are the beliefs, attitudes, values, prejudices of the addressed audience?

What Do They Speak/Write About?

—What topics or issues does the forum consider? What are allowable subjects? What topics are valued?

—What methodology or methodologies are accepted? Which theoretical approach is preferred: deduction (theoretical argumentation) or induction (evidence)?

—What constitutes "validity," "evidence," and "proof" in the forum (e.g., personal experience/observation, testing and measurement, theoretical or statistical analysis)?

How Do They Say/Write It?

Form

—What types of discourse does the forum admit (e.g., articles, reviews, speeches, poems)? How long are the discourses?

—What are the dominant modes of organization?

—What formatting conventions are present: headings, tables and graphs, illustrations, abstracts?

Style

—What documentation form(s) is used?

—Syntactic characteristics?

—Technical or specialized jargon? Abbreviations?

—Tone? What stance do writers/speakers take relative to audience?

—Manuscript mechanics?

Other Considerations?

Questions for Discussion and Journaling

1. After reading the first page of the article, define *intertextuality*. When you're finished reading the entire article, define it again. How, if at all, do your two definitions differ?

2. Do you agree with Porter that *intertext* — the great web of texts built on and referring to each other — makes individual writers less important? Why or why not?

3. Why does Porter call the idea of an autonomous writer "romantic"? If you've read Ridolfo and DeVoss's article in this chapter (p. 512), do you think "romantic" is being used the same way in both articles? If not, how does the term seem to differ?

4. Porter argues that the key criterion for evaluating writing should be its "acceptability" within the reader's community. How is this different from the way you might have assumed writing should be evaluated prior to reading his article? How is it different from the way(s) your own writing has been evaluated in the past?

5. If Porter is right about intertextuality and its effects on originality, then his article must not be "original," and he must not be writing as an "autonomous individual." How does his own work reflect — or fail to reflect — the principles he's writing about?

6. What harm is there, according to Porter, in imagining writing "as individual, as isolated, as heroic" (para. 39)? What problems does it cause?

7. The chapter introduction and Downs's reading earlier in this chapter (p. 457) employ the concept of rhetorical *ecology*. How does Porter's explanation of intertextuality align with, relate to, or help you better understand the idea of rhetorical ecology?

Applying and Exploring Ideas

1. Choose a commercial or advertisement you've seen recently and search for traces of intertextuality in it. How many texts can you find represented in it? How do you find *cultural* intertext represented in it?

2. If we accept Porter's argument, then the typical school definition of *plagiarism* seems oversimplified or inaccurate. Rewrite the plagiarism policy for the course you're in now so that it accounts for Porter's notion of plagiarism but still keeps students from cheating. When you're finished, compare the original and your revised version. How much and in what ways do they differ?

3. If you have also read Ridolfo and DeVoss's article on "Rhetorical Velocity," apply both their idea of rhetorical velocity and Porter's idea of intertextuality to a text of your choice. Explain how Porter would talk about your text's inter-textuality and how Ridolfo and DeVoss would talk about its rhetorical velocity, and then note the differences and similarities between the two concepts of how the text works.

- -

META MOMENT   Many of us have been taught to imagine "writers" as people who work more or less alone to get their ideas down in print. Has Porter's study changed the way *you* imagine writers and writing? Would adopting his notion of writers and writing change the way you write?

- -

Rhetorical Reading Strategies and the Construction of Meaning

Christina Haas

Courtesy of Linda Flower

CHRISTINA HAAS
LINDA FLOWER

Framing the Reading

In the late 1980s and early 1990s, Christina Haas and Linda Flower were doing research on how reading contributes to writing at Carnegie Mellon University's Center for the Study of Writing. Specifically, they were trying to understand what experienced readers do differently from less-experienced ones. What they found was that more-experienced readers used what they called **rhetorical** reading strategies to more efficiently come to an understanding of difficult texts.

Haas and Flower's research makes use of a somewhat imperfect method of investigation called a *think-aloud protocol*. Because we can't see what people think, we can at least try to hear some of what they're thinking by asking them to "think out loud." So research participants are asked first to read aloud and then to describe what they're thinking while they try to understand what the text means. The researchers make tapes of this talk, which are later transcribed for further study. The method is a good way of capturing some of what's going on in people's heads, but you may be able to see potential drawbacks to it as well.

If you read Keith Grant-Davie's article on rhetorical situations (p. 484), you'll remember our discussion of the term **rhetoric** as descriptive of texts that *accomplish* or *do* things (like get you to buy a car or get you married or get you into war).

Haas, Christina, and Linda Flower. "Rhetorical Reading Strategies and the Construction of Meaning." *College Composition and Communication*, vol. 39, no. 2, May 1988, pp. 167–83.

Haas and Flower help us think about another angle of rhetoric: the *motivation* of the **rhetors** (speakers and writers) and the **context** in which the texts they create are written and read.

It may help you to know, in reading this piece, that Carnegie Mellon has been the scene of a lot of research on artificial intelligence — how to make machines able to think like humans. In research conducted around the time the article was written, human brains were often thought of as "information processors" much like computers — working with memory, central processors, inputs and outputs, and sensory data. Because this way of understanding the human mind was "in the air" (everyone was talking more or less this way) at that time, Haas and Flower's article carries some of that sense, too, and, for better or worse, they tend to talk about minds as quite machine-like. Knowing that, you understand a little more of the context of this article, and (Haas and Flower would say) that means you're a little better equipped to make sense of it.

Getting Ready to Read

Before you read, do at least one of the following activities:

- Ask a couple of friends how they read: When do they pay attention to who is the writer of what they're reading? When do they look up information like definitions or background on the subject? What strategies do they use to keep track of what they're reading, like highlighting, notes in the margins, or a reading notebook? When they encounter material they don't understand, what do they do to try to understand it? Keep notes of your friends' answers and compare them with what you do as a reader.

- Make an audio or video recording of yourself reading an unfamiliar and hard-to-read text aloud and talking aloud as you try to figure out what it means. When you play back the recording, make notes about what you heard that you didn't expect to and what you learn about yourself as a reader from doing this.

- Make a quick self-assessment of your reading abilities by answering the following questions: What are you good at, as a reader? What do you think you're not good at when it comes to reading? Is there anything you wish you had been taught better or differently?

As you read, consider the following questions:

- How does the reading style that Haas and Flower recommend compare with your own habits of reading and understanding texts?

- What does it mean to *construct* the meaning of a text rather than to "extract" it or find it "in" the text?

- What, according to Haas and Flower, are more-experienced readers doing that less-experienced readers aren't?

- How do Haas and Flower actually study their question? What do you think of their methods?

THERE IS A GROWING consensus in our field that reading should be thought 1 of as a constructive rather than as a receptive process: that "meaning" does not exist in a text but in readers and the representations they build. This constructive view of reading is being vigorously put forth, in different ways, by both literary theory and cognitive research. It is complemented by work in rhetoric which argues that reading is also a discourse act. That is, when readers construct meaning, they do so in the context of a discourse situation, which includes the writer of the original text, other readers, the rhetorical context for reading, and the history of the discourse. If reading really is this constructive, rhetorical process, it may both demand that we rethink how we teach college students to read texts and suggest useful parallels between the act of reading and the more intensively studied process of writing. However, our knowledge of how readers actually carry out this interpretive process with college-level expository texts is rather limited. And a process we can't describe may be hard to teach.

> There is a growing consensus in our field that reading should be thought of as a constructive rather than as a receptive process: that "meaning" does not exist in a text but in readers and the representations they build.

We would like to help extend this constructive, rhetorical view of reading, 2 which we share with others in the field, by raising two questions. The first is, how does this constructive process play itself out in the actual, thinking process of reading? And the second is, are all readers really aware of or in control of the discourse act which current theories describe? In the study we describe below, we looked at readers trying to understand a complex college-level text and observed a process that was constructive in a quite literal sense of the term. Using a think-aloud procedure, we watched as readers used not only the text but their own knowledge of the world, of the topic, and of discourse conventions, to infer, set and discard hypotheses, predict, and question in order to construct meaning for texts. One of the ways readers tried to make meaning of the text was a strategy we called "rhetorical reading," an active attempt at constructing a rhetorical context for the text as a way of making sense of it. However, this valuable move was a special strategy used only by more experienced readers. We observed a sharp distinction between the rhetorical process these experienced readers demonstrated and the processes of freshman readers. It may be that these student readers, who relied primarily on text-based strategies to construct their meanings, do not have the same full sense of reading as the rhetorical or social discourse act we envision.

Some of the recent work on reading and cognition gives us a good starting point 3 for our discussion since it helps describe what makes the reading process so complex and helps explain how people can construct vastly different interpretations of the same text. Although a thinking-aloud protocol can show us a great deal, we must keep in mind that it reveals only part of what goes on as a reader is building a representation of a text. And lest the "constructive" metaphor makes this process sound tidy, rational, and fully conscious, we should emphasize that it may in fact be rapid, unexamined, and even inexpressible. The private mental representation that a reader constructs has many facets: it is likely to include a representation of propositional or content information, a representation of the structure — either conventional or unique — of that information, and a representation of how the parts of the text function. In addition, the reader's representation may include beliefs about the subject matter, about the author and his or her credibility, and about the reader's own intentions in reading. In short, readers construct meaning by building multifaceted, interwoven representations of knowledge. The current text, prior texts, and the reading context can exert varying degrees of influence on this process, but it is the reader who must integrate information into meaning.

We can begin to piece together the way this constructive, cognitive process 4 operates based on recent research on reading and comprehension, and on reading and writing. Various syntheses of this work have been provided by Baker and Brown; Bransford; Flower ("Interpretive Acts"); and Spivey. To begin with, it is helpful to imagine the representations readers build as complex networks, like dense roadmaps, made up of many nodes of information, each related to others in multiple ways. The nodes created during a few minutes of reading would probably include certain content propositions from the text. The network might also contain nodes for the author's name, for a key point in the text, for a personal experience evoked by the text, for a striking word or phrase, and for an inference the reader made about the value of the text, or its social or personal significance. The links between a group of nodes might reflect causality, or subordination, or simple association, or a strong emotional connection.

The process of constructing this representation is carried out by both highly 5 automated processes of recognition and inference *and* by the more active problem-solving processes on which our work focuses. For instance, trying to construct a well-articulated statement of the "point" of a text may require active searching, inferencing, and transforming of one's own knowledge. The reason such transformations are constantly required can be explained by the "multiple-representation thesis" proposed by Flower and Hayes ("Images" 120). It suggests that readers' and writers' mental representations are not limited to verbally well-formed ideas and plans, but may include information coded as visual images, or as emotions, or as linguistic propositions that exist just above the level of specific words. These representations may also reflect more abstract schema, such as the schema most people have for narrative or for establishing credibility in a conversation. Turning information coded in any of these forms into a fully verbal articulation of the "point," replete with well-specified connections between ideas and presented according to the standard conventions of a given discourse, is constructive; it can involve not only translating one kind of representation into another, but reorganizing knowledge and creating new knowledge, new conceptual nodes and connections. In essence, it makes sense to take the metaphor of "construction" seriously.

It should be clear that this image of "meaning" as a rich network of disparate 6 kinds of information is in sharp contrast to the narrow, highly selective and fully verbal statement of a text's gist or "meaning" that students may be asked to construct for an exam or a book review. Statements of that sort do, of course, serve useful functions, but we should not confuse them with the multi-dimensional, mental structures of meaning created by the cognitive and affective process of reading.

If reading, then, is a process of responding to cues in the text and in the 7 reader's context to build a complex, multi-faceted representation of meaning, it should be no surprise that different readers might construct radically different representations of the same text and might use very different strategies to do so. This makes the goals of teacher and researcher look very much alike: both the teacher and the researcher are interested in the means by which readers (especially students) construct multi-faceted representations, or "meaning." The study we are about to describe looks at a practical and theoretical question that this constructive view of reading raises: namely, what strategies, other than those based on knowing the topic, do readers bring to the process of understanding difficult texts—and how does this translate into pedagogy?

Seeing reading as a constructive act encourages us as teachers to move from 8 merely *teaching texts* to *teaching readers*. The teacher as co-reader can both model a sophisticated reading process and help students draw out the rich possibilities of texts and readers, rather than trying to insure that all students interpret texts in a single, "correct" way—and in the same way. Yet this goal—drawing out the rich possibilities of texts and of readers—is easier to describe than to reach.

WHAT IS "GOOD READING"?

The notion of multiple, constructed representations also helps us understand 9 a recurring frustration for college teachers: the problem of "good" readers who appear to miss the point or who seem unable or unwilling to read critically. Many of our students are "good" readers in the traditional sense: they have large vocabularies, read quickly, are able to do well at comprehension tasks involving recall of content. They can identify topic sentences, introductions and conclusions, generalizations and supporting details. Yet these same students often frustrate us, as they paraphrase rather than analyze, summarize rather than criticize texts. Why are these students doing less than we hope for?

To interpret any sophisticated text seems to require not only careful read- 10 ing and prior knowledge, but the ability to read the text on several levels, to build multi-faceted representations. A text is understood not only as content and information, but also as the result of someone's intentions, as part of a larger discourse world, and as having real effects on real readers. In an earlier study, we say that experienced readers made active use of the strategy of rhetorical reading not only to predict and interpret texts but to solve problems in comprehension (Flower, "Construction of Purpose"). Vipond and Hunt have observed a related strategy of "point-driven" (vs. "story-driven") reading which people bring to literary texts.

If we view reading as the act of constructing multi-faceted yet integrated 11 representations, we might hypothesize that the problem students have with critical reading of difficult texts is less the representations they *are* constructing than those they *fail to construct.* Their representations of text are closely tied to content: they read for information. Our students may believe that if they understand all the words and can paraphrase the propositional content of a text, then they have successfully "read" it.

While a content representation is often satisfactory — it certainly meets the 12 needs of many pre-college read-to-take-a-test assignments — it falls short with tasks or texts which require analysis and criticism. What many of our students *can* do is to construct representations of content, of structure, and of conventional features. What they often *fail to do* is to move beyond content and convention and construct representations of texts as purposeful actions, arising from contexts, and with intended effects. "Critical reading" involves more than careful reading for content, more than identification of conventional features of discourse, such as introductions or examples, and more than simple evaluation based on agreeing or disagreeing. Sophisticated, difficult texts often require the reader to build an equally sophisticated, complex representation of meaning. But how does this goal translate into the process of reading?

As intriguing as this notion of the active construction of meaning is, we 13 really have no direct access to the meanings/representations that readers build. We cannot enter the reader's head and watch as the construction of meaning proceeds. Nor can we get anything but an indirect measure of the nature, content, and structure of that representation. What we can do, however, is to watch the way that readers go about building representations: we can observe their use of *reading strategies* and so infer something about the representations they build.

In order to learn something about the construction of meaning by readers, 14 we observed and analyzed the strategies of ten readers. Four were experienced college readers, graduate students (aged 26 to 31 years), three in engineering and one in rhetoric; six were student readers, college freshmen aged 18 and 19, three classified "average" and three classified "above average" by their freshman composition teachers.

We were interested in how readers go about "constructing" meaning and 15 the constructive strategies they use to do so. However, we suspected that many academic topics would give an unfair advantage to the more experienced readers, who would be able to read automatically by invoking their knowledge of academic topics and discourse conventions. This automaticity would, however, make their constructive reading harder for us to see. We wanted a text that would require equally active problem solving by both groups. So, in order to control for such knowledge, we designed a task in which meaning was under question for all readers, and in which prior topic knowledge would function as only one of many possible tools used to build an interpretation. Therefore, the text began *in medias res*, without orienting information about author, source, topic, or purpose. We felt that in this way we could elicit the full range of constructive strategies these readers could call upon when the situation demanded it.

The text, part of the preface to Sylvia Farnham-Diggory's *Cognitive Processes* 16 *in Education*, was like many texts students read, easy to decode but difficult to interpret, with a high density of information and a number of semi-technical expressions which had to be defined from context. The readers read and thought aloud as they read. In addition, they answered the question "how do you interpret the text now?" at frequent intervals. The question was asked of readers eight times, thus creating nine reading "episodes." The slash marks indicate where the question appeared, and also mark episode boundaries, which we discuss later. To see the effect of this manipulation on eliciting interpretive strategies, you might wish to read the experimental text before going further. (Sentence numbers have been added.)

> But somehow the social muddle persists.[s1] Some wonderful children come from appalling homes; some terrible children come from splendid homes.[s2] Practice may have a limited relationship to perfection — at least it cannot substitute for talent.[s3] Women are not happy when they are required to pretend that a physical function is equivalent to a mental one.[s4] Many children teach themselves to read years before they are supposed to be "ready."[s5] / Many men would not dream of basing their self-esteem on "cave man" prowess.[s6] And despite their verbal glibness, teenagers seem to be in a worse mess than ever.[s7] /
>
> What has gone wrong?[s8] Are the psychological principles invalid?[s9] Are they too simple for a complex world?[s10] /

Like the modern world, modern scientific psychology is extremely technical and complex.[s11] The application of any particular set of psychological principles to any particular real problem requires a double specialist: a specialist in the scientific area, and a specialist in the real area.[s12] /

Not many such double specialists exist.[s13] The relationship of a child's current behavior to his early home life, for example, is not a simple problem — Sunday Supplement psychology notwithstanding.[s14] / Many variables must be understood and integrated: special ("critical") periods of brain sensitivity, nutrition, genetic factors, the development of attention and perception, language, time factors (for example, the amount of time that elapses between a baby's action and a mother's smile), and so on.[s15] Mastery of these principles is a full-time professional occupation.[s16] / The professional application of these principles — in, say a day-care center — is also a full-time occupation, and one that is foreign to many laboratory psychologists.[s17] Indeed, a laboratory psychologist may not even recognize his pet principles when they are realized in a day care setting.[s18] /

What is needed is a coming together of real-world and laboratory specialists that will require both better communication and more complete experience.[s19] / The laboratory specialists must spend some time in a real setting; the real-world specialists must spend some time in a theoretical laboratory.[s20] Each specialist needs to practice thinking like his counterpart.[s21] Each needs to practice translating theory into reality, and reality into theory.[s22]

17 The technique of in-process probing tries to combine the immediacy of concurrent reporting with the depth of information obtained through frequent questioning. It can of course give us only an indirect and partial indication of the actual representation. What it does reveal are gist-making strategies used at a sequence of points during reading, and it offers a cumulative picture of a text-under-construction.

18 Aside from our manipulation of the presentation, the text was a typical college reading task. Part of the author's introduction to an educational psychology textbook, it presented an array of facts about the social reality of learning, problems of education, and the aims of research. *Our* reading of the text, obviously also a constructed one, but one constructed with the benefit of a full knowledge of the source and context, included two main facts and two central claims. In a later analysis, we used these facts and claims to describe some of the transactions of readers and text.

Fact: Social problems exist and psychological principles exist, but there's a mismatch between them.

Fact: There are two kinds of educational specialists — real-world and laboratory.

Claim (explicit in text): The two kinds of specialists should interact.

Claim (implicit): Interaction of the two specialists is necessary to solve social problems.

The differences in "readings" subjects constructed of the text were striking 19 and were evidenced immediately. For instance, the following descriptions of three readers' readings of the text suggest the range of readers' concerns and begin to offer hints about the nature of their constructed representations of the text. These descriptions were what we called "early transactions" with the text—an analysis based on readers' comments during reading of the first two paragraphs, or ten sentences, of the text.

Seth, a 27-year-old graduate student in Engineering, by his own account a 20 voracious reader of literature in his own field, of travel books, history, and contemporary novels, is initially confused with the concepts "physical function and mental one" (sentence 4). He then explains his confusion by noting the nature of the materials: "Well, that's got some relationship with something that came before this business."

Kara, a freshman who does average college work, also thinks the text is con- 21 fusing; specifically, she says "I don't know what glibness means" (sentence 7). But whereas Seth sets up a hypothesis about both the content of the text and its source—"I think it's part of an article on the fact that the way you turn out is not a function of your environment"—and reads on to confirm his hypothesis, Kara's reading proceeds as a series of content paraphrases—"It's talking about children coming from different homes . . . and women not being happy." She continues to interpret the text a chunk at a time, paraphrasing linearly with little attempt to integrate or connect the parts. She reacts positively to the text—"I love the expression 'what has gone wrong'" (sentence 8)—and, despite her initial confusion with "glibness," she seems satisfied with her simple reading: "I just feel like you're talking about people—what's wrong with them and the world."

Not all the freshman student readers' transactions with the text were as super- 22 ficial and oversimplified as Kara's—nor were they all as contented with their readings of the text. Bob—an above-average freshman with a pre-med major—paraphrases content linearly like Kara, but he also sets up a hypothetical structure for the text: "It seems that different points are being brought out and each one has a kind of a contradiction in it, and it seems like an introduction. . . ." Unlike Kara, however, he becomes frustrated, unable to reconcile his own beliefs with what he's reading: "Well, I don't think they're too simple for a complex world. I don't think these are very simple things that are being said here. I think the situations—women, children, and men—I think they're pretty complex . . . so I don't understand why it said 'too simple for a complex world'" (sentence 10).

Our more experienced reader, Seth, also sets up a hypothesis about the text's 23 structure: "Maybe he's [the author] contrasting the verbal glibness with caveman

567

instinct." But Seth goes further: "I think the author is trying to say that it's some balance between your natural instinct and your surroundings but he's not sure what that balance is." These hypotheses try to account for not only the propositional content of the text, but also the function of parts ("contrasting"), the author's intent, and even the author's own uncertainty.

Seth continues to read the text, noting his own inexperience with the area of psychology — "I'm thinking about Freud and I really don't know much about psychology" — and trying to tie what he has just read to the previous paragraph: "I guess the psychological principles have something to do with the way children turn out. But I don't know if they are the physical, environmental things or if they're a function of your surroundings and education." 24

In these "early transactions" with the text, we see a range of readings and vast differences in the information contained in the readers' representations: Kara is uncertain of the meaning of a word and somewhat confused generally; she paraphrases content and is satisfied with the text and her reading of it. If we have a hint about the representations of text that Kara is building it is that they are focused primarily on content and her own affective responses and that they are somewhat more limited than those of the other readers. Bob's comments suggest that he may be building representations of structure as well as content, and that he is trying to bring his own beliefs and his reading of the text into line. 25

Seth is concerned with the content, with possible functions — both for parts of the text and for the text as a whole — with the author's intentions, with the experimental situation and with missing text; he also attends to his own knowledge (or lack of it) and to his prior reading experiences. What this suggests is that Seth is creating a multi-dimensional representation of the text that includes representations of its content, representations of the structure and function of the text, representations of author's intention and his own experience and knowledge as a reader of the text. 26

The "texts" or representations of meaning that the readers created as they were wrestling with the text and thinking aloud were dramatically different in both quantity — the amount of information they contained — and quality — the kinds of information they contained and the amount of the original text they accounted for. However, with no direct access to the internal representations that readers were building, we looked instead at the overt strategies they seemed to be using. 27

STRATEGIES FOR CONSTRUCTING MEANING

The initial transactions with text suggested some differences among readers. Our next move was to more systematically analyze these differences. Each protocol contained two kinds of verbalizations: actual reading of the text aloud and comments in which the readers were thinking aloud. About half of these comments 28 were in response to the question, "How do you interpret the text now?" and the rest were unprompted responses. Each comment was sorted into one of three categories, based on what the readers seemed to be "attending to." This simple, three-part coding scheme distinguished between Content, Function/Feature, and Rhetorical reading strategies. These strategies are readily identifiable with some practice; our inter-rater reliability, determined by simple pair-wise comparisons, averaged 82%. Later, after about 20 minutes' instruction in the context of a college reading classroom, students could identify the strategies in the reading of others with close to 70% reliability.

Comments coded as *content strategies* are concerned with content or topic 29 information, "what the text is about." The reader may be questioning, interpreting, or summing content, paraphrasing what the text "is about" or "is saying." The reader's goal in using content strategies seems to be getting information from the text. Some examples of comments coded as content strategies:

> "So we're talking about psychological principles here."
>
> "I think it's about changing social conditions, like families in which both parents work, and changing roles of women."
>
> "I don't know what glibness is, so it's still confusing."

As Table 1 shows, both student and more experienced readers spent a large proportion of their effort using content strategies. On the average, 77% of the reading protocol was devoted to content strategies for students, 67% for the older readers. Building a representation of content seems to be very important for all of the readers we studied.

Function/feature strategies were used to refer to conventional, generic functions 30 of texts, or conventional features of discourse. These strategies seemed closely tied to the text: readers frequently named text parts, pointing to specific words, sentences, or larger sections of text — "This is the main point." "This must be an example," "I think this is the introduction." While content strategies seemed to be used to explain what the text was "saying," function/feature strategies were often used to name what the text was "doing": "Here he's contrasting," "This

TABLE 1 MEAN PROPORTION OF STRATEGIES USED

	STUDENTS	EXPERIENCED READERS
Content Strategies	77% (58.1)	67% (58.0)
Feature Strategies	22% (15.8)	20% (18.0)
Rhetorical Strategies	1%* (.3)	13%* (9.3)

*Difference significant at .05 level. Numbers in parentheses indicate the mean number of protocol statements in each category.

part seems to be explaining. . . ." In short, the use of these strategies suggests that readers are constructing spatial, functional, or relational structures for the text. Some examples of comments coded as function/feature strategies:

> "I guess these are just examples."
>
> "Is this the introduction?"
>
> "This seems to be the final point."

Predictably, these strategies accounted for less of the protocol than did the content strategies: 22% for students, 20% for more experienced readers (see Table 1). And the groups of readers looked similar in their use of this strategy. This, too, may be expected: Identifying features such as introductions, examples, and conclusions is standard fare in many junior high and high school curricula. In addition, these students are of at least average ability within a competitive private university. We might ask if more basic readers—without the skills or reading experiences of these students—might demonstrate less use of the function/feature strategies. Further, these readers were all reading from paper; people reading from computer screens—a number which is rapidly increasing—may have difficulty creating and recalling spatial and relational structures in texts they read and write on-line (Haas and Hayes 34–35).

Rhetorical strategies take a step beyond the text itself. They are concerned with 31 constructing a rhetorical situation for the text, trying to account for author's purpose, context, and effect on the audience. In rhetorical reading strategies readers use cues in the text, and their own knowledge of discourse situations, to re-create or infer the rhetorical situation of the text they are reading. There is some indication that these strategies were used to help readers uncover the actual "event" of the text, a unique event with a particular author and actual effects. One reader likened the author of the text to a contemporary rhetorician: "This sounds a little like Richard Young to me." Readers seem to be constructing a rhetorical situation for the text and relating *this* text to a larger world of discourse. These examples demonstrate some of the range of rhetorical strategies: comments concerned with author's purpose, context or source, intended audience, and actual effect. Some examples of rhetorical reading strategies:

> "So the author is trying to make the argument that you need scientific specialists in psychology."
>
> "I wonder if it [the article] is from *Ms.*"
>
> "I don't think this would work for the man-in-the-street."
>
> "I wonder, though, if this is a magazine article, and I wonder if they expected it to be so confusing."

While the groups of readers employed content and function/feature strate- 32 gies similarly, there is a dramatic difference in their use of the rhetorical strategy category. Less than 1% (in fact, one statement by one reader) of the students' protocols contained rhetorical strategies, while 13% of the experienced readers' effort went into rhetorical strategies. This is particularly striking when we consider the richness and wealth of information contained in these kinds of comments. For instance, setting this article into the context of *Ms.* magazine brings with it a wealth of unstated information about the kind of article that appears in that source, the kind of writers that contribute to it, and the kind of people who read it.

Rhetorical reading appears to be an "extra" strategy which some readers used 33 and others did not. Mann-Whitney analyses show no significant differences in the use of content or function/feature strategies, and an interesting—$p > 0.5$—difference between the two groups in use of rhetorical strategies. The small numbers in parentheses indicate the mean number of protocol statements in each category for each group of readers; the significance tests, however, were performed on the proportions of strategies used by each reader.

An example of two readers responding to a particularly difficult section of 34 text reveals the differences in the use of strategies even more clearly than do the numbers.

> *Student Reader*: Well, basically, what I said previously is that there seems to be a problem between the real-world and the laboratory, or ideal situation versus real situation, whatever way you want to put it—that seems to be it.

> *Experienced Reader*: Ok, again, real world is a person familiar with the social influences on a person's personality—things they read or hear on the radio. . . . And laboratory specialists are more trained in clinical psychology. And now I think this article is trying to propose a new field of study for producing people who have a better understanding of human behavior. This person is crying out for a new type of scientist or something. (Ph.D. Student in Engineering)

While the student reader is mainly creating a gist and paraphrasing content, the experienced reader does this and more—he then tries to infer the author's purpose and even creates a sort of strident persona for the writer. If readers can only build representations for which they have constructive tools or strategies, then it is clear that this student reader—and in fact all of the student readers we studied—are not building rhetorical representations of this text. In fact, these student readers seem to be focused almost exclusively on content. The student reader above is a case in point: her goal seems to be to extract information from the text, and once that is done—via a simple paraphrase—she is satisfied with her reading of the text. We called this type of content reading "knowledge-getting," to underscore the similarity to the knowledge-telling strategy identified by Bereiter and Scardamalia (72) in immature writers. In both knowledge-getting and knowledge-telling, the focus is on content; larger rhetorical purposes seem to play no role.

It is useful to see rhetorical reading not as a separate and different strategy but as a progressive enlargement of the constructed meaning of a text. These student readers seldom "progressed" to that enlarged view. Reading for content is usually dominant and crucial—other kinds of strategies build upon content representations. Functions and features strategies are generic and conventional—easily identified in texts and often explicitly taught. Rhetorical strategies include not only a representation of discourse as discourse but as *unique* discourse with a real author, a specific purpose, and actual effects. This possible relationship between strategies may point to a building of skills, a progression which makes intuitive sense and is supported by what we know about how reading is typically taught and by teachers' reports of typical student reading problems. [35]

The difference in the use that experienced and student readers make of these strategies does not in itself make a convincing case for their value. Rhetorical reading strategies certainly *look* more sophisticated and elaborate, but an important question remains: What does rhetorical reading *do* for readers? We might predict that constructing the additional rhetorical representation—requiring more depth of processing—would be an asset in particularly problematic reading tasks: texts in a subject area about which the reader knows little, or texts complex in structure. It might also be important in those reading tasks in which recognizing author's intention is crucial: propaganda, satire, even the interpretation of assignments in school. [36]

However, let us consider a rival hypothesis for a moment: maybe rhetorical strategies are simply "frosting on the cake." Maybe good readers use these strategies because reading for information is easier for them, and they have extra cognitive resources to devote to what might be largely peripheral concerns of the rhetorical situation. [37]

We suspect that this was not the case, that rhetorical reading is not merely "frosting on the cake" for several reasons: first, in the absence of a rhetorical situation for the text, *all* experienced readers constructed one. Second, the more experienced readers seemed to be using all the strategies in tandem; i.e., they used the rhetorical strategies to help construct content, and vice versa. They did not "figure out" the content, and then do rhetorical reading as an "embellishment." Rhetorical reading strategies were interwoven with other strategies as the readers constructed their reading of the texts. [38]

And third, in the "tug of war" between text and reader which characterizes constructive reading (Tierney and Pearson 34), we found that the rhetorical readers seemed to recognize and assimilate more facts and claims into their reading of the text. Recall that there were two facts and two claims which we felt constituted a successful reading of this text. We used readers' recognition of these facts and claims to gauge and to describe the kind of representation they had constructed. [39]

Fact: Social problems exist and psychological principles exist, but there's a mismatch between them.

Fact: There are two kinds of educational specialists—real-world and laboratory.

Claim (explicit in text): The two kinds of specialists should interact.

Claim (implicit): Interaction of the two specialists is necessary to solve social problems.

In recognizing facts in the text, both groups of readers did well. But there were very interesting differences in the patterns of recognition of claims in the text. Readers who used the rhetorical strategies, first, recognized more claims, and second, identified claims sooner than other readers. As we described earlier, our presentation of the text to the readers created nine reading episodes; each asked for the readers' interpretation of "the text so far" at the end of the episode. This allowed us some measure of constructed meaning by plotting the points at which readers recognized each fact or claim. We said that readers recognized a claim when they mentioned it as a possibility. This "recognition" was often tentative; readers made comments such as "So maybe this section is saying the two kinds of scientists should communicate," or "I guess this could solve the stuff at the beginning about social muddle."

The "episode line" in Figure 1 shows the points at which two readers (a student and a more-experienced reader) recognized Claim 1, plotted in relation to the point at which the text would reasonably permit such recognition. Figure 2 shows this information for the same readers recognizing Claim 2. Claim 2 is never explicitly

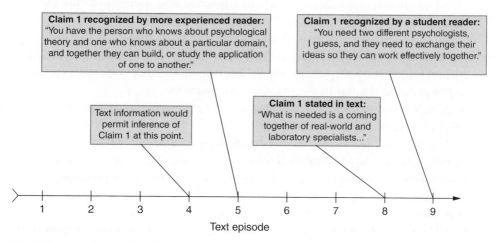

Figure 1 When did a reader recognize Claim 1? "The two kinds of specialists should interact."

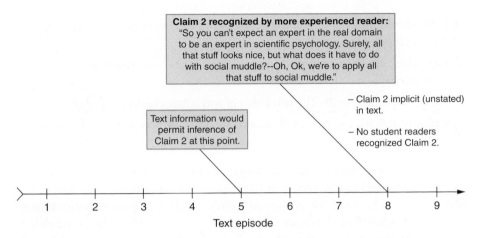

Claim 2 recognized by more experienced reader:
"So you can't expect an expert in the real domain to be an expert in scientific psychology. Surely, all that stuff looks nice, but what does it have to do with social muddle?--Oh, Ok, we're to apply all that stuff to social muddle."

– Claim 2 implicit (unstated) in text.

– No student readers recognized Claim 2.

Text information would permit inference of Claim 2 at this point.

1 2 3 4 5 6 7 8 9

Text episode

Figure 2 When did a reader recognize Claim 2? "Interaction of two kinds of specialists is necessary to solve social problems."

stated, it only becomes easy to infer in the final episode. Of all the implicit meanings the text *could* convey, we saw this second claim as central to the coherence of the argument.

As Figure 3 illustrates, all student readers got Claim 1, but only at episode 9, where it was explicitly stated—for the second time—in the text. (Claim 1 is first stated in episode 8.) More experienced readers, on the other hand, had all inferred Claim 1 much earlier—by episode 7. In addition, student readers did not recognize the unstated second claim at all, although all experienced readers inferred it, some as early as episode 8.

At episode 4 (the first point at which it would be possible to infer Claim 1), 25% of the experienced readers had inferred and mentioned this idea. At episode 5, 50% of these readers recognized it, at episode 6, 75% saw it, and by episode 7, all of the experienced readers had inferred Claim 1. In contrast, none of the student readers recognized this claim until episode 8, when it was cued in the text. At that point, 33% of the students noted it. At episode 9, when Claim 1 was restated, the rest of the students recognized it.

Claim 2 was never explicitly stated in the text, but half the experienced readers had inferred this claim at episode 8 and all had inferred it at episode 9. None of the student readers offered any hints that they had recognized this implicit claim. It seems that the rhetorical readers were better able to recognize an important claim that was *never explicitly spelled out in the text*. In sophisticated texts, many important high-level claims—like Claim 2—remain implicit, but are crucial nonetheless.

This study, because it is observational rather than experimental, does not allow us to conclude that the rhetorical reading we observed in the more experienced readers—and only in the more experienced readers—was the only or even the

42

43

44

45

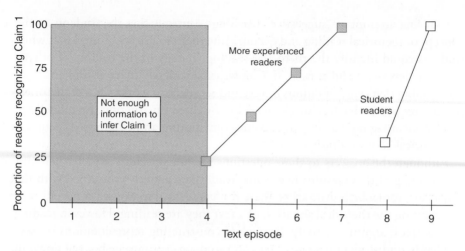

Figure 3 Readers' Recognition of Claim 1

dominant cause for their ability to recognize claims. However, it makes sense that readers who are trying to make inferences about author, context, purpose, and effect, who are trying to create a representation of the text as the result of a purposeful action, would be more likely to recognize the claims — both implicit and explicit — within a text.

THE ROLE OF RHETORICAL READING

This study suggests that the strategy of rhetorical reading may be an important   46 element in the larger process of critical reading. The constructive process we observed in readers actively trying to understand the author's intent, the context, and how other readers might respond appears to be a good basis for recognizing claims, especially unstated ones the reader must infer. Speaking more generally, this act of building a rich representation of text — larger than the words on the page and including both propositional content and the larger discourse context within which a text functions — is the kind of constructive reading we desire our students to do.

However, is rhetorical reading a strategy students could easily adopt if cued to   47 do so? Being able to see one's own text and the texts of others as *discourse acts* — rather than bodies of facts and information — is desirable, useful, and important for reading and writing of all kinds. This is the kind of meaning building we would like students to do, and rhetorical reading is one strategy that may help them do it. In saying this, however, we recognize that this knowledge will do us little good if we can't use it to help students. People must be *able* to construct elaborate representations of meaning, and they must have the strategies to do so. How this is to come about is not clear.

575

Our first attempt at "suggestive" teaching—introducing the students to the 48 concept of rhetorical reading and encouraging them to use it—found that while students could identify the rhetorical reading strategy in the reading of others, they were less successful at using it. Can we expect merely to hand students tools for building rich representations of text and set them to work? Or will rhetorical reading require active teaching—teaching by direct instruction, by modelling, and by encouraging students to become contributing and committed members of rhetorical communities?

Although the answers to these questions are not yet clear, we offer here our 49 own reading of these results: first, some readers are actively concerned with the situations from which texts arise. These readers seemed to expend some effort in representing the rhetorical situation of a text they are reading. However, reading is a complex cognitive activity. It involves constructing representations on several levels, and student readers, even good students, seem to be bogged down in content: they focus on knowledge-getting while reading.

We believe that teaching students to read rhetorically is genuinely difficult. 50 It is difficult in the way that teaching students to *write* rhetorically is difficult. In fact, this work with student and experienced *readers* provides a potential parallel to research results with student and expert *writers*. While expert writers, like those Flower, Hayes, Schriver, Carey, and Haas have studied, work within a rhetorical framework—imagining audience response, acknowledging context, and setting their own purposeful goals—student writers often concentrate on content and information—they "knowledge tell," in Bereiter and Scardamalia's terms. Similarly, these student readers seem to concentrate on knowledge, content, what the text is about—not taking into account that the text is the product of a writer's intentions and is designed to produce an effect on a specific audience.

While experienced readers may understand that both reading and writing are 51 context-rich, situational, constructive acts, many students may see reading and writing as merely an information exchange: knowledge-telling when they write, and "knowledge-getting" when they read. Helping students move beyond this simple, information-exchange view to a more complex rhetorical model—in both their reading and their writing—is one of the very real tasks which faces us as teachers. And research with real readers and writers continues to offer insights into the equally complex ways all of us construct meaning.

Works Cited

Baker, Linda, and Ann L. Brown. "Metacognitive Skills and Reading." *Handbook of Reading Research.* Ed. R. Barr, Michael L. Kamil, and Peter Mosenthal. New York: Longman, 1984. 353–94.

Bereiter, Carl, and Marlene Scardamalia. "Cognitive Coping Strategies and the Problem of Inert Knowledge." *Learning and Thinking Skills: Research and Open Questions.* Ed. Susan Chipman, J. Segal, and Robert Glaser. Hillsdale, NJ: Lawrence Erlbaum Associates, 1985. 65–80.

Bransford, John. *Cognition: Learning, Understanding and Remembering.* Belmont, CA: Wadsworth Publishing Company, 1979.

Farnham-Diggory, Sylvia. *Cognitive Processes in Education: A Psychological Preparation for Teaching and Curriculum Development.* New York: Harper and Row, 1972.

Flower, Linda. "The Construction of Purpose in Writing and Reading." *College English* 50 (1988): 528–50.

Flower, Linda. "Interpretive Acts: Cognition and the Construction of Discourse." *Poetics* 16 (April 1987): 109–30.

Flower, Linda, and John R. Hayes. "Images, Plans, and Prose: The Representation of Meaning in Writing." *Written Communication* 1 (January 1984): 120–60.

Flower, Linda, John R. Hayes, Karen Schriver, Linda Carey, and Christina Haas. *Planning in Writing: A Theory of the Cognitive Process.* ONR Technical Report # 1. Pittsburgh: Carnegie Mellon, 1987.

Haas, Christina, and John R. Hayes. "What Did I Just Say? Reading Problems in Writing with the Machine." *Research in the Teaching of English* 20 (February 1986): 22–35.

Scardamalia, Marlene. "How Children Cope with the Cognitive Demands of Writing." *Writing: The Nature, Development, and Teaching of Written Communication (Vol. 2).* Ed. Carl Frederiksen, M. F. Whiteman, and J. F. Dominic. Hillsdale, NJ: Lawrence Erlbaum Associates, 1981. 81–103.

Spivey, Nancy N. "Construing Constructivism: Reading Research in the United States." *Poetics* 16 (April 1987): 169–93.

Tierney, Robert, and P. David Pearson. "Toward a Composing Model of Reading." *Composing and Comprehending.* Ed. Julie M. Jensen. Urbana, IL: NCTE, 1984. 33–45.

Vipond, Douglas, and Russell Hunt. "Point-driven Understanding: Pragmatic and Cognitive Dimensions of Literary Reading." *Poetics* 13 (June 1984): 261–77.

Questions for Discussion and Journaling

1. What are Haas and Flower trying to find out by doing this research? Why do they want to find it out?

2. Haas and Flower spend a lot of time pointing out that readers "construct" "representations" of a text's content and what it means. Why is this particular language of construction and representation so important to them? How is it different from the ways in which we usually talk about what happens when readers read?

3. One claim this article makes is that when readers try to understand texts, they bring their own knowledge to them. What kinds of knowledge did you bring to this article that helped you make sense of it?

4. Haas and Flower seem to criticize reading that's merely for "information exchange." Why? What do they consider inadequate about using readings simply to convey information?

5. What does it mean to see texts "as purposeful actions" (para. 12)? What are some examples you've seen of texts that serve as actions?

6. Consider how Haas and Flower went about answering their research questions. What were some advantages and some drawbacks to their methods? What do you think might be the biggest weakness of their approach? How would you have done it?

7. Think back to the last time someone gave you some instruction in how to read. When was it? What were you taught? What differences are there between what you were taught and what Haas and Flower say is important to teach about reading?

8. Can you identify instances in the past where you've been a rhetorical reader? If so, what were you reading? How was it similar to and different from your usual reading practice?

9. The chapter introduction argues that rhetoric shows us how texts and discourse are epistemic. What parts of Haas and Flower's explanations of how readers *construct meaning* rather than *receive information* from a text help you better understand what it means for rhetoric to be "epistemic"?

Applying and Exploring Ideas

1. Use a text your teacher gives you to conduct your own read-aloud/think-aloud experiment. After recording yourself reading the text and stopping at predetermined points to talk about how you understand the text at that moment, listen to your recording and try to find patterns that describe how you read and understand while reading. Then write a three- to four-page report discussing what you've learned.

2. Write a summary of Haas and Flower's article that discusses the following: Why was it written? Who was meant to read it (and how can you tell)? What do Haas and Flower seem to be trying to *do* with the article? How can your understanding of the text be improved by identifying the *rhetorical situation*?

3. Make a list of the rhetorical reading strategies that Haas and Flower discuss, trying to include even those they only imply without explicitly stating. Use this list to help you write a set of instructions on reading rhetorically for the next group of students who will take the class you're in now. What should they look for in texts? What questions should they ask about texts to ensure they're reading rhetorically?

4. Locate a text that seems to be purely *informational* (like an instruction manual or directions for taking the SAT). Reading it rhetorically — that is, trying to understand the motivation of the writer and the audience's needs — can you find aspects of the text that go beyond information to claims, opinion, and argument?

- -

META MOMENT   How can you benefit from knowing the results of Haas and Flower's study? How does reading and understanding this article help you achieve the goals of this chapter listed at the end of its introduction on page 456? How do you see it relating to the threshold concepts discussed in the chapter introduction?

- -

Helping Students Use Textual Sources Persuasively

MARGARET KANTZ

Framing the Reading

Given this chapter's focus on rhetoric, several of its pieces suggest that writing and reading are not just about transmitting and receiving information. Texts don't mean the same thing to every reader because, as rhetorical theory shows (and the previous reading by Haas and Flower explored), readers *construct* meaning by *interacting* with texts, putting something of themselves into the text and drawing meaning from the text's context.

Margaret Kantz's work takes us to the next logical step, in discussing how it is that we write a new text from other existing texts. In Kantz's article we follow the learning experiences of a particular student, Shirley. Whereas Shirley had been taught in high school that "research" meant compiling facts and transmitting them to a teacher, she must now learn to use a variety of conflicting sources to make an original **argument** on the subject she's researching. Kantz analyzes how Shirley has moved from the realm of *reporting* "just the facts" to the more sophisticated world of *arguing about what the facts might be*, and she shows readers how many new ideas are involved in that change.

A key concept in this change is learning to recognize that facts aren't so much inherently true statements as they are **claims** — that is, assertions that most of a given **audience** has *agreed* are true because for that audience sufficient proof has already been given. You, like most people, would probably classify the statement "the Earth is round" as a "fact." Its status as a fact, however, depends on our mutual agreement that "round" is an adequate description of the Earth's actual, imperfectly spherical shape. What Kantz wants us to see is that what makes the statement a fact

Kantz, Margaret. "Helping Students Use Textual Sources Persuasively." *College English*, vol. 52, no. 1, Jan. 1990, pp. 74–91.

is not how "true" the statement is but that most people have *agreed* that it's true and treat it as true. Statements about which we haven't reached this consensus remain *claims*, statements that people *argue* about. Kantz's work here demonstrates why it's so important to read texts — even "factual" works like textbooks and encyclopedias — as consisting of claims, not facts.

This idea that textbooks and other "factual" texts aren't inherently true but instead simply represent a *consensus of opinion* is a major conceptual change from the way most students are taught in school before college. It is also a major implication of rhetorical theory. Like the ideas that writing is always personal (not purely factual and objective), which you encountered if you read Murray's article in Chapter 2 (p. 223), and Haas and Flower's findings (in this chapter, p. 559) about how different readers construct their own meanings from texts, the idea of truth built through consensus stems from rhetoric's qualities of being **situated** and **epistemic**, or knowledge-*making*. Rhetorical theory suggests that people are limited to subjective, partial knowledge formed through consensus because we are embedded in particular moments — we can never see an issue from every angle or perspective simultaneously, leaving our knowledge incomplete and provisional. It is this idea that Kantz is working on while exploring the difference between facts and claims.

While Kantz wrote this piece as a professor at Central Missouri State University, she conducted the research for it as a graduate student at Carnegie Mellon University. One of her professors there was Linda Flower and one of her classmates was Christina Haas, whose names you might have noticed earlier in this chapter (and, if you pay close attention, in Kantz's works-cited list). We make this point to remind you that texts are authored by real people, and these people are often connected both inside and outside of their texts — another example of the concept of rhetorical **ecology** and its idea of networks of rhetors.

Getting Ready to Read

Before you read, do at least one of the following activities:

- Think about an argument you've had recently in which people disagreed about the facts of an issue. How did you resolve the factual dispute? Did the arguers ever agree on what the facts were? If not, how was the argument resolved?

- Write down, in a few quick sentences, how *you* define these terms: *fact, claim, opinion*, and *argument*.

- Watch three commercials and count the number of *facts* and the number of *claims* in each. Then think about what's most persuasive in the ads: the facts, the claims, or a combination of the two?

As you read, consider the following questions:

- How does Kantz know what she knows? What is the basis for her claims?

- What is Kantz's research question or problem? What does she want to know, or what is she trying to solve?

- What challenges do the students about whom Kantz writes face in making sense of conflicting sources?

ALTHOUGH THE RESEARCHED ESSAY as a topic has been much written 1 about, it has been little studied. In the introduction to their bibliography, Ford, Rees, and Ward point out that most of the over 200 articles about researched essays published in professional journals in the last half century describe classroom methods. "Few," they say, "are of a theoretical nature or based on research, and almost none cites even one other work on the subject" (2). Given Ford and Perry's finding that 84% of freshman composition programs and 40% of advanced composition programs included instruction in writing research papers, more theoretical work seems needed. We need a theory-based explanation, one grounded in the findings of the published research on the nature and reasons for our students' problems with writing persuasive researched papers. To understand how to teach students to write such papers, we also need a better understanding of the demands of synthesis tasks.

> *We need a theory-based explanation, one grounded in the findings of the published research on the nature and reasons for our students' problems with writing persuasive researched papers.*

As an example for discussing this complex topic, I have used a typical college 2 sophomore. This student is a composite derived from published research, from my own memories of being a student, and from students whom I have taught at an open admissions community college and at both public and private universities. I have also used a few examples taken from my own students, all of whom share many of Shirley's traits. Shirley, first of all, is intelligent and well-motivated. She is a native speaker of English. She has no extraordinary knowledge deficits or emotional problems. She comes from a home where education is valued, and her parents do reading and writing tasks at home and at their jobs. Shirley has certain skills. When she entered first grade, she knew how to listen to and tell stories, and she soon became proficient at reading stories and at writing narratives. During her academic life, Shirley has learned such studying skills as finding the main idea and remembering facts. In terms of the relevant research, Shirley can read and summarize source texts accurately (cf. Spivey;

581

Winograd). She can select material that is relevant for her purpose in writing (Hayes, Waterman, and Robinson; Langer). She can make connections between the available information and her purpose for writing, including the needs of her readers when the audience is specified (Atlas). She can make original connections among ideas (Brown and Day; Langer). She can create an appropriate, audience-based structure for her paper (Spivey), take notes and use them effectively while composing her paper (Kennedy), and she can present information clearly and smoothly (Spivey), without relying on the phrasing of the original sources (Atlas; Winograd). Shirley is, in my experience, a typical college student with an average academic preparation.

Although Shirley seems to have everything going for her, she experiences 3 difficulty with assignments that require her to write original papers based on textual sources. In particular, Shirley is having difficulty in her sophomore-level writing class. Shirley, who likes English history, decided to write about the Battle of Agincourt (this part of Shirley's story is biographical). She found half a dozen histories that described the circumstances of the battle in a few pages each. Although the topic was unfamiliar, the sources agreed on many of the facts. Shirley collated these facts into her own version, noting but not discussing discrepant details, borrowing what she assumed to be her sources' purpose of retelling the story, and modelling the narrative structure of her paper on that of her sources. Since the only comments Shirley could think of would be to agree or disagree with her sources, who had told her everything she knew about the Battle of Agincourt, she did not comment on the material; instead, she concentrated on telling the story clearly and more completely than her sources had done. She was surprised when her paper received a grade of C–. (Page 1 of Shirley's paper is given as Appendix A.)

Although Shirley is a hypothetical student whose case is based on a real event, 4 her difficulties are typical of undergraduates at both private and public colleges and universities. In a recent class of Intermediate Composition in which the students were instructed to create an argument using at least four textual sources that took differing points of view, one student, who analyzed the coverage of a recent championship football game, ranked her source articles in order from those whose approach she most approved to those she least approved. Another student analyzed various approaches taken by the media to the Kent State shootings in 1970, and was surprised and disappointed to find that all of the sources seemed slanted, either by the perspective of the reporter or by that of the people interviewed. Both students did not understand why their instructor said that their papers lacked a genuine argument.

The task of writing researched papers that express original arguments presents 5 many difficulties. Besides the obvious problems of citation format and coordination of source materials with the emerging written product, writing a synthesis can vary in difficulty according to the number and length of the sources, the abstractness or familiarity of the topic, the uses that the writer must make of the material, the degree and quality of original thought required, and the extent to which the sources will supply the structure and purpose of the new paper. It is usually easier to write a paper that uses all of only one short source on a familiar topic than to write a paper that selects material from many long sources on a topic that one must learn as one reads and writes. It is easier to quote than to paraphrase, and it is easier to build the paraphrases, without comment or with random comments, into a description of what one found than it is to use them as evidence in an original argument. It is easier to use whatever one likes, or everything one finds, than to formally select, evaluate, and interpret material. It is easier to use the structure and purpose of a source as the basis for one's paper than it is to create a structure or an original purpose. A writing-from-sources task can be as simple as collating a body of facts from a few short texts on a familiar topic into a new text that reproduces the structure, tone, and purpose of the originals, but it can also involve applying abstract concepts from one area to an original problem in a different area, a task that involves learning the relationships among materials as a paper is created that may refer to its sources without resembling them.

Moreover, a given task can be interpreted as requiring an easy method, a diffi- 6 cult method, or any of a hundred intermediate methods. In this context, Flower has observed, "The different ways in which students [represent] a 'standard' reading-to-write task to themselves lead to markedly different goals and strate- gies as well as different organizing plans" (*Role* iii). To write a synthesis, Shirley may or may not need to quote, summarize, or select material from her sources; to evaluate the sources for bias, accuracy, or completeness; to develop original ideas; or to persuade a reader. How well she performs any of these tasks — and whether she thinks to perform these tasks — depends on how she reads the texts and on how she interprets the assignment. Shirley's representation of the task, which in this case was easier than her teacher had in mind, depends on the goals that she sets for herself. The goals that she sets depend on her awareness of the possibilities and her confidence in her writing skills.

Feeling unhappy about her grade, Shirley consulted her friend Alice. Alice, 7 who is an expert, looked at the task in a completely different way and used strat- egies for thinking about it that were quite different from Shirley's.

"Who were your sources?" asked Alice. "Winston Churchill, right? A French 8 couple and a few others. And they didn't agree about the details, such as the sizes of the armies. Didn't you wonder why?"

"No," said Shirley. "I thought the history books would know the truth. When 9 they disagreed, I figured that they were wrong on those points. I didn't want to have anything in my paper that was wrong."

"But Shirley," said Alice, "you could have thought about why a book entitled 10 *A History of France* might present a different view of the battle than a book subtitled *A History of British Progress*. You could have asked if the English and French writers wanted to make a point about the history of their countries and looked to see if the factual differences suggested anything. You could even have talked about Shakespeare's *Henry V*, which I know you've read—about how he presents the battle, or about how the King Henry in the play differs from the Henrys in your other books. You would have had an angle, a problem. Dr. Boyer would have loved it."

Alice's representation of the task would have required Shirley to formally 11 select and evaluate her material and to use it as proof in an original argument. Alice was suggesting that Shirley invent an original problem and purpose for her paper and create an original structure for her argument. Alice's task is much more sophisticated than Shirley's. Shirley replied, "That would take me a year to do! Besides, Henry was a real person. I don't want to make up things about him."

"Well," said Alice, "You're dealing with facts, so there aren't too many choices. 12 If you want to say something original you either have to talk about the sources or talk about the material. What could you say about the material? Your paper told about all the reasons King Henry wasn't expected to win the battle. Could you have argued that he should have lost because he took too many chances?"

"Gee," said Shirley, "That's awesome. I wish I'd thought of it." 13

This version of the task would allow Shirley to keep the narrative structure 14 of her paper but would give her an original argument and purpose. To write the argument, Shirley would have only to rephrase the events of the story to take an opposite approach from that of her English sources, emphasizing what she perceived as Henry's mistakes and inserting comments to explain why his decisions were mistakes—an easy argument to write. She could also, if she wished, write a conclusion that criticized the cheerleading tone of her British sources.

As this anecdote makes clear, a given topic can be treated in more or less 15 sophisticated ways—and sophisticated goals, such as inventing an original purpose and evaluating sources, can be achieved in relatively simple versions of a task. Students have many options as to how they can fulfill even a specific task (cf. Jeffery). Even children can decide whether to process a text deeply or not, and purpose in reading affects processing and monitoring of comprehension (Brown). Pichert has shown that reading purpose affects judgments about what is important or unimportant in a narrative text, and other research tells us that attitudes toward the author and content of a text affect comprehension (Asch; Hinze; Shedd; Goldman).

One implication of this story is that the instructor gave a weak assignment and 16 an ineffective critique of the draft (her only comment referred to Shirley's footnoting technique; cf. Appendix A). The available research suggests that if Dr. Boyer had set Shirley a specific rhetorical problem such as having her report on her material to the class and then testing them on it, and if she had commented on the content of Shirley's paper during the drafts, Shirley might well have come up with a paper that did more than repeat its source material (Nelson and Hayes). My teaching experience supports this research finding. If Dr. Boyer had told Shirley from the outset that she was expected to say something original and that she should examine her sources as she read them for discrepant facts, conflicts, or other interesting material, Shirley might have tried to write an original argument (Kantz, "Originality"). And if Dr. Boyer had suggested that Shirley use her notes to comment on her sources and make plans for using the notes, Shirley might have written a better paper than she did (Kantz, *Relationship*).

Even if given specific directions to create an original argument, Shirley might 17 have had difficulty with the task. Her difficulty could come from any of three causes: (1) Many students like Shirley misunderstand sources because they read them as stories. (2) Many students expect their sources to tell the truth; hence, they equate persuasive writing in this context with making things up. (3) Many students do not understand that facts are a kind of claim and are often used persuasively in so-called objective writing to create an impression. Students need to read source texts as arguments and to think about the rhetorical contexts in which they were written rather than to read them merely as a set of facts to be learned. Writing an original persuasive argument based on sources requires students to apply material to a problem or to use it to answer a question, rather than simply to repeat it or evaluate it. These three problems deserve a separate discussion.

Because historical texts often have a chronological structure, students believe 18 that historians tell stories, and that renarrating the battle casts them as a historian. Because her sources emphasized the completeness of the victory/defeat and its decisive importance in the history of warfare, Shirley thought that making these same points in her paper completed her job. Her job as a reader was thus to learn the story, i.e., so that she could pass a test on it (cf. Vipond and Hunt's argument that generic expectations affect reading behavior. Vipond and Hunt would describe Shirley's reading as story-driven rather than point-driven.) Students commonly misread texts as narratives. When students refer to a textbook as "the story," they are telling us that they read for plot and character, regardless of whether their texts are organized as narratives. One reason Shirley loves history is that when she reads it she can combine her story-reading strategies with her studying strategies. Students like Shirley may need to learn to apply basic organizing patterns, such as cause-effect and general-to-specific, to their texts. If, however, Dr. Boyer asks Shirley to respond to her sources in a way that is not compatible with Shirley's understanding of what such sources do, Shirley will have trouble doing the assignment. Professors may have to do some preparatory teaching about why certain kinds of texts have certain characteristics and what kinds of problems writers must solve as they design text for a particular audience. They may even have to teach a model for the kind of writing they expect.

The writing version of Shirley's problem, which Flower calls "writer-based 19 prose," occurs when Shirley organizes what should be an expository analysis as a narrative, especially when she writes a narrative about how she did her research. Students frequently use time-based organizing patterns, regardless of the task, even when such patterns conflict with what they are trying to say and even when they know how to use more sophisticated strategies. Apparently such common narrative transitional devices such as "the first point" and "the next point" offer a reassuringly familiar pattern for organizing unfamiliar material. The common strategy of beginning paragraphs with such phrases as "my first source," meaning that it was the first source that the writer found in the library or the first one read, appears to combine a story-of-my-research structure with a knowledge-telling strategy (Bereiter and Scardamalia, *Psychology*). Even when students understand that the assignment asks for more than the fill-in-the-blanks, show-me-you've-read-the-material approach described by Schwegler and Shamoon, they cling to narrative structuring devices. A rank ordering of sources, as with Mary's analysis of the football game coverage with the sources listed in an order of ascending disapproval, represents a step away from storytelling and toward synthesizing because it embodies a persuasive evaluation.

In addition to reading texts as stories, students expect factual texts to tell 20 them "the truth" because they have learned to see texts statically, as descriptions of truths, instead of as arguments. Shirley did not understand that nonfiction texts exist as arguments in rhetorical contexts. "After all," she reasoned, "how can one argue about the date of a battle or the sizes of armies?" Churchill, however, described the battle in much more detail than Shirley's other sources, apparently because he wished to persuade his readers to take pride in England's tradition of military achievement. Guizot and Guizot de Witt, on the other hand, said very little about the battle (beyond describing it as "a monotonous and lamentable repetition of the disasters of Crecy and Poitiers" [397]) because they saw the British invasion as a sneaky way to take advantage of a feud among the various branches of the French royal family. Shirley's story/study skills might not have allowed her to recognize such arguments, especially because Dr. Boyer did not teach her to look for them.

When I have asked students to choose a topic and find three or more sources 21 on it that disagree, I am repeatedly asked, "How can sources disagree in different ways? After all, there's only pro and con." Students expect textbooks and other authoritative sources either to tell them the truth (i.e., facts) or to express an opinion with which they may agree or disagree. Mary's treatment of the football coverage reflects this belief, as does Charlie's surprise when he found that even his most comprehensive sources on the Kent State killings omitted certain facts, such as interviews with National Guardsmen. Students' desire for truth leads them to use a collating approach whenever possible, as Shirley did (cf. Appendix A), because students believe that the truth will include all of the facts

————and Annmarie S. Palincsar. *Reciprocal Teaching of Comprehension Strategies: A Natural History of One Program for Enhancing Learning.* Technical Report #334. Urbana, IL: Center for the Study of Reading, 1985.

Churchill, Winston S. *The Birth of Britain*, New York: Dodd, 1956. Vol. 1 of *A History of the English-Speaking Peoples.* 4 vols. 1956–58.

Flower, Linda. "The Construction of Purpose in Writing and Reading." *College English* 50.5 (1988): 528–550.

————. *The Role of Task Representation in Reading to Write.* Berkeley, CA: Center for the Study of Writing, U of California at Berkeley and Carnegie Mellon. Technical Report, 1987.

————. "Writer-Based Prose: A Cognitive Basis for Problems in Writing." *College English* 41 (1979): 19–37.

Flower, Linda, Karen Schriver, Linda Carey, Christina Haas, and John R. Hayes. *Planning in Writing: A Theory of the Cognitive Process.* Berkeley, CA: Center for the Study of Writing, U of California at Berkeley and Carnegie Mellon. Technical Report, 1988.

Ford, James E., and Dennis R. Perry. "Research Paper Instruction in the Undergraduate Writing Program." *College English* 44 (1982): 825–31.

Ford, James E., Sharla Rees, and David L. Ward. *Teaching the Research Paper: Comprehensive Bibliography of Periodical Sources*, 1980. ERIC ED 197 363.

Goldman, Susan R. "Knowledge Systems for Realistic Goals." *Discourse Processes* 5 (1982): 279–303.

Guizot and Guizot de Witt. *The History of France from Earliest Times to 1848.* Trans. R. Black. Vol. 2. Philadelphia: John Wanamaker (n.d.).

Haas, Christina, and Linda Flower. "Rhetorical Reading Strategies and the Construction of Meaning." *College Composition and Communication* 39 (1988): 167–84.

Hayes, John R., D. A. Waterman, and C. S. Robinson. "Identifying the Relevant Aspects of a Problem Text." *Cognitive Science* 1 (1977): 297–313.

Hinze, Helen K. "The Individual's Word Associations and His Interpretation of Prose Paragraphs." *Journal of General Psychology* 64 (1961): 193–203.

Iser, Wolfgang. *The act of reading: A theory of aesthetic response.* Baltimore: The Johns Hopkins UP, 1978.

Jeffery, Christopher. "Teachers' and Students' Perceptions of the Writing Process." *Research in the Teaching of English* 15 (1981): 215–28.

Kantz, Margaret. "Originality and Completeness: What Do We Value in Papers Written from Sources?" Conference on College Composition and Communication. St. Louis, MO, 1988.

————. *The Relationship Between Reading and Planning Strategies and Success in Synthesizing: It's What You Do with Them that Counts.* Technical report in preparation. Pittsburgh: Center for the Study of Writing, 1988.

Kennedy, Mary Louise. "The Composing Process of College Students Writing from Sources," *Written Communication* 2.4 (1985): 434–56.

Kinneavy, James L. *A Theory of Discourse.* New York: Norton, 1971.

Kroll, Barry M. "Audience Adaptation in Children's Persuasive Letters." *Written Communication* 1.4 (1984): 407–28.

Langer, Judith. "Where Problems Start: The Effects of Available Information on Responses to School Writing Tasks." *Contexts for Learning to Write: Studies of Secondary School Instruction.* Ed. Arthur Applebee. Norwood, NJ: ABLEX Publishing Corporation, 1984. 135–48.

Luftig, Richard L. "Abstractive Memory, the Central-Incidental Hypothesis, and the Use of Structural Importance in Text: Control Processes or Structural Features?" *Reading Research Quarterly* 14.1 (1983): 28–37.

Marbaise, Alfred. "Treating a Disease." *Current Issues and Enduring Questions.* Eds. Sylvan Barnet and Hugo Bedau. New York: St. Martin's, 1987. 126–27.

McCormick, Kathleen. "Theory in the Reader: Bleich, Holland, and Beyond." *College English* 47.8 (1985): 836–50.

McGarry, Daniel D. *Medieval History and Civilization.* New York: Macmillan, 1976.

Nelson, Jennie, and John R. Hayes. *The Effects of Classroom Contexts on Students' Responses to Writing from Sources: Regurgitating Information or Triggering Insights.* Berkeley, CA: Center for the Study of Writing, U of California at Berkeley and Carnegie Mellon. Technical Report, 1988.

Pichert, James W. "Sensitivity to Importance as a Predictor of Reading Comprehension." *Perspectives on Reading Research and Instruction.* Eds. Michael A. Kamil and Alden J. Moe. Washington, D.C.: National Reading Conference, 1980. 42–46.

Robinson, Cyril E. *England: A History of British Progress from the Early Ages to the Present Day.* New York: Thomas Y. Crowell Company, 1928.

Schwegler, Robert A., and Linda K. Shamoon. "The Aims and Process of the Research Paper." *College English* 44 (1982): 817–24.

Shedd, Patricia T. "The Relationship between Attitude of the Reader Towards Women's Changing Role and Response to Literature Which Illuminates Women's Role." Diss. Syracuse U, 1975. ERIC ED 142 956.

Short, Elizabeth Jane, and Ellen Bouchard Ryan. "Metacognitive Differences between Skilled and Less Skilled Readers: Remediating Deficits through Story Grammar and Attribution Training." *Journal of Education Psychology* 76 (1984): 225–35.

Spivey, Nancy Nelson. *Discourse Synthesis: Constructing Texts in Reading and Writing.* Diss. U Texas, 1983. Newark, DE: International Reading Association, 1984.

Toulmin, Steven E. *The Uses of Argument.* Cambridge: Cambridge UP, 1969.

Vipond, Douglas, and Russell Hunt. "Point-Driven Understanding: Pragmatic and Cognitive Dimensions of Literary Reading." *Poetics* 13, (1984): 261–77.

Winograd, Peter. "Strategic Difficulties in Summarizing Texts." *Reading Research Quarterly* 19 (1984): 404–25.

- -

Questions for Discussion and Journaling

1. Kantz writes that Shirley "believes that facts are what you learn from textbooks, opinions are what you have about clothes, and arguments are what you have with your mother when you want to stay out late at night" (para. 28). What does Kantz contend that facts, opinions, and arguments *actually* are?

2. Make a list of the things Kantz says students don't know, misunderstand, or don't comprehend about how texts work. Judging from your own experience, do you think she's correct about student understanding? How many of the things she lists do you feel you understand better now?

3. As its title indicates, Kantz's article has to do with using sources *persuasively*. Did her article teach you anything new about the persuasive use of sources to support an argument? If so, what?

4. Do you think Kantz contradicts herself when she says that we should think of sources neither as stories nor as repositories of truth? Explain why or why not.

5. Kantz offers a number of critiques of students thinking of all texts as narratives and using narrative arrangements very frequently in their own writing (see para. 19). How do you think she might respond to the argument in Downs's paper earlier in this chapter (p. 457) that narrative and storytelling are principle modes of human knowing and knowledge-making? Are the two in conflict, and if so, how would you resolve this situation?

6. Which of the students in Kantz's article do you most identify with, and why?

7. Do you think Kantz's ideas will change your own approach to doing research and writing with sources? If so, how?

8. What threshold concepts emphasized in the chapter introduction do you see Kantz's work relating to?

Applying and Exploring Ideas

1. Kantz places some blame for students' writing difficulties on poorly written assignments that don't clearly explain what teachers want. Conduct your own mini review of college writing assignments you've received. How many do you think gave sufficient explanation of what the professor was looking for? As you look at assignments that did give good directions, what do they have in common? That is, based on those assignments, what did you need to be told in order to have a good understanding of what you were being asked to write? Write one to two pages about what you find, and share what you write in class.

2. Write a short reflection on the relationship between creativity and research as you've learned to understand it prior to this class, and as Kantz talks about it. Where do your ideas overlap with hers? Where does her thinking influence yours? And where does it not seem to work for you?

- -

META MOMENT One of our goals for this book is to have you consider constructs or conceptions of writing that don't hold up under close scrutiny. How would you name the constructs that Kantz is calling into question? Why would it be useful for you as a writer in college or in professional settings to understand her findings and claims?

- -

Argument as Emergence, Rhetoric as Love

JIM W. CORDER

Framing the Reading

Culturally, we almost always think of argument as *agonistic*, a term based on the Greek for *oppositional* and implying *competition* — an argument of debate: a two-sided contest, a clash, winners, and losers. Language scholars George Lakoff and Mark Johnson in their book *Metaphors We Live By* point out dozens of metaphors in the English language that position argument as *war*. "He defended his position" and "she pummeled even his strongest case with her evidence" are two examples. In this book, beginning with Stuart Greene's "Argument as Conversation" in Chapter 1 (p. 31), we have resisted this agonistic vision of argument and substituted a cooperative, *dialog-based* model in which people use argument *together* to make new knowledge.

Jim Corder, who was a rhetoric professor for many years at Texas Christian University, offers us a third model of argument in this reading: argument, and therefore rhetoric, as humans *becoming* and learning to love and respect each other as people. "Argument is emergence toward the other," he writes (part 8). The problem Corder is working on is, in contemporary terms, disagreements with and misunderstandings of other people that are so intense that people come to verbal or physical blows, or even actually blow themselves or each other up, rather than try to understand and live with the each other. The limitations of cooperative, dialogic argument become clear, Corder says, when we think about contention so deeply rooted in bodies and mythos that we are left "flushed, feverish, quaky, shaky, angry, hurt, shocked,

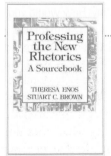

Corder, Jim W. "Argument as Emergence, Rhetoric as Love." *Rhetoric Review*, vol. 4, no. 1, Sept. 1985, pp. 16–32. Reprinted in *Professing the New Rhetorics: A Sourcebook*, edited by Theresa Enos and Stuart C. Brown, Pearson, 1994.

disappointed, alarmed, outraged, even terrified" (part 4) by the threat presented by an Other. In other words, sometimes what we feel and believe is so deeply threatened by who someone else is, what they represent, or what they believe that we are physically unable to hear and dialog with them.

Corder argues here that if we can understand ourselves as constantly emerging narratives, we can use and understand rhetoric as a way to love others before understanding them, and thus have a means of staying in conversation with those who threaten us long enough to truly understand their own emerging narratives. This ability to stay in conversation even when it is uncomfortable and threatening can help reduce our desire to silence, "beat," or even destroy the other before they do so to us.

Getting Ready to Read

Before you read, do at least one of the following activities:

- Read the Wikipedia entry on "Jim W. Corder" to get a feel for Corder's particular ethos and fit within the field of rhetoric studies.

- Write a narrative of the last argument you were in that provoked a physical response from you (like throwing things, trembling with fear/anger/ frustration, or a pit in your stomach).

As you read, consider the following questions:

- How do Corder's frequent statements directly to the reader — like "I'm not ready to go on yet" — impact your reading experience?

- Which of Corder's claims or interpretations are hard for you to accept or believe? Make notes in the margins and keep a list.

- Are you able to grasp what Corder is getting at in the key terms he uses, especially *narrative* and *emergence*?

1

In a recent review in *The New York Times Book Review*, A. G. Mojtabai said, "We are all authors. Adding here, deleting there, we people the world with our needs: with friends, lovers, ciphers, enemies, villains—and heroes" (March 3, 1985, 7). All authors, to be sure, we are more particularly narrators, historians, tale-tellers. Going through experience, hooking some version of it to ourselves, accumulating what we know as evidence and insight, ignoring what does not look like evidence and insight to us, finding some pieces of life that become life for us, failing to find others, or choosing not to look, each of us creates the narrative that he or she is. We tell our lives and live our tales, enjoying where we can, tolerating what we must, turning away to re-tell, or sinking into madness and disorder if we cannot make (or re-make) our tale into a narrative we can live in. Each of us forms conceptions of the world, its institutions, its public, private, wide, or local histories, and each of us is the narrative that shows our living in and through the conceptions that are always being formed as the tales of our lives take their shape. In this history-making, as E. L. Doctorow says, "there is no fiction or non-fiction as we commonly understand the distinction" ("False Documents," *American Review* 26 [1977]: 215–32). There is only our making, sometimes by design, sometimes not. None of us lives without a history; each of us is a narrative. We're always standing some place in our lives, and there is always a tale of how we came to stand there, though few of us have marked carefully the dimensions of the place where we are or kept time with the tale of how we came to be there.

The catch is that, though we are all fiction-makers/historians, we are seldom 2 all that good at the work. Sometimes we can't find all that's needed to make the narrative we want of ourselves, though we still make our narrative. Sometimes we don't see enough. Sometimes we find enough and see enough and still tell it wrong. Sometimes we fail to judge either the events within our narrative or the people, places, things, and ideas that might enter our narrative. Sometimes we judge dogmatically, even ignorantly, holding only to standards that we have already accepted or established. We see only what our eyes will let us see at a given moment, but eventually make a narrative of ourselves that we can enjoy, tolerate, or at least not have to think about too much. Every so often, we will see something we have not seen before, and then we have to nudge, poke, and re-make our narrative, or we decide we can either ignore the thing seen or whittle it to shape the narrative we already have. We are always seeing, hearing, thinking, living, and saying the fiction that we and our times make possible and tolerable, a fiction that is the history we can assent to at a given time. But not only can we not always be good narrators/historians, we also cannot be thorough at the work. We never quite get the narrative all said: we're always making a fiction/history that always has to be re-made, unless we are so bound by dogma, arrogance, and ignorance that we cannot see a new artifact, hear a new opinion, or enter a new experience in our narrative.

When I say that we make the fictions that are our lives, I mean to identify a 3 human activity, not a foolish or evil one. History as fiction may become evil, of course, if we refuse to see any history except the one we've already accepted or if we try to force that history upon others. At any rate, making the fiction of our lives — not at all the same as discovering a way to present an objective, externally verifiable history, which is not possible, anywhere — is not by nature limited, valueless, ignorant, despicable, or "merely subjective." It is human. It is what we do and are, even if we think we are doing and being something else. Even if we imagine that we are learning what can be known "out there," some truths that are fixed and forever, we are after all creating our narratives "in here," ourselves always agents for what can be known. We are always, as the rhetorician might say, inventing the narratives that are our lives.

As I have already suggested, we are always standing somewhere in our nar- 4 ratives when we speak to others or to ourselves. When we use language, some choices have already been made and others must be made. Our narratives, which include our pasts, accompany us and exist in our statements and exercise their influence whether or not we are aware of the influence. Before we speak, we have lived; when we speak, we must continually choose because our mouths will not say two words simultaneously. Whether consciously or not, we always station ourselves somewhere in our narratives when we use language. This means that invention always occurs. The process of invention may occur in a conscious, deliberate way, but it will occur, even if at some subterranean level. Any statement carries its history with it. We may speak without knowing all of our narratives, but the history is there. If the history of a statement someone else makes isn't apparent to us as hearers, then we have to go and find it. If we are talking to someone and that person says something we don't understand, or something that offends us, or something we cannot easily agree to, then we have to start searching that person's history until we begin to understand what led him or her to speak just so. Sometimes we do less well: if the history isn't there for us, we don't learn it, but instead make it up to suit ourselves. If we learn or make up another's narrative so that it becomes part of our narrative, then we can live in some peace with the other. If the other's narrative will not enter our own, then something else happens, to which I'll return in a moment.

While the language that lets us invent our narratives and be human is a great 5 gift, its capacities will not extend infinitely. Language comes out of us a word at a time; we cannot get all said at once. We open ourselves as we can to insight and experience and say what we can, but what we say will invariably be incomplete. Two words cannot occupy the same space at the same time: two messages cannot fully occupy the same space at the same time. Language enforces a closure: we must say one thing or the other; we choose, and make our narrative. To be sure, having lived, thought, and spoken, we can open ourselves again to insight and experience and evidence and try to say it all again. But what will come out will be the fiction we can make at the time. We cannot make all that was and is and shall be into an is of the moment's speaking. Whatever we can get into our heads we will make into the narratives that will be our truths unless we learn again.

2

Each of us is a narrative. A good part of the time we can live comfortably 6
adjacent to or across the way from other narratives. Our narratives can be congruent with other narratives, or untouched by other narratives. But sometimes
another narrative impinges upon ours, or thunders around and down into our
narratives. We can't build this other into our narratives without harm to the tales
we have been telling. This other is a narrative in another world; it is disruptive,
shocking, initially at least incomprehensible, and, as Carl Rogers has shown us,
threatening.

When this happens, our narratives become indeed what they are perpetually 7
becoming — arguments. The choosing we do to make our narratives (whether or
not we are aware of the nature of our choosing)
also makes our narratives into arguments. The
narratives we tell (ourselves) create and define
the worlds in which we hold our beliefs. Our
narratives are the evidence we have of ourselves
and of our convictions. Argument, then, is not
something we *make* outside ourselves; argument
is what we are. Each of us is an argument. We
always live in, through, around, over, and under
argument. All the choices we've made, accidentally or on purpose, in creating our histories/
narratives have also made us arguments, or, I
should go on to say, sets of congruent arguments,
or in some instances, sets of conflicting arguments.

> The narratives we tell
> (ourselves) create and define
> the world in which we hold
> our beliefs. Our narratives
> are the evidence we have of
> ourselves and of our convic-
> tions. Argument, then, is not
> something we make outside
> ourselves; argument is what
> we are.

3

Each of us is an argument, evidenced by our narrative. What happens, then, 8
if the narrative of another crushes up against our own — disruptive, shocking,
incomprehensible, threatening, suddenly showing us into a narrative not our
own? What happens if a narrative not our own reveals to us that our own narrative was wanting all along, though it is the only evidence of our identity? What
happens if the merest glimpse into another narrative sends us lurching, stunned
by its differentness, either alarmed that such differentness could exist or astonished to see that our own narrative might have been or might yet be radically
otherwise than it is? Do we hold our narratives? Keep telling the story we have
been telling? At all costs?

We react, of course, in many different ways. Sometimes we turn away from 9
other narratives. Sometimes we teach ourselves not to know that there are other
narratives. Sometimes — probably all too seldom — we encounter another narrative and learn to change our own. Sometimes we lose our plot, and our convictions

as well; since our convictions belong to our narratives, any strong interference with our narrative or sapping of its way of being will also interrupt or sap our convictions. Sometimes we go to war. Sometimes we sink into madness, totally unable to manage what our wit or judgment has shown us—a contending narrative that has force to it and charm and appeal and perhaps justice and beauty as well, a narrative compelling us to attention and toward belief that we cannot ultimately give, a contending narrative that shakes and cracks all foundations and promises to alter our identity, a narrative that would educate us to be wholly other than what we are. Any narrative exists in time; any narrative is made of the past, the present, and the future. We cannot without potential harm shift from the past of one narrative into the present and future of another, or from the past and present of one narrative into the future of another, or from the future we are narrating into a past that is not readily ours. How can we take that one chance I mentioned just now and learn to change when change is to be cherished? How can we expect another to change when we are ourselves that other's contending narrative?

4

Let there be no mistake: a contending narrative, that is, an argument of genuine 10 consequence because it confronts one life with another is a threat, whether it is another's narrative become argument impinging upon or thundering into ours, or our own, impinging upon the other's. A contending narrative, I'd suggest, is a threat more consequential than Carl Rogers has shown us. In *On Becoming a Person* (Boston: Houghton Mifflin Company, 1961), Rogers proposes that "significant learning . . . takes place when five conditions are met":

- when the client perceives himself as faced by a serious problem;
- when the therapist is a congruent person in the relationship, able to *be* the person he *is;*
- when the therapist feels an unconditional positive regard for the client;
- when the therapist experiences an accurate emphatic understanding of the client's private world and communicates this;
- when the client to some degree experiences the therapist's congruence, acceptance, and empathy.

Rogers had earlier applied his thinking more directly to rhetoric, announcing his 11 belief that a sense of threat usually blocks successful communication. As he put it, "the major barrier to mutual interpersonal communication is our very natural tendency to judge, to evaluate, to approve or disapprove, the statement of the other person" ("Communication: Its Blocking and Its Facilitation," paper delivered at Northwestern University's Centennial Conference on Communication,

Oct. 11, 1951, reprinted in Richard E. Young, Alton L. Becker, and Kenneth L. Pike, *Rhetoric: Discovery and Change* [New York: Harcourt, Brace, and World, 1979], 284–89). If we refrain from evaluating and instead "listen with understanding," according to Rogers, we will "see the expressed idea and attitude from the other person's point of view . . . sense how it feels to him . . . achieve his frame of reference in regard to the thing he is talking about" (285). When we are immersed in the attitudes, ideas, and beliefs of the other person, we "will find the emotion going out of the discussion, the differences being reduced, and those differences which remain being of a rational and understandable sort" (286).

Such insights have been enormously valuable in recent years. Some (Maxine   12
Hairston, for example) believe that Rogers' work has brought a new dimension to rhetoric after all these centuries, changing our way of thinking about argument. Others believe that Rogers' views are assumed by Aristotle, as Andrea Lunsford put it, to be "the foundation which is necessary before successful argumentation begins" ("Aristotelian vs. Rogerian Argument: A Reassessment," *College Composition and Communication* [May, 1979]: 146–51). Lunsford singles out two texts that propose methods of organizing Rogerian argument. Young, Becker, and Pike (283) suggest the following method:

First: an introduction to the problem and a demonstration that the opponent's position is understood.

Second: a statement of the contexts in which the opponent's position may be valid.

Third: a statement of the writer's position, including the contexts in which it is valid.

Fourth: a statement of how the opponent's position would benefit if he were to adopt elements of the writer's position.

In *A Contemporary Rhetoric* (Boston: Houghton Mifflin and Co., 1974, 210-11),   13
Maxine Hairston presents another Rogerian pattern:

1. a brief, objectively phrased statement of the issue.

2. a complete and impartially worded summary of your audience's opinions on the issue, demonstrating that you have made an honest effort to understand how they feel and why they feel that way. It would be useful to mention the values that underlie these opinions.

3. an objective statement of your opinions on the issue, along with your reasons for feeling as you do. Here again it would be useful to give the values on which you base your opinions.

4. an analysis of what your opinions have in common.

5. a proposal for resolving the issue in a way that injures neither party.

Such insights added to those of Carl Rogers, I'll say again, have been highly 14 valuable. They lead to patterns of argument that may even work, part of the time, in some settings. But they won't do. They do not, I believe, face the hushed, feverish, quaky, shaky, angry, scared, hurt, shocked, disappointed, alarmed, outraged, even terrified condition that a person comes to when his or her narrative is opposed by a genuinely contending narrative. Then it is one life or another, perhaps this life or none.

I want to pause a little to suggest some of the reasons that I think Rogers 15 and others who have applied his work have not gone far enough, though this is not the place for a full critique, even if I could give it. First, we should remember, Rogers is talking about the therapist-client relationship, and much of what he says rises from that context. Since it takes two to tango, and since at least one of the participants in this context is already intent upon *not* being an adversary, then conflict may be resolved and mutual communication may ensue. The therapist-client relationship, I'd suggest, even at its prickliest, is simply not going to produce the stress and pain that can occur when contending narratives meet. It is by its nature more amenable to discussion and resolution, and the rules or conditions I cited earlier are, at any rate, *game* rules, as my colleague, Professor James Baumlin, has pointed out. In the passage I cited earlier, Rogers is talking about a client who already has a need (he or she is faced by a serious problem), and the therapist is already a congruent person in the relationship. Rogers proposes for the therapist an "unconditional positive regard," but straight away recommends that all take emotion out of discussions and reduce differences. If one holds another in "unconditional positive regard," that regard, I believe, includes both emotions and differences. They cannot be reduced, though their force may be diminished for a moment; such energy is always conserved. If emotions do go out of the discussion — and I don't think they do — it is only after time and care. What each must face in contention before emotions and differences dwindle is something in the other altogether more startling: a horror, a wrong, a dishonesty (as each sees the other), a shock, an outrage, or perhaps a beauty too startling and stunning to see. As for the texts that propose patterns of Rogerian arguments, I'd say that the recommended designs are altogether commendable and will sometimes work, so long as the argument isn't crucial to the nature of the narratives involved. Where arguments entail identity, the presentation of "a statement of how the opponent's position would benefit if he were to adopt elements of the writer's position" is about as efficacious as storming Hell with a bucket of water or trying to hide the glories of Heaven with a torn curtain. If I cannot accept the identity of the other, his kindness in offering me benefits will be of no avail. As for offering a "proposal for resolving the issue in a way that injures neither party," I'd say that in the arguments that grip us most tightly, we *do* injure the other, or the other injures us, or we seem about to injure each other, except we take the tenderest, strongest care. Paul Bator ("Aristotelian and Rogerian Argument," *College Composition and Communication* [Dec., 1980]: 427–32) acknowledges that Rogerian strategy works most effectively when students "encounter non-adversary writing situations." "Under the Rogerian schema," he continues, "students can be encouraged to view their writing as a communicative first step, one designed to build bridges and win over minds—rather than being prompted to view the essay only as a finished product serving as an ultimate weapon for conversion."

I am suggesting that the arguments most significant to us are just where threat 16 occurs and continues, just where emotions and differences do not get calmly talked away, just where we are plunged into that flushed, feverish, quaky, shaky, angry, scared, hurt, shocked, disappointed, alarmed, outraged, even terrified condition I spoke of a little earlier. Then what do we do?

5

To make the kind of contention or opposition I am trying to discuss a 17 little clearer, I should add another term. I have been talking about contending narratives, or identities. Let me now add what I hope has been suggested all along: let us suppose that in this contention each narrator is entirely *steadfast*, wholly intent upon preserving the nature and movement of his or her narrative, earnest and zealous to keep its identity. I think we have not fully considered what happens in argument when the arguers are steadfast.

If Ms. Smith is steadfast in conviction and is outfitted with what she takes to 18 be good evidence and sound reasoning, that means that she is living a narrative that is congruent with her expectations and satisfying to her needs. But if she speaks to Mr. Jones, who is at opposites and equally steadfast, who is his own satisfying narrative, then it's likely that Ms. Smith's evidence will not look like evidence to Mr. Jones, and Ms. Smith's reasoning will not look like reasoning. Evidence and reason are evidence and reason only if one lives in the narrative that creates and regards them.

That seems to picture a near-hopeless prospect. 19

Sometimes it is, at least for long periods of time. Sometimes we don't resolve 20 oppositions, but must either remain apart or live as adversaries with the other. But the prospect doesn't have to be hopeless, at least not permanently.

What can change it? What can free us from the apparent hopelessness of 21 steadfast arguments opposing each other? I have to start with a simple answer and hope that I can gradually give it the texture and capacity it needs: we have *to see* each other, *to know* each other, *to be present to* each other, *to embrace* each other.

What makes that possible? We have to change the way we talk about argu- 22 ment and conceive of argument.

6

I'm not ready to go on yet. I want to try to place my interest in argument, and 23 perhaps I can do that by comparing my interest to those of Carl Rogers, to whom I am clearly much indebted. Rogers extrapolates from therapist-client relationships to public communication relationships. The base from which he works (the therapist-client relationship) gives him a setting in which civil understanding is a goal to be reached through mutual communication transactions. He does recognize the potentially threatening effect of alien insights and ideas. Young, Becker, and Pike show that the Rogerian strategy "rests on the assumption that a man holds to his beliefs about who he is and what the world is like because other beliefs threaten his identity and integrity" (7). In the Rogerian view, as Paul Bator puts it, carefully reasoned arguments "may be totally ineffectual when employed in a rhetorical situation where the audience feels its beliefs or values are being threatened. No amount of reasoned argument will prompt the audience to consider the speaker's point of view if the audience senses that its opinions are somehow being 'explained away'" (428). Followers of Rogers see in Aristotle's *Rhetoric* an antagonistic speaker-audience relationship; they do not find this in Rogers, for, as Bator says, "Generation and control of audience expectation do not attract Rogers" (428). As I have already suggested, given the therapist-client relationship he starts from, Rogers is appropriately enough interested in rhetorical contexts that do not involve advocacy. As Rogers says, "If I can listen to what [the other person] can tell me, if I can understand how it seems to him, if I can see its personal meaning for him, if I can sense the emotional flavor which it has for him, then I will be releasing potent forces of change in him" (285-86). Since he is customarily talking about a mutual communication transaction, Rogers is often as concerned with the audience as with the speaker. A speaker, Bator says, "must be willing to achieve the frame of reference of the listener even if the values or views held by the other are antithetical to the speaker's personal code of ethics. A necessary correlate of acceptance (of the other's view) is understanding, an understanding which implies that the listener accepts the views of the speaker without knowing cognitively what will result. Such understanding, in turn, encourages the speaker to explore untried avenues of exchange" (428). Looking for the therapist-client relationship, Rogers sees the therapist/communicator as an understanding audience. He expects that the therapist-as-audience will not only accept, but also understand the feelings and thoughts of the client-as-speaker. When the therapist understands the feelings and thoughts that seem so horrible or weak or sentimental or bizarre to the client, when the therapist understands and accepts the client, then the therapist frees the client to explore deep experience freely. As each understands and accepts the other, then they may move toward the truth.

   This, I would gladly agree, is the way we ought to argue, each accepting, under- 24 standing, and helping the other. However, I think the significant arguments that crowd us into each other are somewhat less kindly composed. I want to get to the place where we are threatened and where the setting doesn't seem to give us opportunity to reduce threat and to enter a mutual search for congruence and regard. I want to get to the place where we are advocates of contending narratives (with their accompanying feelings and thoughts), where we are adversaries, each seeming to propose the repudiation or annihilation of what the other lives, values, and is, where we are beyond being adversaries in that strange kind of argument we seldom attend to, where one offers the other a rightness so demanding, a beauty so stunning, a grace so fearful as to call the hearer to forgo one identity for a startling new one.

7

What can free us from the apparent hopelessness of steadfast arguments con- 25 tending with each other, of narratives come bluntly up against each other? Can the text of one narrative become the text of another narrative without sacrifice? If there is to be hope, we have to see each other, to know each other, to be present to each other, to embrace each other.

What makes that possible? I don't know. We can start toward these capacities 26 by changing the way we talk about argument and conceive of argument.

It may be helpful, before I go on, if I try to explain a little more fully the kind 27 of occasion I mean to refer to, the kind of setting in which contention generates that flushed, feverish, quaky, shaky, angry, scared, hurt, shocked, disappointed, alarmed, outraged, even terrified condition I have mentioned. Of course I cannot imagine, let alone explain or describe, all the oppositions that can occur. Perhaps I can by illustration at least suggest the kind of occasion that I want to talk about. I mean such occasions as these: let two people confront each other, each holding views antithetical to the sacred values and images of the other, one an extreme advocate of the current Pro-Life movement, the other an extreme advocate of the current movement to leave free choice open to women in the matter of abortion, each a mockery of the other; let two parties confront each other, zealous advocates of one contending that farmers must learn to stand on their own without government support, and zealous advocates of the other contending that the government, by withdrawing support, will literally kill farmers; let two tribes go to war for ancient reasons not entirely explicable to themselves or to outsiders, each a denial of the other, as in various current Middle East crises; let two nations confront each other in what sometimes appears to be a shocked and total inability to understand or even to recognize each other, as in continuing conflicts between the United States and Russia, wherever these conflicts happen to be located, whether in East Germany or in Nicaragua; let a beautiful Jewish woman encounter an aged captain of guards for Dachau; let some man confront an affirmation of life he has not been able to achieve; let an honest woman encounter cruel dishonesty; let a man encounter a narrative so beautiful but different that he cannot look; let two quite different narratives converge in conflict inside the head of a single lonely man or woman.

Given such occasions, what do we do in argument? Can we hope for happy 28 resolution? I don't know. I do think the risk in argument is greater than we have learned from Aristotle or Rogers. What can we do, then?

We can start, as I suggested earlier, by changing the way we talk about 29 argument.

As we presently understand, talk about, and teach argument, it is, whatever 30 our intentions, *display* and *presentation*. We entice with an exordium and lay in a background. We present a proposition. We display our proofs, our evidence. We show that we can handle and if need be refute opposing views. We offer our conclusion. That is display and presentation. The same thing is true of proposed plans for Rogerian argument, as in the passages I cited earlier from Young, Becker, and Pike and from Maxine Hairston.

But argument is not something *to present* or *to display*. It is something *to be*. It 31 is what we *are*, as I suggested earlier.

We are the argument over against another. Another is the argument over 32 against us. We live in, through, around, and against arguments. To display or to present them is to pretend a disengagement that we cannot actually achieve and probably should not want to achieve. Argument is not display or presentation, for our engagement in it, or identity with it, will out. When argument is taken as display or presentation, then it eventually becomes a matter of my poster against yours, with the prize to the slickest performance.

If we are to hope for ourselves and to value all others, we must learn that 33 argument is emergence.

8

Argument is emergence toward the other. That requires a readiness to testify to 34 an identity that is always emerging, a willingness to dramatize one's narrative in progress before the other; it calls for an untiring stretch toward the other, a reach toward enfolding the other. It is a risky relevation of the self, for the arguer is asking for an acknowledgment of his or her identity, is asking for witness from the other. In argument, the arguer must plunge on alone, with no assurance of welcome from the other, with no assurance whatever of unconditional positive regard from the other. In argument, the arguer must, with no assurance, go out, inviting the other to enter a world that the arguer tries to make commodious, inviting the other to emerge as well, but with no assurance of kind or even thoughtful response. How does this happen? Better, how can it happen?

It can happen if we learn to love before we disagree. Usually, it's the other way 35 around: if we learn to love, it is only after silence or conflict or both. In ancient times, I was in the United States Army. I spent the better part of 1951 and 1952 in Germany. In those years, American troops were still officially regarded as an Occupation Force, with certain privileges extended, such as free transportation. One service provided was a kind of rental agency in many large cities. On pass or on leave, one could go to this agency and be directed to a room for rent (very cheap) in a private home. Since I was stationed only ten or twelve miles away, I often went to Heidelberg when I had just a weekend pass or a three-day pass. On one such occasion I went to Heidelberg, stopped in at the agency, and got directions to a room that was available. I found the address, a large brownstone just a block off the main street, met the matron of the house, and was taken to a small bedroom on the third floor that would be mine for a couple of days. I left shortly thereafter to go places and do things, paying no particular attention to the room except to notice it was clean and neat. The next morning was clear and bright and cool; I opened the windows and finally began to see the room. A picture on one wall startled me, more, stunned me.

36 On the kitchen wall in my parents' home in Texas there was a picture of my older brother, taken while he was in what was known as the Air Corps in World War II. It was a posed shot of the sort that I suppose most airmen had taken at one time or another to send home to the folks. In the picture, my brother is wearing the airman's favorite of that time, a leather jacket with knit cuffs and a knit band about the waist. He is wearing the old-fashioned leather cap with ear flaps and goggles, and there is a white scarf around his neck, one end tossed over his shoulder. Behind him there is a Consolidated Vultee B-24.

37 The picture on the wall in the bedroom in Heidelberg showed a young man wearing a leather jacket with knit cuffs and a knit band about the waist. He wore an old-fashioned leather cap with ear flaps and goggles, and there is a white scarf around his neck, one end tossed over his shoulder. Behind him there was an airplane; it was a Focke-Wulfe 190. He might have been my brother. After a while, I guess I realized that he *was* my brother.

38 The television news on March 7, 1985, showed a memorial service at Remagen, Germany, marking the fortieth anniversary of the American troops' capture of the Remagen bridge, which let them cross the Rhine. No major world leaders were there, but veterans from both sides had come to look and take notice of the day. American and German veterans who had fought there wept and hugged each other and shook hands.

39 In the mid-fifties, another group of veterans met, to commemorate the fortieth anniversary of the end of battle at Verdun, that hellish landscape where over a million men died to gain or to preserve two or three miles of scrubby country, where no birds sang. They shook hands; they embraced; they wept; they sang an old song that begins, "Ich hatte ein kamaraden."

40 After a while, the hated dead can be mourned, and the old enemy can be embraced.

In these instances, we waited to love (or at least to accept) until long after 41
silence and grim conflict. (I've not lost my head altogether: some conflicts will
not be resolved in time and love—there's always that captain of guards from
Dachau.) Often, we don't learn to love (or at least to accept) at all. All precedents and examples notwithstanding, I'll still insist that argument—that rhetoric itself—must begin, proceed, and end in love.

9

But how is this to happen? How will we argue, or teach argument taken in this 42
way? I don't know, but I'll chance some suggestions.

a. The arguer has to go alone. When argument has gone beyond attempts 43
made by the arguer and by the other to accept and understand, when those early
exploratory steps toward mutual communication are over, or when all of these
stages have been bypassed altogether—as they often will be—then the arguer is
alone, with no assurance at all that the other or any audience will be kindly disposed. When argument comes to advocacy or to adversarial confrontation, the
mutuality that Rogers describes will probably not occur. At the point of advocacy, most particularly at the crisis point in adversarial relationships, the burden
is on the maker of the argument as he or she is making the argument. At the
moment of heat (which may last twenty seconds or twenty years and which may
be feverish and scary), the arguer in all likelihood will not know whether or not
the other, the audience, will choose to take the role of the well-disposed listener
or the kindly therapist. The arguer, alone, must see in the reverence owed to the
other, discover and offer all grace that he or she can muster, and, most especially,
extend every liberty possible to the other. The arguer must hold the other wholly
in mind and yet cherish his or her own identity. *Then*, perhaps, the arguer and
the other may be able to break into mutuality.

b. The arguer must at once hold his or her identity and give it to the 44
other, learning to live—and argue—provisionally. In "Supposing History Is
a Woman—What Then?" (*The American Scholar*, Autumn, 1984), Gertrude
Himmelfarb remarks:

> Whatever "truth or validity" adheres to history . . . does not derive, as the
> conventional historian might assume, from an "objective" world, a world
> of past events waiting to be discovered and reconstructed by the historian.
> For there is no objective world, no historical events independent of the
> experience of the historian, no events or facts which are not also ideas.

We must keep learning as speakers/narrators/arguers (and as hearers). We can
learn to dispense with what we imagined was absolute truth and to pursue the
reality of things only partially knowable. We can learn to keep adding pieces of
knowledge here, to keep rearranging pieces over yonder, to keep standing back

and turning to see how things look elsewhere. We can learn that our narrative/ argument doesn't exist except as it is composed and that the "act of composition can never end," as Doctorow has said.

c. As I have just suggested, we arguers can learn to abandon authoritative positions. They cannot be achieved, at any rate, except as in arrogance, ignorance, and dogma we convince ourselves that we have reached authority. We should not want to achieve an authoritative position, anyway. An authoritative position is a prison both to us and to any audience. [45]

d. We arguers can learn the lessons that rhetoric itself wants to teach us. By its nature, invention asks us to open ourselves to the richness of creation, to plumb its depths, search its expanses, and track its chronologies. But the moment we speak (or write), we are no longer open; we have chosen, whether deliberately or not, and so have closed ourselves off from some possibilities. Invention wants openness; structure and style demand closure. We are asked to be perpetually open and always closing. If we stay open, we cannot speak or act; if we stand closed, we have succumbed to dogma and rigidity. Each utterance may deplete the inventive possibilities if a speaker falls into arrogance, ignorance, or dogma. But each utterance, if the speaker having spoken opens again, may also nurture and replenish the speaker's inventive world and enable him or her to reach out around the other. Beyond any speaker's bound inventive world lies another: there lie the riches of creation, the great, unbounded possible universe of invention. All time is there, past, present, and future. The natural and the supernatural are there. All creation is there, ground and source for invention. The knowledge we have is formed out of the plentitude of creation, which is all before us, but must be sought again and again through the cycling process of rhetoric, closing to speak, opening again to invent again. In an unlimited universe of meaning, we can never foreclose on interpretation and argument. Invention is a name for a great miracle—the attempt to unbind time, to loosen the capacities of time and space into our speaking. This copiousness is eternally there, a plentitude for all. Piaget remarked that the more an infant sees and hears, the more he or she wants to see and hear. Just this is what the cycling of rhetoric offers us: opening to invention, closing to speak, opening again to a richer invention. Utterances may thus be elevated, may grow to hold both arguer and other. [46]

e. We still need to study. There is much about argument that we still have not learned, or that we have not acknowledged. If we are accurate in our evaluation of what happens in conflict, I think we will have to concede that most of what happens is bad. If we know that accurately, we'll be a step farther than we were toward knowing how to deal with contention and the hurts that rise from conflict and argument. We have not at any time in our public or personal histories known consistently how to deal with conflicts, especially when each side or party or view arises normally according to its own variety of thought—and there is no arguer who does not believe that his or her view is a just consequence of normal [47] thought and need. In discourse and behavior, our ways of resolving conflicts have typically been limited and unsatisfactory. When opposing views, each issuing by its own normal processes from its own inventive world, come together in conflict because each wants the same time and space, we usually have only a few ways of handling the conflict:

1. one view prevails, the other subsides;

2. advocates of the two views compromise;

3. the need for action prompts arbitrary selection of one of the two views, even if both are appealing and attractive;

4. we are paralyzed, unable to choose;

5. we go to war; or

6. occasionally, the advocates of one side learn gladly from those of the other and gladly lay down their own views in favor of the other.

To be sure, there are other patterns for resolving conflicts that I haven't had wit enough to recognize; I'd reckon, however, that most are unrewarding to some or all. Once a view emerges—that is, once an inventive process has become structure and style—it cannot wholly subside, as in (1), though it must seem to do so; required by force or expediency to subside, it does not subside but persists underground, festering. Compromise, as in (2), is likely to leave parts of both views hidden away and festering. Deliberate choice between two appealing views, as in (3), leaves the unchosen to grow and compete underground, generating a cynicism that undercuts the chosen argument. Paralysis, as in (4), clearly gives no view gain, though each remains, eating away at the paralyzed agent. War, physical or psychological, is plainly not an appropriate human resolution. In most of these instances there is a thwarted or misplaced or submerged narrative, a normality that may grow wild because it is thwarted, misplaced, or submerged. We have not learned how to let competing normalities live together in the same time and space. We're not sure, we frail humans, that it is possible.

f. The arguer must go alone, unaided by any world of thought, value, and 48 belief except the one that he or she composes in the process of arguing, unassisted by the other because the other is over in a different place, being realized in a different narrative. In my mind, this means that the burden of argument is upon the *ethos* of the arguer. *Ethos*, of course, is a term still poorly understood. Among others, Bator objects to any concentration upon *ethos* because it seems to be "related primarily to adversary situations calling for argumentative strategies designed to persuade others," because "the speaker may be concerned particularly with enhancing her own image or character rather than addressing the issue at hand" (428). Ideally, Bator believes, the subject or problem "is viewed within the audience's framework of values, not simply from the writer's assumptions or premises. The *ethos* of the writer is not the main focus of attention, nor is it the primary means of appeal" (431). This view omits considering the likelihood that *ethos* occurs in various ways; the term does not require to be defined as it has formerly been defined. A genuinely provocative and evocative *ethos* does, in fact, hold the audience wholly in mind, does view matters both as the arguer sees them and as others see them. The self-authenticating language of such an *ethos* issues an invitation into a commodious universe. Argument is partial; when a speaker argues a proposition or develops a theme or makes an assertion, he or she has knowingly or not chosen one proposition, one theme, one assertion from all available. When we speak, we stand somewhere, and our standing place makes both known and silent claims upon us. We make truth, if at all, out of what is incomplete or partial. Language is a closure, but the generative *ethos* I am trying to identify uses language to shove back the restraints of closure, to make a commodious universe, to stretch words out beyond our private universe.

g. We must pile time into argumentative discourse. Earlier, I suggested that 49 in our most grievous and disturbing conflicts, we need time to accept, to understand, to love the other. At crisis points in adversarial relationships, we do not, however, have time; we are already in opposition and confrontation. Since we don't have time, we must rescue time by putting it into our discourses and holding it there, learning to speak and write not argumentative displays and presentations, but arguments full of the anecdotal, personal, and cultural reflections that will make us plain to all others, thoughtful histories and narratives that reveal us as we're reaching for the others. The world, of course, doesn't want time in its discourses. The world wants the quick memo, the rapid-fire electronic mail service; the world wants speed, efficiency, and economy of motion, all goals that, when reached, have given the world less than it wanted or needed. We must teach the world to want otherwise, to want time for care.

10

Rhetoric is love, and it must speak a commodious language, creating a world full 50 of space and time that will hold our diversities. Most failures of communication result from some willful or inadvertent but unloving violation of the space and time we and others live in, and most of our speaking is tribal talk. But there is more to us than that. We can learn to speak a commodious language, and we can learn to hear a commodious language.

Questions for Discussion and Journaling

1. In your own words, what is the problem that Corder is taking up or trying to solve in this article?

2. Consider other pieces you've read so far in this book: Who does Corder sound most like, of the authors you've read? Whom does he sound most unlike? (You can consider either his ideas or his voice and tone in addressing this question.)

3. Corder argues that "each of us is a narrative" (para. 1). What are the main reasons or pieces of evidence supporting this claim?

4. What does Corder mean by the term "steadfast" (para. 17) and how does that term relate to his idea of *emergence*?

5. If you read Downs's article earlier in this chapter (p. 457), you encountered the idea of *adherence* as an alternative to "persuasion." What in Corder's thinking sounds like "adherence" or is reminiscent of that concept?

6. Corder's perspective on argument is that "argument is not something *to present* or *to display*. It is something *to be*. It is what we *are*" (para. 30). What does this perspective have to do with you as a *writer*? How does it connect to other readings you've encountered in this chapter?

7. Corder argues that we have to learn to both hold our identity and to "give it to the other," living and arguing *provisionally* (para. 43). What does "provisional" mean and why would both holding and giving away one's identity be provisional?

8. Can you say the narrative and argument that you are? Can you say how you are emerging, or how you have emerged so far? Can you say how the argument that you are shapes how you interact with the people around you? Can you say how it shapes your choice to come to college, what you want to do while you're here, and where you want to go afterward?

Applying and Exploring Ideas

1. Pay attention to your body: What is your visceral reaction to Corder's argument that people are actually narratives? Do you *like* the idea or not, and how does your body reflect your felt sense about the idea? Write a one- to two-page "felt reflection" that expresses your visceral reactions to the piece and its ideas and considers the values that lead to those feelings. If Corder's ideas sound and feel "right" to you, what values of your own do they align with? If they don't feel good to you, can you see which values of your own they conflict with?

2. Make a list of conflicts you're aware of in the world that seem to be the kind Corder is referring to. (For example, an easy one to think of is the Israel/Palestine conflict.) Choose one conflict from your list and research it in sufficient depth that you can write knowledgeably, respectfully, and meaningfully about it. Now try to write the arguments-as-narratives of three kinds of people involved in the conflict. These may be actual people you've met and talked to,

or people you imagine based on your reading. (You might be involved in the conflict so one of those narratives might be yours, though it doesn't have to be.) Be thoughtful, respectful, and open, trying your best to follow Corder's advice in parts 9(b), (c), and (d) (paras. 44–46). Your class can compare what trying to write the narratives was like and what you've learned about the difficulties and possibilities of doing so.

3. Corder is creating an argument for a very narrow set of readers — teachers and students of rhetoric — who he hopes can be sufficiently convinced of his argument to spread it to other people. Create a plan for introducing your friends and family to this perspective. Apart from (or including) having them read Corder's piece itself, how would you introduce other people to these ideas in ways that could help change their model of argument from agonistic to loving emergence?

- -

META MOMENT   What are some ways that you would behave differently toward others if you adopted Corder's ideas?

- -

Impression Management on Facebook and Twitter

Where Are People More Likely to Share Positivity and Negativity wIth Their Audiences?

ANNALISE SIGONA

Devon Vasquez

Framing the Reading

Annalise Sigona, who wrote this piece as a first-year student at the University of Central Florida, creates a classic study in the social-science mode of research to ask whether (1) college students use Facebook and Twitter for different purposes, (2) whether they are more likely to make negative or positive posts to one or the other social media platforms, and (3) whether they are doing so in order to manage their electronic images. Through surveys and interviews, she is able to develop reasonably concrete answers to these questions, some of which are predictable and some of which are not.

Sigona's study is particularly interesting from a rhetorical perspective because it connects to important principles of contemporary rhetoric, which you will have encountered if you read the chapter introduction or Downs's selection earlier in the chapter. If we look at Sigona's study through the lens of **ecologies**, we can consider media platforms like Twitter or Facebook (or Instagram or Pinterest) as separate and relatively independent rhetorical ecologies. Similarly, while Sigona does not frame her research in terms of *identification* or *ethos*, the questions she raises clearly link to these rhetorical principles. She shows that a significant part of what people are

Sigona, Annalise. "Impression Management on Facebook and Twitter: Where Are People More Likely to Share Positivity and Negativity with Their Audiences?" *Young Scholars in Writing*, vol. 12, 2015, pp. 134–41.

up to on social media is projecting particular self-images — *and*, even more interestingly, not being very self-aware, or at least forthcoming, that they are doing so. So Sigona's work provides a useful platform to wonder about what kinds of *ethos* work social media do for us as rhetors.

You may decide that Sigona's research doesn't involve enough people to be completely reliable. But we think it's important for you to look at the *shape* and *moves* that her study makes because of how good they are for demonstrating how survey- and interview-based research can work and how well they can be written about. Sigona's piece is an excellent model of meaningful, efficient, and highly readable writing about research, and it tells an interesting story.

Getting Ready to Read

Before you read, do at least one of the following activities:

- List the social media you have accounts on, and from among that list, those which you actively use. Then consider *why* you use each of the ones you do. What does each one that you use actively offer you that the others don't?

- Turn to paragraph 7 on page 622, which lists Sigona's eight survey questions, and complete them yourself before you begin.

As you read, consider the following questions:

- Review Swales's CARS model of research introductions (p. 21). Can you trace these "moves" in Sigona's article? Where do you find the territory introduced, the niche in the territory offered, and the niche occupied? (We've also identified some of these moves in articles with the Genre Cue tags; see Assist Tags on pp. 58–59 or Grant-Davie's article in this chapter, starting on p. 484.)

- Which parts of the article are harder for you to make sense of and which are easier? Can you find a pattern in your reactions and reasons for the pattern?

DIGITAL TECHNOLOGY IS UNAVOIDABLE in much of today's world, and   1
it is shaping how people interact with literacy. In this digital age people read
the daily news online, use tablets to read books instead of paperbacks, send text
messages instead of handwritten letters, and spend a lot of their reading time
on social media sites. There has been strong curiosity about literacy and social
media, in particular, especially as social media becomes increasingly prevalent.

According to *The New York Times*, "Now that first impressions are often made in cyberspace, not face-to-face, people are not only strategizing about how to virtually convey who they are, but also grappling with how to craft an e-version of themselves that appeals to multiple audiences"(Rosenbloom). With so many people engaging in social media, its users are left with various audiences to interact with, which may influence how they present themselves.

Numerous researchers have found that typically users do, in fact, manage their impressions on social media. According to communication experts Younbo Jung, Hayeon Song, and Peter Vorderer, impression management, or self-presentation, can be defined as managing how one presents his or herself to others in a desirable way, due to social evaluation and how the impression that others have influence one's social behavior (1627). This idea of impression management on social media sites has been the topic of many in-depth studies, as well as the broader topic behind my own personal research. In looking at why people blog and read others' blogs in the first place, Jung, Song, and Vorderer discovered that impression management was one of two main psychological causes, and that "personal blogs have successfully provided users with a virtual space where they strategically construct their desired identities" (1632), which is applicable to various other types of social media as well.

This idea of strategically constructing desired Identities can also be found in people's postings on Twitter, for example. Researchers Olivier Toubia and Andrew T. Stephen found that image-related utility, which assumes that users are motivated by others' perceptions and is influenced by the number of "followers," was the larger factor in peoples' postings, meaning people who contribute to Twitter often times do so due to image-related causes (368–369). When looking at social media in general terms, communication researchers also found similar evidence of impression management. According to Jian Raymond Rui and Michael A. Stefanone, people who based their self-esteem on how they are judged on social media tactically managed their wall posts and tagged photos (1286). Through studies such as these, it is evident that impression-management exists and is even a common behavior.

It is also apparent that people manage their impressions to appear in a "positive" light at times. In an examination of self-presentation on Facebook, researchers Bazarova, Taft, Choi, and Cosley discovered that in most of the study's participants, status updates contained less negative emotion words than did wall posts and private messages, and that when concern with self-presentation increased, so did the use of positive emotion words in statuses (133). Status updates are shared with the entire audience, so people made fewer negative posts, but were more negative—possibly more honest in their thoughts—when they were able to choose their audience, illustrating that people are careful regarding what they share with their audience as a whole.

Similarly, Baiyun Chen and Justin Marcus discovered that culture and per- 5
sonality play a role in impression management as well. In their study of college
students' self-presentation on Facebook, members of collectivist cultures posted
more to please their audiences than those of individualist cultures, and extro-
verts shared more about themselves than introverts (2091). While Chen and
Marcus focused on collectivist and individualistic cultures, Natalie Pennington,
a graduate student at Kansas State University, looked at the digital native culture.
She analyzed the managing and posting of images, finding that her participants
each had conflicting online identities. She even concluded that these conflicting
identities, likely due to posting for various audiences, depict the Digital Native
generation as a "no consequences" generation, caring more about appearances
than other factors.

Researchers have been able to make strong observations about impression 6
management and how it is influenced by various factors, but there is still much
to be discovered in this field. Despite these robust observations, few researchers have compared impression management on Facebook and Twitter directly,
especially at the college level. This led me to my own research questions: Are
people, particularly first-year students attending my university, more likely to
share positive or negative life events on particular social media sites, particularly
when comparing Facebook and Twitter? If so, is it due to audience? I expected
to find that people would be more comfortable posting freely on Twitter, due to
a more casual audience type than on Facebook. I discovered that not only was
impression management evident, but Twitter and Facebook each have their own
unique audience types, and how people post on each site in regard to positivity
and negativity is different.

METHODS

To address my research questions, I chose to use surveys and personal interviews, 7
which I administered within the first-year student population at my university.
In accordance with University of Central Florida's policy for research conducted
in first-year writing classes, survey respondents and interviewees were informed
of the scope of my project and signed informed consent forms. I posted my
survey of eight questions to an official Facebook group comprised of close to six
thousand first-year students. I used this method because while it only reached
those that were members of this group, the actual participants would be randomly reached within this population, reaching out through social media guar-
anteed Facebook use, and gathering my information from this source would
be sufficient in providing me with the type of data I needed. I also knew that I
would get enough responses from students to be able to draw conclusions from
the data. I collected twenty-four sets of survey data via this Facebook group, plus
an additional three sets of survey results from my three follow-up interviews,

providing me with twenty-seven in total. These twenty-seven surveys addressed the following questions:

1. Who is your typical audience (your "followers") on Twitter? Check all that apply. (*Answer choices included: friends, family, coworkers, classmates, strangers, other (please specify)*)

2. Who is your typical audience (your "friends") on Facebook? Check all that apply. (*Answer choices included: friends, family, coworkers, classmates, strangers, other (please specify)*)

3. Are you concerned with how people perceive you based on your online social media postings? Why or why not?

4. If you lost your job, where would you be more inclined to post about it in any manner? Why? (*Answer choices included: Twitter, Facebook, both, neither*)

5. If you entered into a new relationship you were very excited about, where would you be more inclined to post about it in any manner? Why? (*Answer choices included: Twitter, Facebook, both, neither*)

6. In your opinion, would you say you post more about positive or negative events/thoughts/etc. on Twitter?

7. In your opinion, would you say you post more about positive or negative events/thoughts/etc. on Facebook?

8. Have you ever started to type a status, post a photo, etc. on Facebook or Twitter, but decided not to post it? If so, is it due to what others might think?

I began each of the three interviews with the same survey I posted to the Facebook group, providing me with the three additional sets of survey data, before moving into the actual interview questions. Through the interviews, I was able to get more explanation as to why people post various things on social media, and I was able to look at examples of their posts firsthand. The participants classified their last ten posts on Twitter and Facebook as of the day of the interview as positive, negative, or neutral, in their own opinion. I went back to their social media sites at a later time and also classified their postings as positive, negative, or neutral, as an outside observer. Since how people view positivity and negativity can be slightly different, I did so to see if our classifications were similar or not, and if their perceptions of their postings matched how their audiences may be perceiving them. I conducted these interviews in locations that were convenient for the participant, such as quiet areas in the student union. They took place over the course of a week, and each interview lasted approximately thirty minutes. The questions addressed in the interview were as follows:

1. What do you typically use Twitter for?

2. What do you typically use Facebook for?

3. Have you ever untagged yourself from a post, such as a status, wall post, or photo? Please explain.

4. Think about a time something negative, whether large or small, happened in your life. Did you post about it on social media, and if so, on which sites?

5. As of today's date, look through your last ten posts on Twitter, and your last ten posts of Facebook and classify them as either positive, negative, or neutral, to the best of your ability.

Some of the limitations to my methods included some lack of randomiza- 9 tion in classifying posts and possible bias on the participants' end. The lack of randomization in classifying posts stemmed from the fact that by looking at the ten most recent posts it was random, but not as much as it could have been if there was some way for me to randomly select posts throughout the participants' entire social media history. This would have been difficult to fix since the participants had such high activity and possibly years of use. With regard to bias, people may not have wanted to admit they post negatively. Typically, people engage in self-serving bias, in which they view themselves more favorably than they view others, so they may not have even realized it if they are sharing any negativity. This was a limitation that was difficult to control. Nonetheless, the fact that the results are completely anonymous and are not attached to the participants in this final document should help reduce that potential bias.

RESULTS

Surveys

As displayed in Table 1, the first two survey questions, "Who is your typical 10 audience (your 'followers') on Twitter?" and "Who is your typical audience (your 'friends') on Facebook?" addressed audience types. The *Socialnomics* website states that Facebook is based more on offline relationships and connects people to family, friends, coworkers and acquaintances, while Twitter is based less on personal relationships and more on keeping up with trending topics (Aedy). I wanted to see if this would be reflected in my participants' social media accounts, so that I could later analyze the data to determine any impression management based on audience. My participants tended to have more family and coworkers as "friends" on Facebook than as "followers" on Twitter, and they had more strangers as "followers" on Twitter than as "friends" on Facebook.

When asked the third survey question, "Are you concerned with how people 11 perceive you based on your online social media postings? Why or why not," sixteen participants (59.3%) said no, and eleven (40.7%) said yes. While the fifteen responses varied as to why, there were several typical responses. The typical "no" was

TABLE 1 AUDIENCE TYPES (QUESTIONS ONE AND TWO OF SURVEY)

SITE	FRIENDS	FAMILY	COWORKERS	CLASSMATES	STRANGERS
Twitter	26/27	7/27	2/27	17/27	16/27
	96.3%	26%	7.4%	63%	59.3%
Facebook	27/27	26/27	10/27	18/27	3/27
	100%	96.3%	37%	66.7%	11.1%

because the participant is not concerned with what others think of him or her, and the typical "yes" was because he or she does not want to post anything that would hurt others or him/herself in the future. A few participants answered "yes" or "no," but when asked to explain, they said they really saw both sides. For instance, one survey participant stated, "Both yes and no. I'm not afraid to be myself on social media, but I try not to post things that could hurt me in the future."

Like question three, survey question eight also addressed concern over what   12
others think, but focused on such concerns in a less direct manner. Participants were asked, "Have you ever started to type a status, post a photo, etc. on Facebook or Twitter, but decided not to post it? If so, is it due what others might think?" Fifteen participants (55.6%) answered "yes," four participants (14.8%) answered "no," while five participants (18.5%) answered "depends," and three participants (11.1%) answered that the situation did not apply to them. This question yielded potentially conflicting results when compared to question three, which will be addressed in the discussion section of this article.

Tying back to the study by Bazarova, et al. regarding positivity and negativity   13
on Facebook, questions four and five addressed a positive event and a negative event and whether or not the participant would post about it and, if so, where he or she would post. When asked, "If you lost your job, where would you be more inclined to post about it in any manner? Why?" as the negative event, seven participants said they would post about it on Twitter, one said Facebook, two said both sites, and seventeen said neither. When asked, "If you entered into a new relationship you were very excited about, where would you be more inclined to post about it in any manner? Why?" as the positive event, five participants said they would post about it on Twitter, fourteen said Facebook, three said both sites, and five said neither. Most answered "Facebook." More participants would post solely about the negative event on Twitter than on Facebook, 25.9% compared to 3.7%, and more participants would post solely about the positive event on Facebook than on Twitter, 51.9% compared to 18.5%.

Questions six and seven addressed how the participants perceive themselves   14
to post on Facebook and Twitter, whether positively or negatively. In regard to posting on Twitter, twelve (44.4%) said they post more positive, six (22.2%)

said more negative, and nine (33.3%) said equally negative and positive events/thoughts/etc. In regard to posting on Facebook, twenty-two (81.5%) said they post more positive, zero said more negative, and five (19%) said equally negative and positive events/thoughts/etc. More people said they post negatively or equally negatively and positively on Twitter than on Facebook.

Interviews

Interview participants said they use Twitter to vent, share thoughts or funny 15 occurrences, or simply to retweet others' posting about topics of interest. They use Facebook to keep people up to date with their lives and communicate with certain people. They tended not to untag themselves from posts, although one participant said she would untag herself from a photo if she did not like how she looked, but not for any other reason. The first two participants said that when negative events happen, they may post about them on Twitter. Participant one stated, "Usually when anything bad happens, I'll just post about it on Twitter, but try to be funny about it so it doesn't come off too negatively," but the third participant said he probably would not post about it on social media at all.

The results of their self-classification of their ten most recent posts on each 16 site show that the third participant is an outlier when compared to the other two. Participants one and two showed that while these ten postings on Twitter did not vary much numerically in positivity versus negativity, they varied a lot when compared to Facebook. Facebook tended to have almost all positive postings. My own classifications of these posts were extremely similar, in fact almost identical, more precisely. When classifying their ten most recent posts on Facebook and Twitter themselves, the results, out of ten posts, are indicated in Table 2.

TABLE 2 SELF-CLASSIFICATIONS OF POSTS (QUESTION FIVE OF SURVEY)

TWITTER	POSITIVE	NEGATIVE	NEUTRAL
Participant 1	3	3	4
Participant 2	5	4	1
Participant 3	10	0	0
FACEBOOK	POSITIVE	NEGATIVE	NEUTRAL
Participant 1	8	0	2
Participant 2	9	0	1
Participant 3	9	1	0

DISCUSSION

The findings of this study fortify the theories from numerous other impression 17
management studies, in that significant evidence of impression management
was found. Not only was impression management evident showing that people
care about how they are perceived online, but I discovered that Twitter and
Facebook each have their own unique audience types. Similarly, how people
post on each site, positively or negatively, is very different. These findings imply
that what people see about others on social media may be strategically planned,
whether consciously or somewhat unconsciously. It is important to be aware of
these results, as people choose which social media to interact on and with whom.

Concern with Perception

Like the research mentioned in my literature review, I also discovered through 18
my participants that people care about how others perceive them online. Based
on the robust findings of impression management research discussed previously, I
anticipated a trend in which people engage in a good deal of impression management on Facebook and Twitter. When asked directly, "Are you concerned with
how people perceive you based on your online social media postings?" 59.3% of
participants said "no," and 40.7% said "yes." This is close to a 6:4 ratio, so there
was a definite distinction. More people claimed to not care about what others
think of them based on what they post online, but when asked less directly
with the question, "Have you ever started to type a status, post a photo, etc. on
Facebook or Twitter, but decided not to post it? If so, is it due what others might
think?" 55.6% of participants answered "yes." 59.3% of participants claimed not
to care about others' perceptions in the previous question, but in the later questions 55.6% admitted that they chose not to post something due to what others
may think. Only 14.8% said "no," that is not why they did not post; 18.5% said
it "depends;" and 11.1% said they had never even been in that situation. There
is a contradiction between the results of the two questions. In the earlier question, only 40.7% said they were concerned with how people perceive them on
social media, but in the later question, 55.6% said they did not post something
due to what people would think. Because the earlier question was more direct,
people could easily provide an answer to appear a certain way for the study, but
in the later question they were probably more honest. This leads me to believe
that people may want to appear like they do not care about others' perceptions
of them based on social media postings, but that they probably really do care.

Audience Types

I found that my hypothesis about audience types on each site was accurate. I 19
hypothesized that Twitter users would tend to have an audience of more friends

and strangers than family members and coworkers, and that due to this, people would post more negatively on Twitter than on Facebook because they might be more comfortable being open and honest with the audience. People might be more careful about what they post when family and coworkers can see it than when it is mostly friends and strangers because of harsher judgment or because people could possibly get into trouble if their postings were seen by particular people. These ideas can be reflected in the comments of some of my participants. For instance, one survey participant stated, "Facebook is more of a photo outlet than anything for me. Twitter is where I express my opinions/ feelings." It is likely that this person shares photos of positive life events on Facebook, while he or she speaks true thoughts through Twitter. Another participant stated, "[Twitter is] more casual; Facebook is more for family," showing a level of comfort in sharing on Twitter that may not exist on Facebook, due to audience type. Steve Aedy, one of *Socialnomics'* journalists, stated, "Facebook users connect with friends, family, colleagues and other acquaintances," and the results directly support this idea.

My thoughts about the types of audiences each site would have were accurate 20 for my population. Out of the twenty-seven people who completed the survey, only seven had "followers" on Twitter that were family, while twenty-six had family members as "friends" on Facebook. On Twitter, only two had coworkers as "followers" but on Facebook, ten had coworkers as "friends." As a whole, participants had more strangers as "followers" on Twitter than as "friends" on Facebook—sixteen out of twenty-seven participants when compared to just three out of twenty-seven. These are big differences that were reflected in a small population. Knowing that these differences in audience exist, I analyzed the rest of the data to determine if the differences correlated to types of postings in any way.

Facebook Versus Twitter: Positivity and Negativity

There was a significant difference in how people posted on Facebook versus 21 how they posted on Twitter. Like Bazarova and her colleagues, who concluded that people were careful about sharing positive and negative status updates, wall posts, and private messages, I found that most of my participants were careful about posting positive and negative events, as noted in survey questions four and five. More participants would post about the negative event on Twitter than on Facebook, and more participants would post about the positive event on Facebook than on Twitter. Since participants tended to use Twitter to share thoughts or sometimes even vent, and Facebook is so family-centered, it makes sense that the outcome was as such. A limitation to these results, though not very significant, is that the specific negative and positive event examples I used have different connotations for different people. Had I used different events, such as failing a test and winning the lottery, for example, maybe results would be slightly different. Even so, I do believe the trend would ultimately be similar.

The survey also indicated that more participants felt that posts about neg- 22 ative thoughts and events belonged on Twitter than on Facebook. Questions six and seven directly asked how the participant thought he or she posted on each site—more positive, negative, or equally positive and negative thoughts, events, etc. Six participants (22.2%) said they post more negatively on Twitter, and nine (33.3%) said equally positive and negative. While on Facebook, absolutely no participants said they post more negative things on Facebook, and only five (19%) said they post equally positive and negative things. This, too, is an astounding difference between the two social media sites. To further exhibit this trend within the study, when the interview participants classified their own postings as positive, negative, or neutral, they posted negatively more on Twitter than on Facebook. When combining the ten results of each of the three participants, Facebook had twenty-seven out of thirty posts as positive, and only one negative, while Twitter had seven negative posts and only eighteen positive posts in total.

CONCLUSION

The results of this study indicate that within the first-year student population 23 at my university, impression management takes place on both Facebook and Twitter, which is comparable to results found in prior research studies. These students tended to post more negatively on Twitter than on Facebook, which I have discovered has a strong correlation with audience type. More participants had family members and coworkers as "friends" on Facebook than on Twitter, making it less likely that they would share negative thoughts, events, and other postings on Facebook. Participants, even if they did not realize it at times, were trying to appear in different ways to different audience groups.

The findings of this study can be applicable to society as a whole, and fur- 24 ther research can be done to see if these results hold true in other settings and with larger data pools. Both my research and the research of those prior have found that culture and personality, as well as audience type, influence impression management, but it would be worthwhile to see if gender plays a role in whether someone posts more positively or negatively. This thought arose when I realized that the male interview participant was significantly more positive in his postings than the two female interview participants. It would be interesting to see if this would be a consistent finding in others or if it merely ties back to personality's role in impression management, as studied by Chen and Marcus.

By looking at the results of not only my study, but the previous impres- 25 sion management studies, it is clear that how we perceive others online is not always reality. It is easy to show others what we want to show them, such as

Zilla van den Born's 2014 experiment in which she faked vacation photos from a five-week trip to Southeast Asia, fooling most of her friends and family through social media (Cooper). People typically want to appear exciting and interesting and choose the best photos of themselves to post. These types of actions, which vary on different social media sites, can create false expectations of what we should be like and can make us wonder why we are not as "happy" or "attractive" as others. While people put their best "cyber face" forward, the best way to get to really know a person's online identity would be to interact with them on multiple sites, as they post to please their multiple audiences. By "friending" someone on Facebook and "following" someone on Twitter, for instance, you will get not only the positive experiences, but possibly the more honest, and sometimes not so happy ones as well.

> *While people put their best "cyber face" forward, the best way to get to really know a person's online identity would be to interact with them on multiple sites, as they post to please their multiple audiences.*

Works Cited

Aedy, Steve. "Facebook vs. Twitter: Know Whom You're Writing For." *Socialnomics.* Erik Qualman. 15 Mar. 2013. Web. 8 Mar. 2014.

Bazarova, Natalya, Jessie Taft, Yoon Hyung Choi, and Dan Cosley. "Managing Impressions and Relationships on Facebook: Self-Presentational and Relational Concerns Revealed Through the Analysis of Language Style." *Journal of Language and Social Psychology* 32.2 (2012): 120–41. Print.

Chen, Baiyun and Justin Marcus. "Students' Self-presentation on Facebook: An Examination of Personality and Self-construal Factors." *Computers in Human Behavior* 28.6 (2012): 2091–99. Print.

Cooper, Brittany Jones. "Fake it 'Til You Make it: Woman Uses Photoshop to Create Phony Vacation Photos." *Yahoo! Travel.* Yahoo! 9 Sep. 2014. Web. 16 Sep. 2014.

Jung, Younbo, Hayeon Song, and Peter Vorderer. "Why do People Post and Read Personal Messages in Public? The Motivation of Using Personal Blogs and its Effects on Users' Loneliness, Belonging, and Well-being." *Computers in Human Behavior* 28.5 (2012): 1626–33. Print.

Pennington, Natalie R. D. *No Consequences: An Analysis of Images and Impression Management on Facebook.* MA thesis. Kansas State University, 2010. Web. 8 Mar. 2014.

Rosenbloom, Stephanie. "Putting Your Best Cyberface Forward." *NY Times.* The New York Times. 3 Jan. 2008. Web. 8 Mar. 2014.

Rui, Jian Raymond, and Michael A. Stefanone. "Strategic Image Management Online: Self-presentation, Self-esteem and Social Network Perspectives." *Information, Communication & Society* 16.8 (2013): 1286–1305. Print.

Toubia, Olivier, and Andrew T. Stephen. "Intrinsic versus Image-Related Utility in Social Media: Why Do People Contribute Content to Twitter?" *Marketing Science* 32.3 (2013): 368–92. Print.

Questions for Discussion and Journaling

1. How does Sigona explain where her research question emerges from and how it relates to the existing research? What is the connection?

2. How do your own answers to Sigona's questions (if you are a social media user) align with those of her respondents? Are yours typical of the responses she got? If not, how do they differ?

3. How good is Sigona's evidence for her claim that "people may want to appear like they do not care about others' perceptions of them based on social media postings, but . . . they probably really do care" (para. 18)? How did she arrive at this conclusion?

4. Do you think that Sigona is suggesting that people are more willing to show their "true," not-completely-positive selves to strangers than to family and friends? If so, do you agree with her? Do you think there is something about the particular rhetorical work of these social media ecologies that make this the case?

5. As a rhetorical thinker who is therefore concerned with what image you present for others to identify with, what kinds of strategies, "rules," or habits do you have for presenting yourself on social media?

6. Research like Sigona's suggests that social media are a very powerful tool for managing our images. How does rhetorical theory, as you understand it, predict that we would use it this way?

Applying and Exploring Ideas

1. Pick your favorite (or preferred) social media platform and describe it as a rhetorical ecology. An *ecology* is an interrelated network of elements that all rely on each other, shape each other, and interact with each other to make the overall ecology what it is. The network makes the sustenance of each of its elements possible. How would you describe your social media platform in these terms? What are its elements — both human and material? How are they related to and dependent on each other?

2. Write an analysis of "social contracts" that exist on your social media. Are there ideals or "rules" or "standards" that you and your friends or followers have for what should or shouldn't be posted, or how? How did those ideals emerge? How did you come to be aware of or learn them? How often are they broken, and under what circumstances can this happen?

META MOMENT   How does Sigona's research help you think about the ways that rhetoric can apply to all of your interactions, not just those in specific locations or moments like school or work?

From Pencils to Pixels

The Stages of Literacy Technologies

DENNIS BARON

Photograph by Rachel Baron

Framing the Reading

Dennis Baron is a linguist who has studied **literacy**, communication technologies, and the laws countries make about language use (like making English the "official" language of the United States). In this essay, which developed material he later used in his 2009 book *A Better Pencil: Readers, Writers, and the Digital Revolution*, Baron examines the history of a few writing technologies that we are unlikely to even recognize *as* "technology" anymore. In thinking, for example, about how pencils were once state-of-the-art technology, Baron suggests that writing was never *not* technological, that every writing technology has taken time to become established, and that writing technologies must be learned.

We consider writing technologies in a chapter that explores rhetorical theory because taking a rhetorical perspective on writing technology is crucial to several threshold concepts in this book. *All writers have more to learn*, in part because writing technologies now change almost too quickly to keep up with, and so do each technology's own rhetorical implications. *What makes writing "good" in a given rhetorical situation depends* in part on what writing technologies are available. That is, technology is part of rhetorical **contingence**. Technology is also one of the *constraints which accompany all writing and rhetorical situations*. And so we look at writing technologies as a rhetorical phenomenon: motivated, situated, contingent, interactional, epistemic, and embodied. Technology is what turns ephemeral thoughts into tangible, material writing.

Baron's work raises more questions than it answers, but in doing so it shows us how comparatively limited the research has been at the intersection of technology

Baron, Dennis. "From Pencils to Pixels: The Stages of Literacy Technologies." *Passions, Pedagogies, and 21st Century Technologies*, edited by Gail Hawisher and Cynthia Selfe, Utah State UP, 1999, pp. 15–33.

and literacy. When Baron wrote in the late 90s, he could argue that literacy research-ers had largely failed to understand writing *as a technology*; as a result, he argued, they didn't really understand what we're actually doing when we write. (His argu-ment, among others, has prompted much more research along these lines in the ensuing two decades.) In using historical explanations and discussion of writing tools that many of us no longer recognize as technological to begin with, Baron raises interesting questions about the future of writing. What will happen when the computers we use now are no longer really recognized as "unnatural" technolo-gies? As we write this edition, smartphones, tablets, and "phablets" are now ubiq-uitous, our televisions and other screen-based devices are beginning to watch *us*, and "wearable technology" that brings computer processors directly onto and into the body are beginning to emerge — all altering our perception of the relationship between humanity and technology. How will that altered perception influence how we write?

Getting Ready to Read

Before you read, do at least one of the following activities:

- Write your own definition of "technology," and provide some examples. What kinds of things count as technology, and what don't?

- Make a quick list of all the technologies you use for writing.

- Talk with a parent or grandparent about what writing technologies were dominant when they were in school. How do those technologies compare with the ones you use today?

As you read, consider the following questions:

- For Baron, what counts as a technology?

- How do literacy technologies empower some people and disempower others?

- What does Baron seem to want us to learn from his work?

- How does the authenticity Baron talks about relate to literacy?

THE COMPUTER, THE LATEST development in writing technology, promises, 1 or threatens, to change literacy practices for better or worse, depending on your point of view. For many of us, the computer revolution came long ago, and it has left its mark on the way we do things with words. We take word processing as a given. We don't have typewriters in our offices anymore, or pencil sharpeners, or even printers with resolutions less than 300 dpi. We scour *MacUser* and *PC World* for the next software upgrade, cheaper RAM, faster chips, and the latest in connectivity. We can't wait for the next paradigm shift. Computerspeak enters ordinary English at a rapid pace. In 1993, "the information superhighway" was voted the word—actually the phrase—of the year. In 1995, the word of the year was "the World Wide Web," with "morph" a close runner-up. The computer is also touted as a gateway to literacy. The Speaker of the House of Representatives suggested that inner-city school children should try laptops to improve their performance. The Governor of Illinois thinks that hooking up every school classroom to the Web will eliminate illiteracy. In his second-term victory speech, President Clinton promised to have every eight-year-old reading, and to connect every twelve-year-old to the National Information Infrastructure. Futurologists write books predicting that computers will replace books. Newspapers rush to hook online subscribers. The *New York Times* will download the Sunday crossword puzzle, time me as I fill in the answers from my keyboard, even score my results. They'll worry later about how to get me to pay for this service.

I will not join in the hyperbole of predictions about what the computer will 2 or will not do for literacy, though I will be the first to praise computers, to acknowledge the importance of the computer in the last fifteen years of my own career as a writer, and to predict that in the future the computer will be put to communication uses we cannot now even begin to imagine, something quite beyond the word processing I'm now using to produce a fairly conventional text, a book chapter.

I readily admit my dependence on the new technology of writing. Once, called 3 away to a meeting whose substance did not command my unalloyed attention, I began drafting on my conference pad a memo I needed to get out to my staff by lunchtime. I found that I had become so used to composing virtual prose at the keyboard I could no longer draft anything coherent directly onto a piece of paper. It wasn't so much that I couldn't think of the words, but the physical effort of handwriting, crossing out, revising, cutting and pasting (which I couldn't very well do at a meeting without giving away my inattention), in short, the writing practices I had been engaged in regularly since the age of four, now seemed to overwhelm and constrict me, and I longed for the flexibility of digitized text.

> *Whether it consists of energized particles on a screen or ink embedded in paper or lines gouged into clay tablets, writing itself is always first and foremost a technology, a way of engineering materials in order to accomplish an end.*

When we write with cutting-edge tools, it is 4 easy to forget that whether it consists of energized particles on a screen or ink embedded in paper or lines gouged into clay tablets, writing itself is always first and foremost a technology, a way of engineering materials in order to accomplish an end. Tied up as it is with value-laden notions of literacy, art, and science, of history and psychology, of education, of theory, and of practicality, we often lose sight of writing as technology, until, that is, a new technology like the computer comes along and we are thrown into excitement and confusion as we try it on, try it out, reject it, and then adapt it to our lives—and of course, adapt our lives to it.

New communications technologies, if they catch on, go through a number 5 of strikingly similar stages. After their invention, their spread depends on accessibility, function, and authentication. Let me first summarize what I mean, and then I'll present some more detailed examples from the history of writing or literacy technologies to illustrate.

THE STAGES OF LITERACY TECHNOLOGIES

Each new literacy technology begins with a restricted communication func- 6 tion and is available only to a small number of initiates. Because of the high cost of the technology and general ignorance about it, practitioners keep it to themselves at first—either on purpose or because nobody else has any use for it—and then, gradually, they begin to mediate the technology for the general public. The technology expands beyond this "priestly" class when it is adapted to familiar functions often associated with an older, accepted form of communication. As costs decrease and the technology becomes better able to mimic more ordinary or familiar communications, a new literacy spreads across a population. Only then does the technology come into its own, no longer imitating the previous forms given us by the earlier communication technology, but creating new forms and new possibilities for communication. Moreover, in a kind of backward wave, the new technology begins to affect older technologies as well.

While brave new literacy technologies offer new opportunities for producing 7 and manipulating text, they also present new opportunities for fraud. And as the technology spreads, so do reactions against it from supporters of what are purported to be older, simpler, better, or more honest ways of writing. Not only must the new technology be accessible and useful, it must demonstrate its trustworthiness as well. So procedures for authentication and reliability must be developed before the new technology becomes fully accepted. One of the greatest concerns about computer communications today involves their authentication and their potential for fraud.

My contention in this essay is a modest one: the computer is simply the 8 latest step in a long line of writing technologies. In many ways its development parallels that of the pencil—hence my title—though the computer seems more complex and is undoubtedly more expensive. The authenticity of pencil writing is still frequently questioned: we prefer that signatures and other permanent or validating documents be in ink. Although I'm not aware that anyone actually opposed the use of pencils when they began to be used for writing, other literacy technologies, including writing itself, were initially met with suspicion as well as enthusiasm.

HUMANISTS AND TECHNOLOGY

In attacking society's growing dependence on communication technology, the Unabomber (1996) targeted computer scientists for elimination. But to my chagrin he excluded humanists from his list of sinister technocrats because he found them to be harmless. While I was glad not to be a direct target of this mad bomber, I admit that I felt left out. I asked myself, if humanists aren't harmful, then what's the point of being one? But I was afraid to say anything out loud, at least until a plausible suspect was in custody. 9

Humanists have long been considered out of the technology loop. They use technology, to be sure, but they are not generally seen as pushing the envelope. Most people think of writers as rejecting technological innovations like the computer and the information superhighway, preferring instead to bang away at manual typewriters when they are not busy whittling new points on their no. 2 quill pens. 10

And it is true that some well-known writers have rejected new-fangleness. Writing in the *New York Times*, Bill Henderson (1994) reminds us that in 1849 Henry David Thoreau disparaged the information superhighway of his day, a telegraph connection from Maine to Texas. As Thoreau put it, "Maine and Texas, it may be, have nothing important to communicate." Henderson, who is a director of the Lead Pencil Club, a group opposed to computers and convinced that the old ways are better, further boasts that Thoreau wrote his anti-technology remarks with a pencil that he made himself. Apparently Samuel Morse, the developer of the telegraph, was lucky that the only letter bombs Thoreau made were literary ones. 11

In any case, Thoreau was not the complete Luddite that Henderson would have us believe. He was, in fact, an engineer, and he didn't make pencils for the same reason he went to live at Walden Pond, to get back to basics. Rather, he designed them for a living. Instead of waxing nostalgic about the good old days of hand-made pencils, Thoreau sought to improve the process by developing a cutting-edge manufacturing technology of his own. 12

The pencil may be old, but like the computer today and the telegraph in 1849, it is an indisputable example of a communication technology. Henderson, unwittingly concedes as much when he adds that Thoreau's father founded "the first quality pencil [factory] in America." In Thoreau's day, a good pencil was hard to find, and until Thoreau's father and uncle began making pencils in the New World, the best ones were imported from Europe. The family fortune was 13 built on the earnings of the Thoreau Pencil Company, and Henry Thoreau not only supported his sojourn at Walden Pond and his trip to the Maine woods with pencil profits, he himself perfected some of the techniques of pencil-making that made Thoreau pencils so desirable.

The pencil may seem a simple device in contrast to the computer, but although 14 it has fewer parts, it too is an advanced technology. The engineer Henry Petroski (1990) portrays the development of the wood-cased pencil as a paradigm of the engineering process, hinging on the solution of two essential problems: finding the correct blend of graphite and clay so that the "lead" is not too soft or too brittle; and getting the lead into the cedar wood case so that it doesn't break when the point is sharpened or when pressure is applied during use. Pencil technologies involve advanced design techniques, the preparation and purification of graphite, the mixing of graphite with various clays, the baking and curing of the lead mixture, its extrusion into leads, and the preparation and finishing of the wood casings. Petroski observes that pencil making also involves a knowledge of dyes, shellacs, resins, clamps, solvents, paints, woods, rubber, glue, printing ink, waxes, lacquer, cotton, drying equipment, impregnating processes, high-temperature furnaces, abrasives, and mixing (Petroski 12). These are no simple matters. A hobbyist cannot decide to make a wood-cased pencil at home and go out to the craft shop for a set of instructions. Pencil-making processes were from the outset proprietary secrets as closely guarded as any Macintosh code.

The development of the pencil is also a paradigm of the development of lit- 15 eracy. In the two hundred fifty years between its invention, in the 1560s, and its perfection at John Thoreau and Company, as well as in the factories of Conté in France, and Staedtler and Faber in Germany, the humble wood pencil underwent several changes in form, greatly expanded its functions, and developed from a curiosity of use to cabinet-makers, artists and note-takers into a tool so universally employed for writing that we seldom give it any thought.

THE TECHNOLOGY OF WRITING

Of course the first writing technology was writing itself. Just like the telegraph 16 and the computer, writing itself was once an innovation strongly resisted by traditionalists because it was unnatural and untrustworthy. Plato was one leading thinker who spoke out strongly against writing, fearing that it would weaken our memories. Pessimistic complaints about new literacy technologies, like those made by Plato, by Bill Henderson, and by Henderson's idol, Henry David Thoreau, are balanced by inflated predictions of how technologies will change our lives for the better. According to one school of anthropology, the invention of writing triggered a cognitive revolution in human development (for a critique of this so-called Great Divide theory of writing, see Street 1984). Historians of print are fond of pointing to the invention of the printing press in Europe as the second great cognitive revolution (Eisenstein 1979). The spread of electric power, the invention of radio, and later television, all promised similar bio-cultural progress. Now, the influence of computers on more and more aspects of our existence has led futurologists to proclaim that another technological threshold is at hand. Computer gurus offer us a brave new world of communications where we will experience cognitive changes of a magnitude never before known. Of course, the Unabomber and the Lead Pencil Club think otherwise.

Both the supporters and the critics of new communication technologies like 17 to compare them to the good, or bad, old days. Jay Bolter disparages the typewriter as nothing more than a machine for duplicating texts—and as such, he argues, it has not changed writing at all. In contrast, Bolter characterizes the computer as offering a paradigm shift not seen since the invention of the printing press, or for that matter, since the invention of writing itself. But when the typewriter first began to sweep across America's offices, it too promised to change writing radically, in ways never before imagined. So threatening was the typewriter to the traditional literates that in 1938 the *New York Times* editorialized against the machine that depersonalized writing, usurping the place of "writing with one's own hand."

The development of writing itself illustrates the stages of technological 18 spread. We normally assume that writing was invented to transcribe speech, but that is not strictly correct. The earliest Sumerian inscriptions, dating from ca. 3500 BCE, record not conversations, incantations, or other sorts of oral utterances, but land sales, business transactions, and tax accounts (Crystal 1987). Clay tokens bearing similar marks appear for several thousand years before these first inscriptions. It is often difficult to tell when we are dealing with writing and when with art (the recent discovery of 10,000-year-old stone carvings in Syria has been touted as a possible missing link in the art-to-writing chain), but the tokens seem to have been used as a system of accounting from at least the 9th millennium BCE. They are often regarded as the first examples of writing, and it is clear that they are only distantly related to actual speech (see figure 1).

We cannot be exactly sure why writing was invented, but just as the gurus of 19 today's technology are called computer geeks, it's possible that the first writers also seemed like a bunch of oddballs to the early Sumerians, who might have called them cuneiform geeks. Surely they walked around all day with a bunch of sharp styluses sticking out of their pocket protectors, and talked of nothing but new ways of making marks on stones. Anyway, so far as we know, writing itself begins not as speech transcription but as a relatively restricted and obscure record-keeping shorthand.

As innovative uses for the literacy technology are tried out, practitioners may 20 also adapt it to older, more familiar forms in order to gain acceptance from a wider group. Although writing began as a tool of the bean counters, it eventually added a second, magical/religious function, also restricted and obscure as a tool

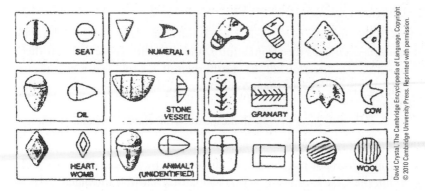

Figure 1 Clay Tokens and Sumerian Inscriptions Some of the commonest shapes are here compared with the incised characters in the earliest Sumerian inscriptions (only some of which have been interpreted) (Crystal 1987, 196).

of priests. For writing to spread into a more general population in the ancient world, it had first to gain acceptance by approximating spoken language. Once writers—in a more "modern" sense of the word—discovered what writing could do, there was no turning back. But even today, most written text does not transcribe spoken language: the comparison of script and transcript in figure 2 makes this abundantly clear.

Of course writing never spread very greatly in the ancient world. William 21 Harris (1989) argues convincingly that no more than ten percent of the classical Greek or Roman populations could have been literate. One reason for this must be that writing technology remained both cumbersome and expensive: writing instruments, paints, and inks had to be hand made, and writing surfaces like clay tablets, wax tablets, and papyrus had to be laboriously prepared. Writing therefore remained exclusive, until cheap paper became available, and the printing press made mass production of written texts more affordable and less labor-intensive.

WHAT WRITING DOES DIFFERENTLY

As a literacy technology like writing begins to become established, it also goes 22 beyond the previous technology in innovative, often compelling ways. For example, while writing cannot replace many speech functions, it allows us to communicate in ways that speech does not. Writing lacks such tonal cues of the human voice as pitch and stress, not to mention the physical cues that accompany face to face communication, but it also permits new ways of bridging time and space. Conversations become letters. Sagas become novels. Customs become legal codes. The written language takes on a life of its own, and it even begins to influence how the spoken language is used. To cite an obvious example, people

Scripted dialogue:

Thersites: The common curse of mankind, folly and ignorance, be thine in great revenue! heaven bless thee from a tutor, and discipline come not near thee! Let thy blood be thy direction till thy death! then, if she that lays thee out says thou art a fair corpse, I'll be sworn and sworn upon't she never shrouded any but lazars. Amen.

Shakespeare, Troilus and Cressida, II, iii, 30.

Unscripted dialogue (ostensibly):

Lt. Col North: I do not recall a specific discussion. But, I mean. It was widely known within the CIA. I mean we were tracking that sensitive intelligence. I—I honestly don't recall, Mr. Van Cleve. I mean it—it didn't seem to me, at the time, that it was something that I was trying to hide from anybody. I was not engaged in it. And one of the purposes that I thought we had that finding for was to go back and ratify that earlier action, and to get on with replenishing. I mean, that was one—what I understood one of the purposes of the draft to be.

from Taking the Stand: The Testimony of Lt. Col. Oliver North, 15

Figure 2 Script and Transcript

begin to reject traditional pronunciations in favor of those that reflect a word's spelling: the pronunciation of the "l" in falcon (compare the l-less pronunciation of the cognate name Faulkner) and the "h" in such "th" combinations as *Anthony* and *Elizabeth* (compare the nicknames *Tony* and *Betty,* which reflect the earlier, h-less pronunciation).

In order to gain acceptance, a new literacy technology must also develop 23 a means of authenticating itself. Michael Clanchy (1993) reports that when writing was introduced as a means of recording land transfer in 11th-century England, it was initially perceived (and often rightly so) as a nasty Norman trick for stealing Saxon land.

As Clanchy notes, spoken language was easily corroborated: human witnesses 24 were interactive. They could be called to attest whether or not a property transfer had taken place. Doubters could question witnesses, watch their eyes, see whether witnesses sank when thrown bound into a lake. Written documents did not respond to questions—they were not interactive. So the writers and users of documents had to develop their own means of authentication. At first, seals, knives, and other symbolic bits of property were attached to documents in an attempt to give them credibility. Medieval English land transfers also adopted the format of texts already established as trustworthy, the Bible or the prayer book, complete with illuminations, in order to convince readers of their validity.

Questions of validity came up because writing was indeed being used to 25 perpetrate fraud. Monks, who controlled writing technology in England at the time, were also responsible for some notorious forgeries used to snatch land from private owners. As writing technology developed over the centuries, additional ways of authenticating text came into use. Individualistic signatures eventually replaced seals to the extent that today, many people's signatures differ significantly from the rest of their handwriting. Watermarks identified the provenance of paper; dates and serial numbers further certify documents, and in the absence of other authenticators, stylistic analysis may allow us to guess at authorship on the basis of comparative and internal textual evidence. In the digital age, we are faced with the interesting task of reinventing appropriate ways to validate cybertext.

THE PENCIL AS TECHNOLOGY

Just as writing was not designed initially as a way of recording speech, the pen- 26 cil was not invented to be a writing device. The ancient lead-pointed stylus was used to scribe lines—the lead made a faint pencil-like mark on a surface, suitable for marking off measurements but not for writing. The modern pencil, which holds not lead but a piece of graphite encased in a wooden handle, doesn't come on the scene until the 1560s.

The 16th-century pencil consists of a piece of graphite snapped or shaved 27 from a larger block, then fastened to a handle for ease of use. The first pencils were made by joiners, woodworkers specializing in making furniture, to scribe measurements in wood. Unlike the traditional metal-pointed scribing tools, pencils didn't leave a permanent dent in the wood. By the time Gesner observed the pencil, it had been adopted as a tool by note-takers, natural scientists, or others who needed to write, sketch, or take measurements in the field. Carrying pens and ink pots outdoors was cumbersome. Early pencils had knobs at one end so that they could be fastened with string or chain to a notebook, creating the precursor to the laptop computer.

Pencils were also of use to artists. In fact the word pencil means "little tail," 28 and refers not only to the modern wood-cased pencil but to the artist's brush. Ink and paint are difficult to erase: they must be scraped off a surface with a knife, or painted over. But graphite pencil marks were more easily erased by using bread crumbs, and of course later by erasers made of rubber—in fact the eraser substance (caoutchouc, the milky juice of tropical plants such as ficus) was called rubber because it was used to rub out pencil marks.

THOREAU AND PENCIL TECHNOLOGY

It is true that Thoreau rejected modern improvements like the telegraph as 29 worthless illusions. In *Walden* he says, "They are but improved means to an unimproved end." Thoreau did not write much of pencils. He even omitted the pencil in his list of items to take into the Maine woods, though like naturalists

De figuris lapidum, &c.

&titij puto, quod aliquos Stimmi An-
glicum voca-
re audio) ge-
nere, in mu-
cronem dera·
fi, in manubri
um ligneum
inferto.

L. Lateres
è luto finguntur & coquuni, ad ædi-
ficiorum parietes, pauimenta, cami-
nos: item ad furnos, aliosꝗ vfus.

Lithoftrota dicuntur loca lapidibus ftrata: vt apud Varronem pauimenta nobilia lithoftrota, fiebant au-
tem è cruftis paruis, marmoreis præ-
cipuè, quibus folum pauimeti incru-
ftabatur. Vide Agricolam libro 7. de
nat. fofsilium.

M. Menfæ fiunt nó folùm è ligno:
fed etiam lapidibus & marmore, fiue
folidæ: fiue marmore aut lapide fifsili
incruftatæ duntaxat.

Molaris lapidis icon pofita eft Ca-
pite

The New York Public Library/Art Resource, NY

Figure 3 De Figuris Lapidum Translation: "The stylus . . . is made . . . from a sort of lead (which I have heard some call English antimony), shaved to a point and inserted in a wooden handle." From *De rerum fossilium lapidum et gemmarum maxime, figuris et similitudinibus liber*, a book on the shapes and images of fossils, esp. those in stone and rock. Gesner wrote a Greek-Latin dictionary, was a doctor, lectured on physics, and, obviously, was a rock hound.

before him, he certainly carried one on his twelve-day excursion in order to record his thoughts. Despite this silence, Thoreau devoted ten years of his life to improving pencil technology at his family's pencil factory. It was this pencil technology, not inherited wealth or publication royalties, that provided the income for one of the greatest writers of the American renaissance.

As Petroski tells it, the pencil industry in the eighteenth century was buffeted 30 by such vagaries as the unpredictable supply of graphite, dwindling cedar forests, protective tariffs, and, for much of its history, an international consumer preference for British-made pencils. All of this affected John Thoreau and Co., manufacturers of pencils. Until the nineteenth century, the best pencil graphite (or plumbago, as it was often called), came from Borrowdale, in England. There were other graphite deposits around the world, but their ore was not particularly pure. Impure ore crumbled or produced a scratchy line. In the later eighteenth century, the Borrowdale deposits began to run low, and exports were curtailed. After the French Revolution, with his supply of English graphite permanently embargoed, the French pencil-maker Nicholas-Jacques Conté learned to produce a workable writing medium by grinding the local graphite, mixing it with clay and water, and forcing the mixture into wooden casings.

This process allowed the French to produce their own pencils, and it also permitted manufacturers to control the hardness of the lead, which in turn controlled the darkness of the mark made by the pencil. (The more clay, the harder the lead, and the lighter and crisper the mark; less clay gives a darker, grainier mark.) So successful was Conté's process that Conté became synonymous with pencil, and Conté crayons are still valued by artists. In Nuremberg, Staedtler teamed to mix ground graphite with sulfur. He and his rival, Faber, founded German pencil dynasties that also survive to this day. 31

The superiority of Borrowdale English graphite was evident to American consumers as well, and they regularly preferred imports to domestic brands. American pencil manufacturers had a hard time convincing the public that they could make a good native pencil. In 1821 Charles Dunbar discovered a deposit of plumbago in Bristol, New Hampshire, and he and his brother-in-law, John Thoreau, went into the pencil business. By 1824 Thoreau pencils were winning recognition. Their graphite, however, was not as pure as Borrowdale, and since the Conté process was unknown in the United States, American pencils, though cheaper than imports, remained inferior. 32

Henry Thoreau set about to improve his father's pencil. According to Petroski, Thoreau began his research in the Harvard Library. But then, as now, there was little written on pencil manufacture. Somehow, Thoreau learned to grind graphite more finely than had been done before and to mix it with clay in just the right proportion, for his improvements on the pencil-making process, combined with the high import duty imposed on British pencils after the War of 1812, led to great demand for Thoreau pencils. 33

Thoreau did not ascribe transcendent value to pencils. As Petroski sees it, Thoreau's purpose was simply to make money. Once he developed the best pencil of the day, Thoreau saw no sense in trying to improve on his design. His pencils sold for seventy-five cents a dozen, higher than other brands, a fact which Emerson remarked on, though he still recommended Thoreau pencils to his friends. It is easy for us to think of Thoreau only as a romantic who lived deliberately, disobeyed civil authority, and turned Walden Pond into a national historic site. But to do these things, he was also an engineer and marketing expert. When pencil competition grew, shaving his profit margin, Thoreau stopped pushing 34 pencils and sold his graphite wholesale to electrotypers because this proved more lucrative (Petroski 122).

Perhaps, then, Thoreau, despite his technological expertise, opposed Morse's telegraph just to protect the family business. It is more likely, though, from the absence of references to pencil-making in any of his writings, that Thoreau honestly thought pencils were better for writing than electrical impulses, and he simply kept his business life and his intellectual life in separate compartments. In any case, Thoreau's resistance to the telegraph didn't stop the project. 35

THE TELEPHONE

The introduction of the telephone shows us once again how the pattern of communications technology takes shape. The telephone was initially received as an interesting but impractical device for communicating across distance. Although as Thoreau feared, the telegraph eventually did permit Maine and Texas and just about everywhere else to say nothing to one another, Samuel F. B. Morse, who patented the telegraph and invented its code, saw no use for Alexander Graham Bell's even newer device, the telephone. Morse refused Bell's offer to sell him the rights to the telephone patent. He was convinced that no one would want the telephone because it was unable to provide any permanent record of a conversation. 36

Indeed, although we now consider it indispensable, like writing, the uses of the telephone were not immediately apparent to many people. Telephone communication combined aspects of speaking and writing situations in new ways, and it took a while to figure out what the telephone could and couldn't do. Once they became established, telephones were sometimes viewed as replacements for earlier technologies. In some cities, news and sports broadcasts were delivered over the telephone, competing with the radio (Marvin 1988). Futurologists predicted that the telephone would replace the school or library as a transmitter of knowledge and information, that medical therapy (including hypnosis) could be delivered and criminals punished over the phone through the use of electrical impulses. The telephone even competed with the clock and the thermometer: when I was growing up in New York in the 1950s, my family regularly called MEridian 6-1212 to find out the time, and WEather 7-1212 for the temperature and forecast. 37

Of course the telephone was not only a source of information. It also threatened our privacy. One early fear of putting telephones in people's homes was that strangers could call up uninvited; people could talk to us on the phone whom we would never wish to converse with in person — and no one predicted then that people selling useless products would invariably call at dinner time. Today, as our email addresses circulate through the ether, we find in our electronic mailboxes not just surprise communications from long-lost acquaintances who 38 have tracked us down using Gopher and other Web browsers, but also unwelcome communiqués from intruders offering get-rich-quick schemes, questionable deals, and shoddy merchandise. Even unsolicited religious messages are now circulating freely on net news groups.

The introduction of the telephone for social communication also required 39 considerable adaptation of the ways we talk, a fact we tend to forget because we think of the modern telephone as a reliable and flexible instrument. People had to learn how to converse on the telephone: its sound reproduction was poor; callers had to speak loudly and repeat themselves to be understood, a situation hardly conducive to natural conversation. Telephones were located centrally and publicly in houses, which meant that conversations were never private. Telephones emulated face-to-face communication, but they could not transmit the visible cues and physical gestures that allow face-to-face conversation to proceed smoothly, and this deficiency had to be overcome. Many people still accompany phone conversations with hand and facial gestures; very young children often nod into the phone instead of saying "Yes" or "No," as if their interlocutor could see them.

Initially, people were unsure of the appropriate ways to begin or end phone 40 conversations, and lively debates ensued. The terms "hello" and "good-bye" quickly became standard, despite objections from purists who maintained that "hello" was not a greeting but an expression of surprise, and that "good-bye," coming from "God be with you," was too high-toned and serious a phrase to be used for something so trivial as telephone talk. As people discovered that telephones could further romantic liaisons, guardians of the public morality voiced concern or disgust that sweethearts were actually making kissing noises over the phone. Appropriate language during conversation was also an issue, and phone companies would cut off customers for swearing (like today's computer Systems Operators, or Sysops, the telephone operators, or "hello girls" as they were called in the early days, frequently listened in on conversations and had the authority to interrupt or disconnect calls).

While the telephone company routinely monitored the contents of telephone 41 calls, when transcripts of telephone conversations were first introduced as evidence in trials, phone companies argued that these communications were just as private and privileged as doctor-patient exchanges (Marvin 68). Phone companies also tried to limit telephone access solely to the subscriber, threatening hotels and other businesses with loss of phone service if they allowed guests or customers to make calls. Telephone companies backed down from their demand that phones only be used by their registered owners once another technological development, the pay telephone, was introduced, and their continued profits were assured (this situation is analogous to the discussions of copy protection and site licensing for computer software today).

THE COMPUTER AND THE PATTERN OF LITERACY TECHNOLOGY

Writing was not initially speech transcription, and pencils were first made for 42 woodworkers, not writers. Similarly, the mainframe computer when it was introduced was intended to perform numerical calculations too tedious or complex to do by hand. Personal computers were not initially meant for word processing either, though that has since become one of their primary functions.

Mainframe line editors were so cumbersome that even computer program- 43 mers preferred to write their code with pencil and paper. Computer operators actually scorned the thought of using their powerful number-crunchers to process mere words. Those who braved the clumsy technology to type text were condemned to using a system that seemed diabolically designed to slow a writer down well below anything that could be done on an IBM Selectric, or even with a pencil. (Interestingly, when the typewriter was developed, the keyboard was designed to slow down writers, whose typing was faster than the machine could handle; initially computers too were slow to respond to keystrokes, and until type-ahead capability was developed, typists were frustrated by loud beeps indicating they had exceeded the machine's capacity to remember what to do.)

Early word-processing software for personal computers did little to improve 44 the situation. At last, in the early 1980s, programs like Wordstar began to produce text that looked more like the typing that many writers had become used to. Even so, writers had to put up with screens cluttered with formatting characters. Word wrap was not automatic, so paragraphs had to be reformatted every time they were revised. Furthermore, printed versions of text seldom matched what was on the computer screen, turning page design into a laborious trial-and-error session. Adding to the writer's problems was the fact that the screen itself looked nothing like the piece of paper the text would ultimately be printed on. The first PC screens were grayish-black with green phosphor letters, displaying considerably less than a full page of text. When it came along, the amber screen offered what was seen as a major improvement, reducing eye strain for many people. Today we expect displays not only with black on white, just like real paper, and high resolution text characters, but also with color, which takes us a step beyond what we could do with ordinary typing paper.

If the initial technical obstacles to word processing on a PC weren't enough to 45 keep writers away from the new technology, they still had to come up with the requisite $5,000 or more in start-up funds for an entry-level personal computer. Only die-hards and visionaries considered computer word processing worth pursuing, and even they held on to their Selectrics and their Bics just in case.

The next generation of word-processing computers gave us WYSIWYG: 46 "what you see is what you get," and that helped less-adventurous writers make the jump to computers. Only when Macintosh and Windows operating systems allowed users to create on-screen documents that looked and felt like the old,

If you type this:

^BCombining Special Effects^B. To combine special effects, simply insert one control character after another. For example, your ^BWordstar^B^VTM^V cursor may look like this: H^HI^HN^HZ.

I^Ba^BI = /(a^Vx^V^T2^T + a^Vy^V^T2^T + a^Vz^V^T2^T)

You (might) get this:

Combining Special Effects. To combine special effects, simply insert one control character after another. For example, your Wordstar™ cursor may look like this: ■

$|a| = / (a_x{}^2 + a_y{}^2 + a_z{}^2)$

Figure 4 Instructions from a Wordstar manual

familiar documents they were used to creating on electric typewriters did word processing really become popular. At the same time, start-up costs decreased significantly and, with new, affordable hardware, computer writing technology quickly moved from the imitation of typing to the inclusion of graphics.

Of course that, too, was not an innovation in text production. We'd been 47 pasting up text and graphics for ages. The decorated medieval charters of eleventh-century England are a perfect parallel to our computerized graphics a millennium later. But just as writing in the middle ages was able to move beyond earlier limitations, computer word processing has now moved beyond the texts made possible by earlier technologies by adding not just graphics, but animation, video, and sound to documents. In addition, Hypertext and HTML allow us to create links between documents or paths within them, both of which offer restructured alternatives to linear reading.

The new technology also raises the specter of digital fraud, and the latest 48 literacy technology is now faced with the task of developing new methods of authentication to ensure confidence and trust in its audience (see figure 5).

Over the years, we have developed a number of safeguards for preventing or 49 detecting fraud in conventionally produced texts. The fact that counterfeit currency still gets passed, and that document forgeries such as the *Hitler Diaries* or hoaxes like the physicist Alan Sokal's spoof of deconstruction, "Transgressing the Boundaries: Toward a Transformational Hermeneutics of Quantum Gravity," come to light from time to time shows that the safeguards, while strong, are not necessarily foolproof. The average reader is not equipped to detect many kinds of document falsification, and a lot of text is still accepted on trust. A writer's reputation, or that of a publisher, predisposes readers to accept certain texts as authoritative, and to reject others. Provenance, in the world of conventional documents, is everything. We have learned to trust writing that leaves a paper trail.

Courtesy of the Estate of Howard Frank

Figure 5 Example of Digital Fraud From Feb. 1994 *Scientific American*, William J. Mitchell, "When is seeing believing?" (68–73). Mitchell explains the process used to create this photograph of Marilyn Monroe and Abraham Lincoln that never existed in the original. The final result can be so seamless that the forgery is undetectable. Examples of the intrusion of such false images include an ABC News broadcast in which correspondent Nina Totenberg was shown on camera with the White House in the background. In actuality, she was miles away in a studio and the montage gave the impression she was reporting from the field. Needless to say, fraudulent computer text is even easier to compose and promulgate across the bandwidth.

Things are not so black and white in the world of digital text. Of course, as 50 more and more people do business on the Internet, the security of transactions, of passwords, credit card numbers, and bank accounts becomes vital. But the security and authenticity of "ordinary" texts is a major concern as well. Anyone with a computer and a modem can put information into cyberspace. As we see from figure 5, digitized graphics are easy to alter. Someone intent on committing more serious deception can with not too much trouble alter text, sound, graphics, and video files. Recently several former Columbia University students were arrested for passing fake twenty-dollar bills that they had duplicated on one of Columbia's high-end color printers. The Treasury Department reported that while these counterfeits were easy for a non-expert to spot, some $8,000 to $9,000 of the bad money had been spent before the counterfeiters attracted any attention. Security experts, well aware of the problems of digital fraud, are developing scramblers, electronic watermarks and invisible tagging devices to protect the integrity of digital files, and hackers are probably working just as hard to defeat the new safeguards. Nonetheless, once a file has been converted to hard copy, it is not clear how it could be authenticated.

Digitized text is even easier to corrupt accidentally, or to fiddle with on 51 purpose. Errors can be inadvertently introduced when print documents are scanned. With electronic text, it may be difficult to recover other indicators that we expect easy access to when we deal with print: the date of publication, the edition (sometimes critical when dealing with newspapers or literary texts), editorial changes or formatting introduced during the digitization process, changes in accompanying graphics (for example, online versions of the *Washington Post* and the *New York Times* use color illustrations not found in the paper editions). And of course digital text can be corrupted on purpose in ways that will not be apparent to unsuspecting readers.

Electronic texts also present some challenges to the ways we attribute exper- 52 tise to authors. When I read newsgroups and electronic discussion lists, I must develop new means for establishing the expertise or authority of a poster. I recently tried following a technical discussion on a bicycle newsgroup about the relative advantages of butyl and latex innertubes. I can accept the advice of a bicycle mechanic I know, because we have a history, but posters to a newsgroup are all strangers to me. They may be experts, novices, cranks, or some combination of the three, and in the case of the two kinds of tire tubes, I had difficulty evaluating the often conflicting recommendations I received. After reading the newsgroup for a while, becoming familiar with those who post regularly, and getting a sense of the kinds of advice they gave and their attitudes toward the subject, I began to develop a nose for what was credible. My difficulty was compounded, though, because the most authoritative-sounding poster, in the conventional sense of authoritative—someone who evoked principles of physics and engineering to demonstrate that flats were no more common or disastrous with latex than butyl tubes, and who claimed to have written books on bicycle repair—was clearly outshouted by posters attesting the frequency and danger of rupturing latex inner tubes. In the end I chose to stay with butyl, since everyone seemed to agree that, though heavier than latex, it was certainly not the worst thing in the world to ride on.

My example may seem trivial, but as more and more people turn to the World 53 Wide Web for information, and as students begin relying on it for their research papers, verifying the reliability and authenticity of that information becomes increasingly important, as does revisiting it later to check quotations or gather more information. As anyone knows who's lost a file or tried to revisit a website, electronic texts have a greater tendency to disappear than conventional print resources.

CONCLUSION

As the old technologies become automatic and invisible, we find ourselves more 54 concerned with fighting or embracing what's new. Ten years ago, math teachers worried that if students were allowed to use calculators, they wouldn't learn

649

their arithmetic tables. Regardless of the value parents and teachers still place on knowing math facts, calculators are now indispensable in math class. When we began to use computers in university writing classes, instructors didn't tell students about the spell-check programs on their word processors, fearing the students would forget how to spell. The hackers found the spelling checkers anyway, and now teachers complain if their students don't run the spell check before they turn their papers in.

Even the pencil itself didn't escape the wrath of educators. One of the major 55 technological advances in pencil-making occurred in the early twentieth century, when manufacturers learned to attach rubber tips to inexpensive wood pencils by means of a brass clamp. But American schools allowed no crossing out. Teachers preferred pencils without erasers, arguing that students would do better, more premeditated work if they didn't have the option of revising. The students won this one, too: eraserless pencils are now extremely rare. Artists use them, because artists need special erasers in their work; golfers too use pencils without erasers, perhaps to keep themselves honest. As for the no-crossing-out rule, writing teachers now routinely warn students that writers never get it right the first time, and we expect them to revise their work endlessly until it is polished to perfection.

The computer has indeed changed the ways some of us do things with words, 56 and the rapid changes in technological development suggest that it will continue to do so in ways we cannot yet foresee. Whether this will result in a massive change in world literacy rates and practices is a question even more difficult to answer. Although the cost of computers has come down significantly enough for them to have made strong inroads into the American office and education environment, as well as in the American middle class home, it is still the case that not every office or every school can afford to computerize, let alone connect to the World Wide Web. And it is likely that many newly-computerized environments will not have sufficient control over the technology to do more than use it to replicate the old ways.

After more than a decade of study, we still know relatively little about how 57 people are using computers to read and write, and the number of people online, when viewed in the perspective of the total population of the United States, or of the world—the majority of whose residents are still illiterate—is still quite small. Literacy has always functioned to divide haves from have nots, and the problem of access to computers will not be easy to solve.

In addition, researchers tend to look at the cutting edge when they examine 58 how technology affects literacy. But technology has a trailing edge as well as a down side, and studying how computers are put to use raises serious issues in the politics of work and mechanisms of social control. Andrew Sledd (1988) pessimistically views the computer as actually reducing the amount of literacy needed for the low end of the workplace: "As for ordinary kids, they will get jobs at Jewel, dragging computerized Cheerios boxes across computerized check-out counters."

Despite Sledd's legitimate fear that in the information age computers 59
will increase the gap between active text production and routine, alienating, assembly-line text processing, in the United States we live in an environment that is increasingly surrounded by text. Our cereal boxes and our soft drink cans are covered with the printed word. Our televisions, films, and computer screens also abound with text. We wear clothing designed to be read. The new computer communications technology does have ability to increase text exposure even more than it already has in positive, productive ways. The simplest one-word Web search returns pages of documents which themselves link to the expanding universe of text in cyberspace.

Computer communications are not going to go away. How the computer 60
will eventually alter literacy practices remains to be seen. The effects of writing took thousands of years to spread; the printing press took several hundred years to change how we do things with words. Although the rate of change of computer development is significantly faster, it is still too early to do significant speculating.

We have a way of getting so used to writing technologies that we come to 61
think of them as natural rather than technological. We assume that pencils are a natural way to write because they are old—or at least because we have come to think of them as being old. We form Lead Pencil Clubs and romanticize do-it-yourselfers who make their own writing equipment, because home-made has come to mean "superior to store-bought."

But pencil technology has advanced to the point where the ubiquitous no. 2 62
wood-cased pencil can be manufactured for a unit cost of a few pennies. One pencil historian has estimated that a pencil made at home in 1950 by a hobbyist or an eccentric would have cost about $50. It would cost significantly more nowadays. There's clearly no percentage in home pencil-making. Whether the

Cartoon by Dennis Baron

In the brave new world virtual text, if you chain an infinite number of monkeys to an infinite number of computers, you will eventually get, not Hamlet, but Hamlet BASIC.

computer will one day be as taken-for-granted as the pencil is an intriguing question. One thing is clear: were Thoreau alive today he would not be writing with a pencil of his own manufacture. He had better business sense than that. More likely, he would be keyboarding his complaints about the information superhighway on a personal computer that he assembled from spare parts in his garage.

- -

Questions for Discussion and Journaling

1. Who is the Unabomber? How did he use writing? What technologies did he use for writing?

2. Sometimes Baron seems to shrug at technology and suggest that it's hard to imagine new technologies as fundamentally changing the shape or nature of writing. Do you agree that this seems to be one of his messages? If so, do you agree with it? Might Baron's outlook from the late 1990s be different if he wrote today?

3. Why might the first class of people to have access to a technology be called "priestly," as Baron describes them near the beginning of his piece (para. 6)?

4. What are some other literacy technologies you can think of that, like the pencil, were once high technology but are now barely recognized as technology at all? What do these technologies have in common?

5. If you read Downs earlier in this chapter (p. 457), consider technology as an element of rhetorical **ecology**. How might technology constitute or influence a given rhetorical ecology?

6. Why does Baron focus so much on *fraud* and *authenticity* in discussing writing technologies?

7. Look back over the illustrations and images in Baron's text. What do they contribute to it? Do you understand the illustrations and images as *writing*? What would considering them to be *writing* require adding to the list of technologies commonly associated with writing and literacy?

Applying and Exploring Ideas

1. Select a writing technology Baron talks about and write a brief history of how it has spread to its current number of users since it was invented. Does Baron's account of how new literacy technologies spread seem to fit the technology you're studying?

2. Baron devotes some time to discussing the "Thoreau pencil," an improvement on previous pencils. What writing technology do you wish someone would improve? Create a brief proposal that chooses a writing technology and recommends improvements you believe it needs.

3. Think about communication technologies that keep a record of a conversation and those that don't, and write a short analysis that considers the advantages of keeping, and not keeping, such records. Can you think of any communication technologies that *don't* keep a record that we would still recognize as writing?

4. Poll your classmates to build a list of knowledge that people need to gain about a particular new writing technology (for example, texting). What do people report needing to learn about how to use the technology, and how to be socially acceptable with it (for example, avoiding cell-yell)?

- -

META MOMENT   Does it help you, as a writer, to think of writing as a technology? What, if anything, changes in how you understand writing if you think of it in these terms?

- -

Document Design and Social Justice

A Universal Design for Documents

NATASHA N. JONES
STEPHANIE K. WHEELER

Natasha Jones

Stephanie Wheeler

Framing the Reading

As the chapter introduction and many other pieces in this chapter suggest, a central aspect of thinking rhetorically is trying to understand the rhetorical **ecology** of a given text or discourse, including **exigence** — what need is calling the text into being, making it necessary, which shapes how it will be *used* — and who other **rhetors** in the ecology are — particularly what needs, values, and expectations they have for what you're writing. Two questions, then, are how we actually carefully identify our other rhetors and their needs, and how we craft texts that include them.

Natasha Jones and Stephanie Wheeler, both assistant professors at the University of Central Florida, work on such questions by focusing on designing documents that include readers who are often excluded by less careful design. In the following article, Jones and Wheeler consider design from the perspective of a whole rhetorical ecology — all the users and uses of a document — rather than just a particular writer's own values. The field of universal design concerns itself specifically with seeing ways that document design can marginalize and disempower some rhetors (readers), and how writer-designers (how writers should always think of themselves) who are more *aware* in their work can increase access to the document for all the rhetors it intends to reach.

When the term *universal* appears in rhetorical theory, it has to do with *questions* or *categories* of thought that are common to all (or nearly all) rhetorical ecologies and situations. For example, in rhetorical theory, *ecology* and *situation* are themselves posed as universals: *What the ecology is* varies, but *that there is an ecology* doesn't vary. (Anywhere there is sentient interaction, there is a rhetorical ecology.) What Jones and Wheeler show in their work is that universal design doesn't guarantee that a rhetor can accommodate every audience in the universe, but rather that it creates a practice and a set of questions that *should be asked* universally, of every rhetorical situation.

Jones and Wheeler show that universal design is an explicitly *critical* discipline. In this context, *critical* refers to questioning and critique with the specific end of analyzing how a culture includes, normalizes, privileges, and thus empowers some participants while marginalizing, disempowering, excluding, and thus oppressing some other participants. Such imbalances of power unfortunately seem to be an inevitable feature of human cultures. What various "critical" fields of study, including universal design, do is carefully track and analyze these power imbalances with the goals of exposing hidden or unacknowledged imbalances, tracing their effects on various members of a culture, protecting marginalized members, and ultimately reducing the inequalities. Together these goals come under the heading of *social justice*. You'll see that Jones and Wheeler explicitly acknowledge these aims in their work, and their paper will make sense more quickly to you if you approach it with this expectation.

Getting Ready to Read

Before you read, do at least one of the following activities:

- Google "assistive technology" to learn more about kinds of products people use to access technology and read texts when they do not have "normate" bodies and abilities (para. 10) or when they need assistance in accessing a type of technology.

- Make a list of the assistive technologies you use on a daily basis. For example, Microsoft classifies *keyboard filtering* as an assistive technology, and lists examples of this technology as spelling auto-correct, predictive typing, and swiping systems, which you very likely use on your smartphone every day.

- Think back to the last "official" document you received that you found difficult to understand or interpret. (Perhaps a document from your college, a tax or a financial aid form, or a notice from your city about parking or jury duty you received.) If you still have a copy of the document, review it. Can you see any design choices that make it difficult to understand, or that could make it easier to understand if they were written differently?

As you read, consider the following questions:

- Since Jones and Wheeler emphasize that design must address both form and content (para. 4), do you see places throughout the document where their design critiques discuss both these aspects of composition? (Mark these places or make a list.)

- What ideas are you encountering about design that conflict with what you had thought or assumed about document design before?

INTRODUCTION

This article examines two traditional frameworks that help you, as writer- 1 designers, structure the design of documents: a usability framework and an accessibility framework. However, both usability and accessibility design frameworks tend to be exclusionary, meaning that these approaches emphasize the needs and desires of an imagined audience from the writer-designer's perspective. Despite information that is available, like usability testing results and accessibility guidelines, this imagined audience is filtered through the experience of the writer-designer and what the writer-designer *thinks* these audiences need. What results is that the writer-designer's experiences are privileged in the design, making the document difficult to engage for readers who do not share the same experiences or values.

With the exclusionary potential of usability and accessibility approaches to 2 document design in mind, we present a better approach for considering best practices of document design. We call this framework *Universal Design for Documents* (UDD). This approach, based on established principles of universal design, gives writer-designers the opportunity to be more aware of *how*, exactly, their document design might be exclusionary and how it can be more inclusive. Instead of assuming abilities and preferences of an imagined audience, employing a UDD framework asks writer-designers to pay close attention to the multiple ways a reader needs or wants to engage with a document. This framework can help writer-designers see how personal values and assumptions influence a design, but also how the proper adjustments to a design can result in documents that are more inclusive.

DESIGNING DOCUMENTS

In 1997, Karen Schriver's foundational textbook, *Dynamics in Document Design:* 3 *Creating Texts for Readers*, explored document design from historical, theoretical and practical perspectives. Schriver defined document design as how a designer "integrate[s] words and pictures" to create a text (p. 10). Redish (2000) also tackled defining document design and information design and argued that both address two major concepts: (1) the invention process involved in creating an effective document and (2) the more practical and aesthetic aspects of how a document looks on the page or in a digital environment. The invention process requires that writer-designers think through the needs of an identified audience. In addition, they must assess what an audience knows about a topic or subject, what information an audience may need in order to complete a task, make a decision, or understand important information. Finally, a writer-designer needs to find out how the audience might use a document in order to address a specific purpose. The aesthetic and practical aspects to which Redish refers is quite often what people think about when they think about the "design" of a document.

It is important to remember that the design of a document must address 4
both form and content. *Content* refers to the information and message being
communicated to an audience. What is being said? *Form* refers to *how* the information and message are being communicated. What does that message look
like? Form includes the format of a document, as well as the visual appearance of
typographical aspects (like font choice and text size) and graphical aspects (like
charts, graphs, drawings, and photographs) of a document. Typographical and
graphical elements of a document constitute the visual components of design
(again, what the message looks like on the page). Some scholars specifically
study and analyze visual elements and persuasion in a document (*visual rhetoric*).
Finally, document design also considers the medium through which a document
is delivered—including but not limited to, printed media (such as a book or
magazine) and technological media (such as a website).

Scholars in varied disciplines (Zhou, 2015; Campbell, 2013; Riley & 5
Mackiewicz, 2010) have proposed a number of practical and theoretical frameworks that examine ways to design by targeting users' needs and helping users
to complete tasks. Two of the most prominent approaches to document design
are designing documents from a usability framework and designing documents
from an accessibility framework.

DESIGNING DOCUMENTS: USABILITY FRAMEWORKS

Schriver (1992, 2010) contended that writers and designers of texts need to be 6
able to anticipate the needs of and processes of readers and users in a methodological and purposeful manner. Schriver and others (Johnson, 1997) acknowledged
the need for writers to address feedback from readers in the document creation
cycle. As this shift in thinking began to take hold in the field of document design,
other writers and designers began to work toward understanding how documents could be more usable. One aspect of creating a usable document is integrating what Johnson (1997) termed "audience knowledge" or "user knowledge"
(pp. 267–268). A document is considered usable when it uses specific design elements to provide users with information that they seek in a manner that is both
effective and efficient. Design elements are both modal and rhetorical choices
that writer-designers can make about content and form: text (alphabetic text and
type), pictures and icons, and technological enhancements (like video and audio).

Most instruction on document design considers the following principles: 7

- **balance:** how elements are organized in order to create a sense of unity
  and equilibrium
- **contrast:** how elements are emphasized or differentiated
- **repetition:** how elements are used in a consistent manner to create
  cohesion

657

- **alignment:** how elements line up in order to create structure
- **proximity:** how related elements are visually grouped together

Redish noted that document design considerations should also include "lay- 8
out, typography, and color" (p. 163). *Layout* includes textual and visual design
elements. *Typography* is the study of typefaces and fonts (in written text both
digital and printed). Considerations of color include how color is used to
persuade and communicate a message. Writer-designers use the principles of
balance, contrast, repetition, alignment, and proximity when making choices
about a document's layout, typography choices, and use of color. For example,
a writer-designer may decide to use white text on a black background to create
contrast. Or, a writer-designer might use repetition—for example, Times New
Roman, font size 14, for all major headings in a document.

A usability approach necessarily bases choices about design principles on the 9
analysis of the end-users. As noted above, Schriver (2010) argued for basing
practical design choices on stakeholder analyses and detailed knowledge of what
users and readers want and need (gleaned from approaching design as usability). However, there are some major drawbacks of the usability framework. First,
writer-designers who approach design as a set of criteria for producing a document
or as a checklist of questions for users oversimplify the design process. Second,
even with exposure to user feedback during the
document design process, writers (and student
writer-designers in particular) often do not base
their design choices on the actual feedback from
users and instead rely on more surface-level
implementation of document design elements
(Friess, 2008; Schriver, 2012). In other words,
an understanding of how to apply practical skills
in order to make documents more usable does
not necessarily make writer-designers, particularly students, more attuned to the real needs of a
reader or end-user.

> An understanding of how to apply practical skills in order to make documents more usable does not necessarily make writer-designers, particularly students, more attuned to the real needs of a reader or end-user.

Finally, the practical principles of document design within a usability frame- 10
work, while important, do not necessarily attend to issues of accessibility because
usability practices do not typically include disabled users, and consequently
respond to an imaginary *"normate"* body, a term coined by Thomson (1997) that
refers to what culture thinks is a "normal" or "typical" body. We extend this definition to include what culture thinks are the values, privileges, and experiences
of a "normal" or "typical" person. In the context of document design, then, we
can think of the imagined audience as a version of the normate body constructed
by the writer-designer.

DESIGNING DOCUMENTS: ACCESSIBILITY FRAMEWORKS

While document design with an emphasis on usability is often anchored by 11 practical application of skills and end-user feedback to improve a user's experience, accessibility as a framework centers on *how* those practical applications can help (or the lack of certain applications can hinder) a reader navigating through a document. In this manner, there is a clear distinction between what is considered usable and what is considered accessible. According to Alexander (2006), one of the primary differences in definitions between usability and accessibility is founded in the "goal of design" (p. 3). "The goal of usability is a better experience for the user; better in terms of efficiency, effectiveness, and satisfaction. In contrast, the goal of accessible design is the removal of barriers to access based on disability, technical or environmental limitations" (p. 3). The other aspect that differentiates usability and accessibility lies in how audience is considered. As mentioned above, usability approaches most often do not, on an integral level, consider users with disabilities. On the other hand, accessibility frameworks focus specifically on users with disabilities and "other users of the web are mentioned as secondary beneficiaries" (Alexander, 2006, p. 3).

Though there are unique differences between usability and accessibil- 12 ity approaches to design, there are also some important overlaps. Some authors posited that accessibility is, indeed, an aspect of or "subset" of usability (Thatcher et al., 2003; Petrie and Kheir, 2007). Petrie and Kheir (2007) noted that, according to Thatcher et al. (2003), "usability problems affect all users equally, regardless of ability or disability, whereas accessibility problems hinder access for people with disabilities and put people with disabilities at a disadvantage relative to people without disabilities" (p. 398). In other words, usability is interrelated with accessibility. But the most important difference to note is that accessibility frameworks pay special attention to readers and end-users that may have disabilities.

One area of design that privileges an accessibility framework is the design 13 of websites. Though this paper focuses on document design broadly (and not web design or interface design), the design of websites is a good place to examine how designers attempt to pay special attention to issues of accessibility. For example, web accessibility guidelines have been developed in response to the need for increasing access to the web for disabled users. As noted by WebAIM (2013), designers should address accessibility early in the design process. Many of the suggested considerations for making a site more accessible overlap with document design principles and best practices. For example, WebAIM noted that a designer should "provide good contrast," "use adequate font size," and "watch the use of CAPS" (http://webaim.org/resources/designers/). In regard to document design in general, there are steps that any writer-designer can take to improve accessibility in documents.

- *Separate the foreground from the background.*

  - Use a color template that ensures the background is much lighter or darker than the text, images, and graphics in the foreground.
  - When using background images or watermarks, make sure there is an outline or a "halo" that provides enough contrast for the foreground text color.
  - Avoid using color alone to convey meaning. When using color in documents, be sure the purpose of color is retained if the document is printed or accessed in grayscale (for example, hyperlinks that appear blue on screen appear as a lighter shade of gray on a printout).
  - Attend to *legibility,* which measures "how easy it is to distinguish discrete letters that make up words" (Berger, 2011, p. 63). Use readable typefaces, like sans serif font, and don't use all caps outside of headers and headings.

- *Help readers navigate, find content, and determine where they are.*

  - For larger documents, include a table of contents to help readers get to the information they need quickly.
  - Always include page numbers.
  - Include headings for each new section or subsection.
  - Be sure to identify the difference between headings, subheadings, and normal text through the tools in your word processor. This will ensure that users accessing the document on a screen will be able to use a screen reader.

- *Make text content readable and understandable.*

  - Always spell out abbreviations and acronyms the first time they appear in a document.
  - Ensure that content is left-justified for languages that read from left to right, and avoid center-aligned or full-justified, since it could lead to readability and spacing issues.
  - Create redundancy in your text for the most important information: if a visual is used, include redundant information in text form, and vice versa.

- *Add text descriptions to graphic elements.*

  - Add *alt text* (a word or phrase inserted into HTML that tells a reader what a graphic is) to graphic elements. Alt text provides readers using screen readers with access to information about graphic elements on the page.
  - Always include a text equivalent on or next to a graphic. The related text and graphic should convey the same information.

While accessible design opened new doors of access to people with disabili- 14 ties, it also posed a problem to already existing document design practices that did not adhere to these guidelines. Because of this, accessibility frameworks lends itself to the problem of *retrofitting,* what Dolmage (2008) described as "an accommodation that doesn't change and challenge the mainstream" (p. 27). Too often documents are designed first and altered for accessibility after the fact. In the context of Dolmage's definition, then, accessibility frameworks make us aware of the need for accessibility but run the risk of framing that accessibility in ways that resist change about how we think about accessibility and document design in the first place. In other words, accessibility should be thought about at the outset of document design so as to ensure that the users that benefit most are central to the design process, not an afterthought.

So while making document design accessible is no doubt a critical part 15 of being a writer-designer, so too is thinking more broadly about whom our designs include and exclude. Meloncon's (2013) edited collection addressed these considerations by bringing together concepts from technical and professional communication and disability studies to explore the implications of how the invention, production, delivery, and comprehension of texts and documents impact users with disabilities. Contributors to Meloncon's collection moved us closer to understanding how documents can integrate a universal design framework in order to become more aware of issues of inclusion and social justice.

DESIGNING DOCUMENTS: UNIVERSAL DESIGN FRAMEWORKS

Considering document design from a social justice perspective (concern for how 16 society privileges some and marginalizes others) requires thinking about the practicality and application of design in a different conceptual way. Universal Design (UD) is an ideal approach for re-envisioning document design beyond a collection of practical applications. UD as a theory and a method affords document designers the rhetorical space to interrogate concepts and ideals about document design in relation to the critical implications of marginalization, disempowerment, and oppression in design.

But how, exactly, can writer-designers accomplish this? Usable and acces- 17 sible design frameworks provide great starting points, asking writer-designers to critically think about the needs of the end-user. Thinking about users with disabilities, for example, can help make the value — and limitations — of each clearer: Accessibility asks writer-designers to think about the constraints that users with disabilities might have in reading a document, yet it is difficult to resolve all of these limitations without running the risk of conflating the experiences of people with disabilities as a singular "disabled experience" that can be addressed by "checking off" a list that can make a document accessible. These checklists only allow a writer-designer to check off a "yes" or "no," leaving little to no room for flexibility when considering the needs of users that may not easily fit into those categories. While a great place to start, these checklists tend to be designed with a singular idea of what a disabled end-user's experience is, or what the needs of someone who would benefit from accessible design are. For example, in Figure 1, the checklist accounts for significant issues that end-users who use screen readers might have. However, the checklist does not necessarily accommodate writer-designers who do not have access to Microsoft Word and its accessibility options (such as the Style template), as the checklist below assumes.

Usable design, similarly, considers the easiest and most efficient way to engage with a document; however, usability tests too often do not include people with disabilities and focus more on efficiency (for example, how quickly end-users can use a document to complete a task). A complication with both of these approaches is that while taking into account the needs of users with disabilities, ultimately many documents are authored by writer-designers who reframe the experiences of others through the filter of their own experience. Thus, they are guided by these "checklists" that supposedly account for experiences that are not their own. While accessibility and usability frameworks are fundamental to "good" document design, it puts an enormous amount of pressure on the author to make a document accessible and usable by accounting for every experience he or she can think of. 18

It goes without saying that this is an impossible task, and this is where Universal Design for Documents (UDD) comes in. A UDD framework takes the incredibly useful and important guidelines of usable *and* accessible designs and pushes them a step further. UDD provides a way to acknowledge the impossibilities by 19

ID	2.0. General Layout and Formatting Requirements	Yes (Pass)	No (Fail)	N/A
2.1	Is the document free of scanned images of text?			
2.2	Have bookmarks been included in all PDFs that are more than 9 pages long? And, if bookmarks are present, are they logical?			
2.3	Are decorative images marked as background/artifact?			
2.4	Have all scanned signatures been removed from the PDF? (see http://webstandards.hhs.gov/standards/41)			
2.5	If there is an automated accessibility checker in the program used to create the PDF, has that been run and does it pass?			

Department of Health and Human Services.

FIGURE 1   Checklist for accessible text documents

critically engaging the *writer-designer's* experience as a way to think about how the design of a document reveals the writer-designer's assumptions and values. UDD asks the writer-designer to consider what kind of impact the design of a document might have on the reader or end-user. Putting this level of responsibility on the writer-designer, then, invites a design that is grounded in collective access (making documents to which *anyone* who desires access has access) and participatory design (working closely *with* end-users). This is an approach that Hamraie (2013) quite smartly described as "design *with* and *by* misfitting bodies" (n.p.). That is, this approach asks writer-designers and end-users of all abilities and accesses to design and collaborate on the very documents they will be using, instead of having documents designed for them. To that end, Hamraie thinks about UD as a "form of activism" (n.p.), compelling us to think about how prioritizing UD as we design our documents can be a form of social justice in and of itself. Indeed, Hamraie reminded us that UD requires us to be aware of the "underlying values and ideologies in circulation that support designs" (n.p.) that exclude unwanted participants. In other words, UD is a design strategy that uncovers the ways that the design of documents reveals the values of the designers, and are consequently made with assumed, desirable audiences in mind. So, writer-designers working within a UDD framework should aim to put a high value on inclusiveness, diversity, and equality in their work.

What this means is that a UDD framework requires writer-designers to be 20 adaptable in the design of a document. UDD should be regarded more as a practice than a set of checklists or criteria to adhere to, which means being ready to implement a variety of adaptable strategies in a document to address the needs of as many audiences as possible. What works for one document may not work for another document. Writer-designers may use some of, but not all strategies in a particular document. While it may seem easier (and possibly less overwhelming) to present writer-designers with a checklist of things to make a document universally designed, this approach would put writer-designers right back where they started: attempting to design for every possible circumstance or situation.

As a start, the Center for Universal Design (CUD) provides seven princi- 21 ples (and requisite definitions of each principle) of UD[1] created by a group of architects, product designers, engineers, and environmental design researchers that can aid in the document design process.[2] The fundamental practice of UD is the same across documents, but it is important to remember that the tools being used will determine how practices are implemented. Table 1 outlines the CUD principles and definitions (as articulated by the CUD) and details how these principles can be applied to document design. We present a Universal Design for Documents (UDD) framework that writer-designers can use to critically interrogate the inclusiveness of the design of the documents that they create.

TABLE 1 UNIVERSAL DESIGN FOR DOCUMENTS (UDD)

UD PRINCIPLE	CUD'S UD PRINCIPLE DEFINITIONS	DOCUMENT DESIGN APPLICATION
Equitable use	The design is useful and marketable to diverse people with diverse abilities	• Make document available for universal audiences (including multilingual, braille, electronic) • Identify whose knowledges and experiences are being privileged
Flexibility in use	The design accommodates a wide range of individual preferences and abilities	• Make document available in a variety of formats • Retain accessibility when converting formats
Simple and intuitive	Use of the design is easy to understand, regardless of the user's experience, knowledge, language skills, or current concentration level	• Ensure that document is not overly complex • Use headings and lists • Avoid jargon, undefined acronyms and terms
Perceptible information	The design communicates necessary information effectively to the user, regardless of ambient conditions or the user's sensory abilities	• Remove elements that are purely decorative • Use tables and graphics to emphasize essential information • Ensure that document can be accessed using different types of assistive technologies (for example, screen readers)
Tolerance for error	The design minimizes hazards and the adverse consequences of accidental or unintended actions	• Rephrase information for emphasis and clarity • Revise (content) and redesign (form) information that is useful to users
Low physical effort	The design can be used efficiently, comfortably, and with a minimum of fatigue	• Make document easy on the eyes by sufficient color contrast (black font on white background) and font choice (serif versus sans serif) • Chunk large blocks of text by using *white space* (the absence of typographical or graphical elements) wisely • Use lists to make document more *scannable* (read through quickly)
Size and space for approach for use	Appropriate size and space is provided for approach, reach, manipulation, and use regardless of the user's body size, posture, or mobility	• Make the acquisition of the document straightforward and accessible to everyone • Think carefully about typography, layout, and legibility

APPLICATION OF UNIVERSAL DESIGN FOR DOCUMENTS (UDD)

In Baltimore, Maryland, housing is a major social justice concern. Due to preda- 22 tory and biased lending practices, Baltimore's home foreclosure rate ranks ninth in the nation (Litten, 2015), increasing rental rates and the need for affordable rental units. However, even after individuals are able to secure rental housing, tenants are faced with poor housing standards and a limited understanding of their rights as tenants and the "broken system [that] puts long-standing tenant protections and basic housing standards second to landlords' bottom line" (Public Justice Center, p. vi). In an attempt to force necessary housing improvements, many renters withhold their rent, landing tenants in what is colloquially known as "rent court." Once inside the Rent Court, renters operate from undeniable knowledge deficits (Public Justice Center, p. v), the fundamental issue here that are not informed.

One particular organization that is trying to help is Public Justice Center 23 (PJC). The PJC developed documents meant to provide tenants with much needed information about renting and eviction processes. One such document, the "Evictions in Baltimore City: Procedures for Tenants and Landlords" booklet, aims to explain the eviction process to tenants and landlords in a step-by-step manner. Using excerpts from the booklet, we demonstrate how UDD principles can help the organization reach and inform more Baltimore citizens.

In the document that Figures 2 and 3 are taken from, the intent of the writer- 24 designer is to offer information for tenants about what to expect before, during, and after the eviction process. From a UDD perspective, how effective or ineffective are these excerpts in providing the tenants with the information they might need? Below, we demonstrate how you can use a UDD perspective as a flexible way to assess a document.

Equitable use: Is the document available for universal audiences? Whose knowledges and experiences are privileged?

- The document is only available in English and online as a PDF (which can be printed). At the time of writing, the PDF is not searchable (it has not been scanned using Optical Character Recognition software), which makes it unavailable for audiences that use screen readers. Optical Character Recognition (OCR) software converts data in documents into a searchable and scannable format.

- The document speaks more to landlord rights than to tenant rights. The landlord is spoken to (for example, some headings specifically address the landlord, with phrases like "You should keep a copy of the notice..."), while the tenant is spoken about (for example, "The tenant has no right to the property.").

Flexibility in use: Is the document available in a variety of formats? Does it retain accessibility when converted to different formats?

- While the document is only available online in PDF form, the format is not retained if the document is printed.
- Symbols appear in place of letters in the printed document. See Figure 3.

Simple and intuitive: Does the document use headings and lists? Does the document use active voice and omit unnecessary modifiers?

- The document uses headings and lists. For example, each step serves as a separate heading.

STEP SIX:

Disposal of property after the eviction

When the Sheriff returns possession of the property to the landlord and the landlord changes the locks, any of the tenant's personal property left in or around the rental unit is considered abandoned. The tenant has no right to the property. The landlord's only obligation for abandoned property is to properly dispose of it.

◆ **The landlord is strictly prohibited from putting the abandoned property in the street, the sidewalk, alleys, or on any public property.** Anyone who illegally dumps abandoned property from an eviction is guilty of a misdemeanor and subject to a penalty of up to $1,000 for each day of unlawful dumping.

◆ **The landlord may dispose of the abandoned property by:** (1) transporting it to a licensed landfill or solid waste facility, (2) donating it to charity, or (3) some other lawful means. A landlord may be entitled to a discount on fees charged at City owned or operated landfill or solid waste facilities.

> This prohibition of disposal on public property applies to ALL evictions from leased property.

STEP SEVEN:

Reporting illegal activities

◆ Call 311 to report illegal dumping, including landlords who do not properly dispose of eviction chattel.

◆ Any attempt by the tenant to re-enter the unit after an eviction should be reported to police by calling 911 as a criminal matter.

FIGURE 2 Procedures 6 and 7 online

- Some information is presented in paragraph form that could be revised in bulleted list form. For example, in Figure 3, the section "What the Notice Must Say" is very text-heavy. A bulleted list would make the information stand out.
- The document uses jargon and terms that may be unfamiliar to the reader (for example: "eviction chattel").

STEP THREE:
Landlord Notifies Tenant of Date of Scheduled Eviction

In evictions for nonpayment of rent, special notice requirements apply: the landlord must provide notice to the tenant of the scheduled eviction date in two separate ways:

1. Mail the notice to the tenant by first class mail with a certificate. of mailing at least 14 days in advance of the eviction date; and

2. Post the notice on the premises at least 7 days in advance of the eviction date.

LANDLORD: The best place to post the notice is the front door of the rental unit. It must be posted so that the tenant can easily find it. You should keep a copy of the notice, the certificate of mailing, and a signed affidavit from the person who posted the premises. This evidence must be presented to the Sheriff at the eviction, and may be presented to the Judge if the landlord's compliance with the notice requirements is challenged.

What the Notice Must Say: The notice must tell the tenant certain important information: the District Court case number, the scheduled date of eviction, state that the eviction will occur on that date unless the tenant moves out or pays the amount ordered by the court to redeem, prominently warn the tenant that any property left will be considered abandoned and may be disposed of, and that this is the final notice of eviction. The attached "Notice to Tenant of Eviction Date" is an example of a form a landlord may use to provide the required information.

How to Count Days : Count the day of mailing or posting as Day 1. Day 14 must be the day before the scheduled date of eviction. Count holidays and weekends.

> These notice provisions do not apply to evictions for tenant holding over, breach of lease, nuisance, or wrongful detainer.

FIGURE 3 Procedure 3 printed

Perceptible information: Does all text and visual elements provide the reader with relevant information or visual cues?

- The white on black contrast in the headings can present problems for readers with low vision. Simple black text on a white background would suffice.
- The visual cues are not consistent. Some subheadings are in all-caps (for example, "LANDLORD," despite the fact that the text before it was already prioritizing the landlord's experience), and only some information in the callout boxes is italicized.
- There is inconsistency in the headings, including grammatical structure and visual design.

Tolerance for error: Is important information rephrased for emphasis and clarity? Are there design choices that point to significant or relevant information to the reader?

- No information is rephrased for emphasis or clarity.
- There are design choices that point to relevant information, including the use of all caps, bolding, and callout boxes. This information, however, is primarily for the benefit of the landlord and not the tenant.
- Not all information that is emphasized is necessary for the audience the document addresses.

Low physical effort: Is the document easy on the eyes by sufficient color contrast and font choice? Are large blocks of text chunked by using white space? Is the document scannable, enabling readers to access information quickly?

- In general, the black text on a white background is effective contrast.
- The black boxes around the heading for each new step and reverse contrast (white text on a black background) can pose problems for users with low-vision.
- The size of the black boxes around the heading for each new step can be reduced, increasing the white space in the document.
- The use of bulleted lists makes the document more scannable.

Size and space for approach for use: Is it easy to acquire a copy of the document? Is the typography, layout, and legibility appropriate for the medium of the copy?

- Access to a computer is required to obtain this document.
- It is only available online as a PDF. This means that a user must have access to the internet and/or a printer.

- The sans-serif type is appropriate for reading the document on a screen; however, the type becomes more difficult to read once it is printed out.

Safe, accessible, and affordable housing is a social justice concern. The UDD lens [25] showed us that some elements in the original design can potentially prevent tenants from being able to effectively access and use the information to navigate the housing system. As Dolmage (2008) noted, "UD as praxis is [still] a matter of social justice" (p. 25). It is important to note that UDD is not a checklist and will not guarantee that all audiences will be accommodated. Rather, what UDD does provide is a framework to help writer-designers remember that design is dynamic. UDD encourages the writer-designer to re-envision the document design process through a critical and focused awareness of inclusion, diversity, and equality. Furthermore, while UDD provides the opportunity to increase inclusivity, it is important to remember that no existing framework can address *every* possible audience or situation.

CONCLUSIONS

In this article, we traced two related but different approaches to document design (a [26] usability framework and accessibility framework), highlighting the advantages and disadvantages of each. From these considerations, we offered an alternative approach to document design and developed a framework that emphasized the social justice element of universal design. Using an example of guidelines developed to help assist renters in Baltimore city rent court, we demonstrated how a UDD framework reveals the ways in which document design can disempower and marginalize. Moreover, we offered suggestions that can help writer-designers begin to place a high value on inclusivity, diversity, and equality throughout the design process.

Notes

1. Copyright © 1997 NC State University, The Center for Universal Design.
2. The Principles of Universal Design were conceived and developed by The Center for Universal Design at North Carolina State University. Use or application of the Principles in any form by an individual or organization is separate and distinct from the Principles and does not constitute or imply acceptance or endorsement by the Center for Universal Design of the use or application.

References

Alexander, D. (2006). Usability and accessibility: Best friends or worst enemies? *Available at http:// www. valaconf. org. au/vala2006/papers2006/99_Alexander_Fina l.pdf.*

Berger, L. L. (2011). Document design for lawyers: The end of the typewriter era. *Scholarly Works.* Paper 676. Retrieved from http://scholars.law.unlv.edu/facpub/676

Campbell, K. S. (2013). *Coherence, continuity, and cohesion: Theoretical foundations for document design*. London: Routledge.

The Center for Universal Design (1997). *The principles of Universal Design*, Version 2.0. Raleigh, NC: North Carolina State University.

Dolmage, J. (2008). Mapping composition: Inviting disability in the front door. In C. Lewiecki-Wilson & B.J. Brueggemann (Eds.), *Disability and the teaching of writing: A critical sourcebook* (14–27). Boston, MA: Bedford/St. Martin's.

Friess, E. (2008). *The user-centered design process: Novice designers' use of evidence in designing from data*. Ph.D. rhetoric dissertation, Carnegie Mellon University, Pittsburgh, PA.

Hamraie, A. (2013). Designing collective access: A feminist disability theory of universal design. *Disability studies quarterly, 33*(4).

Johnson, R. R. (1997). Audience involved: Toward a participatory model of writing. *Computers and composition, 14*(3), 361–376.

Klare, G. R. (1977). Readable technical writing: Some observations. *Technical communication, 24*(2), 1–5.

Litten, K. (2015, April 16). Baltimore continues to rank high for foreclosure activity. *Baltimore Business Journal*. Retrieved from http://www.bizjournals.com/baltimore/blog/real-estate/2015/04/baltimore-continues-to-rank-high-for-foreclosure.html

Maceri, K. (2003). *Document design for user with reading disorders*. Retrieved from http://www.angelfire.com/tn3/writing/DesignUsersReadDis.pdf

Meloncon, L. (2013). *Rhetorical accessibility: At the intersection of technical communication and disability studies*. Amityville, New York: Baywood Publishing Company.

Petrie, H., & Kheir, O. (2007, April). The relationship between accessibility and usability of websites. In *Proceedings of the SIGCHI conference on Human factors in computing systems* (pp. 397–406). ACM.

Public Justice Center. (2015, December). *Justice diverted: How renters are processed in Baltimore City rent court*. Retrieved from http://www.publicjustice.org/uploads/file/pdf/JUSTICE_DIVERTED_PJC_DEC15.pdf

Redish, J. C. G. (2000). What is information design?. *Technical communication, 47*(2), 163166.

Reid, L. D., Reid, M. L., & Bennett, A. (2004). Towards a reader-friendly font: Rationale for developing a typeface that is friendly for beginning readers, particularly those labeled dyslexic. *Visible language, 38*(3), 246.

Riley, K., & Mackiewicz, J. (2010). *Visual composing: Document design for print and digital media*. Upper Saddle River, NJ: Prentice Hall Press.

Schriver, K. A. (1992). Teaching writers to anticipate readers' needs: What can document designers learn from usability testing. In H.P. Maat & M. Steehouder (Eds.), *Studies of functional text quality* (pp. 141–157). Amsterdam: Rodopi.

Schriver, K. A. (1997). *Dynamics in document design*. New York, NY: John Wiley & Sons.

Schriver, K. A. (2010). *Reading on the web: Implications for online information design*. Ljubljana Museum of Architecture and Design Lecture Series on Visual communications theory: On information design. Retrieved from http://videolectures.net/aml2010_schriver_rotw

Schriver, K. (2012). What we know about expertise in professional communication. In V. Wise Berninger (Ed.), *Past, present, and future contributions of cognitive writing research to cognitive psychology* (pp. 275–312). New York, NY: Psychology Press.

Thomson, R. G. 1997. *Extraordinary Bodies: Figuring Physical Disability in American Culture and Literature.* New York, NY: Columbia University Press.

United States Department of Health and Human Services. (2013, March). *Word document 508 checklist.* Retrieved from http://www.hhs.gov/web/section-508/making-files-accessible /checklist/word/index.html

United States Department of Justice. (2010). *Americans with disabilities act (ADA) standards.* Retrieved from http://www.access-board.gov/guidelines-and-standards/buildings-and-sites /about-the-ada-standards/ada-standards

WebAIM (2013). *Web Accessibility for Designers.* Retrieved from http://webaim.org/resources /designers/

Zhou, Q. (2015, May). Strategy first, execution second: Teaching design strategy in technical communication. *Communication design quarterly, 3*(3), 53.

Questions for Discussion and Journaling

1. Designing purely from the writer-designer's perspective alone tends to exclude some readers, according to Jones and Wheeler. Why?

2. What are the three *frameworks* for document design that Jones and Wheeler discuss, and how do they differ from each other?

3. Jones and Wheeler argue that the *practice* of universal design applies to all documents but that how the practice is implemented will depend on the documents and the tools used to create them (para. 25). Is their thinking rhetorical, and if so, how?

4. A writer-designer needs to think about his or her own values and expectations for *what readers need and value.* How can this thinking help the writer-designer better understand the rhetorical ecology in which he or she is working?

5. Universal Design for Documents is grounded in "collective access" and "participatory design" (para. 23). In your own words, what do these two principles mean?

6. How can collective access and participatory design enact the ideals and practices of Universal Design for Documents?

7. In discussing *retrofitting* (para. 18), the writers argue that designing documents to be inaccessible and then going back to make them accessible is not a sufficient solution to the problem of accessibility. Why is that? If retrofitting isn't solving the problem, then what actually is the problem?

8. Talking about social justice issues is often difficult because people in privileged cultural groups can feel accused, or guilty, of hurting those in marginalized groups, and people in marginalized groups can feel frustration at the difficulty of being heard and empowered. Yet as writers we *must* talk about power because one of the main points of writing *is* empowerment, to make the writer powerful. So, try talking about it: How did it feel, as you read this

chapter from wherever you are, in terms of identity and status in your culture, to think and talk about these issues? Did you feel relieved? Defensive? Attacked? Supported? Curious? Confused? Take a moment to acknowledge whatever your feelings were and see if you can tell where they came from.

Applying and Exploring Ideas

1. Jones and Wheeler quote Thomson as saying that culture creates "an imaginary 'normate' body" (para. 10). Collect a handful of cultural texts (they might be YouTubes, advertisements, album covers, Pinterest pins, church bulletins, news articles, playbills, Craigslist ads, or others) that create or seem to suppose one kind of normate body in a culture you identify with. Describe what normate body the culture is imagining and explain how the texts you've collected are *designed for* this normate body.

2. "Check your privilege" has become a meme in U.S. culture over the past couple years, a shorthand way of saying "remember that it might be easy for you to say something because of power that culture has given you that others don't have, and that many people don't have the same cultural power to say it." In asking writer-designers to become aware of their own assumptions and values for *what readers should want*, UDD seems to ask for the same thing. Write a one-page analysis of the assumptions you have about your readers. Do you usually assume, for example, that they are sighted rather than blind? (Most sighted people do.) Do you usually assume that your readers' first language is the same as your first language? (Most people who grew up monolingual do.) Do you usually assume that your readers have no difficulties visually processing letters and words? (Most people who don't have dyslexia assume that their readers don't either.) You can ask the same questions of other identity categories such as gender, sexual orientation, ethnicity or race, and age. (How old do you usually think of your audience as being?) What you will create is a map of assumptions you make about your readers' typical identities and normate bodies. Conclude your analysis by reflecting on how what you compose could change if you imagined other kinds of readers as well.

3. Locate a document (either paper or online) such as a flyer, a credit card bill, a bank statement, or a webpage, and compare it to your guidebook (or to Jones and Wheeler's design guidance). Assess the strengths and weaknesses of the document you've chosen. Then, try redesigning the document you selected for usability, accessibility, and universal design.

4. How can you make use of Jones and Wheeler's piece giving you both concrete recommendations for design (e.g., paras. 7 and 14–17, and Table 1) and continual cautions that the categories and elements shown should not be treated as yes/no checklists?

5. Jones and Wheeler demonstrate that universal design practices could enhance social justice in the specific situation of the predatory Baltimore housing market. Do a little research to find three social justice issues that could be impacted

by creating more accessible documents through UDD practices, and explain how these documents could be more universally designed. (Remember that in this context, "social justice" refers to equalizing harmful power imbalances.)

- -

META MOMENT   How will you use what you've learned in Jones and Wheeler's piece to approach reading and writing documents or composing multimedia texts differently?

- -

Digital Literacy and the Making of Meaning

How Format Affects Interpretation in the University of Central Florida Libraries Search Interface

Komysha Hassan

KOMYSHA HASSAN

Framing the Reading

If you're a typical Internet user, the places you most often search online are Google and Amazon.com. If you're not a typical user, then you probably use some other search engine and some other online shopping place — but you still search and shop. If you're a college student, you *might* also use your college's library search page. (Though statistics suggest that a majority of you just go straight to Google for that, too.) Each of these online portals creates its own digital ecology with its users. What interests Komysha Hassan is how the *library* search interface is increasingly designed to resemble other online search interfaces even though it's constructed for a different purpose for users with different constraints (a term that will be familiar if you've read Keith Grant-Davie's article in this chapter, p. 484).

Hassan's article questions this design practice. Published in *Stylus*, the journal for writing students' research at the University of Central Florida (where Hassan wrote this piece as a first-year student majoring in political science/pre-law), it creates an intriguing mix of research methodologies. Hassan blends extensive theoretical framing with rhetorical analysis of her university library's home page and then compares

Hassan, Komysha. "Digital Literacy and the Making of Meaning: How Format Affects Interpretation in the University of Central Florida Libraries Search Interface." *Stylus*, Knights Write Showcase Special Issue, Spring 2015, pp. 55–66.

these with her **autoethnographic** account of using the home page. Her critique contains some striking insights as a result of this blend.

At question is, simply, whether the web page's design actually facilitates the rhetorical use to which students need to put the page. Hassan discovers a form of double-bind the university library finds itself in: The kind of search interface that students will find recognizable, familiar, and usable based on their existing web literacies, built on other uses of the Internet, is not the kind of interface best suited to doing the specific kind of searching academic research requires. Hassan's findings suggest that libraries face an unpalatable choice: attracting students with an effective but unfamiliar and thus initially off-putting style of search interface, or attracting students with a familiar and apparently welcoming interface that then yields poor results and leaves students turning to other, more Google-ish resources.

Hassan's arguments for why this is a relevant issue for college students are persuasive; she makes clear links between various aspects of rhetoric as knowledge-making and the ways in which digital tools shape the knowledge we wind up building.

Getting Ready to Read

Before you read, do at least one of the following activities:

- Think about how you usually find sources for your school research projects. What online resources do you use? Are your search practices for school projects different from your search practices for non–school-related queries?

- Visit your college's library home page. (Have you, before?) Either leave the page open as you read this piece, or take a screenshot for later comparison with Hassan's description of her library's home page.

As you read, consider the following questions:

- How easy is it to follow this article's organization, and how does its organization impact your reading experience?

- How does this article balance between "setup" — laying out various pieces and parts that will later help you interpret its findings — and actually "doing" the research? Which is there more of?

THE LIBRARY: AN EPIC repository of knowledge and information that has 1 endured for centuries. Individuals of all ages have come to these hallowed corridors for enlightenment and discovery, borrowing fragments from so many different sources in order to create their own pieces of work. Work that may one day, too, find its rightful place alongside the pages that once served as their inspiration. Over the centuries, libraries have endured, weathering a diversity of tumultuous events. As such, they have also eased into the 21st century with an embracing, if awkward, welcome. The newest reincarnation of the library has been its modern, digital counterpart—a repository of a different kind that promises to be the grandest collection of knowledge ever put together. Digital collections can be truly vast, encompassing thousands of journals, periodicals, and even e-books, that no library would entertain indexing—and with a growing percentage of authorship taking place in digital spaces, print media can no longer stand alone. Experts in the field of library sciences are at odds on how to better implement digitization and to what extent; however, there is no debate with regards to its necessity. This digitization is, in fact, well under way and has been for quite some time.

We live in an increasingly digital world where a great percentage of our textual production and consumption (reading and writing activity) occurs in digital environments. Clive Thompson, whose book *Smarter Than You Think* examines authorship in the digital age, estimates the amount of online composition as more than 3.6 trillion words daily, or the equivalent of 36 million books *every day.* To provide a better perspective, Thompson writes, "The entire U.S. Library of Congress, by comparison, holds about 35 million books" (256). Libraries have thus joined the digital realm, and with that their overall collection has grown substantially. Each library now has its own section for digital collections where you will find plenty of otherwise print-based publications in digital format. According to research conducted by the Association of Research Libraries, digitization of library collections, or the process of creating a digitally available copy of published works, is no longer the job of major library institutions alone. This practice is gaining prevalence in libraries of all sizes, both public and private. The result has been unprecedented access to vast collections previously unavailable to the browsing masses, and even greater access to general collections, at the tip of one's finger.

All this modernization of the venerable library appears to be most beneficial; however, the wide-reaching implications of such a significant undertaking must be taken into consideration. What has made the library so remarkable is not simply its collection of knowledge, but its means of accessibility to that knowledge that make the library a vast repository open to all and available to all. In general, no special literacy is necessary to browse through its collection or stumble upon epic works of intellectual enlightenment. Random, serendipitous discovery is more the rule than the exception. Within digital environments, however, means of access change. Browsing, a term so synonymous with a library's books, has been usurped by digital terms to convey a more pointed search for a target rather than the casual scanning of material. Search interfaces are our reference desks. Like little e-librarians, they must interpret terms we input in order to provide relevant matches. But these librarians are one-dimensional and cannot know any more than what you allow them to know through a few chosen words about what you hope to find. One-dimensionality in this sense arises from the fact that you, as a user, are its source of information on what can and will be retrieved. Unlike more complex web search engines like Google, library database searches do not collect user information and track their behaviors in order to build complex profiles on the kinds of material a particular searcher may be seeking. The keywords a searcher inputs limit the extent of the information received by the user.

These considerations are of great consequence to what exactly we *can* access, 4 and what limitations exist on the library experience in the digital realm. Whether a search interface is used to locate your object of interest or an actual, physical librarian, your information is processed through a mediator, and thus the mediator becomes an important part of the result. The knowledge, expertise and perceptiveness of your librarian come into play when he or she stands as the mediator, acting as the bridge between you and what you seek. In the same way, accuracy, relevance, and — in the digital realm — speed, govern interaction and results when using a search interface. Both exert influence over interpretation of those results, but digital formats in this case rely entirely on user input. Thus, the receipt of information itself is affected by how it is processed and what conduit was used to access it. However, the manner in which it is received is also worth noting.

Possible influences upon information interpretation have garnered much 5 interest in literacy and writing studies. Gail Hawisher and Cynthia Selfe conclude that digital literacy is shaped by "social contexts; educational practices, values, and expectations; cultural and ideological formations like race, class, and gender; political and economic trends and events; family practices and experiences; and historical and material conditions — among many, many other factors" (644). Ingrid Hsieh-Yee, a library information scientist, argues that the degree of an individual's expertise in searching and in utilizing digital interfaces equally affects the way results are achieved and subsequently processed for repurposing, stating that "findings on the role of subject knowledge, suggest that experienced searchers knew how to cope with their deficiency in this area" (169). While plenty of research is available on how means of access affect information receipt, less attention has been paid to the more critical question: how do these changes influence the interpretation and utilization of the information? How such digital formats affect the meaning constructed from the results is what I wish to examine in this paper.

LITERATURE REVIEW

In this section, I will discuss briefly the theoretical basis for some of the concepts 6 that are used throughout this research which have provided direction and a framework for this particular study. Digital literacy, as discussed earlier, has become a major component of writing studies, and new concepts have emerged about the varied influences of our interaction with digital material. Before addressing digital environments more specifically, however, the concept of construction of meaning needs to be more fully understood. For that, I have relied heavily on a few insightful works whose conceptual breadth allows for further-reaching implications. James Porter and Nancy Spivey both have addressed construction of meaning in similar, if slightly different, terms. Spivey approaches the literary spaces we interact with as a conglomeration of workspaces that are mutually influential, as both the reader and writer exert influence on one another. This is captured in a brief interpretation of authorship, wherein Spivey posits, "What I present reflects my construction of an author and his or her work. . . . The 'author' serves as a means of classification and is a kind of projection of the various connections we make and the commonalities we see" (28). Spivey continues, "When an author is cited, my own readers are cued to bring their own constructions of that author and that text to bear, even though I provide guidance for the sort of selections and inferences that they might make" (28). Here, Spivey suggests that the way information is presented influences the audience in a certain manner, but an audience's interpretation is the final influence that constructs what that piece of information really means.

Porter enriches Spivey's view with his concept of intertextuality, arguing that 7 "ever and always, texts refer to other texts and in fact rely on them for their meaning," suggesting that all texts are interdependent (87). He views the construction of meaning as heavily dependent on other literary influences and further explains that "we understand a text only insofar as we understand its precursors" (87). Influence from the intertext affects the meaning for both the writer and the reader extending that influence to the final interpretation. Exposure to a variety of texts is critical in shaping creative genius, a term which Porter is skeptical of, preferring instead "creative borrower" in an ode to the true skill of a writer's creativity: borrowing from so many other writers and texts to create a single cohesive work. In that vein, we must assess what governs access to those critical sources of information, including environmental, social, and economic factors. Hawisher and Selfe's research captures this intersection well through the term "cultural ecology," with the authors stating that "the specific conditions of access have substantial effect on people's acquisition and development of digital literacy" (644). Taking into consideration these numerous influences, Hawisher and Selfe conclude that "access is a much more complexly rendered social formation than we have heretofore recognized" (673).

Hawisher and Selfe's work offers a good point of transition to construction 8 of meaning in the digital environment, as it addresses digital spaces specifically within the broader context of literacy development. The "cultural ecology" of digital literacy acquirement is one that creates very subjective, experiential interaction with literacy. Levels of accessibility cannot be measured in the same way for different individuals. Access to a certain portal does not mean that it can or should influence the user in the same way. It is, as Hawisher and Selfe suggest, "the specific *conditions* of access (and the timing of these conditions) [that] seem to be important in determining when and how people develop effective sets of technological literacy skills—or, indeed, if they choose to do so" (673, emphasis in original). Digital literacy is not a skill that we can choose *not* to acquire in this day and age, but how we possess it and the ways we utilize it are factors that also determine what we make of information received through that particular medium.

In examining factors of influence on access, and more importantly literacy, 9 we turn to Hsieh-Yee's study of novice and experienced searchers to determine whether digital, and, more specifically, search literacy level are a factor in facilitating a successful search. The study was conducted with 32 "professional" or experienced searchers, and 30 novices; the purpose was to identify whether search experience and subject knowledge made a difference in the results obtained and the success of either group. The data from the study showed that experienced searchers were more successful in obtaining relevant results regardless of subject knowledge, and that they did so faster when the topic was familiar (167). The study further determined that novice searchers did not change their tactics when confronted with topics they were unfamiliar with, and that they relied less on usage of varied terms and thesaurus assistance in comparison with experienced searchers (167). On subject knowledge, Hsieh-Yee comments, "The most intriguing finding about subject knowledge, however, is its lack of effort on novice searchers. Data showed that no matter which topic was searched, novice searchers displayed no difference in their use of search tactics selected for this study" (169). The author goes on to suggest that searchers "need to have a certain amount of search experience for subject knowledge to have any effects on them" (169).

The findings from Hsieh-Yee's study have strong implications on the type of 10 ability that is needed to gain access to information from a search portal. Access here is governed by factors beyond the cultural ecology of the user and their degree of digital literacy in general, but also modal literacy in search tactics and knowledge of the subject being searched. It is not sufficient to be digitally literate, but to be literate in the effective use of search functions and terms. These findings show that search is a more complex act than simply the entering of a keyword or search term, and that many outside factors, unrelated with the search functionality, determine the kind of information that is produced. This issue becomes clearer when the complexity of retrieving information from a digital portal is examined, this time from the algorithmic, computational end. In "A Taxonomy of Web Search," Andrei Broder presents some difficulties in the processing of data entry, and how often what the user intends is not what the search function provides. Broder classifies searches as one of three types: navigational (the intent being to reach a certain site), informational (to acquire some information presumed to exist), and transactional (to perform a web-mediated activity). Though these search determinants are broadly placed, Broder suggests that there is no way for the system to determine "the need behind the search."

The accuracy of search results is in and of itself a matter of individual search systems. Each search provider has their own algorithm that is used to try and mitigate the effect of what I refer to as "intention-blindness" that is inherent in digital systems. This also suggests that each search system brings along with it a unique set of characteristics associated with its environment and sponsors. Broder submits that "human-computer interaction, and the cognitive aspects play a significant role" (4) in the web context and recognizes that this is "a rapidly changing landscape" (8). However, he concludes that for search interfaces to be most successful they will need to "deal with all three types" of queries, instead of interpreting the majority as simply informational, which the data determined, had made up less than 50% of total queries (9).

So far we have looked into how the individual's literacy, authority, and authorial capacity is shaped and influenced, and ultimately how these same factors affect the seemingly inanimate digital environment. Each specific data set and research effort creates a picture of how meaning is constructed and the individual influences on that process. Even in the language of the machine, the making of meaning is a critical element of how it provides answers to our queries. But beyond that, a final determinant of meaning is that of the interface itself. This simple portal that we recognize as a means to an end, barely noticing it beyond that, could well be dictating how researchers make moves within its space and, most importantly, what they get out of that interaction. In "Rhetorical Situations and Their Constituents," author Keith Grant-Davie examines this relationship between user and textual environment, which for our purposes may be digital or otherwise. Like Porter, Grant-Davie finds plenty of intertextual context for the development of certain rhetorical moves and the manner in which they are used. Again, the imperceptible and the implicit are most pervasive. Like Spivey, Grant-Davie finds construction of meaning a conditional relationship between input and output—author and reader, or in the concept for this paper, portal and user.

Grant-Davie provides a framework for his concept: the rhetorical situation. While he is not the first to suggest such a rhetorical construct, he has framed it in a unique and accessible manner that I find most relevant to this particular study. The rhetorical situation, in Grant-Davie's terms, has four constituents: exigence, rhetor, audience, and constraints. Though the first three are most likely familiar to the reader, constraints is one that may require some further defining. Grant-Davie refers to constraints as "factors in the situation's context that may affect the achievement of the rhetorical objectives" (111). Constraints are not necessarily a bad thing; they may be positive constraints, limiting contexts or frames in such a manner as to serve the rhetor's ends. He offers that rhetorical situations should be examined "as sets of interacting influences from which rhetoric arises, and which rhetoric in turn influences" (104). Going beyond that, Grant-Davie sees rhetorical situations as complex, even compound, stating that "exigence, rhetor, audience, and constraints can interlace with each other, and the further one delves into a situation the more connections between them are likely to appear" (115).

Understanding the rhetorical situation is critical in understanding how an 14 interface functions to influence its user. What moves does the rhetor (or rhetors) execute in order to accomplish his or her goal? And, more importantly, what exactly *is* the rhetor's goal? Here, rhetor is indicating the designer(s) or creator(s) of the library search interface. The exigence behind an interface is the primary determinant of how that interface will appear to its relevant audience. Finally, what constraints surround the use of a certain interface? In the same vein, we can also ask what is the audience's exigence—their need—in accessing that search function. What are the constraints that we have by now learned affect an individual's ability to access and use that interface effectively? Hsieh-Yee's study would suggest that digital literacy and search literacy along with subject knowledge are important constraints upon the successful utilization of a given search function. And, even more fundamentally, Hawisher and Selfe's research suggests that the "cultural ecology" of one's literacy development is an equally critical constraint upon an individual's interaction with the digital search interface. A keen rhetor must take these elements of audience into consideration if he or she is to successfully manipulate the rhetorical situation and respond to the exigence of the search page.

I find it necessary to also briefly introduce another author whose research 15 has been enlightening in as far as the sources, influences, and channels of meaning making. Eminent literacy researcher and scholar Deborah Brandt's piece "Sponsors of Literacy" delves into the concept of literacy sponsorship via an expansive, ethnographic study. Brandt finds sponsors taking on many shapes and origins, such as "relatives, teachers, priests, supervisors, military officers, editors, [and] influential authors" (335). Beyond individuals, sponsors may be institutions, as well as events and experiences (339). Although a correlation can be found between Brandt's and Hawisher and Selfe's research, Brandt's particular frame of sponsorship—even the term itself—is very useful in interpreting those background influences on the creation of meaning. One area of Brandt's work that will be revisited later in this research is well-summarized in a quote describing sponsors as entering "a reciprocal relationship with those they underwrite. They lend their resources or credibility to the sponsored, but also stand to gain benefit from their success" (335). This concept plays a role in understanding some elements of purpose and support when considering the roles of the rhetor and exigence.

Finally, a work that has exerted an influence on my own thinking in approach- 16
ing this research and that I find quite powerful in its ability to connect the concepts discussed thus far is Cathy Davidson's book *Now You See It*. This particular
work is relevant to my research not only because of its brain-science approach
to our interaction with digital environments, but because of the extensive work
the author does showing the complex rhetorical moves that are made in order to
influence an audience, and how these influences impact the meaning extracted
from the situation. Davidson focuses on "attention-blindness" as a phenomenon
only exacerbated by the digital world which we now occupy, writing, "[W]e are
in a transitional moment. We are both adopting new information technologies
all the time and being alarmed by them" (16). Davidson continues, "How we
perceive the world, what we pay attention to, and whether we pay attention with
delight or alarm are often a function of the tools that extend our capabilities or
intensify our interactions with the world" (16).

These tools that Davidson speaks of are very much the same ones that, in 17
differing terms, Hawisher and Selfe, Porter, Broder and Hsieh-Yee speak of. They
determine the means of access and control the production of information by
allowing individuals at different corners of it to manipulate attention-blindness
and interpret information in certain ways. What these authors collectively suggest
is that meaning is constructed way before we arrive at the interface from which
we will begin a search. Meaning is very subjec-
tive, yet it is also collective. Decisions are made
that generalize conclusions for all and yet, inevitably, can only satisfy a few. The concepts put
forth by the authors mentioned in this section
are concepts that are neither unheard of nor individually remarkable. I would venture to say that
many readers are already aware of them in one
context or another. But together these concepts
can shed light on a question that is less readily
discussed: what influences do formats have on the making of meaning? And,
more specifically, what influence does the University of Central Florida (UCF)
Libraries search format have on the making of meaning?

> What these authors
> collectively suggest is that
> meaning is constructed
> way before we arrive at the
> interface from which we will
> begin a search.

METHODOLOGY AND DATA COLLECTION

In order to investigate and examine my particular research question, I have chosen 18
to conduct a rhetorical analysis of my research subject, namely the UCF library
search function. I have considered other methods of ethnographic data collection;
however, the constraints of time, accuracy, and accessibility on those methods
led me to conclude that they may hinder or altogether disrupt my ability to conduct research and provide relevant and valid results. A rhetorical analysis involves

the researcher critically examining a certain text, disassembling its cohesive parts, and determining how and why certain actions of speech or visual argument were made. In the case of the UCF library search format, the text here was a visual rhetorical argument, with each of its parts examined wholly and individually to determine its respective role on the page and identify the purpose for which it was placed. The rhetorical examination does not stand alone; it is framed by a certain theoretical lens that helps provide context to the argument I make and the conclusions that are drawn from the information. These lenses allow us to use well-established concepts and to stand on the firm footing of an existing wealth of research in deciphering and interpreting the information gleaned from the rhetorical analysis. It also serves to provide a framework to help conceptualize the data. I have already introduced most of the literature that creates these lenses through which rhetorical analysis is conducted in the literature review section above.

Ideas extracted from the various works that have been used to interpret my data are included in this paper. In addition, since the physical search interface is the subject of my research, commentary and analysis in many cases can be readily observed through viewing the page or using some of its functions. I have also conducted an extensive interview with a UCF research librarian, asking questions about some of the aspects of his specific interaction with the library search format and utilization of its functions. The input from the librarian is helpful in broadening the research perspective to encompass a professional viewpoint of using the library search function and what factors may affect its utility. It is, however, important to note that this is a single case study from one librarian's perspective and therefore no broader generalizations could be drawn from this particular data, neither on librarians in general nor for UCF librarians more specifically. The questionnaire sheet can be found in the appendix. 19

Finally, I will include some of my own observations in the course of using the UCF library search function for the purpose of this research. I have myself taken a single class of library research methods in conjunction with my Composition class, which was very helpful despite the fact that I was already familiar with the concepts discussed. I had also done a few hours of tutorials on the function and navigation of the UCF library search for the same class. This experience was instrumental in creating my individual identity as a researcher, although I identify as someone who is simply using a search engine. The realization that such a specialty affects the success of my own interaction with the interface helped initiate my interest to delve deeper in this subject. 20

OVERVIEW OF SEARCH PAGE

Let us briefly overview the elements of the UCF library search page. The search page contains four major elements immediately visible, placed as individual pieces on the page. The central two, and most visually fixating, are the large banner header and the OneSearch box immediately below it. Less significant in 21 size or distinct in appearance are two bars on each side. To the right, six different buttons appear in plain text, with the various other modes of search function the library has available, including the specific articles and database and books/catalog search functions. The "Ask a Librarian" button is also located among the six buttons. On the left bar, the library hours are posted, also in plain text and regular typeset with emphasis made on the weekday hours. These two are not linked and do not direct the user to any other location. However, a small "more" link is located towards the bottom that navigates the user to a page giving extended information on operational times.

Garnering the most attention at first is the image-transition banner, with its picture format and extra large, colorized text. A quick glance at the images, however, allows the user to recognize that this is a non-function related element, displaying various shots of the library and informing of the availability of study rooms. Moving to the second largest and most prominent element on the page, we find the library OneSearch box. Besides the actual keyword entry box, three radio-buttons appear below allowing the user to select whether he or she is trying to initiate a search by keyword, title, or author. The keyword option is selected by default. Immediately below the term OneSearch are parentheses in faint gray text providing description for this search function: "Searches Catalog, Databases, and Articles." Though the term OneSearch may be, to an extent, self-explanatory, no further information is provided that explains to the user what is the advantage of OneSearch versus, for example, any other search function the library has available, if indeed there are other functions available. There is also an advanced search link to the right of the search and clear navigation buttons for the search box. However, this too is presented quite plainly. 22

The page contains two more elements that, although clearly visible, are easily lost in the more interesting and immediately available elements taking center-stage on the page: a navigation bar at the very top of the page, and a footer. The navigation bar at the top functions as a pull-down menu when the cursor is placed over it, with regular typeset and simple text links to various pages such as "home," "services," and "about." If the cursor is moved over those links, larger, pull-down menus and button links will appear with extensive navigation and search functions. The footer at the bottom contains ways to interact with the library on social media, as well as a few quick-navigation links, disclaimer page, and library news section. The overall color scheme of the page is one of light, unobtrusive hues and, apart from the header banner, contains no images. 23

DISCUSSION

Several rhetorical elements of the search page are immediately identifiable. The centrality of the search function, the recessive nature of the side elements, and the mostly non-functional banner at the top all serve to emphasize the primary 24 function of this page: the search. However, the page itself contains many different search elements. In fact, the entire right sidebar contains links to various *other* ways to search within the library. In fact, by definition, each of these search functions is more specific and specialized, hence more pointed in retrieving a certain result—assuming, of course, the user knows what he or she is looking for. And what if users do not know *exactly* what they are looking for? Equally, both the database and book catalog searches can help narrow results to more specific categories. But these functions are almost imperceptible, as the user's attention is immediately funneled to what appears to be the primary—and to the novice the only—search bar on the page.

Davidson refers to this as the "gorilla in the room," where we focus on the 25 one main element that is deemed, by navigational location and immediacy, most important or most relevant to the purpose of the search—blinded to all other functions. Our literacy in the digital intertext of search modality assists us even further in making that immediate move to the central part of the page, because we are used to locating the search function conveniently in that location in so many other search interfaces used on the Internet. We are already primed, in a sense, to locate the search bar in that central location, and to ignore the usual filler that appears in various parts of the page that most often have no function in assisting someone's research. Web literacy has taught us to ignore most side elements of pages because, beyond possible navigational qualities, they are mostly of no benefit to the user, and, in fact, are usually non-informational, such as solicitations.

In the preceding simplistic analysis of a single rhetorical element of the page, 26 we were able to demonstrate that even users with good, and perhaps even extensive, digital literacy could be influenced by a page's format in several ways, and that this influence may not be entirely beneficial to the user's goal. But, if the function of the page is to conduct a search, what then is truly significant about this particular rhetorical move—the centrality of the primary search function? The question is not whether the search functionality of the page is readily accessible and central to it, but more so why this *particular* one has been pre-selected as the primary search function to which a user will most likely navigate. In that pre-selection, the other search elements that may be more relevant to a given searcher's query are ignored, or possibly not seen. The rhetor's exigence, to use Grant-Davie's terms, must then be examined and reviewed in relation to the audience's purpose in accessing the page and, more specifically, who that audience is.

Because the audience for the UCF library search page primarily consists of 27 students, their perspective queries are more than likely academically related targets, such as a journal or a book related to a homework assignment. Generally, students tend to possess a few characteristics: young, digitally literate, and likely still learning about the subjects they are researching. These specific audience characteristics are ones that a rhetor must take into consideration when developing a space that successfully interacts with them. Knowing this audience is young, digitally literate, and still learning, we could infer that this audience wants quick access and response (young), places importance to certain parts of the page and pays attention to those parts in particular (digital literacy), and is not necessarily aware of what in particular they are looking for, and if they are, where exactly to find it (still learning). To satisfy an audience with these factors, the interface must be simple, focused, and broad in accessibility and results. Note that the "keyword" query option is selected by default, assuming that the purpose of a search is to narrow a topic, rather than having a specific one (e.g., title or author) in mind.

Not being a particularly savvy searcher, my personal observations using 28 OneSearch in this manner are interesting to note. Though I was particularly aware of the subject matter I sought, I did not have particular articles or books in mind. Instead, I was searching for existing research and published work on a specific subject of interest. Finding relevant information was difficult. The significant number of returns to my queries had not provided specific responses that were relevant to the particular search target. I used simple parameters to limit the returns in the "Advanced Search" function of OneSearch. However, the accuracy of the results, though less numerous, was not significantly improved. Instead, the diversity of returns that included some of the terms entered led me to look into several other avenues of research and subject matter that were, on occasion, far removed from the original search target.

Having been made aware of the database search function through my course, 29 I used that next. Though I did not know which database was most appropriate for my search, I selected a few relevant ones, so far as I could identify them. I also entered simpler keywords since I did not have to include terms that limited the focus of search to a general topic area as the database function already did that. The returns were significantly more accurate, with results mostly in line with the specific search target. In a final observation of comparative search methods, I consulted with a librarian regarding the same topic search, asking for assistance in finding relevant journal articles or books. Though my inquiry was the same, no keywords were given to the librarian. Instead, I described with some extensiveness what the subject was, providing background and anecdotal information. The results were even more accurate and relevant, providing more specifics than the other methods used when searching on my own.

Clearly, the exigence — the need — a search page responds to is to provide 30 prompt and accurate results. If it fails to do so, it fails its single function and users would discontinue using it. This cannot be the purpose of the rhetor in directing users to OneSearch. Revisiting Broder, we understand that search functions can only deduce limited value from keywords towards a certain query, and that each search system uses their own algorithmic formulas to determine search results. Thus, we must also consider constraints of sponsorship, in the concept of Brandt, and the environment on the search format. Sponsors, such as UCF and the database engine that operates the search, EBSCO, are two factors among many in determining the databases available for query and the prioritization of search results. Environmental factors such as the size of the university and the diversity in fields of study and overall student body at UCF affect the type of interaction that the rhetor would find most appropriate and effective.

CONCLUSION

We can conclude from the research conducted in this study that, indeed, the 31 UCF search format influences the way in which we interact with it and submit our queries through its portal. But how that affects the meaning we make from the results is the ultimate question. The interaction and response phases say a lot about how we think of information access in the digital library age versus the age of the traditional library. The essence of "quantity over quality" seems to be a theme in digital spaces: higher returns are more valued, perhaps, than accurate ones. And what do simplistic search interfaces say about the *kind* of information we seek? Are we looking for a fast resolution to a problem, to quickly find a study subject? If searchers do not know what they are looking for *exactly*, does that also mean that they do not know what they seek in general? In my own observation, I had a very specific target subject and I was familiar with the subject matter. Hsieh-Yee's study results, however, indicate that a searcher's subject knowledge does not influence effectiveness if they are not also experienced searchers.

What if a very different search interface was used, one that was complex 32 rather than simplistic but that would allow users to interpret the best way to get results to their queries? Interestingly, not many would use it. The UCF librarian I interviewed explained that, in his personal experience, most questions asked were simple but marginally more specific, and were perhaps best found using a subject database. The librarian observed that he rarely uses OneSearch, not because of its quality as a search portal, but because this librarian's queries are never so general.

My research conclusions here are not a critique of the UCF library search's 33 effectiveness per se, but that of the digital environment that surrounds it, and which it is a part of. The format of the UCF search page reflects a certain digital tradition in which the traditional library does not belong. In their study of computer mediated communication in academic settings, Jane Mitchell and Gaalen Erickson noted that such communication has "far-reaching consequences for academic practices, particularly for ways in which knowledge is constructed, communicated, represented, used, learned, and critiqued as part of the processes of research and pedagogy" (21). These consequences, Mitchell and Erickson later conclude, have the potential to "reconfigure the relationship between knowledge and language through how we read, write, and think" (38). That reconfiguration of meaning through the search portal is well under way.

Though inadvertently, the search page encourages this practice: the superficial 34 pursuit of a random subject to complete a task, rather than an in-depth pursuit of a specific area of inquiry in order to gain a fuller understanding. In framing our query from the outset within this context, the search format in and of itself affects how we interpret these results, leading to the discovery of a quick answer or a single part of a greater body. Because the digital space is so much more prevalent and pervasive, we are much more likely to seek it than, for example, a librarian. The answers seem to be at our fingertips and they do not inquire or push us to questions of deeper meaning. But we miss a point that keywords cannot encompass—the nuance of meaning, the inflection, and anecdotes that communicate what we *truly* seek. There is no "you know what I mean" in digital interfaces. The accuracy gap that I encountered between the improved database search and that of my librarian query has less to do with the librarian's advanced knowledge than their ability to process the whole of my query and then utilize their specialized knowledge to target an appropriate search function.

There is no doubt that information and knowledge are available, but access to 35 it is what is inconsistent and the way we interpret it, as this research has found, is influenced by the portals we seek it through. Our exposure to the intertext, too, is affected, changing from open-ended inquiry to targeted keyword search. In the case of the latter, we do encounter many texts, possibly more than those we would on a library's shelves; however, our inquiry is focused on matching results. Results that appear to be inconsistent with the query often end up disregarded, instead of piquing interest.

> There is no doubt that information and knowledge are available, but access to it is what is inconsistent and the way we interpret it, as this research has found, is influenced by the portals we seek it through.

Davidson finds that we need to update our 36 manner of interaction with the digital environment so as not to exacerbate attention-blindness, but to seek complex questions in a way that will allow us to find complex meaning. To gain the most from our digital world, we must make changes to the way we interact with it, rather than trying to fit old ways of information-seeking to new rules of information retrieval. As Davidson suggests, "learning, unlearning, and relearning, require cultivated distraction, because as long as we focus on the object we know, we will miss the new one we need to see" (19). More research will need to be done to record and address the influences of search portal interfaces on the meaning of the results and the gaps that exist between our understanding of traditional and digital information access. Digital libraries, however, are not a thing to fear but rather to embrace. Digital collections will be just as great as their print counterparts, and perhaps greater as their proponents would suggest. It is simply a matter of learning, unlearning, and relearning.

Works Cited

Brandt, Deborah. "Sponsors of Literacy." Wardle and Downs 331-51. Print.

Broder, Andrei. "A Taxonomy of Web Search." *ACM SIGIR Forum* 36.2 (2002): 3–10. *JSTOR*. Web. 15 Feb. 2014.

Davidson, Cathy N. *Now You See It: How the Brain Science of Attention Will Transform the Way We Live, Work, and Learn.* New York: Viking, 2011. Print.

Grant-Davie, Keith. "Rhetorical Situations and Their Constituents." Wardle and Downs 101–18. Print. Hawisher, Gail E., et al. "Becoming Literate in the Information Age: Cultural Ecologies and the Literacies of Technology." *College Composition and Communication* 55.4 (2004): 642–92. *JSTOR*. Web. 12 Feb. 2014.

Hsieh-Yee, Ingrid. "Effects of Search Experience and Subject Knowledge on the Search Tactics of Novice and Experienced Searchers." *Journal of the American Society for Information Science* 44.3 (1993): 161–74. *JSTOR*. Web. 20 Feb. 2014.

Mitchell, Jane, and Gaalen Erickson. "Constituting Conventions of Practice: An Analysis of Academic Literacy and Computer Mediated Communication." *The Journal of Educational Thought* 38.1 (2004): 19–42. *ProQuest*. Web. 24 Feb. 2014.

Porter, James. "Intertextuality and the Discourse Community." Wardle and Downs 86-99. Print.

Spivey, Nancy Nelson. *The Constructivist Metaphor: Reading, Writing, and the Making of Meaning.* San Diego: Academic, 1997. Print.

Thompson, Clive. *Smarter than You Think: How Technology Is Changing Our Minds for the Better.* New York: Penguin, 2013. Print.

Wardle, Elizabeth, and Doug Downs, eds. *Writing about Writing: A College Reader.* Boston: Bedford/St. Martin's, 2011. Print.

APPENDIX

UCF Librarian Questions

This is a brief questionnaire about the UCF Library search function, for the purpose of a research paper assignment. Replying to this questionnaire is entirely discretionary. You may at any time refuse to answer a question or discontinue the interview without consequence. You are not obligated to answer any or all of the following questions, or others that may arise from discussion surrounding them. This paper is not intended for publication; however, in the event that the author does choose to publish his or her research, you will be notified for approval prior to publication. Your participation is anonymous and you are not asked to give any personal information, including name, for the purpose of this interview.

1. How often do students seek your assistance in finding a text in/from the library?

2. Do you use OneSearch?

> If no, why not?

> If yes, how often?

3. When conducting a search, what function do you seek most often?

4. How would you generally interact with the search interface?

> Go directly to the 'advanced' function?

> Use a Boolean type search?

> Use general, relevant terms?

5. What do you find as the best search feature?

6. What is the worst feature?

7. How would you compare general web search engine function to library search?

- -

Questions for Discussion and Journaling

1. Does Hassan succeed in making a convincing case that how a search interface is designed affects the meaning its users can construct? What reasons lead you to answer as you do?

2. Hassan repeatedly critiques the "intention-blindness" (para. 11) in digital search interfaces. What does she mean by that term? Have you experienced it in your own searches online? What strategies have you developed for getting around it?

3. In her "Methodology and Data Collection" section, how does Hassan define and describe *rhetorical analysis* as a research method? Does her explanation help you think about rhetorical analysis differently than you have before?

4. What do you think Hassan means when she says "Meaning is very subjective, yet it is also collective" (para. 17)? Can you think of other readings where you've encountered this idea, or is this the first you've heard of it? Does it make sense to you?

5. How many separate theoretical frameworks does Hassan weave together to interpret her data? List the frameworks by the author's name and the key concept of the framework that Hassan uses. Which of them have you encountered in your own reading of this book? Does it make sense to combine them in the ways that she does?

6. In her conclusion, Hassan argues that "the format of the UCF search page reflects a certain digital tradition in which the traditional library does not belong" (para. 33). What "certain digital tradition" is she referring to at this point, and do you concur with her argument that college libraries should not be joining this tradition?

Applying and Exploring Ideas

1. Hassan writes that digital search interfaces have no "you know what I mean" interpretive ability. Write a creative nonfiction account of an epically difficult online search you faced because of this limitation. Describe what you were looking for, how this limitation influenced your results, and what resulting meaning you were or were not able to make. Feel free to make your piece as entertaining or funny as you like.

2. Two kinds of "blindness" come up in Hassan's research: *intention* blindness, where an online search interface can't tell what you actually want to find based on just the keywords you enter, and *attention* blindness, where one feature of a text or experience so captures our attention that we ignore everything else in the text or experience. Collaborate with two classmates to make a list of other "blindnesses" that you think might influence how we interact with digital technologies.

3. What is it like trying to use *your* library's search interface? Try replicating Hassan's analysis and write a polite (even if critical) and informative description of your experience that gives your librarians useful feedback on how you're encountering the search interface and how it seems to be shaping your knowledge-making as a result.

- -

META MOMENT   College libraries report finding it increasingly difficult to get students to use *their* search resources rather than general search engines like Google. Did you learn anything in reading this article that would make you more likely to search for sources using your library's resources? What habits would you have to change to do so?

- -

WRITING ABOUT RHETORIC: WRITING ASSIGNMENTS

To help you learn and explore the ideas in this chapter, we suggest four assignment options for larger writing projects: Rhetorical Analysis of a Previous Writing Experience; Rhetorical Reading Analysis: Reconstructing a Text's Context, Exigence, Motivations, and Aims; Mapping a Rhetorical Ecology; and Analyzing Rhetorical Velocity in Social Media.

RHETORICAL ANALYSIS OF A PREVIOUS WRITING EXPERIENCE

Think back: What's the most memorable piece of writing you've ever done? What was the situation? And how did that situation help shape the writing? In this four- to five-page rhetorical analysis of a memorable writing experience, your task as a writer is to reflect on how that particular writing experience was a result of the particular situation it was related to — how the situation helped determine what you wrote and why.

Writers are always responding to the situations they're writing in, from, and for, more or less consciously. But even when you're not aware of it, you're responding to rhetorical situations (and were even before you knew that term or concept). This assignment can show you how you've already been doing that and spur your thinking about what possibilities writing holds if you do it more consciously.

Analysis Description and Object of Study   Your rhetorical analysis will be based on some significant piece of writing or writing experience that you've had in the last several years. That writing could have been for school, work, family, or your personal life. It could have been completely private (like a journaling experience) or all-the-way public, like a blog or other online post. It could have been a single short document, like a poem or song lyrics, or it could have been an extended project or experience that involved multiple pieces of writing. The key requirement here is that it has to have been a memorable or important enough experience that you can *clearly remember the circumstances surrounding the writing.*

Once you know what experience and writing you want to focus on, you need to *reflect on and analyze that experience and writing from a rhetorical perspective.* What does that mean? Remember that your overall research question — what you're trying to find out that you don't already know — is *how did your rhetorical situation help shape that piece of writing?* Based on the principles Grant-Davie demonstrates as well as work you do in class, consider the following about the experience you had and the circumstances surrounding it:

- Why did you *need to write* to begin with (**exigence**)? Since it's easier not to write than it is to write, there had to be some reason or purpose behind your writing, some problem to be solved or addressed. What was that?

- Where did that need *come from* (**context**)? What gave rise to it? This is a *historical* question: To understand the circumstances that demanded writing, you need to know what led to those circumstances.

- What **constraints** did you face as a writer? What were the *givens* in your situation — the aspects of it you could not change that controlled what you could do with your writing?

- Who was meant to *read and use your writing* and *what did you want them to do with it* (**audience**)? How was your writing supposed to do something for, to, or with the readers you imagined it for?

The answers to all of these questions, and others, will help you talk about *why* this piece of writing took the shape that it did.

Planning, Drafting, and Developing through Revision   In order to make your analysis most meaningful and clear both to you and to other readers, it will need to include at least the following features:

- An *introduction* explaining what inquiry your piece does by posing your research question.

- Some *description of the writing you're focusing on and the experience itself.* You might even include an electronic copy of the writing you're talking about, if one is still available, but in many cases that may not be possible. Whether you can do that or not, take whatever space is necessary in your analysis to describe as clearly as possible what this writing and experience were.

- An *extended discussion of the questions above* in order to describe and analyze the rhetorical situation in which the writing or experience occurred.

- A *conclusion including implications* of your reflection: What did you learn from this? What principles can you draw to help you in future writing situations?

What Makes It Good?   While your rhetorical analysis of a writing experience may take a number of different shapes, it will tend to include these traits:

- Meaningful and accurate use of rhetorical terms such as *exigence, constraints, audience* (or *readers*), *purpose, motivation,* and *context*

- A focus on and clear account of how the writing you're analyzing was shaped by the situation and circumstances in which you were writing it

- A main point about the writing, the situation, or rhetorical principles more broadly

- Readable and usable flow through the main parts of the piece (such as a description of the writing itself and the experience of writing it, to the aspects of the rhetorical situation that shaped it)

- Evidence that you understand how rhetorical situations constrain writing (in the broad sense of *constrain* that Grant-Davie offers)

RHETORICAL READING ANALYSIS: RECONSTRUCTING A TEXT'S CONTEXT, EXIGENCE, MOTIVATIONS, AND AIMS

This assignment asks you to practice the rhetorical reading strategies that Haas and Flower describe in "Rhetorical Reading Strategies and the Construction of Meaning" (p. 559). As a college writer, you need to make rhetorical reading a normal habit. To read texts rhetorically is to read them as if they're people talking to you, people with motivations that may not always be explicit but are always present. It means talking about not only what a text *says* or what it *means*, but what it *does*. (Start a war? Make a friend smile? Throw down a gauntlet? Refocus everyone's attention? Woo a lover?) When you read a text trying to figure out what it does or why a person would go to the trouble of writing it, you're reading rhetorically.

For this rhetorical reading project, the object of your analysis will be a scholarly journal article or book chapter. Working in this genre will give you important additional practice for reading scholarly work rhetorically in your later classes, and you'll probably have a lot to learn about how scholarly communities work in order to do the assignment well. Your task is to rhetorically read a text and compose a four- to five-page piece that explains your interpretation of what the writer meant the text to accomplish, and why.

Select a Text Your instructor might simply have you use any of the scholarly articles in this book (or choose from a smaller group of them). Or, you might be required to find a scholarly article of your own, either in writing and rhetoric studies, or in your major. You'll probably be more engaged in the project if the subject is of interest to you, so be sure that if you're choosing an article from this book or in the field of writing studies, you pick one that takes up an issue relating to writing (or rhetoric or literacy) that you care about. The only functional constraint on your choice of article is that you *must* be able to trace its provenance — to know where it was first published, and when, and by whom.

Summarize the Text The first rule of rhetorical reading is, *read*. You need to get a sufficient handle on the text you've chosen to be able to write a summary of it in about a page. Look for these aspects of the text in building your summary:

- The territory the text covers, and the niche it occupies, which may be its research questions or its thesis, if you can identify one. (You might try identifying and labeling these aspects with Assist Tags like we do in this book; see pp. 58–59 for descriptions of the tags.)

- The text's main parts or sections

- The main lines of argument in the piece

- Its theoretical framework — what underlying theories or principles it uses to study or interpret whatever it's focused on

- Any research methods the writer used

- Any findings or discoveries the writer reports

- The writer's discussion of the implications of their work (which will be mostly in the conclusion and potentially in the introduction as well)

When you summarize these aspects of the text, you're creating an account of what the writer *talked about* in the piece — generally speaking, you're trying to gather up what they said. This isn't a full account of the text yet, but you can't figure out what the text *means* or what it *does* if you don't know what it *says*.

Historicize the Text Along with summarizing what the text *says*, you'll need to collect some basic information on the text's provenance. This information is crucial to rhetorical reading because it will help you make inferences later about the exigence and motives that gave birth to the text, helping you understand what it was meant to *do*, and what needs doing so would meet. Most of this information is *contextual*, meaning that it lies *with* but *outside* of the text. Here are things you need to know in order to give a good rhetorical reading of your text:

- *Who wrote it*? You can probably find some basic author information published with the article itself, although sometimes biographies are not provided. In either case, to dig deeper, use your research and Google skills (and potentially consult Wikipedia).

- *Who published it*? What journal or book did it originally appear in, and who publishes that journal or book? What can you learn about that publisher? What kinds of work do they usually publish, and what is the purpose of the journal or book it appeared in? (You'll be looking for the journal's own web page, or the book publisher's catalog, in order to address such questions.)

- *Who reads what this publisher prints?* Often, student readers believe that a text was written with them as the intended audience simply because they're reading the piece. You can avoid this misinterpretation by finding out who a given journal or publisher expects to be reading its work. Most journals' "About" pages will describe their intended readership.

- *When was the text written?* Particularly for writing on scientific or technical subjects, it is imperative to know *when* the writing happened. That information tells you two things: (1) What the writer could and could not have known at that point (given what had been discovered in the field at that time), and (2) where on both a field's and a broader culture's "timeline" a given piece fits — whether it was written during a particular conversation the field or a society was having, or sometime before or after that.

We call this research *historicizing* your text because what you are doing by asking these questions is building your sense of the text's history — how it fit in a particular rhetorical ecology, that web of rhetors, circumstances, events, and material objects that would have originally given rise to the text to begin with. Effective rhetorical reading is impossible without such historicizing.

Write Your Interpretation of the Text's Context, Exigence, Motivations, and Aims The thesis of your rhetorical reading analysis should have to do with *what the article does* (or did at the time) and *why the writer wanted it to do that.* The final step of your project is creating your interpretation of the text's history, and what it says, in order to make these assertions about the exigence, motivations, and aims that fueled the text given the context in which it was written.

While there is no set organization that will work best for all versions of this project, we do know a variety of functions your analysis will need to accomplish in some way in the piece. These functions are in the following list, which is not arranged in a particular order and which you shouldn't try to treat as a map of your analysis.

- Discuss the article's *context*: where and when it appeared, what the historical moment in the field was, and pertinent information about the writer and publisher.

- Discuss the *conversation* in which the article participates: It may be helpful to use Swales's CARS terms of "territory" and "niche" to assist this discussion. (See the summary of his framework on p. 29.)

- Summarize what the article *says*: Incorporate the short (approximately one-page) summary that you created after reading the article.

- Consider the writer's main *argument*: their central claim, their support for that claim, and, importantly, any major warrants that readers must agree with in order to build adherence with the argument. (If any of this language is confusing to you, read or reread Downs, p. 457.)

- Draw conclusions about the *exigence*, *motivations*, and *aims* of the text: What was this text *meant* to accomplish, and why? How do what it *says* and what it *means* relate to what the text actually does or accomplishes?

- Offer *evidence* for your interpretations: When you make a claim about the text or its context, what evidence do you have to support that claim? It could be quotations from the text, or information from external sources that you've found in your research to historicize the text.

An analysis that accomplishes each of these functions should, if it's well organized, be both an interesting rhetorical reading of your article and highly informative for the reader of your analysis. Most importantly, it will be an excellent example of rhetorical reading.

What Makes It Good?

- The main point of your rhetorical reading analysis should be what the text does and why the author meant it to do that.

- Your analysis needs to summarize the text you're interpreting.

- Your analysis has to talk about the context in which the text appeared.

- Your analysis should be organized and include an introduction and conclusion.

- Your analysis should include textual evidence for your claims.

MAPPING A RHETORICAL ECOLOGY

Ecology-mapping helps you trace the elements in a rhetorical ecology to see how they form an interconnected network — a web from which a rhetorical interaction emerges not just by the rhetor's own intention but by the "intentions" of everything and everyone else in the network as well. We want you to get used to this way of *seeing* rhetorical interactions and their roots.

Review Downs's explanation of rhetorical ecology (p. 466) before starting this project.

Choosing the Interaction Choose the rhetorical interaction whose ecology you want to map carefully, because we want a map, not an atlas. You're looking for an interaction between a small number of people in a small time and place. Trying to map the ecology of a large multi-authored document — say, an accident report about a plane crash — would permit only the largest generalizations about the ecology. In contrast, we are after much finer-grained or "higher resolution" mapping of a much more limited interaction. Here are some examples of the types and scale of rhetorical interactions that would make for good mapping:

- An instruction manual or online help file for a device you own

- A Facebook status update, Pinterest pin, or Instagram post with a short string of comments in response

697

- A single round of *Cards Against Humanity* or *Apples to Apples* with several players
- An editorial on a hometown issue in your local newspaper
- A "big decision" conversation you have with two or three friends or family members (choosing a college, buying a car, picking a vacation spot, etc.)
- A chapter in one of your textbooks
- A flyer for a fundraising event of a community organization you're involved in.

All these options have certain features in common (1) a textual or discursive interaction that "exposes" or makes the ecology visible; (2) at least two rhetors (a writer and a reader) who are doing the interacting; (3) a subject of discussion for that interaction that has lots of "threads" or history; and (4) a relatively *small* interaction, limited in time and space. Be creative and have fun in your choice of the interaction whose ecology you want to map. Just remember that it has to be an interaction you *actually observe* or participate in, not simply one that you imagine.

Our example for this assignment guide is a blog post by Shelly, a photo-drone enthusiast who flies a small camera drone to take videos of waterfalls and posts them to a blog.

Finding the Ecology This assignment is about *building awareness* of how our everyday rhetorical interactions emerge from a web of relationships among many elements. Once you know what interaction you want to study, start building your awareness of its rhetorical ecology. To see non-obvious parts, consider the elements explained in the table below. Each is present in some way in every rhetorical interaction.

You'll probably think of other ecological elements as you work on this project, so feel free to add to the list. But remember two limitations. First, *you're not going to be able to capture every element* in the ecology. Even if you noticed them all, you wouldn't have time or space to include them all in your map. Second, you'll have to

ELEMENT	EXPLANATION	SHELLY'S EXAMPLE
Beings	People and other creatures who this interaction touches or emerges from. Think as inclusively as possible about *all* the embodied aspects of an interaction: bodies, moods, habits, needs, values, and expectations.	• Shelly as author, and her readers • Friends who fly drones with her but don't read her blog • The Australian shepherd puppy who never leaves her side • The mosquitoes whose bites made her jerk the controls of her drone and take a different picture

Environment	Any object or condition that can be sensed and can shape the interaction.	• Physical conditions including weather and temperature • Arrangements of objects (including the waterfalls themselves) • Food and drink • Both her flying environment and her video-editing and blog-composing environments
Events	Happenings and circumstances that precede, lead to, surround, and shape an interaction.	• A hard day at work before flying in the evening • A new battery in the drone giving more flying time • A talk with a friend about how to get better waterfall video
Texts	As Porter (p. 542) shows, the network of texts linked to an interaction (or other text). The links might or might not be explicitly noted in the interaction.	• The drone instruction manual • Shelly's past blog posts • The blogs of other drone videographers • FAA printed notices on drone regulations
Structures	Any kind of "preset" rule, pattern, policy, or other "given" that arranges or organizes an interaction. Structures can be social, material, institutional, conceptual, and lingual. Structures make rhetorical interaction possible to begin with by creating a shared symbol system for meaning-making.	• The FAA's drone regulations themselves (institutional) • The genre conventions of drone-video blogs (conceptual) • The meetings of a drone flyers club Shelly participates in (social) • The Forest Service trails, handrails, and boundaries leading to a given waterfall (material) • The languages of drone-flying and videography (lingual)

(*Continued*)

Dispositions	A "leaning" or a tendency, a pre-existing desire or a default expectation of the way something should be. Conditions, activities, or attitudes a being, structure, or interaction is pre-set to favor or disfavor. Rhetorical ecologies are usually complex enough to have multiple sets of competing dispositions.	• Shelly has a cheerful disposition • The light is usually best for shooting outdoor video in the hour before sunset • Particular drone maneuvers always make for the best video shots • Shelly's blog posts usually introduce new waterfall video in the same way

set artificial boundaries on your map. In the same way that the elements in an ecology seem entangled with each other, your ecology will merge into other ecologies. You'll have to decide for yourself where your ecology "ends."

These limitations are okay because we're more interested in your *awareness of the ecology* than the exact map you make of it.

Making Your Map   Your map needs to depict the "web" or "network" you discover as you explore a given ecology: not just its individual elements, but their connections and relations to one another. This need suggests that you compose a *network chart* or *mind map* — an image that shows elements in the ecology as hubs or nodes, and relationships among the elements shown as connecting lines, or by positioning relative to each other. There is a wide range of software and apps that will help you create such diagrams, much of it free. (XMind, FreeMind, Coggle, MindNode, Scapple, and MindMeister are a few examples. Prezi or Visio would also serve the purpose. You may also be aware of animation software that would allow you to create your "fly-through" maps to be "played" as videos.)

You have a lot of choices in how to create your map. Here are some things you can think about:

- Spatially, you'll need to decide how you want to lay out the various elements. You might choose to literally map the ecology onto a photo or diagram of the space of the interaction. Or you might use other conceptual arrangements, like putting the speaking rhetors at the center of the diagram and other elements webbed out from them; or a chart to be read chronologically, either backward or forward in time.
- You'll need to choose design elements such as fonts, colors, the shapes of your element-nodes, and the look of the lines you draw to represent the

web. (See Jones and Wheeler's article, p. 654, for advice on usable and accessible designs.)

- You'll also need to consider what you'll say *about* your nodes and connections: how much you explain them, and how you include that explanation on, or with, your map.

- Your map will also need an introduction explaining your subject — the interaction and ecology you are mapping — and overviewing the ecology. This introduction might include reflection on what you learned or realized in making the map.

What Makes It Good? This is a big project, both in terms of the observation and analysis that will help you decide what to put on your map, and in terms of designing and laying it out. The first thing that will make it good is *time*: Do not expect to do this in half an hour. Here are some other ways to know you're on the right track:

- Get all the *big stuff.* You won't be able to entirely map the ecology, but don't leave out the obvious rhetors and agents, things that very clearly make a big difference to the rhetorical interaction.

- Think at least as much about *relationships* as about *elements.* You will make a more interesting map (and learn more) if you think carefully about the relationships among ten rhetors or elements than if your map includes fifty elements but you don't seriously consider the relationships between them. Ecology is about *influence*, *symbiotics*, and *connectedness*. Give this a lot of attention.

- Take your *introduction* seriously. Your map will show the ecology, but your introduction will explain your map and your learning. Reflection will likely be most interesting if it says specifically how this project has changed your understanding of rhetorical interaction (if it has) and how you might use this awareness in the future. Make sure that your map *design* emphasizes the main points you want your map to make. If you concentrate on really rich descriptions of the elements and their connections, don't make the font that gives those descriptions tiny and unreadable. If one of your main points is how *time* is a major factor in your ecology, make sure you create a map that helps readers visualize time.

ANALYZING RHETORICAL VELOCITY IN SOCIAL MEDIA

This assignment is based on Ridolfo and DeVoss's article "Composing for Recomposition: Rhetorical Velocity and Delivery" (p. 512). It asks you to think, as those authors do, about writing that is created *with the specific goal of being rewritten by other people*. In this assignment, you'll look specifically at social-issue advocacy pieces (blog posts, commentaries, and editorials) written to "go viral" via social media, and how language and links from those pieces show up in other social media. The purpose of the assignment is to further explore, demonstrate, and practice with the concepts of velocity, ecology, and intertextuality in rhetorical interaction.

Choose an Issue, a Social Media Platform, and Texts   Start the project by choosing a social issue of interest to you. Next, decide which social media you want to search for texts related to your issue. Facebook, Pinterest, Instagram, Twitter, or any other sharing-based social media should work fine. (You could also search across platforms.)

What you'll be looking for on these sites is memes, links, images, listicles, blog posts, or other commentaries that make arguments on your issue of interest. Your main task will be to trace the pieces you find in your social media streams back to their original versions and places of publication. Remember that you're not just looking for *repostings* or copies of a piece; you're looking for "transformative" re-creations of the piece, new texts that carry significant portions of the earlier texts.

In this assignment, you're trying to trace the *velocity* of a piece: from its point of origin (if you can find your way back to that from where you first encounter it on social media), what directions it goes, at what rates, and what it becomes. You can accomplish this purpose by finding several rewrites of one piece, or by finding a few original/rewrite pairs. Try to come up with a total of three or four rewrites, one way or another.

Get to Know the Original   Having collected this group or *corpus* ("body") of texts, your next task will be reading the original rhetorically so that you can talk about what genre it is, its context, and its main lines of argument and evidence. As in all rhetorical reading, you need to assess the exigence and motivation underlying the text, how its readers are meant to *use* the text, and what it is trying to accomplish.

Since you're dealing with advocacy for a particular social issue, the text is likely argument-based and may have a "campaign" feel to it. You should, in all of the textual analysis for this project, pay very careful attention to sources of *support* for the advocacy piece. Who does the writer work for? What organization(s) are publishing or funding the piece? What social groups does the text seem to align with (or say that it is)?

As you're getting a firm grasp of the nature of the original — its arguments, context, and sources — also begin paying attention to "portable" elements of the document that could be easily appropriated in later texts. These might be graphical features: What images does the original use? Where do its images come from? Does the piece include a logo or other standard graphical elements? They might also be particularly strong lines or quotable language, chunks of text that will show up in later documents. Especially notice links, which are probably the most frequently forwarded part of social advocacy documents.

Trace Transformations   Your next task is to look at how pieces of the earliest or "original" text you found get recombined in the later texts. Especially if your analysis deals with memes, there's some chance that you'll encounter a ring or web of texts combining elements from each other back and forth. If you're working with longer pieces like blog posts or commentaries, you might just see key lines, paragraphs, or links "forwarding" into later pieces. Because the web makes hypertext more convenient than physical rewriting of one piece into another, sometimes you'll find a later text built entirely around an earlier text, but simply summarizing the original and linking to it, rather than writing large parts of it into the new text. Since there isn't just one kind of velocity or intertextuality, describing specifically the kind you're finding is important.

In analyzing the later texts that have drawn from originals, you'll want to consider the same categories that you did in getting to know the original, plus some additions:

- What *genres* are the new texts and how different or "far" are those from the original? (For example, has a speech turned into a meme? Is a commentary being rewritten into another commentary, or into a fundraising ad?)

- How is material from the original text *attributed* or *acknowledged* in the new texts? Is the original text referenced at all? If so, is it linked? Named? Discussed? Credited?

- Is there a difference in *hook* in the new material versus original? Oftentimes velocity is toward "sharpening" or "sound-biting" or reducing a longer, more thorough, more thoughtful piece into a punchline, headline, or catchphrase. A remix or rewrite might grab only the original's catchiest, highest-impact parts.

- Has the *look* of the new texts changed while the language remains the same? Because memes are visually oriented, often what changes is not the words but the images.

- What is the newer texts' *stance* toward the rewritten material? On Twitter, for instance, a tweet is repeated *critically* in later tweets. The original is recirculating, but in a way that disses it.

- Where do the rewrites *come from* — who is authoring and publishing them? Some social media enterprises do nothing but use and manage rhetorical velocity by republishing speeches, presentations, or texts from notable social advocates with a "honed" message. As of this writing, some of the most prolific are Upworthy, Jezebel, Vox, Buzzfeed, Gateway Pundit, Infowars, and Breitbart.

Examine Velocity, Intertext, and Ecology   The shared elements and differences in the documents will give you ways to talk about their rhetorical velocity. We can't predict everything you might investigate or find about the texts you're looking at, but here are a few questions it will help to ask.

- Think about *timing* and *rate*. How *quickly* have the new texts followed the original? Is it a matter of minutes, hours, days, or weeks? Does the timing seem to pattern itself according to genre, subject, or writer?

- Consider what elements of the original seem *most likely to be forwarded*, repeated, or remixed. Particular kinds of language? Graphics and visuals? Are originals by one person or kind of person likely to be reused differently than those by other people?

- Look for patterns in where the texts come *from* and go *to* — who tends to originate, who tends to reuse? This has to do with the *directionality* aspect of velocity. You are likely to find habits among who rewrites what.

- Consider how rewrites *cross ecologies* and bring new *readership*, if they do. Do you find an original written for one group of rhetors (say, wealthy donors to a cause) and rewrites designed for a completely different group (say, community organizers)?

- Look for *networks of texts* emerging in your analysis. Do you find an "echo chamber," where a small number of texts keep citing and rewriting each other?

- Look for ways the original text seems to have "meant" itself to be able to be rewritten, and for ways that rewrites seem to have "made" the original rewriting when it didn't necessarily "mean" to be.

Remember that ultimately the focus of your research is tracing velocity and looking for patterns in it. Any questions that assist this task are worth asking.

Making Your Report Your research and analysis will lead to a text of your own, but the nature of that text will be up to you and your instructor. Because your analysis is likely to be graphics-intensive, since the texts you'll be studying are themselves multimodal and graphical, it's unlikely you're going to create a traditional alphabetic essay. Instead, your analysis text will need to use modalities that make it easy to include images of the texts you studied, and possible to graphically annotate those images yourself. Because velocity has a *time* component, you may want to design your analysis text in ways that can emphasize and demonstrate time flow — perhaps a flowchart, a network diagram, or even ultimately a video. Because it's possible that the texts you've studied were videos or included videos, your analysis text may need to have audio capacity so that you can embed or link videos and soundfiles. It could be, then, that you compose your analysis text in Prezi or PowerPoint or other software that makes integrating audio/visual material relatively easy.

Because composing in these modalities is much more complex than straightforward alphabetic composing tends to be, we recommend that you don't try to do your analysis of your texts *while* simultaneously composing a text that reports your analysis. But because of the epistemic nature of writing, it would not be unusual for you to discover new things to say in your analysis *while* you're composing your report of it. Try to stay open to new ideas.

What Makes It Good?

- *Study a meaningful group of texts.* To a point, the larger your sample, the more you're going to see and the more faith you and your readers will be able to have in your conclusions. Looking at eight texts is better than looking at three. As important as size is quality: Try to choose texts that are good examples of what you want to focus on.

- *Read rhetorically, smartly, and mindfully.* Better analyses are those that notice more about the texts they study, and make more connections.

- *Come up with an interesting claim.* Make sure that the main point of your piece goes beyond *describing* what the texts you studied are doing to draw some conclusion or make some comment about the *implications* of what your observations mean.

- *Have strong examples.* When you draw a conclusion or make an assertion about a pattern or an effect you see in the texts, you need clear, meaningful examples to show what leads you to your claim.

- *Use images when you need to use images.* There is no point trying to write an artful verbal description of what an image looks like when you could just exercise some velocity of your own and include a copy of the image you're trying to describe in your own text.

- *Compose in modalities that fit what you need to show and what you want to say.* Make your document design align with the points you want to make.

CHAPTER 5

PROCESSES:
How Are Texts Composed?

AP Photo / Marcio Jose Sanchez

While we often think of writing as a solitary activity, the reality is that writers — who are creating texts that help mediate activities — are constantly working with readers and other writers as they write. In this photo, writer Rodes Fishburne hangs his ideas in an office shared by a group of freelancers. The shared office space provides lots of readers and helps the writers' ideas progress. (See Stacey Pigg's piece "Coordinating Constant Invention" for a profile of a writer using the same strategies through social media.)

So far in this book, we have considered how individuals' literate histories influence their current literacy practices and attitudes, how the texts individuals create are constructed and influenced by other people, and how texts are constructed and make meaning. Now we will focus on how people create texts: the processes by which individuals put words on a page and attempt to make meaning — for themselves as well as for and with others. How do writers' individual writing processes vary to respond to changing contexts? Are there aspects of writing process that are typical across many contexts for most writers?

Answering the question, "How do I write?" isn't as easy as it seems. How well do you really understand how you get things written? How would you describe your writing process if asked to do so right now? And is what you *think you do* actually *what you do?*

While many people are quite conscious of "what works for them" in order to get a text written, they tend to have more difficulty explaining *why* it works — or even what they're doing, beyond some basic details like "I write down a lot of ideas until I feel like I know what I want to say and then I just start typing it up." Such a description doesn't actually tell us a lot. Yet it would seem that if you want to become a more versatile, capable, powerful writer, you need to be pretty aware of which activities, behaviors, habits, and approaches lead to your strongest writing — and which ones don't.

Understanding yourself as a writer is complicated by popular conceptions (or misconceptions) of what writing is and how it gets done. As you've seen in earlier chapters of this book, many of our conceptions related to writing (like imagining it to have universal rules, or cultural attitudes toward originality in writing) are inaccurate. These misconceptions are not harmless; they can impact what we do and don't do, what we are willing to try or not, and how we feel about ourselves and our writing — our self-efficacy, how competent and powerful we feel at doing a given activity. In the case of writing processes, several popular but incorrect conceptions seem to be that good writers write alone, using "inspiration" or genius; that writing does not make new knowledge but rather simply transmits existing information; that some people are born writers and others are not; and that good writing is easy and "automatic" for good writers, who don't have to think about what they're doing. If we believe these things about writing, we might be less likely to try to write better, assuming that if we struggle we simply aren't "natural writers." Or we might not ask other people for feedback, assuming that good writers should be able to produce something by themselves without feedback from readers.

These misconceptions happen to be addressed by a number of **threshold concepts** which the readings in this chapter demonstrate:

- Writers do not, in fact, write alone, because writing is extensively collaborative, and some writing scholarship demonstrates ways this is true.
- Writers don't just pass existing knowledge from one place to another; the act of writing helps make new knowledge, in part through intertextuality — bringing existing texts together in new ways. (Because texts get their meaning from other texts.)
- Most good writers neither find writing easy nor "get it right the first time," because revision is central to developing writing and writing is imperfectible.
- Good writers are made, not born, through extensive practice and through circumstance. Writers always have more to learn.
- Writers always have more to learn in part because writing is technological, not natural, and technology is always evolving — and directly shaping writing processes.
- Writing is enhanced by **mindfulness** and reflection — a writer thinking about what they are actually doing, and consciously controlling their process. Researchers on learning and thought call this *metacognition*, thinking about thinking.

Writing researchers have collected useful data on what people are doing when they write, so that they can show novice writers what experienced writers are doing, get them to practice doing similar things, and help them find their own writing groove along the way. We've selected the readings in this chapter to speak to a variety of the concepts above, so we've outlined the readings here to show how they contribute to a greater understanding of process. Writing researchers are particularly interested in where a writer's ideas come from and how they develop over time. So studies of composing processes seriously examine **invention**, or how writers (or **rhetors**) think up ideas over time, whether through multiple drafts, or outlines, or lots of mulling and percolating and interaction with other people. In Stacey Pigg's "Coordinating Constant Invention: Social Media's Role in Distributed Work" (p. 711), readers see the ways in which one professional writer uses social media to think together with other writers and work from existing texts to create new knowledge for other writers to draw on. Pigg's study helps us think about how writers work collaboratively rather than alone, how they use intertextuality (see Porter, p. 542) to develop some of their ideas, and how their texts do not simply send existing knowledge from place to place but actually develop new knowledge. Pigg's research also helps readers see how writing technologies — in this case, social media — shape the writing process, and how writers (and readers!) always have more to learn.

Many writers in this chapter are concerned not only with invention but also with **planning** and **revision**. Sondra Perl examines in great detail the many ways in which her research participants divide their time while writing — and how this influences the quality of what they write. Perl's work engages the threshold concepts of knowledge-making and the importance of revision. In addition, her attention to developing writers emphasizes the concept that all writers have more to learn and that writing *can be* learned. A student researcher, Alcir Santos Neto, follows a similar method of study and adds attention to some aspects of writing that Perl didn't, expanding her code to include distractions and to talk about the inventional challenges of thinking and writing in separate languages. Both Neto and Perl demonstrate the influence of a writer's mindfulness and reflection on their writing as well.

The same is true of Mike Rose's work, in which he explores writers' self-awarenesss of rules they believe apply to writing and how those beliefs can actually block them *from* writing. Compared with writers who treat rules flexibly and say what they want before thinking about following rules, other writers are so busy trying not to break any rules that they have difficulty thinking of anything to say. Rose ultimately emphasizes that part of the way writers need to keep developing is to grow their awareness of the beliefs they have about writing and rules for writing, and to learn how "true" those rules are. Many people come to believe, typically during early schooling, that writing *can* and *should* be perfectible, mistake-free. But Joseph Williams points out that whether people *perceive* the presence of an error in writing sometimes depends less on whether the error is there and more on whether they *expect* a certain kind of writer to make errors — say, student writers versus professional writers. Michael Rodgers, one such student researcher, has created a literacy narrative that emphasizes his learning that, in fact, writing "one's own way" not only may not be opposed to the knowledge-making work of scholarly writing but might actually help it.

Much the same turns out to be true of a professional, award-winning writer. Carol Berkenkotter, in "Decisions and Revisions: The Planning Strategies of a Publishing Writer") observes Donald Murray at work with his writing. (And Murray responds with "Response of a Laboratory Rat — or, Being Protocoled.") Berkenkotter observes that Murray, too, emphasizes the importance of personal investment in writing while still being able to accomplish serious work. The study shows the advantages of closely examining process in order to become mindful of how the various phases of a writing process — such as planning, drafting, reading, and revising — blend together and may not go in order. By studying Murray's process, Berkenkotter found that Murray was doing a lot of planning via revision — returning us to the threshold concept that writing is not easy even for award-winning professional writers, and writing by good writers rarely comes out "right" the first time. Anne Lamott speaks to the same concept in her very popular piece "Shitty First Drafts" — insisting that as writers we have permission to write badly at first, as a necessary step in finding our way to better later drafts. The weight that these writers put on revision and their belief that meaning emerges through multiple drafts leads us to Nancy Sommers's finding that student writers often don't understand that ideas emerge through the act of writing, and thus they tend to see revision as changing words rather than as a chance to continue to find their ideas.

There are a number of other ways to understand the readings in this chapter as well, depending on what aspects of the writing process you are focusing on. For example, because writing is in the realm of thought and ideas, we're dealing with **cognition** — the mental aspect of writing — when we think about process. You'll see a number of the researchers in this chapter thinking about, theorizing about, modeling, and testing problem-solving patterns, or **heuristics,** and other guesses at how our brains process ideas in order to construct meaning in texts (both as writers and readers); see, for example, Rose (p. 787), Berkenkotter (p. 830), and Sommers (p. 858). Along with the cognitive, some researchers consider the *affective* domain — that is, what goes on with the body and with emotions. Berkenkotter (p. 830), Lamott (p. 852), Perl (p. 738), and Murray (p. 846) think about these issues. This is where **context** comes in: Writing depends not only on the ideas in your brain, but on whether you're trying to write in a journal under a tree on a gorgeous sunny afternoon, or in a fluorescent-lit cubicle with a boss breathing over your shoulder who needs your memo on budget cuts right away. It also depends on the history of the writer (think about what you learned in Chapter 2) and his or her previous experiences with writing, with the ideas currently under consideration, with the **genre** being written, etc. Our environment and **rhetorical situation** shape our thoughts, so the cognitive domain never stands apart from what's outside our brains and bodies.

Still, writing is ultimately the meaning we make in our heads, so to understand composing processes, we have to somehow look inside our heads. This is the tricky part of writing research, as you'll see reflected in the numerous **methodologies** (procedures for conducting research) the research studies in this chapter use and demonstrate. The basic problem is this: Researchers can't directly access what's happening in your brain; they have to infer what's happening by looking for external signs. You could *tell* researchers what you're thinking, although (1) you can't talk as fast as you think, and (2) the talking inevitably *changes* what you're thinking. Researchers could look at the mistakes you make and try to explain the rules you're following (which you're probably not even aware of). They could interview you and study the words you use to express yourself. They could ask you to draw about your processes and all of the resources on which you rely while writing. But they would still never know *exactly* what's going on in there. (Not even you know that, really.) So, in these readings, you'll see researchers working to get at something that we can't access directly.

CHAPTER GOALS

- To acquire vocabulary for talking about writing processes and yourself as a writer
- To actively consider your own writing processes and practices and shift them as needed
- To understand writing and research as processes requiring planning, incubation, revision, and collaboration
- To improve as a reader of complex, research-based texts

Coordinating Constant Invention

Social Media's Role in Distributed Work

STACEY PIGG

Stacey Pigg

Framing the Reading

You've probably heard "social media" such as Facebook, Twitter, Instagram, and blogging denigrated as harmful to good writing. Often news media and cultural criticism tell us that social media are shallow, distracting, self-involved, and trite — a waste of time and attention. And, very frequently, these critics discount social media *as writing*. So there is an image of social media, culturally, as getting in the way of writing rather than assisting or *being* meaningful writing.

Stacey Pigg is one of a number of writing researchers who is skeptical of that easy storyline about the negative impacts of social media, and she decided to study what writers *actually* do with it rather than accepting easy cultural jokes about social media only being good for pictures of people's dinners. In actually observing professional writers going about their work while also engaging with social media, Pigg comes to a number of findings that relate to the threshold concepts that writing is not perfectible, that writing helps people make meaning and get things done, and that writing is constrained, in part by technology. In this article, we see **invention** as an **intertextual** activity, and observe a writer who, while working by himself, is not actually solitary. Instead, he works collaboratively with other writers through social media. Further, writers don't simply pass information along from one place to another; they "weave" and "coordinate" from many existing sources of knowledge in order to be "knowledge workers" making new knowledge. Pigg's research also offers a powerful demonstration of not just how writing *is* technological, but how the particular writing technologies that come together in blogging actively shape the texts created by the writer Pigg is observing.

TECHNICAL
COMMUNICATION
QUARTERLY

Pigg, Stacey. "Coordinating Constant Invention: Social Media's Role in Distributed Work." *Technical Communication Quarterly*, vol. 23, no. 2, March 2014, pp. 69–87.

What readers can take from Pigg's work, then, is a thought-provoking description of one way that writers can move among writing and reading on many social media sites in ways that are not simply distracting or time-consuming (although they might be both), but in fact help the writer come up with what to say, create a sense of what is important to write about, and directly inform the writing that's happening. Her work shows us, among other important lessons, that some of the cultural cynicism around social media exists *because* commentators have inaccurate expectations of writing to begin with. If you imagine that writing is supposed to be created by a silent writer working on her own, then you're likely to imagine writing that takes place in constant conversation with other people via social media to be less valuable. But if writing was never actually such a solitary activity to begin with, then writing via social media makes a lot more sense.

Stacey Pigg published this piece while an assistant professor at the University of Central Florida, and she is now an assistant professor at North Carolina State University. Her reseach has long been grounded in examining the impact of new digital writing technologies on writing broadly and on students writing in school. As a graduate student, she was part of the WIDE survey team at Michigan State University; you can read more about their findings on students' use of digital writing technologies in Chapter 2 (p. 245).

Getting Ready to Read

Before you read, do at least one of the following activities:

- Do you have a clear sense of what a blog *is* — what kinds of web pages blogs are, what a page needs to have or be in order to be considered a blog? Write a description of what blogs are, based on what you know, and then make a list of blogs you frequently read or encounter (if you do).

- Make a list of the "social media" you regularly use. Usually we use that term to refer to online applications whose purpose is to share experiences (and objects like photos and music files) of your own with other people, and to talk about those shared things. Blogs are social media, and so are Twitter, Instagram, Pinterest, Facebook, and similar sites. Once you've made your list, write down some of the *reasons* you use the social media sites you do. Why do you use them, or, what do you do with them?

As you read, consider the following questions:

- How do the blogs that people in Pigg's study use compare with the ones you use or read?

- How (and where) does Pigg explain her reasons for designing and conducting her study as she did?

INTRODUCTION

The texture of symbolic work is always shifting. Locations and technologies that would have been considered personal in the past are central to contemporary work life for many people. For instance, today's cafés, coffee shops, and book-stores are often crowded with writers who are also workers: individuals huddled over laptops taking advantage of clean space, wireless networks, and available supplies of caffeine. Many of those workers fit Reich's (1991) definition of the "symbolic analyst," whose work involves creative and critical thinking and man-aging complex information (pp. 177–180). Building on Reich, Johnson-Eilola (2005) described how symbolic analysts "tend to work online, either communi-cating with peers (they rarely have direct organizational supervision) or manip-ulating symbols" (p. 28). Symbolic-analytic work often develops over multiple times and spaces, involves many different people, and requires layers of expertise and communication. 1

Recent scholarship has explored how the "distributed" nature of this work affects career trajectories and work practices of professional and technical com-municators (Spinuzzi, 2007). With knowledge workers increasingly discon-nected from desk and office spaces on the one hand, and with contract and freelance work on the rise on the other, professional communicators whose work is symbolic-analytic often face a dual burden: composing an immediate time and space to conduct their work and overcoming a long-term lack of stability related to future professional opportunities. This alternative positioning requires activities such as locating and constructing rhetorical spaces (virtual and physi-cal) to support multiple writing tasks (see Spinuzzi, 2012; Swarts & Kim, 2007). However, it also requires what might be described as "invention," when that term refers to a general sense of "the creation of what is new in any discipline or endeavor" (LeFevre, 1987, p. 2) and invokes what Grabill (2007) has described as a "problem of knowledge" related to creating discourse in the presence of multiple conflicting epistemologies (pp. 14–15). In contexts where knowledge is distributed and shared, social contexts cannot be assumed; writers must con-struct relational networks among people with shared interests (Swarts, 2011) and sense opportunities for future action and consider when and how to shift practices or discourse in response to them. 2

Drawing on prior research and scholarship, this article begins to trace how social media and digital participatory writing environments are intertwined with the inventive practices of symbolic analysts who work outside traditional orga-nizational structures. Since sites like Facebook, My Space, Flickr, LinkedIn, and Last FM emerged in 2003 and 2004, networked spaces are not only increasingly integrated into many individuals' everyday habits (see Lenhart, Purcell, Smith, & Zickuhr, 2010) but also have become crucial interpersonal communication tools that span personal and work domains (see boyd & Ellison, 2008). Kaplan and 3

Haenlein (2010) defined social media as "Internet-based applications that build on the ideological and technological foundations of Web 2.0 and allow the creation and exchange of User Generated Content" (p. 61). In contrast to early Web sites, in which content was understood to move linearly from designer to audience, a nonhierarchical model of exchange grounds social media. Although this social context is not unique to networked writing environments, social media not only promote decentered exchange but also frequently make social and intertextual connections visible and immediate, and indicate where relationships might exist. For example, blogs frequently include a "blog roll" that lists affiliated writers who share interests as well as hyperlinks to associated content on other sites. Similarly, popular social networking and microblogging sites such as LinkedIn, Twitter, and Facebook display lists of friends or followers such that observers can see relationships concretized. Social media establish proximity as they visualize relationships. As boyd and Ellison state, "They enable users to articulate and make visible their social networks" (p. 211).

Social media offer a means through which individuals can aggregate people 4 and knowledge or, at the least, learn how existing webs of participation are held together. In this article, I first build on recent technical communication scholarship to identify social coordination through digital technologies as a significant rhetorical activity for contemporary symbolic analysts. I further describe why work to build and understand social context is particularly important for professional communicators working outside or across traditional organizational structures. To learn from an example of how coordination intersects with social media, I then turn my attention to the work habits and practices of Dave,[1] a professional communicator whose blogging and microblogging created a traceable location for his professional activity and enabled alliances that grounded ongoing projects. As I illustrate through Dave's case, networked writing environments help knowledge workers gain access to existing communities of practice, maintain a presence within them, and leverage community norms to circulate texts through them. Social media accomplish not only the "textual coordination" that Slattery (2007) identified as the point when writers assemble new texts from written fragments but also social coordination that brings together distributed knowledge needed to invent texts, identities, and careers.

Dave's fast-paced movement across multiple social writing platforms during a time-mapped writing session shows him juggling layered responsibilities of constantly inventing texts, alliances, and his own professional persona.

Although this function of social media is itself 5 worth the note of technical and professional communication teachers and researchers, we can also learn more broadly applicable lessons from Dave's story. Dave's fast-paced movement across multiple social writing platforms during a time-mapped writing session shows him juggling layered responsibilities of constantly inventing texts, alliances, and his own professional persona. To maintain presence in social networks, he must constantly monitor and participate in their symbolic exchange. Investigating and building the social context for professional communication requires more time, effort, vigilance, and forms of symbolic action than we often realize. Social media help knowledge workers perform this work not only because of their design but also because they are ubiquitous in contemporary personal and professional landscapes—a normalized and routine part of many individuals' technological repertoires. Subtle and continual shifts in technology use and organizational structure that reshape the cultural field of professional communication translate to radical changes in individual work practice.

DISTRIBUTED WORK, COORDINATION, AND SOCIAL MEDIA

The decentralization of organizations, the increasing movement of writing into informal locations, and the collaborative nature of writing continue to challenge the foundations of technical and professional communication. Spinuzzi's (2007) introduction to the *TCQ* special issue on distributed work, "Technical Communication in the Age of Distributed Work" defined distributed work as the "coordinative, polycontextual, crossdisciplinary work that splices together divergent work activities (separated by time, spaces, organizations, and objectives) and that enables the transformations of information and texts that characterize such work" (p. 266). Though Spinuzzi's introduction offered technical and professional communication a definition and terminology for a prevalent cultural turn affecting workplaces worldwide, it also captured a sense of ambivalence toward the effects of this changing landscape on the field. On the one hand, distributing expertise, people, and texts has the potential to decenter traditional hierarchies of information flow in ways that can empower publics (see Grasso, Meunier, Pagani, & Pareschi, 1997; Victor & Boynton, 1998; Zuboff & Maxmin, 2002). On the other hand, it also restructures the way professional careers are lived and experienced, as stability and expertise are replaced by ongoing shifts and inventions. Quoting Deleuze (1995), Spinuzzi painted a grim portrait:

> The result is a sort of endless postponement rather than a defined avenue of development; workers travel in continuously changing orbits, they undulate, they find themselves switching jobs and careers and positionalities ([Deleuze], p. 180). The factory is gone, as are unions and lifetime employment; the best way to get a raise is to switch jobs. (p. 270)

The necessary skills for navigating this landscape involve "negotiation" and "agility" in creating, maintaining, and reorganizing alliances (Spinuzzi, 2007, pp. 271–272). The idea of the assemblage (see Latour, 2005) becomes

715

an important unit for understanding what remains stable for now among the fluctuations, as groups of texts, technologies, and people are configured and reconfigured in service of constantly changing goals. The activity that describes the act of making assemblages—coordinating—is a key component of creating momentary stability and overcoming distance. As Spinuzzi described it, "Coordinative work . . . enables sociotechnical networks to hold together and form dense interconnections among and across work activities that have traditionally been separated by temporal, spatial, or disciplinary boundaries" (p. 268).

Coordination has thus emerged as a central activity within theories of distrib- [8] uted work, calling new attention to how people, texts, tasks, and technologies are grouped in ways that enable action. As Slattery (2007) noted, most research on distributed work has aimed its descriptive lens at organizations or society at large, analyzing the flattening of expertise and the use of information technology to facilitate interaction and exchange necessary for assembling. Arguing for a turn toward how individual writers within organizations are affected by distribution, Slattery detailed the fast-paced movement of one technical writer moving across multiple documents that he recombined. Through activity he called "textual coordination" (Slattery, 2005, 2007), assembling texts becomes an antidote to distribution: the means through which writers "undistribute" expertise existing across different people, texts, and technologies, resolidifying it into one document or text assembled from multiple others. For Slattery, the rhetorical skill inherent in this activity involves work to mitigate the effects of distribution through "effective weaving" together of disparate textual elements, as well as the ability to "identify and solicit needed information" (p. 322). However, the status of coordination as a work activity for technical writers remained problematic in Slattery's discussion "not only in that coordination is more difficult to perform, but in that it begins to constitute the area of expertise of the technical writer" (p. 323). For Slattery, understanding coordination as expertise presents problems for two reasons: First, it positions technical communicators as experts "not in what information should be organized and how, but only in the process of bringing it together," an especially difficult situation for contract and freelance writers who often lack authority within organizational structures (p. 323); second, its presence threatens to reduce technical communicators' expertise to functional technological skill (p. 323).

The coordination that individual symbolic analysts practice, however, is [9] already more diverse and supported by a broader range of writing technologies than this description implies. For example, charged with assembling both expertise and infrastructures to support it, symbolic-analytic workers

- layer texts and resources needed to complete projects
- manage multiple competing projects (Gonzalez & Mark, 2004)

- balance personal and work domains (Bay, 2010; Geisler, 2004; Golden & Geisler, 2007)
- assemble component parts of disparate technologies into "functional systems" that work strategically to solve everyday problems (Van Ittersum, 2009).

As Swarts and Kim aptly described it, "Writing becomes an act of building the places in which . . . information is used" (p. 219). The work of "building" also involves learning social and epistemic norms such that one can effectively participate in groups and communities that make knowledge together. That is, when knowledge is understood as "deeply rhetorical, coordinated in its products and communal in its meaning and value," inventing knowledge requires that individuals find ways of connecting to resources that help them understand and build social context (Grabill, 2007, p. 28). We might further refer to the range of rhetorical activities that facilitate this building (e.g., making relationships, gaining access to understanding discursive norms, and listening and learning from ongoing conversations) as forms of coordination. In this sense, coordination is central to invention, particularly for individual knowledge workers who not only assemble fragments into texts, but also assemble projects or assignments into a career. When faced with activities that require communal knowledge building, workers outside traditional organizational structures often cannot assume the presence of established information communication technologies to facilitate exchange. In this case, individual professional communicators bear the burden of constructing a means for bringing together texts, technologies, and people to produce texts in the short term and sustain work practice in the long term.

Social media, with their broad availability and high percentage of use, offer 10 unique affordances for overcoming fragmentation. Discussing Twitter in particular, Zhou and Rosson (2009) argued that short conversational updates "help [employees] sustain a virtual feeling of proximity (i.e., being there, still there), enable more chances of exposure to what is on others' minds and what they have been doing, and provide possibilities to explore similar experiences and attitudes with each other" (p. 250). Zhou, Rosson, Matthews, and Thomas (2011) further demonstrated how social media's connective nature influences workplace collaboration. They argued that microblogging[2] facilitates informal project information sharing that heightens group awareness, creates more common ground in face-to-face project meetings, and provides collaborators with timely feedback and ongoing updates that build social context for collaborative work. Thompson (2008) has referred to this property of social media as cultivating "ambient awareness" that allows for maintaining weaker social ties (para. 11).

Although the relational properties of social media cultivate proximity, McNely 11 (2011) argued that social media practices like microblogging are often not recognized as work, but rather as "informal communication" that happens alongside it.

In spite of participants' categorizations, McNely suggested microblogging is "interstitial" work that "circulates in the in-between spaces of organizational writing work and carries meaning in non-traditional ways" (n.p.). Even this is a somewhat unusual categorization, as social Internet use in work contexts is more frequently constructed as "cyberslacking" (Garrett & Danzinger, 2008; Vitak, Crouse, & LaRose, 2011), "cyberloafing" (Blanchard & Henle, 2008), or non-work-related computing (Bock & Ho, 2009; Pee, Woon, & Kankanhalli, 2008). Although research has shown that control and surveillance protocols (i.e., blocking access to particular sites, monitoring Web usage) have largely negative effects on employees (de Lara, Tacoronte, & Ding, 2006), many workplaces still remove access to portions of the Internet, particularly social media outlets like Facebook, Twitter, and YouTube.

For symbolic analysts working as freelancers, however, organizational directives do not impose the same constraints on what Lanham (2006) called "attention structures" that direct focus or influence "how we pay attention to the world of human information and hence what we can make of it" (p. 14). The concept of attention structures highlights that attention is not merely individually directed but instead is mediated through institutions, technologies, and other social forces. Although Lanham's examples of attention structures range from mobilization of art forms to technological systems like video games, his suggestion that noncognitive forces mediate attention is relevant for understanding how new technologies and ongoing cultural shifts may affect individual work practices. Currently, however, we lack detailed portraits of how individual professional communicators' inventive practices are affected, or attention redirected, by the intersection of social media platforms with the cultural and technological turns pushing contemporary work practice toward continually more distributed contexts. With this backdrop in mind, I formulated the following questions, which are central to the research project from which the remainder of this article is drawn: 12

- How are social media affecting the day-to-day and moment-to-moment unfolding of professional writing work distributed geographically (i.e., outside sanctioned office spaces)?

- How are social media used as inventive coordinative technologies for professional communicators who are assembling professional trajectories from projects that span multiple organizations and interests?

RESEARCHING THE ROLE OF SOCIAL MEDIA IN DISTRIBUTED WORK

The larger study from which this case example was drawn explored everyday practices of distributed work in one informal public place: an independent coffeehouse. Drawing on Sullivan and Porter (1997), who argued for tracing 13 technologically mediated writing outside traditional spaces, this café was an ideal site for exploring the coordination practices of individual writers beyond the boundaries of a single organization or workplace. Once understood as primarily civic institutions, coffeehouses and coworking facilities (Spinuzzi, 2007, 2012) have emerged as important workspaces for mobile writers (Hampton & Gupta, 2008; Varnelis & Friedberg, 2008). With its access to high-speed wireless Internet, its location on a major avenue that links the university and government districts, its ample space for spreading out materials, its numerous power outlets, and, of course, the caffeine, the coffeehouse that was the focus of my study attracted writers who lacked offices or were in positions that made writing while mobile important.

During 6 weeks in 2009, I conducted participant observations within the café 14 for 5 days a week at varied times of the day. During participant observation, I observed the café's macro activity, noting prevalent technologies and software, observing when the café contained the most people writing, and determining where individuals who wrote often located themselves. This phase revealed that mobile technologies such as laptops and mobile phones[3] were important writing devices in this space. In addition, social media use was prevalent as an ongoing activity in the café for writers from different age groups who were writing for different purposes. In addition to focusing on mobile writing devices and social software, I identified café patrons who frequently used the space for writing and would be ideal case study participants.

Following the observation phase, I selected four research participants who 15 used the café frequently and habitually for writing to trace as case studies. These individuals demonstrated what Prior and Shipka (2003) referred to as environmental structuring and selecting practices involving repeated use of this coffee shop as an informal public writing workspace. After identifying participants and obtaining consent, I videotaped a writing work session that participants conducted at the café. My decision to videotape and analyze participants' writing[4] was motivated by Haas (1996), who argued that capturing writing activity in the interaction between bodies and technologies can help elucidate a middle ground of writing practice that illuminates both cognitive and cultural influences. My approach extended Haas's work by conceiving embodied practices as both physical bodily movements and on-screen, virtual practices.

Drawing on these approaches, I disturbed the routine of the writers as little 16 as possible as I videotaped writing in progress using an external video camera positioned to capture a view of their laptop screens, the artifacts present on their tables, and their bodies within the space (from behind). This enabled me to observe and analyze how writers manipulated various physical and virtual objects within their workspaces at multiple levels of scope and to capture tacit practices that potentially would be overlooked in retrospective self-reports. Drawing on

Slattery (2005, 2007), I analyzed these videotaped recordings by coding the data for central mediating artifacts or resources that held participants' attention during the unfolding work session. To categorize the sessions, I divided each work session into time segments based on duration spent working with a particular mediating resource. I used these coded work sessions to create visualizations of writing activity as it unfolded at the micro level. These visualizations identified patterns of use for networked technologies such as microblogs (i.e., Twitter), social networking sites (i.e., Facebook, LinkedIn), blogs, and e-mail as well as other material resources such as word processing programs, phones, and other external technologies.

After analyzing work sessions, I scheduled semistructured, stimulated recall [17] interviews with each participant to discuss his or her work session, focusing on a range of questions involving general habits for organizing writing space and time, as well as specific details related to work accomplished in the session I observed. These questions expanded the story of the writing routines that participants exhibited in their work sessions by contextualizing their micro movements within larger motivations and structures, including their organizational affiliations and professional or career trajectories. I then analyzed the interviews, focusing on social-media use, which I defined at its broadest to mean any act of reading or writing in an internetworked, participatory online system. For purposes of the study, I included e-mail within this category; it often functioned similarly to social networking sites and microblogs because it was checked and monitored frequently.

Each case study participant was engaged in multiple writing projects, rou- [18] tinely communicated with people geographically removed from his or her current physical location, and used social media either moderately or extensively during time spent working. In the remainder of this article, I present findings from one participant, whom I have chosen to discuss in detail because his observation session involved the complete production of one text written for a social media outlet and thus provided a rich example of both how and why social media intersect with inventive practice. My discussion will analyze which particular social media resources he accessed during his writing session, how they were integrated into time spent writing, and how this writer framed the broader purpose of time spent with social media within the context of his professional communication work.

THE ROLE OF SOCIAL MEDIA IN MICROLEVEL WORK PRACTICE

Social media are embedded in the material, technological contexts in which [19] many contemporary symbolic analysts work, and thus play crucial parts in the unfolding scripts of everyday symbolic-analytic practice. This was particularly true for Dave, a technology consultant who writes, consults, and teaches for a number of different academic, community, and nonprofit entities. Dave needed a workspace for undertaking this work; however, as a self-employed contractor, he had no official workspace and writing at home was difficult because he was a stay-at-home dad. Thus, Dave chose to work as often as possible in the local coffeehouse: one full scheduled workday a week and often much more. In this analysis of Dave's writing practice, I begin with the most fine-grained look at how he moves across textual and social resources during one work session that he devoted to producing a blog entry and then extend my analysis outward to more macro-level perspectives on this activity, including (a) how he describes the lifecycle of this particular social media project and (b) how he locates this blog activity and the coordinative work that supports it in relationship to his professional trajectory.

Resources Used

During my observation period in the café, Dave drafted, edited, and published 20 a post to his fatherhood blog, a task that lasted about 54 minutes and involved 119 different time segments (i.e., durations of time spent with a particular resource before moving to work with another). The activity of Dave's session happened almost exclusively within the boundaries of his 13-inch computer screen, drawing on a range of virtual tools that included many free, public, social software platforms. Because his visual screen space was limited, Dave almost never attended to more than one major object or site at a time. Instead, he moved across them in succession, keeping multiple tabs open on his browser that he could easily move across or minimize when needed. Table 1 lists the 15 different resources that Dave utilized. As the table indicates, Dave made the most visits to his WordPress dashboard during the observation, which did not surprise me because his dashboard housed the text editor in which he wrote and edited the blog post. However, Dave also checked Twitter and Gmail extensively and spent ample time reading five different blogs related in theme or content to the post he was producing.

Attending to Drafting, Monitoring, and Researching

The WordPress dashboard, Dave's primary location for drafting, occupied more 21 of his time than did any other resource. For purposes of the work session, Dave typed text directly into its editor, reading and revising text he had just written and inserting and manipulating images. Dave was not assembling this writing from prior materials (with the exception of locating and inserting images he had taken previously), so he was not repurposing existing text but instead was typing, erasing, and rewriting sentences.

TABLE 1 RESOURCES THAT DAVE ACCESSED DURING HIS 54-MIN BLOG-WRITING SESSION

RESOURCE CATEGORY	SPECIFIC RESOURCE	NUMBER OF TIMES ACCESSED	GENERAL USE
Blog text editor	WordPress Dashboard	28	Drafting current post, including metadata and inserting and manipulating images; checking analytics
Browser tab—blank	Google Chrome	4	Transitioning from one blog to another
E-mail	Gmail	16	Primarily monitoring; sending one message
Existing blog sites	Blog 1	6	Accessing information, icon, and community for participating in the Fatherhood Friday event
	Blog 2	7	Reading a past blog posting containing content similar to his own
	Blog 3	7	Reading a past blog posting containing content similar to his own
	Blog 4	11	Reading a past blog posting containing content similar to his own
	Blog 5	8	Reading a past blog posting containing content similar to his own
	Blog 6 (own blog)	1	Reading his recently completed and published posting
External technology	External hard drive	1	Accessing personal image files needed to draft the blog post
Feed reader	Google Toolbar for Chrome	5	Finding prior blog posts with similar content to his own
Microblog	Twitter accessed through Hootsuite	14	Monitoring ongoing activity, circulating final published blog post
Personal computer desktop screen	Mac OS	1	Transitioning from work done online through his browser to programs housed on his laptop
Personal computer folder and file structure	Image files stored on personal computer	7	Locating and choosing among image files previously created and stored
Photo editor	Photoshop	3	Creating a new image file from two previously existing images to include in the post

While WordPress anchored Dave's writing session, his workflow involved 22 fluid movement across multiple networked writing spaces, including those often considered personal. In particular, two dominant uses of social media during the inventive process can be visualized through a time mapping of Dave's writing activity. The first is a repeated, fast-paced movement of checking or monitoring online sites where he generally maintains presence or exchanges information. During time spent drafting, Dave monitored both Twitter and Gmail. In Figure 1, points mapped on the first and second horizontal grid lines represent this monitoring activity. As the figure indicates, when opening Twitter or Gmail on his laptop during the course of drafting, Dave often perused the site for a second or two, checking to see whether he had received new messages or whether an additional microblog update was present on his feed. Once during his writing session, Dave took the time to delete incoming e-mail (during minute 28) and he also posted two Twitter microblog posts during the process of composing: one early in his drafting session (during minute 10) and then later to circulate his recently completed and published blog post (during minute 54). However, nearly all time segments related to Twitter and Gmail were spent monitoring activity, with these sites open for only a second or two at a time before he returned to WordPress or another anchoring resource.

The second dominant use of social media involved reading for content-related 23 reference while writing. During the draft process, Dave first opened a blog posting that provided instructions on how to link his current post to a collection of fatherhood blogs organized on one community site. Joining the blog network curated by this aggregating blogger required that Dave include a "badge" or small icon in his published post, circulate his writing on Twitter accompanied by a particular *hashtag* (i.e., a word added to create a searchable link between multiple posts), and link his post back to this community blog. In addition to visiting this blog to remind himself of the conventions of his task, Dave also had installed a feed reader with a search mechanism in his Internet browser toolbar that enabled him to locate blog postings by other writers about similar topics. Using this search tool, he identified four previously published blog postings that were nearly identical in theme and content to his draft. Dave read these blog postings continually while writing, visiting them multiple times and quickly toggling between his own drafting and scanning existing posts. Dave's activity of reading and interacting with these published posts can be observed in the clusters of movement shown in Figure 1 that involve points plotted on the horizontal lines associated with blogs 2–5 — online locations he visited 5, 6, and 10 times, respectively, over the course of his writing. Although fast paced, this activity was notably different from checking Gmail or Twitter. Dave was not randomly visiting these sites to monitor changing activity; he targeted them because they offered specific information he might reference or use for inventive inspiration.

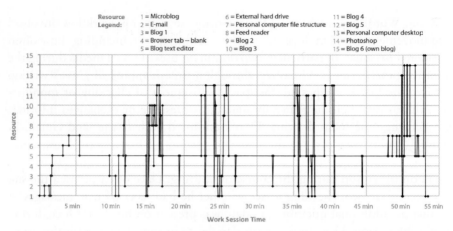

Figure 1 This time-mapping illustrates which resources Dave used and for how long during his drafting session. Numbers across the horizontal axis represent time elapsed in minutes. Numbers labeling the vertical axis represent the 15 resources Dave used. Looking at the chart from left to right indicates which resources Dave used and in what order.

This fine-grained time mapping of Dave's writing session reveals a multilay- 24 ered role for how different social media environments functioned: as production spaces, mechanisms for monitoring change, and resources for generating content by understanding histories related to one's content area. The combination of these three major uses of social media created a cycle during this writing session, as Dave visited the same sites repeatedly, moving from direct content generation to intertextual research to monitoring sites where change is evident. His work habits suggest that he makes use of social media outlets in groupings, much like what Slattery (2005) has called "constellations," or "recurrent patterns of mediating artifacts" accessed together as part of the composing process (p. 356). Furthermore, his use of multiple social media forms together is not surprising, given research showing that online searchers often move across multiple sites, "gathering information and turning that information into knowledge as they share it with others" (Potts, 2009, p. 284).

Visualizing Dave's work practice by grouping together his social media use as 25 constellations reinforces how networked writing environments are a continual presence in the writing session. In particular, as Figure 2 illustrates, the activity between minute 5 and minute 50 of the writing session was spent almost entirely moving back and forth between inventing language in his primary production environment and either monitoring social media or reading it for generating content. In other words, social media are not peripheral but central to producing new text, integrated (even if tacitly) into the processes and practices of written invention.

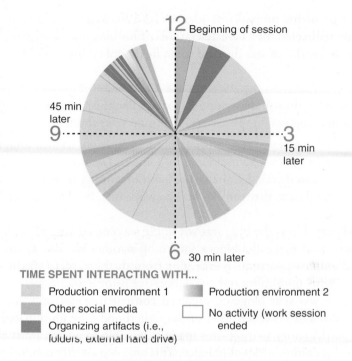

Figure 2 This figure visualizes which resources Dave used and for how long during his drafting session, when social media are grouped rather than differentiated. In this diagram, Dave's movement across inventive resources can be traced by moving clockwise around the circle beginning at 12.

THE LIFE CYCLE AND FUNCTION OF ONE SOCIAL-MEDIA PROJECT: THE ROLE OF THE FATHERHOOD BLOG

Time mapping revealed how networked participatory writing environments 26 functioned as both production and multipurpose research space. Dave's reflections on the life cycle of the particular project he was working on during this observation — his fatherhood blog — give further insight into why social media were important. Social technologies provided him multiple forms of coordinative reach. Social media reading and writing created access to a range of social inventive resources that he needed to understand participatory norms of the community for which he wrote, an activity central to creating knowledge with and for other bloggers.

I wish to pause to explain why Dave was blogging in the first place. Dave 27 revealed that an intricate desire for both interpersonal connection and future professional projects motivated time spent with the fatherhood blog, even as he juggled other, more immediately profitable, writing projects. Keeping a fatherhood blog might seem a personal activity, yet Dave described it as an integral part of his professional identity and work practice. For example, he frequently redirected my characterizations of his blogging as "writing" by referring to it as "work," as was the case when he described his choice to work in the coffee shop:

> STACEY: Why do you do writing in a space like this? Is there one major reason that you would say to sort of sum up your thoughts?
>
> DAVE: Well, when you can't work at home, you've got to find somewhere else to do it as long as you're interested in doing it. I've been actually here for like 3 years, so there's definitely that habit of coming here. Even though the blog is brand new, that coming here to work isn't. So that's just really it.

Dave elaborated how the blog was work: He was considering offers from advertisers that could make the blog a source of income. He also discussed future print and online opportunities emerging from the blog: social media work with children's rights nonprofits and a collaborative print book project to name two. Dave's sense was that blogging involved constructing not only texts but also relationships, and his description of the fatherhood blog illuminated how networked participatory writing sites made it possible to access, learn about, and then leverage communities of practice. This ongoing activity connected with the constant checking, monitoring, and layered reading practice of this writer who built a professional reputation primarily through online presence.

Accessing a Network

Social media create a way for individuals to research the social context surrounding a given writing subject matter. When I asked him directly about whether social media use was a habit, Dave explained his motivation for using networked writing sites by invoking the idea of connectedness: "Part of it is trying to stay connected, because that's how I got the blog to be kind of popular." Elaborating on this idea, Dave detailed how he drew on lines of connection built within Twitter to join others with similar interests:

> Well, what I did before I even launched the blog was that I got on Twitter and I started connecting with people. So then when I launched, I had a little bit of a following from the Twitter. . . . I was gonna wait until I had 100 people following me on Twitter . . . just for that.

In this case, a relatively tight-knit but geographically distributed community already existed around the writing Dave wanted to undertake. Through a combination of Twitter and community blogs that curated posts from multiple contributors, he began to understand which individuals wrote and read one another's writing.

To participate, then, Dave did not understand himself as building a new net- 30 work but instead inventing himself as a genuine member of and contributor to the existing network. Thus, inventing his own persona was key to coordinating a social network in which his writing might circulate. As Hart-Davidson, Spinuzzi, and Zachry (2006) suggested,

> For writers, as important as discovering genres and documents is the ability to explore the social resources they might draw upon to complete a writing task, or the ability to understand the network of recipients that may constitute their "audience" for a given text they are preparing. (p. 76)

Social media resources became tools usable at once to allow him to under- 31 stand where relationships of exchange already existed as well as to perform the introductory work of connecting himself to them. His use of Twitter in the work session observation is closely related to both these functions for social media.

Maintaining a Presence

Work to "stay connected" requires ongoing maintenance through symbolic activ- 32 ity. Keeping up a presence required ongoing participation and extended through the time Dave engaged with the project and this community of fatherhood bloggers. Thus, even after he launched the blog, Dave maintained his presence through a variety of engagement activities. He described a few of them in detail. First, he shared quality content with others, again drawing primarily on Twitter to become an active contributor in this network of exchange. Dave reflected, "Twitter to me was like a resource. . . . I would share and would retweet those links to people." Second, he visualized intertextual connections by keeping up with and linking to others' blogs:

> [A] lot of times in the post, I link to stuff, so I have to be looking up links. So it's like totally a multi-. . . . I think writing online as compared to writing with pen and paper, I think there's more things involved with it than just writing. Because it's really important to me, if I'm writing about something [online], then I'd like to—whether it's a post I wrote or if I'm talking about somebody else—to link back to them. It connects back to them. It helps me, it helps them, it's connected to a whole give-and-take.

Dave's discussions of why his social media practices matter help to provide rationale for why the fine-grained texture of his work practice took the form evident in his observation. His active, persistent presence on Twitter helped to legitimize his blog and his relationship to other writers. Furthermore, the give-and-take that Dave describes is closely connected to the reading and research practice he enacted in the work session: Using a blog search tool to identify prior posts with closely related content allowed him to participate in the exchange of attention that sustained multiple blogs over time. Maintaining his association with these potential and actual blog readers required a great deal of time spent researching current and past activity as well as actively establishing and reestablishing that his relationship to others was active and actual.

Learning and Leveraging Norms

Many symbolic analysts must extend beyond understanding social norms and maintaining a presence in relationship to them; they must leverage them toward future action. What resulted between Dave and other dad bloggers was a reciprocal exchange of readership and knowledge that could be understood as a temporary alliance maintained through shared attention and practices. However, maintaining a presence or becoming part of a community was not the end goal for Dave's work; he learned and practiced participatory norms to use them to launch his writing. For instance, Dave signaled this movement of using group knowledge to construct individual knowledge when he explained that he monitored social networks because it often "sparks an idea for me to write a blog." 33

However, leveraging participatory norms also extended beyond shared content and into shared routines of timing and exchange. Once writing was completed, for example, Dave leveraged social norms to garner notice from other dad bloggers. First, he posted kairotically (see Sheridan, Ridolfo, & Michel, 2012), timing his contribution to coincide with times of high readership. "Fatherhood Fridays," which drew on Twitter's tradition of using Fridays to share recommendations for new followers, were high on his list: "I've had 120 hits on Fridays. I have huge days on Fridays." This sense of timing motivated choices about what work to complete when: He posted in times of high potential activity to garner individual attention from the network. During his observation, for instance, Dave was motivated to finish his blog posting early during the day on Friday to have a new post online during Fatherhood Friday. 34

Participating in other blogs as a close reader and commenter was yet another way to draw attention to his own writing. For instance, Dave frequently left comments on other blogs not only because he found them interesting but also because they increased the chances of another blogger's returning the favor. He recognized that others practiced a similar exchange of attention and used this understanding to interpret others' commenting practices on his blog. Describing a recent review feature he had begun, he explained, 35

> I'm connected to like 200 dads on Twitter. So a lot of the dads . . . now that I'm reviewing blogs, the dads want to be reviewed, but they won't ask me to review them, but they come and the comment on the blog and I can tell like . . . so usually on Friday I announce who I'm going to review so that gives me a lot of traffic.

Checking and reading social media enacted participation in this give-and-take of attention — it maintained the temporary alliance that supported not only Dave's work but also that of others. This give-and-take of making and maintaining connections influenced most choices that Dave made with the blog: from how to approach writing an individual text to how to structure the workflow of a writing session. Social media was central to both how he conducted his symbolic work and why he focused on particular forms of supporting writing.

SOCIAL MEDIA, COORDINATION, AND ATTENTION STRUCTURES OF DISTRIBUTED WORK

Blogging requires a large investment in understanding changing content and participatory norms within communities to which and with whom one writes. As with most forms of writing, writing well for social media platforms requires even more foundational social media reading, research, and writing that functions to support it. In Dave's case, for instance, understanding the temporal rhythms of blog circulation in which Fridays were the most opportune time for posting was only possible because he researched information movements via external blog comments and traced networks visible through Twitter and a blog that aggregated participants in this community. As I have detailed, Dave used multiple, existing, public, free participatory networked writing platforms in ways that were closely interwoven. He moved effortlessly across these resources as he moved from constructing a sentence, to looking at a previously written blog comment that prompted a response, to linking his blog to those that came before it, to circulating his post using microblogging software. 36

The idea that effective social media writing requires and generates more social media writing to support it is an important point for understanding both the microlevel unfolding of Dave's work session and the importance he attaches to this particular blog project within the context of his professional trajectory. Social media platforms are often involved in layers of coordinative activity that are interdependent on one another and impact the texture of work practice. They are technical resources, in the sense that Slattery described coordination as a technological capacity of weaving fragments into new texts. However, social media also provide access to social resources that professional communicators use to weave together projects and professional networks that sustain long-term identities and ongoing career trajectories. Social media coordinate for Dave at two levels of scale: that of a project or task (e.g., creating networks in which to circulate a given text) and that of an ongoing professional trajectory (e.g., building relationships and networks to sustain future work activities). The intersecting and sometimes competing nature of these functions affects professional communicators' unfolding workflow — how attention is directed in moments of work. 37

At the level of social coordination, Dave's activity suggests that some symbolic 38
analysts outside traditional positions and workplaces may lean most heavily on
social media. With professional trajectories echoing the "constantly changing
orbits" that Deleuze (1995) predicted, freelancers like Dave are responsible for
inventing opportunities that will sustain them both affectively and economically.
Dave was inventing his career out of alliances he formed through social media
writing in small, incremental movements. The social coordination that blogging (and its attendant social media practices) afforded was important because
it created new opportunities, such as the recent invitation he had received to
participate in a local conference as a result of the local popularity of his blog.
Only 3 months into his current blog project, Dave had already begun imagining
where it would take him, as he understood his professional trajectory as positioned within a responsive model, always aware of potentialities connected to
current networked participation.

Technical and professional communicators are increasingly tasked with work- 39
ing outside traditional organizational roles and spaces, often juggling multiple
contracts and tasks (see Wilson, 2001). Not surprisingly, Dave continually looked
ahead to his next professional project. Reflecting on the blog project's role, Dave
described its relationship to his professional trajectory with a bit of uncertainty:

> DAVE: I . . . I don't know where this is going to go. Maybe it will go
> somewhere, maybe it won't. I don't know, you know?
>
> STACEY: Wait and see?
>
> DAVE: I'm kinda concentrating on that. I do consult, but that is kinda
> changing.
>
> STACEY: With technology stuff?
>
> DAVE: Yeah. But I can go to blog conferences at some point and talk about
> blogging and how . . . you know or whatever. Or do a class about that. So
> we'll see where that goes.

Social media writing was an integrated part of a linked chain of professional 40
opportunities. Because he was blogging, it would be possible for him later to
offer classes on blogging, or to put together the print collection I referenced
earlier. And, if the chain of events connected to his current social media writing
extended into the future, he could also trace his current project from networks
of the past. For instance, Dave described gaining much of the existing local
support for the fatherhood blog as a result of earlier work with a community
"birth center" affiliated with a nonprofit initiative he described as a separate
ongoing project. His work moved responsively as relationships and knowledge
gained from former projects influenced new ones. Dave's social media writing
was inventive in the sense that it opened professional opportunities, facilitating

slight shifts in alliance that would create and sustain future work. However, these future trajectories were uncertain, and thus it was necessary to continue building and maintaining a range of active connections.

Understanding what networked writing afforded for Dave as a means to access 41 and create provides a view of social media reading and writing as a central component of his work practice. When knowledge work involves constructing "infrastructures to support invention" (Grabill, 2007, p. 90), writers draw on available means to access social context and create shared knowledge. We need to understand the turn to social media as a common practice, in part, so that technical and professional communication teachers, researchers, and practitioners can continue to trace how these infrastructures mediate individuals' attention and impact the fine-grained detail of how symbolic work unfolds. For instance, though Dave worked for several organizations, his individual professional identity was the node that connected the multiple projects, activities, and organizations in his professional network. Thus, for Dave, relying on social media spaces as locations to construct a traceable personal, professional persona continually redirected his attention toward the ongoing maintenance of that identity. Social media are common places not only for creating ideas and texts but where identity and professional trajectory are continually invented—a place where he and others working outside of typical geographies could make a presence and then be found.

> Social media are common places not only for creating ideas and texts but where identity and professional trajectory are continually invented.

The idea that one's individual professional identity might take precedence 42 over organizational affiliations represents just one potential impact on the everyday practice of symbolic-analytic work. Understanding the burgeoning social media cycle also helps account for movement we see in Dave's work session. With attention both to the goal he hoped to garner through his writing and the scarce resource that determined how he spent his work time, Dave's movement across multiple sites was an inherent part of what social coordination brought to his micro work practice. For Dave, social media assembled social and technological resources to sustain and create his current project, but they also helped him to look beyond the current moment and toward the connections, alliances, and presences that could support later inventions. Movement from one to the other was part of the goal—aligning with a bigger social network extended the blog's reach, and blogging in turn extended his own potential social reach.

CONCLUSION

Learning what it means to practice contemporary symbolic-analytic work today 43 is not a simple task. Embodied practices are never static. The cultural contexts, writing technologies, and microlevel movements and routines of contemporary symbolic analysts are coemergent; they are evolving together, with slight shifts in each driving forward new adaptations in the others. Individuals continually invent, adapt, and make do in local scenes with resources they have available. Working for himself while interacting with and across multiple organizations heightened Dave's need for technologies that enabled him to build and understand relevant social context for future writing. As is the case in many current technical and professional writing scenarios, social software offered a means for accessing and interacting with different kinds of publics (see Rauch, Morrison, & Goetz, 2010). Dave represents one account of the multiple ways this current turn to social media impacts everyday practice. Whereas his story stands in neither for all professional communicators nor for all freelance and contract writers, it suggests social media both extend symbolic analysts' reach and direct their attention. Social media facilitate activities that are deeply important to invention: accessing or creating networks of relationships, building and maintaining a presence that can interact with them, and then leveraging them toward future action.

The social coordination that has become a crucial layer of what symbolic analysts do is itself a form of literate activity. It is also intricate, complex, time consuming, and often tacit rather than explicit. This analysis reveals Dave using social media simultaneously as production spaces, mechanisms for monitoring change, and content-related invention aids. However, even his own language reflects ambiguity toward the meaning of his practices in these online locations. Reflecting on the role of social media use in his workflow, he commented, "At the very least, even if I just end up messing around on Twitter, that's something, you know? If I'm just doing something interactive on there." This analysis reveals that Dave is doing more than "messing around," despite the fact that it is difficult for him to put into words exactly what that "something" is that he achieves through this activity. 44

Dave's statement can teach us about how long it takes for our conceptualizations of a phenomenon to catch up to changes in practice already underway. Everyday symbolic practices may shift particularly drastically in moments of rapid cultural and technological change such as that which we are currently experiencing. As the technologies and organizational locations that mediate knowledge work shift on a broad scale, we should continually focus our research lenses to trace symbolic practice in detail. Fine-grained visualizations of the embodied practices of those reinventing its texture, texts, and technologies can help us continually construct emergent theories of symbolic-analytic work. 45

Acknowledgments

I would like to thank the research participant for his time and willingness to share, Amy Koerber and two anonymous reviewers for their excellent feedback, Jim Ridolfo and Jeff Grabill for responding to early drafts, and my colleagues and writing group at the University of Central Florida for their support.

Notes

1. Dave's name has been changed in this article to comply with IRB guidelines. His case example presented is taken from a larger IRB-approved study conducted in 2009 and 2010.

2. The particular social software of focus in this study was Yammer, an informal microblogging application. Working together on projects necessitates not only exchange of official information but also "noncritical" information like ongoing updates of project status or developing feelings or thoughts that may change dynamically during the work process.

3. With data collection taking place in 2009, this study predates the widespread use of tablet PCs like the iPad as mobile writing devices.

4. In this research study, I opted not to use video screen capture (see Geisler & Slattery, 2007), because I felt that it would be too intrusive to ask individuals working in a public space to install software on their computers as well as because I wanted to capture both on-screen and off-screen movement at once.

References

Bay, J. (2010). Networking pedagogies for professional writing students. *The Writing Instructor.* Retrieved from http://www.writinginstructor.com/bay

Blanchard, A. L., & Henle, C. A. (2008). Correlates of different forms of cyberloafing: The role of norms and external locus of control. *Computers in Human Behavior, 24*, 1067–1084. doi: 10.1016/j.chb.2007.03.008

Bock, G.-W., & Ho, S. L. (2009). Non-work related computing (NWRC). *Communications of the ACM, 52*(4), 124–128. doi: 10.1145/1498765.1498799

boyd, d. m., & Ellison, N. B. (2008). Social network sites: Definition, history, and scholarship. *Journal of Computer Mediated Communication, 13*(1). Retrieved from http://jcmc.indiana.edu/vol13/issue/boyd.ellison.html

de Lara, P. Z. M., Tacoronte, D. V., & Ding, J.-M. T. (2006). Do current anti-cyberloafing disciplinary practices have a replica in research findings? A study of the effects of coercive strategies on workplace Internet misuse. *Internet Research, 16*, 450–467. doi: 10.1108/10662240610690052

Deleuze, G. (1995). *Negotiations: 1972–1990.* (M. Joughin, Trans.). New York: Columbia University Press.

Garrett, R. K., & Danzinger, J. N. (2008). On cyberslacking: Workplace status and personal Internet use at work. *CyberPsychology & Behavior, 11*, 287–292. doi: 10.1089/cpb.2007.0146

Geisler, C. (2004). When management becomes personal: An activity-theoretic analysis of palm technologies. In C. Bazerman & D. Russell (Eds.), *Writing selves/writing societies: Research from activity perspectives* (pp. 125–158). Fort Collins, CO: WAC Clearinghouse of Mind, Culture, and Activity. Retrieved from http://wac.colostateedu/books/selves_societies

Geisler, C., & Slattery, S. (2007). Capturing the activity of digital writing: Using, analyzing, and supplementing the video screen capture. In H. A. McKee & D. N. DeVoss (Eds.), *Digital writing research: Technologies, methodologies, and ethical issues* (pp. 185–200). Cresskill, NJ: Hampton Press.

Golden, A. G., & Geisler, C. (2007). Worklife boundary management and the personal digital assistant: Practical activities and interpretive repertoires. *Human Relations, 60*, 519–551. doi: 10.1177/0018726707076698. Retrieved from http://www.sagepub.com/greenhaus4e/study/chapters/articles/Chapter14_Article02.pdf

Gonzalez, V., & Mark, G. (2004, April). "Constant, constant, multi-tasking craziness": Managing multiple working spheres. *CHI '04 Proceedings of the SIGCHI Conference on Human Factors in Computing Systems* (pp. 113–120). doi: 10.1145/985692.985707

Grabill, J. T. (2007). *Writing community change: Designing technologies for citizen action.* Cresskill, NJ: Hampton Press.

Grasso, A., Meunier, J.-L., Pagani, D., & Pareschi, R. (1997). Distributed coordination and workflow on the World Wide Web. *Computer Supported Cooperative Work, 6*(2–3), 175–200.

Haas, C. (1996). *Writing technology: Studies on the materiality of literacy.* Mahwah, NJ: Lawrence Erlbaum.

Hampton, K. N., & Gupta, N. (2008). Community and social interaction in the wireless city: Wi-Fi use in public and semi-public spaces. *New Media and Society, 10*(6), 831–850. doi: 10.1177/1461444808096247

Hart-Davidson, W., Spinuzzi, C., & Zachry, M. (2006). Visualizing writing activity as knowledge work: Challenges & opportunities. *SIGDOC Proceedings of the 24th Annual ACM International Conference on Design of Communication* (pp. 70–77). doi: 10.1145/1166324.1166341

Johnson-Eilola, J. (2005). *Datacloud: Toward a new theory of online work.* Cresskill, NJ: Hampton Press.

Kaplan, A. M., & Haenlein, M. (2010). Users of the world, unite! The challenges and opportunities of social media. *Business Horizons, 53*, 59–68. doi: 10.1016/j.bushor.2009.09.003

Lanham, R. A. (2006). *The economics of attention: Style and substance in the age of information.* Chicago: University of Chicago Press.

Latour, B. (2005). *Reassembling the social: An introduction to actor-network-theory.* Oxford, U.K.: Oxford University Press.

LeFevre, K. B. (1987). *Invention as a social act.* Carbondale: Southern Illinois University Press.

Lenhart, A., Purcell, K., Smith, A., & Zickuhr, K. (2010, February 3). Social media and mobile Internet use among teens and young adults. *PEW Internet and American Life Project.* Retrieved from http://pewinternet.org/Reports/2010/ Social-Media-and-Young-Adults .aspx

McNely, B. J. (2011, October). Informal communication, sustainability, and the public writing work of organizations. In *Proceedings of the IEEE International Professional Communication Conference* (1–7).

Pee, L. G., Woon, I. M. Y., & Kankanhalli, A. (2008). Explaining non-work-related computing in the workplace: A comparison of alternative models. *Information & Management, 45*, 120–130. doi: 10.1016/j.im.2008.01.004

Potts, L. (2009). Using actor network theory to trace and improve multimodal design. *Technical Communication Quarterly, 18*, 281–301. doi: 10.1080/10572250902941812

Prior, P., & Shipka, J. (2003). Chronotopic lamination: Tracing the contours of literate activity. In C. Bazerman & D. Russell (Eds.), *Writing selves/writing societies: Research from activity perspectives* (pp. 180–238). Fort Collins, CO: WAC Clearinghouse and Mind, Culture, and Activity. Retrieved from http://wac.colostate.edu/books/selves_societies

Rauch, M., Morrison, C., & Goetz, A. (2010, July). Are we there yet? An examination of where we've been and where we're headed as technical communicators. *Proceedings of the IEEE Internatonal Professional Communication Conference* (pp. 297–309).

Reich, R. B. (1991). *The work of nations: Preparing ourselves for 21st-century capitalism.* New York: Vintage Books.

Sheridan, D. M., Ridolfo, J., & Michel, A. (2012). *The available means of persuasion: Mapping a theory and pedagogy of multimodal public rhetoric.* Anderson, SC: Parlor Press.

Slattery, S. (2005). Understanding technical writing as textual coordination: An argument for the value of writers' skill with information technology. *Technical Communication, 52,* 353–360.

Slattery, S. (2007). Undistributing work through writing: How technical writers manage texts in complex information environments. *Technical Communication Quarterly, 16,* 311–325. doi: 10.1080/10572250701291046

Spinuzzi, C. (2007). Guest editor's introduction: Technical communication in the age of distributed work. *Technical Communication Quarterly, 16,* 265–277. doi: 10.1080/10572250701290998

Spinuzzi, C. (2012). Working alone together: Coworking as emergent collaborative activity. *Journal of Business and Technical Communication, 26,* 399–441. doi: 10.1177/1050651912444070

Sullivan, P., & Porter, J. E. (1997). *Opening spaces: Writing technologies and critical research practices.* Greenwich, CT: Ablex.

Swarts, J. (2011). Technological literacy as network building. *Technical Communication Quarterly, 20,* 274–302. doi: 10.1080/10572252.2011.578239

Swarts, J., & Kim, L. (2007). Guest editors' introduction: New technological spaces. *Technical Communication Quarterly, 18,* 211–223. doi: 10.1080/10572250902941986

Thompson, C. (2008, September 5). The brave new world of digital intimacy. *New York Times Online.* Retrieved from http://www.nytimes.com/2008/09/07/magazine/07awareness-t .html?pagewanted=all&_r=0

Van Ittersum, D. (2009). Distributing memory: Rhetorical work in digital environments. *Technical Communication Quarterly, 18,* 259–280. doi: 10.1080/10572250902942026

Varnelis, K., & Friedberg, A. (2008). Place: The networking of public space. In K. Varnelis (Ed.), *Networked publics* (pp. 15–42). Cambridge, MA: MIT Press.

Victor, B., & Boynton, A. C. (1998). *Invented here: Maximizing your organization's internal growth and profitability—A practical guide to transforming work.* Boston: Harvard Business School Press.

Vitak, J., Crouse, J., & LaRose, R. (2011). Personal internet use at work: Understanding cyberslacking. *Computers in Human Behavior, 27*(5), 1751–1759. doi: 10.1016/j.chb .2011.03.002

Wilson, G. (2001). Technical communication and late capitalism: Considering a postmodern technical communication pedagogy. *Journal of Business and Technical Communication, 51,* 72–99. doi: 10.1177/105065190101500104

Zhou, D., & Rosson, M. B. (2009). How and why people use Twitter: the role that micro- blogging plays in informal communication at work. *Proceedings of the ACM 2009 International Conference on Supporting Group Work* (pp. 243–252). Retrieved from http://www.pensivepuffin .com/dwmcphd/syllabi/info447_au10/readings/zhao.rosson.Twitter.GROUP09.pdf

Zhou, D., Rosson, M. B., Matthews, T., & Thomas, M. (2011). Microblogging's impact on collaboration awareness: A field study of microblogging within and between project teams. *2011 International Conference on Collaboration Technologies and Systems* (pp. 31–39), Philadelphia, PA.

Zuboff, S., & Maxmin, J. (2002). *The support economy: Why corporations are failing individuals and the next episode of capitalism.* New York: Penguin Books.

Questions for Discussion and Journaling

1. Which threshold concept discussed in the chapter introduction would you say Pigg's article most strongly emphasizes or demonstrates, and why?

2. How does Dave's use of social media for invention compare with your own writing processes? What roles do social media play in how you come up with what to say?

3. If we define *invention* loosely as "figuring out what to say in your writing," then it makes some sense that invention is often about focusing on your own thoughts. Pigg, though, spends a lot of time throughout her article thinking about *coordination* as one aspect of invention. How do you understand these two aspects of invention — coordination among many minds, and your own thinking — happening together?

4. Pigg seems very interested in the *speed* with which Dave moves among the social media sites that he's reading and his own blog writing. Do you think this element of speed or pace is meaningful, and if so, why?

5. Pigg says that her research was motivated in part by Haas's argument that "capturing writing activity in the interaction between bodies and technologies can help elucidate a middle ground of writing practice that illuminates both cognitive and cultural influences" (para. 15). Why is it that seeing people use technology might help us understand how writing is both an internal thinking (cognitive) process and a process influenced by culture?

6. Researchers have long noted that observing research subjects can impact what those subjects do. How well do you think Pigg's research handles this problem? Do you think her research guards well enough against this problem?

7. What were the two "dominant uses of social media" (para. 22) during Dave's invention process, and how similar do they seem to your own uses of social media while figuring out what to say in your writing?

Applying and Exploring Ideas

1. Write your own definition of *symbolic-analytic work*, which should explain two things: First, how it seems different from other kinds of work such as working in restaurants, in retail, or in a factory. Second, what kinds of work "symbolic analysts" might actually be doing — how are they "knowledge workers"?

2. Reread the opening pages of the article that bring Pigg to her two main research questions at the end of the "Distributed Work, Coordination, and Social Media" section; this should allow you to get the best understanding you can of how she arrives at her research questions based on other people's work (in the review of the literature and establishment of the theoretical framework). Then, write two *additional* research questions that you could ask based on that work.

3. Create a description of your favorite or most commonly used social media site or app that explains how it develops, uses, or enhances *coordination* as Pigg uses that term.

4. Based on Pigg's two main research questions in this article, write a one-page analysis in which you put yourself in Dave's shoes as the research subject: Even though you may not consider yourself a "professional communicator" (though what else is a college student?), how would *your* writing experiences provide answers to Pigg's questions?

- -

META MOMENT What are some ways in which reading Pigg's account of a writer using social media makes you more conscious of your own uses of social media while writing?

- -

The Composing Processes of Unskilled College Writers

SONDRA PERL

Framing the Reading

Writing this article in 1979, Sondra Perl argued, "To date no examination of composing processes has dealt primarily with unskilled writers. As long as 'average' or skilled writers are the focus, it remains unclear as to how process research will [help unskilled writers]" (para. 4). Much of the nature of this article is captured in that brief passage.

With the study reported here, Perl attempted to accomplish two important and quite distinct projects in advancing writing research. The first was to create a brand-new way to study writers writing. In the first few pages you'll read Perl's description of the problem with previous research on the writing process: It relied almost entirely on stories researchers told about what they observed. Perl tried to create a more objective system for describing what writers were doing.

The second was to study a group of writers that previous research had ignored. Writers who aren't very good at writing probably aren't the best test subjects for "how writing works," and so they had not been studied much by researchers trying to learn about "the composing process" (which is how composition was described in those times — as a single kind of process writers either mastered or didn't). Yet, as Perl argued, studying people who are already proficient writers would probably not "provide teachers with a firmer understanding of the needs of students with serious writing problems" (para. 4). And what Perl saw her research participants doing connects to our threshold concepts that writing makes knowledge (often through revision) and that writers always have more to learn, no matter how strong or weak they are.

Perl, Sondra. "The Composing Processes of Unskilled College Writers." *Research in the Teaching of English*, vol. 13, no. 4, Dec. 1979, pp. 317–36.

Like a few other articles in this chapter, Perl's is more than 30 years old. It reflects a time of great interest, among writing researchers, about processes writers use to compose texts. That interest waned by the end of the 1980s; even though there was still much to be discovered and understood (most process research findings were provisional at best and needed to be followed up with larger-scale studies that have never been done), the attention of writing researchers went in other directions. Thus there is a major gap between research on process conducted in the late 1970s and 1980s, like Perl's, and when interest in process research returned in the early 2000s, leading to research like Pigg's earlier in this chapter.

Perl's article had a particularly great impact on the field because of her combined focus on a standardized method for observing, recording, and reporting on writers' behaviors while writing and her attention to "basic" writers whose writing was difficult to read and understand. Work such as this has made Perl one of the most significant researchers the field has seen. She went on to study how writers imagine what to say before they quite *know* what they want to say. (In 2004 she published a book called *Felt Sense: Writing with the Body*, which includes a CD that offers "meditations" for writers. It's quite different from the work you'll read here, which we hope might motivate you to look it up.)

This reading is tagged in order to help you navigate it. Remember that the tags are explained in more detail in Chapter 1 (pp. 58–59). You may want to quickly review the tags there before you begin (or read them for the first time).

Getting Ready to Read

Before you read, do at least one of the following activities:

- Ask yourself how you view yourself as a writer. Do you think you are a skilled or unskilled writer? Is writing easy or hard for you?

- Write down exactly what you think you do when you have to write something for school. Have you ever consciously thought about this before?

- Watch a roommate or friend write something for school, and make note of the things he or she does while writing.

As you read, consider the following questions:

- What arguments does Perl make about what research methods are necessary for good studies of writing?

- What attitudes and assumptions does Perl seem to bring to her study that you might not agree with, or at least might question?

- What conclusions is Perl able to reach about the major aspects of the composing process — prewriting, writing, and editing — that she identifies?

- How are Tony's processes as an "unskilled" writer different from those of skilled writers?

THIS PAPER PRESENTS the pertinent findings from a study of the composing processes of five unskilled college writers (Perl, 1978). The first part summarizes the goals of the original study, the kinds of data collected, and the research methods employed. The second part is a synopsis of the study of Tony, one of the original five case studies. The third part presents a condensed version of the findings on the composing process and discusses these findings in light of current pedagogical practice and research design.

GOALS OF THE STUDY

This research addressed three major questions: (1) How do unskilled writers write? (2) Can their writing processes be analyzed in a systematic, replicable manner? and (3) What does an increased understanding of their processes suggest about the nature of composing in general and the manner in which writing is taught in the schools?

In recent years, interest in the composing process has grown (Britton et al., 1975; Burton, 1973; Cooper, 1974; Emig, 1967, 1971). In 1963, Braddock, Lloyd-Jones, and Schoer, writing on the state of research in written composition, included the need for "direct observation" and case study procedures in their suggestions for future research (pp. 24, 31–32). In a section entitled "Unexplored Territory," they listed basic unanswered questions such as, "What is involved in the act of writing?" and "Of what does skill in writing actually consist?" (p. 51). Fifteen years later, Cooper and Odell (1978) edited a volume similar in scope, only this one was devoted entirely to issues and questions related to

GENRE CUES

1 — Forecasting

2 — Research Questions

3 — Conversation

READING CUES

Look Ahead Take a moment to preview the article and see what sections it is divided into. Can you tell how each section will contribute to answering Perl's three research questions?

research on composing. This volume in particular signals a shift in emphasis in writing research. Alongside the traditional, large-scale experimental studies, there is now widespread recognition of the need for works of a more modest, probing nature, works that attempt to elucidate basic processes. The studies on composing that have been completed to date are precisely of this kind; they are small-scale studies, based on the systematic observation of writers engaged in the process of writing (Emig, 1971; Graves, 1973; Mischel, 1974; Pianko, 1977; Stallard, 1974).

> How do unskilled writers write?

For all of its promise, this body of research has yet to produce work that would insure wide recognition for the value of process studies of composing. One limitation of work done to date is methodological. Narrative descriptions of composing processes do not provide sufficiently graphic evidence for the perception of underlying regularities and patterns. Without such evidence, it is difficult to generate well-defined hypotheses and to move from exploratory research to more controlled experimental studies. A second limitation pertains to the subjects studied. To date no examination of composing processes has dealt primarily with unskilled writers. As long as "average" or skilled writers are the focus, it remains unclear as to how process research will provide teachers with a firmer understanding of the needs of students with serious writing problems.

The present study is intended to carry process research forward by addressing both of these limitations. One prominent feature of the research design involves the development and use of a

GENRE CUES

4 — CARS: Territory
5 — CARS: Niche
6 — So What?
7 — CARS: Niche
8 — So What?
9 — CARS: Occupy

meaningful and replicable method for rendering the composing process as a sequence of observable and scorable behaviors. A second aspect of the design is the focus on students whose writing problems baffle the teachers charged with their education.

DESIGN OF THE STUDY

This study took place during the 1975–1976 fall semester at Eugenio Maria de Hostos Community College of the City University of New York. Students were selected for the study on the basis of two criteria: writing samples that qualified them as unskilled writers and willingness to participate. Each student met with the researcher for five 90-minute sessions (see Table 1). Four sessions were devoted to writing with the students directed to compose aloud, to externalize their thinking processes as much as possible, during each session. In one additional session, a writing profile on the students' perceptions and memories of writing was developed through the use of an open-ended interview. All of the sessions took place in a sound-proof room in the college library. Throughout each session, the researcher assumed a noninterfering role.

The topics for writing were developed in an introductory social science course in which the five students were enrolled. The "content" material they were studying was divided into two modes: extensive, in which the writer was directed to approach the material in an objective, impersonal fashion, and reflexive, in which the writer was directed to approach similar material in an affective, personalized fashion. Contrary to Emig's (1971) definitions, in this study it was assumed that the teacher was always the audience.

DATA ANALYSIS

Three kinds of data were collected in this study: the students' written products, their composing tapes, and their responses to the interview. Each of these was studied carefully and then discussed in detail in each of the five case study presentations. Due to limitations of space, this paper will review only two of the data sets generated in the study.

TABLE 1 DESIGN OF THE STUDY

	SESSION 1 (S1)	SESSION 2 (S2)	SESSION 3 (S3)	SESSION 4 (S4)	SESSION 5 (S5)
Mode	Extensive	Reflexive		Extensive	Reflexive
Topic	Society & Culture	Society & Culture	Interview: Writing Profile	Capitalism	Capitalism
Directions	Students told to compose aloud; no other directions given	Students told to compose aloud; no other directions given		Students told to compose aloud; also directed to talk out ideas before writing	Students told to compose aloud; also directed to talk out ideas before writing

Coding the Composing Process One of the goals of this
10 research was to devise a tool for describing the movements that
occur during composing. In the past such descriptions have
taken the form of narratives which detail, with relative precision and insight, observable composing behaviors; however,
these narratives provide no way of ascertaining the frequency,
relative importance, and place of each behavior within an individual's composing process. As such, they are cumbersome and
11 difficult to replicate. Furthermore, lengthy, idiosyncratic narratives run the risk of leaving underlying patterns and regularities
obscure. In contrast, the method created in this research provides a means of viewing the composing process that is:

1. Standardized—it introduces a coding system for observing
   the composing process that can be replicated;
2. Categorical—it labels specific, observable behaviors so that
   12 types of composing movements are revealed;
3. Concise—it presents the entire sequence of composing
   movements on one or two pages;
4. Structural—it provides a way of determining how parts of
   the process relate to the whole; and
5. Diachronic—it presents the sequences of movements that
   occur during composing as they unfold in time.

In total, the method allows the researcher to apprehend a
process as it unfolds. It lays out the movements or behavior
sequences in such a way that if patterns within a student's process or among a group of students exist, they become apparent.

The Code The method consists of coding each composing
behavior exhibited by the student and charting each behavior

GENRE CUES

10 — CARS: Territory

11 — CARS: Niche The niches in this article are usually problems with or weaknesses in existing scholarship.

12 — CARS: Occupy

on a continuum. During this study, the coding occurred after the student had finished composing and was done by working from the student's written product and the audiotape of the session. It was possible to do this since the tape captured both what the student was saying and the literal sound of the pen moving across the page. As a result, it was possible to determine when students were talking, when they were writing, when both occurred simultaneously, and when neither occurred.

The major categorical divisions in this coding system are talking, writing, and reading; however, it was clear that there are various kinds of talk and various kinds of writing and reading operations, and that a coding system would need to distinguish among these various types. In this study the following operations were distinguished:

1. General planning [PL]—organizing one's thoughts for writing, discussing how one will proceed.

2. Local planning [PLL] talking out what idea will come next.

3. Global planning [PLG]—discussing changes in drafts.

4. Commenting [C]—sighing, making a comment or judgment about the topic.

5. Interpreting [I]—rephrasing the topic to get a "handle" on it.

6. Assessing [A(+); A(−)]—making a judgment about one's writing; may be positive or negative.

7. Questioning [Q]—asking a question.

8. Talking leading to writing [T→W]—voicing ideas on the topic, tentatively finding one's way, but not necessarily being committed to or using all one is saying.

9. Talking and writing at the same time [TW]—composing aloud in such a way that what one is saying is actually being written at the same time.

10. Repeating [re]—repeating written or unwritten phrases a number of times.

11

745

11. Reading related to the topic:

   (a) Reading the directions [R$_D$]

   (b) Reading the question [R$_q$]

   (c) Reading the statement [R$_s$]

12. Reading related to one's own written product:

   (a) Reading one sentence or a few words [R^a]

   (b) Reading a number of sentences together [R^{a-b}]

   (c) Reading the entire draft through [R^{W1}]

13. Writing silently [W]

14. Writing aloud [TW]

15. Editing [E]

   (a) adding syntactic markers, words, phrases, or clauses [Eadd]

   (b) deleting syntactic markers, words, phrases, or clauses [Edel]

   (c) indicating concern for a grammatical rule [Egr]

   (d) adding, deleting, or considering the use of punctuation [Epunc]

   (e) considering or changing spelling [Esp]

   (f) changing the sentence structure through embedding, coordination or subordination [Ess]

   (g) indicating concern for appropriate vocabulary (word choice) [Ewc]

   (h) considering or changing verb form [Evc]

16. Periods of silence [s]

By taking specific observable behaviors that occur during composing and supplying labels for them, this system thus far provides a way of analyzing the process that is categorical and capable of replication. In order to view the frequency and the duration of composing behaviors and the relation between one particular behavior and the whole process, these behaviors need to be depicted graphically to show their duration and sequence.

12

The Continuum The second component of this system is the construction of a time line and a numbering system. In this study, blank charts with lines like the following were designed:

A ten-digit interval corresponds to one minute and is keyed to a counter on a tape recorder. By listening to the tape and watching the counter, it is possible to determine the nature and duration of each operation. As each behavior is heard on the tape, it is coded and then noted on the chart with the counter used as a time marker. For example, if a student during prewriting reads the directions and the question twice and then begins to plan exactly what she is going to say, all within the first minute, it would be coded like this:

$$\text{Prewriting}$$
$$\overbrace{\text{R}\cup\text{R}_Q\text{R}\cup\text{R}_Q\text{PLL}}$$
$$\text{10}$$

If at this point the student spends two minutes writing the first sentence, during which time she pauses, rereads the question, continues writing, and then edits for spelling before continuing on, it would be coded like this:

$$\overset{1}{\overbrace{\text{TW}_1\,/\text{s}/\text{R}_Q \quad \text{TW}_1[\text{Esp}]\text{TW}_1}}$$
$$\qquad\quad 20 \qquad\qquad\quad 30$$

At this point two types of brackets and numbering systems have appeared. The initial sublevel number linked with the TW code indicates which draft the student is working on. TW_1 indicates the writing of the first draft; TW_2 and TW_3 indicate the writing of the second and third drafts. Brackets such as [Esp] separate these operations from writing and indicate the amount of time the operation takes. The upper-level number above the horizontal bracket indicates which sentence in the written product is being written and the length of the bracket indicates the amount of time spent on the writing of each sentence. All horizontal brackets refer to sentences, and from the charts it is possible to see when sentences are grouped together and written in a chunk (adjacent brackets) or when each sentence is produced in isolation (gaps between brackets). (See Appendix for sample chart.)

The charts can be read by moving along the time line, noting which behaviors occur and in what sequence. Three types of comments are also included in the charts. In boldface type, the beginning and end of each draft are indicated; in lighter typeface, comments on the actual composing movements are provided; and in the lightest typeface, specific statements made by students or specific words they found particularly troublesome are noted.

16

From the charts, the following information can be determined:

17

1. the amount of time spent during prewriting;

2. the strategies used during prewriting;

3. the amount of time spent writing each sentence;

4. the behaviors that occur while each sentence is being written;

5. when sentences are written in groups or "chunks" (fluent writing);

6. when sentences are written in isolation (choppy or sporadic writing);

7. the amount of time spent between sentences;

8. the behaviors that occur between sentences;

9. when editing occurs (during the writing of sentences, between sentences, in the time between drafts);

10. the frequency of editing behavior;

11. the nature of the editing operations; and

12. where and in what frequency pauses or periods of silence occur in the process.

The charts, or *composing style sheets* as they are called, do not explain what students wrote but rather *how* they wrote. They indicate, on one page, the sequences of behavior that occur from the beginning of the process to the end. From them it is possible to determine where and how these behaviors fall into patterns and whether these patterns vary according to the mode of discourse.

(13) It should be noted that although the coding system is presented before the analysis of the data, it was derived from the data and then used as the basis for generalizing about the patterns and behavioral sequences found within each student's process. These individual patterns were reported in each of the five case studies. Thus, initially, a style sheet was constructed for each writing session on each student. When there were four style sheets for each student, it was possible to determine if composing patterns existed among the group. The summary of results reported here is based on the patterns revealed by these charts.

(14) ***Analyzing Miscues in the Writing Process*** Miscue analysis is based on Goodman's model of the reading process. Created in 1962, it has become a widespread tool for studying what students do when they read and is based on the premise that reading is a psycholinguistic process which "uses language, in written form, to get to the meaning" (Goodman, 1973, p. 4). Miscue analysis "involves its user in examining the observed behavior of oral readers as an interaction between language and thought, as a process of constructing meaning from a graphic display" (Goodman, 1973, p. 4). Methodologically, the observer analyzes the mismatch that occurs when readers make responses during oral reading that differ from the text. This mismatch or miscueing is then analyzed from Goodman's "meaning-getting" model, based on the assumption that "the reader's preoccupation with meaning will show in his miscues, because they will tend to result in language that still makes sense" (Goodman, 1973, p. 9).

18

19

GENRE CUES

(13) — **Making Knowledge** The order in which the coding system was derived and applied is important to understanding how the researchers made knowledge from their data.

(14) — **Framework**

.In the present study, miscue analysis was adapted from Goodman's model in order to provide insight into the writing process. Since students composed aloud, two types of oral behaviors were available for study: encoding processes or what students spoke while they were writing and decoding processes or what students "read"[1] after they had finished writing. When a discrepancy existed between encoding or decoding and what was on the paper, it was referred to as miscue. 20

For encoding, the miscue analysis was carried out in the following manner: 21

1. The students' written products were typed, preserving the original style and spelling.

2. What students said while composing aloud was checked against the written products; discrepancies were noted on the paper wherever they occurred,

3. The discrepancies were categorized and counted.

   Three miscue categories were derived for encoding: 22

1. Speaking complete ideas but omitting certain words during writing.

2. Pronouncing words with plural markers or other suffixes completely but omitting these endings during writing.

3. Pronouncing the desired word but writing a homonym, an approximation of the word or a personal abbreviation of the word on paper.

For decoding, similar procedures were used, this time comparing the words of the written product with what the student "read" orally. When a discrepancy occurred, it was noted. The discrepancies were then categorized and counted. 23

Four miscue categories were derived for decoding: 24

1. "Reading in" missing words or word endings;

2. Deleting words or word endings;

3. "Reading" the desired word rather than the word on the page;

4. "Reading" abbreviations and misspellings as though they were written correctly.

A brief summary of the results of this analysis appears in the findings.

SYNOPSIS OF A CASE STUDY

Tony was a 20-year-old ex-Marine born and raised in the Bronx, New York. Like many Puerto Ricans born in the United States, he was able to speak Spanish, but he considered English his native tongue. In the eleventh grade, Tony left high school, returning three years later to take the New York State high school equivalency exam. As a freshman in college, he was also working part-time to support a child and a wife from whom he was separated.

Behaviors The composing style sheets provide an overview of the observable behaviors exhibited by Tony during the composing process. (See Appendix, page 769, for samples of Tony's writing and the accompanying composing style sheet.) The most salient feature of Tony's composing process was its recursiveness. Tony rarely produced a sentence without stopping to reread either a part or the whole. This repetition set up a particular kind of composing rhythm, one that was cumulative in nature and that set ideas in motion by its very repetitiveness. Thus, as can be seen from any of the style sheets, talking led to writing which led to reading which led to planning which again led to writing.

The style sheets indicated a difference in the composing rhythms exhibited in the extensive and reflexive modes. On the extensive topics there was not only more repetition within each sentence but also many more pauses and repetitions between sentences, with intervals often lasting as long as two minutes. On the reflexive topics, sentences were often written in groups, with fewer

25

26

27

READING CUES

Look Ahead Look through the next few pages to identify titles and categories of the different subsections, which will give you a better sense of the coming description.

rereadings and only minimal time intervals separating the creation of one sentence from another.

Editing occurred consistently in all sessions. From the moment Tony began writing, he indicated a concern for correct form that actually inhibited the development of ideas. In none of the writing sessions did he ever write more than two sentences before he began to edit. While editing fit into his overall recursive pattern, it simultaneously interrupted the composing rhythm he had just initiated.

28

During the intervals between drafts, Tony read his written work, assessed his writing, planned new phrasings, transitions or endings, read the directions and the question over, and edited once again.

29

Tony performed these operations in both the extensive and reflexive modes and was remarkably consistent in all of his composing operations. The style sheets attest both to this consistency and to the densely packed, tight quality of Tony's composing process—indeed, if the notations on these sheets were any indication at all, it was clear that Tony's composing process was so full that there was little room left for invention or change.

30

Fluency Table 2 provides a numerical analysis of Tony's writing performance. Here it is possible to compare not only the amount of time spent on the various composing operations but also the relative fluency. For Sessions 1 and 2 the data indicate that while Tony spent more time prewriting and writing in the extensive mode, he actually produced fewer words. For Sessions 4 and 5, a similar pattern can be detected. In the extensive mode, Tony again spent more time prewriting and produced fewer words. Although writing time was increased in the reflexive mode, the additional 20 minutes spent writing did not sufficiently account for an increase of 194 words. Rather, the data indicate that Tony produced more words with less planning and generally in less time in the reflexive mode, suggesting that his greater fluency lay in this mode.

31

TABLE 2 TONY: SUMMARY OF FOUR WRITING SESSIONS (TIME IN MINUTES) ⟲ Read Later

		S1 TW$_1$				S4 T→W	
	Drafts	Words	Time		Drafts	Words	Time
Extensive mode			Prewriting: 7.8				Prewriting: 8.0
	W1	132	18.8		W1	182	29.0
	W2	170	51.0		W2	174	33.9
	Total	302	Total composing: 91.2*		Total	356	Total composing: 82.0*

		S2 TW$_1$				S5 T→W	
	Drafts	Words	Time		Drafts	Words	Time
Reflexive mode			Prewriting: 3.5				Prewriting: 5.7
	W1	165	14.5		W1	208	24.0
	W2	169	25.0		W2	190	38.3
	W3	178	24.2		W3	152	20.8
	Total	512	Total composing: 76.0*		Total	550	Total composing: 96.0*

*Total composing includes time spent on editing and rereading, as well as actual writing.

Strategies Tony exhibited a number of strategies that served him as a writer whether the mode was extensive or reflexive. Given any topic, the first operation he performed was to focus in and narrow down the topic. He did this by rephrasing the topic until either a word or an idea in the topic linked up with something in his own experience (an attitude, an opinion, an event). In this way he established a connection between the field of discourse and himself and at this point he felt ready to write.

32

READING CUES

○-- **Read Later** First, skip ahead to read what the writer says *about* the data. Coming back later to read the data itself will be quicker and less confusing.

Level of Language Use Once writing, Tony employed a pattern
of classifying or dividing the topic into manageable pieces and
then using one or both of the divisions as the basis for narration.
In the four writing sessions, his classifications were made on the
basis of economic, racial, and political differences. However, all
of his writing reflected a low level of generality. No formal principles were used to organize the narratives nor were the implications of ideas present in the essay developed.

In his writing, Tony was able to maintain the extensive/reflex-
ive distinction. He recognized when he was being asked directly
for an opinion and when he was being asked to discuss concepts
or ideas that were not directly linked to his experience. However,
the more distance between the topic and himself, the more difficulty he experienced, and the more repetitive his process became.
Conversely, when the topic was close to his own experience, the
smoother and more fluent the process became. More writing was
produced, pauses were fewer, and positive assessment occurred
more often. However, Tony made more assumptions on the part
of the audience in the reflexive mode. When writing about himself, Tony often did not stop to explain the context from which he
was writing; rather, the reader's understanding of the context was
taken for granted.

Editing Tony spent a great deal of his composing time editing. However, most of this time was spent proofreading rather
than changing, rephrasing, adding, or evaluating the substantive parts of the discourse. Of a total of 234 changes made in
all of the sessions, only 24 were related to changes of content
and included the following categories:

1. Elaborations of ideas through the use of specification and
   detail;

2. Additions of modals that shift the mood of a sentence;

3. Deletions that narrow the focus of a paper;

4. Clause reductions or embeddings that tighten the structure of a paper;

5. Vocabulary choices that reflect a sensitivity to language;

6. Reordering of elements in a narrative;

7. Strengthening transitions between paragraphs;

8. Pronoun changes that signal an increased sensitivity to audience.

The 210 changes in form included the following:

36

Additions	19	Verb changes	4
Deletions	44	Spelling	95
Word choice	13	Punctuation	35
		Unresolved problems	89

The area that Tony changed most often was spelling, although, even after completing three drafts of a paper, Tony still had many words misspelled.

Miscue Analysis Despite continual proofreading, Tony's completed drafts often retained a look of incompleteness. Words
remained misspelled, syntax was uncorrected or overcorrected,
suffixes, plural markers, and verb endings were missing, and
often words or complete phrases were omitted.

37

The composing aloud behavior and the miscue analysis derived
from it provide one of the first demonstrable ways of understanding how such seemingly incomplete texts can be considered
"finished" by the student. (See Table 3 for a summary of Tony's
miscues.) Tony consistently voiced complete sentences when
composing aloud but only transcribed partial sentences. The same
behavior occurred in relation to words with plural or marked endings. However, during rereading and even during editing, Tony
supplied the missing endings, words, or phrases and did not seem

38

TABLE 3 TONY — MISCUE ANALYSIS

	ENCODING			
	Speaking complete ideas but omitting certain words during writing	Pronouncing words with plural markers or other suffixes completely but omitting these endings during writing	Pronouncing the desired word but writing a homonym, an approximation of the word or a personal abbreviation of the word on paper	Total
S1	1	4	11	16
S2	8	0	14	22
S4	4	0	16	20
S5	3	1	15	19
	16	5	56	77

	DECODING			
	Reading in missing words or word endings	Deleting words or word endings	Reading the desired word rather than the word on the page	Reading abbreviations and misspellings as though they were written correctly	Total
S1	10	1	1	15	27
S2	5	1	2	10	18
S4	3	3	0	13	19
S5	7	1	2	10	20
	25	6	5	48	84

to "see" what was missing from the text. Thus, when reading his paper, Tony "read in" the meaning he expected to be there which turned him into a reader of content rather than form. However, a difference can be observed between the extensive and reflexive modes, and in the area of correctness Tony's greater strength lay in the reflexive mode. In this mode, not only were more words produced in less time (1,062 vs. 658), but fewer decoding miscues occurred (38 vs. 46), and fewer unresolved problems remained in the text (34 vs. 55).

When Tony did choose to read for form, he was handicapped in another way. Through his years of schooling, Tony learned that there were sets of rules to be applied to one's writing, and he attempted to apply these rules of form to his prose. Often, though, the structures he produced were far more complicated than the simple set of proofreading rules he had at his disposal. He was therefore faced with applying the rule partially, discarding it, or attempting corrections through sound. None of these systems was completely helpful to Tony, and as often as a correction was made that improved the discourse, another was made that obscured it.

Summary Finally, when Tony completed the writing process, he refrained from commenting on or contemplating his total written product. When he initiated writing, he immediately established distance between himself as writer and his discourse. He knew his preliminary draft might have errors and might need revision. At the end of each session, the distance had decreased if not entirely disappeared. Tony "read in" missing or omitted features, rarely perceived syntactic errors, and did not untangle overly embedded sentences. It was as if the semantic model in his head predominated, and the distance with which he entered the writing process had dissolved. Thus, even with his concern for revision and for correctness, even with the enormous amount of time he invested in rereading and repetition, Tony concluded the composing process with unresolved stylistic and syntactic problems. The conclusion here is not that Tony can't write, or that Tony doesn't know how to write, or that Tony needs to learn more rules: Tony is a writer with a highly consistent and deeply embedded recursive process. What he needs are teachers who can interpret that process for him, who can see through the tangles in the process just as he sees meaning beneath the tangles in his prose, and

39

40

who can intervene in such a way that untangling his composing process leads him to create better prose.

SUMMARY OF THE FINDINGS

15 A major finding of this study is that, like Tony, all of the students studied displayed consistent composing processes; that
is, the behavioral subsequences prewriting, writing, and editing
appeared in sequential patterns that were recognizable across
writing sessions and across students.

41

This consistency suggests a much greater internalization
of process than has ever before been suspected. Since the written products of basic writers often look arbitrary, observers
commonly assume that the students' approach is also arbitrary.
However, just as Shaughnessy (1977) points out that there is
"very little that is random . . . in what they have written" (p. 5),
16 so, on close observation, very little appears random in *how* they
write. The students observed had stable composing processes
which they used whenever they were presented with a writing
task. While this consistency argues against seeing these students
as beginning writers, it ought not necessarily imply that they are
proficient writers. Indeed, their lack of proficiency may be attrib-
utable to the way in which premature and rigid attempts to correct and edit their work truncate the flow of composing without
substantially improving the form of what they have written. More
detailed findings will be reviewed in the following subsections
which treat the three major aspects of composing: prewriting,
writing, and editing.

42

17 *Prewriting* When not given specific prewriting instructions,
the students in this study began writing within the first few
minutes. The average time they spent on prewriting in sessions

43

GENRE CUES

15 — Making Knowledge

16 — Extending

17 — Making Knowledge

1 and 2 was four minutes (see Table 4), and the planning strategies they used fell into three principal types:

1. Rephrasing the topic until a particular word or idea connected with the student's experience. The student then had "an event" in mind before writing began.

2. Turning the large conceptual issue in the topic (e.g., equality) into two manageable pieces for writing (e.g., rich vs. poor; black vs. white).

3. Initiating a string of associations to a word in the topic and then developing one or more of the associations during writing.

When students planned in any of these ways, they began to write with an articulated sense of where they wanted their discourse to go. However, frequently students read the topic and directions a few times and indicated that they had "no idea" what to write. On these occasions, they began writing without any secure sense of where they were heading, acknowledging only that they would "figure it out" as they went along. Often their first sentence was a rephrasing of the question in the topic which, now that it was in their own handwriting and down on paper in front of them, seemed to enable them to plan what ought to come next. In these instances, writing led to planning which led to clarifying which led to more writing. This sequence of planning and writing, clarifying and discarding, was repeated frequently in all of the sessions, even when students began writing with a secure sense of direction.

Although one might be tempted to conclude that these students began writing prematurely and that planning precisely what they were going to write ought to have occurred before they put pen to paper, the data here suggest:

1. that certain strategies, such as creating an association to a key word, focusing in and narrowing down the topic, dichotomizing and classifying, can and do take place in a relatively brief span of time; and

44

45

TABLE 4 OVERVIEW OF ALL WRITING SESSIONS

Read Later

	PREWRITING TIME*				TOTAL WORDS / TOTAL COMPOSING TIME				EDITING CHANGES		UNRESOLVED PROBLEMS	MISCUES DURING READING
	S1	S2	S4	S5	S1	S2	S4	S5	Content	Form		
TONY	7.8	3.5	8.0	5.7	302 / 91.2	512 / 76.0	356 / 82.0	550 / 96.0	24	210	89	84
DEE	2.5	2.9	5.0	5.0	409 / 55.5	559 / 65.0	91 / 24.5	212 / 29.0	7	24	40	32
STAN	3.5	4.3	14.8	14.7	419 / 62.0	553 / 73.1	365 / 73.0	303 / 68.0	13	49	45	55
LUELLER	2.0	1.5	4.0	13.0	518 / 90.8	588 / 96.8	315 / 93.0	363 / 77.8	2	167	143	147
BEVERLY	5.5	7.0	32.0	20.0	519 / 79.0	536 / 80.3	348 / 97.4	776 / 120.0	21	100	55	30

*Due to a change in the prewriting directions, only Sessions 1 and 2 are used to calculate the average time spent in prewriting.

2. that the developing and clarifying of ideas is facilitated once students translate some of those ideas into written form. In other words, seeing ideas on paper enables students to reflect upon, change and develop those ideas further.

Writing Careful study revealed that students wrote by shuttling from the sense of what they wanted to say forward to the words on the page and back from the words on the page to their intended meaning. This "back and forth" movement appeared to be a recursive feature: at one moment students were writing, moving their ideas and their discourse forward; at the next they were backtracking, rereading, and digesting what had been written. 46

Recursive movements appeared at many points during the writing process. Occasionally sentences were written in groups and then reread as a "piece" of discourse; at other times sentences and phrases were written alone, repeated until the writer was satisfied or worn down, or rehearsed until the act of rehearsal led to the creation of a new sentence. In the midst of writing, editing occurred as students considered the surface features of language. Often planning of a global nature took place: in the midst of producing a first draft, students stopped and began planning how the second draft would differ from the first. Often in the midst of writing, students stopped and referred to the topic in order to check if they had remained faithful to the original intent, and occasionally, though infrequently, they identified a sentence or a phrase that seemed, to them, to produce a satisfactory ending. In all these behaviors, they were shuttling back and forth, projecting what would come next and doubling back to be sure of the ground they had covered. 47

A number of conclusions can be drawn from the observations of these students composing and from the comments they made: although they produced inadequate or flawed products, they 48

GENRE CUES

 18— Making Knowledge

nevertheless seemed to understand and perform some of the crucial operations involved in composing with skill. While it cannot be stated with certainty that the patterns they displayed are shared by other writers, some of the operations they performed

(19) appear sufficiently sound to serve as prototypes for constructing two major hypotheses on the nature of their composing processes. Whether the following hypotheses are borne out in studies of different types of writers remains an open question:

1. Composing does not occur in a straightforward, linear fashion. The process is one of accumulating discrete bits down on the paper and then working from those bits to reflect upon, structure, and then further develop what one means to say. It can be thought of as a kind of "retrospective structuring"; movement forward occurs only after one has reached back, which in turn occurs only after one has some sense of where one wants to go. Both aspects, the reaching back and the sensing forward, have a clarifying effect.

2. Composing always involves some measure of both construction and discovery. Writers construct their discourse inasmuch as they begin with a sense of what they want to write. This sense, as long as it remains implicit, is not equivalent to the explicit form it gives rise to. Thus, a process of constructing meaning is required. Rereading or backward movements become a way of assessing whether or not the words on the page adequately capture the original sense intended. Constructing simultaneously affords discovery. Writers know more fully what they mean only after having written it. In this way the explicit written form serves as a window on the implicit sense with which one began.

Editing Editing played a major role in the composing processes of the students in this study (see Table 5). Soon after students began writing their first drafts, they began to edit, and

49

TABLE 5 EDITING CHANGES

	TONY	DEE	STAN	LUELLER	BEVERLY	TOTALS
Total number of words produced	1720	1271	1640	1754	2179	8564
Total form	210	24	49	167	100	550
Additions	19	2	10	21	11	63
Deletions	44	9	18	41	38	150
Word choice	13	4	1	27	6	51
Verb changes	4	1	2	7	12	26
Spelling	95	4	13	60	19	191
Punctuation	35	4	5	11	14	69
Total content	24	7	13	2	21	67

they continued to do so during the intervals between drafts, during the writing of their second drafts and during the final reading of papers.

While editing, the students were concerned with a variety of items: the lexicon (i.e., spelling, word choice, and the context of words); the syntax (i.e., grammar, punctuation, and sentence structure); and the discourse as a whole (i.e., organization, coherence, and audience). However, despite the students' considered attempts to proofread their work, serious syntactic and stylistic problems remained in their finished drafts. The persistence of these errors may, in part, be understood by looking briefly at some of the problems that arose for these students during editing.

Rule Confusion (1) All of the students observed asked themselves, "Is this sentence [or feature] correct?" but the simple set of editing rules at their disposal was often inappropriate for the types of complicated structures they produced. As a result, they misapplied what they knew and either created a hypercorrection or impaired the meaning they had originally intended to clarify; (2) The students observed attempted to write with terms they heard in lectures or class discussions, but since they were not yet familiar with the syntactic or semantic constraints one word placed upon another, their experiments with academic language resulted in what Shaughnessy (1977, p. 49) calls, "lexical transplants" or "syntactic dissonances"; (3) The students tried to rely on their intuitions about language, in particular the sound of words. Often, however, they had been taught to mistrust what "sounded" right to them, and they were unaware of the particular feature in their speech codes that might need to be changed in writing to match the standard code. As a result, when they attempted corrections by sound, they became confused, and they began to have difficulty differentiating between what sounded right in speech and what needed to be marked on the paper.

Selective Perception These students habitually reread their papers from internal semantic or meaning models. They extracted the meaning they wanted from the minimal cues on the page, and they did not recognize that outside readers would find those cues insufficient for meaning.

52

A study of Table 6 indicates that the number of problems remaining in the students' written products approximates the number of miscues produced during reading. This proximity, itself, suggests that many of these errors persisted because the students were so certain of the words they wanted to have on the page that they "read in" these words even when they were absent; in other words, they reduced uncertainty by operating as though what was in their heads was already on the page. The problem of selective perception, then, cannot be reduced solely to mechanical decoding; the semantic model from which students read needs to be acknowledged and taken into account in any study that attempts to explain how students write and why their completed written products end up looking so incomplete.

53

GENRE CUES

 Making Knowledge

TABLE 6 **THE TALK-WRITE PARADIGM MISCUES — DECODING BEHAVIORS**

	TONY	DEE	STAN	LUELLER	BEVERLY	TOTALS
Unresolved problems	89	40	45	143	55	372
"Reading in" missing words or word endings	25	13	11	44	11	104
Deleting words or word endings	6	2	4	14	9	35
"Reading" the desired word rather than the word on the page	5	6	18	15	8	52
"Reading" abbreviations and misspellings as though they were written correctly	48	11	22	74	2	157
Miscues during reading	84	32	55	147	30	348

Egocentricity The students in this study wrote from an egocentric point of view. While they occasionally indicated a concern for their readers, they more often took the reader's understanding for granted. They did not see the necessity of making their referents explicit, of making the connections among their ideas apparent, of carefully and explicitly relating one phenomenon to another, or of placing narratives or generalizations within an orienting, conceptual framework. ⁵⁴

On the basis of these observations one may be led to conclude that these writers did not know how to edit their work. Such a conclusion must, however, be drawn with care. Efforts to improve their editing need to be based on an informed view of the role that ⁵⁵

editing already plays in their composing processes. Two conclusions in this regard are appropriate here:

1. Editing intrudes so often and to such a degree that it breaks down the rhythms generated by thinking and writing. When this happens the students are forced to go back and recapture the strands of their thinking once the editing operation has been completed. Thus, editing occurs prematurely, before students have generated enough discourse to approximate the ideas they have, and it often results in their losing track of their ideas.

2. Editing is primarily an exercise in error-hunting. The students are prematurely concerned with the "look" of their writing; thus, as soon as a few words are written on the paper, detection and correction of errors replaces writing and revising. Even when they begin writing with a tentative, flexible frame of mind, they soon become locked into whatever is on the page. What they seem to lack as much as any rule is a conception of editing that includes flexibility, suspended judgment, the weighing of possibilities, and the reworking of ideas.

IMPLICATIONS FOR TEACHING AND RESEARCH

One major implication of this study pertains to teachers' conceptions of unskilled writers. Traditionally, these students have been labeled "remedial," which usually implies that teaching ought to remedy what is "wrong" in their written products. Since the surface features in the writing of unskilled writers seriously interfere with the extraction of meaning from the page, much class time is devoted to examining the rules of the standard code. The pedagogical soundness of this procedure has been questioned frequently,[2] but in spite of the debate, the practice continues, and it results in a further complication, namely that students begin to conceive of writing as a "cosmetic" process where concern for correct form supersedes development of ideas. As a result, the excitement of composing, of constructing and discovering meaning, is cut off almost before it has begun.

More recently, unskilled writers have been referred to as "beginners," implying that teachers can start anew. They need not "punish" students for making mistakes, and they need not assume that their students have already been taught how to write. Yet this view ignores the highly elaborated, deeply embedded processes the students bring with them. These unskilled college writers are not beginners in a *tabula rasa* sense, and teachers err in assuming they are. The results of this study suggest that teachers may first need to identify which characteristic components of each student's process facilitate writing and which inhibit it before further teaching takes place. If they do not, teachers of unskilled writers may continue to place themselves in a defeating position: imposing another method of writing instruction upon the students' already internalized processes without first helping students to extricate themselves from the knots and tangles in those processes.

A second implication of this study is that the composing process is now amenable to a replicable and graphic mode of representation as a sequence of codable behaviors. The composing style sheets provide researchers and teachers with the first demonstrable way of documenting how individual students write. Such a tool may have diagnostic as well as research benefits. It may be used to record writing behaviors in large groups, prior to and after instruction, as well as in individuals. Certainly it lends itself

57

58

GENRE CUES

22 — So What?

23 — Making Knowledge

24 — So What?

to the longitudinal study of the writing process and may help to elucidate what it is that changes in the process as writers become more skilled.

[25] A third implication relates to case studies and to the theories derived from them. This study is an illustration of the way in which a theoretical model of the composing process can be grounded in observations of the individual's experience of composing. It is precisely the complexity of this experience that the case study brings to light. However, by viewing a series of cases, the researcher can discern patterns and themes that suggest regularities in composing behavior across individuals. These common features lead to **[26]** hypotheses and theoretical formulations which have some basis in shared experience. How far this shared experience extends is, of course, a question that can only be answered through further research.

A final implication derives from the preponderance of recursive behaviors in the composing processes studied here, and from the theoretical notion derived from these observations: retrospective structuring, or the going back to the sense of one's **[27]** meaning in order to go forward and discover more of what one has to say. Seen in this light, composing becomes the carrying forward of an implicit sense into explicit form. Teaching composing, then, means paying attention not only to the forms or **[28]** products but a!so to the explicative process through which they arise.

59

60

GENRE CUES

[25] — Making Knowledge

[26] — So What?

[27] — Making Knowledge

[28] — So What?

APPENDIX

Composing Style Sheet

Name: Tony   Mode: Extensive TW₁   Date: October 31, 1975

Session: 1   Topic: Society & Culture   Time: 11:00 AM - 12:30 PM

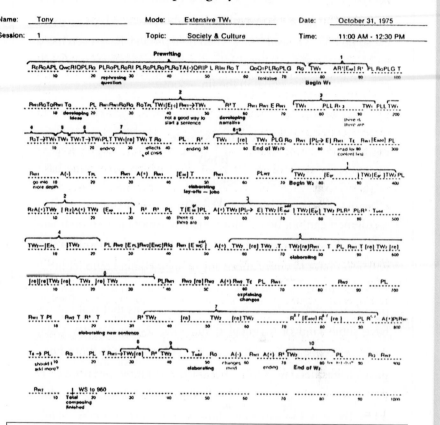

Writing Sample

TONY

Session 1

W1

All men can't be consider equal in a America base on financial situation.[1] Because their are men born in rich families that
will never have to worry about any financial difficulties.[2] And
         are
then theyre / ~~the~~ another type of Americans that is born to a poor
         may
family and alway / have some kind of fina—difficulty.[3] Espeicaly

and all

nowadays in New York city With the bugdit Crisis / .⁴

If he is able

~~He may~~ be able To get a job.⁵ But are now he lose the job just as easy as he got it.⁶ So when he loses his job he'll have to try to get some fina—assistance.⁷ A Then he'll probley have even more

here

fin—diffuicuty.⁸ So right here / you can't see that In ~~Amerian~~, all men are not create equal in the fin—sense.⁹

Writing Sample

TONY

Session 1

W2

All men can not be consider equal in America base on financial situations.¹ Because their are men born in rich families that will never have to worry about any finan~~cial diff~~uel diffuliculties.²

the

And then there are / another type of ameicans that are born to a

may

poor famitly.³ And This is the type of Americans that ~~will~~ / alway have some kind of finanical diffuliculty.⁴ Espeical today ~~today~~

working

~~the~~in new york The way the city has fallen ~~has fallen~~ into fin— debt.⁵ It has become such a big crisis for the ~~people~~ people, in

with the

the ⁶ If the working man is able to find a job, espeicaly ~~for~~ / ~~city~~

the   is

a city The way ~~the way~~ city / fin—sitionu is set up now, ~~h~~He'll probley lose the job a whole lot faster than what he got it.⁷ When he loses his job he'll ~~p~~ have even more fin—difficulty.⁸ And then he'll be force to ~~got~~ to the city for some fini—assi—.⁹ So right here you can see that all men in America are not create equal in the fin—sense.¹⁰

Notes

1. The word "read" is used in a particular manner here. In the traditional sense, reading refers to accurate decoding of written symbols. Here it refers to students' verbalizing words or endings even when the symbols for those words are missing or only minimally present. Whenever the term "reading" is used in this way, it will be in quotation marks.

2. For discussions on the controversy over the effects of grammar instruction on writing ability, see the following: Richard Braddock, Richard Lloyd-Jones, and Lowell Schoer, *Research in Written Composition* (Urbana, Ill.: National Council of Teachers of English, 1963); Frank O'Hare, *Sentence Combining* (NCTE Research Report No. 15, Urbana, Ill.: National Council of Teachers of English, 1973); Elizabeth F. Haynes, "Using Research in Preparing to Teach Writing," *English Journal*, 1978, 67, 82–89.

References

Braddock, R., Lloyd-Jones, R., & Schoer, L. *Research in written composition*. Urbana, Ill.: National Council of Teachers of English, 1963.

Britton, J., Burgess, T., Martin, N., McLeod, A., & Rosen, H. *The development of writing abilities (11–18)*. London: Macmillan Education Ltd., 1975.

Burton, D. L. Research in the teaching of English: The troubled dream. *Research in the Teaching of English*, 1973, 1, 160–187.

Cooper, C. R. Doing research/reading research. *English Journal*, 1974, 63, 94–99.

Cooper, C. R., & Odell, L. (Eds.) *Research on composing: Points of departure*. Urbana, Ill.: National Council of Teachers of English, 1978.

Emig, J. A. On teaching composition: Some hypotheses as definitions. *Research in the Teaching of English*, 1967, 1, 127–135.

Emig, J. A. *The composing processes of twelfth graders*. Urbana, Ill.: National Council of Teachers of English, 1971. (Research Report No. 13) (Ed. D. Dissertation, Harvard University, 1969).

Goodman, K. S. (Ed.) *Miscue analysis: Applications to reading instruction*. Urbana, Ill.: NCTE and ERIC, 1973.

Graves, D. H. Children's writing: Research directions and hypotheses based upon an examination of the writing process of seven year old children (Doctoral dissertation, State University of New York at Buffalo, 1973). *Dissertation Abstracts International*, 1974, 34, 6255A.

Haynes, E. F. Using research in preparing to teach writing. *English Journal*, 1978, 67, 82–89.

Mischel, T. A case study of a twelfth-grade writer. *Research in the Teaching of English*, 1974, 8, 303–314.

O'Hare, F. *Sentence-combining: Improving student writing without formal grammar instruction.* Urbana, Ill.: National Council of Teachers of English, 1973. (Research Report No. 15).

Perl, S. *Five writers writing: Case studies of the composing processes of unskilled college writers.* Unpublished doctoral dissertation, New York University, 1978.

Pianko, S. *The composing acts of college freshmen writers.* Unpublished Ed.D. dissertation, Rutgers University, 1977.

Shaughnessy, M. P. *Errors and expectations: A guide for the teacher of basic writing.* New York: Oxford University Press, 1977.

Stallard, C. K. An analysis of the writing behavior of good student writers. *Research in the Teaching of English,* 1974, *8,* 206–218.

Questions for Discussion and Journaling

1. Perl notes that Tony's writing process and resulting text were markedly different when he was writing about his own experience and when he was trying to write less personally. Describe this difference and explain whether it makes sense to you.

2. Why does Perl take it as such a positive sign that Tony and her other research participants' composing processes are "consistent" rather than scattered or random?

3. Find the section of the article where Perl discusses how she developed her "code" of composing behaviors. What is your sense of how she put it together, and at what point in her research did she do so?

4. Build a list of reasons Perl is critical of previous writing-process research, and explain each of them. How well would you say her research here overcomes or eliminates those problems?

5. Do you think Perl's research methods might have actively shaped the writing her participants produced? That is, if she had changed the design of her study, is it possible she would have gotten different writing from her participants? Explain.

6. Perl appears not to count changes made while drafting sentence-by-sentence as "editing"; instead, she reserves that term for changes made between drafts. Why do you think she makes that distinction?

7. Do you see your own composing as "the carrying forward of an implicit sense into explicit form" (para. 60)? How so, and how not?

8. How does Perl's "restrospective structuring" (para. 60) apply to the threshold concepts emphasized in this chapter — that writing makes new knowledge, and that writers don't usually "get it right the first time"?

Applying and Exploring Ideas

1. Put together a list of the problems Tony had with composing and editing — for example, his tendency to say a sentence one way but write down something else. As you review the list, do you see problems that you've had trouble with in the past, or any you still have trouble with? If so, how did you solve them — or what have you tried that hasn't worked? Discuss this question with one or more classmates: Have they encountered the problem of selective perception, for example? If so, how have they dealt with it?

2. Perl argues that it's a good thing when people don't wait to write until they know everything they want to say — rather, she wants writers to use the clarifying power of the act of writing itself to help them figure out what they want to say. To what extent does this strategy resemble your own writing process?

3. Perl was researching in a time before camcorders. Today, to do the same research, we would not only set up a camera (thus recording the participant's speech, behaviors, and writing activity simultaneously and in real time) but possibly also capture their keystrokes (assuming they composed at a computer) for a microscopically accurate record of exactly how the participant was writing. If you have a device to record digital video, try recording yourself or a volunteer while he or she writes, and then use the recording to help you devise a code to explain the processes you recorded. If that's not possible, consider: If you were doing Perl's study today, how would you design it to take advantage of current technology and your own ideas about the writing process? What kind of code would you devise to explain the activity that your technology recorded?

4. Look through the Assist Tags in this reading. Write an analysis of any patterns that emerge in them, and how those patterns might connect to what you've been learning about writing while using this book.

- -

META MOMENT   Name one thing you now understand about the writing process or will do differently in your own writing after reading about Tony's process.

- -

Tug of War

The Writing Process of a Bilingual Writer and His Struggles

ALCIR SANTOS NETO

Reginaldo Azevedo Filho

Framing the Reading

We expect that many readers of this book are multilingual, and that by reading it in English, they are encountering it in their second or third language. Too often, however, English-speaking researchers of writing look only at native speakers of English when investigating how writers compose and inscribe knowledge and texts. Whatever complications monolingual writing involves, we might expect that multilingual writers face a somewhat more complicated scene and process. But how so?

Using an extension of the protocol process that Sondra Perl developed to trace writing process, Alcir Santos Neto takes up that question by examining his own multilingual writing processes. He writes, "I read information in English, rationalize it in Portuguese, and write it in English" (para. 2). Neto's descriptions of moving between two languages at various points in his writing offer an excellent window into how languages themselves can influence our invention and composing. Neto also offers an interesting demonstration of what it is to be a reflective and mindful writer. Both before his research, and even more as a result of it, he is aware of and able to say a great deal about his writing processes, which demonstrates one of the concepts about process we discussed in the introduction: *Writing is enhanced by metacognition* (mindfulness and reflection). Reading Neto's research gives us an opportunity to see how much control this mindfulness may or may not give him of his composing.

Neto was born in Brazil. At the time this piece was published, he was a first-year international and global studies major at the University of Central Florida, also

Neto, Alcir Santos. "Tug of War: The Writing Process of a Bilingual Writer and His Struggles." *Stylus*, Knight's Write Showcase Special Issue, Spring 2014, pp. 1–8.

minoring in Latin American studies. His experience at the time included a number of student programs in international relations, including the Harvard Secondary School Program for international relations, Junior Statesman Summer School at Princeton University for international relations, and the National Student Leadership Conference for International Diplomacy with the United Nations. His career goals included working as a foreign analyst in Brazil and diplomatic service as an ambassador.

Getting Ready to Read

Before you read, do at least one of the following activities:

- Talk with someone — it may be yourself! — who is multilingual. Ask them how they compose in the languages they know, and what differences they are aware of in how they compose in their first language versus second and later languages.

- If you've read Perl's piece (preceding this one), make a short list of aspects of the writing process that you notice she did *not* look at in the code she created for describing writing processes. What is missing from her work that other researchers could do additional research on?

As you read, consider the following questions:

- What distracts you while you read and write, and how do your distractions compare with Neto's? Do your reading and writing distractions tend to be different from one another?

- How might Neto's self-protocol of his writing process be influencing that process itself?

INTRODUCTION

"WHAT IS INVOLVED IN the act of writing?" asked researcher Sondra Perl 1 (193). This question ignited a desire in the expansion for the academic study of a writer's composing process. According to Perl, "In recent years, interest in the composing process has grown" (193). Instead of academic researchers investigating simply in order to describe and understand literature, they are analyzing the processes related to composing a piece of writing. Various studies have been done on this subject. For example, Perl conducted "a study of the composing processes of five unskilled college writers" (192). Another researcher, Carol Berkenkotter, "wanted to learn more about the planning and revising strategies of a highly skilled and verbal writer," and decided to focus on Donald M. Murray (219). When Berkenkotter conducted her study, she stated that "[t]o date there are no reported studies of writers composing in natural (as opposed to laboratory) settings that combine thinking-aloud protocols with the writers' own introspective accounts" (219). Her study was the first of its kind.

Both studies analyzed the writing styles of native English writers. In order 2 to contribute to this conversation, I decided to take a different approach and analyze my composing process, since I was taught Portuguese before I learned to speak English. Throughout the years, I have personally struggled with the "tug of war" between both languages when I write: I read information in English, rationalize it in Portuguese, and write it in English. To further investigate this complex process, I have decided to analyze my writing process and compare it to two native English writers: to Tony, the unskilled writer in Perl's study, and to Murray, a highly skilled writer. Also, I analyzed the benefits and disadvantages of how the language barrier affects my writing process. To successfully analyze my writing process, I used the thinking-aloud protocol, since both Tony and Murray used the protocol. The strengths and weakness of this protocol and its effects on my process are addressed later on in this study.

METHODS

Each writer, skilled or unskilled, has a unique composing process. But what are 3 the characteristics in my writing process? In order to acquire credible results, a natural setting was used in order to minimize the negative impacts of conducting a study in a laboratory environment, such as unnatural distractions. I filmed myself in my dorm using the think-aloud protocol proposed by Berkenkotter. The method was simple, consisting of an iPhone 4S to record the video and audio, a laptop as a medium for the composing process, and a timer.

In this study, I decided not to focus on the content, but on the process of 4 constructing an essay. I have applied some of Perl's coding system to my study, but I also took the liberty to expand and personalize it. I created a coding system (see Table 1) to substitute every four to nine words with one or more codes corresponding to what I was doing. Each code was assigned to a category: talking, writing, reading, or distractions. For example, on page three of the transcript, I stated, "Okay, so I'm going to do the introduction." In these eight words, I am talking about what I am going to do (T_a) and planning on how to proceed with my essay (W_{pl}). After my coding system was in place, I watched the video and coded the script. This helped me decide when I read the book (R_b) or if I re-read my text aloud (T_{re}), serving as a great aid in finding specific patterns in my writing that I would not have discovered by solely analyzing the script.

Within my writing category, I have codes based on the editing process, such 5 as spelling (W_s) and punctuation (W_p), and on codes based on the writing itself,

TABLE 1 CODING SYSTEM

TALKING	WRITING	READING	DISTRACTIONS
T_r – Random	W_a – Adding	R_w – Reading word count	D_i – Distraction
T_a – Talking about action	W_b – Writer's block	R_b – Reading the book	T_x – Texting
T_{lt} – Losing train of thought	W_c – Citations	R_s – Scanning	C_a – Calling
T_q – Questioning	W_d – Deleting		M – Mumbling
T_{re} – Rereading aloud	W_s – Spelling		
T_t – Talking about thought	W_{lt} – Losing train of thought		
T_w – Talking while writing	W_p – Punctuation		
T_f – Speaking Portuguese	W_r – Red Line		
T_{an} – Analyzing Text aloud	W_{pl} – Planning		
T_{tol} – Relating Text to Essay			

such as planning (W_{pl}) and writer's block (W_b). To clarify, the red line code (W_r) refers to the red line that appears under a misspelled word of the Microsoft Word Spelling Check. In regards to the talking category, talking about an action (T_a) means stating what I will do, like, for example, "Okay, so I'm going to do the introduction," shows that I was talking about an action (writing the introduction).

Script	Codes
"Okay, so I'm going to do the introduction, the introduction has to start out with, has to start broad, so pretty much summarize the article and I'll explain how it relates to me,"	$(T_a, W_{pl})\ W_{pl}\ (T_a, W_{pl})\ (T_a, W_{pl})$ *Note: The (,) means two codes occurring simultaneously.*

Figure 1 **Sample Coded Transcript**

Strengths and Weaknesses

There were strengths and weaknesses with the methods of this study. The natural 6 composing environment strengthens the composer's ability to immerse into his natural process. Each writer has a different environment that helps her brainstorm and construct ideas. This allows for flexibility in each writer, which helps build the credibility of the results. The negative effects of a laboratory environment restrict the writer to an uncommon environment compared to his natural writing environment. This uncommon environment can create unwanted distractions that can negatively affect the writing process, skewing the results. Unwanted distractions include uncommon noises and events that a writer would not be affected by if in a more common writing environment. On the other hand, the thinking-aloud protocol brings out the ability to know what the writer is thinking, which can be very beneficial; however, it had a negative impact on my study. This protocol became a distraction and influenced my natural process. This occurred because I think in Portuguese, and I had to simultaneously translate what I was thinking to speak in English, since the project needed to be in English. This distraction happened because I caught myself censoring and focusing on my words, which distracted me and increased the normal time to process the information in my head. I will address this in greater detail later on in my study. Even with the weaknesses presented, the thinking-aloud protocol contributed to finding patterns within my research that would not have appeared if I didn't use this method, such as discovering the constant need to reread the text. Thus, the strengths outweigh the weaknesses in this study, which makes the results reliable.

RESULTS

Table 2 presents the total of each code as a percentage of all codes. For example, 7 code T_r represented 9.21% of all codes. This table does not include more than one code together (for example, code T_p, T_a, and T_{tol} within the four to nine words). The purpose of presenting Table 2 was to provide organized and clear data of the behaviors analyzed. Each column is divided by each category analyzed in this study, followed by the related codes beneath them. The totals were given in order to facilitate the comparison between sections whereas the percentage of the total is compared to the sum of the behaviors in that section. I have provided the frequency of each behavior along with the percentage to describe how each behavior relates to the total amount of behaviors that occurred (of which there were a total of 805).

DISCUSSION

As I began to organize my data, I was surprised by my patterns of behaviors. 8 There were actions that I tended to do more often that I have never caught

TABLE 2 FREQUENCIES OF BEHAVIORS

TALKING		READING		WRITING		DISTRACTIONS	
T_r	74 – (9.21%)	R_w	6 – (0.74%)	W_a	10 – (1.24%)	D_i	21 – (2.61%)
T_a	122 – (15.19%)	R_b	44 – (5.47%)	W_b	2 – (0.24%)	T_x	2 – (0.24%)
T_{lt}	5 – (0.62%)	R_s	3 – (0.37%)	W_c	6 – (0.74%)	C_a	2 – (0.24%)
T_q	43 – (5.35%)			W_d	9 – (1.12%)	M	10 – (1.24%)
T_{re}	177 – (22.04%)			W_s	5 – (0.62%)		
T_t	4 – (0.49%)			W_{lt}	1 – (0.12%)		
T_w	149 – (18.55%)			W_p	27 – (3.36%)		
T_f	13 – (1.61%)			W_r	2 – (0.24%)		
T_{an}	8 – (0.99%)			W_{pl}	36 – (4.48%)		
T_{tol}	23 – (2.86%)						
Total	= 618 (76.91%)	**Total**	= 53 (6.58%)	**Total**	– 99 (12.16%)	**Total**	= 35 (4.33%)

myself doing, such as talking about an action (T_a). It's also interesting to notice that only certain categories were influenced by my bilingual background. Each category brings out important patterns found by this study, with the talking category as the one with the most interesting patterns.

Talking

Talking significantly affected my writing by influencing the speed and revision, such as rereading my text. Related to writing speed, when I talk while writing (T_w), I do so slowly. That happens because I think in Portuguese. When I brainstorm or analyze text, I do so in Portuguese; however, when I write those ideas on paper, I translate in my head from Portuguese into English. Thinking in Portuguese speeds up my rhetorical analysis of texts and brainstorming because I am more familiar with my native language. Since this project required my transcript to be in English, my writing and process speed was reduced; I had to translate from Portuguese into English in my head and speak English during the thinking-aloud protocol. The benefit of writing and talking

> When I brainstorm or analyze text, I do so in Portuguese; however, when I write those ideas on paper, I translate in my head from Portuguese into English.

9

779

fast while planning (T_{tol}) in Portuguese is that it helps me rationalize the text and brainstorm what to write. Unfortunately, the slow pace during talking while writing (T_w) is sometimes the cause for distractions (D) to happen or "losing my train of thought" (T_{lt}) because I had to quickly analyze in Portuguese, translate, and write it in English.

I also consciously tend to reread aloud (T_{re}) what I wrote and that happened   10 22.04% (177 times) of the time; this was the code that happened most often during my composing process. I reread my writing from the minimum of three to the maximum of 23 times per page. All of the pages in my script contain rereading, with the exception of the last page (the conclusion). Rereading helps me to understand what I wrote and smoothly transition into another concept. Another benefit of rereading is to check whether I'm being faithful to the topic. My foreign language wasn't a factor when I reread the text because I absorb and store the information in my head in English; it is solely the rationalizing part that happens in Portuguese.

The tendency of rereading text is a common factor that I share with unskilled   11 writers. Perl found the same issue in her study, stating, "Often in the midst of writing, students stopped and referred to the topics in order to check if they had remained faithful to the original intent" (207). Therefore, rereading is common not only in my writing, but also with unskilled writers. There are both positive and negative aspects of constantly checking back to the topic to remain faithful. It can be positive by demonstrating that the writer wants to be confident that his piece reflects the topic in the best manner necessary; however, it can be a distraction and negatively affect the writing process, resulting in writer's block (W_b) or even losing the train of thought (T_{lt}).

Talking about an action (T_a) was a frequently occurring code, which emerged   12 122 times (15.19%). One benefit from talking about an action is that it helped me to be organized. For example, when I stated "okay, so I'm going to do the introduction," I was organizing what I would do, which also can be called planning about an action. That would be the same as T_a. Another benefit of talking about an action is that it helped me organize my thoughts in Portuguese, before I would write my ideas on paper in English. When I read, I pay attention to main ideas and key words. Talking about an action allowed me to organize these items in Portuguese and prepare them for translation. The method of planning aloud is similar to a method used by Donald M. Murray, which consists of "the stating of 'process goals'—mentioning procedures, that is, that he developed in order to write" (Berkenkotter 222). Berkenkotter found that "frequently, these procedures led the writer to generate a series of plans for carrying out the larger plan" (222). This planning happens as we write, not prior to writing the essay. In a positive aspect, using this approach helps Murray and I to organize the action needed to fulfill the goal: finishing the essay. However, it could have a negative impact on the natural writing process of other writers. For writers who are not used to this concept, it could lead them into distractions (D), such as writer's block (W_b) or even losing the train of thought (T_{lt}).

Writing

While talking is essential for brainstorming and the organization of my paper, writing is also very important for constructing the meaning of my essay. Within my writing category, I have codes based on two groups: editing processes and composing processes. Spelling (W_s) and punctuation (W_p) are categorized under the editing process group, whereas planning (W_{pl}) and writer's block (W_b) are categorized under the composing group. The writing category was only 12% of the total categories. This surprises me, since I previously thought that I checked punctuation, spelling, and citations frequently. Tony, on the other hand, "spent a great deal of his composing time editing" (Perl 202). I discovered that, according to the statistics, I am more concerned with my ideas connecting to the audience than the grammatical issues of my essay because of the language barrier. If I connect with my audience, then my conversation would have a greater impact than obeying every grammatical rule in the book. With this thought, it led me to check for punctuation less than I expected. [13]

It is also interesting to notice that the majority of codes in the writing category that happened were planning (occurring 36 times, 4.48% of the total transcript) and punctuation (occurring 27 times, 3.36% of the total transcript). I found out that planning happened when I finished writing an idea to go to the other idea. To clarify, the planning done in my process is while I'm writing, not before I begin the essay. This type of planning differs from planning about an action, and consists of planning about the content. For example, when I state in my script, "Okay, so I'm going to do the introduction, the introduction has to start out with, has to start broad, so pretty much summarize the article and I'll explain how it relates to me, then I hit the important points, so how to, how am I going to transition to that important point? I have how my article is the problem, so I'll pretty much going to state." This quote shows planning as I'm writing, a unique pattern identified by this study. This was a natural way for me to move from the translation step into the writing step. Also, it naturally came out as a way to shift ideas within the text, contributing to the organization of my process. Common words that I have found that I use before I begin to plan are "umm," "okay," "so," and "alright." That can happen within a paragraph or before that paragraph begins, a pattern identified through the coding process. It is also interesting to notice that each word serves as a break from a previous idea, allows me to organize what I would write next, and gives me the opportunity to translate ideas into English. [14]

Planning also happened in talking about an action (T_a), such as deciding to do the introduction first, as discussed earlier. This is common with unskilled writers, as pointed out by Perl. She said that unskilled writers "began writing [15] without any secure sense of where they were heading, acknowledging only that they would 'figure it out' as they went along" (205). Since unskilled writers "figure it out" as they go along, this could be an explanation for writer's block. Writer's block is when a writer doesn't know how to proceed with their writing and gets stuck.

I only encountered writer's block twice: once halfway through the essay and 16 once at the end, during the conclusion. One reason could be the lengthy writing process, since I normally don't take any breaks. Naturally, I discovered that, to get over the writer's block, I stop, take a deep breath, question myself, and then tell myself what to do. If I'm reading, I also reread to get my ideas flowing again to restart my composing process. This consequently slows down my process. One would think that writer's block could happen if my translation step "overheats," but the writer's block that happened was in regards with the content and not the process of writing.

Reading

Reading provides me with the text support as a base for my arguments, giving 17 this category its importance. According to the data, the majority of my reading category is directed towards reading the text for information (R_i). This tends to mostly happen in the beginning of my composing process, a pattern that I have found during the coding of the transcript (occurring 44 times, 5.47% of the total transcript). That normally gives me the ability to find a topic and select quotes. There was one exception, and that happened on page 10 of the transcript. During that time, I read the book to verify if a fact was actually included in the text. When that happened, I said, "I guess Mr. Murray was- I guess Mr. Murray was skilled, right? Let me see, let me go back to the page, Mr. Murray, Mr. Murray, Okay. I wanted to learn more about the planning and revising strategies of highly skilled and verbal writers." It can be inferred from this quote that reading the book only gives me the ability to brainstorm ideas. One benefit of gathering information at the beginning of the composing process is that, instead of going back to the text every time, it lets my ideas flow and not be disrupted. Ironically enough, this category was not disrupted by the translation of information in my head. Reading text for information in the beginning of my composing process was merely the act of absorbing information. Since I store information in my head in English, this process was not affected by the language barrier. Like any other writer, however, the flow of the writing process was affected by distractions.

Distractions

Neither Perl nor Berkenkotter analyzed distractions in their study, but I decided 18 to do so. The importance of distractions can best be seen by their disruption of a writer's composing process. In that respect, my distractions occurred when my ideas ceased from flowing, occurring 21 times (2.61%). During that time, I remembered about sending my essay to a friend to help me edit it before I would turn it in, which led me to call (C_x happened two times, being 0.24%) and text him (T_x happened two times, being 0.24%). He would then check for grammatical errors. After that distraction, I would reread what I last typed, take a deep breath, and then continue to write.

Distractions also occurred when I began to get tired of writing. I quickly 19 became frustrated and that is where speaking in a foreign language came in (T_f happened 13 times, being 1.61%). I would complain in Portuguese about being tired and then tell myself to get focused. For example, from the end of page 13 to the beginning of page 14, I got tired and distracted (the translation are in brackets): "– mumbling- So, so carol last name spelled out Astronomy notes, chapter 7, meus Deus eu vou ter que fazer tudo isso ainda hoje que saco [My Gosh, I still need to do all of this today. Darn it] 7:39pm, so depois eu vou fazer statistics [After I'll do statistics] - I would write, I forgot how to say this, I think I'm forgetting something, astronomy study, review statistics for now. Alright, let me go back to the reading journal– mumbling-." Thus, frustration caused by writing fatigue leads me to speak in a foreign language.

As previously stated, the thinking aloud protocol had a negative impact 20 on my study. It caused major distractions and influenced my natural process by censoring words and transferring my focus away from the writing process. Consequently, it increased the time to process the information in my head, something that I didn't expect to happen. I did not think that the translation step actually increased the time it takes to write an essay. One method that I used to help me overcome the negative impact of the thinking-aloud protocol was mumbling, which made up 2.61% (occurring 21 times) of the total behaviors and tendencies. This helped me process my information when I was distracted by the protocol. The mumbling that I did was a way to think quickly in Portuguese and bypass the thinking-aloud protocol. As seen by the previous quote, mumbling happened at the end or at the beginning of the distraction, being a medium for me to go back into writing.

IMPLICATIONS

Through the results acquired by this study, my writing process can be related to 21 Tony's and Murray's composing processes. Certain tendencies that I had, such as reading text for information in the beginning, were tendencies that Tony has. A strength that I shared with Murray in my process was the planning of process goals. By creating these small goals to accomplish within my essay, I was able to keep consistency in the voice and in the structure of my composing process. On the other hand, a weakness that I need to improve on would be planning content beforehand, a similar process that I shared with the unskilled writers examined by Perl. Furthermore, my slow writing process that happens due to my language barrier is a factor that native English speakers do not go through because of the translation that happens in my head. It can be inferred that each writer has strengths and weaknesses in certain areas, such as spelling or transitions. By analyzing the results, I have learned that my style of composing an essay consists of a large amount of rereading and a small quantity of editing.

As a bilingual writer, I experience many difficulties as well as benefits. One 22 difficulty that I encounter constantly relates to untranslatable concepts, the "tug of war" problem. Untranslatable concepts normally appear in the form of "slang" and that happened when I stated "meus Deus eu vou ter que fazer tudo isso ainda hoje que saco [My Gosh, I still need to do all of this today. Darn it]." In this case, the closest word to the definition of "que saco" would be "darn it," but it is not the literal translation. Because of that problem, it takes me longer to find a substitute for that idea. This is a struggle that I encounter when I write; it differentiates me from a native English writer. The benefit of being a bilingual writer is that I would try to incorporate examples and ideas that different cultures can also grasp. I tend to keep a globalized audience in mind when I write because I am aware of the personal difficulties that I had to overcome when I was learning the English language and reading texts. The goal of this study is to help bilingual writers to reflect upon their weaknesses and hopefully be able to apply my findings to their own process in order to improve their writing.

The unexpected data acquired by this study helped me transform my writing 23 process into a healthier one. To reduce distractions, which are a result of fatigue, I will take 20-minute breaks. Also, to improve the organization of my writing, I will formulate an outline before I begin to write, but I will keep the writing process goals to allow room for flexibility when new ideas develop and creativity flows. In regards to improving my writing process due to the language issue, there is no way to change the tendency to think in another language and write in English. The only way that it could change was if English was my first language. I am certain that there are many writers that might be experiencing the same language difficulty, but the only solution to increase the translation speed when transitioning from their native language into English is to continue to practice to write and translate. To improve the planning content process, I should plan before writing as well, which will help by guiding me in the right direction. However, I should keep the "process goals," which Murray and I share because it is an effective method to organize what I will be doing throughout the essay. Planning affected my process by changing the direction I would take to fulfill the goal of writing an essay.

CONCLUSION

As a freshman in college, an unskilled writer, and a non-native English writer, I 24
believe that many could relate my study to their own writing process. One concept that many can relate to is distractions, and I hope that my results can provide
solutions to those who read this study. Certainly, each writer has her own natural
tendencies and behaviors, which normally relates to writing environment. But
if writers would make an introspective "checklist" of their own process, many
would find healthier ways to improve and even build on their composing process.

Works Cited

Berkenkotter, Carol. "Decisions and Revisions: The Planning Strategies of a Publishing Writer."
Wardle and Downs, pp. 218–30.

Perl, Sondra. "The Composing Processes of Unskilled College Writers." Wardle and Downs,
pp. 192–214.

Wardle, Elizabeth, and Doug Downs, editors. *Writing about Writing*. Bedford/St. Martin's, 2011.

- -

Questions for Discussion and Journaling

1. What conversation does Neto position himself as contributing to, and what
   does he mean to add to it?

2. Do you agree with Neto's argument that his research method proved to be
   reliable even though it created a distraction that influenced his writing method?

3. Which categories of activities did Neto think were most influenced by his bilingual background? Considering your own lingualism (mono-, bi-, or multi-), are
   his arguments borne out by your own experience?

4. If you can write in more than one language, how do your challenges writing in
   your second language seem similar to and different from those that Neto reports?

5. If you've read Perl's "The Composing Process of Unskilled Writers" (p. 738) as
   well as Neto's article, compare their organizations: Which is easier to follow,
   and why? ("Neto's, because it's shorter" is not a sufficient answer.)

6. How do Neto's study and findings show that having more than one language
   is powerful?

7. In his implications section, Neto writes that he needs to improve on planning
   content before drafting. What are some ways in which someone who wanted
   to plan more before drafting could do so?

Applying and Exploring Ideas

1. You can study one aspect of your writing process, in a limited way, without needing to do the kind of full-on studies Neto and Perl do. Select one element of Neto's process coding (for example, Planning or Questioning or Citations), and, following his method for noting how much time is spent on a given activity, see what proportion of your writing time is spent on it. Write a one-page analysis, explanation, and reflection on the results. Does the result surprise you, or not? Why?

2. Neto reports that an advantage of being a bilingual writer is heightened empathy: "I tend to keep a globalized audience in mind when I write because I am aware of the personal difficulties that I had to overcome when I was learning the English language and reading texts" (para. 22). Write a reflection on the language experiences you've had that make you empathetic toward learners and users of your first language.

3. Neto's work extends Perl's study by adding Distractions as a category of interest. Write an argument for what other categories of activities and elements of writing process need to be studied, and why. What do you see as the biggest gap left by Perl's and Neto's research?

- -

META MOMENT   Neto relates that his study findings have led him to a healthier writing process. What ideas have you gotten from his study for questioning and potentially modifying your own process?

- -

- What are the relationships among **heuristics**, plans, rules, algorithms, set, and perplexity?

- Where do you see yourself, if anywhere, among the various writers Rose describes?

RUTH WILL LABOR OVER the first paragraph of an essay for hours. She'll write a sentence, then erase it. Try another, then scratch part of it out. Finally, as the evening winds on toward ten o'clock and Ruth, anxious about tomorrow's deadline, begins to wind into herself, she'll compose that first paragraph only to sit back and level her favorite exasperated interdiction at herself and her page: "No. You can't say that. You'll bore them to death."

Ruth is one of ten UCLA undergraduates with whom I discussed writer's block, that frustrating, self-defeating inability to generate the next line, the right phrase, the sentence that will release the flow of words once again. These ten people represented a fair cross-section of the UCLA student community: lower-middle-class to upper-middle-class backgrounds and high schools, third-world and Caucasian origins, biology to fine arts majors, C+ to A– grade point averages, enthusiastic to blasé attitudes toward school. They were set off from the community by the twin facts that all ten could write competently, and all were currently enrolled in at least one course that required a significant amount of writing. They were set off among themselves by the fact that five of them wrote with relative to enviable ease while the other five experienced moderate to nearly immobilizing writer's block. This blocking usually resulted in rushed, often late papers and resultant grades that did not truly reflect these students' writing ability. And then, of course, there were other less measurable but probably more serious results: a growing distrust of their abilities and an aversion toward the composing process itself.

What separated the five students who blocked from those who didn't? It wasn't skill; that was held fairly constant. The answer could have rested in the emotional realm — anxiety, fear of evaluation, insecurity, etc. Or perhaps blocking in some way resulted from variation in cognitive style. Perhaps, too, blocking originated in and typified a melding of emotion and cognition not unlike the relationship posited by Shapiro between neurotic feeling and neurotic thinking.[1] Each of these was possible. Extended clinical interviews and testing could have teased out the answer. But there was one answer that surfaced readily in brief explorations of these students' writing processes. It was not profoundly emotional, nor was it embedded in that still unclear construct of cognitive style. It was constant, surprising, almost amusing if its results weren't so troublesome, and, in the final analysis, obvious: the five students who experienced blocking were all operating

> *It was constant, surprising, almost amusing if its results weren't so troublesome, and, in the final analysis, obvious: the five students who experienced blocking were all operating either with writing rules or with planning strategies that impeded rather than enhanced the composing process.*

either with writing rules or with planning strategies that impeded rather than enhanced the composing process. The five students who were not hampered by writer's block also utilized rules, but they were less rigid ones, and thus more appropriate to a complex process like writing. Also, the plans these non-blockers brought to the writing process were more functional, more flexible, more open to information from the outside.

These observations are the result of one to three interviews with each student. I used recent notes, drafts, and finished compositions to direct and hone my questions. This procedure is admittedly non-experimental, certainly more clinical than scientific; still, it did lead to several inferences that lay the foundation for future, more rigorous investigation: (a) composing is a highly complex problem-solving process[2] and (b) certain disruptions of that process can be explained with cognitive psychology's problem-solving framework. Such investigation might include a study using "stimulated recall" techniques to validate or disconfirm these hunches. In such a study, blockers and non-blockers would write essays. Their activity would be videotaped and, immediately after writing, they would be shown their respective tapes and questioned about the rules, plans, and beliefs operating in their writing behavior. This procedure would bring us close to the composing process (the writers' recall is stimulated by their viewing the tape), yet would not interfere with actual composing.

In the next section I will introduce several key concepts in the problem-solving literature. In section three I will let the students speak for themselves. Fourth, I will offer a cognitivist analysis of blockers' and non-blockers' grace or torpor. I will close with a brief note on treatment.

SELECTED CONCEPTS IN PROBLEM SOLVING: RULES AND PLANS

As diverse as theories of problem solving are, they share certain basic assumptions and characteristics. Each posits an *introductory period* during which a problem is presented, and all theorists, from Behaviorist to Gestalt to Information Processing, admit that certain aspects, stimuli, or "functions" of the problem must become or be made salient and attended to in certain ways if successful problem-solving processes are to be engaged. Theorists also believe that some conflict, some stress, some gap in information in these perceived "aspects" seems to trigger problem-solving behavior. Next comes a *processing period*, and for all the variance of opinion about this critical stage, theorists recognize the necessity of its existence — recognize that man, at the least, somehow "weighs" possible solutions as they are stumbled upon and, at the most, goes through an elaborate and sophisticated information-processing routine to achieve problem solution. Furthermore, theorists believe — to varying degrees — that past learning and the particular "set," direction, or orientation that the problem solver takes in dealing with past experience and present stimuli have critical bearing on the efficacy of solution. Finally, all theorists admit to a *solution period*, an end-state of the process where "stress" and "search" terminate, an answer is attained, and a sense of completion or "closure" is experienced.

These are the gross similarities, and the framework they offer will be use- 7 ful in understanding the problem-solving behavior of the students discussed in this paper. But since this paper is primarily concerned with the second stage of problem-solving operations, it would be most useful to focus this introduction on two critical constructs in the processing period: rules and plans.

Rules

Robert M. Gagné defines "rule" as "an inferred capability that enables the indi- 8 vidual to respond to a class of stimulus situations with a class of performances."[3] Rules can be learned directly[4] or by inference through experience.[5] But, in either case, most problem-solving theorists would affirm Gagné's dictum that "rules are probably the major organizing factor, and quite possibly the primary one, in intellectual functioning."[6] As Gagné implies, we wouldn't be able to function without rules; they guide response to the myriad stimuli that confront us daily, and might even be the central element in complex problem-solving behavior.

Dunker, Polya, and Miller, Galanter, and Pribram offer a very useful distinc- 9 tion between two general kinds of rules: algorithms and heuristics.[7] Algorithms are precise rules that will always result in a specific answer if applied to an appropriate problem. Most mathematical rules, for example, are algorithms. Functions are constant (e.g., pi), procedures are routine (squaring the radius), and outcomes are completely predictable. However, few day-to-day situations are mathematically circumscribed enough to warrant the application of algorithms. Most often we function with the aid of fairly general heuristics or "rules of thumb," guidelines that allow varying degrees of flexibility when approaching problems. Rather than operating with algorithmic precision and certainty, we search, critically, through alternatives, using our heuristic as a divining rod — "if a math problem stumps you, try working backwards to solution"; "if the car won't start, check x, y, or z," and so forth. Heuristics won't allow the precision or the certitude afforded by algorithmic operations; heuristics can even be so "loose" as to be vague. But in a world where tasks and problems are rarely mathematically precise, heuristic rules become the most appropriate, the most functional rules available to us: "a heuristic does not guarantee the optimal solution or, indeed, any solution at all; rather, heuristics offer solutions that are good enough most of the time."[8]

Plans

People don't proceed through problem situations, in or out of a laboratory, with- 10
out some set of internalized instructions to the self, some program, some course
of action that, even roughly, takes goals and possible paths to that goal into consideration. Miller, Galanter, and Pribram have referred to this course of action as a
plan: "A plan is any hierarchical process in the organism that can control the order
in which a sequence of operations is to be performed" (p. 16). They name the fundamental plan in human problem-solving behavior the TOTE, with the initial T
representing a *test* that matches a possible solution against the perceived end-goal
of problem completion. O represents the clearance to *operate* if the comparison
between solution and goal indicates that the solution is a sensible one. The second
T represents a further, post-operation, *test* or comparison of solution with goal,
and if the two mesh and problem solution is at hand the person *exits* (E) from
problem-solving behavior. If the second test presents further discordance between
solution and goal, a further solution is attempted in TOTE-fashion. Such plans
can be both long-term and global and, as problem solving is underway, short-term
and immediate.[9] Though the mechanicality of this information-processing model
renders it simplistic and, possibly, unreal, the central notion of a plan and an
operating procedure is an important one in problem-solving theory; it at least
attempts to metaphorically explain what earlier cognitive psychologists could
not—the mental procedures underlying problem-solving behavior.

Before concluding this section, a distinction between heuristic rules and plans 11
should be attempted; it is a distinction often blurred in the literature, blurred because,
after all, we are very much in the area of gestating theory and preliminary models.
Heuristic rules seem to function with the flexibility of plans. Is, for example, "If the
car won't start, try x, y, or z" a heuristic or a plan? It could be either, though two qualifications will mark it as heuristic rather than plan. (A) Plans subsume and sequence
heuristic and algorithmic rules. Rules are usually "smaller," more discrete cognitive
capabilities; plans can become quite large and complex, composed of a series of
ordered algorithms, heuristics, and further planning "sub-routines." (B) Plans, as
was mentioned earlier, include criteria to determine successful goal-attainment and,
as well, include "feedback" processes—ways to incorporate and use information
gained from "tests" of potential solutions against desired goals.

One other distinction should be made: that is, between "set" and plan. Set, 12
also called "determining tendency" or "readiness,"[10] refers to the fact that people
often approach problems with habitual ways of reacting, a predisposition, a tendency to perceive or function in one way rather than another. Set, which can
be established through instructions or, consciously or unconsciously, through
experience, can assist performance if it is appropriate to a specific problem,[11] but
much of the literature on set has shown its rigidifying, dysfunctional effects.[12]
Set differs from plan in that set represents a limiting and narrowing of response
alternatives with no inherent process to shift alternatives. It is a kind of cognitive

habit that can limit perception, not a course of action with multiple paths that directs and sequences response possibilities.

The constructs of rules and plans advance the understanding of problem solving beyond that possible with earlier, less developed formulations. Still, critical problems remain. Though mathematical and computer models move one toward more complex (and thus more real) problems than the earlier research, they are still too neat, too rigidly sequenced to approximate the stunning complexity of day-to-day (not to mention highly creative) problem-solving behavior. Also, information-processing models of problem-solving are built on logic theorems, chess strategies, and simple planning tasks. Even Gagné seems to feel more comfortable with illustrations from mathematics and science rather than with social science and humanities problems. So although these complex models and constructs tell us a good deal about problem-solving behavior, they are still laboratory simulations, still invoked from the outside rather than self-generated, and still founded on the mathematico-logical. 13

Two Carnegie Mellon researchers, however, have recently extended the above into a truly real, amorphous, unmathematical problem-solving process — writing. Relying on protocol analysis (thinking aloud while solving problems), Linda Flower and John Hayes have attempted to tease out the role of heuristic rules and plans in writing behavior.[13] Their research pushes problem-solving investigations to the real and complex and pushes, from the other end, the often mysterious process of writing toward the explainable. The latter is important, for at least since Plotinus many have viewed the composing process as unexplainable, inspired, infused with the transcendent. But Flower and Hayes are beginning, anyway, to show how writing generates from a problem-solving process with rich heuristic rules and plans of its own. They show, as well, how many writing problems arise from a paucity of heuristics and suggest an intervention that provides such rules. 14

This paper, too, treats writing as a problem-solving process, focusing, however, on what happens when the process dead-ends in writer's block. It will further suggest that, as opposed to Flower and Hayes' students who need more rules and plans, blockers may well be stymied by possessing rigid or inappropriate rules, or inflexible or confused plans. Ironically enough, these are occasionally instilled by the composition teacher or gleaned from the writing textbook. 15

"ALWAYS GRAB YOUR AUDIENCE" — THE BLOCKERS

In high school, *Ruth* was told and told again that a good essay always grabs a reader's attention immediately. Until you can make your essay do that, her teachers and textbooks putatively declaimed, there is no need to go on. For Ruth, this means that beginning bland and seeing what emerges as one generates prose is unacceptable. The beginning is everything. And what exactly is the audience seeking that reads this beginning? The rule, or Ruth's use of it, doesn't provide for such 16 investigation. She has an edict with no determiners. Ruth operates with another rule that restricts her productions as well: if sentences aren't grammatically "correct," they aren't useful. This keeps Ruth from toying with ideas on paper, from the kind of linguistic play that often frees up the flow of prose. These two rules converge in a way that pretty effectively restricts Ruth's composing process.

The first two papers I received from *Laurel* were weeks overdue. Sections 17 of them were well written; there were even moments of stylistic flair. But the papers were late and, overall, the prose seemed rushed. Furthermore, one paper included a paragraph on an issue that was never mentioned in the topic paragraph. This was the kind of mistake that someone with Laurel's apparent ability doesn't make. I asked her about this irrelevant passage. She knew very well that it didn't fit, but believed she had to include it to round out the paper, "You must always make three or more points in an essay. If the essay has less, then it's not strong." Laurel had been taught this rule both in high school and in her first college English class; no wonder, then, that she accepted its validity.

As opposed to Laurel, *Martha* possesses a whole arsenal of plans and rules 18 with which to approach a humanities writing assignment, and, considering her background in biology, I wonder how many of them were formed out of the assumptions and procedures endemic to the physical sciences.[14] Martha will not put pen to first draft until she has spent up to two days generating an outline of remarkable complexity. I saw one of these outlines and it looked more like a diagram of protein synthesis or DNA structure than the time-worn pattern offered in composition textbooks. I must admit I was intrigued by the aura of process (vs. the static appearance of essay outlines) such diagrams offer, but for Martha these "outlines" only led to self-defeat: the outline would become so complex that all of its elements could never be included in a short essay. In other words, her plan locked her into the first stage of the composing process. Martha would struggle with the conversion of her outline into prose only to scrap the whole venture when deadlines passed and a paper had to be rushed together.

Martha's "rage for order" extends beyond the outlining process. She also 19 believes that elements of a story or poem must evince a fairly linear structure and thematic clarity, or — perhaps bringing us closer to the issue — that analysis of a story or poem must provide the linearity or clarity that seems to be absent in the text. Martha, therefore, will bend the logic of her analysis to reason ambiguity out of existence. When I asked her about a strained paragraph in her paper on Camus' "The Guest," she said, "I didn't want to admit that it [the story's conclusion] was just hanging. I tried to force it into meaning."

Martha uses another rule, one that is not only problematical in itself, but 20 one that often clashes directly with the elaborate plan and obsessive rule above. She believes that humanities papers must scintillate with insight, must present an array of images, ideas, ironies gleaned from the literature under examination. A problem arises, of course, when Martha tries to incorporate her myriad "neat little things," often inherently unrelated, into a tightly structured, carefully sequenced essay. Plans and rules that govern the construction of impressionistic, associational prose would be appropriate to Martha's desire, but her composing process is heavily constrained by the non-impressionistic and non-associational. Put another way, the plans and rules that govern her exploration of text are not at all synchronous with the plans and rules she uses to discuss her exploration. It is interesting to note here, however, that as recently as three years ago Martha was absorbed in creative writing and was publishing poetry in high school magazines. Given what we know about the complex associational, often non-neatly-sequential nature of the poet's creative process, we can infer that Martha was either free of the plans and rules discussed earlier or they were not as intense. One wonders, as well, if the exposure to three years of university physical science either established or intensified Martha's concern with structure. Whatever the case, she now is hamstrung by conflicting rules when composing papers for the humanities.

Mike's difficulties, too, are rooted in a distortion of the problem-solving pro-   21
cess. When the time of the week for the assignment of writing topics draws near, Mike begins to prepare material, strategies, and plans that he believes will be appropriate. If the assignment matches his expectations, he has done a good job of analyzing the professor's intentions. If the assignment *doesn't* match his expectations, however, he cannot easily shift approaches. He feels trapped inside his original plans, cannot generate alternatives, and blocks. As the deadline draws near, he will write something, forcing the assignment to fit his conceptual procrustian bed. Since Mike is a smart man, he will offer a good deal of information, but only some of it ends up being appropriate to the assignment. This entire situation is made all the worse when the time between assignment of topic and generation of product is attenuated further, as in an essay examination. Mike believes (correctly) that one must have a plan, a strategy of some sort in order to solve a problem. He further believes, however, that such a plan, once formulated, becomes an exact structural and substantive blueprint that cannot be violated. The plan offers no alternatives, no "subroutines." So, whereas Ruth's, Laurel's, and some of Martha's difficulties seem to be rule-specific ("always catch your audience," "write grammatically"), Mike's troubles are more global. He may have strategies that are appropriate for various writing situations (e.g., "for this kind of political science assignment write a compare/contrast essay"), but his entire approach to formulating plans and carrying them through to problem solution is too mechanical. It is probable that Mike's behavior is governed by an explicitly learned or inferred rule: "Always try to 'psych out' a professor." But in this case this rule initiates a problem-solving procedure that is clearly dysfunctional.

While Ruth and Laurel use rules that impede their writing process and Mike   22
utilizes a problem-solving procedure that hamstrings him, *Sylvia* has trouble deciding which of the many rules she possesses to use. Her problem can be characterized as cognitive perplexity: some of her rules are inappropriate, others are

functional; some mesh nicely with her own definitions of good writing, others don't. She has multiple rules to invoke, multiple paths to follow, and that very complexity of choice virtually paralyzes her. More so than with the previous four students, there is probably a strong emotional dimension to Sylvia's blocking, but the cognitive difficulties are clear and perhaps modifiable.

Sylvia, somewhat like Ruth and Laurel, puts tremendous weight on the craft- 23
ing of her first paragraph. If it is good, she believes the rest of the essay will be good. Therefore, she will spend up to five hours on the initial paragraph: "I won't go on until I get that first paragraph down." Clearly, this rule—or the strength of it—blocks Sylvia's production. This is one problem. Another is that Sylvia has other equally potent rules that she sees as separate, uncomplementary injunctions: one achieves "flow" in one's writing through the use of adequate transitions; one achieves substance to one's writing through the use of evidence. Sylvia perceives both rules to be "true," but several times followed one to the exclusion of the other. Furthermore, as I talked to Sylvia, many other rules, guidelines, definitions were offered, but none with conviction. While she *is* committed to one rule about initial paragraphs, and that rule is dysfunctional, she seems very uncertain about the weight and hierarchy of the remaining rules in her cognitive repertoire.

"IF IT WON'T FIT MY WORK, I'LL CHANGE IT"— THE NON-BLOCKERS

Dale, Ellen, Debbie, Susan, and Miles all write with the aid of rules. But their 24
rules differ from blockers' rules in significant ways. If similar in content, they are expressed less absolutely—e.g., "*Try* to keep audience in mind." If dissimilar, they are still expressed less absolutely, more heuristically—e.g., "I can use as many ideas in my thesis paragraph as I need and then develop paragraphs for each idea." Our non-blockers do express some rules with firm assurance, but these tend to be simple injunctions that free up rather than restrict the composing process, e.g., "When stuck, write!" or "I'll write what I can." And finally, at least three of the students openly shun the very textbook rules that some blockers adhere to: e.g., "Rules like 'write only what you know about' just aren't true. I ignore those." These three, in effect, have formulated a further rule that expresses something like: "If a rule conflicts with what is sensible or with experience, reject it."

On the broader level of plans and strategies, these five students also differ from 25
at least three of the five blockers in that they all possess problem-solving plans that are quite functional. Interestingly, on first exploration these plans seem to be too broad or fluid to be useful and, in some cases, can barely be expressed with any precision. Ellen, for example, admits that she has a general "outline in [her] head about how a topic paragraph should look" but could not describe much about its structure. Susan also has a general plan to follow, but, if stymied, will quickly attempt to conceptualize the assignment in different ways: "If my

original idea won't work, then I need to proceed differently." Whether or not these plans operate in TOTE-fashion, I can't say. But they do operate with the operate-test fluidity of TOTEs.

True, our non-blockers have their religiously adhered-to rules: e.g., "When 26 stuck, write," and plans, "I couldn't imagine writing without this pattern," but as noted above, these are few and functional. Otherwise, these non-blockers operate with fluid, easily modified, even easily discarded rules and plans (Ellen: "I can throw things out") that are sometimes expressed with a vagueness that could almost be interpreted as ignorance. There lies the irony. Students that offer the least precise rules and plans have the least trouble composing. Perhaps this very lack of precision characterizes the functional composing plan. But perhaps this lack of precision simply masks habitually enacted alternatives and sub-routines. This is clearly an area that needs the illumination of further research.

And then there is feedback. At least three of the five non-blockers are an 27 Information-Processor's dream. They get to know their audience, ask professors and T.A.s specific questions about assignments, bring half-finished products in for evaluation, etc. Like Ruth, they realize the importance of audience, but unlike her, they have specific strategies for obtaining and utilizing feedback. And this penchant for testing writing plans against the needs of the audience can lead to modification of rules and plans. Listen to Debbie:

> In high school I was given a formula that stated that you must write a thesis paragraph with *only* three points in it, and then develop each of those points. When I hit college I was given longer assignments. That stuck me for a bit, but then I realized that I could use as many ideas in my thesis paragraph as I needed and then develop paragraphs for each one. I asked someone about this and then tried it. I didn't get any negative feedback, so I figured it was o.k.

Debbie's statement brings one last difference between our blockers and 28 non-blockers into focus; it has been implied above, but needs specific formulation: the goals these people have, and the plans they generate to attain these goals, are quite mutable. Part of the mutability comes from the fluid way the goals and plans are conceived, and part of it arises from the effective impact of feedback on these goals and plans.

ANALYZING WRITER'S BLOCK

Algorithms Rather Than Heuristics

In most cases, the rules our blockers use are not "wrong" or "incorrect"—it is 29 good practice, for example, to "grab your audience with a catchy opening" or "craft a solid first paragraph before going on." The problem is that these rules seem to be followed as though they were algorithms, absolute dicta, rather than the loose heuristics that they were intended to be. Either through instruction, or the power of the textbook, or the predilections of some of our blockers for absolutes, or all three, these useful rules of thumb have been transformed into near-algorithmic urgencies. The result, to paraphrase Karl Dunker, is that these rules do not allow a flexible penetration into the nature of the problem. It is this transformation of heuristic into algorithm that contributes to the writer's block of Ruth and Laurel.

Questionable Heuristics Made Algorithmic

Whereas "grab your audience" could be a useful heuristic, "always make three 30 or more points in an essay" is a pretty questionable one. Any such rule, though probably taught to aid the writer who needs structure, ultimately transforms a highly fluid process like writing into a mechanical lockstep. As heuristics, such rules can be troublesome. As algorithms, they are simply incorrect.

Set

As with any problem-solving task, students approach writing assignments with 31 a variety of orientations or sets. Some are functional, others are not. Martha and Jane (see footnote 14), coming out of the life sciences and social sciences respectively, bring certain methodological orientations with them—certain sets or "directions" that make composing for the humanities a difficult, sometimes confusing, task. In fact, this orientation may cause them to misperceive the task. Martha has formulated a planning strategy from her predisposition to see processes in terms of linear, interrelated steps in a system. Jane doesn't realize that she can revise the statement that "committed" her to the direction her essay has taken. Both of these students are stymied because of formative experiences associated with their majors—experiences, perhaps, that nicely reinforce our very strong tendency to organize experiences temporally.

The Plan That Is Not a Plan

If fluidity and multi-directionality are central to the nature of plans, then 32 the plans that Mike formulates are not true plans at all but, rather, inflexible and static cognitive blueprints.[15] Put another way, Mike's "plans" represent a restricted "closed system" (vs. "open system") kind of thinking, where closed system thinking is defined as focusing on "a limited number of units or items, or members, and those properties of the members which are to be used are known to begin with and do not change as the thinking proceeds," and open system thinking is characterized by an "adventurous exploration of multiple alternatives with strategies that allow redirection once 'dead ends' are encountered."[16] Composing calls for open, even adventurous thinking, not for constrained, no-exit cognition.

Feedback

The above difficulties are made all the more problematic by the fact that they 33
seem resistant to or isolated from corrective feedback. One of the most striking
things about Dale, Debbie, and Miles is the ease with which they seek out, interpret, and apply feedback on their rules, plans, and productions. They "operate"
and then they "test," and the testing is not only against some internalized goal,
but against the requirements of external audience as well.

Too Many Rules — "Conceptual Conflict"

According to D. E. Berlyne, one of the primary forces that motivate 34
problem-solving behavior is a curiosity that arises from conceptual conflict —
the convergence of incompatible beliefs or ideas. In *Structure and Direction in
Thinking*,[17] Berlyne presents six major types of conceptual conflict, the second
of which he terms "perplexity":

> This kind of conflict occurs when there are factors inclining the subject
> toward each of a set of mutually exclusive beliefs. (p. 257)

If one substitutes "rules" for "beliefs" in the above definition, perplexity becomes
a useful notion here. Because perplexity is unpleasant, people are motivated to
reduce it by problem-solving behavior that can result in "disequalization":

> Degree of conflict will be reduced if either the number of compet-
> ing . . . [rules] or their nearness to equality of strength is reduced. (p. 259)

But "disequalization" is not automatic. As I have suggested, Martha and Sylvia
hold to rules that conflict, but their perplexity does *not* lead to curiosity and
resultant problem-solving behavior. Their perplexity, contra Berlyne, leads to
immobilization. Thus "disequalization" will have to be effected from without.
The importance of each of, particularly, Sylvia's rules needs an evaluation that
will aid her in rejecting some rules and balancing and sequencing others.

A NOTE ON TREATMENT

Rather than get embroiled in a blocker's misery, the teacher or tutor might interview 35
the student in order to build a writing history and profile: How much and what
kind of writing was done in high school? What is the student's major? What kind
of writing does it require? How does the student compose? Are there rough drafts
or outlines available? By what rules does the student operate? How would he or she
define "good" writing? etc. This sort of interview reveals an incredible amount of
information about individual composing processes. Furthermore, it ofen reveals
the rigid rule or the inflexible plan that may lie at the base of the student's writing problem. That was precisely what happened with the five blockers. And with

Ruth, Laurel, and Martha (and Jane) what was revealed made virtually immediate remedy possible. Dysfunctional rules are easily replaced with or counter-balanced by functional ones if there is no emotional reason to hold onto that which simply doesn't work. Furthermore, students can be trained to select, to "know which rules are appropriate for which problems."[18] Mike's difficulties, perhaps because plans are more complex and pervasive than rules, took longer to correct. But inflexible plans, too, can be remedied by pointing out their dysfunctional qualities and by assisting the student in developing appropriate and flexible alternatives. Operating this way, I was successful with Mike. Sylvia's story, however, did not end as smoothly. Though I had three forty-five minute contacts with her, I was not able to appreciably alter her behavior. Berlyne's theory bore results with Martha but not with Sylvia. Her rules were in conflict, and perhaps that conflict was not exclusively cognitive. Her case keeps analyses like these honest; it reminds us that the cognitive often melds with, and can be overpowered by, the affective. So while Ruth, Laurel, Martha, and Mike could profit from tutorials that explore the rules and plans in their writing behavior, students like Sylvia may need more extended, more affectively oriented counseling sessions that blend the instructional with the psychodynamic.

Notes

1. David Shapiro, *Neurotic Styles* (New York: Basic Books, 1965).

2. Barbara Hayes-Ruth, a Rand cognitive psychologist, and I are currently developing an information-processing model of the composing process. A good deal of work has already been done by Linda Flower and John Hayes (see para. 14 of this article). I have just received — and recommend — their "Writing as Problem Solving" (paper presented at American Educational Research Association, April 1979).

3. *The Conditions of Learning* (New York; Holt, Rinehart and Winston, 1970), p. 193.

4. E. James Archer, "The Psychological Nature of Concepts," in H. J. Klausmeier and C. W. Harris, eds., *Analysis of Concept Learning* (New York: Academic Press, 1966), pp. 37–44; David P. Ausubel, *The Psychology of Meaningful Verbal Behavior* (New York: Grune and Stratton, 1963); Robert M. Gagné, "Problem Solving," in Arthur W. Melton, ed., *Categories of Human Learning* (New York: Academic Press, 1964), pp. 293–317; George A. Miller, *Language and Communication* (New York: McGraw-Hill, 1951).

5. George Katona, *Organizing and Memorizing* (New York: Columbia Univ. Press, 1940); Roger N. Shepard, Carl I. Hovland, and Herbert M. Jenkins, "Learning and Memorization of Classifications," *Psychological Monographs*, 75, No. 13 (1961) (entire No. 517); Robert S. Woodworth, *Dynamics of Behavior* (New York: Henry Holt, 1958), chs. 10–12.

6. *The Conditions of Learning*, pp. 190–91.

7. Karl Dunker, "On Problem Solving," *Psychological Monographs*, 58, No. 5 (1945) (entire No. 270); George A. Polya, *How to Solve It* (Princeton: Princeton University Press, 1945); George A. Miller, Eugene Galanter, and Karl H. Pribram, *Plans and the Structure of Behavior* (New York: Henry Holt, 1960).

8. Lyle E. Bourne, Jr., Bruce R. Ekstrand, and Roger L. Dominowski, *The Psychology of Thinking* (Englewood Cliffs, N.J.: Prentice-Hall, 1971).

9. John R. Hayes, "Problem Topology and the Solution Process," in Carl P. Duncan, ed., *Thinking: Current Experimental Studies* (Philadelphia: Lippincott, 1967), pp. 167–81.

10. Hulda J. Rees and Harold E. Israel, "An Investigation of the Establishment and Operation of Mental Sets," *Psychological Monographs,* 46 (1925) (entire No. 210).

11. Ibid.; Melvin H. Marx, Wilton W. Murphy, and Aaron J. Brownstein, "Recognition of Complex Visual Stimuli as a Function of Training with Abstracted Patterns," *Journal of Experimental Psychology,* 62 (1961), 456–60.

12. James L. Adams, *Conceptual Blockbusting* (San Francisco: W. H. Freeman, 1974); Edward DeBono, *New Think* (New York: Basic Books, 1958); Ronald H. Forgus, *Perception* (New York: McGraw-Hill, 1966), ch. 13; Abraham Luchins and Edith Hirsch Luchins, *Rigidity of Behavior* (Eugene: Univ. of Oregon Books, 1959); N. R. F. Maier, "Reasoning in Humans. I. On Direction," *Journal of Comparative Psychology,* 10 (1920), 115–43.

13. "Plans and the Cognitive Process of Writing," paper presented at the National Institute of Education Writing Conference, June 1977; "Problem Solving Strategies and the Writing Process," *College English,* 39 (1977), 449–61.

14. Jane, a student not discussed in this paper, was surprised to find out that a topic paragraph can be rewritten after a paper's conclusion to make that paragraph reflect what the essay truly contains. She had gotten so indoctrinated with Psychology's (her major) insistence that a hypothesis be formulated and then left untouched before an experiment begins that she thought revision of one's "major premise" was somehow illegal. She had formed a rule out of her exposure to social science methodology, and the rule was totally inappropriate for most writing situations.

15. Cf. "A plan is flexible if the order of execution of its parts can be easily interchanged without affecting the feasibility of the plan . . . the flexible planner might tend to think of lists of things he had to do; the inflexible planner would have his time planned like a sequence of cause-effect relations. The former could rearrange his lists to suit his opportunities, but the latter would be unable to strike while the iron was hot and would generally require considerable 'lead-time' before he could incorporate any alternative sub-plans" (Miller, Galanter, and Pribram, p. 120).

16. Frederic Bartlett, *Thinking* (New York: Basic Books, 1958), pp. 74–76.

17. *Structure and Direction in Thinking* (New York: John Wiley, 1965), p. 255.

18. Flower and Hayes, "Plans and the Cognitive Process of Writing," p. 26.

- -

Questions for Discussion and Journaling

1. Create a list of all the rules that, according to Rose, interfere with "the blockers'" writing. What rules, if any, do you find yourself forced to follow that seem to get in the way of your writing?

2. Describe the difference between the rules that blockers in Rose's study were following and those that non-blockers were following. What accounts for the difference?

3. What's the difference between an *algorithm* and a *heuristic*? Give a couple of examples of each that you use on an everyday basis.

4. Based on Rose's study and descriptions of writers and their rules, write a "rule" explaining what makes a rule good for writers, and what makes a rule bad for writers. You'll get bonus points if you can tell whether your rule is an algorithm or a heuristic.

5. Can you think of mutually exclusive rules that you've tried to follow in your writing? If you can't easily or quickly think of any, comb through the rules that you follow for writing, and see if they're consistent with each other.

6. Rose writes that the attitude of the non-blocking writers he interviewed is, "If it won't fit my work, I'll change it!" Is it a threshold concept for you that writers can have, or take, this kind of power?

Applying and Exploring Ideas

1. Find the origins of the rules you follow. Start by listing the ten rules that most powerfully impact your writing, whether good or bad. Now stop and think. Where, and when, did you learn each rule? Did it come from personal experience? Teachers? Parents? Observation of what other people were doing? Are there any rules you follow that you *don't* like? What would happen if you abandoned them?

2. Stop and think: Do you encounter rules in writing that flatly contradict your experience as a writer or reader? (For example, we're aware of a rule against beginning a sentence with "and." And we see good, professional writers do it all the time.) Describe one or two of these rules that you know of.

3. Rose concludes his article with a discussion of the difference between *knowing* a rule is ineffective and *acting* on that knowledge. If you find yourself following a rule that Rose suggests has a negative impact on writing, reflect on these questions: If you had permission to, would you stop following this rule? What is the risk of setting aside one rule and starting to use another? Is it possible that, rather than setting aside a rule completely, you might simply treat it more flexibly and have the best of both worlds?

META MOMENT Has anyone ever talked to you about *blocking* before? How might understanding this concept and knowing how to actively deal with it be useful to you in your life?

The Phenomenology of Error

JOSEPH M. WILLIAMS

Framing the Reading

Be forewarned: Your teacher will know if you do not read beyond the first three pages of Joseph Williams's "The Phenomenology of Error." Once you reach the end you'll understand why.

Error, in composition theory, is a technical term, referring to a specific set of mistakes that writers make with syntax and the mechanics and **conventions** of writing. Errors include using *I* where you should use *me*, spelling words incorrectly, and ending a sentence with a comma instead of a period. If you follow baseball, you might think of errors in writing just as you do errors in baseball, as mistakes in a standard, almost automatic, procedure that most people usually get right.

The interesting thing about error in writing is that many people believe the things you can make errors on — grammar, punctuation, spelling — are *all that writing is.* They think that if they learn grammar, punctuation, and spelling, they've learned to write. Compare that to baseball: Nobody thinks you know everything you need to know about how to play baseball just because you can catch the ball and throw it to the right base to tag a runner out. Just as there's a lot more to the game of baseball than catching and throwing, there's a lot more to the game of writing than avoiding grammar, punctuation, and spelling errors.

Of course, you would lose a lot of baseball games if you made a lot of errors, and the same is true of writing: Numerous errors in grammar, punctuation, and spelling can really drag down a piece of writing. That explains why so much of your writing instruction in earlier levels of school tried to help you eliminate errors from your

Williams, Joseph M. "The Phenomenology of Error." *College Composition and Communication*, vol. 32, no. 2, May 1981, pp. 152–68.

writing. But did you ever wish that teachers would have paid a little more attention to what you were trying to say and a little less attention to how you messed up in getting it said? Did you ever feel like maybe they cared a little too much about the errors and not nearly enough about everything else there was to care about in your writing? Did you ever feel the difference between having your writing read and having it corrected? Williams has certainly felt this way, as you will see from his introduction.

In the end, Williams concludes that error is a **construct**, a set of ideas woven together over time until they seem inevitable, the only way of thinking about a problem, when in fact they are not at all inevitable but simply choices in thinking that are constructed to look unavoidable. The concept of error in writing that most people hold is one that people have become accustomed to, but it is *not* one that is necessarily universally "true." Much the opposite, in fact: What is *not* true is that all the error can and thus should be eliminated from writing. Remember one of this chapter's threshold concepts: *Writing is not perfectible*. Williams shows us how the problem of error in writing is not as great as the problem of readers who assume certain writers will make errors simply because of who they are.

Getting Ready to Read

Before you read, do at least one of the following activities:

- Make a list of the errors you most commonly make in your writing. What makes avoiding them difficult for you — why do you still make them even though you know about them?

- Grab your writing or grammar handbook and see if it has a list of "most common errors." See if you can find another handbook, or do a search online, and compare the lists. How similar are they?

- Look up the word *phenomenology*.

As you read, consider the following questions:

- What does Williams mean by the *phenomenology of error*? Do you think a more straightforward title would have been more effective?

- Judging from his introduction, what would you say are the *research problem* and *question* that Williams means to address?

- If an idea that we take for granted turns out to be a construct, that means we can and should revise that idea if we come up with a better one. What is Williams's "better idea"? What do you think of it?

I AM OFTEN PUZZLED by what we call errors of grammar and usage, errors 1
such as *different than, between you and I,* a *which* for a *that,* and so on. I am puzzled by what motive could underlie the unusual ferocity which an *irregardless* or
a *hopefully* or a singular *media* can elicit. In his second edition of *On Writing Well*
(New York, 1980), for example, William Zinsser, an otherwise amiable man I'm
sure, uses, and quotes not disapprovingly, words like *detestable vulgarity* (p. 43),
garbage (p. 44), *atrocity* (p. 46), *horrible* (p. 48); *oaf* (p. 42), *idiot* (p. 43), and
simple illiteracy (p. 46), to comment on usages like *OK, hopefully,* the affix *-wise,*
and *myself* in *He invited Mary and myself to dinner.*

The last thing I want to seem is sanctimonious. But as I am sure Zinsser 2
would agree, what happens in Cambodia and Afghanistan could more reasonably be called horrible atrocities. The likes of Idi Amin qualify as legitimate oafs.
Idiots we have more than enough of in our state institutions. And while simply
illiteracy is the condition of billions, it does not characterize those who use *disinterested* in its original sense.[1]

I am puzzled why some errors should excite this seeming fury while others, 3
not obviously different in kind, seem to excite only moderate disapproval. And
I am puzzled why some of us can regard
any particular item as a more or less serious
error, while others, equally perceptive, and
acknowledging that the same item may in
some sense be an "error," seem to invest in
their observation no emotion at all.

> *I am puzzled why some
> errors should excite this
> seeming fury while others,
> not obviously different in
> kind, seem to excite only
> moderate disapproval.*

4

At first glance, we ought to be able to
explain some of these anomalies by subsum-
ing errors of grammar and usage in a more
general account of defective social behavior,
the sort of account constructed so brilliantly by Erving Goffman.[2] But errors of
social behavior differ from errors of "good usage": Social errors that excite feelings commensurate with judgments like "horrible," "atrocious," "oaf(ish)," and
"detestable" are usually errors that grossly violate our personal space: We break
wind at a dinner party and then vomit on the person next to us. We spill coffee
in their lap, then step on a toe when we get up to apologize. It's the Inspector
Clouseau routine. Or the error metaphorically violates psychic space: We utter an
inappropriate obscenity, mention our painful hemorrhoids, tell a racist joke, and
snigger at the fat woman across the table who turns out to be our hostess. Because
all of these actions crudely violate one's personal space we are justified in calling
them "oafish"; all of them require that we apologize, or at least offer an excuse.

This way of thinking about social error turns our attention from error as a dis- 5
crete entity, frozen at the moment of its commission, to error as part of a flawed
transaction, originating in ignorance or incompetence or accident, manifesting

itself as an invasion of another's personal space, eliciting a judgment ranging from silent disapproval to "atrocious" and "horrible," and requiring either an explicit "I'm sorry" and correction, or a simple acknowledgment and a tacit agreement not to do it again.[3]

To address errors of grammar and usage in this way, it is also necessary to shift 6 our attention from error treated strictly as an isolated item on a page, to error perceived as a flawed verbal transaction between a writer and a reader. When we do this, the matter of error turns less on a handbook definition than on the reader's response, because it is that response — "detestable," "horrible" — that defines the seriousness of the error and its expected amendment.

But if we do compare serious nonlinguistic gaffes to errors of usage, how can 7 we not be puzzled over why so much heat is invested in condemning a violation whose consequence impinges not at all on our personal space? The language some use to condemn linguistic error seems far more intense than the language they use to describe more consequential social errors — a hard bump on the arm, for example — that require a sincere but not especially effusive apology. But no matter how "atrocious" or "horrible" or "illiterate" we think an error like *irregardless* or a *like* for an *as* might be, it does not jolt my ear in the same way an elbow might; a *between you and I* does not offend me, at least not in the ordinary sense of offend. Moreover, unlike social errors, linguistic errors do not ordinarily require that we apologize for them.[4] When we make *media* a singular or dangle a participle, and are then made aware of our mistake, we are expected to acknowledge the error, and, if we have the opportunity, to amend it. But I don't think that we are expected to say, "Oh, I'm sorry!" The objective consequences of the error simply do not equal those of an atrocity, or even of clumsiness.

It may be that to fully account for the contempt that some errors of usage 8 arouse, we will have to understand better than we do the relationship between language, order, and those deep psychic forces that perceived linguistic violations seem to arouse in otherwise amiable people.[5] But if we cannot yet fully account for the psychological source of those feelings, or why they are so intense, we should be able to account better than we do for the variety of responses that different "errors" elicit. It is a subject that should be susceptible to research. And indeed, one kind of research in this area has a long tradition: In this century, at least five major surveys of English usage have been conducted to determine how respondents feel about various matters of usage. Sterling Leonard, Albert Marckwardt, Raymond Crisp, the Institute of Education English Research Group at the University of Newcastle upon Tyne, and the *American Heritage Dictionary* have questioned hundreds of teachers and editors and writers and scholars about their attitudes toward matters of usage ranging from *which* referring to a whole clause to split infinitives to *enthuse* as a verb.[6]

The trouble with this kind of research, though, with asking people whether 9 they think *finalize* is or is not good usage, is that they are likely to answer. As

William Labov and others have demonstrated,[7] we are not always our own best informants about our habits of speech. Indeed, we are likely to give answers that misrepresent our talking and writing, usually in the direction of more rather than less conservative values. Thus when the editors of the *American Heritage Dictionary* asks its Usage Panel to decide the acceptability of *impact* as a verb, we can predict how they will react: Merely by being asked, it becomes manifest to them that they have been invested with an institutional responsibility that will require them to judge usage by the standards they think they are supposed to uphold. So we cannot be surprised that when asked, Zinsser rejects *impact* as a verb, despite the fact that *impact* has been used as a verb at least since 1601.

The problem is self-evident: Since we can ask an indefinite number of questions about an indefinite number of items of usage, we can, merely by asking, accumulate an indefinite number of errors, simply because whoever we ask will feel compelled to answer. So while it may seem useful for us to ask one another whether we think X is an error, we have to be skeptical about our answers, because we will invariably end up with more errors than we began with, certainly more than we ever feel on our nerves when we read in the ways we ordinarily do. 10

In fact, it is this unreflective feeling on the nerves in our ordinary reading that interests me the most, the way we respond—or not—to error when we do not make error a part of our conscious field of attention. It is the difference between reading for typographical errors and reading for content. When we read for typos, letters constitute the field of attention; content becomes virtually inaccessible. When we read for content, semantic structures constitute the field of attention; letters—for the most part—recede from our consciousness. 11

I became curious about this kind of perception three years ago when I was consulting with a government agency that had been using English teachers to edit reports but was not sure they were getting their money's worth. When I asked to see some samples of editing by their consultants, I found that one very common notation was "faulty parallelism" at spots that only by the most conservative interpretation could be judged faulty. I asked the person who had hired me whether faulty parallelism was a problem in his staff's ability to write clearly enough to be understood quickly, but with enough authority to be taken seriously, He replied, "If the teacher says so." 12

Now I was a little taken aback by this response, because it seemed to me that one ought not have to appeal to a teacher to decide whether something like faulty parallelism was a real problem in communication. The places where faulty parallelism occurred should have been at least felt as problems, if not recognized as a felt difficulty whose specific source was faulty parallelism. 13

About a year later, as I sat listening to a paper describing some matters of error analysis in evaluating compositions, the same thing happened. When I looked at examples of some of the errors, sentences containing alleged dangling 14 participles, faulty parallelism, vague pronoun reference, and a few other items,[8] I was struck by the fact that, at least in some of the examples, I saw some infelicity, but no out-and-out grammatical error. When I asked the person who had done the research whether these examples were typical of errors she looked for to measure the results of extensive training in sentence combining, I was told that the definition of error had been taken from a popular handbook, on the assumption, I guess, that that answered the question.

About a year ago, it happened again, when a publisher and I began circulating 15 a manuscript that in a peripheral way deals with some of the errors I've mentioned here, suggesting that some errors are less serious than others. With one exception, the reviewers, all teachers at universities, agreed that an intelligent treatment of error would be useful, and that this manuscript was at least in the ballpark. But almost every reader took exception to one item of usage that they thought I had been too soft on, that I should have unequivocally condemned as a violation of good usage. Unfortunately, each of them mentioned a different item.

Well, it is all very puzzling: Great variation in our definition of error, great 16 variation in our emotional investment in defining and condeming error, great variation in the perceived seriousness of individual errors. The categories of error all seem like they should be yes-no, but the feelings associated with the categories seem much more complex.

If we think about these responses for a moment we can identify one source 17 of the problem: We were all locating error in very different places. For all of us, obviously enough, error is in the essay, on the page, because that is where it physically exists. But of course, to be in the essay, it first has to be in the student. But before that, it has to be listed in a book somewhere. And before that in the mind of the writer of the handbook. And finally, a form of the error has to be in the teacher who resonated—or not—to the error on the page on the basis of the error listed in the handbook.

This way of thinking about error locates error in two different physical loca- 18 tions (the student's paper and the grammarian's handbook) and in three different experiences: the experience of the writer who creates the error; in the experience of the teacher who catches it; and in the mind of the grammarian— the E. B. White or Jacques Barzun or H. W. Fowler—who proposes it. Because error seems to exist in so many places, we should not be surprised that we do not agree among ourselves about how to identify it, or that we do not respond to the same error uniformly.

But we might be surprised—and perhaps instructed—by those cases where 19 the two places occur in texts by the same author—and where all three experiences reside in the same person. It is, in fact, these cases that I would like to examine for a moment, because they raise such interesting questions about the experience of error.

For example, E. B. White presumably believed what he (and Strunk) said in 20 *Elements of Style* (New York, 1979) about faulty parallelism and *which* vs. *that*:

> Express coordinate ideas in similar form. This principle, that of parallel construction, requires that expressions similar in content and function be outwardly similar. (p. 26)
>
> *That, which. That* is the defining or restrictive pronoun, *which* the non-defining or non-restrictive . . . The careful writer . . . removes the defining *whiches,* and by so doing improves his work. (p. 59)

Yet in the last paragraph of "Death of a Pig,"[9] White has two faulty parallelisms, and according to his rules, an incorrect *which*:

> . . . the premature expiration of a pig is, I soon discovered, a departure which the community marks solemnly on its calendar . . . I have written this account in penitence and in grief, as a man who failed to raise his pig, and to explain my deviation from the classic course of so many raised pigs. The grave in the woods is unmarked, but Fred can direct the mourner to it unerringly and with immense good will, and I know he and I shall often revisit it, singly and together, . . .

Now I want to be clear: I am not at all interested in the trivial fact 21 that E. B. White violated one or two of his own trivial rules. That would be a trivial observation. We could simply say that he miswrote in the same way he might have mistyped and thereby committed a typographical error. Nor at the moment am I interested in the particular problem of parallelism, or of *which* vs. *that,* any more than I would be interested in the particular typo. What I am interested in is the fact that no one, E. B. White least of all, seemed to notice that E. B. White had made an error. What I'm interested in here is the noticing or the not noticing by the same person who stipulates what should be noticed, and why anyone would surely have noticed if White had written,

> I knows me and him will often revisit it, . . .

Of course, it may be that I am stretching things just a bit far to point out a 22 trivial error of usage in one publication on the basis of a rule asserted in another. But this next example is one in which the two co-exist between the same covers:

> *Were* (sing.) is, then, a recognizable subjunctive, & applicable not to past facts, but to present or future non-facts. (p. 576)
>
> Another suffix that is not a living one, but is sometimes treated as if it was, is *-al* . . . (p. 242)

> H. W. Fowler. *A Dictionary of Modern English Usage.* Oxford, 1957.

Now again, Fowler may have just made a slip here; when he read these entries, certainly at widely separate intervals, the *was* in the second just slipped by. And yet how many others have also read that passage, and also never noticed?

The next example may be a bit more instructive. Here, the rule is asserted in 23 the middle of one page:

> In conclusion, I recommend using *that* with defining clauses except when stylistic reasons interpose. Quite often, not a mere pair of *that's* but a three-some or foursome, including the demonstrative *that,* will come in the same sentence and justify *which* to all writers with an ear. (p. 68)

and violated at the top of the next:

> Next is a typical situation which a practiced writer corrects for style virtually by reflex action. (p. 69)
>
> Jacques Barzun. *Simple and Direct.* New York, 1976.

Now again, it is not the error as such that I am concerned with here, but rather the fact that after Barzun stated the rule, and almost immediately violated it, no one noticed — not Barzun himself who must certainly have read the manuscript several times, not a colleague to whom he probably gave the manuscript before he sent it to the publisher, not the copy editor who worked over the manuscript, not the proof reader who read the galleys, not Barzun who probably read the galleys after them, apparently not even anyone in the reading public, since that *which* hasn't been corrected in any of the subsequent printings. To characterize this failure to respond as mere carelessness seems to miss something important.

This kind of contradiction between the conscious directive and the unreflex- 24 ive experience becomes even more intense in the next three examples, examples that, to be sure, involve matters of style rather than grammar and usage:

Negative constructions are often wordy and sometimes pretentious.

1. wordy   Housing for married students is not unworthy of consideration.

   concise   Housing for married students is worthy of consideration.

   better   The trustees should earmark funds for married students'
             housing. (Probably what the author meant)

2. wordy   After reading the second paragraph you aren't left with an
            immediate reaction as to how the story will end.

   concise   The first two paragraphs create suspense.

The following example from a syndicated column is not untypical:

Sylvan Barnet and Marcia Stubbs. *Practical Guide to Writing.* Boston, 1977, p. 280.

Now Barnet and Stubbs may be indulging in a bit of self-parody here. But I don't think so. In this next example, Orwell, in the very act of criticising the passive, not only casts his proscription against it in the passive, but almost all the sentences around it, as well:

> I list below, with notes and examples, various of the tricks by means of which the work of prose construction is habitually dodged . . . *Operators* or *verbal false limbs.* These save the trouble of picking out appropriate verbs and nouns, and at the same time pad each sentence with extra syllables which give it an appearance of symmetry . . . the passive voice is wherever possible used in preference to the active, and noun constructions are used instead of gerunds . . . The range of verbs is further cut down . . . and the banal statements are given an appearance of profundity by means of the *not un* formation. Simple conjunctions are replaced by . . . the ends of sentences are saved by . . .
> "Politics and the English Language"

Again, I am not concerned with the fact that Orwell wrote in the passive or used nominalizations where he could have used verbs.[10] Rather, I am bemused by the apparent fact that three generations of teachers have used this essay without there arising among us a general wry amusement that Orwell violated his own rules in the act of stating them.

And if you want to argue (I think mistakenly) that Orwell was indulging in 25 parody, then consider this last example — one that cannot possibly be parodic, at least intentionally:

> Emphasis is often achieved by the use of verbs rather than nouns formed from them, and by the use of verbs in the active rather than in the passive voice.
> *A Style Manual for Technical Writers and Editors,* ed. S. J. Reisman. New York, 1972. pp. 6–11.

In this single sentence, in a single moment, we have all five potential locations of error folded together: As the rule is stated in a handbook, it is simultaneously violated in its text; as the editor expresses in the sentence that is part of the handbook a rule that must first have existed in his mind, in his role as writer he simultaneously violates it. And in the instant he ends the sentence, he becomes a critical reader who should — but does not — resonate to the error. Nor, apparently, did anyone else.

The point is this: We can discuss error in two ways: we can discuss it at a level 26 of consciousness that places that error at the very center of our consciousness. Or we can talk about how we experience (or not) what we popularly call errors of usage as they occur in the ordinary course of our reading a text.

In the first, the most common way, we separate the objective material text 27
from its usual role in uniting a subject (us) and that more abstract "content"
of the object, the text, in order to make the sentences and words the objects of
consciousness. We isolate error as a frozen, instantiated object. In the second
way of discussing error, a way we virtually never follow, we must treat error not
as something that is simply on the surface of the page, "out there," nor as part
of an inventory of negative responses "in here," but rather as a variably experienced union of item and response, controlled by the intention to read a text in
the way we ordinarily read texts like newspapers, journals, and books. If error
is no longer in the handbook, or on the page, or in the writer — or even purely
in the reader — if instead we locate it at an intersection of those places, then we
can explain why Barzun could write — or read — one thing and then immediately experience another, why his colleagues and editors and audience could
read about one way of reflexively experiencing language and then immediately
experience it in another.

But when I decided to intend to read Barzun and White and Orwell and 28
Fowler in, for all practical purposes, the way they seem to invite me to read — as
an editor looking for the errors they have been urging me to search out — then
I inform my experience, I deliberately begin reading with an intention to experience the material constitution of the text. It is as if a type-designer invited me
to look at the design of his type as he discussed type-design.

In short, if we read any text the way we read freshman essays, we will find 29
many of the same kind of errors we routinely expect to find and therefore do
find. But if we could read those student essays unreflexively, if we could make
the ordinary kind of contract with those texts that we make with other kinds of
texts, then we could find many fewer errors.

When we approach error from this point of view, from the point of view of 30
our pre-reflexive experience of error, we have to define categories of error other
than those defined by systems of grammar or a theory of social class. We require
a system whose presiding terms would turn on the nature of our response to
violations of grammatical rules.

At the most basic level, the categories must organize themselves around two 31
variables: Has a rule been violated? And do we respond? Each of these variables has two conditions: A rule is violated or a rule is not violated. And to
either of those variables, we respond, or we do not respond. We thus have four
possibilities:

1a. A rule is violated, and we respond to the violation.

1b. A rule is violated, and we do not respond to its violation.

2a. A rule is not violated, and we do not respond.

2b. A rule is not violated, and we do respond.

	[+ response]	[– response]
[+ violation]		
[– violation]		

Now, our experiencing or noticing of any given grammatical rule has to be 32
cross-categorized by the variable of our noticing or not noticing whether it is or
is not violated. That is, if we violate rule X, a reader may note it or not. But we
must also determine whether, if we do not violate rule X, the same reader will
or will not notice that we have violated it. Theoretically, then, this gives us four
possible sets of consequences for any given rule. They can be represented on a
feature matrix like this:

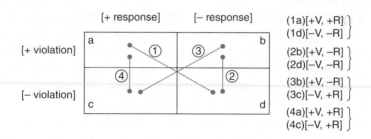

	[+ response]	[– response]	
	a		b
[+ violation]	①	③	
	④	②	
[– violation]			
	c		d

(1a)[+V, +R]
(1d)[–V, –R]

(2b)[+V, –R]
(2d)[–V, –R]

(3b)[+V, –R]
(3c)[–V, +R]

(4a)[+V, +R]
(4c)[–V, +R]

That is, the first kind of rule, indicated by the line marked ①, is of the following
kind: When violated, [+V], we respond to the violation, [+R]. When it is not
violated, [–V], we do not respond, [–R]. Thus the same rule results in combinations of features indicated by (a-d). Rule type ② is characterized by a rule
that when violated, [+V], we do not notice, [–R]. But when we do not violate
it, [–V], we do not notice it either, [–R]. Thus the single rule combines features
indicated by (b-d). The other rules follow the same kind of grid relationships.
(As I will point out later, the problem is actually much more complex than this,
but this will do as a first approximation.)

I do not assert that the particular items I will list as examples of these rules 33
are universally experienced in the way indicated. These categories are based on
personal responses, and it is possible that your responses are quite different than
mine. But in fact, on the basis of some preliminary research that I shall report
later, I would argue that most readers respond in the ways reflected by these
categories, regardless of how they might claim they react.

The most obviousest set of rules be those whose violation we instantly notes, 34
but whose observation we entirely ignore. They are the rules that define bedrock

standard English. No reader of this journal can fail to distinguish these two passages:

> There hasn't been no trainees who withdrawed from the program since them and the Director met to discuss the instructional methods, if they met earlier, they could of seen that problems was beginning to appear and the need to take care of them immediate. (+V, +R)

> There haven't been any trainees who have withdrawn from the program since they and the Director met to discuss the instructional methods. If they had met earlier, they could have seen that problems were beginning to appear and that they needed to take care of them immediately. (–V, –R)

Among the rules whose violation we readily note but whose observance we do not are double negatives, incorrect verb forms, many incorrect pronoun forms, pleonastic subjects, double comparatives and superlatives, most subject-verb disagreements, certain faulty parallelisms,[11] certain dangling modifiers,[12] etc.

The next most obvious set of rules are those whose observation we also entirely ignore, but whose violation we ignore too. Because we note neither their observation nor their violation, they constitute a kind of folklore of usage, rules which we can find in some handbook somewhere, but which have, for the most part, lost their force with our readers. For most readers, these two passages differ very little from one another; for many readers, not at all:

> Since the members of the committee had discussed with each other all of the questions which had been raised earlier, we decided to conduct the meeting as openly as possible and with a concern for the opinions of everyone that might be there. And to ensure that all opinions would be heard, it was suggested that we not limit the length of the meeting. By opening up the debate in this way, there would be no chance that someone might be inadvertently prevented from speaking, which has happened in the past. (+V, –R)

> Because the members of the committee had discussed with one another all the questions that had been raised earlier, we decided to conduct the meeting in a way that was as open as possible and concerned with the opinion of everyone who might be there. To ensure that all opinions would be heard, someone suggested that we not limit the length of the meeting. By opening up the debate in this way, we would not take the chance that someone might be inadvertently prevented from speaking, something which has happened in the past. (–V, –R)

I appreciate the fact that some readers will view my lack of sensitivity to some of these errors as evidence of an incorrigibly careless mind. Which errors go in which category, however, is entirely beside the point.[13] The point is the existence of a *category* of "rules" to whose violation we respond as indifferently as we respond to their observance.

A third category of rules includes those whose violation we largely ignore   36
but whose observance we do not. These are rules which, when followed, impose
themselves on the reader's consciousness either subliminally, or overtly and specifically. You can sense the consequence of observing these rules in this next
"minimal pair":

> I will not attempt to broadly defend specific matters of evidence that
> one might rest his case on. If it was advisable to substantially modify the
> arguments, he would have to re-examine those patients the original group
> treated and extend the clinical trials whose original plan was eventually
> altered. (+V, –R)

> I shall not attempt broadly to defend specific matters of evidence on which
> one might rest one's case. Were it advisable substantially to modify the
> arguments, one should have to re-examine those patients whom the original
> research group treated and extend the clinical trials the original plan of
> which was eventually altered. (–V, +R)

I appreciate that many of you believe that you notice split infinitives as   37
quickly as you notice a subject-verb error, and that both should be equally condemned in careful prose. At the end of this paper, I will try to offer an argument
to the contrary — that in fact many — not all — of you who make that claim are
mistaken.

The exceptions are probably those for whom there is the fourth category of   38
error, that paradoxical but logically entailed category defined by those rules
whose violation we note, and whose observance we also note. I think that very
few of us are sensitive to this category, and I think for those very few, the number of items that belong in the category must, fortunately, be very small. Were
the number of items large, we would be constantly distracted by noticing that
which should not be noticed. We would be afflicted with a kind of linguistic
hyperesthesia, noticing with exquisite pleasure that every word we read is spelled
correctly, that every subject agrees with its verb, that every article precedes its
noun, and so on. Many of us may be surprised when we get a paper with no
mispelled words, but that pleasure does not derive from our noticing that each
word in turn is correctly spelled, but rather in the absence of mispelled words.

In my own case, I think I note equally when an infinitive is split, and when it   39
is not. In recent months, I also seem to be noticing when someone uses *that* in
the way that the "rule" stipulates, and I notice when a writer uses *which* in the
way which the "rule" prohibits. I hope I add no more.

I suspect that some readers put into this category the *regardless/irregardless*   40
pair, *media* as a singular and as a plural, perhaps *disinterested/uninterested.* I offer
no pair of contrasting examples because the membership of the category is probably so idiosyncratic that such a pair would not be useful.

Now in fact, all this is a bit more complicated than my four categories sug- 41
gest, albeit trivially so. The two-state condition of response: [+/−], is too crude to
distinguish different qualities of response. Responses can be unfavorable, as the
ordinary speaker of standard English would respond unfavorably to

> Can't nobody tell what be happening four year from now.

if it appeared in a text whose conventions called for standard English. A response
can be favorable, as in the right context, we might regard as appropriate the
formality of

> Had I known the basis on which these data were analyzed, I should not have
> attempted immediately to dissuade those among you whom others have . . .

(We could, of course, define a context in which we would respond to this
unfavorably.)

Since only the category of [+response] can imply a type of response, we catego- 42
rize favorable and unfavorable response, [+/−favorable], across only [+response].
This gives us four more simple categories:

> [+violate, −favorable]
> [−violate, +favorable]
> [+violate, +favorable]
> [−violate, −favorable]

The first two I have already illustrated:

> [+v, −f]: He knowed what I meaned.
> [−v, +f]: Had I known the basis on which . . . I should not etc.

This leaves two slightly paradoxical categories, which, like Category IV: those 43
rules whose violations we notice and whose observations we notice too, are pop-
ulated by a very small number of items, and function as part of our responses
only idiosyncratically. In the category [−violate, −favorable], I suspect that many
of us would place *It is I,* along with some occurrences of *whom,* perhaps.

The other paradoxical category, [+violate, +favorable] is *not* illustrated by *It's* 44
me, because for most of us, this is an unremarked violation. If it elicits a response
at all, it would almost invariably be [−favorable], but only among those for
whom the *me* is a bête noir. In fact, I can only think of one violation that I
respond to favorably: It is the *than* after *different(ly)* when what follows is a
clause rather than a noun:

> This country feels differently about the energy crisis than it did in 1973.

I respond to this favorably because the alternative,

This country feels differently about the energy crisis from the way it did in 1973.

is wordier, and on principles that transcend idiosyncratic items of usage, I prefer the two less words and the more certain and direct movement of the phrase. My noticing any of this, however, is entirely idiosyncratic.

As I said, though, these last distinctions are increasingly trivial. That is 45 why I refrain from pursuing another yet more finely drawn distinction: Those responses, favorable or unfavorable, that we consciously, overtly, knowingly experience, and those that are more subliminal, undefined, and unspecific. That is, when I read

It don't matter.

I know precisely what I am responding to. When most of us read a *shall* and a shifted preposition, I suspect that we do not consciously identify those items as the source of any heightened feeling of formality. The response, favorable or unfavorable, is usually less specific, more holistic.

Now what follows from all this? One thing that does not follow is a rejection 46 of all rules of grammar. Some who have read this far are undoubtedly ready to call up the underground grammarians to do one more battle against those who would rip out the Mother Tongue and tear down Civilized Western Values. But need I really have to assert that, just because many rules of grammar lack practical force, it is hardly the case that none of them have substance?

Certainly, how we mark and grade papers might change. We need not believe 47 that just because a rule of grammar finds its way into some handbook of usage, we have to honor it. Which we honor and which we do not is a problem of research. We have to determine in some unobtrusive way which rules of grammar the significant majority of careful readers notice and which they do not. One way to do this research is to publish an article in a journal such as this, an article into which have been built certain errors of grammar and usage. The researcher would then ask his readers to report which errors jumped out at them **on the first reading**. Those that you did not notice should then not be among those we look for first when we read a student's paper.

One curious consequence of this way of thinking about error is that we no 48 longer have to worry about defining, rejecting, quibbling over the existence of a rule. We simply accept as a rule anything that anyone wants to offer, no matter how bizarre or archaic. Should anyone re-assert the 19th-century rule against the progressive passive, fine. Upon inspection it will turn out that the rule belongs in the category of those rules whose violation no one notices, and whose observation no one notices either. As I said, it may be that you and I will find that for any particular rule, we experience its violation in different ways. But that is an empirical question, not a matter of value. Value becomes a consideration only when we address the matter of which errors we should notice.

Done carefully, this kind of classification might also encourage some dictio- 49 nary makers to amend their more egregious errors in labeling points of usage. The *AHD,* for example, uses "non-standard" to label

> . . . forms that do not belong in any standard educated speech. Such words are recognized as non-standard not only by those whose speech is standard, but even by those who regularly use non-standard expressions.

The *AHD* staff has labeled as non-standard, *ain't, seen* as the past tense of *see,* and *don't* with a singular subject. It has also labeled as non-standard *irregardless, like* for *as, disinterested for uninterested,* and *see where,* as in the construction, *I see where* . . . Thus we are led to believe that a speaker who would utter this:

> I see where the President has said that, irregardless of what happens with the gasoline shortage, he'll still be against rationing, just like he has been in the past. He seems disinterested in what's going on in the country.

would be just as likely to continue with this:

> I ain't sure that he seen the polls before he said that. He don't seem to know that people are fed up.

Indeed, we would have to infer from this kind of labeling that a speaker who said "I ain't sure he seen . . ." would also be sensitive to mistakes such as *disinterested* for *uninterested* or *like* for *as.* In matters such as this, we see too clearly the very slight scholarly basis upon which so much of this labeling rests.

Finally, I think that most of this essay is an exercise in futility. In these mat- 50 ters, the self-conscious report of what should be counted as an error is certainly an unreliable index to the unself-conscious experience. But it is by far a more satisfying emotion. When those of us who believe ourselves educated and literate and defenders of good usage think about language, our zealous defense of "good writing" feels more authentic than our experience of the same items in unreflective experience of a text. Indeed, we do not experience many of them at all. And no matter how wrong we might discover we are about our unreflective feelings, I suspect we could be endlessly lectured on how we do not respond to a *less* in front of a count noun, as in *less people,* but we would still express our horror and disgust in the belief that *less* is wrong when used in that way. It simply feels more authentic when we condemn error and enforce a rule. And after all, what good is learning a rule if all we can do is obey it?

If by this point you have not seen the game, I rest my case. If you have, I 51 invite you to participate in the kind of research I suggested before. I have deposited with the Maxine Hairston of the University of Texas at Austin (Austin, Texas 78712), a member of the Editorial Board of this journal, a manuscript with the errors of grammar and usage that I deliberately inserted into this paper specifically marked. How can I ask this next question without seeming to distrust you? If you had to report right now what errors you noticed, what would they be? Don't go back and reread, looking for errors, at least not before you recall what errors you found the first time through. If you would send your list (better yet, a copy of the article with errors noted on first reading circled in red) to Professor Hairston, she will see that a tally of the errors is compiled, and in a later issue will report on who noticed what.

If you want to go through a second time and look for errors, better yet. Just 52 make clear, if you would, that your list is the result of a deliberate search. I will be particularly interested in those errors I didn't mean to include. There are, incidentally, about 100 errors.

Notes

1. I don't know whether it is fair or unfair to quote Zinsser on this same matter:

   OVERSTATEMENT. "The living room looked as if an atomic bomb had gone off there," writes the inexperienced writer, describing what he saw on Sunday morning after a Saturday night party that got out of hand. Well, we all know that he's exaggerating to make a droll point, but we also know that an atomic bomb didn't go off there, or any other bomb except maybe a water bomb. . . . These verbal high jinks can get just so high—and I'm already well over the limit—before the reader feels an overpowering drowsiness. . . . Don't overstate. (p. 108)

2. Erving Goffman, *Frame Analysis: An Essay on the Organization of Experience.* (New York: Harper and Row, 1974).

3. Some social errors are strictly formal and so ordinarily do not require an apology, even though some might judge them "horrible": a white wedding gown and a veil on a twice-divorced and eight-month pregnant bride, brown shoes with a dinner jacket, a printed calling card.

4. Some special situations do require an apology: When we prepare a document that someone else must take responsibility for, and we make a mistake in usage, we are expected to apologize, in the same way we would apologize for incorrectly adding up a column of figures. And when some newspaper columnists violate some small point of usage and their readers write in to point it out, the columnists will often acknowledge the error and offer some sort of apology. I think William Safire in *The New York Times* has done this occasionally.

5. Two other kinds of purely linguistic behavior do arouse hostile feelings. One kind includes obscenities and profanities. It may be that both are rooted in some sense of fouling that which should be kept clean: obscenities foul the mouth, the mouth fouls the name of a deity. The other kind of linguistic behavior that arouses hostility in some includes bad puns and baby talk by those who are too old for it. Curiously, Freud discusses puns in his *Wit and the Relation to the Unconscious* (under "Technique of Wit") but does not in "The Tendencies of Wit" address the faint sense of revulsion we feel at a bad pun.

6. Sterling Leonard, *Current English Usage,* English Monograph No. 1 (Champaign, Ill.; National Council of Teachers of English. Chicago, 1932); Albert H. Marckwardt and Fred Walcott, *Facts About Current English Usage*, English Monograph No. 7 (Champaign, Ill.: National

Council of Teachers of English. New York, 1938); Raymond Crisp. "Changes in Attitudes Toward English Usage," Ph.D. dissertation, University of Illinois, 1971; W. H. Mittins, Mary Salu, Mary Edminson, Sheila Coyne, *Attitudes to English Usage* (London: Oxford University Press, 1970); *The American Heritage Dictionary of the English Language* (New York: Dell, 1979). Thomas J. Cresswell's *Usage in Dictionaries and Dictionaries of Usage*, Publication of the American Dialect Society, Nos. 63–64 (University, Alabama: University of Alabama Press 1975), should be required reading for anyone interested in these matters. It amply demonstrates the slight scholarly basis on which so much research on usage rests.

7. William Labov, *The Social Stratification of English in New York City* (Washington, D.C.: Center for Applied Linguistics, 1966), pp. 455–81.

8. Elaine P. Maimon and Barbara F. Nodine, "Words Enough and Time: Syntax and Error One Year After," in *Sentence Combining and the Teaching of Writing*, eds. Donald Daiker, Andrew Kerek, Max Morenberg (Akron, Ohio: University of Akron Press, 1979) pp. 101–108. This is considered a dangling verbal: *For example, considering the way Hamlet treats Ophelia, there is almost corruptness in his mind.* Clumsy yes, but *considering* is an absolute, or more exactly, meta-discourse. See footnote 12. This is considered a vague pronoun reference: *The theme of poisoning begins with the death of old King Hamlet, who was murdered by his brother when a leperous distillment was poured into his ear while he slept.* Infelicitous, to be sure, but who can possibly doubt who's pouring what in whose ear (p. 103)? Counting items such as these as errors and then using those counts to determine competence, progress, or maturity would seem to raise problems of another, more substantive, kind.

9. *Essays of E. B. White* (New York: Harper and Row, 1977), p. 24.

10. Orwell's last rule: *Break any of these rules sooner than say anything outright barbarous*, does not apply to this passage. Indeed, it would improve if it had conformed to his rules:

    > I list below, with notes and examples, various of the tricks by means of which a writer can dodge the work of prose construction . . . such writers prefer wherever possible the passive voice to the active, and noun constructions instead of gerunds . . . they further cut down the range of verbs . . . they make their banal statements seem profound by means of the *not un*-formation. They replace simple conjunctions by . . . they save the ends of sentences . . .

    Should anyone object that this is a monotonous series of sentences beginning with the same subject, I could point to example after example of the same kind of thing in good modern prose. But perhaps an example from the same essay, near the end, will serve best (my emphasis):

    > When *you* think of a concrete object, *you* think wordlessly, and then, if *you* want to describe the thing *you* have been visualizing, *you* probably hunt about till *you* find the exact *words that* seem to fit it. When *you* think of something abstract *you* are more inclined to use words from the start, and unless *you* make a conscious effort to prevent it, the existing dialect will come rushing in and do the job for you . . .

    Nine out of ten clauses begin with *you*, and in a space much more confined than the passage I rewrote.

11. Virtually all handbooks overgeneralize about faulty parallelism. Two "violations" occur so often in the best prose that we could not include them in this Category I. One is the kind illustrated by the E. B. White passage: the coordination of adverbials: . . . *unerringly and with immense good will.* The other is the coordination of noun phrases and WH-clauses: *We are*

studying the origins of this species and why it died out. Even that range of exceptions is too broadly stated, but to explain the matter adequately would require more space than would be appropriate here.

12. Handbooks also overgeneralize on dangling constructions. The generalization can best be stated like this: When the implied subject of an introductory element is different from the overt subject of its immediately following clause, the introductory element dangles. Examples in handbooks are always so ludicrous that the generalization seems sound:

> Running down the street, the bus pulled away from the curb before I got there.

> To prepare for the wedding, the cake was baked the day before.

Some handbooks list exceptions, often called absolutes:

> Considering the trouble we're in, it's not surprising you are worried.

> To summarize, the hall is rented, the cake is baked, and we're ready to go.

These exceptions can be subsumed into a more general rule: When either the introductory element *or* the subject of the sentence consists of meta-discourse, the introductory element will not always appear to dangle. By meta-discourse I mean words and phrases that refer not to the primary content of the discourse, to the reference "out there" in the world, the writer's subject matter, but rather to the process of discoursing, to those directions that steer a reader through a discourse, those filler words that allow a writer to shift emphasis (*it, there, what*), and so on, words such as *it is important to note, to summarize, considering these issue, as you know, to begin with, there is,* etc. That's why an introductory element such as the following occurs so often in the prose of educated writers, and does not seem to dangle (meta-discourse is in bold face):

> To succeed in this matter, **it is important** for you to support as fully as possible . . .

> Realizing the seriousness of the situation, **it can be seen** that we must cut back on . . .

As I will point out later, the categories I am suggesting here are too broadly drawn to account for a number of finer nuances of error. Some violations, for example, clearly identify social and educational background:

> He didn't have no way to know what I seen.

But some violations that might be invariably noted by some observers do not invariably, or even regularly, reflect either social or educational background. Usages such as *irregardless, like* for *as, different than,* etc. occur so often in the speech and writing of entirely educated speakers and writers that we cannot group them with double negatives and non-standard verb forms, even if we do unfailingly respond to both kinds of errors. The usage note in the *American Heritage Dictionary* (Dell Paperback Edition, 1976; third printing, November, 1980) that *irregardless* is non-standard and "is only acceptable when the intent is clearly humorous" is more testimony to the problems of accurately representing the speech and writing of educated speakers. On February 20, 1981, the moderator on *Washington Week in Review,* a Public Broadcasting System news program, reported that a viewer had written to the program, objecting to the use of *irregardless* by one of the panelists. To claim that the person who used *irregardless* would also use *knowed* for *knew* or an obvious double negative would be simply wrong. (I pass by silently the position of *only* in that usage note. See footnote 13, item 9.) The counter-argument that the mere occurrence of these items in the speech and writing of some is sufficient testimony that they are not in fact educated is captious.

13. Here are some of the rules which I believe belong in this Category II: (1) Beginning sentences with *and* or *but;* (2) beginning sentences with *because* (a rule that appears in no handbook that I know of, but that seems to have a popular currency); (3) *which/that* in regard to restrictive relative clauses; (4) *each other* for two, *one another* for more than two; (5) *which* to refer to a whole clause (when not obviously ambiguous); (6) *between* for two, *among* for more than two. These next ones most readers of this journal may disagree with personally; I can only assert on the basis of considerable reading that they occur too frequently to be put in any other category for most readers: (7) *less* for *fewer;* (8) *due to* for *because;* (9) the strict placement of *only;* (10) the strict placement of *not only, neither,* etc. before only that phrase or clause that perfectly balances the *nor.* The usage of several disputed words must also suggest this category for most readers: *disinterested/uninterested, continuous/continual, alternative* for more than two. Since I have no intention of arguing which rules should go into any category, I offer these only as examples of my observations. Whether they are accurate for you is in principle irrelevant to the argument. Nor is it an exhaustive list.

14. The rules that go into Category III would, I believe, include these. Again, they serve only to illustrate. I have no brief in regard to where they should go. (1) *shall/will,* (2) *who/whom,* (3) unsplit infinitives, (4) fronted prepositions, (5) subjunctive form of *be,* (6) *whose/of which* as possessives for inanimate nouns, (7) repeated *one* instead of a referring pronoun *he/his/him,* (8) plural *data* and *media,* singular verb after *none.*

Questions for Discussion and Journaling

1. Return to our earlier question about the title: What does Williams mean by the *phenomenology* of error? What do you think was his purpose in choosing this title instead of a more straightforward one?

2. What have been some of your own experiences with the construct of *error*? Why do they stand out in your mind? How might you react to those experiences now, having read Williams's piece?

3. What, if anything, did you disagree with in this article? Did Williams make any arguments that conflict with your experience or with your sense, as a writer, of how things should be done?

4. Two of Williams's claims are that (a) if we read expecting to find errors, we tend to find them, whereas if we aren't looking for them we are less likely to notice them, and (b) if we were to read student papers as we read "ordinary" texts, we would find far fewer errors in them. If you take these two ideas together, what does Williams seem to be saying? What do you think of what he's saying?

5. How would you describe Williams's **tone** in this piece — that is, if he were reading it aloud, how would he sound? Note how often he repeats the words *puzzled* and *puzzling.* Do you think he really was puzzled?

6. What would you say Williams's text *does*? It might be helpful for you to think about why Williams wrote it, where it was published, and who was meant to

read it. We think that Williams's article *indicts* someone or something. (If you aren't sure what "indict" means, look it up.) If this is true, then what or whom does it indict, and why?

7. Of the various observations that Williams makes in this article, what was most *surprising* to you? Which did you *like* most? Why?

Applying and Exploring Ideas

1. Compile your own list of writing errors that people criticize in others while ignoring in themselves. What will you use to come up with this list? Will you look in handbooks or in the writing of other students? Or will you think back to errors that your teachers have emphasized? Though this is a short assignment, gathering the information for your list can be considered a mini research project.

2. See how many errors you can find in Williams's piece: Mark it up with a red pen — and then make a list of the errors you find. Next, compare your list with those of three of your classmates. Which errors did you all notice? Which ones did only some, or just one, of you notice? Do these results tell you anything about one of Williams's main questions — which errors are bigger problems than others?

3. Write a few informal paragraphs to share with your classmates regarding the research Williams did for this article. What did he study? What data did he collect? How did he analyze the data he collected? Now brainstorm a few research questions of your own that would prompt you to collect and analyze data like these. Why are these interesting questions to you?

META MOMENT Why do you think your teacher and the authors of this textbook are asking you to consider *error* as a construct? Do you think your relationship to writing would be different if all of your previous teachers had understood error as a construct and taught it to you that way?

Expanding Constraints

MICHAEL RODGERS

Framing the Reading

"C most likely stands for Creative," Michael Rodgers suggests in his account of learning to write for good grades in high school, and the tensions that created for him with self-expression and knowledge-making in his writing (para. 7). It is rare to find a clearer account of the threshold concept that writing creates new knowledge than Rodgers provides in his literacy narrative. It's fairly likely you'll recognize some of the scenes he describes from your own school experiences, and perhaps be entertained by his rendering of them.

If you've read the pieces by Mike Rose earlier in this chapter and Keith Grant-Davie in the previous chapter, some of Rodgers's ideas will probably sound familiar to you. He uses Grant-Davie's idea of **constraints** in the way rhetorical theorists intend, to mean not just *re*straints but also situational opportunities that shape writing. And he reflects Rose's idea that when a writing process is wrapped up in rules, it can become much harder for a writer to say what they actually think. Rodgers suggests that writing "one's own way" not only may not be opposed to the knowledge-making work of scholarly writing, but may actually help it.

Rodgers was a first-year student at University of Central Florida, studying animation, when he wrote this piece.

Getting Ready to Read

Before you read, do at least one of the following activities:

- List three of your most memorable writing experiences in school. Are they positive or negative (or a mixture), and how many of them had to do with rules of writing?

a journal of first-year writing

Throw the Notebook at the Wall: What Writing Can Do to the Average Student
AUSTIN LEMASTER

Fanfiction, Poetry, Blogs, and Journals: A Case Study of the Connection between Extracurricular and Academic Writings
MARISSA PENZATO

The Genres of Chi Omega: An Activity Analysis
VICTORIA CHIARO

Volume 3 | Issue 1 | Spring 2012

The Journal of the First-Year Writing Program at the University of Central Florida

Rodgers, Michael. "Expanding Constraints." *Stylus*, vol. 4, no. 1, Spring 2013, pp. 1–4.

- What is your favorite rule about writing from high school that you knew then or have since found out is not entirely true?

As you read, consider the following questions:

- Is it possible that Rodgers is overstating things here — and if so, how?

- What might it be like to have been one of the teachers Rodgers writes about?

IT'S DIFFICULT TO REMEMBER if I wrote my essay about Lewis and Clark's 1 expedition in 5th grade or 6th grade, and ultimately it doesn't really matter. It was the Christmas season, I was young, and I didn't really care about writing one way or another. I didn't follow many writing rules when it came to writing at that age except for the ones that the teacher would give me, which at that time was mainly that essays should have five paragraphs and that paragraphs should have so many sentences in them. I would do some research early on in the assignment if I had to, then wait until the day before the assignment was due to write out my essay. This is something I learned to stop doing pretty fast, as it just builds up stress and would keep me from writing efficiently. I also decided that writing essays with just five paragraphs was pointless, but that wasn't until much later.

I consider winter in Florida to be a bit of a miracle. When the season comes 2 around, going outside becomes a recreational event in itself. I remember the first day the cold front came the year I wrote this paper. I walked outside to put in some mail before my grandma woke up to drive me to school. Being the energetic approximately-ten-year-old that I was, I rarely ever paid attention to the news or weather, so here I was in an undershirt and underwear going out into forty degree weather. Needless to say I was incredibly inspired to go back inside. That day, I was given a very special assignment that would change my views on writing and what it means to me. Everyone in the class moaned as we were assigned a two-page research project about the expedition Lewis and Clark took. It was to be written in five paragraphs with an intro, three body paragraphs, and a conclusion, which is the format that would follow me for a while. What made it special, and what made us moan, was that it had to be written in the perspective of one of the travelers who went with Lewis and Clark on their journey. I decided it would be funny to do the report from the perspective of their dog, Seaman. I laughed all the way to the library where I came to the shocking realization that not a lot of historians really considered dogs to play a huge role in American history. I rationalized that if there was no information on Seaman, then there was no report to be had. I asked my teacher kindly if she would let me change who I wrote the paper on. Seeing this as an opportunity to turn me into an experiment, she said no and told me to write the essay the best I could. So that was it; there was nothing else to do. I couldn't get the research I needed and I couldn't change my subject matter, so where could I go? It was getting close to Christmas Break, the time where hot cocoa comes in large quantities and all anyone can ever think about it was television specials they're going to watch for 24 hours. The last thing I had on my mind was getting around this problem, but it had to be addressed soon otherwise my academic career, and most likely my life, would cease to exist. Finally, with the due date staring me in the face and my mom making hot cocoa in my peripheral vision, I decided I needed to write something. I sat there wrapped up in my blanket, determined to write something cohesive for some sort of grade.

That's when it all hit me. I could make an argument that this was the first 3 time I did any real critical thinking. In reality it definitely wasn't, but it was the first time in my life I felt that I did something I thought was intuitive. "If this is from Seaman's perspective, why do I need to know about Seaman? He's a dog. I just need to write about Lewis and Clark's expedition and how it affects Seaman as a dog." I had no idea that by choosing to write from Seaman's perspective that I had created the best constraint ever, and that this would be the start of many great constraints to come. It allowed me to creatively address the research I had obtained about Lewis and Clark's journey while adding new information into the mix. Of course, being the first essay in which I actually tried to add new information, the new information addresses things such as "What did Seaman think about traveling?" and "What do dogs do when they face troubles on a journey of that caliber?" It's nothing mind-blowing, but it's special to me because of what it did. I started to realize what writing could do. Writing not only answered certain questions, but also asked new ones. Writing didn't have to be this set in stone, grocery list of a medium. I could talk.

> I started to realize what writing could do. Writing not only answered certain questions, but also asked new ones. Writing didn't have to be this set in stone, grocery list of a medium. I could talk.

It started to go downhill after that though. Once all the hot cocoa was gone 4 and it came time to go back to school, I was greeted with the worst thing a private school student with a strict mother could ever imagine: a C. I still remember my face getting as red as a lobster when I saw it. It was actually kind of nice considering how cold it was outside, but that didn't really help the situation much. It wasn't really the fact that my mom was probably going to destroy me that made me sad, it was the fact that I thought I wrote this paper well. The grammar was fine, I thought it was interesting, and it followed the assignment guidelines. What went wrong? Well, it turns out that my teacher just wanted me to state facts about Lewis and Clark and nothing more. I thought about it too hard. I started to question my revelation, and from then on I was average.

From that year until 11th grade, I became efficient with many of the rules 5
that would end up hindering my writing. Five paragraphs only, paragraphs
should be a certain amount of sentences, thesis statements should have three
ideas present in them, and essays must have at least three sources cited in them.
I think the best way for me to summarize my writing from 7th grade to the end
of 11th grade is as follows:

"One time I read a book. It was a lot different from the movie because this 6
reviewer said so (source of review). The book talks about idea 1, 2, and 3. Let
me talk about these ideas in further detail and quote where they come from
occasionally."

If I said that there was anything more to them I would be lying. I never really 7
got to write anything memorable. Well, I did get to write a really cool paper
on Shel Silverstein's influence on my life, but go ahead and guess what I got on
that. C most likely stands for creative. And you know what they (meaning my
teachers) say: ideas can take you anywhere, but good grades get you into college.
Because of this mindset, my love for writing died out as quickly as it came. I
would become so good at writing five paragraphs and expressing three ideas in
a thesis statement for my body paragraphs that writing became an algorithm. It
became a set equation that I could do on the fly, and writing became just another
chore that I did.

It wasn't until I started to write for scholarships — the money that would 8
get me into the aforementioned college — that things got exciting. I specifically
remember the scholarship essay where I talked about how the arts influenced my
life. The prompt for the essay was simply to describe a moment in time where
art changed the way I viewed things. I wanted to be unique this time around,
mainly because I knew a lot of people would apply for the scholarship, but also
because I wasn't in school right then and there, so grades and time weren't a
factor. I would write how I wanted, when I wanted. I started to write about the
first time I cooked eggs. To sum up a four-page paper, the fact that I cooked the
eggs myself made them taste better than any other eggs I had before in my life.
I came to the conclusion that making your own art makes it that much more
special, and if I never made those eggs, I would've never realized that. It got me
to start writing personally, and it was fantastic. The writing I did in school was
still stiff and uninteresting because, if I didn't write in the formulaic way I did,
I wouldn't feel confident that I could get a good grade. At least now I had a way
to express myself in my writing.

The biggest change, however, came this past year. Well, maybe not change, 9
but more confirmation. See, I always thought my first year of college would simply be reconciliation. I would walk in, tell the teacher my sins, the teacher would
tell me to do X amount of prayers, I'd go on my way, and that was it. I realize
now that isn't the case. Sometimes teachers care, and sometimes they like to give
closure to doubts you've had since you were 10. I was told that it was okay to

write the way I do when I'm not being graded. That with a little practice I could turn my voice, this thing I thought may have been a flaw in my writing for all these years, into scholarly inquiry that others could come to respect. I wrote my first essay in the class, sitting in front of my laptop as I am now. I had done the research, now all I had to do was turn on the jazz music and put my heart and soul into what I wanted to say about the discoveries I made during my work on the project. I didn't have to write big five paragraph essays anymore, nor did I have to follow any of the other strict rules that I've faced while I was growing up with writing. Because I'm in college, I was also given more freedom as to when I could write, too. I could write whenever I felt the most creative, which turned out to be during the morning. It didn't matter how personal I got or how many ideas I expressed either. I was actually encouraged to get specific. As long as I elaborated on everything, I was golden. I could essentially say anything I wanted about my subject and it would be seen as work. I was able to analyze and discuss a magazine that talked about my dream job, and it was fun. And it made me fall in love with writing the same way I did when I was writing about a dog's opinion on New World exploration or when I wrote about artful eggs. And I think in the end that's all I ever really wanted: confirmation. Knowing that it's okay to write the way I do through scholarly inquiry made me forget all about the rules that constrained me when I was younger. I could make my own rules that enhanced my writing instead of hindering it.

For me, improving my writing came from the constraints that I encountered 10 during my younger years. I saw the highs and lows of where my writing could go, and this in turn gave me a new appreciation for the medium, and gives me hope for the future. I've had the right ideas about writing since I was in 5th grade, but it took a college professor to tell me that those ideas were right in order for me to start reaching for my full potential. I think, now that I know sharing my thoughts is something smart people do, I can start to really explore the world for what it really is, and express the way I feel about something in a way where someone else might get something out of it. And now that I know what rules work for me, I can start to get more in-depth with my writing. All I ever hope is that I can leave a mark on someone. Make a difference for somebody that will make their day a little better or make them think just a little more than they already do. I hope that, with this newfound confidence in my voice, I can do that in my writing.

- -

Questions for Discussion and Journaling

1. Make a list of the different purposes that Rodgers gives for the various writing he did in his earlier schooling. What were the reasons or motivations from which he was writing?

2. In paragraph 6, Rodgers offers a schematic of his writing from seventh to eleventh grade. What kind of schematic would sum up your experiences with writing in high school?

3. Choose what you regard as the most powerful line in this piece, and explain what makes it so.

4. You may be very early in your college experience when you read this piece and the corresponding questions, but if you can, say whether college courses for you will be more free or equally as constrained as your previous schooling, and why you think that is.

Applying and Exploring Ideas

1. Think of a piece of writing you've created that truly said what you were thinking at the time you wrote it. Write a short description of this piece. What made it true, and what did it feel like to write it?

2. Oftentimes, students remember or count only the writing they do for school as "real" writing. Build a "playlist" of writing that you regularly do outside of school, if you counted everything that uses the alphabet as writing. As an example, *building a playlist* (as on Spotify or iTunes) would count as writing. Put everything on your list you can think of. Then write a reflection on what you learn as you consider the entire list and compare it with your school writing. As part of your reflection, focus on *creativity*. How is your out-of-school writing creative? How is your school writing creative? Does the comparison teach you anything about writing?

- -

META MOMENT Rodgers writes, "Now that I know sharing my thoughts is something smart people do, I can really start to explore the world for what it really is" (para. 10). Do you have a version of that statement—an idea about what you would do if writing were an opportunity for voice and expression and not "just another chore" (in Rodgers' words, para. 7)?

- -

Decisions and Revisions: The Planning Strategies of a Publishing Writer

CAROL BERKENKOTTER

and

Response of a Laboratory Rat — or, Being Protocoled

DONALD M. MURRAY

Courtesy of Carol Berkenkotter

© Gary Samson, University of New Hampshire

Framing the Readings

Earlier in this chapter, you may have read Sondra Perl's 1979 study of "unskilled college writers," which used a "think-aloud" or "talk-aloud" protocol, a technique that at the time was very popular among psychology researchers. This method solved a very basic problem of research on mental operations — that is, how we know what thoughts people are having that lead them to write certain things — by proposing the following simple solution: Have them talk while they think. Another aspect of Perl's design, a "laboratory" setting where students came to the researcher and wrote in response to specific prompts the researcher provided, was quite common in this

Berkenkotter, Carol. "Decisions and Revisions: The Planning Strategies of a Publishing Writer." *College Composition and Communication*, vol. 34, no. 2, May 1983, pp. 156–69.

Murray, Donald M. "Response of a Laboratory Rat — or, Being Protocoled." *College Composition and Communication*, vol. 34, no. 2, May 1983, pp. 169–72.

time and style of research on writing processes. Most researchers publishing studies on writers' processes, including Carol Berkenkotter, author of one of the pieces you are about to read, used such methods.

But there are real problems with this kind of research, chief among them the artificiality of the setting and the writing tasks. In the following selection, you will read Berkenkotter's account of how she engaged a professional writer, Donald Murray, as a participant for a different kind of research, one that tried to keep the writer in his own context — normal surroundings, real projects — rather than bringing him into a lab. Like Perl's article, then, Berkenkotter's has two focuses: a test of a particular methodology and a question about a particular aspect of composing — in this case, the revision process of a professional writer.

Berkenkotter and Murray did something else uncharacteristic of research on writing in the era: Murray was given the opportunity to write a reflection on the experience of being a research subject, his thoughts on what Berkenkotter's study found, and observations on the methodology. For this reason, we strongly recommend that you read the pieces back-to-back; the experience of reading Berkenkotter isn't complete without Murray's rejoinder and the interplay between the two pieces.

While you should pay close attention to any researcher's methods and context, the most interesting part of this article for you will likely be what you can learn about how a professional and award-winning writer goes about writing. His processes are odd, and you likely don't write like Murray did. In 1981, when Berkenkotter and Murray undertook the study, cell phones, the Internet, and personal computers were not in widespread use. Pay close attention, though, to how Murray invents things to say, how he learns from his writing, how he writes for his audience, and how he revises, and ask yourself what his writing gains from his complex planning, drafting, and revising. Consider how his process links to the threshold concepts that this chapter has stressed: that writing makes knowledge, that it often doesn't come out well the first time for experienced writers, and that writers always have more to learn about writing and how their writing is working.

Carol Berkenkotter is currently a professor in the University of Minnesota's Department of Writing Studies. At the time she wrote this piece, about 30 years ago, she was teaching at Michigan Technological University. Over that span of time, her research shifted from the kinds of writing-process questions that shaped this article, to extensive focus on **genre** theory. One of her most significant works is her 1995 book with Thomas Huckin, *Genre Knowledge in Disciplinary Communication: Cognition/Culture/Power.* Her research subject and co-author here, Donald Murray, has an article of his own in this book. You can read more about him in Chapter 2 with his article "All Writing Is Autobiography."

Getting Ready to Read

Before you read, do at least one of the following activities:

- Take fifteen minutes and write in response to this prompt: "Explain death to an eleven-year-old." Then consider how it felt to write this. Was it easy? Hard? What did you wonder or think about while you were writing? Set this aside and come back to it after you have read this article.

- Consider whether you have any writing rituals. For example, do you have to have a cup of coffee while you write? Do you need to write on paper before typing? Do you have to take a nap or clean the house?

As you read, consider the following questions:

- What discoveries do Berkenkotter and Murray make that contradict their expectations?

- What are strengths and weaknesses of this particular way of studying writing processes?

- What have you learned about writing from reading this article that you didn't know before?

DECISIONS AND REVISIONS: THE PLANNING STRATEGIES OF A PUBLISHING WRITER

Carol Berkenkotter

THE CLEAREST MEMORY I have of Donald M. Murray is watching him 1 writing at a long white wooden table in his study, which looks out on the New Hampshire woods. Beside his desk is a large framed poster of a small boy sitting on a bed staring at a huge dragon leaning over the railing glowering at him. The poster is captioned, "Donald imagined things." And so he did, as he addressed the problems writers face each time they confront a new assignment. During the summer of 1981, as I listened to him daily recording his thoughts aloud as he worked on two articles, a short story, and an editorial, I came to understand in what ways each writer's processes are unique and why it is important that we pay close attention to the setting in which the writer composes, the kind of task the writer confronts, and what the writer can tell us of his own processes. If we are to understand

> If we are to understand how writers revise, we must pay close attention to the context in which revision occurs.

how writers revise, we must pay close attention to the context in which revision occurs.

Janet Emig, citing Eliot Mishler, has recently described the tendency of writing research toward "context stripping."[1] When researchers remove writers from their natural settings (the study, the classroom, the office, the dormitory room, the library) to examine their thinking processes in the laboratory, they create "a context of a powerful sort, often deeply affecting what is being observed and assessed."[2] Emig's essay points to the need to examine critically the effects of these practices.

The subject of the present study is not anonymous, as are most subjects, nor will he remain silent. I began the investigation with a critical eye regarding what he has said about revision, he with an equally critical attitude toward methods of research on cognitive processes. To some extent our original positions have been confirmed—yet I think each of us, researcher and writer, has been forced to question our assumptions and examine our dogmas. More important, this project stirs the dust a bit and suggests a new direction for research on composing processes.

I met Mr. Murray at the Conference on College Composition and Communication meeting in Dallas, 1981. He appeared at the speaker's rostrum after my session and introduced himself, and we began to talk about the limitations of taking protocols in an experimental situation. On the spur of the moment I asked him if he would be willing to be the subject of a naturalistic study. He hesitated, took a deep breath, then said he was very interested in understanding his own composing processes, and would like to learn more. Out of that brief exchange a unique collaborative research venture was conceived.

To date there are no reported studies of writers composing in natural (as opposed to laboratory) settings that combine thinking-aloud protocols with the writers' own introspective accounts. Recently, researchers have been observing young children as they write in the classroom. In particular, we have seen the promising research of Donald Graves, Lucy Calkins, and Susan Sowers, who have worked intimately with children and their teachers in the Atkinson Schools Project.[3] By using video tapes and by actively working in the classroom as teachers and interviewers, these researchers were able to track the revising processes of individual children over a two-year period. Studies such as these suggest that there may be other ways of looking at writers' composing processes than in conventional research settings.

There remains, however, the question: to what extent can a writer's subjective testimony be trusted? I have shared the common distrust of such accounts.[4] There is considerable cognitive activity that writers cannot report because they are unable to compose and monitor their processes simultaneously. Researchers have responded to this problem by taking retrospective accounts from writers immediately after they have composed,[5] or have studied writers' cognitive activity through the use of thinking-aloud protocols.[6] These protocols have been examined to locate the thoughts verbalized by the subjects while composing, rather than for the subjects' analysis of what they said. Typically, subjects were instructed to "say everything that comes to mind no matter how random or crazy it seems. Do not analyze your thoughts, just say them aloud." The effect of these procedures, however, has been to separate the dancer from the dance, the subject from the process. Introspective accounts made *in medias res* have not been possible thus far because no one has developed techniques that would allow a subject to write and comment on his or her processes between composing episodes. For this reason I had begun to entertain the idea of asking a professional writer to engage in a lengthy naturalistic study. When Donald Murray introduced himself, I knew I wanted him to be the subject.

METHODOLOGY

The objectives that I began with are modifications of those Sondra Perl identified in her study of five unskilled writers.[7] I wanted to learn more about the planning and revising strategies of a highly skilled and verbal writer, to discover how these strategies could be most usefully analyzed, and to determine how an understanding of this writer's processes would contribute to what we have already discovered about how skilled writers plan and revise. 7

The project took place in three stages. From June 15th until August 15th, 1981 (a period of 62 days), Mr. Murray turned on the tape recorder when he entered his study in the morning and left it running during the day wherever he happened to be working: in his car waiting in parking lots, his university office, restaurants, the doctor's office, etc. This kind of thinking-aloud protocol differs from those taken by Linda Flower and John R. Hayes since the subject's composing time is not limited to a single hour; in fact, during the period of time that Mr. Murray was recording his thoughts, I accumulated over one hundred and twenty hours of tape. The writer also submitted photocopies of all text, including notes and drafts made prior to the study. Thus I was able to study a history of each draft. 8

In the second stage, during a visit to my university, I gave the writer a task which specified audience, subject, and purpose. I asked him to think aloud on tape as he had previously, but this time for only one hour. Between the second and third stages, Mr. Murray and I maintained a dialogue on audiotapes which we mailed back and forth. On these tapes he compared his thoughts on his composing in his own environment over time to those on giving a one-hour protocol in a laboratory setting. 9

During the third stage of the study, I visited the writer at his home for two days. At this time I observed him thinking aloud as he performed a writing task which involved revising an article for a professional journal. After two sessions of thinking aloud on tape for two and one-half hours, Mr. Murray answered 10 questions concerning the decisions he had made. Over the two-day period we taped an additional four hours of questions and answers regarding the writer's perceptions of his activities.

Another coder and I independently coded the transcripts of the protocols made   11
in the naturalistic and laboratory settings. Using the same procedure I employed in my study of how writers considered their audience (i.e., first classifying and then counting all audience-related activities I could find in each protocol), my coder and I tallied all planning, revising, and editing activities, as well as global and local evaluations of text[8] that we agreed upon. I was particularly interested in Murray's editing activities. Having listened to the tapes I was aware that editing (i.e., reading the text aloud and making word- and sentence-level changes) sometimes led to major planning episodes, and I wanted to keep track of that sequence.

The study was not conducted without problems. The greatest of these arose   12
from how the writer's particular work habits affected the gathering of the data and how he responded to making a one-hour protocol. Unlike most writers who hand draft or type, Mr. Murray spends much time making copious notes in a daybook, then dictates his drafts and partial drafts to his wife, who is an accomplished typist and partner in his work. Later, he reads aloud and edits the drafts. If he determines that copy-editing (i.e., making stylistic changes in the text) is insufficient, he returns to the daybook, makes further notes, and prepares for the next dictation. The revision of one of the articles he was working on went through eight drafts before he sent it off. Two days later he sent the editor an insert.

Murray's distinctive work habits meant that all of the cognitive activity occur-   13
ring during the dictation that might ordinarily be captured in a protocol was lost since he processed information at a high speed. During these periods I could not keep track of the content of his thoughts, and became concerned instead with the problem of why he frequently would find himself unable to continue dictating and end the session. There turned out to be considerable value in following the breakdowns of these dictations. I was able to distinguish between those occasions when Murray's composing was, in Janet Emig's terms, "extensive," and when it was "reflexive,"[9] by comparing the relative ease with which he developed an article from well-rehearsed material presented at workshops with the slow evolution of a conceptual piece he had not rehearsed. According to Emig, "The extensive mode . . . focuses upon the writer's conveying a message or communication to another. . . . the style is assured, impersonal, and often reportorial." In contrast, reflexive composing " . . . focuses on the writer's thoughts and feelings. . . . the style is tentative, personal, and exploratory."[10] In the latter case the writer is generating, testing, and evaluating new ideas, rather than reformulating old ones. I could observe the differences between the two modes of composing Emig describes, given Murray's response to the task in which he was engaged. When the writer was thoroughly familiar with his subject, he dictated with great

fluency and ease. However, when he was breaking new ground conceptually, his pace slowed and his voice became halting; often the drafts broke down, forcing him to return to his daybook before attempting to dictate again.[11]

A more critical problem arose during the giving of the one-hour protocol. At the time he came to my university, the writer had been working on tasks he had selected, talking into a tape recorder for two months in a familiar setting. Now he found himself in a strange room, with a specific writing task to perform in one short hour. This task was not simple; nor was it familiar. He was asked to "explain the concept of death to the ten- to twelve-year-old readers of *Jack and Jill* magazine." Under these circumstances, Murray clutched, producing two lines of text: "*Dear 11 year old. You're going to die. Sorry. Be seeing you. P. Muglump, Local Funeral Director.*" Both the transcript and later retrospective testimony of the writer indicated that he did not have pets as a child and his memories of death were not of the kind that could be described to an audience of ten- to twelve-year-old children. He also had difficulty forming a picture of his audience, since he suspected the actual audience was grandparents in Florida who send their children subscriptions to *Jack and Jill.* Toward the end of the hour, he was able to imagine a reader when he remembered the daughter of a man he had met the previous evening. The protocol, however, is rich with his efforts to create rhetorical context—he plotted repeated scenarios in which he would be asked to write such an article. Nevertheless, it seems reasonable to conclude that Mr. Murray was constrained by what Lester Faigley and Stephen Witte call "situational variables":[12] the knowledge that he had only one hour in which to complete a draft, his lack of familiarity with the format of *Jack and Jill* (he had never seen the magazine), his doubts that an audience actually existed, and finally, the wash of unhappy memories that the task gave rise to. "So important are these variables," Faigley and Witte contend, "that writing skill might be defined as the ability to respond to them."[13]

One final problem is intrinsic to the case study approach. Although the tapes are rich in data regarding the affective conditions under which the writer composed (he was distracted by university problems, had to contend with numerous interruptions, encountered family difficulties that he had to resolve, not to mention experiencing his own anxiety about his writing), as Murray reported, the further away he was in time from what he had done, the less able he was to reconstruct decisions he had made.

RESULTS

Planning and Revising

In this study I was primarily concerned with the writer's planning, revising, and editing activities. I had to develop a separate code category for the evaluation of text or content, since the writer frequently stopped to evaluate what he had written.

	JOURNAL OF BASIC WRITING	COLLEGE COMPOSITION AND COMMUNICATION	EDITORIAL FOR CONCORD MONITOR
Planning	45%	56%	35%
Evaluating	28%	21%	18%
Revising	3.0%	3.0%	.0%
Editing	24%	20%	47%

Figure 1 Percentage of Coded Activities Devoted to Planning, Evaluating, Revising, and Editing for Three Pieces of Discourse

Figure 1 indicates the percentage of coded activities devoted to planning, revising, and editing for three pieces of discourse.[14] These three pieces were among the projects Murray worked on over the two-month period when he was making the protocols.

The coded data (taken from the transcripts of the tapes he made during this time) showed that up to 45%, 56%, and 35% of the writer's activities were concerned with planning, 28%, 21%, and 18% with either global or local evaluation, 3.0%, 3.0%, and .0% with revising (a finding which surprised me greatly, and to which I shall return), and 24%, 20%, and 47% with editing.

Murray's planning activities were of two kinds: the first were the stating of "process goals"—mentioning procedures, that is, that he developed in order to write (e.g., "I'm going to make a list of titles and see where that gets me," or "I'm going to try a different lead.").[15] Frequently, these procedures (or "thinking plans" as they are also called)[16] led the writer to generate a series of sub-plans for carrying out the larger plan. The following excerpt is from the first draft of an article on revision that Murray was writing for *The Journal of Basic Writing*. He had been reading the manuscript aloud to himself and was nearly ready to dictate a second draft. Suddenly he stopped, took his daybook and began making copious notes for a list of examples he could use to make the point that the wise editor or teacher should at first ignore sentence-level editing problems to deal with more substantive issues of revision (this excerpt as well as those which follow are taken from the transcript of the tape and the photocopied text of the daybook):

> Let me take another piece of paper here. Questions, ah . . . examples, and ah set up . . . situation . . . *frustration of writer. Cooks a five course dinner and gets response only to the table setting . . . or to the way the napkins are folded* or to the . . . *order of the forks.* All right. I can see from the material I have how that'll go. I'll weave in. Okay. *Distance in focus. Stand back. Read fast. Question writer.* Then *order doubles advocate.* Then *voice. Close in. Read aloud.* Okay, I got a number of different things I can see here that I'm getting to.

I'm putting different order because that may be, try to emphasize this one. May want to put the techniques of editing and teaching first and the techniques of the writer second. So I got a one and a two to indicate that. [Italics identify words written down.]

In this instance we can see how a writing plan (taking a piece of paper and developing examples) leads to a number of sub-plans: "I'll weave in," I'm putting in different order because that may be, try to emphasize this one," "May want to put the techniques of editing and teaching first and the techniques of the writer second," etc.

A second kind of planning activity was the stating of rhetorial goals, i.e., planning how to reach an audience: "I'm making a note here, job not to explore the complexities of revision, but simply to show the reader how to do revision." Like many skilled writers, Murray had readers for his longer pieces. These readers were colleagues and friends whose judgment he trusted. Much of his planning activity as he revised his article for *College Composition and Communication* grew out of reading their responses to his initial draft and incorporating his summary of their comments directly onto the text. He then put away the text, and for the next several days made lists of titles, practiced leads, and made many outlines and diagrams in his daybook before dictating a draft. Through subsequent drafts he moved back and forth between the daybook and his edited dictations. He referred back to his readers' comments twice more between the first and last revised drafts, again summarizing their remarks in his notes in the daybook. 19

To say that Mr. Murray is an extensive planner does not really explain the nature or scope of his revisions. I had initially developed code categories for revising activities; however, my coder and I discovered that we were for the most part double-coding for revising and planning, a sign the two activities were virtually inseparable. When the writer saw that major revision (as opposed to copy-editing) was necessary, he collapsed planning and revising into an activity that is best described as *reconceiving*. To "reconceive" is to scan and rescan one's text from the perspective of an external reader and to continue redrafting until all rhetorical, formal, and stylistic concerns have been resolved, or until the writer decides to let go of the text. This process, which Nancy Sommers has described as the resolution of the dissonance the writer senses between his intention and the developing text,[17] can be seen in the following episode. The writer had been editing what he thought was a final draft when he saw that more substantive changes were in order. The flurry of editing activity was replaced by reading aloud and scanning the text as the writer realized that his language was inadequate for expressing a goal which he began to formulate as he read: 20

(reading from previous page)[18] *It was E. B. White who reminded us,* "Don't write about Man. Write about a man." O.K. I'm going to cut that paragraph there . . . I've already said it. *The conferences when the teacher listens to the student can be short. When the teacher listens to the student in conference . . . when the teacher listens to the student . . .* the conference is, well, *the conference can be short. The student learns to speak first of what is most important to the student at the point. To mention first what is most important . . . what most concerns . . . the student about the draft or the process that produced it. The teacher listens . . . listens, reads the draft through the student's eyes then reads the draft, read or rereads . . . reads or . . .* scans or re-scans the draft to confirm, adjust, or compromise the student's concerns. *The range of student response includes the affective and the cognitive . . . It is the affective that usually controls the cognitive, and the affective responses usually have to be dealt with first* . . . (continues reading down the page) *Once the feelings of inadequacy, overconfidence, despair or elation are dealt with, then the conference teacher will find the other self speaking in more cognitive terms. And usually these comments* . . . O.K. that would now get the monitor into, into the phrase. All right. Put this crisscross cause clearly that page is going to be retyped . . . I'll be dictating so that's just a note. (continues reading on next page) *Listening to students allows the teacher to discover if the student's concerns were appropriate to where the student is in the writing process. The student, for example, is often excessively interested in language at the beginning of the process. Fragmentary language is normal before there is a text.* Make a comment on the text, (writes *intervention*) Now on page ten scanning . . . my God, I don't . . . I don't think I want to make this too much a conference piece. I'm going to echo back to that . . . monitor and also to the things I've said on page two and three. O.K. Let's see what I can do . . . The biggest question that I have is how much detail needs to be on conferences. I don't think they're, I don't think I can afford too much. Maybe some stronger sense of the response that ah . . . students make, how the other self speaks. They've got to get a sense of the other self speaking.

The next draft was totally rewritten following the sentence in the draft: "When 21 the teacher listens to the student, the conference can be short." The revision included previously unmentioned anecdotal reports of comments students had made in conferences, a discussion of the relevant implications of the research of Graves, Calkins, and Sowers, and a section on how the writing workshop can draw out the student's "other self" as other students model the idealized reader. This draft was nearly three pages longer than the preceding one. The only passage that remained was the final paragraph.

Granted that Mr. Murray's dictation frees him from the scribal constraints 22 that most writers face, how can we account for such global (i.e., whole text) revision? One answer lies in the simple, yet elegant, principle formulated by Linda Flower and John R. Hayes.[19] In the act of composing, writers move back and forth between planning, translating (putting thoughts into words), and reviewing their work. And as they do, they frequently "discover" major rhetorical goals.[20] In the episode just cited we have seen the writer shifting gears from editing to planning to reconceiving as he recognized something missing from the text and identified a major rhetorical goal—that he had to make the concept of the other self still more concrete for his audience: "They've got to get a sense of the other self speaking." In this same episode we can also see the cognitive basis for alterations in the macrostructure, or "gist," of a text, alterations Faigley and Witte report having found in examining the revised drafts of advanced student and expert adult writers.[21]

Planning and Incubation

This discussion of planning would be incomplete without some attention to the role of incubation. Michael Polanyi describes incubation as "that persistence of heuristic tension through . . . periods of time in which problems are not consciously entertained."[22] Graham Wallas and Alex Osborn agree that incubation involves unconscious activity that takes place after periods of intensive preparation.[23] 23

Given the chance to observe a writer's processes over time, we can see incubation at work. The flashes of discovery that follow periods of incubation (even brief ones) are unexpected, powerful, and catalytic, as the following episode demonstrates. Mr. Murray was revising an article on revision for the *Journal of Basic Writing*. He had begun to review his work by editing copy, moving to more global issues as he evaluated the draft: 24

> The second paragraph may be . . . Seems to me I've got an awful lot of stuff before I get into it. (Counting paragraphs) 1, 2, 3, 4, 5, 6, 7, 8, 9, 10, ten paragraphs till I really get into the text. Maybe twelve or thirteen. I'm not going to try to hustle it too much. That might be all right.

The writer then reread the first two paragraphs, making small editorial changes and considering stylistic choices. At that point he broke off and noted on the text three questions, *"What is the principle? What are the acts? How can it be taught?"* He reminded himself to keep his audience in mind. "The first audience has got to be the journal, and therefore, teachers." He took a five-minute break and returned to report,

> But, that's when I realized . . . the word hierarchy ah, came to me and that's when I realized that in a sense I was making this too complicated for myself and simply what I have to do is show the reader . . . I'm making a note here . . . *Job not to explore complexities of revision, but simply to show the reader how to do revision.*

From a revision of his goals for his audience, Murray moved quickly into planning activity, noting on his text, 25

Hierarchy of problems. O.K. What I'm dealing with is a hierarchy of problems. *First, focus/content, second, order/structure, third, language/voice . . .* O.K. Now, let's see. I need to ah, need to put that word, hierarchy in here somewhere. Well, that may get into the second paragraph so put an arrow down there (draws arrow from hierarchy to second paragraph), then see what we can do about the title if we need to. Think of things like 'first problems first' (a mini-plan which he immediately rejects). It won't make sense that title, unless you've read the piece. Ah well, come up with a new title.

Here we can observe the anatomy of a planning episode with a number of goals and sub-goals generated, considered, and consolidated at lightning speed: "O.K. What I'm dealing with is a hierarchy of problems." . . . "I need to ah, need to put that word, hierarchy in here somewhere." " . . . so put an arrow down there, then see what we can do about the title . . ." " . . . 'first problems first.' It won't make sense that title . . . Ah well, come up with a new title." We can also see the writer's process of discovery at work as he left his draft for a brief period and returned having identified a single meaning-laden word. This word gave Murray an inkling of the structure he wanted for the article—a listing of the problems writers face before they can accomplish clear, effective revision. In this case, a short period of incubation was followed by a period of intense and highly concentrated planning when Murray realized the direction he wanted the article to take.

Introspection

One of the most helpful sources in this project was the testimony of the writer as he paused between or during composing episodes. Instead of falling silent, he analyzed his processes, providing information I might have otherwise missed. The following segments from the protocols will demonstrate the kinds of insights subjects can give when not constrained by time. At the time of the first, Mr. Murray had completed the tenth list of titles he had made between June 26th and July 23rd while working on the revision of his article for *College Composition and Communication*. Frequently, these lists were made recursively, the writer flipping back in his daybook to previous lists he had composed:

I think I have to go back to titles. *Hearing the student's other self.* Hold my place and go back and see if I have any that hit me in the past. *Teaching the reader and the writer. Teaching the reader in the writer. Encouraging the internal dialogue.* I skipped something in my mind that I did not put down. *Make your students talk to themselves. Teaching the writer to read.*

At this point he stopped to evaluate his process:

All that I'm doing is compressing, ah, compressing is, ah, why I do a title . . . it compresses a draft for the whole thing. Title gives me a point of view, gets

> the tone, the difference between teaching and teach. A lot of time on that, that's all right.

The following morning the writer reported, "While I was shaving, I thought of 28 another title. *Teaching the other self: the writer's first reader.* I started to think of it as soon as I got up." This became the final title for the article and led to the planning of a new lead.

Later that day, after he had dictated three pages of the fourth of eight drafts, 29 he analyzed what he had accomplished:

> Well, I'm going to comment on what's happened here . . . this is a very complicated text. One of the things I'm considering, of course, is incorporating what I did in Dallas in here . . . ah, the text is breaking down in a constructive way, um, it's complex material and I'm having trouble with it . . . very much aware of pace of proportion; how much can you give to the reader in one part, and still keep them moving on to the next part. I have to give a little bit of head to teaching. . . . As a theatrical thing I am going to have to put some phrases in that indicate that I'm proposing or speculating, speculating as I revise this . . .

This last summation gave us important information on the writer's global and 30 local evaluation of text as well as on his rhetorical and stylistic plans. It is unique because it shows Murray engaged in composing and introspecting at the same time. Generally speaking, subjects giving protocols are not asked to add the demands of introspection to the task of writing. But, in fact, as Murray demonstrated, writers *do* monitor and introspect about their writing simultaneously.

SUMMARY

Some of the more provocative findings of this study concern the sub-processes 31 of planning and revising that have not been observed in conventional protocols (such as those taken by Flower and Hayes) because of the time limitations under which they have been given. When coding the protocols, we noted that Mr. Murray developed intricate style goals:

> It worries me a little bit that the title is too imperative. When I first wrote, most of my articles were like this; they pound on the table, do this, do that. I want this to be a little more reflective.

He also evaluated his thinking plans (i.e., his procedures in planning): "Ah, reading through, ah, hmm . . . I'm just scanning it so I really can't read it. If I read it, it will be an entirely different thing."

Most important, the writer's protocols shed new light on the great and small 32 decisions and revisions that form planning. These decisions and revisions form an elaborate network of steps as the writer moves back and forth between planning, drafting, editing, and reviewing.[24] This recursive process was demonstrated time after time as the writer worked on the two articles and the editorial, often discarding his drafts as he reconceived a major rhetorical goal, and returned to the daybook to plan again. Further, given his characteristic habit of working from daybook to dictation, then back to daybook, we were able to observe that Donald Murray composes at the reflexive and extensive poles described by Janet Emig. When working from material he had "rehearsed" in recent workshops, material with which he was thoroughly familiar, he was able to dictate virtually off the top of his head. At other times he was unable to continue dictating as he attempted to hold too much in suspension in short-term memory. On these occasions the writer returned to the daybook and spent considerable time planning before dictating another draft.

One final observation: although it may be impolitic for the researcher to contradict the writer, Mr. Murray's activity over the summer while he was thinking aloud suggests that he is wrong in his assertion that writers only consider their audiences when doing external revision, i.e., editing and polishing. To the contrary, his most substantive changes, what he calls "internal revision," occurred as he turned his thoughts toward his audience. According to Murray, internal revision includes

> everything writers do to discover and develop what they have to say, beginning with the reading of a completed first draft. They read to discover where their content, form, language, and voice have led them. They use language, structure, and information to find out what they have to say or hope to say. The audience is one person: the writer.[25]

The writer, however, does not speak in a vacuum. Only when he begins to discern what his readers do not yet know can he shape his language, structure, and information to fit the needs of those readers. It is also natural that a writer like Murray would not be aware of how significant a role his sense of audience played in his thoughts. After years of journalistic writing, his consideration of audience had become more automatic than deliberate. The value of thinking-aloud protocols is that they allow the researcher to eavesdrop at the workplace of the writer, catching the flow of thought that would remain otherwise unarticulated.

However, *how* the writer functions when working in the setting to which he or she is accustomed differs considerably from how that writer will function in an unfamiliar setting, given an unfamiliar task, and constrained by a time period over which he or she has no control. For this reason, I sought to combine the methodology of protocol analysis with the techniques of naturalistic inquiry.

This project has been a first venture in what may be a new direction. Research on single subjects is new in our discipline; we need to bear in mind that each writer has his or her own idiosyncrasies. The researcher must make a trade-off, forgoing generalizability for the richness of the data and the qualitative insights to be gained from it. We need to replicate naturalistic studies of skilled and unskilled writers before we can begin to infer patterns that will allow us to understand the writing process in all of its complexity.

Notes

1. Janet Emig, "Inquiry Paradigms and Writing," *College Composition and Communication,* 33 (February, 1982), p. 55.

2. Emig, "Inquiry Paradigms and Writing," p. 67.

3. Donald Graves, "What Children Show Us About Revision," *Language Arts,* 56 (March, 1979), 312–319; Susan Sowers, "A Six Year Old's Writing Process: The First Half of the First Grade," *Language Arts,* 56 (October, 1979), 829-835; Lucy M. Calkins, "Children Learn the Writer's Craft," *Language Arts,* 57 (February, 1980), 207–213.

4. Janet Emig, *The Composing Processes of Twelfth-Graders* (Urbana, IL: National Council of Teachers of English, 1971), pp. 8–11; Linda Flower and John R. Hayes, "A Cognitive Process Theory of Writing," *College Composition and Communication,* 32 (December, 1981), 368.

5. See Janet Emig, *The Composing Processes of Twelfth-Graders,* p. 30; Sondra Perl, "Five Writers Writing: Case Studies of the Composing Processes of Unskilled College Writers," Diss. New York University, 1978, pp. 48, 387, 391; "The Composing Processes of Unskilled College Writers," *Research in the Teaching of English,* 13 (December, 1979), 318; Nancy I. Sommers, "Revision Strategies of Student Writers and Experienced Adult Writers," paper delivered at the Annual Meeting of the Modern Language Association, New York, 28 December, 1978. A slightly revised version was published in *College Composition and Communication,* 32 (December, 1980), 378–388.

6. See Linda Flower and John R. Hayes, "Identifying the Organization of Writing Processes," in *Cognitive Processes in Writing,* ed. Lee W. Gregg and Erwin R. Steinberg (Hillsdale, NJ: Lawrence Erlbaum Associates, 1981), p. 4; "The Cognition of Discovery: Defining a Rhetorical Problem," *College Composition and Communication,* 32 (February, 1980), 23; "The Pregnant Pause: An Inquiry into the Nature of Planning," *Research in the Teaching of English,* 19 (October, 1981), 233; "A Cognitive Process Theory of Writing," p. 368; Carol Berkenkotter, "Understanding a Writer's Awareness of Audience," *College Composition and Communication,* 32 (December, 1981), 389.

7. Perl, "Five Writers Writing: Case Studies of the Composing Processes of Unskilled College Writers," p. 1.

8. Evaluations of text were either global or local. An example of global evaluation is when the writer says, "There's a lack of fullness in the piece." When the writer was evaluating locally he would comment, " . . . and the ending seems weak."

9. Emig, *The Composing Processes of Twelfth-Graders,* p. 4.

10. *Ibid.* See also "Eye, Hand, and Brain," in *Research on Composing: Points of Departure,* ed. Charles R. Cooper and Lee Odell (Urbana, IL: National Council of Teachers of English), p. 70. Emig raises the question, "What if it is the case that classical and contemporary rhetorical terms such as . . . extensive and reflexive may represent centuries old understandings

that the mind deals differentially with different speaking and writing tasks. To put the matter declaratively, if hypothetically, modes of discourse may represent measurably different profiles of brain activity."

11. Janet Emig, observing her subject's writing processes, noted that "the *nature of the stimulus*" did not necessarily determine the response. Emig's students gave extensive responses to a reflexive task (*The Composing Processes of Twelfth-Graders*, pp. 30–31, 33). Similarly, Murray gave a reflexive response to an extensive task. Such a response is not unusual when we consider what the writer himself has observed: "The deeper we get into the writing process the more we may discover how affective concerns govern the cognitive, for writing is an intellectual activity carried on in an emotional environment, a precisely engineered sailboat trying to hold course in a vast and stormy Atlantic" ("Teaching the Other Self: The Writer's First Reader," *College Composition and Communication*, 33 [May, 1982], p. 142). For a writer as deeply engaged in his work as Murray, drafting a conceptual piece was as personal and subjective as describing a closely felt experience.

12. Lester Faigley and Stephen Witte, "Analyzing Revision," *College Composition and Communication*, 32 (December, 1981), 410–411.

13. Faigley and Witte, p. 411.

14. These three pieces of discourse were chosen because their results are representative of the writer's activities.

15. Linda Flower and John R. Hayes describe "process goals" as "instructions and plans the writer gives herself for directing her own composing process." See "The Pregnant Pause: An Inquiry into the Nature of Planning," p. 242. However, this definition is not always agreed upon by cognitive psychologists studying problem-solvers in other fields. On one hand, Allen Newell, Herbert A. Simon, and John R. Hayes distinguish between the goals and plans of a problem-solver, considering a goal as an end to be achieved and a plan as one kind of method for reaching that end. See John R. Hayes, *Cognitive Psychology* (Homewood, IL: The Dorsey Press, 1978), p. 192; Allen Newell and Herbert A. Simon, *Human Problem Solving* (Englewood Cliffs, NJ: Prentice-Hall, Inc. 1972), pp. 88–92, 428–429. On the other hand, George Miller, Eugene Galanter, and Karl H. Pribram use the term "plan" inclusively, suggesting that a plan is "any hierarchical process in the organism that can control the order in which a sequence of operations is to be performed." See *Plans and the Structure of Human Behavior* (New York: Holt, Rinehart, and Winston, Inc., 1960), p. 16.

16. Flower and Hayes use these terms interchangeably, as have I. "Thinking plans" are plans for text that precede drafting and occur during drafting. Thinking plans occur before the movements of a writer's hand. Because of the complexity of the composing process, it is difficult to separate thinking plans from "process goals." It is possible, however, to distinguish between *rhetorical goals* and *rhetorical plans*. Murray was setting a goal when he remarked, "The biggest thing is to . . . what I've got to get to satisfy the reader . . . is that point of what do we hear the other self saying and how does it help?" He followed this goal with a plan to "Probe into the other self. What is the other self? How does it function?"

17. Sommers, "Revision Strategies," pp. 385, 387. (See note 5, above.)

18. The material italicized in the excerpts from these transcripts is text the subject is writing. The material italicized and underlined is text the subject is reading that has already been written.

19. Flower and Hayes, "A Cognitive Process Theory of Writing," 365–387.

20. Berkenkotter, "Understanding a Writer's Awareness of Audience," pp. 392, 395.

21. Faigley and Witte, pp. 406–410.

22. Michael Polanyi, *Personal Knowledge: Toward a Post-Critical Philosophy* (Chicago: The University of Chicago Press, 1958), p. 122.

23. Graham Wallas, *The Art of Thought* (New York: Jonathan Cape, 1926), pp. 85–88; Alex Osborn, *Applied Imagination: Principles and Procedures of Creative Problem-Solving*, 3rd rev. ed. (New York: Charles F. Scribner and Sons), pp. 314–325.

24. For a description of the development of a writer's goal structure, see Flower and Hayes, "A Cognitive Process Theory of Writing."

25. Donald M. Murray, "Internal Revision: A Process of Discovery," *Research on Composing: Points of Departure* (See note 10), p. 91.

RESPONSE OF A LABORATORY RAT — OR, BEING PROTOCOLED

Donald M. Murray

1.

First a note on self-exposure, a misdemeanor in most communities. I have long [1] felt the academic world is too closed. We have an ethical obligation to write and to reveal our writing to our students if we are asking them to share their writing with us. I have felt writers should, instead of public readings, give public workshops in which they write in public, allowing the search for meaning to be seen. I've done this and found the process insightful — and fun.

I have also been fascinated by protocol analysis research. It did seem a fruitful [2] way (a way, there is no one way) to study the writing process. I was, however, critical of the assignments I had seen given, the concentration on inexperienced students as subjects, and the unrealistic laboratory conditions and time limitations.

And, in the absence of more proper academic resources, I have made a career of [3] studying myself while writing. I was already without shame. When Carol Berkenkotter asked me to run in her maze I gulped, but I did not think I could refuse.

2.

The one-hour protocol was far worse than I had expected. If I had done that [4] first there would have been no other protocols. I have rarely felt so completely trapped and so inadequate. I have gone through other research experiences, but in this case I felt stronger than I ever had the need to perform. That was nothing that the researcher did. It was a matter of the conditions. I had a desperate desire to please. I thought of that laboratory experiment where subjects would push a button to cause pain to other people. I would have blown up Manhattan to get out of that room. To find equivalent feelings from my past I would have to go back to combat or to public school. I have developed an enormous compassion and respect for those who have performed for Masters and Johnson.

3.

The process of a naturalistic study we have evolved (Can a rat be a colleague? Since 5 a colleague can be a rat, I don't see why not.) soon became a natural process. I do not assume, and neither did my researcher, that what I said reflected all that was taking place. It did reflect what I was conscious of doing, and a bit more. My articulation was an accurate reflection of the kind of talking I do to myself while planning to write, while writing, and while revising. At no time did it seem awkward or unnatural. My talking aloud was merely a question of turning up the volume knob on the muttering I do under my breath as I write.

> Writing is an intellectual activity, and I do not agree with the romantics who feel that the act of writing and the act of thinking are separate.

I feel that if there was any self-consciousness in the process it was helpful. I 6 was, after all, practicing a craft, not performing magic. Writing is an intellectual activity, and I do not agree with the romantics who feel that the act of writing and the act of thinking are separate.

Having this researcher, who had earned my trust, waiting to see what I wrote 7 was a motivating factor. While the experiment was going on she was appropriately chilly and doctoral. But I still knew someone was listening, and I suspect that got me to the writing desk some days.

It is certainly true that debriefing by the researcher at some distance from the 8 time of writing was virtually useless. I could not remember why I had done what. In fact, the researcher knows the text better than I do. I am concentrating almost entirely on the daily evolving text, and yesterday's page seems like last year's. I intend to try some teaching experiments in the future that make it possible for me to be on the scene when my students are writing. I'm a bit more suspicious now than I had been about the accounts that are reconstructed in a conference days after writing. They are helpful, the best teaching point I know, but I want to find out what happens if we can bring the composing and the teaching closer together.

4.

I certainly agree with what my researcher calls introspection. I am disappointed, 9 however, that she hasn't included the term that I overheard the coders use. Rats aren't all that dumb, and I think there should be further research into those moments when I left the desk and came back with a new insight. They called them: "Bathroom epiphanies."

5.

I was surprised by: 10

1. The percentage of my time devoted to planning. I had realized the pen-
    dulum was swinging in that direction, but I had no idea how far it had
    swung. I suspect that when we begin to write in a new genre we have to do
    a great deal of revision, but that as we become familiar with a genre we can
    solve more writing problems in advance of a completed text. This varies
    according to the writer but I have already changed some of my teaching to
    take this finding into account by allowing my students much more plan-
    ning time and introducing many more planning techniques.

2. The length of incubation time. I now realize that articles that I thought
    took a year in fact have taken three, four, or five years.

3. The amount of revision that is essentially planning, what the researcher calls
    "reconceiving." I was trying to get at that in my chapter, "Internal Revision: A
    Process of Discovery," published in *Research on Composing: Points of Departure*,
    edited by Charles R. Cooper and Lee Odell. I now understand this process far
    better, and much of my revision is certainly a planning or prewriting activity.

6.

I agree with my researcher (what rat wouldn't?) that affective conditions are impor-   11
tant in writing. I do think the affective often controls the cognitive, and I feel
strongly that much more research has to be done, difficult as it may be, into those
conditions, internal and external, that make effective writing possible or impossible.

7.

I was far more aware of audience than I thought I was during some of the   12
writing. My sense of audience is so strong that I have to suppress my conscious
awareness of audience to hear what the text demands.

    Related to this is the fact that I do need a few readers. The important role   13
of my pre-publication readers was clear when my revisions were studied. No
surprise here. I think we need more study of the two, or three, or four readers
professional writers choose for their work in process. It would be helpful for us
as teachers to know the qualities of these people and what they do for the writer.
I know I choose people who make me want to write when I leave them.

8.

I worry a bit about the patterns that this research revealed have been laid down   14
in my long-term memory. The more helpful they are the more I worry about

them. I fear that what I discover when I write is what I have discovered before and forgotten, and that rather than doing the writing that must be done I merely follow the stereotypes of the past. In other words, I worry that the experienced writer can become too glib, too slick, too professional, too polished—can, in effect, write too well.

9.

The description of working back and forth from the global to the particular dur- 15 ing the subprocesses of planning and revising seems accurate to me.

There is a great deal of interesting research and speculation about this process, 16 but we need much more. I find it very difficult to make my students aware of the layers of concern through which the writing writer must oscillate at such a speed that it appears the concerns are dealt with instantaneously.

Too often in my teaching and my publishing I have given the false impression 17 that we do one thing, then another, when in fact we do many things simulta- neously. And the interaction between these things is what we call writing. This project reaffirmed what I had known, that there are many simultaneous levels of concern that bear on every line.

10.

I realize how eccentric my work habits appear. I am aware of how fortunate I am 18 to be able to work with my wife. The process of dictation of non-fiction allows a flow, intensity, and productivity that is quite unusual. It allows me to spend a great deal of time planning, because I know that once the planning is done I can produce copy in short bursts. It is not my problem but the researcher's, however, to put my eccentric habits into context.

If I am the first writer to be naked, then it is up to those other writers who 19 do not think they look the same to take off their clothes. I hope they do not appear as I do; I would be most depressed if I am the model for other writers. I hope, and I believe, that there must be a glorious diversity among writers. What I think we have done, as rat and ratee, is to demonstrate that there is a process through which experienced writers can be studied under normal working con- ditions on typical writing projects. I think my contribution is not to reveal my own writing habits but to show a way that we can study writers who are far better writers than I.

11.

Finally, I started this process with a researcher and have ended it with a colleague. 20 I am grateful for the humane way the research was conducted. I have learned a great deal about research and about what we have researched. It has helped me in my thinking, my teaching, and my writing. I am grateful to Dr. Carol Berkenkotter for this opportunity.

Questions for Discussion and Journaling

1. What was your impression of Murray's writing processes as they're described by Berkenkotter? How do they compare to yours? What do you do the same or differently?

2. Murray's relationship with his audience seems complicated. Try to describe it, and then compare it with your own sense of audience: How much are *you* thinking about *your* audience while you write?

3. How did this study change Berkenkotter's understanding of writing processes, particularly planning and revision?

4. What problems with existing methods for studying writing process does Berkenkotter identify? If you read Perl (p. 738), did you notice any of these problems in her methods? What do you think they might mean for Perl's findings? In what ways is Berkenkotter's newer approach to studying writing processes able to solve the weaknesses in other methods? Do any weaknesses remain?

5. Why do you suppose Berkenkotter often refers to Murray as "the writer" and in his response Murray calls Berkenkotter "the researcher"? Why not just use each other's names, since the audience knows them anyway?

6. What do you think of the apparent back-and-forth between the researcher and the researched that occurred as Berkenkotter analyzed her data and drew conclusions? Was it good? Bad? Necessary? Irrelevant? Did anything about it surprise you?

7. As you read this account of Murray's writing, how much (to what extent, or, how often) does he seem to be aware of writing as making new knowledge (one of this chapter's threshold concepts)? Does he seem to imagine all his writing as doing this, or just some pieces?

Applying and Exploring Ideas

1. Less-experienced writers, especially when writing for school, tend to spend comparatively little time on revision (by which we mean *developing the ideas* in a piece rather than **editing**, which is the sentence-level work that improves the style and correctness of a text). Explore your own writing habits: How do you spend your writing time? How would you characterize your level of writing experience? How do you think your level of experience relates to the amount of time you spend on various parts of the writing process? In making these estimates, keep the following in mind: Murray, a highly professional and quite

reflective writer, had an erroneous impression of how much time he spent on various aspects of his writing process.

2. Begin a writing log in which you list all the writing situations you find yourself in on a day-to-day basis: Every time you write over two weeks, note what you write, the audience for that writing, the genre, the technologies employed, and the skills used. At the end of the period, reflect on what you learned about your writing habits.

3. Try your own brief experiment, re-creating Berkenkotter and Murray's dynamic: Pair with a class partner and designate one of you as researcher and the other as researched. Have the researcher observe the researched's writing process on a short (approximately one-page) piece of writing, and then have the researcher write a brief description of that process while the researched writes a piece of similar length on the experience of doing the writing. Compare these descriptions and negotiate the findings: What, put together, do the two accounts reveal about the writer's process?

- -

META MOMENT   Name one thing you learned from the Berkenkotter and Murray readings that you could use to help you write more effectively.

Shitty First Drafts

ANNE LAMOTT

Araya Diaz/Getty Images

Framing the Reading

Anne Lamott is most people's idea and, perhaps, stereotype of a successful writer. She has published fourteen novels and nonfiction books since 1980, probably the best known of which is the book this excerpt comes from, *Bird by Bird: Some Instructions on Writing and Life*. She is known for her self-deprecating humor and openness (much of her writing touches on subjects such as alcoholism, depression, spirituality and faith, and motherhood). This piece is no exception. Characteristically, Lamott's advice in "Shitty First Drafts" draws extensively on her personal experience with writing (it was her sixth book). And you'll probably find it makes its arguments not only reasonably, but entertainingly. Not many writers would disagree with either her overall point or her descriptions in making it. Thus, it's become one of the most widely anthologized pieces of contemporary advice on writing process. Few writers get more directly at the threshold concepts that writing is not perfectible, that writers always have more to learn, and that writing is a process of trying and trying again, not simply for "weak" writers but for *all* writers.

Getting Ready to Read

Before you read, do at least one of the following activities:

- Think back through your writing experiences and education, and make a list of the times you've been told it's okay to write badly, and who told you.

- What advice would you typically give someone who's having a hard time getting started writing?

Lamott, Anne. "Shitty First Drafts." *Bird by Bird: Some Instructions on Writing and Life*. Anchor Books, 1994, pp. 21–27.

As you read, consider the following questions:

- Can you imagine what the shitty first draft of *this piece itself* looked like? Reading the finished prose, can you make any guesses about what the second and third drafts changed from the first?

- How does this piece make you feel about writing?

NOW, PRACTICALLY EVEN BETTER news than that of short assignments is the idea of shitty first drafts. All good writers write them. This is how they end up with good second drafts and terrific third drafts. People tend to look at successful writers, writers who are getting their books published and maybe even doing well financially, and think that they sit down at their desks every morning feeling like a million dollars, feeling great about who they are and how much talent they have and what a great story they have to tell; that they take in a few deep breaths, push back their sleeves, roll their necks a few times to get all the cricks out, and dive in, typing fully formed passages as fast as a court reporter. But this is just the fantasy of the uninitiated. I know some very great writers, writers you love who write beautifully and have made a great deal of money, and not *one* of them sits down routinely feeling wildly enthusiastic and confident. Not one of them writes elegant first drafts. All right, one of them does, but we do not like her very much. We do not think that she has a rich inner life or that God likes her or can even stand her. (Although when I mentioned this to my priest friend Tom, he said you can safely assume you've created God in your own image when it turns out that God hates all the same people you do.)

> *I know some very great writers, writers you love who write beautifully and have made a great deal of money, and not one of them sits down routinely feeling wildly enthusiastic and confident.*

Very few writers really know what they are doing until they've done it. Nor do they go about their business feeling dewy and thrilled. They do not type a few stiff warm-up sentences and then find themselves bounding along like huskies across the snow. One writer I know tells me that he sits down every morning and says to himself nicely, "It's not like you don't have a choice, because you do—you can either type or kill yourself." We all often feel like we are pulling teeth, even those writers whose prose ends up being the most natural and fluid. The right words and sentences just do not come pouring out like ticker tape most of the time. Now, Muriel Spark is said to have felt that she was taking dictation from God every morning—sitting there, one supposes, plugged into a Dictaphone, typing away, humming. But this is a very hostile and aggressive position. One might hope for bad things to rain down on a person like this.

For me and most of the other writers I know, writing is not rapturous. In 3 fact, the only way I can get anything written at all is to write really, really shitty first drafts.

The first draft is the child's draft, where you let it all pour out and then let it 4 romp all over the place, knowing that no one is going to see it and that you can shape it later. You just let this childlike part of you channel whatever voices and visions come through and onto the page. If one of the characters wants to say, "Well, so what, Mr. Poopy Pants?" you let her. No one is going to see it. If the kid wants to get into really sentimental, weepy, emotional territory, you let him. Just get it all down on paper, because there may be something great in those six crazy pages that you would never have gotten to by more rational, grown-up means. There may be something in the very last line of the very last paragraph on page six that you just love, that is so beautiful or wild that you now know what you're supposed to be writing about, more or less, or in what direction you might go — but there was no way to get to this without first getting through the first five and a half pages.

I used to write food reviews for *California* magazine before it folded. (My 5 writing food reviews had nothing to do with the magazine folding, although every single review did cause a couple of canceled subscriptions. Some readers took umbrage at my comparing mounds of vegetable puree with various ex-presidents' brains.) These reviews always took two days to write. First I'd go to a restaurant several times with a few opinionated, articulate friends in tow. I'd sit there writing down everything anyone said that was at all interesting or funny. Then on the following Monday I'd sit down at my desk with my notes, and try to write the review. Even after I'd been doing this for years, panic would set in. I'd try to write a lead, but instead I'd write a couple of dreadful sentences, xx them out, try again, xx everything out, and then feel despair and worry settle on my chest like an x-ray apron. It's over, I'd think, calmly. I'm not going to be able to get the magic to work this time. I'm ruined. I'm through. I'm toast. Maybe, I'd think, I can get my old job back as a clerk-typist. But probably not. I'd get up and study my teeth in the mirror for a while. Then I'd stop, remember to breathe, make a few phone calls, hit the kitchen and chow down. Eventually I'd go back and sit down at my desk, and sigh for the next ten minutes. Finally I would pick up my one-inch picture frame, stare into it as if for the answer, and every time the answer would come: All I had to do was to write a really shitty first draft of, say, the opening paragraph. And no one was going to see it.

So I'd start writing without reining myself in. It was almost just typing, just 6 making my fingers move. And the writing would be *terrible*. I'd write a lead paragraph that was a whole page, even though the entire review could only be three pages long, and then I'd start writing up descriptions of the food, one dish at a time, bird by bird, and the critics would be sitting on my shoulders, commenting like cartoon characters. They'd be pretending to snore, or rolling their eyes at my overwrought descriptions, no matter how hard I tried to tone those descriptions down, no matter how conscious I was of what a friend said to me gently in my early days of restaurant reviewing. "Annie," she said, "it is just a piece of *chicken*. It is just a bit of *cake*."

But because by then I had been writing for so long, I would eventually let myself trust the process—sort of, more or less. I'd write a first draft that was maybe twice as long as it should be, with a self-indulgent and boring beginning, stupefying descriptions of the meal, lots of quotes from my black-humored friends that made them sound more like the Manson girls than food lovers, and no ending to speak of. The whole thing would be so long and incoherent and hideous that for the rest of the day I'd obsess about getting creamed by a car before I could write a decent second draft. I'd worry that people would read what I'd written and believe that the accident had really been a suicide, that I had panicked because my talent was waning and my mind was shot. 7

The next day, though, I'd sit down, go through it all with a colored pen, take out everything I possibly could, find a new lead somewhere on the second page, figure out a kicky place to end it, and then write a second draft. It always turned out fine, sometimes even funny and weird and helpful. I'd go over it one more time and mail it in. 8

Then, a month later, when it was time for another review, the whole process would start again, complete with the fears that people would find my first draft before I could rewrite it. 9

Almost all good writing begins with terrible first efforts. You need to start somewhere. Start by getting something—anything—down on paper. A friend of mine says that the first draft is the down draft—you just get it down. The second draft is the up draft—you fix it up. You try to say what you have to say more accurately. And the third draft is the dental draft, where you check every tooth, to see if it's loose or cramped or decayed, or even, God help us, healthy. 10

What I've learned to do when I sit down to work on a shitty first draft is to quiet the voices in my head. First there's the vinegar-lipped Reader Lady, who says primly, "Well, *that's* not very interesting, is it?" And there's the emaciated German male who writes these Orwellian memos detailing your thought crimes. And there are your parents, agonizing over your lack of loyalty and discretion; and there's William Burroughs, dozing off or shooting up because he finds you as bold and articulate as a houseplant; and so on. And there are also the dogs: let's not forget the dogs, the dogs in their pen who will surely hurtle and snarl their way out if you ever *stop* writing, because writing is, for some of us, the latch that keeps the door of the pen closed, keeps those crazy ravenous dogs contained. 11

Quieting these voices is at least half the battle I fight daily. But this is better than it used to be. It used to be 87 percent. Left to its own devices, my mind spends much of its time having conversations with people who aren't there. I walk along defending myself to people, or exchanging repartee with them, or 12 rationalizing my behavior, or seducing them with gossip, or pretending I'm on their TV talk show or whatever. I speed or run an aging yellow light or don't come to a full stop, and one nanosecond later am explaining to imaginary cops exactly why I had to do what I did, or insisting that I did not in fact do it.

I happened to mention this to a hypnotist I saw many years ago, and he 13 looked at me very nicely. At first I thought he was feeling around on the floor for the silent alarm button, but then he gave me the following exercise, which I still use to this day.

Close your eyes and get quiet for a minute, until the chatter starts up. Then 14 isolate one of the voices and imagine the person speaking as a mouse. Pick it up by the tail and drop it into a mason jar. Then isolate another voice, pick it up by the tail, drop it in the jar. And so on. Drop in any high-maintenance parental units, drop in any contractors, lawyers, colleagues, children, anyone who is whining in your head. Then put the lid on, and watch all these mouse people clawing at the glass, jabbering away, trying to make you feel like shit because you won't do what they want—won't give them more money, won't be more successful, won't see them more often. Then imagine that there is a volume-control button on the bottle. Turn it all the way up for a minute, and listen to the stream of angry, neglected, guilt-mongering voices. Then turn it all the way down and watch the frantic mice lunge at the glass, trying to get to you. Leave it down, and get back to your shitty first draft.

A writer friend of mine suggests opening the jar and shooting them all in the 15 head. But I think he's a little angry, and I'm sure nothing like this would ever occur to you.

- -

Questions for Discussion and Journaling

1. Why is it so hard for many people (maybe you) to knowingly put bad writing on paper?

2. What are your own "coping strategies" for getting started on a piece of writing? Do you have particular strategies for making yourself sit down and start writing?

3. What would you say is the funniest line in this piece? Why did it make you laugh?

4. Most readers find that Lamott sounds very down-to-earth and approachable in this piece. What is she doing with language and words themselves to give this impression?

5. Lamott talks, toward the end of this piece, about all the critical voices that play in her mind when she's trying to write. Most, maybe all, writers have something similar. What are yours?

Applying and Exploring Ideas

1. Lamott obviously knows well what the weaknesses in her SFDs are likely to be. Are you aware yet of any patterns in your first-draft writing — places or ways in which you simply expect that the writing will need work once you actually have words on paper?

2. As you read other "process" pieces in this chapter, what do you find makes Lamott different (from, say, Neto or Rose or Sommers)? What is she saying (or how is she saying it) that others don't — or what does she not say that others do?

3. Lamott says: "There may be something on the very last line of the very last paragraph of page six that you just love . . . but there was no way to get to this without first getting through the first five and a half pages" (para. 4). We might explain this idea about revision with an analogy: When you drive at night, your headlights don't light the whole way to your destination, just the first couple hundred yards. When you drive that far, then you can see the next couple hundred yards — and so on. Drafting works exactly the same way: In your first draft, you write what you know so far. But you discover new ideas while you write, and so, just like being able to see more of the road in your headlights, after you've written one draft, what you wrote in it helps you know *more* to say in the second draft — and so on. What other metaphors or analogies could you make to explain this phenomenon?

- -

META MOMENT   Lamott gives you permission to write badly in order to write well. What else would you like permission to do with/in your writing?

- -

Revision Strategies of Student Writers and Experienced Adult Writers

NANCY SOMMERS

Framing the Reading

We've already introduced you to Nancy Sommers with her piece "I Stand Here Writing" in Chapter 2 (so if you didn't read that piece, take a moment and read the first paragraph of its "Framing the Reading" section on page 212 to get a sense of who Sommers is). In this piece, we move from Sommers's investigation of how writers work on the **invention** phase of their writing to her questioning about how writers handle **revision**, or coming up with what to say in their writing. This article came when Sommers worked at the University of Oklahoma and at New York University in the late 1970s and early 1980s, long before her current work at Harvard.

If you've read Sommers's piece in Chapter 2, you might notice that this piece, in contrast, has a much different, possibly more "scientific" feel to the writing (especially in this piece's "Methods" section). It's worth thinking about how the same writer can handle two very different styles of writing and have both appear in scholarly journals. That makes Sommers's articles an excellent example of the range of work that can count as scholarly to begin with.

This study is one of the most widely anthologized articles in the field (meaning that it is very frequently reprinted in a variety of collections about the study of writing and writing process — including the book you are reading now), and it won a major award. Sommers's basic research question is whether there are differences in how student writers talk about and implement revision in their writing compared

Sommers, Nancy. "Revision Strategies of Student Writers and Experienced Adult Writers." *College Composition and Communication*, vol. 31, no. 4, Dec. 1980, pp. 378–88.

with how experienced professional writers do so. The need for this research, she argued in 1980, was that while other aspects of the writing process were being studied quite carefully, revision wasn't being studied in the same detail; she attributed this lack of research to definitions of the writing process that were dominant at the time — definitions that imagined revision as almost an afterthought to writing. So Sommers studied revision and reached the conclusions you'll read here, finding that revision is central to writing, and that professional and experienced writers understand revision differently than most student writers.

Sommers's work showed us how to think of revision as something like driving with headlights (our metaphor, not hers): Headlights only let you see a couple hundred yards, but once you've driven those, you see new ground that you couldn't at the beginning. Revision lets you write what you know at the beginning, find out what new ground you can see having written that much, and then write again saying what you would have if you'd known in the beginning what you learned while writing the first draft. Revision, Sommers's research shows, isn't a punishment or something writers need to do when they've done badly; the better a writer you are, the more likely you are to revise, because it's so powerful a way to find out what you want to say. This reality again leads us to the threshold concept that *writing is not perfectible* and that *writing is a process in which writers learn more about what they're writing about.*

Something you want to keep in mind while reading this piece (which you will already have encountered if you've read other chapters in this book): Context is important. Remember, for example, that the composing and revising Sommers observed *was not* happening on word-processors, because those largely didn't exist in 1980. Whatever you think of revision today, however you do it, unless you're writing with pencil/pen and paper, you're not experiencing revision the same way that the people Sommers interviewed in 1980 did. (And you're probably aware how much drafting on computer is different than drafting on paper.) Be sure that you're attending to these kinds of contextual differences between a more than 35-year-old study and how you write today, and keep an eye out for others. Still, part of the reason Sommers's article is still so widely read is because it suggested something that all of us involved in the study of writing should look out for as we think about writing process. See if you can get a feel for the importance of this subject as you're reading.

Getting Ready to Read

Before you read, do at least one of the following activities:

- Read the "Framing the Reading" for Sommers's preceding article (p. 212) if you haven't already.

- Make a list of words you use to describe the process of changing what you've written to improve it. What do you call this kind of changing? Do you use different terms for the changing that you do at different times (for example, changes you make to a sentence while you're finishing writing it, changes you make after you finish an entire draft of what you're writing, or changes you make as you're getting ready to turn a draft in for grading or give your final version to readers)?

- Think about where revision fits in your writing process: At what points do you do it? How much, usually?

As you read, consider the following question:

- At what moments in the piece does Sommers's discussion of principles lead to clear, straightforward statements of differences between the student and experienced writers? Make a list of these statements.

ALTHOUGH VARIOUS ASPECTS of the writing process have been stud- 1
ied extensively of late, research on revision has been notably absent. The reason for this, I suspect, is that current models of the writing process have directed attention away from revision. With few exceptions, these models are linear; they separate the writing process into discrete stages. Two representative models are Gordon Rohman's suggestion that the composing process moves from prewriting to writing to rewriting and James Britton's model of the writing process as a series of stages described in metaphors of linear growth, conception — incubation — production.[1] What is striking about these theories of writing is that they model themselves on speech: Rohman defines the writer in a way that cannot distinguish him from a speaker ("A writer is a man who . . . puts [his] experience into words in his own mind" — p. 15); and Britton bases his theory of writing on what he calls (following Jakobson) the "expressiveness" of speech.[2] Moreover, Britton's study itself follows the "linear model" of the relation of thought and language in speech proposed by Vygotsky, a relationship embodied in the linear movement "from the motive which engenders a thought to the shaping of the thought, *first* in inner speech, *then* in meanings of words, and *finally* in words" (quoted in Britton, p. 40). What this movement fails to take into account in its linear structure — "first . . . then . . . finally" — is the recursive shaping of thought by language; what it fails to take into account is *revision.* In these linear conceptions of the writing process revision is understood as a separate stage at the end of the process — a stage that comes after the completion of a first or second draft and one that is temporally distinct from the prewriting and writing stages of the process.[3]

The linear model bases itself on speech in two specific ways. First of all, it is 2
based on traditional rhetorical models, models that were created to serve the spoken art of oratory. In whatever ways the parts of classical rhetoric are described,

they offer "stages" of composition that are repeated in contemporary models of the writing process. Edward Corbett, for instance, describes the "five parts of a discourse" — *inventio, dispositio, elocutio, memoria, pronuntiatio* — and, disregarding the last two parts since "after rhetoric came to be concerned mainly with written discourse, there was no further need to deal with them,"[4] he produces a model very close to Britton's conception [*inventio*], incubation [*dispositio*], production [*elocutio*]. Other rhetorics also follow this procedure, and they do so not simply because of historical accident. Rather, the process represented in the linear model is based on the irreversibility of speech. Speech, Roland Barthes says, "is irreversible":

> "A word cannot be retracted, except precisely by saying that one retracts it. To cross out here is to add: if I want to erase what I have just said, I cannot do it without showing the eraser itself (I must say: '*or rather . . .*' '*I expressed myself badly . . .*'); paradoxically, it is ephemeral speech which is indelible, not monumental writing. All that one can do in the case of a spoken utterance is to tack on another utterance."[5]

What is impossible in speech is *revision:* like the example Barthes gives, revision in speech is an afterthought. In the same way, each stage of the linear model must be exclusive (distinct from the other stages) or else it becomes trivial and counterproductive to refer to these junctures as "stages."

By staging revision after enunciation, the linear models reduce revision in writing, as in speech, to no more than an afterthought. In this way such models make the study of revision impossible. Revision, in Rohman's model, is simply the repetition of writing; or to pursue Britton's organic metaphor, revision is simply the further growth of what is already there, the "preconceived" product. The absence of research on revision, then, is a function of a theory of writing which makes revision both superfluous and redundant, a theory which does not distinguish between writing and speech.

What the linear models do produce is a parody of writing. Isolating revision and then disregarding it plays havoc with the experiences composition teachers have of the actual writing and rewriting of experienced writers. Why should the linear model be preferred? Why should revision be forgotten, superfluous? Why do teachers offer the linear model and students accept it? One reason, Barthes suggests, is that "there is a fundamental tie between teaching and speech," while "writing begins at the point where speech becomes *impossible.*"[6] The spoken word cannot be revised. The possibility of revision distinguishes the written text from speech. In fact, according to Barthes, this is the essential difference between writing and speaking. When we must revise, when the very idea is subject to recursive shaping by language, then speech becomes inadequate. This is a matter to which I will return, but first we should examine, theoretically, a detailed exploration of what student writers as distinguished from experienced adult writers *do* when they write and rewrite their work. Dissatisfied with both the linear model of writing and the lack of attention to the process of revision, I conducted a series of studies over the past three years which examined the revision processes of student writers and experienced writers to see what role revision played in their writing processes. In the course of my work the revision process was redefined as *a sequence of changes in a composition — changes which are initiated by cues and occur continually throughout the writing of a work.*

METHODOLOGY

I used a case study approach. The student writers were twenty freshmen at Boston   5 University and the University of Oklahoma with SAT verbal scores ranging from 450–600 in their first semester of composition. The twenty experienced adult writers from Boston and Oklahoma City included journalists, editors, and academics. To refer to the two groups, I use the terms *student writers* and *experienced writers* because the principal difference between these two groups is the amount of experience they have had in writing.

Each writer wrote three essays, expressive, explanatory, and persuasive, and   6 rewrote each essay twice, producing nine written products in draft and final form. Each writer was interviewed three times after the final revision of each essay. And each writer suggested revisions for a composition written by an anonymous author. Thus extensive written and spoken documents were obtained from each writer.

The essays were analyzed by counting and categorizing the changes made.   7 Four revision operations were identified: deletion, substitution, addition, and reordering. And four levels of changes were identified: word, phrase, sentence, theme (the extended statement of one idea). A coding system was developed for identifying the frequency of revision by level and operation. In addition, transcripts of the interviews in which the writers interpreted their revisions were used to develop what was called a *scale of concerns* for each writer. This scale enabled me to codify what were the writer's primary concerns, secondary concerns, tertiary concerns, and whether the writers used the same scale of concerns when revising the second or third drafts as they used in revising the first draft.

REVISION STRATEGIES OF STUDENT WRITERS

Most of the students I studied did not use the terms *revision* or *rewriting*. In fact,   8 they did not seem comfortable using the word *revision* and explained that revision was not a word they used, but the word their teachers used. Instead, most of the students had developed various functional terms to describe the type of changes they made. The following are samples of these definitions:

> *Scratch Out and Do Over Again:* "I say scratch out and do over, and that
> means what it says. Scratching out and cutting out. I read what I have

written and I cross out a word and put another word in; a more decent word or a better word. Then if there is somewhere to use a sentence that I have crossed out, I will put it there."

Reviewing: "Reviewing means just using better words and eliminating words that are not needed, I go over and change words around."

Reviewing: "I just review every word and make sure that everything is worded right. I see if I am rambling; I see if I can put a better word in or leave one out. Usually when I read what I have written, I say to myself, 'that word is so bland or so trite,' and then I go and get my thesaurus."

Redoing: "Redoing means cleaning up the paper and crossing out. It is looking at something and saying, no that has to go, or no, that is not right."

Marking Out: "I don't use the word rewriting because I only write one draft and the changes that I make are made on top of the draft. The changes that I make are usually just marking out words and putting different ones in."

Slashing and Throwing Out: "I throw things out and say they are not good. I like to write like Fitzgerald did by inspiration, and if I feel inspired then I don't need to slash and throw much out."

The predominant concern in these definitions is vocabulary. The students understand the revision process as a rewording activity. They do so because they perceive words as the unit of written discourse. That is, they concentrate on particular words apart from their role in the text. Thus one student quoted above thinks in terms of dictionaries, and, following the eighteenth century theory of words parodied in *Gulliver's Travels*, he imagines a load of things carried about to be exchanged. Lexical changes are the major revision activities of the students because economy is their goal. They are governed, like the linear model itself, by the Law of Occam's razor that prohibits logically needless repetition: redundancy and superfluity. Nothing governs speech more than such superfluities; speech constantly repeats itself precisely because spoken words, as Barthes writes, are expendable in the cause of communication. The aim of revision according to the students' own description is therefore to clean up speech; the redundancy of speech is unnecessary in writing, their logic suggests, because writing, unlike speech, can be reread. Thus one student said, "Redoing means cleaning up the paper and crossing out." The remarkable contradiction of cleaning by marking might, indeed, stand for student revision as I have encountered it.

The students place a symbolic importance on their selection and rejection of words as the determiners of success or failure for their compositions. When revising, they primarily ask themselves: can I find a better word or phrase? A more impressive, not so clichéd, or less hum-drum word? Am I repeating the same word or phrase too often? They approach the revision process with what could be labeled as a "thesaurus philosophy of writing"; the students consider the thesaurus a harvest of lexical substitutions and believe that most problems in their essays can be solved by rewording. What is revealed in the students' use of the thesaurus is a governing attitude toward their writing: that the meaning to be communicated is already there, already finished, already produced, ready to be communicated, and all that is necessary is a better word "rightly worded." One student defined revision as "redoing"; "redoing" meant "just using better words and eliminating words that are not needed." For the students, writing is translating: the thought to the page, the language of speech to the more formal language of prose, the word to its synonym. Whatever is translated, an original text already exists for students, one which need not be discovered or acted upon, but simply communicated.[7]

The students list repetition as one of the elements they most worry about. 11 This cue signals to them that they need to eliminate the repetition either by substituting or deleting words or phrases. Repetition occurs, in large part, because student writing imitates — transcribes — speech: attention to repetitious words is a manner of cleaning speech. Without a sense of the developmental possibilities of revision (and writing in general) students seek, on the authority of many textbooks, simply to clean up their language and prepare to type. What is curious, however, is that students are aware of lexical repetition, but not conceptual repetition. They only notice the repetition if they can "hear" it; they do not diagnose lexical repetition as symptomatic of problems on a deeper level. By rewording their sentences to avoid the lexical repetition, the students solve the immediate problem, but blind themselves to problems on a textual level; although they are using different words, they are sometimes merely restating the same idea with different words. Such blindness, as I discovered with student writers, is the inability to "see" revision as a process: the inability to "re-view" their work again, as it were, with different eyes, and to start over.

The revision strategies described above are consistent with the students' under- 12 standing of the revision process as requiring lexical changes but not semantic changes. For the students, the extent to which they revise is a function of their level of inspiration. In fact, they use the word *inspiration* to describe the ease or difficulty with which their essay is written, and the extent to which the essay needs to be revised. If students feel inspired, if the writing comes easily, and if they don't get stuck on individual words or phrases, then they say that they cannot see any reason to revise. Because students do not see revision as an activity in which they modify and develop perspectives and ideas, they feel that if they know what they want to say, then there is little reason for making revisions.

The only modification of ideas in the students' essays occurred when they 13 tried out two or three introductory paragraphs. This results, in part, because the students have been taught in another version of the linear model of composing to use a thesis statement as a controlling device in their introductory paragraphs. Since they write their introductions and their thesis statements even before they have really discovered what they want to say, their early close attention to the thesis statement, and more generally the linear model, function to restrict and circumscribe not only the development of their ideas, but also their ability to change the direction of these ideas.

Too often as composition teachers we conclude that students do not willingly revise. The evidence from my research suggests that it is not that students are unwilling to revise, but rather that they do what they have been taught to do in a consistently narrow and predictable way. On every occasion when I asked students why they hadn't made any more changes, they essentially replied, "I knew something larger was wrong, but I didn't think it would help to move words around." The students have strategies for handling words and phrases and their strategies helped them on a word or sentence level. What they lack, however, is a set of strategies to help them identify the "something larger" that they sensed was wrong and work from there. The students do not have strategies for handling the whole essay. They lack procedures or heuristics to help them reorder lines of reasoning or ask questions about their purposes and readers. The students view their compositions in a linear way as a series of parts. Even such potentially useful concepts as "unity" or "form" are reduced to the rule that a composition, if it is to have form, must have an introduction, a body, and a conclusion, or the sum total of the necessary parts. 14

The students decide to stop revising when they decide that they have not violated any of the rules for revising. These rules, such as "Never begin a sentence with a conjunction" or "Never end a sentence with a preposition," are lexically cued and rigidly applied. In general, students will subordinate the demands of the specific problems of their text to the demands of the rules. Changes are made in compliance with abstract rules about the product, rules that quite often do not apply to the specific problems in the text. These revision strategies are teacher-based, directed towards a teacher-reader who expects compliance with rules — with pre-existing "conceptions" — and who will only examine parts of the composition (writing comments about those parts in the margins of their essays) and will cite any violations of rules in those parts. At best the students see their writing altogether passively through the eyes of former teachers or their surrogates, the textbooks, and are bound to the rules which they have been taught. 15

REVISION STRATEGIES OF EXPERIENCED WRITERS

One aim of my research has been to contrast how student writers define revision with how a group of experienced writers define their revision processes. Here is a sampling of the definitions from the experienced writers: 16

> *Rewriting:* "It is a matter of looking at the kernel of what I have written, the content, and then thinking about it, responding to it, making decisions, and actually restructuring it."

Rewriting: "I rewrite as I write. It is hard to tell what is a first draft because it is not determined by time. In one draft, I might cross out three pages, write two, cross out a fourth, rewrite it, and call it a draft. I am constantly writing and rewriting. I can only conceptualize so much in my first draft—only so much information can be held in my head at one time; my rewriting efforts are a reflection of how much information I can encompass at one time. There are levels and agenda which I have to attend to in each draft."

Rewriting: "Rewriting means on one level, finding the argument, and on another level, language changes to make the argument more effective. Most of the time I feel as if I can go on rewriting forever. There is always one part of a piece that I could keep working on. It is always difficult to know at what point to abandon a piece of writing. I like this idea that a piece of writing is never finished, just abandoned."

Rewriting: "My first draft is usually very scattered. In rewriting, I find the line of argument. After the argument is resolved, I am much more interested in word choice and phrasing."

Revising: "My cardinal rule in revising is never to fall in love with what I have written in a first or second draft. An idea, sentence, or even a phrase that looks catchy, I don't trust. Part of this idea is to wait a while. I am much more in love with something after I have written it than I am a day or two later. It is much easier to change anything with time."

Revising: "It means taking apart what I have written and putting it back together again. I ask major theoretical questions of my ideas, respond to those questions, and think of proportion and structure, and try to find a controlling metaphor. I find out which ideas can be developed and which should be dropped. I am constantly chiseling and changing as I revise."

The experienced writers describe their primary objective when revising as finding the form or shape of their argument. Although the metaphors vary, the experienced writers often use structural expressions such as "finding a framework," "a pattern," or "a design" for their argument. When questioned about this emphasis, the experienced writers responded that since their first drafts are usually scattered attempts to define their territory, their objective in the second draft is to begin observing general patterns of development and deciding what should be included and what excluded. One writer explained, "I have learned from experience that I need to keep writing a first draft until I figure out what I want to say. Then in a second draft, I begin to see the structure of an argument and how all the various sub-arguments which are buried beneath the surface of all those sentences are related." What is described here is a process in which the writer is both agent and vehicle. "Writing," says Barthes, unlike speech, "develops like a seed, not a line,"[8] and like a seed it confuses beginning and end, conception and production. Thus, the experienced writers say their drafts are "not determined by time," that rewriting is a "constant process," that they feel as if (they) "can go on forever." Revising confuses the beginning and end, the agent and vehicle; it confuses, *in order to find*, the line of argument.

After a concern for form, the experienced writers have a second objective: a concern for their readership. In this way, "production" precedes "conception." The experienced writers imagine a reader (reading their product) whose existence and whose expectations influence their revision process. They have abstracted the standards of a reader and this reader seems to be partially a reflection of themselves and functions as a critical and productive collaborator — a collaborator who has yet to love their work. The anticipation of a reader's judgment causes a feeling of dissonance when the writer recognizes incongruities between intention and execution, and requires these writers to make revisions on all levels. Such a reader gives them just what the students lacked: new eyes to "re-view" their work. The experienced writers believe that they have learned the causes and conditions, the product, which will influence their reader, and their revision strategies are geared towards creating these causes and conditions. They demonstrate a complex understanding of which examples, sentences, or phrases should be included or excluded. For example, one experienced writer decided to delete public examples and add private examples when writing about the energy crisis because "private examples would be less controversial and thus more persuasive." Another writer revised his transitional sentences because "some kinds of transitions are more easily recognized as transitions than others." These examples represent the type of strategic attempts these experienced writers use to manipulate the conventions of discourse in order to communicate to their reader.

> . . . *experienced writers say their drafts are "not determined by time," that rewriting is a "constant process," that they feel as if (they) "can go on forever."*

But these revision strategies are a process of more than communication; they are part of the process of *discovering meaning* altogether. Here we can see the importance of dissonance; at the heart of revision is the process by which writers recognize and resolve the dissonance they sense in their writing. Ferdinand de Saussure has argued that meaning is differential or "diacritical," based on differences between terms rather than "essential" or inherent qualities of terms. "Phonemes," he said, "are characterized not, as one might think, by their own positive quality but simply by the fact that they are distinct."[9] In fact, Saussure bases his entire *Course in General Linguistics* on these differences, and such differences are dissonant; like musical dissonances which gain their significance from their relationship to the "key" of the composition which itself is determined by the whole language, specific language (parole) gains its meaning from the system of language (langue) of which it is a manifestation and part. The musical composition—a "composition" of parts—creates its "key" as in an overall structure which determines the value (meaning) of its parts. The analogy with music is readily seen in the compositions of experienced writers: both sorts of composition are based precisely on those structures experienced writers seek in their writing. It is this complicated relationship between the parts and the whole in the work of experienced writers which destroys the linear model; writing cannot develop "like a line" because each addition or deletion is a reordering of the whole. Explicating Saussure, Jonathan Culler asserts that "meaning depends on difference of meaning."[10] But student writers constantly struggle to bring their essays into congruence with a predefined meaning. The experienced writers do the opposite: they seek to discover (to create) meaning in the engagement with their writing, in revision. They seek to emphasize and exploit the lack of clarity, the differences of meaning, the dissonance, that writing as opposed to speech allows in the possibility of revision. Writing has spatial and temporal features not apparent in speech—words are recorded in space and fixed in time—which is why writing is susceptible to reordering and later addition. Such features make possible the dissonance that both provokes revision and promises, from itself, new meaning.

For the experienced writers the heaviest concentration of changes is on the 20 sentence level, and the changes are predominantly by addition and deletion. But, unlike the students, experienced writers make changes on all levels and use all revision operations. Moreover, the operations the students fail to use— reordering and addition—seem to require a theory of the revision process as a totality—a theory which, in fact, encompasses the *whole* of the composition. Unlike the students, the experienced writers possess a non-linear theory in which a sense of the whole writing both precedes and grows out of an examination of the parts. As we saw, one writer said he needed "a first draft to figure out what to say," and "a second draft to see the structure of an argument buried beneath the surface." Such a "theory" is both theoretical and strategical; once again, strategy and theory are conflated in ways that are literally impossible for the linear model. Writing appears to be more like a seed than a line.

Two elements of the experienced writers' theory of the revision process are 21 the adoption of a holistic perspective and the perception that revision is a recursive process. The writers ask: what does my essay as a *whole* need for form, balance, rhythm, or communication. Details are added, dropped, substituted, or reordered according to their sense of what the essay needs for emphasis and proportion. This sense, however, is constantly in flux as ideas are developed and modified; it is constantly "re-viewed" in relation to the parts. As their ideas change, revision becomes an attempt to make their writing consonant with that changing vision.

The experienced writers see their revision process as a recursive process—a 22 process with significant recurring activities—with different levels of attention and different agenda for each cycle. During the first revision cycle their attention is primarily directed towards narrowing the topic and delimiting their ideas. At this point, they are not as concerned as they are later about vocabulary and style. The experienced writers explained that they get closer to their meaning by not limiting themselves too early to lexical concerns. As one writer commented to explain her revision process, a comment inspired by the summer 1977 New York power failure: "I feel like Con Edison cutting off certain states to keep the generators going. In first and second drafts, I try to cut off as much as I can of my editing generator, and in a third draft, I try to cut off some of my idea generators, so I can make sure that I will actually finish the essay." Although the experienced writers describe their revision process as a series of different levels or cycles, it is inaccurate to assume that they have only one objective for each cycle and that each cycle can be defined by a different objective. The same objectives and sub-processes are present in each cycle, but in different proportions. Even though these experienced writers place the predominant weight upon finding the form of their argument during the first cycle, other concerns exist as well. Conversely, during the later cycles, when the experienced writers' primary attention is focused upon stylistic concerns, they are still attuned, although in a reduced way, to the form of the argument. Since writers are limited in what they can attend to during each cycle (understandings are temporal), revision strategies help balance competing demands on attention. Thus, writers can concentrate on more than one objective at a time by developing strategies to sort out and organize their different concerns in successive cycles of revision.

It is a sense of writing as discovery—a repeated process of beginning over 23 again, starting out new—that the students failed to have. I have used the notion of dissonance because such dissonance, the incongruities between intention and execution, governs both writing and meaning. Students do not see the incongruities. They need to rely on their own internalized sense of good writing and to see their writing with their "own" eyes. Seeing in revision—seeing beyond hearing—is at the root of the word *revision* and the process itself; current dicta on revising blind our students to what is actually involved in revision. In fact, they blind them to what constitutes good writing altogether. Good writing disturbs: it creates dissonance. Students need to seek the dissonance of discovery, utilizing in their writing, as the experienced writers do, the very difference between writing and speech—the possibility of revision.

Notes

1. D. Gordon Rohman and Albert O. Wlecke, "Pre-writing: The Construction and Application of Models for Concept Formation in Writing," Cooperative Research Project No. 2174, U.S. Office of Education, Department of Health, Education, and Welfare; James Britton, Anthony Burgess, Nancy Martin, Alex McLeod, Harold Rosen, *The Development of Writing Abilities (11–18)* (London: Macmillan Education, 1975).

2. Britton is following Roman Jakobson, "Linguistics and Poetics," in T. A. Sebeok, *Style in Language* (Cambridge, Mass: MIT Press, 1960).

3. For an extended discussion of this issue see Nancy Sommers, "The Need for Theory in Composition Research," *College Composition and Communication*, 30 (February 1979), 46-49.

4. *Classical Rhetoric for the Modern Student* (New York: Oxford University Press, 1965), p. 27.

5. Roland Barthes, "Writers, Intellectuals, Teachers," in *Image-Music-Text*, trans. Stephen Heath (New York: Hill and Wang, 1977), pp. 190-191.

6. "Writers, Intellectuals, Teachers," p. 190.

7. Nancy Sommers and Ronald Schleifer, "Means and Ends: Some Assumptions of Student Writers," *Composition and Teaching*, II (in press).

8. *Writing Degree Zero* in *Writing Degree Zero and Elements of Semiology*, trans. Annette Lavers and Colin Smith (New York: Hill and Wang, 1968), p. 20.

9. *Course in General Linguistics*, trans. Wade Baskin (New York, 1966), p. 119.

10. Jonathan Culler, *Saussure* (Penguin Modern Masters Series; London: Penguin Books, 1976), p. 70.

Acknowledgment: The author wishes to express her gratitude to Professor William Smith, University of Pittsburgh, for his vital assistance with the research reported in this article and to Patrick Hays, her husband, for extensive discussions and critical editorial help.

- -

Questions for Discussion and Journaling

1. Sommers says that the language students use to describe revision is about *vocabulary*, suggesting that they "understand the revision process as a rewording activity" (para. 9). How is that different from the way she argues that revision *should* be understood?

2. Is it important that Sommers elected to identify her two groups of writers as *student* and *experienced* writers rather than as, for example, *novice* and *professional* writers? What alternative terms might *you* choose to identify these groups? Do the terms make a difference?

3. In her introduction and in analyzing students' descriptions of revision, Sommers focuses quite a lot on the difference between speech and writing. In your words, what is she saying that difference is between the two, and why is this difference relevant to how we understand revision?

4. In paragraph 19, Sommers writes that for experienced writers, revision is "a process of more than communication; they are a part of the process of *discovering meaning* altogether." What does she seem to mean by "discovering meaning"? How is "discovering meaning" different from "communication"?

Does Sommers's emphasis on writing as an act of making meaning relate to anything else you've encountered in this book?

5. What do you think Sommers means when she says that for experienced writers, revision is based on a non-linear theory in which a sense of the whole writing both precedes and grows out of an examination of the parts? What does she mean by "the whole writing"? What does it mean for writing processes to be non-linear (not a straight line of progress from beginning to end)? And why do you think that experienced writers see writing as non-linear but student writers tend to see writing as linear (pre-write → write → edit)?

6. One of the experienced writers that Sommers interviews talks about having an "editing generator" and an "idea generator." What do you think that means? Can you think about your own writing experiences and identify any kinds of mental "generators" that help you come up with ideas, edit, etc.? If you haven't had the experience of an "idea generator," why do you think that is?

7. Sommers's research, she says, makes her believe that student revision practices don't reflect a *lack* of engagement, "but rather that they do what they have been taught to do in a consistently narrow and predictable way" (para. 14). Where do you think students got the idea that they should see writing as transcribing and revising as changing words? Does this match what you have been taught about writing and revising? If not, what has been different in your experience?

8. In the closing lines of her article, Sommers asserts that "good writing disturbs; it creates dissonance." What does that mean? Do you think that is always true? Can you think of good writing that *doesn't* disturb, create dissonance, or try to resist other ideas? Sommers is really making a claim about what counts as "good" writing. How does her definition here of good writing compare to those of other scholars you've read in this book? How does it compare to your own idea of good writing?

9. Sommers contrasts writing with a "predefined meaning" (para. 19) versus "writing as discovery" (para. 23). How are these two understandings of writing different? Why does she claim that these are opposing? What does writing as discovery seem to allow that writing with a predefined meaning doesn't? Can you think of examples where you've done each? Was one kind of experience better than the other?

Applying and Exploring Ideas

1. Create a one- to two-paragraph summary of Sommers's report on what student writers say about revision, gathering up her main points about what the students she interviewed thought about revision. Then compare it with your own ideas about revision. How much do these students sound like you? Where your ideas about revision sound different, do they sound more like the professional writers' ideas, or like something else altogether?

2. Sommers begins her article by looking at research by Rohman and Wlecke and Britton that imagines writing as happening in linear *stages*. By the end of her article, she describes research suggesting that writers seem to be concerned with most stages of writing (coming up with ideas, composing text, revising ideas, editing, etc.) all at the same time (see para. 22). Explain each of these views and then argue for one of these views (or a combination of the two) that best explains how you write.

3. Look up the word *recursive* and get a sense of its various definitions. Based on that, and about how you typically think about writing, write an explanation for the class of why writing is a recursive activity. Then stop and think: How is *your* typical writing process *actually* recursive? What does that recursivity look like in your own writing?

4. Sommers identifies four "levels of change" in revision: word, phrase, sentence, and theme — "the extended statement of one idea" (by which she seems to mean, when a single sentence doesn't express a "complete thought" but rather when a couple or several sentences or even a paragraph are required to express an idea). Find two pieces of writing you've completed recently which you revised before submitting, and examine what you actually changed between the first draft and the last. Do you see any changes that aren't accounted for by Sommers's four levels — any levels "higher" than theme, or different from *sentence structure* (which basically contains all her levels)? Write a report on your analysis that focuses specifically on this question.

- -

META MOMENT   Can you think of things you can do, and ways you can imagine writing differently, so that you revise more like an experienced writer and less like the student writers in Sommers's study?

- -

WRITING ABOUT PROCESSES: WRITING ASSIGNMENTS

To help you learn and explore the ideas in this chapter, we are suggesting three assignment options for larger writing projects: Autoethnography, Portrait of a Writer, and Writer's Process Search.

AUTOETHNOGRAPHY

For this assignment, you will conduct a study similar to those conducted by Perl, Neto, and Berkenkotter, but instead of looking at someone else, you will examine yourself and your own writing processes and write an autoethnography in which you describe them. Your method will be to record (preferably with video and audio) your complete writing process as you complete a writing assignment for a class. Your purpose is to try to learn some things about your actual writing practices that you might not be aware of and to reflect on what you learn using the terms and concepts you've read about in this chapter.

Determining Your Object of Study and Collecting Data   To make this assignment as useful as possible, you need to plan ahead, so figure out what you will be writing for this or other classes in the next few weeks, and make a decision about what you will study. Consider the following:

- What kinds of assignments are easiest or most difficult for you to write?
- What kinds of assignments would be the most useful to examine yourself writing?

Before beginning your project, make sure that you know how to use your computer or other device's audio and/or video recording programs.

As you write the assignment that you will study, record yourself every time that you work on it — this includes even times when you are thinking and planning for it, or when you are revising. Keep the following in mind:

- You may not be near your recording device(s) when you are planning; if that is the case, then keep a log in which you note your thoughts about the assignment.
- When you sit down to type the paper, think out loud the entire time. This will feel strange, and it will take some effort. Do your best.
- Try to externalize everything you are thinking. If you have trouble knowing what to say, go back to Perl and to Berkenkotter and look at the kinds of things that Tony and Donald Murray said aloud when they were being studied.

When you have completely finished writing the assignment whose writing process you're studying, listen to or view the recording of yourself and transcribe it. This means typing everything that you said on the tape, even the "ums" and "ahs." It will be helpful to double space (or even triple space) the transcript so that you can make notes on it, if you plan to do so by hand. You might also find Track Changes or its equivalent useful for note-taking as you transcribe.

Analyzing Your Data Alone or with your class, as your teacher directs, come up with a code to help you study your transcript. To see how to make a code, return to Berkenkotter, Neto, or Perl for their descriptions of how they came up with their codes. To consider what categories or elements of writing process you might want to include in your code, look back through the readings you've done in this chapter. What did the various authors choose to study about people's writing processes? Some suggestions for things you might include would be notes about context (where and when you wrote, what distractions you faced, your attitude, any deadlines, etc.), codes for planning, brainstorming, large-scale revision, small-scale revision, pausing, and so on.

What you want is a code that will help you understand what's happening when you write. Beware of the following potential pitfalls:

- If the code is too vague, you won't learn anything at all.
- If the code is too detailed (for example, if you try to do what Perl did and record the exact amount of time you took for each action), you might never get done coding.

We recommend coming up with a code with the rest of your class, and then trying to use that code on a practice transcript that your teacher provides. This will help you see if the code is useful.

Once you have settled on a code, use it to analyze your transcript.

- You might get a box of highlighters of different colors, and use each color to highlight the parts of the text that correspond to parts of the code (for example, pink is for planning).
- You could simply underline parts of the transcript and label them in shorthand (P = planning).
- If you used a computer, you could search for key phrases in the text and mark each occurrence by using the software's "reviewing" feature to insert a comment in the margin.
- You could use free or low-cost coding and data analysis software such as Dedoose to upload your transcript and label different parts of it with codes you input, which allows you to generate helpful visualizations of how your various codes interact with the data.

Once you have coded the transcript, go back and consider these questions:

- What is interesting about what you found? What immediately jumps out at you?

- Did you do some things a lot, and other things rarely or never? Which codes do you see frequently or little at all?

- How does your analysis suggest you compare with Tony or with Murray?

Like some of the authors in this chapter, you might make some charts or tables for yourself in order to visually explore what percentage of time you spent on various activities.

Planning and Drafting   What are you going to write about? You don't need to go into excruciating detail about everything you coded. Instead, you should decide what you want to claim about what you found. For example:

- How would you describe your writing process?

- What are the most important take-home points from your analysis?

- Are there aspects of your process that are definitively impacted by technologies like instant messaging, social networking, Skype, or even word-processing?

Based on the patterns that emerge from your analysis of data, decide what your claims will be and then return to your analysis to select data that give evidence of those claims.

By now, from discussions in class and with your teacher you should have a sense of what genre you'll write your report in, and in deciding that, you should know your audience, purpose, and exigence as well. Will you write about your findings in an informal reflective essay in which you discuss your process and compare yourself to some of the writers in the chapter — something like Sommers does in "I Stand Here Writing" (p. 212) — or write a more formal, researched argument like Perl, Neto, or Berkenkotter did, using an intro/background/methods/analysis/discussion structure? Or will you write in some other genre?

You'll definitely want to plan your genre before you begin drafting, since your drafting processes will vary by genre. If you are writing the reflective essay, you are most likely writing for yourself (writing to learn) and to share what you learn with fellow student writers and your teacher, for the purpose of improving your writing processes and abilities. Such reflection is often best "drafted toward" by knowing the main claims you want to make and striking out on your writing, understanding that you'll be discovering and learning along the way and will probably revise extensively in order to reach a consistent message from beginning to ending of your piece.

If you will be writing a more scholarly research article, you might begin by outlining the various sections of your paper: In your introduction, what other research will you cite? Whose work provides important background information for your study? What is the gap or niche that your study fills? How will you describe your research methods? What are the main claims you want to make in the findings? One trick that some writers use is to write headings for each section, with main claims underneath. Then the writer can go back and write one section at a time in order to break up the writing.

Once you have a "shitty first draft," revise it to make it a little more coherent. Then share it with classmates, being sure to tell them what genre you wrote and what concerns or issues you'd like them to read for.

What Makes It Good? The purpose of this assignment was for you to try to learn some things about your actual writing practices that you might not have been aware of, and to reflect on what you learned using the terms and concepts you've read about in this chapter. Does your paper demonstrate that this purpose was achieved? In addition, your readers will want to learn something from having read your paper. Does your finished text clearly convey your insights and findings?

A caveat: We have found that some students just go through the motions when they complete this assignment, but don't make an attempt to learn something about themselves as writers. When those students write their papers, they have very little to say about "results" or "insights." They tend to say pretty clichéd things like "I am distracted when I write. I should try to write with fewer distractions." In general, if the "insights" of the paper were obvious to you before you ever conducted the autoethnography, then you have not fully engaged in the project and are unlikely to receive a good grade on it.

Alternative Assignment Instead of studying yourself writing one assignment, compare yourself writing two very different kinds of texts (maybe in school and out of school, or humanities and science) and analyze them to see whether — or how — your process changes depending on what you're writing.

PORTRAIT OF A WRITER

The various authors in this chapter clearly believe that good writing takes hard work and multiple drafts, and that many of us are hampered from being better writers by the "rules" and misconceptions we have been taught about writing.

This is true even of very famous people who write a lot every day. For example, U.S. Supreme Court Justice Sonia Sotomayor has been widely criticized for her writing. She even criticizes herself, saying, "Writing remains a challenge for me even today — everything I write goes through multiple drafts — I am not a natural writer."[1]

---

[1]Gerstein, Josh. "Sotomayor: Writing a Challenge 'even today.'" *POLITICO*, 4 June 2009, www.politico.com /blogs/under-the-radar/2009/06/sotomayor-writing-a-challenge-even-today-018902.

Here she conflates being a "good" writer with being a "natural" writer; she seems to believe that some people are born good writers and some people aren't. Her conception is that a "good" writer only has to write one draft; anyone who has to write multiple drafts must be a "bad" writer. Even from this one short quotation, you can see that Justice Sotomayor's conceptions of writing are limiting and would not hold up if closely examined by the researchers and professional writers in this chapter.

Use what you have read in this unit to consider the story you have to tell about yourself as a writer. How do you see yourself as a writer? Is that self-perception helping you be the best writer you can be? The purpose of this assignment is for you to apply what you have learned in this chapter to help you better understand why and how you write — and how you might write differently.

Brainstorming and Planning Try the following to generate material for your assignment:

- Go back to the discussion and activity questions you completed as you read the articles in this chapter. What did you learn about yourself and your writing processes here?
- Consider what you write and don't write.
- Consider how you prepare — or don't prepare — to write a paper.
- Think of any kinds of writing that you enjoy, and any kinds of writing that you dread.
- Freewrite about the writing rules that block you, and the writing rules that aid you.
- Make a list of all the metaphors or similes about writing and revision that you and your friends use.

You should spend a substantial amount of time reflecting on yourself as a writer, using the concepts and ideas that you learned in this chapter. Even if some or most of your brainstorming doesn't end up in your paper, the act of reflecting should be useful to you as a writer.

Looking at all the notes and freewriting from your brainstorming so far, consider what's interesting here. What catches your interest the most? What is new or surprising to you? Settle on a few of these surprises or "aha!" moments as the core of what you will write for this assignment. For each of these core elements of your essay, brainstorm examples, details, and explanations that would help your reader understand what you are trying to explain about yourself.

Drafting and Revising Write a three- to five-page essay in which you describe your view of yourself as a writer, using examples and explanations to strengthen your description. As appropriate, you might refer to the authors of texts in this chapter to help explain your experiences, processes, or feelings. Conclude the essay by considering how or whether the things you've learned in this chapter might change your conception of yourself as a writer or your writing behaviors. Your class should discuss potential audiences for this essay:

- Are you writing to the teacher, to demonstrate what you've learned in this chapter?
- Are you writing for yourself, to help solidify what you've learned?
- Would you like to adapt your essay to write for someone else — maybe your parents, to demonstrate who you are as a writer and what influences you can identify? Maybe to a teacher who had an impact, positive or negative, on who you are as a writer?

Of course, this choice of audience and purpose will have a significant impact on your essay — its form, content, tone, language, level of formality, and so on. You might also talk with your teacher about more creative ways to paint your self-portrait:

- Try writing a play outlining your writing process.
- Transform a metaphor about writing into a visual description — for example, a collage — of who you are as a writer or what you think "good writing" is.
- Create a hypertext essay where readers can look at pictures, watch video, listen to songs, even listen to your own voice, as you describe yourself and your conceptions of writers, the writing process, and "good writing."

Try to get readers for your piece as early in your composing process as possible, and use their feedback on their reading experience to revise for the most reader-friendly document possible. Pay particular attention to whether your readers seem to be experiencing all the ideas you want them to — or whether some of what you want to say is clear in your thoughts but not in what you've composed.

What Makes It Good?   The purpose of this assignment is for you to step back and consider yourself as a writer, applying what you learned in this chapter to help you better understand why and how you write — and how you might write differently, or perhaps even understand yourself differently as a writer. When you've finished it, ask yourself:

- Were you able to apply what you learned in this chapter to understand yourself better? (If not, that will likely show up in the depth of your writing.)
- Did you successfully identify an audience for your piece and write appropriately for those readers?

WRITER'S PROCESS SEARCH

We hope the readings in this chapter have raised some questions for you about how professional writers might go about writing every day, and what language they might choose to talk about and describe writing. It is tempting to offer an assignment where you go find a handful of writers and interview them on their processes and ideas about writing, and then write the results. (And you should feel free to discuss such a project with your teacher if that's interesting to you.) But as it turns out, there are a number of venues where other researchers and reporters *already have* done these sorts of interviews, and posted them in online archives.

The presence of these archives provides the basis for this assignment option: Establish a research question on some aspect of writing process (for example, "Where do professional writers get their ideas?" or "How do professional writers talk about revision?"), and mine the interview archives we list below (and any others you might be aware of or come across in your own reading) seeking writers' accounts that relate to and can help answer your research question. Synthesize whatever commentary you find into a report on your question: What do professional writers of various kinds have to say about the aspect of writing you're wondering about? That is your focus in researching and writing this piece. We call it a "writer's process search" because you'll be searching these interview archives for data (interviews) that address your question(s) on writing processes.

Getting to Know the Archives Your first task in this project will be to familiarize yourself with the data resources available to you. We present here four repositories of interviews with writers. Certainly, more such repositories exist, which you might find with some good Internet searching, but we know these will give you a good start. Together they include interviews from literary writers, other professional writers, playwrights and screenwriters, songwriters, journalists, and research writers. Most take a question-and-answer (Q&A) format with their interview subjects. When used together with a resource like Wikipedia (since many of the people interviewed are likely to have a Wikipedia page) to gain richer background on the interviewees, these archives create a rich repository of professionally recognized writers talking about writing in their own words.

The New York Times — Books, "Writers on Writing"
nytimes.com/books/specials/writers.html

Unlike the other archives we're pointing you to, in the *Times* column "Writers on Writing," the writers were not interviewed; rather, they wrote short essays on some topic related to writing, which were then published in the *Times*. What you'll find at this site, then, are writers — from Joyce Carol Oates, Saul Bellow, Barbara Kingslover to Chitra Divakaruni, David Mamet, and Susan Sontag — writing on a full range of subjects — what makes a good novel, taking a break from writing in order to have more to say (Richard Ford), selecting music for writing (Edmund White), handwriting (Mary Gordon), the relationship between writing and living (Gish Jen), how running assists writing (Joyce Carol Oates), or the role of rewriting in writing (Susan Sontag). Because each essay is thematic, this isn't the place where a single writer will have a wide-ranging discussion on many different aspects of writing process. As is the case with most of these archives, it's easier to search by author than by subject, so you'll need to schedule enough time just to read what's there and make good notes about where you found particular information so that you can locate it again later. On the upside, most of the articles were written between 1999 and 2001 and thus don't require a *New York Times* subscription to access. When you find one that touches on your area of inquiry, it will be a rich source of information about a writer's words on the subject of writing.

Songwriters on Process
songwritersonprocess.com

This website contains an archive of interviews with songwriting musicians. The interviews are conducted by site author Benjamin Opipari, who asks questions of the writers about "their creative process, from beginning to end." Opipari demonstrates an eclectic taste in interview subjects, having spoken with songwriters as diverse as Chris Difford from Squeeze to Neil Finn of Crowded House to Bechtolt and Evans of YACHT and Cohen and Emm of Tanlines. A wide range of other genres are represented as well. The interviews tend to focus on the process by which songwriters get ideas for lyrics and music, and how they move those ideas along to become finished songs. Typical questions include "When it comes to the songwriting process, how do you feel about inspiration?," "How disciplined are you as a songwriter?," and "How much revision do you do to your lyrics?" Readers can learn a lot about songwriting simply by reading the interviews, but they're also good for zooming in on particular aspects of the writing process. The site is arranged by the name of the interviewee and their band, and the format for interviews (with questions bolded and short) makes any given interview easy to glance through to get a sense of subjects covered.

The Paris Review, "Interviews"
theparisreview.org/interviews

The Paris Review is a journal of literary writing (fiction, poetry, and essays) that also publishes some literary criticism. Founded in 1953, it began running interviews with contemporary writers a year later — and it has done so every year for the ensuing sixty years, running more than half a dozen per year. The site is searchable by author or by decade. You'll find interviews with Maya Angelou, Margaret Atwood, Ray Bradbury, Philip Larkin, Doris Lessing, Edna O'Brien, Walker Percy . . . the list is immense, and the range of genres represented is complete (fiction, poetry, plays, essays, journalism), though many of the interviewees are novelists. These interviews are often conducted as public events with audiences, which may influence the responses the writers offer to questions. As with other interview archive sites, this one will be difficult to search by subject — but because of its arrangement by time, it might be especially useful for questions related to change in writing process through time (for example, how processes change as writing technologies do).

The New York Times, "*Why I Write: Q&A with Seven* Times *Journalists.*"
*learning.blogs.nytimes.com/2011/10/17/why-i-write-q-and-a-with-seven
-times-journalists/*

Different from the other three archive sites, this "Learning Network" blog post in the *Times* focused narrowly on a short list of journalists writing for the *Times*, covering a range of story types, and asked each the same questions. The occasion of these interviews was the 2011 "National Day on Writing" (created by the National Council of Teachers of English). Among other questions, each of the writers (such as Web producer Jeffery Delviscio, Styles writer Simone Oliver, and sportswriter Pete Thamel) responded to how they became a reporter, what outside forces influence their writing, what their writing process looks like, and why they write. The whole set of interviews can be read in about half an hour, and is extremely valuable for seeing less famous but very professional writers talk in down-to-earth ways about how they experience writing.

Brainstorming and Selecting a Research Question Explore each of these sites, familiarizing yourself with which writers have been interviewed by each source and considering the best ways to search the sites for material specifically related to the research question you'll choose.

Once you've read some interviews at each site in order to get your inquiry juices flowing, you should be considering what question you might like to focus your project on.

- Did you see something a given writer was talking about that you'd like to investigate further?
- Is there some "writer's problem" such as writer's block or coming up with what to write about that you'd like to find how professional writers deal with?
- Is there a larger aspect of writing process, such as revision, that you'd like to see how various writers talk about?
- Is there some subject related to writing, such as what role music can play during the writing process, that you're curious about?
- Are you seeing trends related to the kind of writing that a person does? For example, do songwriters think about process differently than journalists?
- Do writing technologies come up at all? If so, are there trends across time, genre, or type of writer?

While the focus of your particular question may be somewhat challenging to settle on, given the variety of information in the archives, it's very likely that some of these writers will have discussed your question, whatever it turns out to be. Notice that the broader your question, the more quickly you're likely to find interviews related to it; however, a very broad question might be difficult to write about because of its breadth.

Collecting and Analyzing Data   Once you have settled on a research question, you'll need to begin searching the interview archives to find a set of interviews that touch on your subject of inquiry. You will collect a number of these interviews and begin considering and synthesizing what various writers say about your question.

First you will need a plan for searching the interview archives. There are a number of approaches you could take:

- You could choose which interviews to look at based on your interest in the authors themselves. For example, you could make a list of all the authors names you already recognize in a given archive and choose all those to read; you could also briefly familiarize yourself with authors by searching their names in Wikipedia.

- You could do a "brute-force" search by opening a large number of interviews and using your browser's "Find in page" function (Ctrl-F) to search for keywords related to your subject of inquiry. This method lets you determine in just a second or two whether your subject term appears in the interview, and takes you directly to it in the page if it does. You could easily search fifty to sixty interviews per hour using this method.

- You could select interviews based on a Google search. For example, if your question is on the role of music in the composing process and you want to see which *Paris Review* interviews have landed on the subject of music, you can type *music "paris review" interview* into the search bar and Google will return a list of all the *Paris Review* interviews it finds that term in. (Of course, you will also find a million other unrelated hits. If you use this method, be sure to include the title words of your archive in quotation marks to force Google to return hits only on that specific title rather than on any combination of words from the title.)

- You could always simply read randomly, and if you have five or six hours over a few days to devote to your research, this approach (which relies on what researchers call *serendipity*) might be a very good one, especially combined with one of the other approaches. The interviews are relatively short, quick reads, interesting in and of themselves, and you could cover quite a lot of ground simply by giving yourself some time to be curious and read actively.

You'll also need to decide which archives are the best fit for your research question. You'll find some overlap between *The New York Times — Books* interviews and *Paris Review* interviews but very little overlap in the others.

Once you have a stack of interviews that seem to touch on your subject of inquiry in some way, you'll analyze that data the same way that you do in many of the other projects in this book:

- Watch for patterns that emerge — What gets said repeatedly? — but also be prepared for there to be no pattern. If writers disagree or do things in wildly different ways, that is just as much a finding as discovering that there are similarities across writers. Writing is a very individual process, so finding only one pattern might be difficult. You might also see several patterns — people might do A, B, or C rather than mostly doing A.

- Watch for outliers: Is there something that very few of the writers say? When someone does say this thing, is it striking or unusual in comparison to the emerging patterns?

- Look closely at details in language. When a writer refers to revision as "polishing" versus referring to it as "honing," for example, the terms engage different metaphors for writing that show different assumptions about its nature and how it works.

- Compare what you're reading with your own experience: Compared with your own writing experiences, what are these writers saying that sounds "normal" and what are they saying that sounds unusual to you?

Again as in other projects requiring analysis of observations or a corpus of textual data, take careful notes to keep track of the patterns and interesting ideas you're seeing, and after you've reviewed your interviews at least twice, step back and see what you have to say on your question. Now might also be a good time to do more general Web searching to see if other people have written and commented on the question you're working on.

Planning, Drafting, and Revising Ultimately, you should emerge from your data analysis with some key points to make in your Writer's Process Search report. The purpose of the project has been to discover what professional writers of various kinds have to say about the aspect of writing you're studying; the purpose of your report is to present your findings in a readable and interesting way to your classmates and instructor (or to another audience that you and your teacher might agree upon).

It might be most natural to arrange this piece in typical social-science research-report fashion, where you introduce your subject of inquiry and research question using Swales's CARS model (in Chapter 1, p. 21), detail the archive reviews you used and explain the methods by which you searched them, walk readers through the data you found and how you analyzed it, discuss what you found, and conclude with implications from your study: How do the findings of your study help us?

However, instead of using the typical social-science research report format, you might also leave your imagination open to other ways of making this report. Here are some of many possibilities that you should discuss with your classmates and teacher:

- Combine the interview subjects with similar ideas into one "composite" interview. Margaret Kantz does something like this in "Helping Students Use Textual Sources Persuasively" in Chapter 4 (p. 579). In this way, you might create several "characters" who articulate the main ideas espoused by a number of the writers whose interviews you read. You could also consider drafting some friends to play these characters and produce a short documentary.

- Dramatize your findings through a song, poem, or play. This might be especially relevant if you drew on the songwriters' database.

- Create a hypertext that includes additional background information on the writers whose interviews you used and link back to the interviews themselves.

- Create a (somewhat long) tweet-stream that reduces your findings to 140-character sayings.

Whatever genre and modality you write in, expect to use a fair amount of quotation from the interviews themselves in your piece. Remember, what the interviewees said is your data, and your readers need to be able to see examples of your data in order to judge for themselves how much sense the conclusions that you're drawing from the data make. Quotations from the interviews will become your *reasons* for making the claims you do about your subject of inquiry.

Revise, as always, by getting reader feedback on how much sense the piece makes, how readable it is (in terms of flow and organization, clarity of statements of ideas, and editing quality), and what would improve their experience of the piece.

What Makes It Good?   The best versions of this project will do the following:

- Make a clear point or series of points about your subject of inquiry (in answer to your research question).

- Explain your research question and the sources of it precisely and clearly.

- Use a creative and reliable method of searching the archives.

- Balance use of quotations as examples with analysis of quotations. (They don't speak for themselves; you need to explain what's important about them or what they convey.)

- Report findings in a manner consistent with the genre/modality you've chosen to write in, hopefully being no less interesting and entertaining than the interviews themselves.

GLOSSARY

ACTIVITY SYSTEM In his 1997 article "Rethinking Genre in School and Society: An Activity Theory Analysis," David Russell describes an *activity system* as "any ongoing, object-directed, historically conditioned, dialectically structured, tool-mediated human interaction." In simpler terms, an *activity system* consists of a group of people who act together over time as they work toward a specific goal. The people in the system use many kinds of tools, both physical (like computers or books) and symbolic (like words), to do their work together. The group's behaviors and traditions are influenced by *their* history, and when one aspect of the system changes, other aspects of it change in response.

ACTIVITY THEORY *Activity theory* "was originally a psychological theory that sees all aspects of activity as shaped by people's social interactions with each other and the tools [including writing and language] that they use" (p. 395). In Chapter 3, Kain and Wardle explain the concept further: "The most basic activity theory lens, or unit of analysis, is the activity system, defined as a group of people who share a common object and motive over time, as well as the wide range of tools they use together to act on that object and realize that motive. David Russell (1997) describes an activity system as 'any ongoing, object-directed, historically conditioned, dialectically structured, tool-mediated human interaction'" (p. 398).

APPRENTICESHIP *Apprenticeship* is a term used to describe the relationship between a master and a student, or a mentor and a mentee, in which the student or mentee undergoes training in order to become an expert in a profession or group.

In his 1998 book, *Communities of Practice,* Etienne Wenger argues that apprentices move from peripheral participation to more central participation in a group as they become engaged with and more skilled at the group's practices. (See also **community of practice**.)

ARGUMENT *Argument* can describe any of the many ways by means of which people try to convince others of something.

Mathematically, arguments are the individual propositions of a proof. In a legal context, formal arguments are used to persuade a judge or jury to rule in favor of a particular position. In everyday use, or on talk radio or cable news shows, arguments tend to consist of people yelling at each other but rarely convincing or being convinced. We call all these forms of argument *agonistic,* meaning that they pit people against each other in a win/lose contest.

In an *intellectual* or *academic* context, argument is *inquiry-based* or *conversational,* and it describes the attempt to *build knowledge* by questioning existing knowledge and proposing alternatives. Rather than aiming simply to show who is right or wrong, inquiry-based argument aims to *cooperatively find the best explanation* for whatever is in question.

AUDIENCE   An *audience* is anyone who hears or reads a text — but it is also anyone a writer *imagines* encountering his or her text. This means that there is a difference between *intended* or "invoked" audience and *actual* or "addressed" audience.

For example, when Aristotle composed *On Rhetoric* in about 350 BCE, his intended audience was his students, and for a time they were also his actual audience. (We would also call them his *primary* audience, the ones who first encountered his text.) Today, Aristotle's actual audience — the people who read him in coursepacks, on iPads, and on Kindles — are *secondary* audiences for Aristotle's work.

AUTHORITY   An *authority* is an accepted source, an expert, or a person with power or credibility. *Authority* (as an abstract noun) connotes confidence and self-assurance.

In this book, the term is generally used to refer to people who understand the **conventions** or accepted practices of a **discourse community** and thus are able to speak, write, or act with credibility and confidence. A writer's **ethos** is based in part on his or her authority.

AUTHORSHIP   To "author" a text is to create or originate it; the *authorship* of a text then is a question of *who* created or originated it. Most traditional Western notions of authorship presume that **originality** is one key component of authorship.

The term is seen by some scholars as problematic if it assumes *sole* authorship — invention by just one person — because it seems to discount the importance of social interaction and the fact that virtually every idea we can have already draws from other ideas authored by other people. The question becomes, where do we draw the line on who has authored what? For a related discussion, see **plagiarism**.

AUTOBIOGRAPHY   Literally, *autobiography* is writing about one's own life. ("Auto" = self, "bio" = life, and "graphy" = writing.) The **genre** of autobiography is a book-length text containing a retrospective account of the author's life.

More broadly, *autobiographical* means simply about, or having to do with, one's own life. Donald Murray and others contend that all writing is autobiographical — that is, that one's writing always has some connection to one's own life and that a writer can never completely remove all traces of her life from her writing.

AUTOETHNOGRAPHY   *Autoethnography* is an **ethnography**, or cultural study, of one's own experiences and interaction with the world.

CARS ("CREATE A RESEARCH SPACE") MODEL   The *CARS model* is based on John Swales's description of the three typical "moves" made in the introductions to academic research articles (for more, see Chapter 1). Swales conducted an analysis of research articles in many disciplines and discovered that most introductions in all disciplines do the following:

1. establish a territory (by describing the topic of study);

2. establish a niche (by explaining the problem, gap, or question that prompted the current study); and

3. occupy the niche (by describing the answer to the question or problem, and/or outlining what will be done in the article).

CASE STUDIES *Case studies* are detailed observations and analyses of an event, situation, individual, or small group of people. Case study research, according to Mary Sue MacNealy in her book *Strategies for Empirical Research in Writing,* refers to "a carefully designed project to systematically collect information about an event, situation, or small group of persons or objects for the purpose of exploring, describing, and/or explaining aspects not previously known or considered" (197). Case studies are considered to be qualitative research.

CLAIM A *claim* is an assertion that a writer tries to convince his or her readers of. An example might be "*Wired* magazine is great." To believe or accept a claim, readers need to know the *reasons* why a writer believes the claim or wants readers to accept it — saying, for example, "*Wired* includes really interesting articles about people in the technological world." Readers may also need *evidence* to believe the claim or its reasons, such as "Every month *Wired* has several stories that interview the people who invented netbooks, the iPhone, cloud computing, and the most cutting-edge technological innovations."

COGNITION *Cognition* describes anything having to do with *thought* or *mental activity.*

In Writing Studies, *cognitive* and *cognition* have to do with the internal thinking processes that writers use to write. Scholars in this field have contrasted the *internal, private, personal* nature of cognition with the *social* aspects of writing — that is, with the writer's *external* interactions with their surroundings, culture, and audience. A great deal of research about cognition in Writing Studies was conducted in the 1980s and sought to find and describe the mental processes that writers use to solve problems related to writing.

COMMUNITY OF PRACTICE *Community of practice* is a term coined by sociologists Jean Lave and Etienne Wenger to describe groups of people who participate in a shared activity or activities. In his 1998 book, *Communities of Practice,* Wenger argues that participating in a community of practice also involves "constructing *identities* in relation to these communities" (4).

This term is similar to, but not exactly the same as, the terms **activity system** and **discourse community**, discussed in Chapter 3.

COMPOSITION *Composition* is the process of designing a text and its ideas ("I'm composing my paper") or the product of that design process ("I got an A on that composition"). Writing scholar Paul Prior divides writing into two separate acts, **composition** and **inscription**, where *composing* is designing a text and its ideas, and *inscribing* is using tools and media to set the text on some object.

Composition sums up the first three rhetorical canons of *invention* (coming up with ideas, from memory or from research), *arrangement* (determining the line of reasoning or the flow of ideas in the text), and *style* (fine-tuning expressive choices of language and sentence syntax to best suit the text to its **exigence, audience,** and **context**). One of the unique powers of writing is that *inscription* is often an aid to *composition*: When you do many kinds of writing, the act of inscribing is itself often giving you new ideas — that is, helping you compose.

CONCEPTION A *conception* is a belief about or understanding of something, with the same root as the term *concept,* meaning "something conceived," or an idea formed in the mind. A "conception" is the way in which you perceive or regard a thing. For example, one "conception of writing" might be that "writing typically requires revision."

CONSTRAINTS *Constraints* are factors that limit or otherwise influence the persuasive strategies available to the rhetor. More precisely, in "Rhetorical Situations and Their Constituents," Keith Grant-Davie defines constraints as "all factors in the situation, aside from the rhetor and the audience, that may lead the audience to be either more or less sympathetic to the discourse, and that may therefore influence the rhetor's response to the situation" (p. 500).

CONSTRUCT (conSTRUCT, CONstruct) *Construct,* the verb (pronounced conSTRUCT), means *to build or to put together* ("con" = with, and "struct" = shape or frame). By turning the verb into a noun (pronounced CONstruct), we make the word mean, literally, *a thing that has been constructed.* In everyday use, we use the noun *CONstruct* only in the realm of *ideas or concepts.* The ideas of *freedom, justice, wealth,* and *politics,* for example, are all constructs, or ideas that we have *built up* over time.

What is important to remember about constructs is that, while they may seem to be "natural" or "inevitable," they're actually unchallenged **claims** that can be questioned, contested, redefined, or reinvented.

CONTEXT Literally, a *context* is the substructure for a woven fabric ("con" = with/together, "text" = weaving, fabric). In Writing Studies, *context* typically refers to where a text comes from or where it appears. (A *written work* first started being called a *text* because it's "woven" from words in the same way that *textiles* are woven from threads.) Contexts can consist of other text(s) as well as the circumstances or setting in which a text was created — for example, various contexts for the statement "We hold these truths to be self-evident" include the Declaration of Independence, the meeting of the Continental Congress in spring and summer of 1776, and the broader socio-historical environment that describes pre–Revolutionary War America.

CONTINGENT One of the claims of this book is that meaning is *contingent;* that is, it depends. In other words, meaning is conditional. For example, "good writing" depends upon the context, purpose, and audience. Ideas about meaning as being contingent and conditional are taken up most directly in Chapter 4, where authors claim that meaning depends on context and that principles for good communication depend on the specific situation and are not universal.

CONTRIBUTE, CONTRIBUTION In academic contexts, one makes a *contribution* by adding to an ongoing conversation on a given research subject, issue, problem, or question.

In Writing Studies, *contribution* is commonly discussed in terms of Kenneth Burke's *parlor metaphor,* where Burke describes scholarship as an ongoing conversation at a party: You arrive late and other guests are already in conversation; you join one conversation by listening for a while and then, once you have something to add, making a contribution to the conversation; after a time, you join another conversation, while the first one continues without you.

CONVENTIONS In Writing Studies, writing is understood to be governed by *conventions* — that is, agreements among people about the best ways to accomplish particular tasks (such as starting new paragraphs, or citing sources, or deciding how to punctuate sentences). That people have to come to agreements about such questions means that there is no "natural" or pre-existing way to accomplish the tasks; rather, people simply agreed to do *A* rather than *B.* Tabbing the first line of a paragraph one-half inch is a convention; ending sentences with periods is a convention; citing sources in parentheses is a convention, as are parentheses themselves.

Conventions are a kind of **construct**, and like constructs, they can be questioned, challenged, and changed, if key decision makers agree to alter them or to establish another convention in their place.

CORPUS (ANALYSIS)   A *corpus analysis* is a detailed examination of a collection or *corpus* of related texts, phrases, utterances, etc. (*Corpus* means "body" — the word *corpse* also derives from it.) For example, John Swales conducted a *corpus analysis* of academic writing to discover how people in various fields introduce their research.

CREATE A RESEARCH SPACE MODEL: see *CARS ("Create a Research Space") model*

DISCOURSE/DISCOURSE   At its most basic, *discourse* is *language in action*, or language being used to accomplish something. Discourse can describe either an instance of language (e.g., "His discourse was terse and harsh") or a collection of instances that all demonstrate some quality (e.g., "Legal discourse tries to be very precise"). Because groups of people united by some activity tend to develop a characteristic discourse, we can talk about communities that are identified *by* their discourse — thus, **discourse community**.

James Paul Gee uses *Discourse* with an uppercase D to differentiate his specialized meaning of the term.

DISCOURSE COMMUNITY   Scholars continue to debate the meaning of *discourse community*, as the selections in this book suggest. For the sake of simplicity, we will use John Swales's definition from his 1990 book, *Genre Analysis: English in Academic and Research Settings*. According to Swales, a *discourse community* is made up of individuals who share common goals agreed upon by most members; further, it has "mechanisms of intercommunication among its members," "uses its participatory mechanisms primarily to provide information and feedback," has and uses "one or more genres" that help the group achieve its shared goals, "has acquired some specific lexis," and has "a reasonable ratio" of "novices and experts" (24–27).

ECOLOGY   An *ecology* is, literally, the interactions among groups of living things and their environments (and the scientific study of those interactions). More broadly, "ecology" has come to refer to any network of relationships among beings and their material surroundings. In **rhetorical** terms, ecology refers to the web of relationships and interactions between all the rhetors and all the material in a **rhetorical situation**. Like other meanings of *ecology*, it is difficult to define the boundaries of a rhetorical ecology because elements in an ecology will also connect to elements outside the ecology.

EDITING   *Editing* is the correction of minor errors in a written text. Editing usually comes at the end of the writing process. It should not be confused with **revision**, which involves major rethinking, rewriting, and restructuring of texts.

EMBODIED, EMBODIMENT   Rhetorical interaction happens with, to, and by beings with material bodies. The term *embodiment* reminds us that such interaction is **contingent** on the bodies that give it shape. It is easy to assume that rhetorical interaction is simply ideas worked on mentally apart from bodies; when we look for how rhetorical interaction is *embodied*, we remember that the interaction depends on material bodies as well as ideas.

ENCULTURATE   A newcomer *enculturates* when he or she learns to become a part of a group or "culture" (including an **activity system**, **discourse community**, or **community**

of practice). Becoming successfully enculturated usually requires gaining some level of competence in the activities and language practices of the group. See **apprenticeship** for a definition of a similar term.

EPISTEMIC   The term *epistemic* has to do with the making of knowledge. Research is an *epistemic* pursuit because it is about developing new knowledge. *Epistemology* is the branch of philosophy that deals with human knowledge: where it comes from and how people know what they know. Communication, including *writing*, is also an epistemic activity — it makes new knowledge — as we can see when we read a piece and come away with a new idea that we didn't know before but also that wasn't in the text we just read.

ERROR   *Error* is the term for "mistakes" in grammar (e.g., subject-verb agreement, like "Dogs barks loudly"), punctuation, or usage (e.g., using *that* where some readers would prefer *which*). *Mistakes* is in quotes here because such "errors" are as often differences of opinion regarding convention or taste as they are actual problems that every English speaker or writer would agree are violations of rules.

ETHNOGRAPHY, ETHNOGRAPHIC RESEARCH   *Ethnography* is a research methodology for carefully observing and describing people participating in some activity. At its broadest, ethnography can be written of entire cultures; more narrowly, *ethnographies* may involve writing about a class of students, a church and its members, or a video game arcade and the gamers who play there.

ETHOS   In classical rhetoric, *ethos* is one of the three "pisteis" or persuasive appeals, along with **logos** and **pathos**. In a narrow sense, *ethos* describes the credibility, expertise, or competence that a writer or speaker establishes with an audience through his or her **discourse**. More broadly, *ethos* is a term for the sense of "personality" that rhetors perceive about one another. Ultimately *ethos* describes a rhetor's "way of being in" or "inhabiting" their world. As such, it has to do with a rhetor's *identity* and is a basis for **identification** among rhetors. As a persuasive appeal, ethos derives from **authority**, character (the perceived values, morals, and ethics of a writer), and goodwill (the readers' sense that the writer has the readers' best interests at heart and is not purely self-interested).

EXIGENCE   *Exigence* is the *need or reason* for a given action or communication. All communication exists for a reason. For example, if you say, "Please turn on the lights," we assume the *reason* you say this is that there's not enough light for your needs — in other words, the *exigence* of the situation is that you need more light.

GENERALIZABLE, GENERALIZE   *Generalizable* is a term used to refer to research findings that can apply (or *generalize*) to a larger group than the one that was studied. Generalizable research typically examines a group of statistically significant size under rigorous experimental conditions. Qualitative research is not generalizable, strictly speaking, while quantitative research may be.

GENRE   *Genre* comes from the French word for "kind" or "type" and is related to the Latin word *genus*, which you might remember from the scientific classification system for animals and plants. In the field of rhetoric, genres are broadly understood as *categories of texts*. For example, the poem, the short story, the novel, and the memoir are genres of literature; memos, proposals, reports, and executive summaries are genres of business writing; hiphop, bluegrass, trance, pop, new age, and electronica are genres of music; and the romantic comedy, drama, and documentary are genres of film.

Genres are types of texts that are recognizable to readers and writers and that meet the needs of the **rhetorical situations** in which they function. So, for example, we recognize wedding invitations and understand them to be different from horoscopes. We know that when we are asked to write a paper for school, our teacher probably does not want us to turn in a poem instead.

Genres develop over time in response to recurring rhetorical needs. We have wedding invitations because people keep getting married, and we need an efficient way to let people know and to ask them to attend. Rather than making up a new rhetorical solution every time the same situation occurs, we generally turn to the genre that has developed — in this case, the genre of the wedding invitation.

Genre theorists have suggested that the concept of *genre* actually goes well beyond texts; accordingly, some theorists use *genre* to describe *a typified but dynamic social interaction that a group of people use to conduct a given activity*. (*Typified* means it follows a pattern, and *dynamic* means that people can change the pattern to fit their circumstances as long as it still helps them do the activity.) In "Rethinking Genre," for example, David Russell says that genres are actually "shared expectations among some group(s) of people" (513).

For more on genre and genre theory, see Chapter 1.

HEURISTICS *Heuristics* are approaches or patterns for problem solving. For example, a heuristic for deciding what to have for dinner tonight might be the following: (1) check the fridge; (2) check the pantry; and (3) eat whatever can be assembled most quickly and palatably from the ingredients there.

IDENTIFICATION *Identification* represents the recognition of common ground among rhetors. When someone says "I can identify with that statement," they are saying the statement is in some way equivalent to some part or aspects of themselves. Rhetorical theorist Kenneth Burke suggested that persuasion is actually an act of creating identification, so that one rhetor convinces other rhetors to see themselves in or aligned with the speaker's ideas.

IDENTITY *Identity* comprises your characteristics or personality, consisting of those factors that create a sense of "who you are." Recent theory suggests that individuals may have multiple and/or changing identities, not one "true," stable identity.

INSCRIPTION *Inscription* refers to the act of marking a medium in order to create writing. Writing Studies researcher Paul Prior divides writing into two separate acts, **composition** and inscription, where *composing* is designing a text and its ideas, and *inscribing* is using tools and media to set the text on some object. While inscription can happen without composition (photocopying) and composition can happen without inscription (conversation), what we describe as *writing* cannot happen without both. Prior reminds us that a *medium* (what gets inscribed) can be anything from a t-shirt to a plastic disc to a clay tablet to paper, while *inscribing tools* can be anything from knives and sticks to pencils to printers to DVD burners.

INTERTEXT, INTERTEXTUALITY *Intertextuality* refers to the idea that all texts are made up of other texts — and thus, to the resulting *network* of texts that connect to any given text or idea. At the most basic level, texts share *words*: that is, every text uses words that other texts have used. Sometimes texts use words that, in their combination, are considered unique; in those cases, following Western conventions, those words must be formally marked as *quotations*. *Intertextuality* can go beyond just language, however, by referencing the *ideas and events* that other texts have focused on. If, for example, I claim that people whose governments abuse them have the right to make a better government, I haven't used a quotation from the Declaration of Independence, but most people familiar with that document could "hear it" in my statement. Intertextuality thus is an effect even more than an intention — I don't have to intend to be intertextual in order to *be* intertextual.

INVENTION   *Invention* comprises the processes, strategies, or techniques writers use to come up with what to say in their writing. While the term suggests the notion of "making things up," a significant part of invention is not saying brand-new things but rather combing one's memory and written resources for things that have already been said that will work. Ancient rhetorical theorists such as Aristotle thought carefully about how *stock arguments* they called *common topics* could help a speaker — for instance, the idea "that which has happened frequently before is likely to happen again," which could be recalled through invention and included in many pieces of writing.

KAIROS   *Kairos* represents the element of "being in the right place at the right time" that removes some agency from a **rhetor**. *Kairos* carries a sense of a *moment* when by timely good fortune, circumstances beyond the rhetor's control favor an argument that the rhetor wishes to make. For example, a law enforcement officer in favor of heightened surveillance of U.S. citizens can use the *kairos* of a recent terrorist attack to strengthen her argument by pointing out how the attack demonstrates the need for greater surveillance. The officer is of course not responsible for the attack but can use the "fortunate" occurrence of that particular moment to her advantage.

LEXIS   *Lexis* is a term used for the specific vocabulary used by a group or field of study.

LITERACY, LITERATE   *Literacy* denotes fluency in a given practice. In its original use, literacy referred to *alphabetic literacy* — that is, to fluency in reading and writing "letters," or alphabetic text. This kind of literacy was contrasted with orality, which was characterized as a *lack* of literacy. Over time, however, in academic circles, the meaning of *literacy* and *literate* has broadened to encompass fluency in other areas; most academics therefore now use the term *literacies* (plural) and discuss *digital, electronic, musical, visual, oral, mathematical,* and *gaming* literacies, among many other kinds.

LITERACY SPONSOR   *Literacy sponsor* is a term coined by Deborah Brandt to describe people, ideas, or institutions that help others become **literate** in specific ways. A sponsor could be a parent or sibling who taught you to read, a teacher who helped you learn to love books, or a manufacturing company that requires its employees to be able to read. The sponsors of alphabetic literacy in your life might be very different from the sponsors of visual literacy, musical literacy, or other forms of literacy in your life. (*Pandora,* for instance, can be a musical literacy sponsor for people who use it.)

LITERATURE REVIEW, REVIEW OF THE LITERATURE   A *literature review* (or *review of the literature*) is a text that explains the existing conversation about a particular topic. Literature reviews are usually found at the beginning of research articles or books, but are sometimes written as separate projects. Note that *literature* in this case refers to published research in an area, not to novels or short stories.

LOGOS   *Logos* is one of the three major "proofs" or "appeals" (**pisteis**) identified by Aristotle as central to persuasion. (The others are **ethos** and **pathos**.) In rhetorical theory, Aristotle used *logos* to refer to persuasion by verbal reasoning. In Greek, *logos* literally means "word," referring to language, or "reason," or to kinds of reasoning, including logic. Aristotle did not limit logos appeals to formal logic, but also understood a logos appeal as any an audience would recognize as reasoning by inference or enthymeme.

LONGITUDINAL STUDY   A *longitudinal study* is a research study that examines an individual, group, event, or activity over a substantial period of time. For example, rather than studying a student's writing habits for just a few days or weeks, a longitudinal study might look at his or her habits over several years.

MEDIATE   People use texts in order to get things done. They read in order to learn something (for example, they read instructions in order to figure out how to put together a new desk); they write in order to communicate something (for example, a student might write an e-mail to let her mom know she is short on money). When a text helps people accomplish an activity as in these examples, we say the text *mediates* the activity. To *mediate* is to help make things happen, to play a role in situations and enable communication and activities to take place. In the examples offered above, reading the instructions *mediates* assembly of the desk; sending Mom an e-mail *mediates* receiving $200 to buy much needed school supplies.

METAKNOWLEDGE   *Metaknowledge* is knowledge about knowledge — that is, what we can determine about our learning, its processes, and its products.

METHODOLOGIES   In an academic or scholarly context, *methodologies* are procedures for conducting research — the formalized, field-approved methods used to address particular kinds of research questions. Some examples of methodologies in Writing Studies are **case study, ethnography**, experiment, quasi-experiment, and discourse analysis. *Methodology* can also mean the particular combination of methods used in any particular study. For example, the methodologies used by Sondra Perl in "The Composing Processes of Unskilled College Writers" include case study and discourse analysis.

MINDFULNESS   *Mindfulness* means thinking carefully about what one is doing — that is, purposefully and carefully paying attention. This term derives from Zen Buddhism and has become a key concept in modern psychology. It is often used by researchers interested in helping writers effectively **transfer** knowledge about writing. For a writer to be mindful, for example, means not just to come up with something to say, but to *pay attention to how* she came up with something to say. In the future, she may be able to *mindfully* try that procedure again, adapting it to the new situation.

MODES, MULTIMODALITY   A *mode* (or *modality*) refers to the senses or facilities readers use to experience a text; typical modalities are linguistic (verbal), alphabetic-print, visual/image, aural, color, and kinesthetic/touch. In another sense, *modality* means mode of **inscription** of **texts**, with typical examples being paper, codex/book, or electronic/networked. *Multimodality* refers to texts that combine multiple modes, such as alphabetic, visual, and aural. Technically, *all* texts are multimodal because there are no texts that use just one mode. For example, a novel that is entirely verbal (without any images) inscribed in black alphabetic print engages verbal, print, and color modalities simultaneously.

MOTIVATED   To be *motivated* is to have particular reasons and desires for doing, saying, or thinking something. All rhetorical interaction is motivated — that is, there is a motive behind it. The reasons that motivate a particular interaction also give it a bias or slant: Motivation is inevitably subjective and thus works against neutrality or objectivity.

MULTILITERACIES *Multiliteracies* is a term that reflects the recent, broader understanding of literacy as consisting of more than mastery of the "correct" use of alphabetic language. Multiliteracies include the ability to compose and interpret texts showing **multimodality** (including oral, written, and audio components, among other possibilities), as well as the ability to make meaning in various contexts. A group of scholars known as the New London Group is generally credited with coining the term *multiliteracies*.

MULTIMODAL: see *modes*

MUSHFAKE *Mushfake* is a term used by James Paul Gee to describe a partially acquired **Discourse**, a Discourse that people use to "make do" when they participate in or communicate with a group to which they don't belong. Gee borrows the term from prison culture, in which *mushfake* refers to making do with something when the real thing is not available.

NARRATIVE *Narrative* is most often a synonym for *story* or *storytelling*; the word carries the sense of an accounting or retelling of events, usually in the order they occurred. In the context of writing studies, we focus on narratives as **epistemic**, a way of making knowledge and meaning through rhetorical interaction. Narrative is so central to how people make and convey truth that very few kinds of knowledge-making can happen without it, including scientific research (almost always explained by using narrative) and legal reasoning (which almost always uses narratives of actual events to establish the facts of a case to which the law must be applied, and also uses narrative to explain the development through time of a given law or legal principle).

NORMATE According to Rosemarie Garland Thomson (1996), *normate* refers to a culture's ideal of a "normal" or "typical" body. Wheeler and Jones (p. 654) add what a culture expects to be the values, privileges, and experiences of a "normal" or "typical" person. Some examples of a *normate* body in U.S. culture would be a person who has 20/20 vision (eyesight), has four working limbs with five fingers per hand, can walk up and down stairs with ease, and can eat wheat and dairy products without difficulty.

ORIGINALITY *Originality* is the quality of being singular, unique, and entirely made up or invented, as opposed to imitative or derivative. American culture presumes that writers will have originality — that they will invent work never seen before — and judges the quality of **authorship** in part on its originality. This simplified view of **invention** is assumed by many scholars to be inaccurate in that it fails to describe how people develop ideas through social interaction. This can lead to difficulties in defining and identifying **plagiarism**.

PATHOS *Pathos* is one of the three major "proofs" or "appeals" (**pisteis**) identified by Aristotle as central to persuasion. (The others are **ethos** and **logos**.) In rhetorical theory, Aristotle used *pathos* to refer to persuasion by appeal to emotions and values, which he opposed to appeals to reasoning (*logos*) or to personal credibility (*ethos*). Aristotle recognized that even though emotions are not always "logical" or reason-driven, they are powerful motivators and thus persuasive. Western philosophy has long believed pathos to undermine logos, but current understandings of rhetorical theory recognize that appeals to reasoning are actually simultaneously appeals to values and thus act as pathos appeals in argument. (See Downs, chapter 4, p. 457.)

PEER-REVIEWED JOURNAL Journals are collections of relatively short articles (between five and thirty pages, usually) on a related topic, published periodically (monthly or quarterly, usually) — just like a magazine. Some journals are *scholarly* — meaning that their articles are written by scholars in a field or discipline *to other scholars* studying in the same field. Their purpose is to report on new research: scholarly journals are the main sites in which scholarly conversations (see Greene, page 31) are carried on. Most of the articles collected in this book come from scholarly journals, such as *College Composition and Communication* or *College English*. Some of these scholarly conversations can be *very* specialized — the kind that perhaps only twenty-five or fifty people in the entire world would share enough background knowledge to understand. (Imagine an article on a brand-new branch of theoretical physics or a piece on a new kind of black hole — topics that not many people study.) That specialization poses two problems for a journal: First, how does the editor of a journal — who might be an expert on *a few* specialty areas in a field (say, on "writing process" and on "pedagogy" in composition) but can't be an expert on *all* of them — actually know whether a given article knows what it's talking about? Second, so many people doing research want to publish in any given journal, the journal doesn't have space for them all. In fact, it might only have space for a small percentage of what gets submitted to it. How can it choose which pieces to publish and which not to? The answer to both questions is *peer review:* the editor sends submissions to other experts in the specialty the article is reporting on — usually between two and four other readers. They report back to the journal's editor on the relative *value* of a submission — how significant a contribution it makes, how it fits in the ongoing conversation — and on its *quality* — how well its argument is made, how good its research is. They can make suggestions to the editor about how the piece needs to be improved before publication, and thus guide revisions that most articles are required to make before finally being published. Peer review, then, is a major feature of scholarly journals, and most library databases (along with Google Scholar) let you limit searches to just peer-reviewed journals. (Almost all scholarly *books* are peer-reviewed as well.)

PISTEIS   The Greek term for *proofs* that a rhetor can offer in support of an argument. Most often this term refers to what Aristotle called "artistic" proofs, meaning those that rhetors invent and embed in their discourse. The three such proofs Aristotle identified are **logos, ethos,** and **pathos**.

PLAGIARISM   *Plagiarism* literally means *kidnapping* in Latin; in contemporary English, the word refers to the *theft* of a text or idea. (Authors sometimes think of their writings or ideas as their "children," thus the link to kidnapping.) Definitions of plagiarism tend to come down to *taking another's ideas without giving them credit and thus pretending that you invented the ideas yourself*. In cultures that highly value *intellectual property* — the idea that one's ideas are one's *own* and that use of those ideas by others deserves either credit or payment — plagiarism is an ethical violation punishable by community sanction (such as failing a class or losing one's job). Plagiarism's cousin *copyright infringement* is an actual crime punishable by fine or imprisonment.

A significant difficulty with the idea of plagiarism is that **originality** and **authorship** are technically quite difficult to trace in ways that new digital technologies are making impossible to miss or deny. In *sampling, re-mixing*, and *mash-up* cultures where ideas are freely reused and reincorporated to make new texts, authorship becomes very difficult to trace, and it becomes difficult to tell what counts as original work.

PLANNING   While **invention** focuses on coming up with what to say in one's writing, *planning* focuses more broadly on *how to get a piece written*. Therefore, it includes not only invention but *arrangement*, which is the art of organizing what one has to say to present it most effectively. Planning also includes **process** considerations, such as considering what work needs to be done to complete a piece, what order to do it in, and when to do it in order to meet a deadline.

PROCESS   *Process* refers to the variety of activities that go into writing/composing, including, at minimum,

- *planning* (inventing and arranging ideas),
- *drafting* (creating actual text from previously unwritten ideas),
- *revising* (developing a text or a portion of a text further after an initial draft),
- *editing* (fine-tuning, polishing, or correcting problems in a text), and
- *production* (inscribing a composition in its final, "produced" form, whether in print, online/digital, or some other material format).

Process theory is the study of the methods by which various writers compose and produce texts. The *process movement*, which took place within the field of Composition Studies in the 1970s, was the widespread adoption by writing teachers of instruction that focused on teaching students successful writing processes rather than focusing solely on the quality of their written products.

REGISTER   In the field of linguistics, *register* refers to a type of language used in a particular setting. Changing one's register might mean changing the kinds of words used, as well as the way one says the words. For example, a person might say, "I've finished my homework" to her parents, using one register, while she might say (or text), "I'm finally dooooooooooone!" to her friends.

REVIEW OF THE LITERATURE: see *literature review*

REVISION   *Revision* is the act of developing a piece of writing *by* writing — that is, by adding additional material, shifting the order of its parts, or deleting significant portions of what has already been written. The purpose of revision is to "see again" ("re-vision"), which is necessary because what one could see in originally drafting a piece has been changed *by* the drafting.

   This might become clearer if you think of writing as driving at night. When you begin to write, you know a certain amount about where you're going in your project, just as, when you're driving at night, your headlights let you see two hundred yards (but only two hundred yards) ahead. Writing (or driving) further takes you to new places, where you continually see something different, rethink your position, and decide how to proceed.

   Because revision can go on for some time, for many professional writers *most* writing time is actually spent revising, not creating the first draft. Also, it is important to distinguish revision from **editing,** the correction of minor mistakes in a near-final draft.

RHETOR   Originally (in Greek) a *public speaker, rhetor* means *one who engages in rhetorical interaction or* **discourse**. *Writer* and *speaker* are common synonyms.

RHETORIC   *Rhetoric* is the study or performance of human interaction and communication or the product(s) of that interaction and communication. Because most human interaction is *persuasive* by nature — that is, we're trying to convince each other of things, even when we say something simple like "that feels nice" — one way to think of rhetoric is as the study of persuasion. *Rhetoric* can refer to *a field of knowledge* on this subject, to systematic *explanations for* and *predictions of* how persuasion works, or to the *performance art* of human interaction and persuasion itself.

Rhetoric always has to do with these specific principles:

1. Human communication, or **discourse**, is **situated** in a *moment,* a particular time and place, which is part of a larger **ecology.** That moment and ecology are the **context** of the communication. A particular text takes it meaning in part from its context, so knowledge of the context is necessary in order to know the text's meaning. For example, "Help me!" means one thing when your mom is standing next to a van full of groceries and another when she's standing next to a van with a flat tire. Her *discourse* is *situated* in a particular context.

2. Communication is **motivated** by particular **rhetors'** *purposes,* needs, and values. No communication is *un*motivated.

3. Communication is *interactional,* "back-and-forth" between rhetors. Readers actually *complete* the meaning of a writer's text. Successful writers therefore think carefully about who their **audience** is and what the audience values and needs.

4. Communication is **epistemic,** which means that it *creates new knowledge.* We often talk about "reporting" or "transmitting" information as if we can find information and pass it along unaltered. But we actually *can't* transmit information without altering it, so our communication makes new knowledge as it goes.

5. Communication is **embodied** and material, meaning that it exists not simply in the mental realm of ideas but *takes place via material bodies* that themselves shape the meaning of the communication.

6. Communication is shaped by *technology.* "Technology" simply refers to *use of tools,* and it is certainly possible to communicate without technology (through purely organic means such as by voice). Practically speaking, though, almost all communication in any culture in which you're reading this book is assisted and shaped by technology. Rhetoric teaches us to look for how technology influences even communication that doesn't directly use it.

7. Communication is *contingent,* meaning that what we consider *good* communication depends on the circumstances and context in which it happens. Because communication depends on context, we can't make universal rules about what makes good communication.

RHETORICAL   *Rhetorical* refers to a phenomenon such as human interaction that has the qualities of being situated, motivated, interactive, epistemic, embodied, and contingent. (See the definition of **rhetoric.**) *Rhetorical study,* for example, is the investigation of human communication as situated, motivated, interactive, epistemic, embodied, and contingent. *Rhetorical reading* involves reading a text as situated, motivated, etc. *Rhetorical analysis* is a way of analyzing texts to find what choices their embodied **rhetor** (speaker or writer) made based on their purpose and motivation, their situatedness and context, and how they interact with and make new knowledge for their audience.

RHETORICAL SITUATION   *Rhetorical situation* is the particular circumstance of a given instance of communication or **discourse.** The rhetorical situation includes **exigence** (the *need or reason* for the communication), **context** (the *circumstances* that give rise to the *exigence,* including location in time/history and space/place/position), **rhetor** (the originator of the communication — its speaker or writer), and **audience** (the auditor, listener, or reader of the rhetor's discourse). The rhetorical situation is a moment in a larger rhetorical **ecology**, the network of relationships among rhetors in the situation.

RHETORICAL THEORY *Rhetorical theory* is a set or system of principles for and explanations of human interaction from the perspective of rhetoric, which emphasizes the situated, contingent, and motivated nature of communication. Rhetorical theory has historically emphasized persuasion but can be more broadly understood as explaining and predicting how we make up our minds and how we change them.

SITUATED Located at a particular place and time, and therefore dependent on a specific context and set of circumstances. In everyday language, we use *situated* to describe an object's or person's place: "The piano was situated on the left side of the great room" or "She situated herself between the two potted ferns." In a scholarly, rhetorical sense, we mean roughly the same thing, but use the term to call attention to the uniqueness of the moment and place of situation: "The President's speech is situated at a very tense time of diplomatic relations with Libya." *Situatedness* is a key element of rhetorical activities: When we say a given activity or experience is "rhetorical," we mean that it has the quality of being *situated* in time and space (among other qualities). That is the opposite of being *universal*: A universal rule is one that applies in all times and places. In contrast, most rules are situated, applying only to specific times, places, and circumstances.

SOCIAL CONTEXT *Social context* is the environment, situation, or culture in which something is embedded. Key aspects of the social context of **discourse** might include participants, goals, setting, race, class, gender, and so on.

STASES *Stases* (we often say *the stases*) are a problem-solving pattern (a **heuristic**) that helps writers develop arguments by asking a set of specific questions about the subject. First described in the rhetorical theory of Aristotle, the word *stases* shares the same root as the words *state, status*, and *stasis* (the singular of *stases*), all of which denote *condition* or *being*. Stases have to do with *the state of things*, so that when we consider the stases, we are taking stock, or asking, "What is the state of things?" The stases include (1) questions of fact, (2) questions of value, and (3) questions of policy:

1. What is the *nature* of the thing in question? How would we define or name the thing? What caused the thing? For example, if a four-legged creature with a wagging tail shows up at your back door, your first question might be "What is [the nature of] that?" Your answer might be that it's a "stray dog."

2. What is the *quality* or *value* of the thing? Is it good or bad? Desirable or undesirable? Wanted or unwanted? Happy or sad? Liked or disliked? Your answer to this will depend on a complex set of calculations, taking into account the nature of the thing and the context in which it is encountered. To extend our example, let's say you decide the stray dog is good because you like dogs and this one is appealing.

3. What should *be done* about it? What policy should we establish toward it? What is the best thing to do with respect to it? In the case of our example, you might decide that the best policy would be to take in the stray dog, at least temporarily, and feed it.

SYMBOL A *symbol* is a thing that represents or stands for something else — usually an object standing for an idea or an abstract concept. In the U.S. flag, which is itself a symbol, white stars stand for (symbolize) individual states and the blue field in which they all rest symbolizes unity. Language is a symbol (or sign) system; all words are symbols for the objects or concepts they're associated with.

THEORY   A *theory* is a systematic explanation for some aspect of people's lived experience and observation. For a given experience — say, an apple falling on one's head — people propose explanations, or *theories*, for why the experience happens as it does, or why it doesn't happen some other way (e.g., a theory of gravity). People then test the theory against more observed experiences, seeing if those experiences are consistent with the explanation suggested by the theory, and seeing whether the theory can predict what will happen in future experiences. Theories are, for a long time, not "right" or "wrong" but "stronger/better" or "weaker/poorer" at explaining the phenomenon in question. The better or stronger a theory is, the more completely it accounts for existing phenomena (experiences, events, and objects) and the more accurately it makes testable predictions about future events. For example, a theory that tries to explain how people make up or change their minds has to be able to account for existing cases of this and predict how future cases will work. Theories — such as the theory in Writing Studies that "writing is a process" — become treated as essentially factual when we recognize that though they are still **constructs** (made-up explanations that can only approximate the truth), they're very good explanations widely supported by many kinds of evidence.

THRESHOLD CONCEPTS   *Threshold concepts* are ideas that literally change the way you experience, think about, and understand a subject. Every specialized field of study (or discipline — history, biology, mathematics, etc.) has threshold concepts that learners in that field must become acquainted with in order to fully understand the ideas of that field of study. Threshold concepts, once learned, help the learner see the world differently. They can be hard to learn (what researchers Jan Meyer and Ray Land call "troublesome") for a variety of reasons, including the possibility that they might directly conflict with ideas you already have. Once you're aware of these new and troublesome threshold concepts and you really start to understand them, they are hard to unlearn — Meyer and Land say they are "irreversible." Very often, learning threshold concepts doesn't just change the way you think about the subject, but also the way you think about yourself. But what makes them most powerful is that they help you understand a whole set of other ideas that are hard to imagine without knowing the threshold concept — so they let you do a whole lot of learning at once by helping entire sets of ideas "fall into place." Chapter 1 discusses the main threshold concepts addressed in *Writing about Writing*.

TONE   *Tone* is a reader's *judgment* of what a text sounds like, sometimes also termed the dominant mood of a text. It is important to note that tone is not a characteristic actually *in* a text but rather one constructed in the interaction among the writer, the reader, and the text. Tone emerges not just from the language (word choice and sentence structure) of a text but also from a reader's judgment of the **rhetorical situation** and the writer's **ethos** and motivation.

TRANSFER   Sometimes called *generalization or repurposing*, *transfer* refers to the act of applying existing knowledge, learned in one kind of situation, to new situations. For example, a writer who learns how to write a summary in her College Writing I class in English is expected to *transfer* that summary-writing knowledge to her "history of the telescope" project in astronomy. Transfer, we are learning, is not automatic — people learn many things that they forget and/or don't or can't use in different circumstances. Research suggests that learning in particular ways (for example, being **mindful**) can increase the likelihood of later transfer.

VELOCITY   Based on the term from physics meaning *movement at some rate in some direction*, rhetorical theorists use *velocity* to describe how a text "moves" or is transformed through time and space. A text may be written into new forms or taken to new places. Analysis of velocity attends to both *direction* — where the text "goes" or how it is transformed — and *rate* — how quickly the transformation takes place. The concept of *velocity* is available not just to analysts but to rhetors themselves, who can compose and inscribe a text with a specific velocity in mind to begin with.

VOICE   *Voice* is the way a writer "sounds" in a text, or the extent to which you can "hear" a writer in his or her text. The definition of this term has changed over time. It has been used to refer to *authenticity* in writing, as well as to a written text that seems to be "true" to who its author is and what he or she wants to say. Author bell hooks has argued that finding a voice or "coming to voice" can be seen as an act of resistance. In *Writing about Writing* we use the term *voice* to refer to a writer's ability to speak with some **authority** and expertise deriving from his or her own experiences and knowledge. According to this view, writers have multiple voices, any one of which may find expression, depending on the precise context of utterance.

WRITING STUDIES   *Writing Studies* is one of the terms used to describe a field or discipline that takes writing and composing as its primary objects of study. Another term commonly used to describe this field of study is Rhetoric and Composition. Most of the readings in this book are written by Writing Studies scholars.

WORKS CITED

MacNealy, Mary Sue. *Strategies for Empirical Research in Writing*. Longman, 1999.

Prior, Paul. "Tracing Process: How Texts Come into Being." *What Writing Does and How It Does It*, edited by Charles Bazerman and Paul Prior. Lawrence Erlbaum Associates, 2004, pp. 167–200.

Russell, David. "Rethinking Genre in School and Society: An Activity Theory Analysis." *Written Communication*, vol. 14, no. 4, Oct. 1997, pp. 504–54.

Swales, John. *Genre Analysis: English in Academic and Research Settings*. Cambridge UP, 1990.

Thomson, Rosemarie Garland. *Extraordinary Bodies: Figuring Physical Disability in American Culture and Literature*. Columbia UP, 1996.

Wenger, Etienne. *Communities of Practice: Learning, Meaning, and Identity*. Cambridge UP, 1998.

ACKNOWLEDGMENTS

Baron, Dennis. "From Pencils to Pixels: The Stages of Literacy," from *Passions, Pedagogies, and 21st Century Technologies*. Edited by Gail E. Hawisher and Cynthia L. Selfe. Logan: Utah State University Press, 1999 (pp.15–33). Copyright © 1999. Reprinted by permission.

Berkenkotter, Carol. "Decisions and Revisions: The Planning Strategies of a Publishing Writer." *College Composition and Communication* 34 (1983):156–69. Copyright © 1983 by the National Council of Teachers of English. Reprinted with permission.

Brandt, Deborah. "Sponsors of Literacy." *College Composition and Communication* 49.2 (1998): 165–185. Copyright © 1998 by the National Council of Teachers of English. Reprinted by permission.

Branick, Sean. "Coaches Can Read, Too: An Ethnographic Study of a Football Coaching Discourse Community." Reprinted by permission of the author.

Cisneros, Sandra. "Only Daughter." First published in *Glamour*, November 1990. Reprinted by permission of Susan Bergholz Literary Services, New York and Lamy, NM. All rights reserved.

Corder, Jim W. Copyright © 1985 from "Argument as Emergence, Rhetoric as Love," by Jim W. Corder, *Rhetoric Review* 4(1), 16–32. Reproduced by permission of Taylor & Francis LLC, http://www.tandfonline.com.

Gee, James Paul. "Literacy, Discourse, and Linguistics: Introduction." *Journal of Education* 171.1 (1989): 5–17. Reprinted by permission of James Paul Gee, Mary Lou Fulton Presidential Professor of Literacy Studies, Arizona State University.

Grabill, Jeff, William Hart-Davidson, Stacey Pigg, Paul Curran, Michael McLeod, Jessie Moore, Paula Rosinski, Tim Peeples, Suzanne Rumsey, Martine Courant Rife, Robyn Taska, Dundee Lackey, and Beth Brunk-Chavez. "Revisualizing Composition: Mapping the Writing Lives of First-Year College Students." Writing in Digital Environments Research Center, Michigan State University, 2010. Reprinted by permission.

Grant-Davie, Keith. Copyright © 1997 from "Rhetorical Situations and Their Constituents" by Keith Grant-Davie, *Rhetoric Review* 15(2), 264–279. Reproduced by permission of Taylor & Francis LLC, http://tandfonline.com.

Greene, Stuart. "Argument as Conversation: The Role of Inquiry in Writing a Researched Argument." From *The Subject is Research: Processes and Practices,* edited by Wendy Bishop and Pavel Zemliansky. Copyright © 2001 by Heinemann. Published by Heinemann, Portsmouth, NH. Reprinted by permission of the publisher and Stuart Greene. All rights reserved.

Hass, Christina, and Linda Flower. "Rhetorical Reading Strategies and the Construction of Meaning." *College Composition and Communication* 39:2 (1988): 167–183. Copyright © 1988 by the National Council of Teachers of English. Reprinted with permission.

Hassan, Komysha. "Digital Literacy and the Making of Meaning: How Format Affects Interpretation in the University of Central Florida Libraries Search Interface," produced in Jacob Stewart's Spring 2014 ENC 1102. Reprinted by permission of Komysha Hassan.

Johns, Ann M. "Discourse Communities and Communities of Practice: Membership, Conflict, and Diversity" from *Text, Role, and Context: Developing Academic Literacies.* Copyright © Cambridge University Press, 1997. Reprinted with permission from Cambridge University Press.

Jones, Natasha, and Stephanie Wheeler. "Document Design and Social Justice: A Universal Design for Documents." Reprinted by permission of the authors.

Kain, Donna, and Elizabeth Wardle. "Activity Theory: An Introduction for Writing in the Classroom." Reprinted by permission of the authors.

Kantz, Margaret. "Helping Students Use Textual Sources Persuasively." *College English* 52.1 (1990): 74–91. Copyright © 1990 by the National Council of Teachers of English. Reprinted with permission.

Klass, Perri. "Learning the Language" from *A Not Entirely Benign Procedure*. Copyright © 1987 by Perri Klass. Used by permission of the Elaine Markson Literary Agency.

Lamott, Anne. "Shitty First Drafts," from *Bird by Bird: Some Instructions on Writing and Life* by Anne Lamott. Copyright © 1994 by Anne Lamott. Used by permission of Pantheon Books, an imprint of the Knopf Doubleday Publishing Group, a division of Penguin Random House LLC. All rights reserved.

Malcolm X. "Learning to Read," from *Autobiography of Malcolm X* as told to Alex Haley, copyright © 1964 by Alex Haley and Malcolm X. Copyright © 1965 by Alex Haley and Betty Shabazz. Used by permission of Ballantine Books, an imprint of Random House, a division of Penguin Random House LLC. All rights reserved.

Marro, Victoria. "The Genres of Chi Omega: An Activity Analysis." Reprinted by permission of the author.

McCarthy, Lucille P. "A Stranger in Strange Lands: A College Student Writing Across the Curriculum." *Research in the Teaching of English* 21.3 (1987): 233–65. Copyright © 1987 by the National Council of Teachers of English. Reprinted with permission.

Mellix, Barbara. "From Outside, In." Originally appeared in *The Georgia Review*, Volume XLI, No. 2 (Summer 1987). Copyright © 1987 by The University of Georgia/Copyright ©1987 by Barbara Mellix. Reprinted by permission of Barbara Mellix and *The Georgia Review*.

Mirabelli, Tony. "The Language and Literacy of Food Service Workers." From *What They Don't Learn in School*, edited by Jabari Mahiri. NY: Peter Lang Publishing, 2004. Pages 143–162. Reprinted by permission.

Murray, Donald M. "All Writing Is Autobiography." *College Composition and Communication* 42.1 (1991): 66–74. Copyright © 1991 National Council of Teachers of English. Reprinted with permission.

Murray, Donald M. "Response of a Laboratory Rat–or, Being Protocoled." *College Composition and Communication* 34.2 (1983): 169–172. Copyright © 1983 by the National Council of Teachers of English. Reprinted by permission.

Neto, Alcir Santos. "Tug of War: The Writing Process of a Bilingual Writer and his Struggles," produced in Mary Tripp's Fall 2012 ENC 1101. Reprinted by permission of Alcir Santos Neto.

Pasqualin, Lucas. "Don't Panic: A Hitchhiker's Guide to My Literacy," produced in Vanessa Calkins' Summer 2013 ENC 1101. Reprinted by permission of Lucas Pasqualin.

Perl, Sondra. "The Composing Processes of Unskilled College Writers." *Research in the Teaching of English* 13.4 (1979): 317–36. Copyright © 1979 by the National Council of Teachers of English. Reprinted with permission.

Pigg, Stacey. Copyright © 2014 from "Coordinating Constant Invention: Social Media's Role in Distributed Work," by Stacey Pigg, *Technical Communication Quarterly*, 23(2), 69-87. Reproduced by permission of the Association of Teachers of Technical Writing. http://www.attw.org.

Porter, James E. Copyright © 1986 from "Intertextuality and the Discourse Community," by James E. Porter, *Rhetoric Review* 5(1), 34–47. Reproduced by permission of Taylor & Francis LLC, http://www.tandfonline.com.

Public Justice Center. "Step Six, Step Seven, Step Three," from *Evictions in Baltimore City: Procedures for Tenants and Landlords*. Public Justice Center, 2016. http://publicjustice.org /uploads/file/pdf/Evictions%20brchr%202016a.pdf. Reprinted by permission of the Public Justice Center.

Ridolfo, Jim, and Dànielle Nicole DeVoss. (2009). "Composing for Recomposition: Rhetorical Velocity and Delivery." *Kairos: A Journal of Rhetoric, Technology, and Pedagogy*, 13(2). Reprinted by permission of Jim Ridolfo.

Robertson, Liane, Kara Taczak, and Kathleen Blake Yancey. "Notes Toward a Theory of Prior Knowledge." *Composition Forum* 26, Fall 2012. Copyright © 2012 Liane Roberston, Kara Taczak, and Kathleen Blake Yancey. Reprinted by permission of the authors.

Rodgers, Michael. "Expanding Constraints," produced in Nate Holic's Fall 2012 ENC 1101. Reprinted by permission of Michael Rodgers.

Rose, Mike. "Rigid Rules, Inflexible Plans, and the Stifling of Language: A Cognitivist Analysis of Writer's Block." *College Composition and Communication* 31.4 (1980): 389–401. Copyright © 1980 by the National Council of Teachers of English. Reprinted with permission.

Sigona, Annalise. "Impression Management on Facebook and Twitter: Where Are People More Likely to Share Positivity or Negativity with Their Audiences?" *Young Scholars in Writing*, Department of English, Language & Literature, University of Missouri-Kansas City. Reprinted by permission of the author.

Sommers, Nancy. "I Stand Here Writing." *College English* 55.4 (1993): 420–428. Copyright © 1993 by the National Council of Teachers of English. Reprinted with permission.

Sommers, Nancy. "Revision Strategies of Student Writers and Experienced Adult Writers." *College Composition and Communication* 31.4 (1980): 378–88. Copyright © 1980 by the National Council of Teachers of English. Reprinted with permission.

Straub, Richard. "Responding — Really Responding — to Other Students Writing." From *The Subject Is Writing, 4th Edition: Essays by Teachers and Students,* edited by Wendy Bishop and James Strickland. Copyright © 2006 by Heinemann. Published by Heinemann, Portsmouth, NH. Reprinted by permission of the publisher. All rights reserved.

Swales, John. "The Concept of Discourse Community." In *Genre Analysis: English in Academic and Workplace Settings*, pp. 21–32. Cambridge University Press, Copyright © 1990. Reprinted with the permission of Cambridge University Press.

Tejada, Arturo, Jr., Esther Gutierrez, Brisa Galindo, DeShonna Wallace, and Sonia Castaneda. "Challenging Our Labels: Rejecting the Language of Remediation." *Young Scholars in*

905

Writing, Department of English, Language & Literature, University of Missouri-Kansas City. Used with permission.

Villanueva, Victor. From *Bootstraps: From an American Academic of Color*, pages 66–77. Urbana, IL: National Council of Teachers of English (NCTE), 1993. Copyright © 1993 by the National Council of Teachers of English. Reprinted with permission.

Wardle, Elizabeth. "Identity, Authority, and Learning to Write in New Workplaces." *Enculturation* 5.2 (2004). Reprinted by permission of the author.

Williams, Joseph M. "The Phenomenology of Error." *College Composition and Communication* 32.2 (1981): 152–68. Copyright © 1981 by the National Council of Teachers of English. Reprinted with permission.

Young, Vershawn Ashanti. "'Naw, We Straight': An Argument Against Code Switching." *JAC Online Journal* Volume 29 No. 1/2 (2009). Reprinted by permission of the author.